Warman's®
Antiques and Collectibles
Price Guide
37th Edition

Edited by Ellen T. Schroy

Published by

krause publications
An F&W Publications Company

700 East State Street • Iola, WI 54990-0001
715-445-2214 • 888-457-2873
www.krause.com

Please call or write for our free catalog of publications.
Our toll-free number to place an order or obtain a free catalog is 800-258-0929
or please use our regular business telephone 715-445-2214.

Library of Congress Catalog Number: 82-643543
ISBN: 0-87349-588-8

Printed in the United States of America

INTRODUCTION

Warman's: Serving the trade for more than 50 years

In 1994, *Warman's Antiques and Their Prices* became *Warman's Antiques and Collectibles Price Guide*. The latest edition is bigger than ever—physically, that is. Longtime *Warman's* users will find several new changes to this edition. Hopefully you will agree that they are improvements. The first big change is the three-column format, continued from the last edition. The second, and probably the most noticeable, is the dramatic increase in the number of photographs presented. This edition features close to 2,000 photos. The third change is enhanced introductions to several categories. These new introductions try to help the reader establish what historical period their object was created in through the use of clues, photographs, and line drawings.

In true *Warman's* spirit, we've strived to show different items in each category and include detailed descriptions to help explain what the object is, when it was made, and what it is worth. You can always expect more, never less, from *Warman's*.

Individuals in the trade refer to this book simply as *Warman's*, a fitting tribute to E. G. Warman and the product he created. *Warman's* has been around for more than 50 years. We are proud as peacocks that *Warman's* continues to establish the standards for general antiques and collectibles price guides in 2003, just as it did in 1972 when its first rival appeared on the scene.

Warman's, the antiques and collectibles "bible," covers objects made between 1700 and the present. Because it reflects market trends, *Warman's* has added more and more 20th-century material to each edition. Remember, 1900 was more than 100 years ago—the distant past to the new generation of 20-something and 30-something collectors. The general "antiques" market consists of antiques (for the purposes of this book, objects made before 1945), collectibles (objects of the post-World War II era that enjoy an established secondary market), and desirables (contemporary objects that are collected, but speculative in price). Although *Warman's* contains information on all three market segments, its greatest emphasis is on antiques and collectibles. In fact, this book is the essential field guide to the antiques and collectibles marketplace, which indicates that *Warman's* is much more than a list of object descriptions and prices. It is a basic guide to the field as a whole, providing you with the key information you need every time you encounter a new object or collecting category.

'Warman's is the Key'

Warman's provides the keys needed by auctioneers, collectors, dealers, and others to understand and deal with the complexities of the antiques and collectibles market. A price list is only one of many keys needed today. *Warman's* 37th edition contains many additional keys including histories, marks, and reproductions. Useful buying and collecting hints also are provided. Used properly, there are few doors these keys will not open. *Warman's* is designed to be your first key to the exciting world of antiques and collectibles. As you use the keys this book provides to advance further in your specialized collecting areas, *Warman's* hopes you will remember with fondness where you received your start. When you encounter items outside your area of specialty, remember *Warman's* remains your key to unlocking the information you need, just as it has in the past.

Organization

Listings: Objects are listed alphabetically by category, beginning with ABC Plates and ending with Zsolnay Pottery. If you have trouble identifying the category to which your object belongs, think about what the object is made of, or who made it, what marks are visible, and use the extensive index in the back of the book. It will guide you to the proper category. We have made the listings descriptive enough so that specific objects can be identified. We also emphasize items that are actively being sold in the marketplace. Some harder-to-find objects are included to demonstrate market spread—useful information worth considering when you have not traded actively in a category recently. Each year as the market changes, we carefully review our categories—adding, dropping, and combining to provide the most comprehensive coverage possible. *Warman's* quick response to developing trends in the marketplace is one of the prime reasons for its continued leadership in the field.

History: Collectors and dealers enhance their appreciation of objects by knowing something about their history. We present a capsule history for each category. In many cases, this history contains collecting hints or other useful information.

References: Krause Publications also publishes other *Warman's* titles. Each concentrates on a specific collecting group, e.g., American pottery and porcelain, Americana and collectibles, glass, and jewelry. Several are second or subsequent editions. Their expanded coverage compliments the information found in *Warman's Antiques and Collectibles Price Guide*. Many categories in the 37th edition feature the cover of a *Warman's* book where you can find more information and in-depth coverage on the subject. These books include *Warman's Advertising*; *Warman's American Furniture*; *Warman's American Pottery and Porcelain*, 2nd edition; *Warman's American Records*; *Warman's Coins and Paper Money*; *Warman's Depression Glass*; *Warman's English and Continental Pottery and Porcelain*, 3rd edition; *Warman's Glass*, 4th edition; *Warman's Jewelry*, 3rd edition; *Warman's Native American Collectibles*; and *Warman's Pattern Glass*, 2nd edition.

There are also several good publications collectors and dealers should be aware of to be knowledgeable about antiques and collectibles in general:

- *Antique & The Arts Weekly*, Bee Publishing Company, 5 Church Hill Road, Newton, CT 06470; http://www.thebee.com/aweb
- *Antique Review*, P.O. Box 538, Worthington, OH 43085
- *Antique Trader Weekly*, P.O. Box 1050, Dubuque, IA 52001; http://www.csmonline.com
- *AntiqueWeek*, P.O. Box 90, Knightstown, IN 46148; http://www.antiqueweek.com
- *Antiques* (The Magazine Antiques), 551 Fifth Ave., New York, NY 10017
- *Antiques & Collecting*, 1006 South Michigan Ave., Chicago, IL 60605
- *Maine Antique Digest*, P.O. Box 358, Waldoboro, ME 04572; http://www.maineantiquedigest.com
- *New England Antiques Journal*, 4 Church St., Ware, MA 01082
- *New York-Pennsylvania Collector*, Drawer C, Fishers, NY 14453

Space does not permit listing all the national and regional publications in the antiques and collectibles field. The above is a sampling.

Reproductions: Reproductions are a major concern to all collectors and dealers. Throughout this edition, boxes will alert you to known reproductions and keys to recognizing them. Most reproductions are unmarked; the newness of their appearance is often the best clue to uncovering them. Specific objects known to be reproduced are marked within the listings with an asterisk (*). The information is designed to serve as a reminder of past reproductions and prevent you from buying them, believing them to be period. We strongly recommend subscribing to *Antique & Collectors Reproduction News*, a monthly newsletter that reports on past and present reproductions, copycats, fantasies, and fakes. Send $32 for 12 issues to: ACRN, Box 12130, Des Moines, IA 50312-9403; (www.repronews.com). This newsletter has been published for several years. Consider buying all available back issues. The information they contain will be of service long into the future.

Index: A great deal of effort has been expended to make our index useful. Always begin by looking for the most specific reference. For example, if you have a piece of china, look first for the maker's name and second for the type. Remember, many objects can be classified in three or more categories. If at first you don't succeed, try, try again.

Black-and-white photographs: You may encounter a piece you cannot identify well enough to use the index. Consult the photographs and marks. If you own several editions of *Warman's*, you have available a valuable photographic reference to the antiques and collectibles field.

Price notes

In assigning prices, we assume the object is in very good condition; if otherwise, we note this in our description. It would be ideal to suggest that mint, or unused, examples of all objects exist. The reality is that objects from the past were used, whether they are glass, china, dolls, or toys. Because of this, some normal wear must be expected. In fact, if an object such as a piece of furniture does not show wear, its origins may be more suspect than if it does show wear. Whenever possible, we have tried to provide a broad listing of prices within a category so you have a "feel" for the market. We emphasize the middle range of prices within a category, while also listing some objects of high and low value to show market spread. We do not use ranges because they tend to confuse, rather than help, the collector and dealer. How do you determine if your object is at the high or low end of the range? There is a high degree of flexibility in pricing in the antiques field. If you want to set ranges, add or subtract 10 percent from our prices.

Price research

Everyone asks, "Where do you get your prices?"

They come from many sources. First, we rely on auctions. Auction houses and auctioneers do not always command the highest prices. If they did, why do so many dealers buy from them? The key to understanding auction prices is to know when a price is high or low in the range. We think we do this and do it well. The 37th edition represents a concentrated effort to contact more regional auction houses, both large and small. The cooperation has been outstanding and has resulted in an ever-growing pool of auction prices and trends to help us determine the most up-to-date auction prices.

Second, we work closely with dealers. We screen our contacts to make certain they have full knowledge of the market. Dealers make their living from selling antiques; they cannot afford to have a price guide that is not in touch with the market. More than 50 antiques and collectibles magazines, newspapers, and journals come into our office regularly. They are excellent barometers of what is moving and what is not. We don't hesitate to call an advertiser and ask if his listed merchandise sold. When the editorial staff is doing fieldwork, we identify ourselves. Our conversations with dealers and collectors around the country have enhanced this book. Teams from *Warman's* are in the field at antiques shows, malls, flea markets, and auctions recording prices and taking photographs. Collectors work closely with us. They are specialists whose devotion to research and accurate information is inspiring. Generally, they are not dealers. Whenever we have asked them for help, they have responded willingly and admirably.

Board of advisers

Our board of advisers is made up of specialists, both dealers and collectors, who feel a commitment to accurate information. You'll find their names listed in the front of the book. Several have authored a major reference work on their subject. Our esteemed board of advisers has increased in number and

scope. Participants have all provided detailed information regarding the history and reference section of their particular area of expertise, as well as preparing price listings. Many furnished excellent photographs and even shared with us their thoughts on the state of the market. We are delighted to include those who are valuable members, officers, and founders of collectors' clubs. They are authors of books and articles, and many frequently lecture to groups about their specialties. Most of our advisers have been involved with antiques and collectibles for more than 20 years. Several are retired, and the antiques and collectibles business is a hobby that encompasses most of their free time. Others are a bit younger and either work full time or part time in the antiques and collectibles profession. One thing they all have in common is their enthusiasm for the antiques and collectibles marketplace. They are eager to share their knowledge with collectors. Many have developed wonderful friendships through their efforts and are enriched by them. If you wish to buy or sell an object in the field of expertise of any of our advisers, drop them a note along with a SASE. If time permits, they will respond.

Buyer's guide, not seller's guide

Warman's is designed to be a buyer's guide, suggesting what you would have to pay to purchase an object on the open market from a dealer or collector. It is not a seller's guide to prices. People frequently make this mistake. In doing so, they deceive themselves. If you have an object listed in this book and wish to sell it to a dealer, you should expect to receive approximately 50 percent of the listed value. If the object will not resell quickly, expect to receive even less. Private collectors may pay more, perhaps 70 to 80 percent of our listed price, if your object is something needed for their collection. If you have an extremely rare object or an object of exceptionally high value, these guidelines do not apply. Examine your piece as objectively as possible. As an antiques and collectibles appraiser, I spend a great deal of time telling people their treasures are not "rare" at all, but items readily available in the marketplace. In respect to buying and selling, a simple philosophy is that a good purchase occurs when the buyer and seller are happy with the price. Don't look back. Hindsight has little value in the antiques and collectibles field. Given time, things tend to balance out.

Always improving

Warman's is always trying to improve. Space is freely given to long price descriptions, to help you understand what the piece looks like, perhaps what's special about it. With this edition, we've arranged some old formats, using more bold words to help you find what you're looking for. Some categories have been arranged so that if the only thing you know is how high, you can start there. Many times, identifying what you've got is the hardest part. Well, the first place to start is how big—grab that ruler and see what you can find that's a comparable size. You are still going to have to make a determination about what the object is made of, be it china, glass, porcelain, wood, or other materials. Use all your senses to discover what you've got. Ask questions about your object, who made it, and why, how was it used, where, and when. As you find answers to these questions, you'll be helping yourself figure out just what the treasure is all about. Now take that information and you'll be able to look it up and discover the value.

Eager to hear from readers

At *Warman's* and Krause Publications, we're always eager to hear what you think about this book and how we can improve it. Let us know if you like the "face lift" the old gal has gotten with this edition and how we might continue to improve her outlook. Write to either Ellen Schroy, *Warman's* editor, 135 S. Main St., Quakertown, PA 18951-1119 or e-mail at schroy@voicenet.com. The fine staff at Krause Publications can be reached at 700 E. State St., Iola, WI 54990. It's our goal to continue in the *Warman's* tradition and make it the best price guide available.

STATE OF THE MARKET
2002—A YEAR OF CHANGE

The antiques and collectibles world is always changing, but I think 2002 represented even greater swings than in past years. Reports from auction houses, flea markets, antiques shows, and antiques malls all reflect that the year ended on a nervous note—partially because of the shaky nature of the economy and the tensions of the times, but also because many folks are redefining their collecting interests.

This past year was a very good year to be buying antiques and collectibles as investments, especially if one could find them at bargain prices, whether at auction or through private transactions. The record-breaking attendance at last March's Atlantique City show seemed to reinforce that collectors were there and seeking ways to spend money. Many traveled there as an escape from the dreary winter months, while dedicated collectors searched for something unique to add to their growing collections.

This huge antiques and collectibles show offers something for everyone, from the beginner to the advanced collector. The vendors there carry a wide array of merchandise, from toys from everyone's childhood to fine art glass, to exquisite lamps, to enticing jewelry. Buyers could exchange their dollars for a beautiful doll, a vintage post card, or even a slot machine. In addition to dolls, post cards, and coin-operated items, other hot collectibles include furniture, costume jewelry, table linens from the 1940s and 1950s, and toys, especially Hot Wheels.

Several dealers exhibited dolls from all ages, many countries, and all types of manufacturers. Dealer Dawn Herlocher, author of *200 Years of Dolls: Identification and Price Guide* and *Antique Trader's Doll Makers and Marks: A Guide to Identification*, had a booth brimming with smiling dolls, accessories, and other items that doll collectors love. Her prices ranged from a few dollars to multi-thousands. Dawn is one of those great dealers who not only sells antiques, but also helps educate the buyer as to why a particular example is so special. She will tell you if the hair or dress is original, what kinds of marks may be found, and other points that add to the value of the doll. Every doll she sells is also carefully wrapped for the long trip to its new home, adding a very personal touch to every sale.

Known as "Antiqueslotmachines.com," dealer Bob Levy always offers buyers at Atlantique City a chance to own their very own slot machine. He certainly knows the odds, as well as the history, of all these mechanical wonders. He, too, will gladly discuss his wares with interested folks, telling what makes each one special. Many of his coin-operated machines are eagerly sought by collectors, especially those dedicating a room in their home as a game room, complete with classic vintage pinball machines, perhaps a Coke machine, and other classic coin-operated items. Bob's classic slot machines range in price from $2,000 to $3,000.

The market for jukeboxes was a little soft this past year, however. Some of us prefer our music to be "re-mastered"

Dealer/author Dawn Herlocher explains some finer points to a shopper at Atlantique City.

Warman's adviser Robert Levy with one of his favorite slot machines.

Doll dealer Dawn Herlocher's booth, full of vintage and collectible dolls and accessories.

Posters of all types were available for collectors at the October Atlantique City show.

and perfect on our CDs and DVDs, leaving the colorful old jukeboxes sitting quietly. Those of us who prefer to jitter bug to the old hits can still enjoy our songs played on a jukebox full of tunes and nostalgia.

Lin's Quilt Source had a stunning corner display at the October Atlantique City show. Her large display racks held beautiful quilts. I particularly like her colorful tags where she shows a colored photograph of each quilt, fully spread out, so the potential buyer can get an idea of the overall effect of the quilt. Anyone in the market to buy an antique quilt certainly could have found something of investment quality in this booth, where prices ranged from $60 to thousands of dollars for outstanding examples.

While Lin's quilts were reasonably priced and displayed well, her booth was not as busy as those who were selling jewelry or toys. I've noticed a real hesitancy in quilt buyers at auction lately, too. One of the reasons may be that potential buyers are nervous about the reproductions they hear about in this collecting area. Another reason might be that it is almost too easy, and certainly less expensive, to buy a modern quilt to use. Buying antique quilts can be very rewarding, but when lesser quality, slightly damaged, or

soiled quilts make their way to the auction floor, bidders are not paying top dollar. Bidders, however, are snapping up colorful table linens from the 1940s and early 1950s. Many are happily carried home to kitchens where they lend their special charm and an air of nostalgia. Popular decorating magazines are also encouraging this craze, and vintage textiles are being used in almost every room of the house.

Atlantique City show promoter Ted Jones initiated a very popular service to attendees when he started his "free furniture delivery" policy. The dealers who exhibited quality furniture soon found themselves writing sales receipts and explaining how the delivery policy worked. Many customers then went about the rest of the show looking for accessories to compliment their furniture purchases, such as lamps, framed art, or an interesting piece of glass or china. Finding a good rug to balance with antique furniture often leads folks to consider buying an Oriental rug. Like quilts, this particular area has been hurt by mass-produced

Dealer Jeffrey Kohn's booth, named "With All Due Ceremony," featured fine Americana and beautifully displayed flags.

The displays reached new heights this fall at Atlantique City with dealers using the overhead space to beautifully exhibit fine Oriental textiles.

Lin's Quilt Source featured a booth full of vintage quilts. The stunning display was further enhanced by color photographs attached to every quilt, allowing the viewer to see the entire quilt at a glance.

examples and fears of repairs and copies. But the good news for vintage rug buyers, as well as vintage quilt buyers, is that their treasured examples will probably continue to go up in value, just not as fast as someone who might be investing in more trendy objects.

What I probably should be shopping for at the next Atlantique City show, as well as the flea markets, antiques shops, malls, and auctions I frequent, is probably a big crystal ball—then I could gaze deeply into its mysterious aura and discover what will become the next collecting craze.

For the time being, I guess I'll have to settle for inviting you to join me in reading the pages of this edition of *Warman's Antiques and Collectibles Price Guide* where expanded coverage has been devoted to Barbie, Hot Wheels, coins, furniture, jewelry, and textiles. You'll still find the traditional categories, such as cut glass and Wedgwood, and the same attention to detail and accurate pricing you've grown to expect from Warman's. Together, we'll be buyers of those special collectibles that make us smile and feel good to own because, for collectors, it's all about the search and the passion to own beautiful objects.

Time will tell if the Generation X'ers will be interested in decorating their homes and apartments with antiques and collectibles. They might be more than willing to take the cast-offs from Dad's or Grandma's, but how many are going out searching for more? How the antiques and collectibles marketplace learns to attract those buyers will determine how well it moves forward.

At the Atlantique City Antiques Show in March 2002, I was asked by the promoter, Ted Jones, to walk around and see what was offered for sale. Was the merchandise tagged well, were the goods presented in a pleasing manner, etc. While taking this tour, I spoke to many dealers and also shoppers and tried to gauge their reaction. The March show was a real contrast to the October 2001 show held only a few weeks after September 11, where many dealers felt privileged to be able to show their wares and carry on the tradition of a fine antiques show like Atlantique City. Many felt it was time for Americans to start to get on with their lives again, but feared it would take some time for this collective healing to begin.

The October show went well, but was a bit quiet, with collectors somewhat reserved. The attendance at the March 2002 show was enthusiastic and great numbers of collectors came to view the vast array of antiques and collectibles offered. The dedicated collectors were there, scouting with their telephones, pagers, and other electronic devices, hoping to find that wonderful treasure. Many shoppers left clutching objects to add to their collections and were glad for the opportunity to participate in such a lively antiques show experience.

In general, shoppers found a virtual feast of interesting objects. Many dealers sported a spring or patriotic theme to their booths, giving visual appeal and/or decorating insights to the shoppers. Most dealers told me at the end of the show that they had a good experience, while a few were not quite as optimistic and had hoped for more sales. But, that's the usual response and is nothing really new. Where is that crystal ball we're all looking for to see what the future will hold?

What is certain is that the future will brighten and that antiques and collectibles will always remain the intriguing hobby it has been for decades.

This clever sign was spotted at the October Atlantique City show. It says a lot and perhaps it even inspired some children to try to get a bigger allowance!

Dealer Laurel Bailey explains the fine points of an interesting brooch to a shopper.

BOARD OF ADVISERS

John and Alice Ahlfeld
2634 Royal Road
Lancaster, PA 17603
(717) 397-7313
e-mail: AHFELDS@aol.com
Pattern Glass

Bob Armstrong
15 Monadnock Road
Worcester, MA 01609
(508) 799-0644
Puzzles

Susan and Al Bagdade
The Country Peasants
1325 N. State Parkway,
Apt 15A
Chicago, IL 60610
(312) 397-1321
Quimper

Craig Dinner
P.O. Box 4399
Sunnyside, NY 11104
(718) 729-3850
Doorstops

Roselyn Gerson
P.O. Box 100
Malverne, NY 11565
(516) 593-6746
Compacts

Ted Hake
Hake's Americana &
Collectibles Auctions
P.O. Box 1444
York, PA 17405
(717) 848-1333
e-mail: auction@hakes.com
Disneyana, Political

Mary Harris
221 Scarborough Lane
Millersville, PA 17551
(717) 872-8288
e-mail: marymaj@dejazzd.com
Majolica

Tom Hoepf
P.O. Box 90, 27 Jefferson St.
Knightstown, IN 46148
(800) 876-5135
e-mail: antiqueth@aol.com
Cameras

Joan Hull
1376 Nevada
Huron, SD 57350
(605) 352-1685
Hull Pottery

David Irons
Irons Antiques
223 Covered Bridge Road
Northampton, PA 18067
(610) 262-9335
e-mail:
Dave@ironsantiques.com
Irons

Michael Ivankovich
P.O. Box 2458
Doylestown, PA 18901
(215) 345-6094
e-mail: Wnutting@comcat.com
*Wallace Nutting, Wallace
Nutting Look-Alikes*

Dorothy Kamm
P.O. Box 7460
Port St. Lucie, FL 34985-7470
(561) 465-4008
e-mail:
dorothy.kamm@usa.net
*American Hand-Painted
Porcelain, American
Hand-Painted Jewelry*

James D. Kaufman
248 Highland St.
Dedham, MA 2026
(800) 283-8070
Dedham Pottery

W.D. and M. J. Keagy
P.O. Box 106
Bloomfield, IN 47424
(812) 384-3471
Yard-Long Prints

Ellen G. King
King's Antiques
102 N. Main St.
Butler, PA 16001
(724) 894-2596
e-mail: egking@attglobal.net
Flow Blue, Mulberry China

Samuel Kissee
P.O. Box 3762
Chico, CA 95927-2763
e-mail: skissee@cschico.edu
Pattern Glass

Michael Krumme
P.O. Box 48225
Los Angeles, CA 90048-0225
Paden City

Elizabeth M. Kurella
2133 Davis Ave.
Whiting, IN 46396
(219) 659-1124
Lace and Linens

Mel and Roberta Lader
8212 Glyn St.
Alexandria, VA 22309
(703) 360-6078
e-mail: lader@gwu.edu
Pattern Glass

Robert Levy
The Unique One
2802 Centre St.
Pennsauken, NJ 08109
(856) 663-2554
e-mail:
theuniqueone@worldnet.att.net
Coin-Operated Items

Clarence and Betty Maier
The Burmese Cruet
P.O. Box 432
Montgomeryville, PA 18936
(215) 855-5388
e-mail:
burmesecruet@erols.com
*Burmese Glass, Crown
Milano, Royal Flemish*

James S. Maxwell, Jr.
P.O. Box 367
Lampeter, PA 17537
(717) 464-5573
Banks, Mechanical

Bob Perzel
505 Rt. 579
Ringoes, NJ 08551
(908) 782-9361
Stangl Birds

Evalene Pulati
National Valentine Collectors
Assoc.
P.O. Box 1404
Santa Ana, CA 92702
Valentines

John D. Querry
RD 2, Box 137B
Martinsburg, PA 16662
(814) 793-3185
Gaudy Dutch

David Rago
David Rago Auctions, Inc.
333 N. Main St.
Lambertville, NJ 8530
(609) 397-9374
e-mail:
http://www.ragoarts.com
*Art Pottery, Arts & Crafts,
Fulper Grueby, Newcomb*

Charles and Joan Rhoden
8693 N. 1950 East Road
Georgetown, IL 61846-6254
(217) 662-8046
e-mail: rhoden@soltec.net
Yard-Long Prints

Julie P. Robinson
P.O. Box 117
Upper Jay, NY 12987
(518) 946-7753
Celluloid

Jerry Rosen
15 Hampden St.
Swampscott, MA 01907
Piano Babies

Kenneth E. Schneringer
271 Sabrina Ct.
Woodstock, GA 30188
(707) 926-9083
e-mail: trademan68@aol.com
Catalogs

Susan Scott
882 Queen St. West
Toronto, Ontario Canada
M6K 1Q3
e-mail: Susan@collecting
20thcentury.com
Chintz

Judy Smith
1702 Lamont St. NW
Washington, DC 20010-2602
(202) 332-3020
e-mail:
judy@bauble-and-bibebs.com,
judy@quilt.net
Lea Stein Jewelry

George Sparacio
P.O. Box 791
Malaga, NJ 08328-0791
(856) 694-4167
e-mail: mrvesta1@aol.com
Match Safes

Henry A. Taron
Tradewinds Antiques
P.O. Box 249
Manchester By-The-Sea, MA
01944-0249
(978) 526-4085
e-mail:
taron@tradewinds
antiques.com
Canes

George Theofiles
Miscellaneous Man
P.O. Box 1776
New Freedom, PA 17349
(717) 235-4766
Posters

Lewis S. Walters
143 Lincoln Lane
Berlin, NJ 08009
(856) 719-1513
e-mail: lew69@erols.com
Phonographs, Radios

AUCTION HOUSES

The following auction houses cooperate with *Warman's* by providing catalogs of their auctions and price lists. This information is used to prepare *Warman's Antiques and Collectibles Price Guide*, volumes in the Warman's Encyclopedia of Antiques and Collectibles. This support is truly appreciated.

Sanford Alderfer Auction Company
501 Fairgrounds Road
Hatfield, PA 19440
(215) 393-3000
Web site:
http://www.alderfercompany.com

Andre Ammelounx
The Stein Auction Company
P.O. Box 136
Palantine, IL 60078
(847) 991-5927

Arthur Auctioneering
RD 2, P.O. Box 155
Hughesville, PA 17737
(717) 584-3697

Auction Team Köln
Jane Herz
6731 Ashley Court
Sarasota, FL 34241
(941) 925-0385

Auction Team Köln
Postfach 501168 D 5000
Köln 50, W. Germany

Robert F. Batchelder
1 W. Butler Ave.
Ambler, PA 19002
(610) 643-1430

Bear Pen Antiques
2318 Bear Pen Hollow Road
Lock Haven, PA 17745
(717) 769-6655

Bill Bertoia Auctions
1881 Spring Road
Vineland, NJ 08360
(609) 692-1881

Biders Antiques Inc.
241 S. Union St.
Lawrence, MA 01843
(508) 688-4347

Brown Auction & Real Estate
900 East Kansas
Greensburg, KS 67054
(316) 723-2111

Buffalo Bay Auction Co.
5244 Quam Circle
Rogers, MN 55374
(612) 428-8440
Web site: www.buffalobayauction.com

Butterfield, Butterfield & Dunning
755 Church Road
Elgin, IL 60123
(847) 741-3483
Web site: http://www.butterfields.com

Butterfield, Butterfield & Dunning
7601 Sunset Blvd
Los Angeles, CA 90046
(213) 850-7500
Web site: http://www.butterfields.com

Butterfield, Butterfield & Dunning
220 San Bruno Ave.
San Francisco, CA 94103
(415) 861-7500
Web site: http://www.butterfields.com

C. C. Auction Gallery
416 Court
Clay Center, KS 67432
(913) 632-6021

Cerebro
P. O. Box 327
East Prospect, PA 17317
(717) 252-3685

W. E. Channing & Co., Inc.
53 Old Santa Fe Trail
Santa Fe, NM 87501
(505) 988-1078

Chicago Art Galleries
5039 Oakton St.
Skokie, IL 60077
(847) 677-6080

Christie's
502 Park Ave.
New York, NY 10022
(212) 546-1000
Web site: http://www.christies.com

Cincinnati Art Galleries
635 Main St.
Cincinnati, OH 45202
(513) 381-2128
Web site:
http://www.cincinnatiartgalleries.com

Mike Clum, Inc.
P.O. Box 2
Rushville, OH 43150
(614) 536-9220

Cohasco Inc.
Postal 821
Yonkers, NY 10702
(914) 476-8500

Collection Liquidators Auction Service
341 Lafayette St.
New York, NY 10012
(212) 505-2455
Web site:
http://www.rtam.com/coliq/bid.html
e-mail: coliq@erols.com

Collectors Auction Services
RR 2, Box 431 Oakwood Road
Oil City, PA 16301
(814) 677-6070
Web site: http://www.caswel.com

C. Wesley Cowan Historic Americana
673 Wilmer Ave.
Cincinnati, OH 45226
(513)-871-1670
Fax: (513) 871-8670
e-mail: info@HistoricAmericana.com;
wescowan@fuse.net

Decoys Unlimited, Inc.
P.O. Box 206
West Barnstable, MA 02608
(508) 362-2766
http://www.decoysunlimited.inc.com

DeWolfe & Wood
P.O. Box 425
Alfred, ME 04002
(207) 490-5572

Marlin G. Denlinger
RR3, Box 3775
Morrisville, VT 05661
(802) 888-2775

Dixie Sporting Collectibles
1206 Rama Road
Charlotte, NC 28211
(704) 364-2900
Web site: http://www.sportauction.com

Dorothy Dous, Inc.
1261 University Drive
Yardley, PA 19067-2857
(888) 548-6635

William Doyle Galleries, Inc.
175 E. 87th St.
New York, NY 10128
(212) 427-2730
Web site: http://www.doylegalleries.com

Dunbar Gallery
76 Haven St.
Milford, MA 01757
(508) 634-8697

Early Auction Co.
123 Main St.
Milford, OH 45150
(513) 831-4833

Fain & Co.
P.O. Box 1330
Grants Pass, OR 97526
(888) 324-6726

Ken Farmer Realty & Auction Co.
105A Harrison St.
Radford, VA 24141
(703) 639-0939
Web site: http://kenfarmer.com

Fine Tool Journal
27 Fickett Road
Pownal, ME 04069
(207) 688-4962
Web site: http://www.
wowpages.com/FTJ/

Steve Finer Rare Books
P.O. Box 758
Greenfield, MA 01302
(413) 773-5811

Flomaton Antique Auction
P.O. Box 1017
320 Palafox St.
Flomaton, AL 36441
(334) 296-3059

Fontaine's Auction Gallery
1485 W. Housatonic St.
Pittsfield, MA 01201
(413) 488-8922

Freeman\Fine Arts Co. of Philadelphia, Inc.
1808 Chestnut St.
Philadelphia, PA 19103
(215) 563-9275

Garth's Auction, Inc.
2690 Stratford Road
P.O. Box 369
Delaware, OH 43015
(740) 362-4771

Greenberg Auctions
7566 Main St.
Skysville, MD 21784
(410) 795-7447

Green Valley Auction Inc.
Route 2, Box 434
Mt. Crawford, VA 22841
(540) 434-4260

Hake's Americana & Collectibles
P.O. Box 1444
York, PA 17405
(717) 848-1333

Gene Harris Antique Auction Center, Inc.
203 South 18th Ave.
P.O. Box 476
Marshalltown, IA 50158
(515) 752-0600
Web site: www.harrisantiqueauction.com

Norman C. Heckler & Company
Bradford Corner Road
Woodstock Valley, CT 06282
(203) 974-1634

High Noon
9929 Venice Blvd
Los Angeles, CA 90034
(310) 202-9010
Web site: www.High Noon.com

Randy Inman Auctions, Inc.
P.O. Box 726
Waterville, ME 04903
(207) 872-6900
Web site: www.inmanauctions.com

Michael Ivankovich Auction Co.
P.O. Box 2458
Doylestown, PA 18901
(215) 345-6094
Web site: http://www.nutting.com

Jackson's Auctioneers & Appraisers
2229 Lincoln St.
Cedar Falls, IA 50613
(319) 277-2256
Web site: http://www.jacksonauction.com

James D. Julia Inc.
Rt. 201 Skowhegan Road
P.O. Box 830
Fairfield, ME 04937
(207) 453-7125
Web site: www.juliaauctions.com

J. W. Auction Co.
54 Rochester Hill Road
Rochester, NH 03867
(603) 332-0192

Gary Kirsner Auctions
P.O. Box 8807
Coral Springs, FL 33075
(954) 344-9856
Web site: www.garykirsnerauctions.com

Lang's Sporting Collectables, Inc.
31 R Turthle Cove
Raymond, ME 04071
(207) 655-4265

Joy Luke
The Gallery
300 E. Grove St.
Bloomington, IL 61701
(309) 828-5533
Web site: http://www.joyluke.com

Mapes Auctioneers & Appraisers
1729 Vestal Pkwy
Vestal, NY 13850
(607) 754-9193

Martin Auctioneers Inc.
P.O. Box 477
Intercourse, PA 17534
(717) 768-8108

McMasters Harris Doll Auctions
P.O. Box 1755
Cambridge, OH 43725
(614) 432-4419

Gary Metz's Muddy River Trading Company
P.O. Box 1430
Salem, VA 24135
(540) 387-5070

William Frost Mobley
P.O. Box 10
Schoharie, NY 12157
(518) 295-7978

William Morford
RD #2
Cazenovia, NY 13035
(315) 662-7625

Neal Auction Company
4038 Magazine St.
New Orleans, LA 7015
(504) 899-5329
Web site: http://www.nealauction.com

New Orleans Auction St. Charles Auction Gallery, Inc.
1330 St. Charles Ave.
New Orleans, LA 70130
(504) 586-8733
Web site:
http://www.neworleansauction.com

New Hampshire Book Auctions
P.O. Box 460
92 Woodbury Road
Weare, NH 03281
(603) 529-7432

Norton Auctioneers of Michigan Inc.
50 West Pearl at Monroe
Coldwater, MI 49036
(517) 279-9063

Old Barn Auction
10040 St. Rt. 224 West
Findlay, OH 45840
(419) 422-8531
Web site: http://www.oldbarn.com

Richard Opfer Auctioneering Inc.
1919 Greenspring Drive
Timonium, MD 21093
(410) 252-5035
Web site: www.opferauction.com

Pacific Glass Auctions
1507 21st St., Suite 203
Sacramento, CA 95814
1-800-806-7722
Web site: http://www.pacglass.com

Past Tyme Pleasures
PMB #204, 2491 San Ramon Valley Blvd, #1
San Ramon, CA 94583
(925) 484-6442
Fax: (925) 484-2551
Web site: http://www.pastyme.com
e-mail: Pasttyme@excite.com

Postcards International
2321 Whitney Ave., Suite 102
P.O. Box 5398
Hamden, CT 06518
(203) 248-6621
Web site:
http://www.csmonline.com/postcardsint/

Poster Auctions International
601 W. 26th St.
New York, NY 10001
(212) 787-4000
Web site: www.posterauction.com

Profitt Auction Company
684 Middlebrook Road
Staunton, VA 24401
(540) 885-7369

David Rago Auctions, Inc.
333 S. Main St.
Lambertville, NJ 08530
(609) 397-9374
Web site: http://www.ragoarts.com

Lloyd Ralston Toy Auction
350 Long Beach Blvd
Stratford, CT 06615
(203) 375-9399
Web site: www.lloydralstontoys.com

James J. Reeves
P.O. Box 219
Huntingdon, PA 16652-0219
(814) 643-5497
Web site: www.JamesJReeves.com

Mickey Reichel Auctioneer
1440 Ashley Road
Boonville, MO 65233
(816) 882-5292

Sandy Rosnick Auctions
15 Front St.
Salem, MA 01970
(508) 741-1130

Seeck Auctions
P.O. Box 377
Mason City, IA 50402
(515) 424-1116
Web site:
www.willowtree.com/~seeckauctions

L. H. Selman Ltd
761 Chestnut St.
Santa Cruz, CA 95060
(408) 427-1177
Web site: http://www.selman.com

Skinner Inc.
Bolton Gallery
357 Main St.
Bolton, MA 01740
(978) 779-6241
Web site: http://www.skinnerinc.com

Skinner, Inc.
The Heritage on the Garden
63 Park Plaza
Boston, MA 02116
(978) 350-5429
Web site: http://www.skinnerinc.com

C. G. Sloan & Company Inc.
4920 Wyaconda Road
North Bethesda, MD 20852
(301) 468-4911
Web site: http://www.cgsloan.com

Smith & Jones, Inc., Auctions
12 Clark Lane
Sudbury, MA 01776
(508) 443-5517

Sotheby's
1334 York Ave.
New York, NY 10021
(212) 606-7000
Web site: http://www.sothebys.com

Southern Folk Pottery Collectors Society
220 Washington St.
Bennett, NC 27208
(336) 581-4246

Stanton's Auctioneers
P.O. Box 146
144 South Main St.
Vermontville, MI 49096
(517) 726-0181

Michael Strawser
200 N. Main St., P.O. Box 332
Wolcottville, IN 46795
(219) 854-2859
Web site: www.majolicaauctions.com

Swann Galleries Inc.
104 E. 25th St.
New York, NY 10010
(212) 254-4710
Web site: www.swanngalleries.com

Swartz Auction Services
2404 N. Mattis Ave.
Champaign, IL 61826-7166
(217) 357-0197
Web site: http://www/SwartzAuction.com

The House In The Woods
S91 W37851 Antique Lane
Eagle, WI 53119
(414) 594-2334

Theriault's
P.O. Box 151
Annapolis, MD 21401
(301) 224-3655
Web site: http://www.theriaults.com

Treadway Gallery, Inc.
2029 Madison Road
Cincinnati, OH 45208
(513) 321-6742
Web site:
http://www.a3c2net.com/treadwaygallery

Victorian Images
P.O. Box 284
Marlton, NJ 08053
(609) 985-7711
Web site: www.tradecards.com/vi

Bruce and Vicki Waasdorp
P.O. Box 434
10931 Main St.
Clarence, NY 14031
(716) 759-2361
Web site:
http://www.antiques-stoneware.com

Winter Associates
21 Cooke St. Box 823
Plainville, CT 06062
(203) 793-0288

Woody Auction
Douglass, KS 67039
(316) 746-2694

York Town Auction, Inc.
1625 Haviland Road
York, PA 17404
(717) 751-0211
e-mail: yorktownauction@cyberia.com

ABBREVIATIONS

The following are standard abbreviations, which we have used throughout this edition of *Warman's*.

ABP = American Brilliant Period

ADS = Autograph Document Signed

adv = advertising

ah = applied handle

ALS = Autograph Letter Signed

AQS = Autograph Quotation Signed

C = century

c = circa

Cal. = caliber

circ = circular

cyl. = cylinder

cov = cover

CS = Card Signed

d = diameter or depth

dec = decorated

dj = dust jacket

DQ = Diamond Quilted

DS = Document Signed

ed = edition

emb = embossed

ext. = exterior

eyep. = eyepiece

Folio = 12" x 16"

ftd = footed

ga = gauge

gal = gallon

ground = background

h = height

horiz. = horizontal

hp = hand painted

hs = high standard

illus = illustrated, illustration

imp = impressed

int. = interior

irid = iridescent

IVT = inverted thumbprint

j = jewels

K = karat

l = length

lb = pound

litho = lithograph

ll = lower left

lr = lower right

ls = low standard

LS = Letter Signed

mfg = manufactured

MIB = mint in box

MOP = mother-of-pearl

n/c = no closure

ND = no date

NE = New England

No. = number

NRFB = never removed from box

ns = no stopper

r/c = reproduction closure

o/c = original closure

opal = opalescent

orig = original

os = orig stopper

oz = ounce

pcs = pieces

pgs = pages

PUG = printed under the glaze

pr = pair

PS = Photograph Signed

pt = pint

qt = quart

RM = red mark

rect = rectangular

sgd = signed

S. N. = Serial Number

SP = silver plated

SS = Sterling silver

sq = square

TLS = Typed Letter Signed

unp = unpaged

vert. = vertical

vol = volume

w = width

yg = yellow gold

= numbered

Grading Condition

The following numbers represent the standard grading system used by dealers, collectors, and auctioneers:

C.10 = Mint
C. 9 = Near mint
C.8.5 = Outstanding
C.8 = Excellent
C.7.5 = Fine +
C.7 = Fine
C. 6.5 = Fine – (good)
C. 6 = Poor

ABC PLATES

History: The majority of early ABC plates were manufactured in England and imported into the United States. They achieved their greatest popularity from 1780 to 1860. Since a formal education was uncommon in the early 19th century, the ABC plate was a method of educating the poor for a few pennies.

ABC plates were made of glass, pewter, porcelain, pottery, or tin. Porcelain plates range in diameter from 4-3/8 inches to slightly more than 9-1/2 inches. The rim usually contains the alphabet and/or numbers; the center features animals, great men, maxims, or nursery rhymes.

For more information, see these books.

Glass

Christmas Eve, Santa on chimney, colorless, 6" d **75.00**
Clock face center, Arabic and Roman numerals, alphabet center, colorless and frosted, 7" d **75.00**
Elephant with howdah, three waving Brownies, Ripley & Co., colorless, 6" d **135.00**
Little Bo Peep, center scene, raised alphabet border, colorless, 6" d . .**50.00**
Plain center, white scalloped edge, colorless, 6" d **65.00**
Young Girl, portrait, colorless, 6" d
. . . .**65.00**

Maxim ware, ABC border, boy at open gate, 5-1/4" d, **$185.**

Pottery or porcelain

Aesop's Fables the Leopard and the Fox, black transfer print, pearlware, England, 19th C. **175.00**
Crusoe Finding the Foot Prints, color-enhanced brown transfer, pearlware, England, 19th C, minor discoloration **125.00**
Eye of the master will do no more than his hands, multicolored transfer **145.00**
Federal Generals, black transfer print, pearlware, England, 19th C. . . .**175.00**
Franklin's Provbs, (sic) black transfer print, pearlware, England, 19th C
. . . .**175.00**
Horses for Hire or Sale, brown transfer and polychrome dec, 6-3/4" d . .**145.00**
Old Mother Hubbard, brown transfer, polychrome enamel trim, alphabet border, marked "Tunstall," 7-1/2" d **200.00**

White, embossed alphabet on rims, decal center of organ grinder and children, **$165.**

Robinson Crusoe, multicolored transfer, maroon line. **95.00**
Take Your Time Miss Lucy, black transfer of money and cat, polychrome enamel, titled, molded hops rim, red trim, ironstone, imp "Meakin," 6" d **125.00**
Teach thy dog to be polite, multicolored transfer. **125.00**
Twelve year olds obey their mother, multicolored transfer **145.00**

Tin

George Washington profile, rust spot, minor wear, 6-1/8" d **200.00**
Girl on swing, lithographed center, printed alphabet border, 3-1/2" d
. . . .**60.00**
Two kittens playing with basket of wood, 4-1/2" d. **80.00**
Who Killed Cock Robin, 7-3/4" d
. . . .**120.00**

Staffordshire, embossed alphabet on rims, polychrome printed transfer decoration, pearlware bodies, 5-1/4" d plate impressed "Meakin," 5-1/2" d plate unmarked, with staining and hairline, **$195.** *Photo courtesy of Cowan's Historic Americana Auctions.*

White, embossed alphabet on rims highlighted in green, multicolored center with children watching Punch and Judy show, **$195.**

ADVERTISING

History: Before the days of mass media, advertisers relied on colorful product labels and advertising giveaways to promote their products. Containers were made to appeal to the buyer through the use of stylish lithographs and bright colors. Many of the illustrations used the product in the advertisement so that even an illiterate buyer could identify a product.

Advertisements were put on almost every household object imaginable and constant reminders to use the product or visit a certain establishment.

Additional Listings: See *Warman's Americana & Collectibles* for more examples.

For more information, see these books.

Coffee tins, *"Fairy Dell"* and *"Oakford & Fahnestock, Peoria, Illinois,"* each four pounds, each valued at **$125**; 19 advertising tins and packages, including two Bergner's Soap Flakes boxes, Clabber Girl Baking Powder tin, Packer's Tar Soap and World's Fair Toothpicks, averaging **$15-$25 each**; advertising tin *"Sweet Mist Chewing Tobacco, Manufactured by Scotten Dillon Company, Detroit, Mich,"* **$250**; two peanut butter advertising pails with bail handles, Sultana and Frontenag, each valued at **$65**; coffee advertising tin *"Old Southern Coffee, Net Weight One Pound, Larkin Co. Inc., Buffalo, N.Y.,"* **$75**. *Photo courtesy of Joy Luke Auctions.*

Grading Condition. The following numbers represent the standard grading system used by dealers, collectors, and auctioneers:

> **C.10 = Mint**
> **C. 9 = Near mint**
> **C.8.5 = Outstanding**
> **C.8 = Excellent**
> **C.7.5 = Fine +**
> **C.7 = Fine**
> **C. 6.5 = Fine – (good)**
> **C. 6 = Poor**

Ashtray, Buster Brown, glazed china, figural hat, Buster gesturing towards Tige balancing steaming teapot on nose, 4-7/8" l, 1" h **165.00**

Blotter, unused

Eppens, Smith Co., NY, Coffee and Tea Importer, 1900 seasonal greetings, full-color celluloid, slight use **15.00**

Fairbanks Portable Pumping Outfit, graphics of metal vehicle, road paving machinery, 7-1/4" x 9-1/2" **10.00**

Booklet, Dutch Boy Paint, 20 pgs, 5" x 6" **12.00**

Bookmark, Rally Day, diecut celluloid, Spirit of '76 fife and drummers, large American flag, string tassel, early 1900s **25.00**

Calendar, Red Goose Shoes, 1924, colorful print of mountain goat hunter titled "Getting His Goat," H. C. Edwards, artist, ads for Red Goose Shoes, Friedman-Shelby Shoe Col, Atlantic Shoes, Pacific Shoes, 8" x 19" wall type **25.00**

Candy pail, Novia Kiddie Pops, pail shape, image of pops and children and dog on both sides, 3-3/4" d, 3-1/4" h, C.7.5+ **675.00**

Card game, Going to Market, 1" x 2-3/4" x 3-3/4" boxed game, copyright 1915, 52 illus cards, black and white art of elderly lady plus children headed to market, ads for Pompeian complexion creams, Kelly-Springfield tires, Willys-Overland cars, Post cereals, Welch fruit drinks, Beech-nut food and candy, Knox gelatins, Libby's canned foods, Western Electric appliances and

*Crumb tray, "Use Eagle Lye – Purest & Best – Milwaukee, Wis.," painted tin, **$165**. Photo courtesy of Joy Luke Auctions.*

telephone, Perfection heaters, Ingersoll pocket watches, Walk-Over shoes, Sherwin-Williams paints, local sponsor George E. Keith Co., Walk-Over shoes, hinged box **48.00**

Clicker

Motorcycle Boy, litho tin, youngster in yellow motorcycling outfit with goggles and neckerchief, riding red cycle, holding ice cream cone in one hand, 1930s **25.00**

Poll-Parrot Shoes, litho tin, red, yellow, blue parrot, yellow background, red lettering, 1930s **25.00**

*Coffee tin, Campbell "Bloomington, Illinois," four pounds, **$100**. Photo courtesy of Joy Luke Auctions.*

Fan, Rome, NY, store, diecut thin cardboard, wooden handle, colorful art image on front of boy, long blond hair, plumed hat, chest plate with crest, surrounded by low relief red flowers and green leaves, blue lettered text on back promotes store and "The Fashion," 1890s, 9-1/4" w, $45. Photo courtesy of Hake's Americana & Collectibles.

Twinkie Shoes, litho tin, full-color art of elf character standing on mushroom, dark green background, tiny inscription for "Hamilton-Brown Shoes Co.," 1930s. **30.00**

Dye cabinet, Putnam, tin litho lid with General Putnam, 36 divided compartments, c1920, 19" x 14" **200.00**

Fan

Bradley Knit Wear, 7" x 8" cardboard mounted on wooden 5-1/2" l handle, colorful art pictures for swimsuits for young adult female and male bathers, reverse with customer service text by merchant, late 1920s **30.00**

Qualtop Beverage, 7-1/2" x 10" diecut cardboard photo image of young lady in sepia, flesh tone tint on face and body, orange tint on headband, reverse "Tell The Boy To Serve You A Cold Bottle Of Qualtop-Any Flavor Has Real Food Value-Refreshing-Nourishing-A Rochester Product," back with publisher Geiger Bros., Newark, NY, 1920s **35.00**

The Valley of Fair Play, 9-1/2" x 10-1/2" w diecut cardboard, red on white, half-circle aerial black and white photo view of shoe manuf company, center flesh tone portrait of young man "The Smiling Worker and a cast of 17,000 people," black and white text on back for shoe tanneries and factories, Feb. 1923 patent date **20.00**

Gauge

Standard Roller Bearing Co., 3" x 3" celluloid covers, diecut openings, inner disk wheels to use in determining precise measurements, requirements, etc. for ball bearings, c1920 . . . . **20.00**

Sunkist, pr of 3-1/2" d celluloid disks joined by center grommet, each side with diecut vertical slot opening, disk wheels turn to determine grocer's cost and profit margins for CA orange on one side, CA lemons on other, red and black lettering. **20.00**

Gum tin, Frozen Mints, hinged, satin pebbly finish litho, 1-3/8" x 4" x 2-5/8", C.8. . . . . **150.00**

Gum wrapper, Pulver's Yellow Kid Chewing Gum, paper litho, 15/16" x 2-3/4" **160.00**

Mixing bowl, "Monmouth Savings & Loan Assoc – It Pays to Mix with Us," Western Stoneware, Monmouth, 9" d, 4-3/4" h, $175. Photo courtesy of Joy Luke Auctions.

Lamp shade, Eat L. V. Orsinger's Ice Cream, red, two white opaque glass panels, metal frame, six colored jewels, 6" h **750.00**

Lapel stud

Alaska Stove Trimmings, brown and white celluloid, metal lapel stud fastener, stove lid lifter illus, plus inscription "Mama! Do You Use Alaska Stove Trimmings-Always Cold" **20.00**

Widow Jones Suits Me, 1-1/4", multicolored celluloid on metal, young lady in stylish gray outfit and hat, pale blue to white background, blue lettering, New England clothing store sponsor **40.00**

Match holder

Buster Brown Bread, tin litho, children at table **290.00**

Universal Stove Co., tin litho . . **85.00**

Match safe, Advance Farm Equipment, silvered brass, hinged, celluloid wrapper print in color, one side with medieval figure raising Advance banner on rocky height, opposite side with "Simple Traction Engine," two smaller panels each with lists of offices by city, early 1900s **115.00**

Paperweight mirror, 3-1/2" celluloid on weighted metal, underside mirror insert

C.P.A. Services, brown rim inscribed in white for Indianapolis firm, two officers pictured by inset sepia photos with names, tinted sepia real downtown photo in center, 1920s **30.00**

D. M. Distillery, tinted celluloid, crisp real photo of "Warehouses and Straight American in Yard at D. M. Distillery Juarez, Mexico," names of two distillery officials, ring of whiskey barrels on front, 1920s **40.00**

Paperweights, left: J. R. Leeson & Co., Boston, rectangular, white opaque base, spinning wheel scene, patent date 1882 stamped on back, 4", $35; center: White, Warner & Co., Taunton, Mass, rectangular, white opaque base with scene of two men leaning on stove, 4", $25; right: M. M. Rhodes & Sons Co., Papier Mâché, Buttons, Shoes, rectangular, white opaque base with German cross medallion in center, 4", $40. Photo courtesy of Woody Auctions.

Rossite, can of drain pipe cleansing compound, 1930s **35.00**

Whitewater Flour Mills, tinted sepia scene of Niagara Falls, brown rim lettered in white "Whitewaters, Kansas," 1920s **35.00**

Pencil clip

Ardee Flour, red, yellow, blue logo, celluloid on brass wire clip, Hubbard Milling Co., Mankato, Minn, sponsor, early 1900s . **25.00**

Red Man Cigar Leaf, multicolored, tobacco pack mounted on brass wire spring clip, early 1900s **55.00**

The Metropolitan, black, white, and red celluloid, mounted on brass wire spring clip, sponsor store designates "Hats" and "Furnishings" **20.00**

Pinback button

Clean Shirts of America, red, white, and blue graphic of army of starched shirts marching across North America on world globe, 1920s **20.00**

Davis OK Baking Powder, multicolored, bottle flanked by slogans, black lettering, back paper, c1896 . . . . **20.00**

Empire Cream Separator, black and white image, blue letters, rim inscription "I Chirp for the Empire because it makes the most dollars for me," clicker hanging from bottom rim **50.00**

Farm Boy Bread, red, white, and blue, center bluetone photo of young farm lad posed next to cow and rooster, blue and red lettering, 1930s **15.00**

Hessler Rural Mailbox, illus of sample mailbox, "Approved By Postmaster General" **75.00**

Kar-A-Van Coffee, multicolored, loaded camel, early 1900s . . **20.00**

Lekko Scouring Powder, multicolored, image of product canister, and housewife on knees scrubbing floor, 1920s **35.00**

Mephisto Auger Bits, black and red lettering, white ground **15.00**

Metzer's Milk Infant Keeps Them Smiling, 1" d, tinted fleshtone face, white background, blue and red lettering, c1930 . . . . **12.00**

O.I.C. Hogs, black and white art and inscription, patriotic red, white, blue, and silver outer rim, back paper with lengthy text for "Famous O.I.C. Hogs," c1900 . . . . **50.00**

Orange Crush, black, white, and orange, character squeezing orange juice, 1930s **15.00**

Stetson Hats Best in the World, multicolored logo, celluloid, oval **12.00**

Vote Betty Crocker, red, white, and blue litho, c1960 . . . . **12.00**

Widow Hoffman System-Boys Clothing-Harris Clothing Co., Baltimore, black and white celluloid, young lad in cap and jacket **15.00**

Wilbur's Cocoa, multicolored, cherub trademark stirring Wilbur mug, orig back paper, c1896 . . . . **20.00**

Pocket mirror

California Wine House, full color, tinted portraits of young lady garbed in sheer pale blue bodice, gold lettering **40.00**

Continental Cubes Pipe Tobacco, multicolored, graphic art of young lady in rich red gown, matching hat and gloves, winning cards in hand while seated on product can, briar pipe wafts smoke in foreground, rim curl inscribed "American Tobacco Co." **125.00**

Dr Winters Dentists, rect acetate over brown paper ad for dental services and fixtures **65.00**

Gail Borden Canned Milk, blue on white ground, image of can "Eagle Brand Borden's Condensed Milk," name and facsimile signature of founder Gail Borden, also inscribed "Best For The Nursery-And General Household Purposes" **50.00**

Garland Stoves and Ranges, red on ivory white design, "Largest Makers of Stoves In The World" **45.00**

Harvard Pure Beer, 1-3/4" l, celluloid, inscribed in crimson red and black, "America's Health Beverage" **35.00**

Horlick's Malted Milk, multicolored, gold rim, blue lettering, inscription "The Diet For Infants, Invalids And Nursing Mothers," inscription on side of brown cow "Ask For Horlick's At All Druggists" . . **60.00**

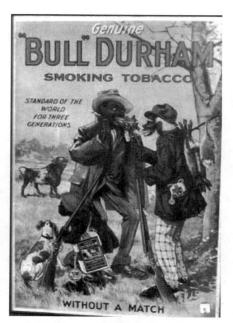

Print, titled "Without a Match," Bull Durham Smoking Tobacco, two African American gentlemen and young boy holding rifles, bull in background, framed, 27-1/2" x 19", **$75.** Photo courtesy of Joy Luke Auctions.

Plate, Compliments, D. S. Harr, Sellersville, PA, green border with gold trim, pretty girl in center, **$65.** Photo courtesy of Ron Rhoades Auctions.

Plate, "Clarke's Pure Rye – Bottled by the Government," decorated with figure of man holding medicine bottle, earthenware, 11" d, **$50.** Photo courtesy of Joy Luke Auctions.

Preserve jar, stoneware, three gallons, impressed "Crawfords & Murdock, Dealers in Dry Goods Groceries, Clothing, Crockery & Hardware, Pulaskie, NY," cobalt blue accent at store mark and script "3" surrounded by brushed plumes, c1875, professional repair to rim, 12-1/2" h, $385. Photo courtesy of Vicki and Bruce Waasdorp.

J. I. Case, multicolored trademark symbol of eagle poised on world glove, red lettering "J. I. Case Threshing Machine Co. Inc., Racine, Wis, U.S.A." **95.00**

Krug Cigars, black and white, photo portrait of cigar maker, sponsor "Sport's Cigar & Confectionery Store, Cohockton, NY"...... **65.00**

Salesman's sample, washing machine and ringer; washer stenciled "The Green Valley Novelty Co.," wringer marked "Gem No. 2, American Wringer Company, New York," 19-1/2" w, $375. Photo courtesy of Joy Luke Auctions.

Margolia Pure Ceylon Tea, diecut thin celluloid covers sandwich celluloid rimmed double-sided mirror, one side with multicolored illus of "Mardi-Gras Coffee" on white, black lettering, multicolored image of tea on reverse with black lettering "Everybody's Drinking It," American Artworks, Ohio, maker **65.00**

Minnehaha, multicolored scenic view of wooded waterfall, foreground wooden bridge, red rim, white lettering **60.00**

New King Snuff, celluloid rect, multicolored image of New King variety of Scotch-King tobacco snuff, red and black lettering on tan bar, margin reads "Good Snuff Packed Tight Keeps Right" . **85.00**

Paris Millinery Shop, multicolored image of lady posed in red evening gown, black background, gold lettering **45.00**

Pennisular Stove Co., blue and white, bluetone picture of cast iron cooking stove........... **65.00**

Queen Quality Shoes, black and white queen posed on interior steps.................. **95.00**

Twin City Barber College, dark brown celluloid, center sepia real photo of "Prof. Gilsdorf-The Man Who Has Successfully Taught The Barber Trade To Thousands of Men and Women"............ **45.00**

Ward Safety Razor, brown celluloid, sepia real photo of man demonstrating razor "The Only Safety Razor With The Natural Sliding Stroke And Thin Concave Blades"................ **65.00**

White House Coffee, blue and white illus of package, red rim, white letters **40.00**

Print, 30" x 15", Falls City Clothing Co., Imperial Clothes, Louisville, Ky, titled *Elsie*, sgd B. Tichman, woman in red duster and bonnet, printed by Meek Co., Coshocton, OH, copyright 1908, framed **235.00**

Sign

Atlas Cement, heavy porcelain enamel, cement bag design in center, 14-3/4" x 10" **550.00**

Beauty Shoppe, porcelain, lightly emb lettering and oval portrait of woman, 9" x 18", C.8+ **375.00**

Sign, Bull Durham, Genuine Bull Durham Smoking Tobacco, Prize Winners, litho tin disc, panoramic farm scene, original gessoed frame and black wood shadow box, 36" square, some scattered small rust spots, slight overall fading to lithography, $3,565. Photo courtesy of James D. Julia, Inc.

Carnation Fresh Milk, porcelain, red and white, center milk bottle, 15" x 14-1/4", C.8 .... **600.00**

Cherry Blush, Cherries Only Rival, beveled tin over cardboard, dark background, 6-1/2" x 9-1/4", C.8+ **550.00**

Eddie's Everlasting Black Dye, diecut hanger, lightly emb tin litho, E-Jay-R Mfg Co., Baltimore, illus of products, c1920, 6-1/2" x 8-1/2" **70.00**

Eureka Vacuum Cleaners, litho beveled tin over cardboard, detailed interior image with lady using cleaner, blue background, 19" x 13", C.8.5+ **1,100.00**

Franklin Mills, Lockport, NY, diecut cardboard, easel back, little girl holding boxes of Wheatlet Cereal and Franklin Flour, 4-3/4" w, 9" h, C.8.5+ **250.00**

Gilt Edge Best Ruhstaller Beer Lager, made by Bacharach & Co, San Francisco, c1900, round, two-sided, electrical, three color glass, metal edging **5,500.00**

"McBurney's For Dry Goods, Carpets and Cloaks, Tipton, Iowa,"

Sign, Hi-Plane Tobacco, metal, 35-1/2" l, 11-1/2" h, $90. Photo courtesy of Joy Luke Auctions.

painted wood, black painted panels, white lettering, 36" x 48", wear **590.00**

Pure Milk for Babies Milk Station of the Visiting Nurse Assoc, two sided, painted wood, white lettering, blue asphaltum ground, white and light blue border, black frame, minor paint losses on frame, 18" **940.00**

Red Goose Shoes, light-up neon, diecut porcelain back, 24" x 12" x 5" **2,100.00**

Ronson Table Lighters, molded hard plastic, 1" recess to hold lighter, 1950s, 7" x 8" **20.00**

Shield Lighters, rigid cardboard easel, holding 12 identical gold luster finish metal lighters, c1950, 9-1/2" x 12-1/2" **60.00**

Snow Drift Fancy Patent Flour, Imperial Enamel Co., NY, heavy porcelain, two-sided 1940s, 15" x 18" **30.00**

Eddie's Everlasting Black Dye, diecut hanger, lightly emb tin litho, E-Jay-R Mfg Co., Baltimore, illus of products, c1920, 6-1/2" x 8-1/2" **70.00**

Eureka Vacuum Cleaners, litho beveled tin over cardboard, detailed interior image with lady using cleaner, blue background, 19" x 13", C.8.5+ **1,100.00**

Franklin Mills, Lockport, NY, diecut cardboard, easel back, little girl holding boxes of Wheatlet Cereal and Franklin Flour, 4-3/4" w, 9" h, C.8.5+ **250.00**

Hudepohl Brewery, Cincinnati, tin litho, self framed, 19-1/4" x 15-1/4", C.8+ **275.00**

Kellogg's Corn Flakes with Bananas, cardboard stand-up, easel back, 30" x 20", C.8+ **275.00**

Mayo's Plug, Smoking Cock O' The Walk, porcelain, large color image of crowing rooster, 6-1/2" w, 13" h **1,250.00**

Phez Loganberry Juice, litho tin, c1920, 9" x 6-1/2" **575.00**

Red Goose Shoes, light-up neon, diecut porcelain back, 24" x 12" x 5" **2,100.00**

Shield Lighters, rigid cardboard easel, holding 12 identical gold luster finish metal lighters, c1950, 9-1/2" x 12-1/2" **60.00**

Snow Drift Fancy Patent Flour, Imperial Enamel Co., NY, heavy porcelain, two-sided, 1940s, 15" x 18" **30.00**

Sign, Sweet-Orr Overalls, porcelain, trademark tug-of-war silhouette in red flanked by blue lettering against yellow ground, 72-1/2" l x 28-3/4" h, wood frame, $460. Photo courtesy of James D. Julia, Inc.

Stone Hill Wine, litho tin, allegory of white, nude woman titled "Autumn," molded wood grain self framed border printed "Compliments of Stone Hill Wine Co., Hermann, MO, U.S.A.," c1910 . . . . **635.00**

Sunoco Motor Oil, porcelain, yellow ground, black letters, C.8- . **350.00**

Waterman's Fountain Pen, porcelain, orig wood frame, dark blue, white lettering, 30" l, 8" h **300.00**

Wings Cigarettes, high gloss paper, model in negligee glamour pose, c1940, 12" x 18", some archival tape repairs on back **70.00**

Wrigley's Double Mint Gum, litho tin, red ground, c1930, 13" x 6" **865.00**

Yeast Foam Is The Best, We Sell Only the Best Goods, heavy porcelain, white lettering, blue ground, 20" l, 4-1/4" h, C.8+ **425.00**

Spinner top

Hurd Shoes, black and white celluloid, wooden red spinner dowel, Parisian Novelty Co., maker name on rim curl, 1930s **20.00**

Poll-Parrot Shoes, litho tin, wooden spinner dowel, red and yellow parrot striding between black shoes, yellow background, red rim, red star logo, 1930s **25.00**

Store bin, Sure Shot Chewing Tobacco, Indian with bow and arrow on front and back panels, 15-1/4" w x 10-1/4" d, 8" h, some scratches, scuffs, and mild dents, $490. Photo courtesy of James D. Julia, Inc.

Woodmen of the World, blue lettering on white celluloid, wooden red spinner dowel, Parisian Novelty Co., maker name on rim curl, 1930s **18.00**

Store mannequin, 42-1/2" h, boy, polychrome painted composition, America, late 19th C, wear . . . **2,960.00**

Tape measure

Fox's Guernsey Dairy, black lettering on yellow ground, red rim, four red carnations on black ground on reverse **25.00**

Sears, Roebuck & Co., white lettering, black ground, lightning bolt-style lettering for "WLS" (World's Largest Store) red, white, blue, and green stylized floral design on back **15.00**

Thermometer

Pepsi, metal, oversize dot logo bottle, c1930, 15-3/8" x 6-1/4" x 3/4", C.8+ **525.00**

White House Coffee, wooden, white ground, black image of man drinking coffee, 4" w, 15" h, light overall wear, C.8- **275.00**

Tin, miscellaneous, tin litho

Donald Duck Pop Corn, Disney cartoon characters on both sides, unopened, 2-7/8" w, 4-7/8" h, C.7.5+ **300.00**

Imperial Shaving Stick, Talcum Puff Co., New York, image of man lathering face, 3-3/8" l, C.8+ **325.00**

Professor Searele's Veterinary Blood Purifier Medicinal, Sommers Bros.,

Thermometer, Dr. Pepper, metal, 25-1/2" h, some paint worn, $90. Photo courtesy of Joy Luke Auctions.

Trade sign, jeweler's watch, painted iron and zinc, America, 19th C, double-sided, gilded cast iron ring, winder, and bezel, painted zinc face with black numerals and "A. J. ROBINSON" on cream-colored ground, wear, a couple of cracks, dents, a few bullet holes, 16" d, 23" h, **$550.** *Photo courtesy of Skinner Auctioneers and Appraisers.*

litho of barnyard animals, 3-1/4" x 2-7/8" x 1-3/4", C.8.5+ **450.00**
Spencerian Pen Points, litho tin, sliding lid, steel pen tips, yellow printed in red and black on lid with tiger head logo, ad text on underside, early 1900s **20.00**
Velvet Tread Foot Powder, green, black, and brown, winged foot and giant winged insect, 4-3/4" x 2-1/4" x 1-3/8", C.8 . . . . **400.00**

Tobacco bin, Game Cut Tobacco, Jon Babley Co., held forty-eight 5 cent packs of tobacco, litho on tin, 11-1/2" w, 7-3/4" d, 7" h **850.00**

Tobacco can, tin litho
Dixie Kid Cut Plug, Nall & Williams, lunch pail type, white kid, 7-3/4" l, 5-1/4" d, 3-3/4" h, C.8.5+ . **1,600.00**
Mayo's Inspector, roly poly, 7" x 5-1/4", C.8+ **1,450.00**
U. S. Marine, lunch pail type, colorful graphics on four sides, 4-3/4" x 7-3/8" x 4-3/8", C.8.5 . . . . . **525.00**

Tobacco tin, pocket, tin litho
Charm of the West, Spaulding & Merrick, horizontal, graphics on both sides, 2-3/8" x 3-3/4" x 5/8" **300.00**
Ensign Perfection Cut Tobacco, vertical, Missouri flag on back, 4-1/2" x 3" x 7/8", C.8+, minor wear, litho chip on back **900.00**

Forest and Stream, Canadian, vertical, 4-1/4" x 3" x 7/8", C.8+ **425.00**
Lord Kenyon, vertical, dark blue and white, 3" x 3-1/2" x 1", C.8. . **375.00**
Old Glory, Spaulding & Merrick, horizontal, red ground, detailed graphics on both sides, 2-3/8" x 3-3/4" x 5/8", C.8.5 . . . . . . **325.00**
Paul Jones Clean Cut Tobacco, vertical, teal ground, multicolored image of Jones on front, sea battle on back, 4-1/2" x 3" x 7/8", C.8.5+ **2,900.00**
Trout-Line Smoking Tobacco, vertical, dark green ground, image of trout fisherman on both sides, 3-3/4" x 3-1/4" x 1-1/8", C.8+ **775.00**

Token, Sambo's Coffee, 1-1/2" d, wooden, printed in red on both sides, one side with patriotic design featuring coffee mug, inscription "What This Country Needs Is A Good 10 Cent Cup of Coffee-Sambo's Has It," reverse inscribed "Sambo's Restaurants Anywhere," late 1970s **10.00**

Tray, Fairy Soap, "Have You A Little Fairy in Your Home," decorated with young girl seated on bar of soap, painted tin, 4" d, **$100.** *Photo courtesy of Joy Luke Auctions.*

Tray, tin litho
Anheuser-Busch, Bevo wagon, team of horses, c1910, 13" x 10-1/2" **115.00**
Cunningham Ice Cream, image of early factory and delivery trucks, 15-1/4" x 18-1/2", C.8 . . . . . **450.00**
Duesseldorfer Beer, toddler clutching beer bottle, inscribed "Grand Prize Winners," 1904, 14" d **95.00**
Falstaff Brewing, merry group of cavaliers, c1920, 24" d **95.00**

J. H. Cutter Whiskey, titled "Sunrise Till Sunrise Gladden's, The Inner Man," oval **750.00**
Velvet Beer, Terre Haute Brewing CO., round, festive banquet scene of men and women in 18th C dress **325.00**

Watch fob
Corby's Canadian Whiskey, silvered white metal frame, four large flower blossoms surround color insert of pretty woman reclining against stone wall, robe falling open, Whitehead & Hoag **175.00**
Savage Arms, emb metal, pointing Indian chief, painted head band, orig patina, 1-5/8" d **325.00**

ADVERTISING TRADE CARDS

History: Advertising trade cards are small, thin cardboard cards made to advertise the merits of a product. They usually bear the name and address of a merchant.

With the invention of lithography, colorful trade cards became a popular way to advertise in the late 19th and early 20th centuries. They were made to appeal especially to children. Young and old alike collected and treasured them in albums and scrapbooks. Very few are dated; the prime years for trade card production were 1880 to 1893; cards made between 1810 and 1850 can be found, but rarely. By 1900, trade cards were rapidly losing their popularity, and by 1910, they had all but vanished.

Uncle Sam Banks, Shepherd Hardware Store, c1886, card trimmed, **$60.** *Photo courtesy of James D. Julia, Inc.*

Beverages
Ayer's Sarsaparilla, "Ayer's Sarsaparilla Makes the Weak Strong," two gentlemen **18.00**
Hires' Root Beer, 5" x 6-1/2", full-color portrait of young lady holding package of powdered Hires Improved Root Beer,

reverse with brown and white design and text, including medical claims "Best Blood Purifier in the World," late 1800s **18.00**

Gibson's Pure Rye Whiskey . . . **35.00**

Mayer Brewing, Palest Brewery, New York, diecut **65.00**

Union Pacific Tea, young lad sailors with American flag, includes Easter greeting **8.00**

Clothing

A. S. Shaw Footwear, floral chromo, c1885, 4-1/2" x 7" **12.00**

Child's & Staples, Gilbertsville, ME, young girl chasing butterfly, 2-3/4" x 4-1/2" **12.00**

Honest Abe Work Shirts-Overalls, black and white, Abe Lincoln type with text, sgd by Abe N. Cohen, diecut hole for hanging, c1910, 2-1/2" x 4-1/2" **12.00**

Solar Tip Shoes, Girard College, Philadelphia, Where Boys Wear Our Solar Tip Shoes **20.00**

Thompson's Glove Fitting Corsets, lady and cupids **35.00**

Farm machinery and supplies

Gale Mfg. Co., Daisy Sulky Hay Rake, folder type, four panels, field scene **75.00**

Keystone Agricultural Implements, Uncle Sam talking to world representatives, metamorphic . . . **75.00**

New Essay Lawn Mower, scene of Statue of Liberty, New York harbor **35.00**

Reid's Flower Seeds, two high wheeled bicyclers admiring flowers held by three ladies **15.00**

Sheridan's, To Make Hens Lay, Use Sheridan's Condition Powder, before and after views of farmer in chicken house **25.00**

Food

Batsford, W. A., Dealer in Milk in Orange Co., NY, floral motif, c1880, 2" x 3-1/2" **7.50**

Czar Baking Powder, black woman and boy with giant biscuit **25.00**

Heinz Apple Butter, diecut, pickle shape **48.00**

Pearl Baking Powder, light blue and sepia, reverse with order blank, c1890 . . . . **35.00**

Royal Hams, Chief Joseph & His Tribe examining barrel of hams **48.00**

Tunison, E., Grocer, elf standing next to pansies **15.00**

Advertising cards for hotels: Delavan House, Albany, NY, 1860s; Morris House, Temperance Hotel, Phila., Pa., 1850s; and Arch Street House, Phila., Pa., late 19th C, each 2-3/4" x 4-1/4" or smaller, **$30**. Photo courtesy of Sanford Alderfer Auction Company.

Woolson Spice, Lion Coffee, young children portraying Cinderella . . . **25.00**

Health and beauty

Ayer's Hair Vigor, four mermaids, ship in background **7.50**

Golf Queen Perfume, Ricksecker Co., c1895, blotter type **12.00**

Hoyt's German Cologne, E. M. Hoyt & Co., mother cat and kittens **25.00**

Laundry and soaps

Empire Wringer Co., Auburn, NY, child helping "I Can Help Mama" **35.00**

Fort Wayne Improved Western Washer, Horton Manufacturing Co., Fort Wayne, Ind., one lady watching as other works new machine **35.00**

Ivorine Cleanser, lettering on side of elephant, other animals **15.00**

Mrs. Potts' Sad Irons, sign painters **35.00**

Soapine, Kendall Mfg. Co., Providence, RI, street scene **12.50**

Medicine

Dr. Kilmer & Co., Binghamton, NY, 36" x 60", Standard Herbal Remedies, detailed graphics **395.00**

Trick Pony Toy Savings Bank, mechanical, trick pony mechanical bank seated on Victorian table, marble top table, background, text on the reverse promoting "Trick Pony Toy Savings Bank," New York News Co., NY, 5" x 3-1/4", paper slightly torn, **$60**. Photo courtesy of James D. Julia, Inc.

King of the Blood Medicine, Automation Musical Band, Barnum's Traveling Museum **45.00**

Perry Davis, Pain Killer for Wounds, armored man of war ships battle scene **25.00**

Quaker Bitters, Standard Family Medicine, child in barrel **17.50**

Scott's Emulsion of Cod Liver Oil, man with large fish over back, vertical format **20.00**

Miscellaneous

Agate Iron Ware, Father Time at stove, 3-7/8" x 2-3/4" **45.00**

American Machine Co., Manufacturers of Hardware Specialties, three women ironing, vertical format **40.00**

Emerson Piano Co., black and white illus **40.00**

Forbes, C. P., Jewelry, Greenfield, MA, Santa in front of fireplace, toys on table **15.00**

Granite Iron Ware, three ladies gossiping over tea **25.00**

Read McCraney, Sonora, Tuolumne Co., CA, Diamonds and Watches, Jewelry & Optical Goods, 1890s, 2-1/2" x 4" **10.00**

Wells Portrait & Landscape Photographer, Sonora, CA, adv on front, ship motif, gold and silver trim, 4-1/4" x 6" **35.00**

Stoves and ranges

Andes Stove, black children . . . **15.00**

Dixon's Stove Polish, Brownies illus **20.00**

Enamieline Stove Polish, paper-doll type, distributed by J. L. Prescott & Co., 11 Jay St., 1900s, Rose, 5" h **30.00**
Florence Oil Stove, colorful illus of two women and two children **40.00**
Rising Sun Stove Polish, folder type, "The Modern Cinderella" **50.00**
Rutland Stove Lining, child talking to parrot **115.00**

Thread and sewing

Brooks' Spool Cotton, three kittens playing instruments made from spools **25.00**
Corticelli Spool Silks, Nonotuck Silk Co., diecut leaf shape with silkworm, green and white, c1888, 2" **10.00**
J. & P. Coats, Best Silk Thread, "We Never Fade," black youngster and spool of thread **12.00**
Singer Manufacturing Co., choir of children singing as birds listen . . . **20.00**
White Sewing Machine Co., elves working at sewing machine **15.00**

New Home Sewing Machines, full color art image on front, Columbia and other allegorical females including Black and Native American, flag banner with shield in center picturing the sewing machine "The Pride Of The World," text: Compliments Of The New Home Sewing Machine Company, Orange, Massachusetts, 1896, grommet at top for hanging, attached pink ribbon bow, probably had slide-out calendar underneath bow, reverse has light glue stains around edges from attachment in album, minor edge damage and creases, 6-3/4" x 9-1/4", **$120.** *Photo courtesy of Hake's Americana & Collectibles.*

Tobacco

Capadura Cigar, two baseball players, "Judgment, Judgment is always decided in favor of the Capadura Cigar" **30.00**
49 Cut Plug, miners' scene . . . **225.00**

AGATA GLASS

History: Agata glass was invented in 1887 by Joseph Locke of the New England Glass Company, Cambridge, Massachusetts.

Agata glass was produced by coating a piece of peachblow glass with metallic stain, spattering the surface with alcohol, and firing. The resulting high-gloss, mottled finish looked like oil droplets floating on a watery surface. Shading usually ranged from opaque pink to dark rose, although pieces in a pastel opaque green also exist. A few pieces have been found in a satin finish.

Vase, crimson New England peachblow body with shiny finish, gold tracery, 4-1/2" h, **$685.** *Photo courtesy of Clarence and*

Bowl, 8" d, 4" h, green opaque body, staining and gold trim **1,150.00**
Celery vase, 7" h, sq, fluted top **685.00**
Finger bowl, 5-1/4" d, 2-5/8" h, crushed raspberry shading to creamy pink, allover gold mottling, blue accents **995.00**
Pitcher, 6-3/8" h, crimped rim . **1,750.00**
Spooner, 4-1/2" h, 2-1/2" w, sq top, wild rose peachblow ground, small areas of wear **400.00**
Toothpick holder, 2-1/4" h, flared, green opaque, orig blue oil spots, green trim **795.00**
Tumbler, 3-7/8" h, peachblow ground, gold tracery, bold black splotches **785.00**
Vase
4-1/2" h, square scalloped top, gold tracery, crimson peachblow ground **695.00**
8" h, lily, shiny surface, crimson peachblow ground, large black splotches **1,100.00**

AMBERINA GLASS

1883

History: Joseph Locke developed Amberina glass in 1883 for the New England Glass Works. "Amberina," a trade name, describes a transparent glass which shades from deep ruby to amber. It was made by adding powdered gold to the ingredients for an amber-glass batch. A portion of the glass was reheated later to produce the shading effect. Usually it was the bottom that was reheated to form the deep red; however, reverse examples have been found.

Most early Amberina is flint-quality glass, blown or pattern molded. Patterns include Diamond Quilted, Daisy and Button, Venetian Diamond, Diamond and Star, and Thumbprint.

In addition to the New England Glass Works, the Mount Washington Glass Company of New Bedford, Massachusetts, copied the glass in the 1880s and sold it at first under the Amberina trade name and later as "Rose Amber." It is difficult to distinguish pieces from these two New England factories. Boston and Sandwich Glass Works never produced the glass.

Amberina glass also was made in the 1890s by several Midwest factories, among which was Hobbs, Brockunier & Co. Trade names included "Ruby Amber Ware" and "Watermelon." The Midwest glass shaded from cranberry to amber, and the color resulted from the application of a thin flashing of cranberry to the reheated portion. This created a sharp demarcation between the two colors. This less-expensive version was the death knell for the New England variety.

In 1884, Edward D. Libbey was given the use of the trade name "Amberina" by the New England Glass Works. Production took place during 1900, but ceased shortly thereafter. In the 1920s, Edward Libbey renewed production at his Toledo, Ohio, plant for a short period. The glass was of high quality.

For more information, see this book.

Marks: Amberina made by Edward Libbey in the 1920s is marked "Libbey" in script on the pontil.

Reproduction Alert: Reproductions abound.

Additional Listings: Libbey, Mount Washington.

Basket, 10-1/2" l, wide flared rim, enameled and gilt dec florals, polished pontil, mounted with finely sculpted gilt bronze dragon form handle, Victorian **690.00**
Biscuit jar, 5" h, Diamond Quilted pattern, polished pontil, lid missing **50.00**

Celery vase, amberina celery vase with scalloped top and vertical ribbing, original silver-plated two-handle holder, 9" h, $1,610. Photo courtesy of James D. Julia, Inc.

Bowl, 4-1/2" d, 2-1/4" h, tricorn, fuchsia shading to amber, Venetian Diamond design **325.00**

Celery vase

6-1/4" h, Diamond Quilted pattern, squared rim, polished pontil **150.00**

6-1/2" h, Thumbnail pattern, scallop cut rim, Victorian. **175.00**

Creamer, 4-1/2" h, Thumbprint pattern, polished pontil, Victorian **85.00**

Cruet

5-1/2" h, Inverted Thumbprint pattern, fuchsia trefoil spout, neck, and shoulder, Mt. Washington **435.00**

Cheese dish, Inverted Thumbprint pattern, applied clear lapidary knob, matching 8" d underplate, 7" h, $200. Photo courtesy of James D. Julia, Inc.

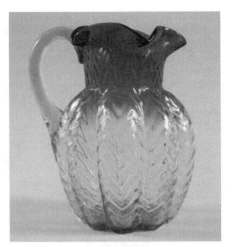

Milk pitcher, melon ribbed, herringbone design, ruffled top, applied amber handle and ruffled top, 8" h, handle appears to be have been ground, $185. Photo courtesy of James D. Julia, Inc.

6" h, Inverted Thumbprint pattern, gilt dec, replaced stopper, wear to gilt **90.00**

6" h, Thumbprint pattern, replaced stopper, Victorian **95.00**

Decanter, 12" h, Optic Diamond Quilted pattern, solid amber faceted stopper **475.00**

Finger bowl, 4-1/2" d, Diamond Quilted pattern, polished pontil, Victorian **75.00**

Jug, 4-1/2" h, Thumbprint pattern, applied amber handle, straight neck, protruding base, polished pontil **150.00**

Nappy, 6" l, handle, enameled dec, polished pontil, Victorian **140.00**

Pitcher

7-3/4" h, Thumbprint pattern, polished pontil, attributed to Hobb's **115.00**

8-1/4" h, Inverted Thumbprint pattern, polished pontil, applied colorless handle **150.00**

8-3/4" h, polished pontil, fluted green tinted handle, attributed to Hobbs **260.00**

10" h, 4-3/4" d, Optic Diamond Quilted pattern, applied amber handle, ground pontil **245.00**

Punch cup, 2" h, applied reeded handle, 16 optic panels **185.00**

Sweetmeat, 6" d, Baby Thumbprint pattern, applied colorless florals, feet, and rim, polished pontil **320.00**

Syrup pitcher, Hobnail pattern, orig pewter top std "Pat. Jan 29 84," Hobbs,

Punch cup, 16 optic panels, reeded handle, 2-1/8" h, $185. Photo courtesy of Clarence and Betty Maier.

Brockunier & Co., three hobs chipped **300.00**

Tankard, 7" h, flared cylinder, Diamond Quilted pattern, applied handle **450.00**

Tumbler, 3-3/4 " h, Hobnail pattern, Hobb's, price for pr **310.00**

Table set, 3-1/2" d x 4" h cream pitcher, 3-1/4" d x 4" h, open sugar, 4-1/2" d x 2-3/4" h waste bowl, optic vertical diamond quilted design, each in silver-plated holder marked "B. Bros. Triple Plate," New England Glass, fracture in pitcher, $1,500. Photo courtesy of Clarence and Betty Maier.

Vase

5" h, Thumbprint pattern, applied petal feet, polished pontil, attributed to Hobbs **75.00**

8" h, Swirl pattern, applied amber rigaree around crown-form top, applied amber petal feet, polished pontil, Victorian **150.00**

Tankard, fuschia shading to amber, applied amberina handle, 9-1/2" h, $1,790. Photo courtesy of James D. Julia, Inc.

Vase, lily, Mt. Washington, deep fuchsia to honey amber, 4-1/4" w tri-fold blossom, wafer base, 16 optic ribs, 9-1/4" h, $565. Photo courtesy of Clarence and Betty Maier.

8-1/4" h, swirled mold, enameled flowers, gilt scrolling, polished pontil, French, c1890......**150.00**

10" h, swirled, applied rim, polished pontil, Victorian.........**150.00**

14-3/4" h, swirled cone, flared base, applied snake, polished pontil, attributed to Harrach, c1890, price for pr.............**600.00**

25-3/4" h, trumpet form, swirl mold, applied amber rim, polished pontil, Victorian...............**350.00**

Water set, 8-1/2" h water pitcher, six similar 3-3/4" h tumblers, Diamond Quilted pattern, attributed to Hobb's **600.00**

Wine set, 14" h Baby Thumbprint pattern decanter, six matching tumblers **250.00**

AMERICAN HAND-PAINTED CHINA

History: The American china painting movement began in 1876 and remained popular over the next 50 years. Thousands of artisans-professionals and amateur-decorated tableware, desk accessories, dresser sets, and many other items with floral, fruits, and conventional geometric designs and occasionally with portraits, birds, and landscapes. Some American firms, such as Lenox and Willetts Manufacturing Co. of Trenton, New Jersey, produced Belleek, a special type of porcelain that china painters decorated, but a majority of porcelain was imported from France, Germany, Austria, Czechoslovakia, and Japan.

Marks: American-painted porcelains bear foreign factory marks. However, the American style was distinctive, whether naturalistic or conventional (geometric). Some pieces were signed and dated by the artist.

Notes: The quality of the artwork, the amount of detail, and technical excellence—not the amount of gilding or the manufacturer of the porcelain itself—are key pricing factors. Unusual subjects and uncommon forms also influence value.

Adviser: Dorothy Kamm.

Bonbon box , 6" d, 3-1/2" h, dec with conventional design of three intertwined peacocks, baby blue base, burnished gold rims and feet, opal luster int., marked "T. & V. Limoges, France," c1892-1907 ....**95.00**

Cake plate, individual, double-handled

7" d, dec with central conventional floral bouquet, sgd "IFP," marked "Schumann, Bavaria"......**20.00**

7-1/8" d, dec with conventional border design, burnished gold rim and handles, sgd "LMC," marked "MADE IN JAPAN," c1925 ..**22.00**

Coffee pot, dec with conventional design in enamel, outline in raised paste covered with burnished gold, burnished gold finial and base, marked "CAC, BELLEEK," 1889-1906 ..**600.00**

Compote, ftd, 8-7/8" d, 4-1/4" h, interior dec with cluster of pink and white morning glories and pink butterfly, rim and foot dec with bands of conventional pink butterflies, burnished gold rim and foot, sgd and dated "CL, April 13th, 1881," marked "CFH" **200.00**

Cream soup cup, 4-3/8" d, double handled, dec with conventional border, burnished gold handles and rim, marked "Bavaria," c1900-1915 ..**25.00**

Creamer, decorated with conventional style border design of moths, opal luster ground, burnished gold border band, rim, and handle, signed "Jennie Katz, 1918," marked "W. C. & G. France," 4-3/16" h, $45.

Creamer and sugar, dec with conventional floral border design in blue and soft green on burnished gold band, burnished gold lips, spout, rims, and handles, ivory ground, sgd "Helen Hurley".....................**55.00**

Cup and saucer

Decorated with conventional Celtic border design in celadon, light blue border, ivory center, cup bottom and interiors, burnished gold rims and handle, sgd "L.E.S.,"

marked with crown in double circle, "Victoria, Austria," 1900-20 ..**30.00**

Decorated with conventional swag design of blue flowers, burnished gold rims and handle, sgd "Jane Bent Telin," marked "Favorite Bavaria," 1910-25 ....**45.00**

Dessert set, three pieces, 7-7/16" d plate, dec with forget-me-not clusters, cup and saucer, opal luster on cup interior, burnished gold rims and handle, plate marked with shield, "Thomas, Bavaria," cup and saucer marked "JAPAN," c1925-30 .....**40.00**

Jam jar, 4-3/8" h, 6-3/4" d plate, dec with border design of grapes and leaves, variegated blue enamels, burnished gold ground, yellow luster border band and knob, sgd "L. Vance-Phillips, 1917," marked with Belleek palette, "Lenox".......**350.00**

Milk pitcher and plate set, 5-11/16" h pitcher, 7-3/8" d plate, dec with conventional design of yellow wild roses, yellow ground, burnished gold rims, handle, and trim, sgd "M.S.C. '90," pitcher marked "H & Co., Limoges," plate marked "CFH/GDM" **75.00**

Olive or bonbon dish, 6" d, ring-handles, dec with conventional border motif in matt antique green, sgd "M.H. Butler," marked "Thomas Bavaria," c1908-15............**35.00**

Perfume bottle, stopper, 4-3/4" h, dec with daisies and greenery, ivory ground, burnished gold lip and stopper, marked "O. & E. G. Austria," 1896-1918 ..**45.00**

Pin tray, 5-3/4" l, 4" w, dec with border design of blue and burnished gold moths, connected by burnished gold and black band, ivory ground,

Perfume bottle, stopper, decorated with daisies and greenery, ivory ground, burnished gold lip and stopper, marked "O. & E. G. Austria," 1896-1918, 4-3/4" h, $45. Photos courtesy of Dorothy Kamm.

Two-in-one salt and pepper shaker, decorated with raised paste garlands covered with burnished gold, accented with turquoise enamel ivory ground, burnished gold tops, handle and foot rim, marked "Germany," c1891-1914, 4-3/4" w, 2-1/2" h, $45.

burnished gold rim, sgd "E. ARRINDELL, 1-2-18," marked "MZ, Austria" 45.00

Plate

6-5/8" d, dec with band of conventional style roses and leaves, ivory ground, pale green center, burnished gold rim, sgd "P. M. T.," marked "Bavaria," c1892-1914 . . . . 20.00

8-1/2" d, dec with clusters of sea shells and sea weeds, black green border band edged with burnished gold scrolls and rim, sgd "C.C.O.," marked with crown and crossed swords, "Bavaria," 1896-1906 . . . . 65.00

Rose bowl, 2-7/8" h, dec with band of conventional-style violets and bands in burnished gold, marked "O. & E.G., Royal, Austria," c1898-1918 . . . . 30.00

Salt and pepper shakers

3" h, dec with conventional blue-winged insects, burnished gold tops, 1905-20, price for pr 35.00

4-3/4" w, 2-1/2" h, two-in-one shaker, dec with raised paste garlands cov with burnished gold, accented with turquoise enamel ivory ground, burnished gold tops, handle and foot rim, marked "Germany," c1891-1914 . . . . 45.00

Teapot stand, 6-3/8" d, dec with border design of forget-me-not-clusters, burnished gold rim, c1900-1920. 45.00

Vase, 7-7/8" h, dec with two Art Deco-style floral panels in various lusters and burnished gold, sgd "M.D.P. 1920" 85.00

AMERICAN HAND-PAINTED CHINA JEWELRY AND BUTTONS

History: The American china painting movement began in 1876, about the time the mass production of jewelry also occurred. Porcelain manufacturers and distributors offered a variety of porcelain shapes and settings for brooches, pendants, cuff links, and shirt-waist buttons. Thousands of artisans painted flowers, people, landscapes, and conventions (geometric) motifs. The category of hand-painted porcelain jewelry comprises a unique category, separate from costume and fine jewelry. While the materials were inexpensive to produce, the painted decoration was a work of fine art.

Marks: American painted porcelain jewelry bears no factory marks, and is usually unsigned.

Notes: The quality of the artwork, the amount of detail, and technical excellence—not the amount of gilding—are the key pricing factors. Uncommon shapes also influence value.

Adviser: Dorothy Kamm.

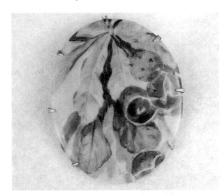

Belt buckle brooch, oval, decorated with horse chestnuts, baby blue ground, gold-plated bezel, 1900-17, 2" x 2-1/2", $100. Photos courtesy of Dorothy Kamm.

Belt buckle brooch

1-11/16", x 2-1/4" oval, dec with white pansy, accented with white enamel, burnished gold ground, gold-plated bezel, 1900-17 . . 75.00

2" x 2-1/2" oval, dec with horse chestnuts, baby blue ground, gold-plated bezel, 1900-17. 100.00

Brooch

7/8" d, pink and ruby rose, leaves, polychrome ground, burnished gold rim, gold-plated bezels, price for pr 50.00

7/8" sq, diamond shape, dec with waterscape with water lilies, white enamel highlights, burnished with gold border, brass bezel, c1920-40 . . . . 35.00

1" d, dec with Colonial dame, burnished gold rim, brass bezel, c1890-1910 . . . . 40.00

1" x 1", cross-shape, dec with pink and ruby roses, polychrome ground, tips dec with raised paste dots, burnished gold gold-plated bezel with tubular hinge. . . . 80.00

1" x 3/4" rectangle, Florida landscape in white on platinum ground, sterling silver bezel, c1920-40 . . . . 75.00

1-1/4" x 1-4/8" oval, dec with woman's portrait surrounded by forget-me-nots, ivory ground, white enamel highlights, framed by burnished gold raised paste scrolls and dots, gold-plated bezel. 80.00

1-7/16" x 1-7/8" oval, dec with pink roses, burnished gold border, sgd "Albrecht," brass bezel65.001-1/2" x 2", oval, dec with Art Nouveau-style woman's head and neck, poppies in her hair, gold-plated bezel 90.00

1-1/2" x 2" oval, dec with stained glass-like conventional design in polychrome colors and burnished gold, gold-plated bezel, 1905-15 . . . . 65.00

1-3/4" d, dec with daisy, burnished gold border, brass bezel, c1900-10 . . . . 45.00

1-7/8" w, crescent shape, dec with dark pink roses, burnished gold tips, brass bezel, 1900-20 . . 45.00

Brooch, cross-shape, decorated with pink and ruby roses, polychrome ground, tips decorated with raised paste dots, burnished gold gold-plated bezel with tubular hinge, 1" x 1", $80.

1-13/16" x 2-3/16" oval, dec with columbine and greenery, polychrome ground, burnished gold trim, gold-plated bezel . **75.00**

1-9/16" x 1-7/8" oval, dec with pink roses and greenery on light blue and yellow, burnished gold ground, scrolls, and dots, sgd "E. GARDE," 1920s, gold-plated setting . . **50.00**

1-11/16" x 2-1/8" oval, dec with a tropical landscape, burnished gold rim, sgd "OC" (Olive Commons, St. John's Island, FL, 1908-1920), gold-plated bezel **105.00**

2" x 1-5/8" oval, dec with Art Nouveau-style poppies, burnished gold border, brass bezel, 1856-1915 . . . . **75.00**

2" x 1-1/2" oval, dec with pink and ruby roses, solid dark blue ground, white enamel highlights, burnished gold border, brass bezel, c1940 . . . . **65.00**

2-1/16" d, dec with violets, burnished gold rim, brass bezel, 1900-1920 . . . . **65.00**

2-1/2" l, horseshoe shape, dec with violets, burnished gold tips, brass bezel **100.00**

Cuff buttons, pr, 3/4" x 1" ovals, dec with lavender flowers, border of burnished gold dots and apple green jewels, burnished gold rims, c1890-1920 . . . . **40.00**

Dress set

Five pieces: 2" x 2-5/8" belt buckle brooch, oval brass bezel, pr 1" d shirt waist buttons with shanks, pr 1" d shirt waist buttons with sew-through backs, dec with forget-me-nots, black green scalloped borders rimmed in burnished gold, c1900-17. . **400.00**

Four pieces: 3/4" d shirt waist collar button, three 5/8" d shirt waist buttons, dec with pink roses, white enamel highlights, burnished gold rims, shank backs **60.00**

Flapper pin, 1-5/8" x 2-1/8" oval, dec with stylized woman, burnished gold border, brass bezel, 1924-28 . . . . **75.00**

Hat pin, 3/4" wide by 1" oval medallion, 6" l shaft, dec with four-leaf clover on burnished gold ground, brass bezel, 1900-20 . . . . **115.00**

Pendant

1-5/8" x 2-1/8" oval, dec with violets, burnished bold border, brass bezel, c1880-1914 . . . . **60.00**

1-3/4" x 1-3/4" oval, dec with forget-me-nots, white enamel

Shirtwaist button, with shank, decorated with violets entwined around burnished gold fancy letter "J," burnished gold border, signed with illegible cipher, 7/8" square, $20.

highlights, burnished gold rim, brass bezel, c1900-20 . . . . . **50.00**

Shirt-waist button

7/8" sq, with shank, dec with violets entwined around burnished gold fancy letter "J," burnished gold border, sgd with illegible cipher **20.00**

1-3/16" d, with eye, dec with single daisy, burnished gold ground **20.00**

1-3/16" d, with shank, dec with conventional floral design, burnished gold ground **35.00**

Set, two 7/8" d, three 5/8" d, with shanks, dec with maidenhair fern, pastel polychrome ground, burnished gold borders, price for five-pc set **80.00**

AMPHORA

History: The Amphora Porcelain Works was one of several pottery companies located in the Teplitz-Turn region of Bohemia in the late 19th and early 20th centuries. It is best known for art pottery, especially Art Nouveau and Art-Deco pieces.

Marks: Several markings were used, including the name and location of the pottery and the Imperial mark, which included a crown. Prior to World War I, Bohemia was part of the Austro-Hungarian Empire, so the word "Austria" may appear as part of the mark. After World War I, the word "Czechoslovakia" may be part of the mark.

Additional Listings: Teplitz.

Center bowl, 2-1/8" h, incised dec outlined in black, enameled blue-green and pink cabochons, mottled tan matte ground, four legs, circular base **200.00**

Greenwood, raised gilded poppies, incised dianthus, gilt trim (minor losses), cobalt blue ground, unmarked, 9-1/2" h, $1,955. Photo courtesy of David Rago Auctions.

Ewer, 14-1/2" h, pink, gold, and green floral dec, gold accents, salamander entwined handle, c1900 . . . . . . **575.00**

Pitcher, 11" h, emb owl sitting on branch **175.00**

Sugar bowl, cov, 6-1/4" d, 4-1/2" h, Art Deco enamel dec, polychrome birds and leaves, stamped mark "15449/30" **280.00**

Vase

5-1/4" h, three buttressed handles dec with naturalistic leafy rose vines, rose hip clusters, matte green rose on mottled brown round, gilt highlights, imp mark and stamp on base **250.00**

6" h, flattened spherical form, shoulder dec with alternating large and small moths in shades of blue, pink, and yellow, raised gilt outline, relief spider webs and enameled disk centers, gilt highlights on green and blue ground, imp "Amphora" in oval, printed "R. S. & K. Turn-Teplitz Bohemia" with maker's device on base . . . **900.00**

10" h, shouldered form, textured green and blue glaze, gilt accents **650.00**

11-1/8" h, pear shape, extended neck, two tri-part handles, mottled matte green and brown glaze, inscribed cipher, R. S. & K, Teplitz, Bohemia, c1900, crazing, base chip **1,035.00**

Wall plaque, 18-1/2" d, Moorish man and woman in relief, red ground, gilt molded frames, marked "Amphora," price for pr **900.00**

ANIMAL COLLECTIBLES

For more information, see this book.

History: The representation of animals in fine arts, decorative arts, and on utilitarian products dates back to antiquity. Some religions endowed certain animals with mystical properties. Authors throughout written history used human characteristics when portraying animals.

The formation of collectors' clubs and marketing crazes, e.g., flamingo, pig, and penguin, during the 1970s increased the popularity of this collecting field.

Additional Listings: See specific animal collectible categories in *Warman's Americana & Collectibles.*

Barnyard

Carving, folk art, wood

7" l, peep, painted, c1900, with stand **9,545.00**

9-1/2" l, 2-1/2" w, 8" h, rooster, polychrome red, mustard yellow, and brown, base with indistinct pencil inscription, PA, c1840 . . . . **4,320.00**

17" l, 15" h, rooster, old cream-colored paint, 3/4 flat body, stand **460.00**

Chopper, 12" l, 7-1/2" d, 7-1/4" h, rooster, iron, fanciful silhouette, incised feather detail, mounted on wooden fragment, with stand, late 18th/early 19th C, lacks wooden handle . **1,035.00**

Figure, sewer tile

5-1/4" l, 5" h, frog on log, hand modeled, tooled bark, inscribed initials "H.S." on base, dark brown, slightly metallic glaze, traces of gold on one end of log **425.00**

7-7/8" h, pig, standing, wearing pants, vest, and bow tie, reddish-brown glaze, few spots of wear **320.00**

Jar, cov, 6" d, 6-1/2" h, stoneware, figure of pig eating from trough on lid, German, some damage to base **115.00**

Painting, 40" w, 32-1/4" h, oil on canvas, big horn sheep on hillside overlooking small fog shrouded lake, sgd "C. O. Williams," back of canvas with preparer's label "Reeves & Sons, London," ornate gilt frame with painted gold highlights **4,100.00**

Tin, Dr. Daniels' Cow Invigorator, 18 oz pry lid tin litho, image of cow on each side, C-8+ **275.00**

Toy, stuffed

Cow, 11-1/2" l, 8-1/2" h, brown, felt covering, glass eyes, black painted nostrils and mouth, fur tip of tail, tin wheels attached to wooden hooves, early 20th C, some soil and wear, break to top of leg **230.00**

Goat, 4-3/4" h, black mohair legs and face, long white mohair body, felt horns, green glass eyes . **60.00**

Figure, Peregrine Falcon, Kaiser Studios, #628/1500, finely detailed porcelain, 13" h, $195. Photo courtesy of Joy Luke Auctions.

Birds

Architectural element, 18-1/2" h, owl, pottery, unglazed, traces of old silver paint, base imp "Owens and Howard, St. Louis, MO," minor hairlines . . **550.00**

Eagle, cast iron, painted, black with white spots, America, late 19th C, 11" l, 5-1/2" d, 3-1/2" h **250.00**

Figure, sewer tile, 10-1/2" h, horned owl, perched on round pedestal base, orange glaze **450.00**

Lamp base, 16" h, owl perched on stump, sewer pipe, hollow body, good detail, dark brown glaze, shallow edge chips. **385.00**

Plaque, 7" x 4" sight, 11-1/2" x 8-1/2" ebonized frame, pietra dura, colorful parrot on perch, Italian, early 20th C **250.00**

Sculpture, 15-1/2" wingspan, 20" h, eagle, carved wood, standing, spread wings **395.00**

Tobacco container, Bob White Tobacco, paper label on cloth pouch, multicolored Bob White on both sides, 1910 tax stamp, 2-3/4" w, 1-1/4" d, 4" h **400.00**

Trivet, parrot, pastel central figure with intricate flower and vine pattern, eight triangular feet, Rookwood marks, 1929, 5-3/4" sq **325.00**

Wall shelf, 16-1/2" w, eagle, carved wood, shaped shelf supported by eagle with spread wings, loss to gilt . . **475.00**

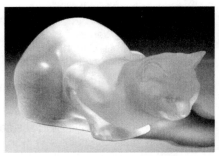

Chat Couche, a Lalique model of a sitting cat, c. 1970, in clear and frosted glass. Engraved Lalique France, 9-1/4" l, $575. Photo courtesy of David Rago Auctions.

Cats

Bank, 11" h, chalk ware, seated, wearing red bow, minor loss . . . **200.00**

Cane

34-1/2" l, 1-3/4" d x 1-3/4" h carved ivory ball handle with cat face emerging from one side, 1/3" sterling collar with Chester hallmarks for 1903, dark Malacca shaft, 3/4" brass ferrule . . . **450.00**

36" l, 2" w x 3-1/2" carved wood head, nicely detailed features, when button on back is pressed, red eyes change to blue, long red tongue shoots out, 1-1/4" dec silver collar, Malacca shaft, 7/8" replaced brass ferrule, German, c1880 . . . . **2,020.00**

Carnival target, kitten, pr **950.00**

Figure

2-5/8" h, carved marble or alabaster, sitting, glass eyes, America, 19th C, chip on base corner . . **1,035.00**

9" l, sewer tile, reclining, hand-tooled eyelashes, white glazed eyes **360.00**

9-1/2" w, 7" d, 17-1/4" h, carved pine, fat cat, incised "E. Sweet," 20th C, cracks **435.00**

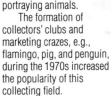

13-1/4" h, sewer tile, elongated form, head cocked to one side, curious look, hand tooled eyelashes, metallic glaze, Ohio **660.00**

Painting

Brown Tabby Kitten with a Rose Bow, John Henry Dolph, sgd "JHDolph" lower left, oil on board, 12" x 9", framed, scattered retouch
. . . . **4,700.00**

Gray Tiger Cat with a Blue Bow, sgd "MABrown" lower right, American School, 19th C, oil on canvas, 17" x 21", framed, minor scattered retouch, varnish inconsistencies
. . . . **2,000.00**

Kittens Playing, sgd indistinctly lower right, titled in pencil on reverse, American School, 19th C, oil on panel, 6-1/4" x 8-1/2", framed, minor retouch upper right . . **530.00**

Sleepy Tabby, Franklin W. Rogers, sgd "F.W. Roger" lower right, label on reverse, oil on canvas, 21" x 17", framed, scattered retouch, varnish inconsistencies, craquelure
. . . . **1,175.00**

The Sleeping Tabby, monogrammed and dated "JLC 1881" lower left, American School, 19th C, oil on canvas, 9" x 12", framed, scattered retouch, craquelure **3,300.00**

Tiger Cat, unsigned, American School, 19th C, oil on canvas, 19-1/2" x 15-1/2", large tiger cat, yellow eyes, framed, minor retouch
. . . . **5,875.00**

Stamp box, 4-3/4" l, carved fruitwood, figural cat lying inside shoe, glass eyes, hinged lid, early 20th C **225.00**

Dogs

Ashtray, Scottish Terrier, sq, porcelain, center black terrier, images of hounds and rabbits, green and white ground, Hermes **50.00**

Cane

35" l, 3-1/2" l x 1-1/2" h carved elephant ivory handle, pug family consisting of father, mother, three pups in line, 1" gold filled collar dec in "C" scrolls, orig owner's elaborate initials, ebony shaft carved with simulated thorns, 1-1/8" burnished brass and iron ferrule, English, c1890 . . **1,570.00**

35-1/4" l, 1-3/4" d x 4-3/4" h carved ivory handle, performing poodle, wearing toy soldier's cap, holding toy gun, 3/4" silver collar, tan Malacca shaft, 1" replaced brass ferrule, English, c1890 . . **1,120.00**

Ashtray, Hermes, "Scottish Terrier," porcelain, square centered by black terrier, further decorated with images of hounds and rabbits on green and white ground, **$50.** *Photo courtesy of Skinner's Auctioneers and Appraisers.*

36-1/2" l, 2-1/2" w x 2" h purple quartz handle carved as French bulldog, upright ears, dec gold plated collar, ebony shaft, 1" brass and iron ferrule, Continental, c1890
. . . . **950.00**

36-7/8" l, 2" w x 2-3/4" h elephant ivory handle carved as mastiff emerging from seashell, brown glass eyes, maccassar ebony shaft, 1-1/2" white metal and iron ferrule, Continental, c1890
. . . . **1,680.00**

Figure, clay

7" w, 3-1/2" d, 9-1/2" h, seated, freestanding front legs, yellow Ohio clay, mottled green glaze on base, brown dec on dog, black eyes, blue ink stamp label "E. Houghton & Co. Dalton, Ohio, 1928," hairline in base **1,450.00**

7-1/4" l, 9-1/4" h, seated, freestanding front legs, gray clay, cream-colored glaze, brown and blue polka dots, long tail with brown, one ear brown, other blue, chips on base **6,270.00**

8-1/8" h, Ohio white clay, seated, short ears and tail, long jowls, grown glaze, chip on back of base, small flake on ear **110.00**

10" h, Newcomerstown, Ohio, pottery, seated, unglazed clay, good detail, shallow front chip
. . . . **3,750.00**

Figure, pearlware, 2-7/8" l, 3-1/4" h, long hair seated dog, white, brown and gold spots, minor flakes on base, short hairline **520.00**

Figure, sewer tile

7-1/2" h, seated, hand modeled, tooled fur and facial features, mat glaze with metallic speckles, traces of white paint **110.00**

Figure, recumbent dog, carved marble, 10-1/2" l, 4-1/2" h, **$135.** *Photo courtesy of Joy Luke Auctions.*

10-1/2" l, 5-1/2" w, 11-1/2" h, Collie, standing, reddish brown glaze, rect molded base, firing separations, small chips on ears **935.00**

11" h, seated, molded with hand tooled details on ears and face, long eye lashes, glaze varies from light tan to dark reddish brown, Ohio, minor flakes on base . **660.00**

Figure, stoneware, 13-1/2" h, Spaniels, tan and brown speckled matte glaze, glass eyes, oval bases, England, c1875, repair to base of one, glaze flakes, price for pr **6,465.00**

Jewelry, brooch

Micromosaic, recumbent King Charles spaniel, gold ropetwist frame, minor lead solder on verso
. . . . **900.00**

Platinum and diamond, terrier, pave setting, green stone eyes **1,725.00**

Reverse painted crystal, standing boxer, oval 14kt gold frame, sgd "W. F. Marcus" **920.00**

Painting, pastel on paper

13-1/4" x 17-1/4", naughty puppy worrying a piece of lace, unsigned,

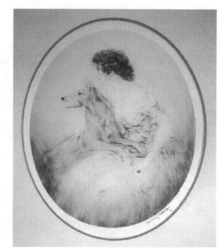

Framed print portrait of lady with dog, signed in plate Louis Icart, 31" x 26-1/2", **$350.** *Photo courtesy of Joy Luke Auctions.*

American School, 19th C, molded gilt frame, rippling **1,295.00**

12-1/2" x 17-1/4", puppy sleeping on green cushion, unsigned, American School, 19th C, gilt frame, small ear at center right edge **1,175.00**

Sculpture, 13" l, 14" h, carved limestone, Ohio, c1920-30, repair to right ear **1,150.00**

Sign, Glovers Dog Remedies, litho tin, bulldog, green ground, c1900, 13" d **1,210.00**

Vase, 10" h, Lenox, marked "Hunter Arms Co., First Prize, Class A," image of pointer in clearing, sgd "Delan," stamped Lenox logo **3,665.00**

Watch fob, four graduated round 14kt gold plaques depicting dog's heads in repoussé, suspended by trace link chains, monogrammed, swivel clasp, 15.0 dwt **575.00**

Horses

Blanket, 68" sq, needlework design of horse, red ground, diamond design in field, black border with cross-stitched multicolored floral design, red yarn fringe, wool backing, reverse stitched with owner's name "Jacob Weber 1871," minor restoration, moth damage in backing **175.00**

Book, *Rodeo, A Collection of Tales & Sketches by R. B. Cunningham Graham,* selected by A. F. Tschiffeley, Literary Guild, 1936 . . . . **10.00**

Cane, 35-3/4" l, 4" l x 2-1/4" h elephant ivory handle carved as two riding horse heads, carved simulated leather tack, 1/2" sterling collar marked "Brigg," London hallmarks for 1897, ebony

Framed oil on canvas, black horse, Pequa, stud from Van Arsdale Stud Farm, Blandinsville, IL, signed "Legrass 1889," gilded frame, 30" x 36", $1,100. Photo courtesy of Joy Luke Auctions.

shaft, 7/8" brass and iron ferrule **1,350.00**

Condiment set, 5" l, 3-5/8" h, electroplate, base formed as horseshoe, spur-form handle, toothpick holder flanked by boot form castor, mustard pot with whip-form spoon, central jockey cap open salt, Elkington & Co., England, late 19th C **175.00**

Figure, carved and painted wood

7-1/2" h, laminated, stylized form, grommet eyes, orig glossy black paint, America, late 19th C, losses to tail **1,610.00**

10-1/2" l, 14-1/2" h, articulated circus figure with red textile shoulder girth, riding horse with glass bead eyes, attributed to Connecticut, c1900-10, stand, minor wear, paint imperfections **2,530.00**

Figure, porcelain

18" l, 20" h, man in colonial dress riding white horse **290.00**

18" l, 20" h, woman in colonial dress riding dappled brown horse **660.00**

Pull toy, 11-1/4" l, painted and laminated carved pine, full stride, horsehair tail, wheeled platform base, America, early 20th C **635.00**

Weathervane, 26-1/2" l, 16-1/2" h, full-bodied trotting horse, copper, verdigris surface, black metal stand, America, late 19th C, minor dents **4,325.00**

Wild animals

Bookends, pr, fox head, 4-3/8" w, 6-5/8" h, carved wood, mahogany backplate mounted with realistically carved and painted head, stepped base, early 20th C **320.00**

Cane

36" l, 2-1/3" w x 3-1/4" h elephant ivory handle carved as American bison, amber glass eyes, finely fashioned features, 1/2" sterling collar with London hallmarks for 1920, heavy ebony shaft, 7/8" brass and iron ferrule . . . **1,120.00**

36-1/4" l, 2" d x 3" h elephant ivory handle carved as six male lions, amber eyes, alternate with mouths open and closed, 1/3" ringed silver collar, thick Malacca shaft, 1-1/2" horn ferrule, English, c1890 . . . . **1,460.00**

Figure

Carved alabaster, reclining rabbit, full relief, rect base, 9" l, 5" d, 6" h **2,185.00**

Figure, sewer tile, squirrel holding nut in paws, brown glaze with white eyes, marked "CM" on base, 6-1/2" t, chip on base and ear, $65. Photo courtesy of Sanford Alderfer Auction Company.

Carved bone, elephant, carved bone, carved wooden armature overlaid with bone tiles in contrasting patterns, India, c1900, 24" l **1,610.00**

Ceramic, white elephant figures, gray and pink enamel detailing, sq bronze bases with gilt rocaille scrollwork to sides, early 20th C, 10" w, 5-3/4" d, 10-1/2" h, price for pr **2,760.00**

Clay, reclining lion, scalloped base, dark brown shiny glaze, Ohio, in-the-making hairlines **250.00**

Polychromed, carved wood

Deer, worn brown paint, white accents on nose and underbelly, green ground stand, America, 19th C, missing one antler and part of right foreleg, 18" l, 3-1/4" d, 17-3/4" h **3,450.00**

Kangaroo, Fred Alten, (1872-1945, Wyandotte, MI), body with traces of brown stain, red glass eyes, shaped base, 3-1/4" w, 7-1/4" h, with stand **575.00**

Sewer tile, lion, reclining position, some hand tooling and molding on face, paws, and oval, stepped base, sgd "J.C.E. July 29, 1901, New York, NY," light glaze varies from putty to reddish brown, 11-1/4" l, 6" h minor edge damage to ears **825.00**

Shooting gallery target, 21" w, 7" d, 31-1/2" h, rabbit, MA, c1940, some paint remaining, with stand **815.00**

Tin, litho

Jumbo Peanut Butter, Frank Tea & Spice Co., one-lb size, 3-3/8" x 3-7/8" **775.00**

Red Wolf Coffee, Ridenour-Baker Co., Kansas City, one-lb size, vacuum pack, trademark wolf, 5" d, 4" h **575.00**

Tiger Bright Sweet Chewing Tobacco, P. Lorillard Co., vertical pocket size, 3" w, 7/8" d, 2-7/8" h **275.00**

ARCHITECTURAL ELEMENTS

For more information, see this book.

History: Architectural elements, many of which are handcrafted, are those items, which have been removed or salvaged from buildings, ships, or gardens. Part of their desirability is due to the fact that it would be extremely costly to duplicate the items today.

Beginning about 1840, decorative building styles began to feature carved wood and stone, stained glass, and ornate ironwork. At the same time, builders and manufacturers also began to use fancy doorknobs, doorplates, hinges, bells, window locks, shutter pulls, and other decorative hardware as finishing touches to elaborate new homes and commercial buildings.

Hardware was primarily produced from bronze, brass, and iron, and doorknobs also were made from clear, colored, and cut glass. Highly ornate hardware began appearing in the late 1860s and remained popular through the early 1900s. Figural pieces that featured animals, birds, and heroic and mythological images were very popular, as were ornate and very graphic designs that complimented the many architectural styles that emerged in the late 19th century.

Fraternal groups, government and educational institutions, and individual businesses all ordered special hardware for their buildings. Catalogs from the era show hundreds of patterns, often with a dozen different pieces available in each design.

The current trends of preservation and recycling of architectural elements has led to the establishment and growth of organized salvage operations that specialize in removal and resale of elements. Special auctions are now held to sell architectural elements from churches, mansions, office buildings, etc. Today's decorators often design an entire room around one architectural element, such as a Victorian marble bar or mural, or use several as key accent pieces.

Arch, 36" l, fragmentary, sandstone, carved figures, including Buddha seated on dais, central India, c15th/16th C **1,495.00**

Bird bath, 19" d, 33-1/2" h, cast iron, shallow basin, gadrooned rim mounted by two doves, fluted baluster form standard on circular base cast with pierced rose design **300.00**

Bird cage, 21" x 19-1/2" x 18", house form, grand entrance, front porch, bay windows, dormers, cupola, painted green, trimmed with red painted wooden buttons, knobs, and perches, some paint loss **230.00**

Bracket, 19-3/4" h, 10-1/2" d, carved wood, mermaids, gilded, bifurcated scrolled tails, America, 19th C, some loss, pr **4,230.00**

Catalog

Hudson Equipment Co., Chicago, IL, 1940, 256 pgs, 6-1/2" x 9-3/4", Hudson Barn Equipment Catalog

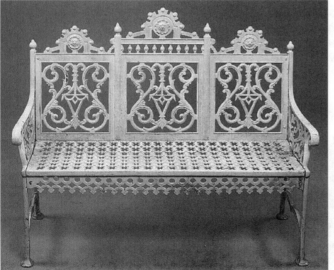

Bench, cast iron, Renaissance Revival, American, ornate scrollwork and rosettes, lattice apron with fleur-de-lis ends, scrolled arms, 46" l, 13-1/4" deep seat, 38" h, $1,830. Photo courtesy of Cowan's Historic Americana Auctions.

No. B-31, stalls, stanchions, bull stall, etc. **30.00**

Little Tree Farm, Framingham Center, MA, 1927, 48 pgs, 8-1/2" x 11-1/2", Section II Year Book, No. 37, Complete Catalog of Evergreens, Shrubs, Trees, Vines, Annuals, Perennials, Landscaping Accessories, etc. **15.00**

Mohawk Carpet Mills, Amsterdam, NY, 1946, 169 pgs, 6" x 9", Woven Floor Covering Retail Sales Manual, hardcover **20.00**

Morgan Sash & Door Co., Chicago, IL, c1953, 180 pgs, 8-1/2" x 11", Catalog & Price List No. 553, Morgan-Anderson Woodwork **35.00**

Chimney pot, terra cotta, tulip top, 48" h **275.00**

Conservatory planter, oak, zinc liner **1,100.00**

Curtain tiebacks, mercury glass, grape dec, pewter collars, price for set of six, some chips, minor wear. .**175.00**

Door

27-1/4" w, 69-1/2" h, raised panel, pegged construction, orig red paint, wrought iron thumb latch, old corner chip **580.00**

31-1/2" w, 78-1/2" h, two molded recessed panels, grain painted to resemble exotic wood, attributed to Maine, early 19th C, very minor surface imperfections **920.00**

Door knocker, 4" w, 11-1/4" h, wrought and hammered copper, tulip shape, monogrammed "IGW," orig dark patina **175.00**

Door pull, 8" d, brass, Arts & Crafts, round, grimacing figure wearing head covering, holding ring in its mouth **270.00**

Eagle

12-3/4" w, 5" h, carved mahogany, bas-relief carving, perched on arrow, gilt highlights, America **530.00**

26" w, 31" l, 25" h, carved giltwood, perched on carved rockery, Pilot House type, America, c1875, old regilding, minor wear . . .**2,415.00**

32-3/4" w, 19-1/4" h, gilded tin, outstretched wings, perched on rockery weighted base, holds scales in beak, metal manufacturer M. F. Frand Co., Camden, NJ, tag on lower base, late 19th C, imperfections **1,880.00**

Finial, 18-1/4" h, granite, gray, urn shape, price for pr **225.00**

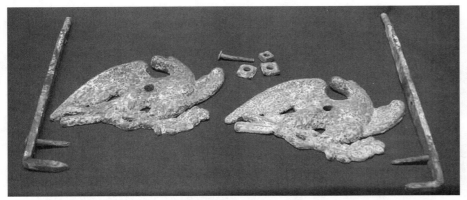

Eagle, cast iron, figural, looking left holding sprig of laurel and arrows in talons, 12-1/2" w, 8" h, $330. Photo courtesy of Sanford Alderfer Auction Company.

Garden edging tiles, set of 10 . . **25.00**

Garden bench, cast iron

36" w, 13-1/2" d, 28" h, openwork vintage design, scrolled seat, worn white paint, price for pr . . . **350.00**

43-1/2" w, 15" d, 31" h, openwork fern design on back and legs, geometric cast designs on seat, old white repaint, two hairlines, chip near front corner. **325.00**

Garden ornament

10" l, 11-5/8" h, rabbit, cast iron, seated figure, traces of white, green, and red paint, late 19th C, wear **345.00**

16-1/2" l, 29-1/2" h, carved and painted wood and gesso, urn with flame, painted tan, putty, and white, traces of gilt, 19th C **2,185.00**

Garden set, bench and chair, cast iron ends with finely detailed griffins, foliage, and scrolling, old replaced beaded mahogany boards, 57" w, 29-1/2" d,

Garden statue, reclining pointer dog, by Janes, Kirtland & Co., metal, possibly zinc, one leg draped over end of cast iron rectangular base, illus as No. 73 in Ornamental Ironwork Catalog of Janes, Kirtland & Co., 1870, 27" l x 16-1/4" h pointer, 26-1/2" l, 16" w, 3" h repainted base, $26,450. Photo courtesy of James D. Julia, Inc.

30-1/2" h bench, 27" w, 28" d, 32" h chair **700.00**

Garden statue, 32" h, cast concrete, cherub, chips **125.00**

Garden urn, cast iron, American

Classical figures, grape and cable handles, orig bases, painted white, c1880, 61" h, pr **9,800.00**

Gadrooned rim and bowl, sq base, 18" d, 12-1/4" h, rusty surface, pr **950.00**

Griffins, winged, stone-cut, English, pr **4,200.00**

Hitching post, 31" h, cast iron, jockey, yellow, red, green, black, and white painted detail, wired for lantern **275.00**

Lock, 8-1/2" w, 11" h, iron, rect plate with male and female silhouettes, key with quatrefoil terminal, 19th C, stand, minor surface corrosion **650.00**

Model, 18" x 13" x 10", carved balsa, temple within enclosure of columns, mounted on pine lid, paper label "Anchor Line India (Steamship) Service," India, 19th/20th C **415.00**

Obelisk, 22" h, marble, gilt incised band of faux hieroglyphics, horizontally fluted base offset with black slate moldings, foot with further incised dec, Egyptian Revival, late 19th/early 20th C, price for pr **950.00**

Pedestal

Birch, poplar, and pine, 48" h carved angel statue with wings on back, 42" sq paneled wood pedestal with Arts & Crafts designs, minor loss to wing. **2,950.00**

Marble, 42" h, white, 11" octagonal top, slightly tapered column with relief stop fluting, round stepped base, lobed urn near bottom, minor edge wear and chips **675.00**

Lantern, bronze, pagoda form sculpture, single door opening to light compartment, three-sided metal grids with crescent moon cut-out, topped with owl, tree trunk base with climbing ivy decorated, 16" square, 54" h, minor losses, weathered patina, $3,025. Photo courtesy of Sanford Alderfer Auction Company.

Marble, 44" h, white, 12" octagonal top, spiral column with beaded center ring, octagonal base with stepped rings and round lobed urn near bottom of column, small edge chips **600.00**

Onyx, 38-1/4" h, cream colored, brown striations, 11" octagonal top, ring turned column, sq block base, small edge chips **450.00**

Planter, stump type, sewer tile

10-1/2" l, 15" w, 12" h, textured surface, stamped medallion "Cambria-Co., C. e. Blackfork, Ohio," few chips. **385.00**

18" h, three branches, hand tooled bark, carved "Gram" plaque, crack **110.00**

Roof finial, 46-1/2" h, zinc, light gray and white oxidized surface, top column tapering down to point, flower petals at center, square to round formed base, removable flag and scrolled wire arrow, 19th C, soldered restorations, late enameled steel stand **1,320.00**

Sphinx, 16" l, 10" h, carved wood, worn surface, good detail on face, carved initials "SV" on base **800.00**

Sundial, 17" d, 34" h, lead, circular, alpha numerics, terra cotta base shaped like three gargoyles, shaped plinth **850.00**

Sundial, stoneware, attributed to Remmy Factory, Philadelphia, hand scribed Roman numerals on perimeter, original shaped brass gnomon, four impressed fleur-de-lis decoration, cobalt blue wash, c1850, 15-1/2" d, $5,500. Photo courtesy of Vicki and Bruce Waasdorp.

Topiary form, 13-1/2" w, 24" h, lyre-shape, wire, conical base, painted green, America, late 19th/early 20th C **150.00**

Window frame, 35-1/2" w, 35" h, arched, mullions in gothic pattern, five small panes remaining, 20th C green paint **55.00**

ART DECO

History: The Art-Deco period was named after an exhibition, "l'Exposition Internationale des Arts Déecorative et Industriels Modernes," held in Paris in 1927. Its beginnings succeed those of the Art-Nouveau period, but the two overlap in time, as well as in style.

Art-Deco designs are angular with simple lines. This was the period of skyscrapers, movie idols, and the Cubist works of Picasso and Legras. Art Deco motifs were used for every conceivable object being produced in the 1920s and 1930s (ceramics, furniture, glass, and metals) not only in Europe but in America as well.

Additional Listings: Furniture and Jewelry. Also check glass, pottery, and metal categories.

Aquarium, 41-1/2" h, 18" h stepped and paneled molded translucent yellow glass bowl, dec with six panels of stylized flowers, set in bronzed metal tripod stand, three enameled green handles, legs terminating in stylized dolphins, central light fixture, tri-part base, dark patina, c1925, chips, wear **2,415.00**

Cane, 36-3/4" l, 2-1/4" x 3" h silver handle, yellow glass eyed stylized bird,

Box, brass, designed by Rockwell Kent, for Chase, rectangular hinged lid, relief decorated with nude figure holding clusters of grapes among leaping goats, impressed "RK," fluted corners, impressed Chase mark on base, fitted interior, 6-3/8" x 5-3/8", $500. Photo courtesy of Skinner Auctioneers and Appraisers.

hidden flask, beak acts as pouring spout, head hinged and unscrews, 8" glass flask with worn cork, 1919 Birmingham hallmarks, black enameled hardwood shaft, 1-1/4" horn ferrule, some wear to finish **1,375.00**

Chair, 31" h, 19-1/2" w, 21-1/2" d, Robert Venturi for Knoll, molded plywood, silk-screen print in polychrome on gray ground, unmarked **630.00**

Chandelier

25" l drop, 13-3/4" d, pod and leaf-form patinated metal ceiling mount and three paperclip chains supporting shade with molded floral and geometric devices **575.00**

26-1/2" l, 30" d, cast bronze ceiling mount and lower shade mount, border of stylized bowl of flowers, geometric, and lapped leaves, four conical frosted glass shades with molded geometric floral designs **2,300.00**

28" l drop, 26-1/2" d, paneled wrought iron framework suspending round, paneled,

Brooch, bow, platinum and diamond, openwork set throughout with 34 old European, transitional and single-cut diamonds, centering line of square-cut sapphires (one missing), millegrain accents, $1,765. Photo courtesy of Skinner's Auctioneers and Appraisers.

etched colorless glass shade with raised center rosette and geometric elements, four matching shades, center shade sgd "Muller Frères Luneville," smaller shades also sgd, c1928 . . . . **2,400.00**

Clock, 16" l, mantle, circular geometric form, green variegated onyx, Whithal electric movement, c1925, some repair, minor loss **100.00**

Coffee set, silver plated, Wilcox, design attributed to Gene Theobald, faceted 10-1/2" h coffeepot, and sugar container with Bakelite finials, matching creamer, 20" l oblong tray, all marked "Wilcox S.P. Co/E.P.N.S./International S.Co./W. M. Wounts/1981N." . **1,150.00**

Desk

30" x 44" x 22-1/2", Plycraft, double pedestal, four drawers on each side, single center drawer, stenciled #331 . . . . **350.00**

66-1/8" l, 36-1/8" d, 29" h, Leopold Corp, Burlington, IA, walnut veneered, semi-oval top over center drawer flanked by pull-out writing surface and two drawers, bronze handles, light brown finish, "Charles S. Nathan Office Equipment New York" distributor's metal tag in drawer, veneer loss, wear **900.00**

Drawings, 13-1/2" x 17", by Alexander Bronson, pencil drawings of two beds by Paul Frankl, other with pedestal table, sgd, mounted in natural wood frames, price for three-pc set. . . **750.00**

Dresser box, 12" l, Egyptian Revival, bentwood Egyptian sarcophagus form, overlaid in emb copper with Egyptian motifs, blue opaque glass scarabs, sides trimmed in tooled leather, silk

Beaded evening purse, green, brown, red and blue Art Deco design, $250. Photo courtesy of Joy Luke Auctions.

Pair of white porcelain heads, man and woman, Lenox, green "Lenox, USA" stamps, 8-3/4" x 4", $325. Photo courtesy of David Rago Auctions.

lining, dark rich patina with verdigris oxidation, c1925 . . . . **460.00**

End table, 16-1/2" w, 14" d, 29" h, mahogany and burlwood, orig marble tops over single drawers, one with two lower shelves, other with shelf and cabinet, raised rosettes on metal hardware, France, c1930, price for pr **1,400.00**

Fireplace screen, 25-1/4" w, 35" h, wrought iron, diagonal grid with spade elements at intersections, dark patina, attributed to Raymond Subes, France, c1925 . . . . **4,200.00**

Lamp base, 21" h, etched brass, silver wash on ovoid brass form, etched nude female figures picking grape clusters from cascading grape vines, weighted round stepped base, France, c1925, wear, scattered corrosion **520.00**

Lamp, boudoir, Danse De Lumiere, 11" h, molded glass figure of woman with outstretched arms, bearing stylized feather drapery, oval platform base with internal light fixture, molded title and patent mark, c1930, mold imperfections **400.00**

Lamp, floor, 65" h, 16" d, wooden base, three bright enameled tubular shafts, three pleated conical shades, Bakelite brace **920.00**

Lamp, table

19" h, 11" d concentric ribbed pink satin shade with stylized rosebud center, shade emb "Vleighe France 1137," nickel-plated brass base with emb geometric designs, minor flakes on shade **520.00**

19" h, 13" d shade, trefoil etched colorless glass shade, rosette and

geometric designs, supported by wrought iron tripod with applied rosette accents and leaf motif, shade sgd "Degue," nicks and chips to shade **920.00**

Microphone, 5-3/4" w, 14" h, bright chrome, stepped metal base, metal tag, Astatic Corp, Ohio **2,890.00**

Night stand, 28-1/4" l, 12-1/2" w, 26-3/4" h, walnut, curvilinear design, walnut and cherry veneers, small drawer with burlwood veneer, chrome and resin handle, flanked by small open shelf over three open shelves, aluminum trim around base, imperfections, price for pr **700.00**

Punch bowl and cordial set, eight-sided finial on paneled cov, 7-1/2" h, 8-1/2" d bowl dec with silver and red geometric design, six 2-1/2" d paneled cordials with similar dec, 14" d round glass tray with multiple star cuts on base, chrome sides, chrome ladle, imperfections **290.00**

Room divider, four panels, black lacquered arched frames inset with canvas, painted abstract gold and black pattern, each panel 24" w, 71-1/2" h, slight damage to hinges **1,725.00**

Salon chair, 28-1/2" w, 26-1/2" d, 24-1/2" h, U-shaped low chair, beige velvet and burlwood, metal tag on bases, "Hotel Le Malandre Modele Depose," c1945, price for pr . **2,185.00**

Server, 10-1/2" l, 10-1/2" w, 13" h, Wiener Werkstatte, Austria, second quarter 20th C, scalloped rim on shallow sq light yellow tinted transparent glass bowl, repeating linear and circle cut glass border, raised on base composed of round silver pan on four colorless glass rod legs over sq platform with four oval bezel-mounted green, pink, purple and black stones, imp marks, few rim chips and scratches **2,185.00**

Sideboard, 54-5/8" w, 16-1/2" d, 43" h, attributed to Jacques-Emile Ruhlmann, France, 1879-1933, inlaid Macassar ebony, elongated rect top with ebony and ivory inlaid trim, three center shelves flanked by cupboards, one fitted with drawer, one with shelf, doors with rect ebony inlay with ivory stringing, applied half-round molding around base, swollen shaped legs, imperfections **920.00**

Side table, 17-1/2" l, 23-1/4" d, 13-1/2" h, wrought iron scrolled frame

and legs, rect mirror top, France, 1930s **375.00**

Tea and coffee service, silver plated, coffeepot, teapot, creamer, cov sugar, serving tray, etched linear dec, rosewood handles, Continental, imp marker's marks with cross flanked by two Ls within octagon, wear . . . **500.00**

Vase

8-1/2" h, cameo glass, black ground, stylized scene of three repeated terriers against bronzed and silvered ground, unsigned, French, c1925 . . . . **300.00**

8-1/2" h, citrine ground, stylized enameled flowers, sgd "Legras," minor heat check **200.00**

11-3/8" h, ceramic, Boch Frères, extended rim, oval form, stylized light green blossoms, stems, and foliage, gold accents, turquoise ground, glossy glaze, painted "BFK/340," imp "708," minor crazing, minor light scratches, price for pr **920.00**

12-1/4" h, 5-1/2" d, Wiener Werkstatte, bulbous, flaring neck, painted white and black geometric pattern, brown ground, stamped "WWW/Made in Austria/HB" **125.00**

12-1/2" h, molded opalescent glass, Art Deco stylized scene of centaur and panther hunting gazelles, foliage background with blue patina, unmarked, attributed to Sabino **635.00**

Wall sconce

7" h, 3" d, nickeled brass plate and curved arm, frosted glass shade with raised geometric design, rim chips to shade, minor dents to sconce **90.00**

Vase, black matte glass, applied silver and turquoise enamel decorated, 8" h, $110. Photo courtesy of Sanford Alderfer Auction Company.

12" h, 5-1/2" w, Art Deco etched colorless glass fanned shades on "V"-shaped silvered metal wall mounts, France, 1928, price for pr **1,150.00**

14-1/2" h, 5-1/4" w, diamond shaped frosted glass inserts, raised geometric design, V-shaped nickeled bronze mounts, France, c1930, minor wear to slip, price for pr.................... **875.00**

Wristwatch, lady's, 6-1/8" l, platinum, rect silvertone dial, black Arabic numerals, bezel and shoulders enhanced with single-cut diamonds, articulated strap set with pave diamonds and calibre-cut emeralds in geometric pattern, further set with single-cut diamond links **3,850.00**

ART NOUVEAU

History: Art Nouveau is the French term for the "new art," which had its beginning in the early 1890s and continued for the next 40 years. The flowing and sensuous female forms used in this period were popular in Europe and America. Among the most recognized artists of this period were Gallé, Lalique, and Tiffany.

The Art-Nouveau style can be identified by flowing, sensuous lines, florals, insects, and the feminine form. These designs were incorporated into almost everything produced during the period, from art glass to furniture, silver, and personal objects. Later wares demonstrate some of the characteristics of the evolving Art-Deco style.

Additional Listings: Furniture and Jewelry. Also check glass, pottery, and metal categories.

Bowl, sterling silver, by George W. Shiebler & Co. flaring shaped rim with pierced work, flower and scrolls, monogrammed, marked "2816" on bottom, 20 troy oz, 12-1/2" w, 2-1/2" h, $460. Photo courtesy of James D. Julia, Inc.

Candlestick, 11-3/8" h, patinated metal, figural, nymph standing on butterfly, holding flower form candle sconce, flower-form base, early 20th C **115.00**

Cane, silver

33-1/2" l, 4" x 3" h "L" shaped handle depicting nude reclining on dec plinth, narrow cloth draped over

Chamberstick, silver plate, Pairpoint, New Bedford, MA, early 20th C, round petal form candlecup, two scrolled arms raised on floral and foliate decorated circular base by four floriform feet, Pairpoint mark, "Quadruple plate, B4 04," 7-1/2" h, $300. Photo courtesy of Skinner's Auctioneers and Appraisers.

thighs, marked "800," German hallmarks, ebony shaft, 1" dark horn ferrule, c1895...... **3,500.00**

35" l, 2/3" w x 6" at arc of crook handle, silver, finished in dull gold in vermeil manner, fashioned like leafy plant stem, 10 silver blossoms emerge at end of stem, each have tiny cabochon emeralds as center, stepped partridge-wood shaft, 1" burnished brass ferrule, French, c1900 .... **1,570.00**

36" l, 7-1/2" across arc, hunting dog head protruding from swirls of marsh reeds, tarnished French hallmarks, lignum vitae shaft, imp below handle "Frizon 5 Av. Del Opera" for Parisian seller, 3/4" white metal ferrule, c1900 ...... **800.00**

Clock

Desk, 3-3/4" w, 4-3/8" h, bronze, Chelsea Clock movement, gilt-metal and glass mount, red enamel dec devices, ftd base, circular face with Arabic chapters, imp "Chelsea Clock Co., Boston, USA, 155252" on inside clock works, worn patina...... **460.00**

Figural, 12-1/2" h, enameled cast white metal, relief of woman's head, flowing hair, leaves, thistles, Seth Thomas movement, circular dial with Roman numerals, c1900, minor wear **300.00**

Wall, 24-1/2" w, 10" d, 38" h, carved walnut, two train movement, floral etched gilt metal dial sgd "Trilla, Barcelona," case topped by bust of young beauty on rocaille shell above iris flower, flanked by poppy roundels, case further carved with stylized florets, writing flower buds at corners, Spanish, early 20th C **490.00**

Door pulls, 3" w, 15" h, bronze, whiplash handles, orig patina, Belgian, price for pr **1,150.00**

Floor vase, 21" h, glass, gray ground internally dec with streaked orange and mottled blue, blown-out into wrought iron armature with scrolled designs, stylized florals, Muller and Chapelle, c1910, glass damaged at base **1,100.00**

Garniture, centerpiece with bronze patina, female spelter figure of "L. Historie," flanked by spelter plinth with clock, enameled dial with painted Arabic numbers, sgd "L. Satre-A Pont. Aven," rect molded marble base with center bronze gilt neoclassical mounting, bronze gilded bun feet, pr of bronze patina spelter Louis XVI style urns, ribbons and swags centering figural medallion, sq marble base, bronze gilded feet **950.00**

Inkwell, 7" x 13", bronze, double inkwells flanking shaped pen tray, raised leaf and berry motif, sgd "C.H. Louchet".................. **460.00**

Lamp, table, 18-1/4" h, opalescent shell held by arched foliage, supported by female figure in white metal, bronze patina, ruffled water-like base, early 20th C, imperfections........ **320.00**

Perfume bottle, 4-1/4" h, paneled slender baluster form bottle painted with blue and gold flowers, gilt-metal hinged lid enclosing glass stopper, lid with short chain **520.00**

Picture frame

4-7/8" h, sterling silver, oval, emb flowers and maiden, Unger Bros., Newark **175.00**

Ewer, Delphin Massier, majolica, baluster form, richly decorated with various foliage, c1910, painted mark, restoration to lip, 21" h, $1,200. Photo courtesy of David Rago Auctions.

8-1/2" w, 11-3/8" h, wood, penwork and colored stained dec of stylized fruiting flowers, easel back. **100.00**

Pitcher, 11-3/4" h, relief wheat dec, mottled blue, brown, and green, imp "Gres Mougin Nancy," by Joseph Victor Xavier, Nancy, France, c1900 . . **865.00**

Stove, coal, 28-1/2" w, 22" d, 36" h, bronze and iron, shaped structure, pierced bronze plaque with "S"-scroll motifs centering pineapple, applied bronze medallions with female profiles, stamped "Deville Pailliette Forest, No. 17, Charlesville, Ardennes," c1900 . . . . **375.00**

Table, side, 24" w, 17" d, 30" h, scallop-edge rect top inlaid with poppies in exotic woods, fluted legs, cabriole feet, lower shelf with variation of poppy motif, orig finish, inlaid "Galle" signature **2,100.00**

Tea kettle, 11" h, sterling silver, floral repousse dec, curved handle, marked "J. E. Caldwell & Co., 925, Sterling, 1000, Philadelphia," 47 troy oz . **550.00**

Vase

7-7/8" h, pottery, painted dec of female profile in central medallion, two medallions of landscapes enhanced by stylized flowers, greens, blues, pinks, and yellows, Continental, glaze chip on rim **150.00**

8-3/4" h, glass, gray ground internally dec with mottled light and dark blue, blown-out into wrought iron reeded armature, base inscribed "Daum Nancy" and "L Majorelle," c1920 . . . . . **1,610.00**

Wine cabinet, 46" w, 18" d, 68-1/2" h, carved walnut, panels elaborately carved with nymphs and grapevines, fitted with two pairs of doors and drawer, early 20th C **5,550.00**

ART POTTERY (GENERAL)

History: America's interest in art pottery can be traced to the Centennial Exposition in Philadelphia, Pennsylvania, in 1877, where Europe's finest producers of decorative art displayed an impressive selection of their wares. Our young artists rose to the challenge immediately, and by 1900, native artisans were winning gold medals for decorative ceramics here and abroad.

The Art Pottery "Movement" in America lasted from about 1880 until the first World War. During this time, more than 200 companies, in most states, produced decorative ceramics ranging from borderline production ware to intricately decorated, labor

intensive artware establishing America as a decorative art powerhouse.

Below is a listing of the work by various factories and studios, with pricing, from a number of these companies. The location of these outlets are included to give the reader a sense of how nationally based the industry was.

For more information, see this book.

Additional Listings: See Clewell, Clifton, Cowan, Dedham, Fulper, Grueby, Jugtown, Marblehead, Moorcroft, Newcomb, North Dakota School of Mines, Ohr, Paul Revere, Peters and Reed, Rookwood, Roseville, Van Briggle, Weller, and Zanesville.

Notes: Condition, design, size, execution, and glaze quality are the key considerations when buying art pottery. This category includes only companies not found elsewhere in this book.

Adviser: David Rago.

Arequipa, vase, bulbous, carved eucalyptus leaves, seafoam green matte glaze, brown clay showing through, stamped AREQ-UIPA/10?/136, incised B.L. 5-1/4" x 3-3/4", $4,315. Photos courtesy of David Rago Auctions.

Arequipa

Bowl, 6-1/2" d, 2-1/4" h, closed-in, emb eucalyptus branches, matte green and dark blue glaze, stamped mark, incised "KH/11" **800.00**

Vase, 3-3/4" d, 5-1/4" h, bulbous, carved eucalyptus leaves, covered in seafoam green matte glaze, brown clay showing through, stamped "AREQUIPA/10?/136," incised B.L. **4,315.00**

Avon, Vance, vase, 5" d, 5-1/2" h, designed by Frederick Rhead, squeezebag stylized trees, orange and green ground, incised "Avon/WPTS.CO./174-1241" . . . **920.00**

Bachelder, O. L., vase, 5" h, 3-3/4" d, bulbous, cobalt blue and teal sheer glossy glaze, incised "OLB/R," ink cipher **500.00**

Bennett, John

Charger

14-1/2" d, dec with polychrome butterfly amidst white azaleas,

John Bennett, charger, decorated with butterfly amidst white azaleas and green leaves, indigo and violet ground, signed J Bennett/412 E24/N.Y., few rim kiln kisses, 14-1/2" d, $5,350.

green leaves, indigo and violet ground, sgd "J. Bennett/412/ E24/NY," few kiln kisses around rim **5,350.00**

14-1/2" d, dec with polychrome daisies and poppies enclosed within hearts, cobalt blue ground, black scroll design, sgd "J. Bennett/412 E24/NY/Oct 9/79," added inscription "Wed last 100 degs in shade" **4,600.00**

Vase, 3-3/4" d, 7-1/2" h, bulbous, painted burgundy phlox and honeybee, ivory ground, minute rim fleck, marked "BENNETT/W2E24/ NJ/artist's cipher" **2,870.00**

Brouwer, vase, 12" x 7-1/4", baluster, flame-painted, orange, yellow, and brown lustered glaze, thick bronze glaze dripping on neck and shoulder, incised wishbone mark and flame, remnants of paper label, firing line and flat chip under base, minor scratches to body, glaze flakes on rim **8,575.00**

Cole, A. R., urn, 18-1/2" h, 9-1/2" d, hand-thrown, three fanciful twisted handles, mirror black glaze, unmarked, shallow scratches **400.00**

Crook, Russel, urn, 16-1/2" h, 10" d, wax-resist, cowboys on horseback, brown clay under glossy, mottled dark blue glaze, incised "John Lampus/ potter/RCrook/92," 1892, restored small rim chip, larger chip at base . . **3,750.00**

Frackelton, Susan, vase, 3-3/4" d, 6-3/4" h, gourd shape, salt-glaze stoneware, dec with abutilon blossoms alternating with stylized leaves and vines in indigo on ivory ground, sgd

"SF/1X/984," chip, nick to rim
.... **20,700.00**

Kenton Hills, vase

4-3/4" d, 7-1/4" h, cylindrical, white prunts cov in mirrored umber glaze, incised "Hentschel" for William Hentschel, imp "KH/124"
.....................**775.00**

6" d, 7-1/2" h, 4-sided, aventurine glaze, imp "KH/171" **650.00**

McLoughlin, Marie Louise

Trivet, 6" d, Losanti Ware, circular, emb with floral motif, celadon glaze, incised cipher, marked "Losanti," clay particles stuck to glaze, firing lines, base chips
.....................**550.00**

Vase, 3-3/4" d, 4-1/4" h, Losanti ware, incised swirling peacock feathers, beige and oxblood crackled glaze, incised cipher/Losanti/97, short, heavy crazing line to rim **2,615.00**

Pewabic

Bookends, pr, 4" w, 4-3/4" h, emb animal, lustered blue and green glaze, stamped "Pewabic," repair to small edge chip.......**415.00**

Miniature, vase, 2" h, crackled turquoise glaze, blue plumes, sgd "Pewabic/Detroit/PP"......**265.00**

Plate, 9-1/4" d, white crackleware, rim dec with squeezebag yellow and red roosters on green field, stamped "Pewabic," some loss of glaze, chips on back.....**920.00**

Vase, 3" d, 3-3/4" h, cylindrical with squatty base, mottled and lustered purple and turquoise glaze, paper label, hand written "Anne/1942," small glaze scale at rim. . . . **265.00**

Vessel, 5-1/4" d, 5-1/2" h, bulbous, ribbed, glossy teal glaze, stamped "Pewabic/Detroit" **520.00**

Pierrefonds, 6" d, 10" h, shouldered ovoid, blue and green crystalline flambé glaze, stamped mark and 602
.....................**575.00**

Pisgah Forest

Tea set, Cameo Ware, wagon and landscape dec, dark matte green ground, raised mark and date 1943, 5-1/4" h teapot **950.00**

Vase, 4-3/4" d, 6-1/4" h, bulbous, white, blue, and yellow crystalline glaze, unmarked **460.00**

Vessel, 5" h, 5-3/4" d, spherical, amber glaze, white and blue crystals, raised potter's mark and date 1947.............. **350.00**

Poillon, Clara, pitcher, 5" d, 4-1/2" h, bulbous, medium green glaze, incised CPI monogram **365.00**

San Jose, charger, 15-1/2" d, cuerda seca dec, polychrome wagon train scene, green semi-matte ground, unmarked, small rim fleck..... **435.00**

Robineau, Adelaide, vase, 4" d, 3-3/4" h, spherical, bright cobalt blue glaze with blooming crystals, incised "AR," hairline to base **6,300.00**

Teco

Vase

5-1/2" d, 6-3/4" h, double gourd shape, four buttressed handles, smooth matte green glaze with charcoaling, stamped "TECO/237," two small glaze flakes
..................**4,600.00**

5-1/2" d, 6" h, bulbous, smooth matte green glaze with charcoaling, stamped "TECO/76," restoration to rim chip
.... **630.00**

7-1/2" d, 15-1/2" h, gourd shape, curdled matte green glaze with charcoaling, stamped "TECO/182" **1,840.00**

Vessel

4-3/4" d, 3-1/4" h, three handles, smooth matte green glaze, stamped "Teco," touch-up to rim bruise **490.00**

10" d, 14-1/2" h, corseted, four handles, smooth matte green glaze with charcoal highlights, stamped "Teco," incised 172, restoration **5,175.00**

Threshold Pottery, Adelaide Robineau, breakfast set, 4" h milk pitcher, 6" d cereal bowl, polychrome enameled rooster, white crackled ground, stamped "Threshold/AR/1924"
.....................**3,375.00**

Volkmar, pitcher, 4" d, 4-1/2" h, bulbous, collared neck, cucumber green matte glaze, incised illegible inscription.................**265.00**

Walley, W. J., vase, 6-1/2" h, bottle shape, sheer light green and gunmetal glaze, imp "W.J.W." **535.00**

Walrath

Cider pitcher, 7" d, 5" h, matte, yellow fruit, green leaves, brown ground, marked "Walrath Pottery/MI"............**1,495.00**

Sculpture, 4" h, 6" l, kneeling nude picking rose, sheer matte green glaze, yellow details, incised "Walrath" **300.00**

Vase, 6-1/4" h, 4" d, painted stylized purple and dark green flowers, light gray-green ground, incised "Walrath Pottery" **4,000.00**

Pewabic, bulbous vase with flaring rim, covered in blue, green, and purple lustered glaze, imp circular mark, small glaze chip to base, 8" x 8", $1,150. Photo courtesy of David Rago Auctions.

Teco, vessel, corseted, four handles, smooth matte green glaze with charcoaled highlights, stamped Teco, incised 172, restoration to few small chips and hairlines, 14-1/2" x 10", $5,175.

Teco, bulbous vase with collar rim, covered in smooth matte green glaze. Stamped "TECO," 7" x 7", $2,100. Photo courtesy of David Rago Auctions.

Wheatley

Lamp base, 14" d, 23" h, emb poppy pods, frothy matte green glaze, new hammered copper fittings, Japanese split-bamboo shade lined with new coral silk, stamped mark **1,380.00**

Sand jar, 15" d, 24" h, high relief sculpted grape leaves and vines from rim, feathered medium green matte glaze, incised mark/722, several glaze nicks restored **2,415.00**

Vase, 6-3/4" d, 12-1/4" h, bulbous, three climbing lizards, feathered medium matte green glaze, remnant of paper label, restoration to drill hole on side **1,380.00**

White, Denver, vase, 6-1/2" d, 3-3/4" h, squatty, smooth matte gold and green glaze, incised "Denver/1916," small bruise under rim **210.00**

ARTS AND CRAFTS MOVEMENT

History: The Arts and Crafts Movement in American decorative arts took place between 1895 and 1920. Leading proponents of the movement were Elbert Hubbard and his Roycrofters, the brothers Stickley, Frank Lloyd Wright, Charles and Henry Greene, George Niedecken, and Lucia and Arthur Mathews.

The movement was marked by individualistic design (although the movement was national in scope) and re-emphasis on handcraftsmanship and appearance. A reform of industrial Society was part of the long-range goal. Most pieces of furniture favored a rectilinear approach and were made of oak.

The Arts and Crafts Movement embraced all aspects of the decorative arts, including metalwork, ceramics, embroidery, woodblock printing, and the crafting of jewelry.

Adviser: David Rago.

Additional Listings: Roycroft, Stickleys, and art pottery categories.

Blanket chest, Greene & Greene, oak and yellow pine, unusually mortised corners fastened with sq dowel pegs, two lift-top doors, good orig finish, from Pratt residence, Ojai, CA, 65" l, 23-3/4" w, 18-1/2" h **22,500.00**

Bookcase, 37" w, 10-1/4" d, 47" h, gallery top, adjustable shelves, small cabinet with leaded glass door, orig finish, Liberty & Co. tag, c1900 . . . . **3,115.00**

Candlesticks, pr, 11-3/4" h, 3-3/4" d, cast copper, imp "1797" with double cross, no patina, unmarked. . . . **195.00**

Chair, dining room, Limbert, side, single broad vertical back slat,

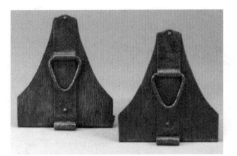

Bookends, pair, hammered copper, woodgrain texturing, V-shaped ring pull, original finish, unmarked, 5-1/4" w, 7" h, $250. Photos courtesy David Rago Auctions.

tacked-on brown leather, orig finish with heavy overcoat, branded mark, 17" w, 37" h, price for set of four **1,610.00**

Chamberstick, 6-1/4" h, hammered copper, cup-shaped bobeche, riveted angular handle, flaring base, stamped "OMS" for Onondaga Metal Shops, old cleaning and verdigris to patina **175.00**

Cigarette box, 2-1/4" x 5" x 4", hammered copper, riveted trim, emb circular medallions, cedar lining, natural patina, unmarked, attributed to England **260.00**

Clock, 14" w, 4-3/4" d, 21-3/4" h, New Haven, Japanese-style, brass hands, keyed through-tenon sides, amber ripple glass, orig ebonized finish, paper label **490.00**

Coal scuttle, 15" x 22", hammered copper, repousse floral motif, riveted seams, rolled rim, new patina, some dents to body, some replaced rivets **575.00**

Charger, hammered copper, in style of Gustav Stickley, repousse spade motif, rolled rim, original dark patina, unmarked. 15" d, $2,070.

Desk clock, pewter, Liberty Tudric, designed by Archibald Knox, embossed stylized leaves, blue and green enameled face, stamped "Tudric Peter/0570," 5-1/2" w, 8" h, $5,175.

Coffee and tea service, coffeepot, teapot, creamer, sugar, and tray, pewter, wicker handles, by Archibald Knox, stamped "Liberty/Tudric," price for five-pc set **3,115.00**

Compote, 8" d, 6-3/4" h, pewter, cluthra green glass liner with opalescent and gold swirls, Liberty Tudric, Archibald Knox **3,115.00**

China cabinet, double-door china cabinet with eight panes per door, four panes on sides, three interior shelves, original finish, stenciled 141, 48-1/4" x 35-3/4" x 13", $2,760.

Inkwell, 5-1/4" sq, 3-1/2" h, faceted copper, curled, riveted feet, enameled green, red, and black, spade pattern, orig patina, unmarked Arts & Crafts Shop, couple of nicks to dec . . . **250.00**

Lamp, ceiling, 8-1/2" d, 11" h, polished hammered brass, four arms, flame-shaped opalescent glass shade with green pulled feather pattern, English **1,355.00**

Lamp, table, 22" h, 22" d shade, D'Arcy Gaw for Dirk Van Erp, hammered copper, four-panel flaring mica shade with bulbous cap, cupped rim, supported by four armatures riveted to tacked-on shoulder, bullet-shaped base, four sockets, orig patina, closed box mark with "D'Arcy Gaw/Dirk Van Erp," re-wired, minor dent removed, missing int. cap **6,900.00**

Lamp, student, 16" h, 13" d, Roycroft brass washed hammered copper base, Stickley Bros. copper and mica shades with silhouetted trees, orig finish, replaced mica, orb and cross mark **1,840.00**

Library table

47-1/2" l, 36-1/4" w, 28-1/2" h, double oval, flaring legs, cut-out stretchers, orig finish, branded Limbert mark, 1" cut off legs **7,475.00**

52" l, 24" w, 29-1/2" h, two arched drawers, corbels, one shelf, orig finish, Lifetime Paine Furniture Co. metal tag **2,300.00**

Magazine stand

18-1/4" w, 14" d, 50-1/2" h, gallery top, vertical slats all around, five tiers, fine orig dark finish, branded "CPM" **2,415.00**

24" w, 12" d, 41-1/2" h, three shelf, two short drawers, arched side rails over slatted sides, light finish, loose joints **630.00**

Music cabinet, 21-1/2" w, 17" d, 42" h, attributed to G. M. Ellwood for J. S. Henry, c1900, English, mahogany, beveled top, paneled door inlaid with fruitwoods and mother-of-pearl, two drawers, brass hardware, good new finish **2,870.00**

Nut set, hammered copper, 8-1/2" d master bowl, six 3" d serving bowls, Benedict, some wear to patina, unmarked **290.00**

Occasional table, 30" d, 29-1/2" h, circular top over flaring legs joined by cut-out stretchers, orig finish, branded Limbert mark, wear and stains to top **2,070.00**

Pitcher, owl shape, pewter, jade cabochon eyes, stamped "TUDRIC/5/05 5," 8" x 6-1/2" **$1,150.** *Photo courtesy of David Rago Auctions.*

Pagoda table, Limbert, corbels under sq top, flaring sides, arched apron, lower shelf, cut-out base, orig finish, heavy overcoat, paper label under top, 34" sq, 30-1/2" h **13,800.00**

Picture frame, 6" w, 9" h, hammered sterling silver, emb daisies, English hallmarks **750.00**

Pillow, 16" x 25", embroidered stylized orange and green poppies, beige linen ground **490.00**

Plant stand, Limbert, quarter-round corbels under sq top, flaring sides, ovoid cut-outs, lower shelf, plank base, fine orig factory finish, factory edge repair to top, no visible mark, 20" sq, 29-1/2" h **6,900.00**

Tabouret, English, copper-clad circular top, turned legs with bun feet, broad cross-stretchers, unmarked, refinished, polished top, 22" d, 16" h, **$300.**

Room divider, 68" h, oak, grid-like top, three-panel, each panel cut-out with fern design, replaced linen panels, orig finish, unmarked, some minor chipping to edges **1,200.00**

Sewing table, 18" l, 18" w closed, 29" h, drop leaf, two drawers with wooden pulls, tapering legs, orig finish, two splits to top **350.00**

String holder, 3-3/4" d, 3-1/2" h, sterling on bronze, bell shape, applied silver leaves and vines, orig patina, stamped "HAMS," Heintz **535.00**

Sideboard, Limbert, large backsplash with plate-rail and shelf, two long drawers flanked by two shorter ones and two doors, open shelf over linen drawer, all with hammered copper pulls, knobs and strap hinges, very good original finish and condition, branded mark, 51" x 60" x 23" **$5,350.** *Photo courtesy of David Rago Auctions.*

A

Tablecloth, 39" d, circular, linen, embroidered red poppies, green leaves
.... 860.00

Table, dining, Limbert, circular, extension, four-sided pedestal base, orig finish with heavy overcoat, 54" d, 27-1/4" h 2,300.00

Tabouret, Limbert, sq top, box construction, sq cut-outs, top refinished, orig finish on base, branded mark, 16-1/2" sq, 18" h 2,615.00

Vase, 5" h, 6" d, bulbous, curtained copper, dimpled and folded sides covered in rare orig red finish, Dirk Van Erp, windmill/San Francisco mark with partial D'Arcy Gaw visible 2,760.00

Wall sconce
   6" d shade, 14-1/2" h, brass, emb stylized poppies, leaded glass period shades, English, price for pr................. 2,530.00
   9" w, 15" l, Jarvie, brass, double, tooled back plate, two riveted candleholders, each with scrolled braces and flaring bobeche, orig patina, stamped "Made By The Jarvie Shop".......... 5,750.00

AUSTRIAN WARE

History: More than 100 potteries were located in the Austro-Hungarian Empire in the late 19th and early 20th centuries. Although Carlsbad was the center of the industry, the factories spread as far as the modern-day Czech Republic.

Many of the factories were either owned or supported by Americans; hence, their wares were produced mainly for export to the United States.

Marks: Many wares do not have a factory mark but only the word "Austrian" in response to the 1891 law specifying that the country of origin had to be marked on imported products.

Additional Listings: Amphora, Carlsbad, Royal Dux, and Royal Vienna.

Vase, face of woman, green hat, two pink flowers as handles, 6" h, $75. Photo courtesy of Joy Luke Auctions.

Vase, two handles, pink, yellow, and red roses, leaves, gilt trim, 8" h, $185. Photo courtesy of Joy Luke Auctions.

Bud vase, bulbous shoulders, cow dec, green ground 45.00

Celery tray, 12" l, scalloped border, pink roses, green leaves, gold trim
.... 75.00

Ewer, 11-3/4" h, 6" d, rococo gold scroll, hp pink and yellow wild roses, gold outlines, four ftd 125.00

Figural group, bronze, cold painted, 13-1/2" w, 14-1/2" h, realistically modeled as small songbird perched on wide leaf in front of tall iris flowers, twig base, late 19th/early 20th C .. 1,840.00

Oyster plate, 9-7/8" d, porcelain, shell-shaped wells to center, scalloped rim, blue and gilt enamel flowers, fish, and birds dec, 19th C 175.00

Perfume set, orange cut glass finials, angular opaque black glass vessels, metal mounts, enameled fan motif, all imp "Austria" on metal, two acid-etched "Austria," 6-1/8" h atomizer, 5-3/8" h

Vase, buttressed, embossed rust, green and gold design on a shaded gray and teal matte ground, raised key mark/JBD/ Austria for Jacques Dressler, cracks to body, 7-1/2" d, 13" h, $150. Photo courtesy of David Rago Auctions.

Vase, Austrian Art Glass Company, cased glass, smoky quartz, decorated with classical figures, unmarked, few minor nicks overall, 8-1/2" x 5" $150. Photo courtesy of David Rago Auctions.

perfume, 5" h cov box, imperfections
.... 500.00

Pokal, glass
   17-1/2" h, green, detailed enameled cavalier holding empty stein, c1890................. 400.00
   18-1/2" h, green, detailed enameled scene of knight on horseback, colorful scrolled acanthus dec, c1890................. 400.00

Table lamp, attributed to Wiener Werkstatte, in the manner of Susi Singer, ceramic, ovoid, flanked by two mermaid figures in high relief, fish, octopus, and starfish in relief, glossy aqua, orange, white, and irid glazes, textured mottled green and brown ground, gilt highlights, four patinated metal dolphins on stepped metal base, 22-1/4" h 375.00

Trinket box, cov, 4-1/4" l, oval, the gilt metal box stamped with continuous bands of anthemion and torches, porcelain set lid with printed scene of two classical beauties on cobalt blue ground, velveteen lining, early 20th C 450.00

Vase
   10" h, divided rim forms two spouts, large dolphin handles, gold scales, raised gold florals, cream ground
   .... 125.00
   10-1/2" h, art pottery, four Art Nouveau style handles, c1900
   .... 230.00

AUTOGRAPHS

History: Autographs appear on a wide variety of formats—letters, documents, photographs, books, cards, etc. Most collectors focus on a particular person, country, or category, e.g., signers of the Declaration of Independence.

For more information, see this book.

Abbreviations: The following are used to describe autograph materials.

ADS	Autograph Document Signed
ALS	Autograph Letter Signed
AQS	Autograph Quotation Signed
CS	Card Signed
DS	Document Signed
FDC	First Day Cover
LS	Letter Signed
PS	Photograph Signed
TLS	Typed Letter Signed

Colonial America

Butcher, John, ALS, Alexandria, VA, Jan. 4, 1800, to daughter, giving lengthy comments on last will and testament of George Washington, whereby he wills 130 Negroes free after Martha's death, two pgs, 12" x 16", integral address leaf........ **1,035.00**

Pickering, Timothy, LS, Department of State, Jan. 11, 1799, as Secretary of State, to Valck and Company, regarding incident between their ship *Aurora* and British Frigate *Latona,* early bibliographic note written on verso by B. Mayer, one page, single 8" x 10", offsetting from portrait engraving, hinged to larger sheet **230.00**

Steuben, Baron Von, March 1782, clipped partly-printed DS, sgd "Steuben Maj General," certifying contents of shipment, one page, 2" x 7-1/2", silked, partially mounted to larger sheet with portrait engraving **750.00**

Foreign

Disraeli, Benjamin, envelope, sgd "Disraeli," addressed to Lady Corneila Guest, 3" x 4" inches, matted and framed **80.00**

Eiffel, Gustave, TLS, Paris, April 19, 1889, sgd "G. Eissel" to E. Hippeau, in French, one page, single 8" x 10" sheet, business stationary, folds..... **375.00**

Leonov, Alexei, Cosmonaut, worn spacesuit **1,997.00**

Peron, Eva, PS, Buenos Aires, Oct. 10, 1950, bust portrait, sgd on mount beneath calligraphic inscription, 9" x 6-1/2" photo on 13-1/2" x 9-1/2" mount, signature light, framed **620.00**

General

Evans, John, document appointing administrate of an estate, March 24, 1704, wax seal, some fold weakness, 9-1/2" x 15"................ **485.00**

Huger, Isaac, ADS, arrest warrant for John Smith, issued by state of South Carolina, Feb. 15, 1785, sgd by Huger as sheriff, some ink bleeding, 8" x 13" **100.00**

Lindbergh, Charles A., TDS, Cuba, Nov. 19, 1932, sgd "C. A. Lindbergh," as Pan American Airways pilot, passenger list for flight from Cuba to Miami, one page, single 8" x 10" sheet, Republica de Cuba Secretaria de Hacienda letterhead, minor chips at edges, corner mounted........... **1,495.00**

McKean, Thomas, document is act authorizing Gov of PA to contract with John Birion to print Laws of the Commonwealth of PA, 3 pgs, March 17, 1806, also sgd by Charles Porter, Speaker of the House of Representatives, and James Brady, Speaker of the Senate, some toning and edge chipping, 20" x 16" **450.00**

Ruth, Babe

Baseball, graded C.9-9.5 .... **17,270.00**

Photo of Babe Ruth with golfer Rudy Jugan, sgd by Ruth **1,430.00**

Wedgwood, Josiah, England, dated 1814, written to W. Howorth, notifying him of salary of 200 pounds a year **980.00**

Literature

Anderson, Sherwood, TLS, Oct. 14, 1939, to Ralph Hartman, regarding autographing books, one pg, oblong 7" sheet, folds, framed with photograph **220.00**

Cooper, James Fenimore, ALS, Cooperstown, Sept. 2, 1845, sgd "J. Fenimore Cooper" to Elliot Cowdin, chair of lecture committee of the Merchantile Library Assoc. of Boston, agreeing to lecture, one page, folded 8" x 10" sheet............... **635.00**

Emerson, Ralph Waldo, ALS, Concord, Sept. 22, 1846, sgd "R. W. Emerson" to Elliot Cowdin, President of Merchantile Library Assoc., agreeing to give lecture, one page, folded 8" x 10" sheet with integral address leaf, usual folds..................... **575.00**

Hemingway, Ernest, ALS, Key West, March 31, 1936, sgd "Ernesto" to Miami Herald fishing columnist Ed Roman, about broadbill swordfish, four pgs, two

James "Jimmy" Harold Doolittle, black and white photo distributed by Mutual of Omaha, inscribed and signed "J. H. Doolittle," 8" x 10", $110. Photo courtesy of Cowan Historic Americana Auctions.

8" x 10" sheets, folds, orig holograph mailing envelope **3,450.00**

Sandburg, Carl, ALS, Chicago Daily News letterhead, Chicago, Dec. 12, 1926, to poet Sara Teasdale, concerning poetry, one page, single oblong sheet, folds, holograph mailing envelope, framed........... **490.00**

Military

Cornwallis, Charles, Earl, ALS, Calcutta, Sept. 17, 1786, sgd as Governor General of the British Indian Government, to Lord Sydney (Thomas Townsend), Home Secretary under William Pitt, concerning arrival in Calcutta, 2-1/2 pgs, folded sheet **1,495.00**

Farragut, David G., LS, New York, Dec. 14, 1863, sgd "D. G. Farragut" to Elliot Cowden, regarding department for station, one page, folded sheet, integral blank, blue-ruled paper, folds .. **350.00**

Ingraham, Duncan, sgd "Dn Ingraham" at top of 7" sheet, faded, mat burn, framed with medal commemorating his naval achievements **175.00**

Mussolini, Benito, PS, close-up bust portrait, looking downwards, sgd on sheet below image, red wax seal affixed to lower left corner, 11" x 7-1/2", minor creases in image, emb stamp on lower right corner of image, framed .. **520.00**

Sherman, William T, PS, sgd "W. T. Sherman, General, New York, Feb. 8, 1889," standing 3/4 portrait, in uniform,

11-1/2" x 7" image size, matted, framed
.......................**2,300.00**

Thomas, Lorenzo, PS, "Brig Genl I. Thomas, Adj. Genl U.S.A.," bust portrait carte-de-visite by Frederick Gutekunst, orig photographer's mount, sgd on recto at bottom of image, bit yellowed and soiled, revenue stamp affixed on verso **260.00**

Yamaashita, Tomoyki, Phillippine one peso banknote, Victory issue, boldly signed in Japanese and English, plus signatures of two of his aides, 2-1/2" x 6-1/4", folds **920.00**

Music

Caruso, Enrico, souvenir illus menu for dinner in his honor, sgd by Caruso and other attendees, including Otto Kahn, Victor Herbert, Winston O. Lord, David Bispham, and Melville E. Stone, New York, Feb. 5, 1916 ....**290.00**

Holst, Gustav, partially printed DS, London, April 19, 1923, signed and initialed five times, contract for publication of opera Savitri, manuscript changes to terms, countersigned by publisher and witness, two pgs, folio sheet, folds, bit toned, signed over revenue stamp.............**320.00**

Melba, Nellie, PS, inscribed "To darling Mr. Shaw with love from Nellie Melba 1917," full-length portrait of soprano standing beside piano, sgd below image, 8-1/2" x 6" image on 14" x 9-1/2" in sheet, minor staining in upper right corner **460.00**

Paganini, Niccolo, ALS, London, July 1, 1831, in Italian, agreeing to take part in benefit for poor musicians, one page

7-1/2" x 7-1/4" sheet, trimmed, minor browning.................**2,300.00**

Presidents

Adams, John Quincy, sgd endorsement, Boston, June 11, 1793, sgd "J. Q. Adams" on verso of partly-printed writ for arrest of debtor, two pgs, single sheet, 6-1/2" x 8", expert restoration closing separations at folds, reinforced corners **260.00**

Grant, Ulysses, ALS, Long Branch, June 28, 1875, sgd as President to Senator Matthew Carpenter, regarding remarks about recent speech, emb personal stationery........**1,380.00**

Johnson, Andrew, check signed, as President, Washington, June 1869, on First National Bank of Washington, endorsed on verso, 3-1/2" x 8", contemporary stamp affixed in the upper right corner **2,100.00**

Kennedy, John F., TLS, as President, White House stationery, Feb. 9, 1962, to Secretary of Labor Arthur Goldberg, thanking him for his role in White House Regional Conference, one page, single tall sheet **1,725.00**

Lincoln, Abraham, ALS, as President, Washington, Sept. 11, 1861, sgd "A. Lincoln," presumably to Secretary of War Cameron, asking him to provide General Sigel's brother with a railroad pass, one page, 4" x 5-1/4", folds, very minor offsetting, minor restoration on verso...................**5,290.00**

Pierce, Franklin, DS, 1854 land grant, awards 40 acres in WI to PA veteran of War of 1812, who in turn transfers it to another individual, orig paper seal,

"Franklin Pierce" sgd secretarially at one place, second larger bolder black signature by words "The President," few folds, 10" x 15-1/2" stiff cream colored paper.....................**150.00**

Taft, William H., ALS, New Haven, Oct. 25, 1919, sgd "Wm H Taft" to Colonel Meekins, apologizing for abrupt end to their visit, four pgs, folded sheet, minor soiling and fading **290.00**

Washington, George, ALS, Mount Vernon, as president, April 13, 1793, demonstrating his loyalty to troops as he seeks to collect French and Indian War claims for deceased comrade
.....................**19,550.00**

Wilson, Woodrow, sepia photo of *S. S. George Washington*, signed by 55 others **1,320.00**

Show business

Crawford, Joan, PS, inscribed "To Maria from Joan Crawford," 14" x 11" portrait by Hurrell, his emb stamp in lower right corner, minor damage at edges, framed..............**320.00**

Grant, Cary, PS, inscribed "To Arnold, with all good wishes, Cary Grant," 13" x 10" portrait by Clarence Bull, MGM stamp on verso, minor creasing, framed....................**580.00**

Holiday, Billie, PS, inscribed "To Norman Stay Happy," souvenir group photo taken in Chicago, showing "Lady Day" with five other people, sgd on mat above image, 5" x 7", presentation folder of Garrick Stage Bar, also inscribed by another, inscriptions in pencil....................**980.00**

Wayne, John, black and white, sgd "Good Luck Tony, John Wayne, 5/27/40," 9" x 7-1/4".........**1,035.00**

Statesmen

Roosevelt, Franklin D., TLS, sgd as Acting Secretary of the Navy, March 27, 1919, on Dept of Navy letterhead, concerning investigation into collision between USS Lake Tahoe and scow W.T.C. #35, 10-1/2" x 8".......**500.00**

Seward, William Henry, ALS, as Secretary of State, Dept of State letterhead, Nov. 14, 1866, letter to David Hoadley, Pres of Panama Railroad Co., regarding dealings with Columbian government, 10" x 7-3/4"
.........................**90.00**

Von Stauffenberg, Count, document of Cavalry Riding School, Hannover, Aug. 11, 1936, official school handstamp, 2-1/4" x 6-3/4" **1,925.00**

Autograph document signed (ADS), Robert Morris (1734-1806), 18th C politician, Signer of the Declaration of Independence, dated March 20, 1795, Certificate #748, one share in North American Land Company, signed as president of the company, 10" x 12", some fold splitting with restoration, **$525.** *Photo courtesy of Sanford Alderfer Auction Company.*

Wilson, Woodrow and John Singer Sargent, Timothy Cole engraving of seated Wilson, sgd in pencil by Wilson and painter Sargent, some foxing and overall toning, reverse of frame with presentation letter dated 1937 regarding raising money for Red Cross, 11-1/2" x 8" **175.00**

AUTOMOBILES

History: Automobiles are generally classified into two categories: prewar, those manufactured before World War II; and those manufactured after the conflict. The Antique Automobile Club of America, the world's oldest and largest automobile historical society, considers motor vehicles, including cars, buses, motorcycles, and trucks, manufactured prior to 1930 "antique." The Contemporary Historical Vehicle Society, however, accepts automobiles that are at least 25 years old. There are also specific clubs dedicated to specific marques, like the Wills/Kaiser/AMC Jeep Club, and the Edsel Owners Club.

Some states, such as Pennsylvania, have devised a dual registration system for older cars—antique and classic. Models from the 1960s and 1970s, especially convertibles and limited-production models, fall into the "classic" designation if they are not used as daily transportation. Many states have also allowed collectible vehicles to sport "year of issue" license plates, thus allowing a owner of a 1964-1/2 Mustang to register a 1964 license plate from their home state.

Notes: The prices below are for cars in running condition, with a high proportion of original parts and somewhere between 60 percent and 80 percent restoration. *Prices can vary by as much as 30 percent in either direction.* Prices of unrestored automobiles, or those not running, or missing original parts can be 50 percent to 75 percent below prices listed.

Many older cars, especially if restored, are now worth more than $15,000. Their limited availability makes them difficult to price. Auctions, more than any other source, are the true determinant of value at this level.

Prices of high-powered 1964 to 1972 "muscle cars" will continue to escalate, while the value of pre-war cars will remain steady for all but unique custom-built roadsters and limousines. There is renewed interest in the original Volkswagen Beetle since the introduction of the updated '90s version. Look for prices of these economical little cars to climb as well.

AMC, 1968 AMX Fastback coupe **8,500.00**
Amphicar, 1962 conv. **19,500.00**
Auburn, 1935, Model 6-653, four-door sedan, 6 cyl **23,000.00**
Bricklin, 1975, Model SV-1, gullwing coupe **12,500.00**
Buick, 1941 Roadmaster, four-door sedan, 8 cyl **17,500.00**
Checker, 1963, Aerobus **6,500.00**

Chevrolet, 1932 Model AE, two-door sedan, 6 cyl **12,000.00**
Chrysler, 1932 Imperial Sedan, 6 cyl **18,000.00**
Crosley, 1950 "Hot Shot" Roadster **8,900.00**
Dodge, 1948 Power Wagon . . **9,500.00**
Essex, 1929 Challenger Series, four-door Town Sedan **9,500.00**
Edsel, 1958 Ranger two-door HT **11,000.00**
Ford
　　1924 Model T coupe. **8,500.00**
　　1956 F-100 pickup **7,500.00**
Hudson, 1951 Hudson Hornet **18,000.00**
International Scout, 4x4, 1966 . . . . **6,500.00**
Jeep, 1966 Wagoneer, four-door, 4x4 . . . . **8,500.00**
Julian, 1922 Model 60 coupe, 6 cyl **9,500.00**
Kaiser, 1953 Manhattan, four-door sedan. **12,000.00**
Lambert, 1909, roadster, 6 cyl **12,500.00**
Mercury, 1969 Cougar XR-7 HT **7,500.00**
Nash, Metropolitan, 1956, conv **8,500.00**
Oakland, 1930 sedan **7,500.00**
Oldsmobile, 1967 Toronado . . **9,500.00**
Packard, 1946 Clipper, sedan **12,000.00**
Plymouth, 1942 Model P14S, two-door sedan, 6 cyl **6,500.00**

*MGP, England, 1935, red and maroon, new top, new tires and leather straps, accompanied by copy of MG Midget Manual, **$18,800.** Photo courtesy of Skinner Auctioneers and Appraisers.*

Pontiac, 1934 two-door sedan **9,500.00**
Rolls Royce, 1951 Silver Wraith **49,000.00**
Studebaker, 1962 Lark **4,500.00**
Volkswagen, 1949 sedan . . **10,500.00**
Willys, 1954, Eagle **8,500.00**

AUTOMOBILIA

History: Automobilia is a wide-ranging category. It includes just about anything that represents a vehicle, from cookie jars to toys. Car parts are not usually considered automobilia, although there are a few exceptions, like the Lalique radiator ornaments. Most sought after are automobile advertising, especially signs and deal promotional models. The number of items related to the automobile is endless. Even collectors who do not own an antique car are interested in automobile, bus, truck, and motorcycle advertising memorabilia. Many people collect only

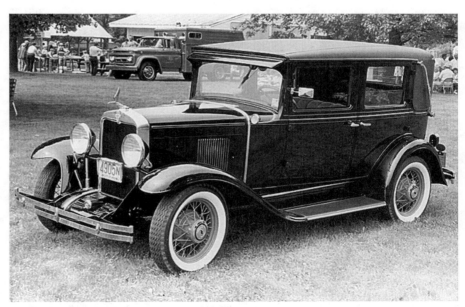
*Chevrolet, 1930, **$8,000.***

items from a certain marque, like Hupmobiles or Mustangs, while others may collect all advertising, like matchbooks or color brochures showing the new models for a certain year. Most material changes hands at automobile swap meets, and specialty auctions held throughout the year. Notably "hot" items on the market are service station and trucking company hat badges.

Advertising button

Auto dealership, Butzer Bros, purple on white, early touring car, early 1900s **25.00**

Best Buick Yet, litho of blue night sky studded by tiny white stars, slogan in white outlined in red, late 1930s **35.00**

Buick Fireball 8, graphic red, white, and blue design, for introduction of high-power engine, 1940s **. . 45.00**

Church Brigade Motor Car, black and white, touring car, associated to "Central Church of Christ Bible School," early 1900s **25.00**

Colburn Automobiles, silver on blue, inscribed "Denver Made". . . **30.00**

Exxon, Conserve Energy, red, white, and blue, early 1970s. **5.00**

Fisk Tires, black, white, and yellow, symbolic youngster ready for bed holding candle and automobile tire, slogan "Time to Re-tire, Get a Fisk," 1930s **20.00**

Flying Red Horse, red on white, symbol for Socony-Vacuum, 1940s **15.00**

Hyvis Motor Oil, black on white, center red figure for "Automobile Contest" sponsored by Kapisco Oil Co., Shakopee, Minn., 1930s **12.00**

Mora Motoring Bonnet, multicolored, young lady modeling bonnet equipped with clear film protection across face, red background, lower third with black and white steering wheel designs for Mora Racytype and Tourer bonnets, early 1900s **25.00**

Nash Airflytes, black inscription on gold, Nash's 50th anniversary year, 1952 . . . . **28.00**

Pyro-Action Spark Plugs, multicolored image of warrior in armor, orange rim inscribed "Crusade Against Spark Plug Paralysis-Sponsored by Robert Bosch," 1930s **10.00**

Advertising tab, 1-1/4" x 2-1/2", Ford Motors Merry Christmas, diecut thin metal tab, two gold lusters, red and green image of Santa in sleigh, red lettering, 1950s. **50.00**

Big Little Book, *Houdini's Big Little Book of Magic*, Whitman, 1927, premium for American Oil and Amoco Gas, 192 pgs **35.00**

Compression tester, Hasting's Piston Ring advertising on dial, orig metal storage box **45.00**

Decanter, figural race car, Lionstone, Al Unser's Johnny Lightning Special, 1970 and 1972 Indianapolis 500 Winner **75.00**

Display cabinet

Auto Lite Spark Plug, 18-1/2" h, 13" w, painted metal cabinet, glass front **125.00**

Schrader tire gauge cabinet, figural tire gauge, opens to reveal parts **350.00**

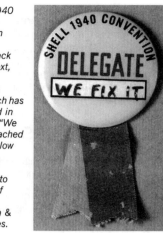

Emblem, Studebaker, red on white litho, late 1930s **20.00**

Grill badge, Sports Car Club of America, black and red wire wheel logo, cloisonné, early 1960s' era **50.00**

Keychain fob

Ford Tractors, dark gold plastic, showing key mechanism for "New Ford Select-O-Speed Tractors," reverse with "Greatest tractor advantage since hydraulics" and Ford logo, late 1940s **12.00**

Shell Oil, silvered metal emblem, painted on reverse with instructions for return if lost, c1930 . . . . . **10.00**

Key ring holder, 3-1/2" h, silvered metal, double ring holder, centered by applied miniature metal 7/8" h figure of smiling and saluting Esso Happy Oil Drop figure finished in porcelain white enamel, copper luster face, Esso logo on chest in red on silver, blue oval logo, 1960s. **25.00**

Lapel stud, brass, spoked automobile wheel, tiny inscription on tire wall "Albany Automobile Show, Feb. 15-22," center engraved "327," c1922 **. . 15.00**

Oil can

Amoco Home Oil, 7/8" x 2-1/4" x 1-3/4" h, tin, 1-1/4" h capped spout, black, white, and red litho logo and design on front, instruction recommendations on back, small quality of orig oil, 1950s. . . . **20.00**

Esso Handy Oil, 1" x 2-1/4" w x 4" h, tin, 1-1/2" capped spout, blue and white litho design, red, white, and blue Esso logo, small yellow accent on Happy Oil Drop, listing of recommended uses on back, 1960s **15.00**

Poster, stunt car show, Adam Forepaugh & Sells Bros. Big United Shows, Lansing Ball Park, Friday, July 29," cars somersaulting through air, framed, 17" x 19" $200. Photo courtesy of Joy Luke Auctions.

Watch, Elgin, eight-day movement, 3" d, **$135.**

Paperweight, Atlantic Richfield, 3" x 3" trapezoid, clear Lucite, small dark amber vial holding liquid "Crude Oil-Prudhoe Bay-North Slope, Alaska," and "Atlantic Richfield Co." with logo in internal blue lettering **15.00**

Pennant, 9" x 23", The People's Choice, Exxon, orange felt, black printing, smiling tiger head, black felt trim band, 1970s **20.00**

Pencil clip, Studebaker, diecut and rolled dark think brass with name diagonally across image of spoked automobile wheel, early 1900s . . . **35.00**

Restroom key tag, 2" x 5" white plastic tag, blue "Happy Motoring Service" emblem, small Esso oval logo in red lettering on white, red background for "Ladies," and blue background for "Men's," brass "S" hook for key attachment, backs with "Return Postage Guaranteed-Drop In Any Mailbox" inscription, c1960, price for pr **20.00**

Stickpin, Kent Grease, diecut thin celluloid, tan and blue pennant on brass stickpin, 1920s **20.00**

Tie bar, Sun Oil, 1939 award, silvered metal spring clip bar, chains suspending metal pendant formed in miniature replica of Sun Oil logo, bronze luster diamond logo inscribed "Bowling-Sun Oil-1939" **30.00**

Tray, Atlantic Richfield, 6-1/4" w, 8-1/4" l, oval, dark glass, gray lettering extending inward from left edge "Atlantic Richfield Company," small logo symbol **15.00**

BACCARAT GLASS

History: The Sainte-Anne glassworks at Baccarat in Voges, France, was founded in 1764 and produced utilitarian soda glass. In 1816, Aime-Gabriel d'Artiques purchased the glassworks, and a Royal Warrant was issued in 1817 for the opening of Verrerie de Vonâoche éa Baccarat. The firm concentrated on lead-crystal glass products. In 1824, a limited company was created.

From 1823 to 1857, Baccarat and Saint-Louis glassworks had a commercial agreement and used the same outlets. No merger occurred. Baccarat began the production of paperweights in 1846. In the late 19th century, the firm achieved an international reputation for cut glass table services, chandeliers, display vases, centerpieces, and sculptures. Products eventually included all forms of glassware. The firm still is active today.

For more information, see this book.

Additional Listings: Paperweights.

Bonbon, 5-3/4" d, amberina, swirled mold, pedestal foot, emb "Baccarat" **150.00**

Candelabra, pr, crystal, 32" h, four light, diamond-cut baluster standard, four scrolling candle arms terminating urn-form sockets, etched glass globes hung with prisms **2,000.00**

Decanter, 11-5/8" h, flattened ovoid, scalloped edge, etched flat sides with hunter on horseback, forest animals, scrolling vine, neck with vine etching, similarly shaped and etched stopper, 20th C, price for pr **550.00**

Compare these three pieces of amberina glass: the two on each end are Baccarat, the jar on the left is 3-1/2", **$95,** *and the bottle on the right is 4",* **$95.** *The center Daisy and Button pattern 3" h toothpick is pattern glass,* **$65.** *Photo courtesy of James D. Julia, Inc*

Perfume bottle, crystal bottle, stopper topped with bronze flower mounts, made for Dior perfume, 8-3/4" h, **$1,850.** *Photo courtesy of Sanford Alderfer Auction Company.*

Finger bowl, 4-3/4" d, 6-3/4" d underplate, ruby ground, gold medallions and flowers dec **350.00**

Lamp, 19-1/2" l, 24-1/2" h, central cut glass urn on short brass stem, two horizontal reeded candle arms, fan cut drip pans suspending cut prisms, ovoid glass knop stem, paneled trumpet foot cut with roundels, brass flat leaf base, one with collar at urn for further prisms, other with collars for two etched-glass shades, electrified, early 20th C, price for pr **2,875.00**

Toothpick holder, 2-1/2" h, Rose Tiente **110.00**

Vase, 9-3/4" h, colorless, tapered cylindrical, slightly everted rim, vertical tapered flutes on body, press-cut, 20th C **165.00**

Wash bowl and pitcher, 12-1/2" h pitcher, 16-1/2" d bowl, colorless, swirled rib design, pitcher with applied handle and polished base, ground table ring on bowl, polished chip **250.00**

BANKS, MECHANICAL

History: Banks which display some form of action while accepting a coin are considered mechanical banks. Mechanical banks date back to ancient Greece and Rome, but the majority of collectors are interested in those made between 1867 and 1928 in Germany, England, and the United States.

Initial research suggested that approximately 250 to 300 different or variant designs of banks were made in the early period. Today that number has been revised to 2,000-3,000 types and varieties. The field remains ripe for discovery and research.

More than 80 percent of all cast-iron mechanical banks produced between 1869 and 1928 were made by J. E. Stevens Co., Cromwell, Connecticut. Tin banks are usually of German origin.

> **Reproduction Alert:** Reproductions, fakes, and forgeries exist for many banks. Forgeries of some mechanical banks were made as early as 1937, so age alone is not a guarantee of authenticity. In the following price listing, two asterisks indicate banks for which serious forgeries exist, and one asterisk indicates banks for which casual reproductions have been made.

Notes: While rarity is a factor in value, appeal of design, action, quality of manufacture, country of origin, and history of collector interest also are important. Radical price fluctuations may occur when there is an imbalance in these factors. Rare banks may sell for a few hundred dollars, while one of more common design with greater appeal will sell in the thousands.

The mechanical bank market is being greatly affected by the on-line auctions found on the Internet. This past year has seen more examples of banks being offered for sale than has been seen in decades. Many of these previously unavailable examples are readily purchased by collectors. Because of large numbers of more common banks also coming into the market, this past year represents a drop in the price of many banks, especially those in the under $3,500 range, but recently the market appears to have stabilized on banks under $3,500. It looks like the market is now poised for potential movement upward on these lower priced banks. Additionally, there have been large sums of investment money coming onto the mechanical bank market, as of late, specifically directed at purchasing banks in the $20,000 to $100,000 and up levels per bank, causing an upward trend in these higher priced banks. It is my theory that much of this money has been moved into mechanical banks by non-collecting investors who have become fed up with the performance of the stock market and are searching for other directions of investment to protect their capital. I strongly suspect that this trend will continue.

The values in the list below accurately represent the selling prices of mechanical banks in the specialized collectors' market. As some banks are hard to find, and the market is quite volatile both up and down in price structure, consultation of a competent specialist in mechanical banks, with up-to-the-moment information, is advised prior to selling any mechanical bank.

The prices listed are for original old mechanical banks with no repairs, in sound operating condition, and with at least 90 percent of the original paint intact.

Adviser: James S. Maxwell Jr.

Price note: Prices quoted are for 100 percent original examples with no repairs, no repaint, and which have at least 90 percent bright original paint. An asterisk indicates casual reproductions; † denotes examples where casual reproductions and serious fakes exist.

Bank building, cast iron, front door opens, animated teller appears to receive coin, 1874, 4-1/4" base, **$490.** *Photo courtesy of James D. Julia, Inc.*

†**Acrobat**	1,050.00
African Bank, black bust, back emb "African Bank"	450.00
American Bank, sewing machine	650.00
*****Artillery**	900.00
Automatic Fortune Bank, tin	3,700.00
Automatic Savings Bank, tin, soldier	270.00
Automatic Savings Bank, tin, sailor	220.00
†**Baby Elephant X-O'clock**, lead and wood	1,200.00
*****Bad Accident**	1,920.00
Bear, tin	220.00
†**Bear and Tree Stump**	3,500.00
†**Bear**, slot in chest	320.00

Bulldog, pat. 1880, J. & E. Stevens, cast iron, 5-1/4" l, trap missing, original paint, **$920.** *Photo courtesy of James D. Julia, Inc.*

†**Bill E. Grin**	400.00
†**Billy Goat Bank**	230.00
Bow-ery Bank, iron, paper, wood	1,850.00
Bowing Man in Cupola	1,700.00
†**Bowling Alley**	4,500.00
†**Boy and bull dog**	4,500.00
†**Boys stealing watermelons**	750.00
British Clown, tin	12,000.00
*****Bull Dog**, place coin on nose	1,800.00
†**Bull and Bear**	75,000.00
†**Bull Dog**, standing	950.00
Bureau, Lewando's, wood	28,000.00
Burnett Postman, tin man with tray	3,500.00
†**Butting Buffalo**	510.00
†**Butting Goat**	1,200.00
*****Cabin**, black man flips	720.00
Caller Vending, tin	2,800.00
†**Calamity**	2,800.00
†**Called Out**	1,500.00
Calumet, tin and cardboard, with sailor	18,000.00
Calumet, tin and Cardboard, with soldier	20,000.00
†**Camera**	750.00
*****Cat and Mouse**	775.00
†**Cat and Mouse**, giant cat standing on top	45,000.00
*****Chief Big Moon**	1,080.00
Child's Bank, wood	450.00
Chocolate Menier, tin	950.00

Creedmore, cast iron, some original paint, 9-3/4" base, fair to good condition, $415. Photo courtesy of James D. Julia, Inc.

†**Chrysler Pig** 750.00
Cigarette Vending, tin 420.00
Cigarette Vending, lead 1,200.00
†**Circus,** ticket collector 300.00
†**Clown on Bar,** tin and iron . . 1,200.00
***Clown on Globe** 3,000.00
Clown with arched top, tin 150.00
Clown with black face, tin 675.00
Clown with white face, tin 125.00
Clown with white face, round, tin 3,700.00
Columbian Magic Savings, wood and paper 12,000.00
Cowboy with tray, tin 210.00
Crescent Cash Register 3,100.00
Crowing Rooster, circular base, tin 6,500.00
†**Cupola** 750.00
***Darktown Battery** 2,200.00
†**Darky Watermelon,** man kicks football at watermelon 7,500.00
Dinah, iron 300.00
Dinah, aluminum 200.00
†**Dog with tray** 300.00
***Eagle and Eaglettes** 450.00
Electric Safe, steel 1,200.00
***Elephant and Three Clowns** . . 850.00

Eagle and Eaglets, 1883, cast iron, original glass eyes, original paint, 6-1/2" base, $1,380. Photo courtesy of James D. Julia, Inc.

***Elephant,** locked howdah 260.00
Elephant, man pops out, wood, cloth, iron 330.00
†**Elephant,** no stars 3,700.00
***Elephant,** pull tail 70.00
†**Elephant with tusks,** on wheels 300.00
English Bulldog, tin 220.00
5 cents Adding 180.00
Football, English football 1,200.00
Fortune Teller, Savings, safe . 1,320.00
†**Freedman's Bank,** wood, lead, brass, tin, paper, etc. 85,000.00
Frog on rock 575.00
†**Frogs,** two frogs 650.00
***Gem,** dog with building 1,700.00
German Vending, tin 1,200.00
†**Giant in Tower** 750.00
Girl Feeding Geese, tin, paper, lead 24,000.00
†**Girl in Victorian chair** 1,200.00
Guessing, woman's figure, iron 1,320.00
Guessing, woman's figure, lead 900.00
Hall's Liliput, with tray 200.00
Hartwig and Vogel, vending, tin 750.00
Highwayman, tin 400.00
***Hindu,** bust 450.00
†**Hold the Fort,** two varieties, each 650.00
Hoop-La 5,500.00
***Horse Race,** two varieties, each 1,200.00
†**Humpty Dumpty,** bust of clown with name on back, iron 1,680.00
***I Always Did 'spise a Mule,** black man on mule 750.00
***Indian and Bear** 875.00
†**Indian Chief,** black man bust with **Indian feathered headdress,** aluminum 450.00
†**Initiating Bank,** first degree . . 650.00
Initiating Bank, second degree 720.00
John R. Jennings Trick Drawer Money Box, wood 16,500.00
***Jolly Nigger,** American 390.00
Jolly Nigger, lettering in Greek . 225.00
Jolly Nigger, lettering in Arabic 1,200.00
***Jolly Nigger,** raises hat, lead . 800.00
***Jolly Nigger,** raises hat, iron . 1,320.00
***Jolly Nigger,** with fez, aluminum 450.00
***Jonah and The Whale Bank,** large rectangular base 1,200.00
†**Jonah and The Whale Bank,** stands on two ornate legs with rect coin box at center 5,500.00
†**Jumbo,** elephant on wheels . . 300.00

Jolly Nigger, Shepard Hardware Co., 1882, cast iron, red clothing, blue tie, brown eyes, 4-3/4" base, chips to lip and coat, $290. Photo courtesy of James D. Julia, Inc.

Kick Inn Bank, wood 1,500.00
†**Leap Frog** 1,320.00
Lehmann Berlin Tower, tin 280.00
Lehmann, London Tower, tin . . 270.00
†**Light of Asia** 270.00
Lion, tin 345.00
†**Lion and Two Monkeys** 1,110.00
***Little Joe Bank** 570.00
Little Moe Bank 210.00
***Magic Bank,** iron house 400.00
Magic Bank, tin 200.00
†**Magician** 950.00
†**Mama Katzenjammer** 900.00
†**Mammy and Child** 900.00
***Mason** 1,500.00
***Merry-Go-Round,** mechanical, coin activates 1,400.00
†**Merry-Go-Round,** semi-mechanical, spin by hand 510.00
Mikado Bank 5,500.00
†**Milking Cow** 1,800.00
Model Railroad Drink Dispenser, tin 15,500.00
***Monkey and Coconut** 875.00
†**Monkey Bank** 650.00
Monkey, chimpanzee in ornate circular bldg, iron 575.00
†**Monkey,** slot in stomach 300.00
Monkey, tin, tips hat 270.00
Mule Entering Barn 775.00
Musical Church, wood 345.00
Musical Savings, tin 195.00
Musical Savings, velvet-covered easel 270.00
Musical Savings, wood house . 570.00
National, Your Savings, cash register 1,680.00

*New Bank, lever at center 240.00
*New Bank, lever at left 180.00
†North Pole Bank 1,200.00
Old Mother Hubbard, tin 400.00
*Organ Bank, boy and girl 570.00
*Organ Bank, medium, only monkey figure 270.00
Organ Grinder and Dancing Bear 410.00
Owl, slot in head 220.00
*Owl, turns head 280.00
*Paddy and the Pig 950.00
Pascal Chocolate Cigarettes, vending, tin 1,080.00
Pay Phone Bank, iron 1,680.00
Pay Phone Bank, tin 450.00
*Pelican, Arab head pops out . 345.00
*Pelican, man thumbs nose . . . 300.00
†Perfection Registering, girl and dog at blackboard 900.00
*Picture Gallery 1,400.00
Pinball Vending, tin 1,320.00
Pistol Bank, iron 250.00
Policeman, tin 300.00
Post Office Savings, steel . . . 1,200.00
†Presto, iron building 570.00
*Presto, penny changes optically to quarter 575.00
Pump and Bucket 2,000.00
*Punch and Judy, iron 1,400.00
Punch and Judy, iron front, tin back 450.00
†Queen Victoria, bust, brass . 1,500.00
†Queen Victoria, bust, iron . . 2,800.00
†Rabbit Standing, large 410.00
†Rabbit Standing, small 225.00
†Red Riding Hood, iron 1,650.00
Red Riding Hood, tin, vending . 700.00
†Rival Bank 1,950.00
Robot Bank, aluminum 390.00
Robot Bank, iron 620.00
Royal Trick Elephant, tin 5,500.00

Speaking Dog, Norman 5170A, "Pat. July 14, 1885 and Oct. 20, 1885," wear to polychrome, trap missing, 7" h, $715. Photo courtesy of Garth's Auction, Inc.

Speaking Dog, 1885, cast iron, 7" base, paint fair, $835. Photo courtesy of James D. Julia, Inc.

Safe Deposit Bank, tin, elephant 800.00
Sailor Face, tin, pointed top . 1,920.00
Sam Segal's Aim to Save, iron 1,080.00
*Santa Claus 750.00
†Schley Bottling Up Cevera . . . 585.00
School Teacher, tin and wood, American 750.00
Seek Him Frisk 2,000.00
†Shoot That Hat Bank 1,600.00
†Shoot the Chute Bank 1,200.00
†Smith X-ray Bank 675.00
*Snap-It Bank 840.00
Snow White, tin and lead 475.00
*Speaking Dog 1,125.00
Spring Jawed Cat, pot metal . . 120.00
Spring Jawed Chinaman, pot metal 550.00
Spring Jawed Felix the Cat, pot metal 3,700.00
Spring Jawed Mickey Mouse, pot metal 13,500.00
Spring Jawed Penguin, pot metal 120.00
Springing Cat 2,820.00
†Squirrel and Tree Stump 410.00
Starkies Aeroplane, aluminum, cardboard 9,500.00
Starkies Aeroplane, aluminum, steel 14,000.00
Stollwerk Bros., two penny, vending, tin 840.00
Stollwerk Bros., Victoria, spar-automat, tin 570.00
*Stump Speaker Bank 1,200.00
Symphonium Musical Savings, wood 1,200.00
†Tabby 250.00
*Tammany Bank 225.00
Tank and Cannon, aluminum 1,200.00
Tank and Cannon, iron 1,680.00
†Target Bank 252.00

†Target In Vestibule 570.00
*Teddy and The Bear 990.00
Tiger, tin 270.00
Time Lock Savings 345.00
*Toad on Stump 400.00
*Trick Dog, six-part base 875.00
*Trick Dog, solid base 400.00
*Trick Pony Bank 750.00
Trick Savings, wood, end drawer 400.00
Try Your Weight, tin, mechanical 1,560.00
†Turtle Bank 1,200.00
Two Ducks Bank, lead 2,000.00
†U.S. and Spain 720.00
†Uncle Remus Bank 765.00
†Uncle Sam Bank, standing figure with satchel 1,125.00
†Uncle Sam, bust 240.00
†Uncle Tom, no lapels, with star 255.00
†Uncle Tom, lapels, with star . 240.00
†Uncle Tom, no star 230.00
Viennese soldier 750.00
Watch Bank, blank face, tin . . . 120.00
Watch Bank, stamped face, tin . 90.00
Weeden's Plantation, tin, wood 510.00
Whale Bank, pot metal 300.00

William Tell, patent June 23, 1896, cast iron, no paint, 10-1/2" l, 6-1/2" h, $750. Photo courtesy of Joy Luke Auctions.

*William Tell, iron 775.00
William Tell, crossbow, Australian, sheet steel, aluminum 875.00
Woodpecker Bank, large, tin, c1910 . . . . 450.00
Woodpecker Bank, small, tin, c1930-1960 . . . . 50.00
*World's Fair Bank 720.00
Zentral Sparkasse, steel 750.00
Zig Zag Bank, iron, tin, papier-mâché 4,120.00
*Zoo 900.00

BANKS, STILL

History: Banks with no mechanical action are known as still banks. The first still banks were made of wood or pottery or from gourds. Redware and stoneware banks, made by America's early potters, are prized possessions of today's collectors.

Still banks reached a golden age with the arrival of the cast-iron bank. Leading manufacturing companies include Arcade Mfg. Co., J. Chein & Co., Hubley, J. & E. Stevens, and A. C. Williams. The banks often were ornately painted to enhance their appeal. During the cast-iron era, banks and other businesses used the still bank as a form of advertising.

The tin lithograph bank, again frequently a tool for advertising, reached its zenith from 1930 to 1955. The tin bank was an important premium, whether a Pabst Blue Ribbon beer can bank or a Gerber's Orange Juice bank. Most tin advertising banks resembled the packaging of the product.

Almost every substance has been used to make a still bank—die-cast white metal, aluminum, brass, plastic, glass, etc. Many of the early glass candy containers also converted to a bank after the candy was eaten. Thousands of varieties of still banks were made, and hundreds of new varieties appear on the market each year.

Trolley bank, rolling wheels, cast iron, wheels painted gold, embossed "Main Street," unmarked, American, minor paint losses, 3" x 6-1/2", $250. Photo courtesy of David Rago Auctions.

Brass, beehive, 4" h, 4-1/2" d, EOS, well detailed, base marked "A. B. Dalames Bank" **385.00**

Cast iron

Building, 2-3/4" to 4-3/4" h, Kyser & Rex, Town Hall and Log Cabin, chimney on left side, "Town Hall Bank" painted yellow, c1882 . . . . **260.00**

Bungalow, 3-3/4" h, Grey Iron Ceiling Co., porch, painted **470.00**

Cab, Arcade, 7-3/4" l, Yellow Cab, painted orange and black, stenciling on doors, seated driver, rubber tires, painted metal wheels, coin slot in roof **935.00**

Cat with ball, 2-1/2" x 5-11/16", A. C. Williams, painted gray, gold ball **190.00**

Circus elephant, 3-7/8" h, Hubley, colorfully painted, seated position **180.00**

Coronation, 6-5/8" h, Syndeham & McOustra, England, ornately detained, emb busts in center, England, c1911 . . . . **200.00**

Buildings, cast iron, Flatiron Building, painted silver, model of house, painted silver and green, "Bank" building, painted red (broken cupola), unmarked, American, minor paint losses, 5-1/2" h tallest, $415. Photo courtesy of David Rago Auctions.

Duck, 4-3/4" h, Hubley, colorfully painted, outstretched wings, slot on back **165.00**

Dutch boy and girl, 5-1/4" and 5-1/8" h, Hubley, colorfully painted, boy on barrel, girl holding flowers, c1930, price for pr **260.00**

Egyptian tomb, 6-1/4" x 5-1/4", green finish, pharaoh's tomb entrance, hieroglyphics on front panel **275.00**

Elk, 9-1/2" h, painted gold, full antlers. **155.00**

Globe safe, 5" h, Kenton, round sphere, claw feet, nickeled combination lock on front hinged door **80.00**

Hall clock, 5-3/4" h, swinging pendulum visible through panel **110.00**

Horseshoe, 4-1/4" x 4-3/4", Arcade, Buster Brown and Tige with horse, painted black and gold . . . **125.00**

Building, bank, cast iron, painted silver, 4" base, paint in fair condition, $45. Photo courtesy of James D. Julia, Inc.

Husky, 5" h, Grey Iron Casting Co., painted brown, black eyes, yellow box, repaired **365.00**

Jewel chest, 6-1/8" x 4-5/8", ornate casting, ftd bank, brass combination lock on front, top lifts for coin retrieval, crack at corner **90.00**

Kodak, 4-1/4" x 5" w, J & E Stevens, nickeled, highly detailed casting, intricate pattern, emb "Kodak Bank" on front opening panel, c1905 . . . . **225.00**

Mailbox, 5-1/2" h, Hubley, painted green, emb "Air Mail," with eagle, standing type **220.00**

Maine, 4-5/8" l, Grey Iron Casting Co., japanned, gold highlights, c1900 . . . . **660.00**

Mammy, 5-1/4" h, Hubley, hands on hips, colorfully painted **300.00**

North Pole, 4-1/4" h, nickeled, Grey Iron Casting Co., depicts wooden pole with handle, emb lettering **415.00**

Pagoda, 5" x 3" x 3", England, gold trim, c1889 . . . . **240.00**

Pershing, General, 7-3/4" h, Grey Iron Casting Co., full bust, detailed casting **65.00**

Pig, 2-1/2" h, 5-1/4" l, Hubley, laughing, painted brown, trap on bottom **120.00**

Professor Pug Frog, 3-1/4" h, A.C. Williams, painted gold, blue jacket, new twist pin **195.00**

Radio, Kenton, 4-1/2" h, metal sides and back, painted green, nickeled front panel in Art-Deco style **445.00**

Reindeer, 9-1/2" h, 5-1/4" l, A. C. Williams, painted gold, full rack of antlers, replaced screw. **55.00**

Rumplestiltskin, 6" h, painted gold, long red hat, base and feet,

Safe, Stevens, 1897, cast iron, nickel plated, 5" h, dark oxidation to entire surface, $60. Photo courtesy of James D. Julia, Inc.

marked "Do You Know Me," c1910
.... **210.00**
Safe, 4-3/8" h, Kyser & Rex, Young America, japanned, intricate casting, emb at top, c1882
.... **275.00**
Sharecropper, 5-1/2" h, A. C. Williams, painted black, gold, and red, toes visible on one foot
.... **240.00**
Spitz, 4-1/4" x 4-1/2" h, Grey Iron Casting Co., painted gold, repaired
.... **165.00**
Steamboat, 7-1/2" l, Arcade, painted gold **190.00**
Stove, 4-3/4" h, Gem, Abendroth Bros., traces of bronzing, back marked "Gem Heaters Save Money" **275.00**
Tank, 9-1/2" l, 4" w, Ferrosteel, side mounted guns, rear spoke wheels, emb on sides, c1919 ..... **385.00**
U.S. Mail, 5-1/8" h, Kenton, painted silver, gold painted emb eagle, red lettering large trap on back panel
.... **180.00**
World Time, 4-1/8" x 2-5/8", Arcade, paper time tables of various cities around the world **315.00**
Celluloid, Keene National Bank, canister, printed in blue, mellowed ivory white ground, one side shows bank building in Keene, NH, other side with dime savings text **65.00**
Chalk
Cat, 11" h, seated, stripes, red bow
.... **200.00**
Winston Churchill, 5-1/4" h, bust, painted green, back etched "Save for Victory," wood base **55.00**
Glass, Charles Chaplin, 3-3/4" h, Geo Borgfeldt & Co., painted figure standing next to barrel slotted on lid, name emb on base **220.00**
Lead
Boxer, 2-5/8" h, Germany, head, painted brown, black facial details, lock on collar, bent in back **130.00**
Burro, 3-1/2" x 3-1/2", Japan, lock on saddle marked "Plymouth, VT"
.... **125.00**
Ocean liner, 2-3/4" x 7-5/8" l, bronze electroplated, three smoking stacks, hinged trap on deck, small hole................. **180.00**
Pug, 2-3/4" h, Germany, painted, stenciled "Hershey Park" on side, lock on collar **300.00**
Pottery
Acorn, 3-1/2" d, 4" h, redware, paper label reads "Tithing Day/At The/ First Methodist Episcopal Church/

Sunday January 2nd 1916/In the Interest of the Improvement Fund"
.... **220.00**
Bulbous, 3-1/4" h, redware, marked with initials "C.R.S.," 3-1/4" h, flakes on base **220.00**
Dresser, 6-1/2" w, 4" d, 4-1/2" h, redware, Empire chest of drawers shape, Philadelphia, PA, loss to feet, roughness on edges .. **220.00**
Hanging persimmon, 5" x 3", redware, yellow and red paint
.... **90.00**
House, 7-1/2" h, redware, Georgian style house, brown glazed accents, good detail on windows and doorways, central chimney, Jim Seagreaves, sgd "JCS".... **425.00**
Jug, 7-1/2" h, redware, bulbous, bird atop mouth, green and yellow sgraffito dev, Jim Seagreaves, sgd "JCS".................. **515.00**

Chi-Chi Victory Bank, green metal ground, decals of Three Men in Tub on lid, Dutch boy pushing child in sled on left, Dutch boy and girl skating on right, divided int., $125.

Steel
Life boat, 14" l, pressed, painted yellow and blue, boat length decal marked "Contributions for Royal National Life Boat Institution," deck lifts for coin removal, over painted
.... **360.00**
Postal savings, 4-5/8" h, 5-3/8" w, copper finish, glass view front panel, paper registering strips, emb "U.S.Mail" on sides, top lifts to reveal four coin slots, patent 1902
.... **95.00**
Stoneware
Dog's head, white clay, yellow glaze, two-tone brown sponging, 4" h, shallow flakes **175.00**
Ovoid, brushed cobalt blue flowers, leaves, and finial, minor flakes at coin slot, 6" h.......... **6,875.00**

Redware, acorn form, paper label reads "Tithing Day At The First Methodist Episcopal Church Sunday January 2nd, 1916 In the Interest of the Improvement Fund," 3-1/2" d, 4" h, **$220.** *Photo courtesy of Sanford Alderfer Auction Company.*

White metal
Amish Boy, seated on bale of straw, 4-3/4" x 3-3/8", U.S., painted in bright colors, key lock trap on bottom **55.00**
Cat with bow, 4-1/8" h, painted white, blue bow **155.00**
Gorilla, colorfully painted in brown hues, seated position, trap on bottom **165.00**
Pig, 4-3/8" h, painted white, decal marked "West Point, N.Y." on belly
.... **30.00**
Rabbit, 4-1/2" h, seated, painted brown, painted eyes, trap on bottom, crack in ear....... **30.00**
Spaniel, seated, 4-1/2" h, painted white, black highlights **470.00**
Uncle Sam Hat, 3-1/2" h, painted red, white, and blue, stars on brim, slot on top, trap on bottom. **135.00**
Wood, burlwood inlaid with exotic woods, top dec with geometric banding, front with sailing vessels, end panels with flags, Prisoner of War, late 19th C, 5" x 8" x 5-1/4", imperfections
.... **1,150.00**

BARBER BOTTLES

History: Barber bottles, colorful glass bottles found on shelves and counters in barber shops, held the liquids barbers used daily. A specific liquid was kept in a specific bottle, which the barber knew by color, design, or lettering. The bulk liquids were kept in utilitarian containers under the counter or in a storage room.

Barber bottles are found in many types of glass—art glass with various decorations, pattern glass, and commercially prepared and labeled bottles.

Note: Prices are for bottles without original stoppers, unless otherwise noted.

For more information, see this book.

Left to right: Cobalt blue, white
enameled decorated, metal
stopper; cranberry, opalescent
hobnails; cranberry opalescent,
white china stopper; cranberry,
enamel floral decorated, metal
stopper, range from 6-3/4" to
9" h, **$635.** Photo courtesy of
James D. Julia, Inc.

Advertising

Koken's Quinine Tonic for the Hair,
7-1/2" h, clear, label under glass
. . . .**195.00**

Lucky tiger, red, green, yellow,
black, and gilt label under glass,
emb on reverse **85.00**

Vegederma, cylindrical, bulbous,
long neck, amethyst, white enamel
dec of bust of woman with long
flower hair, tooled mouth, pontil
scar, 8" h **130.00**

Amber, Hobb's Hobnail **250.00**

Amethyst, Mary Gregory type dec,
white enameled child and flowers, 8" h
. . . .**200.00**

Cobalt blue, cylindrical, bulbous body,
long neck, white enamel, traces of gold
dec, tooled mouth, pontil scar, 7-1/4" h
. . . .**100.00**

Emerald green, cylindrical bell form,
long neck, orange and white enameled
floral dec, sheared mouth, pontil scar,
some int. haze, 8-1/2" h **210.00**

Latticino, cylindrical, bulbous, long
neck, clear frosted glass, white, red,
and pale green vertical stripes, tooled
mouth, pontil scar, 8-1/4" h **200.00**

Milk glass, Witch Hazel, painted letters
and flowers, 9" h **115.00**

Milk glass,
American
shield
decorated,
marked "Bay
Rum," 9" h,
price for pr,
$225. Photo
courtesy of
Joy Luke
Auctions.

Opalescent

Coin Spot, blue **300.00**

Seaweed, cranberry, bulbous
. . . . **465.00**

Spanish Lace, electric blue ground,
sq, long neck, tooled mouth,
smooth base, 7-7/8" h, pr . .**250.00**

Stars and Stripes, cranberry, pale
blue, tooled mouth, smooth base,
7-1/4" h, pr
. . . . **575.00**

Sapphire blue

Enameled white and yellow daisies,
green leaves, 8-5/8" h **125.00**

Mary Gregory-type dec, white
enamel dec of girl playing tennis,
cylindrical bulbous form, long
neck, tooled mouth, pontil scar, 8" h
. . . . **150.00**

BARBIE

History: In 1945, Harold Matson (MATT) and Ruth
and Elliott (EL) Handler founded Mattel. Initially the
company made picture frames but became involved in
the toy market when Elliott Handler began to make doll
furniture from scrap material. When Harold Matson
left the firm, Elliott Handler became chief designer and
Ruth Handler principal marketer. In 1955, Mattel
advertised its products on "The Mickey Mouse Club,"
and the company prospered.

In 1958, Mattel patented a fashion doll. The doll
was named "Barbie" and reached the toy shelves in
1959. By 1960, Barbie's popularity was assured.

Development of a boyfriend for Barbie, named Ken
after the Handlers' son, began in 1960. Over the years,
many other dolls were added. Clothing, vehicles,
room settings, and other accessories became an
integral part of the line.

From September 1961 through July 1972, Mattel
published a Barbie magazine. At its peak, the Barbie
Fan Club was second only to the Girl Scouts as the
largest girls' organization in the United States.

Always remember that a large quantity of Barbie
dolls and related material has been manufactured.
Because of this easy availability, only objects in
excellent to mint condition with original packaging
(also in very good or better condition) have significant
value. If items show signs of heavy use, their value is
probably minimal.

Collectors prefer items from the first decade of
production. Learn how to distinguish a Barbie #1 doll
from its successors. The Barbie market is one of
subtleties.

Recently many collectors have shifted their focus
from the dolls themselves to the accessories. There
have been rapid price increases in early clothing and
accessories.

Barbie is now a billion-dollar baby, the first toy in
history to reach this prestigious mark—that's a billion
dollars per year, just in case you're wondering.

#1 Ponytail Barbie, brunette, green
silk Pak sheath, no box, VG, **$2,200.**
Barbie photos courtesy of McMasters
Harris Auction Co.

Accessories

Barbie Café Today, dated 1970, NRFB,
age discoloration to box, fading, slightly
scuffed **475.00**

Barbie Teen Dream Bedroom, dated
1970, MIB, discoloration to orig box
. . . .**65.00**

Bedspread, twin size, light weight
cotton, red, blue, and gold, red fabric
edging, VG, some age discoloration
. . . .**295.00**

Doll jewelry, Barbie & Midge, #7001,
gold metal necklace, drop earrings with
light blue rhinestones, heart shaped
plastic cover, cardboard backing,
dated 1964, Cleinman & Sons, Inc.,
some age discoloration to cardboard
. . . .**120.00**

Paper doll book, Whitman, uncut
Barbie and Ken Cut-Outs, #1971,
dated 1962, NM **90.00**
Barbie and Ken Cut-Outs, #1976,
dated 1962, NM **100.00**

Barbie and Ken Cut-Outs, #1986, dated 1970, NM **35.00**

Barbie's Boutique, #1954, dated 1973, NM **85.00**

Francie with Growing Pretty Hair, #1982, dated 1973, NM **35.00**

Hi! I'm Skipper, #1969, dated 1973, NM **30.00**

Malibu Skipper, #1952, dated 1973, NM **20.00**

Midge, #1962, dated 1963, NM **145.00**

Photo album, 13-3/4" x 11" black vinyl, dated 1964, construction paper pages, VG **95.00**

American Girl Barbie, brunette, original one-pc swimsuit, gold wire stand, original booklet, original box, NM-VG, swimsuit slightly age discolored, left side waist seam separated, poor condition box, $550.

Barbie Dolls

American Girl Barbie

Brunette, beige lips, fingernails painted, bendable legs, #1655 Under Fashions, pale pink corselet with ribbon straps, ruffled waistline, attached pink plastic supporters, pink nylon bra, beige textured stockings, pink nylon panties and half slip with lace trim, no box, VG **375.00**

Brunette, gold lips, fingernails painted, bendable legs, #1658 Garden Wedding, pink satin sheath, white lacy overdress with ribbon waist bow, rose pointed toe shoes, box, VG **350.00**

American Girl Barbie, side-part, brown hair, Dressed-Up Pak dress, VG, replaced blue ribbon hairband, outfit age discolored, no box, $1,025.

Brunette, peach lips outlined in gold, fingernails painted, bendable legs, nude, no box, VG **325.00**

Brunette, tan lips, fingernails painted, bendable legs, green silk sheath with bow accent, no box, VG **310.00**

Golden blond, beige lips, nostril paint, fingernails painted, orange one-pc swimsuit, no box, VG **350.00**

Light blond hair, orange lips with beige tint, nostril paint, fingernails painted, bendable legs, nude, no box, VG **325.00**

Titian hair, gold lips, fingernails painted, bendable legs, #1665 Here Comes the Bride outfit, white satin sleeveless gown, white tulle long veil, lace trim on gown and veil, ribbon bow accents, white nylon long gloves, blue nylon garter, white pointed toe shoes, box, VG **350.00**

Billions of Dreams Barbie, marked one billionth Barbie sold since 1959, #17641, box dated 1997, serial #00305, orig shipping box, NRFB, box slightly scuffed **225.00**

Bob Mackie design series

Goddess of the Sun, 8th in series, #14056, box dated 1995, orig shipping box, MIB, bottom box flap insert torn **80.00**

Madame du Barbie, #10 in series, #17934, box dated 1997, cardboard shipping box, MIB, top flap insert worn **200.00**

Bubblecut Barbie

Blond, coral lips, nostril paint, fingernails and toenails painted, straight legs, #1610 Golden Evening outfit, gold knit shirt, matching long skirt with gold glitter, gold belt with buckle, mustard open toe shoes, three-charm bracelet, no box, VG, loss to glitter **90.00**

Blond, white lips with pink tint, white nostril paint, fingernails painted, toenails with faint paint, straight legs, 1-pc red nylon swimsuit, red open toe shoes, orig box with gold wire stand, no box, VG **225.00**

Brunette hair, red lips, fingernails painted, light toenails painted, straight legs, nude, no box, VG **115.00**

Brunette, red lips, fingernails and toenails painted lightly, straight legs, Pak outfit, red and white striped knit shirt, blue shorts, no box, VG/G, frayed tag **135.00**

Dark blond, coral lips, fingernails and toenails painted, straight legs, nude, no box, VG **120.00**

Titian hair, coral lips, nostril paint, fingernails and toenails painted, straight legs, black and white striped one-pc swimsuit, pearl earrings, black open toe shoes, white rimmed glasses with blue lenses, black white stand, booklet, orig box, VG **200.00**

Color Magic Barbie, lemon yellow hair, blue metal hair barrette, original diamond pattern nylon swimsuit, original plastic closet and accessories, NM-VG, $675.

Color Magic Barbie

Lemon yellow hair, blue metal hair barrette, pink lips, cheek blush, fingernails painted, bendable legs, #1692 Patio Party, floral print nylon jumpsuit, blue and green satin overdress, blue pointed toe shoes, no box, NM **550.00**

Lemon yellow hair, pink metal hair barrette, pink lips, cheek blush, fingernails painted, bendable legs, #1688 Travel Togethers, yellow dress with red floral pattern, no box, VG **450.00**

Red hair, green metal hair barrette, pink lips, fingernails painted, bendable legs, nude, no box, VG **550.00**

Red hair, pink lips, cheek blush, fingernails painted, toenails with faint paint, bendable legs, nude, no box, NM/VG **525.00**

Enchanted Seasons Collection,
limited edition

Snow Princess, box dated 1994, NRFB, box slightly scuffed . . **75.00**

Spring Bouquet, box dated 1994, NRFB, box slightly scuffed . . **30.00**

Summer Splendor, box dated 1996, NRFB **35.00**

Fashion Queen, painted brunette hair, blue vinyl headband, pink lips, fingernails and toenails painted, straight legs, gold and white striped swimsuit, matching turban cap, pearl earrings in box with white plastic wig stand with brunette pageboy, blond bubblecut, and titian side-part wigs, black wire stand, MIB, orig box . **400.00**

Growin' Pretty Hair, blond, peach lips, cheek blush, rooted eyelashes, bendable legs, pink satin dress, wrist tag, orig box with hair accessories, pink high tongue shoes, orig box, NRFB **475.00**

Hair Happenin's, titian hair, pink lips, cheek blush, rooted eyelashes, fingernails painted, bendable legs, nude, titan long hair piece braided with pink ribbon, no box, VG **225.00**

Happy Holidays, orig box

1988, #1, NRFB **230.00**

1989, NRFB, plastic window and box scuffed. **70.00**

1990, NRFB, plastic window and box slightly scuffed **75.00**

1991, NRFB, box slightly scuffed and discolored **45.00**

1992, NRFB, box slightly scuffed and worn **35.00**

1993, NRFB, box slightly scuffed, edges worn and creased . . . **25.00**

1994, NRFB, box slightly scuffed, sticker residue on plastic window **35.00**

Living Barbie, brunette, pink lips, cheek blush, rooted eyelashes, bendable arms, bendable legs, rotating wrists, orig silver and gold one-pc swimsuit, orange net cover-up with gold trim, booklet, no box, NM **75.00**

Millenium Bride, box dated 1999, orig shipping box, NRFB **160.00**

#2 Ponytail Barbie, blond, original black and white swimsuit, $3,800.

Ponytail

#1 ponytail

Blond, red lips, fingernails and toenails painted, straight legs, black and white striped one-pc swimsuit, silver loop earrings, black #1 open-toe shoes with holes, white rimmed glasses with blue lenses, pink cover booklet, reproduction #1 stand, box with replaced insert, VG **3,400.00**

Blond, reset in ponytail, red lips, nostril paint, fingernails painted, TL, straight legs, black and white striped one-pc swimsuit, gold hoop earrings, one black #1 open toe shoe with hole (unmarked), white rimmed glasses with blue lenses, pink cov booklet, VG, orig box with partial Marshall Field's sticker **3,200.00**

#3 ponytail, brunette, red lips, nostril paint, brown eyeliner, fingernails painted, straight legs, #976 Sweater Girl outfit, orange knit sweater, matching shell, gray skirt, black open toe shoes, pearl earrings, wooden bowl with orange, green and yellow yarn with two needles, metal scissors, *How to Knit* book, black pedestal with plastic base, pink cover booklet, white rimmed glasses with blue lenses, no box, VG/G, hair and banks no box and fuzzy **475.00**

#5 ponytail, brunette, orig set, red lips, nostril paint, fingernails and toenails painted, straight legs, Pak outfit, black and white striped knit shirt, red shorts, no box, NM/VG **225.00**

#4 Ponytail Barbie, brunette, original black and white striped swimsuit, original box, NM-VG, ends of ponytail loose, lips slightly faded, green discolored dot on both ears, box age discolored, $475.

#6 ponytail

Blond, repainted pink lips, fingernails and toenails painted, straight legs, red nylon one-pc swimsuit, red open toe shoes, orig box with cardboard liner, black wire stand, light blue cover booklet, VG **215.00**

Titian hair, orig top knot, beige lips, fingernails and toenails painted, straight legs, blue two-pc pajamas with lace trim, button accents, no box, VG **325.00**

Official Barbie Collector's Club, Embassy Waltz, 1999, box dated 1998, NRFB, box insert flaps worn **40.00**

Society Style Collection, limited edition

Emerald Enchantment, 3rd ed, box dated 1996, NRFB, box slightly scuffed **40.00**

Radiant Rose, 2nd ed, box dated 1996, NRFB, plastic window slightly scuffed **40.00**

Sapphire Dream, 1st ed., box dated 1995, NRFB, box scuffed . . . **35.00**

Standard

Brunette, pink lips, cheek blush, fingernails painted, toenails with faint paint, straight legs, orig pink nylon swimsuit bottoms with plastic flower accent, #1804 Knit Hit blue and pink knit dress, pale blue high tongue shows, no box, VG **. 150.00**

Light brunette, pink lips, cheek blush, fingernails and toenails painted, straight legs, nude, no box, VG, replaced rubber band **190.00**

Swirl ponytail

Brunette hair, beige lips, fingernails painted, toenails with faint paint, straight legs, nude, no box, VG **300.00**

Brunette hair in orig set, yellow ribbon, metal hair pin, coral lips,

Swirl Ponytail, platinum hair, red nylon swimsuit, NMIB, $2,025.

fingernails and toenails painted, straight legs, red nylon one-pc swimsuit, red open toe shoes, pearl earrings, wrist tag, box with gold metal stand, NM **675.00**

Platinum hair in orig set, yellow ribbon, metal hair pin, white lips, fingernails painted, straight legs, nude, no box, NM-VG **475.00**

Talking, brunette, ribbon bow ties, pink lips, cheek blush, rooted eyelashes, bendable legs, red nylon two-pc swimsuit with metal accent on bottoms, white and silver net cover-up with red trim, no box, VG, possible repairs to talker, working condition **275.00**

Twist 'n' Turn

Blond, pink lips, cheek blush, fingernails and toenails painted, bendable legs, multicolored one-pc knit swimsuit, wrist tag, clear plastic stand, booklet, NRFB **425.00**

Blond, pink lips, cheek blush, rooted eyelashes, fingernails painted, bendable legs, nude, no box, VG **95.00**

Brunette, pink lips, cheek blush, fingernails painted, bendable legs, #1485 Gypsy Spirits outfit, pink nylon blouse, aqua suede skirt, matching vest, no box, VG **. 125.00**

Pale blond, pink lips, cheek blush, rooted eyelashes, fingernails painted, bendable legs, two-pc orange vinyl swimsuit, white net cover-up with orange trim, trade-in program doll, no box, VG **. . 475.00**

Friends and family dolls

Allan, painted red hair, peach lips, straight legs, striped jacket, blue swim trunks, wrist tag, booklet, cork sandals with blue straps in cellophane bag, cardboard leg and arm inserts, black wire stand, MIB, orig box **105.00**

Casey, blond hair, clear plastic headband, peach lips, cheek blush, two-pc hot pink nylon swimsuit, orig clear plastic bag, cardboard hanger, NRFP, orig price sticker **295.00**

Chris, Color Magic-type titian hair, green metal hair barrette, pink lips, cheek blush, bendable arms and legs, #3617 Birthday Beauties outfit, pink floral dress, white slip, white fishnet tights, white shoes with molded straps, gold wrapped present with white ribbon and pink flower accents, one pink crepe paper party favor with gold glitter, white paper invitation, orig box, VG **. . . 105.00**

Francie, brunette, two-pc swimsuit, original box, NM-VG, $275.

Christie

Talking, red hair, pink lips, cheek blush, rooted eyelashes, bendable legs, wrist tag, clear plastic stand, NRFM, nonworking, box age discolored, scuffed, and worn **250.00**

Twist 'n' Turn, red hair, pink lips, cheek blush, rooted eyelashes, bendable legs, #1841 Night Clouds, yellow, orange and pink nylon ruffled night gown with ribbon straps, matching yellow nylon robe with ribbon ties and flower accents, no box, VG **.115.00**

Francie

Brunette, clear plastic headband, peach lips, cheek blush, two-pc yellow nylon swimsuit, orig clear plastic bag, cardboard hanger, NRFP, orig price sticker . . . **250.00**

Brunette, pink lips, cheek blush, straight legs, nude, no box, NM/VG **115.00**

Malibu, The Sun Set, blond, pink plastic sunglasses, plastic head cover, peach lips, painted teeth, bendable legs, pink and red nylon swimsuit, yellow vinyl waistband, orange terrycloth towel, box dated 1970, NRFB **235.00**

Twist 'n' Turn, blond, pink lips, cheek blush, rooted eyelashes, bendable legs, orig floral print outfit with lace trim, pink nylon bottoms, no box, VG **165.00**

Ken, brunette, blue jacket, red swim trunks, wrist tag, cork sandals in cellophane bag, black wire stand, booklet, original box, NM-VG, box slightly age discolored, $250.

Jamie, walking, Furry Friends Gift Set, Sears Exclusive, titian hair, pink lips, cheek blush, rooted eyelashes, bendable legs, green, pink, and orange knit dress, orange belt with buckle, orange furry coat with pink vinyl trim, orange boots, gray dot with felt features, pink vinyl dog collar with silver accents, leash, no box, VG **150.00**

Julia, talking, red hair, pink lips, cheek blush, rooted eyelashes, bendable legs, gold and silver jumpsuit with belt, wrist tag, clear plastic stand, NRFB, nonworking, box age discolored, scuffed, and worn. **225.00**

Ken

Brunette flocked hair, beige lips, straight legs, red swim trunks with white stripe, wrist tag, booklet, yellow terrycloth towel, cork sandals in cellophane bag, black white stand, orig box, VG, oily face, worn wrist tag **155.00**

Brunette flocked hair, beige lips, straight legs, #797 Army and Air Force outfit, beige jacket with button accents, arm decal, matching pants, beige belt with buckle, beige socks and cap, brown necktie and shoes, no box, VG **85.00**

Brunette painted hair, beige lips, straight legs, #1426 Here Comes the Groom outfit, gray jacket with tails, white flower, gray felt vest, white shirt, both with button

accents, gray satin ascot with pearl accent, gray and white striped pants, black socks, black shoes, gray flocked plastic gloves, gray plastic top hat, box, VG . . . **500.00**

Painted blond hair, peach lips, straight legs, #789 The Yachtsman outfit, blue denim jacket with zipper closure, matching pants, red and white striped knit shirt, white socks, black shoes, *How to Sail a Boat* book, no box, VG

. . . . **75.00**

Painted brunette, peach lips, straight legs, #790 Time for Tennis outfit, white knit shirt, white sweater with blue and red trim, white shorts, socks, and shoes, tennis racquet and ball, no box, VG **55.00**

Talking, painted brown hair, peach lips, painted teeth, bendable legs, #1435 Shore Lines outfit, blue nylon jacket with zipper closure, blue shorts, vinyl side stripes, multi-print pants with zipper closure, yellow plastic face mask with elastic head strap, swim fins, no box, NM, nonworking, stretched elastic on mask **75.00**

Midge, titian hair, ribbon hair band, pink lips, fingernails painted, bendable legs, orig one-pc striped knit swimsuit, aqua open toe shoes, gold wire stand, VG

In orig box. **560.00**
No box **325.00**

PJ, talking, blond, beaded tie on left pigtail, replaced rubber-band on right pigtail, attached lavender plastic glasses, pink lips, cheek blush, rooted eyelashes, bendable legs, #1796 Fur Sighted outfit, orange jacket with fur

Skipper, Living, trade-in, blond, original set, bendable arms, green, blue, and pink nylon swimsuit, original box, M-NM, $125.

trim, metallic gold tab and button closures, matching pants, zigzag print knit sweater, orange hat with fur trim, metallic gold chin strap, yellow high tongue shoes, no box, NM/VG, non-working **155.00**

Ricky, painted red hair, peach lips, cheek blush, straight legs, striped jacket, blue shorts, cork sandals in bag, black wire stand, orig box with insert, NM, wrist tag torn. **155.00**

Skipper

Blond, pink lips, straight legs, /#1915 Outdoor Casuals, turquoise knit sweater, matching dickey with button closure, pants, white nylon short gloves, white socks, white flat shoes, red wooden yo-yo, no box, VG **55.00**

Color Magic-type dark red hair, pink lips, straight legs, #1902 Silk 'n' Fancy dress, red velvet bodice, white skirt, red lace underskirt, gold braid waistband, white nylon socks, black flat shoes, NM **90.00**

Color Magic-type titian hair, pink lips, straight legs, #1926 Chill Chasers, white fur coat, red cap with blue pompon, red flat shoes, no box, NM. **120.00**

Pose'n Play, blond, blue ribbon ties, clear plastic headband, pink lips, cheek blush, bendable arms and legs, blue and white outfit with button accents, wrist tag, orig clear plastic bag, cardboard hanger, NRFP. **85.00**

Quick Curl, blond hair, blue ribbon bow, pink lips, cheek blush, straight legs, blue and white long dress, orig clear plastic bag, NRFP **150.00**

Skooter

Blond, red ribbon bows, beige lips with tint of pink, cheek blush, straight legs, #1921 School Girl outfit, red jacket with pocket insignia, red and white pleated skirt, white shirt, red felt hat with red and white band and feather accent, white nylon socks, red flat shoes, brown rimmed glasses, arithmetic, geography, and English books, black book strap, red and natural wooden pencils, orig box, VG **90.00**

Brunette, hair in orig set with ribbons, pale pink lips, right cheek blush, straight legs, two-pc red swimsuit, red flat shoes, gold wire stand, pink plastic comb and brush, orig box, NM/VG . . . **155.00**

Brunette, retied with red cord, beige lips, cheek blush, straight legs, wearing Best Buy Fashions #9122, red plaid coat, black belt, matching cap with black ribbon accent, #9122 dress with red plaid skirt, black velveteen top, white nylon shirt, no box, VG.......... **70.00**

Tutti, Me and My Dog, brunette, red ribbon bow, pink lips, bendable arms and legs, red felt coat, fur trim, white fur hat with ribbon ties, red tights, white flat shoes, white dog with felt features, attached red leash, no box, VG, leash worn and knotted............ **75.00**

Outfits
Barbie
#911 Golden Girl, NRFB.... **235.00**
#916 Commuter Set, VG/G.. **400.00**
#972 Wedding Day Set, white satin gown with glitter and floral print tulle overdress, white tulle veil, pearl headband, white nylon short gloves, white #1 open toe shoes with holes, pearl necklace and earrings, blue garter, flower bouquet with lace and ribbon accents, VG **115.00**
#944 Masquerade, NRFB... **265.00**
#0873 Guinevere, royal blue velvet gown, embroidered and gold tri, attached chain belt, red and gold brocade slippers, red and gold brocade crown with navy blue and gold trim edging, attached gold nylon snood, red nylon armlets, NM/VG **105.00**
#0874 Arabian Night, pink satin blouse, pink chiffon long skirt, matching pink sari with gold trim, gold foil slippers, gold plastic lamp, gold and turquoise beaded necklace, gold drop earrings, gold and turquoise plastic bracelets, paper theater program, VG . **95.00**
#1452 Now Knit, green, navy blue, and silver dress, matching green furry hat, blue nylon scarf with attached silver thread ring, NM/VG **50.00**
#1470 Intrigue, metallic gold cot, pink lining, dress with gold skirt, white bodice with gold net, M **295.00**
#1593 Golden Groove, Sears Exclusive Gift Set, pink and gold lame jacket, matching short skirt, gold thigh-high boots, NM . **145.00**
#1612 Theatre Date, NRFB.. **285.00**
#1615 Saturday Matinee, NM/VG **310.00**

#1617, Midnight Blue, NM-VG **150.00**
#1620 Junior Designer, turquoise dress with green design, green pointed toe shoes, metal iron with black handle, *How to Design Your Own Fashion* book, VG **55.00**
#1622 Student Teacher, red and white dress, white bodice inset with button accents, red vinyl belt, red pointed toe shoes, black rimmed glasses with clear lenses, plastic globe, wooden pointer stick, geography book, VG/G.... **175.00**
#1629 Skater's Waltz, pink nylon skating suit, pink felt skirt, sheer nylon hose, white skates, pink fur muff, matching mittens, VG.. **45.00**
#1632 Invitation to Tea, pink chiffon jumpsuit, pink and silver lame sleeveless vest, silver belt with buckle, clear open toe shoes with silver glitter, silver colored teapot with "B" monogram and lid, two pale pink plastic teacups and saucers, VG............. **105.00**
#1640 Matinee Fashion, red sheath with braid trim, matching jacket, plush print trim, red pillbox hat, attached chiffon scarf, red pointed toe shoes, VG **135.00**
#1644 On the Avenue, white and gold sheath with textured skirt, gold lame bodice, matching jacket, white nylon short gloves, cream colored pointed toe shoes, gold clutch purse, NM/VG, jacket tag frayed, P condition belt.... **100.00**
#1645 Golden Glory, gold floral lame long dress, green chiffon waist scarf, matching gold lame long coat with fur trim, white nylon short gloves, green satin clutch purse, VG.................... **120.00**
#1649 Lunch on the Terrace, green and white checkered dress with polka dot bodice, matching hat with white net cover, VG ... **115.00**
#1650 Outdoor Art Show, VG **145.00**
#1652, Pretty as a Picture, VG **115.00**
#1656 Fashion Luncheon, VG/G **225.00**
#1661, London Tour, VG **105.00**
#1663, Music Center Matinee, NM-VG................. **200.00**
#1666 Debutante Ball, aqua satin gown with chiffon skirt panels, flower accents, white fur stole with aqua chiffon ties, clear open toe shoes with gold glitter, white nylon long gloves, single pearl necklace, VG................... **225.00**

#1670 Coffee's On, butterfly print dress, orange pointed toe shoes, white casserole dish with lid, blue and white coffeepot with lid, NM **75.00**
#1687 Caribbean Cruise, yellow jumpsuit with halter top, yellow flat soft shoes, NM........... **35.00**
#1695 Evening Enchantment, red taffeta and chiffon long dress, marabou trim, matching chiffon cape, red pointed toe shoes, VG **135.00**
#1792 Mood Matchers, paisley print nylon sleeveless blouse, matching pants, aqua nylon shirt, hot pink high tongue shoes, M **65.00**
#1814 Sparkle Squares, checkerboard pattern coat with ruffle trim, rhinestone buttons, matching dress with pleated white nylon skirt, white sheet stockings, NM **105.00**
#1848 All That Jazz, satin striped coat, matching dress with pleated skirt, beige sheer stockings, pink shoes with molded bows, VG **140.00**
#1849 Wedding Wonder, white satin gown, sheer white dress with white flocking, flocked headpiece with metal hair barrette, white tulle veil, white pointed-toe shoes, *World of Barbie Fashions* booklet, VG **75.00**
#3401 Fringe Benefits, fuchsia knit dress, orange suede neckline, attached belt with fringe, matching orange suede boots with fringe, M **65.00**
#4041 Color Magic Fashion Fun, NM/VG **145.00**
Dressed Up, Barbie Pak, dress with pale blue satin skirt, gold and white striped bodice, attached belt and buckle accents, pale blue pointed toe shoes, NM/VG **105.00**
Gala Abend, foreign market, white brocade gown, matching long coat with pale blue satin lining and fur collar, white nylon long gloves, white pointed toe shoes, VG **700.00**
Midnight Pink, foreign market, pink satin gown, pink and silver lame bodice, matching long coat with fur cape and collar, one pink open toe shoe, pink pearl necklace, white nylon long gloves, G/P.... **650.00**
Twinkle Togs, green satin dress, blue lame bodice, clear overskirt with lame stripes, green sheer stockings on cardboard forms, blue pointed-toe shoes, hanger, paper label, NRFB, lower right

cellophane corner torn, booklet missing **285.00**

Francie

#1216 The Lace Pace, gold lame and pink coat cov with white lace, satin bow, matching dress with satin straps, pink shoes with molded bows, VG **105.00**

#1222 Gold Rush, orange satin dress, bright orange open toe shoes, VG **35.00**

#1232 Two for the Ball, pink chiffon long coat, black velvet waistband, long dress with pink satin skirt, pink lace overskirt, black velvet bodice, pink soft pumps, VG/G, coat tag frayed **45.00**

#3367 Right for Stripes, blue vest, blue and white striped pants, matching midriff top, floral print shoulder bag, aqua sneakers, VG **65.00**

Pancho Bravo, Francie Pak, blue, pink, green, and white poncho, blue ankle boots, lavender plastic glasses, label, NRFP, some age discoloration to cardboard backing, orig 99 cent price sticker **40.00**

The Bridge Bit, white knit sweater, green and blue stitching, royal blue stretch pants with metal accent, pink pillow with flower design, NM **65.00**

Ken

#788 Rally Day, NRFB **60.00**

#797 Army and Air Force, NRFB **220.00**

#799 Touchdown, NRFB, box in F/P condition **115.00**

#0770 Campus Hero, NRFB . **130.00**

#0772 The Prince, green and gold lame coat, lace trim, rhinestone buttons, green velvet cape with gold lining, green nylon tights, green velvet shoes with gold trim, gold velvet hat with emerald, pearl, and feather accents, white collar with lace trim, velvet pillow with gold trim and tassels, paper program, VG **150.00**

#0773 King Arthur, silver lame pants, shirt, and cap, red satin surcoat with gold griffin, gray plastic helmet and sword, brown scabbard, two red plastic spurs, cardboard shield, paper program, VG . . **95.00**

#0779 American Airlines Captain, NRFB **175.00**

#1404 Ken in Hawaii, VG **25.00**

#1416 College Student, VG . . . **65.00**

#1417 Rovin' Reporter, red jacket, navy blue pants, white shirt, black socks and shoes, plastic camera, NM/VG **75.00**

#1419 TV's Good Tonight, red robe, blue trim, pocket insignia, cork sandals with red straps, brown plastic TV with metal antenna, VG, no tag on robe **50.00**

#1425 Best Man, VG-G **105.00**

Ricky, #1502 Saturday Show, NRFB **75.00**

Skipper

#1738 Fancy Pants, VG **50.00**

#1901 Red Sensation, NRFB **135.00**

#1905 Ballet Class, NRFB . . **100.00**

#1909 Dreamtime, NRFB . . . **145.00**

#1935 Twice as Nice, orange gold felt coat, matching dress, cap with pompon, VG **50.00**

#1972 Drizzle Sizzle, pink and Kelly green knit dress, orange vinyl appliqué flowers, clear plastic raincoat, cap, and boots, VG **35.00**

BAROMETERS

History: A barometer is an instrument that measures atmospheric pressure, which, in turn, aids weather forecasting. Low pressure indicates the coming of rain, snow, or storm; high pressure signifies fair weather.

Most barometers use an evacuated and graduated glass tube that contains a column of mercury. These are classified by the shape of the case. An aneroid barometer has no liquid and works by a needle connected to the top of a metal box in which a partial vacuum is maintained. The movement of the top moves the needle.

Royal Polytechnic, c1900, carved oak case with Victorian style appointments, Admiral Fitzroy paper face and labels in lower section, with two thermometers, 41" h, $1,220.

4-1/2" h, aneroid, Taylor, circular mahogany frame **75.00**

21-1/2" l, wheel, Aneroid, Swedish, late 19th C, part ebonized, arch top with acorn finials, painted milk glass thermometer between turned uprights, open dial with printed enamel bezel signed "C.L. Malmsjo, Guteborg," within turned frame, acorn pendant finial **300.00**

26-1/2" h, wheel, Georgian, mahogany, dial sgd "Dolland, London," rounded pediment over thermometer, urn inlaid central roundel line inlay throughout, early 19th C **1,840.00**

33" d, wheel, carved oak, foliage and C-scrolls, English, late 19th C . . **230.00**

34" l, stick, sgd E. Kendall, N. Lebanon, mahogany, etched steel face, mirrored well cov **550.00**

36-1/2" l, wheel, English, Georgian, early 19th C, mahogany, dial signed "Dolland, London," rounded pediment over thermometer, urn inlaid central roundel, line inlay throughout. **1,840.00**

38" l, wheel, Scottish, mid-19th C, mahogany, swan's neck cresting over later German hygrometer, vertical thermometer, over painted roundel, signature roundel centered by level and sgd "F. Uago, Glasgow" **865.00**

38-3/4" h, banjo, mahogany, dial engraved "P. Nossi & Co. Boston," broken pediment cresting above shaped case with thermometer, circular barometer dial flanked by inlaid patera **690.00**

39" l, wheel, English, early 20th C, mahogany, broken pediment centered by finial, round hygrometer dial over

G. V. Mooney, walnut, shaped backboard with molded wood and brass bezel framing paper dial and brass lever movement above printed paper dial "G.V. Mooney's Barometer Patented May 30th 1865 – Sold by Arnaboldi & Co. 53 Fulton St. New York," mercury tube extending to base with molded wooden boss, 50" h, $1,880. Photo courtesy of Skinner's Auctioneers and Appraisers.

vertical thermometer, convex mirror over barometer dial, ending in dial for level **815.00**

39-3/4" h, banjo, shell inlaid, painted black, Kirner Bros., Oxford, Victorian, mid-19th C **460.00**

40" l, wheel, rosewood veneer, onion top cornice with hygrometer dial over thermometer over convex mirror, large barometric dial, small level at base, English, mid-19th C **350.00**

42" h, 4" w, stick, French, first half 19th C, inlaid mahogany, slender straight case, inlaid to frieze with symmetrical leafage spray above light wood reserves, readings and three gauges, illegibly signed, gauge replaced **600.00**

50" h, barometer and wall clock, G. V. Mooney, NY, walnut, shaped backboard with molded wood and brass bezel framing paper dial and brass lever movement above printed paper dial "G.V. Mooney's Barometer Patented May 30th 1865—Sold by Arnaboldi & Co. 53 Fulton St. New York," mercury tube extending to the base with a molded wooden boss **1,880.00**

BASKETS

History: Baskets were invented when man first required containers to gather, store, and transport goods. Today's collectors, influenced by the country look, focus on baskets made of splint, rye straw, or willow. Emphasis is placed on handmade examples. Nails or staples, wide splints that are thin

For more information, see this book.

and evenly cut, or a wire bail handle denote factory construction which can date back to the mid-19th century. Decorated painted or woven baskets rarely are handmade, unless they are American Indian in origin.

Baskets are collected by (a) type—berry, egg, or field; (b) region—Nantucket or Shaker; and (c) composition—splint, rye, or willow.

Reproduction Alert: Modern reproductions abound, made by diverse groups ranging from craft revivalists to foreign manufacturers.

Half buttocks, woven splint, thick brown paint, bentwood handle, 8" w, 5" h **200.00**

Miniature
Bushel, painted cream-white over red, America, 19th C, 5-3/4" d, 3-1/4" h **760.00**

Nantucket, made by Ferdinand Sylvaro, Nantucket, MA, 1944, round, swing handle, decorated with three bands of darker caning, inscribed paper label and pyrographic inscription "Patricia Bright Jan. 22, '44 Nantucket Lightship Basket From P.B. & B.S. Heywood & Sylvaro," 10-5/8" d, 13-1/2" h, couple of breaks, **$2,115.** *Photo courtesy of Skinner's Auctioneers and Appraisers.*

Woven splint, single handle, painted blue, 1-3/4" d, 2" h **550.00**

Nantucket Light Ship, America

Oval, cov, swing handle, purse, carved ivory whale mounted on walnut oval lid medallion, carved ivory pins and peg, base inscribed "Made in Nantucket Jose Formoso Reyes" with rending of island, 20th C, 8" l, 6-1/4" w, 7" h **3,115.00**

Round, made by Ferdinand Sylvaro, Nantucket, MA, 1944, swing handle, dec with three bands of darker caning, inscribed paper label and pyrographic inscription "Patricia Bright Jan. 22, '44 Nantucket Lightship Basket From P.B. & B.S. Heywood & Sylvaro," 10-5/8" d, 13-1/2" h, couple of breaks **2,115.00**

Native American

Covered, woven splint, attributed to New England Algonkian or Iroquois, early 19th C, round domed lid, round to square form, red and green flowering vine motif, side handles, 15-1/2" h, minor wear, fading **2,000.00**

Covered, woven splint, attributed to New England Algonkian or Iroquois, early 19th C, round domed lid, round to square form, alternating sides painted with baskets of flowers and flowers, shades of salmon green and black, 19-1/2" d, minor wear, fading **2,250.00**

Splint, Schaticoke Tribe, CT, 19th C, rect, two carved handles, decorative bands, polychrome blue, orange, green, and brown splints, 13" l, 10-1/4" w, 7" h **1,725.00**

Oak
Peach basket shape, initials "CMT," 11-1/2" h, 14" d top **235.00**

Sewing, rect, compartments woven into one end, 21" l, 12" d, 6" h, minor cracking **250.00**

Painted
Miniature, tapering cylindrical form, loop handles, old taupe paint, America, 19th C, 5" d, 3" h **1,150.00**

Splint, round shape, sq bottom, old dark red paint over white, New England, mid-19th C, minor paint wear, 12" d, 3-3/4" h **200.00**

Vertical-shaped wooden slats joined by twisted wire banding, wooden circular base, old painted surface, America, early 19th C, 12-1/2" d, 18" h **865.00**

Rye straw
23" d, dough rising, shallow, hickory splint binding, PA, late 19th C **125.00**

24" d, domed lid, wear, edge damage, one bentwood rim handle missing **300.00**

Splint and cane, Guilford, CT, late 19th C, fixed bale handle, circular rim and sq base, old natural color, 3-1/2" d, 4-3/4" h **100.00**

Stave construction, vertical wood staves taper down at base, fixed with wire, dark orig finish over varnish, 13" d, 17" h **250.00**

Storage, cov, splint, painted blue, attributed to New England, late 19th C, 17" d, 24" h **1,380.00**

Splint, gathering, 14" d, 8-1/4" h, **$45.**

Woven splint
Buttocks, 28 ribs, dark patina, bentwood handle, 10-1/4" l, 5-1/4" h **200.00**

Buttocks, 40 ribs, old gray paint, 13-1/2" x 14" x 7" h **65.00**

Rectangular, courses of splint have unfaded dyed color, red, blue,

yellow, and brown, 10-1/2" x 13" x
5-3/4" **385.00**
Ribbed buttocks, painted green, red
handle, America, 19th C, 13-1/2" h,
minor break **1,410.00**
Round, bentwood handle, old gray
weathered surface, 13-3/4" d,
8-3/4" h **115.00**
Round, bentwood handle, rim, and
foot, alternating salmon colored
ribs, 12-1/4" d, 7-1/2" h, minor split
on foot **150.00**

BATTERSEA ENAMELS

History: Battersea enamel is a generic term for
English enamel-on-copper objects of the 18th century.

In 1753, Stephen Theodore Janssen established a
factory to produce "Trinkets and Curiosities Enameled
on Copper" at York House, Battersea, London. Here
the new invention of transfer printing developed to a
high degree of excellence, and the resulting trifles
delighted fashionable Georgian society.

Recent research has shown that enamels actually
were being produced in London and the Midlands
several years before York House was established.
However, most enamel trinkets still are referred to as
"Battersea Enamels," even though they were probably
made in other workshops in London, Birmingham,
Bilston, Wednesbury, or Liverpool.

All manner of charming items were made,
including snuff and patch boxes bearing mottos and
memory gems. (By adding a mirror inside the lid, a
snuff box became a patch box.) Many figural
whimsies, called "toys," were created to amuse a gay
and fashionable world. Many other elaborate articles,
e.g., candlesticks, salts, tea caddies, and
bonbonnières, were made for the tables of the newly
rich middle classes.

*Patch box,
England, c1800,
oval form, lid
decorated with
polychrome por-
trait, inscribed
"WASHINGTON"
on white ground,
brass rim and
collar, cobalt
blue exterior on
base, white
enamel interior,
7/8" x 2" x
1-1/2", lid is
unattached,
minor losses,* **$470.** *Photo courtesy of
Skinner's Auctioneers and Appraisers.*

Bonbonnière, reclining cow, natural
colors, grassy mound, floral lid, Bilston,
c1770 . . . . **3,750.00**
Etui, white tapered column, pastoral
scenes within reserves, gilt scrolling

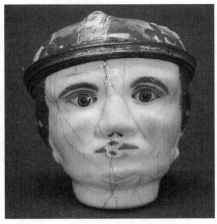

*Snuffbox, knight's head form box, floral
mark at base of neck, 3" h, heavily
restored, loss,* **$45.** *Photo courtesy of
Sanford Alderfer Auction Company.*

and diaper work, int. fitted with perfume
bottle, writing slide, pencil, and bodkin,
Bilston, c1770 . . . . **3,400.00**

Mirror knobs, 2-7/8" d, rural genre
scenes, woman on shore, two restored,
three-pc set **300.00**

Patch box, oval

7/8" x 2" x 1-1/2", lid dec with
polychrome portrait, inscribed
"WASHINGTON" on white ground,
brass rim and collar, cobalt blue
exterior on base, white enamel
interior, c1800, lid is unattached,
minor losses **470.00**

2-1/2" x 1-3/4" x 1-1/2", black and
white King Charles Spaniel, pink
ground, floral dec, around sides
. . . . **2,750.00**

Pill box, cov, 1-1/4" l, lid enameled
"Washington's Name be always in
Fame," some expertly repaired cracks
and restorations. **2,760.00**

*Snuff box, blue enamel box with sailing
ship, lighthouse, and fishermen in
harbor, 2" l,* **$275.** *Photo courtesy of
Sanford Alderfer Auction Company.*

Snuffbox
2-1/4" l, blue enamel, racing scene
. . . . **475.00**
3" l, molded spaniel cover,
landscape painted base, lines
. . . . **1,265.00**
Tiebacks, 2-1/2" d, enamel and brass,
Cupid dec, pr **150.00**
Topsy-turvy box, 2-3/4" l, oval, white,
Before and After Marriage, humorous
drawing of couple whose smiles turn
into frowns with box is turned upside
down, Bilston, c1780 . . . . **1,500.00**

BAVARIAN CHINA

History: Bavaria, Germany, was an important
porcelain production center, similar to the
Staffordshire district in England. The phrase "Bavarian
China" refers to the products of companies operating
in Bavaria, among which were Hutschenreuther,
Thomas, and Zeh, Scherzer & Co. (Z. S. & Co.). Very
little of the production from this area was imported
into the United States prior to 1870.

Bowl, 7-3/8" l, 6" w, ovoid, reticulated
sides, beaded rim, center and sides
painted with scenic roundels en
grisaille, blue ribbon cartouches with
gilt detailing, scenes titled on underside
"Badenburg," "Apolloscumpeil," and
"Schloss Nymphenburg," late 19th C
. . . . **325.00**
Celery tray, 11" l, center with basket of
fruit, luster edge, c1900 . . . . **45.00**
Chocolate set, cov chocolate pot, six
cups and saucers, shaded blue and
white, large white leaves, pink, red, and
white roses, crown mark. **295.00**
Creamer and sugar, purple and white
pansy dec, marked "Meschendorf,
Bavaria" **65.00**

*Plates, pair, wide gilded borders,
central floral panels, marked "Heinrich
Bavarian," 11" d,* **$35.** *Photo courtesy
of Joy Luke Auctions.*

Plates, pair, scenic panels decorated with ladies and birds, 10" d, $90. Photo courtesy of Joy Luke Auctions.

Cup and saucer, roses and foliage, gold handle **30.00**
Dinner plate, 10-1/4" d, gold emb, stippled bands, "A" monogram, marked "Hutshcenreuther selb Bavaria," price for set of 12 . . . . **320.00**
Fish set, 13 plates, matching sauce boat, artist sgd **295.00**
Pitcher, 9" h, bulbous, blackberry dec, shaded ground, burnished gold lizard handle, sgd "D. Churchill" **125.00**
Portrait vase, 10" h, gold enameled flowers and leaves, hp portrait of Naomi, blue beehive mark and "TG Bavaria" mark **520.00**
Ramekin, underplate, ruffled, small red roses with green foliage, gold rim **45.00**
Salt and pepper shakers, pr, pink apple blossom sprays, white ground, reticulated gold tops, pr **35.00**
Shaving mug, pink carnations, marked "Royal Bavarian" **65.00**
Vase, 12" h, hp, red poppies, gold enamel dec, marked "Classic Bavaria" **260.00**

BELLEEK

History: Belleek, a thin, ivory-colored, almost-iridescent porcelain, was first made in 1857 in county Fermanagh, Ireland. Production continued until World War I, was discontinued for a period of time, and then resumed. The Shamrock pattern is most familiar, but many patterns were made, including Limpet, Tridacna, and Grasses.

For more information, see this book.

There is an Irish saying: If a newly married couple receives a gift of Belleek, their marriage will be blessed with lasting happiness.

Several American firms made a Belleek-type porcelain. The first was Ott and Brewer Co. of Trenton, New Jersey, in 1884, followed by Willets. Other firms producing this ware included The Ceramic Art Co. (1889), American Art China Works (1892), Columbian Art Co. (1893), and Lenox, Inc. (1904).

Marks: The European Belleek company used specific marks during given time periods, which makes it relatively easy to date a piece of Irish Belleek. Variations in mark color are important, as well as the symbols and words.

First mark	Black	Harp, Hound, and Castle 1863-1890
Second mark	Black	Harp, Hound, and Castle and the words "Co. Fermanagh, Ireland" 1891-1826
Third mark	Black	"Deanta in Eirinn" added 1926-1946
Fourth mark	Green	Same as third mark except for color 1946-1955
Fifth mark	Green	"R" inside a circle added 1955-1965
Sixth mark	Green	"Co. Fermanagh" omitted 1965-March 1980
Seventh mark	Gold	"Deanta in Eirinn" omitted April 1980-Dec. 1992
Eighth mark	Blue	Blue version of the second mark with "R" inside a circle added January 1993-present

Additional Listings: Lenox.

American
Bowl
7" d, 4-1/4" h, double handles, ruffled rim, gilt trim and handles, gilt and rose-colored flowers dec, brown Willets mark **275.00**
7-1/2" d, green ext., wide gilt textured border, int. with hp floral design, artist sgd "MS" on base, brown Willets mark **100.00**
Candy dish, 8" x 6", shell form, ivory ground, hp floral dec, ruffled gilt rim, marked "Columbia Art Co., Trenton, NJ" **80.00**
Chocolate pot, 10-1/4" h, ivory ground, Art Deco rose design, pale green and yellow wide borders, gilt accents, green Lenox pallet mark **135.00**

Vase, shell shape, coral handle, ivory ground, pink glaze, light gilding, red Willets stamp, 7-1/2" x 8-1/4", $1,920. Photo courtesy of David Rago Auctions.

Cider jug, 6" h, hp, fruit dec, gilt handle, green Lenox pallet mark **50.00**
Cup and saucer, 2" cup, 5-3/4" d saucer, hp, pale pink and green beaded dec, gilt borders, brown Willets mark **60.00**
Dish, 10-1/2" d, hp, lily dec, gold trim, gilt banding and design on ext., sgd "FML," green Lenox pallet mark **145.00**
Jug, 5-1/2" h, hp, pale yellow ground, floral dec, gilt rim and handle, green CAC pallet mark **110.00**
Pitcher, 7" h, hp, white ground, geometric blue floral design, gilt trim, artist sgd "G. L. Urban," green Willets mark **85.00**
Plate, 7-1/4" d, gilt foliate rim, blue enamel beads, red Willets mark, price for pr **45.00**
Salt, 1-1/2" d
    Gilt, ruffled edge, marked "CAC," price for set of six **45.00**
    Pale green, hp pink enamel dec, artist sgd "E.S.M.," Lenox pallet mark, price for set of six . . . **135.00**
Swan, 8-1/2" h, ivory, open back, green Lenox wreath mark **90.00**
Tankard, 5-3/4" h, hand painted
    Brown and blue painted ground, poppy dec, sgd "LM '06," green CAC pallet mark **135.00**
    Multicolored ground, foliage dec, sgd "B.M.A.," brown Willets mark **125.00**
Teapot, 6" h, blue glazed ground, gilt dec, brown Willets mark **135.00**
Vase
    8-1/2" h, sterling overlay, white ground, marked "Rockwell-3175," green Lenox pallet mark . . **145.00**

Goblet, ivory ground, painted yellow poppies, black Lenox and palette stamps, price for five-piece set, 3-1/2" x 2-3/4", $325. Photo courtesy of David Rago Auctions.

15" h, baluster, hp pine cone dec, artist sgd "A.E.G.," green Lenox pallet mark. **450.00**

Irish

Basket, 6-1/2" x 4-1/2", four strand, applied flowers, Belleek Co. Fermangh Ireland pad mark, some repairs, petal missing **80.00**

Bread plate, 10-1/2" l, 9-1/4" w, Shamrock pattern, double handle, 3rd green mark **80.00**

Butter dish, cov, 6-1/2" d top, 8-1/2" d base, Limpet pattern, 1st black mark **475.00**

Cake plate, 10-1/2" d, mask with grape leaves pattern, four looped handles, pale yellow edge, 3rd black mark **155.00**

Creamer

3-1/4" h, Lifford pattern, 3rd green mark **60.00**

3-1/4" h, Ribbon pattern, 3rd green mark **40.00**

3-1/2" h, Cleary pattern, 1st green mark **50.00**

4" h, Rathmore pattern, 3rd green mark **40.00**

4-1/2" h, Undine pattern, 3rd black mark **55.00**

Creamer and sugar, 3-1/2" h creamer, 2" h sugar, Lotus pattern, 3rd black mark, rim chip. **70.00**

Cream jug, 5-1/4" h, blue glazed handle and coral relief, first black mark, c1880, footrim chip. **520.00**

Cup and saucer, 5-3/8" d saucer, Tea Ware, hexagon, pink tint, second black mark, early 20th C, price for pr . **460.00**

Figure

2-1/2" h, pig, 3rd green mark. . **90.00**

6" h, harp, 3rd green mark. . . . **70.00**

Font, 7" h, Sacred Heart, cross form, shaped font, 2nd green mark. . . . **50.00**

Mint tray, 8-1/2" l, shell form, pink highlights on rim, brown mark . . . **70.00**

Bowl, band of fern fronds, scalloped rim and prunted porcelain body, Trenton stamp mark, 9-3/4" d, 4" h, $230. Photo courtesy of David Rago Auctions.

Mustache cup and saucer, 2-1/2" h cup, 6" d saucer, Tridacna, pink rim, 1st black mark. **495.00**

Pitcher

5-1/2" h, Vine and Grape pattern, lavender and green, ivory ground, brown mark **60.00**

5-3/4" h, Ivy pattern, yellow, rope twist handle, 2nd green mark **45.00**

6-1/2" h, Limpet pattern, 3rd black mark. **90.00**

Plate, 10-1/2" d, scalloped edge, woven, three strands, pad mark **200.00**

Spill vase

5" h, Shamrock, 2nd green mark **50.00**

5-1/2" h, Shamrock Daisy, 3rd green mark **65.00**

8" h, owl, 2nd green mark. . . . **55.00**

Sugar bowl, 4" h, Shell, pink tinted edge and coral, first black mark, c1880, footrim chips **575.00**

Swan, 4" h, open back, yellow wings and head, brown mark **55.00**

Tea cup and saucer, 5-3/4" d saucer, gilt trimmed relief of horns, orange peel ground, first black and registry marks, c1870, gilt wear, repaired rim chip on saucer **175.00**

Tea kettle, cov, 6" h, Grass Tea Ware, enamel dec relief, first black mark, c1880, spout lips restored. **230.00**

Teapot, cov

5" h, Shamrock pattern, brown mark **90.00**

6" h, Limpet pattern, 3rd black mark **165.00**

Tea set

Neptune Tea Ware, 5-1/8" h cov teapot, creamer, sugar, six 6-1/8" d plates, six cups and saucers, each pink tinted, third black marks, 20th C. **1,150.00**

Tridacna Tea Ware, 4-1/8" h cov teapot, creamer, sugar, 6-3/4" d plate, six cups and saucers, each pink tinted, second black marks, early 20th C **460.00**

Vase

4-1/4" h, six-sided pot, 3rd green mark **45.00**

4-3/4" h, 5-3/4" d, Cardium, shell form, coral and shell base, 2nd black mark **80.00**

6-1/4" h, tree trunk, 3rd green mark **65.00**

8" h, coral, pink tinted coral and shell int., 1st black mark, c1880 **1,150.00**

Sleigh, brass, set of 16 bells on original leather strap, graduated from 1-1/2" to 2-1/2" d, American, $120. Photo courtesy of Cowan's Historic Americana Auctions.

8" h, Ribbon, applied flowers, ruffled rim, 3rd black mark, minor flakes on flowers **110.00**

8-1/4" h, Dolphin, 1st black mark, chip on tail. **775.00**

9" h, two scrolled and pierced handles, delicate applied bouquet of flowers, 1891 mark, price for pr **690.00**

BELLS

History: Bells have been used for centuries for many different purposes. They have been traced as far back as 2697 B.C., though at that time they did not have any true tone. One of the oldest bells is the "crotal," a tiny sphere with small holes, a ball, and a stone or metal interior. This type now appears as sleigh bells.

True bell making began when bronze, a mixture of tin and copper, was invented. Bells are now made out of many types of materials—almost as many materials as there are uses for them.

Bells of the late 19th century show a high degree of workmanship and artistic style. Glass bells from this period are examples of the glassblower's talent and the glass manufacturer's product.

Brass, hand held, Jacobean, head handle, cast figures on sides, emb inscription, 3-1/4" d, 4" h **95.00**

Ceramic, figural

Anniversary, Florence Ceramics, applied pink Dresden-style flowers, white ground, gold trim, 4-1/2" h **80.00**

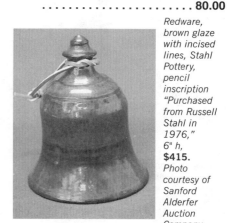

Redware, brown glaze with incised lines, Stahl Pottery, pencil inscription "Purchased from Russell Stahl in 1976," 6" h, $415. Photo courtesy of Sanford Alderfer Auction Company.

School-type, brass, turned wooden handles, left: 11" h, 6-1/2" d, great old patina; right: 9-1/2" h, 4-1/2" d, cast inscription "1813 Colonial 1837," handle striped, nut replaced, price for pair, $120. Photo courtesy of Cowan's Historic Americana Auctions.

Belle O' the Ball, Royal Doulton, HN1997, red and white dress, 1947-79 . . . . **400.00**
Sovereign Bonnet Lady, Gonder, Mold No. 800, 3-1/2" h **60.00**
Desk type, 4-3/8" h, bell enclosed in five polished mother-of-pearl shells, gilt metal surrounds, small mother-of-pearl mounted striker, round alabaster base, late 19th C **185.00**
Dinner, china
Figural, Chinaman, Noritake, 3-1/2" h **210.00**
Rose Tapestry, Royal Bayreuth, three color roses, gold handle, 3-1/4" h **400.00**
Glass
Burmese, Thomas Webb, flaring base, applied amber handle, glossy finish, 6-3/4" h **750.00**
Cranberry, applied clear handle, English, late 19th C, 11" h . . **95.00**
Fostoria, Chintz pattern, orig label **135.00**
Imperial, Candlewick pattern, No. 400/108, 5" h **95.00**
Mount Washington, white satin, pink floral dec, gold trim, 5" h . . **150.00**

School-type, brass, turned wooden handle, 10" h, $70. Photo courtesy of James D. Julia, Inc.

Nickel-plated, railroad engine, arched yoke with U-shaped support, pedestal base, 25" h **2,145.00**
School, 10-1/4" h, turned curly maple handle **385.00**
Sleigh, 55" l, 15 graduated brass bells on leather strap, wear **200.00**
Sterling silver, 4-5/8" h, cupid blowing horn, figural handle, foliate strap work border, frosted finish, Gorham, c1870 . . . . **750.00**

BENNINGTON AND BENNINGTON-TYPE POTTERY

History: In 1845, Christopher Webber Fenton joined Julius Norton, his brother-in-law, in the manufacturing of stoneware pottery in Bennington, Vermont. Fenton sought to expand the company's products and glazes; Norton wanted to concentrate solely on stoneware. In 1847, Fenton broke away and established his own factory.

Fenton introduced to America the famous Rockingham glaze, developed in England and named after the Marquis of Rockingham. In 1849, he patented a flint enamel glaze, "Fenton's Enamel," which added flecks, spots, or streaks of color (usually blues, greens, yellows, and oranges) to the brown Rockingham glaze. Forms included candlesticks, coachman bottles, cow creamers, poodles, sugar bowls, and toby pitchers.

Fenton produced the little-known scroddled ware, commonly called lava or agate ware. Scroddled ware is composed of differently colored clays, which are mixed with cream-colored clay, molded, turned on a potter's wheel, coated with feldspar and flint, and fired. It was not produced in quantity, as there was little demand for it.

Fenton also introduced Parian ware to America. Parian was developed in England in 1842 and known as "Statuary ware." Parian is translucent porcelain that has no glaze and resembles marble. Bennington made the blue and white variety in the form of vases, cologne bottles, and trinkets.

The hound-handled pitcher is probably the best-known Bennington piece. Hound-handled pitchers were made by about 30 different potteries in more than 55 variations. Rockingham glaze was used by more than 150 potteries in 11 states, mainly in the Midwest, between 1830 and 1900.

Marks: Five different marks were used, with many variations. Only about 20 percent of the pieces carried any mark; some forms were almost always marked, others never. Marks include:

- 1849 mark (four variations) for flint enamel and Rockingham
- E. Fenton's Works, 1845-1847, on Parian and occasionally on scroddled ware
- U. S. Pottery Co., ribbon mark, 1852-1858, on Parian and blue and white porcelain
- U. S. Pottery Co., lozenge mark, 1852-1858, on Parian
- U. S. Pottery, oval mark, 1853-1858, mainly on scroddled ware.

Additional Listings: Stoneware.

Bowl, 7-1/8" d, shallow, brown and yellow Rockingham glaze, Fenton's 1849 mark **775.00**
Candlestick, 8-1/4" h, flint enamel glaze **875.00**
Curtain tiebacks, pr, 4-1/2" l, 1849-58, Barrett plate 200, one chipped . **185.00**
Figure, 8-1/2" h, 9" l, poodle, standing, basket in mouth, Barrett plate 367, repairs to tail and hind quarters **2,500.00**
Flask, book, flint enamel, title imp on spine, 1849-58, Barrett plate 411
5-3/4" w, 2-5/8" d, 7-3/4" h, brown and blue flint enamel glaze, "Bennington Battle" on spine **3,300.00**
6" h, titled "Hermit's Life & Suffering" **980.00**
7" h, titled "Ladies Companion" **690.00**
Jug, 10-3/4" h, stoneware, strap handle, imp label "F. B. Norton & Co., Worcester, Mass," cobalt blue slip floral design **220.00**
Marble, 1-1/2" d, blue, some wear **90.00**
Paperweight, 3" h, 4-1/2" h, spaniel, 1849-58, Barrett plate 407 . . . . **815.00**
Picture frame, 9-1/2" h, oval, 1948-58, Barrett plate VIII, chips and repairs, pr **230.00**
Pitcher, 8" h, hunting scene, Barrett pate 26, chips **175.00**

Candleholders, pair, yellow ware with Rockingham glaze, c1850, replaced glass chimneys, 2-1/2" h candleholders, $615. Photo courtesy of Vicki and Bruce Waasdorp..

Foot warmer, yellow ware with Rockingham glaze, relief scroll design at shoulder, c1850, 9" h, minor surface chip on right edge, minor glaze crazing at bottom, $440. *Photo courtesy of Vicki and Bruce Waasdorp.*

Spittoon, 9-1/2" d, flint enamel glaze, rare 1849 mark **450.00**
Sugar bowl, cov, 3-3/4" h, Parian, blue and white, Repeated Oak Leaves pattern, raised grapevine dec on lid
. . . .**150.00**
Teapot, cov, flint enamel, Alternate Rib pattern, pierced pouring spout . **425.00**
Wash bowl and pitcher, flint enamel glaze. **1,100.00**

Bennington-Type
Bank, 3-1/4" h, 3-3/4" h, chest of drawers shape, Rockingham glaze, Barrett plate 428, small chip to front top edge **150.00**
Creamer, 5-1/2" h, 6-3/4" l, figural, cow, Rockingham glaze, Barrett plate 378, chipped cov, repairs. **115.00**
Flask, book, 7" h, titled "Spiritual Manifestations By" imp on spine, Rockingham glaze, mid-19th C, crack
. . . .**260.00**

Crock, J. & E. Norton/ Bennington VT, two-gallon size, cobalt blue flowers decorated, cylindrical form, shaped rim, two applied handles, 7" d top, 11" h, **$500**. *Photo courtesy of Sanford Alderfer Auction Company.*

Spittoon, 8-1/2" d, scallop shell form, Rockingham glaze, 19th C **175.00**
Toby bottle, 9" h, barrel, Rockingham glaze, mid-19th C, rim and base chips
. . . . **175.00**

BISCUIT JARS

History: The biscuit or cracker jar was the forerunner of the cookie jar. Biscuit jars were made of various materials by leading glassworks and potteries of the late 19th and early 20th centuries.

Note: All items listed have silver-plated (SP) mountings unless otherwise noted.

For more information, see this book.

Bristol glass,
6-1/2" h, allover enameled pink, blue, white and yellow floral dec, green leaves, SP top, rim, and handle **125.00**
Cranberry glass, 9" h, 6-1/4" d, two applied clear ring handles, applied clear feet and flower prunt pontil, ribbed finial knob. **195.00**
Nippon China, 7-1/2" h, 4-1/2" w, sq, white, multicolored floral bands, gold outlines and trim **110.00**

Opal glass
7-3/4" h, white opal glass jar, pastel pink and green chrysanthemum dec on bluish-colored ground, metal mount, handle, cover, acorn finials, attributed to Mt. Washington Glass Co., New Bedford, MA, late 19th C, some enamel wear
. . . . **215.00**

Wavecrest, green shading to white body with two horizontal wavy lines, painted floral design, silver plated lid **$245.**

8" h, sq jar with molded bumpy exterior of white opal glass, dec with pink and green enameled clover blossoms, silver-plated cover and rim mount with floral and scroll repousse motifs, attributed to Mt Washington Glass Co, New Bedford, MA, late 19th C, minor enamel wear **290.00**
10" h, white opal glass jar, enameled blue, yellow, pink, and green florals, SP mount, handle, and cov, trefoil finial, attributed to Mt Washington Glass Co., New Bedford, MA, late 19th C . .**230.00**

Royal Bayreuth, Poppy, blue mark
. . . .**650.00**
Satin glass, 7-1/4" h, pink, molded shell base, enameled floral dec, SP lid and handle **315.00**
Wave Crest, 9" h, yellow roses, molded multicolored swirl ground, incised floral and leaf dec on lid, marked "Quadruple Plate" **410.00**

Wedgwood, jasper
5" h, green dip ground, applied white classical figure groups above acanthus leafs, SP rim, handle and cover, imp Wedgwood mark, late 19th C, footrim nick **400.00**

Wedgwood, England, late 19th C, three-color jasper dip, central green ground bordered in lilac ground, applied white classical relief with foliate border, silver plated rim, handle and cover, imp mark partially removed, 5-1/4" h, **$650**. *Photo courtesy of Skinner's Auctioneers and Appraisers.*

5-3/4" h, central dark blue ground bordered in light blue, applied white Muses in relief, banded laurel border, SP rim, handle and cover, imp mark, c1900, slight relief loss **650.00**

5-3/4" h, yellow ground, applied black relief of Muses below fruiting grapevine festoons terminating in lion masks with rings, grapevine border to foot, SP rim, handle and cover, imp mark, c1930 ... **800.00**

6" h, central dark blue ground bordered in light blue ground, applied white classical relief, SP footrim, rim, handle and cover, imp mark, c1900, slight firing lines to relief **600.00**

6-3/8" h, light blue ground, applied white relief of Muses within scrolled foliate frames, silver-plated stand, rim and hinged cover, imp mark, mid-19th C **425.00**

BISQUE

History: Bisque or biscuit china is the name given to wares that have been fired once and have not been glazed.

Bisque figurines and busts, which were popular during the Victorian era, were used on fireplace mantels, dining room buffets, and end tables. Manufacturing was centered in the United States and Europe. By the mid-20th century, Japan was the principal source of bisque items, especially character-related items.

For more information, see this book.

Dish, cov, 9" x 6-1/2" x 5-1/2", dog, brown, and white, green blanket, white and gilt basketweave base **500.00**

Baby girl, three-face fairy lamp, 3-1/2" h, $75 and egg-shaped vase with cupids playing, 6-1/2" h, $35. Photo courtesy of Woody Auctions.

Figural group, 19-1/2" l, 9" w, 13" h, Napoleon and Josephine playing with their daughters, alfresco setting, oval base, flat leaf gilt-metal bands, gilt-metal base mounted with mythic beasts and Napoleon's cipher, Continental, early 20th C **1,725.00**

Figure, boy playing mandolin, marked "Heubach" **75.00**

Match holder, figural, Dutch girl, copper and gold trim **45.00**

Planter, carriage, four wheels, pale blue and pink, white ground, gold dots, royal markings **165.00**

Salt, 3" d, figural, walnut, cream, branch base, matching spoon ... **75.00**

Wall plaque, 10-1/4" d, light green, scrolled and pierced scallop, white relief figures in center, man playing mandolin, lady wearing hat, c1900, pr **275.00**

BITTERS BOTTLES

History: Bitters, a "remedy" made from natural herbs and other mixtures with an alcohol base, often was viewed as the universal cure-all. The names given to various bitter mixtures were imaginative, though the bitters seldom cured what their makers claimed.

The manufacturers of bitters needed a way to sell and advertise their products. They designed bottles in many shapes, sizes, and colors to attract the buyer. Many forms of advertising, including trade cards, billboards, signs, almanacs, and novelties, proclaimed the virtues of a specific bitter.

During the Civil War, a tax was levied on alcoholic beverages. Since bitters were identified as medicines, they were exempt from this tax. The alcoholic content was never mentioned. In 1907, when the Pure Foods Regulations went into effect, "an honest statement of content on every label" put most of the manufacturers out of business.

Cassin Bitters, San Francisco Glass Works, medium golden amber, 1871-75, $44,000. Photo courtesy of Pacific Glass Auctions.

Greeley's Bourbon Bitters, applied top, barrel shape, smoky topaz green, Ring/Ham G101, $1,800. Photo courtesy of Pacific Glass Auctions.

Alpine Herb Bitters, amber, sq, smooth base, tooled lip, 9-5/8" h **175.00**

Bell's Cocktail Bitters, Jas. M. Bell & Co., New York, amber, applied ring, smooth base, 10-1/2" h **450.00**

Browns Celebrated Indian Herb Bitters/Patented Feb. 11, 1868, figural, emb, golden amber, ground lip, smooth base, 12-1/4" h **350.00**

Bryant's Stomach Bitters, dark green, sticky ball pontil **3,600.00**

Caldwell's Herb Bitters/The Great Tonic, triangular, beveled and lattice work panels, yellowish-amber, applied tapered lip, iron pontil **395.00**

Drake's Plantation Bitters, puce, Arabaseque design, tapered lip, smooth base, 9-3/4" h **295.00**

Solomon's Strengthening and Invigorating Bitters, Savannah, Georgia, sapphire blue, applied top, Ring/Ham S139, professionally cleaned, $1,100. Photo courtesy of Pacific Glass Auctions.

Greenley's Bourbon Bitters, moss green, applied top, smooth base
. . . . **4,000.00**

J. C.& Co., molded pineapple form, deep golden amber, blown molded, 19th C, 8-1/2" h **460.00**

Kelly's Old Cabin Bitters, cabin shape, amber, sloping collar lip, smooth base, 9" h **725.00**

McKeever's Army Bitters, amber, sloping collared lip, smooth base, 10-5/8" h **1,700.00**

National Bitters, corn-cob shape, puce amber, applied ring lip, smooth base, 12-5/8" h **350.00**

Red Jacket Bitters, Monheimer & Co., sq, amber, tooled lip, smooth base, 9-1/2" h **100.00**

Simon's Centennial, George Washington bust **3,200.00**

Tippecanoe, Warner & Co., amber, applied mushroom lip, 9" h **95.00**

Warner's Safe Bitters, amber, applied mouth, smooth base, 8-1/2" h . . . **265.00**

Zingan Bitters, amber, applied mouth, smooth base, 11-7/8" h **150.00**

BLACK MEMORABILIA

History: The term "Black memorabilia" refers to a broad range of collectibles that often overlap other collecting fields, e.g., toys and postcards. It also encompasses African artifacts, items created by slaves or related to the slavery era, modern Black cultural contributions to literature, art, etc., and material associated with the Civil Rights Movement and the Black experience throughout history.

The earliest known examples of Black memorabilia include primitive African designs and tribal artifacts. Black Americana dates back to the arrival of African natives upon American shores.

The advent of the 1900s saw an incredible amount and variety of material depicting Blacks, most often in a derogatory and dehumanizing manner that clearly reflected the stereotypical attitude held toward the Black race during this period. The popularity of Black portrayals in this unflattering fashion flourished as the century wore on.

As the growth of the Civil Rights Movement escalated and aroused public awareness to the Black plight, attitudes changed. Public outrage and pressure during the early 1950s eventually put a halt to these offensive stereotypes.

Black representations are still being produced in many forms, but no longer in the demoralizing designs of the past. These modern objects, while not as historically significant as earlier examples, will become the Black memorabilia of tomorrow.

Autograph, Martin Luther King, Jr., 11" x 14" photograph, sgd "with best wishes Martin Luther King" . . . **3,220.00**

Baseball cap, Kansas City Black Royals Negro League, white, gray pinstripes, worn black visor, large black "KC" stitched on front, c1920 . . **930.00**

Book

Argument Before the Supreme Court, Appellants vs Cinque, and Others, Africans, Captured in the Schooner Amistad, John Quincy Adams, New York, 1841, 135 pgs, 8vo, orig shelf wrappers, covers lightly soiled, scattered minor foxing* . . . .

George Washington Carver, An American Biograpny, Rackham Colt, 1943, ex-library copy . . . **5.00**

Who's Who in Colored America, Volume I, J. Joseph Boris, ed., New York, 1927, first edition, portrait plates, small 4to, orig cloth
. . . . **375.00**

Women of Achievement, Benjamin Brawley, Woman's American Baptist Home Mission Society, 1919, portrait plates, small 8vo, orig cloth **375.00**

Bank, mechanical, Jolly Nigger, cast iron, 6-1/4" h, **$775.** *Photo courtesy of Joy Luke Auctions.*

Figure, Eva and Uncle Tom, Staffordshire, 8-1/4" h, **$475.** *Photo courtesy of Joy Luke Auctions.*

Carte-de-visite

Colored Baptist Church, Petersburg, VA, Lazell & McMillin, Petersburg, photographers, 1966, ext. view, men and women sitting on front fence, pencil inscription "Church of Petersburg Negroes burned by rebels, given by Lottie, Feb 9th, 1868," soil, wear, slight crimp
. . . . **345.00**

Frederick Douglas, full-length portrait, c1860, erased pencil marks on top border **550.00**

Sojourner Truth, 3/4 view, seated at table, knitting, "I Sell the Shadow to Support the Substance," 1864, corners clipped, toning, light browning **660.00**

Cigar box label, 6-1/4" x 10", glossy paper label, Booker T., Perfecto Cigars, black and white portrait of Booker T. Washington, red, pale blue, and dark blue border, white stars, c1930s, unused **20.00**

Doll

12" h, Mammy, nut head, painted features, looped plush hair, whisk broom body, orig commercial assemblage, pink print dress, twin black babies in green print organdy outfits, early 20th C
. . . . **635.00**

18" h, Mammy, stuffed cloth, hand-embroidered features, red trimmed dress, blue and white cap, wear, damage **220.00**

20" h, Golliwog, velveteen face, hands, and feet, applied felt eyes and mouth, inked nose, yellow checked shirt, golden crepe pants, red braid trim, removable gray and white checked wool jacket, c1930, some wear and soil **460.00**

Ephemera

Certificate of Freedom, for Thomas Chambers, resident of New York City, September 1814, partly printed document, sgd, small folio, docketed on verso **950.00**

Deposition of Thomas Cook, Shrewsbury, NJ, concerning slave trade and events on the sloop *Fanny*, Jan. 10, 1801, 12-1/2" x 8" **175.00**

Depositions concerning slave trade by sloop *Fanny* between Africa and North America, Oct 8, 1801, 17 pgs, 9-1/2" x 7-1/2" **550.00**

Notice, *The Charleston Daily Courier*, Jan. 5, 1858, regarding issuing of slave badges, giving prices for various trades **1,380.00**

Public instrument of protest by Simon Potter, master of schooner *Sally,* July 16, 1793, regarding payment after loss of ship by unforeseen circumstances, including war between Spain and France, four pgs, 14-1/2" x 9" **90.00**

Receipt, "Negro Apprenticeship 2/6," printed, "Bought of the Anti-Slavery Society, Office, No. 18, Aldermanbury," (England) signed and dated by Francis Wedgwood, Society seal, dated 1838 . . . **490.00**

Nodder, 30" h, black boy, clockwork, head nods up and down, eyes roll, one arm extended upward, other extended forward in greeting manner, papier-mâché **1,500.00**

Perfume bottle, 4-3/4" to 6" h, Golliwogg, stylized faces, black and brown hair covering stoppers, bulbous frosted glass body, painted white collar, black round feet, raised maker's mark for DeVigny, one with partial paper label, c1919, price for three-pc set **575.00**

Pinback button

Baltimore Elite Giants, Negro Leagues, red and white, glossy cello, c1940 . . . . **45.00**

Gold Dust Washing Powder, multicolored trademark of Black twins seated in wash tub, white background, black letters . . . **60.00**

Print

10" x 13", N. Currier, NY, lithograph, titled "Washington at Mount Vernon-1797," shows Washington on horseback conversing with two black field hands, framed . . **295.00**

13-1/4" x 9-3/4", litho, *I'm Not to Blame for Being White Sir,* young white child holding out her hand for coins while passing stranger places coins in hands of black child, c1850, heavily toned **290.00**

Roly poly, Mayo's Roly Poly Tobacco, Mammy, litho tin, 7" x 5-1/4", two pcs, C-8+ **825.00**

Slave tag, 2" sq, copper, Charlestown, 1834

Porter, 171 . . . . **3,065.00**

Servant No. 205, wear, minor dents **1,175.00**

Textile, printed, 32-1/2" x 42", showing Little Black Sambo and tiger, earth tones of red, green, and dark brown, tan linen ground, folded, sewn seam with red ink label "WPA Handicraft Project #10235, Milwaukee, Wisconsin, Sponsored by Milwaukee County and Milwaukee State Teachers College, c1935-43 . . . . **1,350.00**

Store display, Jazzbo Jim, electrified, cabin constructed with tin lithographed sheets over wooden frame, graphic images of Black Mammy and child, front with gentleman playing banjo, children with harmonica and hambones, wide-eyed Pickanninie dancer, all caricatures surrounding cabin have exaggerated Negro facial features, working period electric motor and mechanism in cabin activate large Dancing Black Doll on rooftop, hand-painted composition doll, redressed to match original c1921 Unique Art toy, redressed correctly to match original toy, 23" h doll, 33" h overall, **$3,750.** *Photo courtesy of James D. Julia, Inc.*

Print, Winchester, two black men rousting skunk out of log, old double-barrel muzzleloader leaning on log, dog fleeing in foreground, copyright 1908, oak frame, **$575.** *Photo courtesy of James D. Julia Auctions.*

Token, copper

American, c1838, "Am I Not A Woman and A Sister" **550.00**
English, c1795, "Payable in Dublin or London," reverse struck with handshake and logo "Make Slavery and Opression (sic) Cease Throughout the World" . . **1,380.00**

Token, **silvered brass**, Jefferson Davis, 1861, Death to Traitors **400.00**

BLOWN THREE MOLD

For more information, see this book.

History: The Jamestown colony in Virginia introduced glassmaking into America. The artisans used a "free-blown" method.

Blowing molten glass into molds was not introduced into America until the early 1800s. Blown three-mold glass used a pre-designed mold that consisted of two, three, or more hinged parts. The glassmaker placed a quantity of molten glass on the tip of a rod or tube, inserted it into the mold, blew air into the tube, waited until the glass cooled, and removed the finished product. The three-part mold is the most common and lends its name to this entire category.

The impressed decorations on blown-mold glass usually are reversed, i.e., what is raised or convex on the outside will be concave on the inside. This is useful in identifying the blown form.

By 1850, American-made glassware was relatively common. Increased demand led to large factories and the creation of a technology, which eliminated the smaller companies.

Bowl, 5-3/8" d, colorless, folded rim, pontil, 12-diamond base, McKearin GII-6 . . . . **125.00**

Wines, lot of 12, some with cut designs, some with beveled bowls, 3-3/4" to 4-1/4" h, $350. Photo courtesy of James D. Julia, Inc.

Celery vase, colorless, Pittsburgh, McKearin GV-21 . . . . **650.00**
Creamer, 3-1/2" h, colorless, applied handle **125.00**
Cruet, 7-3/4" h, cobalt blue, scroll scale pattern, ribbed base, pontil, applied handle, French **265.00**

Decanter

6-3/4" h, olive-amber, pint, attributed to Marlboro Street Glass Works, Keene, NH, some abrasions **460.00**
8" h, colorless, three applied rings, McKearin GII-18, replaced wheel stopper **110.00**
8-1/2" h, light sea green, Kent-Ohio pattern, McKearin GII-6 . . **2,415.00**

Dish, colorless, 5-1/2" d, McKearin GII-18 . . . . **50.00**
Flip glass, colorless, 6" h, McKearin GII-18 . . . . **125.00**
Ink bottle, 2-1/4" d, deep olive green, McKearin GII-2 . . . . **195.00**
Mustard, 4-1/4" h, colorless, pontil, cork stopper, orig paper label, McKearin GI-15 . . . . **85.00**
Pitcher, 7" h, colorless, base of handle reglued, McKearin GIII-5 . . . . . . **145.00**
Salt, basket shape, colorless . . **120.00**
Tumbler, 6-1/4" h, colorless, McKearin GII-19 . . . . **165.00**
Vinegar bottle, cobalt blue, ribbed, orig stopper, McKearin GI-7 . . . **285.00**
Whiskey glass, 2-3/8" h, colorless, applied handle, McKearin GII-18 . . . . **285.00**

Toilet water bottle, medium blue, 12 panels, Boston & Sandwich Glass, McKearin GI-7, type 5, 6" h $195.

BOHEMIAN GLASS

History: The once independent country of Bohemia, now a part of the Czech Republic, produced a variety of fine glassware: etched, cut, overlay, and colored. Its glassware, which first appeared in America in the early 1820s, continues to be exported to the U.S. today.

For more information, see this book.

Bohemia is known for its "flashed" glass that was produced in the familiar ruby color, as well as in amber, green, blue, and black. Common patterns include Deer and Castle, Deer and Pine Tree, and Vintage.

Most of the Bohemian glass encountered in today's market is from 1875 to 1900. Bohemian-type glass also was made in England, Switzerland, and Germany.

Reproduction Alert

Bowl, 6" d, green ground, random ruby threading, c1910 . . . . **175.00**
Compote

3-1/2" h, Pallme Konig, green irid ground, random crimson threading, set in three-ftd metal frame **325.00**
9-1/4" h, irid green, threaded glass trim on bowl, pedestal, and foot, c1900 . . . . **175.00**

Fairy lamp, red cut to clear, 3-1/2" d, 4-3/4" h, $200.

Dresser bottle, 8-1/4" h, cut panel body, enameled dec, c1890 .... **90.00**

Goblet, 6-3/4" h, white and cranberry overlay, thistle form bowl, six teardrop panels alternately enameled with floral bouquets and cut with blocks of diamonds, faceted knob and spreading scalloped foot, gilt trim **600.00**

Lampshade, 7-3/4" h, 3-1/4" d, dimpled conical shape, irid green, several minor chips around fitter rims, price for pr **425.00**

Miniature, mantel luster, 3-1/2" h, cobalt blue, enameled florals on gilt ground, four cut crystal pendants...... **150.00**

Rose bowl, 4" h, topaz, enameled figure of man drinking, c1900 .. **115.00**

Urn, cov, 15-3/4" h, colorless, paneled bell-shaped body, tapered octagonal lid with stepped octagonal finial, short baluster stem on octagonal foot, star cut base, late 19th C, price for pr **750.00**

Vase

  3-1/2" h, pink opalescent, irid finish, c1910 .... **90.00**

  3-3/4" h, Pallme Konig, gray ground, light irid finish, dec with heavy random crimson threading, c1910 .... **290.00**

  5" d, green ground, irid finish, c1900 .... **75.00**

  5" h, irid textured amber ground, Art Nouveau stemmed flowers, c1920, some loss to silver dec.... **115.00**

  5-3/4" h, sculptured drape pattern, gray ground, green oil spot dec, irid finish, c1920......... **225.00**

  6-1/2" h, green oil spot irid finish, c1900 .... **175.00**

Vase, agate, similar to lithaline, agate glass exterior is cut through to tan base glass as lotus buds and blossoms, small grinding to corner on a lotus leaf, probably done in the making, 4-1/2" h, Condition: S, $415. Photo courtesy of James D. Julia, Inc.

  8" h, Art Nouveau baluster form, slender neck, enamel dec, stylized wildflowers, gilt details, marked "Turin-Teplitz, Amphora Work Reissner," early 20th C **460.00**

  8" h, Pohl, green translucent body, light irid finish, polychrome enameled daffodil with distant village dec, c1895........ **575.00**

  8-5/8" h, flared rim, double bulbed body, irid red glass, blue-gold irid pulled wavy band dec, polished

pontil, few minor scratches **1,150.00**

  9-1/2" h, inverted rim, tapering body, flaring at base, green irid glass **275.00**

  10" h, Prussian blue, applied amber stemmed flowers, amber rigaree at rim, amber scrolled feet... **175.00**

  10-1/2" h, ruffled rim, tapering body, bulbed ftd base, applied green irid trailing prunts at center ... **300.00**

  13-1/2" h, tricorn rim, hexagonal body, irid translucent amber glass, green irid pulled wavy band dec, large polished pontil **260.00**

  14" h, ruby flashed, enameled florals, c1920................. **220.00**

Wine bottle, 10" h, ruby flashed, engraved florals, matching stopper, c1890 .... **90.00**

Water set, 11-1/2" h green tankard, four matching tumblers, scene of girl with wand and bowl, $250. Photo courtesy of Woody Auctions.

BOOKS, EARLY

History: Collecting early books is a popular segment of the antiques marketplace. Collectors of early books are rewarded with interesting titles, exquisite illustrations, as well as fascinating information and stories. The author, printer, and publisher, as well as the date of the printing, can increase the value of an early book. Watch for interesting paintings on the fore-edge of early books. These miniature works of art can greatly add to the value.

Aelianus, Claudis, *Claudis Aelianus His Various History,* translated by Thomas Stanley, London, Thomas Dring, 1665, first Stanley edition, small 8vo, modern 1/2 sheep gilt, first blank leaf missing, rubbed, some dampstaining in outer corners . **130.00**

Armstrong, John, *The Art of Preserving Health: A Poem,* London, A. Millar, 1774, first edition, 134 pgs, 4to, modern 1/4 calf, title browned .. **70.00**

Pitcher, amethyst, decorated with white figure of young girl, 13-1/4" h, $175. Photo courtesy of Joy Luke Auctions.

Vase, Harrach, satin finish, mother of pearl, dark brown to tan, air traps swirl up and over rips to create striking zipper effect, frosted clear glass fancy rim, four knurled leg attachments, clear glass pontil cap, 11-1/2" h, $1,550. Photo courtesy of Clarence and Betty Maier.

Bentley, Richard, *The Folly and Unreasonableness of Atheism...In Eight Sermons Preached at the Lecture Founded by the Honourable Robert Boyle, Esquire,* London, J. H. for H. Mortlock, 1693, eight parts in one volume, 4to, contemporary mottled sheep, rebacked **410.00**

Bohn, Henry C., *A Catalogue of Books,* London, 1841, engraved frontispiece and title page, thick 8vo, contemporary 1/4 road, front cover detached, frontispiece adhere, heavy foxing
. . . . **150.00**

Burke, Edmund, *Reflections on the Revolution in France,* London, J. Dodsley, 1790, second edition, second impression, 356 pgs, 8vo, contemporary calf, rebacked, hinges reinforced, cloth slipcase **165.00**

Burney, Frances, *Evelina* or *A Young Lady's Entrance into the World,* London, T. Lowndes, 1779, second edition, three volumes, 12mo, contemporary sheep, rebacked **130.00**

Dart, John, *Westmonasterium; or, The History and Antiquities of the Abbey Church of St. Peters Westminster,* London, John Coles, c1723, engraved titles, 148 of 149 plates, two volumes, folio, contemporary calf gilt, red and green morocco lettering pieces, joints cracked, foxing, 19th C armorial bookplate **350.00**

Defoe, Daniel, *The Dyet of Poland, A Satyr,* printed at Dantzick, first edition, 1705, 60 pgs, small 4to, 18th C marbled boards, modern morocco back, contents browned, outer margins trimmed **350.00**

Dodsley, Robert, editor, *A Collection of Poems by Several Hands,* London, J. Hughes, 1748-58, six volumes, 8vo, contemporary calf gilt with red morocco lettering pieces, spine ends chipped, joints reinforced but cracked or starting
. . . . **100.00**

Fairbairn, James, *Fairbairn's Crests of the Families of Great Britain and Ireland, Revised by Laurence Butters,* Edinburgh and London, later 19th C, engraved titles, 148 plates, two volumes, 8vo, contemporary 1/2 levant gilt, rebacked retaining faded orig backstrips **70.00**

Fielding, Henry, *Amelia,* London, A. Millar, 1752, first edition, integral ad leaf at end of Volume 2, four volumes, 12 mo, modern beige calf gilt with morocco lettering pieces **490.00**

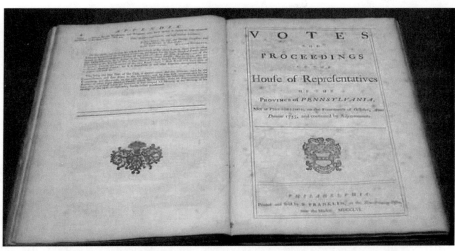

Benjamin Franklin imprint, bound volume including "Votes of the House of Representatives" (Pennsylvania) (1755), "An Act for Raising Fifty Thousand Pounds for the King's Use..." (1755), "Appendix to the Votes of the Assembly, Oct. 1754 to Oct. 1755," "Votes and Proceedings of the House of Representatives of the Province of Pennsylvania" (1756), "printed by B. Franklin, at the new printing office near Market," boards detached with no back flyleaf, original owner's name in ink "William Edmonds, March 1, 1757," ex-lib with library blind stamp, leather covers exhibiting severe wear, **$495.** *Photo courtesy of Sanford Alderfer Auction Company.*

Gay, John, *The Shepherd's Week, In Six Pastorals,* London, Ferd. Burleigh, 1714, first edition, seven full-page etched illus by Louis Du Guernier, 8vo, modern 1/2 calf **865.00**

Gibson, Edward, *The History of the Decline and Fall of the Roman Empire,* London, A. Strahan and T. Cadell, 1782-88, six volumes, three engraved portrait, contemporary tree calf, map of Constantinople missing **320.00**

Godwin, William, *Things as They Are;* or *The Adventures of Caleb Williams,* London, B. Crosby, 1794, first edition, three volumes, 12mo, contemporary marbled boards with red morocco lettering, spines darkened, occasional light browning, armorial bookplates and signatures of SC rice planter Charles Izard Manigault (1795-1874) . . **1,840.00**

Howell, William, *An Institution of General History;* or *The History of the World,* second edition with large additions, London, Thomas Bassett, 1680-80, four volumes in three, folio, modern 1/4 morocco **435.00**

Hume, David, *The History of England,* London, A. Millar, 1754-59-62, six volumes, 4to, contemporary calf gilt with morocco lettering pieces, few joints cracked **980.00**

Johnson, Samuel, *Irene, A Tragedy,* London, R. Dodsley and M. Cooper, 1749, first edition, 8vo, joints rubbed
. . . . **865.00**

Knight, Henrietta, Lady Luxborough, *Letters Written by the Late Right Honourable Lady Luxborough to William Shenstone, Esq.,* London, J. Dodsley, 1775, first edition, 416 pgs, 8vo, contemporary calf, rebacked
. . . . **375.00**

Lackington, James, *Memoirs of the First Forty-Five Years of the Life of James Lackington, the Present Bookseller in Chiswell-street, Moorfields, London, Written by Himself,* printed for and sold by the author, 1791, first edition, engraved frontispiece portrait, 344 pages, 8vo, modern tree calf gilt **215.00**

Milton, John, *Paradise Lost, Paradise Regain'd,* Birmingham, John Baskerville for J. and R. Tonson, London, 1760, together, two volumes, large 8vo, contemporary mottled calf, rebacked
. . . . **575.00**

Priestley, Joseph, *Lectures on History, and General Policy,* London, J. Johnson, 1793, two folding engraved tables, two volumes, 8vo, contemporary calf gilt, joints cracked **200.00**

Salmon, Thomas, *A Critical Essay concerning Marriage...to which is added, An Historical Account of the Marriage Rites and Ceremonies of the Greeks and Romans, and Our Saxon Ancestors, and of Most Nations of the World of this Day,* London, Charles Rovington, 1724, first edition, 8vo, early

19th C 1/2 calf, binding broken, bookplates **320.00**

Shakespeare, William, *The Famous History of the Life of King Henry the Eight(h),* extracted from the second folio, London, 1632, modern cloth, calf lettering piece, some foxing and minor stains, 18th C owner's signature on last page **460.00**

Swift, Jonathan, *A Tale of a Tub*...to which is added *An Account of a Battle between the Ancient and Modern Books in St. James's Library,* fifth edition with author's apology and explanatory notes, London, John Nutt, 1710, first illus edition, eight engraved plates, 344 pgs, 8vo, modern 1/2 calf with morocco lettering piece, spine faded. . . . **375.00**

Walpole, Horace, *A Castle of Otranto, A Gothic Story,* London, William Bathoe and Thomas Lownds, 1765, second edition, 200 pgs, 8vo, contemporary calf, rebacked endpaper renewed **435.00**

Ward, John, *The Lives of the Professors of Gresham College,* to which is prefixed, *The Life of the Founder, Sir Thomas Gresham,* London, John Moore for the author, 1740, first edition, five engraved plates, 156 pgs, folio, late 18th C/early 19th C, 1/2 calf, morocco lettering piece, rebacked, orig backstamp **230.00**

BOOTJACKS

History: Bootjacks are metal or wooden devices that facilitate the removal of boots. Bootjacks are used by placing the heel of the boot in the U-shaped opening, putting the other foot on the back of the bootjack, and pulling the boot off the front foot.

Reproduction Alert

Brass, 10" l, beetle **95.00**

Beetle, cast iron, **$40**

Cast iron, John Van Buren, filigree base, wrench sockets at end, 15-1/4" l, **$50.**

Cast iron

9-3/4" l, Naughty Nellie, painted blond hair, blue ribboned white lingerie, minor wear **150.00**

10" l, Naughty Nellie, unpainted, minor wear **100.00**

10-1/4" l, lyre shape **50.00**

11-1/2" l, intertwined scrolls form letter "M" **35.00**

11-3/4" l, crick, emb lacy design **30.00**

12" l, tree center **35.00**

12-1/2" l, 4-1/2" w, 1-3/4" h, heart-shaped cut-out, America, 19th C, slight corrosion, with stand **220.00**

Wood

10" l, tiger stripe maple **25.00**

13" l, maple, hand hewn **20.00**

22" l, walnut, heart and diamond openwork **40.00**

24" l, pine, rose head nails, pierced for hanging **40.00**

BOTTLES, GENERAL

History: Cosmetic bottles held special creams, oils, and cosmetics designed to enhance the beauty of the user. Some also claimed, especially on their colorful labels, to cure or provide relief from common ailments.

A number of household items, e.g., cleaning fluids and polishes, required glass storage containers. Many are collected for their fine lithographed labels.

Mineral water bottles contained water from a natural spring. Spring water was favored by health-conscious people between the 1850s and 1900s.

For more information, see these books.

Nursing bottles, used to feed the young and sickly, were a great help to the housewife because of their graduated measure markings, replaceable nipples, and the ease with which they could be cleaned, sterilized, and reused.

Beverage

Arny & Shinn, Georgetown, D. C., "This Bottle Is Never Sold," soda water, squat cylindrical, yellow ground, applied heavy collared mouth, smooth base, half pink, professionally cleaned **150.00**

Miller's Extra Old Bourbon, E. Martin & Co., light amber, c1871-75, placed bubbles on front **12,000.00**

Rum, unidentified maker

10-1/2" h, olive amber, globular, crude rolled lip, attributed to New England, 19th C, minor imperfections **650.00**

16-3/4" h, amber, one flattened side, eastern US, 19th C, minor imperfections **550.00**

Sarimento, M. R., soda, Union Glass Works, Phila, teal **2,200.00**

Squarza, V, soda, blue, c1863, crude top, lots of whittle, bubbles . . . **8,500.00**

Thos Taylor & Co., Virginia, Nevada, medium to deep reddish-chocolate color, c1874-80, few scratches **4,400.00**

Cosmetic

Kickapoo Sage Hair Tonic, cylindrical, cobalt blue, tooled mouth, matching stopper, smooth base, 5" h **160.00**

Laxative Velvet Stomach Bitters – Kidney and Liver Tonic, Arrow Distilleries Co., Peoria, **$90.** *Photo courtesy of Joy Luke Auctions.*

Gemel, South Jersey, deep yellow-amber, teardrop shape, applied quilling between two bottles, applied foot, probably Glassboro or Wistarburg, c1780-1800, foot badly damaged, 4-3/4" h, $250. Photo courtesy of Pacific Glass Auctions.

Kranks Cold Cream, milk glass, 2-3/4" h **6.50**

Pompeian Massage Cream, amethyst, 2-3/4" h **9.00**

Household

Ink, Waterman's, paper label with bottle of ink, wooden bullet shaped case, orig paper label, 4-1/4" h **10.00**

Sewing Machine Oil, Sperm Brand, clear, 5-1/2" h **5.00**

Shoe Polish, Everett & Barron Co., oval, clear, 4-3/4" **5.00**

Mineral or spring water

Alburgh A. Spring, VT, cylindrical, golden yellow, applied sloping collared mouth with ring, smooth base, quart **800.00**

Caladonia Spring Wheelock VT, cylindrical, golden amber, applied sloping collared mouth with ring, smooth base, quart **130.00**

Gettysburgh Katalysine Water, yellow olive, applied sloping collared mouth with ring, smooth base, quart . . . **200.00**

Hopkins Chalybeate Baltimore, cylindrical, dense amber, applied double collared mouth, iron pontil mark, pint **130.00**

Middletown Healing Springs, Grays & Clark, Middletown, VT, cylindrical, yellow apricot amber, applied sloping collared mouth with ring, smooth base, quart **1,200.00**

Saratoga (star) Springs, cylindrical, dark olive green, applied sloping

Pickle, E.H.V.B., NY, green, cathedral, Elias H. VanBenschoten, 1849-54, $4,480. Photo courtesy of Pacific Glass Auctions.

collared mouth with ring, smooth base, quart **300.00**

Vermont Spring, Saxe & Co., Sheldon, VT, cylindrical, citron, applied sloping collared mouth with ring, smooth base, quart **600.00**

Nursing

Acme, clear, lay-down, emb **65.00**

Cala Nurser, oval, clear, emb, ring on neck, 7-1/8" h **10.00**

Empire Nursing Bottle, bent neck, 6-1/2" h **50.00**

Mother's Comfort, clear, turtle type **25.00**

Stoneware, six matching bottles in original carrier, relief and cobalt blue decorated goat drinking lager beer on front, original porcelain caps marked "Bock," remaining wording on bottles in French, 12-1/2" h, minor chipping at spouts, $467.50. Photo courtesy of Vicki and Bruce Waasdorp.

BRASS

History: Brass is a durable, malleable, and ductile metal alloy consisting mainly of copper and zinc. The height of its popularity for utilitarian and decorative art items occurred in the 18th and 19th centuries.

Reproduction Alert: Many modern reproductions are being made of earlier brass forms, especially such items as buckets, fireplace equipment, and kettles.

Additional Listings: Bells, Candlesticks, Fireplace Equipment, and Scientific Instruments.

Candlestick, spring-loaded, removable hood with pierced rear vents, top chimney, weighted base, Victorian, split solder joint in top, 14-1/4" h, $250. Photo courtesy of Cowan's Historic Americana Auctions.

Andirons, pr

17-1/2" h, acorn tops, seamed columns, cabriole legs, ball feet **220.00**

18" h, ring-turned columns, scalloped cabriole legs, ball feet **360.00**

Bed warmer, 43-1/2" l, engraved flowers on lid, copper rivers attach pan to turned wooden handle, orig red and black grain dec, wear to handle from use, minor chip **225.00**

Candle sconce

23" h, 17-1/2" d, detailed casting, eight medallions with figures divided by faces, round beveled glass mirror, three branches with single candle sockets **200.00**

23-1/4" h, 8" w, cast, beveled mirror backing with openwork floral medallions, urn crest flanked by two dolphins, two scrolled candle arms below **110.00**

Candlesticks, pr, 9-1/2" h, English, trumpet shaped sticks, raised on circular bases, round socket with drip pan **175.00**

Chandelier, 25" d, 20" h, cast, eight scrolled arms with torch shaped ends, each with small electric socket,

Candlesticks, pair, baluster form, miniature, Victorian, English, 4" h, $65. Photo courtesy of Cowan's Historic Americana Auctions.

simulated candle coverings, 20th C
.... **250.00**
Chestnut roaster, 18-3/4" l, oval, pierced hinged lid, long handle **120.00**
Chimes, 18-1/2" w, 27-1/2" h, mahogany and rosewood frame, eight brass chimes, turned pilasters on either side, striker missing, 20th C ... **220.00**
Coal bin, 18" w, 16" h, hand hammered, polished, Ruskin ceramic cabochons, emb, riveted legs, tulip-shaped finial, orig lacquered finish, unmarked, English **2,100.00**
Coal grate, 19-1/2" l, 10-1/4" d, 27" h, Neoclassical-style, late 19th C, back plate cast with scene of figures in revelry, grate with central horizontal bar over guillouche band, uprights with brass urn finials, rear plinth base, front tapered legs **175.00**
Coal hood, 16-3/4" l, 13-1/8" w, 20" h, Neoclassical-style, late 19th C, rect, two cornucopia handles, lid with mushroom finial, front set with bellflower and paterae pilasters, central urn, pointed feet **375.00**

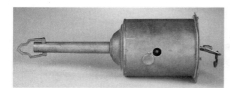

Fireplace clock jack, signed "G. Salter," English, 19th C, clock key missing, minor dents, 4-1/2" d, 15" l, $120. Photo courtesy of Cowan's Historic Americana Auctions.

Dresser mirror, 11" w, 18" h, French, gilt brass, mirrored glass, scrolls, floral pots, and garlands dec, cracks, loss to silvering **525.00**
Easel, late 19th/early 20th C, 61-5/8" h, A-frame topped by girdled round finial
.... **500.00**
Figure, 31-1/2" h, Bodhisattva, dark patina, 10 arms, eight faces, single body, walnut block base **450.00**
Fireplace fender, 54-3/4" l, Rococo-style, 19th C, pierced center with tree flanked by rocaille follies, cartouches engraved with helmets on diapered ground, flanked by leaf scrolls
.... **4,600.00**
Letter sealer, 2" l brass tube, 23 double-sided brass discs with various sentimental seals for wax, 19th C
.... **100.00**
Palace jar, 17" d, 16" h, chased designs of various deities within scrolled field, India, 20th C **420.00**
Plant stand, 14-1/2" d, 35-1/2" h, old gilding, round top with leaf drops and three scrolls, scrolled supports, leaves, and large flowers, eagle talon feet, lacquered **450.00**
Steam whistle, 2-1/2" d, 12" h, single chime, lever control **150.00**
Wood box, 19" l, 12-3/8" w, 13-3/8" h, Neoclassical-style, late 19th C, rect, hinged lid with flat leaf finial, front with band of vertical pierced flutes with three applied rosettes, two pendant handles, four flattened ball feet........ **325.00**

BREAD PLATES

History: Beginning in the mid-1880s, special trays or platters were made for serving bread and rolls.

Weights, waisted, top handles, English, graduated from 1 oz to 7 pounds, 1-1/4" h to 7" h, expected wear, polished, $260. Photo courtesy of Cowan's Historic Americana Auctions.

Designated "bread plates" by collectors, these small trays or platters can be found in porcelain, glass (especially pattern glass), and metals.

Bread plates often were part of a china or glass set. However, many glass companies made special plates which honored national heroes, commemorated historical or special events, offered a moral maxim, or supported a religious attitude. The subject matter appears either horizontally or vertically. Most of these plates are oval and ten inches in length.

Additional Listings: Pattern Glass.

For more information, see this book.

Majolica
Apple and Pear, brown ground, minor wear rim **385.00**
Bamboo and Fern, cobalt blue, Wardles **395.00**
Give Us This Day Our Daily Bread, cobalt border and basket center, wheat handles **360.00**
Pineapple, cobalt blue center
.... **440.00**
Water Lily, 12" l, surface wear
......................**110.00**
Milk glass, Wheat & Barley **70.00**
Mottos, pressed glass, clear
Be Industrious, handles, oval. **50.00**
Rock of Ages, 12-7/8" l..... **175.00**
Waste Not Want Not **35.00**
Pattern glass, clear unless otherwise noted
Actress, Miss Nielson **80.00**
Beaded Grape, sq **35.00**
Cupid and Venus, amber **85.00**
Deer and Pine Tree, amber ..**110.00**
Good Luck **45.00**

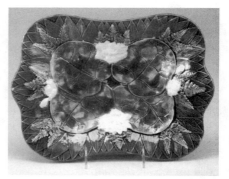

Majolica, Joseph Holdcroft, pond lily design, impressed "J. HOLDCROFT," c1875, 12-3/4" l, $295. Photo courtesy of David Rago Auctions.

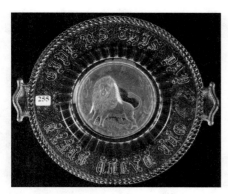

Pattern glass, Frosted Lion, motto, 12" l, $30. Photo courtesy of Woody Auctions..

Lion, amber, lion handles, motto
. . . . **135.00**
Tennessee, colored jewels. . . . **75.00**
Silver
12-3/4" l, 8-1/4" w, oval, molded scroll rim and openwork scroll sides, molded foliate swags, Graff, Washbourne & Dunn, NY, early 20th C, approx 18 troy oz . . **635.00**
15" x 10-1/2", repousse, cartouches of courtship scene, imp German hallmarks and 800, c1920. . **920.00**
Souvenir and Commemorative
Old State House, sapphire blue
. . . . **185.00**
Three Presidents, frosted center
. . . . **95.00**
William J. Bryan, milk glass . . . **65.00**

BRIDE'S BASKETS

History: A ruffled-edge glass bowl in a metal holder was a popular wedding gift between 1880 and 1910, hence the name "bride's basket." These bowls can be found in most glass types of the period. The metal holder was generally silver-plated with a bail handle, thus enhancing the basket image.

Over the years, bowls and bases became separated and married pieces resulted. If the base has been lost, the bowl should be sold separately.

For more information, see this book.

Note: Items listed below have a silver-plated (SP) holder unless otherwise noted.

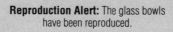

Reproduction Alert: The glass bowls have been reproduced.

8-1/4" w, sq, cased, deep rose and white ext., whit int., dragon, floral, and leaf dec, ruffled edge, Mt. Washington
. . . . **675.00**
8-1/2" d, 12" h, amber, enameled berries and buds, SP holder . . **1,195.00**
9-1/4" d, Peachblow, yellow flowers dec, orig SP holder **225.00**
9-1/2" d, 12" h, satin, deep pink ruffled bowl, white ext., marked "Nemasket Silver Co." SP holder **275.00**
9-3/4" h, opaline cased in pink, ruffled amber rim, married plated holder
. . . . **150.00**
9-7/8" d, 3" h, 3-3/4" base, bowl only, peachblow, glossy finish, deep pink shading to pale **250.00**
10" d, 11" h, Vasa Murrhina, outer amber layer, center layer with hundreds of cream-colored spots, random toffee-colored spots, dark veins, gold mica flakes, mulberry pink lining, crossed rod thorn handles **635.00**
10" w, sq, custard, melon ribbed, enameled daisies, applied Rubena crystal rim, twisted and beaded handle, ftd, emb SP frame, marked "Wilcox"
. . . . **450.00**
10-1/2" h, peachblow, cased rose shading to pink ground, applied amber

Blue glass bowl with deeply crimped ruffled rim, hand-painted enameled flowers, decorated silver plated base, 7" h, $250. Photo courtesy of Joy Luke Auctions.

Pink and white ruffled bowl, fancy silver-plated base, 10-1/2" x 11-1/2", $275. Photo courtesy of Woody Auctions.

stem, green leaves, amber handle, four applied feet, some losses **200.00**

10-1/2" d, 12-1/2" h, sculptured Rubena verde vaseline shading to pink, yellow and green enameled flowers, Benedict SP holder **460.00**

10-3/4" d, 3-1/2" h, bowl only, overlay, heavenly blue, enameled white flowers, green leaves, white underside, ruffled
. . . . **215.00**

11" d, 7-1/2" h, satin, light beige shading to orange ruffled bowl, hp pink, purple and yellow flowers, green leaves, raised gold outlines, blue int., sgd "Simpson, Hall, Miller Co. Quad Plate" holder **895.00**

11-1/8" d, 3-3/4" h, bowl only, satin, brown shaded to cream overlay, raised dots, dainty gold and silver flowers and leaves dec, ruffled **250.00**

Pink opalescent ruffled hobnail bowl, silver plated stand, 11-1/2" d, 9" h, $125. Photo courtesy of Joy Luke Auctions.

Mt. Washington, cased, triangular, white exterior, light blue interior, crimped bowl in signed Pairpoint silver-plated frame, band of grape leaves and grapes, pierced legs of flowers and leaves, base inscribed in German, dated 1888, some wear to plating, 12" w, 11-1/2" h, $460. Photo courtesy of James D. Julia, Inc.

11-1/4" h, opalescent Rubena verde, applied lime stepped flower feet, thorny twist handle, Victorian **425.00**

12" d, 7-1/2" h, white opaline, cased in pink, overall colorful enameled dec, emb Middletown plated holder, applied fruit handles, Victorian, minor losses **525.00**

12-1/2" d, 12" h, maize, amber and crystal crest, hp roses, SP frame, Fenton **275.00**

BRISTOL GLASS

History: Bristol glass is a designation given to a semi-opaque glass, usually decorated with enamel and cased with another color.

Initially, the term referred only to glass made in Bristol, England, in the 17th and 18th centuries. By the Victorian era, firms on the Continent and in America were copying the glass and its forms.

For more information, see this book.

Bowl, light blue, Cupid playing mandolin, gold trim **45.00**

Box, cov, 4-1/8" l, 2-3/4" d, 3-1/2" h, oblong, blue, gilt-metal mounts and escutcheon **550.00**

Cake stand, celadon green, enameled herons in flight, gold trim **135.00**

Wine glass cooler, cobalt blue, blown, double spout stem rests, ground pontil, plain form, late 18th or early 19th C, 5-1/4" w, 3-5/8" h, price for pair, $320. Photo courtesy of Cowan's Historic Americana Auctions.

Candlesticks, pr, 7" h, soft green, gold band **75.00**

Decanter, 11-1/2" h, ruffled stopper, enameled flowers and butterfly . . **75.00**

Dresser set, two cologne bottles, cov powder jar, white, gilt butterflies dec, clear stoppers **75.00**

Ewer, 6-3/8" h, 2-5/8" d, pink ground, fancy gold designs, bands, and leaves, applied handle with gold trim . . . **135.00**

Finger bowl, 4-3/8" d, blue, faceted sides, early 20th C, eight-pc set **500.00**

Hatpin holder, 6-1/8" h, ftd, blue, enameled jewels, gold dec **100.00**

Perfume bottle, 3-1/4" h, squatty, blue, gold band, white enameled flowers and leaves, matching stopper **100.00**

Puff box, cov, round, blue, gold dec **35.00**

Sugar shaker, 4-3/4" h, white, hp flowers **65.00**

Sweetmeat jar, 3" x 5-1/2", deep pink, enameled flying duck, leaves, blue flower dec, white lining, SP rim, lid, and bail handle **110.00**

Urn, 18" h, pink, boy and girl with lamp **550.00**

Vase, 13-3/9" h, moon-flask form, caramel-colored body, attenuated neck, trumpet foot, enamel dec of swallows in flight above floral garlands, line detailing at extremities, late 19th C, price for pr **230.00**

BRITISH ROYALTY COMMEMORATIVES

History: British commemorative china, souvenirs to commemorate coronations and other royal events, dates from the 1600s, with the early pieces being rather crude in design and form. With the development of transfer printing, c1780, the images on the wares more closely resembled the monarchs.

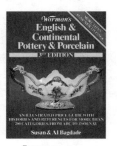

For more information, see this book.

Few commemorative pieces predating Queen Victoria's reign are found today at popular prices. Items associated with Queen Elizabeth II and her children, e.g., the wedding of HRH Prince Andrew and Miss Sarah Ferguson and the subsequent birth of their daughter HRH Princess Beatrice, are very common.

Some British Royalty commemoratives are easily recognized by their portraits of past or present monarchs. Some may be in silhouette profile. Royal symbols include crowns, dragons, royal coats of arms, national flowers, swords, scepters, dates, messages, and monograms.

Additional Listings: See *Warman's Americana & Collectibles* for more examples.

Autograph

Elizabeth I, letter, sgd as Queen, one page, oblong folio, London, Jan. 21, 1592, "Our Trustie and well beloved William Colles," concerning money to be paid toward "...the defense of our Realms...," striking signature, upper right corner of letter missing, integral address intact . . . **7,900.00**

Figure of Queen Victoria, wearing royal robes and crown, Staffordshire, some loss to gilt decorated, 17-1/2" h, $175. Photo courtesy of Cowan's Historic Americana Auctions.

George II, letter, sgd as Prince of Wales, in French, two pages, 4to, Leicester House, Jan. 11/22, 1723, to Madame Marygrove, sympathies over loss of relation **1,200.00**

William IV, document, sgd as king, one page 4to, Bushby House, Sept. 18, 1827, appoints David Davis as his personal surgeon, red wax seal next to signature. . **350.00**

Bottle opener, King Edward, brass, coronation souvenir **8.50**

Box, cov, Elizabeth the Queen Mother, 1980, 80th Birthday, color portrait, Crown Staffordshire, 4" d **85.00**

Cane

35" l, carved entirely out of elephant ivory, "L" handle with circle of Prince of Wales feathers, 1/3" collar of chains and crosses, top of handle with Queen Victoria's "St. Edwards Crown," lower side of handle "E.V." carved in script, remainder carved in doves, vines, and fruit, orig custom leather-cov carrying case, lined with blue velvet and satin, believed to have been made as a gift for Prince of Wales trip to India in late 1875 . . . . **15,680.00**

35-3/4" l, attributed to Queen Victoria's 50th Anniversary Jubilee, 1887, molded gutta percha, 1" w, 8" l handle, top as image of English Royal Crown, on one side, Queen Victoria's profile in oval cartouche, English Rose, Scottish Thistle, and Irish Shamrock and British Isles coat of arms, 3/4" gold gilt collar, black hardwood shaft, 1" horn ferrule **1,235.00**

Cup and saucer, Elizabeth II, portrait flanked by flags, coronation, pairs of

Mug, Edward VIII Coronation, decal decoration, dated May 1937, Minton, $40.

flags inside cup and on saucer, marked "Alfred Meakin England," 3" h x 3-1/4" d cup, 6" d saucer **55.00**

Drinking glass, 3-3/4" h, clear, red and blue illus of George VI and Elizabeth I, 1939 Canadian visit **24.00**

Figure, 5-1/4" h, Elizabeth I, carved ivory, lower section of skirt hinged to reveal triptych of Queen and Sir Walter Raleigh, Continental, 19th C, hairlines **550.00**

Jug

Elizabeth II, 1953 Coronation, emb crowning scene, Burleigh Ware, 8-1/4" h **250.00**

Victoria, 1887 Gold Jubilee, black and white portraits, 5" h . . . **165.00**

Lithophane, cup, crown, and cypher, 2-3/4" h, Alexandra, 1902 . . . . . **195.00**

Loving cup, Elizabeth II and Philip, 1972 Silver Wedding Anniversary, Paragon, 3" h **175.00**

Mug

Edward VIII, Coronation, 1937, sepia portrait of king flanked by

multicolored flags, reverse with Union Jack and Flag of commonwealth, flanking names of some of the nations, topped by crown, gold trim, 2-1/2" h, 2-1/2" d, crest mark and "Empire England" **50.00**

Elizabeth II, Coronation, portrait of Queen facing left, "Coronation of Her Majesty Queen Elizabeth" on reverse, gold trim, 3" h, 3" d, crown and "Radfords Bone China Made in England" mark **55.00**

Paperweight, Edward VIII, 1937 Coronation, black and white portrait, 4-1/4" d **70.00**

Pinback button

King George VI and Queen Elizabeth I, black and white photos, tiny green maple leaf border, red inscription "Welcome to Canada," orig back paper label, 1939 . . . . **20.00**

Queen Elizabeth, 1-3/4" d, black and white cello, coronation portrait photo, red, white, and purple fabric ribbons, miniature gold luster finish metal replica crown pin, c1953 . . . . **15.00**

Queen Elizabeth and Prince Philip, red, white, and blue cello, center black and white portraits, 1951 visit to Canada, waxed fabric red, white, and blue ribbons **20.00**

Pitcher, 8-3/4" h, marriage of Princess Charlotte and Prince Leopold, c1816, relief dec, double scroll handle, Pratt ware, minor enamel loss **1,265.00**

Plate

Edward VII and Alexandra, 1902 Coronation, blue and white, Royal Copenhagen, 7" d **200.00**

George VI and Elizabeth, Canadian visit, 1939, word "Canada" in relief under portraits in center, "King George IV, Queen Elizabeth, 1939" in relief on rim **95.00**

Postcard, Royal Visit to New Zealand, 1953-54, 39" x 29", creased on folds, small tears **20.00**

Program, Prince of Wales Royal Investiture, July 1, 1969, glossy paper, 6-1/2"x 9" **12.00**

Snuffbox, 3" d, round, bronze, round, dark patina, angel riding lion with "Regent," reverse emb inscription "In record of the reign of George III" covered by sunburst and cross, visible on int., engraved paper bust and "H.R.H. George Augustus Frederick Prince Regent...Feb 1811" . . **2,100.00**

Mugs, Coronation King George V and Queen Mary, June 22, 1911 and King Edward VIII, May 12, 1937, $75 each.

Teapot

Charlotte, 1817 In Memoriam, black and white dec, 6" h **275.00**

Victoria, 1897 Diamond Jubilee, color coat of arms, Aynsley **225.00**

Tea set, 8-3/4" l cov teapot, creamer, cov sugar, manufactured for the coronation of Elizabeth II, 1953, applied white relief, solid royal blue ground, Wedgwood imp marks, chip on teapot finial **250.00**

Tin

Queen Elizabeth II, coronation, sq, Queen Elizabeth II on horseback, full view, marked "Sharp Assorted Toffee," stamped "Made In England by Edward Sharp & Sons Ltd. Of Maidstone Kent," 7" x 6" x 2", minor scratches and edge rubbing **40.00**

Prince of Wales, Yardley Invisible Talc for Men, Prince of Wales crest, "By Appointment to HM Queen Elizabeth II Purveyors of Soap Yardley and Co. Ltd.," 5" h . . **15.00**

View master reel set, Queen Elizabeth II coronation, 4-1/2" sq envelope, set of three color stereo view reels, orig fact leaflet for June 2, 1953 coronation **25.00**

BRONZE

History: Bronze is an alloy of copper, tin, and traces of other metals. It has been used since Biblical times not only for art objects, but also for utilitarian wares. After a slump in the Middle Ages, the use of bronze was revived in the 17th century and continued to be popular until the early 20th century.

Notes: Do not confuse a "bronzed" object with a true bronze. A bronzed item usually is made of white metal and then coated with a reddish-brown material to give it a bronze appearance. A magnet will stick to it but not to anything made of true bronze.

A signed bronze commands a higher market price than an unsigned one. There also are "signed" reproductions on the market. It is very important to know the history of the mold and the background of the foundry.

Basket, 10-1/4", trompe l'oeil, folded linen form, woven handle, applied florals and insects, Japanese, 19th C **350.00**

Bookends, pr, 9" h, daffodil silhouette, imp mark of G. Thew, 1928 . . . . **225.00**

Box, chaise lounge form, topped with monkey on pillows, lid lifts to reveal erotic scene of man and woman with carved ivory features, gilt and polychrome dec, marble base, 20th C **1,495.00**

Candlestick, seashore shaft, original patina, inscribed "ETH/1916" for E. T. Hurley, 13-3/4" h, $1,380. Photo courtesy of David Rago Auctions.

Bust, 9-1/2" h, Buddha, serene expression, draped covering, cloud tiara, verdigris finish **195.00**

Charger, 12" d, doré, deeply cast geometric designs on rim, stamped "Tiffany Studios New York #1746", area of discoloration, minor edge dent **330.00**

Figure

4" l, 2-3/4" h, bull, carved ivory horns, early 20th C **350.00**

6" h, dog with game, dark patina, American School, 20th C . . . **90.00**

10" h, two cranes on ftd stool, emb florals, Japanese, Meiji period **125.00**

10-1/2" l, 9-1/2" h, farmer on horseback, greenish-brown patina, oblong naturalistic base, incised "Ruff," (A. Ruff, early 20th C) **750.00**

12" l, standing peacock, long tail, cold painted, Bergmann, loss to comb **175.00**

Cherub, hanging from bronze chain, holding large polished bronze rose in one hand and torch in other, polished bronze ribbon wrap, wings are separate attached pieces, formerly part of a hanging light fixture, rose is replacement for original light socket, minor scratched to patinated surfaces, 18" l, $1,475. Photo courtesy of Cowan's Historic Americana Auctions.

13" h, Farnese Hercules, standing nude figure leaning against outcrop draped with skin, black marble base, early 20th C . **635.00**

24" l, 7-3/4" w, 16-1/2" h, seated nude female, sgd "E. Joé Descomps" on base, subtle wear **1,610.00**

Incense burner, 22" h, Oriental, circular base with relief birds and foliage, center medallions, applied handles, old clock set into one side which has a loose hand, some damage, soldered restorations **525.00**

Lamp, table, 27-3/4" h, Sinumbra, frosted glass shade with cut cherry and floral design, bronze standard with brown paint, electrified, minor chips to shade fitter rim **1,765.00**

Centerpiece, bronze and doré bronze, classical women reclining against floral cache, c1870, 35" w, 10" d, 19" h, $7,840. Photo courtesy of Fontaine's Auction Gallery.

Group, two German Shepherds, by Th. Cartier, 27" w, 22" h, $650. Photo courtesy of Joy Luke Auctions.

Loving cup, 5-1/4" h, gilt, French, 19th C **90.00**

Low bowl, 4" d, shape no. 537, sterling applied geometric designs, imp Heintz logo and "Sterling," c1915 . . . . . **45.00**

Parade helmet, cast

15-3/8" l, 11-1/4" h, 19th C, depicting Hercules battling the hydra with cityscape in background, borders of military motifs and emperors **460.00**

18" l, gladiator's, Continental-style, China, early 20th C, four-part hinged visor comprising two-piece pierced eye guard, over two-piece face guard cast as figures before prison gates, helmet with high relief battle scene, further Roman-style figures **690.00**

Pen vase, 3-1/2" h, gilt, cylindrical vessel, flared base, ribbed swirled design, unsigned, attributed to Tiffany Studios, NY **175.00**

Plaque, 10" h, two Satyrs and enamored nude in relief, gilt, 19th C **690.00**

Sculpture

A Startled Finch on a Perch, Ferdinand Pautrot, gold-green patina, sgd on base "F. Pautrot," 5" h **260.00**

Classical Figures, Gustave Michel, signed lower left, 16" x 12" x 18" **635.00**

Sculpture, P. Philippe, nude woman looking down at frog, mounted on marble base, marked "P. Philippe/910," 7-1/2" bronze, 3" base, $660. Photo courtesy of Sanford Alderfer Auction Company.

Vase, three elephant heads, each with ivory tusks, one with trunk hanging vertically, other two trunks wrapped around side of vase, base with six elephant feet with toenails, textured surface resembles elephant hide, original patina, Chinese or Japanese maker's mark, 13-1/4" h, 6-1/2" turned rosewood base, $2,875. Photo courtesy of James D. Julia Auctions.

Mountain Mother, Mother bear and cubs, sgd "C M Russell (with skull)" dated 1924, inscribed "Roman Bronze Works NY" on base, dark brown patina, low black plinth, casting imperfections, subtle wear to surface **16,100.00**

Pan feeding bear cubs, sgd "E. Fremiet," patinated, 21-1/2" l **2,100.00**

Slave girl, seated on bench, shackles on her wrists, skirt separate piece, sgd "E. Villanis," 10-1/2" h **350.00**

Smoking tray, 6-1/4" d, Doré finish, applied scrolling on ash bowl, cigar rests, matchbox holder, unmarked, c1910 . . . . **70.00**

Stable post finial, 15" h, cast, head of purebred horse, saddle, later polychrome over nickeled finish, early 20th C **520.00**

Standish, 16" l, retriever flanked by pair of foliate molded inkwells, oval verte antico marble base, French, early 20th C **445.00**

Tray, 9" d, band of hammered designs, marked "Apollo Studios, New York" c1910 . . . . **45.00**

Urn, 11-3/8" h, cast, black patinated, everted reeded rim, central band of classical figures, two short handles with male masks, fluted foot, sq black marble base, Classical-style, late 19th/early 20th C, price for pr . **2,530.00**

Vase, 27-5/8" h, Oriental, each section with different creatures in high relief, cranes throughout, two phoenix birds on neck, center with dragons, turtles on base, some dents **425.00**

Wall plaque, 21-1/4" d, shield-form, Classical Revival, raised and pointed center section, continuous battle scene, Continental, late 19th C **500.00**

BUFFALO POTTERY

History: Buffalo Pottery Co., Buffalo, New York, was chartered in 1901. The first kiln was fired in October 1903. Larkin Soap Company established Buffalo Pottery to produce premiums for its extensive mail-order business. Wares also were sold to the public by better department and jewelry stores. Elbert Hubbard and Frank Lloyd Wright, who designed the Larkin Administration Building in Buffalo in 1904, were two prominent names associated with the Larkin Company.

Early Buffalo Pottery production consisted mainly of semi-vitreous china dinner sets. Buffalo was the first pottery in the United States to produce successfully the Blue Willow pattern. Buffalo also made a line of hand-decorated, multicolored willow ware, called Gaudy Willow. Other early items include a series of game, fowl, and fish sets, pitchers, jugs, and a line of commemorative, historical, and advertising plates and mugs.

From 1908 to 1909 and again from 1921 to 1923, Buffalo Pottery produced the line for which it is most famous—Deldare Ware. The earliest of this olive green, semi-vitreous china displays hand-decorated scenes from English artist Cecil Aldin's *Fallowfield Hunt*. Hunt scenes were done only from 1908 to 1909. English village scenes also were characteristic of the ware and were used during both periods. Most pieces are artist signed.

In 1911, Buffalo Pottery produced Emerald Deldare, which used scenes from Goldsmith's *The Three Tours of Dr. Syntax* and an Art Nouveau-type border. Completely decorated Art Nouveau pieces also were made.

Abino, which was introduced in 1912, had a Deldare body and displayed scenes of sailboats, windmills, or the sea. Rust was the main color used, and all pieces were signed by the artist and numbered.

In 1915, the manufacturing process was modernized, giving the company the ability to produce vitrified china. Consequently, hotel and institutional ware became the main production items, with hand-decorated ware de-emphasized. The Buffalo firm became a leader in producing and designing the most-famous railroad, hotel, and restaurant patterns. These wares, especially railroad items, are eagerly sought by collectors.

In the early 1920s, fine china was made for home use. Bluebird is one of the patterns from this era. In 1950, Buffalo made its first Christmas plate. These were given away to customers and employees primarily from 1950 to 1960. However, it is known that Hample Equipment Co. ordered some as late as 1962.

The Christmas plates are very scarce in today's resale market.

The Buffalo China Company made "Buffalo Pottery" and "Buffalo China"—the difference being that one is semi-vitreous ware and the other vitrified. In 1956, the company was reorganized, and Buffalo China became the corporate name. Today, Buffalo China is owned by Oneida Silver Company. The Larkin family no longer is involved.

Marks: Blue Willow pattern is marked "First Old Willow Ware Mfg. in America."

Abino Ware
Candlestick, 9" h, sailing ships, 1913
. . . . **475.00**
Pitcher, 7" h, Portland Head Light
. . . . **700.00**
Tankard, 10-1/2" h, sailing scene
. . . . **900.00**

Advertising Ware
Jug, 6-1/4" h, blue and green transfer print, inscribed "The Whaling City Souvenir of New Bedford, Mass," whaling motifs, staining **355.00**
Mug, 4-1/2" h, Calumet Club . . . **110.00**
Plate, 9-3/4" d, Indian Head Pontiac
. . . . **55.00**
Platter, 13-1/2" l, US Army Medical Dept., 1943 . . . . **65.00**

Deldare
Bowl, 12" l, Ye Olden Days, c1908, small professionally repaired chip under rim **200.00**
Calling card tray, street scene. **395.00**
Cereal bowl, 6" d, Fallowfield Hunt
. . . . **295.00**
Chop plate, 14" d, Fallowfield Hunt
. . . . **795.00**

Deldare Ware, creamer and sugar, pottery ink stamp, restoration to hairlines on creamer, lid missing on sugar, 3", $115. Photo courtesy of David Rago Auctions.

Gravy boat, Willow Ware, blue decoration, buffalo mark, dated 1911, $40.

Cup and saucer, street scene . . **225.00**
Hair receiver, street scene **495.00**
Jardinière, street scene. **995.00**
Mug
   Fallowfield Hunt, 3-1/2" h. . . . **395.00**
   Street Scene, 4-1/2" h **395.00**
   Three Pigeons, 4-1/2" h **350.00**
Pitcher, 12" h, 7" w, The Great Controversy, sgd "W. Fozter," stamped mark **320.00**
Powder jar, street scene **395.00**
Punch cup, Fallowfield Hunt . . . **375.00**
Soup plate, 9" d, street scene . . **425.00**
Tankard, Three Pigeons. **1,175.00**
Tea tile, Fallowfield Hunt **395.00**
Tea tray, street scene. **650.00**
Vase, 7-3/4" h, 6-1/2" d, King Fisher, green and white dec, olive ground, stamped mark, artist signature
. . . . **1,380.00**

Emerald Deldare
Creamer. **450.00**
Fruit bowl **1,450.00**
Mug, 4-1/2" h **475.00**
Vase, 8-1/2" h, 6-1/2" h, stylized foliate motif, shades of green and white, olive ground, stamp mark. **810.00**

Miscellaneous
Jug
   Chrysanthemum **495.00**
   Robin Hood **550.00**
Plate, aqua ground, one "Wild Ducks," other "Gunner", price for pr **65.00**

BURMESE GLASS

History: Burmese glass is a translucent art glass originated by Frederick Shirley and manufactured by the Mt. Washington Glass Co., New Bedford, Massachusetts, from 1885 to c1891.

Burmese glass colors shade from a soft lemon to a salmon pink. Uranium was used to attain the yellow color, and gold was added to the batch so that on reheating, one end turned pink. Upon reheating again, the edges would revert to the yellow coloring. The blending of the colors was so gradual that it is difficult to determine where one color ends and the other begins.

Although some of the glass has a glossy surface, most pieces were acid finished. The majority of the items were free blown, but some were blown molded in a ribbed, hobnail, or diamond-quilted design.

American-made Burmese is quite thin and, therefore, is fragile, and brittle. English Burmese was made by Thos. Webb & Sons. Out of deference to Queen Victoria, they called their wares "Queen's Burmese Ware."

Advisers: Clarence and Betty Maier.

For more information, see this book.

> **Reproduction Alert:** Reproductions abound in almost every form. Since uranium can no longer be used, some of the reproductions are easy to spot. In the 1950s, Gundersen produced many pieces in imitation of Burmese.

Bonbon, 6-1/2" l, 4-3/4" w, 2-3/8" h at handle, Mt. Washington, shiny finish, three applied lemon-yellow prunts, applied handle, re-fired heart shaped rim **835.00**
Cream pitcher, 5-1/2" h, Mt. Washington, shiny finish, lemon-yellow handle, refired yellow spout tip, orig paper label "MT. WG. Co. Burmese Patd. Dec. 15, 1885" **665.00**
Cruet, 7" h, Mt. Washington, shiny finish, butter-yellow body, applied handle, mushroom stopper, each of 30 ribs with hint of pink, color blush intensifies on neck and spout . **1,250.00**

Cream pitcher, lemon-yellow handle, refired yellow tip on spout, original oval paper label "MT. WG.CO. BURMESE PATD. DECO-RATED. 15. 1885." Mt. Washington, 5-1/2" h, $665. Photos courtesy of Clarence and Betty Maier.

Cream pitcher, re-fired yellow border piecrust crimped edge, Shape #154 of Mt. Washington's 1885 catalog, 5-1/2" h, **$485.**

Epergne, 14" h, 8" center floriform vase, Webb, satin finish, pastel yellow stripes, unique pink blush borders, undecorated, shallow bowl-shaped base with muted Burmese color, cone-shaped center rising to support brass fittings that hold three petite Burmese bud vases **1,950.00**

Fairy lamp, Webb

4-3/4" h, pyramid Burmese shade, clear base marked "S. Clarke's Pyramid Fairy" **335.00**

5-1/2" h, Cricklite, satin, dome Burmese shade, 6" sq base with fold-in sides, impressed signature "Thos. Webb & Sons Queens Burmeseware Patented," clear glass candle cup signed, "S Clarke Fairy Trade Mark Patent" . . . **985.00**

6" h, 7-1/2" d spreading, skirt-like, pleated base, two acid etched signatures, "Thos Webb & Sons Queen's Burmeseware Patented" and "S. Clarke's Fairy Patent Trade Mark," clear glass candle cup signed, "Clarke's Criklite Trade Mark" **950.00**

Figure, 3" l, 1-1/2" h, pig, Webb, solid Burmese body, pink tint to hind quarters, curly tail, four feet, ears, and snout **750.00**

Tumbler, shiny finish, eggshell thin satin body, soft blush extends from rim to middle fading to delicate pastel yellow lower half, **$375.**

Milk pitcher, 5" w handle to spout, 4" h, Mt. Washington, satin finish. . . . **850.00**

Rose bowl, 3-1/4" h, Webb, prunus blossom dec, sq top **285.00**

Salt shaker, 4-1/4" h, Mt. Washington, lemon-yellow lower half, intense color on upper half, two-part metal top **265.00**

Toothpick holder, 2-1/2" h, Mt. Washington, flared painted blue rim, mold-in ferns motif, scrolls at base, white blossoms with yellow dot centers **1,085.00**

Tumbler, Mt. Washington, shiny finish, thin satin body, soft color blushes from rim to center then shading to pastel yellow base **375.00**

Vase

6-1/2" h, Mt. Washington, satin finish, 10 scallops with hint of yellow at edges, #52-1/2 S **500.00**

7-3/4" h, Mt. Washington, satin finish, double gourd shape, finely drawn green and coral leafy tendrils, seven nosegays of blossoms, raised blue enamel forget-me-nots, each with pastel center with five coral dots, #147, c1885 . . . **985.00**

8" h, double-gourd shape, roses and forget-me-nots, three lovely peach-colored rose blossoms cling to leafed branch which swirl down rim, around body and down to the base, entwining strands of turquoise-colored forget-me-not blossoms, double gourd shaped **1,250.00**

Whiskey taster, 2-3/4" tall, molded-in elongated diamond quilted design **285.00**

Vase on mirror plateau, flower-form Webb shiny finish 4" h vase, fancy monogram under glass on silver backing of 4" x 2-1/2" w mirror plateau, **$365.**

BUSTS

History: The portrait bust has its origins in pagan and Christian traditions. Greek and Roman heroes dominate the earliest examples. Later, images of Christian saints were used. Busts of the "ordinary man" first appeared during the Renaissance.

During the 18th and 19th centuries, nobility, poets, and other notable people were the most frequent subjects, especially on those busts designed for use in a home library. Because of the large number of these library busts, excellent examples can be found at reasonable prices, depending on artist, subject, and material.

Additional Listings: Ivory, Parian Ware, and Wedgwood.

7-1/2" h, bronze, Nubian Princess, Edrmann Encke, Gladenbeck foundry mark, short socle, marble base . **415.00**

8-1/4" h, lady, carved facial features, ears, and hair style, stepped base with dentil carving, stamped dec, old surface, America, early 20th C. . **650.00**

9" h, bronze, winged cherub, seated on broken column, playing hornpipe, pair of doves perched opposite, after Mathurin Moreau, dark brown patination, green marble socle . **250.00**

Young African-American male, plaster of paris, by Louis Mayer, signed on plinth, inscribed "To Margaret form Louis," c1965, 18-3/4" h, **$1,100.** *Photo courtesy of Cowan's Historic Americana Auctions.*

Young woman, alabaster, mounted on green marble-shaped base, unsigned, 7" w x 8" h, $250. Photo courtesy of James D. Julia, Inc.

9-3/4" h, bronze, Virgin, dark brown patina, Leon Pilet, French, 1836-1916, sgd **575.00**

10" h, black basalt, Cicero, waisted circular socle, imp title and Wedgwood & Bentley mark, c1775, chips to socle rim **2,300.00**

10-7/8" h, bronze, Watteau-style woman, tricorn hat, low décolletage, George (Joris) Van Der Straeten, Paris Bronze Society foundry mark, fluted marble socle, reddish brown and black patination. **460.00**

11-1/4" h, bronze and marble, medieval woman, after Patricia by Roger Hart, young woman, sheer headdress, marked "Mino di Tiesole" on ovoid white marble base, 20th C **575.00**

11-1/2" h, bronze, Mercury, chocolate brown and parcel-gilt patina, short socle, sq base, after the antique, 20th C **410.00**

12-1/2" h, bronze, child, modeled as the head of a young child with curly hair, on cylindrical stone base, 20th C . . **635.00**

13-3/4" w, 9-3/4" d, 26" h, carved marble, Pharaoh's Daughter, John Adams-Acton, snake headdress, beaded necklace, tapered sq section base, carved on front with scene of the discovery of Moses and title, 13-3/8" w, 10-3/4" d, 39" h breche d'alep marble tapered sq section pedestal, England, late 19th C **16,100.00**

15-1/4" w, 6-3/4" d, 15" h, carved marble, Jeanne D'Arc, white marble face and base, pink marble bodice,

incised title on front, early 20th C **700.00**

16-1/4" h, bronze, Ajax, after the antique, helmet, beard, parcel gilt toga, sq base, dark green patination, 20th C **865.00**

17-1/4" h, alabaster, woman in lace headdress and bodice, tapered alabaster socle, early 20th C . . . **450.00**

19" h, Majolica, young boy, French colonial dress, marked "BU 677" **900.00**

20" h, marble, lady with rose, incised "A. Testi," associated partial alabaster pedestal with spiral fluted stem **2,645.00**

20-1/2" h, bronze, Rembrandt, Albert-Ernest Carrier-Belleuse, silvered patination, bronze socle, marble plinth **2,300.00**

22" h, bronze, gentleman, Leo F. Nock, brown-green patina, sgd on base "Leo Nock Sc," dated 1919, stamped "Roman Bronze Works, NY" **320.00**

24" h, bronze, cold painted, Bianca Capello, woman wearing classical clothing, Renaissance Revival motifs, sgd "C. Ceribelli," marble plinth **2,100.00**

Marie Antoinette, early 20th C, white marble bust, variegated green marble bodice, variegated salmon marble socle, 26-5/8" h, $775. Photo courtesy of Skinner Auctioneers and Appraisers.

26" h, marble, young pious woman, lace and flower bodice, hair in long braid, matching 6" h marble socle, Italian, late 19th C **7,475.00**

30-1/2" h, 20" w, white marble, young girl, sgd on back "A. Bottinelli, Roma," detailed, lace dress, braided hair, minor bruise on nose. **2,950.00**

BUTTER PRINTS

History: There are two types of butter prints: butter molds and butter stamps. Butter molds are generally of three-piece construction—the design, the screw-in handle, and the case. Molds both shape and stamp the butter at the same time. Butter stamps are generally of one-piece construction, but can be of two-piece construction if the handle is from a separate piece of wood. Stamps decorate the top of butter after it is molded.

The earliest prints are one piece and were hand carved, often heavily and deeply. Later prints were factory made with the design forced into the wood by a metal die.

Some of the most common designs are sheaves of wheat, leaves, flowers, and pineapples. Animal designs and Germanic tulips are difficult to find. Prints with designs on both sides are rare, as are those in unusual shapes, such as half-rounded or lollipop.

Reproduction Alert: Reproductions of butter prints were made as early as the 1940s.

Butter mold

2" l, oval, warbonnet with feathers, vine border, good patina, handle with age crack, some edge damage to case **200.00**

3-1/2" d, sunflower, carved wood **125.00**

4-3/8" d, pineapple, carved wood **325.00**

5" x 8", roses, carved maple, serrated edges **165.00**

Basswood, circular, knob-turned handle, left: primitive bull with horns, fern leaf arching above; right: thistle flower, both with original worn patina, edge wear, America, 19th C, each 4-1/2" d, price for pair, $330. Photo courtesy of Cowan's Historic Americana Auctions.

Carved wood, circular, one-piece style, left: eagle, zigzag carved edge, $275, center: floral, knob handle, $75; right: small sheaf of wheat, $90.

Butter stamp

1-7/8" d, round, carved flower, one piece handle, 1-7/8" d **175.00**

2-3/8" x 1-3/4", rectangular, backward looking crested peafowl-type bird, sitting on flowering branch, turned inset handle, dark stains **250.00**

2-7/8" d, 4-1/2" l, carved fruitwood, strawberry **50.00**

3" d, speckled rooster, leafy foliage, one-piece handle, small chip on handle **275.00**

3-1/4" d, round, carved wide-eyed cow and fence, threaded insert handle with chip on end **200.00**

3-3/4" d, double sided, oval, peony on one side, tulip on other, carved print on handle, age crack **295.00**

3-3/4" d, stylized eagle with shield, natural finish, blue ink stain **110.00**

3-7/8" d, double sided, geometric design and initials, carved print on handle **250.00**

3-7/8" d, stylized eagle with shield, concentric circle rim, dry surface **110.00**

Sheaf of wheat, square, two-piece mold, 4-1/4" square, $110. Photo courtesy of Sanford Alderfer Auction Company.

4" d, nesting swan, threaded handle, old refinishing, some worm holes, minor edge damage **500.00**

4-1/4" d, pomegranate, concentric circle rim, one-pc handle, dark patina **100.00**

4-1/2" d, eagle on laurel branch, star over it's head, wavy feathers, one pc handle, scrubbed surface **395.00**

4-3/4" d, double sided, flowers, carved print on handle, dark patina . . . **265.00**

4-3/8" d, round, carved primitive eagle, rayed sunbursts, dark patina, worn finish, large one-piece handle, 4-3/8" d **330.00**

4-1/2" d, round, carved strawberries and leaf, threaded handle, age cracks **110.00**

4-5/8" d, round, carved pineapple, turned handle, wear, cracks **95.00**

4-3/4" d, 5-1/2" l, walnut, foliage and flowers **115.00**

5" d, round, carved tulip, good patina, PA, age cracks, 5" d **665.00**

5-7/8" l, lollipop, carved rosette, hardwood **110.00**

6-1/2" l, lollipop, carved heart and leaves, chip carved stars, soft worn finish, hold through handle for cord to hang **1,375.00**

6-3/4" l, sheaf of wheat, stylized design, notched rim band **200.00**

7" l, lollipop style, star, zig-zag band rim, flared end handle, old patina **300.00**

CALENDAR PLATES

History: Calendar plates were first made in England in the late 1880s. They became popular in the United States after 1900, the peak years being 1909 to 1915. The majority of the advertising plates were made of porcelain or pottery and the design included a calendar, the name of a store or business, and either a scene, portrait, animal, or flowers. Some also were made of glass or tin.

Additional Listings: See *Warman's Americana & Collectibles* for more examples.

1907, Santa and holly, 9-1/2" d . . **80.00**

1908, hunting dog, Pittstown, PA **40.00**

1909, woman and man in patio garden, 9" d **35.00**

1911, Souvenir of Detroit, MI, months in center, hen and yellow chicks, gold edge **30.00**

1912, Martha Washington **40.00**

1913, roses and holly **30.00**

1914, Point Arena, CA, 6-3/4" d . . **30.00**

1915, black boy eating watermelon, 9" d **60.00**

1907, Romig's Housekeeping, Quakertown, PA, 1907, pretty girl, green calendar pages, 8-1/4" d, $45.

1916, eagle with shield, American flag, 8-1/4" d **40.00**

1917, cat center **35.00**

1919, ship center **30.00**

1920, The Great War, MO **30.00**

1921, bluebirds and fruit, 9" d . . . **35.00**

1922, dog watching rabbit **35.00**

1969, Royal China, Currier & Ives, green, 10" d **40.00**

CALLING CARD CASES AND RECEIVERS

History: Calling cards, usually carried in specially designed cases, played an important social role in the United States from the Civil War until the end of World War I. When making formal visits, callers left their card in a receiver (card dish) in the front hall. Strict rules of etiquette developed. For example, the lady in a family was expected to make calls of congratulations and condolence and visits to the ill.

The cards themselves were small, embossed or engraved with the caller's name, and often decorated with a floral design. Many handmade examples, especially in Spencerian script, can be found. The cards themselves are considered collectible and range in price from a few cents to several dollars.

Note: Don't confuse a calling card case with a match safe.

Case

2-7/8" x 3-7/8", Chinese Export silver, rect, all over hammered appearance, central monogrammed roundel, attributed to Tuck Chang & Co., late 19th/early 20th C, approx four troy oz **200.00**

3" l, burl wood, Victorian **95.00**

3" w x 4", mother-of-pearl, Victorian **180.00**

Engraved elephant ivory, hinged lid, marked yellow and rose gold mounts, engraving of Italian cathedral, possibly Florence, sides, and real with floral scrollwork engraving, 19th C, wear to gold marks, very short crack in ivory, 1-3/4" w, 3-1/4" h, $625. Photo courtesy of Cowan's Historic Americana Auctions.

3" x 4-1/2", Chinese-Export silver, rect, obverse with emb genre scenes and central cartouche, reverse with emb bamboo shoots, maker's mark "SM," late 19th/early 20th C, approx two troy oz. **300.00**

3-3/8" x 3", white-metal case, enamel dec of harem girl disrobing in exotic int., late 19th/early 20th C, giltwood frame **800.00**

Calling card cases, left: panels of mother-of-pearl decorated with birds and flowers, tortoiseshell outside band, 3" w, 4" h, right: tortoiseshell with cross-hatched and flower mother-of-pearl designs, 2-1/2" w, 3-3/4" h, some inlaid pieces missing, each $125. Photo courtesy of James D. Julia, Inc.

Calling card receiver, figural hand holding removable shell-shaped card tray, attached pen, silver plated, Wilcox, engraved "Silver Wedding 1844," 7-1/2" l, $150. Photo courtesy of Woody Auctions.

3-1/2" x 3-3/4", quadruple silver plate, orig chain, Victorian **125.00**

3-3/4" x 2-3/4", sterling silver, engine turned spiral dec, dark green emerald moiré silk concertina int., hallmarked Birmingham, England. **175.00**

4" l, rect, ivory, wood inlay, block rows, center framed with diamond design rim band **175.00**

4" x 2-3/4", blue and green enamel border around applied spun silver panel with floral dec, unmarked . **250.00**

4" x 3", tortoiseshell with stylized floral plique, hinged metal lid, 19th C . **110.00**

Calling card receiver, Sevres card tray with pink border with royal crest at top, decorated in center with brilliantly colored roses, cherries and strawberries, surrounded by gold enamel wreath, ormolu stand with rim of grapes and leaves, two curving handles with bird sitting upon each, four legs joined by sprays of flowers, 12" l, 6-1/2" w, 6" h, $980. Photo courtesy of James D. Julia, Inc.

5-1/2" x 3", silver filigree work over ivory panels, filigree depicts wild boar hunt n one side, cartouche with monogram framed by filigree border on reverse, engraved brass frame, lid needs regluing, loss to int. **220.00**

Receiver

7" l, figural, bronze, monkey, Victorian **135.00**

7-1/4" l, 5-1/2" h, silver plate, marked "Meriden," wear to plating. **60.00**

9-1/2" l, 6" w, hammered bronze, ovoid, emb comedy and tragedy masks, orig dark patina, crisp details, Gorham stamp mark **650.00**

10" l, porcelain, hand painted, roses, foliage, gold handles. **45.00**

CAMBRIDGE GLASS

History: Cambridge Glass Company, Cambridge, Ohio, was incorporated in 1901. Initially, the company made clear tableware, later expanding into colored, etched, and engraved glass. More than 40 different hues were produced in blown and pressed glass.

The plant closed in 1954 and some of the molds were later sold to the Imperial Glass Company, Bellaire, Ohio.

For more information, see this book.

Marks: Five different marks were employed during the production years, but not every piece was marked.

Banana bowl, Inverted Thistle, 7" l, radium green, marked "Near-cut" **95.00**

Basket, Apple Blossom, crystal, 7" **475.00**

Bonbon, Chantilly, crystal, Martha blank, two handles, 6" **35.00**

Bowl, Wildflower, flared rim, three-ftd, 9-3/8" d **85.00**

Butter dish, cov, Gadroon, crystal **45.00**

Candlestick

Caprice, blue, Alpine, #70, prisms, 7" h **195.00**

Doric, black, 9-1/2" h, pr. . . . **160.00**

Rose Point, crystal, two-lite, keyhole, pr **95.00**

Candy box, cov, crystal, Carmen (ruby) rose finial, 6-3/4" w, 6-1/2" h . . . **175.00**

Candy jar, cov, Rose, green rose-shaped finial, 8" h **250.00**

Celery, Gloria, five-part, 12-1/2" l **70.00**

Decagon pattern, amber, service for six, creamer, sugar, and sandwich tray, $400.

Champagne, Chantilly, crystal . . . **30.00**
Cocktail
    Caprice, blue **45.00**
    Stradivary **50.00**
Cocktail shaker, Chantilly, crystal,
glass lid **250.00**
Comport
    Honeycomb, rubena, 9" d, 4-3/4" h,
    ftd **150.00**
    Nude Stem, #3011, Heatherbloom,
    cupped bowl, 6-1/2" w bowl,
    8" h **1,260.00**
    Rose Point, amber, 7-1/4" d,
    7" h **2,035.00**
Cordial
    Caprice, blue **120.00**
    Chantilly, crystal **75.00**
    Rose Point, #3121 . . . . **78.00**
Cornucopia vase, Chantilly,
9-1/8" h **195.00**
Creamer
    Chantilly, crystal, individual size
    . . . . **22.50**
    Tempo, #1029 . . . . **15.00**
Creamer and sugar, tray, Caprice,
crystal **40.00**
Cream soup, orig liner, Decagon,
green **35.00**
Cup and saucer
    Caprice, crystal **14.00**
    Decagon, pink **10.00**
    Martha Washington, amber . . . **12.00**
Decanter set, decanter, stopper, six
handled 2-1/2 oz tumblers, Tally Ho,
amethyst **195.00**
Dressing bowl, Wildflower, two part,
#1402-95 . . . . **55.00**

Flower frog
    Draped Lady, dark pink,
    8-1/2" h **185.00**
    Eagle, pink **365.00**
    Jay, green **365.00**
    Nude, 6-1/2" h, 3-1/4" d,
    clear **145.00**
    Rose Lady, amber, 8-1/2" h . . **350.00**
    Seagull **85.00**
    Two Kids, clear **155.00**
Fruit bowl, Decagon, pink, 5-1/2" . . **5.50**
Goblet
    Chantilly, crystal, #3625 . . . . . **35.00**
    Diane, crystal, #3122 . . . . **45.00**
    Tempo, #1029/3700 . . . . **15.00**
    Wildflower, gold trim, #3121 . . **45.00**

Goblet, Rose Point, 8-1/2" h, $40.

Ice bucket
    Blossom Time, crystal **125.00**
    Chrysanthemum, pink, silver handle
    . . . . **85.00**
    Wildflower, #3400/851 . . . . . . **225.00**
Ivy ball, Nude Stem, Statuesque
#3011/2, 9-1/2" h, 4-1/4" h d ruby ball,
4" d base **500.00**
Jug, Gloria, ftd, 9-3/4" h **325.00**
Juice tumbler, ftd, Candlelight etch,
5 oz, #3114 . . . . **35.00**
Lemon plate, Caprice, blue, 5" d **15.00**
Martini pitcher, Rose Point, crystal
. . . . **700.00**
Mayonnaise set
    Diane, divided bowl, liner, two ladles,
    #3900/111 . . . . **115.00**
    Wildflower, bowl, underplate,
    #3900/139 . . . . **55.00**
Nut bowl, Diane, crystal, tab handle,
2-3/4" **58.00**
Oyster cocktail, Portia, crystal . . **40.00**
Pitcher, Mt. Vernon, forest green
. . . . **300.00**
Plate
    Apple Blossom, pink, 8-1/2" d . **20.00**
    Chantilly, #3900/22, 8" d **18.00**
    Crown Tuscan, 7" d **45.00**
    Diane, 14" d, rolled edge, #3900/166
    . . . . **75.00**
    Rose Point, crystal, 8" d, ftd . . **70.00**
Relish
    Caprice, club, #170, blue . . . **115.00**
    Mt. Vernon, crystal, five-part . . **35.00**
    Wildflower, 8", three part, three
    handles **45.00**
Salt and pepper shakers, pr
    Rose Point, ball-shaped, silver base,
    marked "Wallace Sterling 100"
    . . . . **550.00**
    Wildflower, chrome tops, one slightly
    cloudy **40.00**

Water set, with pitcher and six tumblers. Pitcher is 10" h; tumblers are 3-3/4" h, $275.

Seafood cocktail, Seashell, #110, Crown Tuscan, 4-1/2" oz **95.00**
Server, center handle, Apple Blossom, amber **30.00**
Sherbet
    Diane, crystal, low **20.00**
    Regency, low **22.00**
    Tempo, #1029 . . . . **12.50**
Sherry, Portia, gold encrusted . . **60.00**
Sugar, Tempo, #1029 . . . . **15.00**
Torte plate, Rose Point, crystal, 13" d, three ftd **95.00**
Tray, Gloria, four part, center handle, 8-3/4" d **70.00**
Tumbler
    Adam, yellow, ftd **25.00**
    Carmine, crystal, 12 oz **25.00**
    Chantilly **30.00**
    Diane, crystal, panel optic, 2 oz
    . . . . **110.00**
    Rose Point, 10 0z, #3500 . . . . **35.00**
Vase
    Diane, crystal, keyhole, 12" h **110.00**
    Rose Point, 3-1/4" d, 10" h, black amethyst **665.00**
    Songbird and Butterfly, #402, 12" h, blue **375.00**
    Tall Flat Panel, swung, 19-1/4" h, sgd
    . . . . **100.00**
    Wildflower, #3400, 10-3/4" h . **175.00**
Whiskey, Caprice, blue, 2-1/2 oz
. . . . **225.00**
Wine
    Caprice, crystal **24.00**
    Diane, crystal, 2-1/2 oz **30.00**

CAMEO GLASS

History: Cameo glass is a form of cased glass. A shell of glass was prepared, and then one or more layers of glass of a different color(s) was faced to the first. A design was then cut through the outer layer(s), leaving the inner layer(s) exposed.

For more information, see this book.

This type of art glass originated in Alexandria, Egypt, between 100 and 200 A.D. The oldest and most famous example of cameo glass is the Barberini or Portland vase found near Rome in 1582. It contained the ashes of Emperor Alexander Serverus, who was assassinated in 235 A.D.

Emile Gallé is probably one of the best-known cameo-glass artists. He established a factory at Nancy, France, in 1884. Although much of the glass bears his signature, he was primarily the designer. Assistants did the actual work on many pieces, even signing Gallé's name. Other makers of French-cameo glass include D'Argental, Daum Nancy, LeGras, and Delatte.

English-cameo pieces do not have as many layers of glass (colors) and cuttings as do French pieces. The outer layer is usually white, and cuttings are very fine and delicate. Most pieces are not signed. The best-known makers are Thomas Webb & Sons and Stevens and Williams.

Marks: A star before the name Gallé on a piece by that company indicates that it was made after Gallé's death in 1904.

Reproduction Alert

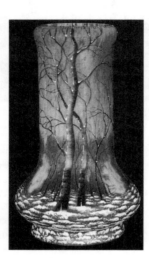

Daum Nancy, vase, cameo carved and enameled leafless trees, snow-covered ground, intense orange and red background shading to yellow, signed "Daum Nancy" with Croix de Lorraine, 10" h, $2,800. Photo courtesy of Fontaine's Auction Gallery.

American
Handel, vase
    8" h, frosted body overlaid in transparent yellow, acid-etched thistle and foliage motif, nicks to base edge **800.00**
    10" h, cylindrical, colorless body overlaid in yellow, acid-etched palm trees and foliage, raised "Handel 4254" on base, sgd "Pamle" on side for Joseph Palme, Meriden, CT **500.00**
Mount Washington
    Bowl, 8" d, 4" h, sq, ruffled edge, two winged Griffins holding up scroll and spray of flowers design, blue over white ground **1,475.00**
    Lamp, 17" h, 10" d shade, fluid font and shade composed of opal white opaque glass overlaid in bright rose pink, acid-etched butterflies, ribbons, and bouquets centering cameo-portrait medallions in classical manner, mounted on silver-plated metal fittings, imp "Pairpoint Mfg. Co. 3013," electrified **3,200.00**

English
Florentine Art, cruet, 6-1/2" h, ruby-red body, textured white enamel meadowland scene, Meadowlark on tall plant stalk, smaller scene on reverse, white rim, trefoil spout, clear frosted handle, teardrop shaped stopper, pontil mark sgd "59" **750.00**
Stevens and Williams, vase, 5-1/2" h, buttercup yellow body shading to cherry blossom-pink, cameo carved twisted Japanese twisted, gnarled, cherry tree branch, pink borders, butterfly on reverse **1,450.00**
Unknown maker
    Vase
        4-1/2" h, conical rim, round body, overlaid in white on blue ground, cameo-cut rose blossom, leafy stems, borders, rim chips, 20th C **920.00**
        9-1/8" h, slender neck and bulbous base, cameo-etched morning glory blossom on leafy vine, white cut to yellow, 20th C, rim chips **865.00**
Webb
    Bonbon, 7-1/2" h, 5" d, morning glory blossoms, white on red on citron, deep yellow base layer, creamy white lining, hammered sterling-silver standard and lid, lid stamped "800," silversmith's mark obscured by finial, attributed to Webb **1,950.00**

Webb, scent bottle, soft yellow body, cameo carved pastel pink apple blossoms and leaves, gold enamel highlighting, "veining." Collar has four stamp marks and is signed "FRM," screw-on cap also signed "FMR," three shallow dents in the cap, 3-1/2" d, 4-1/2" h, $1,750. Photo courtesy of Clarence and Betty Maier.

Cup and saucer, handleless, 2-3/4" h, 5" d, cranberry over crystal, prunus blossom carving, leaves, and branches, 10 blossoms on cup with large butterfly and 25 buds **550.00**

Scent bottle, 3-1/2" d, 4-1/2" h, creamy-yellow ground, pastel pink apple blossom branches, each flower and leaf outlined in gold, tiny gold dots, gold veining on stems and leaves, collar with four stamp marks, sgd "FRM," screw-on cap also sgd "FMR," three shallow dents on cap **1,750.00**

Vase, 7-1/2" h, bulbous baluster, gold ground, carved white geraniums, carved white coral bells on reverse, sgd "Webb" **1,750.00**

French

Arsall, vase, 5" h, flared, pink mottled yellow overlaid ground, green layer etched as decumbent blossoms, buds, and leafy stems, sgd "Arsall" in design **325.00**

Burgen, Schverer, and Cie, Alsace-Lorraine, vase, ftd broad ovoid, frosted colorless glass, amethyst overlay etched and engraved trailing nasturtium blossom, gilt highlights, elaborate gold enamel trademark on base, c1900, enamel wear . . . **2,760.00**

Charder, vase, 5" h, gray ground internally dec with lavender and yellow mottling, overlaid in amethyst, cameo cut lattice and floral design, sgd "Charder" in cameo, c1925 . . . . **815.00**

D'Argental

Vase

10-1/4" h, slender neck, bulbous body, cameo-etched morning glories, amber, red, and orange, sgd "D'Argental (cross)" near base **500.00**

11-3/4" h, dark amber ground, overlaid in plum and burgundy, cut cascading branches of seed pods and leaves, sgd "D'Argental" in cameo, c1910 . . . . **1,610.00**

Daum Nancy

Bowl

8" d, mottled yellow and amethyst-gray ground, overlaid with vitrified green, red, and yellow powders, cameo cut with stemmed leafy red berries, sgd in cameo "Daum Nancy" with

Croix de Lorraine, c1900 . . . . **2,760.00**

10" d, textured opalescent ground, reddish-gold overlay, enameled and cameo cut branching leafy seed pods, tri-fold top with cameo-cut ribbon, sgd "Daum Nancy" in enamel, minor chips . . **1,610.00**

Ewer

7-1/2" h, cranberry ground, highlighted in gold, overlaid in deep purple, cameo cut grapevine motif, metal mount flip lid and handle, emb with matching grape dec, sgd in gold "Daum Nancy," c1895 . . . . **1,380.00**

10-1/2", textured translucent glass, gold highlighted ruby cameo with random trailing flowers, silver-gilt emb collar, handle, and lid with raspberry finial, sgd in gold "Daum Nancy," c1895 . . . . . . **1,955.00**

Flask, 5-5/8" h, tapered cylindrical bottle, translucent colorless body cameo cut with violet blossoms, enameled purple, yellow, orange and white, gilt highlights, inscribed "Daum (cross) Nancy," mounted with bulbed silver cap with emb flower blossoms, engraved "Lola," small cup with raised leaf blade design, emb "SH" in diamond, cap loose **375.00**

Inkwell, 4-1/4" d, 3-1/2" h, mottled green and purple ground, cameo cut falling oak leaves, five jeweled carved insect and acorn

Daum Nancy, lamp, sculpted metal base with leaves at foot and top, shade signed "DAUM NANCY" in the shape of a bowl, cameo carved leaves and flowers and enameled against a pink, yellow and cream background, 14" h, 6" d shade, $4,600. Photo courtesy of James D. Julia, Inc.

cabochons, sgd "Daum Nancy," c1900 . . . . **1,265.00**

Tumbler, 3-1/4" h, gray ground mottled in yellow and amethyst, cameo cut purple and yellow enameled flowers, green leafy stems, sgd in cameo "Daum Nancy" with Croix de Lorraine, c1900 . . . . **1,035.00**

Vase

4-1/8" h, 6-7/8" w, pillow form, quatrefoil rim, yellow, blue, and green landscape, sgd "Daum Nancy (cross)," conjoined "FG" on base **1,265.00**

4-1/4" h, conical, green ground, bands of stylized flower blossoms on etched and polished surfaces, gilt highlights, inscribed "Daum (cross) Nancy" on base, gilt wear **325.00**

4-1/4" h, sq, yellow dawn background, sailboats at sea, inscribed "Daum Nancy (cross)," chips **865.00**

4-1/2" h, gray ground internally dec with amber and frost mottling, cameo carved vitrified leaves, stemmed red bleeding hearts, sgd in cameo "Daum Nancy" with Croix de Lorraine, c1910 . . . . **1,100.00**

4-1/2" h, green ground, alternating bands of cameo and intaglio cut rosettes, gilt highlights, inscribed "Daum Nancy," c1900 . . . . **500.00**

4-3/4" h, gray ground with internal yellow and amethyst mottling, cameo cut and enameled elongated green stemmed red flowers, sgd in cameo "Daum Nancy France," c1900 **1,495.00**

4-3/4" h, opalescent and burgundy textured ground, cameo cut with burgundy gold highlighted thistle, sgd in gold "Daum Nancy," c1910 . . **600.00**

5-1/2" h, three-ftd, gray ground internally dec with lemon yellow mottling, cameo cut and enameled with winter scene of lifeless snowy forest foliage, framed by tall towering trees, sgd in enamel "Daum Nancy" with Croix de Lorraine, c1915 . . . . **4,025.00**

6-5/8" h, slender neck on bulbous base, etched gold and black leafy fines and black enameled landscape scene, inscribed "Daum (cross) Nancy," rim nick **350.00**

8-1/4" h, amethyst and gray mottled ground, cameo cut and enameled with fuchsia buds and flowers, green leafy burgundy stems, scrolling gold highlighted foot, sgd in cameo "Daum Nancy" with Croix de Lorraine, c1900 ...... **3,355.00**

10" h, flared rim, tapered oval ftd vase, opalescent pink glass cased in transparent green, etched dandelions on stems with leaves, wheel carved "hammered" ground, inscribed "Daum (cross) Nancy" on base, early 20th C, minor imperfections **2,185.00**

12-1/4" h, shouldered vessel tapering to flared base, etched leaf design in brown layered over mottled yellow, purple, and green translucent glass, cameo-etched "Daum Nancy (cross)" **1,150.00**

13" h, amber glass overlaid in orange and green, cut mountainous lake scene outlined with towering pine trees, sgd in cameo "Daum Nancy" with Croix de Lorraine, c1910 .... **3,115.00**

13-3/4" h, corset shape, opalescent ground shading to gray, random cameo cut opalescent flowering vines, sgd "Daum Nancy" **1,265.00**

15-3/4" h, ftd, ovoid, gray ground internally dec with white mottling interspread with splashes of lemon yellow and royal blue overlaid with royal blue and pale blue shading to turquoise, cut blue aster blossoms, intertwining buds and large leafy foliage, partial Martelé ground, blossoms with radiating wheel carved petals and Martelé centers in turquoise, circular base cut with floral design in royal blue shading to turquoise, concentric three-ring stem, sgd in cameo "Daum Nancy," c1910 ...... **21,275.00**

21-1/4" h, rose yellow and gray mottled ground, overlaid with vitrified powdered green and red glass, cameo cut with stemmed flowers, sgd in cameo

"Daum Nancy," c1920 .... **5,520.00**

Whiskey jug, 10-1/2" h, textured translucent ground, cameo cut and enameled grapevine and leaves, metal lid and handle in form of knight's helmet, lion finial on flip lid, unsigned, c1895 .... **815.00**

Degue, vase, 10-3/4" h, gray ground internally dec with mottled custard, overlaid in variegated orange and brown, cameo cut leafage and buds, inscribed "Degue," c1925 ..... **750.00**

De Vez, vase, 6" h, maroon and fiery amber oval body, etched cottages, mother, child, under tall trees, sgd "de Vez" at side, polished rim **900.00**

Foussin, vase, 14-3/8" h, cylindrical, cameo cut trailing vines and flowers in green and brown over frosted ground, signature at side, 20th C **500.00**

Galle

Bowl, 7-3/4" d, 4-1/4" h, ftd, four pulled points, pale pink ground, light yellow-green and amber overlay, etched clusters of blossoms on leafy branches, sgd "Galle" among leaves, several bubble bursts and int. wear **690.00**

Decanter, 10-1/4" h, flattened oval body, upturned rim, conical stopper, frosted colorless and purple ground, overlaid in deep purple, etched iris, engraved "Cristallerie de Galle Nancy modele et decor deposes" on base **2,530.00**

De Vez, vase, acid-cut trees, landscape and lake with castle overlooking lake, blue mountains in background with pink sky shading upward to green, signed in cameo "DE VEZ," 8" h, $1,250. Photo courtesy of James D. Julia, Inc.

Galle, vase, peach-colored cameo carved chrysanthemums on a frosted white background, cameo signed "Galle" on side, 13-1/2" h, $2,150. Photo courtesy of James D. Julia, Inc.

Lamp base, 16-3/4" h, blue-gray ground, overlaid with cinnamon and orange, cameo cut cascading leafy stemmed fruit, sgd "Galle" in cameo, lamp fittings **1,330.00**

Tray, 4-1/4" w, sq, translucent light amber ground, etched flowers and buds, pink, cream, deep red, and gilt enameling, cameo-etched "Galle" signature, light wear **150.00**

Vase

3-3/8" h, ovoid, amber shading to cream, overlaid in orange and brown, cameo-etched pond plant life, cameo-etched "Galle" at side **550.00**

5-1/4" h, ftd, pink frosted ground, large amethyst cameo stemmed flowers, sgd "Galle" in cameo, c1920 .... **575.00**

5-3/4" h, flat sided pillow form, frosted ground, overlaid in red, cut random stemmed berries and leaves, sgd "Galle" in cameo, c1900 .... **815.00**

7-1/2" h, frosted gray ground overlaid in chartreuse and white, cut with trailing leaves and seed pods, sgd "Galle" with star in cameo, c1900 .. **1,035.00**

8" h, raised rim, tapered oval body, translucent amber with reddish brown overlay, cameo cut and etched orchid blossoms and foliage, cameo-etched "Galle" signature **900.00**

9-3/4" h, olive green cased to salmon and translucent

colorless glass, cameo cut and etched leaves and pendant seed pods, sgd "Galle" in cameo on side, polished pontil, rim possibly ground, base wear **460.00**

12-3/4" h, oval pillow form, gray ground overlaid with olive, pink, lemon, and opalescent colored glass, six acid cuttings, green umbrella plant leaves, pink and yellow foxglove florals, opalescent shading outline, sgd "Galle" in cameo, c1915 . . . . **5,750.00**

16" h, gray ground, overlaid in green and blue, cameo cut leafy stemmed hyacinths, sgd "Galle" with star in cameo, c1915 . . . . **2,415.00**

Lamartine

Box, 3" h, triangular form sloping from round opening, cameo cut and etched mountain landscape in blues and greens, sterling silver lid, cameo-etched "Lamartine" on side, int. rim nicks **360.00**

Vase

6-1/4" h, mottled blue and green ground, cameo cut and enameled birch trees towering over country stream, etched sgd "Lamartine," c1910 . . . . **1,215.00**

6-1/2" h, oval, frosted ground, green and brown, cameo cut and enameled colorful three filled landscape, sgd "Lamartine" near base and "328/711" on base **980.00**

Legras

Bowl, 10" d, 3-3/4" h, olive-green body, heavily etched and engraved Art-Deco swag and drapery design, fire polished, acid-etched "Legras" near base **825.00**

Floor vase, 24" h, rose amber ground, overlaid in green, cameo cut towering trees above deep forested lake scene, sgd "Legras" in cameo, c1910, price for pr **4,025.00**

Vase

7-3/4" h, textured gray ground with pink hues, overlaid and cameo cut with green enameled mountainous lake scene, sgd "Legras" in enamel, c1915 . . . . **490.00**

10-1/4" h, flared rim, elongated neck, bulbed base, light

Vase, LeGras, rust cut to orange to gray to green, black sunset scene, 5" x 3-1/2" x 4-3/4", **$500.**

lustrous caramel colored glass, cameo cut branches and leaves, brown and green enameled highlights, cameo-etched "Legras" signature on side, minor rim chips **350.00**

11" h, textured translucent shading to crimson ground, cameo cut Art Deco motif, sgd "Legras" in cameo, c1920 . . . . **550.00**

13-1/2" h, stick, gray shading to mauve ground, cameo cut and enameled underwater foliaged scene, sgd "Legras" in cameo, c1915 . . . . **650.00**

14" h, gray shading to mauve ground, cameo cut underwater scene, sgd "Legras" in cameo, c1915 . . . . **825.00**

23-1/2" h, yellow and rose ground, green overly, cameo cut random railing fruit and leaves, sgd "Legras" in cameo, c1910 . . . . **2,645.00**

Le Verre Francais

Floor vase, 12-1/2" h, Décor Rubanier, gray ground with opalescent mottling, overlaid in variegated orange and amethyst, cameo cut with stylized band of spiral design, base inscribed "Le Verre Francais," c1926 . . . . **850.00**

Lamp, hanging, 11" d, mushroom form, gray ground with yellow mottling, overlaid in orange and brown, cameo cut poppies, hand wrought iron from and suspension chain, c1925 . . . . **2,300.00**

Vase

10" h, Décor Pavot, gray ground with internal lemon yellow mottling, overlaid in mottled red and brown, cameo cut floral

design, base inscribed "Le Verre Francais," c1925 **1,610.00**

14-1/2" h, Décor Mirette, gray ground internally streaked with lemon yellow, overlaid in royal blue and orange band, cameo cut long stemmed stylized flowers, base inscribed "Le Verre Francais," c1925-26 . . . . **2,070.00**

15-1/2" h, Décor Yucca A droite, gray ground internally dec with lemon yellow mottling, overlaid in orange and brown, cameo cut stylized flowering yucca, inscribed "Le Verre Francais," c1925-27 . . . . **4,390.00**

17-1/2" h, Décor Papillons, baluster, gray satin ground with internal turquoise mottling, overlaid in mottled crimson and cobalt blue, cameo cut stylized design of butterflies in flight, base inscribed "Le Verre Francais," c1924 . . . . **6,670.00**

Michel, vase, 8" h, ovoid, yellow overlaid in green and brown, cameo cut and etched house and mountainous landscape, sgd "J. Michel Paris" near base **1,035.00**

Muller

Dish, 5-1/2" l, 5" h, boat shape, mottled orange ground, overlaid in brown, cameo cut sailing ships on mountainous lake, sgd "Muller Fres Luneville" in cameo, c1910. **650.00**

Vase, 7-3/4" h, green and gray mottled ground, overlaid with crimson and red, cameo cut stemmed morning glories in various stages of bloom, sgd

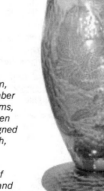

Vase, Richardson, golden amber lily blossoms, shiny golden foliage, signed pontil, 8" h, **$1,350.** *Photo courtesy of Clarence and Betty Maier.*

"Muller Fres Luneville" in cameo, c1915 . . . . **2,990.00**

Pantin, violet vase, 5" h, quatrefoil rim on spherical vase, frosted glass overlaid in lavender, acid-etched violet blossoms, inscribed "Christallerie de Pantin" surrounding "STV & Co" monogram on base **520.00**

Richard, vase

6" h, lemon yellow ground, cameo cut royal blue thistles, sgd "Richard" in cameo, c1915 **320.00**

11-1/2" h, swollen elongated neck, flared base, opaque orange glass overlaid in black, cameo cut and etched tall leafy stems, scrolled lower border, cameo-etched signature **300.00**

21-1/2", gray ground, overlaid with amethyst, cameo cut mountainous lake scene and medieval castle, sgd "Richard" in cameo, c1915, drilled **650.00**

22-1/2" h, gray and rose mottled ground, overlaid in amethyst, cameo cut shoreline castle between towering trees, distant mountains, sgd "Richard" in cameo, c1915 . . . . **1,495.00**

Schneider, vase, 4-1/2" h, mottled orange ground, cameo cut with blue Art Deco design, candy-cane signature, c1920. **490.00**

CAMERAS

History: Photography became a viable enterprise in the 1840s, but few early cameras have survived. Cameras made before the 1880s are seldom available on the market, and when found, their prices are prohibitive for most collectors.

George Eastman's introduction of the Kodak camera in 1888, the first commercially marketed roll-film camera, put photography in the hands of the public.

Most collectors start with a general interest that becomes more defined. After collecting a broad range of Kodak cameras, a collector may decide to specialize in Retina models. Camera collectors tend to prefer unusual and scarce cameras to the most common models, which were mass-produced by the millions.

Because a surplus exists for many common cameras, such as most Kodak box and folding models, collectors are wise to acquire only examples in excellent condition. Shutters should function properly. Minimal wear is generally acceptable. Avoid cameras that have missing parts, damaged bellows, and major cosmetic problems.

Additional Listings: See *Warman's Americana & Collectibles* for more examples.

Adviser: Tom Hoepf.

Ansco, Binghamton, NY

Flash Clipper, 1949, metal roll film camera with rect pop out front **10.00**

Vest Pocket No. 1, c1915, strut-type folding camera **30.00**

Anscoflex II, 1950s reflex-style camera with vertical sliding cover over lens and finder, gray and silver, with flash attachment . **20.00**

Canon Camera Co., Japan

Canon Demi S, c1964, sleek half-frame camera, built-in meter **65.00**

Canonet, series of small 35mm rangefinder cameras introduced in 1960s and continued into 1980s **40.00**

CMC Camera, novelty miniature 16mm roll film camera, made in Japan, blue leatherette. **30.00**

Kodak, No. 2 Brownie, original graphic box shows turn of Brownie Character, original instruction book included, and original price tag of $2.50, 6" l box, **$90.** *Photo courtesy of James D. Julia, Inc.*

Eastman Kodak, Rochester, NY

Brownie Reflex 20, c1959, larger reflex camera using 620 roll film, lift-up viewing hood **10.00**

Duaflex, 1947, first of series (Models I through IV) of inexpensive reflex type cameras using 620 film, snap-on plastic panel to cover lenses and finder **10.00**

Perfex, One-O-One Camera Corp. of America, Wollensak lens, Alphox shutter, F4 5/50 mm, 1947-50, **$35.**

Duo Six-20, c1935 folding camera using 620 film, made in Germany, f3.5/70mm Kodak Anastigmat lens, Compur shutter **45.00**

Jiffy Kodak Six-16, c1935, 616 roll film camera having pop-out Art Deco enameled front **20.00**

Kodak Bantam f8, c1940, Bakelite body with pop-out square front, 40mm Kodalinear lens **25.00**

No. 3A Folding Brownie, c1910, 3-1/4" x 5-1/2" postcard size, maroon bellows **50.00**

Minolta, Osaka, Japan

Minolta Six, c1935, 120 roll film camera, Bakelite body with collapsible front, Coronar Anastigmat f5.6/80mm lens, horizontal format **70.00**

Minolta 16, 1960s subminiature camera using 16mm film cartridge, chrome finish **35.00**

Pho-tak Corp., Chicago, IL

Marksman, 1950s, simple metal box camera using 120 film **10.00**

Scout 120 Flash, metal box camera made for Boy Scouts **15.00**

Polaroid, Cambridge, Mass.

Polaroid 95, 1948, first of Polaroid instant cameras, cast aluminum body, fold-out style, common **25.00**

Polaroid 110A Pathfinder, 1957, Ysarex or Enna-Werk Ennit f4.7/127mm lens, Prontos SVS shutter **45.00**

SX70, 1972, folding single lens reflex, close-up focusing, polished aluminum, tan leather panels, common **40.00**

Time camera, promotional bonus to new subscribers to *Time* magazine, plastic body resembles single lens reflex, weighted bottom. **5.00**

Whitehouse Products, Brooklyn, NY

Beacon II, c1950, black plastic, 127 roll film camera. **10.00**

Charlie Tuna, 1960s, 126 cartridge camera shaped like animated character from Starkist's TV ads **100.00**

CANDLESTICKS

History: The domestic use of candlesticks is traced to the 14th century. The earliest was a picket type, named for the sharp point used to hold the candle. The socket type was established by the mid-1660s.

From 1700 to the present, candlestick design mirrored furniture design. By the late 17th century, a baluster stem was introduced, replacing the earlier Doric or clustered column stem. After 1730, candlesticks reflected rococo ornateness. Neoclassic styles followed in the 1760s. Each new era produced a new style of candlesticks; however, some styles became universal and remained in production for centuries. Therefore, when attempting to date a candlestick, it is important to try to determine the techniques used to manufacture the piece.

Candelabras are included in this edition to show examples of the many interesting candelabras available in today's antiques marketplace. Check for completeness when purchasing candelabras, most are sold in pairs.

Candelabra

11-1/4" h, deep amethyst base and column with cut panels, cut stars around center, detailed brass castings include four branches, all with scrolled acanthus leaves and sockets, emb "Made in France," wear to silver plating, center finial missing **550.00**

Bronze and onyx candelabrum, urn form base with serpent handles, square onyx plinth with applied bronze mounts and paw feet, supporting five scrolled candelabra arms with socket and one central candle socket, 26" h, $385. Photo courtesy of Sanford Alderfer Auction Company.

16-3/4" h, white marble with burgundy striations and ormolu, stepped bases with molded detail, tapered columns, four scrolled branches, turned center column, each with candle socket, small feet below base removed, price for pr **385.00**

20" h, 14-1/2" w, pressed colorless glass, two-light, center faceted prism above drip pan hung with faceted prisms, suspending two chains of prisms to a pair of spiral twisted scrolled arms, flanked by two scrolled candlearms, drip pans hung with further prisms, single knob stem, stepped sq base, late 19th C, bases drilled, price for pr **350.00**

20-1/4" h, brass, hollow stems, adjustable double cross bar arms with serrated ends, seven sockets, domed stepped bases, some discoloration, price for pr **110.00**

22-1/4" h, brass, baluster stems, scrolled tripod bases, cov with highly detailed cast grape vines, center and two branching arms with cast vines with leaves and bunches of grapes, leaves cover sockets, small dents on one, price for pr **1,155.00**

30-1/2" h, bronze, five candle sockets near top, crane finial, Minera heads wearing halo of pine cones below tapering columns, three paw feet and griffins divided by large scrolled leaves around base, engraved signatures "F. Barbedienne," design first exhibited at L'Exposition Universelle in 1867, price for pr **3,100.00**

41" h, gilt bronze, ftd base supporting altar from which a column of clouds mounted with winged angels looking up toward five-arm candelabra, French, 19th C **865.00**

61-1/2" h, oak, dark finish, mortised triangular shaped top, 13 lead sockets, baluster column with ring turnings, shaped X-feet, old age splints, repair near base, one foot old replacement, two sockets missing **250.00**

Candlesticks

5" h, brass, short acorn shaped stem hand riveted to octagonal base, faint copper color, pieced repairs . . . **150.00**

5-1/4" h, 5-1/2" d, brass, Capstan, turned dec on socket, mid-drop pan, base, Dutch, 17th C, wear, scratches, dents **600.00**

5-1/2" h, sterling silver, Neoclassical, England, first half 19th C, emb gadrooned nozzle, campana-shape

Bell metal, Regency, classical column, square base, English, c1820-30, 7" h, $200. Photo courtesy of Cowan's Historic Americana Auctions.

stems, foliate festoons and acanthus dec, waisted pedestal base, emb arms and beaded rims, price for pr . . **280.00**

6-3/4" h, brass, short prickets over baluster, flattened and ball-knopped stem, tiered spreading base, Continental, late 19th/early 20th C **125.00**

7-1/8" h, brass, swirled notched bobeche, swelling at mid-shaft and near base, swirl base, England, c1755, wear, repair **210.00**

7-5/8" h, brass, Queen Anne, push-up, scalloped bases, burnished finish, one has solder underneath at seam, price for pr **770.00**

Brass, King of Diamonds, push-ups, 12-1/2" h, pair, $250. Photo courtesy of James D. Julia, Inc.

8" h, marble, Empire-style, late 19th C, engine turned and beaded ormolu nozzles, gray marble columns hung with gilt-metal chains suspending acorns, stepped white marble base with flat leaf and beaded mounts, flattened ball feet, price for pr **350.00**

8-7/8" h, 3-1/4" d base, pressed glass, emerald green, petal socket joined by wafer to fluted standard, sq base with chamfered corners, attributed to Mt. Washington Glass Works or American Flint Glass Works, both South Boston, MA, 1840-55, large loss to one base, other with imperfections and flaw, price for pr **2,100.00**

9-3/8" h, brass, petal-form bobeche, ruffled swelling under candle cup, conforming base, England, 1740-50, one petal bent, wear **470.00**

9-3/4" h, pressed vaseline glass, dolphins, paneled floriform candle cups, sq stepped bases, America, 19th C, chips, price for pr **1,380.00**

10" h, bell metal, tapered round sticks, raised on steep paneled and beaded sq base, round socket with removable drip-pan insert, pr **175.00**

Glass, blown, colorless, Midwestern, bulbous form, ring turnings on socket, hollow stem, domed round foot, original pewter liners, 10-1/4" h, one with rim chip, $2,825. Photo courtesy of Cowan's Historic Americana Auctions.

10-1/4" h, 3-1/4" d, pressed glass, turquoise, petal socket over dolphin standard with large head, well-defined eye, sq base, attributed to Boston & Sandwich Glass Co., Sandwich, MA, c1845-70, imperfections **4,600.00**

10-5/8" h, porcelain, figural, male and female flower gatherers, against brocage, rocaille base, attributed to Samson, France, late 19th C, price for pr **450.00**

11-1/2" h, wrought iron, scrolled handle and feet, lip handle, notched push-up, price for pr **550.00**

22-3/4" h, pewter, pricket, wide drip pan, double-baluster stem, shaped-tripartite base, three ball feet, Continental, 18th C **700.00**

61" h, cast brass and wrought iron, Gothic Revival, late 19th C, pricket, trefoil-edged drip pan, girdled multi-knopped cast brass standard, wrought-iron trefoil base with serpentine legs, acanthus knees and flowerhead scrolls, price for pr **1,610.00**

CANDY CONTAINERS

History: In 1876, Croft, Wilbur, and Co. filled small glass Liberty Bells with candy and sold them at the Centennial Exposition in Philadelphia. From that date until the 1960s, glass candy containers remained popular. They reflect historical changes, particularly in transportation.

Jeannette, Pennsylvania, a center for the packaging of candy in containers, was home for J. C. Crosetti, J. H. Millstein, T. H. Stough, and Victory Glass. Other early manufacturers included: George Borgfeldt, New York, New York; Cambridge Glass, Cambridge, Ohio; Eagle Glass, Wheeling, West Virginia; L. E. Smith, Mt. Pleasant, Pennsylvania; and West Brothers, Grapeville, Pennsylvania.

Additional Listings: See *Warman's Americana & Collectibles* for more examples.

Notes: Candy containers with original paint, candy, and closures command a high premium, but beware of reproduced parts and repainting. The closure is a critical part of each container; if it is missing, the value of the container drops considerably. Small figural perfumes and other miniatures often are sold as candy containers.

Airplane, P-38 Lightning, orig wire clip, motors, and ground, no closure . **200.00**

Auto, couple, long hood, orig tan snap-on strip, orig gold stamped tin wheels, orig closure **120.00**

Barney Google, bank

Orig paint, orig closure **650.00**
Repainted, orig closure **450.00**

Baseball player, with bat, 50 percent orig paint, orig closure **500.00**

Bear, on circus tub, orig tin, orig closure **500.00**

Boat, USN *Dreadnaught,* orig closure **350.00**

Bulldog, 4-1/4" h, screw closure . **60.00**

Cannon, red tin wheels and carriage hold glass cannon, original candy and tin screw-on cap, 4-1/4" l, $210. Photo courtesy of James D. Julia, Inc.

Bus

Chicago, replaced closure . . **275.00**
New York-San Francisco, orig closure **375.00**
Victory Glass Co., replaced closure **300.00**

Camera on tripod, 80 percent paint, all paint replaced **200.00**

Cannon

Cannon #1, orig carriage, orig closure **375.00**
U. S. Defense Field Gun #17, orig closure **380.00**
Two-Wheel Mount #1, orig carriage, orig closure **220.00**
Two-Wheel Mount #2, orig carriage, orig closure, one replaced wheel **260.00**

Cat, papier-mâché, 3-3/4" h, seated, gray and white paint, pink ribbon, glass eyes, touch up and repairs **375.00**

Chick, composition, 5" h, cardboard, base, Germany **20.00**

Dog, by barrel, 90 percent paint, chip on base, orig closure **220.00**

Elf on rocking horse, 3-1/2" h, pressed glass, no closure **160.00**

Felix the Cat, repainted, replaced closure **550.00**

Fire truck, with ladders **45.00**

George Washington, 3" h, papier-mâché, with tricorn hat, white ponytail and blue coat, standing beside cardboard cabin with deep roof and chimney, unmarked **195.00**

Ghost head, 3-1/2" h, papier-mâché, flannel shroud **150.00**

Goblin head, 60 percent orig paint, orig closure **625.00**

Gun, 5-3/4" l, West Specialty Co. **20.00**

Horse and wagon, pressed glass **35.00**

Hot doggie, traces of paint, orig closure **525.00**

Independence Hall, corner steeple chip, orig closure **250.00**

Man, clear glass, embossed plaid jacket, black plastic hat, 3-3/8" h, $35.

Indian, 5" l, pressed glass, riding motorcycle with sidecar, no closure **350.00**

Jack-o-lantern, open top, 95 percent orig paint, no closure **350.00**

Kettle, 2" h, 2-1/4" d, pressed glass, clear, T. H. Stough, cardboard closure **50.00**

Kewpie on radio, orig paint, orig closure **650.00**

Limousine, orig wheels, orig closure, small chip **600.00**

Little boy, 6" h, papier-mâché head and hollow body, large pink nose, closed smiling mouth, painted brown eyes, molded and painted red vest, green jacket, yellow short pants, purple socks, black shoes, brown tie **210.00**

Locomotive, Mapother's 1892, orig closure **125.00**

Man on motorcycle, side car, repainted, replaced closure **525.00**

Mule, pulling two-wheeled barrel with driver, 95 percent paint, orig closure **85.00**

Nursing bottle, pressed glass, clear, natural wood nipple closure, T. H. Stough, 1940-50 . . . . **20.00**

Puppy, 2-1/2" h, papier-mâché, painted, white, black muzzle, glass eyes **35.00**

Rabbit, glass
    Rabbit pushing chick in shell cart, orig closure **500.00**
    Rabbit with basket on arm, no paint, orig closure **120.00**

Rocking horse, small chips on rockers, no closure **180.00**

Rooster, 6-1/2" h, papier-mâché, pewter feet, orig polychrome paint, marked "Germany" **225.00**

Sailor, 6" h, papier-mâché head and hollow body, large pink nose, closed smiling mouth, protruding lower lip, molded and painted sideburns and hair, molded gray fez, painted blue eyes, molded and painted blue sailor uniform, black belt with knife case and sword, black shoes, unmarked . **275.00**

Santa Claus
    By sq chimney, 60 percent paint, replaced closure **180.00**
    Paneled coat, orig closure . . **150.00**

Stop and Go, replaced switch handle, orig closure **440.00**

Submarine F6, no periscope or flat, orig super structure, orig closure **250.00**

Tank, World War I, traces of orig paint, no closure **90.00**

Telephone, small glass receiver . **55.00**

Turkey, gobbler, small chip under orig closure **100.00**

Village bank, with insert, log-cabin roof **110.00**

Wagon, orig closure **90.00**

Wheelbarrow, orig wheel, no closure **35.00**

Windmill, five windows, ruby-flashed orig blades, orig closure **495.00**

CANES

History: Canes or walking sticks have existed through the ages, first as staffs or symbols of authority, to religious ceremonial pieces. They eventually evolved to the fashion accessory that is the highly desirable antique prized by today's collector for its beauty and lasting qualities. The best were created with rare materials such as carved ivory, precious metals, jewels, porcelain, and enamel, with many being very high-quality works of art. They were also fashioned of more mundane materials, with some displaying the skill of individual folk artists. Another category of interest to collectors is the gadget canes that contained a myriad of hidden utilitarian objects, from weapons to drinking flasks, telescopes, compasses, and even musical instruments, to cite just some.

Adviser: Henry A. Taron.

Agate, English, c1910, 1-3/4" d x 3" h, carved oval cartouche extends to 16 tear-drop shaped sides, blend into smooth panels that extend down to collar, deep rich brown color, white and tan graining, 1/2" silver collar, black enamel shaft, 1" horn ferrule, 36" l **900.00**

Automata
    Continental, c1885, rabbit, carved wood, 3-1/2" l x 2-1/4" h, long-eared rabbit, brown eyes, when lever under chin is depressed, his ears flip upward and mouth opens, 2/3" bright brass collar, smooth partridgewood shaft, holes for wrist cord, 1" brass and iron ferrule, 36" l, minor roughness on nose
    . . . . **1,345.00**
    French, c1890, 2" w x 2-3/4" carved stained elephant ivory handle of furry monkey in floppy hat, when

Cane, gold-filled, American, c1885, 3-1/2" l x 1-3/4" h "L"-shaped handle, finely fashioned deer leg, hoof, and fetlock, ebony shaft, 1-1/4" white metal and iron ferrule, 34-1/2" l, $620. All cane photos courtesy of Henry A. Taron.

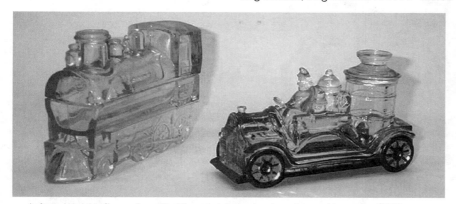

Left: train, right: fire engine with driver, metal wheels, clear glass, sold as pair, $220. Photo courtesy of Joy Luke Auctions.

ivory back lever in back of 3/4" ivory collar is depressed, chin drops, tongue sticks out, glass eyes change from yellow to red, dark bamboo shaft, 7/8" burnished brass ferrule, 36" l **3,360.00**

Enamel, Continental, c1900, 1" d x 1-3/4" h knob handle, pale pink enamel with textured appearance, vermeil ring highlights top rim, 1/3" smooth vermeil collar, Continental hallmarks, stamped "925," black ebonized hardwood shaft, 1" horn ferrule, 36" l **950.00**

Folk Art, R. M. Foster, America, c1870, carved from single piece of hickory, 1" d x 1-1/2" h bark handle, carved in high relief as kangaroo head, upright kangaroo, elephant, flying goose, prong horn deer, rhino, oak leaves, alligator, coiled rattlesnake, padlock, male lion, pelican, gar fish, rabbit head, camel, jackknife, frog, tiger, running doe, flying duck, antelope, full-bodied owl standing on coffeepot, hatchet, sgd in ink on coffeepot "Trade Mark R. M. Foster, Sparta, Mo.," 1/3" lead ferrule, 34-1/2" l **3,360.00**

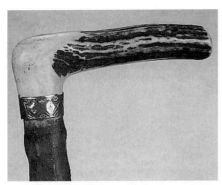

Cane, horn, gadget, undertaker's, 4-1/2" l x 1-1/2" staghorn handle, 1/2" decorated gold-filled collar where long brass internal measuring rod cane can be withdrawn, arm hidden inside measure, graduated in inches, designed to discreetly measure deceased for coffin, briarwood shaft, 1" brass ferrule, English, c1890, 35" l, $1,200.

Gadget

Flag, American, 1889, 1-2/3" d round wood handle, straight pulls reveals 12" x 16" cotton 39 star American flag wrapped around thin black pole, top of handle fashioned with recessed sleeve to allow flag to be attached and displayed, 1" white metal collar, brown shaft pained with black stripes, 35" l . . **2,020.00**

Gout foot rest, Continental, c1885, 1-1/2" d x 2-1/8" h round wood knob removable handle, 1-1/2" sliding brass fitting at middle of hardwood shaft, 1" brass ferrule, when parts are removed, cane become low foot stool, 36" l

. . . . **4,370.00**

Gun

American, c1858-61, Remington, 3-1/4" l x 2-1/4" h gutta percha doghead, 1/3" lined nickel collar on gutta percha veneer shaft enclosing percussion gun, shaft unscrews 3-1/2" down for insertion of powder and 44 caliber ball, notched sight pops up at cocking, percussion nib for loading of percussion cap, 1-1/2" l crack in gutta percha at breech infilled, removable 2" steel ferrule stamped "J. F. Thomas, Patent, Feb'y 9, 1858, Remington & Sons, Ilion, NY, 200," 35-3/4" l **6,160.00**

French, c1890, 4-1/4" l x 1-3/4" h "L" shaped staghorn handle, with quarter turn of handle, nickel pepper-box pistol can be withdrawn from shaft, tiny compartment with swing-open cover for loading and removing 6

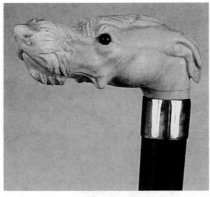

Cane, ivory, bozoi, carved elephant ivory 4-1/4" l x 1-1/2" handle, long-nosed Russian wolfhound, amber glass eyes, 3/4" sterling silver collar, toned rosewood shaft, 1-1/3" white metal and iron ferrule, American, c1890, $1,000.

small caliber shells, 5" stiletto, 1/3" silver collar, marked "Paris, Brevete," and "A. J." (Albert Joubert), black painted hardwood shaft, 1-3/4" white metal ferrule, 35" l **9,500.00**

Harmonica, England, 1885, elephant ivory "L" handle, 4" l x 1-1/3" h, round horn rimmed holes on each side for playing instrument, 1" sterling collar with London hallmarks, thick Malacca shaft, 7/8" white metal ferrule, 35" l . . **2,690.00**

Ladder, attributed to French, c1910, 1-1/2" d x 1" h ebony flat mushroom knob, thick and dark hardwood shaft, 1-2/3" brass ferrule, 3/4" round pin protrudes from ferrule to push into ground to stabilize ladder, at mid-point of shaft is 1" metal ring that removes to open shaft to turn into ladder, four metal crossbars as steps, 37" l . **7,560.00**

Sword, Continental, c1820, 1-1/4" d x 7/8" h elephant ivory knob, whangee bamboo shaft, two horn-rimmed round eyelets, 28-1/2" l blade with partially gilded and engraved blade, 3-1/3" worn brass ferrule, 34-1/2" l . . . **1,570.00**

Violin, Austrian, c1850, mahogany tau handle, 6-1/2" l x 3" h, 3/4" lined nickel collar at which point cane unscrews, chamber with fitted

Cane, ivory, bust of Abraham Lincoln, carved elephant ivory 1-1/4" x 2-1/2" h handle, wearing high-button collar and bow toe, worn 3/8" brass collar, smooth partridgewood shaft, 1-1/4" horn ferrule, American, c1850, 33-1/2" l, $300.

horsehair bow made of exotic dark wood with ebony and ivory fittings, instrument revealed by removing 21-3/4" mahogany panel on side of shaft, internal ebony seats, maple sounding board, bird's eye maple bridge, 1/4" nickel ring that secures panel for closure, 3/4" white metal ferrule, 35" l **10,080.00**

G.A.R., America, c1880, brass "T" handle, 5-1/4" l x 1-7/8" h shaped as Civil War cannon, open touchhole, probably to allow a projectile to be fired from it, thick heavy rosewood shaft, mounted 3" down are brass letters "G.A.R.," brass edge silver shield inscribed "Sergt. Wm. S. Bailey, 3 H. Art., R.I.," 1-1/4" white metal and iron ferrule, 37" l, copies of information about Bailey's life and extensive history of his unit accompany cane . . **1,910.00**

Gold

English, c1860, 1-1/3" d x 1-3/4" h knob, inlaid oval mount on top with painted miniature of young Victorian girl, blue dress, flowers in hand, hair, and on bodice, sides engraved with flowers and shells,

inscribed "G. T. to Y.T.L., 1860," brown hardwood shaft, 1" horn ferrule, 35-3/4" l, marked 14k, but testing shows it is made of very thick layer of rolled gold . . . **620.00**

French, c1900, 1-1/3" d x 2" h rock crystal ball handle, top etched and gold painted with three fancy initials, 1/2" reticulated two-color gold band surrounds ball at midpoint, dec with vine and ribbons, two-color gold cup-shaped collar with French hallmarks, dec with acanthus leaves, raised blossoms, laurel wreath, maccassar ebony shaft, 1" replaced brass ferrule . . . **2,020.00**

Independence Hall Relic, America, 1800-20, 1-1/4" d x 2-1/2" h straight staghorn handle, oblong brass cartouche inlaid on top, 7/8" coil silver collar marked "Independence Hall," oak shaft came from Hall, 3" brass and iron ferrule, 36" l **950.00**

Ivory, carved, figural handle

Continental

Possibly France, c1860, opium pipe, 1-1/3" d x 3-1/2" h

elephant ivory handle, carved and inked on top with fancy initials surmounted by crown, scene around circumference of Napoleonic soldiers at camp in woods, tight rings carved below scene allows handle to unscrew, tiny threaded ivory fitting unscrewed to access vial for opium powder, pipe operates by unscrewing 2-1/2" l ivory ferrule, revealing cork cov horn mouthpiece, when opium powder was ignited, smoke could be drawn down through entire length of cane, fine rosewood shaft, 33" l, strong acrid odor at mouthpiece **7,840.00**

c1895, bulldogs, 3-1/2" l x 3" h elephant ivory, two heads, mouths open, fangs barred, amber eyes, 1" plated gold collar, smooth cartouche and diagonal lines, full bark Malacca shaft, replacement 3/4" grass ferrule, 35-3/4" l **1,120.00**

English

c1884, mermaid, 4-1/3" l x 1" w elephant ivory handle, mermaid sleeping on shell, 2/3" silver collar with owner's name and address, London hallmarks, rosewood shaft, 1" brass ferrule, 36-3/4" l **3,360.00**

c1885, cat, 2" w x 3-1/2" h, yellow glass eyes, prominent whiskers, carved bell peeking out of neck fur, 1/2" silver collar, rosewood

Cane, ivory, falcon and woman, carved elephant ivory 2-1/3" w x 3" h handle, amber glass eyes, 1" silver collar with worn Birmingham hallmarks for 1890s, Malacca shaft, 1-1/8" burnished brass ferrule, $3,400.

Cane, ivory, gargoyle, carved elephant ivory 2" w x 5" h handle, crouching figure, horns, cloven hooves, glass eyes, sitting on stump, hooding pointed tail, thin gold ring collar, ebony shaft with oval gold eyelets, 3/4" brass ferrule, French, c1890, 36" l, $1,100.

Cane, nickel, wax seal, 3-1/4" l x 1-2/3" "T" handle, pointed hound on one end, round textured stamp on other, simulated leather collar marked "Ashford Maker to the Queen," dark bamboo shaft, 1" brass and iron ferrule, Ashford Co, London, c1890, 37-1/3" l, $250.

shaft, 1-1/2" horn ferrule, 38" l
.................**2,360.00**

c1910, Japanese style, octopus, 2-1/4" w x 4-3/4" h elephant ivory, long tentacles extending down ebony shaft and wrapped around it, orange glass eyes, 1-1/8" horn ferrule, 35-1/2" l
.................**4,370.00**

c1919, parrot, 1-1/4" w x 4" h elephant ivory handle, full-bodied, brown glass eyes, perched atop hardwood shaft, 2/3" sterling collar with London hallmarks, shaft worked under finish to simulate snakewood, 1" brass and iron ferrule, 38" l **2,800.00**

French, c1895, boy with rabbit, 1" w x 2-1/3" h elephant ivory handle, finely carved nude child, sitting on plinth, petting rabbit, 1/4" gold collar marked "18 ct" and "Asprey," tan bamboo shaft, 1" brass and iron ferrule, 34-3/4" l **1,680.00**

German, c1880, falconer, 1-1/2" w x 3-1/2" h elephant ivory handle, 18th C nobleman standing under tree holding falcon, dogs at feet staring up at bird, 1/3" gold gilt collar marked "Briggs London," black hardwood shaft, 7/8" horn ferrule, 36" l, handle possibly German, cane fashioned in London
.................**6,385.00**

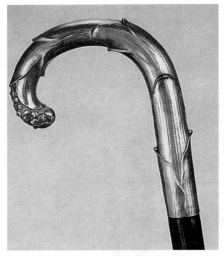

Cane, silver, Art Nouveau vermeil silver, 2/3" w x 6" l crook handle, finished in dull gold in vermeil manner, leafy plant stem motif with 10 silver blossoms at end with cabochon emeralds as their centers, stepped partridgewood shaft, 1" burnished brass ferrule, attributed to France, c1900, 35" l, $1,400.

Japanese

c1885, 1-1/2" w x 5" h elephant ivory handle, three carved monkeys and two rats scrambling among branches, vines, and leaves in confrontation over biwa (loquat fruit), 1/3" silver collar, honey-toned Malacca shaft, 1-1/4" white metal and iron ferrule, 32-1/2" l, cane possibly fashioned in America . **3,360.00**

c1895, thousand faces, 2-1/2" w x 2-1/2" h elephant ivory pistol handle, 25 faces and masks, 3/4" d silver collar initialed for orig owner, figured thick snakewood shaft, 2/3" horn ferrule, 34-1/4" l **2,580.00**

Ivory, silver inlay, American, c1870, 1-1/2" d x 6-1/2" h elephant ivory ball

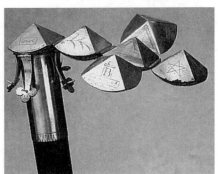

Cane, silver, gadget, c1890, unfolding Masonic ball handle, 1-2/3" d x 3-1/4" h, initialed "R. P." on top for original owner, elaborate "C" scroll decorated, when four silver side latches are opened, ball unfolds to reveal six pyramids, all engraved with secret Masonic symbols, ebonized hardwood shaft, 1" horn ferrule, 35" l, $2,580.

handle, spiral overlaid silver panels with foliate engraving, one inscribed "F. T. Newman" (orig owner), inlay continues down ivory stem with fancy "C" scrolls and bars, 1-1/8" smooth silver collar, ebony shaft, 1-1/8" brass ferrule, 35-1/2" l.................**1,800.00**

Lapis and silver, American, c1900, 7/8" d x 3" h handle, deep blue lapis set in long silver wave-shaped mount marked "Sterling," ebony shaft, 1-1/4" horn ferrule, 35-3/4" l.......**1,915.00**

Porcelain

English, c1860, phrenology head, 1-1/3" w x 2-2/3" h, white, black lettering, gold highlighting, man's head delineated with numbers for different areas, decoder indicating character traits assigned to numbers, rosewood shaft, 7/8" horn ferrule, 36" l **3,250.00**

Meissen, c1885, hand painted, 4-3/4" l x 2" h handle, top painted with scene of lady holding fan, and her hand-maiden, talking to seated gentleman with sword at side, pointing to distant manor, 18th C attire, colorful floral sprays, gold highlights, 1-1/4" gold collar marked by maker, Malacca shaft, 1-1/2" horn ferrule, 34-1/8" h
.................**1,180.00**

Wedgwood, English, c1912, 2" d x 1-1/4" h pale blue and white porcelain knob handle, 1-1/4" sterling silver disk set on top with inscription "Baptist Church Warrington, Presented to Mrs. Margurette Morris, on Placing Foundation Stone, Dec, 12, 1912," Chester hallmarks for 1912, handle sides dec with white raised classical figures, name appears when knob is unscrewed, finely figured snakewood shaft, 2/3" silver collar, 1-1/4" horn ferrule, 34-1/4" l
.................**1,570.00**

Presidential, Grover Cleveland, 6-1/2" l polished staghorn handle, fashioned as arched body of stylized fish, thumb rest carved on one side, 7/8" silver collar inscribed "From James McGowan, Troy, to Grover Cleveland," fine rosewood shaft carved in block letters "Cleveland and Stevenson, Troy, N.Y., The Record," followed by spiral carving in ribbon of all 24 states carried by Cleveland, starting with Alabama and ending with Wisconsin, 1" metal ferrule, 37" l, accompanied by letter of authenticity from grand-daughter Margaret Cleveland **11,200.00**

Russian silver and enamel, c1900, 2/3" d x 4-1/3" long thin silver handle, champleve enamel in red, white, and three shades of blue, dark brown hardwood shaft, 7/8" horn ferrule, 35" l **2,690.00**

Scrimshaw, American, c1864, 1-1/3" d x 1-1/8" h whale ivory knob handle, top with scrimmed spiral sunburst, baleen dot in center, highlighted in red, surrounded by feathery black-inked wreath with red berries, scrimmed around rim "U.S.S. Kearsarge, 1864," with tiny baleen dots, hand fashioned 1/4" ring brass collar on smooth and tapered whalebone shaft with oval brass eyelets, under collar inked scrimshaw "To Capt. John A. Winslow From His Crew," uniform yellow patina, 35-1/4" l, sold with engraved certificate from New York Chamber of Commerce to Captain Winslow and his crew **15,680.00**

Silver

England, attributed to, c1890, 2-1/2" w x 3-3/4" h figural handle, bulging red glass eyes, front legs

Cane, tortoiseshell, crook head of preening swan, 2-1/3" w, 3-1/2" h, 1" gold plated collar with diagonal lines, initialed for original owner, briarwood shaft, 1-1/3" white metal and iron ferrule, American, c1890, minor roughness to tip of beak, some chipping, 35-1/3" l, $650.

tucked under, rear legs extending down black shaft, 1" horn ferrule, 34" l **950.00**

Gorham, Rhode Island, c1900, 1-1/8" d x 6-1/2" l sterling handle, 3/4" faceted amethyst stone inlaid on knob top, stem elaborately chased with fancy dec, Gorham hallmarks, sterling stamp, tightly stepped partridgewood shaft, 3/4" burnished copper ferrule, 36-1/2" l **1,460.00**

Hungarian, c1900, gilt silver, 7/8" d x 5" h handle, small ball top inlaid with 3/8" cabochon garnet, remainder of textured handle fashioned with tiny raised gilt silver balls, dozens of pale blue cabochon turquoise stones, dozens of faceted garnets and amethysts, black enamel shaft, 2-1/8" gilt silver ferrule that matches handle with same inlaid jewels, 35-3/4" l **900.00**

Unger Bros, c1900, 1-1/8" d x 7" h sterling handle, heavily chased in elaborate floral and foliate design, 3/4" ringed collar marked "sterling 925 fine" and round "UB" mark, smooth partridgewood shaft, 1-1/2" white metal and iron ferrule, 34-1/2" l **1,065.00**

Tiffany, American, c1890, 4-1/4" l x 1-1/2" h dark burl "L" handle, 17 smooth solid gold elliptical inlays arranged in lines, 2/3" matching smooth gold collar marked "Tiffany & Co. 18k," stepped partridgewood shaft, 1-1/2" silver and iron ferrule, 34-1/2" l **5,040.00**

Wood, carved, English, c1850, boxwood, thick crook handle, 6" l at arc, top with large male lion holding down snake with one paw while snake wraps around other paw, carving continues at far end with small fox, head and paws protruding from log, 2" further down is carved hand clutching simulated leather top of long twisted cable that continues as rest of shaft, carved cuff with detailed button, ring on hand with small cabochon ring, 3/4" aged metal ferrule, 34" l **5,040.00**

CANTON CHINA

History: Canton china is a type of Oriental porcelain made in the Canton region of China from the late 18th century to the present. It was produced largely for export. Canton china has a hand-decorated light-to dark-blue underglaze-on-white ground. Design

motifs include houses, mountains, trees, boats, and bridges. A design similar to willow pattern is the most common.

Borders on early Canton feature a rain-and-cloud motif (a thick band of diagonal lines with a scalloped bottom). Later pieces usually have a straight-line border.

Early, c1790-1840, plates are very heavy and often have an unfinished bottom, while serving pieces have an overall "orange-peel" bottom. Early covered pieces, such as tureens, vegetable dishes, and sugars, have strawberry finials and twisted handles. Later ones have round finials and a straight, single handle.

Marks: The markings "Made in China" and "China" indicate wares that date after 1891.

Reproduction Alert: Several museum gift shops and private manufacturers are issuing reproductions of Canton china.

Bowl, 9-1/2" d, cut corner, minor int. glaze imperfections, 19th C **900.00**

Box, cov, sq, domed top, cloud-and-rain border on lids, early 19th C, pr **6,270.00**

Coffeepot, 7-1/4" h, mismatched cover **750.00**

Cup, cov, 4" l, 3-1/2" h, handle, repaired lid **165.00**

Dish, leaf shape, 19th C, chips
6-3/4" l **145.00**
8-1/2" l **165.00**

Fruit basket
9-1/4" d, minor chips **690.00**
10-1/2" l, reticulated, undertray **1,100.00**

Milk pitcher, 6-1/8" h, very minor chips **575.00**

Miniature, tureen, underplate, 6-1/2" l, 5" w, 4" h **300.00**

Bottle, bulbous, blue and white, Oriental scene, 9-1/2" h, small rim fleck, $150. Photo courtesy of James D. Julia, Inc.

Plate, Chinese export, blue underglaze decorated on white ground, 6" d, price for pair, $125. Photo courtesy of Sanford Alderfer Auction Company.

Plate, early, c1820-30
  6" d, bread and butter **65.00**
  7-1/2" d, salad **85.00**
  8" d, dessert **95.00**
  9" d, lunch **115.00**
  10" d, cobalt blue underglaze dec, late 19th C **120.00**

Platter
  9-1/2" x 11-1/2", octagonal . . **395.00**
  12-3/4" x 15-3/4", octagonal . **425.00**
  14" x 11-1/2", well and tree, cobalt blue underglaze dec, late 19th C **250.00**
  16" x 19-3/4", octagonal, minor glaze scratches **830.00**

Salt, 3-3/4" l, trench, chips, three-pc set **550.00**

Sauce boat, 6-7/8" w, 8" l, 3-3/8" h, lobed, applied bifurcated handles, rim chips, one handle cracked, price for pr **850.00**

Serving dish
  8-3/4" sq, 19th C, cracks, price for pr **460.00**
  13-1/2" w, 10-3/4" d, 2-1/2" h, oblong, octagonal rim, deep blue dec of

pagodas, boats, and bridge, white ground **110.00**
  15-1/4" x 18-1/4", octagonal, 19th C **650.00**

Shrimp dish, 10-1/4" d, minor edge roughness, pr **690.00**

Tea caddy, cov, 5-1/2" h, octagonal, 19th C **2,645.00**

Tray
  9-3/4" l, 6-3/4" w, rect, 19th C **875.00**
  11-1/4" l, 8-1/4" w, lobed lozenge form, 19th C **875.00**

Tureen, cov, 14" l, 9-3/4" w, 7-3/4" h, stem finial, oval, ftd, hog snout handles **1,265.00**

Vegetable dish, cov, 9-1/2" w, 8" d, 3-1/4" h, diamond shape, scalloped edges, fruit finial, orange peel glaze, unglazed bottom **225.00**

CAPO-DI-MONTE

History: In 1743, King Charles of Naples established a soft-paste porcelain factory near Naples. The firm made figurines and dinnerware. In 1760, many of the workmen and most of the molds were moved to Buen Retiro, near Madrid, Spain. A new factory, which also made hard-paste porcelains, opened in Naples in 1771. In 1834, the Doccia factory in Florence purchased the molds and continued production in Italy.

  Capo-di-Monte was copied heavily by other factories in Hungary, Germany, France, and Italy.

> **Reproduction Alert:** Many of the pieces in today's market are of recent vintage. Do not be fooled by the crown over the "N" mark; it also was copied.

Figure, child with comb, signed "G. Armanis," $165.

Box, cov, 8" d, 4-1/4" h, round, domed lid molded with low relief figures of cherubs with flower baskets, sides similarly molded with cherubs at various artistic pursuits, gilt-metal rim mounts, int. painted with floral sprigs, late 19th C **475.00**

Creamer and sugar, mythological raised scene, dragon handles, claw feet, lion finial, 5-1/2" x 6" creamer, 6-1/4" x 6" cov sugar **250.00**

Dresser set, mythological raised scene, pair of 4" d, 7" h perfume bottles with figural stoppers, 5" d, 4" h cov powder jar, 30" l x 15" w tray . . . **500.00**

Ferner, 11" l, oval, relief molded and enameled allegorical figures, full relief female mask at each end **120.00**

Plate, Chinese export, blue underglaze decorated on white ground, 6" d, price for pair, $125. Photo courtesy of Sanford Alderfer Auction Company.

Figure, old man sleeping on bench, suitcase at his feet, 8-1/2" w, 7" h, $90. Photo courtesy of Joy Luke Auctions.

Stein, half liter, The Lion Hunt, body with figural battle scene in relief, elephant handle, lion finial on lid, $395. Photo courtesy of Sanford Alderfer Auction Company.

Figure, sgd "G. Armani," 7-1/2" l, 6-1/2" h, mare and foal **210.00**

Lamp, table, 25" h, figural Bacchus, female, and grapes **1,300.00**

Plate, 8-3/8" d, each with Capo-di-Monte crest at top, pair of swans, pair of cranes, crimson, blue, yellow, and burnt-orange flowers on border, gold trim, minor wear, price for eight-pc set **1,100.00**

Snuffbox, 3-1/4" d, hinged lid, cartouche shape, molded basketweave and flowerhead ext., painted int. with court lady and page examining portrait of gentlemen, gold mountings, c1740, minor restoration **1,650.00**

Stein, 7-1/2" h, lion-hunt scene, lion on lid, elephant-trunk handle **400.00**

Urn, cov, 21-1/8" h, ovoid, central-molded frieze of Nerieds and putti, molded floral garlands, gadroon upper section, acanthus-molded lower section, socle foot with putti, sq plinth base, applied ram's-head handles, domed cov, acorn finial, underglaze crowned "N" mark, minor chips and losses, pr **1,650.00**

CARLSBAD CHINA

History: Because of changing European boundaries during the last 100 years, German-speaking Carlsbad has found itself located first in the Austro-Hungarian Empire, then in Germany, and currently in the Czech Republic. Carlsbad was one of the leading pottery manufacturing centers in Bohemia.

Plate, Chinese export, blue underglaze decorated on white ground, 6" d, price for pair, $125. Photo courtesy of Sanford Alderfer Auction Company.

Wares from the numerous Carlsbad potteries are lumped together under the term "Carlsbad China." Most pieces on the market are post-1891, although several potteries date to the early 19th century.

Bowl, 14" d, handles, marked "Imperial H&C Carlsbad Austria," numbers "2552" and "18," wear to gold edge, repaired chip **50.00**

Butter dish, cov, 7-1/4" d, pink flowers, green leaves, wavy gold lines, white ground **65.00**

Chocolate pot, cov, 10" h, blue, scenic portrait, marked "Carlsbad Victoria" **115.00**

Creamer and sugar, Bluebird pattern, marked "Victoria Carlsbad" **70.00**

Ewer, 14" h, handles, light green, floral dec, gold trim, marked "Carlsbad Victoria" **85.00**

Game plates, 8" sq, each hand painted with gold trim, light and dark gray corners, center with game birds, gold outlines, mauve circular mark "Carlsbad Mark & Gutherz," price for 11-pc set **700.00**

Hair receiver, 4" d, cobalt-blue flowers, emb basketweave at top, gold trim, white ground **50.00**

Oyster plate, 8-1/4" d, five wells plus center well, stylized pink-and-blue peonies, green leaves, gold accents, marked "Marx & Gutherz" **120.00**

Pin tray, 8-1/2" l, irregular scalloped shape, roses, green leaves, white ground, marked "Victoria Carlsbad Austria" **40.00**

Platter, 13" x 18", hand-painted pink-and-blue flowers, marked "Mark & Gutherz, Carlsbad," imp "LS&S," early 1900s **60.00**

Sugar shaker, 5-1/2" h, egg shape, floral dec **70.00**

Urn, 14-1/2" h, rose bouquet, shaded ivory ground, marked "Carlsbad Austria" **155.00**

CARNIVAL GLASS

History: Carnival glass, an American invention, is colored-pressed glass with a fired-on iridescent finish. It was first manufactured about 1905 and was immensely popular both in America and abroad. More than 1,000 different patterns have been identified. Production of old carnival-glass patterns ended in 1930.

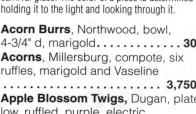

For more information, see this book.

Most of the popular patterns of carnival glass were produced by five companies: Dugan, Fenton, Imperial, Millersburg, and Northwood.

Marks: Northwood patterns frequently are found with the "N" trademark. Dugan used a diamond trademark on several patterns.

Notes: Color is the most important factor in pricing carnival glass. The color of a piece is determined by holding it to the light and looking through it.

Acorn Burrs, Northwood, bowl, 4-3/4" d, marigold **30.00**

Acorns, Millersburg, compote, six ruffles, marigold and Vaseline **3,750.00**

Apple Blossom Twigs, Dugan, plate, low, ruffled, purple, electric purple-and-blue highlights **225.00**

Basket of Roses, Northwood, bonbon, stippled, amethyst **475.00**

Beaded Cable, Northwood
Candy dish, ftd, amethyst.... **70.00**
Rose bowl, aqua opalescent **400.00**

Blackberry Block, Fenton, tumbler,
blue **45.00**

Blackberry Spray, Fenton, hat,
6-1/2" h, Vaseline, sq, four sides up
.... **40.00**

Blackberry Wreath, Millersburg
Bowl, 7-1/2" d, six ruffles, green
.... **65.00**
Bowl, 10-1/2" d, three-in-one edge,
green **165.00**
Ice cream bowl, 8" d, green, some
wear to berries **85.00**
Ice cream sauce, 5-1/2" d, dark
marigold **110.00**
Sauce, 6-1/4" d, six ruffles, green,
satiny finish............. **65.00**

Blossomtime, Northwood, compote,
marigold **200.00**

Bouquet, Fenton
Tumbler, blue **55.00**
Water pitcher, marigold..... **150.00**

Bull's Eye & Beads, Imperial, vase,
7" h, flared, dark marigold...... **40.00**

Bushel Basket, Northwood, round,
sapphire.................**1,350.00**

Butterfly & Fern, Fenton
Tumbler, green **55.00**
Water pitcher, blue, radium finish
.... **800.00**

Cherries, Dugan
Banana boat, electric blue, purple
highlights, three ftd....... **275.00**
Sauce, low, ruffled, 6" d, purple
.... **120.00**

Chrysanthemum, Nu-Art, chop plate,
marigold **450.00**

*Atlantic City Elks, 1911, plate, blue,
$1,200. Photo courtesy of Burns
Auction.*

*Apple Twigs, plate, amethyst, $500.
Photo courtesy of Burns Auction.*

Concave Diamond, Northwood
Tumbler, celeste blue........ **30.00**
Tumble-up, russet green **900.00**
Vase, 6" h, celeste blue **175.00**

Courthouse, Millersburg, ice cream
bowl, 7-1/2" d, amethyst, lettered
example **900.00**

Daisy Wreath, Westmoreland, 8-1/2" d,
ice cream bowl, moonstone **110.00**

Dandelion, Northwood, tumbler, purple
.... **55.00**

Diamond Points, Northwood, vase,
10-1/4" h, aqua opalescent, iridescent
and opalescent from top to base
.... **1,650.00**

Diamond Rib, Fenton, vase, 9" h,
purple..................... **40.00**

Diving Dolphins, Millersburg,
compote, Rosiland int., green **1,700.00**

Dragon and Lotus, Fenton, bowl, red
.... **750.00**

Drapery, Northwood, rose bowl, aqua
opalescent, light butterscotch overlay
.... **250.00**

Embossed Scroll
Bowl, 7" d, Hobstar & Tassel exterior,
electric purple.......... **400.00**
Sauce, 5" d, purple **45.00**

Embroidered Mums, Northwood, Plate,
9" d, ice green **1,100.00**

Enameled Grape, Northwood, water
set, six pcs, blue, enamel dec .. **800.00**

Fanciful, Dugan, bowl, low, ruffled,
frosty white, pink, blue, and green
highlights **115.00**

Fashion, Imperial
Punch cup, marigold........ **28.00**
Tumbler, marigold **90.00**
Water set, marigold, seven-pc
matched set **150.00**

Fine Cut & Roses, Northwood, rose
bowl, purple **135.00**

Fine Rib, Fenton, vase
10" h, powder blue **60.00**
10-1/2" h, blue **85.00**
10-1/2" h, cherry red....... **225.00**
11-3/4" h, vaseline, marigold overlay
.... **70.00**

Fishscale & Beads, Dugan
Plate, 7" d, electric purple .. **575.00**
Plate, 7" d, marigold, satin irid **45.00**
Plate, 7-1/2" d, low, ruffled, purple
.... **325.00**

Flowers, Fenton, rose bowl, blue,
multicolored irid...............**110.00**

Flute, Imperial, toothpick holder, blue
.... **925.00**

Frosted Block, Imperial, rose bowl,
deep marigold................ **30.00**

Fruits & Flowers, Northwood, bonbon,
handled, lavender **200.00**

Good Luck, Northwood
Bowl, 9" d, ruffled, ribbed ext.,
marigold............... **175.00**
Bowl, pie crust edge, blue .. **350.00**
Bowl, ruffled, electric blue .. **435.00**

Grape, Imperial
Decanter, electric purple, stopper
missing................. **85.00**
Punch set, marigold **300.00**
Water carafe, emerald green
.... **4,300.00**

Grape & Cable, Fenton, bowl, 6-1/2" d,
smoky blue **40.00**

Grape and Cable, Northwood
Banana boat, purple....... **195.00**
Cracker jar, cov, handles, amethyst
.... **275.00**
Humidor, amethyst **325.00**
Pin tray, blue............. **400.00**
Plate, ruffled, stippled, sapphire
.... **2,000.00**
Punch bowl set, bowl, base, 12
cups, marigold......... **2,300.00**
Sweetmeat compote, cov, purple
.... **170.00**

*Butterfly, Fenton, bonbon dish, two
handles, purple, 7-1/4" w, $95.*

Farmyard bowl, amethyst, $1,200. Photo courtesy of Burns Auction.

Grape & Gothic Arches, Northwood, tumbler, electric blue **45.00**

Grape Arbor, Northwood
    Tankard pitcher, dark marigold, radium finish **575.00**
    Tankard pitcher, purple, blue irid highlights, bronze highlights at base **400.00**

Grapevine & Lattice, Dugan, tumbler, white **225.00**

Grape Wreath, Millersburg
    Bowl, 8-1/2" d, three-in-one-edge, green, radium finish **135.00**
    Bowl, 9" d, six ruffles, marigold, blue radium finish **65.00**
    Ice cream bowl, 8" d, amethyst, radium finish **155.00**

Grape Wreath Variant, Millersburg, bowl, 7" d, three-in-one edge, Feather center, purple, radium finish **115.00**

Greek Key, Northwood, plate, blue **400.00**

Heavy Grape, Imperial
    Chop plate, 11" d, electric purple **400.00**
    Chop plate, 11" d, helios green, flat, wear on high points **135.00**
    Nappy, 5" d, electric purple . . **110.00**
    Plate, 8" d, electric purple . . . **165.00**

Heavy Iris, Dugan, tumbler, amethyst **75.00**

Heavy Pineapple, Fenton, bowl, ftd, 10" d, amber, satiny iridescence **500.00**

Hobnail, Millersburg, spittoon, marigold **700.00**

Hobnail Swirl, Millersburg, vase, 11" h, amethyst, radium iridescence . . **250.00**

Hobstar & Feather, Millersburg
    Compote, round, clear **75.00**
    Compote, round, frosted **135.00**
    Punch cup, crystal **25.00**
    Rose bowl, large **3,200.00**

    Tumbler, crystal, clear **65.00**
    Tumbler, crystal, frosted **125.00**

Holly, Fenton
    Compote, ruffled, lime green, marigold overlay **100.00**
    Jack-in-the-pulpit hat, crimped edge, marigold **50.00**

Holly Sprig, Millersburg
    Bowl, 6-1/2" d, deep, tight crimped edge, amethyst **120.00**
    Nappy, tri-corn, handle, green **160.00**

Holly Whirl, Millersburg
    Bonbon, Issac Benesch 54th Anniversary adv, marigold . **150.00**
    Bowl, 9-1/2" d, ruffled, marigold, radium finish **85.00**
    Nappy, two handles, deep, flared, amethyst, radium finish . . . **100.00**

Homestead, plate, electric purple **2,300.00**

Horse Head Medallion, Fenton
    Jack-in-the-pulpit bowl, ftd, marigold **75.00**
    Plate, 7-1/2" d, crystal **115.00**

Inverted Strawberry, Cambridge, sauce dish, 5" d, marigold **25.00**

Kittens, Fenton
    Bowl, six ruffles, marigold . . . **135.00**
    Cup and saucer, marigold . . **245.00**
    Toothpick holder, ruffled, marigold, radium finish **115.00**

Leaf and Little Flowers, Millersburg
    Compote, flared, deep, green, radium finish with bright blue highlights **500.00**
    Compote, flared, deep, marigold, radium finish **225.00**
    Compote, six ruffles, amethyst **475.00**
    Compote, six ruffles, dark marigold **300.00**

Hobnail water pitcher, Millersburg, blue, $4,000. Photo courtesy of Burns Auction.

Orange Tree Orchard, pitcher, blue, $2,500. Photo courtesy of Burns Auction.

Leaf Columns, Northwood, vase, 10-1/2" h, radium green, multicolored irid, slightly flared top **135.00**

Leaf Tiers, Fenton, tumbler, ftd, marigold **80.00**

Lotus & Poinsettia, Fenton, bowl, 10" d, ruffled, ftd, dark marigold . **75.00**

Many Fruits, Dugan, punch bowl and base, white **1,500.00**

Many Stars, Millersburg
    Bowl, adv, Bernheimer Bros, blue **3,000.00**
    Bowl, 10" d, blue **3,700.00**

Morning Glory, Imperial
    Funeral vase, 16-1/2" h, 4-3/4" d base, purple **250.00**
    Vase, 6-1/2" h, olive green **60.00**

Night Stars, Millersburg, bonbon, two handles, two sides, olive green, blue radium finish **800.00**

Ohio Star, Millersburg
    Cider pitcher, 11" h tankard, crystal **250.00**
    Cider set, six pcs, 10" h tankard, crystal, chip on one tumbler **625.00**
    Compote, 4-1/2" d, crystal **35.00**
    Punch set, 10 pcs, crystal . **1,550.00**
    Toothpick holder, crystal **115.00**

Open Rose, Imperial
    Bowl, 8-1/2" d, electric purple . **85.00**
    Plate, 9" d, marigold **45.00**
    Rose bowl, electric purple int. and ext. **625.00**

Optic & Buttons, Imperial, rose bowl, marigold **30.00**

Orange Tree, Fenton
    Bowl, 9" d, ruffled, Tree Trunk center, white, blue irid **90.00**
    Mug, standard size, amber, weak impression **55.00**
    Plate, 9-1/2" d, Tree Trunk center, white, frosty irid **185.00**
    Powder box, cov, blue **115.00**
    Punch set, punch bowl, stand, 12 cups, marigold **395.00**
    Wine, blue **60.00**

Peacock, Millersburg

Berry bowl, individual, 5" d, purple, radium finish **115.00**

Berry bowl, master, 9" d, purple, radium finish, small nick . . . **225.00**

Bowl, 10" d, three-in-one edge, green, radium finish, blue highlights **425.00**

Ice cream bowl, 5" d, marigold, satiny irid **200.00**

Peacock at Fountain, Dugan, tumbler, blue **35.00**

Peacock at Fountain, Northwood

Punch cup, white **20.00**

Tumbler, amethyst **25.00**

Water pitcher, amethyst **250.00**

Peacock at Urn, Fenton

Compote, stemmed, celeste blue, marigold overlay **150.00**

Plate, 9" d, blue, bright red, blue, and green highlights **500.00**

Peacock at Urn, Millersburg

Berry bowl, master, 9" d, flared, marigold, radium irid with blue highlights **275.00**

Bowl, 8" d, blue **2,100.00**

Bowl, 10-1/2" d, six ruffles, green, satin finish, bee, no beading **250.00**

Compote, stemmed, ruffled, large, green **1,500.00**

Compote, stemmed, ruffled, large, marigold **2,300.00**

Ice cream bowl, 9-3/4" d, amethyst, radium finish, bee, no beading **225.00**

Sauce, 6" d, ruffled, blue, no bee, no beading **1,050.00**

Peacock Gardens, Fenton, vase, marigold **15,000.00**

Peacocks on Fence (Northwood Peacocks), Northwood

Bowl, aqua opalescent . . . **1,100.00**

Plate, blue **400.00**

Persian Garden, Dugan, plate, 6-1/2" d, marigold **40.00**

Persian Medallion, Fenton

Bonbon, two handles, vaseline, marigold overlay **140.00**

Chop plate, blue **195.00**

Hair receiver, frosty white . . . **130.00**

Plate, 6" d, marigold **25.00**

Petals, Northwood, compote, 7", marigold **30.00**

Peter Rabbit, Fenton, bowl, ruffled **1,800.00**

Pinecone, Fenton, plate, 6" d, marigold **40.00**

Plume Panels, Fenton, vase, 11" h, green **95.00**

Pond Lily, Fenton, calling card tray, two handles, white, weak irid **25.00**

Poppy, Millersburg, compote, flared, dark marigold **475.00**

Poppy Show, Northwood

Bowl, electric blue **2,300.00**

Plate, amethyst **750.00**

Plate, ice blue **1,800.00**

Rays & Ribbons, Millersburg

Bowl, 9-1/2" d, ruffled, crimped edge, Cactus exterior, purple, blue radium irid **175.00**

Bowl, 9-3/4" d, three-in-one edge, marigold **140.00**

Ribbon Tie, Fenton, bowl, three-in-one edge, low, blue **160.00**

Ripple, Imperial, funeral vase, 17" h, marigold **115.00**

Rosalind, Millersburg

Bowl, 10-1/2" d, six ruffles, amethyst **225.00**

Stag & Holly, bowl, purple, 11" d, $195.

Bowl, 10-1/2" d, marigold satin **125.00**

Jelly, stemmed, flared, deep, 8-1/2" h, amethyst **3,500.00**

Rose Show, Northwood

Bowl, ruffled, aqua opalescent **2,000.00**

Bowl, ruffled, sapphire **3,500.00**

Plate, blue **600.00**

Plate, ice blue **2,100.00**

Rose Spray, Fenton

Goblet, marigold **30.00**

Jack-in-the-pulpit, celeste blue **65.00**

Round-Up, Dugan

Bowl, low, ruffled, peach opalescent **250.00**

Plate, 9" d, blue, basketweave back, blue-and-pink highlights . . **275.00**

Rustic, Fenton

Funeral vase, 18-1/2" h, blue, electric-blue highlights **675.00**

Swung vase, 15" h, 4-1/4" d base, green, radium multicolored irid **110.00**

Seacoast, Millersburg, pin tray, amethyst **550.00**

Seaweed, Millersburg

Bowl, 10-1/4" d, three-in-one edge, marigold, satiny irid **350.00**

Plate, 9" d, flared, marigold **1,600.00**

Sauce, 5-1/2" d, ice-cream shape, dark marigold **850.00**

Stag & Holly, Fenton

Bowl, 10" d, ruffled, ftd, powder blue, marigold overlay **200.00**

Bowl, 10-1/2" d, crimped edge, ftd, marigold **125.00**

Bowl, 11-1/4" d, ruffled, ftd, light-blue aqua base, marigold overlay **200.00**

Stippled Petals, Dugan, plate, purple, dome ftd, tightly crimped edge. **750.00**

Stippled Rays, Fenton

Ice cream bowl, 6" d, cherry red **450.00**

Plate, red **750.00**

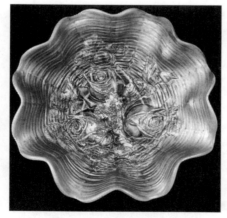

Peacock on the Fence, plate, blue, $400. Photo courtesy of Burns Auction.

Rose Show plate, ice green opal, $7,500. Photo courtesy of Burns Auction.

Strawberry, Northwood

Bowl, 8" d, pie crust edge, purple
. . . .**90.00**

Plate, 9" d, basketweave back, dark marigold, etched "St. Joe, Mich"
. . . .**155.00**

Plate, 9-1/4" d, basketweave back, green **235.00**

Strawberry Wreath, Millersburg

Bowl, 9" d, low-crimped ruffled, purple **185.00**

Compote, six ruffles, dark marigold
. . . .**175.00**

Compote, six ruffles, green . .**400.00**

Sauce, 5" sq, crimped edge, green
. . . .**650.00**

Swirl Hobnail, Millersburg, rose bowl, purple **275.00**

Ten Mums, Fenton

Bowl, 9" d, three-in-one edge, green
. . . .**100.00**

Bowl, 10" d, six ruffles edge, emerald-green base, multicolored irid **350.00**

Three Fruits, Northwood

Bowl, eight ruffles, stippled, green
. . . .**300.00**

Plate, stippled, amethyst **300.00**

Plate, stippled, aqua opalescent
. . . .**3,400.00**

Tiger Lily, Imperial, tumbler, marigold
. . . .**75.00**

Tree Trunk, Northwood

Funeral vase, 10-1/2" h, aqua opalescent, butterscotch overlay, opalescence extending to base
. . . .**950.00**

Funeral vase, 12-1/2" h at back, 10-1/2" h at front, green, radium finish **425.00**

Swung vase, 11" h, blue, radium electric blue highlights **225.00**

Trout and Fly, Millersburg

Bowl, 9" d, three-in-one edge, light amethyst **700.00**

Ice cream bowl, 8-1/4" l, marigold, satiny finish **525.00**

Ice cream bowl, 8-1/2" l, green, satiny finish, bruise on base
. . . .**625.00**

Wild Flower, Northwood, compote, stemmed, light marigold. **65.00**

Wild Rose, Northwood, rose bowl, ftd, stippled rays int., electric purple
. . . .**650.00**

Wild Strawberry, Northwood, plate, 8" d, hand grip, basketweave back, electric purple **325.00**

Windmill, Imperial

Pitcher, marigold **65.00**

Sauce, 5" d, purple **55.00**

Tumbler, purple. **75.00**

Wishbone, Northwood, bowl, low, ftd, ice blue **1,000.00**

Wishbone & Spades, Dugan, chop plate, 10-3/4" d, plain back, purple, with electric purple and blue highlights
. . . .**900.00**

Wreath of Roses, Fenton, punch cups, Vintage interior

Blue. **40.00**

Green **40.00**

Zig-Zag, Millersburg

Bowl, 10" d, three-in-one edge, amethyst. **400.00**

Bowl, tri-corn, crimped edge, amethyst. **1,050.00**

CAROUSEL FIGURES

History: By the late 17th century, carousels were found in most capital cities of Europe. In 1867, Gustav Dentzel carved America's first carousel. Other leading American firms include Charles I. D. Looff, Allan Herschell, Charles Parker, and William F. Mangels.

Notes: Since carousel figures were repainted annually, original paint is not a critical factor to collectors. "Park paint" indicates layers of accumulated paint; "stripped" means paint has been removed to show carving; "restored" involves stripping and repainting in the original colors.

Camel

European, 1890 . . . .**2,400.00**

*Horse, Charles Looff-style jumper, painted dark gray, yellow-trimmed aqua saddle, c1900, displayed on brass Damascus-style pole on pedestal base, from the Whalom Park carousel, Fitchburg, Mass, restored, 58" l, 61" h, **$2,820.** Photo courtesy of James D. Julia, Inc.*

Loeff. **7,000.00**

Morris, E. Joy. **8,000.00**

Chariot bench

Loeff, gilded **625.00**

Parker, C. W. **12,500.00**

Spillman, with flowers **300.00**

Unknown maker, one panel having applied carved flowers, other side with applied carved eagle and horse, 52" x 29" **800.00**

Cow, Bayol, France **5,000.00**

Elephant, fiberglass **600.00**

Giraffe, old mottled painted surface, carved mane, attributed to Ohio, c1880-90, some losses, saddle and tail missing, 39" l, 10" d, 53" h . . .**6,325.00**

Goat, Loeff **7,500.00**

Horse, jumper

Anderson, J. R. **5,000.00**

Bayol, France **3,000.00**

Carmel. **3,700.00**

Dentzel, top knot **5,000.00**

Herschell, Allen, all wood, 1920
. . . .**2,000.00**

Herschell, Allen, metal, restored
. . . .**800.00**

Herschell-Spillman, North Tonawanda, NY, orange, green, and blue, 60" x 56" x 12" cast iron stand **2,750.00**

Illions, from Willow Grove Amusement Park, Willow Grove, PA
. . . .**4,750.00**

Ortega, jumper **300.00**

Parker, C. W., inside jumper, carved, sgd on shoes "C. W. Parker, Leavenworth, Kansas," early worn paint, brown body, black mane and tail, relief-carved saddle blanket, green, yellow, and red saddle, incised stars, red-and-yellow bridle, glass eyes, black-enameled steel base with pole with brass-spiral casing, 62" w, 36" h horse, 101" h pole **5,500.00**

P.T.C. **3,250.00**

Spillman, restored **3,300.00**

Stein & Goldstein. **2,750.00**

Horse, prancer

Dentzel, orig paint **8,000.00**

Hubner, fully restored **4,250.00**

Loeff, Charles, attributed to, outside prancer, carved, repainted in white, carved black mane, horsehair tail, blue-and-gray relief-carved straps and saddle, plaid saddle blanket, red-and-gold detailing, cobalt-blue faceted jewel on outside, glass eyes, 57" w, 55-1/2" h, enameled steel base and pole with brass-spiral casing, 90" h pole . . **2,750.00**

Horse, stander

Dentzel, Gustav, Germantown, PA, c1900-10, flowing mane, double eagle back saddle, outside row, white, green, yellow, and gray over earlier pink paint, 57" l, 12" w, 58" h **10,350.00**

Looff, Charles, c1905-10, cantle carving behind saddle, flowing mane, second row figure, gray and pink over old pale blue paint, 65" l, 13" w, 48" h **3,750.00**

Morris, E. J. **10,500.00**

Spillman, animal pelt **4,600.00**

Stein & Goldstein **10,500.00**

Indian Pony

Parker, C. W., pelt saddle . . **9,000.00**

Spillman **4,500.00**

Panel, carved wood

37-1/2" x 45", cowboy on bucking bronco in panoramic view . **200.00**

63" x 13", cherub at top, carved leaves overall **450.00**

Pig

Dentzel, restored **12,000.00**

Spillman, with pear **5,000.00**

Rooster, carved, c1900 . . . . **18,500.00**

CASTOR SETS

History: A castor set consists of matched condiment bottles held within a frame or holder. The bottles are for condiments such as salt, pepper, oil, vinegar, and mustard. The most commonly found castor sets consist of three, four, or five glass bottles in a silver-plated frame.

Although castor sets were made as early as the 1700s, most of the sets encountered today date from 1870 to 1915, the period when they enjoyed their greatest popularity.

2-bottle, English, two cut-glass condiment jars, rect oak caddy mounted with silver-plate frame, upright

Caster set, two cut glass bottles with original stoppers, silver-plated frame, one bottle stained, 9-1/2" h, $65. Photo courtesy of James D. Julia, Inc.

handle, decorative strapwork and plain central shield, four ball feet, late 19th C, 7-7/8" l, 4-3/8" d, 10-5/8" h **500.00**

3-bottle, Bohemian, three shouldered 14" h decanters, flashed blue, green, and cranberry, cut with circles, etched Greek key band, silver-plated stand with tall central handle above three cylindrical wells, with geometric engine turning, borders with fruiting grapevine, three grapevine feet, late 19th C, 10-1/4" w, 20-1/2" h **865.00**

3-bottle, clear, Daisy-and-Button pattern, toothpick holder center, matching glass holder **125.00**

4-bottle, clear, mold blown, pewter lids and frame, domed based, loop handle, marked "I. Trask," early 19th C, 8" h **320.00**

4-bottle, cranberry bottles and jars, clear pressed-glass frame, silver-plated look handle, two brass caps, one pewter, 9-1/2" h **275.00**

4-bottle, ruby stained, Ruby-Thumbprint pattern, glass frame **360.00**

5-bottle, clear, Bellflower pattern, pressed stoppers, pewter frame with pedestal **295.00**

5-bottle, clear, allover cut linear and geometric design, SS mounts and frame, shell-shaped foot, English hallmarks, c1750, 8-1/2/" h **625.00**

5-bottle, etched, wreath-and-polka-dots pattern, rib-trimmed frame **195.00**

Horse, Philadelphia Toboggan Co., carved and painted, C1918, 70" l, 65" h, **$11,000.**

Caster set, three glass bottles, cranberry, 2" d x 1" h open salt, top of 3" h pepper shaker and 3" mustard pot, and 4" x 4" x 4" holder marked "EPSN," impressed maker's mark on base "J B C & S Ltd," $385. Photo courtesy of Clarence and Betty Maier.

Caster set, five glass bottles, silver-plated stand, engraved "Independence Day 1776 – Centennial 1876," **$300.** *Photo courtesy of Joy Luke Auctions.*

6-bottle, cut, diamond-point panels, rotating sterling-silver frame, allover flowers, paw feet, loop handle, Gorham Mfg. Co., c1880, 11-1/2" h . . . **2,500.00**

CATALOGS

History: The first American mail-order catalog was issued by Benjamin Franklin in 1744. This popular advertising tool helped to spread inventions, innovations, fashions, and necessities of life to rural America. Catalogs were profusely illustrated and are studied today to date an object, identify its manufacturer, study its distribution, and determine its historical importance.

Additional Listings: See *Warman's Americana & Collectibles* for more examples.

Adviser: Kenneth Schneringer.

Atlas Tack Corp, Fairhaven, MA, 1933 to 1947, 27 pgs, 8-3/4" x 11-1/4", add-to catalog and price lists of hardware jobbing items, color illus of cobblers nails, carpet tacks, upholstery nails, clout nails, escutcheon pins, etc. **12.00**

Altbach & Sons, Chicago, IL, 1927, 152 pgs, 8-3/4" x 11-3/4", wholesale jewelers catalog, illus of jewelry, cigarette cases, flasks, etc. **55.00**

Baraca & Philathea Supply, Syracuse, NY, 1923, 32 pgs, 3-1/2" x 6", illus price list of items, memberships, charters, cuts of class pins, watch charms, books, novelties, celluloid goods, class and secretary's helps, rings, banners, festoons, felt banners, etc. **24.00**

Cedar Rapids Pump & Supply, Cedar Rapids, IA, 1924, 524 pgs, 6" x 9", *Cat. No. 14,* plumbing, heating, mill and well supplies, bathtubs, showers, etc., hard cover **32.00**

Dent Hardware Co., Fullerton, PA, c1930, 32 pgs, 6" x 9", Vol. 2, marble and slate stall fittings and trimmings, wardrobe hooks, towel hooks, etc. **18.00**

George H. Wahn Co., Boston, MA, c1920, 84 pgs, 7-3/4" x 10-1/2", *Specialty Catalogue No. 2, Electrical Goods,* hair dryer, vibrators, iron, heating pad, toasters, plate warmer, etc. **45.00**

Geo. W. Peck Co., Bath, ME, 1894, 22 pgs, 5-3/4" x 8-1/2", hardware goods at its five stores, wraps dusted **45.00**

G. I. Sellers & Sons, Co., Elwood, IN, 1930, 16 pgs, 8-1/2" x 11", *Sellers Catalog of Kitchen Furniture & Sales Manual,* two pgs price list laid-in, colored cuts of kitchen ensembles and "klearfront" kitchen cabinets, utility closets, base units, dinettes, buffets, etc. **50.00**

Hendee Manufacturing Co., Springfield, MA, c1916-20, 24 pgs, 7-3/4" x 9-3/4", *Indian Motorcycle,* claiming "The fastest time ever made was an Indian in 35 seconds, 1 mile," introducing Indian Scout, illus of several models **500.00**

J. R. Clancy, Inc., Syracuse, NY, 1928, 64 pgs, 6" x 9", *Cat. No. 36,* theatrical stage hardware, cuts of steel stage screws, extension braces, curtain rigging, etc. **18.00**

Miller Stockman Supply Co., Denver, CO, 1954, 64 pgs, 8" x 10-1/2", mail-out with label, Cat, No. 96, Spring, cowboy and cowgirl clothing, Western style hats, access **32.00**

National Cloak & Suit Co., New York, NY, 1915, 162 pgs, 7-1/4" x 10", *Fall & Winter New York Fashions for Women,* includes some men styles **45.00**

NY Yacht, Launch & Engine, New York, NY, early 1900, 32 pgs, 6" x 9-1/2", 20th C motors, yachts, launches, boat parts **195.00**

Optical Sign Service Co., New York, NY, c1928, 4 pgs, 8-1/2" x 11", Practo canteen-shaped adv Monax glass globes, five color illus **45.00**

Oswego Tool Co., Oswego, NY, 1929, 43 pgs, 6" x 9-1/4", tools for boilermakers, machinists and pipeworkers, wraps loose **35.00**

Rainbo Paper Favor Works, Chicago, IL, c1933, 64 pgs, 5-1/2" x 8-1/4", mail-out envelope, Cat. No. 57, Dance & Party Favors, holiday decs, eight pgs of Halloween dec, party assortments, paper hats, supplies, decorations, flags, bunting, patriotic novelties **35.00**

Roger & Gallet, New York, NY, 1914, 45 pgs, 5-1/2" x 8", *Wholesale Price List of Paris Perfumes,* description and prices on one page, illus of perfume bottles on opposite sheet, toilet waters, colognes, bath salts, hair tonic, etc. **125.00**

Royal Manufacturing Co., Detroit, MI, 1896, 60 pgs, 9-1/2" x 12", *Illustrated Cat. & Price List of Silverware, Book of Rare Bargains,* dishes, cake baskets, pitchers, teapots, casters, butter dishes, carving sets, etc., light tears at edges, shows some use, folded in vertical center. **175.00**

Stewart & McQuire, New York, NY, no date, eight pgs, 8-1/4" x 11", cigarette machines, with protection against slugs and spurious coins, delivers a book of matches with each purchase, seven models illus, highlighted with silver gilt color **45.00**

Syracuse Rubber Co., Syracuse, NY, 1897, 98 pgs, 4-3/4" x 7-3/4", *Rubber & Oil Clothing,* Mackintoches, horse and wagon covers, hats, clothing, nursery and hospital goods, hunting coats, furniture tips, bicycle tires, foot balls, baby items, wraps faded, chips at edges **65.00**

Hendee Manufacturing Co., Springfield, MA, c1916-20, 24 pgs, 7-3/4" x 9-3/4", Indian Motorcycle, claiming "The fastest time ever made was an Indian in 35 seconds, 1 mile," introducing Indian Scout, illus of several models, **$500.** *Photo courtesy of Kenneth Schneringer.*

Thwing Instrument Co., Philadelphia, PA, c1916, 46 pgs, 8" x 11", *General Cat. No. 8,* pyrometers for measuring temperatures, graphic records of temperatures, cuts of thermoelectric, galvanometer, indicators, polarity, thermocouplers, etc. **24.00**

W. H. Frear & Co., Troy, NY, 1903, 152 pgs, 8" x 10-1/4", *Fall & Winter Catalog of Clothing for Women and Girls,* illus of clothing, hand fans, embroideries, bird cages, buttons, toiletries, handkerchiefs, collars, cuffs, trunks, furniture, etc., some roughness to binding **48.00**

Ward-Stilson Co., Anderson, IN, 1920, 112 pgs, 9-1/4" x 12-1/4", *Cat. No. 80, Masonic Lodge Supplies,* cuts of costumes, aprons, jewelry, stereopticans, candlesticks, wigs, beards, tools and gauges, etc. . . **85.00**

White, Van Glahn & Co., New York, NY, 1911, 584 pgs, 8-1/4" x 11", *Cat. No. 99, Merchandise, Clothing & Shoes for the Family,* illus of weather vanes, tools, farm implements, jewelry, silver ware, hollow ware, etc. **100.00**

White Sewing Machine Co., Cleveland, OH, 1897, 32 pgs, 7-3/4" x 7-3/4", very colorful wraps, seven brightly colored farmable pictures, White bicycles, illus **365.00**

Willys-Overland Co., Toledo, OH, 1915, 24 pgs, 8-3/4" x 11", *Overland Motor Cars for 1915,* lightly tinted color,

National Cloak & Suit Co., New York, NY, 1915, 162 pages, Fall & Winter New York Fashions for Women, includes some men styles, 7-1/4" x 10", $45. Photo courtesy of Kenneth Schneringer.

Willys-Overland Co., Toledo, OH, 1915, 24 pages, Overland Motor Cards for 1915, lightly tinted color, cuts of cars, oversized, chips at edges, 8-3/4" x 11", $60. Photo courtesy of Kenneth Schneringer.

cuts of cars, oversized, chips at edges **60.00**

Yale & Towne Mfg. Co., Stamford, CT, 1905, 207 pgs, 6" x 9", *Cat. of Locks & Hardware, No. 18, Handy Edition,* padlocks, rim and mortise night latches, dead locks, sets, keys, cabinet and trunk locks, etc., 12 pgs laid-in, hard cover, light dampening at rear of spine **125.00**

Yale & Towne Mfg. Co., Stamford, CT, 1921, 450 pgs, 7-3/4" x 10-3/4", *Cat. No. 25, Yale Builder's Locks & Trim,* night latches, dead locks, padlocks, cabinet and trunk locks, bank locks, safe locks, prison locks, door closers, chain blocks, electric hoists, industrial trucks, carburetors, hard cover **110.00**

CELADON

History: The term "celadon," meaning a pale grayish-green color, is derived from the theatrical character Celadon, who wore costumes of varying shades of grayish green in Honore d'Urfe's 17th-century pastoral romance, *L'Astree.* French Jesuits living in China used the name to refer to a specific type of Chinese porcelain.

Celadon divides into two types. Northern celadon, made during the Sung Dynasty up to the 1120s, has a gray-to-brownish body, relief decoration, and monochromatic olive-green glaze. Southern (Lung-ch'uan) celadon, made during the Sung Dynasty and much later, is paint-decorated with floral and other scenic designs and is found in forms that appeal to the European- and American-export market. Many of the southern pieces date from 1825 to 1885.

A blue square with Chinese or pseudo-Chinese characters appears on pieces after 1850. Later pieces also have a larger and sparser decorative patterning.

Reproduction Alert

Bowl

5-3/4" d, wide flaring form, dark gray-green color, traces of three spurs on base, surface entirely glazed, Korea, Koryo period, 12th C. **600.00**

7-1/4" d, brownish green, carved phoenixes and lotus dec, Korea, Koryo period **1,200.00**

7-1/2" d, sea green color, inlaid in Sangam technique with clouds and phoenix, Korea, Koryo period, 12th C. **875.00**

7-1/2" d, sea green color, inlaid in Sangam technique with branches and sprigs of flowers, Korea, Koryo period, 12th/13th C **475.00**

9-1/2" d, 4-1/2" h, cut corner shape, Rose Canton dec, hardwood stand, repaired **385.00**

10-1/2" d, scalloped rim, dec with exotic birds, butterflies, and flowers, repairs and gilt losses to edge. **245.00**

Lamp, made from 10" h Chinese celadon glazed porcelain vase, molded floral arabesque design, brass mounts, silk shade, drilled, $65. Photo courtesy of Cowan's Historic Americana Auctions.

Brush box, cov, 7-1/2" w, 3-1/4" d, 2-1/2" h, dec in Rose Medallion palette **400.00**

Center dish, 11-1/4" l, diamond shape, conforming foot, court scenes, central scene contained in vasiform device, Rose Canton pattern, China, 19th C, gilt wear **530.00**

Charger

10" d, Mandarin warrior, One Hundred Antiques border, China, 19th C **210.00**

13-1/2" d, Rose Medallion, court scene within medallion, Famille Rose border, minor glaze wear **725.00**

Ice cream tray, 7" x 13-1/4", rect, flange handles, Rose Canton motif, China, 19th C, minor gilt wear **600.00**

Incense burner, lid surmounted by Buddhist, lion base with lion mask feet, sea-green color, Korea, 12th C **8,000.00**

Plate

5-1/4" d, Rose Canton dec, China, 19th C **90.00**

10-1/4" d, river scene, butterfly and floral border, minor gilt and glaze wear.................**150.00**

10-1/4" d, Rose Canton dec, China, 19th C **120.00**

10-1/4" d, whimsical dogs, butterfly and floral border, minor gilt and glaze wear.............**150.00**

11-1/2" d, pale green color, carved floral springs, China, 18th C **600.00**

Celadon incense burner, lid surmounted by Buddhist, lion base with lion mask feet, sea-green color, Korea, 12th C, $8,000. Photo courtesy of Skinner Auctioneers and Appraisers.

Platter, 13-1/4" x 15-3/4", oval, Rose Canton dec **650.00**

Rice bowl, cov, underplate, 7-1/2" d, 5-3/4" h, dec with various animals, figures, and flowers..........**390.00**

Sauce tureen, cov, undertray, gilt floriform finial, gilt handles, bird, butterfly, and floral motifs, China, 19th C, minor edge wear......**600.00**

Serving dish, cov, 10" d, 6-1/2" h, domed lid, single handle, Rose Canton dec, imperfections **300.00**

Shrimp dish, 10-1/4" x 9-3/4", bird, butterfly, and floral motif, China, 19th C, minor glaze wear............**650.00**

Soap dish, three part, 4-1/8" l, 5-1/4" w, 2-1/2" h, figures in garden on lid, Rose Medallion border, minor edge wear **265.00**

Vase

9-1/2" h, baluster form, raised underglaze blue ornaments, gilt highlights, enamel bird and floral dec, China, 19th C, enamel losses **150.00**

10-3/4" h, Maebyong form, carved floral sprigs on body and lotus petals at base, deep sea-green color, Korea, Koryo period, 12th/13th C, old repair to mouth **1,800.00**

12-3/4" h, hexagonal paneled form, two handles, bird and floral dec, handle chip, gilt wear.....**385.00**

CELLULOID ITEMS

History: In 1869, an Albany, NY, printer named John W. Hyatt developed and patented the world's first commercially successful semi-synthetic thermoplastic. The moldable material was made from a combination of camphor, the crystalline resin from the heart of a particular evergreen tree, and collodion, a type of nitrated-cellulose substance (also called Pyroxylin), which was extremely flammable. Hyatt and his brother, Isaiah, called their invention Celluloid, a name they made up by combining the words cellulose and colloid.

By 1873, the Hyatts were successfully producing raw pyroxylin plastic material at the Celluloid Manufacturing Company of Newark, NJ. In the early days of its commercial development, Celluloid was produced exclusively in two colors: flesh tone, for the manufacture of denture-base material, and off white, which was primarily used for utilitarian applications like harness trimmings and knife handles.

However, during the late 1870s, advances in plastics technology brought about a shift in the ways Celluloid could be used. Beautiful imitations of amber, ivory, tortoise shell, jet, and coral were being produced and used in the fabrication of jewelry, fashion accessories, and hair ornaments. Because the faux-luxury materials were so realistic and affordable,

Celluloid quickly advanced to the forefront of consumerism by the working and middle classes.

Throughout the 1880s and 1890s, competition in the infant plastics industry was rampant and a number of newly organized fabricating companies were aggressively molding their brands of pyroxylin plastic into a variety of consumer products. However, since there was such limited knowledge about the nature of the material, many companies failed due to inferior products or devastating fires.

By the early 20th century, there were four major American manufacturers firmly established as producers of quality pyroxylin plastics. In addition to the Celluloid Company of Newark, NJ, there was the Arlington Manufacturing Company of Arlington, NJ, which produced Pyralin; Fiberloid Corporation of Indian Orchard, MA, makers of Fiberloid; and the Viscoloid Company of Leominster, MA. Even though these companies branded their plastic products with their registered trade names, today the word "celluloid" is used in a general sense for all forms of this early plastic.

Celluloid-type plastic became increasingly popular as an alternative for costly and elusive natural substances. Within the fashion industry alone, it gained acceptance as a beautiful and affordable substitute for increasingly dwindling supplies of ivory and tortoise shell. However, it should be noted that celluloid's most successful application during the late 19th century was realized in the clothing industry; sheet stock in imitation of fine-grade linen was fashioned into stylish waterproof cuffs and collars.

In sheet form, celluloid found other successful applications as well. Printed political and advertising premiums, pinback buttons, pocket mirrors, and keepsake items from 1890-1920 were turned out by the thousands. In addition, transparent-sheet celluloid was ornately decorated by embossing, reverse painting, and lamination, and then used in the production of decorative boxes, booklets, and albums. The toy industry also capitalized on the use of thin-celluloid sheet for the production of blow-molded dolls, animal toys, and figural novelties.

The development of the motion-picture industry helped celluloid fulfill a unique identity all its own; it was used for reels of camera film, as well as in sheet form by animation artists who drew cartoons. Known as animation cels, these are still readily available to the collector for a costly sum, but because of the depreciation of old celluloid, many early movies and cels have been lost forever.

By 1930, and the advent of the modern-plastics age, the use of celluloid began to decline dramatically. The introduction of cellulose-acetate plastic replaced the flammable pyroxylin plastic in jewelry and toys, and the development of non-flammable safety film eventually put an end to its use in movies. By 1950, the major manufacturers of celluloid in the United States had ceased production; however, many foreign companies continued manufacture. Today, Japan, France, Italy, and Korea continue to manufacture cellulose-nitrate plastics in small amounts for specialty items such as musical-instrument inlay, ping-pong balls, and designer fountain pens.

Beware of celluloid items that show signs of deterioration: oily residue, cracking, discoloration, and crystallization. Take care when cleaning celluloid items; it is best to use mild soap and water, avoiding alcohol- or acetone-based cleansers. Keep celluloid from excessive heat or flame and avoid direct sunlight.

Marks: Viscoloid Co. manufactured a large variety of small hollow animals that ranged in size from two to eight inches. Most of these toys are embossed with one of three trademarks: "Made in USA," an intertwined "VCO," or an eagle with a shield.

Adviser: Julie P. Robinson.

Advertising and souvenir keepsake items

Badge, 2" d, printed with "P H" and two intertwined American flags, fraternal organization for Patrons of Husbandry—The Grange, Whitehead & Hoag Co., early 1900s, shaped metal pinbackframe **20.00**

Bookmark, 3 1/4" l, 1/4" w, folded top for slipping over a page, violets dec, "Greetings" on the long flat surface **20.00**

Card, 3-1/16" x 2", engraved "Baldwin & Gleason With Best Wishes," ivory-grained sheet cream-colored celluloid, deep-blue floral motif .. **30.00**

Clothing brush, 3-1/2" d, celluloid-laminated printed paper showing Parisian Novelty Company of Chicago, USA—"Supplies for Making Fiberloid Novelties and Advertising Specialties," rare **175.00**

Compact, 1-3/4" d, imitation ivory-grained celluloid with gold Elk motif and "Third Annual Ball, BPOE, Leominster Lodge No. 1237, Jan. 26, 1917, produced by the Viscoloid Co. of Leominster, MA **65.00**

Fan, 4" tall when closed, mottled turquoise-and-cream celluloid Brise fan, light-blue ribbon, shows the Washington Monument and words, "Washington D.C." in gold-tone paint **15.00**

Game counter, 2-3/4" x 1" ivory-grained celluloid, disks turn to keep baseball score, "Peter Doelger Bottled Beer—Expressly for the Home" **55.00**

Ink blotter, 4 1/8" x 2 7/8" ivory-grained celluloid, front and back covers w/ blotters inside, engraved scene of

Advertising, ink blotter booklet, Jennison Co., Engineers and Contractors, Fitchburg, Mass, 1917 calendars, wood grained celluloid, black lettering, 8-1/2" l, 1-1/2" w, $35. Photo courtesy of Julie Robinson.

Advertising letter opener, ivory grained, sickle-shaped, advertising for Zylonite Novelties, $85. Photo courtesy of Julie Robinson.

Black Diamond File Works, Philadelphia, PA, 1890 calendar, Baldwin & Gleason Co. **45.00**

Match safe, 2-1/2" x 1-1/2", ivory-grained safety-match holder, red outline, blue lettering, "Joseph's Economy Store, 406 Penn St. Reading, PA" **20.00**

Pinback button

3/4" d, red celluloid, white lettering "I'm the Guy that put the oysters in Oyster Bay" **18.00**

1-1/2" d, "Erin Go Braugh," crossed American and Irish flags, center shamrock and lyre motif **25.00**

Pin holder, 1-3/4" d, celluloid disc, metal framework, "F Krupps Steel Works, Thomas Prosser & Son, NY," front shows advertising, back shows small child, engraved ivory-grained celluloid **40.00**

Pocket mirror

1-3/4" d, topsy-turvy image of a smiling man, "This man trades at Hager's Store, Frostburg, MD," turned upside down, the man is frowning and caption reads, "This man does not. For a satisfied customer see other side" .. **110.00**

2-1/4" d, beautiful woman with long red hair, wearing teal-blue dress and cloche, holding a bouquet of roses **45.00**

Advertising, pocket mirrors for Mennen's, left: violets and image of Mennen, $65; right: image of powder tin, pink roses, gold accents, $60. Photo courtesy of Julie Robinson.

Toy, Easter, duck, chick, and big chick, $85. Photo courtesy of Julie Robinson.

Postcard, 5-1/2" x 3-1/2", emb-fan motif with applied fabric and metal-script words, "Many Happy Returns," applied over fabric, circa 1908 .... **10.00**

Tape measure, 1-1/4" d, pull-out tape, colorful pretty girl with flowers, adv for "The First National Bank of Boswell, The Same Old Bank in its New Home," printed by P.N. Co. (Parisian Novelty Co. of Chicago), Patent 7-10-17, emb in the side **65.00**

Animals

Viscoloid Co. of Leominster, MA, manufactured a variety of small hollow toy animals, birds, and marine creatures, most of which are embossed with one of these three trade marks: "Made In USA," an intertwined "VCO," or an eagle with shield. A host of foreign countries also mass-produced celluloid toys for export into the United States. Among the most prolific manufacturers were Ando Togoro of Japan, whose toys bear the crossed-circle trademark, and Sekiguchi Co., which used a three-petal flower motif as its logo. Paul Haneaus of Germany used an intertwined PH trademark, and Petticolin of France branded its toys with an eagle head. Japanese- and American-made toys are plentiful, while those manufactured in Germany, England, and France, are more difficult to find.

Alligator, 3", green, white-tail tip, VCO/USA................... **18.00**

Animal set, six circus animals, garish bright colors, marked "Made In Occupied Japan," elephant, gorilla, giraffe, tiger, lion, and hippo, set. **85.00**

Bear, 5" w, cream bear, pink and gray highlights, VCO/USA......... **20.00**

Bison, 3-1/4" l, dark brown, eagle-and-shield trademark **18.00**

Boar, 3-1/4" l, brown, Paul Haneaus of Germany/PH trademark **75.00**

Camel, 3-1/2" x 2-1/2", peach celluloid, pink and black highlights, marked with crossed circle and "Made in Japan" **18.00**

Cat, 5-1/4", cream, pink and black highlights, molded collar and bell, Made in USA trademark **60.00**

Chick, 7/8", yellow, black eyes and beak, no trademark **8.00**

Chicken, 3" h, standing in grass, cream, gray, yellow feet, VCO/USA trademark **22.00**

Cow, 4-1/2", cream-and-orange cow; intertwined VCO/USA **20.00**

Dog

Airedale, 3" w, 2-1/2" h, white with pink and dark purple highlights, hand-painted collar, plaster filled, nice detailing; Made In Japan trademark **18.00**

Bulldog, 4-3/4" l, 2-1/2" h, spiked neck collar, translucent-green color, rhinestone eyes, intertwined VCO/USA................**30.00**

Hound, 5", long tail, peach celluloid, gray highlights, crossed-circle Japan **15.00**

Scottie, 3-1/4" l, plaster-filled cream-colored celluloid, no detailing, marked JAPAN ...**18.00**

St. Bernard, 3-1/4", tan, black highlights, intertwined VCO/USA **18.00**

Donkey, 4" l, 3-3/4" h, molded harnesses, saddles and blankets, grayish brown, red, and orange highlights, intertwined VCO/USA .**35.00**

Duck, 2-1/4", standing, cream-colored celluloid, hand-painted eyes and bills, original paper label, Made In Japan **20.00**

Elephant, 6-3/4" x 4-3/4", gray elephant, tusks, Made In USA ...**35.00**

Fish, 2-7/8", yellow, brown highlights, molded scales, intertwined VCO, circle **10.00**

Frog, 1-1/4", green or yellow, stripe on back, intertwined VCO/USA **15.00**

Giraffe, 10" h, cream, beaded neck alternating brown and cream, brown and yellow painted highlights, detailed face, crossed-circle mark of Ando Togoro, Made In Japan........**110.00**

Goat, 3", white, curled horns, flower, "N" in circle, Japan...............**18.00**

Hippopotamus, 3-3/4", pink, closed mouth, crossed circle, Japan....**18.00**

Horse

7", cream, purple and pink highlights, Made in USA **24.00**

9-1/4" x 7-3/4", cream, grayish-brown highlights, Made in USA **45.00**

Leopard, 4-1/2", white, orange highlights, black spots, Made in Occupied Japan..............**25.00**

Lion, 3-3/4", tan, brown highlights, TS Made in Japan **20.00**

Swan, cobalt blue, magenta, and teal feathers, red feet and beak, marked "USA," 4" l, 3-1/2" h, **$18.**

Lobster, 1-3/4", bright red, detailed shell, no trademark **55.00**

Pig, 4-1/2", pink, painted eyes, Made in USA......................**35.00**

Polar Bear, 2-1/4" l, white, USA .**12.00**

Ram, 4-1/2", cream, gray highlights, Made in USA................**20.00**

Rhino, 5", gray, fine detail, PH trademark, Paul Haneaus **55.00**

Seal, 4-1/2", gray, balancing red ball, VCO/USA..................**70.00**

Sparrow, 3-1/4", balancing, yellow teal, tail weighted, oval Made in USA trademark near talon **20.00**

Squirrel, 2-7/8", brown celluloid, holding a nut, Made in USA **40.00**

Stork, 6-3/4", standing, white, pink legs, flower mark and Japan **22.00**

Swan, 3-3/8", multicolored purple, pink, yellow, crossed circle **15.00**

Turtle, 1-3/8", two tone, brown top, yellow bottom, USA on foot.....**18.00**

Whale, 4-1/2", curled tail, smooth-molded tails, cream, green, red, and yellow highlights **45.00**

Autograph album, celluloid cover, ocean scene with seagulls, c1907, 5-1/2" x 4", **$75.** *Photo courtesy of Julie Robinson.*

Decorative albums and boxes

Autograph album, 6" x 4", silver and violet clear celluloid-coated paper, central emb oval with beautiful lady in wide-brimmed hat, white dress and fur, maroon-velvet back and binding . **85.00**

Collar box, 6" h, 6" d, covered in gold paper with pink, green, and yellow flowers, clear-celluloid overlay, central image of a pretty woman wearing ruffled dress with corsage **175.00**

Dresser-set box, 8" x 6-1/4" x 3-1/2" d, emb-white celluloid, cornflower motif in two strips across top, blue-satin lining, fitted with brush, mirror, salve box, file and nail cleaner, all original, pieces individually marked "Celluloid" . **250.00**

Hankie box, 7" sq, 3" h, center vignette of pretty girl in hat and gown picking pink flowers, emb Greek-key design on sides, overall pale yellow, green, and blue grapevine with leaf design. **165.00**

Necktie box, 12-1/2" x 4", emb script "Neckties," cream-colored celluloid, emb-circular design on sides ..**145.00**

Photograph album, 8" x 11", Gibson girl, lavender dress, hat with lavender plumes, emb corners, applied-gilt paint **195.00**

Dolls and toys

Baby rattle

2-1/4", peach horse on cream-colored 4-1/2" d ring, two pink and white balls attached to ring, "Japan" on horse **45.00**

4-1/2", bright-red celluloid, clown playing lute, intertwined "VCO/USA" trademark on back, unusual color..............**55.00**

6-1/4", yellow pear, orange-red highlights, brown-twig handle, finely detailed and realistic, no trademark **75.00**

Doll

3-1/4" black baby, strung arms and legs, unidentified lantern trademark, Made in Japan ..**50.00**

5-3/4" Dutch girl, green, pink, yellow, and black details, butterfly trademark—Made In JAPAN, mfg. by Yoshino Sangyo Co......**35.00**

7", molded, moving arms, molded bracelet on right wrist, mermaid in shield trademark on back, DRP Germany, mfg. by Cellba, Celluloidwarenfabrik Co.....**95.00**

16-1/2" realistic baby, movable arms and legs, bright-blue eyes, red hair, smiling face, made in USA by Viscoloid **175.00**

Doll, Uncle Sam, c1915, some age fading, 7" h, $60. Photo courtesy of James D. Julia, Inc.

Roly Poly

2-1/2", Buster Brown winking, cream, brown and black highlights, PH, Paul Hunaeus, Germany .. **225.00**

2-1/2", duckling, peach hat trimmed in flowers, jacket, necktie, green trim, cream celluloid, VCO trademark............... **75.00**

3-1/2", gray man, spectacles; black and white highlights on pink base, emb "Palitoy, Made In England" **85.00**

Toy

4", Bathing Beauty, double figural showing two little girls, pink and green bathing suit, umbrella, floral trademark, Made In Japan, mfg. by Sekiguchi Co............. **75.00**

5", steamer, gray and red, flag, intertwined PH **55.00**

Whistle, 3-1/4" l, 2-1/4" h, Nightingale bird, yellow celluloid, green and red highlights, VCO/USA **24.00**

Fashion accessories

Bar pin, 2-1/2" l, ivory-grained rect shape, orange-brown swirled-pearlescent laminate, center hp florals...................... **28.00**

Belt, 22" l, 3/4" x 1-1/2" rect mottled-green celluloid slabs linked by chain, applied silver-tone filigree dec **35.00**

Bracelet, bangle

Ivory colored, embedded with center row of red rhinestones and flanked by outside rows of clear rhinestones **75.00**

Molded imitation coral, imitation ivory, or imitation jade, allover floral dec, blue-ink stamp "Made in Japan," 3" d, each........ **40.00**

Translucent amber, single row of alternating red and amber rhinestones, further decorated with scored white painted scallop edging around stones **95.00**

Bracelet, link, 3" d, four oblong two-tone cream and ivory links, attached by smaller round cream links **50.00**

Brooch

1-1/4" d thin gold-tint metal frame, blue and white enamel floral embellishment, clear celluloid, designed to hold photo, safety clasp **25.00**

1-3/4" x 3/4", rect pearlized cream celluloid, black stencil silhouette of man and woman conversing over picket fence............. **30.00**

Comb and case

2-1/4" l, folding molded case, emb-rose motif, imitation ivory **25.00**

3" l cream-colored celluloid comb, 3-1/4" x 1" pearlized amber and gray rhinestone-studded case **15.00**

Cuff links, pr

Separable "Kum-a-part" Baer & Wilde Co., 1/4" sq shape divided by purple and black triangular

Toy, wind-up, Wimpy, blue striped pants, red neck tie, black lapelled jacket and bowler hat, Japan, 1930s, cane missing, 7" h, $230. Photo courtesy of James D. Julia, Inc.

shapes of celluloid, center diamond shape, Art Deco, mid-1920s, orig card **55.00**

Toggle back, realistic molded-celluloid lion heads, c1896 .... **95.00**

Dress clips, pr, molded-floral motif, semi-translucent cream celluloid, marked "Japan" **35.00**

Eyeglasses, Harold-Lloyd type, black frames **20.00**

Fan, Brise style, diecut and emb-imitation ivory, silk ribbon, mirrored heart on end stick, pink-floral motif, tassel.................. **45.00**

Hair comb, 4" x 5-1/4", imitation tortoiseshell, 24 teeth, applied-metal trim studded with rhinestones and brad-fastened Egyptian-Revival pink and gold metal floral and beetle dec **145.00**

Hat pin

4" l elephant head, tusks, black-glass eyes, imitation ivory **95.00**

10" l, diecut 1" filigree-hollow egg, pale-green paint applied over grained celluloid **45.00**

12" l, conical, imitation tortoiseshell **30.00**

Hat ornament

3-1/2" h, Art Deco, pearlized red and cream half circles, rhinestone trim **45.00**

4-1/2" h, calla lily, cream-pearlized celluloid, white rhinestones, 1-1/2" l threaded pin with screw-on celluloid point........... **25.00**

Necklace, 2" elegant Art Nouveau-filigree pendant, cream celluloid, oval cameo, profile of a beautiful woman, suspended from 20" cream celluloid-beaded necklace **110.00**

Purse frame

4" l, black pointed-horseshoe shape, rhinestones, white-molded cameo clasp **95.00**

6" l, imitation tortoiseshell, crescent shape, molded filigree and center cameo, celluloid push-button latch and linked chain......... **110.00**

Purse

4" d, round clam shell, imitation tortoiseshell and ivory, leather strap, celluloid findings and finger ring, applied celluloid-leaf decoration **125.00**

4-1/2" x 4-1/2", basketweave, link-celluloid chain, mottled grain ivory and green **185.00**

Dresser set, Fiberloid Fairfax, mottled brown and gold celluloid, floral trim, nine pieces, $85. Photo courtesy of Julie Robinson.

Holiday items

Angels, 1-1/2" h, set of three, one holding cross, star, or lantern, Japan, Mt. Fuji trademark............**25.00**

Christmas decoration, roly poly-type house, opening in back for a small bulb, shows Santa approaching door, red and white, intertwined VCO/USA trademark.................**125.00**

Christmas ornament
3-3/4" little boy on swing, all celluloid, dark-green highlights, holding onto string "ropes" for hanging on tree..........**155.00**
3-3/4", Santa, horn and sack, hole in back for light bulb, trademarked "S" in circle, Japan **100.00**
4" l, stripped green and white Christmas stocking filled with gifts including duck and kitten, crossed-circle trademark, Ando Togoro **145.00**

Figure
3-3/4", Swan Boat, Easter rabbit and chick in eggshell, intertwined VCO/USA...............**145.00**
5-1/4", Uncle Sam, white celluloid, painted red, white, and blue patriotic clothing **175.00**
7-3/4" h, Easter Rabbit, dressed in tails and top hat, holding chicken under arm, cream, pink, and blue highlights, VCO..........**125.00**

Halloween favor, 4" l, orange horn, black witch and trim, intertwined VCO/USA **110.00**

Rattle, 3-3/4" l, standing black cat, orange bow, intertwined VCO/USA **175.00**

Reindeer, 3-1/2", white deer, gold glitter, red eyes and mouth, molded ears and antlers, USA **20.00**

Roly poly, 3-1/2", black cat on orange pumpkin, intertwined VCO/USA.**200.00**

Santa
4", yellow or mint-green translucent celluloid, holding lantern and sack,

Japanese, Mt. in circle trademark **40.00**
5" h, basket of flowers, fur-trimmed suit, nice detail, VCO/USA trademark...............**75.00**

Toy
2-7/8" l, Easter rabbit in harness, attached to cart full of eggs, "Made in Japan" on cart, "Pat.15735" on rabbit **85.00**
3-3/8" x 2", Santa driving house-shaped automobile, white, applied red, yellow, and green painted highlights, VCO/USA trademark..............**125.00**
3-1/2", black Halloween cat pushing a witch in a pumpkin carriage, intertwined VCO/USA......**265.00**
4-3/4" h, Paddy, riding pig, movable legs, little boy with dunce cap riding on back, Japan....**185.00**
5-3/8" x 2", Santa riding on a train laden with holiday decorations and gifts including doll, puppy, and rocking horse, cream, red, and green highlights, VCO/USA on Santa **175.00**

Novelty items

Letter opener
7 3/8" l, ivory grained, magnifying glass in top, coiled-metal snake, red-glass eyes around the handle **85.00**
8" l, blade top by intricately detailed full-figure lady holding a flask **80.00**
9 5/8" l, handle molded with lighthouse and filigree **95.00**

Pin cushion
2" h, rabbit with pin cushion baskets, marked "Germany" **130.00**
2-1/4" h, straight pin holder, brown hen on base.............**65.00**

Tape measure
1-1/4" d, basket of fruit, marked "Made in Germany" **150.00**
1-3/4" h, chariot, horse, and driver, imitation bronze **225.00**
2-1/2" h, Billiken, cream celluloid, applied-brown highlights, marked "Japan".................**185.00**

Utilitarian and household items

Bookends, pr, 4-1/4" h, 3-1/4" w, 2-1/4" d, mottled-pink celluloid, emb ornamental gold neoclassic drape, plaster weighted, no trademark, c1930 ....**35.00**

Candle holders, pr, 5-1/4" h, cylindrical, round flared-weighted bases, unmarked.............**60.00**

Clock
3" sq, New Haven Clock Co., alarm, folding travel case, pearlescent pink laminated over amber celluloid.................**30.00**
5-1/2" x 3", classical Gothic cathedral design, round face, dark-yellow ivory-grained celluloid, Germany **45.00**
9" x 6-1/2", mantle clock, neoclassical design, front molded pearlized gray columns, imitation-ivory weighted base and top, marked "Made in USA," patented clockworks, Apr. 27, 1920 ....**65.00**

Crumb tray set, two dust pan-shaped trays
Ivory celluloid, one large and one small, unadorned, Fuller trademark **20.00**
Ivory celluloid, dark-blue dec border, monogrammed "T" in center of each tray...............**50.00**

Cutlery, solid imitation ivory grained-handle utensils, eight forks, eight knives in orig box, Standard Mfg. Co. **30.00**

Frame
4" d, round, ivory grained, easel back **20.00**
5-1/2" x 7", pearlized-amber celluloid, diecut floral motif, attached over wood frame, celluloid butterflies in each corner **35.00**
6" x 8", plain oval frame, imitation ivory-grained celluloid, glass, easel back **30.00**

Napkin ring
1" w, basketweave strips of celluloid **15.00**
1-1/2" w, plain, pale-green celluloid **5.00**

Pen holder, 3" sq, black base, laminated pearlized top, conical holder attached at center **20.00**

String holder, round sphere on a weighted base, twist apart, center hole in top for string, imitation-ivory grain, no trademark...................**65.00**

Vase
6" h, imitation ivory, conical, fluted weighted base, flange around top **18.00**
7" h, yellow, bulbous bottom, narrow opening, fluted top, painted pink and blue floral motif, no trademark **25.00**
8" h, imitation tortoiseshell, weighted-scalloped base ...**45.00**

Watch holder, 6-1/2" l, pearlescent blue, green, and amber, wall-hanging banjo-clock style, Wilcox trademark, late 1920s **25.00**

Vanity items

Dresser boxes, pr, oval-shaped pearlized peach boxes, dec-shaped lids, marked "Amerith," Lotus Pattern, c1929..................... **25.00**

Dresser set

Three-piece, mirror, brush and comb, green-pearlized celluloid, emb gold-flower motif in center of each item, plaster-filled mirror, orig cardboard box, poor-quality unmarked set **15.00**

Eight-piece, pearlized yellow-laminated amber celluloid, black trim, mirror, brush, shoe horn, button hook, soap box, nail buffer, toothbrush holder, hair-pin holder, marked "Arch Amereth, Windsor," c1928, orig box **65.00**

Seventeen-piece, Fairfax pattern, Fiberloid Company, mottled brown and gold, carved floral trim, comb, brush, mirror, powder box, hair receiver, nail file, scissors, button hook, and clothing brush, c1924 .... **125.00**

Dresser tray, 7-1/2" l, 5" w, oval, pearlized cream color and amber framework, Normandy lace inserted between double-glass bottom, c1925 .... **30.00**

Hair receiver and powder box set

3-1/2" d, pearlized-gray containers, octagonal lids, no trademark **25.00**

4" d, ivory-grained set, scalloped lids laminated in Goldaleur, marked "The Celluloid Co." **45.00**

Hatpin holder, weighted base

5" h center post, round circular disc on top, circular base, cream celluloid, cranberry-colored velvet cushion................. **90.00**

5" h, pale-green celluloid, triangular shape, painted flower...... **20.00**

Manicure set, rolled-up leather pouch fitted with six imitation-tortoiseshell celluloid manicure tools, gold trim, pink-velvet lining **30.00**

Trinket box, 5" l, 2" h, oval, amber, butterfly, grass and milkweed silk under clear-celluloid lid **35.00**

Vanity set, amber, teal-green pearlescent laminate surface, dresser tray, octagonal amber hair-receiver box with pearlized lid, nail buffer, scissors, and button hook, hp-rose motif on all pcs, unmarked, c1930 .... **45.00**

CHALKWARE

History: William Hutchinson, an Englishman, invented chalkware in 1848. It was a substance used by sculptors to imitate marble and also was used to harden plaster of paris, creating confusion between the two products.

Chalkware pieces, which often copied many of the popular Staffordshire items made between 1820 and 1870, was cheap, gaily decorated, and sold by vendors. The Pennsylvania German folk-art pieces are from this period.

Carnivals, circuses, fairs, and amusement parks gave away chalkware prizes during the late 19th and 20th centuries. These pieces often were poorly made and gaudy.

Additional Listings: See Carnival Chalkware in *Warman's Americana & Collectibles.*

Notes: Don't confuse the carnival-chalkware give-aways with the earlier pieces.

Animal

Cat, 5-1/4" h, seated, gray, black spots, ears, and tail, yellow eyes and base, red collar, repaired, some wear, base chips **330.00**

Deer, 5-1/2" h, red, black, and yellow, old worn paint, pr .. **935.00**

Dog, 5-1/2" h, molded detail, painted brown, black spots, red collar, PA, 19th C, pr **375.00**

Hen and rooster, 15" h hen, 20" h rooster, full bodied, comb, wattle, and feather detail, inset glass eyes, quatrefoil base, scrolled acanthus support, repairs, pr **1,495.00**

Lion, 7" l, 4-3/4" h.......... **315.00**

Ram, 2-1/8" l, 2-1/8" h, worn paint **45.00**

Squirrel, worn red and green, base flakes.................. **250.00**

Bank, 11" h, seated cat, wearing red bow, minor loss............. **200.00**

Bust, 10" h, lady, elegant green and gold costume, red beads, raised-letters "Maria" on her shoulders, early 19th C, paint loss **1,495.00**

Mantel ornament

12-1/2" h, fruit and foliage design, American, 19th C, restoration, paint wear, pr **460.00**

16" l, 15-1/2" h, reclining stag, polychrome dec, minor paint loss **300.00**

Figure, lady, wearing off-the-shoulder gown, some wear, 27" h, **$125.** *Photo courtesy of Joy Luke Auctions.*

Match holder, 6" h, figural, man with long nose and beard, Northwestern National Insurance Co. adv, c1890 .... **110.00**

Plaque, 9" h, horse head, orig-polychrome paint **100.00**

Wall pocket, basket shape..... **45.00**

Figure, young girl, holding branches and fruit, damage to toe, 31" h, **$110.** *Photo courtesy of Joy Luke Auctions.*

CHARACTER AND PERSONALITY ITEMS

History: In many cases, toys and other products using the images of fictional comic, movie, and radio characters occur simultaneously with the origin of the character. The first Dick Tracy toy was manufactured within less than a year after the strip first appeared.

The golden age of character material is the TV era of the mid-1950s through the late 1960s; however, some radio-premium collectors might argue this point. Today, television and movie producers often have their product licensing arranged well in advance of the initial release.

Do not overlook characters created by advertising agencies, e.g., Tony the Tiger. They represent a major collecting sub-category.

Additional Listings: See *Warman's Americana & Collectibles* for expanded listings in Cartoon Characters, Cowboy Collectibles, Movie Personalities and Memorabilia, Shirley Temple, Space Adventurers, and TV Personalities and Memorabilia.

Character

Andy Gump, pinback button, 1-1/4" d, "Andy Gump For President/I Endorse The Atwater Kent Receiving Set," red, white, blue, and fleshtone **40.00**

Betty Boop

Book, *Betty Boop Cartoon Lessons,* Fleischer Studios, 1935, 12" x 9" **500.00**

Marble, 11/16", Peltier Glass Co., black and white swirl, black transfer of Betty, c1932 .... **175.00**

Pinback button, 1-1/4" d, celluloid on tin, black and white Betty in front of yellow curtains, copyright Fleischer Studios, c1941 .... **850.00**

String holder, 6-1/2" w, 7-1/2" h, chalk, head and shoulders, orig paint **625.00**

Brownies, Palmer Cox

Book, *The Brownies, Their Book,* Palmer Cox, NY, 1887, first edition, second issue, illus by Cox, 4to, pictorial glazed boards **230.00**

Child's fork and spoon, emb Brownies on handles....... **18.00**

Doll, set of 8" dolls, stuffed cloth, Uncle Sam, Indian, Highlander, Chinaman, German, Sailor, Soldier, Canadian, Irishman, Policeman, John-Bull, and Dude, each has name stitched on back, colorful-printed outfits, marked "Copyright 1892 by Palmer Cox" on back of each, "Brownie's" on right foot of each, set of 12 ..... **775.00**

Pinback button, 1-1/4" d, blue on white, eight Brownies around board fence imprinted with calendar page for January, 1897, Whitehead & Hoag................. **22.00**

Plate, 7" d, octagonal, china, full-color illus of three Brownies, dressed as Uncle Sam, Scotsman, and golfer, soft-blue ground, gold trim, sgd "La Francaise Porcelain" **95.00**

Buster Brown, pinback button, multicolored, original back paper text reads "Look for Buster's Picture on the Sole of Every Shoe," 1-1/2" d, $195. Photo courtesy of Hake's Americana & Collectibles.

Buster Brown

Button, 1/2" d, two pieces, metal, loop shank, price for pr **15.00**

Children's feeding dish, Buster and Tige, wear to gold trim **115.00**

Figure, 2" h, bisque, red hat and suit, blue bow tie, black shoes, c1920 .... **100.00**

Pencil case, 10-1/2" l, Buster Brown Powers Mercantile Co., Minneapolis, MN, wood, cardboard, and tin, orig label **85.00**

Shaving mug, 3-1/2" d, 2-1/2" h, white porcelain, gold trim, Buster Brown with blue and white teapot, filling cup, Tige standing on his hind feet holding blue cup, "Buster Brown" printed near left, marked "Made in Germany"....... **295.00**

Sunday comics, 1914, *St. Paul Daily News*, full section **20.00**

Campbell's Kids

Children's dishes, "Campbell's Lunch Time," 4" x 14" x 17-1/2" unopened display carton, service for six, child's hard-plastic soup bowls and coaster plates, cups, saucers, spoons, and forks, prominent Campbell's marking, sealed in orig clear shrink wrap, six miniature placements on back, ©1984 .... **45.00**

Doll, 16" h, boy, orig clothing, 1970 .... **35.00**

Menu book, 5-1/2" x 7-1/2", softcover, ©1910, 48 pgs, menus for 30 days of the month, full-color Campbell's Kids art on cov **20.00**

Buster Brown, child-size bench, four seats divided by diecut animal shapes, one black and white lion, black and white zebra, and orange tiger, red background, detailed illustration of Buster and Tige on both ends, shown with large stuffed jester dolls, $6,000.

Salt and pepper shakers, pr, 4-1/2" h, painted hard plastic, red and white outfits, yellow-molded hair, ©Campbell Soup **40.00**

String holder, 6-3/4" h, chalk, incised "Copyright Campbell" **395.00**

Charlie the Tuna

Animation cel, 10-1/2" x 12" clear acetate sheet, centered smiling full-figured 4" image of Charlie gesturing toward 4" image of goldfish holding scissors, 10-1/2" x 12-1/2" white paper sheet with matching blue/lead pencil, 4" tall image of Charlie, c1960 . . . **150.00**

Figure, 7-1/2" h, soft vinyl, blue, dark pink-opened mouth, black-rimmed eyeglasses, orange cap inscribed "Charlie," ©1973 . . . . **30.00**

Wristwatch, 1-1/2" d bright gold luster bezel, full-color image of Charlie on silver background, ©1971 Star-Kist Foods, grained purple leather band **60.00**

Dutch Boy, string holder, 14-1/2" x 30",
diecut tin, Dutch Boy sitting on swing painting the sign for this product, White Lead Paint Bucket houses ball of string **300.00**

Elsie the Cow, Borden

Display, mechanical milk carton, cardboard and papier-mâché, figural milk carton rocks back and forth, eyes and mouth move from side to side, made for MN state-fair circuit, 1940s **500.00**

Lamp, 4" x 4" x 10", Elsie and Baby, hollow ceramic figure base, Elsie reading to baby nestled on her lap, brass socket, c1950 . . . . . **125.00**

Mug, 3-1/4" h, white china, full-color image of Elmer, gold-accent line, orig sq box with image of child's alphabet block including panels "E for Elsie" and "B for Borden," Elmer pictured on one side panel, ©1950 . . . . **95.00**

Felix the Cat

Figure, 1" h, dark copper-colored plastic, loop at top, 1950s . . **10.00**

Pinback button, 1" d, Herald and Examiner, c1930s **45.00**

Place-card holder, 1-3/4" h celluloid Felix, arched-back black cat, base, glossy black holder, Japanese, 1930s **85.00**

Valentine, diecut, jointed cardboard, full color, "Purr Around If You Want To Be My Valentine" inscription, ©Pat Sullivan, c1920 . . . . . . **20.00**

Jiggs and Maggie, chalkware figures, multicolored; Jiggs 8-1/2" h, Maggie 9-3/4" h, pair, **$225.**

Happy Hooligan

Figure, 8-1/4" h, bisque, worried expression, tin-can hat, orange, black, blue, and yellow **75.00**

Pin-back button, 11-16" d, brown and cream, profile, inscribed, "Son of Rest," initials below "G.T.A.T.," c1910 . . . . **30.00**

Stickpin, 2-1/4" l, brass **25.00**

Howdy Doody

Belt, suede, emb face **35.00**

Cake-decorating set, unused . **40.00**

Handkerchief, 8" x 8-1/4", cotton **20.00**

Pencil case, vinyl, red **25.00**

Jiggs and Maggie

Pinback button, 3/4" d, *The Knoxville Sentinel*, black and white image of Jiggs, red bow tie, c1920 . . . **15.00**

Salt and pepper shakers, pr, ceramic **48.00**

Katzenjammer Kids

Christmas card, 4-1/4" x 4-1/2", 1951, copyright King Features Syndicate **18.00**

Comic strip, Ovaltine ad on back **15.00**

Li'l Abner

Bank, Schmoo, blue plastic . . **50.00**

Magazine Tear Sheet, Cream of Wheat Breakfast Food, Rastus on front of box illus, 5" w, 11" h **20.00**

Pinback button, 13/16", Li'l Abner, *Saturday Daily News*, black litho, cream ground, newspaper name in red **20.00**

Little Annie Rooney, pinback button,
1-1/4" d, comic-strip contest button, serial-number type, c1930 . . . . . **25.00**

Little Orphan Annie

Big Little Book, *Little Orphan Annie Secret of the Well*, No. 1417. **85.00**

Nodder, bisque, marked "Little Orphan Annie" and "Germany" **150.00**

Toothbrush holder, 4" h, bisque, back inscribed "Orphan Annie & Sandy, © F.A.S., #1565," bottom stamped "Japan," some wear to paint **165.00**

Mr. Peanut

Ashtray, Golden Jubilee, 50th Anniversary, gold-plated metal, figural, orig attached booklet, orig box, 5" h, 5-3/4" h **130.00**

Booklet, *Mr. Peanuts Guide to Tennis*, 6" x 9", ©1960, 24 illus pgs **20.00**

Box, Planters Chocolate Covered Nut Assortment, silver-alligator texture, two early Mr. Peanut figures, 8-1/4" sq **350.00**

Orphan Annie, Captain Secrets folder, 1942, "Official & Confidential," shows other Quaker Puffed Wheat Sparkies cereal premiums, from final radio year, **$250.** *Photo courtesy of Hake's Americana & Collectibles.*

Mr. Peanut, left: green bank, 8-1/4" h, right: mug, green, 3-3/4" h, c1960, sold as pair for ,$35. Photo courtesy of Hake's Americana & Collectibles.

Paint book, *Planter's Paint Book No. 2*, 7-1/4" x 10-1/2", © 1929, 32 pgs **35.00**

Salad set, ceramic tops, wooden fork and spoon, rhinestone monocle, 10" h **170.00**

Toy, trailer truck, red cab, yellow and blue plastic trailer, 5-1/2" l . . **275.00**

Mutt & Jeff

Bank, 4-7/8" h, cast iron, orig paint **125.00**

Book, *The Mutt & Jeff Cartoon Book*, Bud Fisher, black and white illus by author, Ball Pub. Co., 1911 . **100.00**

Sheet music, *Moonlight*, 1911 . **15.00**

Miles Speedy Alka Seltzer, patch, colorful stitched image of smiling Speedy waving his wand, pixie dust accent and Miles name in white at top, 1960s, $35. Photo courtesy of Hake's Americana & Collectibles.

Popeye

Cereal bowl, plastic, white ground, red, blue, and black illus of Popeye and Olive Oyl **5.00**

Charm, 1" h, bright copper-luster plastic figure of Olive Oyl, 1930s **10.00**

Figure, 14" h, chalkware **150.00**

Mug, 4" h, Olive Oyl, figural . . **20.00**

Pencil sharpener, figural, Catalin plastic, dark yellow, multicolored decal, 1930s. **60.00**

Reddy Kilowatt

Hot pad, 6" d, laminated heat-resistant cardboard, textured top surface with art and verse inscription, "My name is Reddy Kilowatt-I keep things cold. I make things hot. I'm your cheap electric servant. Always ready on the spot," c1940 . . . . **40.00**

Pinback button, "Please Don't Litter," blue and white, 1950s **15.00**

Pocketknife, metal cast, red-figure image and title on one side, single-knife blade, Zippo, c1950 . . . . **60.00**

Stickpin, red enamel and silvered-metal miniature diecut figure, c1950 . . . . **30.00**

Smokey Bear

Ashtray, 4" d, tin **55.00**

Doll, 22" h, stuffed, Knickerbocker **75.00**

Hand puppet, 9" h, head incised "1965 Ideal Toy Corp." **195.00**

Little Golden Book, *Smokey Bear and the Campers*, 1971 . . . . . **5.00**

Neck scarf, 22" sq, official Forest Service logo **65.00**

Tab, 2" d, metal, Smokey in center, marked "Green Duck Co., Chicago," unused **15.00**

Yellow Kid

Cap bomb, 1-1/2" h, cast iron, c1898 . . . . **185.00**

Cigar box, 3-1/2" x 4-1/4" x 9", wood, illus and name inscription in bright gold, brass hinges, label inside says, "Smoke Yellow Kid Cigars/Manuf'd by B. R. Fleming, Curwesville, Pa," tax label strips on back, c1896 . . . . **225.00**

Pinback button, #2, 1894, orig paper label **60.00**

Yellow Kid, pin cushion, silvered metal, "I'm Weightin For Yer 'See'," 4-5/8" h, $145.

Personality
Amos and Andy

Ashtray and match holder, plaster **30.00**

Poster, 13" x 29", multicolored, Campbell's Soup ad, radio show listings, framed **145.00**

Toy, Fresh Air Taxi, litho tin wind-up, Marx, 1929 . . . . **425.00**

Autry, Gene

Badge, 1-1/4" d, Gene Autry Official Club Badge, black and white, bright orange top rim, c1940 . . . . **50.00**

Child's book, *Gene Autry Makes a New Friend*, Elizabeth Beecher, color illus by Richard Case, Whitman Tell A Tale, 1952 . . . **12.00**

Watch, orig band **145.00**

Amos, litho tin sparkler toy, glass eyes, lever action, German, flint missing, 4" h, $420. Photo courtesy of James D. Julia, Inc.

Ball, Lucille

Magazine, *Life*, April 6, 1953, five-pg article, full-color cover of Lucy, Desi Arnaz, Desi IV, and Lucy Desiree **30.00**

Movie-lobby card, 11" x 14", full color, 1949 Columbia Picture "Miss Grant Takes Richmond" **40.00**

Cassidy, Hopalong

Coloring book, 1950, large size **30.00**

Tablet, 8" x 10", color-photo cov, facsimile signature, unused. **24.00**

Wallet, leather, metal fringe, multicolored cover, made by Top Secret **35.00**

Chaplin, Charlie

Candy container, 3-3/4" h, glass, Charlie and barrel, small chip **100.00**

Magazine, *Life,* April 1, 1966, Chaplin and Sophia Loren .. **10.00**

Dionne Quintuplets

Advertisement, 5" x 7", Quintuplet Bread, Schultz Baking Co., diecut cardboard, loaf of bread, brown crust, bright red and blue letters, named silhouette portraits, text on reverse **70.00**

Book, *Now We Are Six,* Miline Pub., Dutton, November 1927, orange cover **17.50**

Dolls in Ferris wheel, 18-5/8" h, five 6-1/2" h composition Madame Alexander dolls with brown-painted eyes, closed mouth, orig white organdy dresses, lawn bibs, blue accented yellow and green wooden Ferris wheel, some paint loss, c1936 .... **1,035.00**

Fan, 8-1/4" x 8-3/4", diecut cardboard, titled, "Sweethearts of the World," full-color-tinted portraits, light-blue ground, ©1936, funeral director name on reverse **35.00**

Garland, Judy

Pinback button, 1" h, "Judy Garland Doll," black and white photo, used on c1930 Ideal doll, name appears on curl, also "Metro-Goldwyn-Mayer Star" in tiny letters .. **125.00**

Sheet music, "On the Atchison, Topeka, and the Sante Fe," 1945 MGM movie, "The Harvey Girls," sepia photo, purple, light pink, and brown cov **35.00**

Gleason, Jackie

Magazine, *TV Guide,* May 21, 1955, Philadelphia edition, three-pg article on the Honeymooners **18.00**

Pinback button, 1-5/8" d, "Jackie Gleason Fan Club/And Awa-a-ay We Go!," blue on cream litho, checkered suit, 1950s..... **65.00**

Henie, Sonja,
pinback button, 1-3/4" d, "Sonja Henie Ice Review," orange on blue, illus of skater, c1940s **20.00**

Laurel & Hardy

Movie poster, "Laurel and Hardy in the Big Noise," Fox, 1944, Tooker Litho. **300.00**

Salt and pepper shakers, pr. **230.00**

Lone Ranger

Coloring book, unused **50.00**

Game board, target bull's eye **185.00**

Ring, Cheerios premium, saddle type, filmstrip missing **225.00**

Mix, Tom

Big Little Book, Whitman, *Tom Mix and The Stranger from the Sea,* Pete Daryll, 1936, #1183.... **75.00**

Premium, Tom Mix Ralston Telegraph Set, 1940 .... **95.00**

Ring, magnet, 1946 .... **145.00**

Scarf, Tom Mix Ralston Straight Shooters **195.00**

Rogers, Roy

Bank, Roy on Trigger, porcelain, sgd "Roy Rogers" and "Trigger". **200.00**

Charm, 1" h, blue plastic frame, black and white glossy paper photo **35.00**

Comic book, April, 1958 ..... **60.00**

Guitar, orig box, 1950s **140.00**

Ring, litho tin, Post's Raisin Bran premium, Dale Evans, ©1942 .... **45.00**

Watch, Roy and Dale....... **120.00**

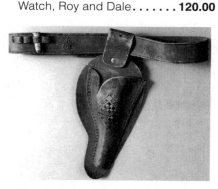

Tom Mix, Ralston Straight Shooters, premium holster set, leather gun belt holding single silver accent wooden bullet, attached 8" tall holster, both have Tom Mix Ralston logo, 1935, rare, $325. Photo courtesy of Hake's Americana & Collectibles.

Roy Rogers on Trigger, Hartland figure, Roy wearing shirt with fringe in "square" design rather than on diagonal, original dark brown guns and white hat, Trigger with mane down, dark blue martingale, 9-1/2" h, $150. Photo courtesy of Hake's Americana & Collectibles.

Temple, Shirley

Child's book, *Shirley Temple's Birthday Book,* Dell Publishing Co., c1934, soft cover, 24 pgs.. **100.00**

Figure, 6-1/2" h, salt-glazed .. **85.00**

Handkerchief, Little Colonel, boxed set of three **200.00**

Magazine tear sheet, Lane Hope Chests adv, 1945 .... **8.00**

Pinback button, 1-1/4" d, brown-tone photo, light-pink rim, Ideal Dolls, 1930s **75.00**

Three Stooges

Autograph, letter, 4-1/2" x 5-1/2" mailing envelope, two folded 6" x 8" sheets of "Three Stooges" letterhead, personally inked response to fan, sgd "Moe Howard," March 10, 1964 Los Angeles postmark **200.00**

Badge, 4" d, cello, black and white upper face image of Curly-Joe on purple background, Clark Oil employee type **20.00**

Photo, 4" x 5" glossy black and white, facsimile signatures of Curly-Joe, Larry, and Moe, plus personal inscription in blue ink by Moe **95.00**

Wayne, John

Magazine, *Life,* Jan. 29, 1972 **25.00**

Magazine tear sheet, 10" x 13", "Back to Bataan," black and white, 1945 .... **15.00**

Movie poster, "McLintock," 1963 .... **250.00**

CHILDREN'S BOOKS

History: Because there is a bit of the child in all of us, collectors always have been attracted to children's books. In the 19th century, books were popular gifts for children, with many of the children's classics written and published during this time. These books were treasured and often kept throughout a lifetime.

Developments in printing made it possible to include more attractive black and white illustrations and color plates. The work of artists and illustrators has added value beyond the text itself.

Additional Listings: See *Warman's Americana & Collectibles* for more examples and an extensive listing of collectors' clubs.

A Child's Garden of Verses, Tasha Tudor, Oxford, 1947, color and black and white illus, 1st ed. **85.00**

A Christmas Carol, Charles Dickens, Garden City Pub, © 1938, color and black and white illus by Everett Shinn, red cover, fancy gold trim **28.00**

Adventures of Tom Sawyer, Mark Twain, American Pub. Co., Hartford, CT, 1899, blue and gold cover **45.00**

Alice's Adventures in Wonderland in Words of One Syllable, Saalfield, © 1908, illus by John Tenniel, dj . . . **18.00**

A Little Freckled Person, A Book of Child Verse, Carolyn Davies, Hough, Miff, 1919, eight plates by Harold Cue, color frontis **18.00**

And To Think That I Saw It On Mulberry Street, Dr. Suess, Vanguard Pub., © 1937, 3rd printing **15.00**

An Old Fashioned Girl, Louisa M. Alcott, Robert Bros. Pub, 1870, 1st ed . . **35.00**

Bob, Son of Battle, Ollivant, 1898, Garden City Pub **12.00**

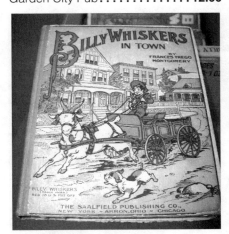

Billy Whiskers In Town, Frances Montgomery, Saalfield, **$30.** *Photo courtesy of Sanford Alderfer Auction Company.*

Bobbsey Twins At The County Fair, The, Grossett & Dunlap, 1922, 1st ed., dj **28.00**

Boys Story of Lindbergh, The Lone Eagle, The, Richard Beamish, 1928, John C. Winston Co., dj **20.00**

Buddy and the Secret Cave, Howard Garis, 1934, Cupples & Leon . . . **10.00**

Burgess Bird Book for Children, The, Thorton Burgess, illus in color by L. A. Fuertes, Little Brown & Co., 1919, 1st ed, water marks along top of pages last quarter of book **40.00**

Children's Missionary Story Sermons, Hugh T. Kerr, DD, Pastor of Shadyside Presbyterian Church, Pittsburgh, 1915, Fleming H. Revell Co., 54 sermons, beige hard cover **7.00**

Danny, the Champion of the World, Ronald Dahl, illus by Jill Bennett, Alfred A. Knopf, 1975, 1st ed. **20.00**

Freckles, Grossett & Dunlap, 1904, illus by E. Stetson Crawford **8.00**

Freckles Comes Home, Grossett & Dunlap, 1929 . . . . **18.00**

Hardy Boys, The Shore Road Mystery, Franklin Dixon, illus by Walter Rogers, Grossett & Dunlap, 1928, 1st ed. **25.00**

Harvester, The, Grossett & Dunlap, 1911, wear to cover **5.00**

Helen's Babies, John Habberton, J. H. Sears & Co., colorful illus by Christopher Rule **10.00**

How the Grinch Stole Christmas, Dr. Suess, Random House, © 1957, Grinch on red and green cover **25.00**

Lawrence and the Arabian Adventure, Robert Graves, illus, Doubleday, Doran, 1928, 2nd ed., some soil on cov. **12.00**

Little Lame Prince, The, Miss Mullock, illus by W Rogers **14.00**

Little Orphan Annie and the Gila Monster Gang, Harold Gray, Whitman

Kupfersannlung Zu J.B. Basedows Elementarwerke Fur Die Jugend Und Ihre Freunde, published Berlin, 1774, 96 copper plate engravings including maps, historical scenes, natural science, leather cover exhibiting some dryness, interior exhibits some minor foxing, 9" x 11-1/2", **$375.** *Photo courtesy of Sanford Alderfer Auction Company.*

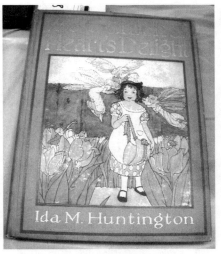

The Garden of Hearts Delight, Ida M. Huntingdon, green cover, gold lettered title, **$25.** *Photo courtesy of Sanford Alderfer Auction Company.*

Publishing, © 1944, licensed by Famous Artists Syndicate, 248 pgs, 5" x 8" **12.00**

Magic Garden, The, Grossett & Dunlap, 1927, green cover **20.00**

Marcella Stories, Johnny Gruelle, M. A. Donohue Co., 1930s, color and black and white illus, dj **95.00**

Mary Frances Garden Book, Adventures Among the Garden People, The, Jane Fryer, illus by Wm Zivimer, John C. Winston, 1916, 7" x 9", 378 pgs **12.50**

Metropolitan Mother Goose, Elizabeth Watson, Metropolitan Insurance Co. promo, 1930s, 20 pgs **18.00**

Mother Goose and Nursery Rhymes, Anthemum Pub., colored wood engravings by Philip Reed, 1963, 1st ed, Mother Goose and gander on orange cover **35.00**

Mother Goose or The Old Nursery Rhymes, Warne, c1900, 44 rhymes, Kate Greenaway illus, pictures on both front and back cov **45.00**

Moving Picture Boys and the Flood, The, Victor Appleton, Grossett & Dunlap, 1914, pictorial cover **15.00**

Mr. Winkle Goes to War, Theodore Pratt, 1943, Duell, Sloan & Pearce, 1st ed, dj **8.00**

Mrs. Appleyard's Year, Louise Andrews Kent, Hough. Mifflin, 1941, 195 pgs, rooster on cover **9.50**

Mrs. Wiggs of the Cabbage Patch, Alice Hegan Rice, Appleton-Century Co., 1941, hard bound, lady in red dress on cover **10.00**

My Very Own Fairy Stories, Johnny Grulle, P. F. Volland Co., 1917, 30th ed, color illus **65.00**

Mystery Hunters on Special Detail, #4, The, Capwell Wyckoff, Saalfield, 1936 . . . . **12.00**

Nancy Drew, The Password to Larkspur Lane, illus by Russell Tandy, Grossett & Dunlap , 1933, some fading to blue cover **65.00**

Nancy Shippen: Her Journal Book-Young Lady of Fashion of Colonial Philadelphia with Letters to Her and About Her, edited by Ames, 1935, 1st ed., colored portrait, illus , maps . **25.00**

Nelly's Silver Mine, Helen Hunt Jackson, 1924, Little Brown & Co., illus by Harriet Richards and Henry Pitz, dj **20.00**

Peter Rabbit and the Little Boy, Linda Almond, Platt & Munk, 1935 . . . . **15.00**

Polly-Anna, Eleanor H. Porter, The Page Co., 1914, eight full-page illus **8.00**

Raggedy Ann's Wishing Pebble, Johnny Gruelle, M. A. Donohue Co., 1930s, color and black and white illus, dj **85.00**

Riley's Songs O'Cheer, James Whitcomb, Bobbs Merrill Pub, 1905, six color illus, black and white illus by Will Vawter **35.00**

Sleeping Beauty, The, Arthur Rackman, black and white illus, two-tone silhouettes, tip-in color frontis replaced **45.00**

Tale of Peter Rabbit, The, Beatrix Potter, Warne Pub., 26 orig color illus, color cover, dj **27.50**

Tarzan and City of the Gold, Edgar Rice Burroughs, Whitman, 1952, dj . . . **15.00**

Uncle Remus His Songs and Sayings, Joel Chandler Harris, 112 illus by A. B. Frost, D. Appleton & Co., 1916 . . **75.00**

Uncle Wiggily and the Runaway Cheese, Howard R. Garis, color illus by A. Watson, Platt & Munk, 1977, oversize **12.50**

White Flag, The, Grossett & Dunlap, 1923, gray cover **12.50**

CHILDREN'S FEEDING DISHES

History: Unlike toy dishes meant for play, children's feeding dishes are the items actually used in the feeding of a child. Their colorful designs of animals, nursery rhymes, and children's activities are meant to appeal to the child and make mealtimes fun. Many plates have a unit to hold hot water, thus keeping the food warm.

Although glass and porcelain examples from the late 19th and early 20th centuries are most popular,

collectors are beginning to seek some of the plastic examples from the 1920s to 1940s, especially those with Disney designs on them.

Bowl, Sunbonnet girls dec, pale orange band, cream colored ground, marked "Roseville," slight wear, inner rim chip **200.00**

Butter pat, 3-1/4" d, "A Present For Ann," blue transfer medallion . . . **125.00**

Cereal set, Nursery Rhyme, amber, divided plate, Humpty Dumpty on mug and bowl, Tiara **125.00**

Creamer, three yellow ducks, yellow band with black outline, cream-colored ground, marked "R12" **125.00**

Cup, Raggedy Ann, Johnny Gruelle, 1941, Crooksville China **65.00**

Cup plate, 4-5/8" d, "Constant dropping wears away stones and little strokes fell great oaks," green transfer, polychrome enamel dec **90.00**

Feeding dish
Kiddieware, pink, Stangl **125.00**
Little Bo Peep, glass, divided, white, red trim **65.00**
Nursery Rhyme, green enamelware, marked "Made in Germany" . **40.00**
Raggedy Ann, Johnny Gruelle, 1941, Crooksville China, 8-3/4" d . . **85.00**
Sunbonnet babies, sweeping, 7-1/4" d **400.00**

Mug
1-3/4" h, "A Rabbit for William," yellow glazed, transfer print, England, c1850, glaze and transfer wear **225.00**

Child's mug, majolica, probably Austrian, c1890, decorated with hurdy-gurdy player with monkey, 4-1/2" h, $230. Photo courtesy of David Rago Auctions.

2-1/8" h, "Keep thy shop and thy shop will keep thee," yellow glazed, transfer print, England, c1850, luster rim, minor chip **195.00**
2-3/8" h, "A new doll for Margaret," yellow glazed, transfer print, England, c1850, glaze and transfer wear, very minor chips **490.00**

Plate
6" d, Buster Brown, 1910, mint center image **135.00**
8" d, nursery rhymes, glass, green **40.00**
8" d, "Where Are You Going My Pretty Maid, See Saw Margery Daw," three parts, transparent-green Depression-era glass. **45.00**

Juvenile set, Roseville, painted chicks, some light wear to decorated, unmarked, 6-1/2" d plate, $290. Photo courtesy of David Rago Auctions.

CHILDREN'S NURSERY ITEMS

History: The nursery is a place where children live in a miniature world. Things come in two sizes: Child scale designates items actually used for the care, housing, and feeding of the child; toy or doll scale denotes items used by the child in play and for creating a fantasy environment which copies that of an adult or his own.

Cheap labor and building costs during the Victorian era encouraged the popularity of the nursery. Most collectors focus on items from 1880 to 1930.

Additional Listings: Children's Books, Children's Feeding Dishes, Children's Toy Dishes, Dolls, Games, Miniatures, and Toys.

Painting fetches nearly $200,000

Skinner's American Furniture & Decorative Arts auction on Feb. 24, 2002 sold a very interesting nursery-related painting. Titled *Little Girl in Red Dress Holding Toys*, it was attributed to Deacon Robert Peckham (1785-1877). The oil on canvas painting was 28" x 24", unframed, and had varnish inconsistencies and possible minor scattered retouch, craquelure, scattered abrasions upper center and lower center. However, despite these minor problems, this charming portrait of a little girl from a long time ago sold for $182,000.

Blocks, boxed set, ABCs, animals, litho of Noah and ark on cov, Victorian
. . . .**185.00**
Boat, play, ice, 24" l, wood with iron runners, c1900 . . . .**460.00**
Bucket, 5-1/2" d, 4-1/4" h, wooden-stave construction, orig yellow paint, blue-painted tin bands, stenciled stars, chick, and eagle, wood and wire bale handle, int. has some crayon marks, bottom band replaced **660.00**
Carriage, 53" l, 37" h, wicker, brown and white hide-covered horse with glass eyes, leather tack, hair mane, horse-hair tail, two-wheeled vehicle pushed by handle, horse sets between shafts on three-wheeled frame, wire wheels with rubber tread, late 19th/early 20th C, some damage to hide, wear to paint **1,380.00**
Chair, child size
English, yew wood, old dark finish, one board sides, wing back, and seat, shaped arms, rose-head nail construction, pierced handle at top, warped sides with insect

Chair, corner, split hickory seat, mixed woods, America, late 19th C, 20th C seat replacement, 12-1/2" h, **$75.** *Photo courtesy of Cowan's Historic Americana Auctions.*

damage and restoration, 7" h seat, 20-1/2" h back **350.00**
Windsor, birdcage, orange paint over earlier green, shield-shaped seat, bamboo turned base, late 19th/early 20th C, wear on one seat, 10-1/4" h seat, 20-3/4" h, price for pr **650.00**

Morris chair, child-size, Stickley Brothers, original black leather-upholstered cushion, Original finish, unmarked, some tears to leather, 21" w, 23" d, 30" h, **$1,450.** *Photo courtesy of David Rago Auctions.*

Chest of drawers, child-size, Hepplewhite-style, curly maple, pine secondary wood, banded inlay around two-board top and base, four graduated dovetailed drawers with dark line inlay, and fans at corners, well-scalloped base, French feet, diamond-shaped escutcheons, emb brasses with cornucopia designs, 27" w, 17" d, 28" h **1,320.00**
Crib, 38-3/4" d, 69-1/2" h, orig 48" l rails, refinished bird, tapered high posts with incised line beading along edges, urn-shaped supports on all sides, narrow vertical slats added for stability
. . . .**220.00**
Cupboard, child-size, step-back
24" w, 11" d, 37-1/4" h, middle Atlantic States, mid-19th C, cherry, flat-molded cornice above cock-beaded case, two cupboard doors with raised panels, two shelves int., arched opening over projecting case with two short drawers with applied molding, two raised-panel cupboard doors, old red-stained surface **1,725.00**
24-1/2" w, 8-1/8" d, 33" h, New England, early 19th C, stained, molded top overhangs case of two drawers opening to two-shelved int., stepped out board overhangs two drawers on legs, side shaping, orig surface **1,265.00**
Desk, 22-3/4" w, 14-1/4" d, 27" h, Queen Anne, southeastern New England, 18th C, cherry and poplar, slant lid, int. with four compartments over drawers, sliding panel revealing well, case with single thumb molded drawers, bracket feet, replaced brasses, old refinish, restorations **4,120.00**

Sleigh, child's, push-type, original robin's egg blue paint, blue line accents, pink rosebuds, oak and iron runners, wooden seat, needlepoint back, bottom lined with old newspaper, some paint and edge wear, 48" l, 18" w, 34" h, **$275.** *Photo courtesy of Garth's Auctions, Inc.*

Doll bed, 28-5/8" l, 16" w, 15-3/4" h, Arts & Crafts, oak, rect headboard with two cartoon-like images of baby dolls, footboard with two sq form cut-outs, imperfections **230.00**

Doll carriage

30" l, 28" h, Heywood Wakefield, woven wicker, natural finish, diamond patternweave, steel wheels, rubber tires, clamshell hood, maker's label on underside, early 20th C **150.00**

30" l, 28" h, natural wicker wooden spoked wheels, original button-upholstered back, red cotton parasol on wire hook, late 19th C **230.00**

32" l, 28" h, American, fringed top surrey, original dark green paint, gold stenciling, wooden wheels, platform top, fringe replaced, c1870 . . . . **350.00**

Doll cradle, 15" l, 8-1/4" w, 13" h, pine, sq and "T" head nails, footboard and part of hood are dovetailed, scrolled end rockers, layers of red paint, age cracks, wear, one rocker glued . **150.00**

Doll crib, 16-1/2" l, 11-1/2" d, 11" h, poplar, orig reddish-brown painted dec, shaped head and footboards, rockers, turned posts with ball finials, edge wear, finial chips **320.00**

Game, ring toss, 16" d, green painted wood backplate set with small hooks, each with gold transfer printed number, four leather tossing rings, England, first quarter 20th C **175.00**

Hobby horse, real horse hide over straw stuffed frame, glass eyes, leather harness, real horsehair mane and tail, mounted on wooden platform with cast wheels (one wheel missing), some old red paint edging, 31" h, $460. Photo courtesy of James D. Julia, Inc.

Rattle, whistle at one end, inset natural polished red coral at other, six small silver bells with floral scrollwork chasing, sterling, maker's mark "G & N," Birmingham, England, 1861-2, 4-1/2" l, $800. Photo courtesy of Cowan's Historic Americana Auctions.

High chair, 22" h seat, 33" h back, pillow-back crest rail, rect splat flanked by raked stiles, scrolled arms, turned supports, rush seat, turned legs joined by stretchers, old beige paint, floral polychrome dec **1,000.00**

Needlework picture, silk threads and watercolor on silk, titled "The Mother's Hope," young girl in landscape setting, MA, early 19th C, framed in oval format, minor scattered staining, small areas of fabric loss, replaced tablet. . . **1,725.00**

Noah's Ark, 18-1/2" l, 5" d, 11-1/2" h, painted red, blue, orange, white, and green wood, roof and one side of base open to inner compartments, six carved and painted animals, Noah, two ladies, one glued leg, some edge wear **750.00**

Quilt, 32-1/2" x 32", printed center fabric with four playful kittens, surrounded by appliquéd parrots, crazy quilt borders, highlighted with decorative embroidery, initials "SBW," imperfections **125.00**

Rattle, 4" l, sterling silver, pink coral handle below knopped body with emb dec, five silver bells, whistle, maker's mark "E.S.B.," Birmingham, England, 19th C **475.00**

Rocking Horse, 40-1/2" l, 14-1/2" w, 21-1/2" h, painted and carved, leather and green velvet saddle, America, mid-19th C, ears, bridle, one stirrup and stirrup leather missing **1,150.00**

Sled, 37" l, 12-1/4" w, 20" h, carved oak and wrought iron, carved horse head, traces of polychrome dec, PA, 19th C **3,110.00**

Rocker, Lincoln style, America, mid-19th C, walnut, caned back and seat, old yellow ochre paint, later caning and paint, small hole in cane back, 10-1/2" h seat, $220. Photo courtesy of Cowan's Historic Americana Auctions.

Sleigh, 19" l, 13-1/2" w, 18" h, high sides, wooden runners, old repaint with scrollwork and foliage, red ground, yellow line borders, blue int., edge wear **385.00**

Tricycle horse, 39" l, 22-1/2" w, 33" h, painted wood horse model, glass eyes, suede saddle, velvet saddle blanket, single front wheel, two rear wheels, chain-driven mechanism, by Jugnet, Lyon, repainted **850.00**

Wheelbarrow, painted red, hand painted scenes with American eagle and flags **2,700.00**

CHILDREN'S TOY DISHES

History: Dishes made for children often served a dual purpose—playthings and a means of learning social graces. Dish sets came in two sizes. The first was for actual use by the child when entertaining friends. The second, a smaller size, was for use with dolls.

Children's dish sets often were made as a sideline to a major manufacturing line, either as a complement to the family service or as a way to use up the last of the day's batch of materials. The artwork of

For more information, see this book.

famous illustrators, such as Palmer Cox, Kate Greenaway, and Rose O'Neill, can be found on porcelain children's sets.

Akro Agate

Tea set, octagonal, large, green and white, Little American Maid, orig box, 17 pcs **225.00**
Water set, Play Time, pink and blue, orig box, seven pcs. **125.00**

Bohemian glass, decanter set, ruby flashed, Vintage dec, five pcs . . **135.00**

China

Cheese dish, cov, hunting scene, Royal Bayreuth **85.00**
Chocolate pot, Model-T car with passengers **90.00**
Creamer, Phoenix Bird. **20.00**
Cup and saucer, Phoenix Bird. **15.00**
Dinner set, Willow Ware, blue and white, Japanese **200.00**
Tea set, Children playing, cov teapot, creamer, cov sugar, six cups, saucers, and tea plates, German, Victorian **285.00**
Tureen, cov, Blue Willow, 3-1/2" w, marked "Made in China" **60.00**

Depression glass, 14-pc set

Cherry Blossom, pink **390.00**
Laurel, McKee, red trim. **355.00**
Moderntone, turquoise, gold . **210.00**

Milk glass

Cheese dish, blue opaque, McKee
. . . . **65.00**
Creamer, Wild Rose. **65.00**
Cup, Nursery Rhyme. **24.00**
Ice-cream platter, Wild Rose . . **60.00**

Pattern glass

Berry set, Wheat Sheaf, seven pcs
. . . . **85.00**

Table set, Oval Star pattern, Indiana Glass Co., $135.

Butter, cov, Hobnail with Thumbprint base, blue **95.00**
Cake stand, Palm Leaf Fan . . **35.00**
Creamer, Lamb. **75.00**
Cup and saucer, Lion **50.00**
Pitcher, Oval Star, clear **20.00**
Punch set, Wheat Sheaf, seven pcs
. . . . **75.00**
Spooner, Tulip and Honeycomb
. . . . **24.00**
Sugar, cov, Beaded Swirl **40.00**
Water set, Nursery Rhyme, pitcher, six tumblers **225.00**

CHINESE CERAMICS

History: The Chinese pottery tradition has existed for thousands of years. By the 16th century, Chinese ceramic wares were being exported to India, Persia, and Egypt. During the Ming dynasty (1368-1643), earthenwares became more highly developed. The Ch'ien Lung period (1736-1795) of the Ch'ing dynasty marked the golden age of interchange with the West.

Trade between China and the West began in the 16th century, when the Portuguese established Macao. The Dutch entered the trade early in the 17th century. With the establishment of the English East India

Company, all of Europe sought Chinese-made pottery and porcelain. Styles, shapes, and colors were developed to suit Western tastes, a tradition which continued until the late 19th century.

Fine Oriental ceramics continued to be made into the 20th century, and modern artists enjoy equal fame with older counterparts.

Additional Listings: Canton, Fitzhugh, Imari, Kutani, Nanking, Orientalia, Rose Medallion, and Satsuma.

Japanese, Oribe pottery, basin, handle, cherry blossom and vine design, greens and brown over cream colored body, 18" x 17", 9-1/2" h, $415. Photo courtesy of Sanford Alderfer Auction Company.

Chinese

Bowl, 6-3/4" d, flared sides, cut foot, molded int. with twin fish medallion at well, pale crackled blue-green glaze, Song Dynasty. **265.00**
Brush washer, 4-3/4" d, compressed circular form, splayed base, incurved rim, thick bluish-gray crackle glaze
. . . . **175.00**

Cup

3-1/2" d, porcelain, turquoise, enamel stylized lotus and bats with gilt, Kuang Hsu mark in gold, 1874-1908. . . . . **2,000.00**
4-1/2" x 3", blue and white, rhinoceros horn-form, molded to resemble Buddha's hand, citron, and foliage, Ch'ien Lung period, 1736-95, five spur marks on the base **3,450.00**
9" l, Blanc de Chine, Te Hua ware, rhinoceros horn-form, carved hardwood stand **825.00**

Dish

9-1/4" d, blue and white porcelain, scalloped, central figural scene surrounded by shaped panels alternating with figures and flowering prunus branches, price for pr **450.00**
11" d, shaped rim, incised floral dec, celadon glaze, Ming dynasty
. . . . **1,200.00**

Tea set, Staffordshire, brown transfer print, May pattern, little girl gathering roses in apron, English cottage in background, teapot, creamer, covered sugar, waste bowl, four 5-1/2" d plates, four cups and saucers, $395. Photo courtesy of Cowan's Historic Americana Auctions.

Figure

9" l, 8" h, mythical animals, porcelain with robin's-egg blue glaze, 19th C
. . . . **500.00**

16" h, horse, standing, draped trappings and saddle, green, chestnut, and honey glaze, Tang style **650.00**

Garden seat, 18" h, porcelain, hexagonal form, blue and white dec, 19th C **900.00**

Ginger jar, cov, 3-1/2" h, blue and white porcelain, figural procession dec, wood cover **300.00**

Incense burner, 15" h, pottery, San Tsai glaze, impressed six-character K'ang Hsi mark on the base, 19th C . . **425.00**

Jar, cov, baluster

26" h, blue ground with roses, surround reserves of flowers and butterflies, lotus finial, China, 20th C, hairline **950.00**

32" h, blue and white dec of Buddhist lion dogs on cloud strewn ground, lion-mask handles, lion finials, 19th C, minor loss
. . . . **3,200.00**

Jardinière, 14" d, iron red and white, dragon chasing flaming pearl of wisdom dec **150.00**

Lamp base, 16" h vase, celadon and blue ovoid form, warriors in landscape dec **150.00**

Moon flask, 8-1/4" h, blue and white porcelain, two central bird- and flower-filled panels, allover scrolling floral and foliate dec, c1830 . . . **425.00**

Plate, 9-3/8" d, Cabbage Leaf and Butterfly, 19th C, minor chips, gilt and enamel wear, cracks, nine-pc set
. . . . **375.00**

Soup plate, 9-5/8" d, Cabbage Leaf and Butterfly, 19th C, minor chips, gilt and enamel wear, four-pc set . . . **175.00**

Teapot, cov, porcelain, Batavia ware, brown glazed ground, enamel flowers and gilt, 18th C **270.00**

Urn, 17" h, baluster, blue and white, scrolling foliate, floral dec, pr . . . **450.00**

Vase

7" h, porcelain, high shouldered, wide neck form, camellia-leaf green glaze with iridescence, China, 18th C **250.00**

20-1/2" h, Tsun-shape, Wu Tsai ware, birds and flowers dec, China, Transitional period, c1640
. . . . **2,000.00**

Chinese export

Basin, 16" d, 5" h, extended rim dec with figures in garden, alternating with reserve of bird on branch surrounded by a border of overlapping blue fans, int. with figures in a garden, 19th C
. . . . **750.00**

Bough pot, 8-1/2" h, 8-1/4" w, 5-1/4" w base, 7-7/8" d, octagonal, applied dec of squirrels among grapes on canted corners which flank shaped lanes, central floral sprays, gilt-dec base, Famille Rose palette, gilt rope-twist handles, inserts with five circular apertures, gilt edges, Chinese Export for European market, c1775-85, gilt wear, three insert handles missing, pr
. . . . **13,800.00**

Charger, 13" d, aqua colored ground, polychrome floral design, Greek key border, six character mark, wear
. . . . **120.00**

Tea and coffee service, gilt shields and monograms "AGM" and "RC," gilt borders, fruit finials, coffeepot, teapot, cov sugar bowl, two mugs, two tea bowls, saucer, small bowl, dessert plate, luncheon plate, minor chips and gilt wear, price for 11-pc set . . **1,265.00**

Tea set, child's, partial, gilt rims, wavy line and dot borders, monogram "CRHL" in oval, teapot, tea caddy, creamer, round tray, three small tea bowls and saucers, larger tea bowl and saucer, 19th C, minor gilt wear, price for 12-pc set **865.00**

Tureen, cov, tray, 13" l, 8-1/2" w, 8-1/2" h tureen, short rabbit head handles, cobalt blue underglaze dec, 14-1/2" x 11-1/2" matching tray, late 18th C **2,100.00**

Warming dish, domed cov, 14-1/4" d, 5-1/2" h, fruit finial, Rose Canton dec, repairs, enamel losses **765.00**

Warming plate, 9-1/2" d, Mandarin figures in Famille Rose palette, lattice border **765.00**

Japanese

Bowl, 9-1/2" d, stoneware, gray crackle ware with various fish in polychrome enamels, Japan, Meiji period, 1868-1911 . . . . **550.00**

Brush washer, 4-3/4" d, compressed circular form, splayed base, incurved rim, thick bluish-gray crackle glaze
. . . . **175.00**

Censer, 3-1/2" h, compressed globular form, splayed raised foot, everted rim, countersunk band dec, two scroll handles, white glaze, 19th C . . . **395.00**

Chinese Export, salt, 5-1/2" h, $350.

Chinese Export, tea set, eggshell porcelain, 4-1/2" h teapot, six matching cups and saucers, intricately painted overglaze decorated, early 19th C, some wear to decorated, short hairline in teapot, tiny rim chips, $220. Photo courtesy of Cowan's Historic Americana Auctions.

Charger, 15-1/4" d, Arita ware, blue and white, scholars in garden vignettes, Japan, late 17th/early 18th C . **1,500.00**

Garden lantern, 10-1/2" h, Bizen ware, stoneware, rustic form with floral piercings, Japan, 19th C **200.00**

Plate, 8-1/4" d, Kakiemon, lobed form, straw rope edge, relief dec of three friends, pine, bamboo, and prunus, center with pair of pheasants and flowers, red, yellow, blue, turquoise, and black enamel, gilt accents, three spur marks on base, late 19th/early 19th C, small chip and hairline. . **520.00**

Vase

7-1/2" h, celadon glaze with band of peach blooms across boy and mouth, sgd in underglaze blue "Tai Nihon Kozan Sei" within square for Makuzu Kozan, c1900. . . . . **575.00**

8-1/2" h, studio pottery, ovoid form, four lug handles, top covered in blue-brown glaze, bottom engraved with Archaic-style horses and fish, sgd with an impressed seal on bottom, Japan, late 19th/early 20th C **395.00**

Wine Ewer, 7-1/2" h, porcelain with underglaze blue and red decoration of an abstract flowering branch, greenish glaze with crackle, Korea, Yi period, 17th C **1,880.00**

Korean

Bottle, 10" h, stoneware, Punchong ware, globular form with decorative slip swirls on a celadon ground, Yi period, 15th/16th C, repair to mouth. . . . **500.00**

Jar, 9" d, 8" h, globular, porcelain, four Bok characters at the sides in underglaze blue, very rare two-character mark on base evidently reading "minister of the right," 18th C, minor rim fretting. **9,500.00**

Oil jar, 3" h, stoneware, underglaze iron decoration, celadon ground, Koryo period, 12th C. **650.00**

Vase, 8-3/4" h, porcelain, underglaze blue and red, decoration of landscapes of the sun, mountains, and trees, Maebyong shape with a wide flaring mouth, Yi period, 17th C. **1,880.00**

CHINTZ CHINA

History: Chintz china has been produced since the 17th century. The brightly colored exotic patterns produced on fabric imported from India to England during this century was then recreated on ceramics. Early chintz patterns were hand painted and featured large flowers, fantastical birds, and widely spaced patterns. The advent of transfer printing resulted in the development of chintz dishes, which could be produced cheaply enough to sell to the masses. By the 1830s, a number of Staffordshire potteries were producing chintzware for everyday use. These early patterns have not yet attracted the interest of most chintz collectors.

Collectors typically want the patterns dating from roughly 1920 until the 1950s. In 1920, A.G. Richardson "Crown Ducal" produced a range of all-over-transfer chintz patterns which were very popular in North America, particularly the East Coast. Patterns such as Florida, Festival, and Blue Chintz were originally introduced as tea sets and then expanded to full dinner services. Florida is the most popular of the Crown Ducal patterns in North America, but Pink Chintz, especially, and Peony has become increasingly popular in the past year or two.

What most collectors consider the first modern chintz was designed by Leonard Grimwade in 1928 and named Marguerite. This pattern was very successful for many years, but has never been highly regarded by collectors. Every year at the British Industries Fair, factories vied with each other to introduce new patterns that would catch the buyers' eye. From the late 1920s until the mid-1950s, Royal Winton produced more than 80 chintz patterns. In some cases, the background color was varied and the name changed: Hazel, Spring, and Welbeck is the same pattern in different colorways. After World War II, Royal Winton created more than 15 new patterns, many of which were more modern looking with large flowers and rich dark burgundy, blue, or black backgrounds—patterns such as May Festival, Spring Glory, and Peony. These patterns have not been very popular with collectors as 1930s patterns, although other 1950s patterns such as Florence and Stratford have become almost as popular as Julia and Welbeck. Some of the more widely spaced patterns, like Victorian Rose and Cotswold, are now attracting collectors.

The 1930s were hard times in the potteries and factories struggled to survive. They copied any successful patterns from any other factories. James Kent Ltd. produced chintzes such as DuBarry, Apple Blossom, and Rosalynde. These patterns were sold widely in North America and complete dinner sets still occasionally turn up. The most popular pattern for collectors is the white Hydrangea, although Apple Blossom seems to be more and more sought after. Elijah Cotton "Lord Nelson" was another factory that produced large amounts of chintz. The workers at Elijah Cotton were never as skilled as the Grimwades' workers, and usually the handles and spouts of teapots and coffeepots were left undecorated. Collectors love the Nelson Ware stacking teapots, especially in Black Beauty and Green Tulip, but prices for all the Lord Nelson have fallen in the past year.

Although a number of factories produced bone china after World War II, only Shelley Pottery seems to be highly desired by today's collector.

By the late 1950s, young brides didn't want the dishes of their mothers and grandmothers, but preferred the clean lines of modern Scandinavian furniture and dishes. Chintz gradually died out by the early 1960s, and it was not until the 1990s that collectors began to search for the dishes their mothers had scorned.

Reproduction Alert: Both Royal Winton and James Kent reproduced some of their more popular patterns. Royal Winton is reproducing Welbeck, Florence, Summertime, and Julia; in 1999 it added Joyce-Lynn, Marion, Majestic, Royalty, and Richmond, Old Cottage Chintz, and Stratford. The company added several new chintz patterns such as Blue Cottage and Christmas Chintz. James Kent reproduced Du Barry, Hydrangea, and Rosalynde, as well as creating several new colorways of old patterns. The company announced in October 2001 that it would be discontinuing the production of chintz ware. The Elijah Cotton backstamp was purchased and new issue Lord Nelson is now on the market. Wade is now producing three chintz patterns—Butterfly, Thistle, and Sweet Pea. Some of the Royal Winton patterns have been copied by Two's Company and Godinger. A number of English ceramic factories are producing a variety of new chintz patterns. Prices for ordinary pieces of vintage chintz have continued to fall as a result of the flood of reproduction chintz, but collectors are still willing to pay for rare shapes in popular patterns.

Warning: Before you buy chintz, ask whether it is new or vintage. Ask to see a photograph of the backstamps. The "1995" on the RW backstamp refers to the year the company was bought, and not the year the chintz was made. Compare old and new backstamps on www.chintz.net.com or in Susan Scott's *Charlton Standard Catalogue of Chintz*, 3rd edition, *New Chintz Section*. Contact the factories for current production lists to avoid confusing old and new chintz.

Adviser: Susan Scott.

Elijah Cotton "Lord Nelson"

Bud vase, 5" h, Rosetime pattern **125.00**

Creamer and sugar, tray, Skylark pattern **95.00**

Cup and saucer, Marina pattern . **50.00**

Mustard pot, cov, underplate, Rosetime pattern **85.00**

Royal Winton, Julia pattern, cup and saucer, $125. Chintz photos courtesy of Susan Scott.

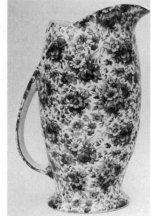

Royal Winton, Summertime pattern, pitcher, $350.

Plate, 8-1/2" sq, Pansy pattern .. **75.00**
Salt and pepper shakers, tray, Black Beauty pattern............... **95.00**
Teapot, stacking, totally patterned Marina **600.00**

Grimwades "Royal Winton"
Biscuit barrel, metal lid, Somerset pattern.................... **525.00**
Breakfast set, Marion pattern.. **750.00**
Bud vase, 5-1/4" h, Royalty pattern **125.00**
Condiment set, five pieces, Royalty pattern.................... **300.00**
Creamer and sugar, Raleigh Shape, English Rose pattern......... **175.00**
Cup and saucer, Spring Glory pattern **65.00**
Eggcup, double, Summertime pattern **95.00**
Jam pot, liner, silver lid, Beeston pattern.................... **150.00**
Jug, 5-1/2" h, Albans shape, Sweet Pea pattern.................... **350.00**
Plate, 6" Ascot, Majestic pattern. **75.00**
Sandwich tray, Crocus pattern. **125.00**
Teapot, stacking
    Julia pattern **1,200.00**
    Old Cottage Chintz pattern.. **450.00**

James Kent, DuBarry pattern, teapot, Melrose shape, $375.

Tennis set, cup and underplate, Florence pattern............. **125.00**
Toast rack, five bars, Julia pattern **250.00**

James Kent Ltd.
Bowl, 5-1/2" d, ruffled, Florita pattern **75.00**
Coffeepot, Granville shape, Primula pattern **300.00**
Compote, ftd, Hydrangea pattern **125.00**
Creamer and sugar, tray, Rapture pattern **95.00**
Cup and saucer, Crazy Paving pattern **45.00**
Nut dish, 3" sq, Apple Blossom pattern **45.00**
Plate, 9" round, Rosalynde pattern **75.00**
Salt and pepper shakers, tray, Du Barry pattern **95.00**
Shaker, Sugar Du Barry pattern. **125.00**

Midwinter Ltd.
Biscuit barrel, chrome lid, Bird Chintz pattern **175.00**
Cake plate, three tiers, Brama pattern **95.00**

A. G. Richardson "Crown Ducal"
Bowl, 5" scalloped edge, Peony pattern **150.00**
Cake plate, 8", metal handle, Primula pattern **95.00**
Comport, 7", Spring Blossom pattern **195.00**
Condiment set, Purple Chintz pattern **250.00**
Cream jug, 3" h, Pink Chintz pattern **125.00**
Demittasse cup and saucer, Florida **75.00**
Eggcup, bucket shape, Pansy pattern **85.00**
Plate, 8-1/2" sq, Blue Chintz pattern **110.00**
Teapot, two cup, Primula pattern **275.00**
Vase, 6-1/4" h, Purple Chintz pattern **150.00**

Shelley Potteries Ltd.
Butter dish, Melody pattern ... **200.00**
Coffeepot, Rock Garden pattern **500.00**
Cake plate, yellow Summer Glory pattern **175.00**
Cup and saucer, Henley shape, Countryside pattern **250.00**
Cup and saucer, Oleander shape, Primrose pattern............. **195.00**

Crown Ducal, vase, pierced cover, purple, A. G. Richardson, $275.

Lamp, Maytime pattern, green Trim **450.00**
Pin dish, 4-1/2" l, Melody pattern **85.00**
Teapot, six cup, Marguerite pattern **375.00**

CHRISTMAS ITEMS

History: The celebration of Christmas dates back to Roman times. Several customs associated with modern Christmas celebrations are traced back to early pagan rituals.

Father Christmas, believed to have evolved in Europe in the 7th century, was a combination of the pagan god Thor, who judged and punished the good and bad, and St. Nicholas, the generous Bishop of Myra. Kris Kringle originated in Germany and was brought to America by the Germans and Swiss who settled in Pennsylvania in the late 18th century.

In 1822, Clement C. Moore wrote "A Visit From St. Nicholas" and developed the character of Santa Claus into the one we know today. Thomas Nast did a series of drawings for *Harper's Weekly* from 1863 until 1886 and further solidified the character and appearance of Santa Claus.

Additional Listings: See *Warman's Americana & Collectibles* for more examples.

Reproduction Alert: Almost all holiday decorations, including Christmas, are now being skillfully reproduced. Only by knowing the source of a possible purchase, trusting the dealer, and careful observation can you be sure you are obtaining an antique.

Advertising

Bank, molded rubber, Santa Clause holding a coin, toys in pack, marked "Christmas Club A. Corp, N.Y. 1972" **6.00**

Booklet, "When All The World Is Kin," 5" x 4", collection of Christmas stories, Christmas giveaway, Fowler, Dick, and Walker, The Boston Store, Wilkes-Barre, PA **7.00**

Catalog, Boston Store, Milwaukee, WI, 1945, 48 pgs, 8-1/2" x 11", "For An American Christmas" **20.00**

Dime bank, celluloid canister, printed in color on one side with Magi offering gifts as Christmas star appears in distant sky, other side with green and red holly wreath, both scenes rimmed in gold, red letter inscription theme to save dimes for Christmas gifts to church **45.00**

Pinback button

American Red Cross, red, green, and white celluloid, Santa carrying toy sack with Red Cross symbol, 1916 .... **60.00**

American Red Cross Health Crusader, red, green, and white celluloid, snow laden pine tree with Red Cross symbol, flanked by red double barred cross symbol for National Tuberculosis Assn, 1917-18 .... **35.00**

Baron's Santa, green portrait, bright white ground, red "Merry Christmas Baron's," 1960s **35.00**

Compliments of the Boston Store, multicolored Santa on village rooftop under full moon, early 1900s **45.00**

Eagle Tribune, 1991 Santa Fund, red, white, and blue portrait, two green holly sprigs **25.00**

Esso, red, white, and blue, centered Santa, 1940 .... **45.00**

Gilmore Brothers Santa, black and white portrait, fleshtone tinted face, red cap, black "Christmas Greetings-Gilmore Brothers," 1940s **60.00**

Gorman's, multicolored, Santa in dark red parka, dark blue not sky dotted by white stars, white lettering and "1904" in black on beard **125.00**

Joske Bros Santason is Here, litho, color design on yellow ground, Santa and child **60.00**

Macy's Santa Knows, red and white, 1950s **35.00**

McCurdy's Santa, 1-1/2" d, multicolored Santa surrounded by children in winter outfits, holly leaves and berries in background, Bastian paper backing, c1910 .... **125.00**

Meet Me In Norman, black and white Santa portrait, green ground, white lettering, c1960s **35.00**

My Headquarters-The Candy Kitchen, multicolored, Santa sighting through telescope, 1920s **125.00**

National Tuberculosis Assn, Health for All, multicolored litho, Santa, 1936 .... **15.00**

Philadelphia Bulletin, multicolored portrait of Santa, accented by holly sprigs, upper pale blue background blending into tan, 1930s **40.00**

Santa Claus at Schipper & Blocks, multicolored, Santa wearing holly leaf and berry crown, nestled by blond child, pale blue blending to white background, early 1900s **85.00**

Christmas tree stand, Europe, c1928, square stand with geometric raised and openwork decorated, bronze patina, minor wear, 13-3/8" w, 4-3/4" h, $175. Photo courtesy of Skinner Auctioneers and Appraisers.

Santa in biplane, 1-1/4" d, Santa steering plane over rooftops, Whitehead & Hoag paper backing, c1912 .... **195.00**

Spiegel Toyland Santa, multicolored litho, black lettering, 1930s .. **50.00**

The Christmas Store, Wolf & Dessauer, multicolored, Santa waving one hand while holding sheaf of holly over opposite shoulder, pale turquoise background, black lettering, early 1900s **95.00**

The May Co. Santa, multicolored Santa surrounded by children in winter outfits, holly leaves and berries in background, red lettering "I Am At The May Co." **95.00**

Stickpin, diecut thin cello multicolored portrait of Santa on short hanger stickpin, back inscribed, "Meet Me At Bowman's," c1920 .... **48.00**

Trade card, child holding snowballs, "The White is King of all Sewing Machines, 80,000 now in use," reverse reads "J. Saltzer, Pianos, Organs, and Sewing Machines, Bloomsburg, Pa." **10.00**

Candy box, cardboard

4-1/2" l, 3" h, Christmas Greetings, three carolers, USA **5.00**

6" x 5", pocketbook style, tuck-in flap, Merry Christmas, Santa in store window with children outside, marked "USA" **15.00**

8" h, four-sided cornucopia, Merry Christmas, Santa, sleigh, and reindeer over village rooftops, string bail, USA **35.00**

Children's books

How Santa Filled the Christmas Stockings, Carolyn Hodman, color illus by F. W. Stecher, Stecher Litho Co., 1916, 13" x 71" **85.00**

Blotter, celluloid, cream colored, one image of Santa in sleigh being pulled by six reindeer across snow-covered field, text "Season's Greetings The Inter-State National Bank Kansas City January First, 1916," box in back of sleigh has text "A.B.A. 1916," probably American Banking Association, two paper blotter pages held to cello cover at left of front oval cello fastener having design of holly bough plus brass tabs on back, 3" x 7-5/8", $95. Photo courtesy of Hake's Americana & Collectibles.

Light bulb, Santa-shape, 9" h, $135. Photo courtesy of Joy Luke Auctions.

Rudolph the Red-Nosed Reindeer, Robert I. May, Maxton Publishers, Inc., 1939. . . . . **12.00**
The Littlest Snowman, Charles Tazewell, Grosset Dunlap, NY, 1958 . . . . . . **18.00**

Feather tree
6" h, red wooden base **35.00**
12" h, green wooden base **95.00**
26" h, red and green wooden base
. . . . **225.00**
4' h, green goose feather-wrapped branches with metal candleholders, painted white with green trim round wooden base, marked "Germany"
. . . . **420.00**

Figures
Belsnickle, 5-1/8" h, chalk, green-hooded coat with clear mica flecks, painted black base, feather tree missing, minor damage to base **275.00**
Father Christmas
　　7" h, composition, pink face, red-cloth coat, painted blue pants, black boots, mounted on mica-covered cardboard base, marked "Japan" **90.00**
　　8" h, papier-mâché, hollow molded, plaster covered, white coat, black boots, sprinkled with mica . **300.00**
Reindeer, 1" h, pot metal, marked "Germany" **20.00**
Santa Claus
　　3" h, cotton batting, red, attached to cardboard house, marked "Japan"
　　. . . . . **48.00**
　　3" l, celluloid, molded, one-piece Santa, sleigh, and reindeer . **35.00**

5" h, hard plastic, Santa on green plastic skis, USA **120.00**
10" h, pressed cardboard, red hat and jacket, black boots **90.00**
Sheep, 3" h, composition body, carved wooden legs, covered with cloth or wool, glass eyes **40.00**

Greeting cards
1892, "Sincere Good Wishes," purple pansy with green leaves, greeting inside, Raphael Tuck & Sons **12.00**
1910, "Loving Greetings," flat card, two girls pictured hanging garland, marked "Germany" **10.00**
1933, "Merry Christmas," series of six envelopes, decreasing in size, small card in last envelope, American Greeting Publishers, Cleveland, USA
. . . . **12.00**

House, cardboard
2" x 2", mica covered, wire loop on top, marked "Czechoslovakia" **10.00**
4" x 5", house and fence, sponge trees, marked "USA" **12.00**
Lantern, 8" h, four sided, peaked top, wire bail, metal candleholder in base, black cardboard, colored tissue paper scenes, 1940s **25.00**
Magazine, *St. Nicholas,* bound edition of 1915 and 1916, color covers, ads, illus, story **15.00**

Ornaments
Angel, 4" h, wax over composition, human-hair wig, spun-glass wings, cloth dress, Germany **60.00**
Ball, 2" d, silvered glass, any color
. . . . **4.00**

Christmas tree light set, manufactured by Royal Electric Co., using G.E. Mazda lamps, original complete set of eight Popeye character lamps with multi-colored Bakelite bases, original cloth covered wiring, original display box which shows Popeye and Wimpy in Christmas setting with tree in background, characters also shown around perimeter of box cover, interior with similar bright graphics, box shows original Filenes price sticker of $1.00, 16-1/2" l, 6-1/2" h, $230. Photo courtesy of James D. Julia, Inc.

Miniature jug, brown and white Bristol glaze, original paper label "A Merry Christmas and Happy New Year," slight wear to label, c1900, 3-1/2" h, $135. Photo courtesy of Vicki and Bruce Waasdorp.

Beads, 72" l, glass, half-inch multicolored beads, paper label marked "Japan" **8.00**
Bulldog, 3" h, Dresden, three-dimensional, marked "Germany"
. . . . **250.00**
Camel, 4" h, cotton batting, Germany
. . . . **160.00**
Cross, 4" h, beaded, two-sided, silvered, wire hanger, paper label marked "Czechoslovakia" **20.00**
Father Christmas on Donkey, 10" h, chromolithograph, blue robe, tinsel trim
. . . . **25.00**
Kugel, 4-1/2" d, round, deep sapphire blue, brass hanger **120.00**
Mandolin, 5" h, unsilvered glass, wrapped in lametta and tinsel . . . **45.00**
Parakeet, 5" h, multicolored glass, spun glass tail, mounted on metal clip
. . . . **20.00**
Pear, 3" h, cotton batting, mica highlights, paper leaf, wire hanger, Japan **15.00**
Santa Claus in Chimney, 4" h, glass, Germany **75.00**
Swan, 5" x 6", Dresden, flat, gold with silver, green, and red highlights **150.00**
Tree top, 11" h, three spheres stacked with small clear glass balls, silvered, lametta and tinsel trim, attached to blown glass hooks **90.00**

Postcards, Germany

Christmas bells and snow scene, marked "Made in Germany," used, one cent stamp, 1911 . . . . 20.00

"Happy Christmas Wishes," Santa steering ship 12.00

"May Your Christmas Be Merry and Gay," photo card, sepia tones, Father Christmas peeking between two large wooden doors, wearing fur cap . . 20.00

Putz

Brush tree, 6" h, green, mica-covered branches, wooden base 8.00

Christmas-tree fence

Cast iron, silver, ornate gold trim, 15 10" l segments with posts, Germany 600.00

Wood, folding red and green sections, 48" l, USA 35.00

Penny wooden, two children on seesaw, hand-carved wood, multicolored, Nurenberg or Erzgebrige 32.00

Toys

Jack-in-the-box, 9-1/2" h, "Santa Pops," hard plastic, red-felt hat, orig box, Tigrette Industries, 1956 . . . . 30.00

Merry-go-round, wind-up, celluloid, green and red base, four white reindeer heads, Santa sitting under umbrella,

Print, Good Morning-Merry Christmas, young girl in white dress, bonnet with red ribbon, narrow painted frame, 15" w, 28-1/2" h, $95. Photo courtesy of Joy Luke Auctions.

Santa spins around, stars hanging from umbrella bounce of bobbing deer heads, orig box, Japan 65.00

Santa, 10" h, battery operated, metal covered with red and white plush suit and hat, soft-plastic face, holding metal wand with white star light, wand moves up and down and lights up while Santa turns head 90.00

Tree stand, 9-3/4" sq, 4" h, cast iron, old worn green, gold, white, and red paint, relief tree trunk, foliage, and stairway design 110.00

CLEWELL POTTERY

History: Charles Walter Clewell was first a metal worker and secondarily a potter. In the early 1900s, he opened a small shop in Canton, Ohio, to produce metal-overlay pottery.

Metal on pottery was not a new idea, but Clewell was perhaps the first to completely mask the ceramic body with copper, brass, or "silvered" or "bronzed" metals. One result was a product whose patina added to the character of the piece over time.

Since Clewell operated on a small scale with little outside assistance, only a limited quantity of his artwork exists. He retired at the age of 79 in 1955, choosing not to reveal his technique to anyone else.

Marks: Most of the wares are marked with a simple incised "Clewell," along with a code number. Because Clewell used pottery blanks from other firms, the names "Owens" or "Weller" are sometimes found.

Candlesticks, pr, 7" h, 3-1/2" d, copper clad, four sided, dark bronzed patina, unmarked 1,300.00

Jardinière, 14" h, ovoid, matte finish 150.00

Vase, copper-clad, reticulated collar embossed with three poppy pods in high relief and blooming poppy, Clewell stamp mark and remnant of paper label, on Weller blank, medium dark patina, 5-1/2" d, 13-1/4" h, $4,890. Photo courtesy of David Rago Auctions.

Mug, 4-1/2" h, copper clad, riveted design, applied monogram, relief signature 65.00

Vase

3-1/2" d, 8-1/2" h, copper-clad, classical shape, bronze and verdigris patina, marked "Clewell 288-256," some surface scarring 800.00

5" d, 11" h, copper-clad, baluster, verdigris patina, incised "Clewell 315-2-6," surface scratches 980.00

7-1/2" h, 4" d, ovoid, copper clad, verdigris to bronze patina, incised "Clewell/351-25" 1,000.00

11" h, 5" d, bulbous, copper clad, bronzed finish, incised "Clewell/357-5," cleaned some time ago 500.00

Vessel, 7-1/2" w, 11" h, copper-clad, verdigris patina, incised "Clewell 72-26" 1,725.00

CLIFTON POTTERY

History: The Clifton Art Pottery, Newark, New Jersey, was established by William A. Long, once associated with Lonhuda Pottery, and Fred Tschirner, a chemist.

Production consisted of two major lines: Crystal Patina, which resembled true porcelain with a subdued crystal-like glaze, and Indian Ware or Western Influence, an adaptation of the American Indians' unglazed and decorated pottery with a high-glazed black interior. Other lines included Robin's-Egg Blue and Tirrube. Robin's-Egg Blue is a variation of the crystal patina line, but in blue-green instead of straw-colored hues and with a less-prominent crushed-crystal effect in the glaze. Tirrube, which is often artist signed, features brightly colored, slip-decorated flowers on a terra-cotta ground.

Marks: Marks are incised or impressed. Early pieces may be dated and impressed with a shape number. Indian wares are identified by tribes.

Biscuit jar, cov, 7" h, 4-1/4" d, gray-brown ground, enameled running ostrich and stork, florals, bail handle 300.00

Bowl, 9" d, Indian cooking ware, black glazed dec, marked, minor rim flake 150.00

Creamer, Crystal Patina, incised "Clifton," dated 225.00

Decanter, 11-1/2" h, rose shading to deep rose, purple flowers, gilt butterfly on neck, applied handle, marbleized rose and white stopper 150.00

Jardinière, 8-1/2" h, 11" d, Four Mile Ruin, Arizona, incised and painted motif, buff and black on brown ground, imp mark and incised inscription, hairline to rim **400.00**

Pedestal, 20" h, Indian, unmarked, small chip to top and glaze **690.00**

Vessel, bulbous with stovepipe neck, Indian, swirls on base, marked "Mississippi," No. 227, 9-1/4" d, 12" h, $1,100. Photo courtesy of David Rago Auctions.

Sweetmeat jar, 4" h, hp ducks and cranes, robin's egg blue ground, cow finial **375.00**

Teapot, 6" h, brown and black geometric design **200.00**

Vase

6-1/2" d, 5-1/2" h, spherical, Crystal Patina, green and mirrored caramel glaze, sgd and dated 1906 . . . . **575.00**

9-1/2" h, 4-1/2" d, bottle shape, Crystal Patina, incised "Clifton/158" **350.00**

10" h, 7" d, angular handles, Crystal Patina, incised "Clifton" . . . **450.00**

Vessel

5-1/4", gourd shape, Indian, swirl pattern, Arkansas, #216, marked **380.00**

7-1/2" x 10", bulbous, Indian, collared rim, geometric chain pattern, "Homolobi, #233," marked, few shallow scratches **925.00**

Vase, spherical, Crystal Patina, unusual green and mirrored caramel glaze, signed and dated 1906, 5-1/2" x 6-1/2", $575. Photo courtesy of David Rago Auctions.

8" x 9", bulbous, Indian, dark birds in flight, "Homolobi, #235," marked **975.00**

12" x 9-1/4", bulbous, Indian, stovepipe neck, swirls on base, "Mississippi #227," marked **1,100.00**

CLOCKS

History: The sundial was the first man-made device for measuring time. Its basic disadvantage is well expressed by the saying: "Do like the sundial, count only the sunny days."

Needing greater dependability, man developed the water clock, oil clock, and sand clock, respectively. All these clocks worked on the same principle—time was measured by the amount of material passing from one container to another.

The wheel clock was the next major step. These clocks can be traced back to the 13th century. Many improvements on the basic wheel clock were made and continue to be made. In 1934, the quartz-crystal movement was introduced.

The first carriage clock was made about 1800 by Abraham Louis Breguet as he tried to develop a clock that would keep accurate time for Napoleon's officers. One special feature of a carriage clock was a device that allowed it to withstand the bumpy ride of a stagecoach. These small clocks usually are easy to carry with their own handle built into a rectangular case.

The recently invented atomic clock, which measures time by radiation frequency, only varies one second in a thousand years.

Notes: Identifying the proper model name for a clock is critical in establishing price. Condition of the works also is a critical factor. Examine the works to see how many original parts remain. If repairs are needed, try to include this in your estimate of purchase price. Few clocks are purchased purely for decorative value.

Advertising, Nature's Remedy, manufactured by Wm. L. Gilbert Clock Co., colorful reverse glass advertising for "Safe – Dependable Vegetable Laxative," original pendulum and key, stain on clock face, 16" w, 31" h, $690. Photo courtesy of James D. Julia, Inc.

Advertising

Chew Friendship Cub Plug, face of man with moving mouth chewing Friendship Tobacco to the tic of the clock, pat'd Mar 2, 1886, 4" h . . **900.00**

Gruen Watch, Williams Jewelry Co. on marquee at bottom, blue neon around perimeter, 15" x 15" **600.00**

Hire's Root Beer, "Drink Hires Root Beer with Root Barks, Herbs," 15" d **250.00**

International Tailoring, Chicago, cast iron, emb design, bronzed, orig working clock, 12" w, 2-1/2" d, 16" h, C.8+ **1,000.00**

Longine's Watches, "The World's Most Honored Watch," brass, 18-1/2" d **300.00**

None Such Mincemeat, pumpkin face, 8-1/2" w, some wear **300.00**

Victrola Records, orig pendulum **2,100.00**

Alarm

Attleboro, 36 hours, nickel-plated case, owl dec, 9" h **75.00**

Bradley, brass, double bells, Germany **40.00**

Advertising, Early Times Hand Made Sourmash, Western Silver Metal Co., Chicago, cast metal, high relief rural scene with figures, cart, and oxen, 14" h, **$125.** *Photo courtesy of Joy Luke Auctions.*

Champion, 30 hours, American movement, metal frame, ornamental feet, 9" h **75.00**

New Haven, c1900, 30 hours, SP case, perfume-bottle shape, beveled-glass mirror, removable cut-glass scent bottle, beaded handle **185.00**

Bracket

Parke, Solomon, Federal case, mahogany veneer, old finish, brass feet, brass hands, brass fusee works, painted steel face with "Strike" and "Silent," labeled "Solomon Parke, Philadelphia," some veneer damage, old veneer repair, pendulum and keys, 17-3/4" h plus top handle **9,350.00**

Regency, Bennett & Co., Norwich, c1810, brass inlaid and gilt bronze mounted mahogany, dial and backplate sgd, oak leaf spandrels, case inlaid with scrolls, gadrooned bun feet, 17" h, chips **4,325.00**

Tiffany & Co., bronze, stepped rect-shaped top, four acorn finials, cast foliate frieze, four capitals with reeded columns, shaped and foliate cast base, beveled glass door and panels, circular face dial with Roman numerals, marked "Famiel Marti Medaille…Paris 1900, Tiffany & Co.", 13" h **600.00**

Carriage

French, oval, brass, four beveled glass panels, fine cut flowers in border to sides, top oval glass panels initialed "M.E.H.," dial painted with woman and cupid, decorative D-shaped handle on top, 5-1/2" h **1,150.00**

Carriage, miniature, English, 1907-08, sterling silver, enameled face with gilded roses, four round feet, hinged handle, stamped "S.O. & Co.," with anchor, lion, h, and registration mark, 2" x 1-1/2" x 3", **$920.** *Photo courtesy of David Rago Auctions.*

Grande Sonnerie, brass, dial marked for "Muiron & Cia., Mexico," phases of the moon, subsidiary day, date, and seconds dial, all enamel, set into brass plate engraved with leafy scrolls and dragons' heads, repeater button, strike/silent quarter strike lever, title on movement engraved in Spanish, made for Mexican market, early 20th C, 7-1/2" h **7,475.00**

New Haven Clock Co., gilded brass case, beveled glass, gold repaint to case, orig pendulum and key, 11-1/2" h **315.00**

Tiffany & Co., early 20th C, brass and glass, French half strike repeater movement marked for Souaillet Freres, enamel dial with Arabic numerals and subsidiary seconds dial, 3-3/8" w, 3" d, 7" h **950.00**

Desk

American, shaped rect, brass case, white enamel bordering cobalt blue, stylized applied monogram, decorative brass corners, central dial with Arabic numerals, 4-3/4" h **150.00**

British United Clock Co., Ltd., Birmingham, England, 20th C, brass, bracket cut-out edges on diamond-shaped brass clock frame, four pierced diamond patterns, floral, bowknot, and fleur-de-lis punch dec, wire easel stand, printed and imp maker's marks, spotty corrosion, 6" w, 4-1/2" h **260.00**

Mantel

Ansonia, French-style, rococo scroll dec, enameled face sgd "Ansonia," bronze colored patina on spelter, orig pendulum, missing finial and key, 14-1/2" h **275.00**

Birge, Mallory, and Co., Bristol, CT, c1830, Classical, mahogany and gilt gesso, scrolled cornice with fruit-filled basket flanked by square plinths, glazed door enclosing white painted and gilt dial, seven-day brass strap weight-driven movement, mirror below, reverse-painted tablet below that, all flanked by gilded engaged and free-standing columns on ball feet, refinished, restoration, imperfections, 17" w, 5" d, 38" h **650.00**

Bradley, Lucius B., Watertown, CT, c1820, mahogany and mahogany veneer, flat molded cornice above glazed door, iron white-painted polychrome and gilt dial with seconds hand, inscribed "Lucius B. Bradley, Watertown, Ct," eight-day brass movement with rack and snail striking mechanism, lower door framing eglomise tablet with classical house by a pond, maker's paper label, both doors flanked by freestanding turned columns, flat veneered base, original finish, minor imperfections, 16-3/4" w, 4-3/4" d, 26-1/4" h **7,050.00**

Desk, E.T. Hurley, bronze, seahorse frame, circular patinated-bronze face, non-functional key-wind movement, original patina, etched numbers, 6" w, 7-1/2" h, **$3,100.** *Photo courtesy of David Rago Auctions.*

Mantel, Black Forest, stag and hunting dogs, foliate woodland scene, c1885, 39" h, $5,040. Photo courtesy of Fontaine's Auction Gallery.

French, late 19th/early 20th C, retailed by Tiffany & Co., bronze and glass, two-train chiming movement, mercury weighted pendulum, rect case with glass on four sides, enamel bezel, partially visible movement, 10-5/8" h
.... **500.00**

French, Louis XVI-style, late 19th C, patinated metal, figural cherub painter with palette and wreath-draped easel, two-train half-striking movement with Japy Fils Medaille D'Argent seal, enamel dial with worn retailer's mark, set into beaded gilt-metal bezel, waisted black marble socle, 17-3/4" w, 7-1/2" d, 22" h **2,990.00**

Germany, white onyx, amber and brown striations, ormolu mounts with shells, paw feet, porcelain dial with chased ormolu center with rampant lions, works marked "Germany," no key, dial damaged, 13" l, 10-3/4" h .. **275.00**

Jugendstil, oak, retailed by Liberty & Co., exposed bell on top, open sides, copper face emb with violets, purple and yellow slag glass window, orig finish, working condition, unmarked, 9-3/4" w, 14-1/4" h **1,840.00**

Leavenworth, Mark, Waterbury, CT, c1825, Federal, pillar and scroll, mahogany, scrolled cresting, three brass urn finials on sq plinths above glazed door, eglomise tablet showing house by lank flanked by freestanding columns, wooden dial with gilt dec housing thirty-hour wooden striking movement, cut-out valanced base, 16-1/2" w, 31-1/4" h, refinished, restoration to tablet......... **3,820.00**

Shreve, Crump & Low, late 19th C, Gothic Revival, carved mahogany, French two-train half-strike movement, engraved silver dial, case formed as Gothic pointed and trefoil arch, paneled turrets, blocked base, 19-1/2" h
.... **850.00**

Terry, Samuel, c1825, Federal, pillar and scroll, mahogany, scrolled cresting, three brass urn finials on sq plinths above glazed door, eglomise tablet showing building in landscape, flanked by freestanding columns, wooden painted and gilt dial, 30-day wooden movement, valanced cut-out base, 17" w, 4-1/2" d, 31-1/2" h, refinished, tablet replaced **1,530.00**

Thomas, Seth, Plymouth Hollow, CT, c1825, Classical, carved mahogany and mahogany veneer, eagle and shield-carved scroll flanked by square plinths above glazed door with eglomise tablet showing public building with floral stenciled border, opening to wooden painted dial, 36 weight-driven movement, flanked by stencil decorated engaged columns on carved acanthus leaf and hairy paw feet, minor imperfections, 17" w, 4-3/4" d, 30" h
.... **775.00**

Tiffany & Co., late 19th C, marble and patinated metal, two-train half-striking movement sgd by Tiffany & Co., pink marble temple form case, pediment set with patinated metal plaque of putti with goat, round bezel set to center of case flanked by patinated pilasters, plinth base mounted with central cartouche and laurel branches, 12-1/4" w, 5-7/8" d, 13-1/8" h **300.00**

Mantel clock with garniture, French, marble and enamel, architectural form clock of beige and brown marble, pediment top over four columns flanking central clock works, stepped down base, gilt metal accents and colorful enamel decorated, two decorative urns of conforming design, losses to marble and gilding, 12-1/2" w, 5-3/4" d, 13-1/2" h clock, 4-1/2" w, 3-1/2" d, 4-1/2" h urns, $770. Photo courtesy of Sanford Alderfer Auction Company.

Mantel, bronze and marble, two dancing cherubs holding sphere, red marble face, engraved open escapement, signed "A. Carrier," 28" h, $3,080. Photo courtesy of Fontaine's Auction Gallery.

Mantel, china, Waterbury, decorated with flowers and leaves, porcelain dial, open escapement, time, and strike, 12" h, $175. Photo courtesy of Joy Luke Auctions.

Victorian, late 19th C, black, rect, two-train strike and bell movement, front with breche d'alep marble pilasters flanking round dial, plinth base with breche d'alep band and diamond inlay, gilt incised line dec, 9-3/4" w, 5-3/4" d, 10-3/4" h **425.00**

Novelty, figural
American, c1880, three stacked rifles supporting drum form pendant housing movement, brass and copper, 10-3/4" h **345.00**
French, 19th C, sedan shape, bronze doré, body with low relief depicting cherubs within low relief within scrolling foliate borders, central enamel dial with Arabic numerals over applied ivory panel depicting cherub, each side with miniature portrait of elegant lady, one sgd "r. peter," other "Renner," 11-1/4" h **1,500.00**

Mantel, Seth Thomas, black marble case, white marble columns, incised decorated highlighted with gold, ornate ormolu trim, $175. Photo courtesy of Joy Luke Auctions.

Pillar and scroll
Downes, Ephraim, Bristol, CT, 1825, mahogany, 30-hour wooden-weight movement, old finish, imperfections, 31" h **950.00**
Leavenworth and Son, Mark, Waterbury, CT, c1825, mahogany, 30-hour wooden movement, imperfections, 16-1/2" w, 4-1/2" d, 29-3/4" h **950.00**
Thomas, Seth, c1825, Federal, mahogany, scrolled cresting joining three brass urn finials above glazed door, 30-hour wooden weight-driven movement, polychrome and gilt dec dial, landscape tablet, flanked by freestanding columns on cut bracket feet, old refinish, minor imperfections, 17-1/4" w, 4-1/2" d, 32" h **2,185.00**

Porcelain
Ansonia, white china scrolled case, painted cherry blossom design, paw feet, works marked "June 14, '81, Ansonia Clock Co., New York," 10-1/4" w, 11-1/2" h, minor imperfections on case **350.00**

Mantel, porcelain, Paris, Honore, 1840-50, rocaille case with peach and gilt glazing, topped by floral bouquet, round steeled dial surrounded by rocaille shells and scrolls, sides with polychrome floral sprays, raised on base with openwork leaves and low rocaille feet, mounted to shaped plateau, further openwork leaves, two train chiming movement, lacking minute hand, 8-3/8" w, 14" h, $950. Photo courtesy of Skinner Auctioneers and Appraisers.

French, possibly Sevres, c1880, architectural stepped-down form, roof with ormolu shell finial, ormolu mounted columns flanking central dial, figural garden scene over scrolled ormolu mounted base, 10-1/2" h, chips, crazing **700.00**

Shelf
Atkins and Downs, eight-day triple, reverse-painted glass with buildings, pendulum window, and split columns, middle section with mirror and full columns, top section with dec dial, split columns, top crest with spread eagle, most of orig label remains, 38" h, 17" w, 6" d **450.00**
Botsford's Improved Patent Timepiece, Coe & Co. 52 Dey St., New York, papier-mâché, scrolled front, gilt, polychrome embellishments, mother-of-pearl floral designs, circular enamel dial inscribed "Saml. S. Spencer," lever spring-driven movement, mounted on dec oval base, brass ball feet, glass dome, 11" h **1,265.00**
Brewster and Ingrahams, Bristol, CT, c1845, Gothic twin steeple, mahogany, peaked cornice, glazed door, stenciled gilt-green on white table showing love birds, enclosing painted zinc dial, double fusee brass movement, flanked by two turned finials and columns, flat base, 19" h, dial replaced, minor veneer loss **1,100.00**
Forrestville Manufacturing Co., Forrestville, CT, c1845, acorn, dial sgd "Forrestville Manufg Co. Bristol County, Co., USA," brass eight-day fusee-type spring-driven movement, reverse painted glass identified as "The State House, Hartford," 24-1/2" h, replaced glass **7,475.00**
North, Norris, Torrington, CT, c1825, Classical, mahogany, flat cornice above glazed door, eglomise tablet of young woman flanked by engaged black paint stenciled columns, polychrome and gilt white painted dial, 30-hour wooden weight-driven movement, 23-3/4" h, 13-1/2" w, 5-1/4" d **4,900.00**
Parker, Gardner, Westborough, MA, c1810, Federal, kidney-shaped iron dial sgd "Warranted by G. Parker" in gilt surround, brass eight-day weight driven movement, mahogany case, box base with inlay, curving skirt and feet, 35" h, old refinish, imperfections . . **26,450.00**
Pomeroy, Noah, Bristol, CT, 1860s, mahogany veneer, movement marked "N. Pomeroy, Bristol, Conn," steeple

Shelf, Ansonia, The Crystal Palace, two spelter standing figures, central mirrored panel, wooden base, under glass dome, 13-3/4" w, 19" h, $450. Photo courtesy of Joy Luke Auctions.

frame encloses glass tablets, lower one with polychrome beehive imagery, 14-3/4" h, imperfections. **1,150.00**

Terry, Eli and Sons, Plymouth, CT, c1810-15, Federal, paper label "Eli Terry and Sons," mahogany, scrolled pediment, wooden painted dial with gilt spandrels, wooden 30-hour movement, eglomise glass, curving case skirt, French feet, 31-1/4" h, restoration **1,955.00**

Thomas, Seth, Plymouth, CT, c1820, Federal, paper label "Seth Thomas," mahogany, wood 30-hour movement, reverse painted glass panels above cyma curved front skirt, thin French feet, 30" h, restoration **1,725.00**

Shelf, Gilbert, oak case, ornately carved floral decorated, glass door, $125. Photo courtesy of Joy Luke Auctions.

Unidentified MA maker

c1805, Federal, mahogany, pierced fret over unsigned painted dial, rocking ship and gilt spandrels, red, white, and blue shields, box base on feet, 38-1/2" h, restorations **12,650.00**

c1810-15, Federal, mahogany, molded cresting above glazed door opening to painted and gilt iron dial, inscribed "I. Curtis, Concord" above design of red drapery and gilt scrolls, eight-day brass weight-driven movement, crossbanded case on cut-out base, flaring French feet, old finish, 35-1/2" h, signature on dial probably spurious, other imperfections **7,635.00**

Willard, Aaron, Jr.

Boston, MA, c1815, Federal, kidney dial sgd "Aaron Willard Boston," pierced crest, eight-day timepiece with recoil escapement, veneered mahogany case with shaped skirt, flaring feet, 37-1/2" h, old refinish, minor imperfections. . . . **32,200.00**

Boston, MA, c1817, Federal, scrolled crest above painted, dished dial, surrounded by reverse painted glass tablet which reads "Aaron Willard Boston" above molding, lower eglomise tablet with "The Escape of the *Constitution*," frontal brass paw feet, rear-turned tapered flat feet, 35" h, restoration **7,475.00**

Wood, David, Newburyport, MA, c1815, Federal, mahogany inlaid, dial sgd "David Wood Newburyport," solid crest with star inlays above painted dial, red and gold spandrels, female neoclassical figure encloses brass 60-hour weight-driven movement, seconds dial aperture, engaged quarter-columns flank satinwood inlaid door, curving skirt, flaring French feet, 33-3/4" h, restoration to case **12,650.00**

Skeleton, French, by Brocot, Rue D'Oleans 15 (Maris), brass, arch form, shaped sides, enamel face, two-train chiming movement with pull repeater, mounted to felt lined giltwood base with bun feet, 10-1/2" h brass and bound glass cover, 7-3/8" h. **650.00**

Table

French, gilt bronze and enamel, case finely molded gilt bronze with hooved feet, translucent maroon panel enameled with cherubs and floral

Shelf, Seth Thomas, walnut case, glass door, double weights, time and strike, original paper label, 25" h, $325. Photo courtesy of Joy Luke Auctions.

sprays, maroon enameled dial with circular florals, gilt numerals, surmounted by matching enameled dome, gilt acorn finial, works stamped "Etienne Maxant, Brevete, Paris made in France," c1900, 14" h **2,590.00**

French, gilt bronze and guilloche enamel, round clock, Swiss movement, enameled in translucent azure blue on engraved radiating ground, enameled and gilt chapter ring, gilt bronze case surmounted by petal forms, 19th C, 4" d **600.00**

Wendell, "Mr. Clock," sq ribbon-mahogany box, tall verdigris-patinated copper legs, sgd and dated 1988, 24" x 6". **1,380.00**

Shelf, E.N. Welch, mahogany ogee case, double weight, glass door decorated with eagle, original paper label, $250. Photo courtesy of Joy Luke Auctions.

Tall Case, Dwarf

Gilmanton, Noah Ranlet, NH, dial sgd "Noah Ranlet Gilmanton 1796," time and strike movement, pine, scrolled solid crest above bonnet that encloses sgd, painted dial, includes side lights, waist door, flanked by quarter-engaged columns above base box, later stenciled eagle dec, pine case with old refinish, 49-1/4" h, replaced crest, other imperfections **18,400.00**

French, 19th C, marble and agate, Egyptian revival style, ormolu anthemion corner pendants, female busts, swans, laurel wreaths, paw feet, 52" h **3,800.00**

Hingham, J. Wilder, c1810-15, dial face indistinctly sgd, reverse dial reads "J. Wilder Hingham" in period script, painted bowl of fruit in arch, gilt spandrels, eight-day timepiece with drop-off strike, mahogany and mahogany veneer, bonnet flanked by free-standing tapering columns above waist door with applied molding, cross-banded veneer box base, curving skirt and feet, 47-1/2" h, replaced crest, other minor imperfections **28,750.00**

Tower, Reuben, Plymouth, MA, c1820-30, alarm dial sgd "Reuben Tower Kingston," pine, pierced fret above bonnet flanked by free-standing mahogany columns, painted iron dial with spandrels and polychrome painted basket of flowers, fruit, and foliage above waist, box base over curing skirt, ogee feet, 40-3/4" h, refinished case, replaced crest and columns, some height loss **12,650.00**

Tall case

Brokaw, Isaac, Federal, mahogany inlaid, dial marked "Isaac Brokaw Bridge Town" (New Jersey), 1800-10, shaped hood with inlaid patera and book-end inlays above glazed door, painted dial, eight-day weight-driven movement, seconds hand, calendar aperture, waist door with serpentine top and elliptical inlay, oval and quarter-fan inlays on lower case, similar embellishments above the bracket feet, refinished, restored, 94-1/2" h
. . . . **10,575.00**

Caldwell, J. E., late 19th/early 20th C, Georgian-Revival, mahogany, dial sgd "Caldwell," subsidiary seconds dial, cast scroll and cherub detailing, phases of the moon, two train chiming movement, hood with swan's neck cresting centered by urn, carved scroll detailing, glass front door flanked by tapering and partially reeded circular section columns, case with beveled glass front door flanked by engaged partially reeded columns, paneled plinth base centered by carved shell, front paw feet, rear ogee feet, 24" w, 15" d, 95" h **2,895.00**

Caldwell, J. E., c1930-40, mahogany, brass and steel face, paint dec moon phase dial, Arabic numeral chapter ring, second and date wheels, works with eight bells and Westminster chimes, case with scrolled bonnet, carved flame finials, scroll work, over case with blind carved fretwork over door with glass panel, fretwork trim, flanked by stylized columns, base with paneled front, ogee bracket feet, 8'6" h **6,650.00**

English, c1790-1820, mahogany veneer and walnut, 12" paint dec dial with landscape panel above Roman numeral clock face, second and dated wheels, hand-painted floral spandrels, arched bonnet over face flanked by full columns with gesso capitals, case with arched door flanked by reeded quarter columns, replaced base with shaped skirt, bracket feet, repaired top plate, crack in foot, 7'3" h **1,550.00**

English Regency, 19th C, mahogany, scrolled cresting above sq door, brass face etched with country scene, two-train movement, date and seconds

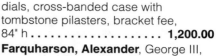

Tall case, William & G. Hutchinson, St. John, New Brunswick, 19th C, mahogany veneer, changing moon dial, name and location on center bottom of dial. Broken arch top with brass eagle finial, pendulum, key and weights present, some veneer flaking and molding chips, 95-1/2" h, $2,875. Photo courtesy of James D. Julia Auction, Inc.

dials, cross-banded case with tombstone pilasters, bracket fee, 84" h **1,200.00**

Farquharson, Alexander, George III, mahogany, gilt bronze mounts, dial signed "Alexander Farquharson, Edinburgh," etched steel face with date aperture and seconds dial, case with broken pediment cresting, dentil molding, two columnar supports with gilt capitals, shaped long door and bracket feet, 89" h **2,760.00**

French, Provincial Renaissance style, quarter strike mobilier**,** 19th C, serpentine cresting above glass door, brass face depicting courting couple, single train movement with quarter chiming on two bells, hour strike on one bell, case carved with strapwork and mask, 94" h **1,400.00**

Hoadley, Silas, Plymouth, CT, c1820-30, grain painted, hood, three plinths, joined by pierced fretwork, flanking urn finials above arched cove-molded cornice, glazed tombstone door flanked by freestanding columns, polychrome and gilt Masonic dial marked "S. Hoadley, Plymouth," floral spandrels and second hand, wooden movement, waist with thumb molded door above molded base, cut-out feet, orig red-under grain paint, simulated stringing on door and base, 89" h **8,820.00**

Mulliken, Joseph, Concord, MA, c1800-10, Federal, cherry, hood with pierced fretwork joining sq plinths and brass ball finials above arched cornice molding, iron painted tombstone dial with bird and floral designs inscribed "J. Mulliken Concord," eight-day weight-driven movement, flanked by free-standing reeded columns, waist with molded rect door flanked by reeded quarter columns on base with inlaid stringing joining corner quarter fans on flat molding, 88-3/4" h, imperfections, lacks hood door and feet **4,700.00**

Mulliken, Nathaniel, Lexington, MA, c1760

Cherry, hood with molded stepped cornice above arched molding, glazed thumb-molded door with flanking engaged columns, brass engraved silvered dial with cast brass spandrels, boss in arch engraved "Nathaniel Mulliken Lexington" above silvered chapter ring, second hand, calendar aperture, thumb-molded

tombstone door, base with molded bracket feet, refinished, restoration, loss of height, 89-1/2" h
.... 12,955.00

Walnut, hood with molded flat cornice above arched molding, glazed tombstone door with flanking engraved columns, engraved brass dial with brass spandrel, boss in arch engraved "Nath Mulliken LEXINGTON" above chapter ring, seconds indicator, and calendar aperture, waist with thumb-molded door, base with applied thumb-molded panel, bracket feet, 87" h, refinished, restored **7,650.00**

Mulliken II, Nathaniel, Lexington, MA, c1770-75, attributed to, mahogany and cherry, hood with broken arched cornice molding, three sq plinths, tombstone glazed door with flanking engaged columns, brass dial with cast

Tall case, Chester County, PA, 18th C, walnut, double scroll top, rosettes, three-flame urn finials, arched brass face with moon phases, engraved leaves and flowers, sweep second hand, signed "Eli Bentley, West Whiteland," rectangular lip molded waist door, recessed panel below, quarter round fluted corners, ogival bracket feet, 96" h, $15,000. Photo courtesy of Freeman/ Fine Arts.

spandrels, silvered banner in arch engraved "Nath. Mulliken + Lexington," above the boss with engraved eagle on branch, silvered chapter ring, seconds indicator, calendar aperture, eight-day weight-driven movement, waist with thumb-molded door, molded base, 88" h, refinished, loss of height, restored
.... **7,650.00**

Munroe, Daniel, Concord, MA, Federal, mahogany

    c1800, hood with pierced fretwork joining reeded plinths with brass finials above arched cornice molding, glazed string inlaid tombstone door, floral polychrome and gilt iron dial, seconds and calendar aperture sgd "Daniel Munroe + Co.," brass eight-day weight-driven movement, flanking reeded brass stop-fluted columns, rect molded and inlaid door flanked by reeded brass stop-fluted quarter columns, inlaid base, ogee bracket feet, refinished
.... **25,850.00**

    c1810, hood with pierced fretwork joining three reeded brass stop fluted plinths above arched cornice molding, glazed inlaid tombstone door enclosing polychrome iron moon phase dial with floral spandrels, polychrome indicator, calendar aperture inscribed "Daniel Munroe," eight-day weight-driven movement, flanked by reeded brass stop-fluted columns, rect inlaid waist door flanked by reeded brass stop-fluted quarter columns on inlaid base ending in molding, 85-1/2" h, feet missing, restored fretwork **17,625.00**

    c1810, hood with pierced fretwork joining reeded plinths with brass ball finials above arched cornice molding, glazed tombstone door, white painted iron dial inscribed "warranted by Nath. Munroe Concord," eight-day weight-driven movement, flanked by standing reeded columns, double-beaded crossbanded waist door on base, double-beaded panel above cut-out feet, 93" h, loss of height, dial repainted, other restoration
.... **5,300.00**

Nash, William, Bridge, England, George III, works signed, brass and steel face with date aperture and seconds dial, inlaid mahogany case

with swan's neck cresting, columnar supports, cross-banded door inlaid with shell, bracket feet, 85" h **6,900.00**

Parke, Soloman, late 18th/early 19th C, Phila, cherry, replaced dial ... **7,700.00**

Read, A. Hepplewhite, country, cherry with old mellow refinishing, bonnet with turned front columns and reeded pilasters in back, broken arch pediment and chip carving on arch, waist with chamfered corners, lamb's tongues and molded edge door, molding between sections, cutout feet and apron, painted wood face labeled "A. Read & Co. Xenia, Ohio," polychrome flowers and vintage dec, wooden works replaced with electric movement, age crack in base, minor pierced repairs, 94-1/2" h
.... **4,400.00**

Smith, Benjamin, Provincial, works signed by Benjamin Smith, Leeds, brass face, steel chapter ring, two-train movement, lunar arch, date dial and subsidiary seconds hand, pierced spandrels, inlaid oak case with broken arch cresting, checkered banding, inlaid with shell and fans, bracket feet, 96" h **7,495.00**

Taber, Elnathan, Roxbury, MA c1815, Federal, dial sgd "E. Taber, Roxbury," painted iron dial with calendar aperture, seconds hand, gilt spandrels, two ships, one flying American flag in the arch of dial, eight-day movement, mahogany veneer inlaid case with pierced fretwork, fluted plinths, brass stop fluted free-standing columns flanking bonnet above waist door with applied moldings, flanked by engaged brass stop fluted quarter columns with brass capitols and bases, waist door opens to reveal early 19th C label "Directions for Setting Up a Clock" above box base with inlay in outline, curving skirt, French feet, 92" h, refinished, imperfections **48,875.00**

Unidentified American maker, Hepplewhite, cherry, inlaid, swan neck pediment with carved rosettes, vase finial, barber pole and vine and berry inlay on hood, barber pole, vine inlay, and inlaid oval a waist, 97" h
.... **15,275.00**

Unidentified maker, attributed to Concord, MA, c1810, Federal, mahogany, hood with pierced fretwork and sq plinths above arched cornice molding, glazed tombstone door, polychrome moon phase dial with floral spandrels and exotic birds flanking seconds hands and calendar aperture, eight-day weight-driven movement, flanked by reeded brass stop-fluted columns, molded tombstone waist door flanked by reeded brass stop-fluted quarter columns, base with inlaid paterae and molding, 87" h, feet missing, other imperfections **14,100.00**

Willard, Benjamin, Lexington, MA, c1771, cherry, brass dial inscribed "Benjamin Willard Lexington," boss inscribed "Tempus fugit," cast brass spandrels, silvered chapter ring, second hand, calendar aperture, eight-day time and strike movement, pagoda style bonnet, fluted plinths above scalloped waist door, molded box base, 82" h, refinished case, restoration to bonnet. **12,650.00**

Willard, Ephraim, Hepplewhite, mahogany with inlay, bonnet with freestanding front columns with brass stop fluting, molded curved cornice with fretwork and brass finials on fluted plinths, fluted quarter columns with brass fittings and brass stop fluting and molded edge door in base, molding between sections, base molding, ogee feet, stringing inlay with invected corners, brass works with second hand and calendar movements, painted steel face with polychrome flowers and birds, labeled "Warranted by Em. Willard," weights, pendulum, and key, repairs to feet, pierced repair where lock was removed on waist door, minor repairs to bonnet, 93-3/4" h **33,000.00**

Willard, Simon, Roxbury, MA, c1800, Federal, dial indistinctly sgd, eight-day time and strike movement, mahogany inlaid case with pierced fret on bonnet, American dial with "S+N" on reverse, rocking ship flying two American flags in arch of dial, painted rose spandrels and gilt outline, flanked by brass stop-fluted free-standing columns above waist door with applied molding, cross-banded veneer, boxed inlaid base, sq feet, 93-1/2" h, refinished, height loss, replaced feet. . . **37,375.00**

Wismer, Henry, Plumstead, Bucks County, PA, c1820, cherry, hood with molded broken-arch resting, carved floral rosettes, three plinths with turned finials, glazed tombstone door, polychrome iron dial, basket of fruit in arch, seashell spandrels, calendar aperture signed "Henry Wismer B.C.," brass weight-driven striking pull-up movement, flanked by turned columns,

waist with door flanked by four ring-turned columns, base with canted corners, flaring French feet, old surface, 95-1/2" h **5,875.00**

Wood, David, Newburyport, MA, c1800-15, Federal, cherry and maple, hood with three reeded plinths above arched molding, glazed tombstone door, polychrome and gilt dial with fruit designs, seconds indicator, calendar aperture inscribed "D. Wood," brass weight-driven movement, flanked by reeded columns, cockbeaded waist door flanked by reeded quarter columns, cove molding, base with reeded band and cut-out feet, engraved label affixed to back of door "David Wood, watch and clockmaker," 89" h, refinished, imperfections **8,820.00**

Polyphon No. 63, unusual coin-operated tall case clock, uses 11-1/4" metal discs to produce music, c1900, $13,300. Photo courtesy of Auction Team Breker.

Wall
Banjo

Abbott, Samuel, Boston, MA, c1815-25, attributed to, Federal, mahogany, painted dial, "A"-shaped brass weight-driven eight-day movement, reverse painted throat glass flanked by gilded rope twist and brass side arms, lower eglomise glass depicting in polychrome "Lafayette the Friend of Liberty," 33-1/2" h, restoration **1,955.00**

Burleigh, Jr., T. F., late 10th C, Federal-style, giltwood and mahogany girandole, eagle finial, gilt bezel enclosing painted metal dial inscribed "L.Curtis patent, reproduction by T. F. Burleigh Jr.," eight-day weight-driven movement, convex throat glass with acorns and oak leaves inscribed "L. Curtis," second convex glass below showing Perry's Victory, both framed by gilt moldings, flanked by brass side pieces all on carved leaf bracket, 47" h **9,400.00**

Cummens, William, Boston, MA, c1820, Federal, dial sgd "warranted by Wm. Cummens," convex painted iron dial enclosed by convex glass and bezel topped

Wall, cartel, bronze, lion and rams head columns, urn pediment, c1880, 30" w, $1,235. Photo courtesy of Fontaine's Auction Gallery.

by acorn finial, molded mahogany veneer case, T-bridge eight-day weight-driven movement, reverse painted throat glass, flanked by side arms, eglomise tablet marked "Patent" in box base, 34" l, restoration. **6,325.00**

Currier, Edmund, Salem, MA, c1820, Federal, dial sgd "E. Currier Salem," eight-day weight-driven movement, throat glass panel reads "Patent," lower reverse painted glass reads "E. Currier Salem" above gilt bracket, 41-3/4" h, restoration **3,335.00**

Curtis and Dunning, Concord, MA, c1815, Federal

Dial sgd "warranted by Curtis and Dunning," eight-day weight-driven movement, mahogany case with brass bezel and convex glass, tapering throat with reverse painted glass flanked by brass side arms, box base with eglomise panel, rope twist giltwood in outline, 33-1/2" l, period throat glass broken **5,175.00**

Eagle and ball finial above mahogany cross-banded case, brass bezel, printed paper dial reading "warranted by Curtis and Dunning," eight-day weight-driven movement, throat glass showing grape vines, lower tablet showing mother and child reading on recamier, both framed by crossbanding, flanked by brass side arms, 35-1/4" h, imperfections **4,700.00**

Curtis, Lemuel, Concord, MA, c1815, Federal

Brass eagle finials, mahogany and gilt gesso case, brass bezel, painted and gilt iron dial inscribed "warranted by L. Curtis," eight-day weight-driven movement, throat glass enclosing thermometer, inscribed "L. Curtis Patent," lower tablet showing figures in farm landscape, both framed by gilt spiral moldings, flanked by brass side arms, 33-1/4" h, restoration, imperfections **7,650.00**

Painted iron dial, brass eight-day weight-driven movement, touch marked "L. Curtis #2," T-bridge

escapement, mahogany case with gilded roping, brass side arms, eglomise lower table of "Venus Resigning Cupid to Calypso," 33-1/2" h, restoration **3,335.00**

Dyar, J., Concord, MA, c1815, Federal, mahogany, brass eagle finial above bras bezel, painted metal dial, reading "Warranted by J. Dyar," eight-day eight-drive movement, foliate throat glass reading "Patent," flanked by rope twist dec, brass side arms, lower tablet with eglomise naval battle framed by applied rope twist moldings, 32-3/4" h, lower tablet replaced, other imperfections **2,820.00**

Munroe, Concord, MA, c1820, Federal, gilt mahogany, brass ball finial over dial, eight-day weight-driven movement, throat glass flanked by brass side arms, lower tablet reading "Munroe's Patent Suspension," classical and foliate devices framed by applied rope twist dec, 33-1/2" h, repainted dial, replaced tablets, other imperfections **1,530.00**

Munroe and Whiting, Concord, MA, c1808-17, Federal, gilt mahogany, acorn-form finial, iron painted dial enclosing eight-day weight-driven movement, foliate throat glass flanked by side arms, lower panel depicting ship battle, both within rope twist dec frames, 33" h, lower tablet replaced, other imperfections **1,880.00**

Noyes, L. W., Nashua, NH, c1825, Federal, mahogany

Ball finial, brass bezel enclosing painted metal dial inscribed "Warranted by L. W. Noyes," eight-day weight-driven movement, throat tablet with scroll design, lower tablet showing ship in village harbor, both framed by half round moldings, flanked by brass side arms, imperfections, tablet replaced, 32" h **2,475.00**

Brass belted ball finial, brass bezel, printed dial, eight-day weight-drive movement, throat glass flanked by brass side arms and tablet with foliate and eagle devices framed by half round moldings, 34" h,

Wall, cuckoo, three-weight, glass eyed game carvings, large deer head crest, c1880, 50" h, **$4,480**. *Photo courtesy of Fontaine's Auction Gallery.*

restoration including tablets **1,765.00**

Sawin, John and John W. Dyer, Boston, MA, c1825, Federal, giltwood and mahogany, dial sgd "Sawin and Dyer, Boston"

Acorn finial above convex glass and brass bezel, brass eight-day weight-driven movement, glass throat panel reads "Patent" flanked by brass side arms over lower glass eglomise tablet which depicts seaside hotel, reads "Nahant," 33" h, minor restoration **4,025.00**

Eight-day weight-driven movement, foliate throat glass flanked by brass side arms, lower tablet with coastal marine and figural scene, both framed by applied rope twist dec, 28-1/2" h, replaced glasses, dial repainted **1,880.00**

Taber, Elnathan, Roxbury, MA, c1810, Federal, dial reads "Warranted by E. Taber," acorn finial above mahogany and cross-banded veneer case, signed, painted dial enclosing brass eight-day weight-driven movement, weight pan inscribed "made by E. Taber, Roxbury, Mafachusetts" (sic), reverse painted throat glass includes "Patent," flanked by brass side arms above lower tablet depicting naval battle, reads "Hornet and Peacock," 33" h, imperfections, note accompanying clock dated June 1961 indicates it was "gift to John May Secretary of State from George Washington" . . . **65,200.00**

Unidentified Concord Massachusetts maker, c1815, Federal, gilt and mahogany

Brass ball finial above brass bezel and dial, eight-day weight-driven movement, foliate throat glass reading "PATENT" flanked by brass side arms, lower tablet depicting battle between the *Constitution* and the *Guerriere,* both framed by applied rope twist dec, 35" h, imperfections **2,475.00**

Brass finial, mahogany and giltwood case, brass bezel, painted iron dial, eight-day weight-driven movement, throat panel showing grapevines, inscribed "A. Willard Jr., Boston," lower tablet showing "La Grange," both framed by gilt spiral moldings, flanked by brass side arms, 33-1/4" h, imperfections, throat glass old but not orig to timepiece
. . . . **1,650.00**

Unsigned painted dial, eight-day brass weight drive movement, gilded carved wooden eagle finial, reverse painted glass panels, brass side arms, gilded bracket, 41-3/4" h, restoration
. . . . **3,740.00**

Unsigned painted dial, Concord-type eight-day brass weight drive movement, carved wooden eagle finial, throat glass panel reading "Patent," flanked by brass side arms over reverse painted glass panel in box base, 33-1/2" h, restoration
. . . . **2,875.00**

Unidentified Massachusetts maker, Federal

c1815, mahogany, unsigned dial, eight-day brass weight drive movement, reverse painted

Wall, long-drop, Connitti of London, mahogany and fruit wood veneer case, open pediment with urn-shaped finial, time and strike, beveled glass door and side panels, $800. Photo courtesy of Joy Luke Auctions.

glass panels surrounded by rope gilt, lower tablet with eglomise ship portrait labeled "President Plantagenet," 32" h, restoration **2,615.00**

c1820, giltwood and mahogany, acorn finial, mahogany and gilt gesso case, brass bezel, painted metal dial, eight-day weight-driven movement, throat glass panel with floral garland, lower panel showing castle on river, both framed by gilt rope twist molding, flanked by brass side arms, 32-1/2" h, indistinct signature on dial, imperfections
. . . . **1,650.00**

c1825, giltwood and mahogany, eagle and shield finial above mahogany and giltwood case, brass bezel, convex painted dial, eight-day weight-driven movement, glass throat panel with gilt scroll, lower panel showing sea battle, both framed by gilt spiral moldings, flanked by brass side arms, 33-3/4" h, restorations **1,550.00**

Willard, Aaron, Jr., Boston, MA, Federal

c1820, mahogany, dial marked "A. Willard Jr., Boston," eight-day weight-driven movement above reverse painted throat glass with thermometer flanked by gilded rope twist and brass side arms, lower eglomise tablet with naval battle between Hornet and Peacock above bracket, 39" h, restoration **13,800.00**

c1820-25, mahogany, acorn form finial, brass bezel and painted dial, eight-day weight-driven movement stamped "A. Willard Jr. Boston," throat glass with scrolling devices, reading "Patent," flanked by brass side arms and lower tablet depicting lakeside church, both framed by applied rope twist dec, applied spherules and carved bracket with pendant, 42-3/4" h, imperfections **3,420.00**

Willard, Simon, Roxbury, MA, Federal

c1805, mahogany, unmarked dial, eight-day weight driven T-bridge movement with stepped train, escapement in case with cross-banded veneer, brass side arms, reverse painted throat glass above lower eglomise tablet which reads "S. Willard's Patent," 33-1/2" h, restoration **10,350.00**

c1815, cast brass eagle finial above mahogany case with circular molded brass bezel, convex glass opening to white painted convex iron dial, brass weight-driven eight-day "T" bridge movement, tapering throat eglomise tablet with flowering vine bordered in light green and black and sunburst all on a white background, lower tablet with "Willard's Patent" and border of conforming design, both framed by crossbanding and stringing, flanked by pierced brass side pieces, some imperfections, 32-3/4" h
. . . . **15,275.00**

Lyre

Chandler, Abiel, Concord, NH, c1825, Classical, dial sgd "A. Chandler," striking brass eight-day weight-driven movement, leaf carved mahogany veneer case with bracket, 43" h, refinished, imperfections **17,250.00**

Sawin, John and John W. Dyer, Boston, MA, mid 1820s, Classical, dial sgd "Sawin and Dyer Boston," eight-day brass weight-driven movement, mahogany case with reverse painted throat and lower eglomise tablets with gilded rope twist surrounds, gilded bracket, 40" l, imperfections **13,800.00**

Mirror

Chadwick, Joseph, Boscawen, NH, c1825, late Federal, painted dial sgd "Joseph Chadwick Boscawen," surrounded by eglomise glass panel that conceals brass eight-day weight-drive movement above mirror glass, flanked by painted and gilded split balusters punctuated by rosettes, 31-1/2" h, case refinished, some re-gilding to case, imperfections **3,335.00**

Morrill, Benjamin, Boscawen, NH, c1825, late Federal

Dial sgd "B. Morrill Boscawen, N.H.," c1825, eight-day wheelbarrow movement surrounded by gilded spandrels above mirror glass, flanked by gilded and painted split baluster columns, 31-3/4" h, restoration **3,740.00**

Paper label, dark stained pine case with unsigned dial, eight-day movement, surrounded by eglomise tablet above mirror glass, flanked by split baluster columns punctuated by rosettes at corners, 30" h, imperfections **10,350.00**

Octagonal

Nelson, George, for Howard Miller, brushed chrome face, walnut case, Roman numerals, paper label, stamped #588, black Howard Miller stamp on front, 12" w, 22" h **920.00**

Spiderweb

Nelson, George, for Howard Miller, wood center, white enameled metal rays, black string, black Howard Miller decal, No. 2214, 18-1/2" d **1,150.00**

Watchman

Morrill, Benjamin, Boscawen, NH, 1860s, rect birch box case, painted iron dial marked "B. Morrill Boscawen, eight-day weight-driven brass movement, 54-1/2" h, imperfections **2,875.00**

CLOISONNÉ

History: Cloisonné is the art of enameling on metal. The design is drawn on the metal body, then wires, which follow the design, are glued or soldered on. The cells thus created are packed with enamel and fired; this step is repeated several times until the level of enamel is higher than the wires. A buffing and polishing process brings the level of enamels flush to the surface of the wires.

This art form has been practiced in various countries since 1300 B.C. and in the Orient since the early 15th century. Most cloisonné found today is from the late Victorian era, 1870-1900, and was made in China or Japan.

Bowl, carp swimming in blue sea, Shotal, $120. Photo courtesy of Cowan's Historic Americana Auctions.

Box, cov, 4-3/4" d, 2-3/4" h, rounded form, butterflies among flowering branches, turquoise ground, Chinese, 19th C **345.00**

Candlesticks, pr, 7-1/8" h, figural, brass, blue mythical animals seated on round dark red base with open work sides, three feet, each animal holds flower in mouth, red candle socket on back **200.00**

Cane, 36" l, 1-1/3" d x 9-1/2" l Japanese cloisonné handle, dark blue ground, long scaly three-toed Japanese dragon in shades of white, pale blue, black, and brown, 1/3" gold gilt collar, black hardwood shaft, 7/8" horn ferrule, fashioned in England, c1890 . **1,460.00**

Cup, 4" h, ftd, butterflies and flowers, lappet borders, Chinese, 19th C **100.00**

Button, red ground, 1-1/4" d, $25.

Desk set, brush pot, pen, pen tray, blotter, and paper holder, Japanese, price for set **130.00**

Figure, 21" h, Tang-style horse, allover phoenix and scrolled florals, turquoise ground, removable saddle exposes int. storage compartment, gilt bronze, 20th C **415.00**

Incense burner, 19-3/4" h, globular, three dragon-head feet, high curving handles, scrolling lotus and ancient bronzes motif, openwork lid, dragon finial, raised Quinlong six-character mark, damage **815.00**

Jar, cov, 6" h, ovoid, even green over central band of scrolling flowers, dome lid, ovoid finial, marked "Ando Jubei," 20th C **230.00**

Jardinière, 13" d, 10" h, bronze, bands of cloisonné designs, golden yellow and blue triangles, polychrome geometric designs on dark blue, chrysanthemums on light blue, cast relief scene of water lily, turtle, and flowering branches on int., soldered repair at foot **220.00**

Planter, 11" l, quatralobe, classical symbol and scroll dec, blue ground, Chinese, pr **200.00**

Scepter, 22" l, three cloisonné plaques inset with wooden cloud-carved frame, China, early 20th C **125.00**

Tea kettle, 10-1/2" h, multicolored scrolling lotus, medium-blue ground, lappets border, waisted neck with band of raised auspicious symbols between key-fret borders, floral form finial, double handles, Chinese, 19th C **690.00**

Teapot, 4-3/4" d, 3-1/4" h, central band of flowering chrysanthemums on pink ground, shoulder with shaped cartouches of phoenix and dragon on floral and patterned ground, lower border with chrysanthemum blossom on swirling ground, flat base with three small raised feet, single chrysanthemum design, spout and handle with floral design, lid with two writhing dragons on peach-colored ground, Japanese, late 19th/early 20th C **4,025.00**

Urn, 23-3/4" h, ovoid, slightly waisted neck, peony dec, black ground, base plaque marked "Takeuchi Chubei," Japanese, late-19th C, Shichi Ho Company, Owari **690.00**

Vase

3 5/8" h, shouldered form, long slender neck flaring at rim, colored enamels, spider chrysanthemums

Vase, left: textured foil under forest green ground, brilliant polychrome flowers and butterflies, shaded broad variegated leaves, French, 7-1/4" h, **$230;** *right: black cloud figured ground encircling dragons, geometric, and floral necks, fish scale foot, Chinese, 7-1/2" h, price for pair,* **$115.** *Photo courtesy of Cowan's Historic Americana Auctions.*

and songbirds, midnight-blue ground, Japanese, Meiji period, pr **550.00**

4-3/4" h, ovoid, continual scene of geese on riverbank, flowering bushes and mountains in distance, Japanese **2,875.00**

6" h, six sided, each side with shield below floral band, alternating dragon and phoenix motif, flecked-blue ground, Japanese, early 20th C **460.00**

8 7/8" h, flattened ovoid, large cartouches of dragon with serpent and phoenix flying among vines, surrounded by flowering vines, black ground, Japanese, Meiji period **8,350.00**

9 1/8" h, angled shoulder, ovoid, waisted neck, multicolored flowering chrysanthemum, bright blue ground, Meiji period, Ota, minor crazing **1,380.00**

10" h, silver wire dec, slender iris, deep-blue ground, Japanese, base sgd "Obei Tsukuru," scratches, fracture **375.00**

12-1/4" h, ovoid, waisted neck, inverted rim, two songbirds among prunus and bamboo, colored enamels with silver wire, dark-blue ground, stamped silver rim, wire Ando Jubei mark on base, Meiji period, orig fitted box . . . **4,975.00**

16" h, finely enameled geometric designs, stylized florals, turquoise ground, Oriental, 20th C, price for pr **230.00**

CLOTHING AND CLOTHING ACCESSORIES

History: While museums and a few private individuals have collected clothing for decades, it is only recently that collecting clothing has achieved a widespread popularity. Clothing reflects the social attitudes of a historical period.

Christening and wedding gowns abound and, hence, are not in large demand. Among the hardest items to find is men's clothing from the 19th and early 20th centuries. The most sought after clothing is by designers, such as Fortuny, Poirret, and Vionnet.

Additional Listings: See *Warman's Americana & Collectibles* for more examples.

Note: Condition, size, age, and completeness are critical factors in purchasing clothing. Collectors divide into two groups: those collecting for aesthetic and historic value and those desiring to wear the garment. Prices are higher on the West coast; major auction houses focus on designer clothes and high-fashion items.

Afternoon dress

Black silk, two-pc, cream star detail, black lace trim, very full skirt with gores, c1880 . . . . **40.00**

Black voile, two-pc, printed rose, green, and black flowers and leaves **150.00**

Dark gray silk, pleated skirt, black lace trim on bodice, c1880 . . **60.00**

White dotted tulle, two-pc, lace yoke, pin tucks, ruffles, lace cuffs, c1890 . . . . **75.00**

White lawn, white cotton embroidery, filet lace insertion, rows of mother-of-pearl buttons on front, c1910 . . . . **225.00**

White linen, elbow-length sleeves, fitted waistline, crocheted buttons up back of bodice, cotton floral embroidery and trim, c1900 . . . . **250.00**

Beaded dress, black silk crepe and silk chiffon over black taffeta, embroidered all over with black glass beads, black silk chiffon drape from waistline, labeled "Best & Co.," c1940 . . . . **200.00**

Bed jacket, pale blue quilted satin, c1950 . . . . **40.00**

Blouse

Black dotted net, long sleeves, pin tucks, lace insertion at neckline, c1910 . . . . **45.00**

Custer's last coat

If you don't mind the small bullet hole in the left side, perhaps you'd like to know what famous clothing items of Gen. George Armstrong Custer brought at SoldUSA.com's June 2002 auction: the final bid was $104,655 for a coat, a war shirt, and supporting documentation. It is believed to be the coat Custer was wearing at the Battle of Little Big Horn, when he was killed on June 25, 1876. Legend has it that Joseph Dietzen of Company E of the 19th Infantry bought the coat in 1880 from an Indian scout. It remained in his family until 1959 when Col. Raymond Vietzen purchased it for $150 to display in his museum at Indian Ridge, where it stayed until his death in 1995. The war shirt was attributed to Chief Rain In The Face and has a map of the battle plan painted on the back. It, too, was displayed in the Indian Ridge Museum.

White lawn, embroidery and lace insertion, c1890, minor edge damage to collar **30.00**

Cape

Black silk velvet, black chantilly lace deep hem, slightly padded, black silk taffeta lining, c1880, lace needs re-attaching at several places............... **100.00**

Black velvet, modified Napoleon collar, single button closure, lined with black quilted satin, c1930 .... **60.00**

Rose silk velvet, fully lined with pale green silk crepe, wide collar, single button closure, c1920..... **195.00**

Capelet, black, glass beaded trim, open work, fringe, c1890....... **40.00**

Chemine, linen, ruffles and lace at cuffs, late 18th/early 19th C..... **25.00**

Collar

Black net, attached yoke, elaborately embroidered with black glass beads, c1890 .... **30.00**

Black silk and velvet, steel beading, c1890 .... **25.00**

Afternoon dress, two-piece, two-tone lilac and mauve silk faille and taffeta, bone-lined bodice, fully lined in ivory silk, ruched silk trim, c1870, labeled "Mlle Marie Traver, Robes, 28 Rue de Mont, Trabor 28, Paris," $1,320. Photo courtesy of Sanford Alderfer Auction Company.

Coat, woman's

Black silk, black fur trim on front, hem, and cuffs, fabric covered buttons, quilted silk lining, c1870 .... **50.00**

Black velvet and brick, blue, and green wool paisley, black soutache, crocheted buttons, black Persian lamb collar, gold taffeta lining, c1940 .... **900.00**

Brown wool, brown silk velvet trim on front, collar, capelet, and cuffs, padded, fully lined in brown silk, c1870 .... **75.00**

Dress

Black silk crepe, scallops at sleeves, cream embroidered silk cuffs and collar, wrap style, labeled "Lucille Ltd., New York," c1915 .... **195.00**

Brown net over rust silk chiffon, elaborately embroidered in cream cotton threads, c1920...... **50.00**

Bustle, two-pc, brown silk damask and brown silk, ruching and ruffles on bustle skirt, tan shell buttons on front, c1870, later added collar **275.00**

Coat, black velvet and brick, blue, and green wool paisley, black soutache, crocheted buttons, black Persian lamb collar, gold taffeta lining, c1940, $900. Photo courtesy of Sanford Alderfer Auction Company.

Navy blue silk and silk chiffon, pin tucks at hipline, beige silk crepe and lace trim, c1930 ...... **45.00**

Pale peach silk chiffon, embroidered blue and clear glass beads in floral and geometric patterns, c1925, several beads missing on bodice **225.00**

Rust silk crepe, detailed at bodice and hem with cream silk, embroidered with pink, tangerine, aqua, and green satin flowers, labeled "New York, Paris, Claire Gowns, Made by Starr and Herbert," c1920 .... **120.00**

Dressing gown, white voile, lace trim, blue and white flowers, c1950 .. **65.00**

Frock, tan cotton print, tangerine and blue paisley detailing, brown carved buttons, c1880, some old repairs, minor fading **65.00**

Gown

Beige lace, light tan silk crepe, lace belt with brass buckle, pleated lace skirt, lace tunic with ruffles at neckline, three-quarter length lace jacket with long sleeves, pin tucks, collar, c1925, some damage to dress shoulder **65.00**

Brown lace full-length, brown chenille embroidery on net over brown net, crepe chartreuse velvet sash with brown carved Bakelite buckle, c1930 .... **125.00**

Charcoal gray and green silk velvet, pin tucks and smoking on sleeves, deep V-neckline, c1930.... **95.00**

Deep aqua silk chiffon, elaborately embroidered with freeform shapes of clear glass beads, blue, rose, and white glass beaded Art Deco motifs, c1920 .... **550.00**

Gold and rust floral printed silk chiffon, cape collar, underpinnings of tan silk crepe, c1930 .... **85.00**

Gray and blue woven silk with cream stripe, pagoda sleeves, ruching on bodice, cream braid on sleeves and bodice, bodice lined with cream linen, c1865 ...... **95.00**

Mauve silk chiffon, sleeveless, elaborately embroidered with lilac satin threads, silver glass beads in Art Deco motif, lilac feather trim at hem, underpinnings of ivory silk chiffon, c1920 .... **275.00**

Pale green silk chiffon, trimmed with pale green silk satin, embroidered at scalloped hem with silver and white glass beads, prong-set rhinestones, c1925....... **175.00**

Pale lilac silk, sq cut steel buttons, cream lace collar, bubble-effect skirt, draped back, c1900, wear **60.00**

Pale pink silk chiffon, embroidered in floral design with heavy satin threads in shades of rose and pink, trimmed with long ombre-dyed rose and pink fringe, c1920, some damage at shoulder straps . **265.00**

Printed blue, yellow, tangerine, and black chiffon, underpinnings of cream silk crepe, matching jacket, c1930 . . . . **195.00**

Pumpkin and lilac silk etched velvet, sleeveless, floral design, fur at hem, c1920 . . . . **275.00**

Sheer cream silk in windowpane weave, overprinted with sepia, rose, and blue floral pattern, silk trim at cuffs, bodice lined with cream muslin, c1820 . . . . . . **500.00**

Tan floral print silk chiffon, back drape, c1930 . . . . **80.00**

Tan silk, long sleeves, dropped waistline, button detailing, embroidery, c1920 . . . . **75.00**

Handbag

Alligator, brown, brass clasp, brown leather lining, c1945 . . . . **45.00**

Black silk faille, embroidered with black glass beads, matching fringe, c1900 . . . . **95.00**

Floral tapestry, rose, green, and blue on cream ground, black border, brass frame with chain handle, c1940, 8-1/2" x 5-1/2" **30.00**

Hermes, Kelly, pressed design in black leather with padlock closure, 10-1/4" l, 13" w, 5" d **995.00**

Purse, painted mesh, butterfly decorated, $160. Photo courtesy of Joy Luke Auctions.

Purse, painted mesh, blue, white, and gold Art Deco-style decoration, $195. Photo courtesy of Joy Luke Auctions.

Mesh, 10kt yg, pierced and scalloped top set with four old mine-cut diamonds, approx 1.12 cts., three oval cabochon turquoise, suspended by trace link chain and gold safety pin, 67.0 dwt., stamped No. "6," European hallmark, c1915 . . . . **1,120.00**

Mesh, 14kt yg, Edwardian, designed with a floral and scroll frame, the bypass-style thumbpiece set with two sugarloaf sapphires joined by a trace link chain, 132.5 dwt. 1,116.75Mesh, 14kt yg, Edwardian, pierced, chased, and engraved floral and foliate closure, suspended from a curb link chain, 96.7 dwt. **835.00**

Silver and enamel, Birmingham, England, 1938, maker's mark

Purse, painted mesh, decorated with vase of flowers, $195. Photo courtesy of Joy Luke Auctions.

Hat, miniature brown Derby hat, original hatbox from "The Brown Derby," Hollywood, $250. Photo courtesy of Joy Luke Auctions.

"EJH," oval, lid with lavender basse taille enamel, leather lined interior, silver link chain, monogrammed, 6-1/4" l, 3-7/8" d **250.00**

Hat, lady's fashion type

Aqua silk pillbox, aqua veil, colorful beads embroidery, c1960 . . . **50.00**

Black velour, wide brim, black feathers, black and white ostrich plumes, c1910 . . . . **95.00**

Wide-brimmed black velvet, under brim of blue velvet, blue ostrich plume, silver stamped on the black silk lining "Dives Pomeroy & Stewart," c1910 . . . . **150.00**

Wide-brimmed natural straw, gold grosgrain ribbon, white cotton daisies, labeled "Jean Allen," c1945 . . . . **35.00**

Hat, man's, top hat, orig box **85.00**

Jacket

Battenburg cream lace, long sleeves, gathering at shoulders, c1890 . . . . **350.00**

Lace, black chantilly, long sleeves, unlined, c1900 . . . . **225.00**

Silk velvet, purple, lined with purple silk, fabric covered buttons, patch pockets, c1890 . . . . **120.00**

Wool flannel, black, bolero, black taffeta lining, black fur tri, c1955 . . . . **65.00**

Lingerie dress

White batiste, embroidery and lace insertion on bodice, and skirt, ruching below waistline, c1910 . . . . **45.00**

White eyelet lace, white lawn, detailed bodice with pin tucks, lace yoke and collar, scalloped hem, c1900 . . . . **65.00**

White lawn, eyelet lace, lace insertion, ruffles at hem, c1790 . . . . **375.00**

Nightgown

Pale pink satin, diminutive roses pattern, cut on bias, c1940 . **35.00**

White cotton, elaborate yoke of ruched white lawn alternating with lace, long lace trimmed sleeves, placket with lace trim, c1910 **20.00**

Oriental robe, pale gold silk, elaborately embroidered with gold and silver metallic threads in bird and dragon with flaming pearl motif, fully lined in pale gold silk, padded slightly, frog closures, c1920, some damage
.... **165.00**

Pajamas

Leopard print flannel, Dora Lee, c1950, unworn **35.00**

Lounging, black silk satin, satin burgundy and tan floral embroidery, sleeve and neckline edged in burgundy silk, c1925
.... **115.00**

Petticoat

Cream organdy, pin tucks, lace, ruffles at hem, train, c1890. . **35.00**

White cotton, scalloped eyelet lace hem, front tucked panel, c1880
.... **40.00**

Robe, printed green, tan, gray, yellow, and ivory silk, swirls, floral, and feather shapes, c1945.............. **60.00**

Shawl

Cream silk, floral cream satin embroidery, knotted fringe, braided dec, back tassel, c1890 ... **150.00**

Ivory silk, floral ivory satin embroidery, knotted satin fringe, Spanish, c1900, 44" sq **75.00**

Woven silk taffeta, light gray plaid, rose and green satin flowers, long knotted silk fringe, c1900, 70" sq
.... **125.00**

Scarf, silk, Hermes

Instructions sur l'art et la maniere de nouer et porter votre carre Hermes (Instructions on the art of tying and wearing your square of Hermes,) blue illustrations on white ground, boxed **235.00**

Sichuan, blue silk background printed with jungle scene, designed by Robert Dallet . **150.00**

Skirt, lace alternating with voile, black, train, underpinnings of cream silk taffeta, pinking and ruffles, c1870, some minor damage on tulle and lining
.... **150.00**

Suit, gray wool tweed, fabric cov buttons, button detailing on jacket pockets, lined with pale gray crepe, flared skirt with gores, "Freiss Orig" label, c1945 .... **110.00**

Umbrella

Black silk, silver handle formed as looped snake, Continental, English import hallmarks for London, 1904, 7-1/8" l handle, 36" l overall **150.00**

Gold, brown, orange, and yellow paisley ruffle, unused, orig gold and black hang tag for "Made in U.S.A., 100% Nylon," orig Strawbridge & Clothier box, c1955
.... **45.00**

Round tapered handle with stamped and engraved vertical bands of leafy scrolls and flowerheads, mother-of-pearl central band, 7-5/8" l handle, 31" l overall
.... **230.00**

Vest, white cotton, mother-of-pearl buttons, c1910 .... **65.00**

Visiting dress

Dark blue silk, dark blue, bodice and sleeves with light gray silk satin in geometric designs, elaborate embroidery on skirt, underpinnings of lace-trimmed cream silk, embroidered organdy collar, labeled "Rendel, Paris, London, New York," c1900........ **100.00**

Pale pink silk, two-pc, pink tucks, lace appliqué, lace cuffs, c1890
.... **65.00**

Purple linen, elaborate fabric-covered button detailing, purple silk net trim at neckline and cuffs, c1910, minor damage to net
.... **40.00**

Waistcoat, gentleman's, silk, embroidered with floral vines and sprigs, two covered pockets, applied cherub-printed roundels below, England or France, late 18th C, restorations **250.00**

Wedding gown, cream silk and cream silk chiffon, bodice, hem, yoke, waistline, and sleeves elaborately bordered with pearls and clear glass beads, additional lace trim, cream silk petticoat with lace at hem, damaged cream tulle veil with flower piece, provenance includes marriage information about Claire M. Mulholland, and also her daughter Claire A. Mulholland, who wore the dress in 1917
.... **190.00**

Left: Oriental robe, pale gold silk, elaborately embroidered with gold and silver metallic threads in bird and dragon motif, c1920, $165; center: gown, lilac silk faille, ivory silk and lace appliqué, ivory satin buttons on bodice, small lace-trimmed capelet and lace at cuffs, slight train, c1880, $250; right: lingerie dress, white eyelet lace, white lawn, bodice detailed with pin tucks, lace yoke and collar, scalloped hem, c1900, $65. Photo courtesy of Sanford Alderfer Auction Company.

COALPORT

History: In the mid-1750s, Ambrose Gallimore established a pottery at Caughley in the Severn Gorge, Shropshire, England.

ENGLAND
COALPORT
A.D. 1750

Several other potteries, including Jackfield, developed in the area.

About 1795, John Rose and Edward Blakeway built a pottery at Coalport, a new town founded along the right-of-way of the Shropshire Canal. Other potteries located adjacent to the canal were those of Walter Bradley and Anstice, Horton, and Rose. In 1799, Rose and Blakeway bought the Royal Salopian China Manufactory at Caughley. In 1814, this operation was moved to Coalport.

A bankruptcy in 1803 led to refinancing and a new name—John Rose and Company. In 1814, Anstice, Horton, and Rose was acquired. The South Wales potteries at Swansea and Nantgarw were added. The expanded firm made fine quality, highly decorated ware. The plant enjoyed a renaissance from 1888 to 1900.

World War I, decline in trade, and shift of the pottery industry away from the Severn Gorge brought hard times to Coalport. In 1926, the firm, now owned by Cauldon Potteries, moved from Coalport to Shelton. Later owners included Crescent Potteries, Brain & Co., Ltd., and finally, in 1967, Wedgwood.

For more information, see this book.

Perfume bottle, bulbous, gilt ground, turquoise beaded decorated, central band of flowers, maroon enamel, crown mark, 4" h, $850. Photo courtesy of Sanford Alderfer Auction Company.

Creamer, Athione, blue **375.00**
Cream soup bowl, two handles, Athione, blue **330.00**
Demitasse cup and saucer, quatrefoil shape, 2-1/4" x 1-1/2" cup with ring handle, 3-1/8" d saucer, pink, gilt trim
. . . . **350.00**

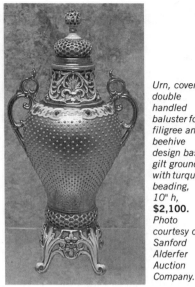

Urn, covered, double handled baluster form, filigree and beehive design base, gilt ground with turquoise beading, 10" h, $2,100. Photo courtesy of Sanford Alderfer Auction Company.

Dessert plate, 9-3/8" d, central gilt flowerhead in holly vine roundel, molded rim with further flowerheads and rocaille, late 19th/early 20th C, set of 12, one damaged **920.00**
Gravy boat with underplate, Indian Tree **480.00**
Place setting, five pcs
    Athione, blue. **360.00**
    Hazelton, white. **315.00**
    Indian Tree **450.00**
Platter
    Athione, blue, 15-3/8" l **750.00**
    Hazelton, white, round **360.00**
    Indian Tree, small **450.00**
Sugar bowl, cov, Athione, blue **385.00**
Vegetable dish, cov, Rosalinda **435.00**

COCA-COLA ITEMS

History: The originator of Coca-Cola was John Pemberton, a pharmacist from Atlanta, Georgia. In 1886, Dr. Pemberton introduced a patent medicine to relieve headaches, stomach disorders, and other minor maladies. Unfortunately, his failing health and meager finances forced him to sell his interest.

In 1888, Asa G. Candler became the sole owner of Coca-Cola. Candler improved the formula, increased the advertising budget, and widened the distribution. A "patient" was accidentally given a dose of the syrup mixed with carbonated water instead of still water. The result was a tastier, more refreshing drink.

As sales increased in the 1890s, Candler recognized that the product was more suitable for the soft-drink market and began advertising it as such. From these beginnings, a myriad of advertising items have been issued to invite all to "Drink Coca-Cola."

Notes: Dates of interest: "Coke" was first used in advertising in 1941. The distinctively shaped bottle was registered as a trademark on April 12, 1960.

Grading Condition. The following numbers represent the standard grading system used by dealers, collectors, and auctioneers:
C.10 = Mint
C. 9 = Near mint
C.8.5 = Outstanding
C.8 = Excellent
C.7.5 = Fine +
C.7 = Fine
C. 6.5 = Fine – (good)
C. 6 = Poor

Binder, 13" x 15-1/2", rigid cardboard, red oilcloth cover, four-ring metal binder to hold advertising sales sheets, c1950, no contents. **48.00**
Bookmark, Romance of Coca-Cola, 1916 . . . . **30.00**
Bottle
    Amber, marked "Lewisburg" . . **30.00**
    Christmas, Williamstown, WV . **15.00**
    Commemorative, NASCAR Series, Bill Elliott, Dale Earnhardt, or Bobby Labonte **5.00**
Bowl, 10" w, Vernon Ware, green, artificial ice, 1930s, C-9.8. . . . . **600.00**
Calendar, 1913, 13-1/2" x 22-1/2", Hamilton King illus **900.00**
Ceiling globe, 14" d, milk glass, four logos, 1930s, C-9.5 . . . . **990.00**
Change tray
    1914, Betty **150.00**
    1941, girl with skates. **48.00**
    1970, Santa Claus **85.00**
Clock, 18" octagonal, neon, silhouette girl, 1939, C-8.5 . . . . **1,800.00**
Door kick plate, litho tin, 11-1/2" x 35", scrolling logo
    Drink Coca-Cola, 1942 couple on right, C-9.9 . . . . **2,600.00**

Boots, black and red rubber, Coca-Cola graphic on heel and topside of boot, one pull on strap has separated, $90. Photo courtesy of James D. Julia, Inc.

Button, left: 4" d, white ground, red text "Welcome Stockholders The Coca-Cola Bottling Co. Of N.Y. Inc.," 1960s, $20; right: 3" d, red ground, white text "UBA & Bands Of Steel With Coke," 1980s, $10. Photo courtesy of Hake's Americana & Collectibles.

Drink Coca-Cola, 1923 bottle on left, C-9.9. . . . . **1,765.00**

Door pull, 8" h, plastic and metal, bottle shape, orig instructions and screws, C-9.3-9.5 . . . . **275.00**

Game board, 11-1/4" x 26-1/2", Steps to Health, prepared and distributed by Coca-Cola Co. of Canada, Ltd., copyright 1938, orig unmarked brown paper envelope **60.00**

Mileage meter, 10" x 7", originating in Statesville, NC, C-8.4 . . . . **1,675.00**

Pin, Hi-Fi Club, gold luster finish, detailed plastic, short metal stickpin, miniature Coke bottle about name in red lettering, phonograph record background inscribed "Sponsored By Your Coca-Cola Bottler," Australian issue, c1950 . . . . **40.00**

Change tray, Hamilton King illustration of woman holding flared glass, 1913, 4-1/4"w, 6" h, $375. Photo courtesy of James D. Julia, Inc.

Clock, figure eight, "Relieves Exhaustion --- Delicious Refreshing," manufactured by Baird, 1893-96, original interior paper label and pendulum, both papier-mâché advertising bezels have been completely restored, typical discoloration on clock face, 16" w, 26-1/4" h, $6,325. Photo courtesy of James D. Julia, Inc.

Pocket mirror, 1-3/4" w, 2-3/4" h oval, celluloid, 1914, pretty girl, dark green ground, white and red lettering . **400.00**

Poster, 1943, two farm girls taking a break, caption "Work Refreshed" **2,750.00**

Prize chance card, 4-1/4" x 5-1/4", printed in red and black on white, c1940, unused **12.00**

Radio

Bottle shape, 24" h, 1930s, C-8.2 . . . . **8,500.00**

Cooler shape, red, 1950s . **2,250.00**

Salesman sample, cooler

By Kay Displays, orig leatherette carrying case, orig cardboard box, 1939, C-9.8 . . . . **10,000.00**

Glasscock Junior, orig carrying case, six small Coke bottles with nickel-plated hardware, 1929, C-8.5 . . . . **33,000.00**

Playing cards, airplane spotter, blue box has image of three purple airplanes on front plus red, white, and yellow Coke logo, painted art on back of Navy nurse in white uniform holding bottle of Coke, card fronts have black silhouettes of planes plus their names, Japanese Zero Fighter, German Dive Bomber, British Spitfire, U.S. Army Flying Fortress, etc., nurse image on back of 52 cards, some loss to box, 2-3/8" x 3-1/2" x 3/4" box, $75. Photo courtesy of Hake's Americana & Collectibles.

Sandwich plate, 7-1/4" d, white ground, script slogan, bottle and glass in center, Knowles, C-9.8 . . . . . **750.00**

Sign

6" x 18", porcelain, diecut, two-color, script, orig box, attaching instructions, screws, C-10 **1,100.00**

11" x 13", diecut, six-pack, 1951, C-9.4 . . . . **1,000.00**

14", countertop, light-up, Art Deco style, 1930s, orig paint, Price Bros decal on back, C-8.5 . . . **15,500.00**

23" x 26", porcelain, diagonal slash, fountain service, 1934, C-9.7 . . . . **4,700.00**

24" d, porcelain, single bottle in center, no slogan, 1950, C-9.2 . . . . **1,800.00**

26" x 25", double-sided, sidewalk, dispenser, 1939, C-9.5 . . . **6,750.00**

60" x 42", porcelain, curb-side service, two-sided, green, red, and white, 1933, C-9.6 . . . . . . **3,000.00**

String holder, two-sided, showing six-lace and logo "Take Home in Cartons," 1940s, C-9.5 . . . . . . **4,000.00**

Thermometer

5" x 17" diecut emb tin, figural Pat'd Dec 25, 1923 bottle, 1930s **150.00**

5-1/2" x 18", Thirst knows no season, Canadian, silhouette girl, porcelain, Canadian, 1939-40, C-9.7 . . . . **4,800.00**

12" d, fishtail logo, C-9.8 . . . **950.00**

12" d, Things Go Better with Coke, 1963, C-9.8 . . . . **650.00**

Tray, Madge Evans, MGM, couple of ring marks from glasses on tray, small amount of wear to trim, $210. Photo courtesy of James D. Julia, Inc.

Tray, The Golfers, 1926, young lady and her beau after a game of golf, he pours her a glass of Coke, blemish in lower right center, few surface scratches on the tray, slight wear to gold trim, $415. Photo courtesy of James D. Julia, Inc.

Toy, van, Corgi, 5" l diecast metal and plastic replica, copyright 1978, 2-3/4" x 6" x 3-1/2" color box with display window **35.00**

Tray

1926, oval, girl handing coke to viewer, 13" x 19", C-10 . . **15,250.00**

1930, bathing beauty, C-8 . . . **195.00**

1935, Madge Evans, C-7.5 . . **165.00**

1942, girl in convertible being waited on by another girl, C-9.5 . . . **450.00**

Vending Machine, 23-5/8" x 21-5/8" x 64" h, Select-O-Matic, Westinghouse, six dial selector, bottle opener set into front, c1960. . . . . **3,200.00**

COFFEE MILLS

History: Coffee mills or grinders are utilitarian objects designed to grind fresh coffee beans. Before the advent of stay-fresh packaging, coffee mills were a necessity.

The first home-size coffee grinders were introduced about 1890. The large commercial grinders designed for use in stores, restaurants, and hotels often bear an earlier patent date.

Arcade, 17" h, wall type, crystal jar, emb design, marked "Crystal" and "Arcade" orig lid rusted **185.00**

Crown Coffee Mill, cast iron, mounted on wood base, decal "Crown Coffee Mill Made By Landers, Frary, & Clark, New Britain, Conn, U.S.A.," number 11 emb on top lid. **525.00**

Early wooden coffee grinder, cast iron grinder, hinged door, metal pan, $225. Photo courtesy of Joy Luke Auctions.

Enterprise

#00, 12-1/2" x 7-1/2" x 8-3/4", two wheels, store type, orig paint, orig decals, C8+ **1,450.00**

#9, orig dec and decals, bright orange/red paint, blue on top of base and edges of wheels, gold detailed lettering, drawer in base stenciled "No. 9," eagle finial, white porcelain knob, minor wear, restored break on lid, 28-1/2" h **1,200.00**

Pine, fingered joints, one drawer, iron pull, iron top cup and handle, wooden knob, c1880, 5-3/4" sq, 6" h **95.00**

Sun Manufacturing, Greenfield, Ohio, worn orig label, round wooden sides, cast iron hardware, directions for use, 12" h. **300.00**

Tin, tole dec of tulip and stars, 12" h **250.00**

X-R, cast iron, mounted on oval board, early 1900s **250.00**

Woodruff Edwards, Elgin, IL, 66" h, store type, 28" d wheels, eagle finial, repainted **1,800.00**

COIN-OPERATED ITEMS

History: Coin-operated items include amusement games, pinball machines, jukeboxes, slot machines, vending machines, cash registers, and other items operated by coins.

The first jukebox was developed about 1934 and played 78-RPM records. Jukeboxes were important to teen-agers before the advent of portable radios and television.

The first pinball machine was introduced in 1931 by Gottlieb. Pinball machines continued to be popular until the advent of solid-state games in 1977 and advanced electronic video games after that.

The first three-reel slot machine, the Liberty Bell, was invented in 1905 by Charles Fey in San Francisco. In 1910, Mills Novelty Company copyrighted the classic fruit symbols. Improvements and advancements have led to the sophisticated machines of today.

Vending machines for candy, gum, and peanuts were popular from 1910 until 1940 and can be found in a wide range of sizes and shapes.

Additional Listings: See *Warman's Americana & Collectibles* for separate categories for Jukeboxes, Pinball Machines, Slot Machines, and Vending Machines.

Adviser: Bob Levy.

Notes: Because of the heavy usage these coin-operated items received, many are restored or, at the very least, have been repainted by either the operator or manufacturer. Using reproduced mechanisms to restore pieces is acceptable in many cases, especially when the restored piece will then perform as originally intended.

Arcade

Fortune Teller, Princess Doraldina, Rochester, NY, c1928, 5 cent, life like, gives fortune. **13,000.00**

Grip Tester, Shake with Your Uncle Sam, Howard, c1904, 1 cent, 66" h **17,250.00**

Photo Viewing Machine, American Mutoscope, NY, c1920, 1 cent, metal, orig photos and paper marquee **1,100.00**

Gum machines

Adams, c1934, four column, tab gum vendor, chrome, decal, 22" h . . . **100.00**

Ford, c1950, round globe, gum balls, large, organizational use, 12" h . . **75.00**

Master, c1923, 1 cent, confection, 16" h **200.00**

Penny King, c1935, four in one, rotates, Art-Deco style, four glass compartments **500.00**

Cash register, brass, candy store type, marked "National Cash Register, Dayton, OH, U.S.A.," $550. Photo courtesy of Joy Luke Auctions.

Slot, Arcade, titled "US Marshall," dime mechanism, game in blue painted wood case, chrome and nickel trim, aluminum saloon façade with various targets that appear in the windows and doors, 28" l, 22" h, $520. Photo courtesy of James D. Julia, Inc.

Pulver, c1930, 1 cent, two-column, porcelain, stick dispenser, policeman figure rotates, 21" h **600.00**

Juke boxes

Seeburg, Model 100R, c1954, high fidelity, classic style, plays 45s
. . . .**2,000.00**

Slot, Mills, Century of Progress, nicknamed "Skyscraper," five-cent machine, 1933, untouched condition, $2,500.

Slot, Mills, Bursting Cherry, 10-cent machine, $2,000.

Wurlitzer, Model 1015, c1946, The Bubbler. **7,500.00**

Miscellaneous

Cash register, National Brass, Model 317, c1910, barber shop size, orig marquee. **800.00**
Pinball, Jolly Roger, four players
. . . .**200.00**
Scale, American Scale, Fortune Model, c1937, 1 cent, health chart **200.00**

Slot, Mills, Cherry, five-cent machine, first one made after WWII, 1946, $2,000.

Slot machines

Caille, Superior, c1929, three reels, fancy design, 5 cent **1,400.00**
Groetchen, Columbia, c1936, three reels, high maintenance, 25 cent
. . . . **500.00**
Jennings, Standard Chief, c1947, three reels, classic design, 10 cent . **1,400.00**
Mills

Jewel Hightop, c1948, three reels, rugged and popular style, 5 cent
. . . .**1,400.00**
Puritan Bell, c1925, cash-register design, 5 cent, 8" h, 8" w . . **700.00**
Pace, All Star Comet, c1936, three reels, side mint vendor, 5 cent **1,400.00**
Watling, Rolatop, c1935, three reels, gold coins on front, 25 cent . .**3,200.00**

Vending machines

Card, slot dispenser, various subjects, exhibit supply, c1930, table top, 12" h, 10" w **225.00**
Cigarettes, Advance, c1930, 15 cent, 30" h, 14" w **100.00**
Coke, Vendo V81, c1955, 6-1/2, 8- or 10-oz bottles, orig condition . . **1,200.00**
Food, Horn and Hardart Automat Dispenser, c1902, four-item unit
. . . .**1,200.00**

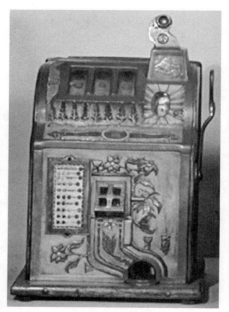

Slot, Mills, Poinsettia, top and front embossed aluminum panels with red and green floral poinsettia motifs, five-cent mechanism, c1930, original reel strips and award card, repainted rear door, 15-1/2" w, 15" d, 24" h, $1,840. Photo courtesy of James D. Julia, Inc.

Matches, Edwards Mfg Co., c1930, Diamond, one to four books, 13-1/2" h **225.00**

Nut, Ajax, Newark, NH, c1947, three-unit vendor, serves hot nuts, 21-1/2" h **300.00**

Pen, Vendorama, Victor Corp, c1962, oak case, 20" h, 14" w **100.00**

Perfume, Perfumatic, c1950, four fragrances, 10 cent spray, pink, 16" h, 18" w **325.00**

Stamp, Dillion Mfg, c1930, two selections, 12" x 12" **75.00**

COINS

For more information, see this book.

History: Coin collecting has long been one of the most respected and honored aspects of the collecting world. Today it still holds its fascination as new collectors come onto the scene every day. And just like the old-time collectors, they should be ready to spend time reading and learning more about this fascinating hobby. The States Quarter Series has spurred many of us to save quarters again and that has encouraged all types of coin collecting.

After the Declaration of Independence, America realized it needed its own coinage. Before that time, foreign coins were used in addition to paper currency. The first real coin of the young America was a copper coin, known as the Fugio Cent. Many of the early states created their own coins until the federal mint was constructed in Philadelphia after 1792. By 1837, the purity of silver was increased from 89.24 to 90 percent with minor adjustments to this weight occurring until 1873. Early dominations included a silver 3-cent piece, a gold $3-piece (1854) $1 and $20 (1849). The coinage law of 1857 eliminated the half-cent, changed the size of some coins, and forbid the use of foreign coins as legal tender. By the time of the Civil War, the two-cent and nickel three-cent pieces and the five-cent nickel were created. The phrase "In God We Trust" was added at this time. From the late 1870s, coins were plentiful. From 1873 to 1918, several laws were passed to force the government to buy silver and strike an abundance of silver dollars. President Theodore Roosevelt is credited with having the Mercury dime, the Walking Liberty half-dollar and the St. Gaudens double eagle, and the buffalo nickel created. Commemorative coins were also becoming very popular at this time. Designs on coins continue to change to reflect events, such as the Bicentennial.

It would be impossible to list values for all types of coins in a general price guide such as *Warman's,* so the following is included to give a general idea of coins. More information about specific coins is available in the various publications, including the *2003 Standard Catalog of World Coins,* published by Krause Publications.

Grading: The value placed on a coin is highly dependent on its "grade" or condition. The general accepted grades are as follows:

Uncirculated (Unc) (Mint State)(Ms) is known as "Very Good." These coins will show no wear at all, and should appear as though they just came from the mint.

Almost Uncirculated (AU) is known as "Good." An *Almost Uncirculated* coin describes coins with slight signs of wear.

Extremely Fine (EX) (Extra Fine) (XF) is known as "Fair." Extremely Fine coins exhibit wear that is readily seen, but still has clear details.

Very Fine (VF) is known as "Poor." A "Very Fine" coin will show obvious signs of wear, but still be clear of defects.

Fine (F) is the lowest grade most people would consider collectible. In this grade, about half the design details will show. The wear should be so slight that the viewer requires a magnifying glass to see it. There are several sub-categories in all these grades.

Very Good (VG). Coins graded at this level will show heavy wear, outlines will be clear.

Good (G). Coins at this grade are considered uncollectible except for novelty purposes.

About Good (AG) and *Fair (Fr).* These grades are for coins with much wear, often the rims are worn down and the outlines of the design are disappearing.

Poor (Pr) is the lowest grade possible; sometimes the coin will barely be identifiable.

Proof (PF) refers not to a grade, but rather a special way of making coins, usually as presentation pieces. A *Proof* will usually be double struck with highly polished coins on polished blanks.

Reproduction Alert: Counterfeit coins of all denominations exist.

Barber Half Dollar, 1892-1915, designed by Charles E. Barber.

1892, VG	23.00
1897S, VF	400.00
1905, VG	19.00
1913, VG	25.00
1915, VF	190.00

Buffalo Nickel, 1913 to 1938

1913, mound, Unc	32.00
1918S, VG	32.50
1936D, VG	25.00

Eisenhower Dollar, 1971-1978

1791D, PF	3.00
1973S, silver, Ms	8.00
1976S, silver, block letters, PF	12.00
1978D, PR	3.50

Franklin Half Dollar, 1948 to 1963

1948, Ms	13.75
1950, XF	6.00
1952, XF	3.00
1961, Ms	4.25

Half Cent. Production ended in 1859.

Braided hair, proof, 1849 . .	3,200.00
Classic head type, 1810, VG	140.00

Draped bust type, 1804, spiked chin version, VG **45.00**
Liberty cap type, 1793, VG **2,000.00**

Kennedy Half Dollar, 1964-2001. Obverse designed by Gilroy Roberts.

1964, XF	2.00
1965, silver clad, BU	1.35
1965-70, XF	1.00
1970S, Proof	7.75
1971-date	.50
1976, Bicentennial reverse, BU.	1.25
1979, filled "S," Proof	2.50
1981S, Proof	2.00
1989D, BU	1.50
1996P, BU	2.00

Indian Head Cent, 1859-1909

1860, copper-nickel allow, F . .	37.00
1867, bronze, XF	155.00
1909S, F	300.00

Jefferson Nickel, 1938 to present

1938, VG	.05
1942-1945, silver, VG	.50
1971S, proof	1.60

Large Cents

Classic head type, 1808-1814, 1810, VG **600.00**
Coronet type, 1816-1857

1817, 13 stars, VG	15.00
1838, VG	14.00
1847, VG	19.50

Draped bust type, 1796 to 1807

1800, VG	350.00
1804, restrike, Unc	450.00

Flowing hair type, 1793, wreath, VG **1,200.00**
Liberty cap type, 1793-1796, 1794, VG **250.00**

Liberty Nickel, 1883 to 1913

1883, no cents, G	3.75
1883-1913, Ms	60.00

Lincoln Cent, 1909-present

1909 to 1958, VG	.05
1943, VG	.15
1959-82, Ms	.15
1982-present	.011

Mercury Dime, 1916-1945, designed by Adolph Weinman.

1916, VF	6.00
1929, D, Ms	25.00
1940, VG	1.10
1944D, Ms	5.50

Morgan Dollar, 1878-1921, designed by George T. Morgan.

1878, 8 tail feathers, VG	20.00
1881S, VG	15.00
1887, Ms	24.00
1889CC, VF	500.00
1899, Ms	100.00
1921S, Ms	26.00

Roosevelt Dime, 1946-2001, designed by John R. Sinnock.

1946, BU	**1.05**
1950S, XF	**1.25**
1953S, XF	**.65**
1964D, BU	**.90**
1970S, proof	**.80**
1980P, BU	**.40**
1995D, BU	**.35**

Seated Liberty Dime, 1837-1891

1837-1838, no stars, G	**30.00**
1838-1860, Ms	**250.00**
1860-1891, G	**8.75**

Seated Liberty Dollar, 1840-1873

1840, G	**100.00**
1846, F	**175.00**
1853, EF	**575.00**
1866, G	**100.00**

Seated Liberty Half Dollar, 1839-1891, designed by Christian Gobrecht, several variations.

1839-1886, G	**16.00**
1840, small reverse letters, VG	**60.00**
1853, arrows and rays, G	**16.50**
1854-55, arrows, G	**16.00**
1857, arrows removed, VF	**45.00**
1873-74, arrows, G	**16.50**
1866-1891, G	**15.00**

Seated Liberty Quarter, 1838-1891, designed by Christian Gobrecht, several variations.

1840O, VG	**25.00**
1852, VG	**145.00**
1853, arrows at date, VG	**20.00**
1856, arrows removed, VG	**20.00**
1860S, arrows removed, VG	**50.00**
1866, motto above eagle, VG	**450.00**
1873, arrows at date, VG	**23.00**
1876, arrows removed, VG	**17.00**

Silver Three Cent

1851-1853, G	**18.50**
1854-1858, Ms	**240.00**
1859-1873, G	**17.50**

Walking Liberty Half Dollar, 1916-1947. Designed by Adolph Weinman.

1918, F	**12.00**
1935, XF	**6.00**
1939, XF	**10.00**

Washington Quarter, 1932-1998. Designed by John Flanagan.

1932, VG	**7.50**
1941, VG	**1.75**
1946, BU	**3.75**
1957D, BU	**2.50**
1972, BU	**.75**

COMIC BOOKS

History: Shortly after comics first appeared in newspapers of the 1890s, they were reprinted in book format and often used as promotional giveaways by manufacturers, movie theaters, and candy and stationery stores. The first modern-format comic was issued in 1933.

The magic date in comic collecting is June 1938, when DC issued Action Comics No. 1, marking the first appearance of Superman. Thus began the Golden Age of comics, which lasted until the mid-1950s and witnessed the birth of the major comic-book publishers, titles, and characters.

In 1954, Fredric Wertham authored *Seduction of the Innocent,* a book that pointed a guilt-laden finger at the comics industry for corrupting youth, causing juvenile delinquency, and undermining American values. Many publishers were forced out of business, while others established a "comics code" to assure parents that their comics were compliant with morality and decency standards upheld by the code authority.

The silver age of comics, mid-1950s through the end of the 1960s, witnessed the revival of many of the characters from the Golden Age in new comic formats. The era began with Showcase No. 4 in October 1956, which marked the origin and first appearance of the Silver-Age Flash.

While comics survived into the 1970s, it was a low point for the genre; but in the early 1980s, a revival occurred. In 1983, comic-book publishers, other than Marvel and DC, issued more titles than had existed in total during the previous 40 years. The mid- and late-1980s were a boom time, a trend that appears to be continuing.

Reproduction Alert: Publishers frequently reprint popular stories, even complete books, so the buyer must pay strict attention to the title, not just the portion printed in oversized letters on the front cover. If there is any doubt, look inside at the fine print on the bottom of the inside cover or first page. The correct title will be printed there in capital letters.

Also pay attention to the dimensions of the comic book. Reprints often differ in size from the original.

Note: The comics listed here are in near-mint condition, meaning they have a flat, clean, shiny cover that has no wear other than tiny corner creases; no subscription creases, writing, yellowing at margins, or tape repairs; staples are straight and rust free; pages are supple and like new; generally just-off-the-shelf quality.

Aaron Strips, #3, 1997	**1.50**
ABC Warriors, #1	**2.00**
Accident Man, #1, Dark Horse	**3.00**
Adventures of Rex the Wonder Dog, #5	**500.00**
Amazing Tales, #2	**275.00**
Amazing Spider-Man, #22	**325.00**

Tarzan #137, August 1963, Edgar Rice Burrough, K. K. Publications, **$8.**

A-Team, 1984	**2.50**
Avengers, #24	**200.00**
Daredevil, #9	**340.00**
DC Super Spectacular, #20	**84.00**
Fantastic Four, #20	**200.00**
Fighting Americans, #1, 1996	**110.00**
Flame, #5	**400.00**
Flash Gordon, #16	**20.00**
Forbidden Love, #2	**325.00**
Forbidden Worlds, #8	**450.00**
GI Joe I Battle, #1	**64.00**

Walt Disney's Comics & Stories, Dell, #131, **$4.50.**

Green Lantern, #27 . . . . **125.00**
Justice League of America, #14. **150.00**
Leave It To Beaver, #1285 . . . . . **310.00**
Little Orphan Annie, #1. . . . . **90.00**
Marvel Premiere, #1 . . . . **160.00**
Modern Comics, #98 . . . . **200.00**
Mystery in Space, #66 . . . . **410.00**
Our Army At War, #21. . . . . **135.00**
Rawhide Kid, #49 . . . . **100.00**
Sea Devils, #54. . . . . **125.00**
Six Gun Heroes, #81. . . . . **12.00**
Strange Tales, #57 . . . . **265.00**
Superman, #109. . . . . **420.00**
Tarzan, Lord of the Jungle, 1995 . **35.00**
Teen Confessions **130.00**
Tip Top Comics, 1938. . . . . **150.00**
Transformers, 1991. . . . . **42.00**
X-Men-14, #18 . . . . **560.00**
X-Men-24, #60 . . . . **75.00**
Zane Grey Stories of the West . . . **10.00**
Zoo Funnies, 1946 . . . . **48.00**
Zorro, 1960. . . . . **36.00**

COMPACTS

History: In the first quarter of the 20th century, attitudes regarding cosmetics changed drastically. The use of make-up during the day was no longer looked upon with disdain. As women became "liberated," and as more and more of them entered the business world, the use of cosmetics became a routine and necessary part of a woman's grooming. Portable containers for cosmetics became a necessity.

Compacts were made in myriad shapes, styles, combinations and motifs, all reflecting the mood of the times. Every conceivable natural or man-made material was used in the manufacture of compacts. Commemorative, premium, souvenir, patriotic, figural, Art Deco, and enamel compacts are a few examples of the types of compacts that were made in the United States and abroad. Compacts combined with other forms, such as cigarette cases, music boxes, watches, hatpins, canes, and lighters, also were very popular.

Compacts were made and used until the late 1950s, when women opted for the "au naturel" look. The term "vintage" is used to describe the compacts from the first half of the 20th century as distinguished from contemporary examples.

Additional Listings: See *Warman's Americana & Collectibles* for more examples.

Adviser: Roselyn Gerson.

Art Deco, 14kt yg, linear engine turned design, black onyx edge dec, mirror and powder puff, matching lipstick case, European hallmarks . . . **1,000.00**
BOAC, British Overseas Airways Corp, 3" d, gold, black leatherette, gold metal logo, framed mirror, BOAC puff, royal blue felt cover. **70.00**
Cartier, 1-7/8" x 2-5/8", 9kt yg, rect form, ribbed case with diamond-set thumbpiece, powder compact with fitted mirror, 61.5 dwt (including mirror), English hallmarks, sgd "Cartier London" **420.00**
Celluloid, unknown maker
  2" sq, metal compact, celluloid top showing pastoral scene with lovers, c1940 . . . . **45.00**
  3" d, orange compact studded with floral rhinestone motif. **45.00**
  5" celluloid diamond shaped purse, 2" tassel and silk cord, mottled cream, green and brown with oval cameo attached to center top, mirror, powder puff and chrome scent vial **275.00**
Coty, #405, envelope box. **65.00**
Djer Kiss, with fairy. **95.00**
European, 14kt gold compact, rect, linear, engine-turned design, channel-set red stone thumbpiece, European hallmarks. **500.00**
Evans, goldtone, heart shape, black twisted carrying cord, lipstick concealed in black tassel suspended from bottom. **250.00**
Fifth Avenue, vanity case "Cosmetist," aquamarine enamel, powder, rouge, lipstick, cleansing cream, and mascara, England. **175.00**
Foster & Bailey, Providence, vanity case, sterling silver and enamel, 3-1/2" x 2", rect, canted corners, lid enameled in center over diamond-shaped starburst ground, vase of roses on white ground, bordered by turquoise enamel cornered by roses, green cabochon thumb piece open to hinged mirror,

off-center hinged double compartment each with cabochon thumb piece, braided wrist chain, c1880. . . . . **800.00**
Italian, hand-mirror shape, sterling silver, stylized floral engraving, lipstick concealed in handle, coral cabochon thumb piece. **325.00**
Jensen, Georg, sterling silver, polished oval case accented with pine cone and leaf motif, hinged cover opens to reveal fitted mirror and powder compact, sgd "Georg Jensen, Inc." **165.00**
Kigu, lady swinging. **45.00**
Lampi, light blue enamel, five colorful three-dimensional scenes from *Alice in Wonderland* enclosed in plastic domes on lid. **180.00**
Max Factor, 2-1/4" d, solid perfume, round faux jade pendant, goldtone twisted braided wire disk, orig Khara fragrance **35.00**
Norida, emb lady, silver tone. . . . **75.00**
Rex Fifth Avenue, vanity-pochette, navy blue, gold polka dots, taffeta drawstring, mirror on outside base **90.00**
Sterling silver, 2-18" d round compact with lid enameled to center with 18th C lady, white basse taille surrounded with black border, opening to mirror and makeup compartment, strung with white chord suspending 2-1/8" l white basse taille lipstick case, American, 20th C. **175.00**
Tiffany & Co., Art Deco, sterling silver, gold, and sapphire, sq engraved lineal design, surmounted by gold and sapphire crescent, mirror and powder compartment, sgd **450.00**

Compact, silver and enameled, top enameled with man and woman sitting under tree, dog and lamb by their sides, chased filigree sides, beveled mirror in lid, three covered compartments for powder, lipstick holder, inside completely gilt with chased design matching outside, marked "800," 3-3/4" by 5", $575. Photo courtesy of James D. Julia, Inc.

Compact, silver and enameled, chased design of flowers and leaves, top enameled with center section of man courting woman with flowers, sitting underneath tree, sheep at her side, border enamel done to resemble green malachite. Beveled mirror, powder puff marked "Miss Bergdorf," marked "800," 3/4" scratch on side, 2-3/4" w, 4-1/4" l, $250. Photo courtesy of James D. Julia, Inc.

Enamel, hexagonal-shaped case made of .935 silver, chased decoration, luminous enamel panel with woman, putti, doves, flowers, and cloudy sky, 3-1/2" x 3", $1,550. Photo courtesy of Sanford Alderfer Auction Co.

Unknown maker, compact

Castanets shape, ebony wood, metal Paris insignia centered on lid, orange tasseled carrying cord **220.00**

Sterling, 2" x 3", enamel panel on one side with landscape and palm trees, rect engraved sterling silver case, chain handle, int. fitted for make-up with mirror, marked "Sterling," minor wear..... **215.00**

Telephone-dial shape, red, white, and blue, slogan "I Like Ike" imprinted on lid, red map of USA on lid center **225.00**

Unknown maker, compact, English, Birmingham, sterling silver and enamel

2-1/2" sq, canted corners, green enamel over "L"-shaped engine-turning, scalloped sunray issuing from scrolls, c1940. **225.00**

2-7/8" sq, canted corners, blue enamel over spiraling engine-turning, central nautical flag with crown **250.00**

Unknown maker, compact, Europe, early 20th C, silver, 800 silver

2-3/8" l, 1-1/2" w, oval, enameled violet on lid, int. mounted with mirrors, losses to int. **290.00**

3" l, quadrangular with shaped edges, engraved lid with polychrome enamel genre scene, underside with engraved foliates, gilt interior with mirror mounted to lid **300.00**

Unknown maker, vanity bag, SS mesh, hallmarked, octagonal, goldtone int. and finger ring carrying chain .. **500.00**

Van Cleef & Arpels, 2-3/4" x 3-1/2", Retro, silver gilt, rect form, thumbpiece set with single-cut diamonds and calibre-cut sapphires in stylized bow motif, fitted mirror, two powder compartments, and lipstick holder inscribed with name and NY address, brown leather Van Cleef & Arpels slip case **750.00**

CONSOLIDATED GLASS COMPANY

For more information, see this book.

History: The Consolidated Lamp and Glass Company was formed as a result of the 1893 merger of the Wallace and McAfee Company, glass and lamp jobbers of Pittsburgh, and the Fostoria Shade & Lamp Company of Fostoria, Ohio. When the Fostoria, Ohio, plant burned down in 1895, Corapolis, Pennsylvania, donated a seven-acre tract of land near the center of town for a new factory. In 1911, the company was the largest lamp, globe, and shade works in the United States, employing more than 400 workers.

In 1925, Reuben Haley, owner of an independent-design firm, convinced John Lewis, president of Consolidated, to enter the giftware field utilizing a series of designs inspired by the 1925 Paris Exposition (l'Exposition Internationale des Arts Décorative et Industriels Modernes) and the work of René Lalique. Initially, the glass was marketed by Howard Selden through his showroom at 225 Fifth Avenue in New York City. The first two lines were Catalonian and Martele.

Additional patterns were added in the late 1920s: Florentine (January 1927), Chintz (January 1927), Ruba Rombic (January 1928), and Line 700 (January 1929). On April 2, 1932, Consolidated closed it doors. Kenneth Harley moved about 40 molds to Phoenix. In March 1936, Consolidated reopened under new management, and the "Harley" molds were returned. During this period, the famous Dancing Nymph line, based on an eight-inch salad plate in the 1926 Martele series, was introduced.

In August 1962, Consolidated was sold to Dietz Brothers. A major fire damaged the plant during a 1963 labor dispute and in 1964, the company permanently closed its doors.

Bonbon, cov, 8" d, Ruba Rhombic, faceted, smoky topaz, catalog #832, c1931 .... **325.00**

Bowl, 5-1/2" d, Coronation, Martelé, flared, blue **75.00**

Box, cov, 7" l, 5" w, Martelé line, Fruit and Leaf pattern, scalloped edge **85.00**

Candlesticks, pr, Hummingbird, Martelé line, oval body, jade green, 6-3/4" h **248.00**

Cocktail, Dancing Nymph, French Crystal...................... **90.00**

Cookie jar, 6-1/2" h, Regent Line, #3758, Florette, rose pink over white opal casing **370.00**

Cup and saucer, Dancing Nymph, ruby flashed.................... **265.00**

Dinner service, Five Fruits, service for six, goblet, plate, sherbet, one large serving plate, purple wash, mold imperfections, wear.......... **375.00**

Goblet, Dancing Nymph, French Crystal...................... **90.00**

Humidor, Florette, pink satin... **225.00**

Jar, cov, Con-Cora, #3758-9, pine cone dec, irid.................... **165.00**

Lamp

Cockatoo, 13" h, figural, orange and blue, black beak, brown stump, black base **450.00**

Flower basket, 8" h, bouquet of roses and poppies, yellows, pinks, green leaves, brown basketweave, black glass base **300.00**

Mayonnaise comport, Martelé Iris, green wash **55.00**

Miniature lamp, 10" h, opalescent blue **380.00**

Night light, Santa Maria, block base **450.00**

Old-fashioned tumbler, 3-7/8" h, Catalonian, yellow............ **20.00**

Boudoir lamp, commemorating Fraternal Order of Elks, elk head form, clock between horns, brown colored glass, chip on threaded fitter ring, 13" h, $320. Photo courtesy of James D. Julia, Inc.

Perfume bottle, 5-1/2" h, Ruba Rombic, gray frosted body, nick on stopper
. . . . **1,420.00**
Plate
8-1/4" d, Bird of Paradise, amber wash **40.00**
10-1/4" d, Catalonian, yellow . . **45.00**
12" d, Martelé, Orchid, pink, birds and flowers **115.00**
Puff box, cov, Lovebirds, blue . . **95.00**
Salt and pepper shakers, pr
Cone, pink **75.00**
Cosmos **115.00**
Guttate, green **85.00**
Sauce dish, Criss-Cross, cranberry opalescent **55.00**
Sherbet, ftd, Catalonian, green . . **20.00**
Snack set, Martelé Fruits, pink . . **45.00**
Sugar bowl, cov, Guttate, cased pink
. . . . **120.00**
Sugar shaker, 3-1/2" d, puff quilted body, pink, brass lid **150.00**
Sundae, Martelé Russet Yellow Fruits
. . . . **35.00**
Syrup, Cone, squatty, pink **295.00**
Toothpick holder, Florette, cased pink
. . . . **75.00**
Tumbler
Catalonian, ftd, green, 5-1/4" h
. . . . **30.00**
Dancing Nymph, frosted pink, 6" h
. . . . **175.00**

Lamp, blown-out floral shade, silvered base, 10" h, $660. Photo courtesy of Jackson's Auctioneers & Appraisers.

Sherbets, Ruba Rhombic, emerald green, few minute nicks, 2-3/4" d, 4-1/4" h, set of four, $350. Photo courtesy of David Rago Auctions.

Guttate, pink satin **65.00**
Katydid, clambroth **165.00**
Ruba Rhombic, faceted, ftd, silver gray, 6" h **210.00**
Umbrella vase, Blackberry **550.00**
Vase
6" h, Regent Line, #3758, cased blue stretch over white opal, pinched
. . . . **175.00**
6-1/2" h, sea foam green, lavender, and tan, floral pattern **150.00**
8-1/2" h, Katydid, blue wash, fan-shaped top **300.00**
10-1/2" h, Love Bird pattern, golden birds, custard ground **600.00**
Whiskey glass, 2-5/8" h, Ruba Rhombic, faceted, transparent jungle green, catalog #823 . . . . **265.00**

CONTINENTAL CHINA AND PORCELAIN (GENERAL)

History: By 1700, porcelain factories existed in large numbers throughout Europe. In the mid-18th century, the German factories at Meissen and Nymphenburg were dominant. As the century ended, French potteries assumed the leadership role. The 1740s to the 1840s were the golden age of Continental china and porcelains.

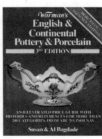

For more information, see this book.

Americans living in the last half of the 19th century eagerly sought the masterpieces of the European porcelain factories. In the early 20th century, this style of china and porcelain was considered "blue chip" by antiques collectors.

Additional Listings: French—Haviland, Limoges, Old Paris, Sarreguemines, and Sevres; German—

Austrian Ware, Bavarian China, Carlsbad China, Dresden/Meissen, Rosenthal, Royal Bayreuth, Royal Bonn, Royal Rudolstadt, Royal Vienna, Schlegelmilch, and Villeroy and Boch; Italian—Capo-di-Monte.

French

Choisy, plate, 8-1/4" d, earthenware transfer printed and hand enameled, each with different numbered scene relating to story of soldier's courtship and military life, naïve enamel accenting, mid-19th C, price for set of 12 . . . . **500.00**
Faience
Bulb pot, 3-1/8" d, sq, molded acanthus-capped scroll feet, conforming handles, front with scene of courting couple, verso landscape, each side with floral sprays, sq form insert, gilt highlights, attributed to Marseilles, last quarter 18th C, pr **900.00**
Inkstand, 13-1/2" l, figural, cartouche-shaped base molded with scrolls, front painted with harbor scene flanked by tower and knight-shaped inkpots, back sections support large figure of lion with raised paw resting on shield with armorial **650.00**
Plate, 9" d, blue and white floral dec, foliate border **115.00**
Sugar caster, 8-1/2" h, brightly polychrome scene of courting couple in landscape, floral sprays borders, dec band of fleur-de-lis border, pierced cov with conforming dec, early 19th C
. . . . **450.00**
Lessore, Emile, platter, 14-1/4" l, oval, earthenware, polychrome figural landscape with putti, artist signed,

Luneville, soup bowl and plate, rooster decorated, marked "K (crown over globe) G Porcelain Opaque, Luneville, France, Hand Painted Under Glaze, F. B. & Cie, Cockade," red, blue and dark green decorated, $45.

printed factory mark for Hautin and Boulenger, France, c1855, rim chip
. . . . **450.00**

Paris

Cache pot, 6" h, ovoid, apple-green ground, floral roundels in leaf surround, two gilt lion's head masks on sides, narrow undertray, late 19th C **115.00**

Candlesticks, pr, 9" h, everted sconce, column-form standard, shaped base with man and woman among rocaille leaves **200.00**

Dessert plate, 9-1/8" d, hand painted, four with flower centers, two with fruit centers, all with peach borders, gilt scrolls, maroon band at molded rim, late 19th C . **750.00**

Vase garniture, 8" h, 8-1/4" h, 9-1/2" h, three vases, each with aqua ground, floral bouquet roundels in gilt surrounds, short scroll handles, domed foot molded with scallop shells, late 19th C
. . . . **500.00**

Veilleuse, 4-1/2" h pot, 9" h overall, hand painted, small pot with black and pink bands, over enameled with gilt scrolls, short gilt spout, angular handle, octagonal pagoda-form stand hp with scenes titled "acqueduque de Buc," showing elevated aqueduct, and

Sampson, table lamp, urn form, figural handles, white ground decorated with polychrome floral design and family crest, mounted on gilt base, 13" h vase, 24" overall height, $365. Photo courtesy of Sanford Alderfer Auction Company.

"a Bonnebose (Calvados)," showing village, 20th C, base missing **475.00**

Samson & Co.

Character figure, 6-3/8" to 7-5/8" h, three figures in masks and caps, two wielding swords, other dagger, bearded figure with guitar, each by vine-covered tree trunk, rect base, guilloche borders, 20th C, price for four-pc set **450.00**

Figure, 12-1/4" h, Neptune, upraised hands standing on scallop shell, dolphin at feet, rocaille base encrusted with shells and seaweed, gilt accents, late 19th C
. . . . **230.00**

Perfume bottle, 2-7/8" l, figural, boy with vessel seated on dolphin, enamel detailing, boy's head as stopper, late 19th C **230.00**

Germany

Hutschenreuther

Plaque, 5-1/8" x 6-7/8", oval, Madonna and Child, giltwood frame, late 19th C **600.00**

Service plate, 10-7/8" d, central dec, summer flowers within heavily gilt cavetto, rim worked with scrolling acanthus, textured ground, underglaze green factory marks, minor rubbing, 12-pc set. **1,600.00**

Nymphenburg, vase, 10-1/2" d, wide baluster form, enamel dec, continuous landscape scene, titled on underside "Vorfrohling in Oberbayorn," signed "R. Sieck," 20th C **750.00**

Tirschenreuth, service plate, 10-3/4" d, gold inner band of Egyptian Revival lotus and roundel, dark apple green edge, gilt rim, price for set of eight
. . . . **225.00**

Unknown maker

Cup and saucer, bucket-shaped 3-5/8" h cup, cerulean blue band over horizontal gilt beaded band above landscape scene, short gilt acanthus scroll handle, three gilt paw feet, similarly beaded and gilded saucer **1,035.00**

Plaque, 5" l, girl with candle, titled "Guten Nahct," oval, reeded giltwood frame, late 19th/early 20th C **1,035.00**

COOKIE JARS

History: Cookie jars, colorful and often whimsical, are popular with collectors. They were made by almost every manufacturer, in all types of materials. Figural

character cookie jars are the most popular with collectors.

Cookie jars often were redesigned to reflect newer tastes. Hence, the same jar may be found in several different variations and these variations can affect the price.

Marks: Many cookie-jar shapes were manufactured by more than one company and, as a result, can be found with different marks. This often happened because of mergers or separations, e.g., Brush-McCoy, which became Nelson McCoy. Molds also were traded and sold among companies.

North Dakota School Of Mines, Mammy, by Margaret Cable, dark brown matte glazes, circular ink stamp, incised "Aunt Susan/dht/M Cable/118A," small nick inside lid rim 6-3/4" d, 10-1/2" h, $1,610. Photo courtesy of David Rago Auctions.

Abingdon Pottery

Bo Peep, No. 694D, 12" h. . . **425.00**

Choo Choo, No. 561D, 7-1/2" h
. . . . **120.00**

Daisy, No. 677, 8" h **50.00**

Fat Boy, No. 495, 8-1/4" h. . . **650.00**

Mother Goose, No. 695D, 12" h
. . . . **550.00**

Pumpkin, No. 674D, 8" h . . . **550.00**

Three Bears, No. 696D, 8-3/4" h
. . . . **245.00**

Windmill, No. 678, 10-1/2" h. **500.00**

Witch, No. 692, 11-1/2" h . . **1,000.00**

Brayton Laguna Pottery

Mammy, turquoise bandanna, burgundy base. **1,300.00**

Partridges, Model No. V-12, 7-1/4" h
. . . . **200.00**

Roseville, Water Lily, brown, raised mark, $400. Photo courtesy of David Rago Auctions.

Provincial Lady, high-gloss white apron and scarf, red, green, and yellow flowers and hearts, marked "Brayton Laguna Calif. K-27," 13" h 455.00

Swedish Maid, 1941, incised mark, 11" h 600.00

Gonder Pottery

Pirate, 8" h 225.00

Sheriff, Mold No. 950, 12" h 1,100.00

Hull Pottery

Barefoot Boy 320.00

Duck 60.00

Gingerbread Boy, blue and white trim 400.00

Gingerbread Man, 12" h 550.00

Little Red Riding Hood, open basket, gold stars on apron 375.00

Unknown maker, Tuggle the Tugboat, $85. Photo courtesy of Joy Luke Auctions.

Metlox Pottery

Bear, blue sweater 100.00

Chef Pierre 100.00

Drummer Boy 750.00

Parrot, tree stump, green and yellow, Model No. 555 .... 425.00

Pine Cone, gray squirrel finial, Model No. 509, 11" h............115.00

Rex Dinosaur, white 120.00

Tulip, yellow and green..... 425.00

Red Wing Pottery

French Chef, blue glaze.... 250.00

Grapes, yellow, marked "Red Wing USA," 10" h............. 125.00

Rooster, green glaze....... 165.00

Shawnee Pottery

Cinderella, unmarked..... 125.00

Cottage, marked "USA 6," 7" h 900.00

Dutch Boy, striped pants, marked "USA," 11" h............ 190.00

Dutch Girl, marked "USA," 11-1/2" h 175.00

Great Northern Boy, marked "Great Northern USA 1025," 9-3/4" h 425.00

Jo-Jo the Clown, marked "Shawnee USA, 12," 9" h........... 300.00

Little Chef 95.00

Muggsy Dog, blue bow, gold trim and decals, marked "Patented Muggsy U.S.A.," 11-3/4" h . 850.00

Owl, eyes repainted 95.00

Smiley Pig, clover blossom dec, marked "Patented Smiley USA," 11-1/2" h.............. 550.00

Winnie Pig, clover blossom dec, marked "Patented Winnie USA," 12" h.................. 575.00

Stoneware, cobalt blue dec, unknown maker

Basketweave and Morning Glory, marked "Put Your Fist In," 7-1/2" h 625.00

Brickers, 8" h............. 475.00

Flying Bird, 9" h..........1,250.00

Watt Pottery

Apple, No. 21, 7-1/2" h 400.00

Cookie Barrel, wood grain, 10-1/2" h 50.00

Goodies, No. 76, 6-1/2" h ... 150.00

Happy/Sad Face, No. 34, wooden lid 165.00

Morning Glory, No. 95, 10" h. 600.00

Policeman, 10-1/2" h......1,150.00

Starflower, No. 503, 8" h 350.00

COPELAND AND SPODE

History: In 1749, Josiah Spode was apprenticed to Thomas Whieldon and in 1754 worked for William Banks in Stoke-on-Trent. In the early 1760s, Spode started his own pottery, making cream-colored earthenware and blue-printed whiteware. In 1770, he returned to Banks' factory as master, purchasing it in 1776.

Spode pioneered the use of steam-powered pottery-making machinery and mastered the art of transfer printing from copper plates. Spode opened a London shop in 1778 and sent William Copeland there about 1784. A number of larger London locations followed. At the turn of the century, Spode introduced bone china. In 1805, Josiah Spode II and William Copeland entered into a partnership for the London business. A series of partnerships between Josiah Spode II, Josiah Spode III, and William Taylor Copeland resulted.

For more information, see this book.

In 1833, Copeland acquired Spode's London operations and seven years later, the Stoke plants. William Taylor Copeland managed the business until his death in 1868. The firm remained in the hands of Copeland heirs. In 1923, the plant was electrified; other modernization followed.

In 1976, Spode merged with Worcester Royal Porcelain to become Royal Worcester Spode, Ltd.

Cabinet plate, 9-1/2" d, artist sgd "Samuel Alcock," 1-3/4" jeweled border, intricate gold, beading, pearl and turquoise jeweling, c1889 ..... 750.00

Plaque, bust of man with beard, titled Shylock, floral border, artist signed "L. Besche," framed, 22-1/2" d, $475. Photo courtesy of Joy Luke Auctions.

Dinner plate, shaped gilt and beaded rim with wide cobalt blue band, interior beaded and printed trefoil gilt band, mid-20th C, 11-piece set, 10-3/8" d, $375. Photo courtesy of Skinner Auctioneers and Appraisers.

Coffee cup and saucer, 2-1/4" h cylindrical cup with allover maroon and gilt scrolled dec, 5" d saucer, retained by Tiffany & Co., late 19th C, price for set of 12 . . . . **325.00**

Demitasse cup and saucer, Heather Rose, marked "Spode's Jewel, Copeland Spode, England," registration, patent numbers, patternname **35.00**

Fish plate, 9-3/4" d, artist sgd "H. C. Lea," four-part gold-swirled design, hp fly in each section, c1891 . . . . . **175.00**

Jug, orange, teal green, and gold dec, matte cream ground, ornate handle with two mythological characters, c1847
. . . . **450.00**

Plate, 9-1/2" d, blue and white, hunting scenes **225.00**

Platter, 18" x 23-1/4" d, Blue Willow pattern, oval, deep, shaped edge, marked "Copeland & Garrett/Late Spode" **375.00**

Service plate, 10-1/4" d, Brompton pattern, floral border, central design of birds and foliage, retailed by Wright, Tyndale & Van Roden, Inc., Philadelphia, marked "Rd. No. 608584," price for set of 10 . . . . **335.00**

Spill vase, 4-3/4" h, flared rim, pale lilac, gilt octagonal panels with portrait of bearded man, band of pearls on rims and bases, Spode, c1920 . . . . . **425.00**

Tea set, Blue Willow, retailed by Tiffany & Co., pattern registered January 1879, printed at rim with quotation from Robert Burns "Auld Lang Syne," 5" h cov hexagonal teapot, creamer, cov sugar, seven cups, six saucers,

20-3/4" d round tray with scalloped gilt rim, gilt handles, gilt foo dog lid finials, price for 17-pc set **950.00**

Tray, 8-1/2" l, black transfer, passion flowers, grape vines border, emb grapes, vines, and leaves on tab handles, c1900 . . . . **200.00**

Tureen, cov, 13" w, 11" h, white, gold and blue accents, marked "Spode New Stone" **1,470.00**

Urn, cov, 15" h, Louis XVI style, cobalt blue ground, medallions on each side with bouquet of roses, majolica, repair to one handle, nick to one lid, pr
. . . . **900.00**

Water pitcher, 8-1/4" h, bulbous, tan acanthus leaf handle and spout, green field dec with white relief classical figures of dancing women, white relief banded floral garland dec at neck, marked "Rd. No. 180288" **250.00**

COPPER

History: Copper objects, such as kettles, teakettles, warming pans, and measures, played an important part in the 19th-century household. Outdoors, the apple-butter kettle and still were the two principal copper items. Copper culinary objects were lined with a thin protective coating of tin to prevent poisoning. They were relined as needed.

Reproduction Alert: Many modern reproductions exist.

Additional Listings: Arts and Crafts Movement and Roycroft.

Notes: Collectors place great emphasis on signed pieces, especially those by American craftsmen. Since copper objects were made abroad as well, it is hard to identify unsigned examples.

Breadbox, 12" l, 7-1/2" w, 11" h, chamfered oblong rect form, hinged cov, paneled domical form, brass finial

Boiler, covered, metal and wood handles, old soldered repair at base, $125. Photo courtesy of Joy Luke Auctions.

Bowl, two iron handles, 21" d, $195. Photo courtesy of Joy Luke Auctions.

raising from lozenge-shaped plaque over brass ring handles, brass bottom, Neoclassical, possibly Dutch, c1800
. . . . **165.00**

Carpenter's pot, 11" l, 8" h, globular, dovetailed body, raised on three plain strap work iron legs, conforming handle
. . . . **70.00**

Charger, 29-1/2" d, hand hammered, emb high relief of owl on branch, naturally-forming patina, Liberty paper label **3,110.00**

Desk set, hammered blotter, letter holder, bookends, stamp box, each with bone carved cabochon, branch and berry motif, Potter Studio, fine orig patina, die-stamp mark **750.00**

Fish poacher, cov, 20-1/2" l, oval, rolled rim, iron swing ball handle, 19th C **350.00**

Inglenook hood, 30" w, 8" d, 34-1/2" h, hammered, emb Glasgow roses, English, small tear at bottom. . **1,610.00**

Pot, cov, 19-1/2" l, 12" w, 16" h, twin handles, oval, raised on four strap work legs, fitted with tubular end handles, shallow domed cov stamped with shield design, center stationary handle, English, 19th C **215.00**

Screen, 24" w, 38-1/4" h, Arts & Crafts, ruffled edges, repousse design of oak tree, acorns, sun behind it, iron supports with copper coils wrapped around on front **495.00**

Snuff box, German, oval form, impressed top, owner's name pierced on outside "Jacob Contre," c1780, 3-1/2" l, $70. Photo courtesy of Sanford Alderfer Auction Company.

Tea kettle, 11-1/2" h, curved spout, upright swing handle, brass lid knob, imp "G. Tyron" on handle, dents, wear, PA, 19th C **690.00**

Tray, 13-1/2" d, Stickley Brothers, hammered copper, loped rim emb with dots, stamped "36" no patina . . . **800.00**

Umbrella stand, 25" h, hand hammered, flared rim, cylindrical body, two-strap work-loop handles, repoussé medallion, riveted flared foot, c1910 . . . . **650.00**

Vase, 5-1/2" d, 7" h, hammered, ovoid, Dirk Van Erp, fine orig mottled patina, D'Arcy Gaw box mark, small shallow dent on rim **8,100.00**

Vessel, 4" d, 3-1/4" h, hammered, ovoid, closed-in rim, orig dark patina, Dirk Van Erp closed box mark **2,300.00**

Wall sconce, 4-1/2" w, 11" h, hammered, flame head, riveted Arts & Crafts details, attributed to Dirk Van Erp, cleaned patina **425.00**

Water urn, 14" h, copper body, int. with capped warming tube, applied brass ram's head handles, urn finial, brass spout, sq base with four ball feet, unmarked, repairs to lid **125.00**

COWAN POTTERY

History: R. Guy Cowan founded the Cowan Pottery in 1913 in Cleveland, Ohio. The establishment remained in almost continuous operation until 1931, when financial difficulties forced closure.

Early production was redware pottery. Later a porcelain-like finish was perfected with special emphasis placed on glazes, with lusterware being one of the most common types. Commercial wares marked "Lakeware" were produced from 1927 to 1931.

Marks: Early marks include an incised "Cowan Pottery" on the redware (1913-1917), an impressed "Cowan," and an impressed "Lakewood." The imprinted stylized semi-circle, with or without the initials "R. G.," came later.

Bookends, pr

6-1/4" h, 4" d, boy and girl, Special ivory glaze, stamped "Cowan" **350.00**

7-1/2" h, Sunbonnet, antique green crystalline glaze, c1925 . . . **375.00**

8-1/2" h, 6" d, flying fish, antique-green glaze, stamped "Cowan" **700.00**

Candleholders, pr, 8-1/2" h, Ming Green glaze, c1928 . . . . **80.00**

Demitasse cup and saucer, 2-1/2" h cup, 4" saucer, block letter logo . . **35.00**

Figure, Nocturne, aka "Radio Figure," attributed to Walter Sinz, 1929, Special Ivory glaze, hand-painted black details, stamped circular mark, 7" d, 9" h, $2,300. Photo courtesy of David Rago Auctions.

Figure

9" x 7", Morning, by Walter Sinz, ivory crackle glaze, inscribed in ink "Walter A. Sinz Sc./Mrs. R. A. Dyer Ceramist," minor nick to top, small flat chip on bottom **1,100.00**

9" x 7", Nocturne, attributed to Walter Sinz, Special ivory glaze, hp black details, stamped circular mark, 1929 . . . . **2,300.00**

9-1/2" x 9", horse, mahogany and gold flambé glaze, imp mark **1,500.00**

Figure, Morning, by Walter Sinz, ivory crackle glaze, Inscribed in ink "Walter A. Sinz Sc./Mrs.R.A. Dyer Ceramist," minor nick to tip, small flat chip to bottom, 7" w, 9" h, $1,100. Photo courtesy of David Rago Auctions.

Flower frog

7" h, figural nude, #698, orig ivory glaze **275.00**

7-3/4" h, 6-1/4" d, Duet, orig ivory glaze, stamped "Cowan" . . **550.00**

10" h, 5-1/4" d, Pan, Special ivory glaze, stamped "Cowan" . . **350.00**

10-3/4" h, 4" d, Swirl Dancer, orig ivory glaze, stamped "Cowan" **850.00**

Lamp base, 11-1/2" h, 9-1/2" d, bulbous, Oriental-red glaze, stamp mark, drilled at side and bottom **300.00**

Match holder, 3-1/2" h, cream color **65.00**

Paperweight, 4-1/2" h, 3-1/4" l, elephant, Special ivory glaze, stamped "Cowan" **300.00**

Snack set, hexagon-shaped plate, solid light blue **115.00**

Trivet, 6-1/2" d, woman's head and flowers, blue, cream, yellow, and pink, die-stamped mark, minor scratches **450.00**

Vase

5" d, 7-1/4" h, classical shape, dripping brown crystalline glaze, mirrored orange glaze, ink mark **300.00**

5" d, 8-1/2" h, blue, emb flowers and leaves **225.00**

10-3/4" h, irid blue, c1925 . . . . **90.00**

CRANBERRY GLASS

History: Cranberry glass is transparent and named for its color, achieved by adding powdered gold to a molten batch of amber glass and reheating at a low temperature to develop the cranberry or ruby color. The glass color first appeared in the last half of the 17th century, but was not made in American glass factories until the last half of the 19th century.

Cranberry glass was blown, mold blown, or pressed. Examples often are decorated with gold or enamel. Less-expensive cranberry glass, made by substituting copper for gold, can be identified by its bluish-purple tint.

For more information, see this book.

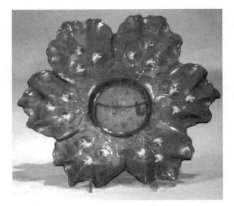

Dish, scalloped rim, decorated with blue flowers, orange leaves, 12-1/2" d, $195. Photo courtesy of Joy Luke Auctions.

Basket, 7" h, 5" w, ruffled edge, petticoat shape, crystal loop handle, c1890 . . . . **250.00**

Bride's basket, 5" h, 3-1/2" d bowl, German silver-filigree frame, plain cranberry bowl **115.00**

Centerpiece, 19-1/2" h, central trumpet-form vase, shallow dish, pedestal foot, gilt Greek-key dec, Victorian **300.00**

Condiment dish, underplate, 6-1/2" h, scrolling vines and grapes dec, Continental **175.00**

Creamer, 5" h, 2-3/4" d, Optic pattern, fluted to, applied clear handle . . . **95.00**

Decanter, 8" h, 3" d, gold mid-band, white-enameled trim, clear-faceted stopper **150.00**

Dresser box, 5" d, blown out melon ribs, enameled scrolling on bronze feet, French, late 19th C **175.00**

Epergne, 19" h, 11" d, five pcs, large ruffled bowl, tall center lily, three jack-in-the-pulpit vases **1,200.00**

Finger bowl, Inverted Thumbprint pattern, deep color **200.00**

Garniture, 14" d bowl, pr 11" h candlesticks, cranberry overlay cut to clear, faceted cut dec, Continental **450.00**

Jack-in-the-pulpit vase, 9" h, Victorian **90.00**

Lamp, 10" h, 5" d, peg, silver-plated base, ruffled-Rubena shade, emb daisies, chimney **265.00**

Miniature, pitcher, elaborate gold trim and handle **75.00**

Pipe, 18" l, hand blown, tapering-bent neck, bulbous bowl, three bulbs at base, white-enamel dec at outer rim of bowl **250.00**

Pitcher

6-1/2" h, 4-1/8" d, Ripple and Thumbprint pattern, bulbous, round mouth, applied clear handle **175.00**

10" h, 5" d, bulbous, ice bladder int., applied clear handle **250.00**

11-3/8" h, 9" w, bulbous, internal vertical ribs, white and blue enameled floral dec, applied clear loop handle, c1895 . . . . **300.00**

Salt, master, ftd, enameled floral dec **200.00**

Tumble-up, Inverted Thumbprint pattern **195.00**

Tumbler, Inverted Thumbprint pattern **65.00**

Water pitcher, ruffled rim, decorated with small blue and white flowers, applied clear glass handle, $195. Photo courtesy of Joy Luke Auctions.

Vase

7-1/2" h, emb ribs, applied clear feet, three swirled applied clear leaves around base **120.00**

8-7/8" h, bulbous, white-enameled lilies of the valley dec, cylindrical neck **150.00**

CROWN MILANO

History: Crown Milano is an American art glass produced by the Mt. Washington Glass Works, New Bedford, Massachusetts. The original patent was issued in 1886 to Frederick Shirley and Albert Steffin.

Normally, it is an opaque-white satin glass finished with light-beige or ivory-colored ground embellished with fancy florals, decorations, and elaborate and thick raised gold. The same glass in shiny finish is Colonial Ware.

Marks: Marked pieces have a purple enamel entwined "CM" with a crown on the base. Sometimes paper labels were used. Since both Mount Washington and Pairpoint supplied mountings, the silver-plated mounts often have "MW" impressed or a Pairpoint mark.

For more information, see this book.

Advisers: Clarence and Betty Maier.

Biscuit jar, cov

7" d, 7" h, squatty, pale green ground, pink and cream roses, naturalistically colored foliage, outlined in gold, replaced lid, base with logo and "520" **975.00**

Epergne, bowl with ruffled rim, trumpet shaped central vase, three clear glass branches each holding cranberry glass basket with ruffled rim, 21" h, $800. Photo courtesy of Joy Luke Auctions.

Miniature lamp, SI-439, slight chips to fitter rim and top rim, 8-3/4" h, $320. Photo courtesy of James D. Julia, Inc.

Biscuit jar, covered, melon-ribbed, chocolate shoulder shading to burnt-orange, raised gold bramble tendrils winding around the burnt-orange-colored body are bedecked with an array of gold colored leaves, gold and silver blossoms, gold and silver berries, leaves with raised gold veins, insect-eaten holes and dabs of oxidized silver, decorated foliage extends up over gold scrollwork border, fancy elongated chocolate-colored rococo scrolls decorate three ribs, oxidized metal fittings, lid with embossed crab and twig finial signed "MW 4415," base is signed with Crown Milano logo and "522," 7" d, 5-1/2" base, 8-1/4" h overall, $1,250. Photo courtesy of Clarence and Betty Maier.

7" d, 8-1/4" h, burnt-orange melon-ribbed body shading to chocolate colored shoulders, raised gold bramble tendrils winding around body, gold colored leaves with raised veins and insect-eaten holes, gold and silver blossoms and berries, fancy elongated chocolate-colored rococo scrolls on three ribs, oxidized metal fittings, emb crab on lid, twig finial, sgd "MW 4415," logo and "522" on base, few in-the-making scratches on two ribs **1,250.00**

Creamer and sugar, melon-ribbed bodies which shade from pale pink to natural white to pale green at base, blue cornflowers and green foliage, silver-plated fittings, sgd "3905/201" **1,500.00**

Demitasse cup and saucer, raised golden vine laden with single-petaled blossoms, buds, and tiny leaves meander around satin white ext., raised gold borders, coral-colored ring of dots centers in four blossoms, black rings in other three blossoms, sepia-colored rococo scrolls entwine floral dec, pale pink tint, sgd with logo, 2" h cup, 5" d saucer **1,750.00**

Ewer, 7-1/2" d, 6-1/2" h, Colonial Ware, shiny white body, two reserves of colorful blossoms framed by rococo borders of raised gold scrolls, gold cross-hatching across cream colored shoulder, some loss to wash of color around rope handle, sgd "0100" **1,250.00**

Lamp, banquet, 23" h, 9" d, Colonial Ware, shiny ground, base and globe-shaped shade dec with sprays of golden roes and blossoms, touches of gold accent molded-in dec of florals, swags, and geometric designs, opaque white chimney, brass burner sgd "Made in United States of America" . . **2,950.00**

Muffineer, melon ribbed, butter yellow tint, swags of dainty powder blue and cream daisies, metal collar, lid emb with butterfly, dragonfly, and blossoms **535.00**

Plate, 7" d, Colonial Ware, glistening white finish, garden of spring flowers that surround centered lush pink cabbage rose, sprays of blue forget-me-nots, yellow daisies, purple chrysanthemums, dark red tulips, coral nasturtiums, white apple blossoms and white begonias, five elaborate raised gold rococo embellishments, sgd **550.00**

Syrup pitcher, Colonial Ware, 15 sprays of Dresden floral bouquets strewn on white melon-ribbed body, fancy gold scrollwork on body, ornate pewter-like collar and lid **950.00**

Vase, sand-colored body, 24 swirling molded-in ribs, rare desert tableau of two cactus in full blossom, hand-painted pink, white and coral blossoms, outlined in raised gold, sharp gold thorns, 7-1/2" h, $2,450. Photo courtesy of Clarence and Betty Maier.

Sweetmeat, cov, 5-1/2" d, 6" h, Colonial Ware, blossoms and scrolls on two tendrils encircle glistening bridal-white body, brilliant gold highlights, gold wash collar, lid and bail, red crown and wreath logo, lid marked "MW Pat. Apld. For 2040" **485.00**

Tumbler, Colonial Ware, shiny body, shades of raised gold, swags of finely detailed roses and daisies descend from free-flowing ribbon, numbered "1026" **585.00**

Vase

4-1/2" h, white satin body with tint of lilac at neck, three fully opened chrysanthemum blossoms, two partially opened buds, raised gold borders, rich gold rim, raised DQ design, sgd **685.00**

7-1/2" h, sand-colored body, 24 swirling molded-in ribs, rare desert tableau, two cactus in full bloom, with five pink, white, and coral blossoms and one bud, outlined in raised gold, gold thorns on branches **2,450.00**

9" h, Colonial Ware, sprays of colorful enamel blossoms, shadow foliate branches of single-petaled roses and buds, neck with gold embellishments, sgd logo and "0615" **945.00**

CRUETS

For more information, see this book.

History: Cruets are small glass bottles used on the table holding condiments such as oil, vinegar, and wine. The pinnacle of cruet use occurred during the Victorian era, when a myriad of glass manufacturers made cruets in a wide assortment of patterns, colors, and sizes. All cruets had stoppers; most had handles.

Art glass, 6" h, opaque white, New England **850.00**

Bluerina, 7-1/4" h, deep royal blue neck fades to clear at shoulder, optic inverted thumbprint design in body, applied clear glass handle, teardrop-shaped airtrap stopper, in-the-making thin elongated bubble in neck **500.00**

Bohemian, amber cut to clear, floral arrangement intaglio carved on ruby flashed ground of three oval panels with carved frames of floral swags, five cut-to-clear panels at neck, three embellished with gold scrolls, all edged in brilliant gold, 16 decorative panels edged in gold, base and stopper both sgd "4"............... **750.00**

Burmese, 7" h, Mt. Washington, shiny finish, butter-yellow ribbed, body, applied handle, and mushroom stopper **1,250.00**

Chocolate, opaque, Greentown
    Cactus, no stopper....... **125.00**
    Leaf Bracket, orig stopper... **295.00**

Cranberry opalescent, Hobnail, Hobbs, Brockunier & Co., Wheeling, WV, 7-1/2" h **485.00**

Custard glass, Wild Bouquet pattern, fired-on dec................ **500.00**

Moser, 6" h, eight raised cabochon-like ruby gems, deep cut edges of burnished gold, mounted on colorless body, eight alternating panels of brilliant gold squiggles and stylized leaves, handle cut in three sharp edges, six gold dec panels on stopper, each set with ruby cabochon, inside of mouth and base of stopper sgd "4," some loss to gold squiggles........... **585.00**

Pattern glass, orig stopper
    Amazon, bar-in-hand stopper, 8-1/2" h............... **185.00**
    Beveled Star, green **225.00**
    Croesus, large, green, gold trim **395.00**
    Daisy and Button with Crossbars **75.00**
    Delaware, cranberry, gold trim **295.00**
    Esther, green, gold trim..... **465.00**

Pattern glass, Thousand Eye-Three Knob, canary, original canary holder, made by Adams & Company, Pittsburgh, PA, circa 1885-95, 6-1/2" h pair cruets, 9" l, 5" w, 7-3/4" h holder, to top of handle, **$750.** *Photo courtesy of Clarence and Betty Maier..*

Satin, heavenly blue raindrop mother of pearl, brilliant clear cut faceted stopper, clear frosted reeded handle, tiny discolored flake, 7-1/2" h, **$385.** *Photo courtesy of Clarence and Betty Maier.*

Fluted Scrolls, blue dec..... **265.00**
Millard, amber stain....... **350.00**
Riverside's Ransom, vaseline **225.00**
Tiny Optic, green, dec..... **150.00**

Peachblow, New England, shiny finish, Wild Rose, pink-white handle, orig white stopper.................. **1,500.00**

Rainbow, 7" h, pastel blue, pink, and yellow swirls from base to trefoil spout, molded-in bulging ribs, polished pontil mark, ribbed applied handle, cut glass stopper.................... **975.00**

Sapphire blue
    7-1/4" h, Hobnail, faceted stopper, applied blue handle, damage to three hobs............. **385.00**
    7-1/2" h, 3-1/4" d, enameled pink, yellow, and blue flowers, green leaves, applied clear handle and foot, cut clear stopper....... **165.00**

Satin, 7-1/2" h, blue Raindrop MOP, clear frosted reeded handle, clear cut faceted stopper, flake........ **385.00**

CUP PLATES

History: Many early cups were handleless and came with deep saucers. The hot liquid was poured into the saucer and sipped from it. This necessitated another plate for the cup, hence the "cup plate."

The first cup plates made of pottery were of the Staffordshire variety. From the mid-1830s to 1840s, glass cup plates were favored. The Boston and Sandwich Glass Company was one of the main manufacturers of the lacy-glass type.

Notes: It is extremely difficult to find glass cup

For more information, see this book.

plates in outstanding (mint) condition. Collectors expect some signs of use, such as slight rim roughness, minor chipping (best if under the rim), and, in rarer patterns, portions of scallops missing.

The numbers used are from the Lee-Rose book in which all plates are illustrated.

Prices are based on plates in average condition.

Advertising, colorless, lacy, retail importer "E. A. & S. R. Filley Importers of China, Glass & Queensware, Saint Louis," Rose/Lee No. 315, tiny pinpoint flakes at scalloped edges, **$330.**

Glass

LR 26, 3-9/16" d, colorless, attributed to Sandwich or New England Glass Co. **175.00**

LR 37, 3-1/4" d, opalescent, attributed to Sandwich or New England Glass Co. **200.00**

LR 61, 3-3/8" d, opalescent, attributed to Sandwich or New England Glass Co. **250.00**

LR 75-A, 3-13/16" d, colorless, attributed to New England Glass Co. **120.00**

LR 81, 3-3/4" d, fiery-red opalescent, New England origin.......... **350.00**

Henry Clay, colorless, lacy, left: Rose/Lee No. 566, very minor rim chips; right: Rose/Lee No. 565, many rim chips, price for pair, **$190.** *All cup plate photos courtesy of Cowan's Historic Americana Auctions.*

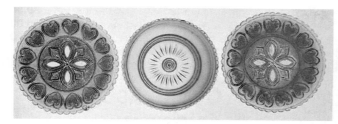

Opalescent, lacy, two Rose/Lee No. 455 with 13 heart border and 48 even scallops, and Rose/Lee No. 503, sunburst, all with very minor pin-point rim chips, price for all three, **$75.**

American, colorless, lacy, Rose/Lee No. 694 with beehive; Rose/Lee No. 695 with beehive; unlisted figurals with Irish harp, butterfly, and nautical anchor, all with small rim chips or pinpoint flakes, price for lot of five, **$125.**

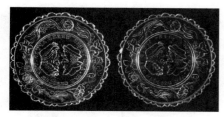

American, colorless, lacy, comic Irish "Before & After Marriage" reversible scene, Rose/Lee No. 697, and 20th C reproduction of Rose/Lee No. 698, both with small rim chips, price for pair, **$70.**

LR 100, 3-1/4" d, colorless, attributed to Philadelphia area, normal mold roughness **115.00**
LR 121, colorless, lacy, Midwestern
. . . . **150.00**

LR 242-A, 3-1/2" d, black amethyst, lacy, Eastern origin, mold underfill and overfill **600.00**
LR 319, 3-5/16" d, colorless . . . **120.00**
LR 459-E, 3-7/16" d, colorless, hearts, 43 even scallops, attributed to Sandwich **75.00**
LR 476, 3-5/16" d, colorless, hearts, 12 plain sides, attributed to Sandwich
. . . . **75.00**

Glass, historical
LR 568, 3-7/16" d, colorless, attributed to Sandwich **175.00**
LR 586-B, colorless, Ringgold, Palo Alto, stippled ground, small letters, attributed to Philadelphia area, 1847-48
. . . . **665.00**
LR695, 3" d, colorless, Midwestern origin, normal mold roughness . **135.00**

Pottery or porcelain
Gaudy Dutch, Butterfly pattern . **750.00**
Leeds, 3-3/4" d, soft paste, gaudy blue and white floral dec, very minor pinpoint edge flakes **250.00**
Majolica, leaf motif **250.00**
Mulberry, cabbage roses, wheat border
. . . . **175.00**
Staffordshire, Historical
  3-1/4" d, Woodlands Estate near Philadelphia, dark blue **475.00**
  3-1/2" d, Franklin Tomb, dark blue, Wood **650.00**
  4" d, The Tyrants Foe, light blue, unknown maker **295.00**

William Henry Harrison, colorless, lacy, two Rose/Lee No. 568 and two Rose/Lee No. 569, all with very tiny pinpoint rim flakes, price for lot of four, **$175.**

American, cobalt blue, lacy, shield breasted American eagle, star and rayed surround, scalloped edge, Rose/Lee No. 670-A, large rim chip, few nicks, **$150.**

Nautical, sapphire blue, American frigate under sail, star and floral scroll surround, Rose/Lee No. 610, numerous rim chips, 3-1/2" d, **$60.**

William Henry Harrison Log Cabin, colorless, lacy, from presidential campaign, one Rose/Lee No. 594, and two Rose/Lee No. 593, all with tiny pinpoint flakes, price for lot of three, **$90.**

CUSTARD GLASS

History: Custard glass was developed in England in the early 1880s. Harry Northwood made the first American custard glass at his Indiana, Pennsylvania, factory in 1898.

From 1898 until 1915, many manufacturers produced custard-glass patterns, e.g., Dugan Glass, Fenton, A. H. Heisey Glass Co., Jefferson Glass, Northwood, Tarentum Glass, and U.S. Glass. Cambridge and McKee continued the production of custard glass into the Depression.

For more information, see this book.

The ivory or creamy yellow-custard color is achieved by adding uranium salts to the molten hot glass. The chemical content makes the glass glow when held under a black light. The more uranium, the more luminous the color. Northwood's custard glass has the smallest amount of uranium, creating an ivory color; Heisey used more, creating a deep yellow color.

Custard glass was made in patterned tableware pieces. It also was made as souvenir items and novelty pieces. Souvenir pieces include a place name or hand-painted decorations, e.g., flowers. Patterns of custard glass often were highlighted in gold, enameled colors, and stains.

Reproduction Alert: L. G. Wright Glass Co. has reproduced pieces in the Argonaut Shell and Grape and Cable patterns. It also introduced new patterns, such as Floral and Grape and Vintage Band. Mosser reproduced toothpicks in Argonaut Shell, Chrysanthemum Sprig, and Inverted Fan & Feather.

Banana stand, Grape and Cable, Northwood, nutmeg stain **315.00**
Berry bowl, individual size, Fan . **45.00**
Berry bowl, master, Diamond with Peg
. . . . **225.00**
Bonbon, Fruits and Flowers, Northwood, nutmeg stain **225.00**
Bowl, Grape and Cable, Northwood, 7-1/2" d, basketweave ext., nutmeg stain **70.00**
Butter dish, cov
    Everglades **375.00**
    Grape and Cable, Northwood, nutmeg stain **450.00**
    Tiny Thumbprint, Tarentum, dec
. . . . **300.00**
    Victoria **300.00**
Compote, Geneva **65.00**
Creamer, Heart with Thumbprint. **85.00**
Cruet, Chrysanthemum Sprig, 7" h, gold dec **485.00**
Goblet, Grape and Gothic Arches, nutmeg stain **80.00**
Hair receiver, Winged Scroll. . . **125.00**
Nappy, Northwood Grape **60.00**

Spooner, Wild Bouquet pattern, Northwood, 4-1/4" h, $90.

Pitcher, Argonaut Shell **325.00**
Plate, Grape and Cable, Northwood
. . . . **45.00**
Punch cup
    Diamond with Peg **40.00**
    Louis XV **35.00**
Salt and pepper shakers, pr,
Chrysanthemum Sprig **165.00**
Sauce, Intaglio **35.00**
Spooner, Grape and Gothic Arches
. . . . **95.00**
Sugar, cov
    Diamond with Peg **175.00**
    Georgia Gem, pink floral dec **185.00**
    Tiny Thumbprint, rose dec. . . **185.00**
Tankard pitcher, Diamond with Peg
. . . . **275.00**
Toothpick holder, Louis XV. . . . **200.00**
Tumbler
    Cherry Scale **50.00**

Toothpick holder, Chrysanthemum Sprig, Northwood, brilliant gold leaves and blossoms, blue ground, gold rim, tiny flake on base, 2-3/4" h, $545. Photo courtesy of Clarence and Betty Maier.

Inverted Fan and Feather. . . . **80.00**
Vermont **90.00**
Wild Bouquet **45.00**
Water set, Ring Band, Heisey, blue floral dec, pitcher, six tumblers . **695.00**

CUT GLASS, AMERICAN

1895–1920

1903–1920

Post–1920

History: Glass is cut by grinding decorations into the glass by means of abrasive-carrying metal or stone wheels. A very ancient craft, it was revived in 1600 by Bohemians and spread through Europe to Great Britain and America.

American cut glass came of age at the Centennial Exposition in 1876 and the World Columbian Exposition in 1893. The American public recognized American cut glass to be exceptional in quality and workmanship. America's most significant output of this high-quality glass occurred from 1880 to 1917, a period now known as the Brilliant Period.

Marks: Around 1890, some companies began adding an acid-etched "signature" to their glass. This signature may be the actual company name, its logo, or a chosen symbol. Today, signed pieces command a premium over unsigned pieces since the signature clearly establishes the origin. However, signatures should be carefully verified for authenticity since objects with forged signatures have been in existence for some time. One way to check is to run a fingertip or fingernail lightly over the signature area. As a general rule, a genuine signature cannot be felt; a forged signature has a raised surface.

Many companies never used the acid-etched signature on their glass and may or may not have affixed paper labels to the items originally. Dorflinger Glass and the Meriden Glass Co. made cut glass of the highest quality, yet never used an acid-etched signature. Furthermore, cut glass made before the 1890s was not signed. Many of these wood-polished items, cut on blown blanks, were of excellent quality and often won awards at exhibitions.

For more information, see this book.

Bowl, geometric design, ABP, unsigned, 9" d, $85. Photo courtesy of Sanford Alderfer Auction Company.

Banana bowl, 11" d, 6-1/2" d, Harvard pattern, hobstar bottom **220.00**

Basket

7-1/2" h, 8-1/2" d, four large hobstars, two fans applied crystal rope-twisted handle. **350.00**

9-1/2" h, 11-1/2" d, five large hobstars, fancy emb floral silver handle and rim **225.00**

Bonbon, 8" d, 2" h, Broadway pattern, Huntly, minor flakes **135.00**

Bowl

8" d, 1-1/2" h, rayed base, diamond point border, sgd "Libbey" in circle **150.00**

8" d, 2" h, brilliant cut, cross bars and flowers, scalloped rim, sgd "Libbey" in circle, some grinding to edge **175.00**

8" d, 4" h, three brilliant cut thistles surround bowl, flower in center, scalloped edge, etched "Libbey" label, price for pr **400.00**

9" d, 4" h, Hartford, stars with button border, scalloped edge, minor edge flakes **125.00**

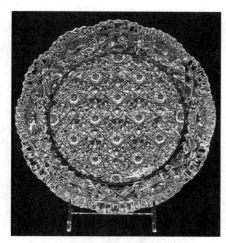

Bowl, Hunt's Royal pattern, 9" d, $295.

10" d, deep-cut buttons, stars, and fans. **220.00**

12" d, 4-1/2" h, rolled-down edge, cut and engraved flowers, leaves, and center thistle, notched-serrated edge. **275.00**

Box, cov, 5" d, 2-3/4" h, cut-paneled base, cover cut with large eight-pointed star with hobstar center surrounded by fans, C. F. Monroe **275.00**

Bread tray, 8" x 12", Anita, Libbey in circle mark. **535.00**

Butter dish, cov, Hobstar. **250.00**

Candlesticks, pr

9-1/2" h, hobstars, teardrop stem, hobstar base **250.00**

10" h, faceted cut knobs, large teardrop stems, ray base. . **425.00**

12" h, Adelaide pattern, amber, Pairpoint. **250.00**

Centerpiece, 10-3/4" d, wheel cut and etched, molded, fruiting foliage, chips **490.00**

Champagne, Kalana Lily, pattern, Dorflinger. **75.00**

Champagne bucket, 7" h, 7" d, sgd "Hoare" **400.00**

Champagne pitcher, 11" h, Prism pattern, triple notch handle, monogram sterling silver top **425.00**

Cheese dish, cov, 6" h dome, 9" d, plate, cobalt blue cut to clear, bull's eye and panel, large miter splints on bottom of plate. **250.00**

Cider pitcher, 7" h, hobstars, zippers, fine diamonds, honeycomb-cut handle, 7" h. **225.00**

Cologne bottle

6" h, Hob and Lace pattern, green cased to clear, pattern-cut stopper, Dorflinger **625.00**

7-1/2" h, Holland pattern, faceted-cut stopper. **275.00**

Compote

6-3/4" d, 5-1/2" h, deep bowl with trefoil, curved edge, three hobstars, and panels with diamond point, fan, and zipper patterns, short pedestal, round base, etched maple leaf mark of T. B. Clark & Co., Honesdale, PA, minor grinding to sawtooth edge **395.00**

7" d, 4-1/4" h, strawberry and chain pattern, serrated edge, low pedestal base, minor roughness and grinding. **95.00**

8-1/4" d, 8-3/4" h, Russian cut, scalloped rim and foot, zipper cut faceted stem teardrop center, minor pinpoints and grinding **500.00**

Bowl, octagonal, crimped edges, hobstar and cane, signed "Niagara," 8-1/4" d, $275.

9-1/8" d, 6-1/4" h, hobstars on scalloped edge bowl, straight paneled stem with zipper cut edges, minor flakes. **400.00**

Creamer and sugar, pr

3-1/4" h, 3-3/4" d, hobstar designs, handles with oval cutting, minor roughness on spout **250.00**

4-1/2" h, pedestal, geometric cuttings, zippered handles, teardrop full length of handle, sgd "Hawkes". **750.00**

5-1/2" h, pedestal, Carolyn variation, notched handles **895.00**

Cruet, 6-7/8" h, round, stars on body, paneled neck with zipper cut edges, scallop cut handle, rayed base, faceted stopper, handle sgd "Tuthill" . . . **250.00**

Decanter, orig stopper

7-7/8" h, pineapple and zipper cut designs, paneled neck with zipper cut designs, diamond pattern on base, faint label of "J. Hoare & Co. Corning 1853". **350.00**

American Brilliant Period examples, left: dish, 10" d, $90; front: oblong dish, 12-1/4" l, $50; right: water pitcher, 10-1/2" h, $115. Photo courtesy of Joy Luke Auctions.

Lamp, mushroom shade, hobstars, prism, strawberry diamond, feathered fan, $3,000. Photo courtesy of Woody Auction.

11-1/2" h, stars, arches, fans, cut neck, star cut mushroom stopper **125.00**

14" d, eight panels, hollow pointed stopper, sgd "Hawkes". . . . **220.00**

Dish

5" d, hobstar, pineapple, palm leaf **45.00**

8" d, scalloped edge, allover hobstar medallions and hobs **175.00**

Dresser box, cov, 7" h, 7" w, Harvard pattern variation, three-ftd, silver-plated fittings, orig beveled mirror on swivel hinge under lid, cut by Bergen Glass Co., couple of minute flakes . . . **750.00**

Fern dish, 3-3/4" h, 8" w, round, silver-plate rim, C. F. Monroe, minor roughness to cut pattern, normal wear on base, no liner **200.00**

Flower center

5" h, 6" d, hobstars, flashed fans, hobstar chain and base . . . **325.00**

7-3/4" h, 12" d, etched and wheel cut motif, honeycomb flared neck, some wear **500.00**

Goblet

7" h, Buzzstar, pineapple, marked "B & B" **40.00**

8-1/2" h, intaglio vintage cut, 8-1/2" h, sgd "Sinclaire" **80.00**

Humidor, cov

7-1/2" d, Middlesex, hollow stopper, sponge holder in lid, Dorflinger **490.00**

9" h, hobstars, beaded split vesicas, hobstar base, matching cut glass lid with hollow for sponge . . **575.00**

Ice bucket

6-5/8" h, colorless, body cut with vertical flutes, beaded silver-mounted rim with sterling silver swing handle marked for Wilcox Silver Plate Co., early 20th C **320.00**

7" h, hobstars and notched prisms, 8" d underplate, double handles **940.00**

Ice cream set, Russian pattern, eight 7" d dishes, 8-1/2" d serving bowl, 11" d cake plate, some chips to edges , price for 10-pc set **500.00**

Jar, cov, 10" h, diamond cut finial on stepped lid, ftd ovoid vessel, four Oriental influenced cut medallions, cane and star-cut ground, 20th C, several nicks **260.00**

Knife rest, 4" l **90.00**

Punch bowl, footed, lidded, colorless, leaded, cross-hatched copper wheel cutting, fall faceted knob finial, round foot with bulbous hollow stem, notch cut for ladle in lid, possibly British, early 19th C, ground base and lid, tiny flakes on foot, $150. Photo courtesy of Cowan's Historic Americana Auctions.

Lamp

24" h, cut glass shade with butterfly and foliage design, inverted compote form base, cut star and geometric design base, ring of cut glass prisms **550.00**

24" h, cut glass rounded shade with pointed top, inverted trumpet form base, both with etched rose dec, wide borders of geometric design, ring of cut glass prisms . . . **525.00**

Loving cup, three handles, sterling top **350.00**

Nappy, two handles

6" d, hobstar center, intaglio floral, strawberry diamond button border **45.00**

9" d, deep-cut arches, pointed sunbursts and medallions . **135.00**

Orange bowl, 9-3/4" x 6-3/4" x 3-3/4" h, hobstars and strawberry diamond **200.00**

Perfume bottle

3-1/2" l, cranberry overlay, shaped sides, notched cuts, S. Mordan & Co., silver-mounted cap . . . **325.00**

6-1/2" h, bulbous, allover cutting, orig stopper **220.00**

Perfume flask, 4-3/4" l, pistol-form, etched silver-gilt mounts, short chain, spring-action trigger opens lid set with maker's medallion, French, late 19th/early 20th C **1,380.00**

Pickle tray, 7" x 3", checkerboard, hobstar **45.00**

Pitcher

8-7/8" h, baluster form body, upper section vertically ribbed and cut, lower section with stylized flowerheads, facet cut handle, silver-plated rim mount with beaded edging, monogrammed, marked "Wilcox Silver Plate Co." **750.00**

12-1/2" h, tapered body with quatrefoil flowers, tiny diamond point surface, surrounded by fans and hobstars, paneled neck with zipper cuts, spout with diamonds, cut ridges on applied handle, spout has been reworked on underside **475.00**

14-1/8" h, baluster, vertical flutes with bead and lozenge cuts, crosshatched and diamond-cut diamonds at base, mounted with sterling bead-edged spout, monogrammed **250.00**

Plate

10" d, Carolyn pattern, J. Hoare
.....................**525.00**

12" d, alternating hobstar and pinwheel **100.00**

Potpourri jar, 6" h, baluster shaped cut glass base, silver lid with portrait medallion and floral banding ...**200.00**

Punch bowl

11" h, 10" w, two pcs, Elgin pattern, Quaker City **600.00**

14" d, 7" h, five large hobstars, central large hobstar......**550.00**

14-3/8" d, 13-1/4" h, round, set into base, cut rim, miter star cut pattern, acid-etched maker's mark for T. G. Hawkes & Co., Corning, NY, on base..........**1,880.00**

Punch ladle, 11-1/2" l, silver plated emb shell bowl, cut and notched prism handle.....................**165.00**

Relish

8" l, two handles, divided, Jupiter pattern, Meriden **120.00**

13" l, leaf shape, Clear Button Russian pattern..........**375.00**

Salad bowl, Russian pattern **90.00**

Salt, open, Russian pattern, master size........................**45.00**

Salt shaker, prism columns **30.00**

Serving dish, 11" d, two layers, apple and pear branches, grape vine dec, Gravic......................**395.00**

Tankard pitcher

10-1/4" h, Harvard cut sides, pinwheel top, mini hobnails, thumbprint notched handle.**200.00**

11" h, hobstar, strawberry diamond, notched prism and fan, flared base with bull's eye, double thumbprint handle.................**275.00**

Punch bowl, pedestal base, ABP, signed "Hawkes," 16" d, 16" h, $3,360. Photo courtesy of Fontaine's Auction Gallery.

Tray

12" d, round, Monarch, sgd "Hoare"
.....................**975.00**

14" x 7-1/2", Sillsbee pattern, Pairpoint..............**335.00**

16" d, 1-1/4" h, round, expanding diamond point border, star centered daisies and leaves, sawtooth edge **315.00**

Tumbler

Clear Button Russian pattern . **95.00**

Harvard, rayed base........**45.00**

Hobstars.................**40.00**

Urn, cov, Russian pattern **175.00**

Vase

8" h, 11" d, squatty body, short flaring neck, scalloped rim.**550.00**

11" h, fan, amber, engraved grape leaves and vines, round disk base, acid-etched Hawkes mark, small chip on base **300.00**

12" h, three cartouches of roses, star and hobstar cut ground ...**225.00**

12-1/2" h, 6-1/2" d, floral and diamond point engraving, sgd "Hawkes" **250.00**

14" h, ruffled edge, cut iris dec, Gravic.................**295.00**

16" h, corset shape, well-cut hobstar, strawberry diamond, prism, flashed star and fan **300.00**

19-1/2" h, lobed rim, alternating vertical cut patterns, star-cut disk base, 20th C...........**750.00**

23-1/4" h, two pcs, trumpet shape, hobstars and paneled ring design, base and top joined with metal post covered with diamond faceted ball **1,350.00**

Water carafe

Harvard pattern **185.00**

Hobstars and notched prisms
.....................**125.00**

Pinwheel and Fan cutting, notched neck, 8" h, 4" w..........**125.00**

Water pitcher

9-1/2" h, Harvard patternpanels and intaglio cut sprays of flowers and foliage.................**300.00**

10" h, Keystone Rose pattern **190.00**

Whiskey jug, 6-1/4" h, bulbous, thistle and grape cutting, orig stopper, sgd "Sinclaire" **295.00**

Wine, 4" h, flint, cut panels, strawberry diamonds, and fans, Pittsburgh . **60.00**

Wine cooler, Russian pattern ..**145.00**

DAVENPORT

History: John Davenport opened a pottery in Longport,   Staffordshire, England, in 1793. His high-quality lightweight wares are cream colored with a beautiful velvety texture.

The firm's output included soft-paste (Old Blue) products, luster-trimmed pieces, and pink luster wares with black transfer. Pieces of Gaudy Dutch and Spatterware also have been found with the Davenport mark. Davenport later became a leading maker of ironstone and early flow blue. His famous Cyprus pattern in mulberry became very popular. His heirs continued the business until the factory closed in 1886.

Charger, 17-1/2" l, oval, Venetian harbor scene, light-blue transfer.......**80.00**

Compote, 2-1/2" h, 8-1/2" d, turquoise and gold band, tiny raised flowers, hp scene with man fishing, cows at edge of lake, c1860, pr **225.00**

Cup plate, Teaberry pattern, pink luster
.........................**40.00**

Dish, ftd, tricorn, Belvoir Castle dec
.........................**90.00**

Ewer, 9" h, floral dec, multicolored, c1930......................**190.00**

Jug, 5-1/2" h, Jardiniere pattern, blue, orange, green, peach, and gold, peach luster rim, c1805-20 ....**450.00**

Plate

7" d, Chinese River Scene, reticulated, medium to dark blue
....................**310.00**

8" d, Imari, orange, blue, purple, and gold, wear..............**165.00**

9-1/2" d, Flying Bird, blue, orange, pink, yellow, and green....**250.00**

Platter

18-1/4", stone china, polychrome dec blue transfer print bird and floral pattern, printed mark, c1810, glaze wear..............**230.00**

Cup and saucer, Amoy pattern, flow blue on white, incised anchor mark, 3-3/4" cup, 6" saucer, $150.

Plate, cobalt blue and orange decorated, gold trim, 10" d, $35.

19-1/8" l, purple transfer, idyllic scene, boat and church, marked "Davenport" **440.00**

Sauce tureen, cov, ladle, creamware, molded leaves, lime green veining, early **450.00**

Serving bowl, cov, 7" w, 9-3/4" l, Chinoiserie Bridgeless pattern, internal bowl with steam holes, c1810 . . **700.00**

Soup tureen, matching stand, 13-1/4" l, stone china, polychrome dec blue transfer printed bird and floral patter, gilded lion mask handles, printed marks, c1810, large hairline on stand, glaze wear **1,610.00**

Tea service, Imari pattern, 18" l tray, teapot, creamer, cov sugar, four cups and saucers. **850.00**

DECOYS

History: During the past several years, carved wooden decoys, used to lure ducks and geese to the hunter, have become widely recognized as an indigenous American folk-art form. Many decoys are from 1880 to 1930, when commercial gunners commonly hunted and used rigs of several hundred decoys. Many fine carvers also worked through the 1930s and 1940s. Individuals and commercial decoy makers also carved fish decoys.

Because decoys were both hand made and machine made, and many examples exist, firm pricing is difficult to establish. The skill of the carver, rarity, type of bird, and age all affect the value.

Reproduction Alert

Notes: A decoy's value is based on several factors: (1) fame of the carver, (2) quality of the carving, (3) species of wild fowl—the most desirable are herons, swans, mergansers, and shorebirds—and (4) condition of the original paint.

The inexperienced collector should be aware of several facts. The age of a decoy, per se, is usually of no importance in determining value. However, age does have some influence when it comes to a rare or important example. Since very few decoys were ever signed, it is quite difficult to attribute most decoys to known carvers. Anyone who has not examined a known carver's work will be hard pressed to determine if the paint on one of his decoys is indeed original. Repainting severely decreases a decoy's value. In addition, there are many fakes and reproductions on the market and even experienced collectors are occasionally fooled. Decoys represent a subject where dealing with a reputable dealer or auction house is important, especially those who offer a guarantee as to authenticity.

Decoys listed below are of average wear, unless otherwise noted.

Atlantic Brant, Mason, Challenge grade, c1910, from the famous Barron rig (Virginia), nearly mint condition, age shrinkage neck crack repair, tight filled factory back crack **4,500.00**

Baldgate Wigeon Drake, miniature, A. Elmer, Crowell, East Harwich, MA, identified in ink, rect stamp on base, 2-1/2" x 4" **635.00**

Black Bellied Bustard, miniature, H. Gills, initialed "H. G. 1957," identified in pencil, natural wood base, 3-1/2" x 4" **230.00**

Black Bellied Plover, unknown American 20th C maker, orig paint, glass eyes, mounted on stick on lead base

12-1/2" h, minor paint loss, small chips to beak **2,530.00**

13-1/2" h, minor paint loss, beak repair **1,725.00**

Black Breasted Plover, Harry C. Shourds, orig paint **2,650.00**

Black Duck

A. Elmer Crowell, East Harwich, MA, orig paint, glass eyes, stamped mark in oval on base, sleeping, wear, crack, 5-1/4" h **525.00**

Ira Hudson, preening, raised wings, outstretched neck, scratch feather paint **8,500.00**

Mason, Challenge, c1910, hollow, fine orig paint, some neck filler replaced **3,500.00**

Mason, Premier, c1905, Atlantic Coast, oversized, solid-bodied special order, most desirable snaky head, excellent orig condition, some professional restoration, filled in-the-making back crack, tail chip on one side of crack, neck filler replacement **4,500.00**

Mason, Standard, c1910, painted eye, dry original paint, all of its original neck filler, invisible professional dry rot repair in the base **750.00**

Unknown maker, carved balsa body, wood head, glass eyes, orig pant, 15-1/2" l **150.00**

Wildfowler, CT, inlet head, glass eyes, worn orig paint, green overpaint on bottom on sides, 13" l, c1900 . . . . **220.00**

Black Drake, miniature

A. Elmer Crowell, East Harwich, MA, identified in ink, rect stamp on base, break at neck, reglued, minor paint loss, 3-1/2" x 4-3/4" . . **635.00**

James Lapham, Dennisport, MA, identified in black ink, oval stamp, minor imperfections, 2-1/2" x 4" **290.00**

Bluebill Drake, Jim Kelson, Mt. Clemens, MI, carved wing detail, feather stamping, glass eyes, orig paint, orig keep and weight, 13-1/2" l, c1930 . . . . **295.00**

Bluebill Hen, Mason Challenge, c1910, hollow, orig paint **3,450.00**

Blue-Winged Teal Drake and Hen Pair, Davey W. Nichol, Smiths Falls, Ontario, Canada, 1960, matched pair, raised wings, scratch feather patterns, sgd on bottom **1,650.00**

Brant, Ward Brothers, MD, carved, hollow body, head turned left, sgd "Lem and Steve," dated 1917 . . . . . **1,650.00**

Broadbill Drake and Hen Pair, Mason, c1910, painted eyes, rare gunning rigmates, untouched original condition, neck filler missing, some shot evidence, hen has small, superficial chip on one side **1,450.00**

Bufflehead Drake

Bob Kerr, carved detail, glass eyes, orig paint, scratch carved signature, 10-1/2" l, c1980 . **250.00**

James Lagham, Dennisport, MA, identified in ink, oval stamp on base, 3" x 4-1/2" **345.00**

Harry M. Shrouds, carved, hollow body, painted eyes **1,800.00**

Bluebill Drake, Rozell Bliss, Stratford, CT, c1910, $290.

Canada Goose

Hurley Conklin, carved, hollow body, swimming position, branded "H. Conklin" on bottom **600.00**

H. Gibbs, identified and initialed "HG 1957" on natural wood base, 2-1/2" x 4-1/2" **290.00**

Unsigned, attributed to Harry Ackerman, MI, old black, gray, and white repaint, glass eyes, incised detail, wear to paint, chips on bill, 11-1/2" h, 23" l **450.00**

Canvasback Pair

Canvasback Pair, Mason, Premier, Seneca Lake, c1910, matched pair, very fine orig paint with strong patterns, drake is excellent with hairline crack in base; hen has filled factory crack on left side of its back, hairline crack part way through neck. **2,950.00**

Curlew

Dan Leeds, Pleasantville, NJ, 1880-1900, carved and painted brown, stand, 13" l **2,415.00**

Harry V. Shrouds, orig paint **2,000.00**

Curlew Oyster Eater

Curlew Oyster Eater, Samuel Jester, Tennessee, c1920, carved and painted, slight paint wear, age crack in body, stand, 16" l, 9" h **1,035.00**

Top: Golden Eye or Whistler, Joe Wooster, signed "Good Hunting, Josef Wooster, '70," original paint, glass eyes, very good detail, 14-1/2" l, $360; middle: Merganser Hen, Joe Wooster, signed "Good Hunting Joseph 'Buckeye Joe' Wooster," original paint, glass eyes, very good detail, minor paint separation, 21-1/2" l, $200; bottom: Merganser Drake, Joe Wooster, mate to one above, signed the same, minor wear edge, $385. Photo courtesy of Garth's Auctions.

Eider Duck

Eider Duck, polychrome-carved wood America, early 19th C, cracks, 15" l **400.00**

Attributed to Maine maritime region, early 20th C, on stand, 19" l **550.00**

Flying Duck

Flying Duck, glass-bead eyes, old natural surface, carved pine, attributed to Maine, c1930, 16" l, 11" h .. **2,300.00**

Goldeneye Duck

Goldeneye Duck, New England, c1900, minor paint wear, 12" l . **2,300.00**

Great Northern Pike

Great Northern Pike, attributed to Menominee Indian, WI, c1900, painted green, glass eyes, ribbed sheet metal fin, tall stand, 36" l, 9" h **3,450.00**

Green Wing Teal Duck

Green Wing Teal Duck, miniature, A. Elmer Crowell, East Harwich, MA, identified in ink, rect stamp on base, 2-1/2" x 4". **865.00**

Heron

Heron, unknown maker, carved wig and tail, wrought iron legs **900.00**

Herring Gull

Herring Gull, attributed to Gus Wilson, c1910-20, used as weathervane, traces of old paint, metal feet, weathered and worn, 18-3/4" l **3,110.00**

Hooded Merganser Drake

Hooded Merganser Drake, William Clarke, Oakville, Ontario, Canada, c1900, transitional plumage, excellent orig condition, minor in-use wear **2,450.00**

Loon

Loon, carved and painted, wooden rudder, America, 19th C, stand, paint wear, 27" l **9,200.00**

Mallard Drake

Ben Schmidt, Detroit, relief carved, feather stamping, glass eyes, orig paint, orig keep, marked "Mallard drake Benj Schmidt, Detroit 1960," 15-1/4" l **450.00**

Bert Graves, carved, hollow body, orig weighted bottom, branded "E. I. Rogers" and "Cleary" **900.00**

James Lapham, Dennisport, MA, sgd and identified in ink on bottom, 4" x 5" **435.00**

Mason, Challenge, c1910, rare hollow model with elaborate Mason Premier style paint patterns, no tail chip, professional repair to some splintering on end of bill, tight neck crack on left side, some shot evidence on right side ... **3,500.00**

Mallard Drake and Hen Pair

Mallard Drake and Hen Pair, Mason, c1905, glass eyes, gunning rigmates, excellent orig condition, some neck filler replaced, drake has filled factory crack on side. **1,750.00**

Mallard Hen

Robert Elliston, carved, hollow body, orig paint **1,800.00**

Mallard, drake, Mason, Premier, c1900, hollow snaky head, superb original condition with no tail chip, $6,500. Photo courtesy of Russ Goldberger, RJG Antiques.

Mason Premier, c1905, hollow, excellent orig paint, rich red breast, professional tail chip repair and neck putty restoration ... **3,900.00**

Merganser Drake

Merganser Drake, Mason Challenge, Detroit, MI, c1910, strong orig paint with no cracks, some shot holes have been filled on one side, branded "C. Simpson" **7,500.00**

Perch

Perch, Heddon, ice-type **800.00**

Pintail Duck

Drake, Paw Paw Bait Co., c1932-36, stenciled company name on bottom. **800.00**

Drake and hen, John H. Baker, Bristol, PA, 20th C, painted in naturalistic tones, glass eyes, sgd, imp maker's signature, lead ingot affixed to bases stamped "John Baker Bristol, PA," paint flakes on hen **1,100.00**

Plover

Plover, Joe Lincoln, winter plumage, feather painting, orig paint..... **800.00**

Red Breasted Merganser Drake

George Boyd, NH, carved, orig paint **8,000.00**

Amos Wallace, ME, inlet neck, carved crest, detailed feathered paint **2,000.00**

Redhead Drake

Redhead Drake, Dan Bartlett, Prince Edward County, Ontario, Canada, c1920, hollow, fine orig paint ... **950.00**

Robin Snipe

Robin Snipe, Obediah Verity, carved wings and eyes, orig paint... **4,400.00**

Ruddy Duck

Ruddy Duck, miniature, maker unknown, identified in ink on base, paint loss to bill, 2" x 2-3/4" **690.00**

Wood Duck, drake, D. W. Nichol, Smiths Falls, Ontario, 1950's, slightly turned head, excellent original condition, $2,450. Photo courtesy of Russ Goldberger, RJG Antiques.

Shorebirds, black, gray, and white, unsigned, 20th C, newer driftwood mounts, 6" and 4-1/2" l, price for pair, $110. Photo courtesy of Cowan's Historic Americana Auctions.

Ruddy Duck Drake, Len Carmeghi, Mt. Clemens, MI, hollow body, glass eyes, orig paint, sgd and dated, 10-3/4" l **250.00**

Ruffled Grouse, miniature, A. Elmer Crowell, East Harwich, MA, rect stamp, mounted on natural wood base, 3-1/2" x 4-1/2". **865.00**

Sea Gull, 14" l, weathered surface, used as weathervane, attributed to WI, late 19th/early 20th C **1,840.00**

Shorebird, Willard C. Baldwin (1890-1979), CT, 1964, carved wing, mounted on mahogany base branded "WCB" and "TBL", inscribed "Baldwin 1964," minor wear to tail **620.00**

Swan, unknown Chesapeake Bay, MD, maker, carved wood, braced neck, white paint, 30" l **900.00**

Widgeon, matted pair, Charlie Joiner, MD, sgd on bottom **800.00**

Wood Duck Drake, miniature, A. Elmer Crowell, East Harwich, MA, identified in ink, rect stamp on base, 3" x 4-1/2" **1,150.00**

Yellowlegs, carved and painted, New Jersey, c1890, stand, 11" l....**2,185.00**

DEDHAM POTTERY

History: Alexander W. Robertson established a pottery in Chelsea, Massachusetts, about 1866. After his brother, Hugh Cornwall Robertson, joined him in 1868, the firm was called A. W. & H. C. Robertson. Their father, James Robertson,

joined his sons in 1872, and the name Chelsea Keramic Art Works Robertson and Sons was used.

The pottery's initial products were simple flower and bean pots, but the firm quickly expanded its output to include a wide variety of artistic pottery. It produced a very fine redware body used in classical forms, some with black backgrounds imitating ancient Greek and Apulian works. It experimented with underglaze slip decoration on vases. The Chelsea Keramic Art Works Pottery also produced high-glazed vases, pitchers, and plaques with a buff clay body, with either sculpted or molded applied decoration.

James Robertson died in 1880 and Alexander moved to California in 1884, leaving Hugh C. Robertson alone in Chelsea, where his tireless experiments eventually yielded a stunning imitation of the prized Chinese Ming-era blood-red glaze. Hugh's vases with that glaze were marked with an impressed "CKAW." Creating these red-glazed vases was very expensive, and even though they received great critical acclaim, the company declared bankruptcy in 1889.

Recapitalized by a circle of Boston art patrons in 1891, Hugh started the Chelsea Pottery U.S., which produced gray crackle-glazed dinnerware with cobalt-blue decorations, the rabbit pattern being the most popular.

The business moved to new facilities in Dedham, Massachusetts, and began production in 1896 under the name Dedham Pottery. Hugh's son and grandson operated the business until it closed in 1943, by which time between 50 and 80 patterns had been produced, some very briefly.

Marks: The following marks help determine the approximate age of items:

- "Chelsea Keramic Art Works Robertson and Sons," impressed, 1874-1880
- "CKAW," impressed, 1875-1889
- "CPUS," impressed in a cloverleaf, 1891-1895
- Foreshortened rabbit only, impressed, 1894-1896
- Conventional rabbit with "Dedham Pottery" in square blue stamped mark along with one impressed foreshortened rabbit, 1896-1928
- Blue rabbit stamped mark with "registered" beneath, along with two impressed foreshortened rabbit marks, 1929-1943

Reproduction Alert: Two companies make Dedham-like reproductions primarily utilizing the rabbit pattern, but always mark their work very differently from the original.

Adviser: James D. Kaufman.

Bowl, 8-1/2" sq
Rabbit pattern, reg. stamp .. **600.00**
Swan pattern, reg. stamp ... **725.00**

Bowl, 9-3/8" d, 3-3/4" h, Poppy pattern, cut edge rim, Oriental-type, sloping poppies, registered blue ink stamp, "D" in red, minor glaze miss near base edge **1,035.00**

Breakfast plate, 8-3/4" d

Crab pattern, blue ink stamp, glaze imperfections **375.00**
Rabbit pattern, assembled set, marks include blue registered stamp, imp foreshortened rabbit, and 1931 stamp, set of six, one with rim chip........... **635.00**

Butter plate, 4-3/8" d, Swan pattern, registered blue ink stamp **260.00**

Candlesticks, pr
Elephant pattern, reg. blue stamp **525.00**
Rabbit pattern, reg. blue stamp **325.00**

Creamer and sugar, 3-1/4" and 4", Rabbit pattern, blue stamp and "1931" on creamer, blue registered stamp on sugar..................... **350.00**

Cup and saucer, Rabbit pattern, 3-7/8" d cup, 6" d saucers with rabbit borders, blue registered stamps, set of six **700.00**

Knife rest, Rabbit form, blue reg. stamp **575.00**

Paperweight, Rabbit form, blue reg. stamp **495.00**

Pickle dish, 10-1/2" l, Elephant pattern, blue reg. stamp............. **750.00**

Pitcher
3-1/4" h, Rabbit pattern **175.00**
5-1/8" h, Chickens pattern, blue stamp.................. **2,300.00**
7" h, Turkey pattern, blue stamp **585.00**
9" h, Rabbit pattern, blue stamp **700.00**
Style of 1850, blue reg. stamp **975.00**

Plate, 6" d
Clover pattern, reg. stamp .. **625.00**
Iris pattern, blue stamp, Maude Davenport's "O" rebus **280.00**

Bread and butter plate, Crab pattern, blue ink stamp, one impressed rabbit, 6-1/4" d, $425. Photo courtesy of Skinner Auctioneers and Appraisers.

Plate, Lobster pattern, blue ink stamp, one impressed rabbit, 8-1/2" d, $535. Photo courtesy of Skinner Auctioneers and Appraisers.

Rabbit pattern, registered blue ink stamp, set of four, foot chips on two **290.00**

Plate, 6-1/8" d

Horse Chestnut pattern, one impressed rabbit mark **150.00**
Magnolia pattern, blue ink stamp mark **115.00**

Plate, 7-1/2" d, Lobster pattern, registered blue ink stamp, two imp rabbits **290.00**

Plate, 8" d, Iris pattern, reg. stamp **230.00**

Plate, 8-1/2" d

Crab pattern, blue stamp . . .**550.00**
Elephant pattern, blue reg. stamp **650.00**
Rabbit pattern, blue stamp . .**175.00**
Rabbit pattern, blue stamp, Maude Davenport's "O" rebus. **235.00**

Vase, experimental, by Hugh Robertson, bulbous, rich lustered oxblood glaze, incised "Dedham Pottery/HCR," 2-1/2" hairline from rim, 5-3/4" d, 7" h, $1,355. Photo courtesy of David Rago Auctions.

Snow Tree pattern, blue stamp **210.00**
Upside down dolphin, CPUS **900.00**

Plate, 10" d

Dolphin pattern, blue reg. stamp **875.00**
Elephant pattern, blue reg. stamp **900.00**
Pine Apple pattern, CPUS . .**775.00**
Turkey pattern, blue stamp, Maude Davenport's "O" rebus **475.00**

Plate, 10-1/4" d, Rabbit pattern, registered blue ink stamp, one imp rabbit **150.00**

Platter, 9-7/8" l, 6-3/8" w, Rabbit pattern, rect, blue ink stamp, two imp rabbits **260.00**

Salt and pepper shakers, pr, Rabbit pattern, 3-1/2" h, glaze miss . . .**200.00**

Sherbet, two handles, Rabbit pattern, blue stamp. **350.00**

Tea cup and saucer

Azalea pattern, reg. stamp. .**130.00**
Butterfly pattern, blue stamp.**345.00**
Duck pattern, reg. stamp . . .**190.00**
Turtle pattern, reg. stamp . . .**680.00**
Water Lily pattern, reg. stamp**130.00**

Teapot, 6-1/8" h, Rabbit pattern, blue stamp. **875.00**

Vase, 5-3/4" d, 7" h, experimental, by Hugh Robertson, bulbous, rich lustered oxblood glaze, incised "DEDHAM POTTERY/HCR," 2-1/2" h hairline from rim **1,355.00**

DELFTWARE

History: Delftware is pottery with a soft, red-clay body and tin-enamel glaze. The white, dense, opaque color came from adding tin ash to lead glaze. The first examples had blue designs on a white ground. Polychrome examples followed.

The name originally applied to pottery made in the region around Delft, Holland, beginning in the 16th century and ending in the late 18th century. The tin used came from the Cornish mines in England. By the 17th and 18th centuries, English potters in London, Bristol, and Liverpool were copying the glaze and designs. Some designs unique to English potters also developed.

In Germany and France, the ware is known as Faience, and in Italy as Majolica.

> **Reproduction Alert:** Since the late 19th century, much Delft-type souvenir material has been produced to appeal to the foreign traveler. Don't confuse these modern pieces with the older examples.

Charger, red body, white ground, blue geometric allover decorated on both front and back, unclear signature, attributed to Italy, 17th C, glaze edge chips, one larger edge chip, $240. Photo courtesy of Cowan's Historic Americana Auctions.

Bowl

12" d, shallow, blue and white, landscape with figure, edge chips **550.00**
13" d, shallow, polychrome dec, minor edge wear, English . .**715.00**

Bowl, attached strainer, 8-3/4" d, 3-1/2" h, blue and white floral dec, hairlines and deteriorating old repair **470.00**

Charger

13" d, floral design, building scene, manganese and blue, edge chips **615.00**
13-1/8" d, blue and white, foliate devices, Dutch, 19th C, chips, glaze wear. **410.00**
13-5/8" d, blue and white, foliate devices, 19th C, chips, glass wear, restoration **320.00**
16 1/2" d, center branch with fruiting blossoms, two birds, conforming florals on wide rim, sgd "G. A. Kleynoven," c1655 . . . . .**2,250.00**

Dish

8-1/4" d, molded rim, blue and white, stylized landscape and floral design, edge chips. **315.00**
12-3/8" l, fluted oval, blue and white floral design, attributed to Lambeth, chips **440.00**

Flower brick, 4-5/8" l, 2-1/2" h, blue and white, Chinese figures in landscape, Dutch, 18th C, chips, cracks . . .**375.00**

Garniture, three bulbous 17-1/4" h cov urns, two octagonal tapered 12-3/4" h vases, polychrome dec foliage surrounding central blue figural panels, Dutch, late 18th/early 19th C .**8,625.00**

Cracker jar, blue Delft lily decorated, silver plated lid and bail, 7" h, $250. Photo courtesy of Woody Auctions.

Inkwell, 4-1/2" h, heart shape, blue and white floral dec, wear and edge chips **495.00**

Jar, 5" h, blue and white, chips, pr **715.00**

Lamp base, octagonal bottle form with continuous blue and white Oriental figural landscape design, England, 18th C, foot rim chips, drilled . . **690.00**

Model, 17-1/2" h, tall case clock, blue dec white ground, panels of figural and architectural landscapes between scrolled foliate borders, 19th C, slight glaze wear **320.00**

Mug, 6-3/8" h, blue and white, armorial surrounded by exotic landscape, palm trees, marked on base, Dutch, 19th C, minor chips, glaze wear **490.00**

Plaque, 19" x 14", emb scrolled acanthus in cartouche form framing hp scene of Dutch windmill and canal, imp "1" and underglaze "A" on verso, c1900 . . . . **550.00**

Plate

8-3/4" d, manganese, iron red, yellow, and underglaze blue floral design, chips **200.00**

9" d, tin glaze, flowering branch behind fence, blue, yellow, green, and pale purple, English, rim chips **550.00**

10-1/4" d, blue and white Bible illustration, small over reserve with bible reference and date "MAT 2:IV.00, 1752," small edge chips **770.00**

13-3/4" d, Oriental-style hand painted floral dec, shades of red, blue, green, and yellow, black outlining, white ground, England, 19th C, rim chips **775.00**

Posset pot, 4-3/4" h, blue and white, birds among foliage, England, 19th C, minor chips and cracks **920.00**

Sauce boat, 8-1/4" l, applied scrolled handles, fluted flaring lip, blue and white Oriental design, edge chips and hairline, later added yellow enamel rim **440.00**

Saucer, 8-3/4" d, table ring, blue, iron-red, yellow, and manganese bowl of flowers dec **825.00**

Strainer bowl, 9-1/8" d, blue and white floral design, three short feet, chips **520.00**

Tea caddy, 5-7/8" h, blue and white floral dec, scalloped bottom edge, marked "MVS 1750," cork closure, wear, edge flakes, old filled in chip on lid **550.00**

Tile, 5" sq, Fazackerly, polychrome dec of floral bouquets, c1760, price for pr, one with edge nicks, other with edge flaking and chips **350.00**

Tobacco jar, 10" h, blue and white, Indians and "Siville," older brass stepped lid, chips **1,870.00**

Vase, 19" h, tapering octagonal, molded lobes, blue, green, and red polychromed continuous band of birds of paradise within foliage, marked "J.V.D.H.," late 19th C, pr **1,200.00**

Vase, cov, 23" h, Delft blue and white, oval paneled sides with Chinese style dec alternating with female figures in courtyard setting, flowers, and fence

Miniature lamp, blue Dutch scenes, Smith #335, 10-1/2" h, $250.

design, hexagonal form rim, foot, and cov, cat finial, unidentified mark, Holland, 18th C, rim damage, footrim chips, chips to cat's ears, typical edge flaking of tin glaze **815.00**

Wall pocket, 6-1/4" w, 4-1/2" d, 7" h, vasiform, ogee backplate, pierced grillwork, blue and white scenes of figures at harbor, scrollwork borders, applied flower buds on sides, 20th C, price for pr **350.00**

DEPRESSION GLASS

History: Depression glass was made from 1920 to 1940. It was an inexpensive machine-made glass and produced by several companies in various patterns and colors. The number of forms made in different patterns also varied.

Depression glass was sold through variety stores, given away as premiums, or packaged with certain products. Movie houses gave it away from 1935 until well into the 1940s.

Like pattern glass, knowing the proper name of a pattern is the key to collecting. Collectors should be prepared to do research.

Reproduction Alert: The number of Depression glass patterns that have been reproduced continues to grow. Reproductions exist in many patterns, forms, and colors. Beware of colors and forms that were not made in the original production of the pattern. Carefully examine every piece that seems questionable and look for loss of details, poor impressions, and slight differences in sizes.

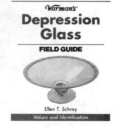

AMERICAN PIONEER

Manufactured by Liberty Works, Egg Harbor, NJ, from 1931 to 1934. Made in amber, crystal, green, and pink.

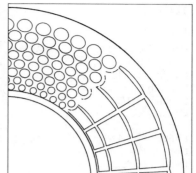

American Pioneer green plate, cup and saucer, **$19.00**

Item	Amber	Crystal	Green	Pink
Bowl				
5" d, handle	45.00	24.00	27.50	24.00
8-3/4" d, cov	—	85.00	125.00	85.00
9" d, handle	—	24.00	30.00	24.00
10" d	—	50.00	70.00	50.00
Candlesticks, pr, 6-1/2" h	—	75.00	95.00	75.00
Candy jar, cov				
1 pound	—	100.00	115.00	110.00
1-1/2 pound	—	70.00	125.00	95.00
Cheese and cracker set	—	50.00	65.00	55.00
Coaster, 3-1/2" d	—	20.00	32.00	30.00
Cocktail	45.00	—	—	—
Console bowl, 10-3/4" d	—	50.00	75.00	60.00
Creamer, 3-1/2" h	60.00	30.00	32.00	30.00
Cup	24.00	10.00	12.00	12.00
Dresser set, two colognes, powder jar, tray	—	300.00	345.00	365.00
Goblet, 8 oz	—	40.00	45.00	40.00
Ice bucket, 6" h	—	50.00	80.00	65.00
Juice tumbler, 5 oz	—	32.00	37.50	35.00
Lamp, 8-1/2" h	—	90.00	115.00	110.00
Mayonnaise, 4-1/4"	—	60.00	90.00	60.00
Pilsner, 5-3/4" h, 11 oz	—	100.00	110.00	100.00
Pitcher, cov 7" h	300.00	175.00	250.00	195.00
Plate				
6" d	—	12.50	17.50	12.50
8" d	28.00	10.00	13.00	14.00
11-1/2" d, handle	40.00	20.00	24.00	20.00
Rose bowl	—	40.00	50.00	45.00
Saucer, 6" sq	11.00	4.00	5.00	5.50
Sherbet, 3-1/2" h	—	18.00	22.00	20.00
Sugar, 2-3/4" h	—	20.00	27.50	25.00
Tumbler, 8 oz, 4" h	—	32.00	55.00	35.00
Vase, 7" h, 4 styles	—	85.00	110.00	90.00
Whiskey, 2 oz, 2-1/4" h	—	48.00	—	48.00

BUBBLE

Bullseye, Provincial

Manufactured originally by Hocking Glass Co., and followed by Anchor Hocking Glass Corp., Lancaster, OH, from 1937 to 1965. Made in crystal (1937), forest green (1937), pink (limited), Royal Ruby (1963), and sapphire blue (1937).

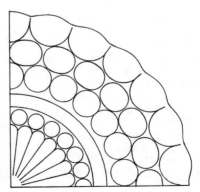

Bubble blue grill plate, **$8.**

BUBBLE (cont.)

Item	Crystal	Forest Green	Royal Ruby	Sapphire Blue
Berry bowl, 4" d	5.00	—	6.50	18.00
Bowl, 9" d, fanged	8.00	—	—	335.00
Candlesticks, pr.	24.00	40.00	—	—
Cereal bowl, 5-1/4" d	8.00	17.00	—	17.50
Cocktail, 4-1/2 oz	4.50	12.50	12.50	—
Creamer	7.50	15.00	18.00	45.00
Cup	4.50	8.75	12.50	15.00
Fruit bowl, 4-1/2" d	5.00	11.00	9.00	12.00
Goblet, 9 oz	7.50	15.00	15.00	—
Iced tea goblet, 14 oz	8.00	17.50	—	—
Iced tea tumbler, 12 oz	12.50	—	19.50	—
Juice goblet, 4 oz	3.00	8.00	—	—
Juice tumbler, 6 oz, ftd	4.00	12.00	10.00	—
Lemonade tumbler	16.00	—	16.00	—
Old fashioned tumbler	6.50	16.00	16.00	—
Pitcher, 64 oz, ice lip	60.00	—	65.00	—
Plate				
6-3/4" d, bread and butter	3.50	4.50	—	3.75
9-3/8" d, dinner	7.50	28.00	27.50	8.00
Platter, 12" l, oval	10.00	—	—	18.00
Sandwich plate, 9-1/2" d	7.50	25.00	22.00	8.00
Saucer	1.50	5.00	5.00	1.50
Sherbet, 6 oz	4.50	9.50	12.00	—
Soup bowl, flat, 7-3/4" d	10.00	—	—	16.00
Sugar	8.00	13.00	—	28.00
Tidbit, two-tier	—	—	35.00	—
Tumbler, 9 oz, water	6.00	—	16.00	—

DOGWOOD

Apple Blossom, Wild Rose

Manufactured by Mac Beth Evans Co., Charleroi, PA, from 1929 to 1932. Made in Cremax, crystal, green, Monax, pink, and yellow (rare). Crystal valued at 50 percent of green.

Dogwood pink sugar, **$24.50**; creamer, **$22.50**; and dinner plate, **$42**.

Item	Cremax or Monax	Green	Pink
Berry bowl, 8-1/2" d	40.00	100.00	65.00
Cake plate, 13" d	185.00	130.00	165.00
Cereal bowl, 5-1/2" d	6.00	32.00	35.00
Coaster, 3-1/4" d	—	—	500.00
Creamer, 2-1/2" h, thin	—	48.00	22.50
Cup			
thin	—	32.00	18.00
thick	36.00	40.00	25.00
Fruit bowl, 10-1/4" d	100.00	250.00	435.00
Pitcher, 8" h			
Am Sweetheart style	—	—	420.00
decorated	—	500.00	265.00
Plate			
6" d, bread & butter	22.00	10.00	9.50
8" d, luncheon	—	9.00	9.00
9-1/4" d, dinner	—	—	42.00
10-1/2" d, grill	—	22.00	25.00

DOGWOOD (cont.)

Item	Cremax or Monax	Green	Pink
Platter, 12" d, oval	—	—	500.00
Salver, 12"d	20.00	—	35.00
Saucer	20.00	10.00	8.50
Sherbet, low, ftd	—	95.00	40.00
Sugar, 3-1/4" h, thick, ftd	—	—	24.50
Tidbit, two-tier	—	—	90.00
Tumbler, 10 oz	—	85.00	53.00
Tumbler, molded band	—	—	25.00

HOBNAIL

Manufactured by Hocking Glass Co., Lancaster, OH, from 1934 to 1936. Made in crystal, crystal with red trim, and pink.

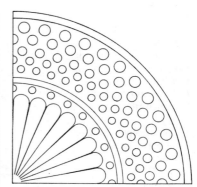

Hobnail pink sherbet, **$5.**

Item	Crystal	Crystal, red trim	Pink
Cereal bowl, 5-1/2" d	4.25	4.25	—
Cordial, 5 oz, ftd	6.00	6.00	—
Creamer, ftd	4.00	4.00	—
Cup	5.00	5.00	6.00
Decanter and stopper	27.50	27.50	—
Goblet, 10 oz	7.50	7.50	—
Iced tea goblet, 13 oz	8.50	8.50	—
Iced tea tumbler, 15 oz	8.50	8.50	—
Juice tumbler, 5 oz	4.00	4.00	—
Milk pitcher, 18 oz	22.00	22.00	—
Pitcher, 67 oz	25.00	25.00	—
Plate			
6" d, sherbet	2.50	2.50	3.50
8-1/2" d, luncheon	5.50	5.50	7.50
Salad bowl, 7" d	5.00	5.00	—
Saucer	2.00	2.00	3.00
Sherbet	4.00	4.00	5.00
Sugar, ftd	4.00	4.00	—
Tumbler, 9 oz	5.00	5.00	—
Whiskey, 1-1/2 oz	5.00	5.00	—
Wine, 3 oz, ftd	6.50	6.50	—

MAYFAIR

Open Rose

Manufactured by Hocking Glass Co., Lancaster, OH, from 1931 to 1937. Made in crystal (limited production), green, ice blue, pink, and yellow.

Reproductions: † This pattern has been plagued with reproductions since 1977. Items reproduced include cookie jars, salt and pepper shakers, juice pitchers and whiskey glasses. Reproductions are found in amethyst, blue, cobalt blue, green, pink, and red.

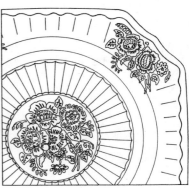

Mayfair Open Rose pink tumbler **$65** *and pink satin-finish covered cookie jar,* **$37.**

MAYFAIR (cont.)

Item	Green	Ice Blue	Pink	Pink Satin	Yellow
Bowl, 11-3/4" l, flat	35.00	75.00	65.00	70.00	195.00
Butter dish, cov	1,295.00	325.00	80.00	95.00	1,295.00
Cake plate					
10" d, ftd	115.00	75.00	40.00	45.00	—
12" d, handles	40.00	70.00	48.00	50.00	—
Candy dish					
cov	575.00	325.00	70.00	85.00	475.00
9" l, divided	155.00	60.00	—		150.00
Celery dish, 10" l, undivided	115.00	80.00	45.00	50.00	115.00
Cereal bowl, 5-1/2" d	24.00	48.00	30.00	35.00	75.00
Claret, 4-1/2 oz	950.00	—	1,150.00	—	—
Cocktail, 3 oz, 4" h	975.00	—	75.00	—	—
Console bowl, 9" d, 3 legs	5,000.00	—	5,000.00	—	—
Cookie jar, cov †	575.00	295.00	47.00	37.00	860.00
Cordial, 1 oz, 3-3/4" h	950.00	—	1,100.00	—	—
Cream soup, 5" d	—	—	65.00	68.00	—
Creamer, ftd			35.00	30.00	
Cup	150.00	55.00	24.00	27.50	150.00
Decanter, stopper, 32 oz	—	—	225.00	—	—
Fruit bowl, 12" d	50.00	100.00	65.00	75.00	215.00
Goblet					
2-1/2 oz, 4-1/8"	950.00	—	950.00	—	—
9 oz, 7-1/4" h	—	225.00	250.00	—	—
Iced tea tumbler, 15 oz	250.00	285.00	65.00	65.00	—
Juice pitcher, 6" h †	525.00	150.00	70.00	65.00	525.00
Juice tumbler, 5 oz	—	120.00	45.00	—	—
Pitcher, 60 oz	475.00	175.00	95.00	100.00	425.00
Plate					
5-3/4" d	90.00	25.00	15.00	15.00	90.00
6-1/2" d, indent	115.00	35.00	30.00	35.00	—
6-1/2" d, sherbet	—	24.00	14.50	—	—
8-1/2" d, luncheon	85.00	55.00	40.00	35.00	80.00
9-1/2" d, dinner	150.00	90.00	65.00	62.00	150.00
11-1/2" d, grill	—	—	—	—	100.00
Platter, 12" l, oval	175.00	60.00	40.00	35.00	115.00
Relish, 8-3/8" d					
undivided	275.00	—	200.00	—	275.00
four parts	160.00	65.00	37.50	37.50	160.00
Salt and pepper shakers, pr†	1,000.00	295.00	65.00	70.00	800.00
Sandwich server	48.00	85.00	65.00	50.00	130.00
Saucer	90.00	30.00	45.00	35.00	140.00
Sherbet, 4-3/4"	150.00	75.00	75.00	75.00	150.00
Sugar, ftd	195.00	85.00	35.00	40.00	185.00
Sweet pea vase	285.00	125.00	140.00	145.00	—
Tumbler, 10 oz	—	145.00	65.00	—	185.00
Vegetable bowl					
7" d	33.00	75.00	65.00	70.00	195.00
9-1/2" l	110.00	70.00	40.00	30.00	125.00
10" d cov	—	120.00	120.00	120.00	900.00
10" d open	—	75.00	20.00	19.00	200.00
Whiskey, 1-1/2 oz †	—	—	58.00	—	—
Wine, 3 oz, 4-1/2" h	450.00	—	120.00	—	—

NEWPORT

Hairpin

Manufactured by Hazel Atlas Glass Co., Clarksburg, WV, and Zanesville, OH, from 1936 to the early 1950s. Made in amethyst, cobalt blue, pink (from 1936 to 1940), Platonite white and fired-on colors, from the 1940s to early 1950s.

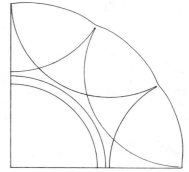

*Newport amethyst plate, **$32**; cream soup, **$25**; sugar, **$20**; and creamer, **$20**.*

Item	Amethyst	Cobalt Blue	Fired-On Color	Pink	Platonite
Berry bowl, 8-1/4" d	50.00	50.00	16.00	25.00	10.00
Cereal bowl, 5-1/4" d	42.00	42.00	—	20.00	—
Cream soup, 4-3/4" d	25.00	25.00	10.00	17.50	8.50
Creamer	20.00	22.00	8.50	10.00	3.00
Cup	12.00	15.00	9.00	6.00	4.50
Plate					
6" d, sherbet	7.50	10.00	5.00	3.50	2.00
8-1/2" d, luncheon	15.00	22.00	9.00	8.00	4.50
8-13/16" d, dinner	32.00	35.00	15.00	15.00	12.00
Platter, 11-3/4" l, oval	42.00	48.00	18.00	20.00	12.00
Salt and pepper shakers, pr	60.00	65.00	32.00	30.00	18.00
Sandwich plate, 11-1/2" d	48.00	50.00	15.00	24.00	10.00
Saucer	5.25	6.00	3.00	2.50	2.00
Sherbet	15.00	18.50	10.00	8.00	4.00
Sugar	20.00	22.00	9.50	10.00	5.00
Tumbler, 9 oz, 4-1/2" h	40.00	48.00	15.00	20.00	—

OLD CAFÉ

Manufactured by Hocking Glass Co., Lancaster, OH, from 1936 to 1940. Made in crystal, pink, and royal ruby.

*Old Café cereal bowl, ruby, **$12**.*

Item	Crystal	Pink	Royal Ruby
Berry bowl, 3-3/4" d	4.50	5.00	6.00
Bowl			
5" d	5.00	6.00	—
9" d, closed handles	10.00	10.00	15.00
Candy dish, 8" d, low	8.00	12.00	16.00
Candy jar, crystal, ruby lid	—	—	20.00
Cereal bowl, 5-1/2" d	9.00	9.00	12.00
Cup	6.00	6.00	10.00
Juice tumbler, 3" h	10.00	10.00	12.00
Lamp	24.00	24.00	35.00
Olive dish, 6" l, oblong	7.50	8.50	—
Pitcher			
36 oz, 6" h	85.00	85.00	—
80 oz	120.00	120.00	—

OLD CAFÉ (cont.)

Item	Crystal	Pink	Royal Ruby
Plate			
6" d, sherbet	4.00	4.00	—
10" d, dinner	35.00	35.00	—
Saucer	4.00	4.00	—
Sherbet, low, ftd	7.00	7.00	12.00
Tumbler, 4" h	12.00	12.00	18.00
Vase, 7-1/4" h	35.00	40.00	45.00

PATRICIAN

Spoke

Manufactured by Federal Glass Co., Columbus, OH, from 1933 to 1937. Made in amber (also called Golden Glo), crystal, green, and pink.

Patrician cream soup bowl, **$28**; *sherbet,* **$13**; *cup,* **$12.50**.

Item	Amber	Crystal	Green	Pink
Berry bowl, 8-1/2" d	50.00	15.00	37.50	35.00
Butter dish, cov	95.00	100.00	215.00	225.00
Cereal bowl, 6" d	32.00	27.50	27.50	25.00
Cookie jar, cov	90.00	80.00	500.00	—
Cream soup, 4-3/4" d	28.00	25.00	24.50	22.00
Creamer, ftd	12.50	9.00	12.50	12.50
Cup	12.50	10.00	12.50	12.50
Jam dish	30.00	25.00	35.00	30.00
Mayonnaise, three toes	—	—	—	165.00
Pitcher				
8" h, molded handle	120.00	125.00	125.00	115.00
8-1/4" h, applied handle	150.00	140.00	150.00	145.00
Plate				
6" d, sherbet	10.00	8.50	10.00	10.00
7-1/2" d, salad	17.50	15.00	12.50	15.00
9" d, luncheon	14.00	12.50	12.00	12.50
10-1/2" d, grill	15.00	13.50	20.00	20.00
10-1/2 d, dinner	10.00	12.75	32.00	36.00
Platter, 11-1/2" l, oval	32.50	30.00	30.00	28.00
Salt and pepper shakers, pr	65.00	65.00	65.00	85.00
Saucer	10.00	9.25	9.50	9.50
Sherbet	13.00	10.00	14.00	16.00
Sugar	12.50	9.00	12.50	12.50
Sugar lid	55.00	50.00	75.00	60.00
Tumbler				
5 oz	30.00	28.50	30.00	32.00
8 oz, ftd	50.00	42.00	50.00	—
12 oz	45.00	—	—	—
Vegetable bowl, 10" l, oval	38.00	30.00	38.50	30.00

QUEEN MARY
Prismatic Line, Vertical Ribbed

Manufactured by Hocking Glass Co., Lancaster, OH, from 1936 to 1948. Made in crystal, pink, and royal ruby.

Queen Mary crystal bowl, **$7.50***; and candlesticks,* **$24.**

Item	Crystal	Pink	Royal Ruby
Ashtray			
3-3/4" l, oval	4.00	5.50	5.00
3-1/2" d, round	4.00	—	—
Berry bowl, 5" d	5.00	10.00	—
Bowl			
4" d, one handle	4.00	12.50	—
5-1/2" d, two handles	6.00	15.00	—
7" d	7.50	35.00	—
Butter dish, cov	42.00	125.00	—
Candlesticks, pr, two lite, 4-1/2" h	24.00	—	70.00
Candy dish, cov	30.00	42.00	—
Celery tray, 5" x 10"	10.00	24.00	—
Cereal bowl, 6" d	8.00	24.00	—
Cigarette jar, 2" x 3" oval	6.50	7.50	—
Coaster, 3-1/2" d	4.00	5.00	—
Coaster/ashtray, 4-1/4" sq	4.00	6.00	—
Comport, 5-3/4"	9.00	14.00	—
Creamer			
ftd	6.00	40.00	—
oval	6.00	12.00	—
Cup			
large	6.50	10.00	—
small	8.50	12.50	—
Juice tumbler, 5 oz, 3-1/2" h	9.50	15.00	—
Pickle dish, 5" x 10"	10.00	24.00	—
Plate			
6" d, sherbet	4.00	5.00	—
6-1/2" d, bread and butter	6.00	—	—
8-1/4" d, salad	6.00	—	—
9-1/2" d, dinner	15.00	60.00	—
Preserve, cov	30.00	125.00	—
Relish			
Clover-shape	15.00	17.50	—
12" d, three part	10.00	15.00	—
14" d, four part	15.00	17.50	—
Salt and pepper shakers, pr	25.00	—	—
Sandwich plate, 12" d	20.00	17.50	—
Saucer	2.00	5.00	—
Serving tray, 14" d	15.00	9.00	—
Sherbet, ftd	6.50	10.00	—
Sugar			
ftd	—	40.00	—
oval	6.00	12.00	—
Tumbler			
9 oz, 4" h	6.00	19.50	—
10 oz, 5" h, ftd	35.00	70.00	—

Royal Ruby

Manufactured by Anchor Hocking Glass Corporation, Lancaster, PA, from 1938 to 1967. Made only in Royal Ruby.

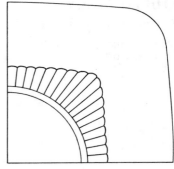

Royal Ruby sugar, **$8**; *creamer (on pedestal),* **$10**; *cup and saucer,* **$12.50**.

Item	Royal Ruby
Apothecary jar, 8-1/2" h	22.00
Ashtray	
4-1/2", leaf	5.00
5-7/8", sq	9.00
7-3/4"	32.00
Beer bottle	
7 oz	30.00
16 oz	35.00
32 oz	40.00
Berry	
4-5/8" d, sq	9.50
8-1/2" d, round	25.00
Bonbon, 6-1/2" d	20.00
Bowl	
7-3/8" w, sq	18.50
12" l, oval, Rachael	50.00
Cereal bowl, 5-1/4" d	12.00
Cigarette box	90.00
Cocktail	
3-1/2 oz, Boopie	8.50
3-1/2 oz, tumbler	10.00
Cordial, ftd	15.00
Creamer	
flat	10.00
ftd	10.00
Cup	
round	6.00
square	7.50
Dessert bowl, 4-3/4" w, sq	9.00
Fruit bowl, 4-1/4" d	6.50

Item	Royal Ruby
Goblet	
9-1/2 oz	14.00
ball stem	12.00
Ice bucket	55.00
Iced tea goblet, 14 oz, Boopie	20.00
Iced tea tumbler, 13 oz, 6" h, ftd	10.00
Ivy ball, 4" h, Wilson	12.00
Juice tumbler	
4 oz	7.00
5 oz, flat or ftd	12.00
Juice pitcher	39.00
Lamp	35.00
Marmalade, ruby top, crystal base	22.00
Pitcher	
3 qt, tilted	45.00
3 qt, upright	38.00
42 oz, tilted	35.00
42 oz, upright	40.00
Pitcher, 86 oz, 8-1/2"	35.00
Plate	
6-1/4" d, sherbet	4.50
7" d, salad	5.50
8-3/8" w, sq, luncheon	12.00
9-1/8" d, dinner	14.00
13-3/4" d	35.00
Popcorn bowl	
5-1/4" d	12.50
10" d, deep	40.00
Puff box, crystal base, ruby lid	28.00
Punch bowl and stand	75.00
Punch set, 14 pieces	200.00
Punch cup	3.50

Item	Royal Ruby
Relish, 3-3/4" x 8-3/4", tab handle	16.00
Salad bowl, 8-1/2" d	19.00
Saucer	
5-3/8" w, sq	4.00
round	4.00
Set, 50 pcs, orig labels, orig box	350.00
Sherbet	
6-1/2 oz, stemmed	7.50
6 oz, Boopie	8.50
Shot glass	4.50
Soup bowl, 7-1/2" d	15.00
Sugar	
flat	8.00
footed	8.00
Sugar lid, notched	11.00
Tray, center handle, ruffled	16.50
Tumbler	
5 oz, 3-1/2" h	6.00
9 oz, Windsor	8.50
10 oz, 5" h, ftd	7.00
14 oz, 5" h	9.00
15 oz, long boy	15.00
Vase	
3-3/4" h, Roosevelt	7.50
4" h, Wilson, fancy edge	12.00
6-3/8" h, Harding	15.00
6-5/8" h, Coolidge	20.00
9" h, Hoover, plain	20.00
9" h, Hoover, white birds on branch dec	25.00
10" h, fluted, star base	35.00
10" h, ftd, Rachael	50.00
Vegetable bowl, 8" l, oval	45.00
Wine, 2-1/2 oz, ftd	12.50

Swirl

Petal Swirl

Manufactured by Jeannette Glass Co., Jeannette, PA, from 1937 to 1938. Made in amber, Delphite, ice blue, pink, and Ultramarine. Production was limited in amber and ice blue.

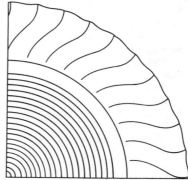

Swirl ultramarine sugar and creamer, **$18 each.**

SWIRL (cont.)

Item	Delphite	Pink	Ultramarine
Berry bowl	—	—	18.00
Bowl, 10" d, ftd, closed handles	—	25.00	30.00
Butter dish, cov	—	175.00	245.00
Candleholders, pr			
2-lite	—	40.00	45.00
1-lite	115.00	—	—
Candy dish			
cov.	—	130.00	150.00
open, three legs	—	20.00	29.50
Cereal bowl, 5-1/4" d	14.00	10.00	15.00
Coaster, 1" x 3-1/4"	—	15.00	14.00
Console bwl, 10-1/2" d, ftd	—	20.00	35.00
Creamer	12.00	9.50	18.00
Cup and saucer	17.50	14.00	22.50
Plate			
6-1/2" d, sherbet	6.50	5.00	8.00
7-1/4" d, luncheon	—	6.50	12.00
8" d, salad	9.00	8.50	12.00
9-1/4" d, dinner	12.00	13.00	22.50
10-1/2" d, dinner	18.00	—	30.00
Platter, 12" l, oval	35.00	—	—
Salad bowl			
9" d	30.00	18.00	35.00
9" d, rimmed	—	20.00	30.00
Salt and pepper shakers, pr	—	—	50.00
Sandwich plate, 12-1/2" d	—	20.00	27.50
Sherbet, low, ftd	—	13.00	23.00
Soup, tab handles, lug	—	25.00	35.00
Sugar, ftd	—	12.00	18.00
Tray, 10-1/2" l, two handles	25.00	—	—
Tumbler			
9 oz, 4" h	—	18.00	42.00
13 oz, 5-1/8" h	—	45.00	90.00
Vase			
6-1/2" h, ftd, ruffled	—	22.00	—
8-1/2" h, ftd	—	—	36.00

WINDSOR

Windsor Diamond

Manufactured by Jeannette Glass Co., Jeannette, PA, from 1936 to 1946. Made in crystal, green, and pink with limited production in amberina red, Delphite and ice blue.

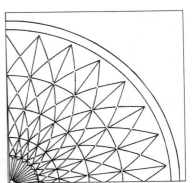

*Windsor crystal chop plate, **$24**; and pink pitcher, **$25**.*

Item	Crystal	Green	Pink
Ashtray, 5-3/4" d	15.00	45.00	45.00
Berry bowl, 8-1/2" d	7.50	18.50	22.00
Bowl			
5" l	10.00	—	25.00
7" x 11-3/4", boat shape	18.00	35.00	32.00
7-1/2" d, three legs	8.00	—	24.00
8" d, two handles	9.00	24.00	20.00
8" l, pointed edge	10.00	—	48.00
10-1/2" l, pointed edge	25.00	—	32.00

WINDSOR (cont.)

Item	Crystal	Green	Pink
Butter dish, cov	27.50	95.00	60.00
Cake plate, 10-3/4" d, ftd	12.00	22.00	20.00
Candlesticks, pr, 3" h	22.00	—	85.00
Candy jar, cov	18.00	—	—
Cereal bowl, 5-3/8" d	10.00	32.50	25.00
Chop plate, 13-5/8" d	24.00	42.00	50.00
Coaster, 3-1/4" d	8.50	18.00	25.00
Comport	9.00	—	—
Cream soup, 5" d	6.00	30.00	25.00
Creamer	5.00	15.00	20.00
Creamer, holiday shape	7.50	—	—
Cup	7.00	22.00	12.00
Fruit console, 12-1/2" d	45.00	—	115.00
Pitcher			
16 oz, 4-1/2" h	25.00	—	115.00
52 oz, 6-3/4" h	20.00	55.00	35.00
Plate			
6" d, sherbet	3.75	8.00	5.00
7" d, salad	4.50	20.00	18.00
9" d, dinner	9.00	25.00	25.00
Platter, 11-1/2" l, oval	7.00	25.00	25.00
Powder jar	15.00	—	55.00
Relish platter, 11-1/2" l, divided	10.00	—	200.00
Salad bowl, 10-1/2" d	12.00	—	—
Salt and pepper shakers, pr	20.00	48.00	42.00
Sandwich plate			
closed handles	10.00	—	24.00
open handles	12.50	18.00	20.00
Saucer	2.50	5.00	4.50
Sherbet, ftd	3.50	15.00	13.00
Sugar			
cov	10.00	40.00	30.00
cov, holiday shape	12.00	—	100.00
Tray			
4" sq	5.00	12.00	10.00
4" sq, handles	6.00	—	40.00
4-1/8" x 9"	5.00	16.00	10.00
4-1/8" x 9", handles	9.00	—	50.00
8-1/2" x 9-3/4"	7.00	35.00	25.00
8-1/2" x 9-3/4", handles	14.00	45.00	85.00
Tumbler			
4" h, ftd	7.00	—	—
12 oz, 5" h	11.00	55.00	32.50
Vegetable bowl, 9-1/2" l, oval	7.50	29.00	25.00

DISNEYANA

History: Walt Disney and the creations of the famous Disney Studios hold a place of fondness and enchantment in the hearts of people throughout the world. The 1928 release of "Steamboat Willie," featuring Mickey Mouse, heralded an entertainment empire.

Walt and his brother, Roy, were shrewd businessmen. From the beginning, they licensed the reproduction of Disney characters on products ranging from wristwatches to clothing.

In 1984, Donald Duck celebrated his 50th birthday, and collectors took a renewed interest in material related to him.

Additional Listings: See *Warman's Americana & Collectibles* for more examples.

Adviser: Theodore L. Hake.

Bambi

Charm bracelet, 6" l gold luster metal link bracelet, five figural gold luster charms of red/brown Bambi and Faline, blue Thumper, black and white Flower, yellow/green Friend Owl, 1950s **20.00**

Figure, 4" x 6" x 7-1/2" h, painted and glazed ceramic, by American Pottery Co., Bambi with head tilted upward, 1940s. **65.00**

Studio fan card, 7" x 9", stiff buff paper, brown design, Walt Disney facsimile signature, small copyright, 1940s **35.00**

Cinderella

Costume, 8-1/4" x 11" x 2-3/4" orig box, two pcs, Ben Copper, copyright Walt Disney Productions, late 1960s, box illus include Spider-Man, Hulk, Thor, and Wonder Woman, wear to box, costume bright **30.00**

Soaky, 10-1/2" h, soft plastic body, hard plastic head, blue dress, movable arms **20.00**

Disneyland

Book, *A Visit to Disneyland,* Whitman Big Tell-A-Tale, copyright 1965, 6" x 8-1/2", 28 pgs, color photos . **20.00**

Game, Disneyland Riverboat Game, 8" x 16" x 1-3/4" deep box, Parker Bros, copyright 1960, 14-3/4" sq board, 6-3/4" full-color cardboard movable tack, four different colored metal boat playing pcs **50.00**

Poster, 19" x 26-1/2", Disneyland Haunted Mansion, full color, glossy, copyright 1982, mansion at twilight, inset photo of mother and child being scared by ghost, tightly rolled **25.00**

Donald Duck, Walt Disney's Donald Duck and his Cat Troubles, Whitman "845," copyright 1948, slight wear, $60.

Disney Studios, Christmas card, 7-1/4" x 9-1/4", copyright 1936, orig mailing envelope, Los Angeles Dec. 22, 1936 postmark, front illus of Mickey, Minnie, Donald, and Pluto in snowstorm, small copyright text on back. **300.00**

Disney World

Convention badge, 4" d, black printing, gold background, "110 Club '79/Disney World" **10.00**

Flicker, I Like Walt Disney World, red metal case, text on reverse including "Vari-Vue" and Walt Disney World logo, black, white, and red image of Mickey wearing blue bow tie, changes to slogan in white on red background . . . **15.00**

Donald Duck

Clerk's button, 2-1/2", Donald Duck Bread, color image of Donald, yellow background, black text, image matches bread label used in the 1950s **75.00**

Comic book, *Donald Duck,* Whitman/K.K. Publications, Inc., copyright 1938, 80 pgs, black and white illus featuring Sunday strip reprints from 1936 and 1937, very fine **500.00**

Egg cup, 2-1/4" x 4" x 3-1/2" h, color image of Donald pushing wheelbarrow, brown/iridescent tan, unmarked, 1950s. **145.00**

Fast Action book, *Donald Duck Out of Luck,* Dell Publishing Co., copyright 1940, 192 pgs, black and white story pictures, ad on back for Donald Duck Comics, near mint, 4" x 5-1/2" **100.00**

Glass, 4-5/8" h, Donald Duck Beverages, blue, white, and yellow

wrap-around design, Donald and three nephews, each holding glass with their name on it and word "More!" repeated three times, 1950s **65.00**

Night light, 3-1/4" x 5-1/2", pink, purple, and white display card, 2-1/2" hard plastic figural night light, General Electric, blue, white, and yellow Donald head, red plug-in base, purple text for Mickey Mouse Club membership . . . **25.00**

Orig art

Model sheet, 9-3/4" x 11", tan paper cov by lead pencil art and text by Frank Follmer, sgd at bottom margin, 12 different images of Donald, accompanied by document regarding Follmer **200.00**

Pencil drawing, from Lonesome Ghosts, 10" x 12" sheet of animation paper, 3" x 3-1/2" image in lead pencil, red pencil outline under Donald, 1937, #153 from numbered sequence, full figure Donald walking, angry expression **250.00**

Toothbrush holder, 2" x 3-1/4" x 5" h, marked "Made in Japan," copyright on back with Disney spelled "Disny," 1930s, high relief image of Donald, head turned to one side, long bill open, restored paint **145.00**

Dumbo

Premium button, 1-1/4" d, black, white, red, and gray, "D-X" printed on platform, reverse Kay Kamen back paper includes small image of running Mickey, 1942 . . . . **24.00**

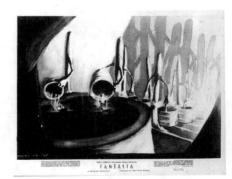
"Fantasia," movie still, 8" x 10" glossy black and white for film's second release in 1944, brooms ascending steps to dump buckets of water, $40. Photos courtesy of Hake's Americana & Collectibles.

Toothbrush holder, 3-1/2" x 5-1/2" x 3-3/4", painted ceramic, matte finish, three openings for toothbrushes, incised 1942 copyright **150.00**

Elmer Elephant, book, *Elmer Elephant*, David McKay Co., copyright 1936, hardcover, 48 pgs with color illus, full color Donald Duck bookplate . . . **95.00**

Fantasia

Plate, 9-1/2" d, Flower Ballet, Vernon Kilns, dark maroon, yellow, green, and blue, copyright 1940 . . . **75.00**

Souvenir movie program, 9-1/2" x 12-1/2", softcover, from orig 1940 release, Western Printing Co., black and white photos of Walt Disney and other contributors, full color plates of scenes from film **50.00**

Flip the Frog

Ashtray, 2-1/2" x 5" x 3-1/4" h, china, marked "Made in Japan," early 1930s, image of Flip seated on edge of basket, surrounded by grapes and leaves, holding bass fiddle, small piece of fiddle missing **175.00**

Coloring book, 10-1/2" x 15", 28 pgs, Saalfield, copyright 1932, black and white illus, full color sample pictures, one page colored, slight wear to covers, 6" split at spine **90.00**

Goofy

Blotter, 4" x 7", Sunoco Oil, Goofy and angry polar bear, broken-down car, copyright 1939, unused **40.00**

Mickey Mouse, Whitman big little book #717, copyright 1933, second cover design, Floyd Gottfredson story and art, penciled inscription on first blank page plus inked inscription on back cover, $125.

Mickey Mouse, mug, image of Mickey riding Henry Horse on front, issued as Canadian souvenir for "Grand Falls, N.B." (New Brunswick), hand-painted text at bottom of image, marked "Made in Japan," early 1930s, 2-1/2" h, $250.

Cel, 10-1/2" x 12-1/2" acetate sheet, 4" x 5-1/2" cel image of Sport Goofy, color laser background of stadium, #A-76 from numbered sequence, from 1980s Disney TV show **150.00**

Glass, 4-1/4" h, Goofy and Wilbur 1939 Walt Disney All Star Parade, green wrap-around design, black title, Goofy in boat with Wilbur the grasshopper and fish **60.00**

Mickey Mouse

Ashtray, 3-1/2" x 4" x 3-1/4" h, china, marked "Made in Japan," 1930s, Mickey and Minnie seated on back edge **250.00**

Bank, 3-14" x 3-1/2" x 6", movable head, painted composition, Crown Toy Mfg Co., 1938, standing next to chest with coin slot on front, orig trap, key missing **175.00**

Better Little Book, *Mickey Mouse and the Dude Ranch Bandit*, Whitman #1471, copyright 1943, 352 pgs **45.00**

Big Little Book, *Mickey Mouse Sails for Treasure Island*, Whitman, copyright 1935, premium imprint for Kolynos Dental Cream on back cover, very fine **85.00**

Book

Mickey Mouse Movie Stories Book 2, by David McKay, copyright 1934, hardcover, 200 pgs, black and white art, scattered wear and aging to cover, 2-1/2" splint in spine **145.00**

Mickey Mouse Presents Santa's Workshop, 7-1/4" x 10", Collins, England, late 1930s, hardover,

80 pgs, black and white and color illus, full color cover art repeated on dust jacket **175.00**

Mickey Mouse Storybook, 6-1/4" x 8-1/2", softcover, by David McKay, 64 pgs, 1931, black and white illus from early cartoons, wear **65.00**

Child's umbrella, 23" l, 33" d, black metal frame, shaft with fabric covering, plaid design, mostly red, black, white, blue, green, and yellow accent stripes, 3-1/4" h 3-D pained composition figure of Mickey as handle, back of head "Mickey Mouse, copyright," 1930s **100.00**

Mickey Mouse, pocket watch, earliest issue of first pocket watch by Ingersoll, 1933, longer stem, 2" d dial features image of Mickey, hands point at numerals, second hand disk features three additional small images of Mickey running, chromed metal case has incised image of Mickey on back, recently overhauled, runs, $375.

Compact, 1-1/2" x 1-3/4" x 3/8" h, chromed metal, red, black, and yellow enamel paint design of Mickey standing next to Minnie on lid, from series by Cohn & Rosenberger, c1934 . . . . **90.00**

Composition book, 6-3/4" x 8-1/4", Mickey Mouse Composition Book, by Powers Paper Co., brown, black and red illus of Mickey and Minnie walking, carrying school books, multiplication tables on back, some penciled school work on pages, dated 1934 . . . . **60.00**

Figure, 8-1/2" h, 2-3/4" sq base, bisque, marked "Made in Japan," 1930s, two movable arms, name incised on front edge of base, string tail missing **850.00**

Magazine, *Mickey Mouse Magazine*, Vol. 1, #2, December 1933 issue, 16 pgs, red and green Christmas cover, green and white contents, imprint for Highland Dairy, near mint, 5-1/4" x 7-1/4" **250.00**

Orig art panel, 6-1/4" x 6-3/4", Mickey Mouse and the Bat Bandit, by Floyd Gottfredson, single panel trimmed from 1934 daily strip, pen and ink, blue pencil accents, thin art board, penciled by Gottfredson, inked by Ted Thwaites, scene of Mickey and bandit on horseback running across cliff, exchanging gunfire, word balloon "Step On It, Steamboat! We Gotta Head 'im Off!" **650.00**

Stuffed toy, Mickey Mouse, red paints, yellow shoes, 17" l, $40.

Pencil box, 5-5/8" x 5" x 1-1/4" h, painted composition, figural, with high relief details on each side, Dixon #2770, 1930s, excellent **600.00**

Sand pail, 5-3/4" h, 5-3/4" d at top, tin litho, attached carrying handle, Ohio Art, copyright 1938, golf theme, wrap-around illus with Mickey, Donald, Goofy, and black cat, play wear **300.00**

Toothpick holder, 1-1/4" x 1-3/4" x 2-5/8" h, china, black and white, Mickey standing next to basket, opening for toothpicks, German, registration number, 1930s. **150.00**

Toy, 9" h, diecut cardboard toy, 5" x 9-1/2" x 2-1/4" h orig box, Dolly Toy Co., 1930s, graphics on box with Mickey climbing rope to meet Minnie, castle background, figural toy, wire tail, attached 36" l string which Mickey climbs when tension is applied, very fine **600.00**

Wristwatch, Ingersoll, 1-1/4" d chromed metal case, dial with large black, white, and yellow Mickey, hands point to numerals, second wheel with three tiny Mickey images, vintage replacement strap, 1933, working order and clean dial **325.00**

Minnie Mouse

Bottle, 9" h, heavy glass, Rochester Healthful Beverages, 2" x 2-1/2" black and white silk screened label on front, 1930s **135.00**

Salt and pepper shakers, 2" x 2" x 5-1/4" h, painted and glazed ceramic, 1950s, Dan Brechner Exclusive foil sticker, ink stamp copyright, WD-52, standing on top of wood crates which house noisemakers, names on front of base, orig stoppers **75.00**

Pinocchio

Book, *Pinocchio Linen-Like, #1061,* Whitman, copyright 1940, 7" x 7-3/4", 12 pgs, full color art on each page **45.00**

Candy bar wrapper, 3-1/4" x 8-1/4", Schutter Candy Co., copyright 1940, black, white, yellow, and red image of Jiminy and premium "Official Conscience Medal" **50.00**

Game, 10" x 15" x 1-3/4" h, Pinocchio Race Game, Chad Valley, c1940, scene of Pinocchio and Jiminy Cricket encountering Foulfellow and Gideon leaving Geppetto's workshop on box lid, some fading

Pinback button, Good Teeth, Pinocchio and Jiminy Cricket, pair marching down road past "Good Teeth" sign, copyright initials "W.D.P." on bottom edge, backpaper "Distributed by The Bureau of Public Relations American Dental Assoc., Chicago," 1-1/4" d, $300. Photo courtesy of Hake's Americana & Collectibles.

to box, 14-1/2" sq board, game pcs **140.00**

Planter, 3" x 5-1/2" x 4-1/2", painted and glazed ceramic, Figaro dipping paw into aquarium planter, raised image of fish on front, c1940 . . . . **35.00**

Soaky, 9-3/4" h, soft plastic body, hard plastic head, Pinocchio sitting on top of tree stump, holding school slate, 1960s **20.00**

Silly Symphonies

Book, *Mickey Mouse Presents His Silly Symphonies Babies in the Woods, King Neptune,* 48 stiff paper pages, four full-color pop-ups, full-color art on front and back hardcovers, tape repairs **165.00**

Record, 78 rpm, 7" d, RCA Victor label, from 1934 set of three black and white picture disks, #226, Lullaby Land of Nowhere/Dance of the Bogey Man, art on each side, very fine **300.00**

Snow White

Autographed photo, Adriana Caselotti, 8" x 10" glossy black and white publicity photo, voice of Snow White, vintage image of her next to film scene, boldly inscribed and sgd in blue **45.00**

Birthday card, 4-1/4" x 5-1/2", White & Wyckoff, copyright 1938, black, white, red, blue, and green design, front with Doc and Sleepy in front of doorway, opens to Snow White dancing with Doc as others play instruments **30.00**

Book

Masks of the Seven Dwarfs and Snow White, Whitman, copyright 1938, 10-1/2" x 10-3/4", eight stiff paper sheets with punch-out masks, near mint, unpunched **400.00**

Snow White and the Seven Dwarfs Big Golden Book, Golden Book Press, copyright 1952, 9-1/2" x 12-3/4", hardcover, 28 pgs, full color story art **35.00**

Figure, 1-1/2" x 2-1/4" x 4-1/2", celluloid with plaster filling, marked "Foreign" on back, "Celluloid" on underside, c1938, some pulling at seams **75.00**

Glass, 3-1/4" h, brown Dopey image, text "Dopey/Snow White & the Seven Dwarfs," back marked "Bosco Glass," 1938 . . . . . . **45.00**

Orig art, pencil drawing of Happy, 10" x 12" sheet of animation paper, 2-3/4" x 4" centered image in lead pencil, 1937, #54 of numbered sequence **100.00**

Song folio, *Snow White and the Seven Dwarfs,* 9" x 12", 52 pgs, Bourne Inc. Music Publishers, copyright 1938, 1950s printing **25.00**

Three Pigs

Ashtray, 3-1/4" x 5" x 3-1/4" h, china, marked "Made in Japan" with copyright, 1930s, iridescent blue base, cream inside, black details, three pigs seated on back . **140.00**

Snow White, alarm clock, Bayard, marked "Made in France, Par Autorisation Walt Disney," $120.

Figure set, 3-1/2" Big Bad Wolf, three pigs and Red Riding Hood 3" to 3-1/8" h, bisque, color accents, some paint loss **350.00**

Postcard set, set of 12 numbered 3-1/2" x 5-1/5" cards, marked "Paris," French text, backs also marked "Disney," each with full-color art telling story, sent by soldier to daughter in US, each with typed or handwritten note, sent on consecutive days in April 1945 . . . . **150.00**

Tin, 6" d, 2" d tin litho, marked "By Arrangement with Walt Disney-Mickey Mouse Ltd.," scene of Wolf hiding behind tree, spying on pigs, wrap-around design on side in red and bright gold luster, English. **175.00**

Walt Disney, postcard, 5" x 7", glossy stiff paper, full color portrait of Walt in center, surrounded by character images of Mickey, Donald, Ludwig, Pluto, Goofy, and Tinker Bell, blue background, unused, 1960s **20.00**

Zorro

Costume, 16" x 37", unused, attached to orig diecut cardboard hanger display, Lindsay, late 1950s, black diecut leatherette mask, black fabric cloak/sash, silver image of Zorro on rearing Toronado, 3-1/4" d Member Lindsay Ranch Club badge . **50.00**

Figure, 3" x 4" x 7" h, painted and glazed ceramic, Enesco, orig foil sticker, copyright, "WDE.140," attached foil-covered cardboard string tag, replaced metal sword **125.00**

Game, 8" x 15-1/2" x 1-1/2" deep box, Whitman, copyright 1965, 15-1/2" sq board, complete set of picture letter cards, one generic plastic marker missing **75.00**

Pencil by Number Coloring Set, 9-1/4" x 12-1/4" x 1" deep color box, Transogram, late 1950s, 11 of 12 orig black and white pictures to color, wear to box **40.00**

DOLLHOUSES

History: Dollhouses date from the 18th century to modern times. Early dollhouses often were handmade, sometimes with only one room. The most common type was made for a young girl to fill with replicas of furniture scaled especially to fit into a dollhouse. Specially sized dolls also were made for dollhouses. All types of accessories in all types of styles were

available, and dollhouses could portray any historical period.

American

21" w, 43" h, ivory-painted gable and center hallway, five large rooms and attic bedroom, attached garage, separate blue shutters and window boxes, most furnishings from same period as house, approx. 40 items, made by John Leonard Plock, NY architect, c1932 . . . . **250.00**

21-1/4" l, 28-3/4" h, Victorian, last quarter 19th C, two-story house, modified Federal style, mansard roof with widow's walk, fenced-in front garden, simulated grass and fountains, polychrome details **400.00**

28-1/4" w, 17-1/4" d, 32-1/2" h, gambrel roof, painted off-white, red paste board scalloped shingles, front opening half doors, six rooms, original paper wall and floor coverings, hinged door in rear roof, front steps, orig furniture, bisque dolls, accessories, and rugs, some paint and paper wear. **920.00**

Bliss, chromolithograph paper on wood

13" h, two-story, litho blue roof, red wood base, two opening windows, working front door, orig litho walls and floors, marked "R. Bliss" on front door, some wear, stains, and discoloration. **900.00**

14" h, two-story, blue litho paper on roof, blue wood on back, red wood chimney and base, two open lower windows and two upper windows, house opens in front, litho wall and floor coverings inside, marked "R. Bliss" on door, some wear, one wall slightly warped. **575.00**

14" h, two-story, stable, red shingle roof, painted green roof and red spire on cupola, painted red base and side poles of stable, single opening door on second floor, brown papier-mâché horse, marked "R. Bliss" **900.00**

16-1/2" h, two-story, front porch with turned columns, working front door, overhanging roof with lattice-work balcony, blue-gray roof with dormer windows, hinged front, int. with two rooms, printed carpeting and wallpaper, celluloid windows with later lace curtains, electric lights, two scratch-built chairs . . **1,725.00**

Elastolin, Germany, 29" w, farmyard, house, barn, fencing, trees, and various figures. **1,150.00**

German, 35" w, 11-1/4" d, 17" h, Nuremberg Kitchen, dark yellow walls with deep red trim, red and black checkerboard floor, cream stove hood, green furniture, tin stove, tin and copper pots, set of scales, wash boiler, baking pans, utensils, pottery, porcelain, and pewter tableware, late 19th C, some paint wear and imperfections **2,300.00**

McLoughlin, 12" x 17" x 16", folding house, two rooms, dec int., orig box **950.00**

Schoenhut, 20" x 26" x 30", mansion, two-story, eight rooms, attic, tan brick design, red roof, large dormer, 20 glass windows, orig decal, 1923 . . . **1,750.00**

Tootsietoy, 21" w, 10-1/8" d, 16" h, house, furniture, and accessories, printed Masonite, half-timbered style, two rooms down, two up, removable roof, open back, orchid and pink bedroom sets, orchid bathroom, brown dining room set, flocked sofa and chairs, green and white kitchen pcs, piano, bench, lamps, telephone, cane-back sofa, rocker, some damage and wear to 3/4 scale furniture . . **525.00**

DOLLS

History: Dolls have been children's play toys for centuries. Dolls also have served other functions. From the 14th through 18th centuries, doll making was centered in Europe, mainly in Germany and France. The French dolls produced in this era were representations of adults and dressed in the latest couturier designs. They were not children's toys.

During the mid-19th century, child and baby dolls, made in wax, cloth, bisque, and porcelain, were introduced. Facial features were hand painted, wigs were made of mohair and human hair, and the dolls were dressed in the current fashions for babies or children.

Doll making in the United States began to flourish in the 1900s with companies such as Effanbee, Madame Alexander, and Ideal.

Marks: Marks of the various manufacturers are found on the back of the head or neck or on the doll's back. These marks are very important in identifying a doll and its date of manufacture.

Additional Listings: See *Warman's Americana & Collectibles* for more examples.

Alt, Beck & Gottschalk, 19" h, bisque shoulder head, set blue eyes, multi-stroke brows, painted upper and lower lashes, closed shapely mouth, pierced ears, molded café au lait hair with jeweled tiara, molded braid across top, looped bun in back with black ribbon, molded white lace-trimmed

Alt, Beck & Gottschalk, bisque shoulder head, lady, 19" h, $1,350. Photo courtesy of McMaster Harris Auction Co.

collar on shoulder plate, cloth body with leather lower arms, red check lower legs with red leather boots, blue and beige lace dress and slip, unmarked **1,350.00**

Amberg

12-1/2" h, Bottle Babe Twins, solid-dome bisque heads, light blue sleep eyes, softly blues brows, painted upper and lower lashes, open mouths, molded tongues, lightly molded and painted hair, cloth bodies with non-working criers, composition arms, right arms molded to hold celluloid bottles, orig white lace-trimmed baby dresses, slips, crocheted bonnets, diapers, and socks, hold orig celluloid baby bottle, blue and white celluloid rattle, marked "A.M./Germany/341/3" on back of heads, "Amberg's/Bottle Babe/Pat. Pending/Amberg Dolls/The World Standard" on dress, both dolls have light rubs on cheeks or hair, cloth bodies are aged, some flaking on arms, paint flaked off right arm of one, price for pr **500.00**

15" h, New Born Babe, solid dome bisque head, blue sleep eyes, softly blushed brown, painted upper and lower lashes, closed mouth, lightly molded and painted hair, cloth body with composition hands, white lace-trimmed antique baby dress, slip and diaper, light

McLoughlin folding dollhouse, two rooms, highly decorated interiors, original box, 16" h, 17" l, 12" d, $950.

A.M., 310 Just Me, 9" h, $1,050. Photo courtesy of McMasters.

dust in bisque, tiny run on upper lip, left side seam split near bottom of torso **315.00**

Armand Marseille

6-1/2" h, Googly, bisque socket head, large slide glancing blue sleep eyes, single strike brows, closed smiling mouth, dark mohair wig, crude composition 5-pc toddler body, lace-trimmed organdy baby dress, matching bonnet, slip, diaper, stockings, crocheted booties, marked "G. 253 B Germany A. 11/0 M" on back of head, repainted body **675.00**

10" h, character baby, bisque socket head, blue sleep eyes, open mouth, two upper teeth, blond mohair wig, bent-limb composition body, orig gauze shift, imp "251 GB, Armand Marseille for George Borgfeldt," 1920s **415.00**

10" l, 9" d head circumference, Dream Baby, brown bisque socket head, brown sleep eyes, closed mouth, black painted hair, brown bent limb composition baby body, fine lawn christening gown with tucks, ruffles, and lace trim, c1920 . . . . **300.00**

11" h, 1894, bisque socket head, set blue eyes, single stroke brows, painted upper and lower lashes, open mouth, four upper teeth, orig mohair wig, jointed wood and composition body with

well-modeled parts, orig clothing, light blue lace-trimmed print dress, lace-trimmed bonnet, orig underclothing, black cotton socks with garters attached to chemise, orig handmade shoes, marked "1894/A.M. 3/0 DEP" on back of head **400.00**

23" h, 990 baby, bisque socket head, brown sleep eyes, feathered brows, painted upper and lower lashes, open mouth, well-accented lips, two upper teeth, antique human hair wig, composition bent-limb baby body, antique baby dress, slip, diaper, new crocheted sweater, cap and booties, marked "Armand Marseille/Germany/990/A 12 M" on back of head, heavy French-style body, arms repainted and have rough finish, right big toe missing, other toes repaired and repainted, normal wear at joints **275.00**

24" h, bisque head, blue sleep eyes, open mouth, dark blond mohair wig, fully articulated composition body, unsullied, orig white cotton cutwork dress, imp "AM 390," early 20th C, chip on inner edge of mouth rim, orig stringing loose **230.00**

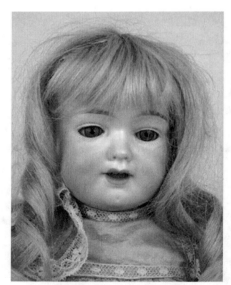

Armand Marseille, #590, character, bisque socket head, blue sleep eyes, open mouth, replaced blond human hair wig, old dress, marked "590 A5M (Armand Marseille) Germany DRGM," torso stamped "Heinrich Handwerck," 17-1/2" h, $460. Photo courtesy of James D. Julia, Inc.

Belton-type, bisque socket head, light blue paperweight eyes, red human hair wig, 15" h, $1,200. Photo courtesy of McMaster Harris Auction Co.

Arranbee

17" h, Nancy Lee, composition head, brown sleep eyes with real lashes, painted lower lashes, single stroke brows, closed mouth, orig human-hair wig in orig set, five-pc composition body, orig brown-flannel belted dress, white ruffle trim, orig underwear combination, orig socks and brown-suede shoes with fringe tongue, marked "R & B" on back of head, unplayed with condition **300.00**

21" h, Nanette, hard plastic head, blue sleep eyes with real lashes, single-stroke brows, painted lower lashes, closed mouth, saran wig, five-pc hard-plastic walking body, orig red and white striped dress with red organdy sleeves and apron, blue vinyl wide belt with charms attached, wrist tag, curlers on card, comb, marked "R & B" on head, "Nanette/An R & B Quality Doll/R & B Dolly Company New York 3, NY" on label on end of box, "R & B/Nanette/Walks/Sits/Stands/ Turns Her Head/R & B Doll Company New York City" on wrist tag, near mint in aged box, lid damaged and repaired . . . **700.00**

Averill, Georgene

20" h, Bonnie Babe, solid dome bisque flange head, brown sleep eyes, softly brushed brows, painted upper and lower lashes, open mouth, two lower teeth, molded tongue, cloth mama doll body, composition lower arms and legs, antique long baby dress, marked "Copr by Georgene Averill 1005 3652 4 Germany" on back of head, body recovered. **475.00**

17" h, solid dome bisque flange head, blue sleep eyes, softly blushed brows, painted upper and lower lashes, open laughing mouth, two lower teeth, molded tongue, deeply molded dimples, lightly molded and painted curly hair, cloth mama-doll body, composition arms and lower legs, non-working crier, dressed in possibly orig white lace-trimmed baby dress, slip, underwear, socks, and knit booties, silk and lace bonnet, marked "Copr by Georgene Averill 1005 3652 3 Germany" on back of head, cloth body aged and lightly soiled **600.00**

Bahr & Proschild, 23" h, 585 baby, bisque socket head, blue sleep eyes, feathered brows, painted upper and lower lashes, open mouth with accented lips, two upper teeth, paper tongue, orig human hair wig, composition baby body, long white baby dress, lace-trimmed bonnet, marked "BP (in heart) 585 M 14 I Germany" on back of head, eyes reset, body shows wear **450.00**

Barrois, E., 17-1/2" h, Poupee, pale bisque swivel head on shoulder plate, set blue eyes with threaded detail, fine multi-stroke brows, painted upper and lower lashes, closed mouth with accented lips, orig blond mohair wig with orig tortoiseshell comb, kid body with kid over wood upper arms, mortise-and-tenon type knee joints, white dotted Swiss dress, possibly orig underclothing, socks, and shoes, marked "E 4 B," at rear edge of bisque shoulder plate, lower bisque arms replaced **1,200.00**

Bisque

4-1/2" h, Oriental pair, olive-tone bisque socket heads, dark brown pupil-less set eyes, single stroke brows, painted upper and lower lashes, closed mouth, orig black mohair wigs, male with orig queue, five-pc olive-tone bisque bodies jointed at shoulders and hips, Oriental embroidered silk clothing, unmarked, price for pr **825.00**

8-1/2" h, bisque socket head, set brown eyes, blush over eyes, heavy feathered brows, painted upper and lower lashes, open mouth, one lower and two upper sq teeth, pierced ears, orig mohair wig with partial plaster pate, all bisque body with heavy proportions, bent left arm, molded and painted socks and black boos, possibly orig ecru satin dress with lace overlay, marked "102/12" on back of head, large chip on left hip, tips of three fingers missing **775.00**

10" h, Just Me, painted bisque socket head, blue side-glancing sleep eyes, single stroke brows, closed mouth, orig mohair wig, five-pc composition body jointed at shoulders and hips, orig white dress with orange and green felt trim, orig white cotton socks and white paper shoes with buckles, marked "Just Me/Registered/Germany/A 310/6/0 M" on back of head, needs to be restrung **900.00**

18" h, Miss Liberty, bisque shoulder head, painted blue eyes with molded lids, multi-stroke brows, tiny painted upper and lower lashes, closed mouth, molded earrings, molded and painted blond hair with copper molded earrings, molded and painted

Bisque, Oriental couple, 4-1/2" h, $825. Photo courtesy of McMaster Harris Auction Co.

Bru Jne, bisque socket head on bisque shoulder plate, blue paperweight eyes, replaced mohair wig, antique fabric outfit, 19" h, $12,700. Photo courtesy of McMaster Harris Auction Co.

blond hair with copper tiara, two black ribbons across top of head and lay against left side of neck, molded bun with waterfall effect, cloth body, leather lower arms, red leather boots as part of lower leg, antique ecru wool dress with lace trim, antique underclothing, small holes in dress **1,650.00**

Bru Jne, 19" h, bisque socket head on bisque shoulder plate with molded breasts, blue paperweight eyes, two-toned feathered brows, painted upper and lower lashes, closed mouth with tip of tongue showing, pierced ears, replaced mohair wig, kid body with bisque lower arms, wooden lower legs, dressed in outfit made from antique fabric and trims, marked "Bru Jne/6" on back of head, "Bru Jne" on back of left shoulder, "No. 6" on back of right shoulder, partial paper label on chest, "6/Bru Jne/Paris" on sole of one shoe **12,700.00**

Century Doll Co., Kestner, Character Baby, c1920, 17" l, 12-1/2" d bisque head, brown sleep eyes, open/closed smiling mouth with two upper molded teeth and tongue, deep modeling across bridge of nose, light dimples, flange neck on cloth body with side-swivel cloth legs, non-working squeaker, mechanism in body waves composition hands, long white lawn baby gown, imp mark "Century Doll Co Kestner Germany" **550.00**

Chase, Martha, 13" h, baby, oil-painted stockinette head, painted brown eyes, single-stroke brows, painted upper lashes, closed mouth, applied ears, oil-painted hair, cloth body with sateen-covered torso, antique white baby dress, slip and diaper, marked "Chase/Stockinet Doll/Trade Mark" in round stamp on left hip, "Feb. 20, 1912/Polly" hand written on front of torso, some wear **325.00**

China, unmarked

11-1/2" h, Frozen Charlie, pink tint, painted blue eyes with blue accent line, single-stroke brows, closed mouth, accent line between lips, painted blond hair with brush strokes around face, un-jointed body with arms extended, hands held with fingers curled, finger nails and toe nails outlined, color flaw on right side of forehead at edge of hair, couple spots of inherent roughness on right back of head and right shoulder, light color wear on edges of feet and hands, small flake off right finger **450.00**

18" h, open mouth, low brow, china shoulder head with turned head, painted blue eyes, red accent line, single-stroke brows, open mouth, molded teeth, molded and painted wavy hair, cloth body, china lower arms and lower legs, painted garters, molded and painted brown shoes with heels, possibly orig beige print dress, underclothing **850.00**

China shoulder head, black painted eyes and one strong brows, rosy cheeks, red lips, black painted Covered Wagon-style hairdo, $1,350. Photo courtesy of McMaster Harris Auction Co.

Cloth, 21" h, Philadelphia Baby, painted head and shoulders, heavily lidded brown painted eyes, deeply modeled mouth, brown hair, cloth body, painted lower limbs, gray and white striped cotton shift, white undergarments, c1900, overall wear, paint rubs and loss **1,100.00**

Cuno & Otto Dressel

14" h, bisque head, blue sleep eyes with lashes, open mouth, two upper teeth, replaced auburn mohair wig, fully articulated composition body, blue dress, imp "Cuno & Otto Dressel," early 20th C, some repair to body **200.00**

15-1/2" h, girl, painted bisque socket head, blue sleep eyes with real lashes, feathered brows, shading around eyes, open mouth, four upper teeth, orig human hair wig, jointed wood and composition teen-age body with high knee joints, orig clothing, short dress, slip, teddy, socks, and leather shoes, marked "Cuno & Otto Dressel/Germany" on back of head **450.00**

Demalcol, 9-1/2" h, Googlie, bisque socket head, blue eyes set to side, single-stroke brows, painted upper and lower lashes, closed smiling mouth, human-hair wig, new jointed composition body, blue and white flowered dress, matching bonnet, new underclothing, socks and shoes, marked "Demalcol/5/0/Germany" on back of head **525.00**

Eden Bebe, 16-1/2" h, bisque socket head, blue paperweight eyes, feathered brows, painted upper and lower lashes, open mouth, six upper teeth, pierced ears, replaced mohair wig, jointed wood and composition French body, redressed, pale blue and ecru outfit, blue and beige jacket, antique underclothing, new stockings, and old shoes, marked "Eden Bebe/Paris/7/Depose" on back of neck, "7" on front of neck, light kiln dust on left cheek, flaking at neck socket of body and on both lower legs, normal wear at joints and on hands **1,200.00**

Effanbee

11" h, Grumpy Cowboy, composition shoulder head, painted blue eyes to side, single-stroke brows, closed pouty mouth, molded and painted hair, cloth body, composition arms and feet, cowboy outfit with plaid shirt, gold pants, green bandanna, imitation-leather chaps, holster with gun, replaced felt hat, marked "Effanbee/Dolls/Walk Talk Sleep" on back of shoulder plate, light crazing, light wear back of head, few flakes off shoulder plate, wear on edges of feet **475.00**

12" h, Candy Kid, composition head, blue sleep eyes, real lashes, single stroke brows, closed mouth, molded and painted hair, five-pc composition toddler body, orig red and white gingham sunsuit and bonnet, orig socks, red leatherette tie shoes, marked "Effanbee" on back of head and on back, "An Effanbere Durable Doll, The Doll with Satin-Smooth Skin" in heart on end of box, unplayed with condition, orig box **375.00**

17" h, American Child Boy, composition head, painted blue eyes, multi-stroke brows, tiny painted upper and lower lashes, closed smiling mouth, orig human-hair wig, five-pc composition child body, orig blue wool two-pc suit, jacket and shorts, white shirt, multicolored tie, orig socks and black leatherette shoes, unmarked, light facial crazing, few light lines of crazing on legs **1,050.00**

Effanbee, Skippy Policeman, rare original outfit and accessories, 14" h, $1,950. Photo courtesy of McMasters.

19-1/2" h, American Child, composition head, blue sleep eyes with real lashes, multi-stroke brows, painted lower lashes, closed mouth, orig human hair wig with orig curlers, five-pc composition child body, orig blue and white striped zippered dress, nylon panties, orig white socks with blue trim, blue leatherette tie shoes, marked "Effanbee/American Children" on back of head, "Effanbee/Anne-Shirley" on back, unplayed with condition . **1,500.00**

Gaultier, Francois

10-1/2" h, Poupee, bisque socket head, bisque shoulder plate, light blue paperweight eyes, feathered browns, painted upper and lower lashes, closed mouth, pierced ears, orig mohair wig, cloth body with kid arms, individually stitched fingers, dressed in probably orig blue and white 2-pc outfit with train, marked "2/0" on back of head, "F. G." on right shoulder, illegible mark on left shoulder, some age discoloration to body, one left finger missing **1,250.00**

21" h, Bebe, bisque socket head, large blue paperweight eyes, feathered browns, painted upper and lower lashes, full-closed mouth, molded tongue, pierced ears, replaced mohair wig, jointed wood and composition body with straight wrists, new blue silk dress with matching bonnet, new underclothing, socks and lace-up boots, marked "F. G. (in scroll)/8" on back of head, fingers touched up, minor repairs **2,200.00**

Halbig, Simon

7" h, Oriental, bisque, medium skin tone, dark pupil-less stationary eyes, closed mouth orig black mohair Oriental-style wig, swivel neck, kid-lined neck socket and legs, long black stockings, brick red one-strap shoes, imp "852 3," late 19th C, some mottling/soil to bisque **920.00**

8" h, bisque head, blue sleep eyes, open mouth, four molded teeth, pierced ears, blond mohair wig, chunky straight wrist articulated composition body, orig finish and stringing, new red faille dress, imp "1079 DEP," c1900, tiny chip to right ear hole **550.00**

Handwerck, bisque socket head, brown sleep eyes, open mouth, pierced ears, replaced blond human hair wig, redressed appropriately, incised "11-1/2 99 DEP Germany Handwerck 3," hands do not match, 20" h, $415. Photo courtesy of James D. Julia, Inc.

21" h, C M Bergmann bisque head, brown sleep eyes with lashes, open mouth, synthetic auburn wig, jointed composition body, period white lawn dress with lace insertion, sprinkling of pepper spots primarily to the right cheek, early 20th C **260.00**

28" h, 949, bisque head, late 19th century, brown stationary eyes, closed mouth, pierced ears, blond mohair wig, fully articulated composition body stamped "Made in Germany," yellow cotton faille dress, imp "949," late 19th C **2,530.00**

Hamburger & Co., 22-1/2" h, Viola, bisque socket head, blue sleep eyes, feathered brows, painted upper and lower lashes, open mouth, four upper teeth, synthetic wig, jointed wood and composition body, antique dress with lace trim, underclothing, new socks and leather shoes, marked "Made in/Germany/Viola/H & Co./7" on back of head, several wig pulls on right side of forehead, light rub on nose, small inherent cut on H in back of head, repairs at neck socket of body, bottom of torso and left upper arm, normal wear at joints, finish of legs slightly different color than rest of body **300.00**

Handwerck, 16" h, bisque head, blue sleep eyes, open mouth, pierced ears, orig blond mohair wig, fully articulated composition body, Alice in Wonderland blue dress and white pinafore, dark brown shoes, imp "109-6 Germany Handwerck" **460.00**

Handwerck, Heinrich

25" h, bisque socket head, brown sleep eyes with real lashes, molded and feathered brows, painted lower lashes, open mouth with accented and well-modeled lips, four upper teeth, pierced ears, orig human-hair wig, jointed wood and composition body, possibly orig white lace-trimmed dress, underclothing, white cotton socks, marked Handwerck shoes, marked "Germany/Heinrich/Handwerck/ Halbig/4-1/2" on back of head, "Heinrich Handwerch/Germany/ 4-1/2" stamped on back of left hip, "4-1/2 /HH" in heart on shoes, light rubs on cheeks, touch-up around neck socket of body and on right side seam of torso, normal wear at joints, sole of left shoe damaged **450.00**

32-1/2" h, bisque socket head, blue sleep eyes, molded and feathered brows, painted upper and lower lashes, open mouth, accented lips, four upper teeth, pierced ears, orig human-hair wig, jointed wood and composition Handwerck body with orig finish, antique white child's dress, antique underclothing, cotton socks, black patent leather shoes, marked "Germany/Handwerck/Simon & Halbig/7" on back of head, "Heinrich Handwerck/Germany/7" stamped in red on lower back, finish flaking on lower left arm and knees, left knee ball replaced **1,025.00**

Handwerck, Max, 21" h, bisque head, blue sleep eyes, open mouth, inset teeth, pierced ears, jointed-composition body, orig finish, newly made pink linen dress and hat, imp "421 10 Germany M HANDWERCK 2-1/2", bisque speckling, small chin pit **320.00**

Harmann, Kurt, 26" h, bisque head, brown sleep eyes, open mouth, replaced blond mohair wig, fully articulated composition body, new blue satin and lace dress, worn period blue leather shoes, imp mark "30 5 K (over script H) 4," early 20th C, white scratch line each cheek **230.00**

Hertel, Schwab & Co.

9" l, 7" d head circumference, twin character babies, blue sleep eyes, open mouths, two upper teeth, wispy blond tufts of hair, composition bent-limb bodies, matching period long white baby gown, one with pink, one blue ribbon trim, imp marks "152/2/0," early 20th C, price for pair . **635.00**

11" l, 8" d head circumference, Character Baby, bisque head, gray-blue sleep eyes, open/closed mouth, two molded upper teeth and tongue, newer auburn mohair wig, bent-limb composition baby body, period white baby slip, dress, knit sweater, and booties with pompoms, imp "152," early 20th C, paint chips to legs, fingers with repainted areas...... **200.00**

15" h, 140 character, bisque socket head, painted brown eyes, red accent line, feathered brows, closed mouth, accented lips, mohair wig, jointed wood and composition body, straight wrists, white factory chemise, dark green pants, matching cap, cotton socks, and new leather shoes, marked "140/4" on back of head, light rub

Gebruden Heubach, walking doll, 11" h, **$2,000.** *Photo courtesy of McMasters.*

on right cheek, minor repair at neck socket of body, light flaking on right upper leg............. **4,200.00**

20" h, bisque socket head, blue paperweight eyes, feathered brows, painted upper and lower lashes, open mouth with accented lips and six upper teeth, pierced ears, replaced human-hair wig, jointed composition body with straight wrists, separate balls at shoulders, elbows, hips and knees, nicely redressed in pale pink French-style dress, new underclothing, socks and shoes, marks "8/0" on back of head and "Jumeau Medaille d'Or Paris" stamped in blue on lower back, replaced antique paperweight eyes, tiny flake at each earring hole, tiny fleck on upper rim at inside corner of right eye, body has good orig finish with wear at all joints, on toes and heels . **1,100.00**

Heubach, Ernest

12-1/2" h, 399 baby, solid dome painted bisque socket head, brown sleep eyes, single stroke brows, painted upper and lower lashes, closed mouth, lightly molded and painted hair, composition bent-limb baby body, orig multicolored "grass" skirt, marked "Heubach* Koppelsdorf/399*9/0/Germany" on back of head...........**350.00**

21" h, 300 baby, bisque socket head, set brown eyes, feathered brows, painted upper and lower lashes, open mouth, accented lips, four upper teeth, replaced wig, composition bent-limb baby body, antique white long baby dress, lace-trimmed antique baby bonnet, underclothing, diaper, and booties, marked "Heubach * Koppelsdorf/ 300 * 6/Germany" on back of head, arms and legs repainted, cracks in finish under repaint, neck socket touched up, repair on right arm joint and right wrist **275.00**

Heubach, Gebruder, 17" h character, bisque head and shoulder plate, blue intaglio eyes, single stroke brows, open-closed mouth with accent colors, two painted lower teeth, molded and lightly painted hair, kid body with gussets at hips and knees, bisque lower arms, cloth lower legs, antique two-pc boy's outfit with belt, new socks and shoes, marked "5/Germany" on

Hertel, Schwab & Co., Patsy Baby, bisque head, five-piece composition body, 18" h, **$1,400.** *Photo courtesy of McMasters.*

back of shoulder plate, arms replaced, repairs on upper legs **475.00**

Heubach, Koppelsdorf

10-1/2" h, Screamer, bisque head, painted hair, painted blue intaglio eyes, open-closed screaming mouth, furrowed brow, straight-limb composition toddler body, maroon velvet short overalls, white shirt, imp "7684," sunburst mark **690.00**

24" h, bisque head, blue sleep eyes with lashes, open mouth, brown human-hair wig, fully jointed wood and composition body, period underwear, new print cotton dress, imp mark "312," early 20th C, rub on cheek **220.00**

Horsman, 15" h, toddler, composition socket head, brown sleep eyes, single stroke brows, painted upper and lower lashes, mohair wig, jointed composition toddler body, straight wrists, diagonal hip joints, old white organdy dress with lace trim, underclothing, socks, high button boots, marked "E.I.H./Co." on back **650.00**

Ideal

13" h, Shirley Temple, composition head, hazel sleep eyes with real lashes, painted lower lashes, feathered brows, open mouth, six upper teeth, orig mohair wig in orig set, five-pc composition body, orig plaid "Bright Eyes" dress, underwear combination, replaced socks, orig shoes, marked "13/ Shirley Temple" on head, "Shirley Temple/13" on back **700.00**

20" h, Shirley Temple, composition head, hazel sleep eyes, real lashes, painted lower lashes, feathered brows, open mouth, six upper teeth, molded tongue, orig mohair wig in orig set, five-pc composition child body, orig dotted organdy dress with pleats from "Curly Top" movie, orig underwear, combination socks and shoes, marks: "20/Shirley Temple/Co. Ideal/N & T Co." on back of head, "Shirley Temple/20*" on back, and "Genuine/Shirley Temple/registered U.S. Pat. Off/Ideal Nov & Toy Co./ Made in U.S.A." on dress tag **500.00**

28" h, Lori Martin, vinyl socket head, blue sleep eyes with real lashes, painted lower lashes, feathered brows, closed smiling mouth, rooted hair vinyl body jointed at waist, shoulders, hips, and ankles, orig tagged clothing, plaid shirt, jeans, vinyl boots with horses, marked "© Metro Goldwyn Mayer Inc./Mfg by/Ideal Toy Corp/80" on back of head, "© Ideal Toy Corp./6-30-5" on back, "National Velvet's/Lori Martin/© Metro Goldwyn Mayer, Inc./All Rights Reserved" on shirt tag **550.00**

Jumeau

9" h, Great Ladies series, bisque socket head, blue paperweight eyes, single stroke brows, painted upper and lower lashes, closed mouth, orig mohair wig, five-pc composition body, painted flat black shoes, orig white brocade gown with gold "diamond" jewelry, orig underclothing, marked "221/3/0" on back of head, "fabrication/Jumeau/Paris/Made in France" on front of paper tag, "Marie-Louise/2, Femme de/ Napoleon Ier/Epogue 1810" hand written on back of paper tag," **475.00**

9-1/2" h, Bebe, bisque head, blue paperweight eyes, closed mouth, pierced ears, blue earrings, orig cork pate and blond mohair wig, fully articulated wood and composition body, orig stringing, undressed, orig Jumeau Bebe marked brown leather shoes,

France, c1890, string loose, paint flaking on lower leg **6,325.00**

14-1/2" h, Portrait Jumeau, bisque socket head, dark brown almond paperweight eyes, multi-stroke brows, painted upper and lower lashes, closed mouth with accented lips, pierced ears, replaced human-hair wig, jointed wood and composition body with separate balls at shoulders and elbows, hips, and knees, straight wrists, well redressed in turquoise silk dress with ecru silk and lace trim, matching bonnet, antique underclothing, new socks and shoes, marked "2/0" on back of head, "Jumeau Medaille d'Or Paris" stamped in blue on lower back, head has been broken and repaired, crack on right forehead to eye, at corner of right eye to below ear, on left forehead down to ear and to crown in back, body finish worn on arms, hands, lower legs, and around neck socket . . **800.00**

18" h, 1907, bisque socket head, blue paperweight eyes, long painted upper and lower lashes, open mouth, accented lips, six upper teeth, pierced ears, replaced mohair wig, jointed wood and composition late-French body, redressed in peach silk French-style dress, white silk

Jumeau, 31" h, bisque head, brown sleep eyes, open mouth, human-hair wig, $2,900. Photo courtesy of McMasters.

bonnet, antique underclothing, old socks and white leather shoes, marked "1907/7" on back of head, light nose rub, small flakes at each earring hole, hands repainted, repairs and wear at knees touched up, right upper arm has paint flaked to wood **1,700.00**

20" h, Bebe, bisque head, brown paperweight eyes, mauve eye shadow, closed mouth, pierced applied ears, orig red Jumeau earrings, imp DEPOSE E.9J, cork pate, orig blond mohair wig, jointed straight wrist, eight-ball composition body marked "Jumeau Medaille d'Or," vintage commercial dress of aqua satin and ecru silk faille, brown leather shoes, marked "E.J., France," c1885, tiny red age line side of nose **5,475.00**

20" h, bisque socket head, blue paperweight eyes, feathered brows, painted upper and lower lashes, open mouth with accented lips and six upper teeth, pierced ears, replaced human-hair wig, jointed composition body with straight wrists, separate balls at shoulders, elbows, hips, and knees, nicely redressed in pale pink French-style dress, new underclothing, socks and shoes, marked "8/0" on back of head, "Jumeau Medaille d'Or Paris" stamped in blue on lower back, replaced antique paperweight eyes, tiny flake at each earring hole, tiny fleck on upper rim at inside corner of right eye, body has good orig finish with wear at all joints, on toes and heels . **1,100.00**

20" h, bisque socket head, large blue paperweight eyes, painted upper and lower lashes, feathered brows, closed mouth, accented lips, pierced ears, replaced human-hair wig, jointed wood and composition Jumeau adult body with jointed wrists, antique ecru and blue dress with lace overlay, new underclothing, black stockings, orig Jumeau shows, " Depose Tete Jumeau Bte. S.G.D.G. 7" on back of head, "Bebe Jumeau/Diplome d'Honneur" on oval label on back, "9/Paris/(bee)/ Depose" on soles of shoes **3,100.00**

Jumeau, bisque head, blue glass sleep eyes, closed mouth, brunette wig, pierced ears, 16-1/2" h, marked "E.D.," $2,600. Photo courtesy of McMasters.

23" h Jumeau, Bebe Soleil box, bisque socket head, blue paperweight eyes, feathered brows, painted upper and lower lashes, open mouth, accented lips, six upper teeth, human-hair wig, jointed wood and composition French body, dressed in factory chemise pants, "Tete Jumeau" stamped in red, "9" incised on back of head, "Bebe due Bon Marche" partial paper label on lower back, "10700" written upside down on upper back, "S.F.B. J. Paris Bebe Soleil Yeux Mobiles Formes Naturelles Entierement Articule" on label on end of box, 2" hairline on right side of forehead, body finish flaking or loose in places, wear on edges of feet, at joints and on hands, box bottom repaired, lid missing **1,400.00**

24" h, bisque socket head, brown paperweight eyes, feathered brows, painted upper and lower lashes, open mouth, accented lips, six upper teeth, pierced ears, replaced human-hair wig, jointed wood and composition French body, redressed in brown velvet and beige dress with lace trim,

straw bonnet trimmed with flowers, antique underclothing, and antique high-button baby shoes, marked "X/9 on back of head," V-shaped hairline on back of head above mark, small repair on right knee and left toes, hands repainted, finish of right hand rough, neck socket of body lined with kid, normal wear to joints of body **1,100.00**

26" h, Tete Jumeau, bisque socket head, large blue paperweight eyes, heavy feathered brows, long painted upper and lower lashes, closed mouth, accented lips, pierced ears, human-hair wig, jointed wood and composition body with straight wrists, orig ribbon dress, matching hat, orig underclothing, socks, and shoes, marked "Depose Tete Jumeau 12" and artist marks on back of head, "12/Paris/bee/Depose" on bottom of shoes **3,000.00**

Kamkins, 19" h, girl, cloth, molded face with painted features, blue eyes, orig brown mohair wig, cloth body and limbs, blue cotton dress, orig undergarments, purple Kamkins stamp mark on back of head, early 20th C, some soil and wear on face . . **1,150.00**

Kammer & Reinhardt

10" h, 115A baby, bisque socket head, blue sleep eyes, feathered brows, painted upper and lower lashes, closed mouth, orig mohair wig, five-pc composition baby body, antique-style white baby dress, slip, lace-trimmed panties, eyelet bonnet, marked "1/K*R/ Simon & Halbig/115A/30" on back of head, wear to orig finish, arms mostly repainted, touch-up around neck socket, on toes, and feet **1,300.00**

11" h, baby, bisque socket head, brown sleep eyes, feathered brows, painted upper and lower lashes, open mouth, two upper teeth, spring tongue, orig mohair wig, bent limb composition baby body, antique white baby dress, underclothing, marked "K*R/28" on back of head, "W" at crown in front, few flakes off body on lower front of torso and back of neck socket, normal wear at joints, light wear on fingers and toes, arms repainted **350.00**

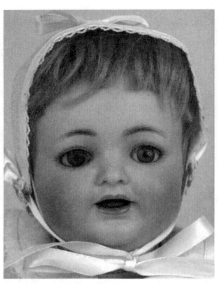

*K * R Simon & Halbig, bisque socket head, open mouth with two teeth and tongue, blue sleep eyes, blond human hair wig, five-piece, bent leg body, incised "K (star) R Simon & Halbig 126 36," 15-1/2" h, $350. Photo courtesy of James D. Julia, Inc.*

18" h, dark brown bisque socket head, brown sleep eyes, feathered brows, open mouth, four upper teeth, pierced ears, antique human hair wig, jointed wood and composition brown body, antique white dress, antique underclothing,

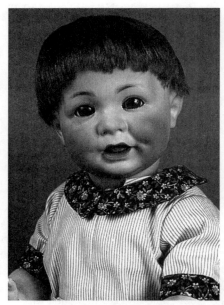

*K * R, 116/A Baby, 16" h, bisque socket head, boyish haircut, brown paperweight eyes, open mouth with tongue, toddler body, $1,750. Photo courtesy of McMaster Harris Auction Co.*

socks, oilcloth shoes, marked "S & H, K * R 50" on head, minor wig pulls, light nose rub **1,150.00**

18-1/2" h, 126 toddler, bisque socket head, blue sleep eyes, feathered brows, open mouth, two upper teeth, wobble tongue, old mohair wig, jointed wood and composition body with diagonal hip joints, white dress, replaced socks and shoes, marked "K*R Simon & Halbig 126 42" on back of head **575.00**

19" h, 115/A character toddler, bisque head, brown sleep eyes, closed pouty mouth, reddish-blond caracul wig, side-jointed composition toddler body, red and green plush jester's costume, also orig pink gingham outfit, imp "K*R Simon & Halbig 115/A, 48," c1910 . . . . **4,320.00**

Kestner

10" h, 150, bisque head with stiff neck, brown sleep eyes, feathered brows, painted upper and lower lashes, open mouth with four upper teeth, orig blond mohair wig, all bisque body jointed at shoulders and hips, mold and painted blue shirred socks and black one-strap shoes, antique white dress, imp "150.5" in back of head and inside upper arms **575.00**

12" h, pouty child, bisque head, brown sleep eyes, closed mouth, characteristic fat roll on back of neck, no pate, new strawberry-blond human-hair wig, early classic straight wrist mitt-fingered body, pink china silk dress, imp "7," late 19th C, cinder to left of mouth **2,070.00**

13-1/2" h, character, bisque head, blue sleep eyes, open mouth, two upper teeth, replaced blond mohair wig, fully articulated Kestner body, pink cotton print dress, extra green print dress, imp "143," red stamp "Germany," one finger broken **635.00**

14-1/2" h, 257 baby, bisque socket head, blue sleep eyes, feathered brows, painted upper and lower lashes, open mouth, accented lips, two upper teeth, spring tongue, synthetic wig, composition Kestner baby body, antique-style long baby dress and bonnet, slip, diaper and new booties, marked "Made in/Germany/J.D.K./257/Germany/35" on back of head, "Made in

Germany" stamped in red on upper back, real lashes missing, worn body finish, moisture damage on lower right near torso and back of right arm **600.00**

15" h, 154, bisque shoulder head, brown sleep eyes, feathered brows, painted upper and lower lashes, open mouth, four molded upper teeth, orig human-hair wig over plaster pate, kid body, bisque lower arms, gussets at elbows, pin joints at hips and knees, possibly orig dress with embroidered design, underclothing, socks and shoes, marked "154 dep. 5" on back of head, minor inherent firing lines on side seams of head, soiled body shows general wear, repair at right shoulder of body **375.00**

23" h, Hilda, solid dome bisque socket head, blue sleep eyes, feathered brows, painted upper and lower lashes, open mouth, accented lips, two upper teeth, lightly molded and painted blond hair composition bent-limb Kestner baby body, antique white baby dress, matching slip, diaper, new pink knit booties, antique baby bonnet, marked "Hilda/C/J.D.K. Jr. 1914/ges.gesch.N. 1070/made in 18 Germany" on back of head **4,000.00**

Kestner, 128, 19" h, bisque socket head, brown paperweight eyes, brunette wig, multi-stroke brows, closed mouth, antique dress, **$2,100.** *Photo courtesy of McMaster Harris Auction Co.*

32" h, 164, bisque socket head, blue sleep eyes, molded and feathered brows, painted upper and lower lashes, open mouth, shapely accented lips, four upper teeth, skin wig, jointed wood and composition Kestner body, faded dark blue velvet sailor suit, white shirt, old socks and shoes, marked "M1/2 made in Germany 16 1/2/164" on back of head, "Excelsior/Germany/7" stamped in red on right lower back, body has orig finish with light wear, normal wear at joints, right finger repaired **1,200.00**

Kley & Hahn, 11-1/2" h, 525 Baby, solid dome bisque socket head, blue sleep eyes, feathered brows, painted upper and lower lashes, open-closed mouth, lightly molded and brush stroked hair, composition baby body, antique baby dress, marked "4/Germany/K&H (in banner)/525" on back of head, repainted **275.00**

Knickerbocker, 11" h, Mickey Mouse, cloth swivel head, white facial, black oilcloth pie eyes, large black nose, painted open/closed smiling mouth with accent lines, black felt ears, un-jointed black cloth body, orange hands with three fingers and a thumb, red oversized composition feet, black rubber tail, orig shorts with two buttons on front and back, some fading . **650.00**

Konig & Wernicke, Germany, early 20th C

17" h, character toddler, bisque head, brown sleep eyes, open mouth, two upper teeth, tongue, orig dark brown mohair wig, fully articulated side hip-joint composition toddler body marked "Made in Germany," period cotton sailor outfit, blue pants, white overblouse, white fabric shoes, imp "Made in Germany 99/7," some wear to finish of limbs, repaint to hands **750.00**

27" l, 16-1/2" d head circumference, character baby, bisque head, early 20th century, blue sleep eyes, open mouth, two upper teeth, wobble tongue, orig brown mohair wig, bent limb composition baby body, red circle stamp "K & W," minor wear **815.00**

Kruse, Kathe

13" h, Schlenkerchen, all-stockinette, pressed and oil-painted double-seam head, painted

Kathe Kruse, Rose X, painted facial features, original clothing and tags, 14" h, $1,050. Photo courtesy of McMasters.

features, brown hair, shaded brown painted eyes with eyeliner, light upper lashes, closed mouth in smiling expression, cloth neck ring, stockinette covered, padded armature frame body, mitten hands, rounded feet, unlaundered off-white undergarments, soles stamped "Kathe Kruse, Germany," c1922, paint rub tip of nose, soil
...................5,475.00

14" h, Rose X, oil-painted swivel head with single seam in back, painted hair, painted brown eyes with highlights, single-stroke brows, closed mouth, cloth body, stitched fingers, jointed hips, orig pink linen dress and kerchief, blue print jacket, nylon teddy, orig socks and shoes, marked "Kathe Kruse 1687" on left foot, "Made in Germany US Zone Original gekleidet, Kathe Kruse Rose X Original gekleidet" on paper tag around neck, "Kathe Kruse Germany Art Dolls Unique" on paper wrist tag 1,050.00

Lenci

8" h, Mascotte, pressed felt swivel head, painted brown "surprise" eyes to side, single-stroke brows, painted upper lashes, open-closed two-tone mouth, orig red mohair wig in braids, cloth body with felt arms and legs, orig blue and white polka dot nylon dress, white felt collar, red felt belt, orig one-pc underwear, red felt sandals, light display soil, front of dress faded
.....................150.00

12" h, girl, pressed felt swivel head, painted brown side-glancing eyes, painted upper lashes, closed mouth with two-tone lips, orig mohair wig, cloth torso, felt limbs, orig pink felt dress with blue trim, blue felt coat with matching hat, orig underclothing, socks, blue felt shoes, marked "2" on bottom of right foot, "Lenci/Made in Italy" on cloth label inside coat.....400.00

28" h, lady, "Mary Pickford" felt face, light gray-blue painted eyes to right, long nose, closed mouth, long bare felt arms, classic Lenci fingers, white and green organdy summer frock, felt wide-brimmed bonnet, all trimmed with felt flowers and ruffles, silk stockings, pale green felt shoes with felt flowers, orig Lenci tag sewn to dress, c1930, small stain back of skirt
...................1,840.00

Limbach, 23" h, character, bisque socket head, blue sleep eyes with real lashes, painted upper and lower lashes, open mouth, accented lips, six upper teeth, human-hair wig, jointed wood and composition body, new white lacy dress, underclothing, new socks and shoes, marked "W/crown/17 72 in shamrock/Limbach" on back of head, two right fingers and three left fingers repaired, finish flaking around neck socket of body, cracks in finish on side seams of torso, wear at all sockets on torso 625.00

Madame Alexander

14" h, Marme from the *Little Women* Series, hard plastic head and body, gray sleep eyes, closed mouth, dark brown wig in snood, gray and pink print dress with orig tags, organdy shawl, shoes and socks, c1955 ....200.00

17" h, Maggie Walker, hard plastic head, blue sleep eyes with real lashes, painted lower lashes, feathered brows, closed mouth, orig wig, five-pc hard plastic body with walking mechanism, orig blue and white taffeta dress, white collar and cuffs, white taffeta slip and panties, orig stockings, black center snap shoes, marked "Madame Alexander/All Rights Reserved/New York U.S.A." on dress tag 700.00

18" h, Sweet Violet, hard plastic head, blue sleep eyes with real lashes, painted lower lashes, feathered brows, closed mouth, orig synthetic wig, hard plastic body jointed at shoulders, elbows, wrists, hips, and knees, walking mechanism, orig tagged blue cotton dress, underclothing, flowered bonnet, white gloves, black side-snap shoes, carrying orig pink Alexander hat box, marked "Alexander" on back of head, "Madame Alexander/All Rights Reserved/New York, U.S.A.," c1954, unplayed-with condition comb and curlers missing...............1,700.00

21" h, Cissy, #2099, hard plastic, blue sleep eyes, closed mouth, orig synthetic wig, hard plastic body jointed at hips and knees, vinyl arms jointed at elbows, orig tagged brocade gown with pale blue sash, jeweled tiara, earrings, long gloves, and, jeweled bracelets, marked "Alexander" on back of head "Cissy by Madame Alexander" on dress tag, c1955
....................600.00

23" h, Special Girl, composition head, composition shoulder plate, blue sleep eyes with real lashes, painted lower lashes, feathered brows, closed mouth, orig human-hair wig in orig set, cloth torso with composition arms and legs, orig pale blue taffeta dress with lace and ribbon trim, attached blue panties, orig socks and center snap shoes, "Madame/Alexander/New York U.S.A." on dress tag
....................750.00

Menjou, Adolph, 32" h, composition shoulder head, painted brown eyes with accent line, molded monocle on right eye, feathered brows, molded and painted mustache, open-closed mouth, seven upper teeth, molded white shirt collar with hole, presumably for a tie, molded and painted hair, excelsior-stuffed cloth body with long limbs, composition white hands as gloves, composition lower legs as socks and shoes, orig black two-pc suit with satin lapels **725.00**

Parian, 24" h, untinted bisque shoulder head, painted blue eyes with red accent line, single stroke brows, closed mouth, pierced ears, molded and painted café au lait hair, molded blue tiara trimmed with gold, molded braid across top, on lower sides, and down middle of back of head, old cloth body with red leather boots as part of leg, new arms by Emma Clear, white dotted Swiss and lace dress, antique underclothing, unmarked, old repair to tiara, body aged **1,900.00**

Petzold, Dora, 16-1/2" h, composition head, painted blue eyes with eye shadow, single-stroke brows, accented nostrils, closed mouth, orig mohair wig, stockinette body stitch-jointed at shoulders and hips, mitten-type hands with stitched fingers, possibly orig white velvet dress with embroidery and lace trim, white teddy, orig socks and marked shoes, marked with girl in circle, "D P/7/7/0" on back of head, girl in circle with "D P" on bottom of shoes **275.00**

Poupee Bois, 17-1/2" h, bisque socket head, bisque shoulder plate, pale blue threaded paperweight eyes, feathered brows, painted upper and lower lashes, closed mouth, pierced ears, orig human hair wig, wooden fashion body articulated at shoulders, elbows, wrists, hips, and knees, swivel joint on upper arms and upper legs, nicely redressed with antique fabric and lace, possibly orig stockings and high button boots, marked "4" on back of head . . **4,400.00**

Poupee Raynal, 19" h, pressed felt swivel head, painted blue eyes, single-stroke brows, painted upper lashes, closed mouth with three-tone lips, orig mohair wig in orig set, five-pc cloth body with stitched fingers, orig light blue organdy dress with pink flower appliqués, matching hat, orig teddy, blue organdy slip, socks, white leather shoes, "Paris" typed on piece of paper pinned to back, unplayed with condition **725.00**

Putnam, Grace

8" h, Bye-Lo Baby, solid dome bisque swivel head, tiny blue sleep eyes, softly blushed brows, painted upper and lower lashes, closed mouth, lightly molded and painted hair, all bisque baby body jointed at shoulders and hips, orig knit pink and white two-pc baby outfit with matching cap, marked "Bye-Lo Baby/©/Germany/G.S. Putnam" on label on chest, "6-20/Copr. By/Grace S. Putnam/Germany" incised on back, "6-20" on hips and right arms, "20" on left arm, chip on right back of neck edge of head, minor firing line behind left ear **525.00**

11" h, 10-1/2" d head circumference Bye-Lo Baby, solid dome bisque head, brown sleep eyes, softly blushed brows, painted upper and lower lashes, closed mouth, lightly molded and painted hair, cloth body with celluloid hands and "frog" legs, redressed in white lace-trimmed baby dress, old baby sweater, slip, diaper, socks, marked "Copr. by/Grace S. Putnam/Made in Germany" on back of head, illegible faint stamp on body, rubs on cheeks, nose, and back of head, light kiln dust on head **425.00**

21" h, 17" d head circumference, Bye-Lo Baby, solid dome bisque head, blue sleep eyes, softly blushed brows, painted upper and lower lashes, closed mouth, lightly molded and painted hair, cloth body with "frog" legs, celluloid hands, orig white Bye-Lo dress, slip, and flannel diaper, marked "Copr. By/Grace S. Putnam/Made in Germany" on back of head, turtle mark on wrists of celluloid hands, light bur on right cheek, body lightly soiled and aged **600.00**

Recknagel, 9" h, character, bisque socket head, tiny painted blue squinty eyes, single-stroke brows, open-closed mouth, five painted upper teeth, four lower teeth, molded tongue, molded

Poupee Bois, 17-1/2" h, bisque socket head on bisque shoulder plate, blue paperweight eyes, $4,400. Photo courtesy of McMaster Harris Auction Co.

*K * R, 116/A Baby, 16" h, bisque socket head, boyish haircut, brown paperweight eyes, open mouth with tongue, toddler body, $1,750. Photo courtesy of McMaster Harris Auction Co.*

and painted short hair with molded pink bow, five-pc chubby composition body, crude unpainted torso, molded and painted socks and shoes, redressed in pink lace-trimmed dress, matching hair ribbon, lace pants, marked "R 57 A/8/0" on back of head, light dust in bisque, light wear on orig body finish .. **675.00**

S & Q, 28" h, 201 baby, bisque socket head, set brown eyes, feathered brows, painted upper and lower lashes, open mouth, two upper teeth, molded tongue, mohair wig, composition baby body, navy blue velvet boy's shorts, jacket, and matching hat, white shirt, stockings, white baby shoes, marked "+ 201 SQ" (superimposed) Germany 14" on back of head **700.00**

Schmidt, Bruno, 22" h, 2042, solid dome bisque socket head, painted brown eyes, two-tone single-stroke brows, open-closed mouth, accented lips, brush-stroked hair, jointed composition body, redressed in maroon velour two-pc suit, ecru satin shirt with lace trim, black cotton socks, new black shoes, marked "5/B.S.W. in heart/2042" on back of head, "Handwerck" stamped in red in middle of lower back **1,500.00**

Schmidt, Franz, 33-1/2" h, child, bisque head, open mouth, brown glass eyes set stationary, pierced ears, replaced long blond human-hair wig, chunky fully jointed composition body, period undergarments, strong blue silk twill dress, imp "S & C 7 1/2 85," late 19th/early 20th C, light soil, repairs, some repaint **1,035.00**

Schoenau & Hoffmeister, 13-1/2" h, Masquerade set, bisque socket head, set brown eyes, single stroke brows, painted upper and lower lashes, open mouth, four upper teeth, antique mohair wig, five-pc composition body, walking mechanism, orig pastel dress with pale green ribbon trim, orig gauze-type underclothing, socks, leather shoes with black pompons, marked "4000 5/0/S PB (in star) H 10" on back of head, "F" on back of legs, "Germany" stamped on bottom of shoes, tied in red cardboard box with two lace-trimmed compartments, blue pierrot costume brimmed with black, white, and ruffled collar, matching cone-shaped hat, black face mask with lace trim, light rub on nose **525.00**

Schoenhut

12" h, composition head, painted blue eyes, lightly molded and single-stroke brows, closed mouth, molded and painted hair, five-pc composition body with bent right arm, pale pink dotted Swiss dress, panties, replaced socks and shoes, marked "Schoenhut/Toys/Made in/U.S.A." on label on back, light wear on fingers, chipped left first finger **1,300.00**

15" h, Tootsie Wootsie, wooden character socket head, brown intaglio eyes, feathered brows, open-closed mouth, two upper teeth, molded tongue, old mohair wig, spring-jointed wooden body with joints at shoulders, elbows, wrists, hips, knees, and ankles, redressed in copy of Schoenhut two-pc sailor suit, new socks and tie shoes, illegible partial imp mark on head, "Schoenhut Doll/Pat. Jan 17, '11, U.S.A. & Foreign Countries" imp on back, repaint on face, touch up, normal wear at points, paint worn and flaking on legs and feet, hands repainted **1,500.00**

19" h, 19/308 girl, wooden socket head, brown intaglio eyes, feathered brow, closed mouth with excellent modeling, orig mohair wig, spring-jointed wooden body jointed at shoulders, elbows, wrists, hips, knees, and ankles, white dress with red dots in Schoenhut style, slip, knit union suit, replaced cotton socks and red flocked shoes, marked "Schoenhut Doll/Pat. Jan 17th 1911/U.S.A." on oval label on back, very light touch up on left cheek, nose, edge of lips, craze lines on front of lower neck, light crazing on right cheek and outer corner of left eye, body has "suntan" color with normal wear at joints and light overall soil, few flakes off ankles **450.00**

Schoenhut & Hoffmeister, 20" h, 13-1/2" d head circumference, character baby, bisque head, blue sleep eyes with lashes, hint of smile, open mouth, 2 upper teeth, pointy chin, orig dark brown mohair wig, bent-limb composition baby body, white cotton slip, imp "SHPB" in a star, "5, Germany," early 20th C, white spot back of head at rim. **325.00**

S.F.B.J.

11" h, 301, bisque socket head, blue sleep eyes with real lashes, open mouth, 4 painted upper teeth,

Simon & Halbig, #939, bisque socket head, blue paperweight eyes, 17-1/2" h, $2,700. Photo courtesy of McMaster Harris Auction Co.

pierced ears, human-hair wig, jointed wood and composition body, jointed wrists, antique white lace dress and bonnet, marked "S.F.B.J./301/Paris/1" on back of head, "2" incised between shoulders, "2" on bottom of feet, good original body finish .. **600.00**

11-1/2" h, 60 Bluette, bisque socket head, blue sleep eyes with real lashes, feathered brows, painted lower lashes, open mouth with four upper teeth, replaced human hair wig, jointed wood and composition body with jointed wrists, pale green silk dress, oversized light green straw hat, marked "D/S.F.B.J./60/Paris/8/0/ on back of head, "Fabrication Francaise/SFBJ/Paris" in colorful round label on back, "2" imp between shoulders .. **1,025.00**

17" h, 226, solid dome bisque socket head, blue "jewel" eyes, single-stroke brows, painted upper and lower lashes, open-closed mouth, molded and painted hair, orig finish wood and composition French toddler body with diagonal hip joints, old white top, sweater, maroon velvet pants, new black socks and shoes, marked "S.F.B.J./226/Paris/6" on back of

head, flaking, normal wear at joints
· · · · · · · · · · · · · · · · · · 1,100.00

Steiner

17-1/2" h, Gigoteur, bisque head, blue threaded paperweight eyes with blush over eyes, delicate feathered brows, painted upper and lower lashes, open mouth and accented lips, four upper and three lower teeth, orig blond mohair wig, papier-mâché torso with walking and crying mechanism, kid covering on lower torso, replaced composition arms, kid-covered upper legs, wax-over composition lower legs, possibly orig white openwork and lace dress, antique underclothing, socks and white leather shoes, unmarked, worn torso, seams taped, kid covering on lower torso and upper legs is deteriorating on left leg, arms replaced, limited movement in legs
· · · · · · · · · · · · · · · · · · 1,050.00

18" h, Figure B, bisque socket head, blue eyes made to sleep with lever left back of head, feathered brows, painted upper and lower lashes, blush over eyes, open smiling mouth, seven upper and seven lower teeth, pierced ears, human-hair wig, jointed composition Steiner body with jointed wrists, torso cut for (non-working) crier, pale blue silk dress with lace trim, matching hat,

Simon & Halbig, 1078, bisque, paperweight eyes, open mouth, 11-1/2" h, $875. Photo courtesy of McMasters.

underclothing, socks and old shoes, marked "Figure B No 2/Steiner Bte S.G.D.G./Paris" on back of head, "Bebe Steiner/Le Petit Parisien" purple stamp on left hip, orig body finish has light wear on lower arms and hands and lower legs, normal wear at joints
· · · · · · · · · · · · · · · · · · 2,900.00

23" h, Figure A, bisque socket head, large blue paperweight eyes, feathered brows, painted upper and lower lashes, closed mouth, pierced ears, orig mohair wig, orig cardboard pate, jointed composition body, jointed wrists, dark brown and beige French-style dress made with antique fabric, antique underclothing, beige/black-striped bonnet, brown cotton socks, brown shoes, marked "J. Steiner/Bte S.G.D.G./Paris/Fire A 15" on back of head, small triangular piece broken out at rim on left front and repaired, hairline to corner of left eye, body repainted, right thumb repaired · · · · 2,000.00

24" h, Figure C, bisque socket head, blue paperweight eyes, blush over eyes, feathered brows, painted upper and lower lashes, closed mouth with accented lips, pierced ears, antique human hair wig, jointed wood and composition French body, jointed wrists, pink silk dress made of antique fabric, underclothing, and straw bonnet with flower trim, new socks and shoes, marked "Figure C No. 3/J. Steiner Bte SGDG/Paris" on back of head, rub on nose, few small flakes at each earring hole, couple small flakes edge of left ear, small flake at edge of cut for eye mechanism, replaced antique paperweight eyes· · · · · · 1,600.00

Terri Lee

12" h, Buddy Lee, hard plastic head with stiff neck, eyes painted to side, single-stroke brows, painted upper lashes, closed mouth, molded and painted hair, hard plastic body jointed at shoulders only, molded and painted black boots, orig Phillips 66 suit with labeled shirt and pants, black imitation-leather belt, marked "Buddy Lee" on back, "Union Made/Lee/Sanforized" on label on back of pants, "Phillips/66" on label on front of shirt · · · 215.00

16" h, bride, hard plastic head, painted brown eyes, single-stroke brows, painted upper and lower lashes, closed mouth, orig brunette wig, five-pc hard plastic body, orig tagged bride dress, matching veil, panties, satin shoes, marked "Terri Lee" on back and dress tag, accompanied by nine orig outfits in a trunk, including yellow Southern Belle with black shoes, Girl Scout uniform with brown and white shoes, nurse uniform with white shoes, tagged pants outfit with shirt, tagged pajamas with rabbit slippers, sweater, beret, shirt, blouse; school dress with pinafore, cowgirl costume with gauntlets and boots, hat missing, also booklets and papers, as well as extra accessories, unplayed with condition · · · · · · · · · · · · 2,400.00

16" h, Terri Lee, hard plastic head, oversized painted brown eyes, single-stroke brows, long painted upper and lower lashes, closed mouth, synthetic wig, five-pc hard

Terri Lee, hard plastic head, painted brown eyes, wig in original style, five-piece hard plastic body, red plaid outfit, 16" h, $500. Photo courtesy of McMaster Harris Auction Co.

Tete Jumeau, 20" h, bisque socket head, blue paperweight eyes, brunette hair, natural linen outfit with red and white trim, large hair bow, $4,300. Photo courtesy of McMaster Harris Auction Co.

plastic body jointed at shoulders and hips, orig yellow Evening Formal, #3570D orig socks and shoes, long white coat, #3690A, matching hat, 1954, marked "Terri Lee" on back, Terri Lee tag on coat **475.00**

18" Connie Lynn, hard plastic head, blue sleep eyes with real lashes, single-stroke brows, painted lower lashes at corners of eyes, closed mouth, orig skin wig, hard plastic baby body, orig two-pc pink baby outfit, plastic panties, orig socks and white baby shoes, Terri Lee Nursery Registration Form and three Admission Cards to Terri Lee Hospital, Connie Lynn tag on clothing, orig box, unplayed with condition.............. **625.00**

Unis France, 9-1/2" h, 60, bisque socket head, light blue sleep eyes, single stroke brows, open mouth with 4 upper teeth, orig mohair wig, crude five-pc composition body, dressed in orig ethnic costume of Pont-l'Abbe in Brittany, France, marked "Unis/France/71 60 140/11/0" on back of head **175.00**

Vogue, Ginny, Red Riding Hood, hard plastic, elastic strung, painted lashes, blue eyes in downcast position, strong cheek color, side-part blond hair, red

polka dot dress, red suede-like cape and hat, red straw basket, red shoes, white socks, orig hinged lid pink box #52, illegible Gilchrest's price tag, c1952 .... **490.00**

Walker, Izannah, 18" h, oil cloth, painted features, brown eyes with highlights, pink mouth and cheek coloring, brown hair, two long curls in front of applied ears, four curls down her back onto shoulders, cloth body, oil-painted hands, stockings stitched on, gray-green plaid silk taffeta dress, blue leather shoes, carries period red leather strap slip-on ice skates, Rhode Island, c1870, some paint wear, rubs **24,150.00**

Wax, unmarked, 18" h, reinforced poured-wax shoulder head, set blue glass eyes, multi-stroke brows, painted upper and lower lashes, closed smiling mouth, pierced ears, orig mohair wig, cloth body, wax-over composition lower arms and lower legs, antique red/white gingham dress, orig underclothing, socks and leather shoes, color worn on lips, eyelashes and brows, minor crack in wax on right front of shoulder plate, cracks on right leg, body is aged, soiled, and repaired **475.00**

Wislizenus, Adolph, 18" h, girl, bisque socket head, brown sleep eyes, feathered brows, painted upper and lower lashes, open mouth, accented

Unis France, bisque socket head, open mouth, blue sleep eyes, replaced auburn human hair wig, partially redressed in old clothing. Impressed "Unis, France 71 149 251 9," eyes possibly replaced, chipping to body, 20-1/2" h, $1,100. Photo courtesy of James D. Julia, Inc.

lips, pierced ears, replaced human-hair wig, jointed composition body with orig finish, possibly orig clothing, white low-waisted dress, antique underclothing, socks and shoes marked "8," blue velvet coat and matching hat with ribbon trim, marked "8/A.W./Germany/6" on back of head, "46" stamped in red on bottom of feet **550.00**

DOORSTOPS

History: Doorstops became popular in the late 19th century. They are either flat or three dimensional and were made out of a variety of different materials, such as cast iron, bronze, or wood. Hubley, a leading toy manufacturer, made many examples.

All prices listed are for excellent original paint unless otherwise noted. Original paint and condition greatly influence the price of a doorstop. To get top money, the original paint on a piece must be close to mint condition. Chipping of paint, paint loss, and wear reduce the value. Repainting severely reduces value and eliminates a good deal of the piece's market value, thereby reducing its value. A broken piece has little value to none.

Adviser: Craig Dinner.

Reproduction Alert: Reproductions are proliferating as prices on genuine doorstops continue to rise. A reproduced piece generally is slightly smaller than the original unless an original mold is used. The overall casting of reproductions is not as smooth as on the originals. Reproductions also lack the detail apparent in originals, including the appearance of the painted areas. Any bright orange rusting is strongly indicative of a new piece. Beware. If it looks too good to be true, it usually is.

Notes: Pieces described here contain at least 80 percent or more of the original paint and are in very good condition. Repainting drastically reduces price and desirability. Poor original paint is preferred over repaint.

All listings are cast-iron and flat-back castings unless otherwise noted.

Doorstops marked with an asterisk are currently being reproduced.

Bear, 15" h, holding and looking at honey pot, brown fur, black highlights **1,500.00**

Bellhop, 8-7/8" h, blue uniform, with orange markings, brown base, hands at side **300.00**

Bowl, 7" x 7", green-blue, natural colored fruit, sgd "Hubley 456". **125.00**

Boy, 10-5/8" h, wearing diapers, directing traffic, police hat, red scarf, brown dog at side **665.00**

Caddie, 8" h, carrying brown and tan bag, white, brown, knickers, red jacket* **725.00**

Cat
8" h, black, red ribbon and bow around neck, on pillow* **155.00**
10-3/4" h, licking paw, white cat with black markings, marked "Sculpture Metal Studios" **425.00**
13-5/8" h, reaching, full figure, two-piece hollow casting, green eyes, off-white body **675.00**

Child, 17" h, reaching, naked, short brown curly hair, flesh color .. **1,375.00**

Clipper ship, 5-1/4" h, full sails, American flag on top mast, wave base, two rubber stoppers, sgd "CJO" . **65.00**

Cosmos Flower Basket, 17-3/4" h, blue and pink flowers, white vase, black base, Hubley **1,350.00**

Cottage, 8-5/8" l, 5-3/4" h, Cape type, blue roof, flowers, fenced garden, bath, sgd "Eastern Specialty Mfg Co. 14" **150.00**

Dancer, 8-7/8" h, Art Deco couple doing Charleston, pink dress, black tux, red and black base, "FISH" on front, sgd "Hubley 270" **1,475.00**

Dog
7" h, three puppies in basket, natural colors, sgd "Copyright 1932 M. Rosenstein, Lancaster, PA, USA" **350.00**
8" x 7-1/2", Beagle pup, full figure, cream with darker markings **685.00**
9" h, Boston Bull, full figure, facing left, black, tan markings ...**175.00**
10-1/2" x 3-1/2", St. Bernard, lying down, full figure, cream with brown markings, Hubley **775.00**

Two iron Boston Bulldogs: left, repainted black and white, $95; right, original paint, $175. Photo courtesy of Joy Luke Auctions.

14" x 9", Sealyham, full figure, Hubley, cream and tan dog, red collar................. **675.00**

Dolly, 9-1/2" h, pink bow in blond hair, holding doll in blue dress, white apron, yellow dress, Hubley **365.00**

Doorman in Livery, 12" h, twin men, worn orig paint, marked "Fish," Hubley **1,760.00**

Drum major, 12-5/8" h, full figure, ivory pants, red hat with feather, yellow baton in right hand, left hand on waist, sq base................... **225.00**

Duck, 7-1/2" h, white, green bush and grass **335.00**

Elephant, 14" h, palm trees, early 20th C, very minor paint wear .. **335.00**

Fisherman, 6-1/4" h, standing at wheel, hand over eyes, rain gear **185.00**

Frog, 3" h, full figure, sitting, yellow and green **50.00**

Giraffe, 20-1/4" h, tan, brown spots, squared off lines to casting .. **2,850.00**

Golfer, 10" h, overhand swing, hat and ball on ground, Hubley* **475.00**

Halloween Girl, 13-3/4" h, 9-3/4" l, white hat, flowing cape, holding orange jack-o-lantern with red cutout eyes, nose, and mouth* **2,000.00**

Indian chief, 9-3/4" h, orange and tan headdress, yellow pants, and blue stripes, red patches at ankles, green grass, sgd "A. A. Richardson," copyright 1928............. **295.00**

Lighthouse, 14" h, green rocks, black path, white lighthouse, red window and door trim................... **385.00**

Mammy
8-1/2" h, full figure, Hubley, red dress, white apron, polka-dot bandanna on head **225.00**
10" h, full figure, one piece hollow casting, white scarf and apron, dark blue dress, red kerchief on head* **325.00**

Monkey
8-1/2" h, 4-5/8" w wrap-around tail, full figure, brown and tan .. **265.00**
14-3/8" h, hand reaching up, brown, tan, and white **650.00**

Old Mill, 6-1/4" h, brown log mill, tan roof, white patch, green shrubs . **425.00**

Owl, 9-1/2" h, sits on books, sgd "Eastern Spec Co" **285.00**

Pan, 7" h, with flute, sitting on mushroom, green outfit, red hat and sleeves, green grass base..... **165.00**

Peasant woman, 8-3/4" h, blue dress, black hair, fruit basket on head . **250.00**

Penguin, 10" h, full figure, facing sideways, black, white chest, top hat

Cat, reaching, full figure, two-piece hollow casting, green eyes, off-white body, 13-5/8" h, $675. Photos courtesy of Craig Dinner.

Dutch Boy, full figure, hands in pockets, blue suit and hat, red belt and collar, brown shoes, blond hair, 11" h, $425.

Mammy, full figure, one-piece hollow casting, white scarf and apron, dark blue dress, red kerchief on head, 10" h, $325.

Turkey, unmarked Bradley & Hubbard, old black, red, silver, and white painted decorated, areas of repaint, 12-1/4" h, $1,375.

and bow tie, yellow feet and beak, unsgd Hubley **435.00**

Policeman, 9-1/2" h, leaning on red fire hydrant, blue uniform and titled hat, comic character face, tan base, "Safety First" on front **725.00**

Prancing horse, 11" h, scrolled and molded base, "Greenlees Glasgow" imp on base, cast iron **175.00**

Quail, 7-1/4" h, two brown, tan, and yellow birds, green, white, and yellow grass, "Fred Everett" on front, sgd "Hubley 459"* **365.00**

Rabbit, 8-1/8" h, eating carrot, red sweater, brown pants **350.00**

Rooster, 13" h, red comb, black and brown tail **360.00**

Squirrel, 9" h, sitting on stump eating nut, brown and tan **275.00**

Storybook

4-1/2" h, Humpty Dumpty, full figure, sgd "661" **375.00**

7-3/4" h, Little Miss Muffett, sitting on mushroom, blue dress, blond hair **175.00**

9-1/2" h, Little Red Riding Hood, basket at side, red cape, tan dress with blue pattern, blond hair, sgd "Hubley" **450.00**

12-1/2" h, Huckleberry Finn, floppy hat, pail, stick, Littco Products label **475.00**

Sunbonnet Girl, 9" h, pink dress **235.00**

Whistler, 20-1/4" h, boy, hands in tan knickers, yellow striped baggy shirt, sgd "B & H" **2,750.00**

Windmill, 6-3/4" h, ivory, red roof, house at side, green base* **115.00**

Woman, 11" h, flowers and shawl* **285.00**

Zinnias, 11-5/8" h, multicolored flowers, blue and black vase, sgd "B & H" **185.00**

DRESDEN/MEISSEN

History:
Augustus II, Elector of Saxony and King of Poland, founded the Royal Saxon Porcelain Manufactory in the Albrechtsburg, Meissen, in 1710. Johann Frederick

Boettger, an alchemist, and Tschirnhaus, a nobleman, experimented with kaolin from the Dresden area to produce porcelain. By 1720, the factory produced a whiter hard-paste porcelain than that from the Far East. The factory experienced its golden age from the 1730s to the 1750s under the leadership of Samuel Stolzel, kiln master, and Johann Gregor Herold, enameler.

The Meissen factory was destroyed and looted by forces of Frederick the Great during the Seven Years' War (1756-1763). It was reopened, but never achieved its former greatness.

In the 19th century, the factory reissued some of its earlier forms. These later wares are called "Dresden" to differentiate them from the earlier examples. Further, there were several other porcelain factories in the Dresden region and their products also are grouped under the "Dresden" designation.

Marks: Many marks were used by the Meissen factory. The first was a pseudo-Oriental mark in a square. The famous crossed swords mark was adopted in 1724. A small dot between the hilts was used from 1763 to 1774, and a star between the hilts from 1774 to 1814. Two modern marks are swords with a hammer and sickle and swords with a crown.

For more information, see this book.

Dresden

Compote, 14-1/4" h, figural, shaped pierced oval bowl with applied florets, support stems mounted with two figures of children, printed marks, late 19th/early 20th C, pr **350.00**

Cup and saucer, hp medallion, marked "GLC Dresden" **150.00**

Dessert plate in frame, 8" d printed and tinted plate, scenes of courting couples, insets, and floral sprigs, gilt details, 15-3/4" sq giltwood shadowbox frame, early 20th C, set of four . . **175.00**

Demitasse cup and saucer, Classical Revival, 2" h ovoid cups with gilt interior and beading, sides with pale yellow ground, and gilt scrolls, two roundels with black ground, one with gilt silhouette of courting couple, the other with rosehead, eighteen matching saucers, early 20th C, $90. Photo courtesy of Skinner's Auctioneers and Appraisers.

Figural group

5-3/4" h, 5-1/2" w, Putti charting the heavens, putto seated at table, peering through telescope, another putto studying celestial globe, ovoid base, late 19th/early 20th C, loss, crazing **375.00**

8-1/4" h, Spaniel, seated, scratching chin with back leg **525.00**

11" h, two ladies, modeled as mischievous maidens in 18th C dress, ovoid base, early 20th C **460.00**

Loving cup, 6-1/2" h, three handles, woodland scene with nymph, gold trim **475.00**

Perfume bottle, 3-3/8" l, cylindrical, enamel dec with scene of courting couple, floral sprays, gilt-metal lid enclosing cut glass stopper, early 20th C **115.00**

Portrait vase, 6" h, front with oval roundel printed with portrait bust of 18th C lady, gilt floral surround, central band of beaded landscape cartouches and foliate scrolls, faux jeweled diapered ground, two short gilt flying-loop handles **635.00**

Urn, cov, 14-1/2" h, domed lid with fruit finial, body with two gilt flying-loop handles, trumpet foot on sq base, rose Pompadour ground, painted scenes of courting couples and floral bouquets, late 19th/early 20th C, price for pr, one damaged **700.00**

Vase, 13-1/4" h, alternating panels of figures and yellow floral bouquets, Thieme factory, late 19th C **115.00**

Vase, green and white costumed figures in garden setting, marked "C. Thieme," $150. Photo courtesy of Jim and Susan Harran.

Vase, cov, 14" h, alternating panels of lowers and turquoise ground floral bouquets, c1900, minor damage, pr 375.00

Whatnot shelf, 13-1/2" w, 13-1/3" h, figural and foliate porcelain posts, mirrored back, shaped ebonized wood tiers, 20th C 200.00

Meissen

Basket, 12" l, shaped oval, molded rococo cartouches, scrolling foliage, heavy gilt highlights, gilt bronze swing

Cup, handleless, c1730-60, detailed landscape decorated, figures with horses, flowering urn, village in the distance, flowers on reverse, 2-1/2" h, $220. Photo courtesy of Sanford Alderfer Auction Company.

handles, late 19th/early 20th C, pr 850.00

Bowl, 9" d, 5" h, double handled form, reticulated sides, ftd base, polychrome floral dec, gilt accents, wear and damage...................295.00

Cabinet plate, 9-5/8" d, enameled center with cupid and female in wooded landscape, gilt dec pink and burgundy border, titled on reverse "Lei Wiedergut"..................490.00

Chandelier, 23" h, baluster-form shaft with hand-painted flower and leaf motifs, similar applied motifs on white ground, six S-scroll arms with conforming applied floral dec, candle cups, suspending tassels with applied floral bouquets.............900.00

Clock, 18-3/4" h, Rococo style, clock face surrounded by applied floral dec, four fully molded figures representing four seasons 3,400.00

Cup and saucer, flower-filled basket dec 90.00

Dessert service, partial, pink floral dec, gilt trim, five 8" d plates with pierced rims, two 11-1/2" h compotes with figures of boy and girl flower sellers in center of dish, pierced rims, 20th C 1,850.00

Dinner service, partial, Deutsche Blumen, molded New Dulong border, gilt highlights, two oval serving platters, circular platter, fish platter, 8-1/2" cov tureen with figural finial, two sauce boats with attached underplates, two serving spoons, sq serving dish, two small oval dishes, cov jam pot with attached underplate and spoon, 20 dinner plates, 11 teacups and saucers, nine salad plates, 10 bread plates, 10 soups, 74-pc set 8,500.00

Dish, cov, 6-5/8" h, female blackamoor, beside covered dish with molded basketweave and rope edge, modeled on freeform oval base with applied florets, incised #328, 20th C ... 575.00

Figure

3-1/4" h, 6-1/4" l, seated child feeding small dog from plate, 20th C................1,100.00

5-1/4" h, Motto, modeled as figure of Eros seated on cloud, three-sided base with central cartouche inscribed "Le prends menesser," late 19th/early 20th C 980.00

5-3/8" h, Putto in cloak, modeled in stride, purple floral and fur lined cloak, 20th C 320.00

6-1/4" h, Commedia Dell'Arte, man with red robe and pointed beard,

Miniature double-handled vase, ruffled rim, turquoise and gilt ground, portraits of ladies and gentlemen, gilt swag decoration, minor restoration, 5" h, $135. Photo courtesy of Sanford Alderfer Auction Company.

on flower-strewn base, Germany, late 19th C...........1,150.00

14-1/4" h, cockatoo, perched on tree stump, flower and leaves at base, early 20th C..........2,300.00

Mirror, 9-1/2" l, oval, heavily applied with leaves and flowers, top adorned with two cherubs supporting floral garland, Germany, c1900 ...1,380.00

Plate, 9" d, molded with four cartouches of bunches of fruit, shaped edge with C-scroll and wings, gilt dec, late 19th C, price for pr 250.00

Tea set, partial, brown, pink, green, blue, gray, purple, and orange enameled birds in center, dragons on rim, gilt accents, seven teacups, seven 6" d saucers, nine 7" plates, 23 pcs 700.00

Tray, 17-3/8" l, oval, enameled floral sprays, gilt trim, 20th C 400.00

Urn on pedestal, 21" h, figural cartouches, scattered floral dec, two handles in form of pair of entwined snakes, mounted as lamps, pr 4,000.00

Vase

10-1/2" h, floral dec, bands of molded gilt dec, each handle molded as two entwined snakes, gilt highlights............475.00

15-1/2" h, scrolled snake handles, cobalt blue ground, gold and silver floral dec, 19th C, new gold trim to handles..............2,300.00

Wall garniture, 12-5/8" w, 19" l two-light girandole in rococo-style frame topped by putto figure, two figures of children among flowers on sides, brackets for two serpentine candle arms, two 15-1/2" w, 15-3/4" h scenic plaques with center painted scenes of bustling harbor, similar styled frames, sockets for candle arms, two 15-3/4" w, 15-3/4" h rococo-style three-light wall sconces, framed as rocaille scroll with three floral-encrusted serpentine candle arms, 19th C **3,100.00**

DUNCAN AND MILLER

For more information, see this book.

History: George Duncan, and Harry B. and James B., his sons, and Augustus Heisey, his son-in-law, formed George Duncan & Sons in Pittsburgh, Pennsylvania, in 1865. The factory was located just two blocks from the Monongahela River, providing easy and inexpensive access by barge for materials needed to produce glass. The men, from Pittsburgh's south side, were descendants of generations of skilled glassmakers.

The plant burned to the ground in 1892. James E. Duncan Sr. selected a site for a new factory in Washington, Pennsylvania, where operations began on February 9, 1893. The plant prospered, producing fine glassware and table services for many years.

John E. Miller, one of the stockholders, was responsible for designing many fine patterns, the most famous being Three Face. The firm incorporated and used the name The Duncan and Miller Glass Company until the plant closed in 1955. The company's slogan was, "The Loveliest Glassware in America." The U.S. Glass Co. purchased the molds, equipment, and machinery in 1956.

Additional Listing: Pattern Glass.

Animal
 Heron, crystal **125.00**
 Swan, 6-1/2" h, opal pink . . . **115.00**
Ashtray, Terrace, red, sq **35.00**
Bowl, First Love, crystal, 11" d, scalloped. **72.00**
Bud vase, First Love, crystal, 9" h **75.00**

Candleholders, pair, ebony (black,) Art Deco, #16, 6-1/2" h, **$75.** *Photo courtesy of Michael Krumme.*

Candleholder, Canterbury, #115-121, price for pr **55.50**
Candy box, cov, Canterbury, crystal, three parts, 6" d **70.00**
Coaster, Sandwich, crystal **15.00**
Cocktail, Caribbean, blue, 3-3/4 oz **45.00**
Compote, Spiral Flutes, amber, 6" d **20.00**
Console bowl, 11" d, Rose etch, crystal **37.50**
Cornucopia, #121, Swirl, blue opalescent, shape #2, upswept tail **75.00**
Creamer and sugar, Passion Flower, crystal. **42.00**
Cup, Sandwich, crystal **9.00**
Finger bowl, Astaire, red. **65.00**
Goblet, water
 First Love, crystal, 10 oz **35.00**
 Plaza, cobalt blue **40.00**
Ice cream dish, Sandwich, crystal, 4-1/4" d **12.00**
Juice tumbler, Sandwich, crystal, 3-3/4" h, ftd **12.00**
Mint tray, Sylvan, 7-1/2" l, crystal, ruby handle. **35.00**
Nappy, Sandwich, crystal, two parts, divided, handle. **14.00**
Oyster cocktail, Canterbury, citrone **18.00**

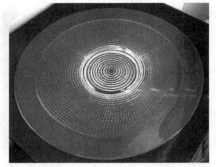

Punch bowl underplate, Teardrop pattern, 23" d, **$200.** *Photo courtesy of Matt Freier.*

Plate
 Canterbury, 8" d, crystal **8.00**
 First Love, 8-1/2" d **25.00**
 Full Sail, amber, 8-1/2" d **18.00**
 Radiance, light blue, 8-1/2" d. **17.50**
 Spiral Flute, crystal, 10-3/8" d. **15.00**
 Terrace, cobalt blue, 7-1/2" d . **30.00**
Relish
 First Love, three parts, #115, two handles, 10-1/2" x 1-1/4", minor wear **60.00**
 Language of Flowers, three parts, three handles, #115 . . . . **37.50**
 Terrace, four parts, 9" d, crystal **55.00**
 Tear Drop, three parts, applied handle, crystal **24.00**
Seafood-sauce cup, Spiral Flutes, green, 2-3/8" h **20.00**
Sherbet
 Canterbury, chartreuse **15.00**
 Sandwich, crystal **20.00**

Cake plate, Snail pattern, 9-3/8" d, 5" h, **$375.**

Punch bowl, Teardrop pattern, 13-3/4" across top, 8-1/2" h, **$350.** *Photo courtesy of Matt Freier.*

Punch bowl, Teardrop pattern, 13-3/4" across top, 8-1/2" h, **$350.** *Photo courtesy of Matt Freier.*

Sugar

Caribbean, crystal **12.00**
Tear Drop, crystal, 8 oz **10.00**
Sugar shaker, Duncan Block, crystal
. . . . **42.00**
Tray, Sandwich, crystal, 8" l, two
handles **18.50**
Whiskey, sea horse, etch #502, red
and crystal **48.00**
Wine, Sandwich, crystal, 3 oz . . . **20.00**

DURAND

History: Victor Durand (1870-1931), born in Baccarat, France, apprenticed at the Baccarat glassworks, where several generations of his family had worked. In 1884, Victor came to America to join his father at Whitall-Tatum & Co. in New Jersey. In 1897, father and son leased the Vineland Glass Manufacturing Company in Vineland, New Jersey. Products included inexpensive bottles, jars, and glass for scientific and medical purposes. By 1920, four separate companies existed.

For more information, see this book.

When Quezal Art Glass and Decorating Company failed, Victor Durand recruited Martin Bach Jr., Emil J. Larsen, William Wiedebine, and other Quezal men and opened an art-glass shop at Vineland in December 1924. Quezal-style iridescent pieces were made. New innovations included cameo and intaglio designs, geometric Art-Deco shapes, Venetian Lace, and Oriental-style pieces. In 1928, crackled glass, called Moorish Crackle and Egyptian Crackle, was made.

Durand died in 1931. The Vineland Flint Glass Works was merged with Kimble Glass Company a year later, and the art glass line was discontinued.

Marks: Many Durand glass pieces are not marked. Some have a sticker with the words "Durand Art Glass," others have the name "Durand" scratched on the pontil or "Durand" inside a large V. Etched numbers may be part of the marking.

Bowl, 9-3/4" d, butterscotch, partial silver sgd **345.00**
Candlesticks, pr, mushroom, red, opal pulled florals, pale yellow base . **725.00**
Compote, 5-1/4" h, green cased with opal int., washed in silvery irid, sgd "Durand 2050" in silver **990.00**
Decanter, 12" h, blue cut to clear, mushroom shaped stopper, unsigned
. . . . **600.00**
Jar, cov, 7-1/4" h, ginger jar form, King Tut, green, irid gold dec, applied amber glass dec on cov **3,100.00**
Lamp shade, 6-3/4" h, spherical, blue and white craquelle, replacement single brass hanging fixture **625.00**

Vase, stylized baluster form, blue Aurene, signed "L.C. Tiffany Favrile," but is actually Durand piece, 10-1/4" h, $990. Photo courtesy of Sanford Alderfer Auction Company.

Mantle lamp, 10-3/4" h, Moorish crackle red and white paneled glass over irid amber lustered body, metal base, c1920 . . . . **815.00**
Sherbet, 3-1/2" h, ambergris, gold luster finish, unsigned **150.00**
Table torchieres, pr, 15-1/2" h, Egyptian crackle, trumpet form, green and white striated glass with irid gold crackle dec, bronze acanthus leaf electrified bases, c1926, pr . . . **1,725.00**

Vase

4-1/4" h, amber, washed with gold luster irid finish, sgd "V Durand 1710-4" in silver **320.00**
8" h, ambergris, green King Tut dec, overall gold irid finish, sgd "V Durand 1722-8," c1915 . . **1,265.00**

Vase, beehive form, marigold Aurene, signed "Durand/20172-5," 5" h, $425. Photo courtesy of Sanford Alderfer Auction Company.

8-1/4" h, flared rim, ovoid form, blue irid body, applied gold irid disk base, painted "Durand" on base
. . . . **1,265.00**
8-1/2" h, amber, gold luster finish, white pulled feathers tipped in green, overall threading, unsigned, c1920 . . . . **2,185.00**
8-1/2" h, 4-3/4" d, irid gold, sgd "Durand" on base **400.00**
9-1/4" h, Moorish crackle, blue and white crackle panels over ambergris lustered body, c1920
. . . . **2,300.00**
9-3/4" h, gold-orange, irid silvery finish, overall gold threading, sgd "V. Durand 1990-10" in silver, c1920, threading losses . . . **750.00**
10" h, blue, gold disk foot, washed in irid finish, white King Tut dec, sgd "Durand 2011-10 R" in silver, c1920
. . . . **2,990.00**
11-1/2" h, amber, irid gold finish, dec with white pulled feather bordered in green, overall gold threading, sgd "Durand" in silver . . . **3,565.00**
12" h, shouldered, opal, green and gold heart and vines, overall irid gold threading, c1920, minor losses **750.00**
12-1/4" h, ftd, opal, blue pulled feather dec tipped in gold, irid gold overall threading, foot and int. sgd in silver "V Durand 20 120-12," c1920 . . . . **2,185.00**
12-1/2" h, beehive form, ambergris, reddish gold luster finish, c1915
. . . . **2,300.00**
12-1/2" h, opal, irid green and gold hearts, overall gold threading, c1920, drilled for lamp **375.00**
18-1/4" h, bulbous, ambergris, silvery irid finish, c1925 . . **2,530.00**

EARLY AMERICAN GLASS

History: The term "Early American glass" covers glass made in America from the colonial period through the mid-19th century. As such, it includes the early pressed glass and lacy glass made between 1827 and 1840.

For more information, see this book.

Major glass-producing centers prior to 1850 were Massachusetts (New England Glass Company and the Boston and Sandwich Glass Company), South Jersey, Pennsylvania (Stiegel's Manheim factory and many

Pittsburgh-area firms), and Ohio (several different companies in Kent, Mantua, and Zanesville).

Early American glass was popular with collectors from 1920 to 1950. It has now regained some of its earlier prominence. Leading auction sources for early American glass include Garth's, Heckler & Company, James D. Julia, and Skinner, Inc.

Additional Listings: Blown Three Mold; Cup Plates; Flasks; Sandwich Glass; Stiegel-Type Glass.

Candlesticks, pair, free blown, leaded, bulbous, jointed to stem and base by wafers and knobs, shaft hollow with bowl for oil or candle, original pewter insets, snapped pontil, Pittsburgh, c1810-20, one perfect, second with glued break at candle socket, 10" h, $1,100. Photo courtesy of Cowan's Historic Americana Auctions.

Blown

Bottle, globular

3-1/8" h, Zanesville, dark amber **1,320.00**

3-1/8" h, Zanesville, light aqua **325.00**

5" h, Midwestern, aqua, 22 swirled ribs, pontil, flared lip **550.00**

6" h, Kent/Mantua, aqua, 16 slightly swirled ribs, flattened lip, tiny pot stones **200.00**

7-3/8" h, Zanesville, olive green, applied lip, few pot stones . **385.00**

7-1/2" h, Zanesville, aqua, 24 swirled ribs, pot stones and scratches **330.00**

7-1/2" h, Zanesville, citron, 24 tightly swirled ribs, one pot stone **4,500.00**

7-5/8" h, Zanesville, aqua, 24 melon ribs, few pot stones **285.00**

8" h, attributed to Kent, brilliant aqua, three-mold, applied collar lip **3,200.00**

8" h, Zanesville, dark amber, 24 swirled ribs, tiny pot stones, broken blister **770.00**

8-1/2" h, Zanesville, olive green, tiny pot stones, overall wear . . . **825.00**

Bowl

4-1/4" d, 2-7/8" h, brilliant amethyst, 16 ribs, flared rim with folded lip, applied foot **550.00**

12-5/8" d, 14-1/2" h, colorless, cylindrical shaped bowl, outward turned rim, raised on flared trumpet base with hollow knop, under-folded rim, light scratches **2,000.00**

Candlesticks, pr, 9-1/2" h, Pittsburgh, tulip sockets, round, domed bases with paneled stems with egg shaped int. drop, some roughness at socket attachments **295.00**

Compote, cov, 6-1/4" d, 10-1/4" h, Pittsburgh, clear, prominent swirled ribs on bowl and lid, applied foot and wafer finial, McKearin Plate 55-2 . . **10,175.00**

Compote, open, 8-1/4" d, 8-1/2" h, Ribbon, brilliant amethyst, sawtooth edge, reticulated flared sides, hexagonal base with rayed bottom, straw marks, Lee 153 . . . . . . **22,000.00**

Creamer

3-7/8" h, brilliant cobalt blue, 20-diamond, applied foot and handle **550.00**

4" h, brilliant cobalt blue, 21 slightly swirled ribs, applied handle **450.00**

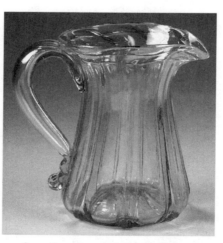

Cream jug, blown, colorless, leaded, vertical tooled ribbed body, treads at flaring lip, applied hollow airtrap C-scroll handle with rigaree end, snap pontil, Midwest, tiny flake on spout, 5-3/4" h, $200. Photo courtesy of Cowan's Historic Americana Auctions.

Cruet, colorless, leaded, 16 ribbed body, applied ribbed hollow airtrap rigaree scroll C-shaped handle, pronounced spout, snap pontil, Midwest, 8-1/2" h, $190. Photo courtesy of Cowan's Historic Americana Auctions.

4-1/2" h, Zanesville, brilliant violet blue, applied handle **2,650.00**

4-3/4" h, brilliant peacock blue, applied foot and handle . . . **450.00**

Cruet, 7-1/4" h, cobalt blue, 16 vertical ribs, Pittsburgh stopper, applied handle, tiny pot stone **800.00**

Fish bowl, 9-3/4" h, colorless, rolled outward rim, trumpet form foot with under-folded rim **215.00**

Flask

3" h, chestnut, cobalt blue, 18 swirled ribs, pontil, sheared and fire polished lip **425.00**

3-3/8" h, Mantua, sea green, 16 swirled ribs, few pot stones and residue **500.00**

5" h, Zanesville, deep amber, chestnut, 10 diamond . . . **3,960.00**

Decanter, pillar-molded, colorless leaded glass, balloon-shaped ribbed stopper, ground graphite pontil, Midwest, 10-1/4" h decanter, 4" h stopper, $125. Photo courtesy of Cowan's Historic Americana Auctions.

Flask, pattern molded, citron green, vertical ribs, sheared lip pontil, Midwestern, 4-3/4" h, $1,400. Photo courtesy of Pacific Glass Auctions.

5-3/4" h, amber, pint, scroll **. . 635.00**

5-3/4" h, Midwestern, light green, chestnut, 16 vertical melon ribs, flared lip, minor scratches, trace of residue. **275.00**

6-3/4" h, dark amber, 24 vertical ribs, wear, pot stones **1,265.00**

Flip glass, cov, 11-3/4" h, cone shaped finial applied to lid, three rows of way lines etched dec on lid, tapering body dec with two sprays of stylized flowers, minor imperfections **550.00**

Mug, 4" h, brilliant cobalt blue, applied handle. **1,155.00**

Pan

5-3/8" d, 2" h, Zanesville, aqua, 10 diamond, flared sides, folded-in rim **8,470.00**

5-3/4" d, 2" h, Pittsburgh, amethyst, 12 ribbed-panel bowl, applied foot, folded rim **4,400.00**

6-1/4" d, 1-1/4" h, Zanesville, dark amber, 24 ribs, folded-in rim, very minor scratches. **4,850.00**

8-7/8" d, 2-1/8" h, Zanesville, golden, flared sides, fold-out rim, pot stone **1,045.00**

10-3/8" d, 2" h, Pittsburgh, pale amethyst, eight panels, folded out lip, in-the-making imperfection in one panel **1,750.00**

Pitcher, 6" h, Zanesville, pale green, 24 swirled ribs, applied ribbed handle **21,725.00**

Salt, master, 2-1/2" d, 3" h, dark cobalt blue, diamond quilted pattern . . **250.00**

Sugar, cov, 4-1/4" d, 6-1/2" h, dark cobalt blue, diamond quilted, applied foot, cone-shaped finial **1,925.00**

Wine glass, 7-1/4" h, clear, cotton stem, early 19th C, price for pr **1,380.00**

Lacy

Bowl, 7-3/8" d, 1-5/8" h, Nectarine, chips. **100.00**

Spill vase, octagonal paneled colorless flint, scalloped top, 10-1/4" h, $125. Photo courtesy of Cowan's Historic Americana Auctions.

Candlesticks, pr, 6" h, reeded and ribbed socket attached with wafer, reeded stem, sq stepped base, chips, checks in socket **450.00**

Compote, cov, 9-1/2" h, 8-1/4" d, Sawtooth, flint, chips **155.00**

Dish, 9-1/4" d, beehive, scalloped, octagonal sides, Sandwich, flakes, roughness **115.00**

Miniature lamp, 4" h, lacy cup-plate base, blown spherical font, knob stem, chips on base **385.00**

Plate, 7" d, eagle, chips **175.00**

Toddy, 5-3/8" d, brilliant dark amethyst, lacy, Roman Rosette, Sandwich, edge chips **330.00**

Pillar mold

Candlestick, 7-5/8" h, teal green, hexagonal, center wafer, small flake on socket, base flakes, chipped corner **1,925.00**

Spill vase, Pittsburgh, blown, clear leaded glass, footed, acid etched ferns, tooled lip, 9-3/4" h, $300. Photo courtesy of Cowan's Historic Americana Auctions.

Cologne bottle, 5-5/8" h, cobalt blue, eight ribs, two applied rings, flared lip, mushroom stopper, stopper base shipped **400.00**

Decanter, 9-3/4" h, cobalt blue, applied handle and collar, pewter jigger cap **7,950.00**

Pitcher, 5-5/8" h, colorless, applied handle, Pittsburgh, bottom ground flat, minor wear **275.00**

Vase

9-5/8" h, 5-3/4" d, Pittsburgh, clear, applied stem and foot. **660.00**

10" h, Pittsburgh, brilliant amethyst, white edging applied on ribs, baluster stem, applied foot **4,750.00**

ENGLISH CHINA AND PORCELAIN (GENERAL)

History: By the 19th century, more than 1,000 china and porcelain manufacturers were scattered throughout England, with the majority of the factories located in the Staffordshire district.

For more information, see this book.

By the 19th century, English china and porcelain had achieved a worldwide reputation for excellence. American stores imported large quantities for their customers. The special-production English pieces of the 18th and early 19th centuries held a position of great importance among early American antiques collectors.

Bow

Bowl, 4-1/2" d, blue trailing vine, white ground, c1770 . . . . **175.00**

Candlesticks, pr, two birds on flowering branches, dog and sheep on grassy base, wood stand, c1755 . . . . **1,200.00**

Egg cup, 2-1/2" h, two half-flower panels, powder blue ground, pseudo Oriental mark, c1760 . . . . **900.00**

Plate, 9" d, Turk's Cap Lily, dragonfly and moths, c1755 . . . . **850.00**

Chelsea

Bowl, 8-3/4" d, swirled ribs, scalloped, foliage and floral dec **75.00**

Candlesticks, pr, 7-1/2" h, figural, draped putti, sitting on tree stump holding flower, scroll-molded base, encircled in puce, gilt, wax pan . **850.00**

Teapot, Castleford, blue trim, 5-1/4" h, $250.

Cup and saucer, multicolored exotic birds, white ground, gold anchor mark, c1765 . . . . **750.00**

Plate, 8-1/2" d, multicolored floral design, scalloped rim, gold anchor mark **475.00**

Derby

Beaker, 3-1/8" h, two short shell-shaped handles, two painted landscape roundels in gilt borders, scenes titled "Near Spondon" and "Near Breadshall," both Derbyshire scenes, pale yellow ground, late 18th/early 19th C . **1,265.00**

Figure, 8" h, 8-1/2" h, pastoral, boy resting against tree stump playing bagpipe, black hat, bleu-do-roi jacket, gilt trim, yellow breeches, girl with green hat, bleu-du-roi bodice, pink skirt, white apron with iron-red flowerheads, gilt centers, leaves, scroll molded mound base, crown and incised iron-red D mark, pr . . . **2,200.00**

Jar, cov, 22" h, octagonal, iron-red, bottle green and leaf green, alternating cobalt blue and white grounds, gilding, grotesque sea-serpent handles, now fitted as lamp with carved base, 19th C, pr **10,000.00**

Plate, 10-1/8" d, enamel dec, stylized Imari-type designs of birds in three, shaped molded rim, Bloor mark, second quarter 19th C, price for set of seven **300.00**

Flight, Barr & Barr

Crocus pot, 9" w, 4" d, 6-1/4" h, D-form, molded columns and architrave, peach-ground panels, ruined abbey landscape reserve, gilding . . . **2,400.00**

Pastille burner, 3-1/2" h, cottage, four open chimneys, marked, c1815 . . . . **425.00**

Tea service, gilt foliate, orange ground banded border, 9-1/2" h cov teapot (finial restoration), 7" l teapot stand, 4-3/4" h creamer, 4-1/2" h sugar bowl, 6-5/8" d waste bowl, two 8" deep dishes, 10 coffee cans, 11 tea cups, 11 saucers, minor chips to cups and saucers, incised "B" mark, c1792-1804, light wear to gilt at rim throughout **1,320.00**

Herculaneum

Jug, 10" h, creamware, black transfer printed, obverse "Washington," oval design with medallion portrait on monument surmounted by wreath, birth, and death dates below, flanked by eagle and grieving woman, upper ribbon inscribed "Washington in Glory," lower ribbon "America In Tears," reverse transfer of American sailing vessel, American eagle beneath spout, inscription "Herculaneum Pottery Liverpool," incised mark on base, imperfections **1,100.00**

Jackfield

Creamer, 4-1/4" h, bulbous, emb grapes design, leaves, and tendrils, gilt highlights, three pr paw feet, ear-shape handle **185.00**

Pitcher, 6-1/2" h, applied handle, black, traces of enameling, bird, initials and "1763," wear, small flakes **125.00**

Sugar bowl, cov, 4-1/2" h, 3-3/4" d, scalloped SS rims, SS-mounted cov and ornate pierced finial **250.00**

Longwy

Lamp, 25" h, pink and red roses dec, green leaves, turquoise ground, orig brass burner, etched glass shade, font marked "Hinks & Sons," orig glass chimney, electrified **665.00**

Masons

Creamer, 4" h, Oriental-style shape, marked "Mason's Patent Ironstone" **85.00**

Jug, 8" h, octagonal, Hydra pattern, waisted straight neck, green-enameled handle, lion-head terminal, underglaze blue and iron-red flowers and vase, two imp marks and printed rounded crown mark, c1813-30 . . . . **320.00**

Platter, 13-1/2" x 10-3/4", Double-Landscape pattern, Oriental motif, deep green and brick red, c1883 . . . . **265.00**

Potpourri vase, cov, 25-1/4" h, hexagonal body, cobalt blue, large gold stylized peony blossom, chrysanthemums, prunus, and butterflies, gold and blue dragon handles, and knobs, trellis diaper-rim border, c1820-25 . . . . **1,750.00**

New Hall

Creamer, Chinese figure on terrace, c1790 . . . . **190.00**

Breakfast set, Lowestoft Border pattern, marked "Booths Silicon China, England," retailed by Tiffany & Co., covered pancake server and underplate, cereal and underplate, fruit/sauce bowl, cup, egg cup, coffeepot, teapot, creamer, sugar, hp cobalt blue border, gold trim, price for set, $950.

Dessert set, two oval dishes, eight plates, printed and colored named views, lavender-blue borders, light-blue ground, c1815 . . . . **450.00**

Tea set, interwoven ribbon and leaf trails, blue and gilt oval-medallion border, c1790, minor repairs, 44 pcs **1,500.00**

Plymouth-type

Sauce boat, 8" l, oval shape, fluted sides, enamel floral dec, c1770, firing lines **175.00**

Rockingham

Tea set, rococo-style, each with central pale buff band, enamel decorated landscape cartouche, gilt scrolled foliate trim, 10-1/2" l cov teapot with scrolled foliate handle and serpent-form spout, rim hairline, light gilt wear to spout and handle; 4-3/8" h creamer, slight chip to side of handle; 6" h cov sugar bowl; 7-1/8" d waste bowl, c1820 . . . . **220.00**

Swansea

Tea set, floral pattern, underglaze blue, black transfer, gilt trim, 12 8" d plates; 11 each teacups, coffee cups, saucers; teapot; creamer; three trays; 7-1/2" d bowl, some professional repair, worn gilt, several pcs with chips and hairlines **590.00**

Woods

Cup and saucer, handleless, Woods Rose **65.00**

Dish, 8" l, 6" w, dark blue transfer of castle, imp "Wood" **165.00**

Jug, 5-3/4" h, ovoid, cameos of Queen Caroline, pink luster ground, beaded edge, molded and painted floral border, c1820 . . . . **425.00**

Plate, 9" d, Woods Rose, scalloped edge **125.00**

Bowl, New Hall, oriental decorated on ext., small painted decorated on inside bottom, some wear to decorated, 6" d, $175. Photo courtesy of James D. Julia, Inc.

Stirrup cup, 5-1/2" l, modeled hound's head, translucent shades of brown, c1760 . . . . **2,200.00**

Whistle, 3-7/8" h, modeled as seated sphinx, blue accents, oval green base, c1770 . . . . **600.00**

Worcester

Cream jug, cov, 5" h, floral finial, underglaze blue floral and insect dec, shaded crescent mark, 18th C, cover possibly married, slight finial chips, shallow flake to cover **175.00**

Deep dish, 9-1/2" l, oval, underglaze blue Chantilly sprig pattern, shaded crescent mark, 18th C, foot-rim chips **320.00**

Miniature, cup and saucer, handleless, blue and white three-flower and butterfly design, Dr. Wall underglaze blue crescent mark **150.00**

Sauce boat, 5-1/4" l, molded body, panels of underglaze blue flowers, cell border, open crescent mark, 18th C **300.00**

Sweetmeat dish, 3" l, molded leaf shape, under glazed blue floral and inset design int., 18th C, rim chip repair **115.00**

Teapot, cov, globular, 5-5/8" h, underglaze blue dec of Waiting Chinaman, floral finial, open crescent mark, 18th C, slight spout nick, chips to finial **865.00**

Tureen, cov, 10-1/2" l, oval, underglaze blue pine cone pattern, artichoke finial, shell handles, shaded crescent mark, 18th C, one handle restored, int. rim flake **800.00**

ENGLISH SOFT PASTE

History: Between 1820 and 1860, a large number of potteries in England's Staffordshire district produced decorative wares with a soft earthenware (creamware) base and a plain white or yellow glazed ground.

Design or "stick" spatterware was created by a cut sponge (stamp), hand painting, or transfers. Blue was the predominant color. The earliest patterns were carefully arranged geometrics that generally covered the entire piece. Later pieces had a decorative border with a central motif, usually a tulip. In the 1850s, Elsmore and Foster developed the Holly Leaf pattern

King's Rose features a large, cabbage-type rose in red, pale red, or pink. The pink rose often is called "Queen's Rose." Secondary colors are pastels— yellow, pink, and, occasionally, green. The borders vary: a solid band, vined, lined, or sectional. The King's Rose exists in an oyster motif.

Strawberry China ware comes in three types: strawberries and strawberry leaves (often called strawberry luster), green featherlike leaves with pink flowers (often called cut-strawberry, primrose, or old strawberry), and relief decoration. The first two types are characterized by rust-red moldings. Most pieces have a cream ground. Davenport was only one of the many potteries that made this ware.

Yellow-glazed earthenware (canary luster) has a canary yellow ground, a transfer design that is usually in black, and occasional luster decoration. The earliest pieces date from the 1780s and have a fine creamware base. A few hand-painted pieces are known. Not every piece has luster decoration.

Because the base material is soft paste, the ware is subject to cracking and chipping. Enamel colors and other types of decoration do not hold well. It is not unusual to see a piece with the decoration worn off.

Marks: Marked pieces are uncommon.

Additional Listings: Gaudy Dutch, Salopian Ware, Staffordshire Items.

Softpaste, sugar bowl, covered, blue stripes with cranberry colored design in central white band, 6" h, $250. Photo courtesy of Sanford Alderfer Auction Company.

Creamware

Basket, 7-1/2" x 6-1/2", 9-1/2" x 7-1/2" undertray, green trim, open sides, woven bottom, undertray with conforming pattern, reticulated border, green trim, hairline on basket side, wear on sides of underplate **950.00**

Coffeepot, cov, 10" h, pear shape, polychrome dec black transfer of Tea Party and Shepherd prints, leaf-molded spout, chips, restoration to body, attributed to Wedgwood, c1775 . . . . **350.00**

Jug, 5-1/8" h, reeded lapped handle, emb floral applications, sides dec with red and green floral sprays, 19th C, glaze wear, small rim nicks **260.00**

Mug, 3-1/3" h, Orange Institution, red transfer printed symbols with verse above "Holiness to the Lord" and verse below "May the Orange Institution stand as firm as the Oak and the Enemies fall off like the leaves in October," England, early 19th C **300.00**

Pitcher, 6-1/4" h, two oval reserves with black transfer printed scenes of naval engagements, "The Wasp Boarding the Frolic," sgd "Bentley, Wear, and Bourne Engravers and Printers Shelton, Staffordshire," reverse depicting "The Constitution taking the Cyane and Livant," light green ground, luster embellishments, imperfections **2,760.00**

Plate, 9-1/2" d, shaped edge, cutout floral design, unmarked, flakes on rim, price for pr **715.00**

Platter, 18" l, 14-1/2" w, oval, scallop dec rim, chips, restorations **300.00**

Sugar bowl, 5-1/8" d, 2-3/4" h, int. with red and green enamel floral dec, purple luster and underglaze blue, ext. marked "Be Canny with the Sugar" flanked by small flowers **385.00**

Teapot

4-3/4" h, molded acanthus spout, ribbed handle, small flakes **385.00**

6-1/2" h, flower knop, floral dec entwined reeded handle with touches of gilt, rim chip, restored spout, gilt loss, 19th C **230.00**

Design Spatterware

Bowl, 7-1/2" d, 4" h, polychrome stripes **95.00**

Creamer, 4-3/8" h, gaudy floral dec, red, green, blue, and black, marked "Baker & Co., England" **75.00**

Cup, oversize, gaudy floral dec, red, blue, and green, 6-1/8" d **200.00**

Jug, 7" h, barrel shape, blue, rosettes and fern prongs **185.00**

Miniature

Cup and saucer, green and black, polychrome center flower . . . **75.00**

Tea set, five pieces, 5-3/4" h teapot, creamer, sugar, two handleless cups and saucers, blue and white design spatter, teapot finial restored, chips **440.00**

Plate, 8-5/8" d, red, blue, green, and black, imp "Elsmore & Foster," minor wear and scratches, price for set of six **385.00**

Sugar bowl, cov, 5" h, white, blue, and red flowers, green leaves, closed ring and shell handles **120.00**

King's Rose

Bowl, 7-3/4" d, Rose, broken solid border, flakes **55.00**

Cup and saucer, handleless

Oyster pattern, hairline cracks **40.00**

Rose, vine border **150.00**

Plate

5-5/8" d, pink border, wear . . . **55.00**

6-1/2" d, broken solid border, flakes **55.00**

7-3/8" d, some flaking **90.00**

8-1/4" d, scalloped borders and edges, some flakes, six pcs **275.00**

8-1/4" d, pink border, wear . . . **70.00**

8-1/4" d, vine border, three pcs **255.00**

9-3/4" d, scalloped border, four pcs **220.00**

Pitcher, 5-5/8" h, dark red rose, blue and yellow flowers, green leaves, some wear **220.00**

Soup plate, 9-1/2" d, broken solid border, scalloped edges, some flakes, three pcs **360.00**

Teapot, 5-3/4" h, broken solid border, some flakes **140.00**

Pearlware

Bowl

4-3/4" d, black and brown slip-filled rouletted band at rim, field of rust with blue, black, and white scroddled dots, early 19th C, repaired **940.00**

8-3/8" d, 3-7/8" h, upper band inscribed repeatedly with dark brown letters in white band "God Save The King," blue, black, and brown slip-filled checkered band, lower band of blue extending to base, incised maker's mark for "Wood & Caldwell," two stapled repairs, glaze wear to int. **7,050.00**

8-1/2" d, cream top band, rust, dark brown, and buff marbling, repaired **825.00**

Coffeepot, cov, 13" h, baluster form, dome lid, ochre, green, brown, and blue floral dec, early 19th C, imperfections **200.00**

Creamer, cup shape, straight sides, applied handle, light brown stripes, yellow band, gilt and light brown foliage band, slight bubbles to yellow, minor spout rim flake **125.00**

Cup and saucer, handleless, 3-1/2" d cup, 5" d saucer, black transfer scene of horse-drawn chariot, flying putti set of six **525.00**

Figure

3" l, sheep, brown, blue, and yellow ochre sponging, small edge flakes **275.00**

3-1/4" h, squirrel, nut and collar with ring, polychrome, orange coat, attributed to Derby, minor wear and small flakes on base **635.00**

8-1/4" h, Peace, overglaze enamel dec sanding figure modeled holding torch to helmet and battle gear, mounted on sq plinth, England, c1800, restoration **200.00**

Jar, 12" h, cobalt blue underglaze design of wave formed by diamonds and scrolls, animal form handles, hp red and green flowers **250.00**

Jug, 4-3/4" h, barrel-form, orange, blue, green, white, medium brown, and dark brown marble slip dec, extruded handle, early 19th C, repaired. **1,175.00**

Mug, 5" h, hp floral bunches, bands of brown and yellow, craquelure, hairline, chip **200.00**

Pitcher, 6-3/4" h, black transfer printed with polychrome enamel and luster dec, oval reserve depicting "a West View of the Cast Iron Bridge over the River Wear built by R. Burdon Esq.," Sailor's Farewell on reserve, sailor's verse beneath spout, rim dec with floral border, minor rim chips, staining **550.00**

Plate

6-1/2" d, early depiction of Seal of US, central whimsical eagle in blue, gold, and brown, two brown rim lines **1,410.00**

7-1/2" d, octagonal, polychrome enamel depiction of Seal of US, central figure and floral sprays painted in dark brown, blue, and gold with olive branches in green, the blue feather-edge, minor imperfections, price for lot of one soup and one luncheon plate **2,470.00**

Punch bowl, 9-5/8" d, 4-3/8" h, stylized floral bands on int., floral bands and central medallion on ext., polychrome enamel dec, late 19th C **1,265.00**

Salt, open, 2-3/4" d, rounded form, dark brown banding, dark brown dendritic dec on rust field, narrow green glazed reeded band, early 19th C, cracked, rim chip **590.00**

Teapot, 5-3/4" h, octagonal, molded designs, swan finial, Oriental transfer, polychrome enamel, attributed to

T. Harley, some edge flakes and professional repair **425.00**
Vase, 7" h, five-finger type, underglaze blue, enameled birds and foliage, yellow ochre, brown, and green, silver-luster highlights, chips and crazing, pr **500.00**
Wall plaque, 8-1/2" w, 12-1/4" l, oval, molded, polychrome dec, female Harvest figure, late 18th C, minor chip
. . . . **435.00**

Queen's Rose, teapot, covered, squatty shell form, pink rose decoration, extra lid with matching decoration, loss to teapot, $200. Photo courtesy of Sanford Alderfer Auction Co.

Queen's Rose
Cream pitcher and sugar, cov, vine border, some flakes **250.00**
Cup and saucer, handleless, broken solid border **495.00**
Plate
6-1/2" d, broken solid border . . **50.00**
7-1/2" d, solid border **75.00**
8-1/4" d, vine border, scalloped edge
. . . . **85.00**
10" d, vine border **110.00**
Tea set, assembled, Strawberry and Queen's Rose, 7" h teapot, creamer, cov sugar, handleless cup and saucer, waste bowl, professional repairs
. . . . **550.00**

Strawberry China
Bowl, 4" d **165.00**
Cup and saucer, pink border, scalloped edge **225.00**
Plate **145.00**
Platter, large **450.00**
Soup bowl, 8-1/4" d, red, green, pink, and yellow flower and strawberry border, basket of strawberries and roses in center **880.00**
Sugar bowl, cov, raised strawberries, strawberry knob **175.00**
Tea bowl and saucer, vine border
. . . . **250.00**
Tea set, two 7" h teapots, 4" h cream jug, 6" h cov sugar, pink flowers, vines,

Yellow glazed earthenware, bowl, 7-1/4" d, 3-1/4" h, $400.

iron-red trim, restoration to cream jug and sugar, chips, cracks, discoloration on teapots **995.00**

Yellow Glazed
Child's mug
2-1/8" h, silver resist, large florets on field of leaves, rim lines . . . **200.00**
2-1/8" h, silver rest, foliate banding, hairline **175.00**
2-1/8" h, titled "John," silver luster dec, repaired **345.00**
2-5/8" h, black banding with black and gray earthworm dec on green field, extruded handle with foliate terminals, impressed partial maker's mark on bottom, England, early 19th C, chips to base edge, glaze wear to rim **2,990.00**

Yellow glazed earthenware, tea service, red printed tea party and shrimper decorated, 4-3/4" h teapot with married cover, (chips to spout lip, glaze blemish to body, chip restored to cover rim); 4" h cream jug; 4-5/8" h covered sugar, (bowl with hairline, cover as is); 12 1-3/4" h tea bowls; and 12 5" d saucers with imp mark "Sewell," (surface wear); c1820, $1,675. Photo courtesy of Skinner's Auctioneers and Appraisers..

Pitcher, 4-3/4" h, transfer dec of foliate devices, reserve of shepherd with milk maid, hand-painted dec, c1850. **635.00**
Plate, 8-1/4" d, brown transfer print, Wild Rose pattern, imp "Montread"
. . . . **250.00**
Sugar bowl, cov, 5-1/2" h, printed transfer of The Tea Party, fishing scene, iron-red painted rims **1,250.00**
Tea bowl and saucer, iron-red print of two cupids, marked "Sewell" . . . **250.00**
Teapot, 5-1/2" h, printed transfer of The Party, iron-red painted rims, minor hairline, spout damage **850.00**

FAIRY LAMPS

History: Fairy lamps, which originated in England in the 1840s, are candle-burning night lamps. They were used in nurseries, hallways, and dim corners of the home.

For more information, see this book.

Two leading candle manufacturers, the Price Candle Company and the Samuel Clarke Company, promoted fairy lamps as a means to sell candles. Both contracted with glass, porcelain, and metal manufacturers to produce the needed shades and cups. For example, Clarke used Worcester Royal Porcelain Company, Stuart & Sons, and Red House Glass Works in England, plus firms in France and Germany.

Fittings were produced in a wide variety of styles. Shades ranged from pressed to cut glass, from Burmese to Nailsea. Cups are found in glass, porcelain, brass, nickel, and silver plate.

American firms selling fairy lamps included Diamond Candle Company of Brooklyn, Blue Cross Safety Candle Co., and Hobbs-Brockunier of Wheeling, West Virginia.

Two-piece (cup and shade) and three-piece (cup with matching shade and saucer) fairy lamps can be found. Married pieces are common.

Marks: Clarke's trademark was a small fairy with a wand surrounded by the words "Clarke Fairy Pyramid, Trade Mark."

Reproduction Alert: Reproductions abound.

3-1/2", bisque, tri-face baby girl **. 70.00**

3-3/4", blue satin mother-of-pearl shade, clear Clarke Fairy pyramid insert **225.00**

4", blue hobnail shade, blue satin ruffled base, married **30.00**

4", Burmese, dec shade, clear Clark's Cricklite base.............. **900.00**

4", yellow satin swirl shade, clear S. Clark's Fairy pyramid base **150.00**

4-1/2", clear molded flame shade, controlled bubbles, clear S. Clarke's Fairy pyramid base **60.00**

4-1/2", figural green glass shade in shape of monk, set on frosted shoulders base..................... **110.00**

Rare Clarke pyramid light, holder, and mug, frosted shade, finger loop signed base, signed pyramid food warmer with white porcelain mug, Clarke advertise slogans, 8-1/2" h, $125. Photos courtesy of Woody Auctions.

Fairy lamps, left: satin, pink ruffled top, frosted pedestal base, marked "Desmarais & Robitaille Limitee," 10-1/2" h, $125; right: Burmese shade, white opaque base signed "S. Clarke's Fairy," 6-1/2" h, $425.

4-1/2", metal, colored inset jewels, reticulated shade with bird designs **185.00**

5", blue satin swirl shade, matching base, ruffled top and edge..... **325.00**

5", green glass molded leaves, clear emb angel head's base **60.00**

5-1/2", green Nailsea shade, porcelain Doulton Lamplih dec base, sgd "S. Clarke's Fairy" in center **1,300.00**

5-1/2", lavender and frosted white shade, matching ruffled base, zigzag design..................... **150.00**

Fairy lamps, left: green opaque shade with gold and blue enamel, clear pressed glass pedestal base, 8-3/4" h, $275; center: white and yellow striped shade, clear S. Clarke Fairy insert nestled on matching ruffled base, 6" h, $500; right: white shade, green flower and branch transfer, Clarke's Cricklite peg holder, brass base, 11" h, $375.

5-3/4", ruby red, profuse white loopings, bowl shaped base with eight turned up scallops, clear glass candle cup holder marked "S. Clarke Patent Trade Mark Fairy".................... **1,250.00**

6", blue and white frosted ribbon glass dome top shade, ruffled base, clear marked "S. Clarke" insert, flakes on shade **490.00**

6" h, white and yellow striped shade, clear S. Clarke Fairy insert, nestled on matching white and yellow ruffled base **500.00**

6-1/4", yellow satin shade, matching ftd base, clear sgd "S. Clarke Fairy" insert **650.00**

6-1/2", Webb, blue shade dec with bird and branch, clear Clarke's Cricklite insert, sq blue satin base **1,500.00**

8" Burmese, egg-shaped shade, crystal insert, colorful porcelain bowl, stamped S. Clark's patent trademark, English trademark backstamp....... **1,380.00**

8-1/2", Clarke Pyramid, light, holder, and white porcelain mug, frosted shade set on finger loop base, sgd "Clarke Food Warmer," adv slogans on mug **125.00**

8-3/4", green opaque shade, gold and blue enamel dec, clear pressed glass pedestal base **275.00**

FAMILLE ROSE

History: Famille Rose is Chinese export enameled porcelain on which the pink color predominates. It was made primarily in the 18th and 19th centuries. Other porcelains in the same group are Famille Jaune (yellow), Famille Noire (black), and Famille Verte (green).

Decorations include courtyard and home scenes, birds, and insects. Secondary colors are yellow, green, blue, aubergine, and black.

Rose Canton, Rose Mandarin, and Rose Medallion are mid- to late- 19th century Chinese-export wares, which are similar to Famille Rose.

Bowl, 8" d, shallow, polychrome birds and butterflies, pink flowers, fruit, and vegetables, gilt rims, few rim chips, price for set of six **395.00**

Bride's lamp, 14" h, hexagonal form, reticulated panels, electrified .. **345.00**

Cache pot, stand, 11" l, 7-1/4" w, 6" h, clusters of flowers on plain ground, 10-1/2" l, 7-1/2" w, 1-1/2" h stand, repaired, reglued foot **1,100.00**

Charger, 12" d, central figural dec, brocade border............. **265.00**

Dish, cov, 11" d, figural dec, Qing dynasty **200.00**

Snuff bottle, 2" w, 2-1/2" h, $175.

Figure

13" h, peacocks, pr **275.00**
16" h, cockerels, pr **550.00**
Garden set, 18-1/2" h, hexagonal, pictorial double panels, flanked and bordered by floral devices, blue ground, 19th C, minor glaze loss
. . . . **1,100.00**
Ginger jar, cov, 10-1/2" h, ovoid, foo dog beside sea reserve, floral and butterfly patterned ground, Famille Verte, Kangxi **420.00**

Vase, large Mandarin panels with people and allover decorated, large foo dog handles, gecko decorated, Chinese Export, 35-1/2" h. Photo courtesy of James D. Julia, Inc.

Jar, cov, 19" h, baluster form, domed lid, ovoid finial, birds on rocky outcrop, flowering branches dec, early 20th C, price for pr. **500.00**
Jardinierè, 9-3/4" h, flowering branches dec, Jiaqing. **700.00**
Lamp base, 17" h, figural and crane dec, molded fu-dog mask and ring handles **175.00**
Mug, 5" h, Mandarin palette, Qianlong, 1790. . . . . **425.00**
Plate, 10" d, floral dec, ribbed body, Tongzhi mark, pr **275.00**
Tea caddy, 5-1/2" h, Mandarin palette, arched rect form, painted front, figures and pavilion reserve, c1780 . . . **550.00**
Tea set in basket, teapot with hinged lid, two cups, fitted into 10-1/2" x 8" x 7" h oval basket, brass hardware
. . . . **125.00**
Tray, 8" l, oval, multicolored center armorial crest, underglaze blue diaper and trefoil borders, reticulated rim, late 18th C **550.00**
Vase, 17-1/2" h, Rouleau form, molded fu-dog handles, scene of figures picking fruit from large vines, verso with butterflies, traditional borders, late 19th C **250.00**
Vase, cov, 26" h, shouldered ovoid, large cartouches with scenes of warriors on horseback, dignitaries holding court, molded fu-dog handles, conforming cartouches on lid, fu-dog finial, c1850-70, pr. **2,400.00**

FENTON GLASS

History: The Fenton Art Glass Company began as a cutting shop in Martins Ferry, Ohio, in 1905. In 1906, Frank L. Fenton started to build a plant in Williamstown, West Virginia, and produced the first piece of glass there in 1907. Early production included carnival, chocolate, custard, and pressed glass, plus mold-blown opalescent glass. In the 1920s, stretch glass, Fenton dolphins, jade green, ruby, and art glass were added.

For more information, see this book.

In the 1930s, boudoir lamps, Dancing Ladies, and slag glass in various colors were produced. The 1940s saw crests of different colors being added to each piece by hand. Hobnail, opalescent, and two-color overlay pieces were popular items. Handles were added to different shapes, making the baskets they created as popular then as they are today.

Through the years, Fenton has beautified its glass by decorating it with hand painting, acid etching, and copper-wheel cutting.

Marks: Several different paper labels have been used. In 1970, an oval-raised trademark also was adopted.

Additional Listing: Carnival Glass.

Ashtray, #8482 ruby, three feet . . **20.00**
Basket
  #3839MI, milk glass, 12" oval . **60.00**
  #7237SC Silvercrest, 7" **50.00**
Bell, milk glass, #3667MI **20.00**
Bonbon
  #3937MI, milk glass, handle . . **17.50**
  #8230 Rosalene Butterfly, two handles **35.00**
Bowl
  Peach Crest, Charleton dec . **105.00**
  #846 Pekin Blue, cupped **40.00**
  #848 8 Petal, Chinese Yellow . **45.00**
  #1562 Satin etched Silvertone, oblong bowl **55.00**
  #7423 Milk glass bowl, hp yellow roses **65.00**
  #8222 Rosalene, basketweave
  . . . . **30.00**
Bride's basket, Cranberry Opalescent Hobnail, 10-1/2" d bowl, 11-1/2" h SP frame **300.00**
Bud vase, #3950MI, milk glass, 10" h **22.50**
Candlestick, single
  #318 Pekin Blue, 3" h **40.00**
  #951 Silvercrest Cornucopia . . **37.50**
Candy box, cov
  Hobnail, 6-1/2" sq, white, ... **40.00**
  Ruby Iridized, Butterfly, for FAGCA
  . . . . **100.00**

Basket, Burmese, hp pink flowers, green leaves, $40.

*Butterfly, #5170, chocolate, FAGCA, $55.
Photo courtesy of Ferill Rice.*

#1980CG Daisy and Button .. **45.00**
#7380 Custard hp pink daffodils,
Louise Piper, dated March 1975
.... **160.00**
Compote, #8422 Waterlily ftd, Rosalene
.... **30.00**
Cocktail shaker, #6120 Plymouth,
crystal **55.00**
Cracker jar, Lilac Big Cookies, no lid,
handle **250.00**
Creamer
#1502 Diamond Optic, black . **35.00**
#6464 RG Aventurine Green w/Pink,
Vasa Murrhina **45.00**
Creatures (animals and birds)
#5174 Springtime green iridized
blown rabbit **45.00**
5193 RE Rosalene fish, paperweight
.... **25.00**
#5197 Happiness Bird, cardinals in
winter **32.50**
Cruet, #7701 QJ, 7" Burmese, Petite
Floral **175.00**
Cup and saucer, #7208 Aqua Crest
.... **35.00**
Epergne
#3902 Petite Blue Opal, 4" h. **125.00**
#3902 Petite French Opal, 4" h
.... **40.00**

*Happiness Birds, #5197, ruby, hand
painted by Louis Piper, $85 each.
Photo courtesy of Ferill Rice.*

Fairy light
#1167 RV Rose Magnolia Hobnail
three pcs, Persian Pearl Crest, sgd
"Shelly Fenton" **80.00**
#3380 CR Hobnail, three pcs,
Cranberry Opal **75.00**
#3680 RU Hobnail, three pcs . **55.00**
#3804 CA Hobnail three pcs,
Colonial Amber **25.00**
#8406 WT Heart, Wisteria **65.00**
#8408 VR Persian Medallion, three
pcs, Velva Rose-75th Anniv. . **75.00**
Ginger jar, #893 Persian Pearl w/base
and top **150.00**
Goblet, #1942 Flower Windows Blue
.... **55.00**
Hat, #1922 Swirl Optic, French Opal
.... **110.00**
Jug, #6068 Cased Lilac, handled,
6-1/2" **50.00**
Lamp, Blue Coin Dot, Gone with the
Wind, 31" h **300.00**
Liquor set, #1934 Flower Stopper, floral
silver overlay, eight-pc set **250.00**
Lotus bowl, #849 Red **25.00**
Miniature lamp, Cranberry Coin Spot,
4-5/8" d, 11" h **600.00**
Nut bowl, Sailboats, marigold carnival
.... **50.00**
Pitcher
Amber Crest **115.00**
Plum Opal, Hobnail, water, 80 oz
.... **190.00**
Powder box, #6080, Wave Crest, blue
overlay **95.00**
Plate
Lafayette & Washington, light blue
iridized, sample **80.00**
#107 Ming Rose, 8" **30.00**
#1621 dolphin handled, Fenton
Rose, 6" **25.00**
Punch bowl set, Silver Crest, 15" d,
7-5/8" h ftd punch bowl, 12 4" d, 2-3/4" h
cups, 12-3/4" l handle........ **800.00**
Rose bowl, #8954TH hanging heart
.... **95.00**
Salt and pepper shakers, pr, #3806
Cranberry Opal, Hobnail, flat **47.50**
Sauce, Pinecone, 5" d, red **35.00**
Sherbet
#1942 Flower Windows, crystal
.... **35.00**
#4443 Thumbprint, Colonial Blue
.... **20.00**
Sugar and creamer, #9103 Fine Cut &
Block (OVG) **20.00**
Temple jar, #7488 Chocolate Roses on
cameo satin **25.00**

*Rose bowl, Burmese, trees decorated,
signed "Louise Piper," 3-1/2" h, $95.
Photo courtesy of Joy Luke Auctions.*

Tumbler
#1611 Georgian, Royal Blue, 5-1/2",
ftd, 9 oz **18.00**
#1634 Diamond Optic, Aqua .. **6.00**
#3700, Grecian Gold, grape cut
.... **15.00**
#3945MI Hobnail, 5 oz **10.00**
Tumble-up, Blue Swirl, 8" h, 5-1/2" w,
applied handle, c1939 .... **900.00**
Vase
Aristocrat Bud Vase, #98 cutting,
Fenton Rose............. **45.00**
Butterfly & Berry, red, tightly crimped
edge, 7" h............... **65.00**
Ivory Crest, 10"........... **65.00**
#847 Periwinkle Blue, fan.... **62.50**
#3759 Plum Opal, Hobnail, swung
.... **150.00**
#4454OR Thumbprint, swung **45.00**
#5858 Wild Rose, wheat..... **85.00**
#6457 GA Vasa Murrhina, fan **85.00**
#7460 Amberina Overlay crimped,
6-1/2" h................. **80.00**
#7547 Burmese, hp pink Dogwood,
5-1/2" h................. **75.00**

*Vase, pinched-in sides, mother-of-pearl,
polka dot, green, white lining, 8" h,
price for pair, $150. Photo courtesy of
James D. Julia, Inc.*

Water pitcher, 8-1/2" h, custard, hand-painted fall scene with red barn, chickens, rooster, birds flying, sgd "Jan Curtis," applied ribbed handle . . **395.00**

Water set, Blue Opalescent, 8-1/4" h cannonball-shaped pitcher, six 5" h tumblers **550.00**

FIESTA

History: The Homer Laughlin China Company introduced Fiesta dinnerware in January 1936 at the Pottery and Glass Show in Pittsburgh, Pennsylvania. Frederick Rhead designed the pattern; Arthur Kraft and Bill Bensford molded it. Dr. A. V. Bleininger and H. W. Thiemecke developed the glazes.

The original five colors were red, dark blue, light green (with a trace of blue), brilliant yellow, and ivory. A vigorous marketing campaign took place between 1939 and 1943. In mid-1937, turquoise was added. Red was removed in 1943 because some of the chemicals used to produce it were essential to the war effort; it did not reappear until 1959. In 1951, light green, dark blue, and ivory were retired and forest green, rose, chartreuse, and gray were added to the line. Other color changes took place in the late 1950s, including the addition of a medium green.

Fiesta ware was redesigned in 1969 and discontinued about 1972. In 1986, Homer Laughlin China Company reintroduced Fiesta. The new china body shrinks more than the old semi-vitreous and ironstone pieces, thus making the new pieces slightly smaller than the earlier pieces. The modern colors are also different in tone or hue, e.g., the cobalt blue is darker than the old blue. Other modern colors are black, white, apricot, and rose.

For more information, see this book.

Reproduction Alert

Ashtray

Cobalt blue	55.00
Ivory	55.00
Red	60.00
Turquoise	50.00
Yellow	48.00

Bowl, 5-1/2" d, green **60.00**
Cake plate, green **1,950.00**
Candlesticks, pr, bulb

Cobalt blue	125.00
Ivory	125.00
Red	120.00
Turquoise	110.00
Yellow	105.00

Coffeepot, green, 10-1/2" h, **$50.**

Candlesticks, pr, tripod, yellow
. . . . **550.00**
Carafe

Cobalt blue	495.00
Ivory	385.00

Casserole, cov, two handles, 10" d

Ivory	195.00
Red	200.00
Turquoise	145.00
Yellow	160.00

Chop plate, 13" d, gray **95.00**
Coffeepot

Cobalt blue	235.00
Ivory	390.00
Red	250.00
Turquoise	250.00
Yellow	185.00

Compote, 12" d, low, ftd

Cobalt blue	175.00
Ivory	165.00
Red	185.00
Turquoise	160.00
Yellow	165.00

Creamer

Cobalt blue	35.00
Ivory	30.00
Red	65.00
Turquoise	24.00
Yellow	30.00

Creamer and sugar, figure-eight server, yellow creamer and sugar, cobalt blue gray **315.00**
Cream soup bowl

Cobalt blue	60.00
Ivory	55.00
Red	65.00
Turquoise	48.00
Yellow	45.00

Cup, ring handle

Cobalt blue	35.00

Ivory	30.00
Red	30.00
Turquoise	25.00
Yellow	25.00

Demitasse cup, stick handle

Cobalt blue	75.00
Ivory	80.00
Red	85.00
Turquoise	75.00
Yellow	65.00

Demitasse pot, cov, stick handle

Cobalt blue	650.00
Ivory	535.00
Red	575.00
Turquoise	650.00
Yellow	465.00

Dessert bowl, 6" d

Cobalt blue	50.00
Ivory	45.00
Turquoise	40.00
Yellow	40.00

Egg cup

Cobalt blue	75.00
Ivory	72.00
Red	80.00
Turquoise	55.00
Yellow	70.00

Fruit bowl, cobalt blue, 11-5/8" d, 2-3/4" h, **$485.**

Fruit bowl, 5-1/2" d

Ivory	33.00
Turquoise	25.00
Yellow	25.00

Fruit bowl, 11-3/4" d, cobalt blue
. . . . **485.00**
Gravy boat

Cobalt blue	75.00
Ivory	65.00
Red	85.00
Turquoise	45.00
Yellow	50.00

Juice tumbler

Cobalt blue	40.00
Rose	65.00
Yellow	40.00

Pitcher, yellow, **$195.**

Marmalade jar, cov
Cobalt blue	335.00
Ivory	325.00
Red	345.00
Turquoise	325.00
Yellow	250.00

Mixing bowl
 # 1, 5" d
Cobalt blue	325.00
Ivory	350.00
Red	375.00
#2, cobalt blue	195.00
#2, yellow	140.00
#4, green	195.00
#5, ivory	275.00
#7, ivory	580.00

Mixing bowl lid, #1, red **1,100.00**

Mug
Dark green	90.00
Ivory, marked	125.00
Rose	95.00

Mustard, cov
Cobalt blue	325.00
Turquoise	275.00

Nappy, 8-1/2" d
Cobalt blue	55.00
Ivory	55.00
Turquoise	42.00
Red	55.00
Yellow	45.00

Nappy, 9-1/2" d
Cobalt blue	65.00
Ivory	65.00
Red	70.00
Turquoise	55.00
Yellow	60.00

Onion soup, cov, turquoise . . **8,000.00**

Pitcher, disk
Chartreuse	275.00
Turquoise	110.00

Pitcher, ice lip
Green	135.00
Turquoise	195.00

Plate, deep
Gray	42.00
Rose	42.00

Plate, 6" d
Dark green	15.00
Ivory	7.00
Light green	9.00
Turquoise	8.00
Yellow	5.00

Plate, 7" d
Chartreuse	12.00
Ivory	10.00
Light green	8.50
Medium green	30.00
Rose	14.00
Turquoise	8.50

Plate, 9" d
Cobalt blue	15.00
Ivory	14.00
Medium green	75.00
Red	15.00
Yellow	13.00

Plate, 10" d, dinner
Gray	42.00
Light green	28.00
Medium green	125.00
Red	35.00
Turquoise	30.00

Platter, oval
Gray	35.00
Ivory	25.00
Red	45.00
Yellow	22.00

Relish
Ivory base and center, turquoise inserts	285.00
Red, base and inserts	425.00

Salad bowl, large, ftd
Cobalt blue	375.00

Pitcher, ice lip, orange, **$325.**

Vegetable dish, turquoise, 11" d, **$45.**

Red	460.00
Turquoise	335.00
Yellow	400.00

Salt and pepper shakers, pr
Red	24.00
Turquoise	135.00

Saucer
Light green	5.00
Turquoise	5.00

Soup plate
Ivory	36.00
Turquoise	29.00

Sugar bowl, cov
Chartreuse	65.00
Gray	75.00
Rose	75.00

Syrup
Green	450.00
Ivory	600.00
Red	695.00

Sweetmeat compote, high standard
Cobalt blue	95.00
Ivory	85.00
Red	100.00
Turquoise	125.00
Yellow	400.00

Tea cup, flat bottom, cobalt blue
	100.00

Teapot, medium green, **$175,**

Teapot, light gray, medium, $295.

Grapes, colorless, glass, some internal discoloration, black caps, price for pair, $25.

Teapot, cov

Cobalt blue, large	335.00
Red, large	245.00
Rose, medium	350.00

Tumbler, cobalt blue 75.00

Vase

8" h, green	825.00
8" h, ivory, c1936-42	550.00
12" h, cobalt blue, c1936-42	1,275.00
12" h, light green, c1937-42	1,195.00

FIGURAL BOTTLES

History: Porcelain figural bottles, which have an average height of three to eight inches and were made either in a glazed or bisque finish, achieved popularity in the late 1800s and remained popular into the 1930s. The majority of figural bottles were made in Germany, with Austria and Japan accounting for the balance.

Empty figural bottles were shipped to the United States and filled upon arrival. They were then given away to customers by brothels, dance halls, hotels, liquor stores, and taverns. Some were lettered with the names and addresses of the establishment, while others had paper labels. Many were used for holidays, e.g., Christmas and New Year's.

Figural bottles also were made in glass and other materials. The glass bottles held perfumes, food, or beverages.

Bisque

Cowboy, 7-1/2" h, little black boy dressed in cowboy hat, vest, chaps, marked "Made in Japan" 125.00

Farmer's Relief, 5-1/2" h, marked "Made in Japan," wear to paint .. 45.00

Man, 4-1/" h, toasting, "Your Health," flask style, tree bark back....... 85.00

Sailor, 6-1/2" h, white pants, blue blouse, hat, high-gloss front, marked "Made in Germany" 115.00

Glass

Ballet dancer, 12" h, milk glass, pink and brown paint dec highlights, sheared mouth, removable head as closure, pontil scar, attributed to America, 1860-90 .... 525.00

Barrel, 4-7/8" h, yellow olive green, fancy rigaree trailing around body, two sleigh runner feet serve as base, each emb with repeating sunburst motif, tooled mouth, pontil scar, Europe, 18th C 450.00

Bear, 10-5/8" h, dense yellow amber, sheared mouth, applied face, Russia, 1860-80, flat chip on back..... 400.00

Big Stick, Teddy Roosevelt's, 7-1/2" h, golden amber, sheared mouth, smooth base, flat flake at mouth 170.00

Portrait, standing figure of Paul Ohm, smoking pipe which forms the spout, wearing top hat as stopper, majolica, impressed "BB" and numbers, French, c1895, restoration to stopper, 12-1/4" h, $495. Photo courtesy of David Rago Auctions.

Cabin, 9" h, two stories, Kelly's Old Cabin Bitters, dark olive green 5,675.00

Cherub, holding medallion, 11-1/8" h, blue opaque milk glass, sq collared mouth, ground pontil scar, attributed to America, 1860-90............ 120.00

Fish, 11-1/2" h, Doctor Fisch's Bitters, golden amber, applied small round collared mouth, smooth base, America, 1860-80, some ext. high point wear, burst bubble on base......... 160.00

Garfield, James, President, 8" h, colorless-glass bust set in turned-wood base, ground mouth, smooth base, America, 1880-1900........... 80.00

Indian maiden, 12-1/4" h, Brown's Celebrated Indian Herb Bitters, yellow amber, inward rolled mouth, smooth base, America, 1860-80...... 600.00

Pig, 10-3/8" l, Berkshire Bitters, golden amber 1,200.00

Queen Mary, ocean liner, c1936 .... 155.00

Shoe, dark amethyst, ground mouth, smooth base................ 125.00

Washington, George, 10" h, Simon's Centennial Bitters, aquamarine, applied double-collared mouth, smooth base, America, 1860-80............ 650.00

Pottery and porcelain

Camel, 4" h, mother of pearl glaze, os 45.00

Canteen, painted bust of Lincoln, Garfield, and McKinley, half pint 375.00

Cucumber, 11-3/4" l, stoneware, green and cream mottled glaze...... 100.00

Fox, reading book, beige, brown mottled dec 95.00

Mermaid, 7-1/4" h, brown and tan Rockingham-type glaze....... 125.00

Pretzel, brown 85.00

FINDLAY ONYX GLASS

History: Findlay onyx glass, produced by Dalzell, Gilmore & Leighton Company, Findlay, Ohio, was patented for the firm in 1889 by George W. Leighton. Due to high production costs resulting from a complex manufacturing process, the glass was made only for a short time.

For more information, see this book.

Layers of glass were plated to a bulb of opalescent glass through repeated dippings into a glass pot. Each layer was cooled and reheated to develop opalescent qualities. A pattern mold then was used to produce raised decorations of flowers and leaves. A second mold gave the glass bulb its full shape and form.

A platinum luster paint, producing pieces identified as silver or platinum onyx, was applied to the raised decorations. The color was fixed in a muffle kiln. Other colors such as cinnamon, cranberry, cream, raspberry, and rose were achieved by using an outer glass plating, which reacted strongly to reheating. For example, a purple or orchid color came from the addition of manganese and cobalt to the glass mixture.

Toothpick holder, $350. Photo courtesy of Clarence and Betty Maier.

Celery vase, cream **450.00**
Cream pitcher, platinum-colored blossoms, creamy-white background, opalescent clear-glass handle . **435.00**
Dresser box, cov, 5" d, cream . **675.00**
Pitcher, 7-1/2" h, cream, applied opalescent handle, polished rim chip **800.00**
Spooner, 4-1/2" h, satin surface, bright silver dec **525.00**
Sugar, cov, 6" h, Onyx, platinum blossoms, cream-white ground, silver medallion on base of bowl, rim chip and roughness to cover **485.00**
Sugar shaker, raspberry **495.00**
Syrup, 7" h, 4" w, silver dec, applied opalescent handle **1,150.00**
Toothpick holder, cream **350.00**

Mustard jar, covered, raspberry, SP cover, 3-3/8" h, $1,350.

FINE ARTS

History: Before the invention of cameras and other ways to mechanically capture an image, paintings, known as portraits, served to capture the likeness of an individual. Paintings have been done in a variety of mediums and on varying canvases, boards, etc. Often it was what was available in a particular area or time that influenced the materials. Having one's portrait painted was often a sign of wealth and many artists found themselves in demand once their reputations became established. Today art historians, curators, dealers, and collectors study portraits to determine the age of the painting and often use clues found in the backgrounds or clothing of the sitter to determine age, if no identification is available. Many portraits have a detailed provenance that allows the sitters, and often the artists, to be identified.

In any calendar year, tens, if not hundreds of thousands, of paintings are sold. Prices range from a few dollars to millions. Since each painting is essentially a unique creation, it is difficult to compare prices.

At Full Sail, sgd "Crowell, 1880" lower left, American School, oil on canvas, framed, 10" x 14", surface grime, craquelure **635.00**
Barque sailing off the coast, unsigned, English, 19th C, oil on canvas, framer's label attached to stretcher, framed, 21-1/4" x 31" **2,875.00**
Entering Boston Harbor, Lemuel D. Eldred, sgd "L. D. Eldred's '80" lower left, oil on canvas, 20" x 29-3/4", framed **8,625.00**
Gloucester Harbor, James McCorkindale, sgd "McCorkindale" lower right, oil on canvas, 20" x 24", framed **650.00**
Harbor Inlet, Sunset, initialed and dated "JF 1862" lower right, attributed to James Fairman, oil on canvas, 7" x 13", framed, repaired, retouched

Jacob Greenleaf, titled Surf at Andrews Point, oil on board, signed lower left "J. Greenleaf," 16" x 20", $350. Photo courtesy of Sanford Alderfer Auction Company.

punctures, surface grime, craquelure **1,725.00**
Harbor scene, John K. Thurston, watercolor on paper, sgd lower right "J. K. Thurston," 10" x 14" **435.00**
Laguna Surf & Sky, Roy Ropp, sgd "Royal M. Ropp" lower right, inscribed titled and sgd on reverse, oil on canvas, 30" x 48", framed **1,500.00**
Mending the Nets, Vladmir Pavlosky, sgd "Vladmir Pavlosky" lower left, oil on canvas, 28" x 34-1/4", framed . **8,625.00**
Midnight Sail, sgd "James G. Tyler" lower right, identified on presentation plaque affixed to frame, oil on canvas, 24" x 20", framed, lined, scattered retouch **1,100.00**
On Rough Seas, unsigned, attributed to Chalrs Louis Verboeckhoven, identified on reverse, oil on panel, 8-1/2" x 11-3/4", prevalent craquelure . **865.00**

Portrait

American steamer *El Rio,* sgd, dated, and inscribed "A. Jacobsen 1893...705 Palisade Av. West Hoboken NJ" lower right, oil on canvas, framed, 22" x 36", scattered retouch, craquelure **12,650.00**

British two-masted schooner *Fanny,* unsigned, oil on canvas, vessel identified on bow, framed, 21-1/4" x 36-1/4", tear center left, scattered losses and punctures, surface grime **2,185.00**

Four masted schooner *Thomas S. Dennison,* sgd, inscribed, and dated "Antonio Jacobsen 1910 31 Paliade av West Hoboken NJ" lower left, vessel identified on bow,

Abraham Hulk, coastal scene with boats, oil on mahogany panel, signed "A. Hul" lower left, sailboat flying Dutch flag with people, row boat with people in choppy seas, coastline with six people on shore next to lighthouse, gilt replacement frame, 12" h, $1,725. Photo courtesy of James D. Julia, Inc.

Alice Kent Stoddard, seascape, oil on canvas, signed lower right: "Alice Kent Stoddard," 18" x 26", $1,600. Photo courtesy of Sanford Alderfer Auction Company.

stern, and flag, oil on board, 35-1/4" w, 21-3/4" h, prevalent flaking and loss, varnish inconsistencies **11,500.00**

Ship *George Thomas* West Master From Calcutta, Off Cap Ann Bound to Salem Mass, 1820, unsigned, ink and gouache on paper, titled beneath image, framed, 13-1/2" x 16-3/4", stabilized tears, staining **1,725.00**

Ship *Republic*, unsigned, attributed to William Pierce Stubbs, vessel identified on bow and stern, oil on canvas, mounted onto masonite, framed, 42" w, 26" h, retouched, scattered flaking and losses **5,465.00**

Steamer *United States,* sgd, dated, and inscribed "A. Jacobsen 257 8 Av NY 1879" lower right, oil on canvas, framed, 22" x 36", slight damage to tacking edge, tears center left, surface grime, and craquelure **13,800.00**

Preparing the Boat, sgd indistinctly lower left, Dutch School 19th C, oil on panel, 10" x 13-3/4", surface grime, craquelure **5,750.00**

Pulling the Boats Ashore, Rockport, unsigned, attributed to Harry Aiken Vincent, oil on board, 11" x 14", framed **2,300.00**

Rough Seas Ahead, John Mundell, sgd "J. Mundell" lower left, oil on canvas, 10" x 18", framed, scattered retouch, craquelure **1,495.00**

Sailboats at Wharf-Holland, unsigned, attributed to Charles Herbert Woodbury, oil on canvas, 8-1/4" x 10-1/4", framed, cut down, lined, minor scattered retouch **1,265.00**

Sailing vessels off the coast, lighthouse in distance, sgd and dated

"W. Plummer 1886" lower right, oil on canvas, framed, 14" x 26", repaired, retouched, craquelure **1,035.00**

Seaport, Rotterdam, sgd, dated, and inscribed "W. C. Ripp 1894, Rotterdam," lower right, watercolor and gouache on board, 20-3/4" x 28-1/2", framed, toning and fading **500.00**

Septembre, La Meuse a Dordrecht, Marie Joseph Leon Clavel, sgd "Iwill" lower right, sgd, inscribed, and titled "Iwill, Marie Joseph I quai Voltaire Paris…" and partial label from Exposition de Strasbourg on reverse, oil on canvas, 13-1/4" x 19-1/2", framed **2,650.00**

Still Harbor, Sunset, sgd "P. Solant" lower right, American School, 19th C, oil on canvas, 9-3/4" x 15", framed, varnish inconsistencies **920.00**

Sunday Morning on the Harbor, sgd and dated "Vladmir Pavlosky 1930" lower right, watercolor on paper, 16-1/4" x 21-1/2", framed **1,380.00**

Sunset Sailing, Archibald Cary Smith, sgd "A. Cary Smith '74" lower right, oil on canvas, 12-1/4" x 23", framed **25,300.00**

Surf, Israel Doskow, oil on board, sgd lower left "Israel Doskow," 12" x 16" **300.00**

Two masted vessel at sea, unsigned, American School, 19th C, oil on canvas, 20" w, 12" h, lined, minor retouch, scattered flaking and losses, craquelure **6,440.00**

Vessels in a Harbor, Robert Salmon, initialed and dated "R. S. 1839" lower right, sgd and dated "Painted by R. Salmon 1839 No. 4" on reverse, oil on panel, 9-3/4" x 12", framed, surface grime, craquelure **52,900.00**

Henry H. Nichols, titled After the Storm, '95, oil on canvas, signed lower right "H. Nichols," relined, 15" x 25", $750. Photo courtesy of Sanford Alderfer Auction Company.

Waves Crashing Ashore, Henry A. Duessel, sgd "Duessel" lower right, oil on board, 9" x 12", framed, subtle surface grime, craquelure **815.00**

Yachts, A Marine Scene, Clement Drew, sgd "C. Drew" lower right, sgd, titled, and dated 1878 on reverse, oil on canvas, 7" x 10", framed **3,750.00**

FIREARM ACCESSORIES

History: Muzzle-loading weapons of the 18th and early 19th centuries varied in caliber and required the owner to carry a variety of equipment, including a powder horn or flask, patches, flints or percussion caps, bullets, and bullet molds. In addition, military personnel were responsible for bayonets, slings, and miscellaneous cleaning equipment and spare parts.

During the French and Indian War, soldiers began to personalize their powder horns with intricate engraving, in addition to the usual name or initial used for identification. Sometimes professional horn smiths were employed to customize these objects, which have been elevated to a form of folk art by some collectors.

Cody's Colt

SoldUSA.com sold Wild West's Buffalo Bill's Colt single-action Army revolver, c1886, in June 2002 for $25,000. This presentation piece features Colt black hard rubber grips depicting an eagle with shield on the lower end, and a bucking colt near the upper side. It's a 44/40 caliber, 4-3/4" barrel, nickel plated, with 99 percent of the original blue finish. Legend has it that William Cody authorized the refinishing and nickel plating before it was presented to C. R. Filkins, son of Lidia Sarah Cody, Bill's cousin. Included with the lot were five original documents relating to the gun, original bills of sale, etc.

In the mid-19th century, cartridge weapons replaced their black-powder ancestors. Collectors seek anything associated with early ammunition—from the cartridges themselves to advertising material. Handling old ammunition can be extremely dangerous because of decomposition of compounds. Seek advice from an experienced collector before becoming involved in this area.

Reproduction Alert: There are a large number of reproduction and fake powder horns. Be very cautious!

Notes: Military-related firearm accessories generally are worth more than their civilian counterparts.

Bullet board, 55-3/4" x 40", Union Metallic Cartridge Co., Bridgeport, CT, 1907, canvasback ducks in snowstorm, litho on cardboard, orig oak frame **9,500.00**

Calendar, 1918, Marble Arms & Mfg Co., artwork by Philip R. Goodwin, top image of two hunters, one with gun raised at animal across river, bottom

Advertising poster, Hercules Powder Co., 1920, titled "Don't You Fool Me, Dog!" image of shabbily dressed black man holding old muzzle loading fowler, standing on snow covered log, skinny dog sniffing in foreground, rabbit escaping in the background, by F.M. Spiegle, advertisement for Hercules Powder Co. and their various smokeless and black powders at bottom, 15-1/2" w, 25" h, $2,875. Photo courtesy of James D. Julia Auctions.

Bowie knife, stag grip, blade marked "Kingman & Hassam Boston," some chips, few nicks, $4,670. Photo courtesy of Jackson's Auctioneers & Appraisers.

image with man by campfire, docked canoe **5,230.00**

Canteen, 7" d, 2-5/8" deep, painted, cheese-box style, dark red paint overall, one side painted gold with a large primitive eagle with shield breast, the top of the shield red with cream lettering "No. 37," other side painted in gold letters, "Lt. Rufus Cook," pewter nozzle, sq nail construction, strap loops missing **1,650.00**

Cartridge board, 22" x 25", Winchester, New Haven, CT, 1874, showing range of rimfire cartridges, wood frame, some shelf spoiling, corner repair to frame **12,915.00**

Cartridge box

3-7/8" x 2" x 1", Hall and Hubbard, .22 caliber, green and black label "100 No. 1/22-100/Pistol Cartridges," cov with molded cream and black paper, empty, missing about half green side label **300.00**

4" x 2-1/8" x 1-1/4", Union Metallic Cartridge Co., .32 caliber, cream and black label "Fifth .32 caliber/No. 2/Pistol Cartridges," engraving of Smith & Wesson 1st Model 3rd Issue, checked covering, orange and black side labels, unopened **210.00**

Catalog

Colt's-The Arm of Law and Order, 5-3/4" x 7-3/4", 42 pgs, black and white illus and specifications of 16 models of Colt revolvers and automatic pistols **25.00**

Savage Arms Corp., Chicopee Falls, MA, 1951, 52 pgs, 8-1/2" x 11", No. 51, *Component Parts Price List for Savage, Stevens, Fox Shotguns & Rifles* **35.00**

Winchester Repeating Arms, New Haven, CT, 1918, 215 pgs, 5-1/2" x 8-1/2", Cat No. 81, illus of repeating and single-shot rifles, repeating shotguns, cartridges, shells, primers, percussions caps, shot **250.00**

Flask, 8" l, brass, dead game, emb, stamped "Am. Flask & Cap Co." **200.00**

Knapsack, 13-5/8" x 13-1/4", painted canvas, flap having American eagle with shield among stars and surrounded by oval cloud border, scrolled banner inscribed "RIFLE CADET," painted in red, white, blue, and gold on black ground, two leather strap and iron buckles, reverse with ink inscription, "Benjamin Pope Bridgewater July 4th 1820," minor paint losses, wooden hanger and twine attached to the back **31,725.00**

Painting, 24" x 33", Blazing the Trail, by Philip R. Goodwin, oil on canvas **110,000.00**

Poster, store type, 41-1/2" x 32", Winchester Rifles, Shotguns and Ammunition For Sale Here, two bear dogs in foreground, bloodhounds in back **6,300.00**

Powder horn

11" l, engraved town surrounding upper part of horn, harbor and ships around plug, sgd "Benjamin Hills Horn, c1760 .... **1,760.00**

12" l, engraved coat of arms above house with hunter, deer, and dog, unengraved banner at top **1,550.00**

12" l, engraved large tree with many birds flanked by hunter and deer, flowering tulip vine and geometric border, tip paneled extending to two raised rings, smooth area extending to dec, inscribed "IVORY SOULE Horn November: y 25 1776," the butt fitted with domed pine plug attached with copper nails, genealogical info accompanying horn traces MA family, and service of Ivory Soule as soldier in Revolutionary War, old 1" crack **3,525.00**

13" l, engraved Adam and Eve with village and lion dec, initialed "G. S. M." **1,760.00**

16" l, engraved, initialed "S B 1790, JHB 1840," top fitted with carved

Combination bullet mold-loading tool, Ideal, cal. 38-55M, nickel finish, standard tool, missing expander plug, one line of deep pitting on outside, $55. Photo courtesy of James D. Julia Auctions.

wooden plug, incised ring at tip, incised band at the throat, recessed portion extends to engraved area with scalloped edge, fine sawtooth border, engraved American eagle with shield and banner inscribed "E Pluribus Unum," axe wielding figure, various other animal and stylistic geometric devices, highlighted with blue, mustard, and brown stains, attached with brass tacks to domed wooden butt plug having brass knob, New England, five small old holes **3,100.00**

18" l, engraved, initialed "Wm M. 1799," also "J. M. 1814," surrounded by series of inscribed circles, flat pine plug **1,200.00**

18" l, engraved, "stil not this horn for fear of shame for hear doth stand the oner name jacob lewis 1785, (sic)" two rows of geometric devices round bottom, carved and incised lines at spout,

Powder horn, engraved, signed and dated "I. Wakefield 1760," and "Oswego 1757," man shooting deer scrimshawed by horn's maker, buildings, double headed eagle, and floral decorated with people by different hand, but of the same period, 14-1/2" l, $1,430. Photo courtesy of Garth's Auctions, Inc.

dome-shaped wooden plug, America, late 18th C, small age crack, wear **1,610.00**
Primer, 7" l, engraved, New York scene, primitively engraved men and animals, date "1852" added later, c1800
. . . . **1,155.00**
Product leaflet
Western Silvertip Ammunition, 3-1/2" x 6" closed, glossy paper, color printing, diecut upper corner, one side shows 18 variations of brass cartridges in differing gauges for large game hunting, one panel devoted to three Winchester hunting rifles, 1956 . . . . **25.00**
Western-Winchester, 3-1/4" x 6-1/2" closed, full color printing, illus and describes western Super-X and Xpert shotgun shells and cartridges, 1957 . . . . **15.00**
Shotgun box, empty
Austin Cartridge Co., Crack-Shot, 16 gauge, full-color scene of three hunting dogs on front **2,310.00**
Chamberlin Cartridge Co., 12 gauge, Blue Rocks **1,100.00**
Chamberlin Cartridge Co., 12 gauge ruffled grouse, c1870 . . . . **3,885.00**
J. F. Schmelzer & Sons Arms Co., 12 gauge carver cartridges, illus of hunter and pointed on front
. . . . **1,750.00**
Peters Quick Shot, 12 gauge shotgun shells **5,835.00**
Robin Hood Eclipse Cartridge, 12 gauge, near smokeless powder shells **2,550.00**
Tin, Oriental Smokeless Gunpowder, half pound, four litho labels with full-color ducks **1,810.00**
Tinder box, 4-3/8" d, tin, candle socket, inside damper, flint, and steel . . **330.00**
Tinder lighter, flintlock
5-1/2" l, rosewood pistol grip, tooled brass fittings **750.00**
6-1/2" l, compartment for extra flint, taper holder **550.00**
Water keg, 9" x 7-1/2" x 9", wooden, American, late 18th/early 19th C, oval, flattened bottom, two Shaker-style wide-tongued wooden straps, large hand-forged nail on each end for carrying cord, orig wood stopper
. . . . **400.00**

FIREARMS

History: The 15th-century Matchlock Arquebus was the forerunner of the modern firearm. The Germans

refined the wheelock firing mechanism during the 16th and 17th centuries. English settlers arrived in America with the smoothbore musket; German settlers had rifled arms. Both used the new flintlock firing mechanism.

A major advance was achieved when Whitney introduced interchangeable parts into the manufacturing of rifles. Refinements in firearms continued in the 19th century. The percussion ignition system was developed by the 1840s. Minie, a French military officer, produced a viable projectile. By the end of the 19th century, cartridge weapons dominated the field.

Notes: Two factors control the pricing of firearms—condition and rarity. Variations in these factors can cause a wide range in the value of antique firearms. For instance, a Colt 1849 pocket-model revolver with a five-inch barrel can be priced from $100 to $700, depending on whether all the component parts are original, some are missing, how much of the original finish (bluing) remains on the barrel and frame, how much silver plating remains on the brass trigger guard and back strap, and the condition and finish of the walnut grips.

Be careful to note a weapon's negative qualities. A Colt Peterson belt revolver in fair condition will command a much higher price than the Colt pocket model in very fine condition. Know the production run of a firearm before buying it.

Laws regarding the sale of firearms have gotten stricter. Be sure to sell and buy firearms through auction houses and dealers properly licensed to transact business in this highly regulated area.

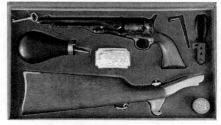

Commemorative, Colt Model 1860, Army, cased, revolver with shoulder stock, 44.caliber, 8" round bbl, French recessed case with replica accessories and belt buckle, unused, $615. Photos courtesy of James D. Julia, Inc.

Carbine

Burnside Precision, 21" round barrel, orig dark finish, bold inspectors' marks and signatures, 39-1/2" l, as found condition **1,320.00**
Hall-North, Model 1843, percussion, 52 caliber, rifled 21" barrel, bold metal stampings, signature and 1849 on receiver, traces of old brown finish, walnut stock with old split between trigger guard and barrel, small repairs near breech, 40" l **935.00**

Joslyn Model 1862, .52 caliber, 22" round barrel, walnut stock, clear inspector's markings, brass buttplate, trigger guard and barrel band, stamped signatures on lock and breech block, 38-5/8" l **650.00**

C. S. Richmond, .58 caliber, 25" barrel, all-steel hardware, brass nose cap, butt plate stamped "U.S.," Type 3, humpback lock, "C. S. Richmond, 1864" mark, no sling swivels, 43" l **3,300.00**

Sharp's New Model 1863, breech loading, walnut stock and forearm, double inspectors markings, 22" blued barrel, areas of very light case coloring on lock, butt plate, hammer, barrel band, and receiver, clear stampings on lock, 34" l **1,980.00**

Spencer, Civil War Model, .52 caliber rimfire, 22" round barrel, overall brown finish on all metal surfaces, worn walnut stick, faint inspector's mark, forearm with additional coat of varnish, 39" l **2,100.00**

Springfield, Model 1884 Trapdoor, saddle ring, mint bore, Buffington sight, stamped "C. Proper," range with inspector's cartouche **825.00**

Wesson, Frank, 28" octagonal barrel, folding rear peep sight, walnut stock with orig dark finish, rear open sight missing, 43" l overall **275.00**

Colt, martially marked, third model dragoon, cal. 44, usual configuration and markings, 7-1/2" bbl, German silver front sight, three-leaf bbl sight, cut for shoulder stock with four-screw frame, one-piece walnut grips with brass trigger guard and iron back strap. All matching numbers, iron has been cleaned and artificially aged with a light brown patina, broken mainspring is broken, hammer will not fall, **$2,070.**

Commemorative

Browning American Mallard, over under shotgun, cal 12 ga, Belgian made engraved superposed Browning with 28" vent rib barrels, choked FULL/MOD with double ivory beads, highly figured oil finished wood finely checkered with long tang and round knob stock, 14-3/8" over checkered

Colt, model 1902 military long slide semi-auto pistol, cal 38, blued finish, 6" bbl with front slide checkering, fixed sights, checkered round hammer, slide lock and lanyard swivel on left side of frame, Rampant Colt black hard rubber grips, all blued eight-round magazine with patent date on bottom, bright shiny bore, **$1,210.**

butt, fitted with single selective gold trigger and ejectors, engraved Angelo Bee style French gray receiver and trigger guard, full coverage Arabesque patterns and game scenes of Mallard ducks in high relief gold in great detail in gold ovals on both sides, each panel has two full-bodied Mallards in flight with two more high relief flying Mallards on bottom, trigger guard with high relief Mallard head on bow, bottom of receiver inlaid in gold in rib and "AMERICAN MALLARD ANAS PLATYAHYNCHOS" and "062 OF 500," orig red velvet lined walnut presentation case with full-length piano hinge and three latches with leather carrying handle, new, unfired **5,175.00**

Sam Colt, single action revolver, cal. 44-40, all blued finish, 7-1/2" bbl, gold dec on bbl, cylinder and frame, inscriptions on both sides of bbl and "1 of 1000" on frame, unfluted cylinder has likenesses of Colt as young sailor on one side and traditional bearded Sam Colt, accompanied by second fluted cylinder, fitted with eagle on other side, rampant Colt black composition grips, gray velvet-lined fitted oak case with Lucite block containing hand forged nail, statement that it was removed from Colt Armorers' residences during restoration, appears to be new and unfired with only the hint of cylinder line **920.00**

Dueling pistols, percussion lock

English, London, second quarter 19th C, dolphin hammer, belt clip, engraved scrollwork on frame, checkered burl-wood grip, barrel engraved "London," 8-1/2" l, price for pr . .**650.00**

Flintlock pistol, Johnson Model 1836, cal 54. 8-1/2" round bbl, dated 1844 on lock, Sharp "JH" and "W.A.T" inspector marks on left side of stock, **$2,415.**

English, Queen-Anne style, London, for J. Wilson, late 18th C, scrolled mask butt, grip set with small monogrammed cartouche, plain stylized dolphin hammer, cannon barrel engraved with cartouches, and maker's mark on underside, 8" l, price for pr **500.00**

Flintlock long arms

French, Model 1766 Charlesville Musket, 44-3/4" l orig barrel length, lock plate only partially legible, matching ramrod, top jaw and top screw period replacements **1,250.00**

Golcher, Joseph, Philadelphia, PA, c1800, .54 caliber, octagonal barrel, brass patch box, butt plate, trigger guard, carved and brass-fitted pick compartment, brass and silver inlays along tiger maple stock, lock plate marked, barrel initialed, 54" l, 38-1/2" l **4,750.00**

Kentucky, R. E. Leman, cal. 38, 37-3/8" oct. bbl with small brass front sight and fixed rear sight, top flat in front of chamber area is marked "R.E. LEMAN/LANCASTER PA/WARRANTED," unmarked flat lock plate, applied grain tiger striped stock, simple brass trigger guard, two-pc patch box with crescent butt plate and dbl. set triggers, ovoid forestock with integral ramrod groove and two small brass guides, dark heavy patina on iron and wood **920.00**

Pennsylvania, attributed to W. Haga, Reading School, 50-1/2" l octagon to round barrel, maple stock, relief carving, incised details, brass hardware with flintlock, some age cracks, glued repair, good patina, replaced patch box lid. **1,760.00**

U. S. Model 1819, Hall, breech loading, second-production type, Harpers Ferry Armory, John Hall's patents, .52 caliber, single shot, 32-5/8" round barrel, three barrel bands, breechblock deeply stamped **1,200.00**

Pepperbox, Cooper Under Hammer, cal. 36. 3-1/4" fluted bbls, marked "J.R. COOPERS/PATENT" on left side of lightly engraved frame, Birmingham proof marks on bbl group, $375.

Virginia, curly-maple stock with good figure, relief carving, old mellow varnished finish, brass hardware, engraved and pierced patch box, Ketland lock reconverted back to flint, silver thumb piece inlay, 41-1/2 l barrel and fore-end shortened slightly, small pierced repair at breech area, top flat engraved "H. B." **3,300.00**

Flintlock pistols-single shot
English

Blunderbuss, 29-1/2" overall, 14" round iron barrel with Birmingham proofs, fitted with 12-1/2" triangular snap bayonet, walnut full stock with lightly engraved brass furniture, two ramrod pipes, butt plate, trigger guard, small shield-shaped wrist plate, two lock-plate screw escutcheons, attributed to John Whitehouse, early 19th C, metal parts complete and orig throughout, missing sliver of wood along right side at muzzle **1,500.00**

Tower, .60 caliber, 12" round barrel, full-length military stock, brass trigger guard, butt cap and sidelined, lock plate marked "Tower" behind hammer and crown over "GR" forward of hammer, proofed on left side of barrel at breech, crown on tang behind tang screw, good condition, re-browned and cleaned, replaced front sight, working order **700.00**

French, military, 16" overall length, 9" round iron barrel, flat beveled lock plate with faceted pan fitted with flat beveled reinforced hammer, brass furniture, unmarked **800.00**

Halsbach & Sons, Baltimore, MD, holster pistol, c1785 to early 1800s, 9" brass part round, part octagon barrel, .65 caliber, lock marked "Halsbach & Sons," large brass butt cap with massive spread wing eagle (primitive) in high relief surrounded by cluster of 13 stars, large relief shell carving around tang of barrel, full walnut stock, pin-fastened **1,750.00**

Kentucky, T. B. Cherington, 12-1/2" octagonal smoothbore barrel, stamped "T. P. Cherington" on barrel and lock plate, .45 caliber, brightly polished iron parts, walnut stock **2,500.00**

U. S. Model 1805, 10" round iron barrel with iron rib underneath holding ramrod pipe, lockplate marked with spread eagle and shield over "US" and vertically at rear "Harper's Ferry" over "1808," .54 caliber, walnut half stock with brass butt plate and trigger guard, Flayderman 6A-008 . . . . **3,000.00**

Musket
Colt, Model 1861, .58 caliber, 39" barrel, "17th N.Y.V." beneath stock, good signature, date, and stampings on metal, inspector's cartouche on stock, bright gray metal, areas of pitting around bolster and lock **1,375.00**

Enfield, dated 1856, cal 58, unmarked, percussion, 39" bbl, square base front sight/bayonet lug with 800 meter military sight, lock plate has markings of acrown over "VR" and date "1856," right side of butt stock carries cartouche of circle with broad arrow and date "1856," three bbl bands with sling swivels and slotted head ramrod, upper bbl band and sling loop, as well as sling loop on trigger and ramrod, appear to be recent replacements, bbl retains smooth gray-brown patina with heavy pitting over breech end, light refinish to wood, worn and damaged nipple. **815.00**

Harper's Ferry, Model 1816 Conversion Musket, cal 69, standard 1816 Model, makers' name and date 1837 vertically behind hammer, small eagle over "US" in front of hammer on lock plate, 42" bbl with top bayonet lug and front sight on rear strap of split front band, iron mounted with three bands and tulip head ramrod, left flat has inspector's initials "JAS," conversion accomplished by mounting nipple at breech end of bbl and filling flash pan cut-out with brass, fine condition, iron retains dark smoky patina with light pitting around nipple area, fine hand-rubbed patina, broken away nipple **690.00**

Parker Snow & Co., Miller conversion, 40" round barrel, bold stampings include signature, eagle, and 1864 on lock, 56" overall **1,375.00**

Springfield, Model 1863 Musket, cal 58. 40" bbl, heavily rusted, deeply pitted except for replacement ramrod, stock is sound, but has some scorching damage, bolster is battered from lack of nipple, lock works **815.00**

Tower, percussion, sling, triangular bayonet, orig browned surfaces on barrel, lock, and barrel bands, signature with 1862 and crown on lock plate, walnut stock stamped "Birmingham small arms trade" with stamped crown, brass butt plate, trigger guard, sling with two tompons for barrel, 55-1/4" l **2,100.00**

U.S. Moro, large bore, 31-1/2" round barrel, single shot, center fire, may have been made to shoot shot shells, pulls apart at center for loading, walnut stock with fine figure, 45" l **250.00**

Percussion pistol
English

Folding bayonet, simple engraving on frame, stands of flags and "Lenning," old hairlines in grip, 4" l barrel, 8-1/2" l **250.00**

Single shot, sgd "W. Parker" on lock, "Maker to His Majesty, London" on barrel, finely checkered bag grip, narrow pierced repair just below lock, 8-1/4" l **715.00**

U. S. Springfield, lock stamped with signature and 1856, eagle on Maynard primer door, 12" barrel dated 1855, brass hardware with iron back strap, walnut shoulder stock, brass hardware, few hairlines, pierced repair on hammer, 28-1/2" l **1,750.00**

Vincent, target, cal. 52, Belgium made, 9-1/8" oct. damascus bbls, marked on

Springfield, model 1795 flintlock musket, cal. 69, 42-1/2" bbl. Lock plate marked "Springfield" in downward curing arch behind hammer, eagle over "US" in front, bbl has been slightly shortened, breech bushed or re-converted, lock with original parts, stock has slight "flame grain" appearance toward the front, $1,265.

top flat with makers name, iron mounted in one-pc half stock with carved fore end tip and fluted butt, secured with single wedge through German silver escutcheons, trigger guard has short finger rest, set triggers, all mounts, hammer and lock plate lightly engraved in arabesque patterns, front action locks with makers' name behind hammer, number 7747 inside trigger guards and bottom of bbls, bbls retain 65-70 percent orig pattern, cleaned to near bright with scattered light surface pitting, wood is sound and retains most of old refinish, gray metal colored fittings, nipple on one damaged, hammer spur on other repaired
. . . . **1,380.00**

Waters, 8-1/2" round barrel, bright metal, stamped address and "1838" on lock, double inspector markings on stock, 14" l **660.00**

Pistol

Colt Model 1911 Army, .45 caliber auto, orig blued finish, checkered walnut grips, good signature and other stampings, 8-1/2" l **825.00**

Sharp's Pepperbox, four shot, .22 caliber, 3" barrels, traces of orig bluing, stamped signature, patent information around hammer screw, gutta percha grips with checkered design, 5-1/2" l
. . . . **220.00**

Volcanic Lever Action, Navy, .38 caliber, 8" barrel, signature "The Volcanic Repeating Arms Co." on top, walnut grips, brass frame with old patina, minor pitting on one side, tab for magazine tube broken, spring missing, 14-1/2" l **9,900.00**

Revolver, pocket, Colt Model 49, cased, factory engraved, cal. 31, style of Gustav Young, full frame coverage arabesque patterns mixed in over bbl lug, up side flats, and loading lever, engraved hammer, arrow at sight notch, wolves heads on other side, engraved grips, small shield on trigger bow and back strap with full coverage gold wash, highly figured one-piece walnut grips, original purple velvet lined compartmented case with brass bullet mold, small eagle flask, Eley's cap box, packet of skin cartridges, **$6,325.**

Revolver, Smith & Wesson, model 1917 Army, cal. 45, blued finish, 5-1/2" bbl, usual markings, missing "US Property" on bottom of bbl, white plastic grips and grip adapter, **$375.**

Revolver

Baby Dragoon, cal. 31, standard 5" oct. bbl without rammer, cylinder has round stop holes, brass grip frame with one-pc wood grips, top flat of bbl is devoid of orig Colt markings, very faintly visible word "Orleans," presumably stamp of New Orleans retailer, medium gray-brown patina on iron, repaired and refinished grip, shoulder repairs on back strap, accompanied by hand-written letter stating that this revolver was owned and used by Confederate Col. Henry C. Kellogg **4,025.00**

Colt

Model 1849 Pocket, 4" barrel, .31 caliber, faint New York address, all serial numbers matching, replaced catch **495.00**

Model 1851 Navy, .36 caliber, percussion, all serial numbers matching, Hartford address on barrel, one screwhead damaged below barrel, grip chips, 13" l
. . . . **1,320.00**

Model 1860 Army, matching serial numbers, butt signature, New York address, overall light brown to gray surface on metal, brass trigger guard, iron grip straps, 8" barrel, 14" overall, old corner chips on grips, period black leather holster with raised "U. S." design and eight or three over stamped "G" on front flap, worn to grain, 13" l . . . **675.00**

Model 1861 Navy, cal. 36, 7-1/2" round bbl, case color frame with silver-plated trigger guard and back strap, Naval battle cylinder scene with one-pc fine old ivory grips, very deep relief Mexican eagle on left side, accompanied by orig Colt casing containing Colt's patent short angle spout flask and iron bullet mold, packet of Johnston & Dow's skin cartridges, Eley cap tin **9,500.00**

Revolver, Crosman 38T CO2 Pellgun, 22 caliber single and double-action eight shot, original box, complete with original box of Crosman Golden Powerlets and original box of Crosman Superpells, **$125.**

Lefaucheux Pin Rimfire, old bright surface on barrel, frame, and cylinder, bold signature and proofmarks, walnut grips finely alligatored varnish, 6-3/8" octagon to round barrel, one Lefaucheux cartridge on mount, 12-1/2" l **450.00**

Remington

Beals, 7-3/4" barrel, 13-1/2" l, old dark finish **825.00**

Model 1858, .44 caliber, 8" octagonal barrel, good signature with faint inspector's stamp on grips, 14" l
. . . . **880.00**

Model 1861 Navy, 7-3/8" octagon barrel, allover matte gray finish, signature stamp **990.00**

Warner, pocket, cal. 28. 3-3/4" round bbl, cased with small flask and incorrect accessories, gray-brown patina overall, faint Warner markings on top of frame, light surface rust overall, grips badly chipped at base, gun does not fit partitions in case very well **920.00**

Rifle

Allin Conversion Model 1866, 40" round barrel, worn browned finish, three bands, "U. S. Springfield" lock with eagle and 1865 date, walnut stock, in-the-making file marks, 56" l . . **250.00**

Conestoga Rifle Works, half-stock Kentucky, cal. 36, bbl cut to 34-1/4", fixed sights, tiger striped stock, pewter nose cap, dbl. set triggers, two-pc patch box, brass furniture, dark brown iron, polished brass, fine dark wood, set trigger won't hold, hammer won't cock
. . . . **410.00**

Percussion, half stock

Partial stamped signatures on lock and barrel for J. Henry & Son, 36-3/8" octagon barrel with browned surface, walnut stock, stepped beaver tail, steel butt plate, brass trigger guard, nickel silver inlays, small "U. S." stamp

Rifle musket, Springfield Civil War, cal. 58, standard, 40" bbl, usual Springfield markings, 1864 dated lock and bbl, with socket bayonet with dark patina, 13" triangle blade believed to be cadet bayonet, $690.

just below trigger guard, 52-1/2" l, orig 8-1/2" l powder horn **. . . 950.00**
Very faint signature possibly J. Henry & Son, 37 octagon barrel with browned surface, curly-maple stock, engraved brass hardware, engraved cap box, beavertail cheek piece, hammer restoration, some deterioration behind bolster, 54" l **. 220.00**

Remington, rolling block

Military, approx .45 caliber, full stock, three barrel bands, 35" tapered round barrel with adjustable rear sight, clear signature on tag, ramrod missing, 50-1/2" l **. . 220.00**
Remington signature and address on tang, crown proofs, "G" stamp on buttstock, old dark finish, brass handle bayonet, dents, one band spring mission, 50" l **. 330.00**

Spencer Repeating, 30" round barrel with three bands, walnut stock, old refinish, traces of inspector's stamp, brass inlay added to top of comb, few chips, 47" l **. 2,310.00**

Springfield, Model 1873 Trapdoor, 45-70 caliber, cadet model, 29-1/2" round blued barrel, three click tumbler,

eagle mark and signature on lock with eagle's head and "V. P." on breech area, minor dents on stock, ramrod, 48-3/4" l **. 450.00**

Winchester, Model 1873 Special Order, cal. 44 WCF, standard grade, 24" oct. bbl, half-nickel front sight, slot blank in rear dovetail, early Lyman tang sight, button magazine with uncheckered wood, straight stock and crescent steel butt plate with trap **. 1,610.00**

Shotgun

European, double barrel, 12 gauge, 30-1/2" Damascus barrels, silver band overlay, sgd "R. Baumgarter in Bernburg" on barrel, engraved stag on tang, "Hubertus Geweher," figured walnut stock, horn trigger guard, 47" l **. 275.00**

Fox Sterlingworth, 16 gauge, double barrel, 26" barrel, top lever break-open, hammerless, double trigger, blued, checkered walnut pistol grip stock and forearm **. 400.00**

Ithaca, Grade 2E NID, four-barrel set, cal. 10 gauge, 32, 30, and two 28" barrels, all numbered to receiver and all fitted with ejectors and marked 3-1/2" chambers, one set of 28" barrels

appears to be of later origin (marked SB & Co.), all four sets marked with Grade 2 designation, double beads, received fitted with single trigger and cocked indicators, typical Grade 2 engraved with standing quail on left side and woodcock on right with light coarse floral engraving to back and bottom, professional replacement wood with wide carved and checkered beavertail forearm, heavy carved and checkered cheek piece butt stock, 14-7/8" over an Ithaca recoil pad, refinished trigger guard **. 2,000.00**

Savage Model 720, 12 gauge, 4-shot tubular, 30" cylinder bore, Browning patent, semi-automatic, hammerless, blued, checkered walnut pistol grip stock and forearm, plain receiver **. 200.00**

Stevens, Model 970, 12 gauge, single shot, 32" l round barrel with octagonal breech, top lever break-open, hammerless, automatic shell ejector, automatic safety, blued, case hardened frame, checkered walnut pistol grip stock and forearm **. 95.00**

FIREHOUSE COLLECTIBLES

History: The volunteer fire company has played a vital role in the protection and social growth of many towns and rural areas. Paid professional firemen usually are found only in large metropolitan areas. Each fire company prided itself on equipment and uniforms. Conventions and parades gave the fire companies a chance to show off their equipment. These events produced a wealth of firehouse-related memorabilia.

Additional Listings: See *Warman's Americana & Collectibles* for more examples.

Advertising button

Clifton Heights Firehouse, sepia real photo, F.P.A. No. 1, 1908 dedication ceremony **. 15.00**
Rescue scene, multicolored, firemen rescuing infant from burning building, pre-1920s **. 20.00**
Sidewalk Fire Chiefs, Holley, NY, red on white, 1940s **. 15.00**
Woodbury Fire Dept, black on gold, center pumper wagon, Friendship No. 1, 1930 event, attached to small red, white, and blue fabric ribbon **. 20.00**

Badge

Allentown Fire Dept 15, silvered brass, engraved serial number, 1930s **. 35.00**

Rifle, Winchester, pre-war model 70 bolt action, cal. 30-06, standard grade, 24" tapered, round bbl, ramp front sight with replaced hood, bbl blank in rear sight dovetail, receiver mounted with Lyman 48WJS sight, factory swivels, military-style leather sling, $1,210.

Rifle, early Kentucky flintlock, cal. 46 smooth bore, 45" oct. bbl, top flat marked with script "P," small brass front sight, fixed rear sight, both sights have engraving before and after on top flat, applied striping to full-length stock, brass furniture, two ramrod guides, faceted nose pipe, full-length saddle guard, plain side plate, two-piece patch box with small floral top, raised center on lid with simple engraving on top and down edges, lock, brass pan, marked "BIRD PHILADELPHIA," single trigger, $2,070.

Fleming Fire Dept, silvered metal, fire hydrant on left, hook and ladder on right, 1930s **25.00**

New Hampshire State Firemen's Assn, delegate, 1925 convention, black and white celluloid attachment with Sunapee Lake lighthouse, fabric ribbon . . . **20.00**

Wilmington, DE, 1907, fabric with celluloid pin **15.00**

Bell, 11", brass, iron back **125.00**

Belt, red, black, and white, 43" l, marked "Hampden" **85.00**

Fire bucket, leather, paint dec 10-3/4" h, "Boston Street Fire Club W. Poor Salem 1826" in diamond

and oval, handle replaced, paint loss **2,415.00**

11" h, 9-1/4" d, "Jesse Smith active, 1806" in oval, surrounding winged Goddess with trumpet, handle unattached, damaged, paint losses **1,880.00**

12" h, "Mechanic Fire Society Ezra Young," reverse "No. 2 1811," eagle and shield depicting symbols of boot maker, probably Portsmouth, NH, broken handle, minor paint wear **54,625.00**

12" h, "Warren Fire Club J. Shove Danvers 1829" in oval cartouche surrounded by foliate scrolls and drapery, broken handle, paint loss **4,415.00**

12-1/2" h, green leather, gilt stencil "C. H. Reed," replaced handle, wear, crack **150.00**

13" h, "Leonidas H. Titcomb Jr. 1820 Bid Vulcan Yield to Neptunes Powr" in oval, wreath and drapery, handle replaced, paint loss **3,220.00**

Fire extinguisher

Babcock, American La France Fire Engine Co., Elmire, NY, grenade, amber glass **500.00**

Hayward's Hand Fire Grenade, yellow, ground mouth, smooth base, 6-1/4" h, c1870 . . . . . . **85.00**

Red Comet, red metal canister, red glass bulb **50.00**

Fire mark, cast iron, oval

8" x 11-1/2", relief molded design, pumper framed by "Fire Department Insurance," polychrome paint
. . . . **495.00**

8" x 12", black, gold eagle and banner dec, marked "Eagle Ins. Co. Cin O" **950.00**

Helmet

Leather, 9" x 14-1/4" x 11", Anderson + Jones, Broad St., NY, emb and ribbed leather, brass trumpetered holder, painted tin front piece lettered "cataract hose 2 j.g.," manufacturer's stamp on underside of brim, repaint, leather losses
. . . . **635.00**

Stamped aluminum, black enameling, leather front panel marked "Chopmist, F.D.," interior makers label for Cairns & Brothers, Clifton, N.J." **200.00**

Ink blotter, Fireman's Fund 75th Year, Allendale, CA, fireman with little child, 1938, 4" x 9" **7.50**

Ledger marker, Caisse General Fire Insurance, statue of Liberty illus, multicolored, tin litho, 12-1/4" l, 3" w
. . . . **275.00**

Medal, Jacksonville Fire Co., silvered brass, firefighting symbols circled by "I.A.F.E.-1917-Jaconsville, Fla.," reverse "Compliments of N. Snellenburg & Co. Uniforms, Philadelphia, Pa," looped ring
. . . . **15.00**

Nozzle, hose, 16" l, brass, double handle, marked "Akron Brass Mfg. Co., Inc." **165.00**

Parade hat, 6-1/2" h, painted leather, polychrome dec, green ground, front with eagle and harp, banner above "Hibernia," back inscribed "1752" in gilt, "1" on top, red brim underside, some age cracks, small losses to brim edge **3,335.00**

Print, Currier and Ives, publishers, lithograph on paper, hand coloring, each identified in inscription in the matrix, 1858

The American Fireman, Facing the Enemy, Conningham, 153, sheet size 25-3/4" x 20", framed, laid down, repaired tear center left margin, tear upper corner, minor loss to margin upper corner, slight overall toning, scattered foxing, inpainting to tear **450.00**

The American Fireman, Prompt to the Rescue, Conningham 154, sheet size 25-3/4" x 20", framed, laid down, repaired tear left margin,

Print, titled The Old Phila. Fire Department. Period of 1850. Print manufactured in 1882 by H. Schede and shows the Great Engine Contest on July 7, 1850 at 5th and Market Streets in Philadelphia. Print measures 21" x 25.5" and exhibits minor staining and has been trimmed. Print is housed in gilt and birds eye maple frame, $350. Photo courtesy of Sanford Alderfer Auction Company.

staining, toning, scattered foxing **450.00**

The American Fireman, Rushing to the Conflict, Conningham, 155, sheet size 25-3/4" x 19-7/8", framed, laid down, three repaired tears, two small losses to upper edges, a few small tears to edges, light toning, scattered foxing **450.00**

Print, art by James Queen, lithography by Duval and Sons, Philadelphia, Hibernia Fire Engine Company, No. 1 of Philadelphia-Instituted 1752-Assembling for Parade on Oct 5 1857, shows 27 firemen, wearing parade uniforms, in front of station house, dec pumping and reel cart, large US flag flies from roof, trimmed at top, ink stamp in margin stating it came from James Queen's file, 29-1/2" x 21-1/2" **665.00**

Print, J. H. Buffords, lithographer, *Warren Engine No. 4 Charlestown*

Toy, Fire Chief car, Girard, pressed steel red coupe, windup siren action, battery operated head and taillight system, black rubber tires marked "Girard Balloon," collapsible luggage rack, front bumper missing, 14" h, $175. Photo courtesy of James D. Julia, Inc.

Mass, chromolithograph on paper, 27-5/8" x 19-3/4", framed, staining, toning. **1,645.00**

Sales sheet, 8-1/2" x 11" glossy paper, Iron Horse Metal Ware Products, Rochester Can Co., NY, pictures five galvanized red fire pails **20.00**

Stickpin, 7/8" celluloid button on 1-3/4" stickpin, Honor To Our Brave, fireman portrait, red shirt, blue helmet, 1900s **15.00**

Toy

Arcade, fire pumper, 1941 Ford, cast iron, painted red, emb sides, cast fireman, hose reel on bed, rubber tires, repaired fender, 13" l **440.00**

Arcade, ladder truck, cast iron, painted red, two cast fireman, rubber tires, bed contains ladder supports, open frame design, 9-1/4" l **440.00**

Hubley, Ahrens Fox fire engine, cast iron, rubber tires, 7-1/2" l . . **475.00**

Kenton, fire pumper, cast iron, painted red, gold highlights on boiler, and ball, emb sides, disc wheels with spoke centers **615.00**

Kingsbury, horse-drawn ladder wagon, sheet metal, pained red, wire supports, holding yellow wooden ladders, two seated drivers, pulled by two black horses, yellow spoke wheels, bell on frame rings as toy is pulled, 26" l **2,150.00**

Williams, A. C., fire pumper, cast iron, painted red, gold highlights, cast driver, bell, and boiler, rear platform with railing, rubber tires, 7-1/2" l **315.00**

FIREPLACE EQUIPMENT

History: In the colonial home, the fireplace was the gathering point for heat, meals, and social interaction. It maintained its dominant position until the introduction of central heating in the mid-19th century.

Because of the continued popularity of the fireplace, accessories still are manufactured, usually in an early-American motif.

Reproduction Alert: Modern blacksmiths are reproducing many old iron implements.

Andirons, brass and iron

Belted ball-top, ring-turned baluster shaft, conforming log stops, spurred knees, attributed to Boston, c1800, repair to logs, dents in one ball finial **530.00**

Double lemon-top, baluster form shaft, spurred cabriole legs and ball feet, 9-3/4" w, 16-1/2" d, 21" h, minor pitting **400.00**

Double lemon-top, beaded belting on finials, ring-turned and swollen hexagonal plinths, spurred cabriole legs, ball feet, 9" w, 18" d, 19" h, minor dents and pitting, small crack on shaft **560.00**

Double lemon-top, baluster form shaft, spurred cabriole legs, ball feet, America, 19th C, 9" w, 17-1/4" d, 19-1/8" h, minor pitting . . **885.00**

Engraved belted lemon-tops, columnar shafts over sq plinths, engraved meandering vine motifs, cabriole legs, ball and claw feet, America, late 18th/early 19th C, imperfections **1,120.00**

Faceted acorn finials, acorn finials surmounting faceted acorn, column, ring-turned shaft, spurred cabriole legs, slipper feet, conforming log stops, minor wear, America, late 18th/early 19th C, 12" w, 22-1/2" d, 19-1/4" h **1,175.00**

Urn top, knife blade, arched legs, penny feet, America, late 18th C, 11" w, 20" d, 19-3/4" h, minor rust **600.00**

Andirons and matching tools, Federal, 24" h brass ring-turned shaft andirons with spurred legs, ball feet, similarly turned fireplace 32" h tongs and 33" h shovel. **1,100.00**

Andirons, pair, brass and iron faceted acorn-top, America, late 18th/early 19th C, acorn finials surmounting faceted acorn, column, and ring-turned shaft, spurred cabriole legs and slipper feet with conforming log stops, minor wear, 12" w, 22-1/2" d, 19-1/4" h, $1,175. Photo courtesy of Skinner's Auctioneers and Appraisers.

Bellows, flat, hand painted design of "North Wind," leather sides and trim, impressed maker's name "Marer??," 19" l, $90. Photo courtesy of Sanford Alderfer Auction Company.

Bellows, turtleback

12" w, 20-1/4" d, 26-3/4" h, engraved metal and iron, Chippendale, urn-on-urn finials, engraved tassel bows an swags over turned columns, sq plinth, engraved edges, spurred cabriole legs ending with ball and claw feet, urn top, turned column and plinth log stops, attributed to Philadelphia, c1775 . . . . **6,900.00**

17-1/4" l, orig yellow paint, green edging, red, green, and copper colored fruit, brass nozzle, leather has wear, some damage, minor wear to paint. **615.00**

18-1/4" l, orig black over cream smoke dec on both sides, fruit and foliage on front, gold and black stenciled border, touch-up on green leaves and handle, expertly restored leather **385.00**

Coal grate, 26" w, 9-1/2" d, 16" h, George II, brass-mounted iron, bowed central section of four rails over grate, ash drawer between bow front side panels, applied brass starbursts, surmounted with brass urn finials, English, last quarter 19th C. . . . **200.00**

Fireboard, 36" x 44-3/8", wide central raised panel, paint dec to depict seaside village, ships, and houses, surround painted to depict tiles with numerous ships, houses, and trees,

America, early 19th C, wear, fading
. . . . **7,650.00**

Fire dogs, pr

7-1/2" w, 6-1/2" h, brass, central horizontal reeded orb raised on three reeded legs, reeded horizontal bar on top, Aesthetic Movement, English, third quarter 19th C **150.00**

15" h, cast iron, rampant lion bearing twisted horizontal bars, seated on rope twist rounded and octagonal base, late 19th/early 20th C
. . . . **700.00**

Fire fender, brass and wire, America or England, late 18th/early 19th C

45-1/2" l, 18" h, D-shaped, brass rim, vertical wirework dec with brass swag and scroll work . . . **2,235.00**

49" l, 14" d, 24" h, D-form brass top rail over conforming wirework screen, swag and scroll work, minor wear. **2,350.00**

49-5/8" l, 11-3/8" h, brass rim, entwined wirework, minor pitting
. . . . **560.00**

Fire screen

23" w, 36" h, brass, lifting handle and foliate repousse frieze above stained glass trelliswork panel depicting foliage about central panel with bird, trestle support with spindles, Aesthetic Movement, c1875-80 . . . . **4,000.00**

24" w, 39" h, walnut frame, Persian embroidered panel in center, c1930 . . . . **225.00**

52" h, mahogany, satin stitch and metallic thread upholstered green felt screen, tripod base with fluting and foliate carving, claw and ball feet, Victorian, late 19th C. . **800.00**

Fire tools, 30-7/8" and 31-3/8" l, brass and iron, ball finial on belted ball top, shovel and tongs, minor dents, scattered pitting **420.00**

Footman, 18" w, 15" d, 12" h, brass, Georgian-style, rect top, turned side

handles, pierced apron, cabriole front legs, straight round rear legs, English
. . . . **365.00**

Hearth broom, 8-1/4" w, 22" l, hardwood handle, bristle holder, carved and painted face of black man, handle end stamped with rocket, inscribed "Forward Biltmore, NC," wear . . **445.00**

Kettle stand, 12-1/2" w, 14-1/4" d, 13" h, pierced brass top, wrought iron base, hearts, club, and scalloped hand hold on top, multiple crosses on front apron, two cast hinged handles, back legs with curved feet, curved front legs with penny feet, two short splits in top
. . . . **275.00**

Mantelpiece, faux marble painted, attributed to Vermont, early 19th C

60" w, 6-3/4" d, 48-1/4" h, rect shelf above cove molding, flanking rect capitals on pilasters and plinths, orig white paint with gray veining, surface wear **715.00**

61" w, 6-1/2" d, 49-1/4" h, projecting shelf above molding, rect capitals on pilasters and plinths, orig gray-green paint with white veining, paint wear **1,000.00**

Pole screen

English, Chippendale-style, mahogany, early petit point panel of urn with flowers, urn turned column, high tripod base with cabriole legs, scroll feet, relief rococo carving at knees, late 19th or 20th C, 54" h **440.00**

English, 1760-80, mahogany, pole with shaped top, turned tapering urn-shaped pillar, cabriole leg base ending in arris pad feet on platforms, orig needlework panel, gold and blue floral pattern, brown ground, outlined with applied wood moldings, old surface, imperfections **5,175.00**

Irish, Chippendale, inlaid walnut and fruitwood veneers, oblong panel

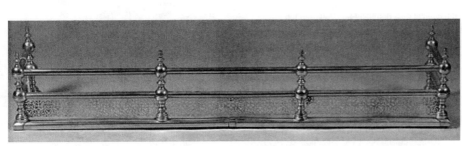

Fender, brass, pierced, turnings, finials, English, late 19th C, polished, 48" w, 12-1/2" deep, $160. Photo courtesy of Cowan's Historic Americana Auctions.

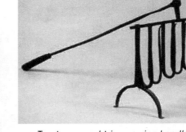

Toaster, wrought iron, swing handle, eight u-shaped holders with open spike, early, 15" w, 7" h, 22" l handle, $300. Photo courtesy of James D. Julia, Inc.

with scalloped edges, orig silk needlework of a dragon, saber legs with line border inlay graduate into triangular block with three turned supports, tripod base, short turned feet below applied blocks, some stains on fabric, few veneer chips missing, 53-1/2" h **470.00**

Tinder lighter, pistol shape, flintlock striker

> 5-1/8" l, mahogany, brass tinderbox, lyre-shaped front support, small candle socket with drop pan, etched scrollwork on the side **1,430.00**

> 8" l, walnut, steel tinder box, candle socket, simple curved support, front end with compartment for tinder/candles, inscribed "Laurent Gille" **935.00**

FISHING COLLECTIBLES

History: Early man caught fish with crude spears and hooks made of bone, horn, or flint. By the mid-1800s, metal lures with attached hooks were produced in New York State. Later, the metal was curved and glass beads added to make them more attractive. Spinners with painted-wood bodies and glass eyes appeared around 1890. Soon after, many different makers were producing wood plugs with glass eyes. Patents, which were issued in large numbers around this time, covered the development of hook hangers, body styles, and devices to add movement to the plug as it was drawn through the water. The wood plug era lasted up to the mid-1930s when plugs constructed of plastic were introduced.

With the development of casting plugs, it became necessary to produce fishing reels capable of accomplishing the task with ease. Reels first appeared as a simple device to hold a fishing line. Improvements included multiplying gears, retrieving line levelers, drags, clicks, and a variety of construction materials. The range of quality in reel manufacture varied considerably. Collectors are mainly interested in reels made with high-quality materials and workmanship, or those exhibiting unusual features.

Early fishing rods, which were made of solid wood, were heavy and prone to breakage. By gluing together tapered strips of split bamboo, a rod was fashioned which was light in weight and had greatly improved strength. The early split-bamboo rods were round and wrapped with silk to hold them together. As glue improved, fewer wrappings were needed, and rods became slim and lightweight. Rods were built in various lengths and thicknesses, depending upon the type of fishing and bait used. Rod makers' names and models can usually be found on the metal parts of the handle or on the rod near the handle.

Badge, 1-3/4" d, Fishing, Trapping, Hunting License, NY, 1930 . . . . . **55.00**

Bait bucket, painted blue, stenciled "Falls City-Magic-Minnow Bucket" **1,980.00**

Bait trap, Katch-N-Karry, Glassman Mfg. Co., Jackson, TN, patented 1941, wood, 4" dia wire mesh circle, litho of bluegill and roach **375.00**

Bank, 3-1/2" x 4" x 7" h, painted composition, bobbing head, round fisherman in hat and sunglasses, mermaid by side, coin slot in back, 1960s, felt covering over base . . **30.00**

Bobber, hand painted

> 5" l, panfish float, black, red, and white stripes **12.00**

> 12" l, pike float, yellow, green, and red stripes **24.00**

Book

Complete Book of Fresh Water Fishing, P. Allen Parsons, 1965, 332 pgs, illus **15.00**

Lures: The Guide to Sport Fishing, Keith C. Schuyler, Stackpole Co., 1955, dj **20.00**

McClaine's Standard Fishing Encyclopedia and International Angling Guide, A. J. McClaine, Holt, Rinehart, Winston, 1965, 2nd printing, 1,057 pgs, color and black and white illus by R. Younger, dj **22.00**

Box, leather-covered wood, original owned by George W. Berry, Wolfeboro, NH, **$1,100.** *All fishing photos courtesy of Lang's Sporting Collectables, Inc.*

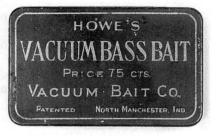

Box, tin, Howe's Vacuum Bait, empty, **$880.**

New Fisherman's Encyclopedia, Ira Gabrielson, Stackpole Co., 2nd ed., 759 pgs **24.00**

Practical Black Bass Fishing, Mark Sosin and Bill Dance, Crown Pub., 1977, illus **10.00**

Spinfishing, The System That Does It All, Norman Strung and Milk Rosko, Macmillian, 1973, 1st ed, 339 pgs 9.75 *The Complete Angler: or Contemplative Man's Recreation: A Discourse on Rivers, Fish-Ponds, Fish & Fishing in 2 Parts,* Issac Walton and Charles Cotton, supplementary and explanatory Sir John Hawkins **125.00**

The Origin of Angling And A New Printing of "The Treatise of Fishing With An Angle," John McDonald, paintings by John Langley Howard, Doubleday, 1963, 271 pgs . . **12.50**

The Treasure of Angling, Larry Koller, 1963, Ridge Press **15.00**

Cane

37" l, gaff, with pouch, 1-1/8" d x 1" h silver knob handle, oak shaft, brass fitting 2/3" way down, when button is depressed, cane can be folded, 2-3/4" ferrule machined with threads to accept 3" pointed steel gaff which is carried in separate leather pouch, English, c1890 . . . . **1,120.00**

37-3/4" l, 1-3/4" d x 2-1/4" h thick wood dec carved knob handle, 1-1/2" silver disc on top inscribed "New Draft, 150 Fish," relating to angler's winning achievement in rural English village, handle unscrews to withdraw sq wooden spool wound with line and hook to attach to fishing line, unscrews at bottom and attaches to 3" brass ferrule to allow assembly into fishing rod, 1" brass collar, brown hardwood shaft dec at top and bottom with matching black and

red cord whipping, English, c1890
.....................**1,250.00**

Canoe, Old Town Sponson, 16'
.....................**1,430.00**

Catalog

Creek Chub Bait Co., Garrett, IN,
1934 .... **330.00**

Evinrude Motors, Milwaukee, WI,
1961, Catalog of Outboard Motors
.... **32.00**

Garcia Fishing Equipment &
Supplies, Garcia Corp., Teaneck,
NY, c1955, accordion fold large
11-1/4" x 30" sheet **20.00**

Hardy Brothers, 1910 ...... **495.00**

Martin Bradford, Boston, 1847,
tackle **2,415.00**

Montague Rod & Reel Co.,
Montague City, MA, c1949, Catalog
No. 49-M................ **55.00**

Orvis, c1900 .... **330.00**

Penn Fishing Tackle Mfg.,
Philadelphia, PA, 1952, Catalog
No. 17 of Penn Reels **32.00**

Shakespeare Co., Kalamazoo,
Catalog No. 27, 1927, some pages
uncut **175.00**

Shakespeare Co., Kalamazoo,
Catalog of Fine Wonerod Fishing
Tackles, 1951 .... **32.00**

Wallsten Tackle Co., Chicago, IL,
1940s, Fishing Tips, Courtesy of
Cisco Kid Lures **21.00**

Weber Lifelike Fly Co., Stevens
Point, WI, 1941, Catalog No. 22,
Flies & Fly Tackle **70.00**

Catalog, Martin L. Bradford, Boston,
MA, 1847, fishing tackle, blue cover,
$2,475.

Creel, Turtle Trade Mark, leather
trimmed rattan, $2,640.

White, E. M. & Co., Old Town, ME,
c1922, E. M. White Builders of
White Canoes **40.00**

Cigarette card, King of England
deep-sea fishing, New Zealand, 1937
.... **12.00**

Clock, mechanical, fish punching hole
in side of boat with moving hammer,
Hero Clock Co., wind-up, marked
"Made in China" **40.00**

Creel

9-1/2" w, 8" d, 8" h, wicker, rear
hinged door, repairs **110.00**

12" w, 6" d, 8-1/2" h, painted splint,
carved wooden wire-hinged top,
forest green, America, early 19th C
.... **920.00**

32" w, 6" h, wicker, leather latch with
netted fish head, silver tail on other
end, late 1940s **275.00**

35" x 32", wicker, orig 2-1/2" x 1-1/4"
paper label "Bestmade, Insist on
the Genuine, Occupied Japan,
3616/4 15".............. **750.00**

Size 15, Tillamook Model, George
Lawrence, Portland, OR, split
willow, leather trim, half leather lid,
leather pocket on front, c1950, with
orig catalog, unused.... **9,020.00**

Dealer display, Swimmy Bait Co., 12
boxed lures................. **175.00**

Decoy, fish, wood

6-1/2" l, Leroy Howell, gray body,
black metal fins.......... **115.00**

7" l, Ice King, perch, painted, Bear
Creek Co. **75.00**

31-1/2" l, wood, paint dec, America,
early 20th C, minor paint wear and
losses **1,495.00**

Fishing license, for resident use

Connecticut, 1935, yellow, black,
and white................ **65.00**

Pennsylvania, 1945, blue and white,
black serial number........ **18.00**

Flask, pewter, emb on both sides, one
side with fisherman landing trout, other
side with fisherman netting catch,
marked "Alchemy Pewter, Sheffield,
England" **175.00**

Float, Ideal **200.00**

Fly, Carrie Stevens **440.00**

Fly fishing display

c1910, C. J. Frost, Stevens Point, WI,
9' l.................... **3,080.00**

c1911, painted wood trout replica, fly
fishing reel, flies, net, wood case,
39-3/4" l, 3-3/4" d, 13-1/4" h **195.00**

Folk art, 25" h, 40-1/4" l, wood carving,
titled "Two Fish and a Frog," sgd "L. A.
Plummer, 1904" in lower right,
polychrome dec, minor cracks
.... **17,250.00**

Knife, Marbles Woodcraft..... **385.00**

License holder, paper envelope,
Florida Game and Fresh Water
Commission, stamped with County
Judge's name **22.00**

Lure

Al Foss Dixie Wiggler, #13, 1928,
metal box, extra hook, pocket
catalog, 3-1/2" l **100.00**

Allen, Vamp, stripy finish ... **550.00**

Blee, Charles, submarine bait, all
metal **2,000.00**

Carters Bestever, red and white,
pressed eyes, 3" l......... **10.00**

Creek Chubb Bait Co., 200 baby
chub, white head, black body
.... **230.00**

Creek Chubb Bait Co., Giant Pike,
12-1/2" x 2-3/4" orig box... **195.00**

Creek Chubb Bait Co., glitter beetle,
red and white........... **615.00**

Creek Chubb Bait Co., jigger 4100,
red side **140.00**

Creek Chubb Bait Co., mouse
.... **470.00**

Creek Chubb Bait Co., pikie minnow,
early orig box........... **440.00**

Creek Chubb Bait Co., plunking
dinger, all black **100.00**

Creek Chubb Bait Co., red beetle
.... **315.00**

Creek Chubb Bait Co., Sarasota,
#3317, c1927-31, luminous yellow
head.................. **800.00**

Lure, Harkauf, fly rod, 1-1/8" l, $550.

Lure, Heddon, Underwater Minnow, model 150, wooden, with original flyer, original box, $935.

Detroit Glass, minnow tube, fish form, four treble hooks, orig box, c1914 .... **3,500.00**

DeWitt, Bil, minnow, orig box with papers................... **90.00**

Dunk's Double Header, black plug, c1931 .... **125.00**

Four Brothers, Neverfail Minnow, orig box **615.00**

Hanson, GE pull-me-slow, two hooks **90.00**

Hanson, Muskegon spoon jack minnow, green back, five-hook **275.00**

H. Comstock, 1883, Flying Helgramite........... **4,400.00**

Heddon, baby lunny frog, c1928 .... **90.00**

Heddon, black sucker **3,300.00**

Heddon, Dowagiac Minnow, series 100, wood, red and yellow stripes, olive green strip down back, glass eyes, 2-3/4" l **300.00**

Heddon, swimming minnow, 1910 .... **800.00**

Heddon, underwater minnow, model 150, perch scale, orig box .**935.00**

Meadow Brook, rainbow, 1-1/4" l, orig box, flyrod type **120.00**

Moonlight Bay #1, c1904, 4" shallow cup **400.00**

Musky, crazy crawler 2510 mouse **250.00**

Musky, giant vamp 7350, jointed, natural scales, c1930..... **130.00**

Musky Minnow **900.00**

Musky, Surfasser 300, two hooks, rainbow................ **150.00**

Paw-Paw, sucker, perch finish, tack eyes **30.00**

Pfleuger, metal, May-Bug spoon **3,190.00**

Pfleuger, Never Fail Minnow, three hooks, early perch finish, hand painted gill marks, large glass eyes, unmarked props, never-fail take hangers **300.00**

Pfleuger, Never Fail Minnow, five-hook, orig box marked "Neptune Wooden Minnow" **495.00**

Pflueger for Sears, No. 9007 new winner wood minnow, five-hook, wine colored box **325.00**

Sam-Bo, 4" l, bass, pike, pickerel, orig box **215.00**

Shakespeare, mouse white and red, thin body, glass eyes, 3-5/8" l **30.00**

Shakespeare, underwater minnow, five-hook, c1907........ **150.00**

South Bend Tackle Co., Panatellia, green crackle-back finish, glass eyes, boxed **50.00**

South Bend Tackle Co., Truck-Oreno, red and white wood **2,970.00**

South Bend Tackle Co., Vacuum Bait, red and white dec ... **100.00**

Souvenir, Lucky Lure, Souv of Indian Lake, OH, 3-1/2" l, nude black female, MOC **130.00**

Strike-It-Lure, green, yellow, and red spots, glass eyes **40.00**

W. D. Chapman, Theresa, NY, metal minnow and propeller ...**2,200.00**

Winchester, 9011, three-hook **500.00**

Winchester, green plug, repainted by Dale Roberts **130.00**

Minnow bucket, green collapsible canvas, wire bail, orig black painted

Reel, B. F. Meek & Sons, Louisville, KY, Blue Grass Model 4, bait casting, $660.

wooden handle, stamped "No. 08 Mfg for the Planet Co. Patent"...... **155.00**

Painting, 13" x 16", oil on canvas, still life with fish and creel, monogrammed and dated "1882" upper right, American School, framed, lined, retouched................. **1,265.00**

Patch, 3-3/4" x 5", Atlantic City Surf Fishing Tournament **12.00**

Pinback button, Johnsburg Fish & Game Club, red and white, forest safety theme, 1930s **10.00**

Poacher's gig, hand forged five pronged rake-type device, long worn wooden handle, from Eastern Shore, MD or VA, 63" l **145.00**

Reel

Abraham Coates, Watertown, NY, 1888 patent........... **2,200.00**

Ambassador 5500C Silver, counter balance, handle, high-speed gear rates **120.00**

Anson Hatch, New Haven, CT, side-mount, brass, c1866 .... **7,150.00**

B. C. Milam, Frankford, KY, #2, casting **1,760.00**

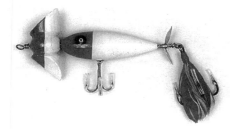

Lure, South Bend Fishing Tackle Co., red and white wooden Truck-Oremo, $2,970.

Prototype reel, C. F. Orvis, Manchester, VT, prototype for 1874 patent trout fly reel, original wooden box, $1,870.

Reel, H. L. Leonard, model 44A, trout fly, $2,970.

Reel, Horton Mfg., Bristol, CT, Blue Grass Model 7, bait casting, $880.

B. C. Milam & Sons, #3, casting 1,430.00
B. F. Meek & Sons
   #2, casting 935.00
   #3, Bluegrass......... 330.00
   #4................. 660.00
   #33 Bluegrass, suede bag 450.00
William Billinghurst, Rochester, NY, brass, patent 1859, birdcage-style, fixed handle 2,750.00
Bogdan, large trout....... 1,100.00
Charles M. Clinton, Ithaca, NY, German Silver, c1900.... 6,820.00
Dr. Allonzo H. Fowler, Ithaca, NY, hard rubber, Fowler's Improved Gem Fly Reel 6,600.00
Hardy, Hercules, c1890, trout 1,430.00
Hardy, Perfect Fly Reel, English, 3-3/8" x 1-1/4"........... 165.00
Hendryx Safety Reel, trout .. 995.00
H. L. Leonard
   Model 44A, fly 2,970.00
   Model 50B, wide spool, fly 1,760.00
   Patent 1877, upright trout 3,080.00
Horton Mfg.
   #3, suede bag 425.00
   #7 Blueglass 880.00
   #33 Bluegrass Simplex, suede bag 425.00
Edw. Vom Hofe
   German silver, c1870, tiny upright trout 7,810.00
   Edw. Vom Hofe, Perfection, size 3, upright trout....... 6,820.00
   Peerless, size 3, upright trout 3,300.00
   Model 621, size 4/0 ..... 250.00
   Salmon, Cascapedia ... 4,290.00
Julius Vom Hofe
   Fly, plain, early size 3.... 880.00

Freshwater, casting, Pat. Nov. 17, 85, Oct. 8, 1887, torn bag 165.00
German silver and hard rubber, size 3 .... 550.00
Ocean, 3/0B 300.00
J. T. Baker, 1871, German silver 1,925.00
Morgan James, side mount, pillbox style, brass, c1860 ..... 9,350.00
Niangua, casting 660.00
Orvis 1874 prototype, fly .. 1,870.00
Otto Zward, 2/0 size 1,540.00
Penn-Jic Master No. 500, 3" d. 65.00
Pflueger
   #1993L, Summit, casting, 1940-50 .... 100.00
   1429-3/4 templar, number engraved on side 125.00
   1420-1/2 templar, owner's name lightly scratched....... 175.00
Restigouche
   1896 patent.......... 1,540.00
   1897 patent.......... 1,320.00
   1902 patent.......... 1,540.00
Shakespeare
   Standard............... 150.00
   Standard, professional ... 150.00
   Tournament............ 110.00
South Bend, #1131A, casting, shiny finish, orig box........... 18.00
Talbot Star 385.00
Thos. J. Conroy, NY, Wells model, c1889, trout 3,300.00
Union Hardware Co., raised pillar type, nickel and brass...... 25.00
Unmarked, wood, brass fittings, c1880-1920, 6" d.......... 85.00
Walker, TR-4, fly......... 1,210.00
Wilkerson Quadruple, 1900... 95.00
Winchester, Model #1135, fly, black finish 65.00
Wm. H. Talbot Eli, casting ... 880.00

Reel, Meek & Milam (1653-1880), German silver, size #6, bait casting, $3,520.

Rod, Goodwin Granger, Denver, Aristocrat model, 7', $1,100.

Rod
Bamboo, fly fishing, orig reel, wear 125.00
Clarence Carlson, split bamboo, early 7' 4,400.00
Clarence Carlson, split bamboo, Carlson Four, 7-1/2' 4,400.00
Everett Garrison, 8'....... 4,180.00
F. E. Thomas, three piece fly rod, extra tip, metal case, marked "Special, Bangor, Maine," 8-1/2' 275.00
George Halstead, Danbury, CT, split bamboo, 7-1/2', trout 3,410.00
Goodwin Granger, split bamboo, 7' 1,100.00
Hardy Brothers, Marvel, split bamboo, 7-1/2' 715.00
Hardy's of England Salmon Deluxe Rod, extra tip, aluminum case, 9' 175.00
Hardy's of England, split bamboo fly, 7' 2", one tip 200.00
Harold Gillum, Ridgefield, CT, split bamboo, 6-1/2' and 7-1/2', sold as pr 7,700.00
H. L. Leonard
   Fly, 6-1/2" 1,450.00
   Fly, Leonard Tournament, extra tip, metal case, 9' 300.00
   Red wrap, 7-1/2' 1,925.00
   Split bamboo, model 50DF, 8' 880.00
   #37ACM-6'........... 3,025.00
   #37-6'............... 1,925.00
Horrocks & Illotson, 9' 3", two tips, split-bamboo fly, maroon wraps 50.00

Rod, George H. Halstead, Danbury, CT, split bamboo, c1940, 7-1/2', restored, $3,410.

Jim Payne
  #94-7' **2,530.00**
  #96-6-1/2' **3,850.00**
  #97-7' **5,500.00**
Kingfisher, brown and red, orig
  wraps, red agate eyes, paper label
  . . . . **125.00**
Lyle Dickerson
  7' **5,225.00**
  7-1/2' **3,850.00**
  8' **4,180.00**
Montaque, bamboo, two tips, orig
  case **135.00**
Orvis Impregnated Battenkill, 8-1/2',
  two tips, splint-bamboo fly, cloth
  bag, aluminum tube **250.00**
Orvis, Wes Jordan, 8-1/2' . . . **550.00**
Paul H. Young, 6' 3" Midge **2,470.00**
Payne, salmon **1,320.00**
Shakespeare, Premier Model, 9',
  three pcs, two tips, split-bamboo
  fly, red silk wrappings, cloth bag,
  metal tube **75.00**
Shakespeare Springbrook, fly
  fishing, orig bag **100.00**
S. J. Small, split bamboo, three-rod
  set **2,640.00**
Superlight, 5' spinning rod . . . **660.00**
Thomas & Thomas, Fountainhead
  . . . . **3,300.00**
Union Hardware Co., 7-1/2',
  Kingfisher, saltwater boat rod,
  split-bamboo fly, dark brown wraps
  . . . . **35.00**
Scale, brass, "Chamllons Improved,
New York, Pat. Dec 10 1967" **30.00**
Sign, The Flatfish, World's largest
selling fishing plug," Helen Tackle Co.,
Detroit, metal framed glass, 8" x 16"
. . . . **350.00**
Tackle box, leather **450.00**
Tie clip, articulated fish, 1-3/4" l . . **18.00**
Tobacco tin, Forest & Stream, pocket
size, 4-1/4" x 3" x 7/8" **600.00**
Tray, aluminum, lady fishing, catches
skirt with hook and lifts it up in the back,
red and black dec, scalloped edge
. . . . **165.00**
Trout net, 22-3/4", nice wood, orig net
. . . . **100.00**
Vise, fly tying
  7" l, 2-1/2" w, steel and brass, bolts
  to table **210.00**

Rod, Lyle Dickerson, 1948, trout, 8',
$2,750.

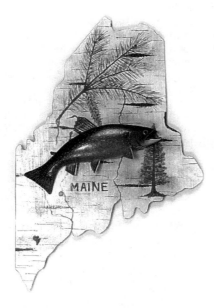

Wall plaque, Lawrence Irvine,
Winthrop, ME, caved wooden brook
trout centered on plaque shaped like
state of Maine, $750.

7-1/2" l, 6" h, cast iron and steel, can
be used free standing or bolted
down **240.00**
Wall plaque, 13" x 9", large mouth bass
. . . .**115.00**

FLASKS

For more
information,
see this book.

History: A flask, which
usually has a narrow neck,
is a container for liquids.
Early American glass
companies frequently
formed them in molds that
left a relief design on the
front and/or back.
Historical flasks with a
portrait, building, scene, or
name are the most
desirable.
  A chestnut is
hand-blown, small, and has a flattened bulbous body.
The pitkin has a blown globular body with a spiral rib
overlay on vertical ribs. Teardrop flasks are generally
fiddle shaped and have a scroll or geometric design.

Notes: Dimensions can differ for the same flask
because of variations in the molding process. Color is
important in determining value—aqua and amber are
the most common colors; scarcer colors demand
more money. Bottles with "sickness," an opalescent
scaling that eliminates clarity, are worth much less.

Chestnut, 4-3/4" h, Zanesville, OH,
blown, 24 vertical ribs, amber, half pint,
minor wear **250.00**

Scroll and two stars, green, pontil
mark, **$75.**

Historical
  Columbia, Liberty cap, eagle,
    Kensington and Union on reverse,
    pale aqua, bubbles **800.00**
  Eagle-Cornucopia, early Pittsburgh
    district, 1820-40, light
    greenish-aquamarine, sheared
    mouth, pontil scar, pint, McKearin
    GII-6 . . . . **475.00**
  Eagle-Willington/Glass Co.,
    Willington glass Works, West
    Willington, CT, 1860-72, bright
    medium yellowish-olive, applied
    double-collared mouth, smooth
    base, half pint, McKearin GII-63
    . . . . **210.00**
  For Pike's Peak Prospector-Hunter
    Shooting Deer, attributed to
    Ravenna Glass Works, Ravenna,

Baltimore
Glass Works,
reversed
embossed
phoenix and
RESURGAM,
pale aqua,
GXIII-53,
$230. Photo
courtesy of
Pacific Glass
Auctions.

OH, 1860-80, aquamarine, applied
mouth with ring, smooth base,
quart, McKearin GXI-47, 1/4"
shallow flake **325.00**

Masonic-Eagle, Zanesville, emb
"Zanesville, J. Sheppard & Co.,"
golden amber, pint, McKearin
GIV-32 . . . . **2,975.00**

Success to the Railroad, Keene
Marlboro Street Glassworks,
Keene, NH, 1830-50, light yellow
amber with olive tone, sheared
mouth, pontil scar, pint, McKearin
GV-3 . . . . **250.00**

Pattern molded

4-5/8" l, Midwest, 1800-30, 24 ribs
swirled to the right, golden amber,
sheared mouth, pontil scar. **190.00**

7-3/8" l, Emil Larson, NJ, c1930,
swirled to the right, amethyst,
sheared mouth, pontil scar, some
exterior high point wear . . . **250.00**

Pictorial

Cornucopia, eagle, emerald green,
pint, applied top, pontil, made by
Lancaster, NY, int. stain . . . **850.00**

Monument-Sloop, Baltimore Glass
Works, Baltimore, MD, 1840-60,
medium variegated yellow green,
sheared mouth, pontil scar, half
pint, McKearin GVI-2, some
exterior high point wear, overall
dullness **1,100.00**

*New England, chestnut shape, light
yellow, applied string lip and pontil,
1780-1820, $325. Photo courtesy of
Pacific Glass Auctions.*

Pitkin type

Midwest, 1800-30, 6-1/4" l, ribbed
and swirled to the right, 16 ribs,
olive green with yellow tone,
sheared mouth, pontil scar, some
int. stain **300.00**

New England, 1783-30, sheared
mouth, pontil scar, 5-1/4" l, ribbed
and swirled to the left, 36 ribs, light
olive yellow **375.00**

Portrait

Adams-Jefferson, New England,
1830-50, yellow amber, sheared
mouth, pontil scar, half pint,
McKearin GI-114 . . . . **325.00**

General Jackson, Pittsburgh district,
1820-40, bluish-aquamarine,
sheared mouth, pontil scar, pint,
McKearin GI-68 . . . . **1,500.00**

Lafayette-DeWitt Clinton, Coventry
Glass Works, Coventry, CT,
1824-25, yellowish-olive, sheared
mouth, pontil scar, half pint, 1/2"
vertical crack, weakened
impression, McKearin GI-82
. . . . **2,100.00**

Rough and Ready Taylor-Eagle,
Midwest, 1830-40, aquamarine,
sheared mouth, pontil scar, pint,
McKearin GI-77 . . . . **1,200.00**

Washington, Albany Glass Works,
sailing ship, deep green, pint,
McKearin GI-28, 5-7/8" h . . . **110.00**

Washington-Sheaf of Wheat,
Dyottville Glass Works,
Philadelphia, PA 1840-60, medium
yellow-olive, inward rolled mouth,

*Sunburst, GVIII-29, pint,
bluish-green, teardrop shape,
$325. Photo courtesy of
Pacific Glass Auctions.*

pontil scar, half pint, McKearin
GI-59 . . . . **9,000.00**

Washington-Taylor, Dyottville Glass
Works, Philadelphia, PA 1840-60,
bright bluish-green, applied double
collared mouth, pontil scar, quart,
McKearin GI-42 . . . . **400.00**

Majolica, 4-1/2" h, polychrome dec
bulldog, landscape, and crest design,
Italy, 19th C **200.00**

Pewter, 14" h, Pilgrim, shaped figural
handles, moon-shaped body, molded
foliage, pierced base, losses, 16th C
. . . . **345.00**

Scroll, pink, golden-amber, applied
collar, iron pontil **1,600.00**

Silver, sterling

4-1/4" l, America, late 19th/early 20th
C, ovoid, emb foliates on textured
ground, domed lid with attached
chain, approx two troy oz . . **175.00**

9" h, Clarence Vanderbilt, New York,
c1909-35, rect, overall textured
finish, reeded circular screw cap,
approx 10 troy oz **260.00**

FLOW BLUE

History: Flow blue, or
flown blue, is the name
applied to china of cobalt
blue and white, whose
color, when fired in a kiln,
produced a flowing or
blurred effect. The blue
varies from dark royal
cobalt blue to navy or steel
blue. The flow may be very
slight to a heavy blur,
where the pattern cannot
be easily recognized. The
blue color does not
permeate through the body
of the china. The amount of flow on the back of a piece
is determined by the position of the item in the sagger
during firing.

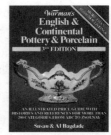

*For more
information,
see this book.*

Known patterns of flow blue were first produced
around 1830 in the Staffordshire area of England.
Credit is generally given to Josiah Wedgwood, who
worked in that area. Many other potters followed,
including Alcock, Davenport, Grindley, Johnson
Brothers, Meakin, Meigh, and New Wharf. They were
attempting to imitate the blue and white wares brought
back by the ship captains of the tea trade. Early flow
blue, 1830s to 1870s, was usually of the pearl ware or
ironstone variety. The later patterns, 1880s to 1900s,
and the modern patterns after 1910, were of the more
delicate semi-porcelains. Most flow blue was made in
England but it was made in many other countries as
well. Germany, Holland, France, Spain, Wales, and
Scotland are also known locations. Many patterns
were made in the United States by several companies,
Mercer, Warwick, Sterling, and the Wheeling Pottery
to name a few.

Adviser: Ellen G. King.

Educational Alert: The Flow Blue International Collectors' Club, Inc. has been studying and discussing new versus reproduction flow blue and mulberry. There are still areas of personal judgment as yet undetermined. The general rule accepted has been "*new*" indicates recent or contemporary manufacture and "*reproduction*" is a copy of an older pattern. Problems arise when either of these fields is sold at "*old*" flow blue prices.

In an effort to help educate its membership, the Club continues to inform of all known changes through its conventions, newsletters, and the Web site: www.flowblue.com.

Warman's is working to those ends also. The following is a listing of "*new*" flow blue, produced since the 1960s.

Blossom, Ashworth Bros, 1962, wash bowl and pitcher.

Blossom: Ashworth Bros., Hanley, 1962. Wash bowl and pitcher made for many years now, in several items.

Vinranka: Upsala-Ekeby, Sweden, 1967-1968. Now discontinued and highly collectible, a full dinnerware set.

Romantic Flow Blue: Blakeney Pottery, 1970s. Resembles Watteau, but not exact. The old patterns never had the words "flow blue" written on them.

Victoria Ware: mark is of lion and uniform, but has paper label "Made in China," 1990s. Made in various patterns and design, but the give-away is the roughness on the bottoms, and much of it has a pea green background. Some of this line is also being made in Mulberry.

Floral pitchers (jugs) and teapots bearing a copied "T. Rathbone England" swan mark.

Williams-Sonoma and Cracker Barrel are also each releasing a vivid blue and white line. Both are made in China. One line is a simplified dahlia flower on white; the other has summer bouquets. Both are well made and readily available, just not old.

The reproductions are more of a threat to collectors.

Waldorf by New Wharf cups and saucers are out, but missing "England" from their mark and are made in China.

Cracker Barrel, pitcher, made in China.

Iris by Dunn, Bennett, Burslem, has been reproduced in a full chamber set.

Touraine, Stanley, teapot, made in China.

Touraine by Stanley, by far the most prolific reproduction made recently, in 2002. Again, the "England" is missing from the mark, and it is made in China. Nearly the entire dinnerware set has been made and is being sold on the market.

In all cases, regarding new pieces and reproductions, be aware of unglazed areas on the bottoms. The footpads are rough and just too white. The reproductions, particularly the Touraine, are heavier in weight, having a distinctive thick feel. The embossing isn't as crisp and the pieces are frequently slightly smaller in over-all size than the originals.

Check the Flow Blue International Collectors' Club, Inc., Web site and also www.repronews.com. Join the Club, study the books available, and always, always, KNOW your dealer! Good dealers guarantee their merchandise and protect their customers.

Albany, Grindley

Plate, 10" d. 95.00

Platter, 20" l 350.00

Amoy, Davenport

Child's creamer, 3-1/4" x 3" . . 550.00

Foot bath, 18" x 13-1/2" . . . 6,500.00

Fruit bowl, pedestal, 9-3/4" x 5"

. . . . 1,400.00

Pitcher, 11-1/4" h 1,500.00

Platter, well and tree, 16" x 20-1/2"

. . . . 1,200.00

Razor/toothbrush box, cov 1,000.00

Relish, mitten shape, 9" l 225.00

Soap dish, cov, insert 650.00

Arabesque, Mayer, teacup and saucer

. . . . 250.00

Argyle, Grindley

Butter dish, cov, insert 475.00

Cake plate, handles 325.00

Plate, 10" d 95.00

Platter, 15" l 225.00

Soup tureen, cov, undertray, ladle

. . . . 1,300.00

Spoon holder 275.00

Vegetable tureen, cov, oval . 350.00

Balmoral, Venables

Butter pat 55.00

Hot water plate, in metal frame, also

known as invalid's dish. . . . 400.00

Beaufort, Grindley, sugar bowl, cov

. . . . 275.00

Bleeding Heart, unknown maker, plate, 10-1/2" d 125.00

Brushstroke, unknown maker, child's mug, polychromed dec 250.00

Bryonia, Utzscheider, gravy boat, attached undertray. 265.00

Buccleuch, unknown maker, tea set, cov teapot, creamer, and cov sugar

. . . . 1,100.00

Campion, Grindley, wash bowl and pitcher set, pitcher, wash bowl, cov slop jar, toothbrush holder 1,250.00

Carnation, Furnivals, plate, 8" d . 45.00

Acme, Hancock, 1880, cheese dish, slant top, gold sponged decorated, $495. Photos courtesy of Ellen G. King.

Cashmere, Morley
  Child's cup and saucer, restoration
    to cup rim 750.00
  Creamer, 16 panels, restoration
    . . . . 350.00
  Posset cup, handleless, panels,
    pedestal, rim chip 1,200.00
  Soup plate, rimmed 175.00
  Teacup and saucer 300.00
Chapoo, Wedgwood
  Plate, 8-1/4" d 175.00
  Sugar, cov, 7-3/4" 450.00
  Teapot, cov, finial restored . . 800.00
Chelsea, Doulton, biscuit jar, cov
  . . . . 375.00
Colonial, Meakin
  Plate, 7" d 40.00
  Platter, 14" d 265.00
  Teacup and saucer 95.00
Conway, New Wharf
  Butter pat (scarce) 75.00
  Plate, 10" d 110.00
  Vegetable bowl, oval, open, 9"
    . . . . 95.00
Coral, Furnivals, vegetable tureen, cov,
  oval 295.00
Delft, Warwick, tea caddy with lid,
  restoration to lid 850.00

Buccleuch, unknown maker, tea set, covered teapot, creamer, covered sugar, $1,100.

Chapoo, Wedgwood, 1850, 10" d, $225.

Dorothy, Corn, teapot, cov 355.00
Duchess, Grindley, plate, 10" d . . 85.00
Flora, Grindley, gravy/sauce boat, 9"
  . . . . 75.00
Florida, Johnson Brothers
  Butter dish, cov 425.00
  Plate, 10" d 120.00
  Teacup and saucer 125.00
Formosa, Mayer, platter, 10-1/2" x
  13-1/2" 450.00
Gironde, Grindley
  Creamer, 5" 250.00
  Dessert bowl, 4-3/4" 40.00
  Gravy/sauce boat 95.00
  Plate, 10" d 110.00
Glenmore, Grindley, platter, 16" l
  . . . . 165.00
Glenwood, Crown Pottery, wash bowl
  and pitcher set 750.00
Gothic, Furnivals, soup bowl, 10-1/2" d
  . . . . 150.00
Haddon, Mayer
  Double salt with attached center
    handle 250.00
  Jardiniere 275.00
Hong Kong, Meigh
  Dessert/individual vegetable dish
    . . . . 150.00
  Syrup pitcher with metal lid . . 750.00
Indian, Pratt, ewer, 9-1/2" h, small
  restoration 350.00
Janette, Grindley
  Butter pat 50.00
  Creamer 235.00
  Plate, 10" d 110.00
  Teacup and saucer 135.00
Jeddo, Adams, soap dish, cov, insert
  . . . . 285.00
Keele, Grindley
  Creamer and sugar, set 550.00
  Plate, 10" d 110.00
  Vegetable tureen, cov, oval . . 375.00

LaBelle, Wheeling
  Bowl, 10-1/2" d, free form, handled
    . . . . 400.00
  Chamber pot, cov 550.00
  Charger, 13" d 225.00
  Demitasse cup and saucer . 375.00
  Ice cream dish 450.00
  Milk pitcher, dolphin handle . 275.00
  Plate
    6" d 85.00
    10-1/4" d, turkey pattern . 150.00
  Platter, 19-1/4" l, turkey pattern
    . . . . 1,600.00
Lily, Adderly, tea caddy, lid 225.00
Linda, Maddock, egg cup 145.00
Lugano, Ridgways, plate, 10" d . 90.00
Madras, Doulton, plate, 6-1/2" d . 40.00
Marechal Niel, Grindley, fruit bowl, ftd
  . . . . 500.00
Marie, Grindley
  Creamer 235.00
  Plate, 10" d 75.00
  Sugar, cov 245.00
  Teapot, cov 800.00
Melbourne, Grindley
  Bone dish 75.00
  Butter pat 55.00
  Cake plate with handles 250.00
  Egg cup 175.00
  Plate, 8" d 50.00
Mongolia, Johnson Brothers,
  Plate
    6-1/4" d 45.00
    10" d 95.00
  Platter, 12-1/2" l 150.00
  Relish tray 55.00
  Teapot, cov 625.00
Morning Glory, unknown maker,
  creamer 375.00
Nankin, Edwards, plate, 9-1/2" d
  . . . . 100.00

Linda, Maddock, egg cup, $145.

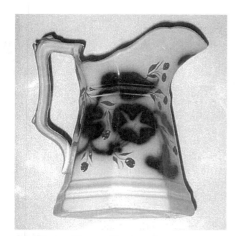

Morning Glory, unknown maker, creamer, **$375.**

Normandy, Johnson Brothers
    Butter pat **60.00**
    Gravy boat **195.00**
Oregon, Mayer
    Creamer **350.00**

Oriental, Ridgways, teapot, covered, restored spout, **$475.**

Pelew, Challinor, teapot, 1840, **$850.**

Scinde, Alcock, soup plate, 10-1/2" d, **$190.**

    Plate, 7-1/2" d **100.00**
    Teapot, cov, 8-1/2" **1,150.00**
Oriental, Ridgways, teapot, cov, restored spout **475.00**
Pansy, Warwick
    Dresser tray, 8" **150.00**
    Nut dish, rect **155.00**
    Pitcher, 6" **200.00**
Persian Moss, Utzschneider
    Dessert/individual vegetable dish
    . . . . **45.00**
    Pitcher, 7" h **135.00**
    Plate, 8" d **50.00**
Poppy, New Wharf, wash bowl and pitcher set, bowl restored **950.00**
Portman, Grindley
    Butter dish, cov, insert **450.00**
    Butter pat **45.00**
    Fruit bowl, pedestal, 12-1/2" x 9" x 4"
    . . . . **500.00**
    Plate, 10" d **100.00**
    Platter, 18" l **350.00**
Scinde, Alcock
    Plate, 9-1/2" d **175.00**
    Platter, 18-1/2" x 10-3/4" **650.00**
    Soup plate, 10-1/2" d **190.00**

Pelew, Challinor, teapot, 1840, **$850.**

Unknown pattern, unknown maker, teacup and saucer, green polychrome decorated, **$145.**

    Vegetable bowl, open, 10-3/4" d
    . . . . **625.00**
Sobraon, unknown maker
    Platter, 10-3/4" x 13-3/4" **350.00**
    Relish, shell shape, 8-3/4" x 5"
    . . . . **550.00**
Sylva, Till & Sons, pitcher, 10-1/2" h
    . . . . **475.00**
Temple, Podmore Walker
    Pitcher, 13-1/2" h **450.00**
    Teacup and saucer **175.00**
Thistle, Burroughs, biscuit jar, cov, undertray, hairline in lid **250.00**

Unknown pattern, unknown maker, matched pair of vases, multicolored polychrome decorated, **$775.**

Unknown patterns, all with polychrome dec, unknown maker

Cake plate, coral coloring. . . **275.00**
Child's mug, henna red coloring
. . . . **155.00**
Teacup and saucer, green coloring
. . . . **145.00**
Vase, matched pair, multicolored
. . . . **775.00**

Watteau, New Wharf

Butter dish, cov, insert **375.00**
Cereal bowl, 7" d. **40.00**
Plate, 8" d **50.00**
Teacup and saucer. **110.00**
Teapot, cov, restoration to lid
. . . . **300.00**

Waverly, Grindley

Bone dish **55.00**
Gravy boat **165.00**
Plate, 10" d **120.00**
Soup bowl, 8" d. **45.00**
Teacup and saucer. **95.00**
Vegetable tureen, cov, round
. . . . **325.00**

FOLK ART

History: Exactly what constitutes folk art is a question still being vigorously debated among collectors, dealers, museum curators, and scholars. Some want to confine folk art to non-academic, handmade objects. Others are willing to include manufactured material. In truth, the term is used to cover objects ranging from crude drawings by obviously untalented children to academically trained artists' paintings of "common" people and scenery.

Contemporary, watercolor, Verna Seagraves, Belsnickel, blue coat, signed lower left "Verna," dated 10-95, 14-1/2 x 11" sight, **$195.** *Photo courtesy of Sanford Alderfer Auction Company.*

Sculpture of bird bath, by Carl Peterson, completed between 1895-1900, constructed of concrete over steel, large concrete shallow bowl sits atop shaft with yellow ring on top and green ring below, resting on stepped square base, central shaft is light colored with painted flower, finial of up stretched green claw holding white sphere, yellow ring base, 30-1/2" d, 57" h, **$4,025.** *Photo courtesy of James D. Julia, Inc.*

Bank, 3-1/4" h, gourd form, paint decorated with face **115.00**
Bird tree, carved and painted wood, 9" h, America, c1900, mother robin with nest, two chicks perched on tree branch, imperfections **1,380.00**
Box, cov, 6" w, 3-1/2" d, 4-1/2" h, carved oak, America, late 19th/early 20th C, figure of man wearing cap with visor, sitting cross-legged on large dog, both have tails, border of turned finials joined by spiral rails, dovetailed box, leaf-carved drawer, paneled sides, old variegated varnish finish **1,265.00**
Candle stand, make-do, 18-3/4" w, 18" d, 26" h, New England, early 19th C, sq top, pedestal fashioned from parts of a yarn winder, tripod cabriole leg base on pads, old cream-colored paint, minor surface imperfections. . **1,150.00**
Carving

Angel

28" l, 17" h, relief carved angel holding star of Bethlehem and scroll, faded inscription begins "Glory to God in the ...," right arm with old iron work repair, American, 19th C **1,100.00**
41" l, 9" h, pine plank naively carved with face of angel,

outstretched wings, radiating layered feathers, remnants of orig polychrome dec, light weathering to gray patina, possibly PA, 19th C **900.00**
Bulls heads, life-size, real horns, glass eyes, old weathered paint, carved by Noah Weiss (1842-1907, Northampton County, PA), dated 1870, price for pr **38,500.00**

Drawing, pen and ink, Universalist Church, Leesburg, Ohio, drawing on heavy paper, glued to cardboard, orig inscription along bottom edge, title cut out and glued on front, dec beveled frame painted to resemble flame graining, 15" l, 10-3/4" h **525.00**

Family record, watercolor

17" x 22", for family of Abraham Brunson and Laura Aries, c1840, dec with watercolor floral and column design, tears, staining
. . . . **335.00**
20" x 15", for family of Joshua Washburn and Sylvia Mosman, written and drawn by Martha Ann Washburn, March 1841, marriage date and names of their children, birth and death dates, dec with floral and foliage designs in green, blue, and white, some stains
. . . . **295.00**

Figure

4-3/4" h, carved burlwood, lady, carved facial features, hair styled in bun, ruffled collar, old dark stained surface, America, late 19th/early 20th C. **425.00**

Token, watercolor, flower garland wrapped around stone monument with poem, signed "D. D. Carlisle January 30th 1841" at base, paper exhibits minor foxing, 9" x 6-1/2", **$160.** *Photo courtesy of Sanford Alderfer Auction Company.*

Toy, dancing, Uncle Sam, tin and wood, Uncle Sam figure extending from red, white and blue and stars and stripes post, San Antonio, Texas, 1885, 15-1/2" x 28" x 8-1/2", **$1,955.** *Photo courtesy of James D. Julia, Inc.*

6" l, 2" d, 9-1/4" h, fantail rooster, yellow, brown, and red polychrome, PA, c1800-20, one feather repaired........ **5,175.00**

13" l, 2-1/4" w, 10-1/4" h, carved and polychrome, horse and groom, leather Western saddle, America, early 20th C........... **5,175.00**

19-3/4" l, 3-1/2" w, 14" h, trotting horse, polychrome-molded copper over wood, attributed to Louis Jobin (1870-90, Quebec City,) twilled mane and tail, worn red paint, black hooves, stand, losses **11,500.00**

26" h, root, glass eyes, applied shell and minerals dec, attributed to Moses Ogden (1844-1919, Angelica, NY,) stand **1,495.00**

Grotesque face jug, stoneware, 5-1/2" h, brown-speckled glaze, found in Ohio, 19th C, imperfections **14,950.00**

Hammer, 13" l, oak and iron, figural, handle surmounted by carved man's head and upper torso, found in PA, 19th C.................... **1,955.00**

Memorial, 31" x 23" x 6-1/2", incised gilt and ebonized deep recessed shadow box frame, white painted cast iron profile of Lincoln surrounded by wreath of wire stemmed wax silk flowers, grouped with ribbon tied and waxed silk roses and calla lilies, surmounted by white dove with wings spread in flight, c1875 .... **700.00**

Picture frame, 12-5/8" w, 15-3/4" h, painted and incised wood, meandering vine and dot border, corner bosses, one corner boss missing.......... **920.00**

Plaque, 14" d, sun face, carved polychrome, molded edge, America, early 19th C, minor imperfections, stand **16,100.00**

Scherenschnitte, 11-1/2" x 14-1/2", birth certificate, dated Sept. 5, 1780, for

Anna Elizabeth Lauerin, Berks County, PA, Tolpehaden Tow ship, cut-work and painted dec border of flowers, tulips, and hearts attached with vine-work, black ink text, glued down, staining, loss **925.00**

Still life, watercolor on paper, American School, 19th C, framed

10-3/4" x 9-1/2", fruit and foliage in gray bowl, shades of red, green, and blue, pinprick dec, general toning, tiny scattered stains **1,150.00**

15" x 13", *Bouquet of Spring Flowers in a Vase*, sgd "Frances Thompson, 1841," tulips, narcissus, and other spring flowers, white handled urn-form vase dec with sea shells, very minor toning **2,715.00**

Theorem

6" x 6-1/2", watercolor on velvet, American School, early 19th C, unsigned, flowers, shades of blue, gold, green, and brown, ivory ground, period gilt frame, toning, losses to frame......... **440.00**

10-1/2" x 13-7/8", watercolor on velvet, still life of fruit in basket, molded black lacquered frame, toning, scattered foxmarks, note on reverse inscribed "This painting on white velvet was done by Grandma Ballard when she was a young girl. She herself hadn't much respect for it but Aunt Fannie saved it. E. W. B."................... **1,645.00**

21-1/4" x 26-3/4", watercolor stencil on card paper, rose bush, American School, 19th C, framed, minor scattered foxing, laid down **2,715.00**

Theorem, watercolor on velvet, flowers in shades of blue, gold, green, and brown, ivory ground, period gilt frame, American School, early 19th C, 6" x 6-1/2", **$440.** *Photo courtesy of Skinner's Auctioneers and Appraisers.*

Tinsel picture, 22" x 17", flower arrangement, reverse-painted glass backed with foil and paper, American School, late 19th C, Victorian frame, repaired **180.00**

Whimsey, wood, 2-5/8" sq base, 20-1/8" h, polychrome carved, gray, blue, and salmon paint, sgd "M. M. Watts, 1881," found in New York state, some wear to paint........ **2,760.00**

FOOD BOTTLES

History: Food bottles were made in many sizes, shapes, and colors. Manufacturers tried to make an attractive bottle that would ship well and allow the purchaser to see the product, thus giving assurance that the product was as good and as well made as home preserves.

Horseradish, dark green, **$8.**

Celery salt, 8" h, Crown Celery Salt, Horton Cato & Co., Detroit, yellow amber, smooth base, ground lip, orig shaker type cap **175.00**

Codd, Lehigh & Sons, Salford, olive-amber, emb globe **50.00**

Extract

Baker's Flavoring Extracts, 4-3/4" h, aqua, sq ring lip **15.00**

Red Dragon Extract, emb dragon **20.00**

Ginger, Sanford's orig label **12.00**

Horseradish, As You Like It, pottery, clamp **25.00**

Lime juice, 10-1/4" h, arrow motif, olive amber, smooth base, applied mouth **85.00**

Milk

Dellinger Dairy Farm, Jefferson, IN **25.00**

Milk bottle, RM Deger, Phoenixville, PA, Pure Milk, clear glass, 9-1/2" h, $20.

Holsgern Farms Dairy, quart, tin top
and closure. **90.00**
Purity Dairy, pint **60.00**
Scott's Dairy, quart, emb. **30.00**
Wonsidlers Dairy, quart. **25.00**
Mustard, Giessen's Union Mustard,
4-3/8" h, clear, eagle **85.00**
Olive oil, 7-1/2" h, Bertin Brand Pure
Olive Oil, dark green **18.00**
Peanut butter, 5" h, Bennett Hubba
. . . . **20.00**
Pepper sauce
8" h, S & P Pat. Appl. For, teal blue,
smooth base, tooled lip **50.00**
8-7/8" h, W & E Peppersauce, sq,
aqua **165.00**
Pickle, cathedral, America, 1845-80,
sq, beveled corners
11-1/2" h, three fancy cathedral
designs, greenish-aqua, tooled
rolled mouth, smooth base. **150.00**
13-5/8" h, sq, medium green, tooled
collared mouth, pontil scar,
Willington Glass Works, CT
. . . . **2,200.00**
Syrup, 12-1/4" h, Boston Cooler, clear,
blue and gold label, tooled mouth,
metal cap, smooth base, c1900 **350.00**
Vinegar, Weso Biko Co. Cider Vinegar,
jug shape. **45.00**

FOOD MOLDS

History: Food molds were used both commercially and in the home. Generally, pewter ice-cream molds and candy molds were used commercially; pottery and copper molds were used in homes. Today, both types are collected largely for decorative purposes.

The majority of pewter ice-cream molds are individual-serving molds. One quart of ice cream would make eight to 10 pieces. Scarcer, but still available, are banquet molds which used two to four pints of ice cream. European-made pewter molds are available.

Marks: Pewter ice-cream molds were made primarily by two American companies: Eppelsheimer & Co. (molds marked "E & Co., N.Y.") and Schall & Co. (marked "S & Co."). Both companies used a numbering system for their molds. The Krauss Co. bought out Schall & Co., removed the "S & Co." from some, but not all, of the molds, and added more designs (pieces marked "K" or "Krauss"). "CC" is a French mold mark.

Manufacturers of chocolate molds are more difficult to determine. Unlike the pewter ice-cream molds, makers' marks were not always used or were covered by frames. Eppelsheimer & Co. of New York marked many of their molds, either with their name or with a design resembling a child's toy top and the words "Trade Mark" and "NY." Many chocolate molds were imported from Germany and Holland and were marked with the country of origin and, in some cases, the mold-maker's name.

Additional Listing: Butter Prints.

Chocolate mold
Basket, 3-1/2" x 6", one cavity . . . **50.00**

Cookie mold, carved fruitwood, floral and foliate carved design in heart shape, 19th C, minor wear, 6-5/8" x 7", $355. Photo courtesy of Skinner's Auctioneers and Appraisers.

Catalog, Anton Reich, 13" x 17", 86 pgs
. . . . **2,420.00**
Chick and egg, 3-1/2" h, two parts,
folding, marked "Allemagne," Germany
. . . . **65.00**
Easter Rabbit, 18-1/2" h, standing,
two-part mold, separate two-part molds
for ears and front legs, "Anton Reiche,
Dresden, Germany" **220.00**
Elephant, tin, three cavities **95.00**
Fish. **95.00**
Heart, 6-1/2" x 6", two cavities . . **70.00**
Hen on basket, two pcs, clamp type,
marked "E. & Co./Toy". **60.00**
Pig. **95.00**
Skeleton, 5-1/2" h, pressed tin . . **60.00**
Witch, 4-1/2" x 2", four cavities . . **75.00**

Food mold
Cake mold, 9-3/4" l, 11-1/2" h, cast iron,
two-part full-figure seated rabbit,
Griswold, Erie, PA, late 19th C . **260.00**
Cheese, 5" x 13", wood, relief-carved
design and "Bid," pinned, branded
"Los," carved scratch date 1893 **60.00**
Cookie, 6-5/8" x 7", carved fruitwood,
floral and foliate carved design in heart
shape, 19th C, minor wear **355.00**
Pudding, tin and copper
4-1/2" d, round, star, ribbed sides
. . . . **175.00**
6" l, oval, trimmed copper eagle
. . . . **195.00**
6-1/2" d, round, fruit design . **125.00**
8" l, oval, lion. **220.00**
9" l, rect, oval sheaf **175.00**
Pudding, white ironstone, corn, marked
"Made in USA," chips, hairline . . **35.00**

Ice cream mold, pewter
Basket, replaced hinge pins . . . **25.00**

Pudding, tin, set of five graduated English 19th molds, all with hinged sides, 4-3/4" l to 9" l; and, American lidded melon-shaped mold marked "Kreamer," $115. Photo courtesy of Cowan's Historic Americana Auctions.

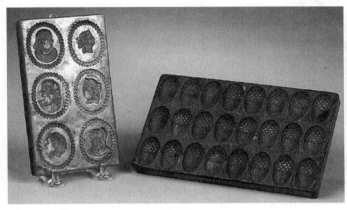

Maple candy, left: pewter mold with walnut back, six different oval bust portraits, including Miss Liberty, 6" x 3-1/2", right: tinned cast steel mold with three rows of eight acorns, stamped "Handle & Smith Birmingham," 4-1/2" x 7-1/2", sold as pair, $70. Photo courtesy of Cowan's Historic Americana Auctions.

Camel, pewter, marked "E & Co. NY, #681" **75.00**
Cherub riding Easter Bunny, 4" h. **45.00**
Easter Lily, three parts **75.00**
Egg, 2-3/4" d, marked "E & Co. NY" **35.00**
Flag, 13 stars **125.00**
Heart with Cupid, 4" h **65.00**
Man in the Moon, 5-1/2" h, marked "E & Co. copyright 1888" **95.00**
Pear, banquet size, marked "S & Co. 17" **325.00**
Rose, two parts, 3-1/2" d **125.00**
Ship, banquet size, two quarts .**265.00**
Steamboat **115.00**
Tulip, 4-1/8" h, marked "E. & Co. NY" **45.00**
Wedding Bells, 3" h **45.00**

Ice cream, Christmas tree, pewter, marked "E & Co. 1154," $85.

FOSTORIA GLASS

Warman's **GLASS** A Value & Identification Guide **4TH EDITION**

Edited by Ellen T. Schroy

For more information, see this book.

History: Fostoria Glass Co. began operations at Fostoria, Ohio, in 1887, and moved to Moundsville, West Virginia, its present location, in 1891. By 1925, Fostoria had five furnaces and a variety of special shops. In 1924, a line of colored tableware was introduced. Fostoria was purchased by Lancaster Colony in 1983 and continues to operate under the Fostoria name.

Ashtray
American, 2-7/8" sq **7.50**
Coin, crystal **30.00**
June, blue **75.00**
Baker, June, topaz, oval, 9" l **95.00**
Bell, Chintz, orig label **130.00**
Berry bowl, June, blue, 5" d **50.00**
Bouillon, Versailles, topaz **30.00**
Bowl
American, oval, 10" l **30.00**
Baroque, blue, 4" sq, one handle **22.00**
Century, 10-1/2" d **35.00**
Coin, emerald, 8" d **110.00**
June, 12" d, blue **125.00**
Bread and butter plate, Trojan, topaz, 6" d **10.00**
Cake salver
Century, crystal **60.00**
Coin, crystal **98.00**
Corsage, 10-1/2" d **32.00**

Candlestick, American pattern, 6-1/2" h, $20.

Navarre, crystal, handles, 10" d **60.00**
Candleholders, pr
Baroque, 4" h, one-lite, silver deposit Vintage dec on base, #2496. **75.00**
Baroque, 8-1/2" h, 10" w, two-lite, removable bobeche and prisms, #2484 . . . . **375.00**
Buttercup, 8" h, 8" w **150.00**
Coin, red, tall **150.00**
Meadow Rose **185.00**
Trindle, #2594, three-lite, Buttercup etch, 8" h, 6-1/2" w **250.00**
Candy dish, cov
Baroque, crystal **40.00**
June, yellow **370.00**
Navarre, three parts **175.00**
Versailles, blue, three parts . . **345.00**
Card tray, Brocaded Daffodil, two handles, pink, gold trim **40.00**
Celery tray, five parts, Lido **100.00**
Cereal bowl, June, rose, 6" d . . . **85.00**
Champagne
Chintz **20.00**
Dolly Madison **18.00**
June, saucer, petal stem **27.00**
Versailles, pink **40.00**
Cheese and cracker
Chintz **70.00**
Colony **55.00**
Cigarette box, cov
Morning Glory etching **65.00**
Oriental **170.00**
Claret
Camelia **30.00**
June, pink **175.00**
Navarre **80.00**
Trojan, yellow, 6" h **100.00**
Cocktail
Baroque, yellow **15.00**
Vesper, amber **30.00**
Compote
Baroque, crystal, 6" **18.00**
Century, 4-1/2" **20.00**
Condiment set, American, pr salt and pepper shakers, pr, cloverleaf tray, pr cruets **200.00**
Console set, Versailles, pink, 12" d bowl, pr 2" h candlesticks **225.00**
Cordial, Dolly Madison **30.00**
Cosmetic box, cov, American, 2-1/2" d, flake on bottom **900.00**
Courting lamp, Coin, amber . . . **150.00**
Creamer, individual size
Century **9.00**
Raleigh **8.00**
Creamer, table size
American, hexagon, 4-3/4" w, rare form **1,400.00**
Chintz **20.00**

Raleigh **10.00**
Trojan, topaz **22.00**
Creamer, sugar, tray, individual size
Camelia.................. **45.00**
Century **30.00**
Cream soup
Colony **95.00**
Versailles, pink **65.00**
Vesper, amber............. **30.00**
Cruet, June, yellow **700.00**
Crushed fruit jar, cov, America,
c1915-25, 5-7/8" d, 6" h...... **1,600.00**
Cup and saucer
Baroque, blue............. **35.00**
Buttercup **21.00**
Camelia.................. **20.00**
June, azure **45.00**
Rose **25.00**
Dinner plate
Versailles, pink, slight use.... **75.00**
Vesper, amber............. **30.00**
Figure
Deer, standing, crystal, 4-1/2" h
.... **45.00**
Lute and Lotus, ebony, gold
highlights, 12-1/2" h, price for pr
.... **975.00**
Mermaid, crystal, 10-3/8" h.. **225.00**
Goblet, water
Dolly Madison............. **20.00**
Golden Lace, gold trim...... **24.00**
Meadow Rose............. **30.00**
Navarre.................. **40.00**
Grapefruit, Coronet........... **9.00**
Gravy boat, liner, Kasmir, blue . **180.00**
Ice bucket, Versailles, pink.... **155.00**
Iced-tea tumbler, Navarre, pink . **75.00**

Plate, milk glass, multicolored decal with fruit, original red, white, and blue label, 8-1/4" d, **$20.**

Goblet, Colonial Mirror, c1930, **$45.**

Jelly, cov
Coin, amber.............. **30.00**
Meadow Rose, 7-1/2" d..... **90.00**
Juice tumbler, June, topaz, ftd .. **30.00**
Lily pond, Buttercup, 12" d **55.00**
Marmalade, cov, American **125.00**
Mayonnaise, liner, Navarre **90.00**
Milk pitcher, Century **60.00**
Nappy, handle
Century, 4-1/2" d **12.00**
Coin, blue, 5-3/8" d **30.00**
Nut cup, Fairfax, amber........ **15.00**
Oil cruet, Versailles, yellow **550.00**
Old-fashioned tumbler, Coin, crystal
.... **30.00**
Oyster cocktail, Colony........ **12.00**
Parfait, June, pink........... **180.00**
Pickle castor, American, ornate silver
plated frame, 11" h.......... **900.00**
Pickle tray, Century, 8-3/4" **15.00**
Pitcher, Lido, ftd **225.00**
Plate
Baroque, green, 7-1/2" d..... **28.00**
Century, 9-1/2" d **30.00**
Rose, 9" d **15.00**
Platter
June, topaz, 12" l, oval...... **145.00**
Trojan, topaz, 12" l, oval..... **80.00**
Punch bowl, ftd, Baroque, crystal, orig
label **425.00**
Relish dish, cov, Brocaded Summer
Gardens, three sections, white... **75.00**
Relish dish, open, June, topaz, two
parts, 8-1/4" l **40.00**
Ring holder, American, 4-1/2" l, 3" h
.... **800.00**
Rose bowl, American, small **18.00**
Salad plate, Buttercup......... **12.00**
Salt and pepper shakers, pr
Coin, red **60.00**
Coronet **15.00**
Versailles, topaz, ftd **200.00**

Sandwich server, Trojan, yellow, center handle, **$40.**

Sauce boat, Versailles, pink, matching
liner **300.00**
Sherbet, June, azure **40.00**
Snack plate, Century, 8" d **25.00**
Sugar, individual size, Baroque, blue
.... **4.00**
Sugar, cov, table size, Trojan, topaz
.... **22.00**
Syrup, American, Bakelite handle
.... **200.00**
Torte plate
Century, 14" d............. **30.00**
Colony, 15" d.............. **80.00**
Heather, 13" d............. **45.00**
Tray, Navarre, 8" l **100.00**
Tumbler, water
June, ftd **55.00**
Trojan, topaz, 5 oz, 4-1/2" h .. **30.00**
Urn, cov, Coin, amber, 12-3/4" h. **68.00**
Vase
Flying Fish, teal, 7" h........ **65.00**
Oak Leaf Brocade, c1929-31, 8" h
.... **240.00**
Versailles, yellow, 8" h, flip .. **395.00**

Sherbet, Navarre pattern, **$24.**

Whipped-cream pail, Versailles, blue
.........................**270.00**
Whiskey, June, yellow **85.00**
Wine
    Chintz.....................**40.00**
    Coin, red **90.00**

FRAKTUR

History: Fraktur, the calligraphy associated with the Pennsylvania Germans, is named for the elaborate first letter found in many of the hand-drawn examples. Throughout its history, printed, partially printed/partially hand-drawn, and fully hand-drawn works existed side by side. Schoolteachers or ministers living in rural areas of Pennsylvania, Maryland, and Virginia often made frakturs. Many artists are unknown.

Fraktur exists in several forms—geburts and taufschein (birth and baptismal certificates), vorschrift (writing examples, often with alphabet), haus sagen (house blessings), bookplates and bookmarks, rewards of merit, illuminated religious texts, valentines, and drawings. Although collected for decoration, the key element in fraktur is the text.

Notes: Fraktur prices rise and fall along with the American folk-art market. The key marketplaces are Pennsylvania and the Middle Atlantic states.

Birth certificate (Geburts and Taufschein)

    7-1/2" h, 8" w, Jesse Snyder, Towamencin Twp, PA, born in 1812, Schwenkfelder, 1873, orange, yellow, and green, two birds on branches **275.00**
    9" h, 11" w, watercolor, pen and ink on paper, heart with vintage, birds, flowers, orange, green, blue, black,

and yellow, penciled birth entries for 1878 and 1886, edge sgd "Henry E. Witmer," stains and minor edge damage, framed **220.00**
11-3/4" w, 7-3/4" h, attributed to Fredrich Krebs, scalloped heart, flowers, and two long necked birds, shades of brown, red, yellow/tan, records birth of Anna Barbara Huinelsin, Bethlehem Township, PA, 1805, fold lines, stains, damage **1,155.00**
12" h, 15" w, hand-colored printed form, Frederick Krebs, watercolor elements, red and green parrots, tulips, sun faces and crown, for Henrich Ott, Bucks County, Bedminster Township, PA, dated Oct. 29, 1800 ....**990.00**
12-1/4" h, 15-1/2" w, watercolor, pen, and ink on paper, Berks County artist, winged angels, paired birds, and mermaids, for Frederick Heverling, dated 1784 ...**2,100.00**
12-3/4" h, 15-1/2" w, watercolor, pen, and ink on paper, Flat Parrot artist, for Susana Gensemer, dated 1811
.....................**1,265.00**
13" h, 15-7/8" w, hand-colored printed form, printed by Gottleib Jungmann, Reading, 1795, Friedrich Krebs imprint, paired parrots, blossoms, and sun faces, for Johannes Ries, Paxton Township, Dauphin County, PA, dated Aug. 28, 1799 ....**2,185.00**
13" h, 16" w, hand-colored printed form, watercolor elements,

Frederick Speyer, paired angels, parrots, blossoms, and mermaids, for Sarra Grill, Lehigh County, PA, dated April 18, 1789 ....**1,380.00**
Bookplate
2-1/4" w, 4-1/2" h, red and green watercolor German verse, crown, heart, and red, green, and yellow bird with flower, German New Testament, published 1796, gold tooling on cover "J. G. St. 1807," loose from book, few stains **220.00**
3-7/8" w, 6-3/4" h, for Jacob Hekler, calligraphy, verse, and pot of flowers, red, yellow, blue, shades of green watercolor, brown ink, leather bound German New Testament book, published in Philadelphia, 1813, stains, some damage to both bookplate and book **110.00**
4-1/8" w, 7-1/8" h, for Anna Borpholder, born 1798, colorful watercolor, red, yellow, blue, and green tulips, daisy, and grapes, yellow heart, leather bound German Psalm book, published in Lancaster 1820, minor wear, leather book straps missing
...................**1,375.00**
4-1/4" w, 3-3/4" h, pen and ink inscription, "Catharina Barbara Heinlenin," watercolor floral garland below in red and yellow, black ink, light foxing, 5-7/8" w x 5-1/2" h burl frame........**360.00**
4-3/8" w, 5-7/8" h, watercolor red, yellow, and dark green flower, paid paper, date appears to be 1800, stains, light wear, taped split in middle, black painted frame with minor wear **615.00**
5-5/8" w, 6-7/8" h, ink and watercolor on laid paper, two long necked blue birds with red wings, yellow and red tulip with green leaves, German script, later frame with some curl **2,475.00**
Child's Book of Moral Instruction (Metamorphis), watercolor, pen and ink on paper
5-3/4" x 7-1/2", dec on both sides of four leaves, each with upper and lower flaps showing different versus and color illus, unknown illustrator **345.00**
6" x 7", printed form on paper, hand colored elements, The Great American Metamorphosis, Philadelphia, printed by Benjamin Sands, 1805-06, printed on both sides of four leaves, each with

Birth and baptismal certificates for brothers Daniel Raup (1784) and Peter Raup (1791), by Frederick Krebs, Adam and Eve, Apple Tree and Serpent in Garden of Eden, printed cut-out birds, watercolor, pen, and ink on paper, gilded decoupage elements, 15-1/2" h, 12-1/4" w, pair, **$3,740.** *Photo courtesy of Southeby's.*

upper and lower flaps, engraved collar illus by Poupard **420.00**
6-1/4" x 7", dec on both sides of four leaves, when folded reveals different versus and full-page color illus, executed by Sarah Ann Siger, Nazareth, PA, orig string hinges **575.00**

Confirmation certificate, 6" x 7-3/4", watercolor, pen and ink on paper, David Schumacher, paired tulips and hearts, for Maria Magdalena Spengler, dated 1780.................... **4,600.00**

Copybook, Vorschrift, 8" w, 5-5/8" h, pen and ink, red watercolor, laid paper, German text with ornate Gothic letters in heading, blocked cut area in lower left unfinished, minor edge damage, 11-3/8" w, 9-1/2" h yellow and red leather covered frame **250.00**

Drawing, watercolor, pen and ink
4" h, 2-3/4" w, red yellow and blue rooster with bushy tail, American School, 19th C **865.00**
5-3/8" h, 7-3/4" w, pen and ink and watercolor on heavy paper, Daniel Sehaey, Smithville, Wayne County, OH, Oct. 11th, A.D. 1854, written by T.H.C.B., black, red, and greenish yellow, 8-3/4" h, 10-3/4" w walnut beveled frame..... **590.00**
15-3/8" w, 12-1/2" h, central heart bordered in blue, orange, and light brown, flowering tulip plant with four buds in blue, red, black, and light brown, compass star flowers, brown and white foliate at upper

Dated 1839, Richland Township, Bucks County, Pennsylvania, verse in German, hand drawn and colored angels, eagle, and birds eating berries on vines, 16" x 13" sight, **$525.** *Photo courtesy of Sanford Alderfer Auction Company.*

Daniel Peterman, Manheim Township, York County, PA, wove paper, watermark, colored decoration, bird, distelfink, and floral motifs, two women, 15-3/4" x 12-1/2", **$1,750.**

corners, six pointed starts in lower corners, colors similar to those found on Shenandoah Valley, VA, examples, foxing, stains, and tears, contemporary frame **495.00**

Family register, 19-3/4" w, 16" h, hand drawn, blue-green and red border with stars and flowers in corners, hearts, cherubs, and cross hatch work at center, German names, written in old brown ink, dates from 1814 to 1870, heart and hand medallion with inscription "Orphans Home and Ft. Wayne Hospital, Allen Co., Ind," sgd "John Cornelius Martin," old taped tear near top margin, small piece of corner missing.................. **1,100.00**

House blessing (Haus Segen), 15-1/2" h, 11-3/4" w, printed by Johann Ritter, Reading, hand colored, orange, green, blue, yellow, brown, and black, professionally repaired and rebacked on cloth, 18-1/4" h, 14-3/8" w old stenciled dec frame **500.00**

Marriage certificate, 8" x 12-1/2", watercolor, pen and ink on paper, Daniel Schumacher, paired red, yellow and green birds flanking an arch with crown, for Johannes Haber and Elisabeth Stimmess, Windsor Township, Berks County, PA, dated 1777 .... **1,035.00**

Reward of merit, American School, early 19th C, watercolor, pen, and ink on paper
3-5/8" x 3-1/8", red, yellow, and blue-tailed bird perched on flowering branch **1,092.00**
4-1/8" x 3-1/4", red and yellow birds, green and yellow pinwheel flower **345.00**

FRATERNAL ORGANIZATIONS

History: Benevolent and secret societies played an important part in America from the late 18th to the mid-20th centuries. Initially, the societies were organized to aid members and their families in times of distress. They evolved from this purpose into important social clubs by the late 19th century.

In the 1950s, with the arrival of the civil rights movement, an attack occurred on the secretiveness and often discriminatory practices of these societies. Membership in fraternal organizations, with the exception of the Masonic group, dropped significantly. Many local chapters closed and sold their lodge halls. This resulted in the appearance of many fraternal items in the antiques market.

Pinback button, Elks Congress of Nations, 1908, multicolored, **$120.** *Photo courtesy of Hake's Americana & Collectibles.*

Benevolent & Protective Order of the Elks, (BPOE)

Beaker, 5" h, cream, black elk head, marked "Mettlach, Villeroy & Boch" **110.00**

Book, *National Memorial,* 1931, color illus **35.00**

Bookends, pr, bronzed cast iron, elk in high relief................... **75.00**

Pinback button, orange, lavender, and green, white accents, gold rim, brown elk symbol, tiny inscription "Souvenir Elks Convention Los Angeles 1909" **25.00**

Shaving mug, pink and white, gold elk head, crossed American flags and floral dec, marked "Germany" on bottom **90.00**

Tip tray, Philadelphia, 21st Annual Reunion, July 1907, rect, 4-7/8" x 3-1/4" **135.00**

Eastern Star

Demitasse cup and saucer, porcelain **25.00**

Doorstop, cast iron, red base, white bird, gold chain, **$125.**

Pendant, SP, rhinestones and rubies
. . . . **45.00**

Ring, gold, Past Matron, star-shape stone with diamond in center . . . **150.00**

Independent Order of Odd Fellows (I.O.O.F)

Ceremonial staff, 3" w, 1-1/2" d, 64" h, polychrome carved wood, reverse tapering staff surmounted by carved open hand in cuffed sleeve holding heart in palm, old red, gold, and black painted surface, mounted on iron base, minor surface imperfections. . **2,300.00**

Gameboard, reverse painted black and gold metallic squares bordered by "I.O.O.F" chain links and other symbols, areas of flaking, 20-1/2" x 20-1/2" black oak frame **350.00**

Shaving mug, 3-3/4" h, B. F. Smith, insignia, gold trim, wear **165.00**

Vignette, 7-3/4" x 14-1/2", oil on board, hand beneath three links holding heart and card bearing archery scene, molded gilt gesso frame, flaking, subtle surface grime **920.00**

Wall hanging, 75" l, 47-1/2" h, painted canvas, from Odd Fellows Lodge #4 in Whitehall, NY, 19th C, several symbols reflecting high ideals, imperfections
. . . . **2,990.00**

Watch fob, 94th Anniversary, April 12, 1913 . . . . **30.00**

Knights Templar

Business card, Reynolds, J. P., Columbia Commandery No. 18 (K of P) Sturgis, MI, color logo, c1890 . . . . **6.00**

Loving cup, china, three handles, green and white, gold tracery, Knights Templer insignia and Pittsburgh, 1907, marked "American China Co." . . **75.00**

Shot glass, bowl supported by three golden swords, dated 1903, Pittsburgh
. . . . **25.00**

Tumbler, emb Indian head, dated 1903, Pittsburgh **45.00**

Masonic

Advertising button, Illinois Masonic Hospital, black and white litho, c1920
. . . . **10.00**

Apron, 14" x 12", leather, white, blue silk trim, white embroidery, silver fringe
. . . . **35.00**

Book, *Morals & Dogma of the Ancient & Accepted Scottish Rite of Freemasonry*, Albert Pike, L. H. Jenkins, 1949, 861 pgs **20.00**

Bookends, pr, patinated metal, "appl'd for" on back **200.00**

Box, cov, 5" x 16-1/4" x 12-1/2", Chinese Export black lacquer, molded top with mother-of-pearl and lacquer Masonic devices, sides with floral dec, top loose, lock mechanism missing, minor lacquer loss **920.00**

Patriotic Order Sons of America, top pin printed celluloid, center portrait of George Washington, gold trim, center medallion with image of Washington kneeling in prayer, made by Whitehead & Hoag, 7" l, $125. Photo courtesy of Julie Robinson.

Ring, 14K white gold Masonic ring, 32nd degree, ring size 10-3/4, $100. Photo courtesy of Sanford Alderfer Auction Company.

Ceremonial cane, 33-1/2" l, carved lizards, rounded top knop with emblem and eagle, metal top, several age cracks. **350.00**

Fob, silvered brass, June 14-15, 1927 event, inscription for "Grand Lodge, F & A.M. Wisconson," blank reverse . **18.00**

Goblet, St. Paul, 1908 . . . . **70.00**

Jug, 5-5/8" h, lusterware, transfer printed and painted polychrome enamels, horseman, inscribed "James Hardman 1823," Masonic dec, royal coat of arms, minor wear **410.00**

Match holder, 11" h, wall type, walnut, pierce carved symbols. **75.00**

Painting, 23-1/4" h, 20" w, oil on canvas, "Our Motto," framed, retouched, craquelure **2,645.00**

Pendant, 1" l, 14K rose gold, enameled blue and white **110.00**

Ring, 14K rose gold, enameled cross on one side, enameled 32 degrees on other, double eagle head set with 10-point diamond, hand engraved 1900-20 . . . . **175.00**

Sign, 28-3/4" w, 34" h, shield shape, polychrome wood, several applied wood Masonic symbols, including All-Seeing Eye, sun, moon, stars, large central "G," pillars, etc., gilt highlights, blue field, red and white stripes below, molded gilt frame, wear and losses
. . . . **3,055.00**

Tobacco jar, 4-7/8" l, 3-7/8" w, 7-1/4" h, cast iron, brass, and lead, oval brass finial on domed octagonal cover, fitted onto conforming container plated with lead, sides decorated with various engraved designs: "Daniel Hall" over a foliage-filled pitcher flanked by tobacco pipes and goblets, shield with Masonic symbols encircled with "FRIENDSHIP LOVE AND TRUTH," ship at sea and anchor; the lid and base painted dark red with black, green, and yellow highlights, wear **1,175.00**

Shriner

Cup and saucer, Los Angeles, 1906
.... **70.00**
Dinnerware, Rajah, partial set, various
marks, 52 pcs **150.00**
Goblet, St. Paul, 1908, ruby stained,
pedestal foot **70.00**
Ice-cream mold, 4-1/4" d, pewter,
crescent with Egyptian head, marked
"E & Co., NY"............... **30.00**
Mug, Syria Temple, Pittsburgh, 1895,
Nantasket Beach, gold figures . **125.00**
Shot glass, cranberry and clear,
symbols and officers' names, St. Louis,
1909...................... **300.00**

FRUIT JARS

History: Fruit jars are canning jars used to preserve food. Thomas W. Dyott, one of Philadelphia's earliest and most innovative glassmakers, was promoting his glass canning jars in 1829. John Landis Mason patented his screw-type canning jar on November 30, 1858. This date refers to the patent date, not the age of the jar. There are thousands of different jars and a variety of colors, types of closures, sizes, and embossings.

Additional Listings: See *Warman's Americana & Collectibles* for more examples.

Advance, Pat. Appl'd For, aqua, ground
lip, qt **95.00**
Atlas Mason's Patent, medium yellow
green, ABM lip, qt **50.00**
Ball, Ideal, colorless, bottom emb
"Pat'd July 14, 1908," wire closure **7.50**
Ball, Mason, yellow green, amber
striations, qt............... **75.00**
Belle, Pat. Dec. 14th, 1869, aqua, three
raised feet, ground lip, metal neck
band, wire bail, qt **75.00**
Canton Domestic, Patent 1889, clear
.... **85.00**

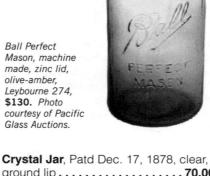

Ball Perfect Mason, machine made, zinc lid, olive-amber, Leybourne 274, $130. Photo courtesy of Pacific Glass Auctions.

Crystal Jar, Patd Dec. 17, 1878, clear,
ground lip **70.00**
Dillion G. Co., Fairmont, IN, green,
quart, wax seal, long crack **12.50**
Dodge Sweeney & Co.'s California,
aqua, ground lip, glass insert, zinc
band, 1-1/2 qt **425.00**
Excelsior, aqua, ground lip, insert, zinc
band, qt **575.00**
Fahnestock Albree & Co., aqua,
applied mouth, qt............ **35.00**
Franklin Fruit Jar, aqua, ground lip,
zinc lid, qt................. **225.00**
Friedley & Cornman's Patent Oct.
25th, 1958, Ladies Choice,
aquamarine, ground mouth, iron rim,
gutta percha or leather insert, smooth
base, half gallon, iron rim lid rusty,
L #1039.................. **1,200.00**
Good Luck, Hazel Atlas, four-leaf
clover on front, glass lid, half gal . **50.00**
Helmen's Railroad Mills, amber,
ground lip, insert, zinc band, pt . . **70.00**

High Grade, aqua, ground lip, zinc lid,
qt **150.00**
Johnson & Johnson, New York, cobalt
blue, ground lip, orig insert, screw
band, qt................... **325.00**
Keystone Mason, Patent Nov. 3, 1858,
quart, aqua **50.00**
Lafayette, aqua, tooled lip, orig
three-pc glass and metal stopper, qt
.... **200.00**
Mason Crystal Jar, clear, ground lip,
zinc lid.................... **65.00**
Mason's Patent Nov. 30th, 1858, light
green, profuse amber striations,
machined mouth, zinc lid, smooth base,
half gallon, some int. stain, L#1787
.... **325.00**
Midget, T. M. Improved, pint,
green-aqua **20.00**
Moore's Patent Dec. 3, 1861,
aquamarine, applied collared mouth,
glass lid, iron yoke clamp, smooth
base, qt, L #2204 .... **120.00**
Peerless, aqua, applied mouth, iron
yoke, half gallon **85.00**
Pet, aqua, applied mouth, qt ... **55.00**
Protector, aquamarine, ground mouth,
unmarked tin lid, smooth base, qt, L
#2420 .... **70.00**
Star, aqua, emb star, ground lid, zinc
insert and screw band, qt..... **300.00**
Sun, aquamarine, ground mouth, glass
lid, iron clamp, smooth base, qt **130.00**
The Pearl, aqua, ground lip, screw
band, qt................... **40.00**
Union N1, Beaver Falls Glass Co.,
Beaver Falls, PA, aqua, applied wax
seal ring, half gallon **45.00**
Woodbury Improved (monogram),
aquamarine, ground mouth, quart, L
#3029 .... **40.00**

FULPER POTTERY

History: The Fulper Pottery Company of Flemington, New Jersey, made stoneware pottery and utilitarian ware beginning in the early 1800s. It switched to the production of art pottery in 1909 and continued until about 1935.

The company's earliest artware was called the Vasekraft line (1910-1915), featuring intense glazing and rectilinear, Germanic forms. Its middle period (1915-1925) included some of the earlier shapes, but they also incorporated Oriental forms. Their glazing at this time was less consistent but more diverse. The last period (1925-1935) was characterized by water-down Art-Deco forms with relatively weak glazing.

Pieces were almost always molded, though careful hand glazing distinguished this pottery as one of the

All Right Patd Jan. 28, 1868, rare variant with reconstructed No. 6, light aqua, Leybourne 16-1, repro metal dome lid and wire closure, $150. Photo courtesy of Pacific Glass Auctions.

Sun, trademark JP Barstow on base, original closure, quart, very light aqua, Leybourne 2761, $130. Photo courtesy of Pacific Glass Auctions.

premier semi-commercial producers. Pieces from all periods are almost always marked.

Marks: A rectangular mark, FULPER, in a rectangle is known as the "ink mark" and dates from 1910-1915. The second mark, as shown, dates from 1915-1925; it was incised or in black ink. The final mark, FULPER, die-stamped, dates from about 1925 to 1935.

For more information, see this book.

Adviser: David Rago.

Clock, architectural table clock, Waterbury clockworks, sheer white and amber glossy glaze, Vasekraft, rectangular ink mark, 4" w, 5-1/2" h, $2,400. Photos courtesy of David Rago Auctions.

Bowl, 8" d, 5" h, flower holder, blue-green crystalline glaze, rect ink mark **110.00**
Bud vase, 9" h, baluster, Butterscotch flambé glaze, ink racetrack mark **275.00**
Console set, 7-3/4" d floriform bowl, pr 4-1/4" h candlesticks, cov in turquoise and clear crystalline flambé glaze, ink racetrack mark, touch-up on one candlestick rim **100.00**
Effigy bowl, 10" d, 8" h, blue, ivory, and green flambé int., matte blue glaze base, rect ink mark **8,050.00**
Ibis bowl, 10-1/2" d, 5-1/2" h, green and blue flambé over Copperdust Crystalline, ink racetrack mark . . **815.00**

Jug, stoneware, cobalt blue squeezebag decorated of three bathing beauties, stamped FULPER BROS./FLEMING TON N.J./3, 1890s, restoration to drilled hole near base, 8-1/2" d, 13" h, $750.

Urn, nubbed handles, mirrored green flambé glaze, bold incised racetrack mark, few small shallow scratches and firing line halfway around foot ring, 8-1/2" d, 11-1/2" h, $3,250.

Jug, 7-3/4" d, 11-1/2" h, loop handle, bulbous, covered in perfectly-fired Copper Dust Crystalline glaze, incised racetrack mark, 1/4" grinding chip **3,775.00**
Lamp, table
  15-1/4" d, 18-1/2" h, mushroom-shaped lamp shade, covered in strong Leopard Skin Crystalline glaze, inset with leaded slag glass pieces, two orig sockets, rect ink mark on both pcs, hairline between two inset pcs **5,750.00**
  17" d, 21-1/2" h, mushroom-shaped shade covered in brown, celadon and blue glaze, inset with green and amber slag glass, on Cucumber Green matte base, rect ink mark on both, possibly married piece **1,610.00**

Vase, barrel-shaped, Chinese Blue glaze dripping over frothy medium green and matte white ground, rectangular ink mark, 5" d, 8-1/2" h, $575.

Urn
  7-1/2" d, 12" h, two handles, fine Mirrored Green, Mahogany, and Ivory flambé glazes, rect ink mark **1,200.00**
  11-3/4" d, 11-3/4" h, hammered, frothy indigo and light bleu glaze, incised racetrack mark, stilt-pull bruise **865.00**
Vase
  3" d, 10-3/4" h, cylindrical, Leopard Skin Crystalline glaze, early rect ink stamp, small stilt-pull or grinding chip **860.00**
  3-1/4" d, 5" h, shouldered, Chinese Blue flambé glaze, speckled blue glaze, rect ink mark **230.00**
  4-3/4" d, 7" h, bullet, frothy Leopard Skin Crystalline glaze, ink racetrack mark, two small opposing bursts at rim, grinding chips on base **520.00**
  5" d, 5-1/2" h, bulbous, brown and Chinese Blue glaze, raised racetrack mark **290.00**
  6-1/4" h, 5-3/4" w, pillow, Cat's Eye flambé glaze, ink racetrack mark **175.00**
  8-3/4" h, 3-3/4" d, four flaring sides, cov in gunmetal green and frothy blue glaze, rect Prang mark, short rim hairlines **460.00**
  11-1/2" h, 7-3/4" d, Cattail, covered in Leopard Skin crystalline glaze, rect ink mark, rim minor burst bubble **2,300.00**
  11-1/2" h, 9" d, bulbous floriform, emb panels, covered in exceptional mirrored Cat's Eye flambé glaze, raised racetrack mark **2,990.00**
  12" h, 9" d, bulbous, covered in frothy blue, ivory, and Mirror Black flambé glaze, incised racetrack mark **1,400.00**

Vase, bullet-shaped vase, ivory, brown, blue and olive flambé glaze, incised racetrack mark, 6" d, 10" h, $575.

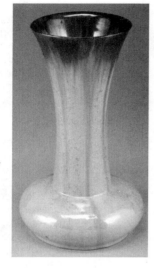

Vase, trumpet, Butterscotch flambé glaze, ink racetrack mark. Light abrasion rim, 7" d, 13-1/2" h, $5,000.

12-1/2" h, 7" d, tapering, cov in Mirror Black to Copper Dust crystalline flambé glaze, incised racetrack mark **2,990.00**

Vessel

6" d, 5" h, squatty, two angular handles, frothy blue flambé glaze, ink racetrack mark, restoration to one handle **195.00**

6" d, 6-1/2" h, bulbous, three horn-shaped handles, ivory, blue, and Mirror Black flambé glaze, vertical ink mark **860.00**

7-1/2" d, 6-1/4" h, spherical, two buttressed handles, mirrored Cat's Eye flambé glaze, ink racetrack mark **435.00**

11-1/2" d, 13-1/4" h, bulbous, four short handles, covered in Leopard Skin Crystalline glaze, incised racetrack mark, restoration to drill hole in bottom **2,990.00**

Vase, tapering, Mirror Black-to-Copper Dust crystalline flambé glaze, incised racetrack mark, 7" d, 12-1/2" h, $2,990.

FURNITURE

History: Two major currents dominate the American furniture marketplace—furniture made in Great Britain and furniture made in the United States. American buyers continue to show a strong prejudice for objects manufactured in the United States. They will pay a premium for such pieces and accept them above technically superior and more aesthetically appealing English examples.

For more information, see this book.

Until the last half of the 19th century, English examples and design books dictated formal American styles. Regional furniture, such as the Hudson River Valley (Dutch) and the Pennsylvania German styles, did develop. Less-formal furniture, often designated as "country" or vernacular style, developed throughout the 19th and early 20th centuries. These country pieces deviated from the accepted formal styles and have a charm that many collectors find irresistible.

America did contribute a number of unique decorative elements to English styles. The American Federal period is a reaction to the English Hepplewhite period. American designers created furniture that influenced, rather than reacted to, world taste in the Gothic-Revival style and Arts and Crafts, Art Deco, and Modern International movements.

Furniture Styles

Furniture styles can be determined by careful study and remembering what design elements each one embraces. To help understand what defines each period, here are some of the major design elements for each period.

William and Mary, 1690-1730. The style is named for the English King William of Orange and his consort, Mary. New colonists in America brought their English furniture traditions with them and tried to translate these styles using native woods. Their

Chair, arm, William and Mary, well-carved shaped crest rail, three-slat banister back, turned legs. Bold stretcher to front legs, replaced rush seat, seat height 18" h seat, 47-1/2" h back, $1,150. Photo courtesy of James D. Julia, Inc.

furniture was practical and sturdy. Lines of this furniture style tend to be crisp, while facades might be decorated with bold grains of walnut or maple veneers, framed by inlaid bands. Moldings and turnings are exaggerated in size. Turnings are baluster-shaped and the use of C-scrolls was quite common, giving some look of moment to a piece of furniture. Feet found in this period generally are round or oval. One exception to this is known as the Spanish foot, which flares to a scroll. Woods tend to be maple, walnut, white pine, or Southern yellow pine. One type of decoration that begins in the William and Mary period and extends through to Queen Anne and Chippendale styles is known as japanning, referring to an imitation lacquering process.

Spanish

Queen Anne, 1720-1760. Evolution of this design style is from Queen Anne's court, 1702 to 1714, and lasted until the Revolution. This style of furniture is much more delicate than its predecessor. It was one way for the young Colonists to show their own unique style, with each regional area initiating special design elements. Forms tend to be attenuated in New England. Chair rails were more often mortised through the back legs when made in Philadelphia. New England furniture makers preferred pad feet, while the

Claw and Ball   **Triffid**   **Pad**

Chair, side, Queen Anne, eastern MA, walnut, carved crest rail, curved vasiform back, replaced balloon seat, block and turned stretcher, good carved Queen Anne legs, some repairs, 40" h, seat height 17" h seat, 40" h back, price for pair, $4,025. Photo courtesy of James D. Julia, Inc.

makers in Philadelphia used triffid feet. Makers in Connecticut and New York often preferred slipper and claw and ball feet. The most popular woods were walnut, poplar, cherry, and maple. Japanned decoration tends to be in red, green and gilt, often on a blue-green field. A new furniture form of this period was the tilting tea table.

Chippendale, 1755-1790. This period is named for the famous English cabinetmaker, Thomas Chippendale, who wrote a book of furniture designs, *Gentlemen and Cabinet-Makers Director*, published in 1754, 1755, and 1762. This book gave cabinetmakers real direction and they soon eagerly copied the styles presented. Chippendale was influenced by ancient cultures, such as the Romans, and Gothic influences. Look for Gothic arches, Chinese fretwork, columns, capitals, C-scrolls, S-scrolls, ribbons, flowers, leaves, scallop shells, gadrooning, and acanthus. The most popular wood used in this period was mahogany, with walnut, maple, and cherry also present. Legs become straight and regional differences still exist in design elements, such as feet. Claw and ball feet become even larger and more decorative. Pennsylvania cabinetmakers used Marlborough feet, while other regions favored ogee bracket feet. The center of furniture manufacturing gradually shifts from New England and Mid-Atlantic city centers to Charleston. One of the most popular form of this period was a card table that sported five legs instead of the four of Queen Anne designs.

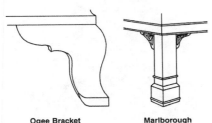

Ogee Bracket   **Marlborough**

Candlestand, Chippendale, American, mahogany, serpent feet, 18" d, 27-1/2" h, **$1,850.**

Sideboard, Hepplewhite, inlaid mahogany, bowfront center section with central door having inset panel and center inlay, flanked by two bottle drawers, top of center section has center drawer flanked by two smaller drawers, side sections have large door and drawer above, shaped backsplash, line inlay, tapered short square legs, L. N. Arnall Richmond, VA, label on reverse, refinished, some restoration, 71" l, 21-1/2" d, 53" h, **$2,550. JDJ.**

Federal (Hepplewhite), 1790-1815. This period reflects the growing patriotism felt in the young American states. Their desire to develop their own distinctive furniture style was apparent. Stylistically it also reflects the architectural style known as Federal, where balance and symmetry were extremely important. Woods used during this period were first and foremost mahogany and mahogany veneer, but other native woods, such as maple, birch, or satinwood, were used. Reflecting the architectural ornamentation of the period, inlays were popular, as was carving, and even painted highlights. The motifs used for inlay included bellflowers, urns, festoons, acanthus leaves, and pilasters to name but a few. Inlaid bands and lines were also popular and often used in combination with other inlay. Legs of this period tend to be straight or tapered to the foot. The foot might be a simple extension of the leg or bulbous, or spade shaped. Two new furniture forms were created in this period. They are the sideboard and the worktable, reflecting forms that came into favor as they served a very functional use. Expect to find a little more comfort in chairs and sofas, but not very thick cushions or seats.

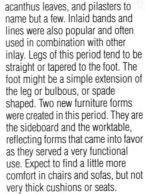

Spade

When a piece of furniture is made in England, or styled after an English example, it may be known as Hepplewhite. The time frame is the same. Robert Adam is credited with creating the style known as Hepplewhite during the 1760s and leading the form. Another English book heavily influenced the designers of the day. This one was by Alice Hepplewhite, and titled *The Cabinet Maker and Upholsterer's Guide,* with publisher dates of 1788, 1789, and 1794.

Straight Tapered

Chair, arm, Sheraton, lyre back, balloon seat, tiger maple arms and crest, 17-1/2" h seat, 34" h back, **$425.** *Photo courtesy of James D. Julia, Inc.*

Sheraton, 1790-1810. The style known as Sheraton closely resembles Federal. The lines are somewhat straighter and the designs plainer than Federal. Sheraton pieces are more closely associated with rural cabinetmakers. Woods would include mahogany, mahogany veneer, maple, and pine, as well as other native woods. This period was heavily influenced by the work of Thomas Sheraton and his series of books, *The Cabinet Maker and Upholster's Drawing Book,* from 1791-1794, and his *The Cabinet Directory,* 1803, and *The Cabinet-Maker, Upholsterer, and General Artist's Encyclopedia* of 1804.

Empire (Classical), 1805-1830. By the beginning of the 19th Century, a new design style was emerging. Known as Empire, it had an emphasis on the classical world of Greece, Egypt, and other ancient European influences. The American craftsmen began to incorporate more flowing patriotic motifs, such as eagles with spread wings. The basic wood used in the Empire period was mahogany. However, during this period, dark woods were so favored that often mahogany was painted black. Inlays were popular when made of ebony or maple veneer. The dark woods offset gilt highlights, as were the brass ormolu mountings often found in this period. The legs of this period are substantial and more flowing than those found in the Federal or Sheraton periods. Feet can be highly ornamental as when they are carved to look like lion feet, or plain when they extend to the floor with a swept leg. Regional differences in this style are very apparent, with New York City being the center of the design style as it was also the center of fashion at the time.

New furniture forms of this period include a bed known as a sleigh bed, with the headboard and footboard forming a graceful arch, similar to that found on a sleigh, hence the name. Several new forms of tables also came into being, especially the sofa table. Because the architectural style of the Empire period used big open rooms, the sofa was now

Desk, Empire, French, flame grain mahogany veneer, black marble top, thin long drawer, fall front, interior fitted with bird's eye maple veneer, leather writing surface, valanced shelf over eight drawers with line inlay, two-door base with three interior shelves, 32-1/2" w, 16" d, 57-1/2" h, $1,800. Photo courtesy of Sanford Alderfer Auction Co.

Stand, étagère, Victorian, walnut, beveled, arched top, central mirror, five shelves on each side, white marble top, cupboard in base, 43" w, 85" h, $880. Photo courtesy of Joy Luke Auctions.

allowed to be in the center of the room, with a table behind it. Former architectural periods found most furniture placed against the outside perimeter of the walls and brought forward to be used.

Victorian, 1830-1890. The Victorian period as it relates to furniture styles can be divided into several distinct styles. However, not every piece of furniture can be dated or definitely identified, so the generic term "Victorian" will apply to those pieces. Queen Victoria's reign affected the design styles of furniture, clothing, and all sorts of items used in daily living. Her love of ornate styles is well known. When thinking of the general term, Victorian, it is best to think of a cluttered environment, full of heavy furniture, and surrounded by plants, heavy fabrics, and lots of china and glassware.

French Restauration, 1830-1850. This is the first sub-category of the Victoria era. This style is best simplified as the plainest of the Victorian styles. Lines tend to be sweeping, undulating curves. It is named for the style that was popular in France as the Bourbons tried to restore their claim to the French throne, from 1814 to 1848. The Empire (Classical) period influence is felt, but French Restauration lacks some of the ornamentation and fussiness of that period. Design motifs continue to reflect an interest in the classics of Greece and Egypt. Chair backs are styled with curved and concave crest rails, making them a little more comfortable than earlier straight back chairs. The use of bolster pillows and more upholstery is starting to emerge. The style was only popular in clusters, but did entice makers from larger metropolitan areas, such as Boston, and New Orleans, to embrace the style.

The Gothic Revival period, 1840-1860, is one relatively easy to identify for collectors. It is one of the few styles that celebrates elements found in the corresponding architectural style: turrets, pointed arches, and quatrefoils—things found in 12th and 16th centuries that were adapted to this interesting mid-century furniture style. The furniture shelving form known as an étagère is born in this period, allowing Victorians to have more room to display their treasured collections. Furniture that had mechanical parts also was embraced by the Victorians of this era. The woods preferred by makers of this period were walnut and oak, with some use of mahogany and rosewood. The scale used ranged from large and grand to small and petite. Carved details gave dimension and interest.

Rococo Revival, 1845-1870. This design style features the use of scrolls, either in a "C" shape or the more fluid "S" shape. Carved decoration in the form of scallop shells, leaves, and flowers, particularly roses, and acanthus further add to the ornamentation of this style of furniture. Legs and feet of this form are cabriole or scrolling. Other than what might be needed structurally, it is often difficult to find a straight element in Rococo Revival furniture. The use of marble for tabletops was quite popular, but

Cabriole

expect to find the corners shaped to conform to the overall scrolling form. To accomplish all this carving, walnut, rosewood, and mahogany were common choices. When lesser woods were used, they were often painted to reflect these more expensive woods. Some cast iron elements can be found on furniture from this period, especially if it was cast as scrolls. The style began in France and England, but eventually migrated to America where it evolved into two other furniture styles, Naturalistic and Renaissance Revival.

Elizabethan, 1850-1915. This sub-category of the Victorian era is probably the most feminine-influenced style. It also makes use of the new machine turned spools and spiral turnings that were fast becoming popular with furniture makers. New technology advancements allowed more machined parts to be generated. By adding flowers, either carved, or painted, the furniture pieces of this era had a softness to them that made them highly suitable. Chair backs tend to be high and narrow, having a slight back tilt. Legs vary from straight to baluster turned types to spindle turned. This period of furniture design saw more usage of needlework upholstery and decoratively painted surfaces.

Sideboard, late Victorian, Elizabethan, c1910, mahogany, full-length beveled glass mirror, gallery supported by fluted columns, molded cornice, resting on four drawer cabinet base with two carved panel doors with stylized florals, original hammered bronze fittings, original finish, rich patina, 77" l, 24" w, 72" h, $1,610. Photo courtesy of Jackson's International Auctioneers & Appraisers.

Louis XVI, 1850-1914. One period of the Victorian era that flies away with straight lines is Louis XVI. However, this furniture style is not austere; it is adorned with ovals, arches, applied medallions, wreaths, garlands, urns, and other Victorian flourishes. As the period aged, more ornamentation became present on the finished furniture styles. Furniture of this time was made from more expensive woods, such as ebonized woods or rosewood. Walnut was popular around the 1890s. Other dark woods were featured, often to contrast the lighter ornaments. Expect to find straight legs or fluted and slightly tapered legs.

Naturalistic, 1850-1914. This furniture period takes the scrolling effects of the Rococo Revival

Chair, Fauteuils, Louis XV, satin-type rose upholstery, carved frame, cream and rust colored re-paint, 34"h. Photo courtesy of James D. Julia, Inc.

designs and adds more flowers and fruits to the styles. More detail is spent on the leaves—so much that one can tell if they are to represent grape, rose, or oak leaves. Technology advances enhanced this design style as manufacturers developed a way of laminating woods together. This layered effect was achieved by gluing thin layers together, with the grains running at right angles on each new layer. The thick panels created were then steamed in molds to created the illusion of carving. The woods used as a basis for the heavy ornamentation were mahogany, walnut, and some rosewood. Upholstery of this period is often tufted, eliminating any large flat surface, as the tufting creates curved peaks and valleys. The name of John Henry Belter is often connected with this design period, for it was when he did some of this best design work. John and Joseph W. Meeks also enjoyed success with laminated furniture. Original labels bearing these names are sometimes found on furniture pieces from this period, giving further provenance.

Hall bench, Naturalistic, Black Forest, c1880, two full standing glass eyed bears supporting detailed curved seat, 55" w, 18" d, 32" h, $8,960.

Renaissance Revival, 1850-1880. Furniture made in this style period reflects how cabinetmakers interpreted 16th and 17th century French designs. Their designs range from curvilinear and florid early in the period to angular and almost severe by the end of the period. Dark woods, such as mahogany and walnut, were primary with some use of rosewood and ebony. Walnut veneer panels were a real favorite in the 1870s designs. Upholstery, usually of a more generous nature, was also often incorporated into this design style. Ornamentation and high relief carving included flowers, fruits, game, classical busts, acanthus scrolls, strapwork, tassels, and masks.

Renaissance Revival, c1875, walnut, step-back, three doors, arched center door, burled trim, 79" w, 20" d, 85" h, $6,720. Photo courtesy of Fontaine's Auction Gallery.

Architectural motifs, such as pilasters, columns, pediments, balusters, and brackets are another prominent design feature. Legs are usually cabriole or pretty substantial turned legs.

Néo-Greek, 1855-1885. This design style easily merges with both the Louis XVI and Renaissance Revival styles. It is characterized by elements reminiscent of Greek architecture, such as pilasters, flutes, column, acanthus, foliate scrolls, Greek key motifs, and anthemion high relief carving. This style originated with the French, but was embraced by American furniture manufacturers. Woods are dark and often ebonized. Ornamentation may be gilded or bronzed. Legs tend to be curved to scrolled or cloven hoof feet.

Eastlake, 1870-1890. This design style is named for Charles Locke Eastlake who wrote a very popular book in 1872, called *Hints on Household Taste*. It was originally published in London. One of his principles was the relationship between function,

Side table, Eastlake, walnut, white marble top, ornate base, 29" l, 21" d, 31" h, $350. Photo courtesy of Joy Luke Auctions.

form, and craftsmanship. Shapes of furniture from this style tend to be more rectangular. Ornamentation was created through the use of brackets, grooves, chamfers, and geometric designs. American furniture manufacturers were enthusiastic about this style since it was so easy to adapt for mass production. Woods used were again dark, but more native woods, such as maple and pine were incorporated. Legs and chair backs are straighter, often with incised decoration.

Art Furniture, 1880-1914. This design period represents furniture designs gone mad, almost an "anything goes" school of thought. The style embraces both straight and angular with some pieces that are much more fluid, reflecting several earlier design periods. This period sees the wide usage of turned moldings and dark woods, but this time stained to imitate ebony and lacquer. The growing Oriental influence is seen in furniture from this period, including the use of bamboo, which was imported and included in the designs. Legs tend to be straight; feet tend to be small.

Straight

Arts and Crafts, 1895-1915. The Arts and Crafts period furniture represents one of the strongest periods for current collectors. Quality period Arts and Crafts furniture is available through most of the major auction houses. And, for those desiring the look, good quality modern furniture is also made in this style. The Arts and Crafts period furniture is generally rectilinear and a definite correlation is seen between form and function. The primary designers of this period were George Stickley, Leopold Stickley, J. George Stickley, George Niedeken, Elbert Hubbard, Frank Lloyd Wright, and the Englishman William Morris. Their furniture designs often overlapped into architectural and interior design including rugs, textiles, and other accessories. Woods used for Arts and Crafts furniture is primarily oak. Finishes

Cabinet, vice, Arts & Crafts, Limbert, pull-out bar shelf inset with hammered glass, single drawer, two cabinet doors, and square brass pulls, branded mark, leaned finish and hardware, 36" x 31" x 19", $2,300. Photo courtesy of David Rago Auctions.

were natural, fumed, or painted. Upholstery is leather or of a fabric design also created by the same hand. Hardware was often made in copper. Legs are straight and feet are small, if present at all, as they were often a simple extension of the leg. Some inlay of natural materials was used, such as silver, copper, and abalone shells.

Art-Nouveau style mirror, mahogany, old finish and gilding, age cracks, 47-1/2" h, 38" w, $175. Photo courtesy of Garth's Auctions, Inc.

Art Nouveau, 1896-1914. Just as the Art Nouveau period is known for women with long hair, flowers, and curves, so is Art Nouveau furniture. The Paris Exposition of 1900 introduced furniture styles reflecting what was happening in the rest of the design world, such as jewelry and silver. This style of furniture was not warmly embraced, as the sweeping lines were not very conducive to mass production. The few manufacturers that did interpret it for their factories found interest to be slight in America. The French held it in higher esteem. Woods used were dark, stylized lilies, poppies, and other more fluid designs were included. Legs tend to be sweeping or cabriole. Upholstery becomes slimmer.

Art Deco, 1920-1945. Furniture of the Art Deco period reflects the general feel of the period. The Paris *"I Exposition International des Arts Décorative et Industriels Modernes"* became the mantra for designs of everything in this period. Lines are crisp, with some use of controlled curves. The Chrysler Building in New York City remains the finest example of Art Deco architecture and those same straight lines and gentle curves are found in furniture. Furniture makers used expensive materials, such as veneers, lacquered woods, glass, and steel. The cocktail table first enters the furniture scene during this period. Upholstery can be vinyl or smooth fabrics. Legs are straight or slightly tapered; chair backs tend to be either low or extremely high.

Straight

International Movement, Dux sofa, fully-upholstered in orange fabric, four loose seat and back cushions, bright chrome base, 88" l, 34" w, 29-1/2" h, $865. Photo courtesy of David Rago Auctions.

International Movement, 1940-present. Furniture designed and produced during this period is distinctive as it represents the usage of some new materials, like plastic, aluminum, and molded laminates. The Bauhaus and also the Museum of Modern Art heavily influenced some designers. In 1940, the museum organized competitions for domestic furnishings. Designers Eero Saarien and Charles Eames won first prize for their designs. A new chair design combined the back, seat, and arms together as one unit. Tables were designed that incorporated the top, pedestal, and base as one. Shelf units were also designed in this manner. These styles could easily be mass-produced in plastic, plywood, or metal.

Different types of feet found on furniture

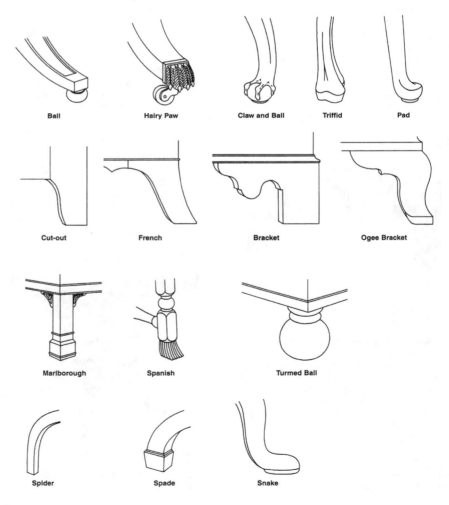

Ball

Hairy Paw

Claw and Ball

Triffid

Pad

Cut-out

French

Bracket

Ogee Bracket

Marlborough

Spanish

Turmed Ball

Spider

Spade

Snake

Different types of legs and hardware found on furniture

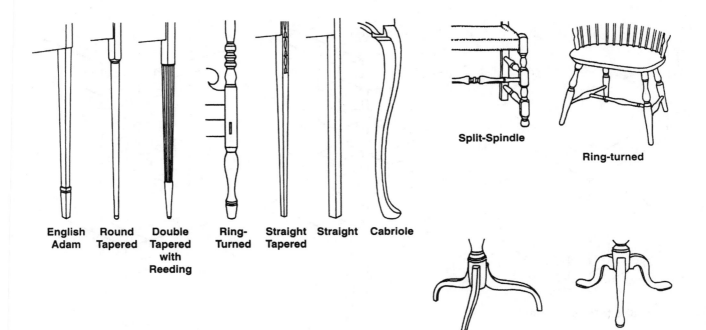

English Adam   **Round Tapered**   **Double Tapered with Reeding**   **Ring-Turned**   **Straight Tapered**   **Straight**   **Cabriole**

Split-Spindle

Ring-turned

Spider

Snake

Hardware

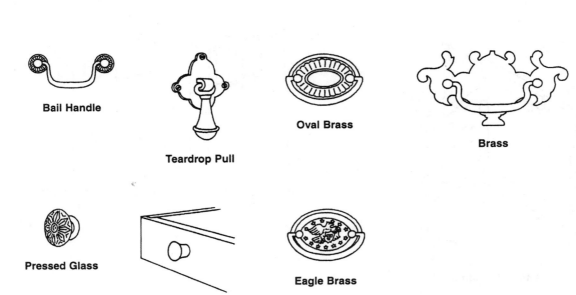

Bail Handle

Teardrop Pull

Oval Brass

Brass

Pressed Glass

Wooden Knob

Eagle Brass

Construction details

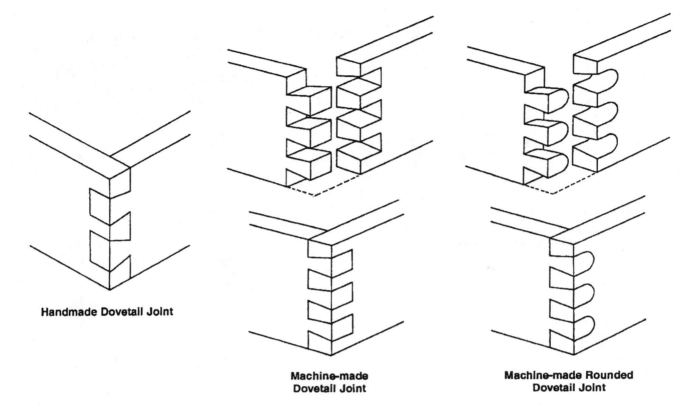

Handmade Dovetail Joint

Machine-made Dovetail Joint

Machine-made Rounded Dovetail Joint

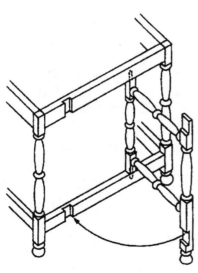

Typical Gateleg Construction

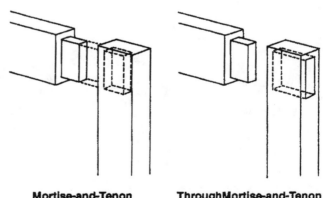

Mortise-and-Tenon Joint

ThroughMortise-and-Tenon Joint

Additional Listings: Arts and Craft Movement, Art Deco, Art Nouveau, Children's Nursery Items, Orientalia, Shaker Items, and Stickley.

Notes: Furniture is one of the types of antiques for which regional preferences are a factor in pricing. Victorian furniture is popular in New Orleans and unpopular in New England. Oak is in demand in the Northwest, but not as much so in the middle Atlantic states.

Prices vary considerably on furniture. Shop around. Furniture is plentiful unless you are after a truly rare example. Examine all pieces thoroughly—avoid buying on impulse. Turn items upside down; take them apart. Price is heavily influenced by the amount of repairs and restoration. Make certain you know if any such work has been done to a piece before buying it.

The prices listed here are "average" prices. They are only a guide. High and low prices are given to show market range.

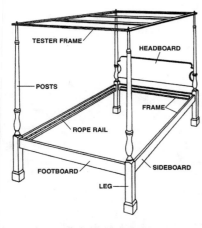

Typical Parts of a Bed

Beds

Arts and Crafts

Limbert, #651, daybed, angled headrest with spade cut-out, orig finish, recovered cushions, branded, numbered, 74" w, 25" d, 23" h **650.00**

Stickley Bros, attributed to, headboard with narrow vertical slats and panels, tapered feet, orig side rails, orig finish, minor

Bed, Arts & Crafts, Gustav Stickley, pyramidal posts, nine spindles to the head- and footboard, original side rails, branded "Stickley," single size, 49-1/4" x 43-3/4" x 79-1/2", **$8,575.** *Photo courtesy of David Rago Auctions.*

scratches, stenciled "9001-1/2," 80-1/2" l, 56-1/2" w, 30" h . **1,355.00**

Stickley, Gustav, single size, pyramidal posts, nine spindles to the head and footboard, complete with side rails, branded mark, 79 1/2" l, 43 3/4" w, 49 1/4" h . **8,575.00**

Baroque, Italian, simulated marble high scrolling headboard dec in patiglia with vacant cartouches and foliage, carved scrolling feet, painted, green and blue marbleized dec, losses to paint and gilt, pr, 45-3/4" w, 84" h **3,750.00**

Biedermeier, figured mahogany veneer, octagonal posts, turned feet and finials, paneled head and footboards, orig rails, some veneer damage, 38" w, 72" l, 45" h, pr. . **750.00**

Chippendale, tall post, curly maple, turned posts, scrolled headboard with poplar panel, orig side rails, old mellow refinishing, minor repairs to posts, 60" w, 72" l, 80" h **3,000.00**

Classical

Massachusetts, c1825-35, carved mahogany, tall post, scrolled mahogany headboard flanked by reeded, carved, and ring-turned posts, acanthus leaf, beading, gothic arches, and foliage carving, reeded and turned feet, orig rails later fitted for angle irons and bed bolts, orig surface, central finial missing, 59" w, 81" d, 98" h **6,900.00**

Middle Atlantic States, 1835-45, carved mahogany veneer, low post, scrolled and paneled

headboard, leaf-carved finials flanked by posts with pineapple finials, acanthus leaves above spiral carved and ring-turned posts, orig rails, bed bolts, and covers, refinished, imperfections, 58-1/2" w, 78" d, 56-1/2" h **1,100.00**

New England, c1820, painted, turned tall post, turned and tapering head posts flanking shaped headboard, spiral-carved foot post joined by rails fitted for roping, accompanying tester, old red paint, restored, 54" w, 79" l, 60-1/2" h **1,400.00**

Country, American, rope, high post, curly maple, areas of tight curl, evidence of old red wash, turned and tapered legs, boldly turned posts taper toward the top, paneled headboard with scrolled crest, turned top finial, 53-1/2" w, 70" l rails with orig bolts, pierced restorations **1,890.00**

Country, American, trundle, southwestern PA, walnut, mortised joints, turned posts, and finials, shaped corners along top edge of head, foot, and sideboards, refinished, 71-1/2" l, 44" d **125.00**

Empire, American

Single, fitted as daybed or sofa, mahogany and mahogany figured veneer, turned and acanthus carved posts, upholstered cushion, 31-1/2" x 80" x 43-3/4" h . . . **825.00**

Bed, canopy, mahogany, front posts are turned and carved with leaf design, resized to accommodate standard queen size bedding with new chamfered, rollback headboard in cherry, bow canopy frame and extensions to post, refinished, 80" l, 60" w, 64" h posts. Photo courtesy of James D. Julia, Inc.

Tall post, curly maple posts, poplar scrolled headboard with old soft finish, turned detail, acorn finials, rails and headboard replaced, 57-1/4" w, 72-1/2" l rails, 89" h **1,650.00**

Empire-style, sleigh, red painted, scrolled ends, bronze mounted foliate and mask mounts, 20th C, price for pr **1,650.00**

Federal

American, first half 19th C, cherry, tester, three-quarter, rect headboard with concave side edges, footboard lower, baluster-turned posts continuing to turned legs, rails with rope pegs, 81-1/2" l, 53-1/2" w, 78-1/4" h **500.00**

New England, c1810, tester, maple, vase and ring-turned foot posts continuing to tapering sq legs and molded spade feet joined to sq tapering head posts continuing to sq legs, arched headboard, later arched canopy, refinished, 51" w, 83-3/4" h **815.00**

New England, c1810-15, mahogany, turned and carved, tall post tester, arched canopy frame on vase and ring-turned spiral carved fluted tapering foot posts, joined to the turned tapering head posts with shaped headboard, ring-turned tapering feet, 45-1/2" w, 72" d, 61" h **1,775.00**

Salem, MA, c1810, mahogany, tall post, vase and ring-turned swelled fluted foot post with leaf carving on fluted plinths continuing to vase and ring-turned legs joined to ring-turned tapering head posts, shaped headboard, old surface, 51" w, 71" d, 650" h **3,175.00**

George III, four poster, carved walnut, brass mounted, circular tapered head posts, shaped mahogany headboard, reeded and acanthus-carved foot posts, ring-turned feet, casters, 9-1/2" h **10,000.00**

Gothic Revival, American, c1850, carved mahogany, tall headboard with three Gothic arch panels, leaf-carved crest rail, flanked by heavy round ribbed posts topped by ring-turned finials, arched and paneled footboard flanked by lower foot posts, heavy bun feet......................**4,750.00**

Hepplewhite-style, Philadelphia, c1943, mahogany, four tall posts each with reeded slender vasiform section

Bedroom suite, Renaissance Revival, c1875, walnut, rounded corner marble tops on dresser and washstand, original condition, 65" w, 89" bed, 44" w, 20" d, 91" h dresser, **$7,280.** *Photo courtesy of Fontaine's Auction Gallery.*

over short vasiform turned carved with continuous swag designs, upholstered tester, 82" l, 62" w, 93" h **1,550.00**

Modern, George Nelson for Howard Miller, Thin Edge, caned headboard, 34" x 76" x 35"............**1,610.00**

Queen Anne, Pennsylvania, early 19th C, low poster, turned and painted pine, head and footposts with flattened ball finials, shaped head and footboards, tapered feet, orig rope rails, orig green paint, 48-1/2" w, 74-3/4" h **3,600.00**

Renaissance Revival, walnut, double, high headboard topped by rounded pediment, pointed finial......**1,700.00**

Sheraton, canopy

Carved mahogany, headboard posts simple turned with ring and block turnings, simple headboard, heavily carved footboard posts with

Bedroom suite, Eastlake, three-piece walnut set, bed with burl veneer, floral carved crest rail, panel headboard, shell and floral carving; dresser and washstand with conforming carvings; dresser with brown marble top (cracked), three secret drawers over three drawers over two drawers; wash stand with long drawer over one door and two drawers, replaced white marble top; bed 62" w, 39" h footboard, 86-1/2" h; dresser 54" w, 23" d, 86" h, wash stand 35" w, 17-1/2" d, 66-1/2" h, **$4,400.** *Photo courtesy of Sanford Alderfer Auction Company.*

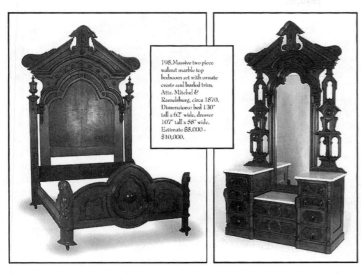

198.Massive two piece walnut marble top bedroom set with ornate crests and burled trim. Attr. Mitchel & Ramelsburg, circa 1870. Dimensions: bed 130" tall x 62" wide, dresser 107" tall x 58" wide. Estimate $8,000 - $10,000.

Bed and chest of drawers, Renaissance Revival, attributed to Mitchel & Ramelsburg, c1870, walnut, 62" w, 130" h bed, 58" w, 107" chest, $9,520. Photo courtesy of Fontaine's Auction Gallery.

spiral turnings and acanthus leaf bell, sq tester with curtains, 58" w, 73-1/2" l, 88" without finials **3,200.00**

Painted, headboard with D-type cut outs on side, footboard with reeded and turned posts, canopy frame, painted red, 52" w, 76" l, 68" h **750.00**

Victorian

American, refinished walnut, paneled head and footboards with applied scroll and fruit detail, matching crest, orig 73" l side rails, 54" w, 71-1/2" h **450.00**

Bed, Sheraton, cherry, American, four turned bedposts, carved flame finials, scroll cutout headboard with turned top crest terminating in acorn finials, converted to standard double side, old refinishing, original bed bolts, one finial slightly damaged, $475. Photo courtesy of Cowan's Historic Americana Auctions.

Brass, c1900, straight top rail, curved corners, ring-shaped capitals, cast iron side rails, 55" w, 61" h **1,200.00**

Half Tester, attributed to Prudent Mallard, New Orleans, LA, c1850, carved rosewood, tall arched headboard, shell carved crest, fruit and nuts, scroll carved borders, shaped bordered panels flanked by tall tapering turned head posts supporting upholstered half tester, scroll carved crest, turned finials, paneled sideboards and footboard, turned and carved details, scroll carved corner braces . . **15,000.00**

Benches

Arts & Crafts, settle

Stickley Bros, cube, vertical slats, orig drop-in seat covered in new green leather, excellent orig finish, stenciled number, 50" l, 22-1/2" d, 33" h **2,530.00**

Stickley, Gustav, No. 208, even arm, vertical slats all around, top rail mortised through legs, drop-in spring seat covered in new green leather, red Gustav decal, 76-1/2" l, 32" d, 29-1/4" h, light standing, some color added to orig finish **6,900.00**

Stickley, Gustav, No. 222, tapering posts, tightly spaced canted slats to back and sides, leather upholstered drop-in seat, fine orig finish, red decal, minor veneer chips, 36" x 80" x 32" . . . **11,500.00**

Stickley, Gustav, No. 225, single board horizontal back panel, vertical side slats, recovered brown leather drop-in seat, over-coated

orig finish, unmarked, 59-3/4" l, 31" d, 29-1/4" h **7,475.00**

Stickley, L. & J. G., cube, border vertical panels on back and under each arm, brown leather cushion, orig condition and finish, orig upholstery, "The Work of L. and J. G. Stickley" label, 72" l, 27" w, 28" h **3,450.00**

Stickley, L. & J. G., open arm, cloud lift top rail, horizontal backslat and corbels, new tan leather upholstered seat cushion, new finish, The Work of L & J. G. Stickley label, 53" l, 26" w, 36" h, some looseness **1,650.00**

Young, J. M., cube, capped top rail, vertical slats all around, fabric cov drop-in spring seat, refinished, unmarked, 78" l, 29-1/2" h, 34" h **2,870.00**

Bucket, pine, old worn green paint, sq nail construction, bootjack cut outs on ends, two shelves, shaped tops, 41-1/2" w, 12-1/2" d, 30-3/4" h . . **660.00**

Classical, window

Boston, 1835-45, carved mahogany veneer, upholstered seat, veneered rail, leaf-carved cyma curved ends, joined by ring-turned medial stretcher, 48" w, 16-1/4" d, 17-1/2" h **2,185.00**

New York, 1815-25, mahogany veneer, curving upholstered seat flanked by scrolled ends, scrolled base, old refinish, some veneer cracking and loss, 20th C olive green velvet upholstery, 39-1/2" w, 14" d, 23-5/8" h **3,500.00**

Bench, Arts & Crafts, three applied medallions to cut-out sides, over-coated original finish, some looseness, 13-1/2" w, 17" h, $325. Photo courtesy of David Rago Auctions.

Bucket bench, Pennsylvania, painted, apple green paint over red paint, backsplash over three shelves, mortised sides, shaped sides and cut-outs, 43-1/2" w, 12" d, 44" h, $990. Photo courtesy of Sanford Alderfer Auction Company.

Classical Revival, mahogany, carved paw feet and lion's heads, maroon velvet cushion, old finish, 16-1/2" l, 29-1/4" w, 23" h **600.00**

Country

96" l, 18-1/4" w, 13" h, pine, orig red paint, PA, early 19th C **750.00**

104" l, 13-1/2" w, pine, old worn and weathered green repaint, one board top with rounded front corners, beaded edge apron, cut-out feet mortised through top, age crack in one end of top **325.00**

Decorated, orig dark green with reddish brown paint, yellow line dec, mortised construction, some sq nails, arched end panels, replaced shoe feet, some later nails added, 33" w, 14" d, 23-1/4" h **275.00**

Mammy bench, America, early 19th C, country, mixed woods, rocker, spindle-back, scrolled arms, single-piece plank seat, removable cradle gate, turned legs, stripped and refinished, 19-3/4 deep, 30-1/2" h, $625. Photo courtesy of Cowan's Historic Americana Auctions.

Federal

New England, c1810, window, mahogany, upholstered seat and rolled arms, sq tapering legs, H-form stretchers, refinished, minor repair to one leg, 39-1/2" l, 16" d, 29" h **900.00**

New York, c1825, window, figured mahogany, each end with rect crotch-figured crest centering removable slip seat, matching seat rail, saber legs, 40-1/2" l . **3,500.00**

George III, English, mid-18th C, window, mahogany, rect seat, scrolling arms, later velvet cov, straight legs, blind fret craved, H-form stretcher, pr, 38" l **4,750.00**

Gothic Revival, American, c1820-40, carved mahogany, angled over-upholstered seat, carved seat rails centering quatrefoil, facet lancet-carved legs, molded faceted feet, 65" l, 20" d, 15-1/2" h **1,750.00**

Louis XVI-style, window, carved cherry, overstuffed seat, channeled rails, flanked by molded, overscroll arms carved with be-ribboned foliate sprays, turned, tapered, and leaf-capped legs **200.00**

Piano, Arts & Crafts, Gustav Stickley, cut-out handles on plank sides, plank top, broad up-ended cross-stretcher, orig finish, red decal, 36" l, 12-3/4" w, 22" h **4,600.00**

Victorian-style, chaise lounge, Chesterfield, early 20th C, tufted brown leather, adjustable backrest, casters, 62" l **3,000.00**

Wagon seat, New England, late 18th C, painted, two pairs of arched slats joining three turned stiles, double rush seat flanked by turned arms ending in turned hand-holds, tapering legs, old brown paint over earlier gray, 15" h seat, 30" h **1,200.00**

Primitive bench, poplar, one-board rectangular top with pit saw marks on underside, hand whittled maple splayed legs, refinished, 45" l, 14-1/2" h, $375. Photo courtesy of Cowan's Historic Americana Auctions.

Primitive, bench, pine, mortise, Chester Co., PA, possibly from Westtown School, long bench with single mortise, shaped supports, traces of yellow paint, 88-1/2" long, 20" h, $330. Photo courtesy of Sanford Alderfer Auction Company.

Wicker, painted white, hooped crest rail flanked by rows of dec curlicues, spiral wrapped posts and six spindles, pressed-in oval seat, dec curlicue apron, wrapped cabriole legs, X-form stretcher, 35" w, 31" h **500.00**

Windsor, settle, 20th C green paint, yellow in turnings, 29 spindles with bamboo turnings across back with turned arms, well-shaped seat with incised rain gutter around back, eight splayed legs joined by cross stretchers, splits in seat, old iron braces added underneath for support, 77-1/2" w, 22" d, 36-3/4" h **2,100.00**

Bentwood

In 1856, Michael Thonet of Vienna perfected the process of bending wood using steam. Shortly afterward, Bentwood furniture became popular. Other manufacturers of Bentwood furniture were Jacob and Joseph Kohn, Philip Strobel and Son, Sheboygan Chair Co., and Tidoute Chair Co. Bentwood furniture is still being produced today by the Thonet firm and others.

Box

5-3/4" w, 4-1/4" d, 2-3/16" h, attributed to C. Hersey, Higham, MA, oval, single finger construction on lid and base, old green paint, traces of earlier green underneath **475.00**

8" d, 7" h, round, worn orig paint resembles wallpaper, yellow and black foliage scrolls on blue ground, some edge damage to lid **750.00**

Bench, window seat, George IV, c1830, "X" form, oak, tapestry drop-in seat, 49-1/2" l, 18" d, 17" h, $1,800. Photo courtesy of Sloan's Auctioneers & Appraisers.

Bentwood, pantry box, maple, hickory, and pine, old wallpaper lined int., NY 1869 newspaper lining lid, iron tack construction, old refinishing, interior varnished, split in lid, 18-1/2" d, 9" h, $65. Photo courtesy of Cowan's Historic Americana Auctions.

17-1/4" l, band, pine, orig blue paint, unusual decoupage paper scene of black man, woman, and child, foreign inscription, wear and loose bottom board **550.00**

Chair, Austrian, Vienna Secession-style, c1910, side, back splat with three circular perforations, three slender spindles, painted black, set of eight **5,500.00**

Cradle, 41" l, 39" h, ivory fittings **440.00**

Hall tree, Thonet, c1910, bentwood frame, contrasting striped wood inlay, coat hooks with central beveled mirror above one door, metal drip pan, orig label, 57" w, 13" d, 76" h **2,750.00**

Plant stand, Thonet, Austria, late 19th C, round top with black printed classical urn and flower motif, bentwood tripod base, imp "Thonet," paper label, wear, couple of breaks on feet, 18-5/8" d, 30-5/8" h **210.00**

Rocker, Thonet, arched twined top rail, cut-velvet fabric fitted back, armrests, and seat, elaborate scrolling frame, curved runners, 53" l **750.00**

Stool, Thonet, attributed to Marcel Kammerer, Austria, 1901, beech, sq seat, four legs, U-shaped braces forming spandrels, shaped bronze sabot feet, 14-1/4" sq, 18-1/2" h **1,500.00**

Table, Josef Hoffman, c1905, circular top, wooden spheres dec below rim, 21-1/4" h **500.00**

Blanket chests

Chippendale, country, pine, molded rect and hinged top, storage well, front with two simulated drawer fronts over two drawers, molded surrounds, outset molded base with bracket feet, 37-1/2" w, 20" d, 41" h **750.00**

Decorated

American, poplar, orig black over red sponge dec, one board top, molded trim, arched cut-outs on end aprons, scalloped front apron, int. fitted with covered till, dovetailed drawer, cast iron hinges, minor touch-up, later coat of varnish, 43-1/4" w, 17" d, 21-1/4" h **495.00**

New York, Schohaire County, early 19th C, six board, painted blue, molded top, dovetailed constructed base with painted diamond and draped frieze with Chinese export punchbowl and ladle, dotted, banded, vine, and diamond border flanked by enamel Stiegel flip glasses with circular borders, minor imperfections, 37" w, 17" d, 15" h **6,900.00**

Ohio, c1820-40, pine and poplar, six-board construction, eagle dec, cover with considerable paint wear, restoration, 49-1/2" w, 21" d, 23-3/4" h **2,300.00**

Ohio, attributed to Knox County, dovetailed poplar, orig sponged circles and meandering borders, two board top with molding, scalloped base painted black, beveled aprons, fitted int. with covered till, early iron casters, 39" w, 29-1/2" d **825.00**

Pennsylvania, attributed to Somerset County, poplar, green stenciled signature for "Hiram Gardner, 1852," salmon, light and dark green, stenciled foliage and scroll detail, freehand heart just below keyhole, green trim on lid and base, dovetailed case and feet,

Blanket chest, grain painted, Pennsylvania, c1840-50, original green on yellow ground graining, red trim, dovetailed case, turned feet mortised through bottom, int. till with lid, 51" l, 22-1/4" w, 27" h, $1,695. Photo courtesy of Cowan's Historic Americana Auctions.

molded apron and scrolling, int. till, replaced hinges, restorations, split in lid, corner chips, 43-1/2" w, 18" d **825.00**

Pennsylvania, Mahatonga Valley, early 19th C, pine and poplar, molded lift top painted with American flag, lattice and banded border above recessed paneled sides with banded borders, joined by stiles continuing to feet, dec attributed to third quarter 19th C, 33" w, 19" d, 21" h **17,250.00**

Dowry, Mahantango Valley, Pennsylvania, "Samuel Grebiel 1799," orig paint dec, red, blue, mustard, black, and white, two shaped polygons painted in blue grain painting, identical polygons on each side, two in front with banner above with name and date, int. lidded till, black painted dovetailed bracket base, off-set strap hinges, orig lock, 48-1/2" w, 21" d, 23-1/2" h **3,000.00**

Federal, PA, early 18th C, pine and cherry, molded lift top, well with till, case with two thumb-molded graduated drawers, dovetailed bracket feet, old refinish, minor imperfections, 40" w, 20-1/2" d, 43" h **1,880.00**

Grain painted, New York state, c1830, molded hinged lift top, lidded till, molded bracket black painted base, orig fanciful ochre and raw umber graining, 48" w, 22" d, 29" h . . **1,265.00**

Jacobean, oak, paneled construction with relief carving, drawer and feet replaced, repairs to lid and molding, old dark finish, 44-1/2" w, 19-1/2" d, 31-3/4" h **825.00**

Miniature, England, early 19th C, mahogany, molded lift-top with wire hinges, dovetail constructed box base, mid molding trim, heavy molded bracket base, worm holes, wear, 14-1/4" l, 6-3/4" h **1,035.00**

Mule, America, pine, thumb-molded top, two overlapping dovetailed drawers, bracket feet, old dark finishing, int. lined with 1875 Boston newspaper, pierced repairs to feet and drawer fronts, 40" w, 18" d, 34-3/4" h **700.00**

Painted

Massachusetts, first quarter 19th C, molded hinged top, case of two drawers, tall cut-out feet with valanced skirt, orig red-brown grain paint with contrasting beige grained drawers, orig pulls, 36-3/4" w, 17-1/4" d, 37-3/4" h **11,750.00**

New England, early 19th C, hinged top, well with till, case with single drawer, cut-out base, orig mustard-brown graining resembling wood, minor imperfections, 39-1/4" w, 18-1/4" d, 40" h **850.00**

New England, early 19th C, six-board, rect top, case with two drawer, cut-out feet joined by straight skirt, all-over orig reddish brown and yellow grain paint resembling exotic wood, old brass pulls, minor imperfections, minor paint wear, 41-1/4" w, 18-1/2" d, 32-1/4" h **2,115.00**

Ohio, wide poplar boards, orig red paint, traces of silvery white star designs on lid and front, dovetailed case, molded top edge, bracket feet, small scalloped returns, molded base, int. till with lid, hinges and narrow hinge rail old replacements, minor edge wear, 49-1/4" w, 21" d, 26" h **650.00**

Pennsylvania, Bucks County, dated 1770, red moldings and base, mottled reddish-brown ground, large triple banded hearts on front and sides, corners with half-hearts, over lozenges with names and date, two lower drawers, molded skirt with central drop, cut-out bracket feet, int. till, secret drawers, orig paint, minor losses, one side foot and back braces replaced, 49" l, 24" d, 29-1/2" h **18,750.00**

Pennsylvania, York County, c1820, blue and white curly grain dec, contrasting molding, turned feet painted red, two drawers with sponged dec **19,500.00**

Queen Anne, New England, c1750, marriage chest, pine, hinged rect lift lid, upper half faced with faux drawer fronts, brown paint, 35" **4,000.00**

Sheraton, country, pine and poplar, orig red paint, molded edge top, paneled front and ends, sq corner posts, mortised and pinned frame, scalloped apron, turned feet, 44" w, 19-1/2" d, 25-1/2" h **900.00**

William and Mary, New England, c1700, oak and yellow pine, joined, drawer base, old finish, minor imperfections, 48-1/2" w, 22" d, 32-3/4" h **4,500.00**

Bookcases

Arts & Crafts

English, double door, corbelled overhanging top, inlaid pewter, ebony, and fruitwood tulips, leaded glass panels with green tear-shaped inserts, curvilinear backsplash, emb strap handles, orig finish, unmarked, some corbels loose, 46" w, 12-1/2" d, 52-1/2" h **2,615.00**

Limbert, Grand Rapids, MI, early 20th C, oak, two elongated glass panels on each of two doors, three adjustable shelves on each side, round copper pulls, medium brown finish, branded mark on reverse, imperfections, 40-1/2" l, 14" d, 57-1/2" h **2,775.00**

Stickley Bros, quarter-sawn oak, double door, slatted gallery top, single panes of glass, orig medium finish, brass tag, 35-1/2" w, 12" d, 50" h **4,875.00**

Stickley, Gustav, quarter sawn oak, double door, eight glass panes to each door, gallery top, hammered copper V-pulls, three int. shelves, top and bottom mortised thru sides, red decal and paper Craftsman label, refinished, 42-3/4" w, 13" d, 56-1/4" h **5,175.00**

Bookcase, Arts & Crafts, Gustav Stickley, gallery top, eight glass panes in each of two doors, three interior shelves, top and base mortised through the sides, faint red decal, refinished, filled-in holes to front divider and to doors around hardware, 42-3/4" w, 13-1/4" d, 56-1/4" h, $5,750. Photo courtesy of David Rago Auctions.

Bookcase, Arts & Crafts, Lifetime, single-door with six small panes, through-tenons and mullion at top of door, good original finish, four drill holes to back, unmarked, 28-1/4" w, 12-1/2" d, 55-3/4" h, $4,500. Photo courtesy of David Rago Auctions.

Stickley, Gustav, quarter sawn oak, double door, 12 panes per door, gallery top, brass V-pulls, mortised top, paper label, 54" w, 13" d, 55" h, refinished, warp in right door, stripped hardware **5,175.00**

Stickley, L. & J. G., quarter sawn oak, double door, 12 panes per door, gallery top, three shelves, keyed through-tenons on sides, orig medium finish, "The Work of L. & J. G. Stickley" decal, 49" w, 12" d, 54-1/2" h, stain on top . . . **6,275.00**

Stickley, L. & J. G., quarter sawn oak, single door, 16 mullioned panes, gallery top, keyed through tenons, refinished, hardware replaced, L & J. G. Stickley Handcraft label, 29-3/4" w, 12" d, 55-1/4" h **4,875.00**

Biedermeier-style, inlaid cherry, outset molded cornice with ebonized bead, front with two recessed glazed doors, four shelves, outset molded base raised on black feet, burr poplar panels, ebonized stringing, 53-1/2" w, 21" d, 72" h **700.00**

Chippendale, New England, southern, late 18th C, mahogany and maple, scroll top, top section with molded

Renaissance Revival, c1875, burled walnut, breakfront, three shaped doors, carved columns, 71" w, 20" d, 64" h, $3,420. Photo courtesy of Fontaine's Auction Gallery.

scrolled cresting, carved pinwheel terminals centering carved fan and bordered with punchwork flanked by flame urn-turned finials, two thumb-molded recessed panel doors opening to compartmented shelved int., lower section with fall front desk opening to stepped multi-drawer compartmented int. above case of four graduated scratchbeaded drawers, bracket feet, replaced brasses, refinished, imperfections, 39" w, 21" d, 84-3/4" h **7,100.00**

Chippendale-style, New England, mahogany, broken arch pedestal over two arched-paneled doors, fitted secretary int. with pigeonholes, six small drawers, lower section with fall front, stepped fitted int., straight front, two small and two wide drawers, brass bail handle, escutcheons, lock plates, straight bracket feet, 42" w, 24" d, 93-3/4" h **3,200.00**

Classical, Boston, 1830s, carved mahogany veneer, cove molded cornice above two glazed doors flanked by columns with leaf carved tops and turned bases, fold-out felt lined writing surface, sectioned for writing implements, two small cock-beaded drawers over two long drawers, flanked by similar columns with carved tops, four reeded and carved bulbous feet, glazed doors open to bird's eye maple veneered int. with two adjustable shelves, valanced open compartments, five small drawers, brasses and wooden pulls appear to be orig, old refinish,

imperfections, 44-3/4" w, 22-1/4" d, 88" h **11,500.00**

Eastlake, America, c1880, cherry, rect top, flaring bead trimmed cornice, pair of single-pan glazed cupboard doors, carved oval paterae and scrolls across top, adjustable shelved int., stepped base with line-incised drawers, bail handles, 47-1/2" w, 15-1/4" d, 69-1/4" h **1,200.00**

Empire, crotch mahogany veneers, top section: large architectural type cornice, two large glass doors with cathedral top muttons, three adjustable shelves; base: 11 drawers, oval brass knobs, applied base molding, two panes of glass cracked, 66" w, 83" h **5,500.00**

Empire-style, mahogany, two-door bookcase top with cathedral-type door, base with one top drawer over two doors, three smaller drawers under doors, shelved int., 43-1/2" w, 83-1/2" h **1,700.00**

Federal, Southern States, attributed to, 1790-1810, mahogany, veneered pediment embellished with inlaid floral vines and leaves above mullioned glazed doors, int. adjustable beaded shelves, lower case as hinged butler's desk with int. of valanced compartments and small drawers outlined with stringing, case of three graduated string inlaid drawers, skirt with inlaid vines and leaves, French

Renaissance Revival, c1880, carved oak, step-back, six ornate paneled doors, lion head columns, 72" w, 21" d, 91" h, $5,880. Photo courtesy of Fontaine's Auction Gallery.

Victorian, c1895, carved oak, double door, floral and reeded columns, claw feet, 61" w, 18" d, 47" h, $1,960. Photo courtesy of Fontaine's Auction Gallery.

feet, old refinish, replaced brasses, restored, 40-1/2" w, 21-1/2" d, 93-1/2" h **4,700.00**

George III, third quarter 18th C, inlaid mahogany, dentil-molded cornice above two paneled doors, shelved interior, two candle slides, slant front enclosing fitted interior, two short and three graduated drawers, bracket feet, 37" w, 22" d, 85-1/2" h **4,600.00**

George III-style, with 18th century elements, mahogany, later swan's neck cresting above pair of paneled doors opening to shelves, fitted with candle rests, lower section with slant lid enclosing a fitted int., all above three long drawers, ogee bracket feet, 35" w, 20" d, 95" h **2,650.00**

Louis XV-style, block front, ormolu mounts, floral marquetry, banded inlay, top surface worn, scratches, 56" w, 16" d, 55" h **2,500.00**

Louis XVI-style, 19th C, inlaid mahogany, parquetry top, low three-quarter gallery and center oval panel inlaid with fleur-de-lis, open shelf raised on sq-section tapered legs, conforming sabots, 24" w, 8-1/4" d, 27-1/4" h, pr **900.00**

Modern

Baker, George III-style, bookcase/breakfront, mahogany, c1950 . . . . **4,510.00**

Beacon Hill, bookcase/breakfront, mahogany, Gothic-arch accents, c1950 . . . . **5,170.00**

Regency, late, early 19th C, mahogany, bookcase/breakfront, concave fronted cornice, frieze carved with anthemion, upper section fitted with four arched and glazed doors; lower section fitted with fall front writing surface and fitted int., all above two pedestals fitted with shelves and drawers, 84" w, 26" d, 93" h **7,475.00**

Revolving, American, second half 19th C, oak, molded rect top, five compartmentalized shelves with slatted ends, quadruped base with casters, stamped "Danners Revolving Book Case...Ohio," 24" w, 24" d, 68-1/4" h **1,200.00**

Rococo-style, Italian, late 19th C, serpentine front with three shelves, cabriole legs, dec with Chinoiserie scenes, green ground, 38" w, 14" d, 49" h **690.00**

Victorian, Globe-Wernicke, barrister type, stacking, three sections, oak, glass fronted drawers, drawer in base, metal bands, orig finish **900.00**

Boxes

Band

Oblong, wallpaper covered

11-1/8" l, 9" w, 6-3/8" h, cov in various floral patterns, lid centered with figures by manor **250.00**

15" l, 11-3/4" w, 10-1/4" h, oblong, printed "Sandy Hook" lighthouse, ships motif, shades

Boxes, left: hanging pipe box, poplar with old grayish-blue over red paint, detailed scalloped backboard and crest, one nailed drawer, 19-1/2" h, $16,500; right: hanging salt box, attributed to Pennsylvania, mahogany, hinged slant front lid, shaped crest, applied base molding, old finish, old replaced pine bottom board, 7-3/4" w, 6-1/2" d, 10" h, $450; upper right shows wax portrait of Ben Franklin in red shadowbox frame with gilded liner, 5-5/8" w, 6" h, $900. Photo courtesy of Garth's Auctions, Inc.

of red, green, white, and brown, blue ground, America, mid-19th C, fading, tears, sewn repairs to lid and base **1,410.00**

Oval, wallpaper covered

11-1/2" l, 9-3/8" w, 6-1/4" h, beaver pattern, black, brown, and green, blue ground, wear **765.00**

14-3/4" h, floral drapery motif, blues, greens, and browns, tears, separations, fading **940.00**

17" l, 14" w, 12" h, large eagle motif, trees in background, green, white, and brown on blue field, wear, losses, fading **355.00**

19-1/4" l, 14" w, 12-1/4" h, fire brigade motif, green, brown, and tan, yellow ground, losses, wear, fading **1,880.00**

19-1/4" l, 17" w, 13-1/2" h, Castle Garden pattern, brown, yellow and green, blue field, cover missing, wear, fading . . . **470.00**

Bible, chestnut, some curl in lid, molded edges, front panel with punched design, initials and date "L. T. 1705," int. with cov till and single drawer, wrought-iron lock, old dark patina, hasp missing, some edge damage, pulls added to drawer, 27" l **650.00**

Book, Maine, carved spruce gum, sliding lids, carved rosette and triangle motifs, chip-carved embellishments, gilt highlights, minor wear, late 19th/early 20th C, 4-3/4" w, 6" h **420.00**

Bride's, oval, bentwood, overlapping laced scenes, orig painted dec, couple in colonial dress, white, red, brown, and black on brown stained ground, German inscription and 1796 in white, edge damage, 15-7/8" l, 10" w, 6-1/2" h **495.00**

Candle, hanging

Poplar, orig dry red paint, peaked back two-board back, base board extends beyond lower front and includes six cut-outs for spoons, reeded sides, wire nail construction, small chip on front, 12" w, 7" d, 6" h **285.00**

Walnut, poplar secondary wood, dovetailed case, hinged lid, good figure on front and lid, arched backboard, one drawer in lower front with orig turned walnut pull, mellow old finish, minor glued split, 14" w, 7-14" d, 8-3/4" h **600.00**

Pantry box, c1830, walnut, dovetailed case, three drawers, acorn shaped pulls, 14" w, 12-1/2" d, 18" h, $375. Photo courtesy of Sanford Alderfer Auction Company.

Cheese, 6-1/2" h, 12-1/8" d, pine, circular, incised "E. Temple" on lid, painted blue, America, 19th C, cracks, paint wear, minor losses **175.00**

Collar, 13" l, 5" h, wallpaper covering, oval, marked "E. Stone no. 116 1/2 William Street, New York" **575.00**

Cutlery, Victorian, 19th C, mahogany, brass lifting handle, three divisions, later sq tapered legs, 11" w, 14" d, 23" h **260.00**

Decorated, dovetailed, pine, orig grain painting, rect, dovetailed, conforming hinged lid, ochre ground paint with red putty or vinegar painted seaweed-like designs, orig lock, wallpaper lined int., New England, 1820s, missing top bail handle, later waxing of surface, 14-5/8" w, 7-1/8" d, 6-3/4" h **690.00**

Document

America, mid to late 19th C, walnut, dovetailed, rect, hinged lid, side till, turned feet, 14" w, 8" d, 10-1/2" h **385.00**

America, late 19th/early 20th C, walnut, dovetailed, inlaid maple star flower on top, brass hinges, int. lock, minor stains, edge damage, 11-1/2" w, 6-3/4" d, 5-1/4" h **150.00**

America, 19th C, hinged lid with central diamond motif, rect, bird's-eye maple, mahogany, and satinwood veneers, minor wear, a couple of small edge losses, 7-1/2" l, 4-3/8" d, 3-1/8" h . . **500.00**

America, 19th C, paint dec pine, rect, hinged lid decorated with a stenciled basket of fruit in green, yellow, and white with gilt highlights on a green ground, yellow and green borders, heart-shaped brass escutcheon, minor wear, 12-1/4" l, 7-7/8" d, 4-3/4" h **600.00**

Dome top

America, 19th C, grain painted, pine, wire hinges, iron handles and latch, dovetailed joinery, minor cracks, 19-3/4" l, 11" d, 8-7/8" h. . . . **990.00**

Vermont, Shaftsbury, 1820s, attributed to Matteson family, whitewood, green and yellow vinegar painted central dec surrounded by simulated inlaid quarter round fans, cross banded tiger maple veneers and circles, repeated on four areas of six-board form, orig surface, varnished, imperfections, 24" w, 12-1/2" d, 12" h **5,465.00**

Pennsylvania, Lancaster County, decorated, orig blue paint, incised compass start designs painted red and white, orig punched tin latch, tin and wire hinges, some damage, few holes where hinges attach, 5-1/2" w, 3-7/8" d, 4-3/4" h **11,550.00**

Dough, pine and poplar, rect removable top, tapering well, splayed ring-turned legs, ball feet, Pennsylvania, 19th C, 38" w, 19-3/4" w, 29-1/2" h **500.00**

Grain painted, America, 19th C, pine, rect, brass ring pull on lid, minor wear, small loss on one corner, 10-1/2" l, 6-1/2" d, 3-1/8" h **250.00**

Knife

9" w, 10" d, 15-3/4" h, English, inlaid flame mahogany veneer over pine, bow front, scalloped corners with banded inlay, brass handles on both sides, star inlay on int. of lid, old refinish, contemporary, dovetailed int. lifts out, slotted for letters, hidden compartment below, some sections of inlay missing, age splits in veneer **550.00**

14-1/2" h, mahogany veneer with inlay, edge veneer damage, int. incomplete, inlaid oval on inside of lid. **225.00**

16" h, 9-3/4" w, 14-1/2" d, Federal, flamed grained mahogany, serpentine and block front, reeded front columns, fitted int., orig keys, pr **2,500.00**

Letter, Gothic Revival, English, late 19th/early 20th C, oak, sloped lid with brass trefoil strapwork, two handles on sides, front doors opening to fitted int.,

Pipe box, stained red, one drawer, constructed with rose head nails, shaped top with hanging hole, drawer has ring handle and dovetails, 5-1/2" w x 4-1/2" d, 18" h, $4,315. Photo courtesy of James D. Julia, Inc.

single drawer in base, maker's tag for "Lechars," London and Paris, 16" w, 12-1/4" d, 15-1/4" h **635.00**

Pantry, circular, nailed construction, swing handle

7-1/2" d, 3-1/2" h, green, two-finger construction, orig paint . . . **250.00**

12" d, 6-3/4" h, orig green painted surface, 19th C, minor surface abrasion **550.00**

Pencil, 10-1/2" l, swivel lid, carved from one piece of pine, old red paint **175.00**

Pipe

16-3/4" h, pine, red stain, molded bottom edge, one dovetailed drawer, two compartments with later, but finely cut, scalloped edges, three cut-out hearts and elaborately scrolled crest, back of drawer with scratch carved inscription "January 13, 1813, John _," minor repairs and small hole added for hanging **1,320.00**

19-1/2" h, 8-3/8" w, 5-1/4" d, carved cherry, painted red, metal lined int., old finish, CT River Valley, late 18th/early 19th C **6,000.00**

21-1/4" h, 6" w, 4-1/4" d, yellow pine, traces of red paint, old finish, southern New England, early 19th C, very minor losses, crack, minor insect damage to base . . **2,650.00**

Salt, 11-1/2" w, 7-1/4" d, 9" h, oak, dovetailed, lift lid, crest, divided int., old finish **120.00**

Sewing

America, 19th C, mahogany inlaid, hinged lid, center inlaid oval reserve with shell motif, ext. with inlaid borders and corners, int. lid centered with diamond motif, lift-out tray with several

compartments, minor imperfections, 12-1/4" w, 7-1/4" d, 5-5/8" h **1,000.00**

Chinese Export, 19th C, lacquered, Chinoiserie dec, scenic panels surrounded by mosaic patterns, Greek key border, brass bail handles on each end, int. with mirrored lid and fitted compartments, single fitted drawer, containing various sewing implements, minor wear and crackling, 17-1/4" w, 11-1/2" d, 5-3/4" h **475.00**

Sliding lid, America, early 19th C, polychrome paint, dovetailed, rect pine box, lid dec with red, white, and blue diamond pattern basket filled with strawberries, surrounded by grapes, leaves, flourishes, and scrolls, striped border, box having central shell design on three sides with similar scrolling, leafy vines and geometric star devices, red, white, blue, gold, and salmon colors on black ground, repair to lid, minor wear, 12" l, 8" d, 4" h. . . **1,880.00**

Spice, America, 19th C, pine, six drawers, turned wooden knobs, old surface, wear, 15" l, 7-1/2" d, 13" h **940.00**

Storage

8-1/2" l, 6-1/2" w, 3-1/2" h, America, late 19th C, pine, painted red, floral and linear dec, int. paper lined **635.00**

18-7/8" l, 8-3/4" h, Massachusetts, early 19th C, ochre-painted pine,

Box, traveling, oak, brass bound with side handles, angled front opens up with two doors revealing calendar date paper inset area, multiple slots for stationery, pen tray and inkwell, secret drawer to bottom has presentation plaque, 15-3/4" w, 11-3/4" d, 15-1/2" h. Photo courtesy of James D. Julia, Inc.

six board, dovetailed, thumb molded lid dec with flags, shield, and banner inscribed "Mass. Militia 2nd Regt. 1st B. 2nd D," partial paper tag tacked to lid inscribed "...K Rogers Boston," minor imperfections **1,150.00**

Tea bin, 24-1/8" h, 17-1/2" w, 25" d, dec of gentleman toasting lady, dec by Ralph Cahoon, oil on wood, with certificate of authenticity from Cahoon Museum of American Art **2,530.00**

Wall

7-7/8" w, 3-1/4" d, 15" h, attributed to New York State, early 19th C, painted, shaped top, open rect compartment with worn dark gray patina **2,760.00**

14" x 11-1/2" x 6-3/4", New England, mid-19th C, red stained chestnut, rect open box, two compartments, extended back board, round hanging loop, stamped initials "J. M." and several other scribed circles, wear **250.00**

Work, 12" w, 10-1/2" d, 7-1/4" h, European, marquetry inlaid mahogany veneer, pine secondary wood, slant top lid with pincushion covered in old burgundy velvet, paper lined int., till with lid, engraved strap hinges, old finish, repairs **275.00**

Cabinets

Apothecary, pine, yellow grain dec, 29 drawers over two open shelves, cut-out base and sides, bracket feet, open back, 62" l, 12" d, 54" h **1,550.00**

Bar, Art Deco, walnut, sarcophagus form, two doors, sq top with drop-front cabinet on left, mirrored bar, small drawer on right between two open bays, 48" w, 21" d, 54-1/2" d . . . **600.00**

China

Art Moderne, mahogany, double doors, floral-carved relief panels, int. shelves, two drawers below, 45" w, 17" d, 62" h **2,000.00**

Arts & Crafts, Limbert, #428, trapezoidal form, two doors, each with four windows at top over one large window, orig copper pulls, sides with two windows over one, refinished, branded, 40" w, 19" d, 63" h **4,250.00**

Edwardian-style, curved glass sides, single flat glazed door, illuminated int., mirrored back, 42" w, 16" d, 64" h, pr **1,675.00**

International Movement, Gilbert Rhode, manufactured by Herman

Miller, glass-sided china cabinet top over two doors with burled fronts, brushed steel pulls, refinished, glass doors and shelves missing, 36" w, 17" d, 58" h . **800.00**

Victorian, American, c1900, shaped crest with lion's head and carved foliage, curved central door flanked by curved glass to either side, four ball and claw feet, 48" w, 16" d, 72" h **1,500.00**

Chinoiserie, two drawers, double doors, two adjustable int. shelves, walnut veneer with inlay and black lacquer, gilded detail, attached base with turned legs, 20th C, 43" w, 15-1/2" d, 63" h **625.00**

Corner, display, Georgian-style, c1880, mahogany and inlay, swan's crest, pair of glazed mullioned doors, int. shelves, pair of cabinet doors with marquetry, bracket feet **2,415.00**

Curio, French

Bombé-shaped base, ornate, old gold repaint, carved rococo dec and gesso, beveled glass front, glass side panels, high scrolled feet, scalloped base aprons, 35" w, 15" d, 71-1/2" h **950.00**

China cabinet, Arts & Crafts, rare L. & J.G. Stickley, double-door china cabinet, 12 panes to each door over two-door cabinet with hammered copper strap hinges and tab pulls, original finish with overcoat, "Work of..." decal inside door, drill holes through back to accommodate later int. lighting, veneer lifting, along with some chips and repairs, 47" w, 16" d, 70" h, $18,400. Photo courtesy of David Rago Auctions.

China cabinet, Arts & Crafts, rare Limbert, single-door china cabinet, arched backsplash, three glass panes to door over one large, and open shelf on either side supported by long corbels, three interior shelves, casters, good original finish, faint stenciled number, 44-1/2" w, 16-1/2" d, 59" h, $6,275. Photo courtesy of David Rago Auctions.

Serpentine front, flowers around case, courting scene on lower case and door, metallic gold ground, ormolu dec around edges and arched crest, two removable glass shelves, worn red velvet covering bottom shelf, mirrored back, 33-1/2" w, 17" d, 74" h **850.00**

Display

Biedermeier-style, poplar and burr-poplar, single door, outset molded cornice, three-pane glazed door flanked by similar stiles and sides, three mirror-backed shelves supporting shaped half shelves, block feet, 41" w, 16" d, 68" h **800.00**

Edwardian, late 19th C, rosewood, dentil molded cornice, two glazed doors and projecting lower section fitted with three drawers, sq tapered legs joined by shelf stretcher, 25" w, 15" d, 56" h **2,415.00**

Empire-style, gilt metal mounted mahogany, rect case fitted with arched glass door, stemmed bun feet, foliate cast mounts, 33" w, 16" d, 68" h **1,975.00**

Rococo, South Germany, 18th C, walnut, scrolling heavily molded open pediment, center gilt-bronze cartouche plate, two arched doors

Cabinet, Chinese, red lacquered elm, mountainous landscape decorated, Qing dynasty, c1850, 23-1/2" w, 14-1/2" d, 32-1/4" h, $700. Photo courtesy of Sloan's Auctioneers & Appraisers.

of fielded panels, mahogany figures of court ladies, basal-molded and conforming stand, shaped apron, cabriole legs, 46" w, 19-1/2" d, 71-1/2" h
.... **4,750.00**

Filing, Arts & Crafts

American, c1910, golden oak, plain vertical stack, five drawers, orig brass nameplates and pulls
.... **650.00**

Stickley, L. & J. G., Manlius, NY, re-issue, two-drawer, rect, hammered copper hardware, branded "Stickley," round yellow and red decal in int. drawer, wear to top finish, 21-3/8" w, 28" l, 31" h **360.00**

Ledger, American, 19th C, walnut and mixed hardwoods, poplar secondary wood, dovetailed case, single paneled door, int. with divided compartments, later salmon paint, pr, 15-1/2" w, 12" d, 24" h **600.00**

Music, two door, full relief figures carved into front, 1920s, 48" h .. **950.00**

Side

Arts & Crafts, oak, single door, orig sq copper pull, notched toe-board, refinished, 22" w, 22" d, 38" h
.... **700.00**

Baroque, Dutch, oak, rect case fitted with three paneled doors, borders carved in shallow relief with

scrolling tulip vines, stemmed bun feet, 82" w, 20" d, 53" h ... **1,380.00**

Biedermeier, late 19th C, fruitwood parquetry, rect top, canted corners, pr of cabinet doors enclosing shelves, bracket feet, 55-1/4" w, 24-3/4" d, 40-1/2" h **1,725.00**

Empire-style, late 19th/early 20th C, gilt bronze mounted mahogany, rect marble top, conforming case fitted with cabinet door, pull-out shelves, plinth base, 20-3/4" w, 16-1/4" d, 52-1/4" h **750.00**

Gothic-style, late 19th/early 20th C, oak, rect case fitted with two doors, upper door carved with gothic tracery, lower with linenfold paneling, sides with linenfold paneling, block feet, 22" w, 19" d, 52" h **450.00**

Louis XVI, Provincial, late 18th/early 19th C, oak, paneled door carved with urns, 41" w, 18-1/2" d, 73" h
.... **1,380.00**

Napoleon III, c1850-70, brass and mother-of-pearl inlaid, ormolu mounts, white serpentine marble top, conforming case, fitted with

Étagère, Japanese, c1900, extensive fretwork, cameo carving, and wire inlay throughout, comprised of multiple compartments and shelves, designs include floral and fowl, landscape panels, accented with carved ivory pulls, minor losses to carvings and inlay 86" t, 51" w, 22" d, 86" h, $4,675. Photo courtesy of Sanford Alderfer Auction Company.

door, bracket feet, 35-1/2" w, 16" d, 41" h **2,645.00**

Renaissance Revival, attributed to New York, c1865-75, ebonized, marquetry, and parcel-gilt, central elevated cupboard flanked by two similar cupboards, 75" w, 15" d, 64" h **4,900.00**

Spice

Counter-type, poplar, old brown sponge dec, vertical stack with four sq nailed drawers with beveled edges, turned wooden pulls, chamfered side moldings, tongue and groove boards on sides of case, one drawer front split, 8-3/8" w, 17-1/2" d, 19-5/8" h
.... **495.00**

Hanging, second half 20th C, rope twist top molding over geometric border flanking eight drawers, inlaid star and heart dec, porcelain knobs, inlaid with ivory and mixed woods, minor losses, 15" w, 8" d, 18" h **475.00**

Vitrine

George III-style, early 20th C, mahogany, open swan's neck cresting, glazed doors, lower section with glass top shelf, sq legs joined by stretchers, 22" w, 18-1/2" d, 68" h **1,495.00**

Filing cabinet, oak, 36 small drawers, two large filing drawer at base, 42" w, 79" h, $495. Photo courtesy of Joy Luke Auctions.

Parlor cabinet, Renaissance Revival, c1875, rosewood and satinwood marquetry inlaid, hand painted porcelain and bronze mounted plaque, 63" w, 18" d, 49" h, $2,185. Photo courtesy of Fontaine's Auction Gallery.

Louis XV-style, late 19th/early 20th C, giltwood, boxed glass on each side, cabriole legs, 19" w, 17" d, 38" h **800.00**

Louis XVI-style, c1850, giltwood, outset molded rect top, frieze with beribboned floral garlands, front with glazed door with inset corners, flanked by fluted stiles, opening to two shelves, glazed sides, paneled skirt with swags, turned, tapered,

Parlor cabinet, Renaissance Revival, c1885, figural carved mahogany, winged griffin shelf supports, elaborate carved doors, beveled mirror back, 54" w, 18" d, 76" h, $4,480. Photo courtesy of Fontaine's Auction Gallery.

and fluted legs with paterae, 27-1/4" w, 16" d, 61-1/2" h **1,200.00**

Wall, hanging, Arts & Crafts, Liberty, softwood, overhanging top, side shelves, door stenciled with panel titled "Spring," pre-Raphaelite maiden with irises, refinished, some breaks to back panel, ivorine Liberty tag, 22" w, 8" d, 23" h **1,610.00**

Candlestands
Chippendale

Boston or Salem, MA, late 18th C, mahogany, carved oval tilt top, vase and ring-turned post, tripod cabriole leg base ending in arris pad feet on platforms, refinished, one leg repaired, 16-1/2" w, 22-3/4" d, 27-1/2" h **1,535.00**
Connecticut River Valley, late 18th C, cherry, old refinish, minor imperfections, 17" w, 16-1/2" d, 25-1/2" h **16,100.00**
New England, late 18th C, tilt-top, walnut, circular molded top, vase and ring-turned post and tripod cabriole leg base, arris pad feet, old refinish, imperfections, minor repair, 17" d, 28" h **2,500.00**
New Hampshire, attributed to Lt. Samuel Dunlap, old refinish, birch, painted red, imperfections, 16-1/2" w, 16-1/8" d, 26-1/2" h **2,950.00**
Pennsylvania, late 18th C, walnut, circular molded top, turned birdcage support, vase and ring-turned post, tripod cabriole leg base, pad feet on platforms,

Candle stand, Chippendale, mahogany, one-board dish turned top, turned column, tripod base with snake feet, old finish, minor repairs, 15-1/2" d, 26" h, $2,900. Also shown are brass Queen Anne candlestick, $660, and English brass honor box, 5-3/4" l, $4,620. Photo courtesy of Garth's Auctions, Inc.

old refinish, 20-1/2" d, 29" h **3,450.00**
Chippendale-style, America, early 20th C, inlaid mahogany, round tilt top with small raised edge, circular inlaid center fan, reeded urn shaped column, tripod base, well carved claw and ball feet, orig dark finish, 23-3/4" d top, 28-1/2" h **225.00**
Country, cherry and maple, southeastern New England, late 18th C, circular top, vase and ring turned post and tripod base, three tapering legs, remnants of old dark green paint, imperfections, 12" d, 25" h . . . **1,150.00**
Federal
Connecticut River Valley, attributed to, c1800-15, cherry, octagonal top with beaded edge, tilts on vase and ring turned post and tripod shaped leg base, old refinish, minor imperfections, 15-3/4" w, 25" d, 27-1/2" h **1,100.00**
Dunlap School, Antrim, New Hampshire area, late 18th century, painted, octagonal top with shaped underside, turned tapering pedestal ending in turned cap flanked by cabriole leg base ending in pad feet, Victorian polychrome dec with gilt highlight, minor imperfections, 13-5/8" x 13-1/2" top, 26-1/2" h . . . **25,850.00**
New England, attributed to, c1810-20, stained cherry, octagonal top tilting over vase and ring-turned post, tripod base, curved legs, ball feet, worn stain, 21-1/2" x 17" top, 27-1/4" h. **475.00**
New Hampshire, early 19th C, birch, painted, sq top with rounded corners, urn shaped turned

Candle stand, country, American, early 19th C, original allover floral stenciled decorated, baluster turned post with cut-out S-carved legs, decoration on top worn, one leg reattached, 22-1/2" d round top, 28-1/4" h, $500. Photo courtesy of Cowan's Historic Americana Auctions.

Candle stand, Federal, MA, 1790-1810, oval tilt top, pedestal with urn shaping, cabriole legs, arris pad feet, old surface, 19-1/2" w, 12-3/4" d, 26-3/4" h, $9,500. Photo courtesy of Skinner's Auctioneers and Appraisers.

pedestal, high arched cabriole tripod base, pad feet, old red paint, imperfections, 13-3/4" w, 13-1/4" d, 26-1/4" h **7,475.00**

Rhode Island, late 18th century, cherry, circular top with scratch-beaded edge, ring-turned tapering column, tripod cabriole leg base ending in arris pad feet, old finish, minor imperfections, 17-1/2" d, 27-3/4" h **1,100.00**

Hepplewhite, American, cherry, one-board octagonal top, turned column with chip carving, tripod base,

Candle stand, Victorian, walnut, needlework under round glass top, four turned columns, supported by carved four leg base with urn finials, staining to needlework, trim loss, 20" d, 32" h, $660. Photo courtesy of Sanford Alderfer Auction Company.

spider legs, old refinishing, minor damage, old repair, 17-1/4" x 18-1/8" top, 27" h **500.00**

Painted and decorated, Connecticut, late 19th C, cherry, octagonal top with molded edge, turned pedestal with urn shaping over high-arched cabriole leg base ending in pad feet, early black paint with 19th C yellow striping on pedestal and legs, minor imperfections, 15-1/4" w, 15-3/4" d, 29-1/2" h . **4,025.00**

Primitive, 40" h, wooden, adjustable candle arm, dark brown patina, early 19th C **715.00**

Queen Anne, attributed to Vermont, 18th C, cherry, circular top, vase and ring turned post, tripod cabriole leg base ending in arris pad feet on platforms, old refinish, 15-1/4" d top, 25-3/4" h **1,150.00**

Regency, English, mahogany, tilt-top, scalloped one board top, boldly turned column, tripod base, saber legs with beaded edges, old refinish, repairs and restoration to top, label underneath "From the summer home (1890-1929) Goshen, NY of Charlotte Beardsley (1852-1914) and George Van Riper (1845-1925), 24" w, 17-1/2" d, 28" h **595.00**

Windsor, pine, one board top with old patina and traces of finish on underside, circular platform at center, tapered column, old gold and dark brown repaint on tripod base, 16" x 16-3/4" top, 27-1/2" h **725.00**

Chairs

Arm

Adirondack-style, rustic twig construction, including small arms,

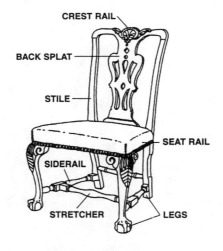

CREST RAIL

BACK SPLAT

STILE

SEAT RAIL

SIDERAIL

STRETCHER   **LEGS**

Typical Parts of a Chair

Chair, arm, Arts & Crafts, rare Limbert, angled back, corbels under flat paddle arms, scooped apron, brown leather-upholstered seat and back cushions, (back cushion not shown), original medium-brown finish, worn on arms, branded mark, 31-1/2" w, 34" d, 32-1/2" h, $3,105. Photo courtesy of David Rago Auctions.

green paint, roped seat, c1910 . . . . **2,300.00**

Aesthetic Movement, after Philip Webb's Sussex chair for Morris & Co., c1885, new natural rush seat, turned spindles, orig black paint, unmarked, 21-1/4" w, 19" d, 36-1/4" h . . . **1,045.00**

Art Deco, France, c1925, giltwood, sloping U-form back rail ending in gently swollen reeded arm supports, D-shaped seat upholstered seat cushion, pr **15,750.00**

Art Nouveau, L. Majorelle, France, c1900, carved mahogany, horseshoe-shaped back rail, upholstered back, front of arm supports carved with pine cones and needles, continuing to form molded front legs with similar carving, dark green leather upholstery. **7,000.00**

Arts & Crafts

Indiana Hickory, twig construction, orig hickory splint seat, weathered finish, branded signature, 26" w, 17" d, 37" h **50.00**

Olbrich, Joseph Marie, Jugendstil, mahogany, small back panel inlaid with fruitwood floral pattern, inset upholstered seat, unmarked, good old refinish, 23-1/2" w, 19" d, 41-1/2" h **1,840.00**

Stickley, Charles, four back slats, recovered spring cushion seat, orig finish, remnant of decal, 26" w, 22" d, 41" h **230.00**

Chair, arm, Arts & Crafts, Gustav Stickley, inverted-V crest rail, broad second slat, arched front and back stretchers, flaring legs, burgundy leather-upholstered seat, original finish, unmarked, some looseness, 23-1/4" w, 21-1/2" d, 37-1/2" h, $19,550. Photo courtesy of David Rago Auctions.

Stickley, Gustav, Model no. 2604, oak, arched crest rail over three horizontal back slats, shaped flat open arms, prominent front leg posts, offset front, back, and side stretchers, dark brown finish, red decal under arm, c1902, wear, 26-3/4" w, 26" d, 37" h. . . . **1,840.00**

Stickley, Gustav, Thornden, two horizontal back slats, narrow arms, 1902-04 red decal, replaced seat, orig finish, minor edge wear, 37" x 21" x 21-1/2" **3,105.00**

Stickley, Gustav, V-back, vertical back slats, replaced leather seat, orig faceted tacks, good orig finish, red decal, 27" w, 20-1/2" d, 37" h **1,045.00**

Stickley, L. & J. G., fixed back, drop arm, slats to seat, corbels, replaced drop-in green leather spring seat and back cushion, waxed finish, L & J. G. Stickley Handcraft label, 32-1/2" w, 33" d, 41" h **5,750.00**

Stickley, L. & J. G., spindled back, open arms, corbels, seat recovered in leather, refinished, unmarked, 24-1/2" w, 21" d, 38-1/2" h **690.00**

Banister-back, New England, 1760-80, painted, shaped crest flanked by turned finials over banisters and

serpentine arms, over-upholstered seat, boldly turned front legs and stretchers, old black paint with gold trim, red velvet seat, imperfections, 17" h seat, 46" h
. . . . **1,175.00**

Centennial, Colonial Revival, Queen-Anne Style, wing back, hardwood cabriole legs, turned stretcher, upholstery removed, old dark finish, 46" h **900.00**

Chippendale, Hartford, CT, area, late 18th C, painted, scrolling crest above pierced splat with center urn, old black paint with traces of yellow striping, 14-3/4" h seat, 40" h, minor paint wear
. . . . **2,100.00**

Chippendale-style, walnut, light green leather upholstery, brass tack borders, shaped arms, sq molded legs, stretcher bases, wear, some splits in leather seats, 18-3/4" h seat, 38-1/4" h, price for six-pc set **1,200.00**

Egyptian Revival, American, c1865, ebonized and parcel-gilt, upholstered scrolling back and seat, matching upholstered arm pads, sphinx head arm supports, claw feet, 39-1/2" h
. . . . **8,050.00**

Empire-style, mahogany, rect padded back, padded arms, ormolu-mounted classical busts, bowed padded seat, sq tapering legs with brass caps, white striped upholstery **850.00**

George III, late 18th C, in the French taste, giltwood, beaded oval backrest carved with anthemion, scrolled arms similarly beaded, serpentine seat raised on circular reeded legs **8,100.00**

Gothic Revival, America, walnut, old finish, reupholstered in damask, age cracks, 52-1/2" h. **200.00**

Chair, arm, Chippendale, 18th C, carved mahogany, pierced back splat, square molded front legs, re-upholstered slip seat, 17-1/2" seat, 37" h back, $650. Photo courtesy of James D. Julia, Inc.

Chair, arm, George III, English, c1760-80, mahogany, shaped crest rail, pierced splat, curving arms, straight legs with canted corners, serpentine front seat rail, old, possibly original, finish, newly upholstered seat, $275. Photo courtesy of Cowan's Historic Americana Auctions.

Louis XIV, early 18th C, fauteuil, giltwood, serpentine cresting, scrolled and reeded arms, over upholstered seat, scrolled legs joined by stretchers
. . . . **2,990.00**

Louis XIV-style, Baroque, late 19th C, walnut, rect backrest, foliate carved arms and legs, X-form stretcher, price for pr **2,650.00**

Modern, Verner Panton, heart chair, by Plus-Linji, orig red fabric upholstery over metal frame, swivel chrome base, 40" w, 24" d, 36" h **10,350.00**

Neoclassical, Italian, late 18th/early 19th C, walnut, urn and wheat carved splat, downswept arms, raised sq tapering legs, 34-1/4" h **1,100.00**

Queen Anne

Middle Atlantic states, last half 18th C, arched crest with square corners, raked stiles, scrolled arms on vasiform supports, trapezoidal seat, frontal cabriole legs ending in pad feet, raked rear legs, imperfections, 16-1/2" h seat, 49" h
. . . . **21,150.00**

New Hampshire, hardwood with old black repaint, molded and curved back posts with vase splat and carved crest, turned posts support molded and scrolled arms, turned legs, Spanish feet, turned rungs with bulbous front stretcher, old rush seat, some loss of paint to feet, 15-3/8" seat, 41" h . . **4,125.00**

Renaissance Revival, attributed to Pottier & Stymus, New York, 1865, walnut, scrolled arms, upholstered back and seed, spherules on seat rail, 38" h
. . . . **1,100.00**

Rococo Revival, John H. Belter, rosewood, Rosalie pattern, laminated, solid back, crest carved with large rose, fruit, and grape clusters, yellow silk

upholstery, tufted back, 42-1/2" h
.... **3,500.00**
Rococo-style, Italian, late 19th/early
20th C, grotto, scallop shell seat,
dolphin-shaped arms, rusticated legs
.... **1,725.00**
Savonarola-style, mahogany, Old Man
of the North carved in crest rail . **230.00**
Shaker, attributed to Canterbury, NH,
c1835, birch and pine, concave rect
back rail, turned stiles, four spindles,
shaped seat, splayed turned tapering
legs joined by stretchers, old refinish,
traces of red stain, minor imperfections,
17" h seat, 24-1/2" h **600.00**
Victorian, George Huntzinger, NY,
patent March 30, 1869, walnut, pierce
carved crest, rect upholstered back
panel flanked by turned and curved
slats and stiles, low upholstered
barrel-back, arm frame carved with
classical heads, upholstered seat,
pierced and scroll-carved front drop
under seat connected to turned rung
joining carved and turned front legs,
ball feet, front leg stamped. . . **2,100.00**

Windsor

   Bowed back, New England,
   attributed to, c1790, bowed incised
   crest rail continuing to
   scroll-carved handholds, nine
   spindles and swelled incised arm
   supports, shaped saddle seat,

*Chair, arm, Art Nouveau, elliptical
shaped back splat and arm decoration,
woven rush seat, whiplash style
extended legs, shaped front stretcher,
$350.*

Chair, arm, Victorian, walnut, blue velvet upholster, carved fruit on top back rail, **$425.** *Photo courtesy of Joy Luke Auctions.*

splayed and incised turned legs
joined by conforming turned
stretchers, old refinish, minor
imperfections, 18" h seat, 40" h
.... **1,300.00**
Braced fan back, Pennsylvania, late
18th C, serpentine crest rail with
carved terminals, five spindles
vase and ring-turned stiles flanked
by shaped incised arms with
scrolled hand-holds, vase and
ring-turned supports, shaped
circular seat, splayed vase and
ring-turned legs joined by swelled
stretchers, 19th C rosewood
grained paint with gilt striping,
17" h seat, 43" h **3,415.00**
Comb back, attributed to
Philadelphia, PA, mixed woods,
areas of old dark green paint,
arched top with finely scrolled ears,
nine back spindles, bentwood arm
rain ending in shaped hand rests,
D-shaped seat with incised line
borders around edges, baluster
and ring turned legs, blunt arrow
feet, stretcher base, old pegged
restoration on arm rail, 23-1/2" w,
17-1/2" h seat, 42" h **11,275.00**
Continuous arm, New England,
c1815, nine-spindle back, saddle
seat, stamped "J Ash," 36" h
.... **1,100.00**
Continuous arm, Pennsylvania, early
19th C, nine-spindle back, bamboo
turnings, 38" h **275.00**
Double bow-back, New England,
c1800-15, maple, ash, and pine,
incised crest rail above seven
spindles, applied scrolled arm,
writing surface to right, both with
bamboo-turned supports on
shaped seat, centering drawer
mounted on underside, splayed
bamboo-turned feet joined by

stretchers, orig red-brown stained
surface, imperfections, 16" h,
45-1/2" h **3,525.00**
Sack back, America, painted,
bowed crest over six spindles
joining shaped arms with vase and
ring-turned supports, incised seat,
four splayed vase and ring-turned
legs joined by H-form bulbous
stretchers, old dark brown over red
paint, minor imperfections, 17" h
seat, 37-3/4" h **4,995.00**
Sack back, America, painted, early
green paint, yellow line dec, small
yellow leaves on front legs and arm
supports, seven-spindle back,
well-shaped arms, shaped oval
seat, baluster and ring turned legs,
H-stretcher base, old damage to
backs of front legs, old
"Providence, RI" warehouse label
beneath seat, 17" h seat, 37" h
.... **1,700.00**
Sack back, New England, c1790,
bowed crest rail above seven
spindles and arms, vine and
ring-turned supports, saddle seat,
splayed legs joined by stretchers,
painted yellow, later coat of salmon
paint and green, 17-1/2" h seat,
40-1/2" h, price for pr .. **72,900.00**
Slough-back, English, George III,
late 18th C, yew and elm, back with
turned spindles, center vasiform
splat framed by pair of flattened
stoles surmounting serpentine
crest rail, shaped arm rail on plain
spindles, saddle shaped seat,
cabriole legs, pad feet, repairs,
refinished, 29" w, 15-1/2" d, 46" h
.... **500.00**

Chair, arm, Windsor, sack back, early green paint, yellow line decorated, small yellow leaves on front legs and arm supports, seven-spindles back, well-shaped arms, shaped oval seat, baluster and ring turned legs, H-stretcher base, old "Providence, RI" warehouse label beneath seat, wear to front legs, 17" h seat, 37" h, **$1,700.** *Photo courtesy of Garth's Auctions, Inc.*

Chair, arm, wicker, Wakefield Rattan Co, high scrolled back continues form ornate sides, $200. Photo courtesy of Joy Luke Auctions.

Corner

Chippendale, walnut, rolled back rest with stepped detail, pierced harp shape splats, serpentine arm supports, scrolled handholds, molded seal frame, slip seat covered in worn upholstery, scalloped aprons, cabriole legs with relief carved shells on knees, claw and ball feet, old dark surface, restorations and replacements **1,870.00**

Chippendale-style, 20th C, mahogany, shaped arms, openwork splats, rush slip seat raised on cabriole legs, claw and ball feet. **575.00**

Country, New England, late 18th/early 19th C, maple, arms with scrolled terminals, shaped crest, scrolled horizontal splats attached to swelled and turned baluster forms continuing to turned legs, joined to similar stretchers, old surface, replaced rush seat, minor imperfections, 16-3/8" h seat, 30-1/2" h back. **1,610.00**

Queen Anne, New England, walnut, shaped seat rail with turned stiles, vasiform splats inlaid with cartouche of Roman warriors, deep shaped skirt, sq legs, sq slip seat with needlepoint upholstery, replaced inlay, 33" h **550.00**

William and Mary, New England, 18th C, shaped backrest and chamfered crest, scrolled handholds, three vase and ring-turned stiles continuing to turned legs, joined to front leg by turned double stretchers, old dark brown paint, replaced wood seat, 30" h. **1,380.00**

Dining

Arts & Crafts

Stickley, Gustav, ladder-back, four slats, cloud-lift aprons, drop-in seats recovered in leather, 37" h, overcoat finish, roughness to edges, some with red Gustav decal, set of eight **6,300.00**

Stickley, L. & J. G., arched vertical back slats, drop-in spring seat, covered in new green leather, good new finish, orig labels, 37-1/2" h, 17" w, price for set of four **3,335.00**

Assembled set, English, c1800-60, turned ash and alder, open spindle back with two or three tiers of short turnings between flattened stiles, rush seat, tapered round legs, pad feet, bulbous turned front stretcher, plain turned side and rear stretchers, two-arm chairs, 10-side chairs, some with feet ended out, 19" w, 16" d, 38" h, price for set of 12 . . . . **1,875.00**

Biedermeier, fruitwood and part ebonized, black faux-leather upholstery, 36" h, restorations, set of four **2,500.00**

Centennial, Colonial Revival, Sheraton-style, mahogany, two arm, eight side, shield back, reeded front legs, corner posts with carving of urns, needlepoint slip seats, 19-1/2" w, 17-1/4" d, 37-1/2" h **3,000.00**

Chippendale-style, Baker, CT, black lacquer, saber-leg, c1960, set of eight **2,100.00**

Classical, New England, c1830-40, figured maple, concave crests above vasiform splats and rails, scrolled and raked stiles, caned seats with serpentine fronts, saber legs joined by stretchers, old refinish, 17-1/4" h seat, 32" h, set of six **950.00**

Eastlake, American, c1870, mahogany, one armchair, six side chairs, fan-carved crest rail, reeded stiles and stretchers, block-carved front legs,

Chair, dining, Arts & Crafts, Stickley Brothers, each with corseted crest rail, three vertical back slats, tacked-on brown leather seat pad, skinned medium finish, Quaint decal, stenciled number on several, two arm 25" w, 19" d, 39" h chairs four 18-1/4" w, 16" d, 37-1/2" h side chairs, $2,990. Photo courtesy of David Rago Auctions.

35" h, minor damage, set of seven **850.00**

Federal, Rhode Island or Salem, MA, c1795, mahogany carved, set of four side and matching arm chair, shield back with molded crest and stiles above carved kylix with festoons draped from flanking carved rosettes, pierced splat terminating in carved lunette at base above molded rear seat rail, seat with serpentine front rail, sq tapering legs joined by stretchers, over-upholstered seats covered in old black horsehair with scalloped trim, old surface, 16-1/2" h seat, 37-3/4" h **23,000.00**

George III, c1800, carved mahogany, yoke back, upswept reeded terminals, carved openwork vasiform splat with center pendant tassels over three flowerheads, green leather over upholstered seat, nailhead trim, fluted, molded, and chamfered front supports, H-form stretchers, swept rear supports, set of six **5,500.00**

George III-style, late 19th C, mahogany, anthemion pierced backrest, over upholstered seat, cabriole legs, claw and ball feet, set of six side chairs, associated arm chair **2,100.00**

Regency-style, late 19th/early 20th C, mahogany and inlay, two armchairs, six side chairs, curved inlaid crest rail, dec horizontal splats, pale blue silk upholstery, Greek key design, 33-3/4" h **10,350.00**

Renaissance Revival, America, c1870, oak, two arm and eight side chairs, each with foliate and beast carved cresting, paneled seat rail and turned legs, set of 10 . . . . **3,105.00**

Chair, dining, Regency, English, light fruit wood, back with oval central panel with original cane work, bamboo turned front legs, turned and fluted scrollwork arms, wide upholstered seats in period style printed silk, set of two arm chairs, four side chairs, $3,675. Photo courtesy of Cowan's Historic Americana Auctions.

Sheraton, Hitchcock type, two arm chairs, six side chairs, old red and black repaint, yellow striping, stenciled and freehand dec, replaced rush seats, 18" h seat, 33-1/2" h **2,500.00**

Easy, Chippendale, New England, 18th C, mahogany, shaped crest and wings above the rolled arms, cushioned seat, molded Marlborough front legs joined by sq stretchers to the raking rear legs, old refinish, imperfections, 16" h seat rail, 45-1/2" h. **3,650.00**

Folding, Austrian, Thonet, late 19th C, bentwood, oval backrest and seat, scrolling arms and legs **600.00**

Highchair, child's

Ladderback, early dark green paint with traces of earlier green beneath, well-defined turnings on arms, three slat back, turned legs with blunt arrow feet on front, tapered rear feet, old worn woven tape seat, 20-1/2" h seat, 38-1/2" h **3,850.00**

Windsor, New England, 1825-40, rect crest above three spindles and outward flaring stiles, turned hand-holds on shaped seat, splayed turned tapering legs joined by stretchers, vestiges of stippled red and black paint, "M.H. Spencer, N.Y." in script on bottom of seat, 22-1/2" h seat, 31-1/2" h. . . **775.00**

Ladderback, five-splat, attributed to Delaware Valley region, c1760, orig red painted surface **25,300.00**

Library, George III, c1800, mahogany and caned, pink upholstered loose cushion, 33-1/2" h. **2,070.00**

Lolling, Federal

Massachusetts, 1790-1800, mahogany, serpentine crest above half serpentine molded shaped arms, concave supports,

Chair, high, Arts & Crafts, Limbert, single backslat, saddle seat, branded mark and stenciled number, refinished, old repair to leg, split to seat, plugged holes to arms, 14-3/4" w, 14-1/2" d, 38-3/4" h, $400. Photo courtesy of David Rago Auctions.

Chair, high, Windsor-style, bow back, Ohio, late 19th C, original red paint, black pin striping, underside of plank seat marked "J. R. MacCormick Mt Vernon, Ohio," 25 percent paint loss, foot rail missing, 24-1/2" h seat, 36-1/2" h overall, $125. Photo courtesy of Cowan's Historic Americana Auctions.

over-upholstered serpentine seat on sq tapering frontal legs, raked rear legs, casters missing, minor imperfections, 16-1/2" h seat, 42" h **4,700.00**

New England, c1790, mahogany, reverse serpentine crest over upholstered back joining shaped arms and molded concave supports on four tapering sq legs, joined by sq stretchers, old refinish, imperfections, 17" h seat, 43-1/4" h **6,900.00**

Morris chair, Arts & Crafts

Stickley, Gustav, no. 332, slats to the floor under flat arms, orig brown leather cushions, orig finish, red decal, arms re-pegged and re-glued, 31-1/2" w, 36" d, 37" h **6,275.00**

Stickley, L. & J. G., Fayetteville, NY, c1915, chair model no. 411, matching model no. 397 footstool, four carved slats on adjustable back, flat open arms with through tenon leg posts and four corbel supports with upholstered spring cushion seat and back, light brown finish, 29-1/4" w, 35" d, 40-1/4" h; footstool with, spring cushion, 20" w, 14" d, 16-1/2" h, both with red and yellow decal "The Work of L. & J. G. Stickley" **1,725.00**

Potty, Queen Anne, country, corner, maple and pine, old red repaint, shaped crest and arms, three turned posts, heart-shaped pierced splats, slip seat with base recovered in green leather upholstery, turned legs, button feet, deep aprons, 16" h, 31" h . **770.00**

Side

Arrowback, 19th C mustard paint, tan, brown, red, and black dec of cornucopias on crest, leaves on back and front stretcher, incising around seat, brushed detain between, evidence of earlier green, bamboo turned base, 15-3/4" h, 32" h . . . **935.00**

Art Deco, Europe, wooden gondola backs, ivory sabots on front legs, cream striped fabric upholstery, pr, 25" h **2,000.00**

Arts & Crafts

Stickley, Gustav, H-back, drop-in seat recovered in burgundy leather, red decal, over-coated orig dark finish, roughness to leg edges, 17" w, 16" d, 40" h **690.00**

Stickley, L. & J. G., Fayetteville, NY, model no. 350, c1910, oak, three horizontal back slats, orig leather seat, wide front stretcher, double side stretchers, red handcraft decal, imperfections, 16-5/8" w, 18-3/4" d, 35" h **300.00**

Banister back

New England, mid to late 18th C, painted black, shaped crest flanked by vase and ring-turned stiles, urn-form finials over three split banisters, trapezoidal cane seat, ring-turned frontal legs joined by double turned stretchers, minor imperfections, 16-3/4" h seat, 41-1/4" h **360.00**

Chair, lounge, International Movement, George Nakashima, 1978, walnut spindle-back, single free-edge arm, broad saddle seat, signed "George Nakashima/February 1978" and original owner's name, 31" w, 26" d, 31-1/2" h, $6,000. Photo courtesy of David Rago Auctions.

Chair, side, Arts & Crafts, L .& J.G. Stickley, No.1313, three vertical backslats, original dark brown leather covered seat, unmarked, over-coated original finish, minor roughness to edges, 16" w, 16" 3, 36" h, $275. Photo courtesy of David Rago Auctions.

New England, last half 18th C, painted black, shaped crest above four split banisters flanked by urn finials, vase and ring-turned stiles, trapezoidal rush seat, turned legs joined by double sausage-turned stretchers, imperfections, 17" h seat, 47" h. **1,300.00**

New Hampshire, coastal, mid to late 18th C, painted black, flaring fishtail carved crest over three split banisters flanked by vase and ring-turned stiles with ball finials, trapezoidal rush seat over ring-turned frontal legs joined by double turned stretchers, rear legs with old piecing, 17" h seat, 43" h **1,425.00**

Biedermeier, fruitwood, lyre back, incurvate seat rail with rosettes, carved lyre splats, sq tapered legs, upholstered slip seats, repairs, replacements, 35" h, price for set of three. **350.00**

Centennial, Colonial Revival, Chippendale-style, walnut, pierced ribbon back, molded seat frame, legs, orig dark finish, slip seat is period replacement with old rush covering, restorations to mortise joints of stretcher base, 17-1/2" h seat, 37-1/2" h . **200.00**

Chippendale

Boston or North Shore, c1760-80, carved mahogany, leaf carved lunettes and C-scrolls centered in shaped crests, raked molded terminals above pierced splats and over-upholstered seats, cabriole front legs terminating in scratch carved high pad feet, old refinish, 18" h seat, 37-1/4" h, price for pair **13,800.00**

Boston or Salem, MA, 1760-80, carved walnut, raked terminals of crest above pierced splat with C-scrolls, compass slip seat, cabriole legs, high pad feet, old refinish, restoration to stiles, 16-1/2" h seat, 38-1/2" h . **2,185.00**

Connecticut River Valley, tiger maple, serpentine crest with raked molded terminals above pierced splat, old rush seat, block and vase turned front legs joined by turned stretcher, old refinish, 17-1/4" h seat, 39" h **900.00**

Country, maple with some curl, pierced spat and shaped crest with carved ears, sq legs, mortised and pinned stretchers, old mellow refinishing, damage to paper rush seat because of breaks in front seal rail, 39" h **110.00**

Massachusetts, Boston, 1750-70, carved mahogany, crest rail centers demi-lune carved fan, ends in raked terminals above pierced splat with C-scrolls, over-upholstered seat, frontal cabriole legs with arris knees, ending in high pad feet, rear legs

Chair, side, Chippendale, Philadelphia, c1760, mahogany, carved crest rail, scrolled ears, carved and pierced back-splat, carved shell knees, claw and ball feet, possible original finis, one scroll on splat replaced, glued break in crest, minor cat scratches, $1,695. Photo courtesy of Cowan's Historic Americana Auctions.

rake to rear, some old surfaces, imperfections, 17-1/2" h seat, 38" h **10,575.00**

Massachusetts, Boston or Salem, c1760-80, mahogany, serpentine crest with molded and beaded terminals, scrolling pierced splat flanked by slightly raked stiles, trapezoidal slip seat with 19th C needlework cover in molded frame, frontal arris cabriole legs ending in claw and ball feet, joined to chamfered rear legs by H-form block, vase, and ring-turned stretchers, old surface, minor imperfections, 16-1/2" h seat, 37" h **4,700.00**

New London, CT, 1760-95, carved cherry, serpentine crest rails, pierced splats with C-scrolls and beaded edges, molded shoes, flanked by stiles and rounded backs, molded seat frames and straight legs with beaded edges, pierced brackets joined by sq stretchers, old refinish, set of five, 17" h seat, 39" h **10,350.00**

New York, 1755-65, carved mahogany, carved crest ending in raked molded terminals above pierced splat with C-scrolls, slip seat, molded seat frame, front carved cabriole legs ending in ball and claw feet, rear raked legs, old surface, imperfections, 18" h seat, 39-1/2" h **2,990.00**

Pennsylvania, 1760-80, carved walnut, serpentine crest with center shell, scrolled-back terminals, pierced splat, molded and shaped seat rail, front cabriole legs with shell carving, through tenons, rear rounded legs, ball and claw feet, old surface, red velvet slip seat, minor imperfections, 17-1/4" h seat, 40" h. **6,465.00**

Rhode Island, c1765-95, mahogany, shaped and carved crest rail, pierced splat, raked stiles, trapezoidal slip seat, molded front legs joined to raked rear legs by sq stretchers, old finish, imperfections, 18" h seat, 38" h **1,100.00**

Chippendale-style, late 19th C, carved mahogany, foliate and C-scroll carved baluster splat, over upholstered seat, cabriole legs ending in scrolled toes, price for set of six **2,990.00**

Classical

Baltimore, painted and dec, scrolled crest above inverted vase-shaped splat, cane seat, dec front legs joined by medial stretcher, stencil dec, orig gilt classical motifs on black ground, 34-1/2" h **750.00**

Connecticut, 1830-50, tiger maple, curving shaped crests, curving front rail, Grecian legs, branded "A. G. Case," refinished, seats missing caning, other imperfections, 17-3/4" h seat, 33-1/2" h, set of six **3,200.00**

Middle Atlantic States, 1830s, mahogany veneer, curving veneered crests, similar horizontal splats, upholstered seats, Klismos-type legs, old refinish, 17-3/4" h seat, 33-1/2" h, set of seven **1,850.00**

New York, 1810-20, carved mahogany veneer, scroll back, beaded edges, horizontal splats carved with leafage and other classical motifs, slip seat, curving legs, old surface, 16-1/2" h, 32" h, set of six **5,200.00**

Chair, side, Louis XV, fruitwood, carved open back, serpentine front seat rail, scroll carved apron, upholstered seat, removable cushion, cabriole legs, carved knees, scrolled feet, probably German, mid-18th C, old refinishing, re-upholstered, back repaired, $165. Photo courtesy of Cowan's Historic Americana Auctions.

Decorated, attributed to Carlisle, PA, plank seat, orig black over red dec, floral panels surrounded by gold stencils, bordered with salmon and yellow line border dec, carefully cleaned, applied coat of protective varnish, professionally executed slight touch-up, 17" h seat, 31" h, price for set of six **3,650.00**

Federal

Massachusetts, early 19th C, carved mahogany, shaped crests and stiles above stay rails, beaded edges, seat with serpentine front, sq tapering molded legs, beaded edges, joined by sq stretchers, old surface, over-upholstered needlepoint seats, 17" h seat, 36" h, set of three **1,150.00**

Massachusetts or Rhode Island, c1780, mahogany inlaid, shield back, arched molded crest above 5 molded spindles and inlaid quarter fan, over-upholstered seats with serpentine fronts, molded tapering legs joined by stretchers, 17-1/2" h seat, 37" h, pr . . **5,475.00**

New England, attributed to, maple, rush seat, dec with polychrome flowers on yellow ground, 18" w, 16" d, 35" h, price for pr . . . **500.00**

New Hampshire, Portsmouth, attributed to Langley Boardman, 1774-1833, mahogany, sq back, reeded on rest rail, stiles, and stay rail, over upholstered serpentine seat, molded sq tapering front legs, sq stretchers and rakes rear legs, refinish, minor imperfections, 18" h seat, 36" h **1,035.00**

George III, English, mahogany, ladder back, swelled crest rail over three graduated ribbon form pierced slats, broad over-upholstered seat in blue fabric, sq legs joined by H-stretcher, 23" w, 19" d, 36" h **500.00**

Gothic Revival, New York City, 1850s, mahogany veneer, trefoil pierced splats, curved stay rails, veneered seal rails, curving rococo legs, old refinish, 20th C upholstery, 16-1/2" h seat, 33-1/2" h, set of eight **6,900.00**

Hepplewhite, American, mahogany, shield back, rush seat **325.00**

Hitchcock, Hitchcocksville, CT, 1825-32, rosewood grained surface, orig gilt dec, urn centering cornucopia splat, old rush seats, ring-turned legs, orig surface, 35-1/2" h, price for set of four **1,265.00**

Neoclassical

American, attributed to workshop of Duncan Phyfe, New York City, 1810-15, carved mahogany and tiger maple veneer, spiral carved crest rail flanked by curving beaded stiles, flanking carved scrolls above horizontal splat with oval tiger maple veneer reserve flanked by carving, beaded seat rail, klismos-type molded legs, 17" h seat, 32-1/4" h, price for set of three **4,900.00**

Italian, early 19th C, fruitwood, shaped trapezoidal backrest, serpentine over-upholstered seat, flared legs, price for set of four **1,275.00**

Plank, northern New England, 1830s, side, arrow-back, yellow ground, stencil dec with dark green and blue leafage and fruit, gold accents, shaped plank seat, splayed bamboo turned legs, paint loss, minor imperfections, 17-3/4" h seat, 35" h, set of five **1,725.00**

Queen Anne

American, early 18th C, burl walnut, shaped cresting, serpentine slat, slip-seat raised on shell carved cabriole legs, hoof feet, price for pr **1,650.00**

Country, maple, arched crest, vase splat, replaced paper rush seat, turned front legs, bulbous turned front stretcher (partially worn), tapered rear posts, refinished, restorations, 16-1/4" h seat, 39-1/2" h **225.00**

Chair, side, Renaissance Revival, attributed to John Belter, c1855, rosewood laminated, floral crests, intricate pierced curved backs, 40" h, price for pair, $5,040. Photo courtesy of Fontaine's Auction Gallery.

Massachusetts, attributed to, mid to late 18th C, red stained maple, yoke back, carved beaded crest continuing to beaded stiles flanking vasiform splat on beaded stay rail over trapezoidal rush seat, block, ball, and ring-turned frontal legs joined by bulbous stretchers, old red stain with varnish, minor repairs and imperfections, 17" h seat, 41" h **425.00**

Newport, RI, 1750-75, black walnut, curving crest above vase-shaped pierced splat, compass seat, front and side rail shaping, cabriole front legs joined to rear sq tapering legs by block and vase-swelled side stretchers, swelled and turned medial stretchers, rear feet without chamfering, old refinish, minor repairs, affixed brass plaque reads "Ebenezer Storer 1730-1807," 17" h seat, 38-1/4" h **2,990.00**

Pennsylvania, Philadelphia, c1760-80, walnut, bow shaped crest rail, solid vasiform splat, scrolled ears, trapezoidal slip seat, plain cabriole legs, pad feet, patch repair, 22" w, 18" d, 40" h . **2,750.00**

Rococo Revival, John H. Belter, rosewood, Rosalie without the Grapes pattern, laminated, solid back, crest carved with large rose and fruit, red silk upholstery, casters, pr, 37-1/2" h **2,550.00**

William IV, England, carved rosewood, foliate carved backrest with central diamond shaped upholstered panel, slip seat, leaf carved circular legs, c1835, price for pr **700.00**

Windsor

Birdcage, attributed to MA, c1810-15, red painted, birdcage, concave crest above seven spindles on incised shaped seats, bamboo-turned swelled and splayed legs joined by stretchers, old worn red paint, minor imperfections, 17-1/2" h, 34-1/2" h **1,100.00**

Birdcage, small ink signature on bottoms of seat for "Fitch," one has later painted name, seven-spindle back, bamboo turnings, shield shaped seat with incised detail, refinished, small corner chip on one crest, edge of seat chip on other, 17" h, 33-1/2" h, price for pr **750.00**

Bow back, New England, late 18th/early 19th C, bowed crest

Chair, side, Windsor, bow back, America, early 19th C, mixed wood, one with added rockers, both refinished, price for pair, $250. Photo courtesy of Cowan's Historic Americana Auctions.

over nine spindles, incised shape seat, splayed swelled legs joined by swelled stretchers, green over older black paint, surface and other minor imperfections, 19" h, 39" h **600.00**

Bow back, reproduction, well executed by L. E. Partridge, nine spindles, incised molding around bow, deeply scooped sets, boldly turned legs and stretchers, mellow light brown finish, surface wear, 18" h seat, 39-1/4" h, price for pr **550.00**

Brace back, nine spindles bow back, well shaped seat with incised detail around spindles, vase and ring turned legs, turned "H" stretcher, old mellow refinish, restorations, 17-1/2" h, seat, 36-3/4" h **385.00**

Butterfly, Pennsylvania, seven-spindle back, bamboo turnings, poplar seats, hickory legs and spindles, refinished, price for pr, one with crack in top rail **285.00**

Clerk's, attributed to New England, c1790, ash, shaped concave crest above seven spindles, vase and ring-turned stiles, shaped saddle seat, splayed vase and ring-turned legs joined by turned, swelled stretchers, old refinish, imperfections, 26" h, 41-1/2" h **1,430.00**

Comb back, mixed woods, arched crest with flared ears, seven-spindle back, turned arms, bentwood arm rail, shield shaped seat, vase and ring turned legs, stretcher base, light refinish, 17" h seat, 38-1/4" h **800.00**

Fan back, America, black repaint, light yellow line detail, shaped crest, eight spindles, well-shaped shield seat, baluster and ring turned legs, stretcher base **250.00**

Fan back, New England, c1780-90, concave serpentine crest rail above seven spindles, vase and ring-turned stiles, shaped seat, splayed vase and ring-turned legs joined by swelled stretchers, old dark finish, 18" h seat, 37" h **1,530.00**

Rod back, New England, early 19th C, bamboo carved crest and stiles flanking seven spindles over rounded seats, four swelled bamboo-turned legs joined by H-form swelled stretchers, dark brown stain, very minor imperfections, price for pr . **600.00**

Slipper

Arts & Crafts, Gustav Stickley, spindled back, drop-in spring seat recovered in brown leather, orig finish, black decal, 17-3/4" w, 16" d, 37" h **1,150.00**

Victorian, c1875, rosewood, angular foliate carved backrest with urn form splat, over upholstered seat and circular turned legs **300.00**

Victorian, late, c1880, ebonized and bobbin turned needlepoint upholstery, foliate dec seat **175.00**

Chair, slipper, Arts & Crafts, Gustav Stickley, laced brown hard leather seat, footrest with corbelled supports, and stretchers, branded mark, original finish and leather, metal brackets added under footrest, 15-1/2" w, 15" d, 24-1/2" h, $475. Photo courtesy of David Rago Auctions.

Chair, wing, Centennial, well formed wings and arms, cabriole front legs with shell carved knees with eagle's head, carved ball and claw feet, re-upholstered, 20" h seat, 44-1/2" h back, $990. Photo courtesy of James D. Julia, Inc.

Wingback

Chippendale, country, birch base, old dark finish, sq slightly tapered legs with molded corners, H stretcher, reupholstered, glued split on one foot, 47-1/2" h **1,650.00**

Louis XV-style, late 19th C, old dark gold painted surface, butterfly wing, finely carved acanthus leaves and ribbon designs around frame, later velvet upholstery, 19" h seat, 47" h **700.00**

Modern, upholstered in athletic award letters mounted on Amish wool **4,200.00**

Vintage, red, white, and blue flag fabric covering **950.00**

Chests of drawers

Art Deco, Quigley, France, c1925, parchment covered, rect top, three tapering drawers, pyramid mirrored stiles, bracket feet, back branded, 44-1/2" x 35" **2,750.00**

Arts & Crafts, English, dresser, orig pivoting mirror with chamberstick shelves, glove boxes, copper repoussé panels, two drawers over one long drawer, orig medium-dark finish, unmarked, split to side, 42-3/4" w, 21-1/2" d, 64" h **1,725.00**

Biedermeier, c1820, maple, rect case fitted with two drawers, splayed sq legs, 36" w, 19" d, 31" h **1,725.00**

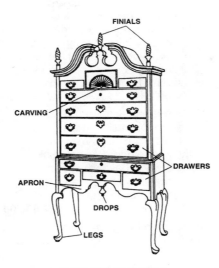

Typical Parts of a Highboy

Chippendale

Boston, 1750-90, mahogany, block front, thumb-molded shaped top, conforming case, four graduated drawers, molded base, bracket feet, old refinish, replaced brass, rear foot missing, backboard inscribed "G. Russell" (George Russell, 1800-1866, born in Providence, RI, married Sarah Shaw, and died in Manchester, MA,) 33" w, 19-1/4" w, 29-1/4" h **46,000.00**

Colchester, CT, c1770-90, mahogany, molded serpentine top, conforming cock-beaded case of four graduated drawers, four scrolling ogee bracket feet joined by straight skirt, old surface, possibly orig brasses, minor repairs and losses, 36" w, 19-1/2" d, 32-1/2" h **23,500.00**

Connecticut, c1760-80, cherry, overhanging oblong top with projecting quarter round corners, case of four scratch-beaded graduated drawers flanked by lambrequin corners, rope twist engaged quarter columns, four claw and ball carved feet, joined by shaped returns, replaced brasses, refinished, minor restoration, 42" w, 21-3/4" d, 37-1/2" h **9,400.00**

Connecticut, Litchfield, 1760-80, cherry, overhanging top, three scratch-beaded drawers, flanked by reeded quarter- engaged columns with lambs' tongues, ball and claw feet with shaped brackets, old refinish and color,

probably original brasses, 38-1/2" w, 19" d, 35" h . . . **7,050.00**

Country, curly maple, four dovetailed drawers, bracket feet, refinished, bottom backboard and feet replaced, brasses replaced, 41-1/4" w, 19-1/2" d, 37-1/2" h **2,450.00**

Massachusetts, Boston, 1770-95, serpentine, carved mahogany, overhanging molded serpentine top with blocked ends, conforming case of four graduated drawers separated by cock-beaded dividers, heavy molded base, intricately shaped bracket ending in ball and claw feet, some original brasses, old refinish, repairs, imperfections, 36-3/4" w, 20-3/4" d, 32-3/4" h **116,000.00**

Massachusetts, Salem, late 18th C, serpentine, inlaid mahogany, overhanging serpentine top with end-blocking and string inlaid edges, case of four drawers with cock-beaded surrounds and quarter-fan inlays, molded base with fan inlaid drop pendant and front feet, old replaced brass, old refinish, imperfections, 38-3/4" w, 22-3/4" d, 33-1/4" h **21,150.00**

Massachusetts, late 18th C, cherry, oblong top with serpentine front,

Chest of drawers, Arts & Crafts, Gustav Stickley, nine-drawer chest with backsplash, six small drawers over three graduated ones, all with hammered copper V-pulls, arched apron and sides, stripped finish, red decal inside drawer and paper label, veneer lifting and chipping and two drill holes on right side, 36" w, 20" d, 50" h, $4,315. Photo courtesy of David Rago Auctions.

case with four graduated scratch-beaded drawers, bracket feet, old brasses, refinished, minor imperfections, 35-1/4" w, 20" d, 32-1/2" h **4,115.00**

New England, southern, 1780-1800, maple, flaring molded cornice, case of six thumb-molded graduated drawers, molded base with shaped bracket feet, old replaced brasses, minor imperfections, 40-3/8" w, 18-1/2" d, 50-5/8" h **9,990.00**

Pennsylvania, c1760-80, attributed to Jonathon Shoemaker, Philadelphia, mahogany, molded top carved with invected corners over quarter-round fluted columns, four graduated thumb-molded drawers, period brasses, shaped ogee bracket feet, refinished, replaced hardware, illus in William Macpherson Horner, Jr, *Blue Book of Philadelphia Furniture, William Penn to George Washington,* provenance included, 38-1/2" w, 21" d, 32" h **55,500.00**

Pennsylvania, c1760-80, walnut, rect overhanging top with applied

Chest of drawers, Chippendale, attributed to Boston, Massachusetts, serpentine, mahogany, thumb-molded top, four dovetailed drawers set in beaded frame, well shaped scroll work, high bracket feet, old finish, old replaced period brasses, minor repairs to feet, 37-3/4" w, 20-1/2" d, 32-1/2" h, $23,100. Also shown are pair of 5-3/8" h brass candlesticks, $385, and Hepplewhite bowfront mahogany shaving mirror, 23-3/4" h, $900. Photo courtesy of Garth's Auctions, Inc.

molded edge, case of four thumb-molded graduated drawers flanked by reeded quarter columns, ogee bracket feet on platforms, possibly orig brasses, refinished, 37-5/8" w, 22" d, 34-1/2" h **30,550.00**

Rhode Island, late 18th C, carved tiger maple, tall, cornice with dentil molding, case of seven graduated thumb-molded drawers, molded tall bracket base with central drop, top drawer with fan-carving, orig brasses, early surface, 38" w, 18-3/4" d, 63-3/4" h **27,600.00**

Chippendale to Hepplewhite Transitional, attributed to the Chapius family, CT, cherry, bowfront, line inlay around two-board top, four dovetailed drawers with beaded edging, reeded quarter columns, ogee feet with boldly scalloped returns, molded base, orig oval emb brasses, drawer glides fitted through the backboards and pegged, restorations to feet **17,160.00**

Chippendale-style, America, late 19th/early 20th C, black walnut, mahogany, pine secondary wood, two board top, five finely dovetailed drawers with beaded edges, two drawers with divided interiors, bracket base with thin molded edge, brass bale

Chest of drawers, Chippendale, New England, c1770-90, original red painted finish, cove molded dovetailed top, five graduated overlapping thumb molded drawers, high scroll cut bracket base, original brass bale handles, oval keyhole escutcheons, faint chalk signature on rear boards of top drawer "? Alexander," 38-1/4" w, 18" d, 45" h, $9,100. Photo courtesy of Cowan's Historic Americana Auctions.

pulls, wire nails, 42" w, 20" d, 41-1/2" h **900.00**

Classical

New England, 1825-30, bird's eye maple, rect top, case with projecting cock-beaded bird's-eye maple veneered drawers, above three graduated drawers with flanking engaged vase and ring-turned spiral carved columns continuing to turned feet, opalescent pattern glass pulls, refinished, 41" w, 20" d, 47-1/2" h **1,530.00**

Ohio, attributed to, 1830s, tiger and bird's-eye maple, backsplash above overhanging top, case with recessed panel sides, cock-beaded graduated drawers flanked by spiral carved columns and colonettes above dies, turned tapering legs and feet, shaped skirt, refinished, replaced glass pulls, imperfections, 46" w, 19-3/4" d, 57-1/4" h **2,000.00**

Eastlake, curly walnut, burl veneer, carved detail, scrolled crest, four dovetailed drawers, two handkerchief drawers, well detailed molded panel fronts, refinished, 39" w, 17-1/2" d, 46" h **750.00**

Empire

America, c1830, cherry, orig dark red flame graining over salmon ground on façade, worn orig red on sides, maple and poplar secondary woods, two-board top with old chip along back edge, serpentine pilasters on either side of four dovetailed drawers, old clear glass pulls, inset panels on ends, turned feet, age splits in top, 43" w, 22-5/8" d, 46-3/5" h . **500.00**

America, c1830, tiger maple, rect top, protruding frieze section fitted with single wide drawer over three drawers between applied half-round turnings, vase and ball turned feet, period round brass pulls, 42-1/2" w, 21-1/2" d, 44-1/2" h **2,750.00**

Maine, attributed to, cherry, mahogany veneer, pine secondary wood, two-board top with shaped back splash, four dovetailed drawers with orig brass pulls and key escutcheons, high crisply turned feet, refinished, veneer repairs, pulls cleaned with minor dents, 41-1/4" w, 20" d, 41-1/2" h **1,100.00**

Chest of drawers, Empire, attributed to western PA or OH, butler's, cherry, curly maple and pine, mahogany veneering, high scrolled broken crest, interior of top drawer with three solid curly maple drawers, five pigeon holes, two flat paper slots, paneled ends, with half turned and carved pilasters on either side of lower dovetailed drawers, carved hairy paw front feet, turned rear feet, original dark surface, 45-3/4" w, 22-3/4" d, 57-3/4" h, $1,100. Photo courtesy of Garth's Auctions, Inc.

Federal

America, bowfront, mahogany, flame mahogany veneer, pine secondary wood, old replaced top with biscuit corners, four dovetailed drawers with applied beading, replaced brass pulls, rope twist carvings on front pilasters, high boldly turned feet, refinished, pierced restorations, one rear foot replaced, 40-1/2" w, 19" d, 36-3/4" h **770.00**

Baltimore, MD, c1810, mahogany veneered and inlaid, serpentine, top with veneered edge overhangs conforming case of four graduated drawers outlined in narrow banding and stringing with ovolo corners, shaped skirt, flaring French feet connected to shaped sides, replaced brasses, old refinish, imperfections, 45-3/4" w, 22-1/4" d, 38" h **5,585.00**

Connecticut, attributed to, c1790-1810, cherry, rect overhanging top with string inlaid edge, case with four scratch-beaded graduated drawers, bracket base, replaced brasses, refinished, minor imperfections, 37-3/4" w, 19-1/2" d, 35" h **4,415.00**

Massachusetts, Boston area, early 19th C, bowfront, mahogany veneer, figured mahogany top with lunette inlaid edge overhangs case of four cock-beaded veneered graduated drawers, serpentine veneered skirt flanked by flaring French feet, drawers include cross banded mahogany veneer bone inlaid escutcheons, orig brasses, old refinish, veneer losses, 41-1/2" w, 22-1/2" d, 35-3/4" h **24,150.00**

Massachusetts or New Hampshire, late 18th/early 19th C, mahogany and mahogany veneer, bow front top with ovolo corners above engaged columns which have colonettes and reeding, flank cock-beaded drawers embellished with quarter-fan inlays, turned, swelled, tapering legs and feet, old refinish, imperfections, 43-3/4" w, 24" d, 41" h **4,420.00**

Middle Atlantic states, 1815-25, mahogany, mahogany veneer, and cherry, rect, top above case of four graduated, cock-beaded drawers, upper drawer with cross banded mahogany inlay, shaped veneered skirt, slightly flaring French feet, refinished, replaced brasses, restored, 44-1/4" w, 19-7/8" d, 45-1/2" h **2,115.00**

New England, southern, c1820, maple, bird's eye maple, and birch, rect top with scratch-beaded edge, rounded front corners, four scratch-beaded graduated drawers flanked by rounded reeded stiles, vase and ring-turned legs, refinished, replaced brasses, minor imperfections, 41" w, 20" d, 36-3/4" h **1,200.00**

New England, c1820-25, mahogany, birch, and bird's eye maple inlaid, rect top with ovolo corners, case with four drawers with bird's eye maple panels bordered by mahogany cross banding with flanking quarter engaged vase and ring-turned, spiral carved columns continuing to vase and ring-turned feet, replaced brasses, refinished, minor imperfections, 37" w, 19" d, 42" h **3,300.00**

New England, c1820-25, wavy birch, bird's eye maple, and mahogany veneer, overhanging rect top with scrolled backboard, case with four graduated drawers flanked by fluted pilasters, vase and ring-

Chest of drawers, Federal, cherry, bird's eye maple veneer, six dovetailed drawers, one with mahogany crossbanding, paneled ends, turned legs, refinished, top and turned pulls replaced, 43" w, 19-3/4" d, 46" h, $800. Also shown are pewter candlesticks, tumblers, teapot, and charger, Photo courtesy of Garth's Auctions, Inc.

turned legs, replaced pulls, refinished, imperfections, 41-1/2" w, 20" d, 40-1/2" h **1,775.00**

New Hampshire, c1790-1810, mahogany veneer inlaid and birch, overhanging top with swelled front, inlaid edge, conforming case of four cock-beaded and string inlaid graduated drawers on base of flaring French feet joined by shaped inlaid skirt centering contrasting rect drop panel bordered by inlay, old oval eagle brass pulls, old refinish, restoration, imperfections, 39" w, 21-1/4" d, 37-1/2" h **4,115.00**

Portsmouth or Greenland, New Hampshire, 1810-14, bow front, mahogany and flame birch veneer, bow front mahogany top with inlaid edge overhanging conforming case, four cock-beaded three-paneled drawers, divisions outlined with mahogany cross banded veneer and stringing above skirt, central veneered rect drop panel, high bracket feet joined by shaped side skirts, similar rear feet, turned pulls appear to be orig, old refinish, minor repairs, 40-1/4" w, 21-1/4" d, 39" h **28,750.00**

Rhode Island, c1800-10, maple, rect top, molded edge, case of four thumb-molded graduated drawers, valanced skirt joining shaped French feet, orig oval brasses, old refinish, imperfections, 42" w, 18-1/4" d, 38-3/4" h **1,765.00**

George III, 19th C, cross banded mahogany, serpentine, four graduated drawers, bracket feet, 36" w, 22-1/2" d, 31-1/2" h **3750.00**

George III-style, 19th C, mahogany, serpentine-front, thumb-molded top above four graduated and cock-beaded drawers, channel-carved bracket feet, 43" w, 24" d, 43" h
. . . . **4,415.00**

Hepplewhite

America, c1800, mahogany, straight front, four cock-beaded drawers, eagle-punched brasses, plain plant sides, bracket feet, shaped interiors, replaced top band, repairs to feet, lightly refinished, 42-1/2" w, 21" d, 37" h **1,550.00**

America, c1810, mahogany, poplar secondary wood, two-board top, four dovetailed drawers with beaded edges, older replaced emb brasses, scalloped fan inlay on lower apron, banding around lower case, French feet, refinished, restorations, replacements, 39" w, 19-3/4" d, 42-5/8" h **1,475.00**

Country, refinished pine, red stain, solid bird's eye maple drawer fronts with natural finish, four dovetailed drawers, cut out feet and apron, old brass knobs, age cracks in front feet, 37-3/4" w, 35-3/4" h
. . . . **1,100.00**

Chest of drawers, International Movement, George Nelson for Herman Miller, "Thin-Edge" rosewood veneer, five graduated drawers next to cabinet door of rare book-matched veneer, all with conical white pulls on brushed chrome tapering legs, Herman Miller foil label, 55-3/4" l, 18 1/2" d, 40-3/4" h, $5,500. Photo courtesy of David Rago Auctions.

Louis Philippe, second quarter 19th C, walnut, later rect top, conforming case fitted with three drawers, shaped bracket feet, 47" w, 20" d, 31" h . **425.00**

Queen Anne, Southeastern New England, c1700, painted oak, cedar, and yellow pine, rect top with applied edge, case of four drawers each with molded fronts, chamfered mitered borders, separated by applied horizontal moldings, sides with two recessed vertical molded panels above single horizontal panel, base with applied molding, four turned ball feet, old red paint, minor imperfections, 37-3/4" w, 20-1/2" w, 35" h . . **26,450.00**

Renaissance, Italian, walnut, composed of antique elements, fitted with three long drawers, foliate and shield shaped carved drawer pulls, paw feet, 36" w, 17" d, 37" h . . **2,450.00**

Sheraton, curly and straight grain maple, pine secondary wood, one board top, four dovetailed drawers with replaced brass pulls, reeded stiles, high well turned legs, refinished, couple of age splits on side panels, minor chips on feet, 41-1/2" w, 18-1/2" d, 41-1/2" h **2,100.00**

Victorian, American, poplar, mahogany veneer facade, serpentine top drawer, two serpentine stepback drawers, five dovetailed drawers, applied beading, worn finish, 40" w, 19-3/4" d, 47" h
. . . . **330.00**

William and Mary

American, burl veneer, bachelor's, five dovetailed drawers, pull-out shelf, worn finish, veneer damage,

Chest of drawers, Sheraton, bird's eye maple, cookie-corner top, four graduated drawers, decorative carved skirt, reeded front lead legs, high turned feet, refinished, 41" h x 41" w x 18" d, 41" h, $2,530. Photo courtesy of James D. Julia, Inc.

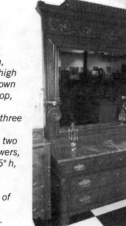

Chest of drawers, Victorian, walnut, high back, brown marble top, candle shelves, three small drawers, two long drawers, 56" w, 95" h, $1,800. Photo courtesy of Joy Luke Auctions.

replaced base molding, turned feet, and backboards, orig brasses, 30" w, 19" d, 35" h
. . . . **1,980.00**

Southern Massachusetts or Rhode Island, tiger maple, graduated drawer construction, two over four drawers, applied moldings to top and bottom, turned turnip feet, old grunge finish, three escutcheon plates present, rest of hardware missing, some repair, 36-1/4" w, 18-1/4" d, 48" h **2,950.00**

Chests of drawers, other

Apothecary, painted blue, 32 drawers, 96" l **2,900.00**

Bachelor, late George III, English, early 19th C, mahogany, rect top with molded edge, slide, four graduated cock-beaded drawers, bracket feet, veneer damage, restoration to feet, 37" l, 33-1/2" h **2,750.00**

Campaign, mahogany, pine secondary wood, brass trim, dovetailed case, int. with lift-out tray, one dovetailed drawer, some shrinkage to lid, 30-3/4" w, 18-1/4" d, 19" h **385.00**

Chamber, Federal, attributed to the Seymour Workshop, Boston, c1915, mahogany inlaid, rect top with inlaid edge overhangs case with single tripartite drawer above six smaller drawers flanking central cabinet on arched inlaid skirt, four turned reeded and tapering legs, similar arched side skirts, upper drawer with oval central stringing reserve, all drawers are outlined in ebonized inlay, missing dressing mirror from int. drawer, minor imperfections, 44-3/4" w, 19-1/2" d, 34-1/4" h **42,550.00**

Chest of drawers, other, bonnet, attributed to shop of Matthew Patton, Montgomery Co., Ohio, c1830, cherry, three drawers over three graduated drawers with central bonnet drawer, inlaid walnut panels on upper stiles, nicely scalloped apron, tapered Hepplewhite-style feet, original hidden till in base, turned walnut knobs with oval brass escutcheon plates, left foot slightly ended, old refinishing, original top reattached, 43-1/2" w, 18" d, 46-1/2" h, $1,475. Photo courtesy of Cowan's Historic Americana Auctions.

Chests of drawers, other, chest on chest, George II, English, c1780, mahogany and kingwood, banded, two small drawers over three graduated drawers in top section, base with three graduated long drawers, 43" w, 21-1/2" d, 70-1/2" h, $5,000. Photo courtesy of Sloan's Auctioneers & Appraisers.

Chest on Chest

Chippendale, Dunlap School, NH, c1770-80, cove molded cornice over case of four thumb-molded long drawers, upper with five short drawer façade centrally carved with pinwheel and fan motif, three graduated drawers below, lower case of four graduated long drawers, four short cabriole legs ending in ball and claw feet, centering central fan-carved drop, refinished, some orig red staining, possibly orig brasses, minor imperfections. **18,800.00**

George III, c1790, mahogany, upper section with dentil-molded cornice, fitted with three short over three long drawers, lower section fitted with three graduated long drawers, bracket feet, 43" w, 21" d, 67" h **7,000.00**

Queen Anne

Salem, MA, attributed to, c1740-60, tiger maple, upper case with molded cornice, five graduated thumb-molded drawers, lower case with one long drawer with two drawer façade, and one long drawer with three short drawer façade, centrally caved fan, four arris cabriole legs with high pad feet on platforms, joined by cyma-curved skirt centering scrolled drops, possibly old brasses, old refinish, minor imperfections, 38-3/4" w, 19-1/2" d, 73-3/4" h **16,450.00**

Southern NH, late 19th C, maple, upper case with cove molded cornice, five graduated thumb-molded drawers, lower case with three graduated drawers, valanced frame joining four short cabriole legs on high pad on platform feet, old refinish, replaced brasses, drawers with chalk and pencil inscriptions, vestiges of old red paint, minor imperfections, 40-1/2" w, 20" d, 80" h... **11,750.00**

Chest on Frame

Queen Anne, Connecticut, 1740-70, painted, flaring cornice with cove molding, case of thumb-molded drawers, arranged in two over four graduating pattern, frame with vigorously scrolling front and side skirts joined to cabriole legs with arris knees, arris disc feet, old red repaint, imperfections, 40" w, 23-1/4" d, 63-1/2" h **9,200.00**

Queen Anne-style, English, walnut and burl veneer, mahogany secondary wood, case with four dovetailed drawers, brass teardrop pulls, cabriole legs, duck feet, 20th C, 19-1/4" x 33-1/2" base, 38-1/2" h **825.00**

Commode

Biedermeier, north Germany or Scandinavia, c1840, pearwood, stepped rect top, three drawers, shaped apron, 35" w, 20" d, 31" h **2,000.00**

Directorie, c1800, fruitwood, rect to, two long drawers, sq tapered legs, restored, 36-1/2" w, 32" h **2,500.00**

French Provincial, Neoclassical, early 19th C, gray and white mottled marble top, conforming case fitted with three drawers, sq tapered legs, 44" w, 21" d, 34-1/2" h **2,300.00**

Louis XV-style, 19th C, marquetry, gilt bronze mounts, bombe, serpentine molded edge marble top, exotic wood floral marquetry on rosewood panels, mahogany cross banding, two drawers, legs ending in scroll and cabochon cast sabots, 53" w, 22" d, 33" h ... **1,350.00**

Victorian, walnut, carved pilasters, open scrolling and leaves, three graduated drawers with fruit carved pulls, light refinishing, back splash missing, 36" w, 19" d, 32" h **400.00**

Credenza

Chippendale-style, Kittinger, mahogany and mahogany veneer, oak secondary wood, four dovetailed drawers down left, smaller center drawer with cabinet below, longer drawer over open compartment flanking on right with adjustable shelf, molded edge and base trip, branded label, emb metallic emblem in drawer, 81-1/2" l, 19-1/2" d, 30" h **900.00**

Chests of drawers, other, lowboy, Queen Anne/George II, walnut, figured veneer, three drawers, small center drawer flanked on each side by one square drawer, restored, replaced handles, 26" l, 15-1/4" d, 28-3/4" h, $2,650. Photo courtesy of James D. Julia, Inc.

Highboy

Chippendale, associated with John Goddard and Job Townsend, Newport, RI, 1760-80, carved mahogany, enclosed scrolled pediment centering fluted plinth surrounded by urns and flame finials above two applied plaques over two short and three long graduated thumb molded drawers, set into lower case of one long and three short drawers above cyma curved skirt, centered carved shell, frontal cabriole legs ending in ball and claw feet, similar rear legs ending in pad feet, old replaced brasses, refinished, repairs, 39" w, 20-1/2" d, 84" h **36,550.00**

Chippendale-style, America, late 19th/early 20th C, mahogany, broken arch pediment, flame finials, reeded quarter columns at corners, inset panels on either end of top, eight dovetailed drawers with brass pulls, gadrooning around base and edges of base and lower section, cabriole legs with scrolled returns, raised acanthus leaf carvings, claw and ball feet, old reddish brown finish, 48-1/2" w, 24-1/4" d, 81" h **1,200.00**

Chest of drawers, other, tall, Hepplewhite, cherry, curly maple banding on front of top, four dovetailed drawers with ivory stringing with invected corners, shaped apron with oval inlay medallion, high French feet, old worn varnish finish, original oval brasses with embossed flowers and foliage, edge damage, old repairs, 36" w, 20-3/4" d, 43-1/2" h, $3,500. Also shown are two brass chambersticks, $135 each, and mahogany writing box with one dovetailed drawer, original brass bail, fitted interior, writing surface recovered in green felt, $615. Photo courtesy of Garth's Auctions, Inc.

Queen Anne

America, cherry, poplar and pine secondary wood, top dovetailed case, circular fan at top, replaced molded cornice, seven graduated drawers on top, four drawers on base, base with pegged construction, molded trim on dovetailed drawers, carved fan at lower center, scalloped aprons, shaped returns, well shaped cabriole legs, pad feet, mellow refinish, replaced bat wing brasses, pierced restorations to some drawer fronts, replaced returns and waist molding, 35" w top, 40" w base, 22" d, 71-1/2" h **6,200.00**

Connecticut, attributed to, c1760-80, cherry and maple, broken arch pediment with three flame finials on fluted plinths, upper case with fan carved thumb-molded short drawer flanked by two shaped short drawers, four graduated long drawers, lower case with long drawer over two short drawers flanking fan carved drawer, carved scrolling skirt joining four cabriole legs, pad feet, replaced brasses and finials, old refinish, repairs and imperfections, 38-1/4" w, 19" d, 86" h **24,675.00**

Dunlap School, NH, c1770-80, carved maple, cove-molded cornice over upper case of five graduated long drawers, lower case of three graduated thumb-molded long drawers, upper and lowermost drawers each fan carved, cyma-curved skirt centering scrolling drops, joining four cabriole legs with shaped returns, pad feet on platforms, dark stained surface, possibly orig brasses, minor imperfections, chalk inscriptions on drawer backs, 39-1/4" w, 21-1/2" d, 78-3/4" h **14,100.00**

Massachusetts or southern New Hampshire, 1760-80, tiger maple, flaring cornice above four thumb-molded drawers on lower case of one long drawer and three small drawers, the central one with fan carving above three flat-headed arches, cabriole legs, high pad feet, replaced brasses, refinished, minor imperfections, 37-3/4" w at mid molding, 19-5/8" d at mid-molding, 72" h .. **16,450.00**

North Shore, MA, 18th C, maple, flaring cove-molded cornice with concealed drawer above four thumb-molded graduated drawers in upper case over mid-molding, two long drawers, lower case visually divided into three drawers centering by carved fan over cyma-curved side skirts, cabriole legs and high pad feet, old surface, old brasses, imperfections, 35-1/2" w, 17-5/8" d, 71" h **31,050.00**

Rhode Island, c1730-60, attributed to Abram Utter, tiger maple and cherry, top section with flat molded cornice, case of two thumb-molded short drawers, three long drawers, lower section with projecting molding above case of central thumb-molded short drawer flanked by deeper drawers, four arris cabriole legs, pad feet, all joined to deeply valanced skirt with applied cock beading and two turned drop pendants, replaced brasses, old refinish, minor imperfections, 37" w, 19-1/4" d, 63-3/4" h **29,375.00**

Chest of drawers, other, tall chest, Pennsylvania or Maryland, 1830s, red stained cherry, cove-molded cornice, case of eight cock-beaded drawers flanked by triple beading in recessed panel continuing to beaded skirt on turned tapering legs, original brass with stalks of wheat, early dark red stained surface, minor surface imperfections, 44-1/2" w cornice, 40-5/8" w case, 22-1/2" d, 65-3/4" h, $2,950. Photo courtesy of Skinner's Auctioneers and Appraisers.

William and Mary-style, 18th C, cross banded walnut, upper section with two short over three long drawers, base with three drawers on trumpet turned legs, 40" w, 21" d, 69" h **1,850.00**

Liquor Chest, early 19th century, mahogany veneer, chest with brass swing handles opens to reveal compartmented int., 12 blown molded wine and spirit bottles, each with inscribed paper labels and dec with gilt flowers, bowknots, and borders about the neck and shoulders, lift out tray fitted with tumblers, funnel and stemware with similar gilt decoration, one tumbler cracked, some veneer loss, 17" w, 12-1/2" d, 11-1/2" h **1,410.00**

Lowboy, Rhode Island, maple, pine secondary wood, case dovetailed at rear, pegged at sides, old replaced two-board curly maple top, four dovetailed drawers with beaded edges, batwing brasses, scalloped aprons, cabriole legs, slipper feet, refinished, small insect holes, restorations with some alterations, 32-1/2" w, 22-1/2" d, 30-1/4" h **1,760.00**

Mule chest, New England, pine, old dry red paint, one board top with shaped edge, wire hinges, bootjack ends with wooden peg construction, dovetailed drawer in base with molded edge, turned wooden pulls, slight warp to top, 38" w, 19-1/4" d, 35" h **1,350.00**

Spice

Ohio, attributed to, walnut, poplar secondary wood, mortised and paneled front door, small brass pull, three drawers with orig turned walnut pulls, turned feet, 14-1/2" w, 12-1/4" d, 18-3/4" h **2,400.00**

Pennsylvania, 1780-1800, walnut, dovetailed, cove-molded cornice, raised panel hinged door, opens to int. of 11 small drawers, brass pulls, molded base, old surface, 15-1/2" w, 11" d, 18-1/4" h
. . . . **14,950.00**

Tall, Federal, New England, late 18th C, tiger maple, cove molded top, case with six thumb-molded drawers, central fan carved drop pendant flanked by high bracket feet, orig brasses, old refinish, repairs, 41" w, 54-5/8" h
. . . . **8,625.00**

Wardrobe, Classical, mid Atlantic states, 1840, mahogany veneer, two recessed panel doors, similar sides, int. with veneered drawers, base with platform feet, small int. drawers added, 65" w, 26" d, 79-1/2" h **3,200.00**

*Hooded cradle, mahogany, cut-out rockers, dovetailed case, scrolled detail on foot and hood, pine bottom board, brass end handles, old finish, old repairs, 44" l, **$1,210**. Also shown is serpentine wire gilt and brass fireplace fender, **$660**. Photo courtesy of Garth's Auctions, Inc.*

Cradles

Chippendale-style, birch, canted sides, scalloped headboard, turned posts and rails, refinished, 37-1/2" l
. . . . **400.00**

Country

America, Tiger maple, dovetailed, heart cut-outs, large rockers, 36" l, 26" w, 16" h **675.00**

New England, 18th C, painted pine, arched hood continuing to shaped and carved dovetailed sides, rockers, old light green paint, old repairs, 40" l **300.00**

Pennsylvania, late 18th C, dovetailed, refinished curly maple, cut-out hearts, age cracks and shrinkage, 41" l **550.00**

Eastlake, 1875, walnut, paneled headboard, footboard, and sides, scrolling crest above short turned spindles, platform support, orig finish, dated **495.00**

Rustic, twig construction, rocker base, unsigned, 33" l, 22" d, 22" h
. . . . **120.00**

Victorian, cast iron, painted black, wooden slat bottom, finial missing, 37" l, 21" d, 36" h **200.00**

Windsor, New England, c1800-20, bamboo turned spindles, worn finish **850.00**

Cupboards

Armoire

Arts & Crafts, English, single-door, overhanging top supported by corbels, mirror, emb copper panels of stylized flowers, unmarked, refinished, new back and shelves, one corbel missing, 40" w, 18" d, 75" h **1,050.00**

Classical, New York, c1835, mahogany, bold projecting molded Roman arch cornice, two paneled doors flanked by tapered veneered columns, ogee bracket feet, 74" w, 31" d, 94" h **3,200.00**

Empire-style, Continental, early 19th C, mahogany, shaped cornice above two paneled doors opening to shelves, ribbed lunette-shaped feet, 42" w, 17" d, 74" h . . **1,610.00**

Louis XV/XVI-style, transitional, 19th C, kingwood and parquetry, molded marble top with serpentine sides, pair of doors, each with two shaped and quarter-veneered flush panels, serpentine sides, coated stiles with gilt-brass chutes, sq-section cabriole legs joined by shaped skirt, stamped "Dubreuil," 44" w, 18-1/2" d, 59" h **950.00**

Restoration, New York, c1830, mahogany, flat top with cornice molding, two doors, birds' eye maple lined int., concealed drawer below, ribbed blocked feet, 56" w, 19-1/2" d, 90" h **2,800.00**

Victorian, American, c1840, walnut, bold double ogee molded cornice, two arched paneled doors, shelved int., plinth base, ogee bracket feet, 62" w, 24" d, 89" h **1,400.00**

Bee keeper's hutch, Canadian, pine, orig red and black painted top panel, paneled door on lower front, door on either end, drop front covers interior workshelf, hinged lid, pegged construction, lid marked "Patent Union, Bee Hive, W. Phelps Pat." 47" w, 19" d, 43-1/4" h **750.00**

Chifforobe, Art Deco, 1935, herringbone design waterfall veneer, arched center mirror, dropped center section, four deep drawers flanked by tall cupboard doors, shaped apron
. . . . **450.00**

CORNICE — PLATE GROOVES — TOP — MIDSECTION MOLDING — BASE — DOORS — FEET

Typical Parts of a Cupboard

Cupboard, armoire, Victorian, walnut with burl veneer, bold cornice molding, three column front case with two arched beveled glass mirrored doors, two drawer base with raised panel, take-down construction, interior contains bird's eye panels and fitted shelves, loss to upper right portion of door, 66" w, 24-1/2" d, 90-1/2" h, $2,200. Photo courtesy of Sanford Alderfer Auction Company.

Chimney, decorated, poplar, pine shelves, ash backboards, orig dark red over lighter red dec, one door with four panes of glass at top over two raised panels, white mullions, white porcelain knob, surface wear, doors have restoration at hinges, price for pr
. . . .**2,365.00**

Corner

Blind door, painted, c1830, pine, blind door, bird's eye maple paint dec, two paneled doors, base with two paneled doors, bracket feet, 29" w, 83" h. **2,750.00**

One piece, Chippendale, Southern states, 1760s, pine, heavy projecting cornice molding above arched molded surround, flanking similarly shaped raised panel doors opening to two shelves above two additional fielded panel doors, flanked by fluted pilasters, opening to single serpentine shelf, refinished, hardware replaced, repairs, 64" w, 30" d, 93-3/4" h
. . . .**7,475.00**

One piece, paneled pine, New England, 19th C, flat ogee molded cornice, arched opening flanks three painted scalloped shelves, two fielded panel cupboard doors,

single int. shelf, old refinish on ext., old red color on shelves, 50" w, 20" d, 88" h **4,255.00**

Two piece, cherry, two doors, orig six wavy glass panes over two doors with four tin panels punch dec with cornflower motif, replacement wooden knobs, repairs, restoration, refinished. **1,425.00**

Two piece, Lancaster County, PA, cherry, documented to Jacob Kintz family, East Stroudsburg, PA, c1810-20, broken arch, molded cornice terminating in rosettes, center plinth with flame finial, fluted quarter columns, arched doors with molded mullions, orig glass, yellow int. with shaped shelves, spoon slots, double plat rails, 39" w, 90" h **14,800.00**

Two piece, painted, c1790, green, architectural design, fluted pilasters, arched doors, 52" w, 93" h **19,500.00**

Corner cupboard, Berks or Lebanon County, PA, c1850, red grain decorated, smoke decorated 12 light door, turned feet, square stepped out column, interior painted blue, two shelves with spoon cut-outs, 32" corner, 7'6" h, $4,950. Photo courtesy of Sanford Alderfer Auction Company.

Court, European, oak, two-pc, mortised construction, top section with two doors and central panel

Incised diamonds and pinwheels, free standing turned pilasters on either side, scrollwork with date "16MIVI" below cornice, two doors with three inset panels each on lower case doors and ends separated by molded T-shaped cross pieces, well executed replaced scrolled wrought iron butterfly hinges, old dark finish, restorations, old alterations, age splits, 63" w, 19-1/4" d, 62-1/2" h
. . . .**2,950.00**

Relief flowers, scrolled vining, matching vining below cornice, leaf and arch carvings across center, three inset panels each on lower case doors and ends separated by molded T-shaped cross pieces, well executed replaced scrolled wrought iron butterfly hinges, old dark finish, restorations, old alterations, 49-1/2" w, 20-1/8" d, 67" h. **1,200.00**

Kas, pine and poplar, old mustard paint, stepped and cove molded cornice, mortise construction on raised panel doors, sq nails in case, dovetailed drawer in base with applied molding around edges, original brass pulls, bracket feet with scalloped returns, molded base, eight turned clothing pegs on int., 42" w, 20" d, 67" h, $880. Photo courtesy of Garth's Auctions, Inc.

Desk top, New England, pine, old grain painted dec, two solid doors with relief carved vertical panels, brass hinges, moldings at top and bottom, shaped feet are extensions of case, 10 cubby holes in int., orig green paint on ext. and int., 29" w, 12" d, 27-1/4" h ... **1,750.00**

Hanging, attributed to PA, first half 19th C, pine, orig red translucent stain flat overhanging cornice above hinged door with two recessed panels opening to shelves, applied beveled base, 24" w, 9-3/4" d, 30-1/2" h...... **775.00**

Jelly, pine, old dark red over orange grained dec, one paneled front door, orig brass pull, turn buckle near top, shaped bracket feet with cut-outs on ends of base, three int. shelves, top right end of top board and back splash missing, 37" w, 14" d, 53-1/2" h . **550.00**

Kas, Long Island, NY, c1730-80, cherry, pine, and polar, architectural cornice molding, two raised panel thumb-molded doors flanked by reeded pilasters, applied moldings, single drawer, painted detachable disc and stretcher feet, replaced hardware, refinished, restored, 65-1/2" w, 26-1/4" d, 77-1/4" h........ **4,500.00**

Kitchen, orig blue paint, six center drawers with porcelain pulls, two side bins, one bin lid sgd "Ezra Woodside Montare, April 20, 1905," cutting board, continuous scalloped face board covering lower front and feet, back

shaped like picket fence, 72" l, 21" d, 54" h...................... **7,200.00**

Linen press, Federal, Boston, 1820-25, mahogany veneer, three parts, veneered entablature with central rect outlined in stringing above veneered frieze, pair of recessed panel doors which open to five pull-out drawers with shaped sides, lower case with molding and three cock-beaded drawers, flaring high bracket feet, inlaid escutcheons, orig brasses, feet restored, surface imperfections, 48" w, 22-1/4" h, 83-1/2" h **6,900.00**

Miniature, hanging, step-back, cherry and poplar, well executed step-down cornice, two paneled doors at top, divided interior, shaped shelves, paneled sides, molded base with five drawers, turned wooden pull on larger drawer to left of four stacked small drawers with brass pulls, all with applied border moldings, wire nail construction, minor base chips, 17-1/2" w, 11-1/4" d, 33" h **1,650.00**

Pewter, two part, top: cornice molding, two six-glass pane doors, two shelves, open pie shelf; base: two drawers over raised panel doors, one shelf int., short turned feet, 56" w, 20" d, 87" h **2,250.00**

Pie safe

Paint decorated, attributed to Shenandoah Valley, poplar, old

Pie safe, southeastern United States, early 19th C, walnut, rectangular top above long drawer and two hinged cupboard doors, each with two pierced tin panels with designs of hearts and initials "J.B." flanked by leafy branches, ends with three conforming decorated panels, square tapering legs, refinished, minor imperfections, 39-1/2" w, 17" d, 49-1/2" h, $5,300. Photo courtesy of Skinner's Auctioneers and Appraisers.

worn blue paint on front, reddish-brown on sides, areas of earlier mustard paint, 12 punched tins, well-executed pots of flowers with scrolled handles, diagonal line punched borders, double doors, one drawer in base, high sq legs, few tins damaged, 38" w, 16-3/4" d, 54-1/2" h **2,300.00**

Poplar, 12 punched tins, three tins in each side, matching doors on front, punched stars surrounded by circles, three-line borders with corner fans, dovetailed drawer in base, turned wooden pulls, areas of pitting on some of the tins, old finish, front lightly cleaned, 41-1/2" w, 17-1/2" d, 57-1/4" h **1,000.00**

Southeastern United States, early 19th C, walnut, rect top above along drawer, two hinged cupboard doors each with two pierced tin panels with designs of hearts and initials "J.B." flanked by leafy branches, ends with three conforming decorated panels, sq tapering legs, refinished, minor imperfections, 39-1/2" w, 17" d, 49-1/2" h **5,300.00**

Slant back, New England, late 18th C, pine, flat molded cornice above beaded canted front flanking shelves, projecting base with single raised panel door, old refinish, doors missing from top, imperfections, 37-1/2" w, 18" d, 73" h.................... **2,300.00**

Spice, northern Europe, last half 18th C, wall-type, painted, flat molded cornice, hinged cupboard door, molded recessed panel opening, compartmentalized int., molded base, old dark green paint bordered by red, int. drawers missing, imperfections, 16" w, 8" d, 17" h........... **1,500.00**

Step-back, wall

America, Empire, c1830, mahogany and mahogany veneer, molded cornice top, three eight-light doors, adjustable shelves, cabinet base with three cupboard doors, sliding center doors in top and base, 73-1/2" w, 21" d, 93" h ...**11,100.00**

Pennsylvania, attributed to, one piece, curly maple, mellow golden color, two mortised and paneled doors on top, one int. shelf, two board top with high pie shelf, five dovetailed drawers in base in three-over-two configuration, turned legs with excellent figure, replaced brass pulls, one glued

Linen press, Gothic-style, English, 19th C, carved walnut, paneled construction, hand carved linen fold panels, two matching linen fold carved doors with hand wrought iron strap hinges, two drawers deeply carved with Gothic-style floral and arches, front corner stiles ornamented with four wrought iron rosettes, 71" l, 20" w, 59" h, $1,725. Photo courtesy of Jackson's International Auctioneers & Appraisers.

break on the lower corner of door, 44-1/2" w, 19-1/2" d, 60-1/4" h **8,525.00**

Pennsylvania or Ohio, attributed to, 1830-40, painted cherry, flaring cornice molding above fluted frieze, pair of glazed doors open to two-shelf int., flanked by fluting above stepped out surface, two drawers over two recessed panel doors opening to single shelf int., recessed panel sides, four short turned legs, all over red paint, brass pulls, imperfections, 50" w, 21-1/2" d, 88" h **18,400.00**

Storage, Montgomery County, PA, poplar, dovetailed case, molded top, two paneled doors, French bracket feet, int. shelves, scraped finish down to red, replaced back boards, moldings, 49" w, 18" d, 72" h **1,100.00**

Wall

America, two pieces, pine and walnut, old mustard paint and faint brown grain dec, traces of earlier red in some areas, brown sponging to three curved front drawers and on raised panels of lower doors, cove molded cornice, two-door top with six panes of glass in each door, vertical central panel with three panels, all top panes are tombstone shaped, chamfered corners, turned feet with applied half turned pilasters, blue painted

Wardrobe, Renaissance Revival, c1875, burled walnut, three arched doors, step out center, 84" w, 28" d, 100" h, $3,080. Photo courtesy of Fontaine's Auction Gallery.

int. with cut-outs for spoons, 61" w, 21" d, 85-3/4" h 5,500.00

Canadian, Hepplewhite, two pieces, pine, beveled and cove molded cornice, two doors in top section with two panes of glass each, two int. shelves with red and white paint, molded waist, five drawers in base with incised beading, turned wooden pulls, well scalloped base, high bracket feet, refinished, evidence of earlier red paint, edge chips, couple of glued splits to feet, 48" w, 23-1/2" d, 78-1/2" h **935.00**

Jacobean, oak and part painted, two parts, upper section with pegs and shelves, projecting lower section with two doors, each with geometric and floral carving, 64" w, 20" d, 80" h **3,000.00**

New England, late 18th C, painted pine, molded cornice, two scalloped shelves, raised panel door, three-shelved interior, old blue paint, 33-3/4" w, 26-1/4" d, 75-1/2" h, minor imperfections **24,150.00**

New England, early 19th C, painted pine and cherry, rect case, single door with four recessed panels, scratch-beaded left edge, int. of 21 scratch-beaded drawers, seven compartments of assorted sizes, sides of case continuing to shaped cut-out feet, early red paint, minor imperfections, 27-3/4" w, 11-1/4" d, 59" h **4,370.00**

New York, upstate, early 19th C, painted, flat cornice, case with two hinged doors each with two recessed vertical panels, shelved int., old gray paint, imperfections, 43" w, 18" d, 78" h **1,000.00**

Wardrobe, Ohio, unknown maker, curly maple, broad striped figure, walnut, maple, ash, and pine secondary woods, wooden peg and nail construction, broad cove molded cornice, two paneled doors, double end panels with chamfered edge detail, scalloped base aprons, two drawers in base, int. shelf near top, mellow brown refinish, orig architectural cupboard, back boards and cornice added later, 60" w, 21-3/4" d, 84" h **2,100.00**

Desks

Aesthetic Movement, Herter Brothers, Washburn Commission, mahogany, fall front, top section: shelf with gallery top

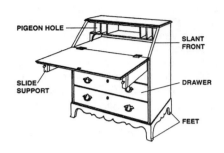

PIGEON HOLE
SLANT FRONT
SLIDE SUPPORT
DRAWER
FEET

Typical Parts of a Desk

supported by turned and blocked posts, back panel with dec gold threaded material; middle section: slant lid, two supporting pull-out arms, central panel of marquetry inlaid with garland of flowers ending in bows, int. with two drawers, five cubbyholes, supported by two turned front legs, two bottom section with shelf and paneled back, missing orig writing surface, raised panel back, needs restoration, commissioned by Hon. William Drew Washburn for MN Greek Revival house, copy of orig bill of sale, 30" w, 20" w, 53-1/2" h **9,000.00**

Art Deco, Leopold Corp, Burlington, IA, walnut veneered, semi-oval top over center drawer flanked by pull-out writing surface and two drawers, bronze handles, light brown finish, "Charles S. Nathan Office Equipment New York" distributor's metal tag in drawer, veneer loss, wear, 66-1/8" l, 36-1/8" d, 29" h **900.00**

Arts & Crafts, Stickley, Gustav, Syracuse, NY, lady's, c1912, model no. 720, cabinet with four vertical shelves,

Desk, Arts & Crafts, Rittencraft, single drawer with copper drop pulls, two open bookshelves on each side with rectangular cut-out panels to front and back, decal mark, original finish, some looseness, 42" l, 26 w", 30" h, $650. Photo courtesy of David Rago Auctions.

Desk, Arts & Crafts, Gustav Stickley, drop-front, gallery top, paneled door over single drawer with cast bronze pulls, and lower shelf, original finish, large red decal, 25-3/4", 15" d, 47-1/4" h, $4,025. Photo courtesy of David Rago Auctions.

two small drawers, three horizontal shelves, rect top, two short drawers, paper Craftsman label, 38" w, 23" d, 37" h **1,725.00**

Chippendale

Connecticut, late 18th C, mahogany, block front, slant front lid, fitted tiered int. with nine dovetailed drawers, pigeonholes, two pull-out letter drawers with fluted columns, flame-carved finials and door with blocking and fan carving, dovetailed case, four dovetailed drawers, conforming apron, bracket feet, replaced brasses, old refinishing, feet replaced, repairs to case, 41-3/4" w, 21-1/2" d, 42-3/4" h **3,850.00**

Massachusetts, Marblehead, c1770-80, slant lid, mahogany, thumb-molded slant lid, stepped interior of shell carved drawer above two concave drawers flanked by document drawers with baluster fronts flanked by four valanced compartments, two blocked drawers, above two drawers centering carved shell, cock-beaded case of four thumb-molded graduated drawers, cut-out bracket feet, brasses appear orig, old mellow surface, minor repairs, 38" w, 20" d, 44-1/2" h **30,550.00**

Massachusetts, c1770-80, slant lid, mahogany, lid opens to int. of central fan, concave caved drawer, two conforming drawers flanked by document drawers with half-baluster fronts, four valanced compartments, two drawers, cock-beaded case of four graduated drawers, ogee bracket feet, center drop pendant, old brass bail pulls, refinished, imperfections, 40" w, 20" d, 43" h **9,400.00**

Massachusetts, Salem, 1780-1800, oxbow, carved mahogany, slant lid opens to int. of small drawers and valanced compartments flanking central fan-carved drawer with two others below, all with end-blocking, above case of reverse serpentine drawers with cock-beaded surrounds, heavy molded base with central fan carved pendant, shaped ogee bracket feet ending in platforms, original brasses, minor imperfections, 41-1/2" w, 22-1/2" d, 44" h **17,625.00**

Massachusetts, attributed to, late 18th C, slant lid, maple, lid opens to int. of two central valanced compartments and concave carved drawer flanked by four valanced compartments with scrolled dividers above two drawers, case of four thumb-molded drawers, bracket feet, orig brasses, old finish, imperfections, 36-1/4" w, 19" d, 42" h **4,700.00**

New England, 18th C, slant lid, maple, pine secondary wood, dovetailed case, stepped interior with six drawers, blocked fronts, fan carving on top three, four pigeon holes, two dovetailed drawers on lower tier, four dovetailed drawers with molded trim, replaced batwing brasses and lock escutcheons, bracket feet with scalloped returns, molded base, refinished, some restorations, 36" w, 20" d, 41-1/4" h. . . . **3,575.00**

Rhode Island, late 18th C, cherry, slant front, stepped int. of small drawers, central one with shaping, case of beaded graduated drawers, ogee bracket feet, orig brasses, old refinish, restoration, 39" w, 20" d, 43" h **3,800.00**

Chippendale-style, Kittinger, mahogany and mahogany veneers, oak

secondary wood, four dovetailed drawers on both sides, center drawer, thing applied moldings create decorative panels on sides and front, shaped bracket feet, molding around bases, emb metallic label, 72" w, 36-1/4" d, 30-1/2" h **1,695.00**

Eastlake, lady's, walnut, two parts, top section sits on pegs, top: mirror with two columns supported shelves, fancy carving, pressed dec; base section: double hinged writing surface with dec floral carving, writing surface with two panels of green felt, lifts to reveal compartment desk int. with two drawers, one side fitted with two long drawers, gallery shelf in base, dec applied pieces, shoe foot base, metal asters, 31-1/2" w, 19" d, 57" h. **1,150.00**

Edwardian, c1900, kneehole, mahogany, rect cross banded top with central oval medallion, front canted corners, long frieze drawer, two banks of three drawers, center cupboard door, foliate marquetry dec, 37-1/2" w, 31" h **600.00**

Edwardian-style, 20th C, marquetry inlaid mahogany, U-shaped superstructure fitted with drawers and doors, serpentine case fitted with drawers, sq tapered legs, 35" w, 24" d, 37" h **2,645.00**

Empire, butler's, cherry and curly maple, poplar secondary wood, scrolled crest with turned rosettes, pull-out desk drawer with arched pigeon holes and three dovetailed drawers, three dovetailed drawers with applied edge beading, turned and carved pilasters, paneled ends, paw feet, old finish, some edge damage, 44-1/2" w, 23" d, 57-3/4" h . . . **1,925.00**

Federal

America, butler's, mahogany and mahogany veneer, rect top, case of three cock-beaded short drawers, pull-out desk with cock-beaded drawer façade flanked by wide drawers opening to prospect door over short drawer flanked by document drawer, two short drawers, two compartments, one long drawer, allover pull-out shelf, three graduated cock-beaded long drawers, cut-out feet joined by shaped skirt, old refinish, 47" w, 19" d, 45-1/2" h **1,300.00**

Massachusetts, North Shore, 1795-1815, mahogany, inlaid, reverse serpentine, the slant lid opens to int. of small drawers, valanced compartments which flank the inlaid prospect door with cross banded inlay opening to three small drawers, case of four graduated cock-beaded drawers, top one arched, shaped bracket feet, original brasses, old surface, repairs and losses, 41-3/4" w, 23-5/8" d, 43" h **5,300.00**

Massachusetts, eastern, c1800-10, tambour, mahogany and mahogany veneer inlaid, upper section with tambour doors flanked by pilasters with chevron inlay enclosing two short drawers over three valanced compartments centering prospect door with inlaid stringing enclosing two short drawers over double valanced compartments, lower section with folding lid over case of two cock-beaded string inlaid long drawers, legs inlaid with bellflowers and stringing tapering to inlaid cuffs, old replaced brasses, old refinish, blue painted int., repairs and imperfections, 38" w, 19-1/4" d, 34-1/2" h **11,750.00**

New England, early 19th C, mahogany and mahogany veneer inlaid, top section shaped gallery above flat molded cornice, two glazed doors enclosing compartments and drawer, flanking door and small drawer; projecting base with fold-out writing surface, two cock-beaded short drawers, two graduated long drawers, four sq tapering legs, inlaid cross-banding, old refinish, some restoration, inscribed "22 Geo. L. Deblois Sept. 12th 1810," 37-1/8" w, 20" d, 51-1/2" **3,000.00**

New Hampshire, early 19th C, slant lid, wavy birch, lid opens to two-stepped int. case of drawers with four cock-beaded surrounds, serpentine skirt, tall arched feet, orig brasses, old refinish, repairs, 37-1/2" w, 18-1/4" d, 45" h . **2,760.00**

New York State, early 19th C, mahogany veneer inlaid, slant lid and three graduated drawers outlined in stringing with ovolo corners, int. of veneer and outline stringing on drawers, valanced compartments, prospect door opening to inner compartments and drawers, flanking document drawers, orig brasses, old surface, veneer cracking loss and patching,

other surface imperfections, 41-1/2" w, 21-1/2" d, 44" h **2,550.00**

Pennsylvania, early 19th C, walnut inlaid, slant front, lid and cock-beaded drawers outlined in stringing, base with band of contrasting veneers, int. of small drawers above valanced compartments, scrolled dividers flanking prospect door which opens to two small drawers, three drawers, old refinish, repairs, 40" w, 20" d, 44-1/2" h **3,550.00**

George III, c1780, mahogany, slant lid, int. fitted with drawers, pigeonholes and door, case fitted with four graduated drawers, bracket feet, 42" w, 22" d, 43" h **2,250.00**

George III-style, partner's, third quarter, 19th C, burl elm, rect top, gold tooled green leather writing surface, molded edge, four cross banded cock-beaded frieze drawers, two banks of three cross banded cock-beaded and opposing cupboard doors, plinth base, 72" w, 31" h **2,875.00**

Hepplewhite, America, cherry, slant front, dovetailed case, four dovetailed drawers with edge beading, fitted int. with eight dovetailed drawers, two letter drawers and center door, scrolled apron, French feet, replaced brasses, old mellow refinishing, old pieced repairs, 41-1/2" w, 19" d, 35" h writing surface, 46" h **3,350.00**

Desk, Hepplewhite-style, English, lady's, mahogany, boxwood line inlay, slide out writing surface, back compartment covered by tambour roll hiding four small drawers and four cubby holes, lift top storage area on each side, two drawers, tapered square legs, brass furniture label "Colonial Manf. Co," 32" w, 20" d, 35" h, $690. Photo courtesy of James D. Julia, Inc.

Queen Anne

America, early 18th C, cross banded walnut, slat front, fitted int. of wells and drawers, three frieze drawers, cabriole legs, pad feet . . . **5,750.00**

Northern Maine, 19th C, maple, slant front, int. with valanced compartments above small drawers, end drawers separated by scrolled dividers, case of three thumb-molded drawers, molded bracket base with central drop pendant, old darkened surface, 35-1/2" w, 17-1/2" d, 40-1/4" h **5,175.00**

Vermont, c1750, tiger maple and cherry, slant front, int. with central fan-carved drawer, two valanced compartments flanked by molded document drawers, four valanced compartments, three drawers, case with four thumb-molded graduated drawers, bracket feet, replaced brasses, old refinish, imperfections, and repairs, 36" w, 18" d, 41-1/2" h **3,220.00**

Regency, English, c1850, lady's, cylinder, mahogany, tambour top, fitted int., slide-out writing surface, over two drawers, lyre base, 30" h writing surface, 35-1/2" w, 20" d, 38" h **3,000.00**

Desk, Windsor, small desk on frame, slant front, two part desk, seven interior pigeon hole compartments, natural finish, on turned leg pegged base, desk has old label on back which reads "Property Society for Prevention New England Antiquities Sold August 8th 1982," 26" w, 16" d, 38" h, $3,165. Photo courtesy of James D. Julia, Inc.

Renaissance Revival, English, partner's, carved oak, rect top with rounded corners, molded edge, front and back each carved with three frieze drawers, one pedestal with three drawers, other with paneled door opening int. with drawers and shelves, canted corners with figural pilasters, conforming molded plinth base, compressed bun feet, profusely carved with fruiting swags, grotesque masks, and heraldic devices, 72" w, 39-1/2" d, 30" h **5,500.00**

Sheraton

American, stand-up, walnut, slant front, four graduated drawers, turned feet, ivory escutcheons, Sandwich glass pulls, flanked by paint dec columns, simply fitted int. with secret drawers, one pull replaced, repair to lid, hinges replaced, int. refitted, 35" h writing surface, 35" w, 43" h **1,200.00**

Country, slant lid, cherry, pine and poplar secondary wood, two dovetailed drawers behind slant lid, two large compartments, three dovetailed drawers in base, turned feet, orig oval brasses with emb pineapple in basket design, refinished, alternations, restored break on one back leg, 37" w, 19-1/4" d, 38-1/2" h **990.00**

Victorian, America, second half 19th C, partner's, mahogany, gilt tooled leather writing surface, two frieze drawers on each side, pedestals fitted with four drawers opposed by cabinet doors, plinth base, 66", 54" d, 29" h. . **6,200.00**

William and Mary, attributed to CT, early 18th C, tulipwood and oak, fall-front lid with raised panel, int. of four compartments, three drawers, well with

Desk, Wooton, Wells Fargo, c1875, standard grade, carved gallery, raised burl panels, 40" w, 27" h, 68" h, $11,200. Photo courtesy of Fontaine's Auction Gallery.

sliding closure, double arched molded front, base with long drawer, four turned legs, joined by valanced skirt, shaped flat cross stretchers, turned feet, replaced brasses, old refinish, minor imperfections, 24-3/4" w, 15" d, 42-1/2" h **17,250.00**

William and Mary-style, American, 20th C, oak, seven dovetailed drawers, applied moldings, molded edge top, brass tear drop pulls, old finish, turned legs and stretchers, one piece of molding missing from drawer, 27-3/4" x 59" x 31" h **500.00**

Dry sinks

Curly maple, rect well, work surface on right with small drawer, two poplar wood cupboard doors, short bracket feet, hardwood edge stripes, minor repairs, refinished, 55" w, 34-1/2" h **2,400.00**

Grain painted, New England, rect well with tin lining, rounded splashboard, two small drawers, two cupboard doors, shelf int., bracket feet, brown and yellow pine graining, 49" w, 38" h **900.00**

Painted, attributed to PA, early 19th C, rect overhanging top, well, cut-out ends with exposed tenons, joined by medial shield fitted with later copper insert, painted red, 44-3/4" w, 18-1/2" d, 32" h **2,645.00**

Pine, three drawers on high back, sink with back-curved sides, paneled doors opening to self, stile feet, c1900, 43" w, 18-1/2" d, 33-1/2" h **900.00**

Pine and poplar, galleried well, one small dovetailed drawer, two paneled doors, cut-out feet, 46" w, 18-1/4" d, 37-3/4" h **600.00**

Poplar, painted, rect well above pair of paneled cupboard doors, scroll-cut apron continuing to low bracket feet, cast iron thumb latch replaced, layers of old worn green paint, 39-1/2" w, 16-13/4" d, 33" h **650.00**

Hall trees and hat racks

Bench

Gothic Revival, oak, composed of some antique elements, tall backrest inset with foliate and figural panels, lift seat and foliate carved lower panels, 34" w, 73" h **690.00**

Gothic-style, late 19th C, oak, tall backrest fitted with three figural, foliate, and seraph carved panels, lift seat, chip-carved sq legs, 60" w, 66-1/2" h **1,855.00**

Chair

Arts & Crafts, Limbert, #79, hall chair, unique "bicycle" shape, orig leather back and shaped seat over slab leg with keyed construction, orig finish, branded and numbered, orig leather has been reinforced, 19" w, 20" d, 42" h **1,100.00**

Cast iron, Union Army motif, patch boxes on base, belt with buckle carved for cane holder, swords and rifles forming back, topped with Union shield, piece found in PA GAR hall **10,500.00**

Hall rack

Art Nouveau, France, early 20th C, mahogany, flaring mahogany panel, five brass curved coat hooks centered by mirror, umbrella stand below, 47" w, 85" h **1,200.00**

Arts & Crafts, attributed to Charles Rohls, early 20th C, oak, tall sq shaft, two tiers of four wooden hooks, each near the top, half buttresses running up from the cross base on all four sides, sq wafer feet, 64" h **1,100.00**

Colonial Revival, Baroque-style, American, 1910, cherry, shell carved crest over cartouche and griffin carved panel back, lift seat, high arms, mask carved base, paw feet, 39-1/2" w, 21-1/2" d, 51" h **700.00**

Hall chair, Arts & Crafts, Charles Rohlfs, 1900, tall back, carved and cut-out details, faceted pegs, semi-circular seat, branded "CR 1900," old, very light overcoat and chip to finial, 18" w, 15" d, 57" h, $2,400. Photo courtesy of David Rago Auctions.

Hall bench, Renaissance Revival, attributed to R. J. Honer, c1885, two parts, mahogany, mirror, griffin arms, winged angel crest, 65" w, 23" d, 98-1/2" h, $15,120. Photo courtesy of Fontaine's Auction Gallery.

Hall tree, Renaissance Revival, c1875, burled walnut, marble top, mirrored door opens to reveal coat compartment, $4,820. Photo courtesy of Fontaine's Auction Gallery.

Victorian, American, burl walnut, ball finials above paneled and shaped cornice, rect mirror flanked by turned garment holders, marble top drawer supported by turned legs, shaped base, painted metal plant holders, 29" w, 14" d, 93" h **1,400.00**

Hat rack

Arts & Crafts, wrought steel, hat and coat style, our sided, double hooks and spindles, unmarked, 21" w, 21" d, 75" h **865.00**

International Movement, Charles Eames, "Hang-It-All," manufactured by Tigrett Enterprises, c1953, white enameled metal frame, multicolored wooden balls, 20" w, 6" d, 16" h **800.00**

Windsor, American, pine, bamboo turned, six knob-like hooks, orig yellow varnish, black striping, 33-3/4" w **200.00**

Hall tree, Renaissance Revival, c1890, walnut, lift-seat, winged griffins, claw feet, leaf carving, full length beveled mirror, 42" w, 16" d, 88" h, $7,840. Photo courtesy of Fontaine's Auction Gallery.

Stand, Arts & Crafts, coat and umbrella type, wrought steel, cut-out apron, spindles, brass hooks, unmarked, 27" w, 10-1/2" d, 73" h **850.00**

Umbrella stand, Black Forest, Germany, early 20th C, carved walnut, figural bear, fierce expression, loose chain around neck, holding tray in raised paw, porcelain base liner, 48" h **5,750.00**

Mirrors

Aesthetic Movement, America, c1880, overmantel, gilt, central cornice supported by two small columns over frieze dec with scene of snake attaching bird in tree, mirror plate highly dec with leaves, orig label of L. Utler, 47 Royal St., New Orleans, 64" w, 6" d, 84" h **3,600.00**

Art Deco, French, c1930, giltwood, frame closed at bottom and sides, carved chevrons, stylized sundials and Chinese scrolls, hung by gilt thread rope, tapered rect beveled mirror plate, 27" w, 37" h **1,500.00**

Arts & Crafts

Boston Society of Arts and Crafts, 1910, carved wood, rect, carved and gilded frame, ink mark, initials, orig paper label, 11-1/4" w, 18-1/2" h **700.00**

Limbert, oak, frame with geometric inlaid design over rect cane panel shoe-foot base, recoated orig frame, orig glass, 20" w, 8" d, 22" h **600.00**

Baroque, Continental, second quarter 18th C, giltwood, fruit filled cartouche form resting, mirrored borders with

Cheval mirror, Arts & Crafts, broad stretcher keyed-through shoe feet and square posts, rectangular pivoting frame, original finish, unmarked, 33" w, 8" d, 71" h, $1,450. Photo courtesy of David Rago Auctions.

Cheval mirror, Victorian, c1900, oval oak, carved crest and knees, original finish, 30" w, 70" h, $2,350. Photo courtesy of Fontaine's Auction Gallery.

grapevines and scrolls, foliate carved pendant, 63" h **5,750.00**

Biedermeier, c1830, walnut, ogee molded cresting, paneled sides, 26" w, 37" h **350.00**

Centennial, Queen Anne-style, American, late 19th C, mahogany faced, scalloped, shell pendant, 32" h **250.00**

Cheval, German, ebonized, swivel rect mirror, rounded ends, low sq mount, artist sgd, 70" h **425.00**

Chippendale

America, late 18th C, mahogany, domed crest, jig sawed symmetrical scrolls, scrolling ears, conforming shallow apron, 21" w, 39" h **990.00**

America, early 19th C, pine, figured mahogany veneer, arched crest, tightly scrolled ears, molded frame around glass, gilt inner liner, minor ear damage, 17-3/4" w, 33-3/4" h **1,775.00**

England, mid-18th C, walnut and parcel-gilt, gilt-gessoed carved phoenix on leafy branch above scrolled frame with applied gilt leafy floral and fruit devices, gilt incised liner framing beveled glass, restoration, 20-1/2" w, 44" h **6,465.00**

New England, late 18th C, mahogany and gilt gesso, scrolled frame centering gilt gesso eagle in crest above gilt incised molded liner, imperfections, 18-1/2" w, 40" h **500.00**

Pennsylvania, label for retailer John Elliott, Jr., 1739-1810, Philadelphia, mahogany, domed crest, shallow apron both jig sawed with symmetrical leafy scrolls, molded upright rect frame, rounded upper corners, enclosing early mirror plate, refinished, 21-1/2" w, 40-1/2" h **1,100.00**

Chippendale-style, cheval, late 19th C, carved mahogany, oval plate, four-legged base carved with foliage, claw and ball feet, 75" h **635.00**

Classical

Dressing, America or England, 1810-20, carved mahogany and mahogany veneer, cylinder top opens to reveal four drawers, centering one door, ivory pulls, above single divided long drawer, restoration, 19" w, 10-5/8" d, 32" h **1,610.00**

Girandole, America or England, 1810-20 gilt gesso, crest with eagle flanked by acanthus leaves, convex glass, ebonized molded liner with affixed candle branches,

Mirror, Chippendale, mahogany, nicely decorated mirror, interior gold painted border, large crest on top and gold painted center round decoration, some gold paint missing and mirror showing age, some outside edge veneer missing or cracked, 22" w, 44" h, $1,560. Photo courtesy of James D. Julia, Inc.

foliate and floral pendant, imperfections, 23" w, 35" h **5,175.00**

Overmantel, New England, c1820-40, painted and giltwood, rect mirror frame with sq corner blocks, applied floral bosses joined by vase and ring turned split baluster columns, molded black liner, old gilt surface, replaced mirror glass, surface imperfections, 46" w, 23" h **920.00**

Wall, New York, 1830s, carved and eglomise, entablature overhangs veneered frieze, reverse painted land and waterscape flanked by leaf carved split balusters, orig eglomise and mirror glass, old refinish, minor losses and crazing, 38" h **460.00**

Courting, wooden frame, reverse painted glass inserts and crest with bird and flowers, orig mirror glass with worn silvering, penciled inscription on back with "restored 1914," touch-up to

Mirror, Empire, American or Continental, c1830-50, crotch grain mahogany, pediment top with recessed arch, large gilt rosette on ebonized ground, ebonized cove molding above, flanked by ebonized half columns, brass ormolu mounts, stepped base, replaced mirror glass, cleaned, 23-1/2" w, 46" h, $1,100. Photo courtesy of Cowan's Historic Americana Auctions.

reverse painting, brass back corner braces, 10-7/8" w, 16-1/2" h.... **935.00**

Edwardian, late 19th C, overmantel, boxwood marquetry inlaid, arched cresting inlaid with musical still life and scrolling vines, shaped mirror plate flanked by cross banded stiles, 60" w, 68" h...................... **900.00**

Empire, flame mahogany veneer over pine, scalloped crest with scrolled ends, inset oval panel at top, applied half turned pilasters, ogee base, worn silvering, glue repairs at ends of crest, old alligatored varnish finish, 21" w, 51" h..................... **770.00**

Federal

Architectural, two parts, pine, old alligatored white paint over orig gilding, stepped cornice with applied ball dec, molded pilasters on sides, applied corner blocks at bottom, reverse dec with ribbons, silver, and black leaves on white ground, edge damage, 15-1/4" w, 24-1/4" h.............. **450.00**

America, gilt, eglomise panel with resting hunter in landscape, green border, gilt foliage, over rect mirror, cove molded frame, applied gesso

Mirror, Federal, America, c1830, gilt, reverse painted glass panel of American merchant ship, top molding with spherical drops, half turned columns at sides and bottom, 13" w, 26" h, repainted over original gilt, heavy flaking of reverse painting, $160. Photo courtesy of Cowan's Historic Americana Auctions.

moldings and dec, minor restoration, 17" w, 28-1/2" h **450.00**

America, over mantel, classical frieze, paterae, anthemion, garlands, and bows, three sections, 35" h........ **4,990.00**

New England, c1800, mahogany inlaid, scrolled frame, rect mitered string-inlaid liner, 18" w, 31" h **1,530.00**

New England, c1820-25, mahogany and mahogany veneer, molded cornice above sq and reeded capitals, half engraved vase and ring-turned, acanthus leaf, diamond faceted columns on sq plinths, refinished, replaced glass, imperfections, 18-1/2" w, 40-1/2" h **355.00**

New York City, c1780-1800, mahogany, swan's neck crest, carved urn, bouquet-type finial with carved florets on wires, veneered frame flanked by wire-bound wood vine work pendants, scrolled apron, heavily reworked, refinished, gold paint, 21-1/2" w, 53" h **675.00**

Tabernacle, attributed to New York or Albany, 1795-1810, gilt gesso, molded cornice with pendant spherules over frieze with applied sunflower and wheat sheaf device, flanked by checkered panels over two-part looking glass, flanked by applied double half columns, gilt surface, replaced glass tablet, 14" w, 30-1/2" h **865.00**

Wall, giltwood, labeled "Parker and Clover Looking Glass and Picture Frame Makers 180 Fulton St. New York," molded cornice with applied spherules above eglomise table of girl in pasture landscape holding dove, mirror flanked by spiral carved pilasters, 13-3/4" w, 29-1/8" h **2,875.00**

Federal, late, attributed to New England, c1820-30, gilt gesso, molded cornice with acorn form drops over frieze centering carved leaf motif flanked by vine and leaf applied devices, two-part mirror glass with grape and leaf designs, flanked by vase, ring, and spiral turned split balusters, old gilt surface, minor imperfections, including replaced mirror glass, 19" w, 37" h **700.00**

Federal-style, America, c1900, mahogany, swan's neck crest, carved

urn-form finial with carved wood flowers on wires atop mirror, flanked by wired wood vine work drop, eglomise panel above mirror, elaborately jig sawed domical scrollwork apron, replaced gold work, restoration, damage, 23" w, 52" h **900.00**

Folk Art, America, 1902, possibly prisoner made, pine, carved hearts, stars, and various numerals and patterns, year "1902," minor wear, 29-1/2" x 29-7/8" **1,410.00**

George II-style, English, 19th C, carved gesso and giltwood, C-scroll and shell carved arched crest, serpentine and rect mirror plate, scrolled foliate corner pendants, C-scroll, shell, and acanthus carved shaped apron, 29" w, 65-1/2" h **1,800.00**

Hepplewhite, shaving, mahogany, inlay, two dovetailed drawers, feet, posts, and mirror are old replacements, 17-3/4" h **225.00**

Louis XV-style, pier, 19th C, carved giltwood, large rect mirror topped by crest carved with leafy scrolls and rocaille, marble-topped ovolo 19-1/4" h shelf, flat leaf edge, gilt metal brackets, reeded scrolls with anthemion and female mask terminals, 33" w, 73" h **1,725.00**

Mirror, International Movement, George Nakashima, wall-hanging mirror, free-edge cherry top and bottom rail, mortised-through uprights, 22" w, 3-3/4" d, 44" h, $2,900. Photo courtesy of David Rago Auctions.

*Over-mantel mirror, Victorian, c1860, gilded, figural heads, floral carvings, claw feet, original condition, 63" w, 50" h, **$4,480**. Photo courtesy of Fontaine's Auction Gallery.*

Neoclassical, English, c1810-15, giltwood, flat molded cornice above eglomise tablet with center sailing vessel within a black oval, red and silver lattice panel bordered by black and white, mirror below flanked by reeded columns on sq plinths with rosettes, 18-1/8" w, 36" h **1,725.00**

Neoclassical-style, early 20th C, giltwood, topped by an urn draped with husk swag, frame surround with lozenge detailing, ending in central patera flanked by further swags, 17-1/2" w, 37-1/2" h **700.00**

Queen Anne, English

Mahogany, top carved round shell with gold highlights, scrolled crest, bottom with small shell carved circle, gold dec gesso liner, replaced beveled glass, 26" l
. . . . **60.00**

Oak, old finish, old glass with some wear to silvering, old replaced backboards, 13" w, 21-1/4" h
. . . . **330.00**

Scroll, mahogany, old finish, molded frame, detailed scrolled crest, minor split in bottom edge of frame, 9" w, 16-1/4" h **550.00**

Walnut, scrolled crest above molded rect frame enclosing beveled mirror glass, backboard inscribed "Capt S Cobb," refinished, glass resilvered, 10-1/2" w, 22-1/2" h
. . . . **1,175.00**

Renaissance Revival, c1870, ebonized and parcel-gilt, elaborate pediment carved with cornucopia, dentil molding and foliage, arched mirror plate and anthemion carved borders, 50" w, 79" h **2,695.00**

Rococo, Continental, third quarter 18th C, giltwood, shaped mirror plate, arched top, frame carved with foliage and C-scrolls, 28" w, 54" h **4,025.00**

Sheraton, mahogany, spiral turned split columns and bottom rail, inlaid panels of mahogany, rosewood, and cherry, architectural top cornice, split mirror, 24-1/2" w, 47" h **300.00**

Victorian, English, Pier, burl columns, base with white marble, incised vine dec on base and top highlighted in gilt, 8-1/2" h **1,500.00**

Rockers

Art Nouveau, American, c1900, oak, fumed finish, carved arms, saddle seat, three splats with floral-type capitals
. . . . **400.00**

Arts & Crafts

American, oak, four vertical back slats, corbel supports under arms, recovered orig spring cushion, orig finish, 29" w, 34" d, 36" h . . **200.00**

Limbert, #580, oak, T-back design, orig recovered drop-in cushion, recent finish, branded, 24" w, 29" d, 34" h **150.00**

Plail, oak, slatted barrel back, D-shaped recovered seat, refinished, unsigned, 26" w, 28" d, 31" h **2,500.00**

Stickley Brothers, oak, six vertical back slats, recovered orig spring cushion, worn orig finish, branded, 25" w, 27" d, 35" h **220.00**

Boston, American, 19th C, maple, spindle back **200.00**

*Rocker, Arts & Crafts, L. & J.G. Stickley, early slats to back and sides, original cane seat support and cushion, original finish, Handcraft decal. Some scratches to back, tears to leather, 28-1/2" w, 31" d, 38-1/2" h, **$1,610**. Photo courtesy of David Rago Auctions.*

*Rocker, Arts & Crafts, L. & J.G. Stickley, six vertical back slats, open arms, and fabric covered seat, original finish, "The Work of..." decal, 27" w, 29" d, 35" h, **$1,100**. Photo courtesy of David Rago Auctions.*

Colonial Revival, Windsor-style, Colonial Furniture Co., Grand Rapids, MI, comb back, birch, mahogany finish, turned legs, 21" w, 17" d, 27-1/2" h
. . . . **200.00**

Decorated

America, orig black over red dec, gold stenciled urn of fruit and flowers on crest, shaped seat, scrolled arms, well turned legs, repaired damage to arms, 15" h seat, 40" h **220.00**

*Rocker, International Movement, George Nakashima, 1979, walnut spindle-back, paddle arms, saddle seat, signed "George Nakashima/May 1979" and original owner's name, 25" w, 26" d, 35-1/2" h, **$3,250**. Photo courtesy of David Rago Auctions.*

Pennsylvania, dark green, gold foliate on crest, slats, and seat, traces of red border with yellow line detail, turned legs, shaped medallion stretcher, scrolled arms, repaired break in one arm, 17" h seat, 42" h.............. **220.00**

International Movement, Charles Eames, manufactured by Herman Miller, salmon fiberglass zenith shell, rope edge, black wire struts, birch runners, c1950, 25" w, 27" d, 27" h **1,400.00**

Ladderback, Portsmouth, NH area, late 18th C, turned finials above arched slats joined to down turned natural arms with carved Indian faces on terminals, old dark brown paint, imperfections, 16" h seat, 46-1/2" h........ **4,600.00**

Wicker, painted white, sq back, basket weave pattern over openwork back, rect armrests with wrapped braces, openwork sides, braided edge on basketweave seat and skirt, X-form stretcher, 32" w, 33" h **200.00**

Windsor

American, c1850, grain painted, stencil dec, scrolled crest, tail spindle back, shaped seat, bamboo turned legs, box stretcher **450.00**

New Hampshire, upholstered, birch splayed legs, dark orig finish, pine base, coarsely woven light green

Rocker, Renaissance Revival, Huntzinger, oak, arms, spring-type, upholstered back and seat with rope turned spindles, large spindle type balls for arms, 34" h, $600. Photo courtesy of James D. Julia, Inc.

Windsor rocker, American, shaped crest with paint decoration, bamboo turned legs, box stretcher, cheese-cutter-type rockers, $375.

fabric, rounded back, slightly rolled arms, few later rails added at tops of legs for support, 17-1/2" h seat, 43-1/2" h **880.00**

Secretaries

Biedermeier-style, inlaid walnut, molded rect top, four drawers, top drawer with fall front, fitted int. with ebonized writing-surface, molded block feet, 50-1/4" w, 23-3/4" d, 35-1/2" h **1,000.00**

Centennial, inlay mahogany, two parts: top with four drawers over six cubbyholes center, line inlay door opening to reveal two cubbyholes and large drawer, sliding tambour doors flanked by inlay panels with simulated columns; lower: fold-over line inlay lid, two drawers with line inlay, diamond inlay on legs, some lifting to veneer, replaced cloth writing surface, 37-1/4" w, 19-3/4" d, 46" h..... **800.00**

Chippendale

Massachusetts, c1770-90, carved mahogany, scrolled and molded pediment above tympanum with projecting shell and arched raised panel doors flanked by fluted pilasters, candle slides, raised panel slant lid with blocked facade, molded conforming base, bracket feet, int. of upper bookcase divided into ine open compartments above

four small drawers, int. of lower case with two fan-carved blocked drawers, similar prospect door, small blocked and plain drawers, scrolled compartment dividers, replaced brasses, old finish, restored, 39" w, 22" d, 93-1/2" h **19,550.00**

New England, late 18th C, block front, two pieces, upper section: flame finial, two blind doors, cyma-carved panels, various-sized open compartments on int., lower section with fur front drawers, plain slant front, fitted int., some later replacements, 91" h **38,180.00**

Rhode Island, Providence area, 1765-85, carved cherry, scrolled molded pediment flanks central plinth and finial above applied shell carving atop central fluted and stop-fluted column flanked by raised panel doors, shelved int. enclosed by quarter-engaged fluted and stop-fluted columns, lower case of two stepped int, of serpentine end-blocked drawers with serpentine dividers, valanced compartments, central document drawers with applied columns,

Secretary, Biedermeier, Continental, first half 19th C, mahogany, brass ormolu mounts, lion mask pulls, light staining to marble top, drop front does not retract properly, face of drawer divide cracked, missing small portion on left side, small repair to back feet, old refinishing, 39" w, 19" deep, 55-3/4" h, $1,475. Photo courtesy of Cowan's Historic Americana Auctions.

above four graduated thumb-molded drawers flanked by fluted and stop-fluted engaged quarter-columns, shaped bracket feet ending in platforms, old surface, some original brasses, presumed owners' names scratched on underside of case: "Abner Lampson, 1743-1797 and Ward Lampson, 1773-1850, Washington N.H." imperfections, 38-1/4" w, 21" d, 80" h . . **55,815.00**

Classical, Boston, 1820-25, secretaire a'abattant, carved mahogany and mahogany veneer, marble top above cove molding, mahogany veneer facade flanked by veneered columns topped by Corinthian capitals, terminating in ebonized ball feet, recessed panel sides, fall front opens to

Secretary, Chippendale, two-piece, mahogany, slant front lid, fitted interior with six dovetailed drawers, eight pigeonholes, center drawer with shell carving and blocking, double doors with geometric arrangement of glass, adjustable shelves, four dovetailed overlapping drawers, bracket feet, old finish, original brasses, replaced brass eagle finial, repairs to feet, other restorations, 41-1/2" w, 19-1/2" d, 92-1/4" h, **$6,875.** *Photo courtesy of Garth's Auctions, Inc.*

desk int. over two cupboard doors, old refinish, 35" w, 17-1/2" d, 57-1/2" h **16,100.00**

Colonial Revival, Colonial Desk Co., Rockford, IL, c1930, mahogany, broken arch pediment, center finial, two glazed mullioned doors, fluted columns, center prospect with acanthus carving flanked by columns, four graduated drawers, brass eagle, carved claw and ball feet, 41" w, 21" d, 87" h **1,000.00**

Eastlake, American, burl walnut and mahogany, shaped cornice, pair of glazed cabinet doors, cylinder front, writing surface, two doors in base, shaped apron, 27" w, 22" d, 66" h **1,500.00**

Empire, America, c1840, mahogany veneer, fall-front, dovetailed construction, two sections, top with two four-light cathedral glass doors, base with fall-front deck, five-drawer int., over three drawers flanked by curved columns, turned feet, 41-1/2" w, 20" d, 7'4" h **1,425.00**

Empire-style, late 19th C, gilt bronze mounted mahogany, rect top, fall front with fitted int., over pr of recessed cupboard doors, flanked by columns, paw feet, 44-1/4" w, 23-1/2" d, 49-1/4" h **1,955.00**

Federal

Massachusetts, Boston or North Shore, early 19th, mahogany inlaid, top section: central panel of bird's eye maple with cross banded mahogany veneer border and stringing joined to the plinths by a curving gallery above flat molded cornice, glazed beaded doors with Gothic arches and bird's eye maple panels and mahogany cross-banding and stringing enclosing shelves, compartments, and drawers; lower: projecting section with fold-out surface inlaid with oval bird's eye maple panel set in mitered rect with cross banded border and cock-beaded case, two drawers veneered with bird's eye maple panels bordered by mahogany cross-banding and stringing, flanked by inlaid panels continuing to sq double tapered legs, lower edge of case and leg cuffs with lunette inlaid banding, old finish, replaced brasses, imperfections, 41" w, 21-3/4" d, 74-1/2" h **9,775.00**

Massachusetts, coastal southern, c1816, inscribed "Wood" in chalk,

mahogany, three pcs, molded cornice with inlaid dentiling above diamond inlaid frieze over two paneled cupboard doors with quarter-fan inlays opening to eight-compartment int., center case with tambour doors centering oval veneered prospect door, flanked by inlaid and reeded applied pilasters, valanced compartments, prospect door opens to single valanced compartment with drawer below, lower case with string inlaid fold-out writing surface, similarly inlaid drawers flanked by stiles, panel inlays, skirt, inlaid dentiling above legs with inlaid bellflowers, line inlay and inlaid cuffs, early surface, replaced pulls, minor veneer loss, 40" w, 20-1/2" d, 81-3/4" h **34,500.00**

Secretary, Classical, Boston, two-piece, bookcase top with large cornice, six-panel glazed doors, fold-over writing surface, compartments for inkwells and pen tray, base with ripple-top drawer over two drawers with Sandwich opalescent knobs, full columns under top drawer supported by short melon feet. Fold-over writing surface with compartments for inkwells and pen tray, 42-1/2" w, 21" d, 80" h, **$1,725.** *Photo courtesy of James D. Julia, Inc.*

New Hampshire, paint decoration, two pieces, pine, old alligatored reddish-brown and yellow dec over earlier red, chamfered corners on dovetailed cases, molded cove cornice, tree dec on two paneled doors, slant front with tree dec, int. with 13 dovetailed drawers with central prospect door, four dovetailed drawers in base with applied beading, slightly shaped bracket feet with applied base molding, replaced wooden pulls, replaced H hinges, touch-up to top doors **7,425.00**

George III, English, early 19th C, japanned, swan neck pediment, rosette carved terminals, two glazed cupboard doors, fitted int. of compartments and small drawers, fall front writing surface with cubbyholes and drawers, four graduated drawers, shaped apron, bracket feet, gilt and polychrome warrior and figural landscape scenes, birds, and flowering trees, green ground, over painting and minor reconstruction, 40-1/4" w, 21-1/2" d, 96-1/2" h **5,000.00**

George III/Early Federal, America, third quarter 18th C, mahogany, two sections, upper: shaped architectural pediment with gilt-metal ball and spike finials, cavetto cornice over cross banded frieze, chequer-banding, front with pair of 13-pane astragal doors, two adjustable shelves; base: outset fall-front opening, fitted int., four graduated cock-beaded oxbow-fronted drawers, conforming molded plinth base, molded and spurred bracket feet, 44-1/4" w, 24-1/4" d, 93-1/2" h **17,000.00**

Hepplewhite, North Shore, MA, mahogany, bookcase upper section, slant front desk **6,250.00**

International Movement, Gilbert Rhode, manufactured by Herman Miller, upper bookcase with drop front desk over four doors, carved wooden pulls in burl and paldio veneers, refinished, c1940, 66" w, 15" d, 72" h **2,600.00**

Louis XV/XVI, c1860, tulipwood and kingwood parquetry, serpentine marble top, case fitted with three drawer sham fall front, fitted interior, four long drawers, foliate cast mounts, 24" w, 14" d, 50-1/2" h **1,035.00**

Renaissance Revival, American, c1865, walnut, two sections, upper: bookcase section, S-curved pediment with center applied grapes and foliage carving, two arched and molded glazed doors, shelved int., three small drawers with applied grapes and foliage carved pulls; lower: fold-out writing surface, two short drawers over two long drawers with oval molding and applied grapes and foliage carved pulls, matching ornamentation on skirt, 48" w, 21" d, 95" h **5,000.00**

Sheraton, New England, mahogany and mahogany flame veneer, cove molded cornice, three drawers across top with oval brasses, two paneled doors in top with fine flame veneer, three interior drawers, four pigeon holes with adjustable shelf, three dovetailed drawers with applied beading, figured book page veneer, reeded legs with ring turnings and molded surround at base of case, refinished, few repaired veneer splits, pierced repairs, stains in bottom, replaced brasses, 42" w, 20" d, 50-1/2" h **1,760.00**

Victorian, two pieces, walnut, top: crown molding cornice, two glazed doors with burl and walnut buttons; base: burl cylinder roll with two-drawer walnut int., pigeon holes, slide-out writing surface, base: three long

drawers with burl dec, tear drop pulls, refinished, 40" w, 23" d, 86" h **1,850.00**

William III, English, c1700-10, burl walnut veneer, two sections, recessed upper with double-domical crest, pair of domically crested doors mounted with beveled glass mirror panels of conforming upper outline, plain int. of three adjustable wood shelves above pr of candle slides; lower section with canted front, hinged fall-front writing board, shaped desk int. with valanced central cubby hole between two pairs of valanced narrow cubby holes over two shaped drawers each, horizontal sliding door, flanked by two-tier side units with single-drawer bases, straight front of two graduated narrow drawers over two graduated wide drawers, highly figured burl on drawers match writing board and doors, engraved period brasses, later short straight bracket feet, minor veneer damage, 40" w, 23-1/2" d, 84" h **18,750.00**

Settees

Art Deco, attributed to Warren McArthur, c1930, tubular aluminum frame, sheet aluminum seat and back

Secretary, Federal, Salem, MA, 1793-1811, gentleman's, mahogany and mahogany veneer inlaid, glazed, sold for **$556,000** *at Skinner's June 9, 2002 auction, setting a new world record price for a piece of American federal furniture sold at auction. Photo courtesy of Skinner Auctions.*

supports, removable vinyl cushions, 68" l **5,750.00**

Arts & Crafts

Limbert, #939, oak, 11 back slats, corbels under arm, recovered orig drop-in cushion, branded, refinished, 75" w, 27" d, 40" h **800.00**

Stickley, Gustav, No. 222, tapering posts, tightly spaced canted slats to back and sides, leather upholstered drop-in seat, fine orig finish, red decal, minor veneer chips, 36" x 80" x 32" . . . **11,500.00**

Stickley, L. & J. G., oak, drop-arm form, 12 vertical slats to back and drop-in orig spring cushion, recovered in brown leather, refinished, unsigned, 65" w, 25" d, 36" h **1,800.00**

Unknown America maker, 20th C, even arm, oak, crest rail over nine wide vertical slats, three on each side, joined by sq vertical posts, medium brown finish, replaced seat, joint separation, 65" w, 25-3/4" d, 32" h **2,650.00**

Biedermeier-style, beechwood, curved open back, three vasiform splats, out-curved arms, caned seat raised on six sq-section sabre legs **650.00**

Classical, American, c1850, mahogany, serpentine front, carved crest, transitional rococo design elements, 82" l **600.00**

Colonial Revival, William and Mary style, American, c1930, loose cushions, turned baluster legs and stretcher, 48" l **750.00**

Settee, Arts & Crafts, Charles Stickley, heavy square posts, back and side slats under rounded rail, new tan leather drop-in seat and two loose cushions, cleaned original finish, branded mark on center back stretcher, two rub spots inside center back slats, 76" l, 31-1/2" w, 31" h, $5,175. Photo courtesy of David Rago Auctions.

Settee, George III, late 18th C, camelback, mahogany, typical form, out-scrolled arms and over-upholstered seat on square legs headed by scrolled returns and joined by stretchers, 72" l, $2,500. Photo courtesy of Skinner's Auctioneers and Appraisers.

Empire-style, late 19th/early 20th C

Gilt bronze mounted mahogany, settee, pair of side chairs, each with foliate and figural mounts, 80" l settee, price for three pieces **1,725.00**

Mahogany, two seats, curved backs, each armrest ending on ram's head, hoof-foot feet **2,100.00**

French Restauration, New York City, c1840, rosewood, arched upholstered back, scrolled arms outlined in satinwood terminating in volutes, rect seat frame with similar inlay, bracket feet, 80" l, 27" d, 33-1/2" h **1,200.00**

George III, early 19th C, black lacquer and faux bamboo, settee, pair of arm chairs, price for three pieces . **1,265.00**

Gothic Revival, American, c1850, carved walnut, shaped crest rail surmounted by center carved finial, stiles with arched recessed panel and similarly carved finials, upholstered back and seat, open arms with padded armrests and scrolled handholds, carved seat rail, ring turned legs, ball feet, 67-1/2" w, 23-1/2" d, 49-3/4" h **800.00**

Settee, Victorian, oval medallion back with button trim, olive brocade upholstery, 58" l, $600. Photo courtesy of Joy Luke Auctions.

Louis XVI-style, third quarter 19th C, gilt bronze mounted ebonized maple, Leon Marcotte, New York City, c1860, 55-1/2" l, 25" d, 41-1/2" h **2,185.00**

Renaissance Revival, America, c1875, carved walnut, triple back, each having carved crest and ebonized plaque inlaid with musical instruments, red floral damask upholstery **1,200.00**

Rococo Revival

Attributed to John Henry Belter, c1885, 65" l settee, pair of lady's chairs, pair of side chairs, each with laminated rose and foliate carved cresting, grapevine openwork sides, cabriole legs, price for three pieces . . **14,375.00**

Attributed to J. & J. Meeks, rosewood, laminated curved backs, Stanton Hall pattern, rose crest in scrolled foliage and vintage, tufted gold velvet brocade reupholstery, age cracks and some edge damage, 65-1/2" l . **5,500.00**

Victorian, carved rosewood, c1870, shaped and padded back, two arched end sections joined by dipped section, each with pierced foliate crest, over upholstered serpentine front seat, flanked by scroll arms, conforming rail continue to cabriole legs, frame leaf carved **850.00**

Wicker, tightly woven rect back, inverted triangle-dec, tightly woven arms, rect seat with woven diamond herringbone pattern, continuous braided edging from crest to front legs, turned spindle apron, 43" w, 36" h **500.00**

Windsor, New England, early 19th C, birdcage, maple, ash, and hickory, bamboo turned birdcage crest over 27 turned spindles flanked by stiles joining bamboo-turned arms and supports over bench seat, eight bamboo-turned legs joined by stretchers, old refinish, imperfections, 72" l, 14-1/2" h seat, 31-1/2" h **2,415.00**

Sideboards

Art Deco, attributed to Jacques-Emile Ruhlmann, France, 1879-1933, inlaid Macassar ebony, elongated rect top with ebony and ivory inlaid trim, three center shelves flanked by cupboards, one fitted with drawer, one with shelf, doors with rect ebony inlay with ivory stringing, applied half-round molding around base, swollen shaped legs, imperfections, 54-5/8" w, 16-1/2" d, 43" h **920.00**

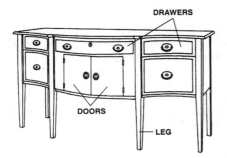

Typical Parts of a Sideboard

Art Nouveau, Louis Majorelle, 1900, oak and mahogany, rect, bowed front, inset marble top, tow long drawers, undulating brass pulls cast with sheaves of wheat, tow cupboard doors with large applied brass sheaves of wheat and undulating leaves, molded apron, four lug feet, 65" w, 39-1/8" h
.................**6,000.00**

Arts & Crafts

English, attributed to, with two "V" backsplashes, two drawers with ring pulls, bottom shelf, casters, orig finish, marked "S79FUM90," 42" l, 20" d, 45-1/4" h **1,150.00**

Limbert, Charles P., Grand Rapids, MI, c1910, oak, oblong top, mirrored back above case, three short drawers flanked by paneled cupboard doors over long drawer, cooper pulls and strap hinges, sq legs, chamfered tenons, branded mark, 49-1/2" w, 53-1/2" h. . **900.00**

Stickley Brothers, backsplash, single drawer with hammered brass hardware, lower shelf, good orig finish, branded "Stickley Brothers," stenciled "B735," light edge wear, 36" l, 19" d, 37" h **2,185.00**

Stickley Brothers, paneled plate rack, four drawers, three panel doors with hammered brass hardware, good orig finish, branded "Stickley Brothers," stenciled "8833," wear to copper patina on iron hardware ..**4,025.00**

Stickley, Gustav, designed by Harvey Ellis, backsplash, plate rest, six drawers, hammered copper pulls, arched apron, lower shelf, orig finish, red decal, replaced back paneling, minor nicks to legs, 42" x 54" x 21"
...................**11,500.00**

Stickley, Gustav, model no. 967, gallery top over two short drawers

Sideboard, Aesthetic Movement, in the manner of Herter Brothers, NY, c1880-90, ebonized, parcel gilt, marquetry, foliate carved panel cupboard doors enclosing shelves, 68" l, 18" d, 69" h, $2,700. Photo courtesy of Sloan's Auctioneers & Appraisers.

and long drawer, two cupboard doors below, iron strap hinges and door pulls, red decal, 1902, imperfections, 59-3/4" w, 23-3/4" w, 43-3/4" h **32,300.00**

Centennial, Chippendale-style, America, late 19th C, mahogany, block front with shell carving, four drawers, front cabinet doors, gadrooned apron, cabriole legs, claw and ball feet, 68" w, 24" d, 40" h.................**950.00**

Classical

Mid Atlantic States, 1840-45, carved mahogany and cherry veneer, rect top over mahogany veneered drawer, two recessed panel doors

Sideboard, Arts & Crafts, Gustav Stickley, plate rail, two cabinets and three drawers over linen drawer, all with hammered copper hardware, Craftsman paper label, refinished, veneer damage on left side, some edge roughness, 66" l, 23-3/4" d, 47-1/2" h, $4,600. Photo courtesy of David Rago Auctions.

opening to one shelf int., flanked by veneered scrolled supports, veneered base, old refinish, hardware changes, splashboard missing, 40" w, 18-3/4" d, 40-1/8" h
..................**2,550.00**

New York, 1830s, carved mahogany veneer, splashboard with molded edge and four spiral carved and turned columns, topped by urn-shaped finials, rect top overhands recessed paneled case, cock-beaded drawers and cupboards outlined with crass banded mahogany veneer, two top drawers with dividers above short drawers, bottle drawers flanked by end recessed panel doors, left one with single shelf int., right one with two-shelf int., flanked by columnar leaf carved supports over frontal carved paw feet, rear feet are heavily turned and tapering, old refinish, imperfections, 60-1/4" w, 23-5/8" d, 56-3/4" h......**2,760.00**

Empire, American, carved mahogany and figured veneers, break front, three drawers, four doors across base with inset gothic panels of figured veneer, well carved paw feet, orig brass hardware, old dark finish, 73-1/2" l, 23" d, 42" h **1,650.00**

Federal

Massachusetts, Boston, 1810-20, mahogany, maple, and rosewood veneer, two-tiered case, demilune superstructure, maple inlaid panels surrounded by cross banded rosewood veneer above

Sideboard, Biedermeier, Continental, first half 19th C, black marble top, flame mahogany case with full columns, ormolu mounts and poles, four drawers, repairs, feet missing, some veneer damage at base, old refinishing, 51" l, 22-1/2" d, 37" h, $2,150. Photo courtesy of Cowan's Historic Americana Auctions.

Sideboard, Hepplewhite, attributed to New York, mahogany and figured mahogany veneer with inlay, serpentine case, five dovetailed drawers, double doors, tapered legs with stringing and banding with husk and bookend inlay, inlaid diamond escutcheons, replaced brasses, minor veneer repairs, 71" w, 30-1/4" d, 40-1/4" h, $12,650. Also shown are pair of Hepplewhite mahogany knife boxes, $2,310; table top mahogany writing box, $660, and steel fireplace fender, $500. Photo courtesy of Garth's Auctions, Inc.

cock-beaded end drawers, small central drawer flanked by end cupboards, six ring turned tapering legs, case with concentric turnings, reeding, cock beading, and scenic landscape jointed on underside of arched opening, old surface, replaced pulls, replaced leg, veneer loss, later landscape painting, 74-1/2" l, 24-1/2" d, 44-3/4" h **9,200.00**

Massachusetts, Boston, 1820-25, carved mahogany and mahogany veneer, molded rect top with convex and concave bowed front with sq corners, conforming case, one long cock-beaded drawer flanked by short drawers above central cupboard doors flanked by bottle drawers, reeded cupboard doors flanked by bottle drawers, reeded pilasters, beaded paneled drawers above beaded skirt, central fan carved pendant, six ring turned and reeded legs, carved hairy paw feet, old finish, imperfections, 71-3/4" w, 25-1/2" d, 42" h **25,300.00**

Massachusetts, c1810, mahogany inlaid, shaped top outlined in inlay, conforming case with central drawer with reserve, flanked by

end drawers outlined in Greek key inlays, two central cupboard doors with beaded ovals, flanked by cupboard doors, legs with bellflower inlays on front of the upper and lower sections, replaced brasses, old surface, 71-1/2" w, 26-1/2" d, 42" h **21,850.00**

Middle Atlantic States, c1790, attributed to, mahogany and cherry inlaid, overhanging top with canted corners and serpentine front, central cock-beaded door inlaid with cherry panel with quarter fan inlays and mahogany mitered border, cock-beaded wine drawer with three-drawer facade at one end, three cock-beaded graduated drawers on other, ends with cherry veneered panels, four sq inlaid tapering legs ending in molded spade feet, lower edge of case with molding, old finish, minor imperfections, 48-1/2" w, 21-5/8" d, 37" h **19,950.00**

New England, c1790, mahogany and mahogany veneer, overhanging top with shaped front, conforming case, central pullout surface, bowed cock-beaded drawers, two cupboard doors flanked by concave drawers and

cupboard doors, six sq tapering legs, replaced brasses, old refinish, imperfections, 64" w, 20-1/8" d, 37-1/2" h **5,500.00**

Southern States, attributed to Francis Marion Kay 1816-87, cherry and other hardwoods, yellow pine secondary wood, replaced rest, three drawers over two doors, another drawer over prospect door at center, lower doors divided by half turned pilasters, six turned legs, one door is restored, hinges replaced, 60-1/4" w, 21-1/4" d, 49" h **3,410.00**

Virginia, 1790-1810, walnut and yellow pine, molded rect top, cock-beaded case with end drawers, right drawer visually divided into two drawers, left with two working drawers, central cupboard cock-beaded door, four square tapering legs, old brass pulls, old refinish, repairs, inscription on drawer reads "Virginia Hunt Board, early 19th cent. from family of Admiral Todd, Naval Commander prior to and during the Civil War, Virginia," 56" w, 22" d, 39" h **5,520.00**

Federal-style, Southern States, huntboard, yellow pine, overhanging rect top, case with three drawers, skirt with central shaping, four sq tapering legs, orig brasses, refinished, 21" w, 19-1/2" h **1,840.00**

George III-style, late 19th C, mahogany, bowed front, three central drawers, flanked by short drawer over cupboard door on sq legs, 71" w, 24" d, 42" h **2,185.00**

George III/Hepplewhite, mahogany, flame grain mahogany, satinwood, and

Sideboard, George III-style, Baker Furniture, 20th C, inlaid mahogany, serpentine top, five drawers, square tapered legs, inlaid with foliage and flowerheads, 72" l, 26" d, 36" h, $2,200. Photo courtesy of Skinner's Auctioneers and Appraisers.

oak, paterae and shell inlay, 36" h
.... **11,160.00**

Gothic, Kimbel & Cabus, New York, c1875, design no. 377, walnut, galleried top over two cupboard doors over open self over slant front over central drawer over open well flanked by two cupboard doors, galleried base shelf, bracket feet, 39-1/4" w, 17-3/4" d, 73" h
.... **9,775.00**

Hepplewhite, mahogany and mahogany veneer with inlay, bowed center section with conforming doors and dovetailed drawer, two flat side doors, sq tapered legs, banding and stringing with bell flowers on legs, corner fans on doors and drawers, reworked, repairs, replaced brasses, 58-1/4" w, 18-1/2" d, 37-3/4" h
.... **2,200.00**

Neoclassical, Boston, 1820-25, mahogany veneer, corner style, paneled and scrolled splashboard over top with veneered molded edge, curving front which overhangs conforming case of three veneered drawers over two recessed paneled doors, single shelved int., similar recessed panel sides above flattened ball feet with brass banding, replaced brass pulls, old surface with some imperfections, 60" w, 35" d, 42" h
.... **55,200.00**

Sideboard, Victorian, c1875, figural walnut, ebonized trim, fruit carved crest, 52" w, 21" d, 74" h, $1,570. Photo courtesy of Fontaine's Auction Gallery.

Regency-style, 19th C, inlaid mahogany, two pedestals, central drawer, silver drawer, 58" w, 24" d, 36" h
.... **1,610.00**

Renaissance Revival, America, cherry, curled mahogany drawer fronts, burled arched panel doors **900.00**

Sheraton, country, walnut and curly maple, beaded edge top, four dovetailed drawers, scalloped aprons, turned legs, line inlay around apron and drawer fronts, old varnish finish, replaced glass pulls, wear and edge damage, one heart inlay missing, large water stain on top, 69-1/2" w, 21-1/2" d, 43-1/2" h **5,500.00**

Victorian, American, late 19th C, pine, serpentine crest, rect top, four small drawers over two banks of four drawers, center cupboard, 65" w, 19" d, 51-1/2" h **750.00**

Sofas

Art Nouveau, Carlo Bugatti, 1900, ebonzied wood, rect back, mechanical seat, slightly scrolling rect arms, parchment upholstery, painted swallows and leafy branches, hammered brass trim, four block form feet, 68-3/8" l **1,900.00**

Centennial, Chippendale-style, American, late 19th C, mahogany, shaped back, rolled arms, yellow velvet upholstered seat, gadrooned apron, cabriole legs with carved knees, claw and ball feet, 62" l **1,500.00**

Chippendale, country, step down back with step down arms, bowed front with large down filled cushions, eight molded carved legs, cup caster feet, reupholstered, 76" w, 32" d, 36" h
.... **3,000.00**

Classical

Mid Atlantic States, 1805-20, carved mahogany and bird's eye-maple veneer, Grecian style, scrolled and reeded arm and foot, punctuated

Classical, America, c1900, walnut frame fully carved with large scrolled acanthus, stippled ground, carved columns at corners, later silk period style upholstery and bolsters, 74" l, 29" d, 36" h, $2,650.

Federal, mahogany frame, carved fruit and leaf decorated on top back rail, carved skirt, gold brocade upholstery with allover leaf design, 81" l, $600. Photo courtesy of Joy Luke Auctions.

with brass rosettes, continuing to similar reeded seat rail with inlaid dies, reeded saber legs flanked by brass flowerettes, brass paw feet on casters, old surface, 75" l, 14-1/2" h seat, 35" h **3,680.00**

New England, 1820-40, carved mahogany veneer, cylindrical crest ends, leaf carved volutes, upholstered seat and rolled veneer seat rail, leaf carved supports, carved paw feet, 92" w, 16-1/2" h seat, 34-3/4" h **1,650.00**

Empire, mahogany and figured mahogany veneer frame, well-detailed carving with sea serpent front legs, turned back legs, lyre arms with relief carved flowers and cornucopia, rope turned crest rail, refinished, reupholstered in floral tapestry on ivory ground, bolster pillows, 107" l . **3,850.00**

Federal

America, carved mahogany, mahogany veer paneled top crest with scrolled sides, front carved with rosette and leaf dec, carved paw feet with front stylized wings, red flower dec upholstery, 96" w, 19-1/2" d, 32" h **1,000.00**

Massachusetts or New Hampshire, c1810, mahogany and bird's eye-maple veneer, raked veneered crest divided into three panels by cross banded mahogany inlay, flanked by reeded arms, similar supports terminating in down-scrolling terminals, ring turned baluster forms, slip seat, bird's eye maple veneered seat rail, four frontal reeded turned legs ending in casters, old refinish, minor re-veneering, 75-1/2" l, 32-1/2" h **6,900.00**

New Hampshire, c1815, carved mahogany, upholstered, straight

International Movement, Sling, George Nelson for Herman Miller, six loose black leather cushions, tubular bright chrome frame, unmarked, 36" w, 29" h, $2,300. Photo courtesy of David Rago Auctions.

crest continuing to shaped sides with carved arms on vase and ring reeded and swelled posts and cock-beaded panels, bowed seat rail, vase and ring-turned legs with cock-beaded rect inlaid dies, old finish, minor imperfections, 78" w, 24" d, 17" h seat, 34" h back **2,415.00**

George III-style, English, carved oak, double arched upholstered high backrest, scrolled arms, loose cushion seat, acanthus carved legs, claw and ball feet, 58" l **1,200.00**

Louis XVI-style, late 19th or early 20th C, upholstered arms with ornate carved cornucopia filled with fruit and flowers, turned and tapered legs with reeding, floral band beneath scrolled tops, raised floral carved borders around framework, old dark finish, dark gold painted detail, contemporary golden brocade upholstery, 44" h.... **2,950.00**

Neoclassical, Baltic, c1825, carved mahogany, paneled cresting, padded arms with lions heads and anthemia, upholstered seat and back, shaped feet, 68" l................. **2,185.00**

Empire, swan carved sofa, mahogany, carved rolled arms detailed carved front with swan decorated, feather, leaf and tear drop carving, carved claw feet, back of sofa with two carved cornucopias and deep pronounced dips along back, cream-colored upholstery with floral decorated, 75" w, 27" d, $1,265. Photo courtesy of James D. Julia, Inc.

Sofa, Victorian, mahogany, rolled arms, raised center back with carved crest, mahogany front with carved swan decoration to front of rolled arms, recently professionally upholstered, 78" w, 37" h to top of back crest, $920. Photo courtesy of James D. Julia, Inc.

Rococo Revival, John B. Belter, carved rosewood, triple back, carved central rose and fruit on sides, scroll band underneath, carved segmented scroll, tufted back red silk upholstery, brass caster feet, old restoration to central crest, worn seat fabric, 62" w, 42" h **4,500.00**

Sheraton to Empire, transitional, carved mahogany, scrolled arms with molded detail, applied rosettes, relief carved leaf supports, brass caps on turned front legs, relief twist carvings, applied moldings on front panels, casters on base, dark refinish, glued break in one scroll, reupholstered, 70" w, 17-1/2" h seat, 34-1/2" h back **550.00**

Victorian, late, American, c1890, camel back, reupholstered, turned legs, 60" l **750.00**

Stands

Baker, wrought iron, 48" h, 14-1/2" d, 84" h..................... **500.00**

Basin, Federal, attributed to Seymour Workshop, Boston, c1810-15, mahogany and bird's eye-maple veneer, small round table with concentric incised circles around basin opening above three veneered and cock-beaded drawers, two of which are hinged, turned and reeded legs joined to the round incised platform, ending in brass paw feet, orig brasses, old refinish, 18-1/8" d, 28-1/4" h . **36,800.00**

Bird cage, wicker, painted white, tightly woven quarter moon-shaped cage holder, wrapped pole standard, tightly woven conical base, 74" h..... **225.00**

Book, Gothic Revival, manufactured by Betjamann's, retailed by Tiffany & Co., Union Square, late 19th C, burlwood veneer, pointed arch uprights pierced

with trefoils, beveled rect base, 13-1/2" l, 5-3/4" w **350.00**

Canterbury, Regency, early 19th C, mahogany, drawer with paper label for "G. Ibison Furniture Broker & Appraiser, Cumberland Place, Near the Elephant & Castle," restoration, 19-1/4" l, 14" d, 22-1/2" h................. **1,380.00**

Cellarette

Arts & Crafts

Stickley, Gustav, flush top, pull-out copper shelf, single drawer, cabinet door, copper pulls, orig finish, large red decal, veneer lifting on sides and back, 22" w, 16" d, 39-1/2" h **4,315.00**

Stickley, L. & J. G., arched backsplash, pull-out copper shelf, two-door cabinet, hammered copper strap hinges, ring pulls, top refinished, orig finish on base, "The Work of ..." decal, 35-1/2" x 32" x 16" **13,800.00**

Federal, attributed to Middle Atlantic states, c1790-1800, mahogany inlaid, octagonal top, conforming case, both inlaid with contrasting

Drink stand, Arts & Crafts, L. & J.G. Stickley, circular copper-covered overhanging top, circular apron, cross stretchers, branded mark, original finish, replaced z-clamps under top, drill holes to underside, finishing nails to bottom of skirt into legs, 18" d, 28" h, $2,300. Photo courtesy of David Rago Auctions.

stringing, interior well with removable lead liner, four sq tapering legs inlaid with bellflowers and stringing, brasses appear to be orig, old refinish, sun faded top, imperfections, 22-1/4" w, 17-1/4" w, 25-1/4" h **28,200.00**

George III, English, mid-19th C, mahogany, lozenge form, brass bands, twin loop carry handles, racked chamfered tapering legs, 24" w, 17-1/2" d, 27-1/2" h **7,500.00**

Chamber, Federal

New England, early 19th C, painted and dec, dec splashboard above wash stand top with round cut-out for basin, medial shelf with drawer below, orig yellow paint with green and gold stenciling and striping, paint wear, imperfections, 18-1/4" h, 1" d, 39-1/4" h . . . **350.00**

North Shore, MA, c1815-25, carved mahogany, shaped splashboard, veneered cabinet door flanked by ovolu corners, carved columns of leaves and grapes on punchwork ground, ring turned tapering legs, brass casters, old replaced brasses, old refinish, minor restoration, 21-1/2" w, 16" d, 35-5/8" h **2,300.00**

Portsmouth, NH, c1800, mahogany inlaid, shaped splashboard with center quarter round shelf, pierced

Library pedestals, Regency, English, left: fruitwood, white marble inset top, octagonal base, fluted column, doors open to reveal three shelves, 16" d at top, 29-1/2" h, old refinishing, hinges reset on door, replaced interior shelves, minor veneer damage, $300; right: mahogany, white marble inset top, octagonal base, fluted column, door opens to reveal three shelves, 14-1/2" d at top, old refinishing, hinges reset on door, one int. shelf replaced, minor veneer damage, $370. Photo courtesy of Cowan's Historic Americana Auctions.

top with bow front, square string inlaid supports continue to outward flaring legs with patterned inlays, medial shelf, satinwood skirt, small center drawer with patterned inlaid lower edge, shaped stretchers with inlaid paterae, old finish, minor imperfections, 23" w, 16-1/2" d, 41" h **5,750.00**

Dumbwaiter

George III style, 19th C, mahogany, three-tier, typical form, graduated dished tiers, baluster turned supports, tripod base, 43" h **985.00**

Queen-Anne style, walnut, three circular shelves, splayed legs, pad feet, 21" d, 39" h **300.00**

Easel

Aesthetic Movement, attributed to Cincinnati furniture maker, cherry, intricate carved sunflowers and oak leaves, orig finish, 23" w, 36" d, 75" h **2,500.00**

Louis XVI-style, mahogany and parcel-gilt, picture support hung with berried laurel swags, trestle-end frame carved with acanthus, imbrications, and dolphins, 25" w, 23-1/2" d, 82" h **950.00**

Étagère

Classical, New England, 1860s, mahogany and mahogany veneer, spool turned gallery, ball finials, three shelves with similar supports, two recessed panel cupboard doors, single shelf int., ball turned feet, old refinish, imperfections, 35-1/4" w, 15-3/4" d, 66" h . . **990.00**

Regency, late, English, early 19th C, six tiers, corner, columnar supports, basal drawer, brass casters, 18" w, 14" d, 62" h **3,000.00**

Victorian, late, English, bamboo and Japanese lacquer, three tiers, corner, scalloped form shelves, raised, colored and gilt Chinoiseries, 16-1/2" w, 45" h **800.00**

Folding, Chippendale

New York State or Pennsylvania, 1755-775, cherry, dished top rotates and titles, birdcage support, swelled and turned pedestal, cabriole tripod base, pad feet, old refinish, imperfections, 17-1/2" d, 26" h **3,220.00**

Magazine stand, Arts & Crafts, Gustav Stickley, beveled square top, paneled sides, and four shelves, signed under top, refinished, stains to top, 15" square, 35" h, $4,025. Photo courtesy of David Rago Auctions.

Pennsylvania, 1760-80, walnut, molded dish top, inscribed edge tilts, tapering pedestal with suppressed ball, cabriole legs ending in pad feet, imperfections, 22" d, 29" h **4,600.00**

Magazine

Arts & Crafts

Stickley, Gustav, paneled sides, four shelves under arched apron, refinished, tacks missing, 15" w, 14-1/4" d, 35-1/4" h **2,415.00**

Stickley, Gustav, Tree of Life, carved sides, four shelves, orig finish and tacks, unmarked, minor edge wear, 14" sq, 43-1/2" h **1,610.00**

Stickley, L. & J. G., single broad slat on either side, arched toe board, new finish, "The Work of L. & J. G. Stickley" decal, 36" w, 12" d, 30" h **2,990.00**

Renaissance Revival, third quarter 19th C, mahogany, walnut, parcel-gilt, and ebonized gilt-metal, hanging, back plate with acanthus crest flanked by fleur-de-lis and bellflowers, uprights mounted on top with gilt-metal bust roundels, central hinged magazine folio set with gilt composition oval bust of Mercury, gilt incised detailing, 19-3/4" w, 21-1/2" h **300.00**

Music

New England, c1840, painted ash and pine, adjustable, two canted sides, vertical slats on cylindrical shaft, chamfered rect post, chamfered cross legs, painted blue-green, 15-1/2" w, 14" w, 78" h **635.00**

Sheet music, Victorian, inlaid mahogany, turned handle on top, two fold out sheet music holders, allover spoon carving, burl panels with different inlaid musical decorated, 17" w, 32" h, **$300.** Photo courtesy of James D. Julia, Inc.

Plant

Arts & Crafts

Limbert, ebon-oak line, overhanging top, four caned panels on each side, recent finish, branded signature, 14" w, 14" d, 34" h **2,100.00**

Stickley, Gustav, sq top flush with cloud-lift apron, narrow board mortised through corseted stretchers with tenon and key, orig finish, 1902-04 red decal, crack in one stretcher, 14" sq, 27" h **3,450.00**

French-style, 20th C, black lacquered finish, turtle-shaped top with open well, ormolu wreath and quiver designs, acanthus leaves, hoof-shaped caps on feet, 19-1/4" w, 14-1/2" d, 30" h **275.00**

Folk Art, carved and painted root, America, polychrome painted animal heads radiating from entwined root base, inscribed

Nightstand, International Movement, George Nelson, open birch cases over ebonized legs, foil labels, 18" square, 24-1/2" h, price for pair, **$2,100.** Photo courtesy of David Rago Auctions.

Parlor stand, Renaissance Revival, c1880, onyx and bronze mounts, decorated champleve panels and legs, 20" d, 31" h, **$3,930.** Photo courtesy of Fontaine's Auction Gallery.

"MAS 1897," 23" w, 38-1/2" h **1,725.00**

Victorian, wirework, painted, late 19th C, demilune, three-tier, each tier with ornately curled rim, fout slender legs heading by scrolled wire design, joined by single stretchers, X-bracing at back, casters, 45" l, 40" h **750.00**

Portfolio, William IV, English, c1830, carved rosewood, folding mechanism **3,500.00**

Reading, Federal, Albany, NY, early 19th C, mahogany, reading stand above ring-turned tapering post on rect shaped canterbury, turned tapering spindles, casters, 22-1/4" w, 14" d, 47-1/2" h **3,200.00**

Sewing, Sheraton, country, black walnut, poplar secondary wood, lift top, fitted int. compartment with four int. dovetailed drawers and pigeon holes, single dovetailed drawer with figured front and incised beading, well-turned legs with ring turnings, replaced brass pull, pegged construction, lock missing, one leg with well-executed repair, 20" w, 19-1/2" d, 29" h . . **1,155.00**

Side

Classical, southern New England, c1825, tiger maple, sq overhanging top over base having single beaded drawer, four swelled and tapering ring-turned legs joined by beaded skirt, opalescent glass pull, refinished, 19-3/4" x 20" top, 29" h **2,115.00**

Empire, mixed hardwoods, flame mahogany veneer, one board top with drop leaves, two dovetailed drawers with pressed-glass pulls, flanked by half turned columns, apron with gadrooning at bottom, carved pineapple column, platform base with scrolled leaf returns to

carved paw feet, 15-1/5" w, 16-3/4" d, 28" h **450.00**

Federal

New England, c1820-30, sq slightly overhanging top, base with single drawer, four sq tapering legs, allover yellow grain paint, drawer with red and green floral and foliate device flanked by dies painted with trailing vines continuing to simulate stringing, possibly orig brass pulls, very minor imperfections, 16" x 18" top, 28-1/2" h **27,025.00**

Northern New England, c1800, birch and bird's eye maple veneer, sq top, conforming base, single drawer, four tapering sq legs joined by straight skirt, replaced brass pull, refinished, 16" w, 15-1/2" d, 27" h **1,175.00**

Hepplewhite, cherry, poplar and pine secondary woods, replaced two-board top, one dovetailed drawer, sq tapered legs, mellow varnished finish, old replaced oval brass pull, 22" w, 18" d, 29-1/4" h **450.00**

Sheraton, country

Cherry, two-board top with biscuit corners, dovetailed drawer, well defined ring-turned legs, orig brass pull, refinished, 19" w, 18-3/4" d, 26-1/2" h **990.00**

Sewing stand, Arts & Crafts, rare L. & J. G. Stickley, drop-leaf, two drawers, lower shelf and hammered copper pulls, excellent original finish and condition, "Work of L. & J. G. Stickley" label, 21 1/2" w, 16" d, 29" h, **$25,000.** Photo courtesy of David Rago Auctions.

Side stand, Sheraton, America, c1830-40, cherry, one slightly recessed drawer with applied thumb molding, drop leaf, tapered turned legs, open, refinished, 27-3/4" l, 38-1/2" wide, 28-3/4" h, $850. Photo courtesy of Cowan's Historic Americana Auctions.

Curly maple and cherry, poplar secondary wood, one board top, two dovetailed drawers with fine curl, internal lock on top one, turned walnut pulls, ring turned legs with paneled detail, refinished, 21" w, 17-3/4" d, 29" h
.... **800.00**

Curly maple, later top, dovetailed drawer, small brass pull with cast stars, turned legs with good figure, golden varnished finish, interior staining on aprons, top, and drawer, 17-3/4" w, 17-1/2" d, 27-3/4" h
.... **880.00**

Curly maple, two-board top, dovetailed drawer fitted with turned wooden pull, well turned legs, golden refinish, replacements, minor restoration, 21-3/8" w, 17-1/4" d, 28-3/4" h
.... **935.00**

Tilt-Top, Federal
Massachusetts, 1790-1810, cherry, oval top tilts above pedestal with urn shaping, cabriole legs ending in arris pad feet, old surface, 19-1/2" x 12-3/4" top, 26-3/4" h
.... **940.00**

Massachusetts, Salem, c1790-1805, mahogany, oval top, urn and ring-turned post, tripod cabriole legs, arris pad feet on platforms, refinished, repairs, 21-1/2" x 14-1/2" top, 27-1/2" h **2,300.00**

Pedestal, paint grained, pine, square tops over hourglass cone configuration, 16-1/2" square top, 42" h, $660. Photo courtesy of Sanford Alderfer Auction Company.

New England, late 18th/early 19th C, mahogany, octagonal top, vase and ring turned post, tripod cabriole leg base, pad feet, refinished, imperfections, 21-1/2" x 15-1/2" top, 26-1/2" h.... **1,265.00**

Umbrella, Arts & Crafts, early 20th C, oak, sq form, four posts, top and bottom stretchers with mortise and tenon joinery, one dark brown finish, other medium brown finish, marked "Cedric S. Sweeter Jan 23, 1920," 12" w, one 28-3/4" h, other 29" h, price for pr
.....................**230.00**

Vitrine, Mahogany, line border inlay, satinwood panels, top with drop front, molded edges, tapered sq legs, brass casters, joined by stretcher base, 21-1/2" w, 16-1/2" d, 28" h......**600.00**

Wash stand, Empire (Classical), c1830-40, mahogany, spool sides, single drawer, lower shelf, 35" l, 17" d, 34" h, $600. Photo courtesy of Sloan's Auctioneers & Appraisers.

Wash
Empire, figured mahogany veneer, poplar secondary wood, dovetailed gallery fitted with narrow shelf, bowed top with cut-outs for wash bowl and two jars, serpentine front supports, turned rear posts, dovetailed drawer in base with brass pulls, high well turned legs, refinished, edge chips, 18" w, 16" d, 37-3/4 h **385.00**

Federal
American, mahogany and figured mahogany veneer, bow front with two small drawers, cutout for bowl, cutout sides, single dovetailed drawer in base, turned legs, worn finish, some water damage, replaced top and two small drawers, 20-1/4" w, 17-1/4" d, 30-1/4" h
.... **275.00**

Wash stand, Hepplewhite, English, country, c1810-30, mixed woods, mustard yellow ground, polychrome stenciled fruit and floral decorated on drawer front and back splash, tan and black pin-striping, scalloped dovetailed splash back with two quarter round shelves, cut-outs for bowls and cups, drawer below shelf with original brass rosette pulls, graceful tapered legs, very minor wear to paint, two short cracks in top, 18" l, 16" d, 37" h, $800. Photo courtesy of Cowan's Historic Americana Auctions.

Rhode Island, c1790, mahogany veneer, top with four shaped corners, canted corners, engaged ring-turned columns ending in reeded legs flanking cock-beaded drawers outlined in cross banded veneer, top two drawers with sections, replaced brasses, old refinish, imperfections, 20-3/4" w, 15-1/2" d, 28-1/2" h . . . **4,025.00**

Hepplewhite, country, pine, worn brown paint over earlier red, dovetailed gallery on top, narrow shelf along back, sq legs, shaped two-board base shelf, 26-3/4" w, 18-1/2" d, 39-1/4" h **800.00**

Whatnot, Corner, Victorian, late 19th C, Chinoiserie bamboo and lacquer, frame set with two diamond-shaped mirrors and shelves, 22" w, 13" d, 56" h **250.00**

Work

Classical, early 19th C, carved maple and rosewood veneer, top outlined with rosewood veneer banding above sectional veneered drawer, lower drawer flanked by short columns, tapering pedestal joining four leaf carved legs ending in carved hairy paw feet on castors, old refinish, 20-3/4" w, 18-1/2" d, 28-3/4" h **500.00**

Hepplewhite, New England, c1810, cherry inlaid, sq top, outline stringing and quarter fan inlays on ovolo corners, line inlaid drawer and skirt, line inlaid sq tapering legs, cross banded cuffs, brass drawer pull, refinished, 19" w, 19" dc, 27" h **2,650.00**

Renaissance Revival, American, c1860, lift top opening to real satinwood interior fitted with compartments, narrow drawer above semi-circular bag drawer, pair of stylized lyre form ends jointed by arched stretcher surmounted by turned finial **875.00**

Sheraton, New England, 1805-15, mahogany, veneered, outset rounded corners, shaped top, pull-out suspended fabric bag below single drawer, ring-turned and reeded round tapering legs ending in ring-turned tapering vasiform feet, old refinish, 16-1/2" w, 18-1/2" d, 28-1/4" h 3,500.00

Steps

Bed, New England, early 19th C, pine and tulipwood, two steps, thumb-molded drawer below bottom one, flanked by shaped sides, demilune base, old color, repaired, 15-1/2" w, 10" d, 17-1/2" h **575.00**

Circus, America, early 20th C, painted white stringers, red, yellow, and blue treads, 25" w, 90" d, 27" h **435.00**

Library

George III, English, late 18th C, mahogany, rect molded hinged top, eight steps, 49-1/2" w, 53-1/2" h **2,500.00**

Regency, English, early 19th C, mahogany, three steps, inset green leather treads, scrolling banister, sq balusters, feet with brass casters, 46" w, 27" w, 56" h **2,400.00**

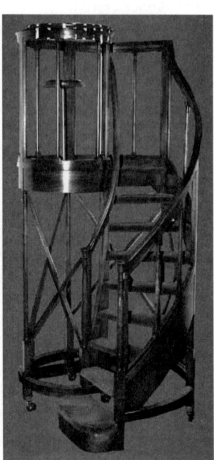

*Library steps, English, 20th C, spiral, mahogany, upper platform with leather upholstered stool and hinged reading surface, 52-1/2" w, 106" h, **$4,000**. Photo courtesy of Sloan's Auctioneers & Appraisers.*

*Foot stool, Arts & Crafts, Harden, arched apron and slatted sides, original drop-in leather seat, original finish, unmarked, some edge wear and glue drips, 20" w, 14" d, 16" h, **$920**. Photo courtesy of David Rago Auctions.*

Stools

Cricket, Arts & Crafts, Limbert, #205-1/2", rect top covered with new leather, splayed sides, inverted heart cut-out, single stretcher with through-tenon, replaced keys, orig finish, branded, 20" w, 15" d, 18" h **950.00**

Foot

Arts & Crafts, oak

Barber Brothers, oak, nicely replaced leather seat, some color added to orig finish, paper label, 13" w, 13" d, 11" h **110.00**

Limbert, cricket, #205-1/2, rect orig leather top and tacks, splayed sides with inverted heart cut-out having single stretcher with through-tenon construction, orig finish, branded and numbered, 20" w, 15" d, 19" h **2,000.00**

Orig leather and tacks, slightly arched rails, orig finish, 12" sq, 8" h **90.00**

Worn orig drop-in leather cushion with 4 vertical slats to side, orig finish, 16" w, 14" d, 14" h **260.00**

Queen Anne, 18th C, walnut, rect frieze, 4 cabriole legs each with shell carving on knees, pad feet, slip seat, 22-1/2" w, 17" d, 17" h **1,950.00**

Sheraton, curly and bird's eye maple, old finish, cane top, minor damage to top, 7-3/4" w, 13" l, 6-1/2" h **440.00**

Victorian, late 19th C, carved walnut, short cabriole legs carved at knees with shells, shaped skirting carved

Foot stool, Victorian, mid-19th C, beaded needlepoint, circular, three brass and wood claw and ball feet, worked with flowers within geometric surround, shades of green, brown, gray and white, losses, 11-1/2" d, $325. Photo courtesy of Sloan's Auctioneers & Appraisers.

with acanthus, velveteen upholstery, 12-3/4" w, 16" l, 11" h **175.00**

Windsor, attributed to Maine, early 19th C, rect top, four swelled legs joined by X-form stretchers, orig dark brown grain paint which resembles exotic wood, yellow line accents, paint imperfections, 12" 2, 8" d, 7" h **625.00**

Joint

Early, oak, old finish, wear and age cracks, 11" w, 16-1/2" l, 17-3/4" h **990.00**

Jacobean-style, oak, rect plank top, shaped skirt, block and ring-turned legs joined by box stretcher, 18" w, 11-1/4" d, 21" h **700.00**

Ottoman, Classical, attributed to Boston, MA, c1830, mahogany veneer, overstuffed cushions rest inside mitred frame atop molded base, ogee bracket feet, wooden casters, refinished, minor imperfections, 20" w, 18" d, 17-1/2" h, price for pr **2,235.00**

Piano

Louis XVI-style, late 19th C, carved beech, circular, adjustable, close-nailed over stuffed top, petal-carved frieze, leaf-capped turned, tapered, and fluted legs, wavy cross-stretcher **850.00**

Foot stool, Victorian, walnut, red velvet cushion top, veneer decorated, side knob handle, wear to velvet, $115.

Renaissance Revival, American, 1870, walnut, sq upholstered seat, acanthus carved baluster supports, four outswept legs, hoof feet **350.00**

Seat-type

Country, folk art, attributed to Fredericksburg, PA, late 19th/early 20th C, painted and dec, octagonal seat, chamfered edge, trimmed with border band of carved hearts, tall splayed and chamfered legs also trimmed with carved hearts and joined by slender rungs, overall polychrome **1,850.00**

George III, late 19th C, mahogany, gold floral satin upholstered rest seat, sq tapering supports, molded H-form stretchers, pr, 19-1/2" l, 17" h **1,650.00**

International Movement

Eames, Charles, manufactured by Herman Miller, Time-Life, walnut, concave seat, 13" d, 15" h **1,000.00**

Platner, Warren, manufactured by Knoll, bronze wire base, peach fabric upholstered seat, 17" d, 21" h **325.00**

Windsor, American, 19th C, oblong plant seat raised on three tall, turned and slightly swelled legs joined by T-stretcher, traces of old green paint, 15" w, 24-1/2" h **200.00**

Piano stool with spiral turned supports, ball and claw feet, $125. Photo courtesy of Joy Luke Auctions.

Typical Parts of a Table

Tables

Architect's, George III, English, late 19th C, mahogany, hinged tooled leather work surface above opposing hinged work surface, turned pedestal on three splayed legs, pad feet, some reconstruction, 29" w, 19-1/4" d, 29-1/2" h **2,300.00**

Breakfast

Chippendale to Hepplewhite, transitional, walnut, one board top, beaded edge apron, sq legs with slight taper, molded corner, and inside chamfer, H stretcher, old finish, stains on top, 19" w, 29-1/4" l, 28-1/4" h **8,250.00**

Classical, New York, 1820-30, carved mahogany inlaid, top with brass inlay in outline, stamped brass on edge of shaped leaves, one working and one faux drawers, flanked by drop pendants, fout pillar curved platform support, leafage carved legs, carved paw feet, casters, replaced pulls, old finish, repairs, losses, 39" w, 24" d, 28" h **2,450.00**

Federal

Massachusetts, central, c1810, inlaid cherry, rect hinged top with ovolo corners, base with straight skirt, edged with lunette inlay, flanked by sq tapering legs outlined in stringing, topped with icicle inlay, old refinish, 36" w, 17" d, 29" h **1,150.00**

Massachusetts or New England, 1815, mahogany oval top, hinged leaves, flanking two drawers, one working, one faux, both outlined in stringing and have central panel of figured mahogany veneer above

Breakfast table, Victorian, c1870, 46-1/2" l, 33-1/2" w, 27" h, figured walnut, ebony banded, $950. Photo courtesy of Sloan's Auctioneers & Appraisers.

chevron-style inlaid banding, reeded, turned, tapering legs, turned feet, old refinish, surface imperfections, 35-3/8" w, 20-1/4" d, 29-3/4" h . . . **8,225.00**

New York City, c1815, carved mahogany veneer, rect top, shaped leaves, one working and one faux end drawers, cross banded mahogany veneer, turned acanthus leaf carved pedestal, four acanthus leaf carved legs, brass hairy paw feet, old refinish, repairs, 25" w closed, 38-1/2" l, 30-1/4" h **1,725.00**

Card

Classical

Attributed to firm of Isaac Vine and Isaac Vine Jr., Boston, 1819-24, carved mahogany and mahogany veneer, rect top with beaded edges, skirt with recessed panel, C-scrolls and carved volutes over tapering pedestal accented by carved leafage above serpentine veneered platform with carved and scrolled feet on casters, old refinish, imperfections, 37" w, 17-1/2" d, 28-1/2" h . . . **1,840.00**

Attributed to Thomas Astens, New York City, 1822, carved

mahogany and satinwood, rect swivel top with rounded ends, outlined in cross banded mahogany veneer, satinwood veneered skirt, faceted pineapple-like carving above acanthus leaf carving on pedestal, shaped legs, carved paw feet on casters, old refinish, imperfections, 36" w, 18-1/4" d, 28" h **3,335.00**

New York, 1820-30, carved mahogany, mahogany veneer rect swivel top with rounded front carved corners, leaf carved and shaped shaft, curving platform which joins four scrolling leaf caved legs ending in carved paw feet, refinished, minor imperfections, 36" w, 17-1/2" d, 30" h **1,495.00**

Federal

Massachusetts, c1790-1800, mahogany inlaid, D-form hinged top, cross banded and string inlaid edge, conforming base with central mitered panel enclosing wavy birch oval flanked by rect panels bordered by contrasting stringing with cross banded edge, four sq

Card table, Hepplewhite, mahogany and figured mahogany veneer with inlay, exaggerated serpentine apron with ovolo corners with inlaid banding and stringing, conforming top with inlaid stringing on edge, square tapered legs with bellflower and stringing inlay, old finish, feet lost some height, added brass castors, initials "W.P." carved inside apron, 35-1/2" w, 17-1/2" d, 27" h, $3,850. Also shown are Queen Anne brass candlesticks, $550 each, and pair of Oriental porcelain plates in celadon with polychrome flowers, birds, and butterflies, $200. Photo courtesy of Garth's Auctions, Inc.

tapering legs with paneled dies and stringing, dart inlaid cuffs, orig surface, skirt underside stamped "W. Leverett," imperfections, 36" w, 16-3/4" d, 29-1/2" h **2,115.00**

Massachusetts, c1790-1800, mahogany inlaid, rect folding top with ovolo corners, string inlaid edge, conforming skirt, central oval panel and rect panels on corners and ends defined by stringing, four sq tapered legs with string inlaid panels and borders, refinished, minor restoration, 34-1/4" w, 17" d, 30" h **2,600.00**

Massachusetts, c1810-15, mahogany and mahogany veneer, folding top with serpentine front, half serpentine ends, corners and scratch-beaded edge, conforming cock-beaded skirt joining half-engaged vase and ring-turned legs, ball feet, old refinish, 36-3/4" w, 18-1/2" d, 29-3/4" h **1,120.00**

Middle Atlantic States, c1790-1810, mahogany inlaid, string inlaid D-form top with recessed elliptical front on base inlaid with panels and stringing on four sq legs, all inlaid with bellflowers tapering to inlaid cuffs joined by straight inlaid skirt, old refinish, repairs and imperfections, 36" w, 16-3/4" d, 29-3/4" h **11,750.00**

New England, early 19th C, painted rect, rect slightly overhanging folding top, conforming base, four sq tapering legs joined by straight skirt, old red-painted surface, minor surface imperfections, 35-3/4" w, 17-1/2" d, 30-1/4" h **1,300.00**

Newburyport, MA, c1800, mahogany veneer, elliptic shaped top with inlaid edge, overhangs divided skirt with panels of stringing and figured maple dies at top of sq tapering legs, outline stringing on legs with cuff inlays, old surface, veneer losses, 36" w, 17-5/8" d, 30" h **3,335.00**

New York, c1810, mahogany and mahogany veneer, folding rect top with canted corners, conforming base, single long cock-beaded drawer, dies inlaid with fiddle back mahogany veneered panels, five reeded tapering legs ending in brass ball feet joined by straight cock-beaded skirt, repairs, 36" w, 18-1/4" d, 30-1/2" h **1,955.00**

Philadelphia, c1800, mahogany and satinwood veneer, serpentine top, string inlaid skirt flanking rect satinwood center, sq tapering legs outlined in stringing with diamond-shaped die, terminating in cuff inlays, refinished, imperfections, 36" w, 18-3/8" d, 29-3/4" h ...**5,600.00**

Providence, RI, c1790-1800, mahogany inlaid, demilune, folding top with string inlaid edge above conforming skirt joining five sq tapering legs with bookend, icicle, diamond, and string inlay continuing to inlaid cuffs, old refinish, imperfections, 35" w, 17-1/4" d, 28-1/2" h **1,880.00**

Georgian-style, late 19th C, carved mahogany, foliate carved top, polished playing surface, foliate carved circular legs, pad feet, 27-1/2" w, 13" d, 29" h....**1,495.00**

Hepplewhite, figured mahogany, mahogany veneer, ovolo-cut corners on top and aprons, line border inlay on edges of top, aprons, and tapered legs, old dark finish, few age splits, minor veneer chip on apron, slight warp in top, 34-1/4" w, 17" d, 30-1/2" h **3,300.00**

Neoclassical, New York City, c1825, carved mahogany veneer, shaped swivel top with cross banded veneer in outline above inlaid edges and veneered skirt, central raised plaque above scrolled and waterleaf carved supports, fluted curving platform, similarly carved legs, carved paw feet on casters, old refinish, imperfections **4,600.00**

Sheraton, attributed to Salem, MA, faint signature on bottom "J. E. Skelton" (or Shelton), mahogany and mahogany veneers with banded inlay, figured top boards with ovolo corners, banded inlay around edges, half serpentine side aprons, serpentine front with banded inlay along bottom edges, figured satinwood panel on front with mahogany diamond, ring turned legs taper at base, reeded bands at centers, refinished, minor veneer loss, 36" w, 17-1/2" d, 29" h **5,500.00**

Center

Biedermeier, inlaid walnut, shaped rect top, molded frieze with drawer, canted, sq-section cabriole legs, 25" w, 37" l, 27-3/4" h....**1,100.00**

Classical

Boston, attributed to, c1825, carved mahogany and mahogany veneer, circular top with inset leather surface, cross banded border, conforming base with four drawers, gilt brass lion's head ring pulls, vase and ring-turned spiral carved center support, gadrooned circular platform,

four scrolled reeded and paneled legs, gilt brass hairy paw feet and casters, refinished, minor imperfections, 27-3/4" d, 28" h **12,925.00**

Philadelphia, c1827, carved mahogany veneer, rect top with molded edge, cock-beaded frieze with single central working drawer flanked by faux drawers, turned and carved pedestal ending in gadrooning above stepped, curved pedestal, four belted ball feet, old surface, minor imperfections, carving similar to work of Anthony G. Quervelle (1789-1856), Philadelphia, 45-1/4" w, 20" d, 34-3/4" h **2,550.00**

Gothic Revival, attributed to New York State, 1935-45, mahogany veneer, hexagonal top with molded edge overhangs shaped frieze, three faceted columns atop flat base with concave sides on scrolled feet, old refinish, restored, 34-1/4" d, 31" h........**1,120.00**

International Movement, Wienerwerkstatte, c1930, mahogany and brass, circular top with cross banded edge,

Center table, Renaissance Revival, c1875, walnut, parcel ebonized, gold incised base, marquetry inlaid top with musical instruments, portrait medallions and birds, 44" l, 27" w, 29" h, $7,280. Photo courtesy of Fontaine's Auction Gallery.

Card table, Sheraton, mahogany, serpentine front, swing top with storage compartment below, reeded, tapered legs, some stains on top, 36-3/4" w x 18-1/2" d, 29-3/4" h, $2,530. Photo courtesy of James D. Julia, Inc.

Center table, Renaissance Revival, attributed to Alexander Roux, NY, c1855, rosewood rococo, carved apron, pierced carved stretcher base, 44" x 32" top, 29" h, $2,240. Photo courtesy of Fontaine's Auction Gallery.

conforming frieze, sq-section support flanked by four further cylindrical supports, raised on truncated pyramidal base, 25-1/4" d, 30-1/2" h **550.00**

Louis XV-style, 19th C, mahogany inlaid, ormolu mounted walnut, shaped rect top, one short drawer, opposite faux drawer, cabriole legs, cast sabots, 35" w, 22" d, 28" h **600.00**

Renaissance Revival, American, c1875-80, burl walnut, top with rounded ends, turned pendants, trestle supports, carved stylized foliage and urns, 55" w, 31" d, 30" h **1,610.00**

Chair

American, late 18th C, cherry, three-board top, hinged seat lid, scalloped edge sides, apron, shoe feet, black paint on underside of top, old refinishing on base, minor repairs, 45-1/2" d top, 28-1/2" h **9,350.00**

New England, late 18th C, pine and birch, top tilts above plant seat flanked by sq tapering arm supports which continue to chamfered legs, four sq stretchers, old refinish, 40-1/2" w, 42" d, 28-3/4" h **1,100.00**

New England, early 19th C, pine, maple, and walnut, three-board top tilts above plank seat, walnut arms with turned tapering supports, similar legs terminate in ball and pad feet, old stained red brown surface, repairs, 48-1/4" w, 46-3/4" d, 27-3/4" h **3,300.00**

Coffee, Chippendale-style, Kittinger, mahogany, large tray top, folding sides with cut-out handles, molded legs, stretcher base, branded label, 40" w, 20-1/4" d, 25" h **660.00**

Coffee table, International Movement, George Nakashima, 1962, walnut, two free-edge planks joined by three rosewood joints, unmarked, 36" l, 38" w, 13" h, $6,500. Photo courtesy of David Rago Auctions.

Console

French-style, white, gold, and cream colored paint, gold glass insert on top, apron with applied gesso leaves, rococo scrolling over latticework with ornate floral swags, four cabriole legs ending in scrolled feet, joined by arched stretchers at center, 71-1/2" l, 22-1/2" d, 34-1/2" h **750.00**

George III, c1790, japanned pine, serpentine top dec with black japanned scenes of Chinese landscapes, fluted frieze on fluted sq legs, 34" w, 20" d, 32" h, price for pr. **3,105.00**

Regency, painted and parcel gilt-, rect marble top with outset corners, frieze carved with foliage, legs headed by masks and ending in hoof feet, plinth base, 44" w, 21" d, 31" h **1,955.00**

Second Empire, French, second quarter 19th C, marble-top mahogany, rect speckled black marble top, frieze drawer, applied with wreaths, sq tapered legs headed by herm busts, plinth base, 37-1/2" w, 17" d, 34" h **2,300.00**

Dining

Arts & Crafts

Limbert, #403, cut-corner top over intricate base, slab supports with three spindles in an oval cut-out keyed stretchers connecting to a center leg, one leaf, orig finish, numbered, 50" w, 50" d, 30" h **2,500.00**

Stickley, Gustav, c1920, variant of model 634, oak, oval top, six

Dining table, Arts & Crafts, L. & J.G. Stickley, extension, circular top, five legs, refinished top, original finish on base, some roughness to legs, branded "The Work of ...," 48" d closed, 30-1/2" h, $2,070. Photo courtesy of David Rago Auctions.

Dining, International Movement, George Nelson for Herman Miller, #5559, swag leg, extension, white micarta top, two integral leaves, white enameled legs, some losses to enamel and discoloration, 72" l, 40" w, 29" h, $750. Photo courtesy of David Rago Auctions.

leaves, sq leg posts with mortise and tenon joinery, 46" w, 54-3/4" to 120-3/4" d, 30" h . . .**11,500.00**

Empire-style, Continental, 19th C, walnut, quarter-veneered top with cross banded border, conforming frieze, four canted scroll supports, rect platform stretcher with concave sides, gilt lion-paw feet, octagonal center support, one leaf, 46-1/4" w, 94-3/4" l extended, 31-1/4" h **2,300.00**

Federal, New England, c1820-25, cherry and bird's eye maple, two parts, two rect ends each with hinged drop-leaf, ring-turned tapering legs ending in ball feet, orig surface, minor surface mars, 82" w, 44-1/2" d, 28-3/4" h **1,725.00**

Federal-style, 20th C, mahogany, rect cross banded top, two pedestal bases each with foliate carved posts on four downswept leaf carved legs, casters, three leaves, 72" l without leaves, 48" w, 29" h **3,220.00**

George III-style, mahogany, D-shaped top with rounded corners and reeded edge, twin pedestal bases of column raised on tripod base, downswept legs, brass toe caps and casters, 120" l, 44" w, 29-1/4" h **2,100.00**

International Movement, Paul Evans, manufactured by Directional, sculptured bronzed metal abstract design base, plate-glass top, 72" w, 37" d, 29" h **2,300.00**

Regency, Late, early 19th C, inlaid mahogany, three parts, D-shaped ends, rect center section, all cross banded in satinwood, checker cross banded frieze and sq

Dining table, Arts & Crafts, Stickley Brothers, No. 2424, extension type, circular top and apron, cross-stretchers with pyramidal block finial, casters, paper label, recent dark finish, three later 8" leaves, 48" d, 30" h, $2,990. Photo courtesy of David Rago Auctions.

tapered legs ending in spade feet, four leaves, 155" l, 54" w, 29" h
. . . . **5,175.00**
Regency-style, late 19th C, mahogany, rect top, reeded edge, rounded corners, three ring-turned pedestals, molded cabriole legs, casters, two leaves, 48" w, 177" l, 29" h **17,250.00**

Dressing
Classical, New England, c1820-40, grain painted and dec, scrolling crest over two short drawers, projecting top with rounded corners on conforming base, single drawer, ring-turned and incised tapering legs, allover grain paint resembling rosewood, highlighted by stencils of fruit bowls and scrolling leaves and flowers, gold, green, and black line dec, minor imperfections, 30" w, 15-1/4" d, 39" h **1,550.00**
Empire, mahogany, small case top with drawer, dovetailed drawer in center, thin molding around lower apron, figured mahogany veneer over pine, high ring turned legs with relief rope twist carvings, small pieced restorations, 35-1/2" w, 17-3/4" d, 36-1/2" h. **1,650.00**
Federal
New England, c1825, mahogany and mahogany veneer, scrolled backboard, two cock-beaded short drawers, projecting rect top, cock-beaded long drawer, straight beaded skirt joining fout vase and ring-turned tapering legs, refinished, 32" w, 17-1/4" d, 37-1/4" h **1,175.00**

New York state, c1825, carved mahogany and mahogany veneer, brass inlaid, cock-beaded rect mirror, scrolled acanthus leaf carved supports with brass emb rosettes above three short drawers, projecting case of two short drawers, one long drawer joining four vase and ring-turned acanthus carved legs, casters, refinished, repaired, 36-1/4" w, 21-1/2" d, 55" h **1,725.00**
George I/II, English, c1725, walnut veneer, banded rect top with rounded front corners overhanging shallow straight front fitted with five shallow drawers of banded treatment, plain cabriole legs, pad feet, veneer losses, worm damage, 32" w, 17" d, 30" h **1,875.00**
Mid-Georgian, English

c1760, mahogany, rect case fitted with one long drawer, seven short drawers and recessed kneehole fitted with door, bracket feet, 35" w, 19" d, 30" h
. . . . **1,110.00**
Mid-18th C, mahogany, rect top, conforming case fitted with one long drawer above six short drawers, central kneehole with recessed door, bracket feet, 36" w, 20" d, 32" h. . . . **1,495.00**

Dressing, Sheraton, mahogany veneer, two-tiers, short back splash, stepped top with two-drawer deck over two drawers, reeded and turned legs, Sandwich opalescent glass knobs, 31" w, 21" d, 42" h. Photo courtesy of James D. Julia, Inc.

Painted, New England, c1830, scrolled backboard, two short drawers, projecting top, long drawer, straight skirt joining four ring-turned and swelled tapering legs, old yellow paint with mustard and green pin striping and floral dec, minor imperfections, 36" w, 17-1/2" d, 38" h **1,765.00**
Queen Anne

Connecticut, attributed to, last half 18th C, cherry, rect top with molded edge, shaped corners, case of two thumb-molded half drawers, three drawers with shell and foliate carved fans on valanced apron joining four cabriole legs, pad feet, old refinish, old replaced brasses, imperfections, 29-1/2" w, 20" d, 36-1/2" h **5,875.00**
Pennsylvania, Philadelphia, c1740-60, walnut, overhanging top with thumb-molded edge, straight front fitted with three thumb-molded drawers, single wide drawer over two narrow drawers, shaped apron, cabriole legs, drake feet, refinished, 35-1/2" l, 21" d, 30-1/2" h **14,350.00**

Drop Leaf
Chippendale
New England, southern, c1760-80, cherry, oval overhanging drop leaf top, cut-out apron, scrolled returns, four cabriole legs ending in claw and ball feet, imperfections, 44-1/2" l open, 15-1/2" w, 27" h
. . . . **4,410.00**

Drop-leaf table, Arts & Crafts, attributed to Lifetime, stretchers keyed through posts, original finish, unmarked, 36" w, 24" d, 38" h open, $700. Photo courtesy of David Rago Auctions.

Drop-leaf table, Chippendale, mahogany, wide drop leaf, tapered legs, carved ball and claw feet, 16-1/23" w (closed), 50-1/2" w (open), 41-3/4" d, 28" h, $2,100. Photo courtesy of James D. Julia, Inc.

Pennsylvania, late 18th C, walnut, shaped skirt, molded Marlborough legs, old surface, minor imperfections, 15-1/2" w, 46-3/4" l, 29" h **550.00**

Rhode Island, c1780, carved mahogany, rect drop leaf top, four sq molded stop fluted legs joined by cut-out apron, repairs, 47-3/4" w, 38-1/4" d, 29" h **2,100.00**

Classical, attributed to NY, c1820, carved mahogany and mahogany veneer, rect top, overhanging shaped leaves, conforming base with single drawer, beaded skirt, suspending four circular drops on leaf carved pedestal, four curved scrolling acanthus leaf carved and molded legs, brass paw feet on casters, possibly orig glass drawer pull, old refinish, very minor imperfections **1,650.00**

Federal, New England, early 19th C, tiger maple, rect leaves, straight skirt, sq tapering legs, old refinish, repairs, 46-1/2" w, 14" d, extends to 44-1/2", 26-3/4" h **1,150.00**

Hepplewhite, cherry, one board top, finely tapered legs, old mellow finish, pieced restorations at rule joints, replaced hinges, 48-3/4" l, 15-1/4" d, 28" h **1,100.00**

Queen Anne

America, c1780, walnut, top with shaped corners, shaped skirt, cabriole legs, pad feet, early refinish, replaced batons, one replaced glue block, 44-1/2" l, 4-2" open, 27-1/2" h . . **2,200.00**

New England, c1750-70, maple, overhanging circular drop leaf top, fout cabriole legs, pad feet

on platforms, shaped apron, refinished, imperfections, 47-1/2" w, 46-1/4" d, 27-3/4" h **7,675.00**

Sheraton, Country

Birch, old red on one board top and leaves, later black on base, crisply turned legs pegged at aprons, crack in top of one leg, 36-1/4" w, 14" d, 10-7/8" l leaves, 28-3/4" h **495.00**

Walnut, 20-1/2" d x 48" l one board top, 20-3/4" d leaves, six turned legs, one foot chipped, refinished **300.00**

Game

Arts & Crafts, Miller Furniture Co., removable circular top, four plank legs inlaid with stylized floral design, paper label, felted gaming surface missing, overcoated top, 36" d, 31" h **1,150.00**

Empire, tilt-top, mahogany and mahogany flame veneer, top with ogee aprons on sides, turned drops, carved pineapple column, platform base with scrolled leaf returns to carved paw feet, one drawer on side, old dark finish, 40-1/2" w, 20" d, 30" h **450.00**

George III, English

c1790, cross banded mahogany, D-shaped, plain frieze, sq tapered and molded legs, 35" w, 17" d, 28" h **1,150.00**

18th C, mahogany, concertina-action, rect top, suede int., blind

Game table, Arts & Crafts, McHugh, circular top, cross-banding to apron, keyed-through tenon ornamentation, two serving as drawer pulls, and two decorative, arched cross-stretchers mortised through legs, original finish, partial paper label, crack to applied tenons, 44-1/2" d, 30-1/2" h, $1,955. Photo courtesy of David Rago Auctions.

fret carved legs, 36" w, 17-1/2" d, 29" h **1,495.00**

Hepplewhite, American, 19th C, inlaid cherry, hinged demilune to, conforming apron, sq tapering legs **400.00**

Phyfe, Duncan, c1820, mahogany, top with band of line inlay on edge, urn pedestal, saber legs, top loose, minor veneer loss, 39" w top open, 29" h **1,875.00**

Queen Anne, English, mahogany, hinged two-board top with molded edge, dovetailed drawer, shaped returns, relief carved detail at knees, well shaped cabriole legs, pad feet, rear swing legs, old dark finish, old replaced brass pulls, minor restoration, side returns missing, old splits in top, 35-1/2" w, 16" d, 28-3/4" h **1,550.00**

Renaissance Revival, A. Cutler & Son, Buffalo, NY, c1874, ebonized and parcel-gilt, drop leaf, orig paper label, wear to baise surface, 36" w, 13-3/4" d, 28-3/4" h . . **700.00**

Sheraton, mahogany, shaped top, cookie corners, shaped frieze, turned reeded legs, replaced supports under top, 36" w, 30-1/2" h **1,225.00**

William and Mary-style, with antique elements, seaweed marquetry inlaid walnut, D-shaped top with concave front, frieze similar shaped, frieze drawer, turned legs joined by stretchers, 32" w, 14" d, 30" h **2,875.00**

Game table, George II, English, c1740, mahogany, fold-over top, baize playing surface, counter wells, 27-1/2" w, 13-3/4" d, 28" h, $2,500. Photo courtesy of Sloan's Auctioneers & Appraisers.

Harvest

English, early, yew and oak, dark finish, old replaced thick five-board top with breadboard ends, beaded aprons, large turned legs, stretcher base, mortise and peg construction, age splits and alterations, 71-1/2" w, 28" d, 29" h
.... **1,500.00**

New England, early 19th C, drop-leaf, pine, scrubbed top, hinged leaves, olive green painted base, ring turned tapering legs, early surface, 102-34" l, 18-1/4" d, 39-3/4" extended, 20-1/2" h
.... **11,500.00**

New England, mid-19th C, drop-leaf, painted pine, rect hinged leaves with rounded corners flanking single drawer at each end, ring turned bulbous legs, orig olive-yellow surface, turned pulls, legs pierced, 72-1/2" l, 26-1/2" w, 26" w extended, 29-1/2" h
.... **19,550.00**

Lamp, Arts & Crafts

Brooks, attributed to, four-sided top, flaring legs, floriform lower shelf, new finish, unmarked, seam separation on side, 20" w, 19-3/4" d, 29-3/4" h **2,300.00**

Stickley, Gustav, No. 644, circular top, arched cross-stretchers topped by finial, mortised legs, good new finish, replaced finial, Als lk Kan brand, 29-1/2" d, 28-3/4" h
.... **2,300.00**

Library

Arts & Crafts

English, overhanging top, arched apron, legs carved with stylized tulips, unmarked, refinished, seam separation to top, minor

Library table, Gothic Revival, carved walnut, c1880, 42" l, 27" d, 28" h, $1,300. Photo courtesy of Sloan's Auctioneers & Appraisers.

nicks and edge roughness at feet, 46" w, 27" d, 30" h
.... **1,955.00**

Robertson Co., H. P., Jamestown, NJ, early 20th C, oak, oval top over single drawer, flanked by side shelves, lower median shelf, imperfections, 48" w, 29-1/4" d, 29-1/4" h..... **950.00**

Stickley, Gustav, three drawers, hammered copper pulls, sq posts, broad lower shelf, red decal, refinished, 66" l, 36" w, 30-1/2" h **3,775.00**

Stickley, L. & J. G., Fayetteville, NY, similar to model no. 520, oak, rect top, single drawer, corbel supports, low median shelf with through tenons, red and yellow decal "The Work of L. & J. G. Stickley" on int. drawer, imperfections, 42" w, 28-1/8" d, 29-1/4" h... **1,265.00**

Georgian-style, Morris and Co., late 19th/early 20th C, mahogany, tooled red leather top and gadrooned edge, two end drawers, boldly carved cabriole legs, claw and ball feet, 90" l, 53" d, 30" h
.... **3,450.00**

Renaissance Revival, third quarter 19th C, carved oak, rect top, two frieze drawers with mask form pulls, griffin form legs, shaped plinth, 54" w, 28" d, 30" h . **3,910.00**

Occasional

Arts & Crafts, Gustav Stickley, circular overhanging top, faceted finial over arched cross-stretchers, very good orig finish, red decal, 24" d, 29" h **2,185.00**

Biedermeier, early 19th C, birchwood, solid gallery top, inset petit point needlework panel, plain frieze, turned legs joined by stretchers, casters, inscription underneath reading "J. J. Werner, Paris," 21-1/2" w, 18-1/2" d, 29-3/4" h............. **2,760.00**

Parlor

Gothic Revival, walnut, rosewood veneer apron, replaced top, 20" x 36" x 29-1/4" h **500.00**

Victorian, walnut, molded detail, white marble turtle top, carved dog on base shelf, old dark finish, old repairs, top cracked, 23" x 3" x 29" h................. **770.00**

Pedestal

Aesthetic Movement, French, c1875-80, brass and pottery, sq top with recessed tile, dec with

Gateleg table, Queen Anne, English, c1750, oval, Marlborough-style legs, oak secondary wood, three boards, old mellow refinishing, drop-leaf hinges all reset, some loss of height to legs, 62" l, 49" w, 28-1/2" h, $2,000. Photo courtesy of Cowan's Historic Americana Auctions.

Library table, Arts & Crafts, Gustav Stickley, two drawers, hammered copper pulls, long corbels, and lower shelf, original finish, paper label and partial red decal, 36" l, 24" d, 30" h, $3,775. Photo courtesy of David Rago Auctions.

Parlor table, Renaissance Revival, ebonized wood with incised gilt decorated, white marble top with faux black graining, turned base with rosette and floral carving, 36" w, 25" d, 32" h, $625. Photo courtesy of Sanford Alderfer Auction Company.

foliage, pedestal with pottery cylinder, four angular legs, foliate dec, 14" w, 34" h **8,100.00**
Biedermeier-style, cherry and burr poplar, circular top with cross banded edge, conforming apron, hexagonal support rising from triangular platform base with concave sides, three scroll supports, 29-1/2" d, 27-1/2" h **600.00**
Second Empire-style, walnut, marquetry, and parcel-gilt, quarter-veneered circular top, polychrome floral marquetry, gilt-metal gadrooned edge, sq section tapered pedestal with concave sides and canted corners, gilt hairy-paw feet, 33-1/2" d, 28-1/4" h **1,000.00**

Pembroke
Chippendale, New England, late 18th C, mahogany, rect overhanging top, drop leaves, straight skirt, four sq tapering legs with inside chamfering, joined by "X" form sq stretchers, old refinish, imperfections, 29" w, 16" d, 30" extended, 27-3/4" h **1,840.00**
Federal
New England, 1795-1810, inlaid mahogany, oval top with outline stringing, conforming base with

Table, Pembroke, Hepplewhite, refinished cherry, serpentine drop-leaf top, serpentine end aprons, conforming drawer, square tapered legs with inside chamber, stringing inlay on legs and aprons with fans and oval paterae, fretwork brackets, 35-3/8" w, 16-3/4" d, 8-3/4" leaves, 28"h, $6,500. Photo courtesy of Garth's Auctions.

string inlaid drawer flanked by inlaid paterae in the dies, four sq tapering legs with stringing, pendant bellflowers, and inlaid cuffs, old refinish, minor imperfections, 32" w, 18-1/2" d, 27-1/2" h **10,925.00**
New York, c1810-15, mahogany, rect overhanging drop leaf top with canted corners, conforming base, single drawer, paneled dies on four tapering reeded legs ending in casters joined by cock-beaded skirt, refinished, 36" l, 20-3/4" w, 28-1/4" h **850.00**
George III, c1785, mahogany, diminutive drop leaves, frieze drawer, sq fluted and tapered legs, casters, 28" l, 34" w, 28" h **1,175.00**
Hepplewhite, English, mahogany, figured veneers, dovetailed drawer in one end, tapered sq legs, line border inlay, oval medallions at tops, brass casters, old refinishing, 29-1/4" l, 18-1/2" d, 9-1/2" l leaves, 27-1/2" h **1,595.00**
Sheraton, New York, mahogany, double drop shaped leaves, single end drawer, well proportioned tapering turned elongated legs fitted with brass ferrules and casters, inlaid mahogany tombstone panels beside drawer, fine reeding to legs, 43" w open, 21" closed, 35-1/2" d, 29" h **6,500.00**
Pier, Classical, Boston, 1835-40, mahogany veneer, replaced carrara marble top, straight paneled veneered frieze above scrolled and carved frontal supports with flattened veneered columns flanking pier glass, old refinish, feet missing, some veneer loss, 41" w, 17-3/4" d, 36" h, price for matched pair **10,925.00**
Refectory, late 19th or early 20th C, oak, 1-1/2" thick three-board top, two large turned and carved supports, stretcher base, shoe feet, old dark finish, 71-1/2" l, 27-1/2" d, 30-1/2" h **1,550.00**
Rent, George III-style, Kittinger, mahogany and figured veneer, oak secondary wood, circular drum top with four drawers alternating with false fronts, leather inset top, single pedestal cabinet base with door, applied trim on sides, metallic label

Reading table, Victorian-style, walnut, revolving, top with an inset brass panel depicting exotic birds and foliage, 20" w, 27" h, $950. Photo courtesy of Sloan's Auctioneers & Appraisers.

inside drawer, minor burns on top, old pieced veneer restorations, 48" d, 30-1/2" d **1,775.00**

Serving
Federal, New England, c1800, inlaid mahogany, band inlay around top and leaves, large satinwood oval on top, single dovetailed drawer with satinwood band inlay, bow-front top with end-blocking and serpentine sides with string-inlaid edge above conforming base, single drawer outlined in veneer banding flanked by rect dies above similar banding and string inlaid legs, brasses appear original, old refinish, imperfections, 34-1/2" w, 17" d, 32" h **16,450.00**
George III, c1800
Mahogany, slightly bowed top, pair of drawers, sq tapering legs **1,725.00**
Satinwood and marquetry, demilune, later fitted with spring action drawers, restoration, 62-1/4" w, 23-1/2" d, 32-3/4" h **19,550.00**

Sewing
Federal
Boston, MA, c1805, mahogany veneer, mahogany top with

outset corners above two veneered cock-beaded drawers, sliding bag frame, flanked by legs with colonettes above reeding, ending in turned tapering feet, old brass, old finish, 20-3/4" w, 15-3/4" d, 28-1/4" h **1,610.00**

New England, mahogany veneer, mahogany top with hinged drop leaves, reeded edge, flanking three veneered drawers, top fitted for writing, bottom with sliding sewing bag frame, ring-turned and spiral carved legs, casters, old refinish, replaced brasses, 18-1/2" w, 18-1/8" d, 29-1/4" h . . . **1,150.00**

French-style, early 20th C, inlaid mahogany, hinged scalloped top finely inlaid with flowers and scrolled leaves, scalloped aprons, delicate cabriole legs with beaded edging, applied ormolu on apron, knees, and feet, shallow int. compartment, old refinish, some alterations, 25" w, 18-1/2" d, 30-1/2" h **600.00**

Sheraton, mahogany, drop leaf, two drawers over one drawer, ring and spiral turned legs, brass cup and caster feet, 20-1/2" closed, 27-3/4" open, 18" d, 28-1/2" h **1,200.00**

Side

Classical, New York, 1835-45, mahogany, rect marble top with rounded corners, conforming ogee molded skirt, pierced and scrolled supports, pillar and scroll bases, applied ripple molding joining scrolled medial shelf, casters, old finish, minor imperfections, 31" w, 18-1/2" d, 31" h **3,750.00**

Federal, attributed to southern New England, c1800-10, mahogany and tiger maple veneer inlay, serpentine top with elliptic ends, conforming base, frieze drawer, inlaid tiger maple veneer panels outlined with crossbanding and stringing, four sq tapering legs with conforming inlay continuing to inlaid cuffs, restored, 23-1/4" w, 17" d, 28-1/4" h **10,575.00**

Louis XV-style, Provincial, 19th C, walnut, rect thumb-molded top, frieze drawer, shaped skirt, cabriole legs, 27" w, 21-1/2" d, 26-1/2" h **980.00**

Renaissance Revival, America, c1870, walnut, inset marble top,

Side table, Arts & Crafts, Stickley Brothers, single-drawer table with flush top, three slats to each side, and lower shelf. Unmarked, some wear to original finish, stain and seam separation to top, 24" w, 22" d, 30" h, $3,100. Photo courtesy of David Rago Auctions.

maidenhead carved frieze raised on angular legs, X-stretcher, 35" l, 22" d, 30-1/2" h **1,495.00**

Silver, George III, c1765, carved mahogany, galleried tray top, low relief carved everted lip, repeating border of C-scrolls and foliage, swirling scroll bordered apron, molded sq cabriole supports with trailing acanthus carving at knees, Spanish feet, alterations to top, repairs, 31-3/4" l 28-3/4" h **2,000.00**

Sofa, Edwardian, c1895, painted satinwood, rounded drop leaves, two frieze drawers, trestle supports

Side table, Victorian, mahogany, scalloped top, lower shelf with carved reclining dog, 35" w, 23" d, 29" h, $250. Photo courtesy of Joy Luke Auctions.

ending in brass paw casters, 36" w closed, 26-1/2" d, 28-1/2" h **8,100.00**

Tavern

Chippendale, Massachusetts or New Hampshire, late 18th/early 19th C, cherry top, thumb molded edge overhangs maple base with straight molded skirt, sq tiger maple legs with beaded front edges, chamfered rear ones, early surface, minor surface stains, 34" w, 25" d, 27-5/8" h . . . **4,600.00**

Hepplewhite, two-board breadboard top, large overhang, one drawer base, tapered sq legs, grungy finish, 42-1/2" w, 29-3/4" d, 28" h **750.00**

Queen Anne, America, maple with some curl, old mellow surface, oval top with old pierced restoration at center, turned feet and legs, stretcher base, molded edges on bottoms of aprons and stretchers with pegged mortise joints, age splits, 23-1/2" w, 21-1/2" d, 26" h **2,350.00**

William and Mary, New England, 18th C, maple and pine, rect overhanging top, straight skirt with drawer, joining block base and ring turned legs, feet joined by square stretchers, old refinish, minor imperfections, 33" w, 21" d, 27" h **1,610.00**

William and Mary-style, oak, rect thumb-molded top, frieze drawer, turned legs joined by box stretcher, 33" w, 24" d, 29" h **575.00**

Windsor, New England, early 19th C, black painted, oval overhanging top, four vase and ring-turned splayed legs, turned feet, joined by stretchers, old paint, imperfections, 26-3/4" l, 21-3/4" d, 22-1/4" h **1,100.00**

Tea

Chippendale

America, possibly Philadelphia, piecrust tilt top, figured mahogany one-piece circular top, ogee and crescent form carving, birdcage support, fluted column, compressed ball knop, three legs with plain knees, ball and claw feet, 28-1/2" h **10,575.00**

Pennsylvania, c1760-80, cherry, circular tilt top with molded edge, birdcage mechanism,

Tea table, Queen Anne, carved walnut, tilt-top, circular top with carved design, birdcage support, carved knees and feet, 30-1/2" d, 28-1/2" h, $500. Photo courtesy of James D. Julia, Inc.

ball and ring-turned post, tripod cabriole legs, arris pad feet, old refinish, very minor restorations, 27-1/4" d, 28-3/4" h . . . **3,820.00**

Philadelphia, 1760-80, cherry, molded and carved bird cage, round top with molded rim, tilts and rotates above pillar, suppressed belted ball over knees carved with C-scrolls and leafage on cabriole legs, pad feet, early surface, minor imperfections, provenance: bought from Mary Ball Washington, 21" d, 28-1/4" h **409,500.00**

Philadelphia, c1760-80, mahogany and walnut, circular tilt top with pie crust edge, bird cage support, carved pedestal with fluted cylindrical section over bun–shaped section carved with leafage to upper half above billet and beat perimeter, plain bottom half, fillet molding above collar of guilloche, cabriole legs carved with scrolling leaves, each with rococo cartouche on upper knee surface, slender claw and ball feet, top replaced, refinished, 33" d, 28" h **19,800.00**

Chippendale-style, America, mahogany, round tilt-top, well turned column, cabriole legs,

snake feet, orig dark finish, minor edge wear, block needs stabilization, 32" d top, 27-1/2" h **500.00**

Mid-Georgian, possibly Irish, walnut, rect top with inset corners, slightly raised paneling in center, serpentine frieze, angular cabriole legs ending in pointed feet, 32-1/2" w, 23-1/2" d, 23-1/2" h **1,100.00**

Hepplewhite, tilt top, poplar one board top with cut corners, birch tripod base with spider legs, turned column, old refinishing with painted foliage border designs in shades of gold and black, top replaced, repairs, 15-1/2" w, 23-1/2" l, 28-3/4" h **440.00**

Queen Anne, New England, c1760-80, cherry, circular tilt top, vase and ring-turned post and tripod cabriole leg base, pad feet, refinished, minor imperfections, 34-1/4" d, 27-1/2" h **1,175.00**

Shaker, attributed to Mt Lebanon, NY, c1830, birch, circular tilt top with bull-nose edge, tilts on platform, tapering turned pedestal, tripod cabriole legs, pad feet, old refinish, 34-1/4" d, 26-3/4" h **6,465.00**

Tilt-Top

Federal, New England, mahogany inlaid, octagonal top with string inlay in outline, urn shaped pedestal, cabriole legs, arris pad feet on platforms, orig surface, very minor imperfections, 22" w, 14-3/4" d, 29-1/2" h **3,750.00**

Georgian, late 18th C, mahogany, plain circular top over turned baluster standard, three cabriole

Trestle table, Arts & Crafts, L.& J.G. Stickley, overhanging top, double-column sides and broad lower shelf keyed-through the sides, unmarked, original finish to base, cleaned finish with color added to top, seam separations to ends, dents and chipping around stretcher, 72" l, 45" d, 29" h, $4,890. Photo courtesy of David Rago Auctions.

legs ending in shaped pad feet, 32" d, 27-3/8" h **1,100.00**

Tray, Edwardian, c1900, satinwood and inlay, two oval tiers, removable wood and glass tray, slightly splayed sq tapering legs joined by stretcher, 36" w, 20-1/4" d, 32" h **1,150.00**

Vitrine, Louis XVI-style, c1880, gilt bronze mounted mahogany, beveled glass panels and turned legs joined by stretchers, foliate cast bronze mounts, 26" w, 16" d, 30" h **3,450.00**

Work

Biedermeier-style, cherry wood and burr popular, rect top, molded frieze with drawer, inverted, pierced, and lyre-form supports joined by pole stretcher, 22-1/2" l, 15-3/4" w, 25-1/4" h **650.00**

Classical, Boston, 1830, mahogany veneer, solid top, hinged rounded drop leaves with beaded edges, flank two convex veneered drawers, top one fitted for writing, lower with replaced fabric sewing fabric bag, turned tapering legs which flank shaped veneered platform, ebonized bun feet, orig stamped brass pulls, imperfections, minor warp in leaf, 19" w, 19" d, 28-3/4" h **980.00**

Federal, New England, first quarter 19th C, cherry, rect top overhangs two drawers, swelled and ring-turned legs, pegged feet, old refinish, one glass knob missing, 19-7/8" w, 14-1/2" d, 28-1/4" h **500.00**

Federal, late, MA, c1825, carved mahogany and mahogany veneer, rect top with molded edge, rounded drop leaves, two working

Work table, Federal, cherry, scrubbed rectangular top overhangs single drawer, ring-turned legs, old refinish, $475.

drawers and false drawer, four vase and ring-turned spiral carved legs ending in turned feet on casters, old refinish, replaced brass pulls, imperfections, bottom drawer missing, 18" w, 18" d, 28-1/4" h **900.00**

George III, early 19th C, mahogany, rect top, canted corners, fitted int., sq tapered and slightly splayed legs joined by stretchers . **2,380.00**

Hepplewhite, country

Walnut and pine, wooden peg construction, one board top, tapered and splayed legs, later blue paint, thin coat of varnish, minor hairlines, split, minor insect damage on legs, 25" x 33" top, 29-1/2" h **650.00**

Walnut, pegged construction, three-board top, dovetailed drawer, turned wooden pull, tapered legs, old dark mellow finish, evidence of earlier blue paint, restoration and replacements, 55-3/4" w, 35-3/8" d, 27" h **450.00**

Queen Anne

Black walnut and pine, painted, PA, c1760-1800, removable blank three-board pine top, supported by cleats and four dowels, two thumb-molded drawers, straight skirt with breaded edge above straight cabriole legs ending in pad feet, orig apple green paint, old replaced wooden pulls, surface imperfections, cracked foot, 48-1/2" w, 32" d, 27" h **2,500.00**

Maple and pine, New England, late 18th C, scrubbed top, straight skirt with beaded edge, turned tapering legs ending in turned button feet, old surface, remnants of red on base, 28" w, 28-1/2" l, 27" h **2,530.00**

Walnut, removable three-board top, two dovetailed overlapping drawers, mortised and pinned apron with edge beading, turned legs, weathered duck feet, old refinishing, period replaced brasses, pieced repairs to top, age cracks, 32" w, 49-1/2" l, 28" h . . **2,750.00**

Sheraton, mahogany and mahogany veneer, three dovetailed drawers, turned legs with ring turned detail, orig gilded lion head brasses, old

finish, top drawer is fitted with tilt-up writing surface, age cracks in sides, some veneer damage to writing tablet, 16" w, 18" l, 27-3/4" h **1,430.00**

William and Mary-style, walnut, ebonized trim, two-board top, one dovetailed drawer, turned stretchers and legs, repairs and old replacements, 22-3/4" w, 34" d, 27-1/4" h **935.00**

GAME BOARDS

History: Wooden game boards have a long history and were some of the first toys early Americans enjoyed. Games such as checkers, chess, and others were easy to play and required only simple markers or playing pieces. Most were handmade, but some machine-made examples exist.

Game boards can be found in interesting color combinations. Some include small drawers to hold the playing pieces. Others have an interesting molding or frame. Look for signs of use from long hours of enjoyment.

Today, game boards are popular with game collectors, folk art collectors, and decorators because of their interesting forms.

Reproduction Alert

Checkerboard

10-1/2" w, 19-1/2" h, painted green and yellow, late 19th C, paint imperfections **1,955.00**

Game board, double sided, America, 19th C, 20-1/2" square applied frame, one side checkerboard painted yellow, black, green, and red, the other side backgammon game in the same colors, wear, $1,645. Photo courtesy of Skinner's Auctioneers and Appraisers.

12-1/2" w, 12-3/4" h, painted black and white, tan colored ground, sgd "F. Smith," PA, c1870 . . . . **1,955.00**

13-7/8" w, 13-3/4" h, painted hunter green and iron red, black frame, yellow grain paint on reverse, America, 19th C, minor paint war **1,380.00**

14" w, 20-1/4" h, oak and mahogany squares, galleried edge with two reserves on sides with sliding lid compartments to hold checkers, two sets of checkers, one round, one square, minor wear, light alligatoring to old black paint on lids and gallery **330.00**

15-1/4" sq, painted black and salmon, New England, 19th C **2,300.00**

16" sq, blue and white, yellowed varnish, New England, 19th C. **3,335.00**

16" w, 17-1/2" h, painted red and white checkerboard, orig cherry frame, Newburyport, MA, c1850 . . . . . **980.00**

17" w, 16" h, painted green and white, unfinished, inscribed on reverse, late 19th/early 20th C **460.00**

17-3/4" w, 17-5/8" h, painted salmon red with ochre and black checkerboard, indistinct pencil inscription on reverse, America, 19th C, scratches and minor paint wear **800.00**

18" w, 21" h, painted red and black, yellow dec, Michigan, c1880 . **2,415.00**

18-1/2" sq, painted yellow and black, green detailing, c1880 . . . . . . **5,465.00**

19-1/2" sq, painted slate, incised geometric design, hand painted to resemble hardstones, shades of marbleized green and red, solid dark red checks, shaded yellow ground, mottled black border, New England, late 19th C, minor paint wear at margins **1,645.00**

20" w, 18-3/4" h, painted and gilt dec, molded edge, reverse marked "Saco Lodge No. 2," Saco, Maine, 19th C **5,175.00**

21-1/2" x 17-1/2", incised checkerboard under glass, red, lime green, yellow, and black, reverse painted in red, white, and blue, framed, America, 20th C, minor paint wear **650.00**

25" w, 19" h, painted red and black, gilt trim, second half 19th C **2,300.00**

Double-sided

7-1/4" w, 7" h, painted pine, brown and black checkerboard on one side, painted brown Old Mill game inscribed on reverse, two sliding panel compartments, New York State, early 19th C **1,150.00**

12-1/4" w, 12" h, painted apple green, brown, and black, obverse with checkerboard, reverse with snake-motif game, America, mid-19th C . **36,800.00**

14" sq, painted salmon, green, and yellow, New England, 19th C, loss to frame **3,740.00**

14-1/4" sq, painted black and red, obverse with checkerboard, reverse with Old Mill, applied molded edge, New England, c1850-70 . . . . . **4,890.00**

14-7/8" w, 15-7/8" h, painted deep blue-green, red and black, checkerboard on obverse, backgammon on reverse, America, 19th C **2,530.00**

15" w, 16" h, painted mustard, red, and green, checkerboard on obverse, backgammon on reverse, America, 19th C **3,335.00**

17" sq, obverse with Parcheesi, painted red, teal, orange, and green, checkerboard on reverse with orange, black, and yellow paint, c1900, paint wear to obverse at edges **2,530.00**

18-1/2" w, 20" h, New Hampshire, Parcheesi game scribed and painted in eight colors, checkerboard on reverse, New Hampshire, 19th C, minor wear, crack **21,850.00**

20-1/8" x 20-1/2", painted wood, sq board with applied frame, one side checkerboard painted yellow, black, green, and red, other side backgammon game in the same colors, America, 19th C, wear **1,645.00**

The Owl, table-top type, Chicago, $65. Photo courtesy of Joy Luke Auctions.

22" x 28-3/4", painted wood, rect, polychrome Parcheesi game on one side, red and black checkerboard on reverse, wear **1,880.00**

23" w, 17-1/4" h, painted apple green, black, and red, checkerboard on obverse, backgammon on reverse, game piece compartments, America, c1870-80 . . . . **3,750.00**

Folding

12-1/2" w, 31" h, painted avocado green, colorful raised segmented tracks, opens for storage, mid-20th C, wear **575.00**

Numbered

14-1/2" w, 16-1/2" h, painted red and black, gold striping and numbers 1 through 32, New York, c1870 . **4,350.00**

Parcheesi

18" w, 17-3/4" h, folding, patriotic red, white, and blue stars and dec, New England, late 19th C **4,350.00**

18-1/2" sq, folding, painted American flag and spade, heart, diamond, and club motifs, MA, c1870, minor paint imperfections **46,000.00**

19-1/2" sq, folding, painted green, white, black, and yellow, varied geometric designs on game corners, America, 19th C **2,875.00**

25" w, 24-1/2" h, painted, center rosette, bull's eye corners, attributed to Maine, 19th C, wear **4,600.00**

27-1/2" w, 27" h, painted red, yellow, and green, New England, 1870-80 . . . . **5,750.00**

Three-panel board

33" x 36", painted pine, red, green, and yellow playing field, light blue ground **825.00**

GAME PLATES

History: Game plates, popular between 1870 and 1915, are specially decorated plates used to serve fish and game. Sets originally included a platter, serving plates, and a sauce or gravy boat. Many sets have been divided. Today, individual plates are often used as wall hangings.

Birds
Plate

9-1/4" d, hp, set of 12 with different center scene of shore birds in natural setting, apple green edge, printed gold scrolled rim dec, artist sgd "B. Albert," Theodore Haviland & Co., France, early 20th C **865.00**

Set, turkey, hand painted, artist signed "Gasri," 20-3/4" platter with strutting tom turkey, 9" gravy boat, 12 10" plates with different turkey designs, green "LDBC Hambeau Limoges" mark, $700. Photo courtesy of James D. Julia, Inc.

9-1/2" d, duck, pastel pink, blue, and cream ground, duck flying up from water, yellow flowers and grasses, sgd "Laury," marked "Limoges," not pierced for hanging . . . **120.00**

10-1/2" d, game bird and two water spaniels, crimped gold rim, sgd "RK Beck" **95.00**

13-1/4" d, game bird and pheasant, heavy gold, scalloped emb rococo border, marked "Coronet Limoges, Bussilion" **250.00**

Platter

11" l, Limoges, artist sgd "Raly," marked "Coronet" with crown and "Limoges, France," script mark, gold trim, shows two ducks, pierced for hanging **410.00**

16" l, two handles, quail, hp gold trim, Limoges **150.00**

Wall plaque, hand-painted, flying grouse, scrolled gilt rim, signed by artist "A. Brousselton," marked "Limoges/ Crown/Coronet/France," 18" d, $615. Photo courtesy of Sanford Alderfer Auction Company.

Set

Seven pcs, wild game birds, pastoral scene, molded edges, shell dec, Fazent Meheim, Bonn, Germany............... **250.00**

Twelve pcs, 10-1/2" d plates, game birds in natural habitat, sgd "I. Bubedi" **3,500.00**

Deer

Plate, 9" d, buck and doe, forest scene **60.00**

Set, 13 pcs, platter, 12 plates, deer, bear, and game birds, yellow ground, scalloped border, "Haviland China," sgd "MC Haywood".........**3,200.00**

Fish, 10-3/4" x 23-3/4" platter, 12 9-1/2" d plates, gravy boat and under-plate, peach shading to ivory ground, gold trim, fish school decoration, unmarked, gravy boat damaged, flakes to some plates, $550. Photo courtesy of Alderfer Auction Company, Inc.

Fish
Plate

8" d, bass, scalloped edge, gray-green trim, fern on side of fish, Limoges **65.00**

8-1/2" d, colorful fish swimming on green shaded ground, scalloped border, gold trim, sgd "Lancy," "Bairritz, W. S. or S. W. Co. Limoges, France," pierced for hanging **50.00**

Platter

14" l, bass on lure, sgd "RK Beck" **125.00**

23" l, hp, Charoone, Haviland **200.00**

Set

Seven pcs, platter, six serving plates, each with different fish dec, white ground, gold trim, Italian **125.00**

Eight pcs, four plates, 24" l, platter, sauce boat with attached plate, cov tureen, Rosenthal..... **425.00**

Eleven pcs, 10 plates, serving platter, sgd "Limoges" **360.00**

Fifteen pcs, 12 9" plates, 24" platter, sauce boat with attached plate, cov tureen, hp, raised gold design edge, artist sgd, Limoges..**800.00**

GAMES

History: Board games have been commercially produced in this country since at least 1822, and card games since the 1780s. However, it was not until the 1840s that large numbers of games were produced that survive to this day. The W. & S. B. Ives Company produced many board and card games in the 1840s and 1950s. Milton Bradley and McLoughlin Brothers became major producers of games starting in the 1860s, followed by Parker Brothers in the 1880s. Other major producers of games in this period were Bliss, Chaffee and Selchow, Selchow and Righter, and Singer.

Today, most games from the 19th century are rare and highly collectible, primarily because of their spectacular lithography. McLoughlin and Bliss command a premium because of the rarity, quality of materials, and the extraordinary art that was created to grace the covers and boards of their games.

In the 20th century, Milton Bradley, Selchow and Righter, and Parker Brothers became the primary manufacturers of boxed games. They have all now been absorbed by toy giant Hasbro Corporation. Other noteworthy producers were All-Fair, Pressman, and Transogram, all of which are no longer in business. Today, the hottest part of the game collecting market is in rare character games from the 1960s. Parker Brothers and All-Fair games from the 1920s to 1940s also have some excellent lithography and are highly collectible.

Additional Listings: See *Warman's Americana & Collectibles.*

Notes: While people collect games for many reasons, it is strong graphic images that bring the highest prices. Games collected because they are fun to play or for nostalgic reasons are still collectible, but will not bring high prices. Also, game collectors are not interested in common and "public domain" games such as checkers, tiddlywinks, Authors, Anagrams, Jackstraws, Rook, Pit, Flinch, and Peter Coodles. The game market today is characterized by fairly stable prices for ordinary items, increasing discrimination for grades of condition, and continually rising prices for rare material in excellent condition. Whether you are a dealer or collector, be careful to buy games in good condition. Avoid games with taped or split corners or other box damage. Games made after about 1950 are difficult to sell unless they are complete and in excellent condition. As games get older, there is a forgiveness factor for condition and completeness that increases with age.

These listings are for games that are complete and in excellent condition. Be sure the game you're looking to price is the same as the one described in the listing. The 19th century makers routinely published the same title on several different versions of the game, varying in size and graphics. Dimensions listed below are rounded to the nearest half inch.

Auto Race, Alderman, Fairchild Co., Rochester, NY, patent date April 20, 1922, chromolithograph, six automobile playing pieces, 17-1/2" x 17-3/4", $75. Photo courtesy of Cowan Historic Americana Auctions.

Big Chief, Milton Bradley, 1938, 8" x 17" **125.00**

Bull in a China Shop, Milton Bradley, 1937 .... **100.00**

Chiromagia Game, McLoughlin, three answer sheets, two question discs, lid missing **100.00**

Clue, Parker Brothers, c1949, separate board and pieces box......... **25.00**

Dixie Pollyana, Parker Brothers, c1952, 8" x 18", all wooden pcs, four orig dice and dicecups **100.00**

Elsie and Her Family, Selcrow & Righter Co., 1941 .... **250.00**

Fish Pond, McLoughlin Bros., c1898, 8" x 18", children on cover..... **125.00**

Flying the United States Air Mail Game, Parker Bros, 1929 copyright, 17" x 27-1/2" playing board, orig playing pcs, deck of cards, 1-1/2" x 14-1/2" x 18" box **55.00**

Game of Battles or Fun For Boys, McLoughlin Bros., c1900, 23" x 23", cardboard soldiers and cannons **2,500.00**

Game of Billy Possum, c1910, 8" x 15" **600.00**

Game of Bo Peep, J. H. Singer, 8-1/2" x 14"...................... **275.00**

Game of Moon Tag, Parker Brothers, c1950, 10-1/2" x 20" **50.00**

Game of Snow White and the Seven Dwarfs, The, Milton Bradley, Walt Disney Enterprises, 1937 ..... **100.00**

Game of the Wizard of Oz, The, Whitman, c1939, 7" x 13-1/2" .. **300.00**

Gilligan's Island Game, Game Gems, c1965, 9-1/2" x 18-1/2" **350.00**

Uncle Sam's Mail, Milton Bradley Co., Springfield, Mass, c1910, 16-1/4" x 15" x 1-1/4", $115. Photo courtesy of James D. Julia, Inc.

Hi Ho Silhouette Game, 1932...**30.00**

Jolly Darkie Target Game, Milton Bradley, c1900, 10-1/2" x 19" ...**750.00**

Limited Mail and Express Game, The, Parker Brothers, c1894, 14" x 21", metal train playing pieces **250.00**

Lone Ranger Hi Yo Silver Game, Parker Brothers, 1938.........**200.00**

Mansion of Happiness, The, W. & S. B. Ives, c1843................**950.00**

Mickey Mantle's Big League Baseball Game, Gardner Games **195.00**

Monopoly, Parker Brothers, c1935, white box edition #9, metal playing pieces and embossed hotels...**150.00**

Young America Target, Parker Brothers, dart board and waxed feathers, original box, $75. Photo courtesy of Joy Luke Auctions.

Monopoly, Parker Brothers, 1946 Popular Edition, separate board and pieces box.................**25.00**
Motorcycle Game, Milton Bradley, c1905, 9" x 9"..............**250.00**
New Board Game of the American Revolution, Lorenzo Borge, 1844, colored scenes and events, 18-1/2" w opened **690.00**
One Two, Button Your Shoe, Master Toy Company, 11" x 12".......**145.00**
Peter Coddles Trip to New York, Milton Bradley, orig instruction sheet, 6" x 8-1/2"..................**65.00**
Radio Amateur Hour Game, 10" x 13" **145.00**
Razzle Dazzle Football Game, Texantics, 1954, 10" x 17" **225.00**
Strange Game of Forbidden Fruit, Parker Brothers, c1900, 4" x 5-1/2" **35.00**
Truth or Consequences, Gabriel, c1955, 14" x 19-1/2"..........**75.00**
Whirlpool, McLoughlin Brothers, 1899, #408, 7-1/4" sq, instructions on cover **40.00**

GAUDY DUTCH

History: Gaudy Dutch is an opaque, soft-paste ware made between 1790 and 1825 in England's Staffordshire district.

The wares first were hand decorated in an underglaze blue and fired; then additional decorations were added over the glaze. The over-glaze decoration is extensively worn on many of the antique pieces. Gaudy Dutch found a ready market in the Pennsylvania German community because it was inexpensive and extremely colorful. It had little appeal in England.

For more information, see this book.

Marks: Marks of various potters, including the impressed marks of Riley and Wood, have been found on some pieces, although most are unmarked.
Adviser: John D. Querry.

Reproduction Alert: Cup plates, bearing the impressed mark "CYBRIS," have been reproduced and are collectible in their own right. The Henry Ford Museum has issued pieces in the Single Rose pattern, although they are porcelain rather than soft paste.

Plate, Butterfly pattern, 9-3/4" d, $800.

Butterfly
Coffeepot, 11" h........ **9,500.00**
Cup and saucer, handleless, minor enamel flakes, chips on table ring **950.00**
Plate, 7-1/4" d **645.00**
Sugar bowl, cov..........**900.00**
Teapot, 5" h, squat baluster form **2,400.00**

Carnation
Bowl, 6-1/4" d **925.00**
Creamer, 4-3/4" h..........**700.00**
Pitcher, 6" h **675.00**
Plate, 9-3/4" d **1,265.00**
Saucer, cobalt blue, orange, green, and yellow, stains, hairline, minor flake on table ring, 5-1/2" d.**115.00**
Teapot, cov **2,200.00**
Waste bowl **675.00**

Dahlia
Bowl, 6-1/4" d **1,800.00**
Plate, 8" d **2,800.00**
Tea bowl and saucer.....**8,000.00**

Double Rose
Bowl, 6-1/4" d **545.00**
Creamer.................**650.00**
Gravy boat...............**950.00**
Plate, 8-1/4" d **675.00**
Sugar bowl, cov..........**750.00**
Tea bowl and saucer......**675.00**
Toddy plate, 4-1/2" d **675.00**
Waste bowl, 6-1/2" d, 3" h ...**850.00**

Dove
Creamer.................**675.00**
Plate, 8-1/8" d, very worn, scratches, stains..................**245.00**
Plate, 8-1/2" d **770.00**
Tea bowl and saucer......**500.00**
Waste bowl **650.00**
Flower Basket, plate, 6-1/2" d.. **375.00**
Grape
Bowl, 6-1/2" d, lustered rim ..**475.00**

Plate, 8-1/4" d, cobalt blue, orange,
    green, and yellow, minor stains
    .... **450.00**
  Sugar bowl, cov **675.00**
  Tea bowl and saucer **475.00**
  Toddy plate, 5" d......... **475.00**
Leaf, bowl, 11-1/2" d, shallow . **4,800.00**
No Name
  Plate, 8-3/4" d **17,000.00**
  Teapot, cov **16,000.00**

Plate, Oyster pattern, 9-1/2" d, $575.

Oyster
  Bowl, 5-1/2" d **675.00**
  Coffeepot, cov, 12" h..... **10,000.00**
  Plate, 10" d **1,550.00**
  Soup plate, 8-1/2" d **550.00**
  Tea bowl and saucer **1,275.00**
  Toddy plate, 5-1/2" d...... **475.00**
Single Rose
  Coffeepot, cov **8,500.00**
  Cup and saucer, handleless, minor
    wear and stains **330.00**
  Plate, 7-1/4" d **550.00**
  Plate, 10" d **975.00**
  Quill holder, cov **2,500.00**
  Sugar bowl, cov **700.00**
  Teapot, cov **1,200.00**
  Toddy plate, 5-1/4" d...... **250.00**

*Creamer, Strawberry pattern, pearlware
body, slight discoloration, $125. Photo
courtesy of Cowan's Historic Americana
Auctions.*

Sunflower
  Bowl, 6-1/2" d............ **900.00**
  Coffeepot, cov, 9-1/2" h .. **6,500.00**
  Cup and saucer, handleless, wear,
    chips **575.00**
  Plate, 9-3/4" d **825.00**
Urn
  Creamer................. **475.00**
  Cup and saucer, handleless . **550.00**
  Plate, 8-1/4" d **910.00**
  Plate, 9-7/8" d, very worn, scratches,
    stains, rim, chips........ **225.00**
  Sugar bowl, cov, 6-1/2" h, round, tip
    and base restored....... **295.00**
  Teapot **895.00**
War Bonnet
  Bowl, cov............... **225.00**
  Coffeepot, cov.......... **9,500.00**
  Plate, 8-1/8" d, pinpoint rim flake,
    minor wear............ **880.00**
  Teapot, cov **4,400.00**
  Toddy plate, 4-1/2" d **975.00**
Zinna, soup plate, 10" d, impressed
"Riley".................. **4,675.00**

GAUDY IRONSTONE

History: Gaudy Ironstone was made in England
around 1850. Ironstone is an opaque, heavy-bodied
earthenware which contains large proportions of flint
and slag. Gaudy Ironstone is decorated in patterns and
colors similar to those of Gaudy Welsh.

Marks: Most pieces are impressed "Ironstone" and
bear a registry mark.

Bread plate, 10-1/4" l, 5-1/4" w, marked
"Tunstall, England, by Enoch
Wedgwood" **65.00**
Coffeepot, cov, 10" h, Strawberry
pattern **650.00**
Creamer and sugar, 6-3/4" h, fruit finial,
Blackberry pattern, underglaze blue,
yellow, and orange enamel and luster,
wear, small flakes, int. chip on sugar
.... **990.00**
Cup and saucer, Blackberry pattern,
handleless, underglaze blue, yellow,
and orange enamel and luster, imp
label or registry mark with "E. Walley,"
price for set of 10 .... **1,375.00**
Jug, 7-1/2" h, yellow, red, white, and
blue tulips on sides, light blue pebble
ground, luster trim, rim outlined . **350.00**
Pitcher, 11" h, six-color floral dec, blue,
green, burgundy, mauve, black, and
yellow, molded serpent handle, dec has
been enhanced, then reglazed, spider
.... **320.00**
Plate
  6-1/4" d, Morning Glories and
    Strawberries pattern, underglaze

*Left: plate, floral with eye, underglaze
blue, red, and green enamel and luster,
impressed "E. Walley, Niagara Shape,"
registry mark, wear and scratches,
8-1/2" g, $120; center: Strawberry plat-
ter, underglaze blue with red, pink, and
green enamel luster, wear, stains, some
enamel flaking, 13-1/2" l, $770; right:
plate, Pinwheel, underglaze blue with
red and green enamel and luster,
impressed "ironstone," minor wear,
8-3/8" d, $175. Photo courtesy of
Garth's Auctions.*

blue, polychrome enamel and
    luster trim **80.00**
  9-1/2" d, Blackberry pattern,
    underglaze blue, yellow, and
    orange enamel and luster, some
    wear, set of seven **1,320.00**
Platter, 13-3/8" l, Gaudy blue and white
floral dec, scalloped border, molded
fish scale and feather design, minor
wear..................... **1,540.00**
Soup plate, 9-7/8" d, Blackberry
pattern, underglaze blue, yellow, and
orange enamel and luster, one imp
"Elsmore & Forster, Tunstall," price for
set of three **650.00**
Sugar bowl, cov, 8-1/2" h, Strawberry
pattern.................... **425.00**
Teapot, 9-3/4" h, domed cov, floral
finial, paneled body, blue flower, red
and green strawberries, gilt highlights,
c1850 .... **2,300.00**
Vegetable, open, 8-3/4" d, Blackberry
pattern, underglaze blue, yellow, and
orange enamel and luster..... **350.00**

Soup plate, unmarked, 7-5/8" d, $65.

Wash basin and pitcher, 14" d bowl, 13" h pitcher, hexagonal, blue morning glories and leaves, copper accents, hp red, green, and yellow berries, hairlines **1,225.00**

GAUDY WELSH

History: Gaudy Welsh is a translucent porcelain that was originally made in the Swansea area of England from 1830 to 1845. Although the designs resemble Gaudy Dutch, the body texture and weight differ. One of the characteristics is the gold luster on top of the glaze. In 1890, Allerton made a similar ware from heavier opaque porcelain.

For more information, see this book.

Marks: Allerton pieces usually bear an export mark.

Carnation, 6-1/4" h........... **550.00**
Chinoiserie, teapot, c1830-40 . . **750.00**
Columbine
   Bowl, 10" d, 5-1/2" h, ftd, underglaze blue and polychrome enamel floral dec **400.00**
   Plate, 5-1/2" d **65.00**
   Tea set, c1810, 17-pc set . . . **625.00**
Conwys, jug, 9" h............ **750.00**
Daisy and Chain
   Creamer................. **175.00**
   Cup and saucer........... **95.00**
   Sugar, cov **195.00**
   Teapot, cov **225.00**
Flower Basket
   Bowl, 10-1/2" d........... **190.00**
   Mug, 4" h **90.00**
   Plate.................... **65.00**
   Sugar, cov, luster trim **195.00**
Grape
   Bowl, 5-1/4" d............ **50.00**
   Cup and saucer........... **75.00**
   Mug, 2-1/2" h **65.00**
   Plate, 5-1/4" d **65.00**
Grapevine Variant, miniature pitcher and bowl, 4-1/4" h pitcher, 4-1/2" d bowl, cobalt blue, orange, green, and luster, scalloped edges **250.00**

Cup and saucer, peppermint transfer, Shan We See, **$75.**

Plate, green holly leaves, red berries dec, 6" d, **$125.**

Oyster
   Bowl, 6" d **80.00**
   Creamer, 3" h **100.00**
   Jug, 5-3/4" h, c1820 .... **85.00**
   Soup plate, 10" d, flange rim . **85.00**
Primrose, plate 8-1/4" d **350.00**
Strawberry
   Cup and saucer **75.00**
   Mug, 4 1/8" h............. **125.00**
   Plate, 8-1/4" d **150.00**
Tulip
   Bowl, 6-1/4" d **50.00**
   Cake plate, 10" d, molded handles **120.00**
   Creamer, 5-1/4" h **125.00**
   Plate, tea size............ **95.00**
   Tea cup and saucer, slight crazing in cup..................... **115.00**
   Teapot, 7-1/4" h........... **225.00**
Wagon Wheel
   Cup and saucer **75.00**
   Mug, 2-1/2" h **95.00**
   Pitcher, 8-1/2" h.......... **195.00**
   Plate, 8-3/4" d **85.00**
   Platter **125.00**

GIRANDOLES AND MANTEL LUSTRES

History: A girandole is a very elaborate branched candleholder, often featuring cut glass prisms surrounding the mountings. A mantel lustre is a glass vase with attached cut glass prisms.

   Girandoles and mantel lustres usually are found in pairs. It is not uncommon for girandoles to be part of a large garniture set. Girandoles and mantel lustres achieved their greatest popularity in the last half of the 19th century both in the United States and Europe.

Girandoles
9-7/8" w, 17" h, Longwy, Aesthetic Movement, third quarter 19th C, two-light, rect, central beveled mirror plate, surrounded by Islamic-inspired tiles in brass frame, scrolled candle arm with two acorn-shaped nozzles, removable bobeches **750.00**
16-3/4" h, Louis XIV-style, late 19th/early 20th C, three-light candelabra style, brass wirework lyre form standard, scrolled arms hung with colorless and amethyst glass drops, three short serpentine candle arms with tulip-shaped nozzles, offset with further drops, tripartite wirework base, price for pr **875.00**
18" h, 15" w, cast brass, high relief rococo scrolling and vintage detail, applied flowers on base, columns shaped like large leaves about to burst into blossom, three sockets each with clear cut glass prisms, orig gilding and bobeches, soldered restorations on branches, price for pr **990.00**

Mantel garnitures
10-1/4" h, urn form, two short scroll handles, incised on side with Japonesque florals in silver and gold coloration, trumpet foot further dec with Japonesque patterning and insects, sq section marble base, inset to front with mixed metal-style patinated plaque depicting drummer and dancer, Aesthetic Movement, third quarter 19th C, price for pr.............. **690.00**

White opaline glass, gilded enamel dec, glass hurricane shade with etched and enamel work, cut glass prisms, 26" h, **$175.** *Photo courtesy of Joy Luke Auctions.*

Green satin glass luster, cut crystal prisms, 9-1/2" h, $75. Photo courtesy of Joy Luke Auctions.

14" h, 12" h, three cov baluster jars and two vases, Hundred Antiques dec, in famille rosé enamels, China, 19th C, price for five-pc set **2,185.00**
20-5/8" h, bronze and crystal, three-light candelabra, stylized lyre form garniture hung with cut and pressed glass prisms, above three scrolled candle arms, trefoil base, price for pr . . **980.00**

Mantel lusters
9" h, overlay glass, white cut to pink, enamel flowers, gilt accents, cut glass prisms, Bohemian, price for pr . **425.00**
9-1/2" h, brass, three dolphin-form uprights supporting leafy spray, glass prisms, 19th C, replacements . . **320.00**
12" h, ruby glass, overlay and enameled plaques, fluted, heavy gilt, cut glass prisms, France, 19th C, price for pr **2,645.00**

GOOFUS GLASS

History: Goofus glass, also known as Mexican ware, hooligan glass, and pickle glass, is a pressed glass with relief designs that were painted either on the back or front. The designs are usually in red and green with a metallic gold ground. It was popular from 1890 to 1920 and was used as a premium at carnivals.

It was produced by several companies: Crescent Glass Company, Wellsburg, West Virginia; Imperial Glass Corporation, Bellaire, Ohio; LaBelle Glass Works, Bridgeport, Ohio; and Northwood Glass Co., Indiana, Pennsylvania, Wheeling, West Virginia, and Bridgeport, Ohio.

Goofus glass lost its popularity when people found that the paint tarnished or scaled off after repeated washings and wear. No record of its manufacture has been found after 1920.

Marks: Goofus glass made by Northwood includes one of the following marks: "N," "N" in one circle, "N" in two circles, or one or two circles without the "N."

Animal dish, cov, turkey, Westmoreland **125.00**
Ashtray, red rose dec, emb adv . **18.00**
Basket, 5" h, strawberry dec **50.00**
Bonbon, 4" d, Strawberry pattern, gold, red, and green dec **40.00**

Bowl, red roses, embossed fern-type foliate, gold ground, scalloped edge, $25.

Bowl
6-1/2" d, Grape and Lattice pattern, red grapes, gold ground, ruffled rim **45.00**
7" d, thistle and scrolling leaves, red dec, gold ground, ruffled rim **35.00**
10-1/2" d, 2-1/2" h, Cherries, gold leaves, red cherries. **35.00**
Bread plate, 7" w, 11" l, Last Supper pattern, red and gold, grapes and foliage border. **65.00**
Candy dish, 8-1/2" d, figure-eight design, serrated rim, dome foot. . **60.00**
Charger, grape and leaves center **125.00**
Coaster, 3" d, red floral dec, gold ground **12.00**
Compote
4" d, Grape and Cable pattern **35.00**
6" d, Strawberry pattern, red and green strawberries and foliage, ruffled **40.00**
6-1/2" d, Poppy pattern, red flowers, gold foliage, green ground, sgd "Northwood" **40.00**
Decanter, orig stopper, La Belle Rose **50.00**
Dresser tray, 6" l, Cabbage Rose pattern, red roses dec, gold foliage, clear ground. **35.00**
Jar, cov, butterflies, red and gold **35.00**

Jewel box, 4" d, 2" h, basketweave, rose dec **50.00**
Mug, Cabbage Rose pattern, gold ground. **35.00**
Nappy, 6-1/2" d, Cherries pattern, red cherries, gold foliage, clear ground **35.00**
Perfume bottle, 3-1/2" h, pink tulips dec **20.00**
Pickle jar, aqua, molded, gold, blue, and red painted floral design . . . **50.00**
Pin dish, 6-1/2" l, oval, red and black florals. **20.00**
Plate
6" d, Sunflower pattern, red dec center, relief molded **20.00**
7-3/4" d, Carnations pattern, red carnations, gold ground. . . . **20.00**
11" d, Cherries, some paint worn off **35.00**
Platter, 18" l, red rose dec, gold ground **65.00**
Powder jar, cov, 3" d, puffy, rose dec, red and gold **40.00**
Salt and pepper shakers, pr, Grape and Leaf pattern **45.00**
Syrup, relief molded, red roses dec, lattice work ground, orig top **85.00**
Toothpick holder, red rose and foliage dec, gold ground **40.00**
Tray, 8-1/4" d, 11" d, red chrysanthemum dec, gold ground **45.00**
Tumbler, 6" h, red rose dec, gold ground. **35.00**
Vase
6" h, Cabbage Rose pattern, red dec, gold ground **45.00**
9" h, Poppies pattern, blue and red dec, gold ground **45.00**
10-1/2" h, Peacock pattern. . . **75.00**

Plate, Wheel and Block, Dugan, 1905, blue opalescent, 10-1/4" square, $40. Photo courtesy of S. Louis Rouse.

GOUDA POTTERY

History: Gouda and the surrounding areas of Holland have been principal Dutch pottery centers for centuries. Originally, the potteries produced a simple utilitarian tin-glazed Delft-type earthenware and the famous clay smoker's pipes.

When pipe making declined in the early 1900s, the Gouda potteries turned to art pottery. Influenced by the Art Nouveau and Art Deco movements, artists expressed themselves with free-form and stylized designs in bold colors.

Reproduction Alert: With the Art Nouveau and Art Deco revivals of recent years, modern reproductions of Gouda pottery currently are on the market. They are difficult to distinguish from the originals.

Bowl

7" h, Art Nouveau scrolled floral and foliage dec, shades of green, brown, and blue, cracked white semi-matte glazed ground, black rooster mark on base, Arnhem factory, c1910, repairs to rim
..................**100.00**

10-1/4" d, 2-1/2" h, dec with three clusters of flowers in symmetrical pattern, matte glaze, shades of orange, yellow, and blue, black ground, blue painted maker's mark, c1927 ....**225.00**

11-3/4" d, 2-3/4" h, stylized floral design, matte glaze, yellow, orange, green, and blue, black ground, black painted Regina marks, c1927, rim repair ...**185.00**

Candlesticks and vase set, pr 9-1/2" h candlesticks, 10-3/4" h vase, Art

Nouveau style dec, matte glaze blue, orange, turquoise, brown, and yellow, painted "Westland (house) Gouda Holland," date and artist's initials
.... **400.00**

Candlesticks, pr, 18" h, bulbed cup, ruffled rim drop pan, tall ribbed flared standard, Art Nouveau-style motif, high glaze, shades of blue, green, yellow, and black, underglaze mark "Gouda Blauw (house)," date mark, artist's initials, and "Made in Holland, 872, 893," dec attributed to Franciscus Ijsselstein, c1926, base chip on one
.... **435.00**

Clock garniture, 20-1/2" h clock, 16-3/4" h pr candlesticks, circular clock mouth with painted ceramic face supported by four ceramic arms on baluster-shaped body and flared base, candlesticks of similar form, all dec with Art Nouveau-style flowers, glossy glaze pink, purple, blue, green, and tan, sgd "Zuid Holland" and imp house and "R" on base, repairs to candlesticks
.... **2,875.00**

Charger, 12" d, multicolored flowers, rope border, black trim **150.00**

Compote, 7 5/8", black ground, geometric design, multicolored scroll int. **175.00**

Ewer

7" h, handle, floral and foliage design, high glaze, shades of purple, mauve, green, blue, and taupe, base painted "Made in Zuid Holland (house)", and artist's initials **325.00**

7-5/8" h, handle, stylized floral and foliage design, high glazes, shades of green, pink, and purple on tan and brown ground, painted "Made in Zuid, Holland" ... **350.00**

Incense burner, 8" h, Roba, flowers and geometric designs, green ground
.... **120.00**

Jug, 5-3/4" d, Rosalie, cream ground, green handle, turquoise interior, marked "Rosalie, #5155," and "Zuid-Holland, Gouda," c1930 .... **195.00**

Lamp base, 11-3/4" h, flared rim, tapered oval form, butterfly design, matte glaze, shades of green, blue, gold, red and cream, base painted "380 Butterfly (tree, house) AJK Holland," c1920 .... **290.00**

Miniature, vase, 2-1/4" h, floral and foliate design, high glaze, shades of green, purple, red, brown, and black
.... **125.00**

Pitcher, 10-1/2" h, angled handle, flared form, stylized flower design, semi-matte soft green, rust, and blue tones, cream colored ground, maker's mark "Marantha" and artist's initials on base, Arnhem factory, c1910, minor crazing
.... **250.00**

Plate, 8-1/4" d, Unique Metallique, scalloped edge, deep blue-green ground, irid copper luster dec .. **350.00**

Shoe, 4-7/8" h, floral and foliate design, high glaze, shades of green, purple, red, brown, and black **125.00**

Urn, 7-3/8" h, two handles, stylized flowers and leaves, high glaze, blue, brown, pink, and green, painted "Distel 27/24," and artist's initials...... **325.00**

Vase

4-1/2" h, raised rim, squatty form, flower blossoms dec, semi-matte glaze, yellow, brown, blue, and cream, black ground, painted and paper labels **200.00**

6" h, Art Nouveau style, elongated neck, squat form, stylized flowers

Chamberstick, matte green, yellow, blue, and cream decoration, marked "1039 DAM III Holland," c1885, 6-1/2" d, 3" h, $115.

Tobacco humidor, covered, Verona pattern, 5" h, $200.

Gotton urn-form vase, 8-1/8" h, 1923; 8-1/4" h Henley pitcher, 1923; 9-3/4" h Breetvelt double handle vase, all with stylized designs in shades of green, blue, rust and gold on black ground matte glaze, all with maker's marks, crazing, $425. Photo courtesy of Skinner Auctioneers and Appraisers.

and leaves, high glaze, white, green, and rust, taupe ground, painted "Holland Utrecht" on base **200.00**

7-1/4" h, two handles, ftd, bulbous, brown, blue, and green butterflies dec, crackled white matte ground, black stamped rooster mark on base, Arnhem factory, c1910 .... **150.00**

7-3/4" h, two handles, bulbed neck flanked by arched handles on squatty body, tulip and foliate designs, high glaze gray, green, yellow, and brown tones, painted "Distel," Distel factory, early 20th C **520.00**

8-3/4" h, waisted, floral and foliage design, high glaze, shades of purple, mauve, green, blue, and taupe, base painted "Made in Zuid Holland (house)", and artist's initials **325.00**

9-3/4" h, elongated neck, bulbous body, incised ice skaters and countryside, matte and high glazes in blue and brown tones, incised maker's marks for Distel Factory, early 20th C, scratches ... **200.00**

10" h, two handles, ovoid, ftd, floral and foliage design, high glaze, shades of purple, mauve, green, blue, and taupe, base painted "Made in Zuid Holland (house)", and artist's initials **350.00**

10-1/2" h, tapered oval, flowers and leaves, semi-matte glaze, gold, brown, turquoise, cream, and black, painted maker's marks **200.00**

10-3/4" h, flared rim, ovoid form, stylized flowers and foliage, matte glaze, shades of yellow, green, blue, orange, and brown, painted mark "Del Breetvelt (house) Zuid Holland Gouda" **420.00**

13-1/4" h, elongated neck on bulbous body, Art Nouveau stylized lilies, foliage, high glaze purple, green, yellow, and black, base painted with wooden shoe "NB Faience du (illegible) Holland 504 Dec A" **865.00**

19" h, tall tapered vessel, Impressionist country scene with figures, trees, and flowers, glossy glaze, naturalistic tones, underglaze painted "Made in Z Holland" with house mark, c1906-17 .... **1,265.00**

20-1/4" h, flared, stylized lily dec, high glaze, purple, brown, green,

dark blue, yellow, and cream, painted mark "Made in Holland (house)," c1898, price for pr **575.00**

GRANITEWARE

History: Graniteware is the name commonly given to enamel-coated iron or steel kitchenware.

The first graniteware was made in Germany in the 1830s. Graniteware was not produced in the United States until the 1860s. At the start of World War I, when European companies turned to manufacturing war weapons, American producers took over the market.

Gray and white were the most common graniteware colors, although each company made its own special color in shades of blue, green, brown, violet, cream, or red.

Older graniteware is heavier than the new. Pieces with cast-iron handles date between 1870 to 1890; wood handles between 1900 to 1910. Other dating clues are seams, wooden knobs, and tin lids.

> **Reproduction Alert:** Graniteware still is manufactured in many of the traditional forms and colors.

Additional Listings: See *Warman's Americana & Collectibles* for more examples.

Batter jug, 6" h, gray mottled, tin lid, tin spout cover, seamed body, wire handle with wood carrying grip **425.00**

Child's set, green ground, decal decoration, Dutch, set, **$85.**

Kitchen tool holder, gray, hand-painted floral decoration, **$165.**

Berry pail, cov, 7" d, 4-3/4" h, gray and black mottled **50.00**

Bowl, 11-3/4" d, 3-3/4" h, green and white **50.00**

Cake pan, 7-1/2" d, robin's egg blue and white marbleized **45.00**

Child's feeding set, cup and dish, white, chickens dec, worn...... **35.00**

Coffeepot, 10" h, gray, tin handle, spout, and lid **525.00**

Colander, 12" d, gray, pedestal base **30.00**

Cup, 2-3/4" h, blue and white medium swirl, black trim and handle **50.00**

Frying pan, 10-1/4" d, blue and white mottled, white int. **135.00**

Funnel, cobalt blue and white marbleized, large **50.00**

Grater, medium blue.......... **115.00**

Hotplate, two burners, white graniteware, Hotpoint **165.00**

Kettle, cov, 9" h, 11-1/2" d, gray mottled **50.00**

Measure, one cup, gray **45.00**

Mixing bowls, red and white, nested set of four, 1930s............ **155.00**

Muffin pan, blue and white mottled, eight cups **250.00**

Pie pan, 6" d, cobalt blue and white marbleized **25.00**

Pitcher, 11" h, gray, ice lip **110.00**

Refrigerator bowls, red swirl, four-pc set **585.00**

Roaster, emerald green swirl, large **250.00**

Skimmer, 10" l, gray mottled.... **25.00**

Pitcher, gray and white, **$195.**

Teapot, 9-1/2" w, 5" h, enameled dec, small chips **525.00**
Tube pan, octagonal, gray mottled **45.00**
Utensil rack, 14-1/2" w, 22" h, shaded orange, gray bowls, matching ladle, skimmer, and tasting spoon **400.00**
Wash basin, 11-3/4" d, blue and white swirl, Blue Diamond Ware **150.00**
Water pail, lime green, brown, and white swirl, early 1900s **225.00**

GREENAWAY, KATE

History: Kate Greenaway, or "K.G.," as she initialed her famous drawings, was born in 1846 in London. Her father was a prominent wood engraver. Kate's natural talent for drawing soon was evident, and she began art classes at the age of 12. In 1868, she had her first public exhibition.

Her talents were used primarily in illustrating. The cards she decorated for Marcus Ward are largely unsigned. China and pottery companies soon had her drawings of children appearing on many of their wares. By the 1880s, she was one of the foremost children's book illustrators in England.

Reproduction Alert: Some Greenaway buttons have been reproduced in Europe and sold in the United States.

Advertisement, 5" x 10" print, black and white, for Kate Greenaway fashions, two little girls dressed in Spanish Plaids **12.00**
Butter pat, transfer print of boy and girl **35.00**

Button, 3/4" d, girl with kitten on fence **12.00**
Calling card holder, 6-1/4" w, 6" h, silver plated, little girl holding puppy, marked "Rogers" **300.00**
Child's book, *Mother Goose or The Old Nursery Rhymes,* Warne, c1900, 44 rhymes, Kate Greenaway illus, pictures on both front and back cov **45.00**
Figure, 5-3/4" h Emma, pink and white, Royal Doulton **375.00**
Handkerchief, 11-1/2" sq, sunbonnet girl, "Love's gentle touch means so much," lace trim **5.00**
Inkwell, bronze, emb, two children **200.00**
Match safe, SP, emb children . . . **50.00**
Napkin ring, SS, girl feeding yearling **160.00**
Perfume bottle, 2" l, SS, low relief of girls, orig stopper **200.00**
Picture frame, 10-7/8" w, 13-1/2" h, wood frame applied with stamped sheet of pewter, shepherdess and sheep, birds and flowering tree, easel back, England or America, early 20th C **150.00**
Salt and pepper shakers, pr, 2-3/4" h, incised "5103," wear to gold trim **95.00**
Tape measure, figural, girl holding muff **45.00**
Tile, each 6-3/8" d, transfer print, four seasons, one spacer, brown and white dec, blue border, stamped mark, produced by T & R Boote, 1881, framed, five-pc set **325.00**

Pie bird, bisque girl, 5" h, **$50.**

Toothpick holder, 1-5/8" d, 2-1/4" h coral shading to opaque white Boston & Sandwich glass holder with hand-painted orange crane in green marsh, 4-3/4" h silver-plated Kate Greenaway holder, figural girl holding toothpick holder in outstretched arms, holder signed "James W. Tufts Warranted Quadruple Plate 3404," incised, "LRA/225," c1895-1908, **$750.** *Photo courtesy of Clarence and Betty Maier.*

Toothpick holder, 3-3/8" h, silver plated, girl with low-cut ball gown standing beside barrel holder, marked "2302/Derby Silver Co." **125.00**

GREENTOWN GLASS

History: The Indiana Tumbler and Goblet Co., Greentown, Indiana, produced its first clear, pressed glass table and bar wares in late 1894. Initial success led to a doubling of the plant size in 1895 and other subsequent expansions, one in 1897 to allow for the manufacture of colored glass. In 1899, the firm joined the combine known as the National Glass Company.

In 1900, just before arriving in Greentown, Jacob Rosenthal developed an opaque brown glass, called "chocolate," which ranged in color from a dark, rich chocolate to a lighter coffee-with-cream hue. Production of chocolate glass saved the financially pressed Indiana Tumbler and Goblet Works. The Cactus and Leaf Bracket patterns were made almost exclusively in chocolate glass. Other popular chocolate patterns include Austrian, Dewey, Shuttle, and Teardrop and Tassel. In 1902, National Glass Company bought Rosenthal's chocolate glass formula so other plants in the combine could use the color.

In 1902, Rosenthal developed the Golden Agate and Rose Agate colors. All work ceased on June 13, 1903, when a fire of suspicious origin destroyed the Indiana Tumbler and Goblet Company Works.

After the fire, other companies, e.g., McKee and Brothers, produced chocolate glass in the same

K.G.

pattern designs used by Greentown. Later reproductions also have been made, with Cactus among the most heavily copied patterns.

Additional Listings: Holly Amber and Pattern Glass.

Reproduction Alert

Animal-covered dish
   Dolphin, chocolate **225.00**
   Rabbit, dome top, amber . . . **250.00**
Bowl, 7-1/4" d, Herringbone Buttress, green **135.00**
Butter, cov, Cupid, chocolate . . **575.00**
Celery vase, Beaded Panel, clear
. . . . **100.00**
Compote, Teardrop and Tassel, clear, 5-1/4" d, 5-1/8" h **50.00**
Creamer
   Cactus, chocolate **85.00**
   Indian Head, opaque white . **450.00**
Cruet, orig stopper, Leaf Bracket, chocolate **275.00**
Goblet
   Overall Lattice **40.00**
   Shuttle, chocolate **500.00**
Mug, indoor drinking scene, chocolate, 6" w, 8" h **500.00**
Mustard, cov, Daisy, opaque white
. . . . **75.00**
Paperweight, Buffalo, Nile green
. . . . **600.00**
Pitcher, cov, Dewey, chocolate, 5-1/4" h
. . . . **115.00**
Plate, Serenade, chocolate **85.00**

*Spooner, Leaf Bracket pattern, opaque chocolate, rim chip, 4" h, **$130**. Photo courtesy of James D. Julia, Inc.*

*Salt and pepper shakers, pair, Cactus pattern, opaque chocolate, one metal top repainted, 3-1/4" h, **$120**. Photo courtesy of James D. Julia, Inc.*

Relish, Leaf Bracket, 8" l, oval, chocolate **75.00**
Salt and pepper shakers, pr, Cactus, chocolate **150.00**
Sugar, cov, Dewey, cobalt blue . **145.00**
Syrup, Cord Drapery, chocolate, plated lid, 6-3/4" h **350.00**
Toothpick holder
   Cactus, chocolate, hairlines . . **75.00**
   Hobnail and Shell, chocolate . **185.00**
Tumbler
   Cactus, chocolate **60.00**
   Dewey, canary **65.00**
Vase, 8" h, Austrian **55.00**

*Tumbler, Cactus pattern, opaque chocolate, 4" h, **$295**.*

GRUEBY POTTERY

History: William Grueby was active in the ceramic industry for several years before he developed his own method of producing matte-glazed pottery and founded the Grueby Faience Company in Boston, Massachusetts, in 1897.

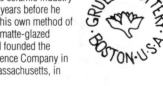

The art pottery was hand thrown in natural shapes, hand molded, and hand tooled. A variety of colored glazes, singly or in combinations, was produced, but green was the most popular. In 1908, the firm was divided into the Grueby Pottery Company and the

Grueby Faience and Tile Co. The Grueby Faience and Tile Company made art tile until 1917, although its pottery production was phased out about 1910.

Minor damage is acceptable to most collectors of Grueby Pottery.

Adviser: David Rago.

*Vase, bulbous, tooled panels, leathery matte brown glaze, circular pottery mark, 5" d, 8" h, **$4,025**. Photos courtesy of David Rago Auctions.*

Jardinière, 7-1/2" x 9", two-color three rows of curled leaves below nine light blue five-petaled flowers, oatmeal matte green glaze, stamped "Grueby Faience/174" and "EG," couple of minor flecks **575.00**
Lotus bowl, 7" d, 6" h, tooled and applied leaves, glossy green int. glaze, matte green ext., circular pottery mark/ER, rim glaze flake, couple of glaze misses **1,610.00**
Tile, cuenca dec
   6" sq, large oak tree against blue sky, puffy white clouds, #28 on reverse **1,150.00**
   6" sq, "The Pines," polychrome cuenca, marked "FH" **1,485.00**
   6" sq, "The Pines," polychrome cuenca, unmarked, 1/2" chip to one corner **860.00**
   6-1/4" sq, yellow tulip on matte green ground, mounted in sterling silver trivet base by Karl Leinonen (Boston League of Arts & Crafts), tile unmarked, mount stamped "Sterling" and "L," very light abrasion to surface **2,990.00**
Vase
   3-1/4" d, 6-1/2" h, ovoid, tooled and applied broad leaves alternating with yellow trefoils, matte green glaze, circular pottery mark, 1" rim hairline **7,475.00**
   4-1/4" d, 10" h, cylindrical, tooled and applied stylized chartreuse flowers alternating with broad leaves, leathery dark green matte

Vase, corseted shoulder, incised vertical ribs, matte ochre glaze, stamped Faience mark, incised "BA,"two paper labels, 5" w, 9-1/2" h, $14,000.

glaze, circular pottery mark
ER/12/3/. **9,780.00**
4-1/2" d, 7" h, squatty, flaring rim, tooled and applied leaves, feathered matte green glaze, paper lapel and HP **2,415.00**
5" d, 8" h, bulbous, tooled panels, leathery matte brown glaze, circular pottery mark **4,025.00**
5" d, 11" h, ovoid, floriform rim, dec with tooled and applied yellow, blue, and burgundy daffodils, narrow leaves, frothy matte green glaze, paper label and "LFH"
. . . . **13,550.00**
7-3/4" d, 12" h, barrel-shaped, by Wilhelmina Post, 1906, crisply tooled and applied yellow daffodils, green leaves, covered in fine pulled leathery matte green glaze, sgd by artist, dated 5/27/06, professional invisible restoration to drilled holes under base, 1" kiln kiss near base. **460.00**

Vessel
4-1/2" d, 4-1/4" h, spherical, crisply dec, tooled and applied pointed

Vase, flaring rim, squat base decorated with tooled and applied leaves, feathered matte green glaze. Paper label and "HP," 4-1/2" d, 7" h, $2,415.

Vessel, squat, three-color, tooled and applied water lilies and lily pads in yellow and green against leathery dark green ground, circular pottery mark/JE/1-14, 1914, 9-1/2" d, 4-1/4" h, $53,500.

leaves, dark green matte glaze, remnant of paper label. . . **4,600.00**
9-1/2" d, 4-1/4" h, three-color, tooled and applied yellow and green waterlilies and lilypads, leathery dark green ground, circular pottery mark "JE/1-14," 1914, very short tight rim bruise **53,500.00**

HALL CHINA COMPANY

History: Robert Hall founded the Hall China Company in 1903 in East Liverpool, Ohio. He died in 1904 and was succeeded by his son, Robert Taggart Hall. After years of experimentation, Robert T. Hall developed a leadless glaze in 1911, opening the way for production of glazed household products.

For more information, see this book.

The Hall China Company made many types of kitchenware, refrigerator sets, and dinnerware in a wide variety of patterns. Some patterns were made exclusively for a particular retailer, such as Heather Rose for Sears.

One of the most popular patterns was Autumn Leaf, a premium designed by Arden Richards in 1933 for the exclusive use by the Jewel Tea Company. Still a Jewel Tea property, Autumn Leaf has not been listed in catalogs since 1978, but is produced on a replacement basis with the date stamped on the back.

Additional Listings: See *Warman's Americana & Collectibles* for more examples.

Cookie jar, cov
Autumn Leaf, Tootsie. **275.00**
Blue Blossom, Five-Band shape
. . . . **300.00**
Chinese Red, Five-Band shape **150.00**
Gold Dot, Zeisel. **95.00**
Meadow Flower, Five-Band shape
. . . . **260.00**

Autumn Leaf, berry bowl, 5-1/2" d, $7.50.

Owl, brown glaze **120.00**
Red Poppy **50.00**

Kitchen ware
Bean pot, New England, #1, Orange Poppy. **100.00**
Casserole, cov, Chinese Red, Sundial, #4, 8" w. **125.00**
Coffeepot, Great American, Orange Poppy. **65.00**
Jug, Primrose, rayed **20.00**
Reamer, lettuce green **450.00**

Patterns
Autumn Leaf
Bean pot, cov **700.00**
Bowl, 5-1/2" d **7.50**
Bud vase, 5-3/4" h **300.00**
Butter dish, cov, one-pound size
. . . . **500.00**
Candy dish, pedestal, 4-5/8" h, 5-13/16" sq top **600.00**
Coffeepot, electric. **500.00**
Cup and saucer. **18.00**
Juice reamer **300.00**
Plate, 8" d **15.00**

Autumn Leaf cup and saucers, $18. Photo courtesy of R Rhoads Auctions.

Water jug, Westinghouse, blue, **$55.**

Teapot, cov, automobile shape, 1993
. . . . **500.00**
Tidbit tray, three tiers **125.00**
Utensil holder, 7-1/4" h, marked
"Utensils" **275.00**

Blue Bouquet
Creamer, Boston. **25.00**
Cup and saucer **28.00**
French baker, round **35.00**
Platter, 13" l **35.00**
Soup, flat. **30.00**
Spoon **100.00**
Teapot, Aladdin infuser. **200.00**

Cameo Rose
Bowl, 5-1/4" d **3.00**
Butter dish, 3/4 lb. **30.00**
Casserole **25.00**
Creamer and sugar. **10.00**
Cream soup, 6" d **7.00**
Cup and saucer **9.00**
Plate, 8" d **2.50**
Teapot, cov, six cup **35.00**
Tidbit, three tier. **40.00**

Fuji
Coffee server **40.00**
Creamer and sugar. **25.00**

Gamebirds
Percolator, electric **140.00**
Teapot, cov, two-cup size, ducks
and pheasant **200.00**

Little Red Riding Hood
Butter dish, cov, 6-3/4" w, 5-1/2" h
. . . . **490.00**
Mustard, cov, 3-1/2" w, 5-1/8" h, orig
wood spoon **390.00**

Mount Vernon
Coffeepot **125.00**
Creamer **12.00**
Cup. **10.00**
Fruit bowl **8.00**
Gravy boat **20.00**
Saucer **4.00**
Soup bowl, 8" d, flat **16.50**
Vegetable bowl, 9-1/4" l, oval . **20.00**

Red Poppy
Bowl, 5-1/2" d **5.00**
Cake plate **17.50**
Casserole, cov **25.00**

Coffeepot, cov **12.00**
Creamer and sugar **15.00**
Cup and saucer. **8.00**
French baker, fluted. **15.00**
Jug, Daniel, Radiance **28.00**
Plate, 9" d. **6.50**
Salad bowl, 9" d. **14.00**
Teapot, New York. **90.00**

Silhouette
Bean pot **50.00**
Bowl, 7-7/8" d. **50.00**
Coffeepot, cov. **30.00**
Mug **35.00**
Pretzel jar. **75.00**
Trivet **125.00**

Tulip
Bowl, 10-1/4" l, oval **36.00**
Coffee maker, drip, Kadota, all china
. . . . **115.00**
Condiment jar **165.00**
Fruit bowl, 5-1/2" d **10.00**
Mixing bowl, 6" d **27.00**
Plate, 9" d, luncheon **16.00**
Platter, 13-1/4" l, oval **42.00**
Shakers, bulge-type, price for pr
. . . . **110.00**
Sugar, cov **25.00**

Teapots
Blue Blossom, airflow. **950.00**
Cadet, Radiance **350.00**
Chinese Red, donut, 9-1/2" w, 7-1/2" h
. . . . **600.00**
Cleveland, turquoise and gold. . **165.00**
Los Angeles, cobalt blue **160.00**
Radiance & Wheat **390.00**

HAMPSHIRE POTTERY

History: In 1871, James S. Taft founded the Hampshire Pottery Company in Keene, New Hampshire. Production began with redwares and stonewares, followed by majolica in 1879. A semi-porcelain, with the recognizable matte glazes plus the Royal Worcester glaze, was introduced in 1883.

Until World War I, the factory made an extensive line of utilitarian and art wares including souvenir items. After the war, the firm resumed operations, but made only hotel dinnerware and tiles. The company was dissolved in 1923.

Bowl, 5-1/2" d, 2-1/2" h, matte green glaze over foliate-forms, imp "Hampshire, M.O." **320.00**

For more information, see this book.

Vase, bulbous, fine mottled blue and rose matte glaze, stamped "Hampshire Pottery/1813," 4-1/2" d, 7" h, **$750.** *Photo courtesy of David Rago Auctions.*

Chocolate pot, 9-1/2" h, cream, holly dec **275.00**

Compote, 13-1/4" d, ftd, two handles, Ivory pattern, light green highlights, cream ground, red decal mark . **175.00**

Inkwell, 4-1/8" d, 2-3/4" h, round, large center well, three pen holes . . . **125.00**

Lamp base, 15" h, 9" d, tall cylindrical form, vertical leaves, stems, and flowers, matte green glaze . . . **2,185.00**

Stein, 7" h, 1/2 liter, transfer printed scene of Pine Grove Springs resort **110.00**

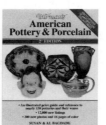

Vase, flaring rim and two handles, covered in a fine dark green matte glaze, impressed "J.S.T. & Co./Keene NH," stamped "Hampshire Pottery, Keene, New Hampshire," 5-1/2" d, 15" h, **$1,355.** *Photo courtesy of David Rago Auctions.*

Tankard, 7" h, band of stylized dec, green matte glaze, imp "Hampshire"
. . . .**100.00**

Vase

3-1/4" h, 4-1/4" d, squat, leathery matte green glaze, imp mark
. . . .**375.00**

4-5/8" h, cylindrical, matte green, designed by Cadmon Robertson, inscribed "Hampshire" and "M" within and "O" cipher, "17/1" on base **250.00**

7-1/2" h, 4" d, cylindrical, feathered matte blue glaze, imp mark "A.O."
. . . .**520.00**

8-1/2" h, 6-1/2" d, bulbous, leathery matte green, blue, and brown dripping glaze, imp mark **1,000.00**

11" h, green matte, squared off handles at shoulder. **1,200.00**

14-5/8" h, inverted rim, cylindrical form tapering to flared base, relief dec lily pads on trailing stems, matte green glaze, "Hampshire Pottery 87," "M" in circle in relief on base, designed by Cadmon Robertson **1,380.00**

HATPINS AND HATPIN HOLDERS

History: When oversized hats were in vogue, around 1850, hatpins became popular. Designers used a variety of materials to decorate the pin ends, including china, crystal, enamel, gem stones, precious metals, and shells. Decorative subjects ranged from commemorative designs to insects.

Hatpin holders, generally placed on a dresser, are porcelain containers that were designed specifically to hold these pins. The holders were produced by major manufacturers, among which were Meissen, Nippon, R. S. Germany, R. S. Prussia, and Wedgwood.

Hatpin

Brass

1-1/4" d, 9" l pin, Victorian Lady, cameo type profile, round, Victorian, orig finish. **110.00**

1-1/2" x 1-3/4", 9" l pin, child with flowing hair, flanked by sunflowers, Victorian, orig finish. **125.00**

2" d, 9-1/2" l pin, military button
. . . .**125.00**

2-1/4" l, oxidized, four citrine-colored stones in each of four panels, citrine-colored stones on 1/2" bezel
. . . .**315.00**

Enamel, black tracery, surmounted by small pearl, 14kt yg, pr. **150.00**

Hand-painted china, violets, gold trim
. . . .**35.00**

Lalique, Scarabees, c1912, clear and frosted glass with sepia patina, $2,070. Photo courtesy of David Rago Auctions.

Glass, 2" l faceted amber glass bead, 13-1/4" l japanned shaft. **125.00**

Ivory, ball shape, carved design **65.00**

Jet, 1-1/4" elongated oval knobby bead, 8" l pin **200.00**

Metal, 9-1/4" l, round disk, Art-Nouveau style lady with flowing hair. **125.00**

Satsuma, Geisha Girl dec **245.00**

Sterling silver

1-1/4" d, 11" l pin, Arts & Crafts motif of ivy leaf in circle, Charles Horner, hallmarks for Chester, England, 1911. . . . . **195.00**

6-1/2" l, elongated tear shape, marked "Horner" **95.00**

Hatpin holder

Belleek, 5-1/4" h, relief pink and maroon floral dec, green leaves, gold top, marked "Willets Belleek," dated 1911. . . . . **125.00**

Limoges, grapes, pink roses, matte finish, artist sgd **60.00**

Hatpin holder, Belleek, African violets decoration, Willet mark, 5" h, $90.

Nippon, 4-7/8" d, hp blue daisy flowers, marked "E. O. China". **185.00**

Royal Bayreuth, tapestry, portrait of lady wearing hat, blue mark. . . . **575.00**

R. S. Germany, 4-1/2" d, pink roses, green foliage, pink luster trim. . . **315.00**

R. S. Prussia, 7" h, 3" d, peach flowers, green foliage **180.00**

HAVILAND CHINA

History: In 1842, American china importer David Haviland moved to

H&C°
L

H&C°
L
FRANCE

Limoges, France, where he began manufacturing and decorating china specifically for the U.S. market. Haviland is synonymous with fine, white, translucent porcelain, although early hand-painted patterns were generally larger and darker colored on heavier whiteware blanks than were later ones.

David revolutionized French china factories by both manufacturing the whiteware blank and decorating it at the same site. In addition, Haviland and Company pioneered the use of decals in decorating china.

David's sons, Charles Edward and Theodore, split the company in 1892. In 1936, Theodore opened an American division, which still operates today. In 1941, Theodore bought out Charles Edward's heirs and recombined both companies under the original name of H. and Co. The Haviland family sold the firm in 1981.

Charles Field Haviland, cousin of Charles Edward and Theodore, worked for and then, after his marriage in 1857, ran the Casseaux Works until 1882. Items continued to carry his name as decorator until 1941.

For more information, see this book.

Thousands of Haviland patterns were made, but not consistently named until after 1926. The similarities in many of the patterns makes identification difficult. Numbers assigned by Arlene Schleiger and illustrated in her books have become the identification standard.

Bone dish, 8-1/4" l, hp

Crab dec **60.00**

Turtle dec. **65.00**

Bouillon, underplate, Rajah pattern, marked "Theo Haviland" **25.00**

Bowl, 8" d, hp, yellow roses **35.00**

Butter dish, cov, Gold Band, marked "Theo Haviland" **45.00**

Butter pat, sq, rounded corners, gold trim **12.00**

Cake plate, 10" d, gold handles and border. **35.00**

Celery dish, scalloped edge, green flowers, pale pink scroll **45.00**

Chocolate set, Norma pattern, chocolate pot, set of six cups and six saucers, $250. Photo courtesy of Joy Luke Auctions.

Chocolate pot, cov, 10-1/2" l, Countess pattern, green mark, c1893 .... **475.00**

Cream soup, underplate, cranberry and blue scroll border **30.00**

Creamer and sugar, small pink flowers, scalloped, gold trim **65.00**

Cup and saucer, Etoile **470.00**

Dinner set, Gold Band, service for 12 .... **1,000.00**

Game plate, 9-1/4" d, hp, center scene of shore birds in natural setting, apple green edge, printed gold scrolled rim dec, artist sgd "B. Albert," Theodore Haviland & Co. blanks, early 20th C, price for set of 12 .... **865.00**

Gravy boat, attached underplate
Chantilly **270.00**
Monteray **315.00**
Schleiger #57 .... **250.00**

Milk pitcher, 8" h, 4-3/4" d, pink flowers, green branches, underglaze green

Dinner service, red roses and green leaves, Johann Haviland, 49 pieces, $190. Photo courtesy of Joy Luke Auctions.

Haviland mark, red "Haviland & Co., Limoges for PDG, Indianapolis, Ind." **450.00**

Oyster plate, five wells
Forget-me-not dec, white ground, brushed gold trim **250.00**
Mussels, brushed gold trim .. **800.00**
Seascape, shellfish and aquatic plants dec **975.00**
Wave design, mauve, brushed gold trim **325.00**

Pitcher, 7-1/2" h, Rosalinde **280.00**

Plate, dinner
Etoile **400.00**
Golden Quail **275.00**

Platter
Chantilly **275.00**
Golden Quail **350.00**

Relish dish, blue and pink flowers **25.00**

Sandwich plate, 11-1/2" d, Drop Rose pattern **275.00**

Sugar bowl, cov, Golden Quail . **435.00**

Teacup and saucer, small blue flowers, green leaves **30.00**

Teapot, Portland **250.00**

Tea set, 8-1/2" d, 8" h teapot, rope and anchor pattern, transfer-printed, hand tinted blossoms, stamped "Haviland-Limoges" mark, restoration to lids, price for three-pc set **200.00**

Tureen, cov, pink roses, green ivy, 12" l, 6-1/2" h **360.00**

Vase, 5-1/2" h, 3-5/8" d, tan, brown, pink, and rose, two oval scenes of lady in large hat, baskets and flower garlands, Charles Field Haviland and GDA Limoges mark **275.00**

Vegetable dish, open, Golden Quail, 9-1/2" x 7-1/2" **435.00**

HEISEY GLASS

1900–58

History: The A. H. Heisey Glass Co. began producing glasswares in April 1896, in Newark, Ohio. Heisey, the firm's founder, was not a newcomer to the field, having been associated with the craft since his youth.

Many blown and molded patterns were produced in crystal, colored, milk (opalescent), and Ivorina Verde (custard) glass. Decorative techniques of cutting, etching, and silver deposit were employed. Glass figurines were introduced in 1933 and continued in production until 1957 when the factory closed. All Heisey glass is notable for its clarity.

For more information, see this book.

Marks: Not all pieces have the familiar H-within-a-diamond mark.

Dinner service, border of pink roses, two cups and saucers, platter, and dinner plate shown from 119 pieces sold as lot, $550. Photo courtesy of Joy Luke Auctions.

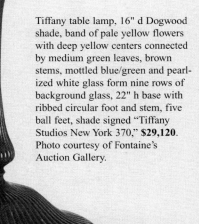

Fulper pottery, table lamp, 18" h two-socket baluster base, 15" d mushroom-cap shade inset with organically shaped blue, green, and red leaded-slag glass pieces, entire piece covered in Chinese Blue Flambé glaze, rectangular ink mark, shade has a few very minor scratches and four short hairlines between leaded glass pieces, probably from firing, **$11,150**. Photo courtesy of David Rago Auctions.

Tiffany floor lamp, 20" d classic Greek Key design shade, butterscotch mottled glass, key in blue-green, onyx used on stem varies from cream to dark brown veining, three metal bands wrap stem, two with ornate leaves and vines, third with beading, vasiform section with two handles and two more bands, four very ornate feet on base incorporating scrollwork, shade signed "Tiffany Studios New York 1907," **$31,160**. Photo courtesy of Fontaine's Auction Gallery.

Tiffany art glass panel, stylistic twin peacocks hovering over urn of fruit and colorful foliage, deep royal blue, rose pink, purple, light blue, and white feathers, plated round chunk of amber glass in upper center, row of blue, green, and yellow chunks border bottom edge, surrounded by pink and blue sections of similar texture, all lead work finished in black patina, c1890-1900, unframed, 19" x 23", **$15,240**. Photo courtesy of Fontaine's Auction Gallery.

Tiffany table lamp, 16" d Dogwood shade, band of pale yellow flowers with deep yellow centers connected by medium green leaves, brown stems, mottled blue/green and pearlized white glass form nine rows of background glass, 22" h base with ribbed circular foot and stem, five ball feet, shade signed "Tiffany Studios New York 370," **$29,120**. Photo courtesy of Fontaine's Auction Gallery.

Pairpoint table lamp, 12" d azalea puffy shade, red and pink flowers, light green leaves, dark green background, 17" h ornate base and stem covered with floral designs, four decorated arms support shade, shade signed "Pairpoint Mfg Co. 3011 1/2" and "P" in diamond, **$20,160**. Photo courtesy of Fontaine's Auction Gallery.

George III silver tea urn, Paul Storr, London, 1809 and 1810, base fully marked, partially marked on cover, cover also inscribed with Latin signature of Rundell, Bridge and Rundell, ovoid vessel, chased with stiff leaves, mounted with fluted spigot terminating in lion's head with ivory tap, gadrooned socle base with guilloche border, square base with canted corners, fully sculpted dolphin feet, neck with applied grapevine, two bold beaded scroll handles chased with leaves and rosettes continuing to snake terminals, pine cone finial on slightly domed cover with guilloche rim, 249 oz 2 dwt, 20-1/2" h, **$16,000**. Photo courtesy of Sloan's Auctioneers & Appraisers.

Here are some nice examples of Mount Washington glass: top: 8" h biscuit jar, square, cream-colored ground, gold enamel floral decoration, signed Mount Washington, silver plated lid, **$150**; front left: 1-1/2" x 3-1/4" Burmese shell-shaped salt dip, satin finish, applied frosted feet, **$75**; right: 3-3/4" unmarked syrup pitcher, white ground, small enamel floral decoration, silver-plated spout and handle, **$100**. Photo courtesy of Woody Auctions.

Pickle castor, vaseline Button & Daisy pattern insert, Boston silver plate holder, oversized lid, 11" h, **$150**. Photo courtesy of Woody Auctions.

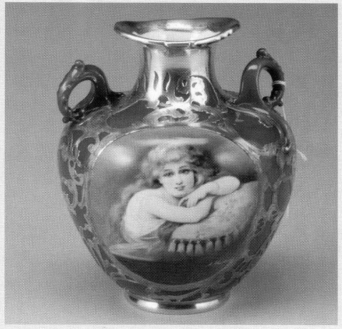

Willets Belleek urn, by G.G. Houghton, 1903, hand-painted pink and yellow roses, brown snake stamp, artist-signed, dated, 9" d, 17-1/2" h, **$1,850**. Photo courtesy of David Rago Auctions.

Presentation urn, bulbous, whiplash handles, covered in Art Nouveau silver overlay, beautifully painted by A. Heinrich with portrait of young girl, inscribed "First Prize/Handicap Lawn Tennis Tournament of the New York Athletic Club, 1896," purple Ceramic Art Co. stamp, restoration to both handles, 7-1/4" d, 9-1/2" h, **$1,355**. Photo courtesy of David Rago Auctions.

Wavecrest umbrella stand, Indian chief in full headdress on one side, scout on horseback on reverse, 19" h, **$22,400**. Photo courtesy of Fontaine's Auction Gallery.

Art pottery, Susan Frackelton, gourd-shaped salt-glazed stoneware vase, c1905, abutilon blossoms alternating with stylized leaves and vines, indigo on ivory ground, chip and rim nick, signed "SF/1X/984," 3-3/4" d, 6-3/4" h, **$20,700**. Photo courtesy of David Rago Auctions.

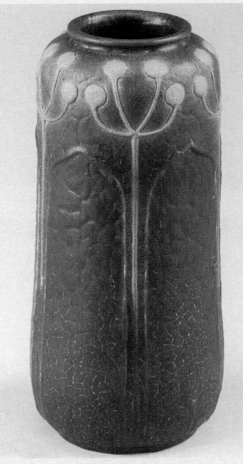

Candelabra, gilt bronze, French, 19th C, altar form, column of clouds mounted with pair of winged angels looking toward five-arm candelabra, footed base, 41" h, **$900**. Photo courtesy of Jackson's International Auctioneers & Appraisers.

Grueby vase, cylindrical, tooled and applied stylized flowers in chartreuse alternating with broad leaves, leathery dark green matte glaze, circular pottery mark/ER/12/3/4, 4-1/4" d, 10" h, **$9,780**. Photo courtesy of David Rago Auctions.

Holy water font, French, 19th C, sculpted bronze figure of Guardian Angel filling font composed of bank of clouds supported by winged cherubs, entire figure set on carved and beveled slab of alabaster, mounted to bronze back, suspension loop, 20" h, **$1,380**. Photo courtesy of Jackson's International Auctioneers & Appraisers.

Dedham, experimental vase by Hugh Robertson, bulbous, rich lustered oxblood glaze, incised "Dedham Pottery/HCR," 2-1/2" hairline from rim, 5-3/4" d, 7" h, **$1,355**. Photo courtesy of David Rago Auctions.

Satsuma vase, Japan, Meiji period (1868-1911), drum-shaped body with a trumpet mouth and foot, molded decoration of various birds and flowering cherry branches (minor loss), 18-1/2" high, **$950**. Photo courtesy of Skinner Auctioneers and Appraisers.

Cane, Faberge, lapis, 1-1/2" w, 1-3/4" h egg-shaped deep blue lapis knob, elaborate gold collar decoration with festoons of two-color gold laurel leaves surmounted by five mine-cut diamonds, fragmented Russian hallmarks, honey-toned Malacca shaft, 1-1/2" horn ferrule, 34-1/2" l, **$8,400**. Photo courtesy of Henry A. Taron.

Wrought iron candelabra made by the Globe Ironworks, Cleveland, Ohio, 18" h, six-light, each candleholder consists of snapped and polished neck of a champagne bottle used to christen a Great Lakes steamship built by Globe Ironworks, foil and wire-held cork of each bottle still in place, silver tag soldered on each engraved with name of ship and date it was launched, each neck has a matching removable 2-3/4" sterling silver drip cut with ornate beaded rim, engraved around the circumference of the interior with ship's name and launching date. Ships represented: *North Star,* Feb. 12, 1889; *Matoa,* June 12, 1890; *Seneca,* June 8, 1889; *Vulcan,* July 10, 1889; *Saxon,* Oct. 15, 1890; *Manola,* June 21, 1890; *Northern Wave,* Jan. 3, 1889; *Northern Queen,* Nov. 1, 1888; *Castalia,* Oct. 31, 1889; *Maruba,* May 17, 1890; *Saronac,* June 21, 1889; and *Cayuga,* April 2, 1889, **$1,600**. Photo courtesy of Cowan's Historic Americana Auctions.

Meissen, two seated ladies in classical attire, one tying ribbon around Cupid's wings, other feeding pigeons, oval base, late 19th C, underglaze blue crossed swords mark, incised 970, imp "51" and "95," enameled "42," 14" w, **$5,500**. Photo courtesy of Sloan's Auctioneers & Appraisers.

KPM plaque, oval, mother feeding child, impressed KPM with scepter and numerals, gilt and gesso frame, **$2,300**. Photo courtesy of Sloan's Auctioneers & Appraisers.

Fishing creel, George Lawrence, Portland, Oregon, size 15, Tillamook Model, leather trimmed, split willow, 1950, **$9,020**. Photo courtesy of Lang's Sporting Collectables, Inc.

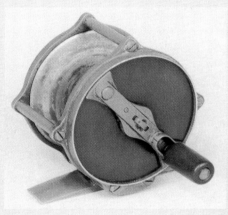

Fishing reel, George W. Gates, Athol, Massachusetts, 1885 patent, trout, **$2,320**. Photo courtesy of Lang's Sporting Collectables, Inc.

Flow Blue pitcher, Sylva, Till & Sons, 10-1/2" h, **$475**. Photo courtesy of Ellen G. King.

Holt Howard Pixieware, condiment jars—mustard, ketchup, and Jam 'n Jelly—1958, **each $75**. Photo courtesy of Walter Dworkin.

Mulberry, Berry, Ridgways, plate, 10" d, **$145**. Photo courtesy of Ellen G. King.

Flow Blue, Unknown pattern, unknown maker, cake plate, coral polychrome decoration, **$275**. Photo courtesy of Ellen G. King.

L. & J. G. Stickley double-door china cabinet, 12 panes to each door, over two door cabinet with hammered copper strap hinges, tab pulls, original finish with overcoat, "Work of L. & J. G. Stickley" decal inside door, back drilled to accommodate interior lighting, some veneer lifting, some chips and repairs, 47" w, 16" d, 70" h, **$18,400**. Photo courtesy of David Rago Auctions.

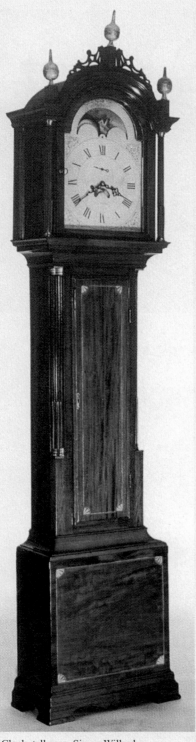

Clock, tall case, Simon Willard, Hepplewhite Roxbury mahogany case, bonnet with freestanding fluted columns, molded arch pediment with fretwork, gilded wooden finials, fluted quarter columns, molded edge door, molding between sections, bracket feet, stringing inlay with corner fans, brass trim with brass stop fluting on columns, brass works with phases of the moon dial, calendar movement, second hand, painted steel face labeled "Simon Willard," Roman numerals hour marking repainted, wear to face, with weights, pendulum, and key, 97" h, **$77,000**. Photo courtesy of Garths Auctions, Inc.

Étagère, Renaissance Revival, c1850, rosewood, mirrored top with floral and scroll carvings, elaborate carved cabriole apron and legs, 73" w, 26" d, 118" h, **$16,800**. Photo courtesy of Fontaine's Auction Gallery.

327

Brooch, Retro, feather, bi-color, center calibré-cut ruby stem with applied circular accent enhanced by old European-cut diamonds, **$1,000**. Photo courtesy of Sloan's Auctioneers & Appraisers.

Brooch, Victorian, yellow gold, circular design, centering applied horseshoe, accented with round graduated lapis bordered by small graduated turquoise within two-tier gold bead and twisted rope border, adapted for pendant, **$450**. Photo courtesy of Sloan's Auctioneers & Appraisers.

Jacquard coverlet, one piece, double weave, eagles with "Liberty," peacocks on fruited tree, floral border, corners with bust of Gen. Washington, tomato red, navy blue, and natural white, minor wear, small holes, edge damage, 70" x 83", **$3,200**. Photo courtesy of Garths Auctions, Inc.

Brooch, Retro, bow, bi-color 14kt green and pink gold bow centering line of channel-set square-cut rubies flanked by four single-cut diamonds, hallmark, 16.9 dwt., **$950**. Photo courtesy of Skinner Auctioneers and Appraisers.

Earrings, Art Deco, 18k white gold, architectural design, calibré-cut rubies and mixed-cut diamonds, **$500**. Photo courtesy of Sloan's Auctioneers & Appraisers.

Catalog, White Sewing Machine Co., Cleveland, Ohio, 1897, 32 pages, 7-3/4" x 7-3/4", very colorful wraps, seven brightly colored farmable pictures, White bicycles, illustrated, **$365**. Photo courtesy of Kenneth Schneringer.

Animal
Gazelle **1,450.00**
Plug horse, Oscar **115.00**
Pony, kicking **175.00**
Sealyham terrier **145.00**
Sparrow **150.00**

Ashtray
Old Sandwich, #1404, moongleam,
   individual size **67.50**
Ridgeleigh, #1469, club shape **10.00**

Bitters bottle, #5003, tube **165.00**

Bowl
Empress, #1401, Alexandrite,
   dolphin foot, 10-7/8" w **735.00**
Queen Anne, 8" d, light use . . . **25.00**

Buffet plate, Lariat, #1540, 21" . . **70.00**
Butter dish, cov, Rose **200.00**
Cake plate, Rose, 15" d, pedestal
. . . . **325.00**
Camellia bowl, Lariat, #1540, 9-1/2" d
. . . . **40.00**
Candelabra, crystal, 10" w, 16-1/2" h,
price for pr **695.00**

Candlesticks, pr
Lariat, two-lite, #1150 . . . . . . **95.00**
Mercury, #122 . . . . **70.00**
New Era, #3877 . . . . **90.00**
Orchid, Trident, two-lite **155.00**
Patrician, 7-1/2" h, cut pattern,
   hexagon shape **425.00**
Pinwheel, #121 . . . . **90.00**
Regency, two-lite, #1504 . . . . . **98.00**
Thumbprint and Panel, #1433
. . . . **140.00**
Trophy, #126, flamingo **275.00**
Windsor, #22, 7-1/2" h **140.00**

Caramel, cov, Lariat, #1540, 7" . . **75.00**
Celery, Empress, Sahara, 10" l . . . **45.00**
Centerpiece bowl, Ridgeleigh, #1469,
11" d **225.00**

Sherbet, Victorian pattern, footed, signed, $20.

Champagne, Duquesne, tangerine,
saucer **235.00**
Cheese dish, cov, Lariat, #1540, ftd
. . . . **40.00**
Cheese plate, Twist, #1252, Kraft,
moongleam **62.50**
Cigarette holder, Crystolite **25.00**

Claret
Carassone, Sahara, 4 oz **68.00**
Orchid, Tyrolean line, 4-1/2 oz
. . . . **150.00**

Coaster
Colonial **10.00**
Plantation **50.00**

Cocktail
Lariat, #1540, moonglo cut . . . **12.00**
Orchid Etch, 4 oz **40.00**
Rose Etch **32.50**
Rosealie, 3 oz **10.00**

Cocktail shaker
Cobel, #4225, quart **55.00**
Orchid Etch, sterling foot . . . **200.00**

Compote, Rose, #1519, low, ftd, 6-1/2"
. . . . **65.00**

Cordial
Carcassone, #390, Sahara . . . **115.00**
Orchid, #5025 Tyrolean line . . **50.00**
5th Avenue-Mitchell, #829 . . . **45.00**

Creamer, Ridgeleigh, #1469 . . . . **20.00**

Creamer and sugar
Twist, #1252, oval, Sahara . . **165.00**
Waverly, #1519, orchid etch . . **75.00**

Cream soup, Queen Anne, etching
. . . . **20.00**
Cruet, Plantation, crystal, #1567
. . . . **155.00**

Cup and saucer
Empress, Sahara yellow, round
. . . . **40.00**
Twist, #1252, flamingo **55.00**

Custard cup, Queen Anne **15.00**

Orchid pattern, large sandwich plate, 14" d, $80. Photo courtesy of Sanford Alderfer Auction Company.

Orchid pattern, tall water pitcher, $500. Photo courtesy of Sanford Alderfer Auction Company.

Floral bowl, Orchid, Waverly, crimped,
12" d, 4" h, some scratches **55.00**
Gardenia bowl, Orchid, Waverly, 13" d
. . . . **90.00**

Goblet
Galaxy, #8005 . . . . **25.00**
Narrow Flute, #393 . . . . **28.50**
Old Dominion, #3380, marigold,
   8-3/4" **55.00**
Orchid, #5025 Tyrolean line . . . **50.00**
Provincial, #1506 . . . . **15.00**
Spanish, #3404, cobalt blue . **155.00**
Tudor **12.00**

Honey, Plantation, #1567, ivy etch,
6-1/2" **80.00**
Hurricane lamp base, Lariat, #1540, pr
. . . . **85.00**
Iced-tea tumbler, ftd, Orchid, #5025,
Tyrolean line **70.00**
Jug, Old Sandwich, #1404, Sahara, half
gallon **225.00**
Mayonnaise bowl, Orchid, two-part,
Queen Anne **65.00**
Mayonnaise ladle, #6, Alexandrite
. . . . **245.00**
Muffin plate, Octagon #1229, 12" d,
moongleam **47.50**

Nut dish
Empress, #1401, individual,
   Alexandrite **175.00**
Narrow Flute, #393, moongleam
. . . . **15.00**

Oyster cocktail, Pied Piper **15.00**
Paperweight, rabbit **225.00**
Parfait glass, Orchid, 5-1/2" h, 2-7/8" d,
price for set of eight **480.00**
Pitcher, Orchid, tankard **625.00**

Plate
Colonial, 4-3/4" d **4.75**
Empress, yellow, 10-1/4" d, dinner
. . . . **110.00**

Minuet, 8" d **19.75**
Orchid, Waverly, 8" d **40.00**
Ridgeleigh, #1469, 8" d **10.00**
Punch bowl set, Crystolite, punch
bowl, 12 cups, ladle **400.00**
Relish
Normandie etch, star, #1466 . **95.00**
Orchid, three-part, three handles,
7-1/4" d **55.00**
Provincial, #1506, 12" **35.00**
Twist, #1252, flamingo, 13" l . . **40.00**
Waverly, two-part **25.00**
Rose bowl, Plateau, #3369, flamingo
. . . . **65.00**
Salt shaker, Old Sandwich, #1404
. . . . **30.00**
Sandwich plate, Rose **220.00**
Serving tray, center handle, Orchid
Etch **150.00**
Sherbet, Yeoman, Sahara **10.00**
Soda
Coronation, #4054, 10 oz **9.50**
Duquesne, #3389, 12 oz, ftd,
tangerine **210.00**
Newton, #2351, 8 oz, Fronetnac etch
. . . . **20.00**
Old Dominion, #3380, 12 oz, ftd,
diamond optic Alexandrite . . **90.00**
Stanhope, #4083, 8 oz, ftd, zircon
bowl and foot **155.00**
Strawberry dip plate, Narrow Flute,
#393, with rim **195.00**
Sugar, Crystolite, individual **17.50**
Tankard, Orchid, ice lip, 9-1/2" h, 7" w
. . . . **480.00**
Toothpick holder, Fancy Loop,
emerald, small base flake, wear to gold
trim **120.00**

*Punch bowl, pedestal, fluted design,
scalloped edge, two-piece, 15" d,
12-3/4" h, chips, roughness on rim and
base, $90. Photo courtesy of Sanford
Alderfer Auction Company.*

Tumbler, Carassone, Sahara, ftd, 2 oz
. . . . **72.00**
Vase
Prison Stripe, #357, cupped, 5"
. . . . **55.00**
Ridgeleigh, #1469, Sahara, cylinder,
8" h **245.00**
Water bottle, Banded Flute, #150
. . . . **125.00**
Wine, Orchid etch, 3 oz **75.00**

HOLT-HOWARD COLLECTIBLES

History: Three young entrepreneurs, Grant Holt and brothers John and Robert Howard, started Holt-Howard from their apartment in Manhattan, in 1949. All three of the partners were great salesman, but Robert handled product development, while John managed sales; Grant was in charge of financial affairs and office management. By 1955, operations were large enough to move the company to Connecticut, but they still maintained their New York showroom and later added their final showroom in Los Angeles. Production facilities eventually expanded to Holt-Howard Canada; Holt-Howard West, Holt-Howard International.

The company's first successful product was the Angel-Abra, followed closely by its Christmas line. This early success spurred the partners to expand their wares. Their line of Christmas and kitchen-related giftware was popular with 1950s consumers. Probably the most famous line was Pixieware, which began production in 1958. Production of these whimsical pieces continued until 1962. Other lines, such as Cozy Kittens and Merry Mouse brought even more smiles as they invaded homes in many forms. Three things that remained constant with all Holt-Howard products were a high quality of materials and workmanship, innovation, and good design.

The founders of this unique company sold their interests to General Housewares Corp. in 1968, where it became part of the giftware group. By 1974, the three original partners had left the firm. By 1990, what remained of Holt-Howard was sold to Kay Dee Designs of Rhode Island.

Holt-Howard pieces were marked with an ink-stamp. Many were also copyright dated. Some pieces were marked only with a foil sticker, especially the small pieces, where a stamp mark was too difficult. Four types of foil stickers have been identified.

Adviser: Walter Dworkin.

Christmas
Air freshener, Girl Christmas Tree
. . . . **65.00**
Ashtray/cigarette holder, Starry-eyed
Santa **45.00**
Bells, Elf Girls, pr **55.00**
Candle climbers, Ole Snowy,
snowman, set **48.00**
Candleholders
Camels **38.00**
Elf Girls, NOEL, set of four **38.00**

Pitcher and mug set, Cloud Santa, **$85.**

Ermine Angels with snowflake rings,
set **48.00**
Reindeer, pr **38.00**
Santa King **85.00**
Totem Pole, Santa **25.00**
Wee Three Kings, set of three **60.00**
Cookie jar, pop-up, Santa **150.00**
Cookie jar/candy jar combination,
Santa **155.00**
Creamer and sugar
Reindeers **48.00**
Winking Santas **55.00**
Head vase, My Fair Lady **75.00**
Letter and pen holder, Santa . . . **55.00**
Napkin holder, Santa, 4" **25.00**
Pitcher and mug set, Winking Santa
. . . . **70.00**
Planter
Camel **40.00**
Elf Girl in Sleigh **58.00**
Ermine Angel **38.00**
Punch bowl set, punch bowl and eight
mugs, Santa **145.00**
Salt and pepper shakers, pr
Cloud Santa **38.00**
Rock' N' Roll Santas, on springs
. . . . **75.00**
Snow Babies **35.00**
**Santa and snowman salt and pepper
shakers**, in NOEL candleholder . **95.00**
Server, divided tray, Santa King . **55.00**
Wall pocket, Santa ornament . . . **58.00**

Cozy Kittens
Bud vase, pr **105.00**
Butter dish, cov **105.00**
Cookie jar, pop-up **250.00**
Cottage cheese crock **60.00**
Kitty catch clip **38.00**
Match dandy **75.00**
Memo minder **90.00**
Meow mug **35.00**
Meow oil and vinegar **175.00**
Mustard condiment jar **180.00**
Salt and pepper shakers, pr . . . **20.00**
Spice set **110.00**
Sugar pour **85.00**

Pitcher and mug set, Merry Whiskers, $90.

Totem pole stacking seasons . . **65.00**

Jeeves, butler
Ashtray **70.00**
Chip dish **80.00**
Liquor decanter **165.00**
Martini shaker set **195.00**
Olives condiment jar **135.00**

Merry Mouse
Cocktail kibitzers mice, set of six
. . . . **120.00**
Corner coaster ashtray **55.00**
Crock, "Stinky Cheese" **50.00**
Desk pen pal **85.00**
Match mouse **70.00**
Salt and pepper shakers, pr . . . **35.00**

Miscellaneous
Ashtray
 Golfer Image **110.00**
 Li'l Old Lace **50.00**
Bank, bobbing, Dandy Lion **135.00**
Bud vase, Daisy Dorable **70.00**
Candelabra, Li'l Old Lace, spiral . **50.00**
Candle climbers, Honey Bunnies, with
bases, set **85.00**
Candle rings, Ballerina, set **48.00**
Cookie jar, pop-up, Clown **225.00**

**Salt and pepper shakers with napkin
holder,** Winking Wabbits **60.00**
Salt and pepper shakers, pr
 Bell Bottom Gobs (sailors) . . . **50.00**
 Chattercoons, Peppy and Salty
 . . . . **38.00**
 Daisy Dorables, ponytail girls . **35.00**
 Goose 'N' Golden Egg **35.00**
 Pink cat, white poodle **65.00**
 Rock 'N' Doll Kids, on springs **75.00**

Pixiewares, 1958
Bottle bracelets
 Bourbon **100.00**
 Gin **100.00**
 Scotch **100.00**
 Whiskey **100.00**
Child's Pixie spoon
 Carrot nose, flesh-colored Pixie
 . . . . **125.00**
 Green head Pixie **125.00**
 Orange head Pixie **125.00**
 Yellow chicken beak Pixie . . **125.00**
Condiment jar
 Cherries **115.00**
 Cocktail Cherries **135.00**
 Cocktail Olives **130.00**
 Cocktail Onions **155.00**
 Instant Coffee **255.00**
 Jam 'N' Jelly **75.00**
 Ketchup **75.00**
 Mustard **75.00**
 Olives **100.00**
 Onions **145.00**
L'il sugar and cream crock . . . **145.00**
Liquor decanter
 "Devil Brew" **580.00**
 "300 Proof" **580.00**
 "Whisky" **580.00**
Oil cruet, Sally **185.00**

Oil cruet, Sam **185.00**
Stacking seasons, shakers, set of four
. . . . **85.00**

Pixiewares, 1959
Ashtray Pixie
 Blue stripe **160.00**
 Green stripe **160.00**
 Pink stripe **160.00**
 Red stripe **160.00**
Condiment jar
 Chili Sauce **365.00**
 Honey **700.00**
 Mayonnaise **180.00**
 Relish **225.00**
Hanging planter, rare **450.00**
Party Pixies hors d'oeuvre dish
 Green stripe boy pixie **200.00**
 Orange stripe girl pixie, Australian
 . . . . **475.00**
 Pink stripe girl pixie **200.00**
Salad dressing jar
 Flat head, French Pixie **140.00**
 Flat head, Italian Pixie **140.00**
 Flat head, Russian Pixie **140.00**
 Round head, French Pixie . . . **125.00**
 Round head, Italian Pixie **125.00**
 Round head, Russian Pixie . . **125.00**
Salty & Peppy shakers **350.00**
Snack Pixie bowl
 Berries **675.00**
 Goo **750.00**
 Ketchup Katie **675.00**
 Mustard Max **675.00**
 Nuts **575.00**
 Onion Annie **675.00**
 Oscar Olives **575.00**
 Peanut Butter Pat **675.00**
 Pickle Pete **675.00**
 Tartar Tom **675.00**

*Pixieware condiment jars, left: instant coffee, 1958, **$255**; middle: ketchup, 1958, **$75**; right: mustard, 1958, **$75**. All Holt-Howard photos courtesy of Walter Dworkin.*

Pixieware, condiment jar, chili sauce, 1959, $365. Photo courtesy of Walter Dworkin.

Teapot candleholder hurricane vase, complete with glass globe

Blue stripe boy	285.00
Pink stripe girl	285.00

Towel hook

Brother	150.00
Dad	150.00
Mom	150.00
Sister	150.00

Red Rooster, "Coq Rouge"

Butter dish, cov	65.00
Candleholders, pr	30.00
Coffee mug	14.00
Coffee server, 36 oz	65.00
Cookie jar	100.00
Creamer and sugar	55.00
Dinner plate	18.00
Electric coffee pot, six cups	70.00
Mustard condiment jar	55.00

Pitcher

12 oz	45.00
32 oz	60.00
48 oz	75.00

Salt and pepper shakers, pr, 4-1/2"

	25.00
Snack tray	18.00
Spoon rest	25.00

Wooden

Canister set, four pcs	85.00
Cigarette carton holder	45.00
Recipe box	70.00
Salt and pepper shakers, pr	23.00

HORN

History: For centuries, horns from animals have been used for various items, e.g., drinking cups, spoons, powder horns, and small dishes. Some pieces of horn have designs scratched in them. Around 1880, furniture made from the horns of Texas longhorn steers was popular in Texas and the southwestern United States.

Ale set, silver plate mounted cov 9-3/4" h jug, two 5-1/2" h beakers, fitted 17-3/4" l x 15" h plated frame with twisted gallery and upright handle, tripartite circular base with Greek Key border, raised on stepped block feet, English, early 20th C 850.00

Arm chair, steer horn, leather upholstered seat, four pairs of matched horns form base, American, 20th C 575.00

Cane

33-3/4" l, 4" w x 5-1/4" h staghorn "L"-shaped handle, high relief carved hunting scene, detailed family crest on top round portion, scene spirals around handle starting at bottom continuing to top, medieval hunt with dogs, men with spears and lances pursing two bears, thin coin silver spacer, Malacca shaft with round silver eyelets, 2-1/4" polished staghorn ferrule, attributed to Germany, c1880 .... 2,800.00

34-1/8" l, 7-1/2" l wild boar's tusk handle, pointed silver cap with leaf dec, marked "sterling" on one end, other end with sq cap inscribed "Judge Henry Bank Jr. from KeoKuK Bar Feb. 15, 1919," 1-1/8" dec silver collar, dark briarwood shaft, 1-1/4" white metal and iron ferrule 1,100.00

35" l, 1-3/4" w, 4" h dark horn handle, carved as perched eagle, clear and black glass eyes, lighter horn beak, 2/3" woven silver thread

Chair, various horns and antlers used in arms and back, wooden seat frame, carved animal legs with hoofs, old dark finish, seat reupholstered in brown moire silk, 36" h, pair, $825. Photo courtesy of Garth's Auctions, Inc.

Cup, shallow relief carved portrait of Naval officer from early 19th C, probably meant to portray Admiral Perry, early 19th C, very minor insect damage at base, tiny old lip chip, 3" h, $70. Photo courtesy of Cowan's Historic Americana Auctions.

collar, blond Malacca shaft, 1-1/2" horn ferrule, Continental, c1895 .... 490.00

35" l, 7-1/2" l x 2" w staghorn handle, carved as Chinese maiden in full ceremonial dress, holding charm on cord with one hand, long stems of lotus leaf and blossom with other, additional blossoms in hair, pink tint to blossoms, black ink highlights, brown hardwood shaft, 3/4" horn ferrule, England, c1890 .... 1,570.00

Cup, 5" h, rhinoceros, carved as magnolia flower, base of branch and leaves, carved wood stand, 18th C or earlier, losses 1,100.00

Plaque, wall mounted, water buffalo horns, brass caps on ends, engraved dec, 33" l 275.00

Snuff box, 2" l, 2-3/4" w, 3/4" h, rect, carved PA motifs, floral dec, red paint on hinged lid, birds carved on sides, star on bottom 450.00

Scottish Snuff Mull, Dark horn bound in silver, c. 1810, hinged lid, 3" l, $300. Photo courtesy of Sanford Alderfer Auction Company.

Tea caddy, cov, 14-1/2" w, 9" d, 7-1/2" h, Ango-Indian, Vishapatnam, early 19th C, antler veneer, steer horn, ivory, int. cov compartments, etched scrolling vines, restorations......... **1,850.00**

Vinaigrette, Victorian, late 19th C, staghorn, 2-1/2" l rough-textured horn mounted with thistle-cast lid, quatrefoil neck band, horn with guilloche strapping, short link chain **350.00**

HULL POTTERY

History: In 1905, Addis E. Hull purchased the Acme Pottery Company, Crooksville, Ohio. In 1917, the A. E. Hull Pottery Company began making art pottery, novelties, stoneware, and kitchenware, later including the famous Little Red Riding Hood line. Most items had a matte finish, with shades of pink and blue or brown predominating.

After a disastrous flood and fire in 1950, J. Brandon Hull reopened the factory in 1952 as the Hull Pottery Company. New, more-modern-style pieces, mostly with glossy finish, were produced. The company added dinnerware patterns, and glossy finished pottery. The company closed its doors in 1986.

Marks: Hull pottery molds and patterns are easily identified. Pre-1950 vases are marked "Hull USA" or "Hull Art USA" on the bottom. Many also retain their paper labels. Post-1950 pieces are marked "Hull" in large script or "HULL" in block letters.

Each pattern has a distinctive letter or number, e.g., Wildflower has a "W" and a number; Waterlily, "L" and number; Poppy, numbers in the 600s; Orchid, in the 300s. Early stoneware pieces are marked with an "H."

Additional Listings: See *Warman's Americana & Collectibles* for more examples.

Adviser: Joan Hull.

Pre-1950 Matte
Bowknot
B-4 6-1/2" h vase **250.00**
B-7 cornucopia **325.00**
B-12, 10-1/2" h basket...... **750.00**
B-17 candleholders, pr **225.00**
Calla Lily
500-32 bowl............. **200.00**
520-33, 8" h vase.......... **150.00**
Dogwood (Wild Rose)
501, 8-1/2" h basket........ **300.00**
508 10-1/2" window box **195.00**
513, 6-1/2" h vase **125.00**
Little Red Riding Hood
Creamer and sugar, side pour
.... **400.00**
Dresser or cracker jar **800.00**
Lamp **2,500.00**
Salt and pepper shakers, pr, small
.... **120.00**
Teapot, cov **395.00**

Hull Ware pottery "Little Red Riding Hood" lidded cracker jar, 13" h and two salt shakers, 5-1/2" h, $325. Photo courtesy of Joy Luke Auctions.

Magnolia
3 8-1/2" h vase **125.00**
9 10-1/2" h vase **200.00**
14 4-3/4" h pitcher **75.00**
20 15" floor vase.......... **500.00**
Open Rose/Camellia
106 13-1/2" h pitcher **650.00**
119 8-1/2" h vase **175.00**
127 4-3/4" h vase **75.00**
Orchid
302 6" h vase **175.00**
304 10-1/2" h vase **350.00**
310 9-1/2" jardinière **450.00**
Poppy
601 9" h basket........... **800.00**
610 13" pitcher **900.00**
613 6-1/2" h vase **200.00**

Vase, Magnolia, matte, 1946-47, 10-1/2" h, $200.

Rosella
R-2 5" h vase **35.00**
R-6 6-1/2" h vase **45.00**
R-15 8-1/2" h vase **75.00**
Tulip
101-33 9" h vase **245.00**
107-33 6" h vase **125.00**
109-33-8" pitcher......... **235.00**
Waterlily
L-14, 10-1/2" basket **350.00**
L-16, 12-1/2" vase **395.00**
Wild Flower, No. Series
53 8-1/2" h vase.......... **295.00**
61 6-1/2" h vase.......... **175.00**
66 10-1/4" h basket **2,000.00**
71 12" h vase............ **450.00**
Woodland
W9 8-3/4" h basket **245.00**
W11 5-1/2" flower pot and saucer
.... **175.00**
W13 7-1/2" l wall pocket, shell
.... **195.00**
W14 10-1/2" window box.... **200.00**

Post 1950
Blossom Flite
T4 8-1/2" h basket **125.00**
T13 12-1/2" h pitcher **150.00**
Butterfly
B9 9" h vase.............. **55.00**
B13 8" h basket **150.00**
B15 13-1/2" h pitcher **200.00**
Continental
C29 12" h vase **95.00**
C55 12-1/2" basket **150.00**
C62 8-1/4" candy dish....... **45.00**
Ebb Tide
E-1 7" h bud vase **75.00**
E-8 ashtray with mermaid ... **225.00**
E-10 13" h pitcher **275.00**

Ewer, Parchment and Pine, 1952-53, 14-1/4" h, $215.

Parchment and Pine

S-3 6" h basket **95.00**
S-11 and S-12 tea set **250.00**
S-15 8" h coffeepot **175.00**

Serenade

S1 6" h vase **55.00**
S-15 11-1/2" d fruit bowl, ftd . **125.00**
S17 teapot, creamer and sugar
. . . . **275.00**

Sunglow

53 grease jar **60.00**
82 wall pocket, whisk broom . **75.00**
85 8-3/4" h vase, bird **60.00**

Tokay/Tuscany

3 8" h pitcher **95.00**
8 10" h vase **150.00**
10 11" l cornucopia **65.00**

Tropicana

T53 8-1/2" h vase **550.00**
T55, 12-3/4" h basket **750.00**

Woodland (glossy)

W1 5-1/2" h vase **45.00**
W15 8-1/2" h vase, double . . . **75.00**
W19 14" d console bowl **100.00**

HUMMEL ITEMS

History: Hummel items are the original creations of Berta Hummel, who was born in 1909 in Massing, Bavaria, Germany. At age 18, she was enrolled in the Academy of Fine Arts in Munich to further her mastery of drawing and the palette. Berta entered the Convent of Siessen and became Sister Maria Innocentia in 1934. In this Franciscan cloister, she continued drawing and painting images of her childhood friends.

In 1935, W. Goebel Co. in Rodental, Germany, began producing Sister Maria Innocentia's sketches as three-dimensional bisque figurines. The Schmid Brothers of Randolph, Massachusetts, introduced the figurines to America and became Goebel's U.S. distributor.

In 1967, Goebel began distributing Hummel items in the U.S. A controversy developed between the two companies, the Hummel family, and the convent. Law suits and counter-suits ensued. The German courts finally effected a compromise: the convent held legal rights to all works produced by Sister Maria Innocentia from 1934 until her death in 1946 and licensed Goebel to reproduce these works; Schmid was to deal directly with the Hummel family for permission to reproduce any pre-convent art.

Marks: All authentic Hummel pieces bear both the signature "M. I. Hummel" and a Goebel trademark. Various trademarks were used to identify the year of production:

Crown Mark (trademark 1)	1935 through 1949
Full Bee (trademark 2)	1950-1959
Stylized Bee (trademark 3)	1957-1972
Three Line Mark (trademark 4)	1964-1972
Last Bee Mark (trademark 5)	1972-1979
Missing Bee Mark (trademark 6)	1979-1990
Current Mark or New Crown Mark (trademark 7)	1991 to the present

Additional Listings: See *Warman's Americana & Collectibles* for more examples.

Festival Harmony, #172, first bee mark, 11" h, $300. Photo courtesy of Woody Auctions.

Bookends, pr, Chick Girl, #618, full bee, trademark-2 . . . . **320.00**
Candleholder, Watchful angel, #194, trademark 2 . . . . **400.00**
Candy box, cov, Happy Pastime, #III/169, trademark 4 . . . . **125.00**
Christmas Angel
   Boy, #117, trademark 3 . . . . . . **45.00**
   Girl, #116, fir tree, 3" h, trademark 3
   . . . . **40.00**

Wash Day, 5-1/2" h, and Kiss Me, 6" h, both mark 5, each, $200. Photo courtesy of Joy Luke Auctions.

Figure

Apple Tree Girl, #141, 6" h, stamped full bee, incised crown mark
. . . . **425.00**
Band Leader, #129, trademark 5
. . . . **120.00**
Chimney Sweep, #122/10, trademark 5 . . . . **70.00**
Daily News, #184, 5" h **400.00**
Farm Boy, #66, trademark 2, 1950-57, 5-3/4" h **375.00**
Goose Girl, #47/0, trade mark 3, 4-3/4" h **425.00**
Happiness, #86, trademark 3 . **110.00**
Just Resting, #112/13/0, trademark 4
. . . . **90.00**
Kiss Me, #311, trademark 3 . **150.00**
Merry Wanderer, #11/0, trademark 2
. . . . **215.00**
Photographers, #178, trademark 4
. . . . **215.00**

Waiter, 6" h, and Little Fiddler, 5" h, both mark 5, each, $160. Photo courtesy of Joy Luke Auctions.

Merry Wanderer, 6" and 4-1/2" h, both mark 5, each, $75. Photo courtesy of Joy Luke Auctions.

Umbrella Boy, mark 5, 5" h, $200; Umbrella Girl, mark 4, 5" h, $200, and Stormy Weather, mark 5, 6" h, $175. Photo courtesy of Joy Luke Auctions.

Strolling Along, #5, full bee mark, 5-3/4" h **550.00**
Umbrella Boy, #152, c1960-72, 8" h **500.00**
Wayside Harmony, #111/3/0, trademark 4 . . . .**100.00**
Font
Child Jesus, #26/0, MK 4 . . . . .**35.00**
Holy Family, #246, trademark 2 . . . .**85.00**
Seated Angel, #10/1, trademark 3 . . . .**420.00**
Lamp, table, Culprits, #44, 9-1/2" h, c1930 . . . .**475.00**
Nativity set, Virgin Mary, Carpenter, Wisemen, Shepherd and lamb, Baby Jesus in manger, stable, Robson, bee in V mark, 4-1/2" h figures, c1959-61 . . . .**795.00**
Plaque, Madonna, #48/0, trademark 7 . . . .**250.00**

IMARI

History: Imari derives its name from a Japanese port city. Although Imari ware was manufactured in the 17th century, the pieces most commonly encountered are those made between 1770 and 1900.

Early Imari was decorated simply, quite unlike the later heavily decorated brocade pattern commonly associated with Imari. Most of the decorative patterns are an underglaze blue and overglaze "seal wax" red complimented by turquoise and yellow.

The Chinese copied Imari ware. The Japanese examples can be identified by grayer clay, thicker glaze, runny and darker blue, and deep red opaque hues.

The pattern and colors of Imari inspired many English and European potteries, such as Derby and Meissen, to adopt a similar style of decoration for their wares.

Reproduction Alert: Reproductions abound, and many manufacturers continue to produce pieces in the traditional style.

Boat dishes, 11" l, Japan, late 19th C, price for set of five **1,350.00**
Bottle vases, 11" h, lobated form, underglaze blue with red, green, aubergine enamels and gilt, Japan, late 19th C, price for pr **775.00**
Bowl
8-1/2" d, 3-1/4" h, red, blue, white, and gold dec **425.00**
13-1/2" d, 5-1/2" h, blue and white, edge chips **715.00**
16" d, 8-1/2" h, scalloped edge, int. dec with fish and water plants, ext.

Charger, fans with warriors and dragons, signed "Koransha," late 19th C, 22" d, $1,650. Photo courtesy of Skinner's Auctioneers and Appraisers.

with dragons and phoenixes, Japan, late 19th C **1,200.00**
Charger
14-1/2" d, underglaze blue and enamel dec, central reserve of planter with flowers, grape and brocade borders, Japan, late 19th/early 20th C **250.00**
20-1/4" d, 4-3/4" h, hp, cinnabar red, underglaze dark blue, green, and gilt, dragons in clouds circle border, leaves and clouds below, two phoenixes in center, ext. cov with blossoming vines, center base with cinnabar and gilt flower, glued repair to edge, gilt imperfections **715.00**
22" d, fans with warriors and dragons dec, sgd "Koransha," late 19th C **1,645.00**
Creamer and sugar, 5-1/2" h creamer, 5-7/8" cov sugar, ovoid, dragon form handles, gilt and bright enamels, shaped reserves, dragon-like beasts, stylized animal medallions, brocade ground, high dome lid, knob, cipher mark of Mount Fuji, Fukagama Studio marks, Meiji period **500.00**
Dish
8-3/8" d, central scene with fence and flowering tree dec, shaped cartouches enclosing flowers and hares on crackle blue ground at rim, gilt highlights, Meiji period, price for pr **650.00**
9-1/2" d, shaped rim, allover flowering vine dec, gilt highlights **150.00**
Food box, 6" h, three section, ext. and lid with phoenix and floral design, underglaze blue, iron-red, and gilt enamels, 19th C **400.00**
Jar, cov, 26" h, ribbed forms with shishi finials, Japan, late 19th C, price for pr **2,000.00**

Meat platter, 19-1/2" x 16", English, $450. Photo courtesy of Sanford Alderfer Auction Co.

Jardinière, 10" h, hexagonal, bulbous, short flared foot, alternating bijin figures and immortal symbols, stylized ground **250.00**

Planter and stand, 17" d, 43" h, lobed form, floral dec, brocade patterns, Japan, late 19th C **460.00**

Plate

8-1/2" d, scalloped edge, rib banding, polychrome dec, floral panels, surrounding floral medallions, bats on reverse, character mark, gilt loss.... **55.00**

10-1/4" d, scalloped edge, rib banding, polychrome gilt dec, floral panels, surrounding floral medallion, bats on reverse, rim chip **65.00**

Platter, 18" d, alternating panels of figures and foliage, trellis work ground, Japanese, late 19th C **475.00**

Punch bowl, 12" d, rubbed, c1870 .... **1,650.00**

Teabowl and saucer, 5" d, floriform, floral spray dec, gilt highlights on saucer **200.00**

Umbrella stand

23" h, ribbed form, Imari underglaze blue with red dec, gilt, Japan, late 19th C **775.00**

25" h, allover hexagonal panels with gold pheasants and orange drawings, flowers, and plant, orange, tomato red, yellow, green, and cobalt blue, old shield shaped "U.S. Customs" label underneath **550.00**

Urn, 36-1/2" h, tomato red, light green, mauve, and cobalt blue, dark gold details, floral panels on sides with pheasants and cranes, geometric band of dec around base, minor roughness around rim **2,100.00**

Vase, 14-1/2" h, baluster, late Meiji period, c1900 .... **775.00**

IMPERIAL GLASS

History: Imperial Glass Co., Bellaire, Ohio, was organized in 1901. Its primary product was pattern (pressed) glass. Soon other lines were added, including carnival glass, Nuart, Nucut, and Near Cut. In 1916, the company introduced Free-Hand, a lustered art glass line, and Imperial Jewels, an iridescent stretch glass that carried

the Imperial cross trademark. In the 1930s, the company was reorganized into the Imperial Glass Corporation, and the firm is still producing a great variety of wares.

Imperial recently acquired the molds and equipment of several other glass companies— Central, Cambridge, and Heisey. Many of the retired molds of these companies are once again in use.

Marks: The Imperial reissues are marked to distinguish them from the originals.

Engraved or hand cut

Bowl, 6-1/2" d, flower and leaf, molded star base................**25.00**

Candlesticks, pr, 7" h, Amelia ...**35.00**

Celery vase, three-side stars, cut star base **25.00**

Pitcher, tankard, Design No. 110, flowers, foliage, and butterfly cutting **60.00**

Plate, 5-1/2" d, Design No. 12 ...**15.00**

Jewels

Bowl, 6-1/2" d, purple Pearl Green luster, marked...............**75.00**

Compote, 7-1/2" d, irid teal blue .**65.00**

Rose bowl, amethyst, green irid .**75.00**

Vase

5" h, stretch, amber shading to light irid finish, early 20th C.....**150.00**

7-3/4" h, classic baluster, white body, mirror bright tray-blue surface, deep orange irid int. rim ...**320.00**

Candlewick, #400/50 Handled Cream Soup bowl, 6-1/2" handle to handle, **$48.** *Photo courtesy of Michael Krumme.*

Lustered (freehand)

Candlestick, 10" h, slender baluster, cushion foot, clear, white heart and vine dec, tall cylindrical irid dark blue socket, orig paper label **440.00**

Hat, 9" w, ruffled rim, cobalt blue, embedded irid white vines and leaves **120.00**

Ivy ball, 4" h, Spun, red, crystal foot **90.00**

Vase

6" h, opal glass, glossy orig irid finish, c1920 ....**150.00**

Art glass, vase, flared rim, bright orange iridescent, cream-colored lip, 6-1/2" h, **$100.** *Photo courtesy of James D. Julia, Inc.*

8-1/2" h, cylindrical, irid green heart and vine design, white ground, marigold lining, some wear **385.00**

10" h, tall slender form, irid orange ext., deep orange throat ..**195.00**

Nuart

Ashtray...................**20.00**

Lamp shade, marigold........**50.00**

Vase, 7" h, bulbous, irid green .**125.00**

Nucut

Berry bowl, 4-1/2" d, handles...**15.00**

Celery tray, 11" l.............**18.00**

Creamer **20.00**

Fern dish, 8" l, brass lining, ftd..**30.00**

Orange bowl, 12" d, Rose Marie **48.00**

Pressed

Baked apple, Cape Cod, 6".....**9.00**

Bar bottle, Cape Cod........**150.00**

Basket, Cape Cod, No. 160/73/0 ....**350.00**

Birthday cake plate, Cape Cod **325.00**

Bowl

Cape Cod, 11" l, oval **90.00**

Windmill, amethyst, fluted, 8" d, 3" h **45.00**

Bread and butter plate, Cape Cod **7.00**

Canapé plate, matching tumbler, #400/36 ....**36.00**

Center bowl, Cape Cod, No. 160/751, ruffled edge................**65.00**

Champagne, Cape Cod, azalea. **22.00**

Coaster, Cape Cod, No. 160/76. **10.00**

Creamer, #400/30.............**9.00**

Cruet, orig stopper, Cape Cod, No. 160/119, amber...............**28.00**

Decanter, orig stopper, Cape Cod, No. 160/163....................**75.00**

Fruit bowl, Cape Cod, 4-1/2" ...**12.00**

Rose bowl, Molly pattern, pink, short foot, four wide toes, eight scalloped top, light ribbed body, 4-1/2" h, 5-1/2" w, $25. Photo courtesy of Johanna Billings.

Goblet

Cape Cod, No. 1602, Verde green **20.00**
Traditional **15.00**
Juice tumbler, Cape Cod, 6 oz . . **10.00**
Mug, Cape Cod **58.00**
Nappy, Quilted Diamond, marigold, ring handle........................ **35.00**
Pitcher, Cape Cod, No. 160/19, ice lip **85.00**
Plate, Windmill, glossy, green slag, IG mark **45.00**

Relish

Candlewick, two-part, 6-1/2" . . **25.00**
Cape Cod, three-part **35.00**
Rose bowl, Molly, black, silver deposit floral dec, 5" h................ **45.00**
Salad plate, 8" d, Cape Cod, use scratches **11.00**

Sherbet

Cape Cod **10.00**
Traditional **10.00**
Sugar, #400/30................ **9.00**
Tea cup, #400/35............. **8.00**
Toothpick holder, 2-1/2" h, carnival or milk white, IG mark............ **30.00**
Tumbler, Georgian, red **18.00**
Whiskey set, Cape Cod, No. 160/280, metal rack, clear bottles, raised letters Bourbon, Rye, and Scotch..... **650.00**

INDIAN ARTIFACTS, AMERICAN

History: During the historic period, there were approximately 350 Indian tribes grouped into the following regions: Eskimo, Northeast and Woodland, Northwest Coast, Plains, and West and Southwest.

American Indian artifacts are quite popular. Currently, the market is stable following a rapid increase in prices during the 1970s.

For more information, see this book.

Awl case

17" l with fringe, Southern Plains, Mescalero Apache, c1900, tapered hide body and cap beaded with bold zigzag pattern in amber, dark blue, yellow, and light blue seed beads, red stained buckskin fringe with tin crimps hang from bottom **765.00**

18" l, Plains, last quarter 19th C, tapered hide body and end cap wrapped with Kiowa red, yellow and white seed beads, long edge beaded hide drop with tin cone danglers, large hollow brass beads on thong.............. **850.00**

Bag

5-1/2" l, Great Lakes, Ojibwa, polychrome wool, finger-woven rect form with red and dark brown geometric devices on tan ground, old yellow tag reads in part "Ojibway Yarn bag from Tom Stone (sow-cug-ifish) 89 years old of Danbury Wisconsin on St. Croix River coll. 1935"........ **825.00**

7" h, Northwest, c1900, U-shaped hide bag partially beaded on front in unusual abstract floral devices using multicolored glass and metallic seed beads, pink ribbon edging **200.00**

11" l, Central Plains, Sioux, c1900, hide, fringed horseshoe shape beaded on both sides with multicolored geometric devices on blue ground, white border . **715.00**

14" l, Plains, Ute, c1870, rect buffalo hide, beaded on both sides, flap with unusual Ute style linear geometric devices, bottom fringe **2,875.00**

16" x 9-1/2", Plateau, c1900, hide, rect form, beaded on front with warrior in profile, wearing feather headdress and necklace with heart-shaped medallion, various colored beads on light blue ground, contour overlay stitch, fringe at bottom, framed, not examined out of frame ... **1,725.00**

Basket

3-3/4" d, California, Pomo, late 19th C, gift, coiled, small compressed form, tightly woven with geometric devices, very fine feather tufts **1,265.00**

7" l, Northwest Coast, Tlingit, twined polychrome rattle top, lidded jar form, woven with bold false embroidered geometric devices using five colors **2,415.00**

Basketry bowl, coiled

7" d, Western, Washo, c1900, slightly flared, simple stacked wedge devices **375.00**

21-1/2" d, California, Yokus, flaring, two bands of interlocking diamonds, minor stick loss, small rim break............. **2,990.00**

Belt, child's, 26" l, Plains, 19th C, commercial leather belt with roller buckle and 18 remaining German silver discs....................... **185.00**

Blanket, 2' 10" x 2' 10", Chimayo, hand woven, red, black, and white stripes and crillo design elements, gray ground, small holes **90.00**

Blanket strip, 58" l, Central Plains, Lakota, late 19th C, beaded hide, repeated cross roundel devices separated by barred zigzag devices, green, royal blue, white-center red, and metallic beads, white ground, water damage, bead loss **1,035.00**

Bottle, twined basketry cover, 9-1/4" h, Northwest Coast, Tlingit, c1900, bands of repeated birds, simple fretz, openwork, glass decanter, minor fading **750.00**

Bow, 47-1/2" l, Central Plains, last quarter 19th C, ash, tapered hand grip, double notch, twisted sinew string **750.00**

Bow case and quiver, 44" l, Southwest, Plains Apache, last quarter 19th C, hide bow case, red and yellow details, orig

Basket, Bridgeport tribe, woven decoration, two handles, shallow, $300.

Bowl, San Ildefonso, pottery, black on black, signed Marie – Julian, 4-1/4" d, 2-1/2" h, $275. Photo courtesy of Joy Luke Auctions.

sinew-backed bow, well-worn quiver with eleven steel-tipped arrows, hide loss, stiffness to leather **2,415.00**

Bowl, pottery, Southwestern, Hopi, polychrome, red and dark brown slip, cream-colored ground, 12" d, high rounded form, highly abstract avian devices, cross-hatching, two encircled stylized butterflies, corn logo at bottom **1,955.00**

Cane, 31" l, Central Plains, probably Lakota, late 19th C, polychrome wood, carved as twined diamond-form snakes, traces of black and green pigments **320.00**

Charm bag, 2-1/2" x 2-1/2", Western Great Lakes, late 19th C, small sq bag, two thunderbirds beaded on one side and diagonal sawtooth pattern on reverse, multicolored glass seed beads on white ground, beaded neck strap and tassels **1,300.00**

Club, Skull Cracker, 26-1/2" l, Central Plains, last quarter 19th C, stone-headed club with rawhide covered wood handle, handle wrapped with plaited polychrome quillwork, quilled strap holding pointed stone head in place with remnant white bead edging, minor bead and quill loss, includes metal stand **2,950.00**

Cradle, 31" l, Plains, probably Cheyenne, c1880, buffalo hide form beaded with classic Cheyenne pattern, white-center red, green, and dark blue beads, white ground, hide board attachments remaining on back, orig tag reads "Crow Indian Baby cov from 'Spotted Tail' Crow Agency Montana, Ter. May 30th, 1888," collected on Crow Reservation **1,500.00**

Cradleboard, 27" l, Central Plains, probably Cheyenne, beaded buffalo hide form attached to later boards, large stepped diamond devices, bottle

green, greasy yellow, translucent rose, black, and white seed beads, bead loss **18,400.00**

Doll

8" h, Southern Plains, Comanche, c1900, hide, male form wearing partially beaded fringed buckskin shirt and leggings, yarn hair wrapped in calico cloth, red pigment **2,000.00**

12" h, Central Plains, probably Lakota, late 19th C, cloth and hide, female form with calico petticoat, partially beaded buckskin dress and beaded moccasins, hair missing, bead loss **1,880.00**

Dress, woman's, 52" l, Central Plains, Lakota, late 19th C, blue trade cloth, ribbon work above selvage edging on sleeves and bottom, large metal sequins sewn to ribbon, yoke dec with rows of cowry shells, cloth belt beaded in "salt and pepper" beadwork . **950.00**

Dress, woman's, Northern Plains, deerskin, 21" w at the chest, raglan type shoulders, short cape type sleeves, shoulder yolk is deerskin laced as are the side seams, center, front and back of yolk have mall decorative area with deer hair still on, neck opening front and back have a narrow band of dark blue cloth and wide band of red trade cloth, scalloped skirt, very fine fringe, dec on each side with rectangles of trade cloth and deerskin, two small spots of red trade cloth on center, opposing side has two 2-1/4" d beaded rosettes of red trade cloth center and white and blue circles surrounding, side seams have very fine fringe, fine hide strings front and back at chest area and on lower part of skirt, attached to one string is old manila tag bearing the quill ink inscription "Indian Woman's Dress/Presented To Col. E. Rice, U.S.A./By White Bull, War Chief Of The Northern Sioux," at the bottom of tag in same writing, but very tiny "Col. Edmund Rice, U.S.A., February 12, 1884," leather soft, great old patina, 48" l, $9,775. Photo courtesy of James D. Julia Auctions.

Effigy ladle, 9-1/4" l, Western Great Lakes or Prairie, carved wood, shallow shovel-shaped scoop with handle terminating in stylized bear's head, heart shape is carved on back of head, small brass eyes, medium brown patina **4,115.00**

Effigy pipe bowl, 5" l, Eastern Plains, Dakota, late 19th C, red pipestone hooked form representing stylized (possibly) panther head, incised linear devices, usual projecting fin is broken and missing **150.00**

Fetish figure, carved stone, Southwest

5-1/2" l, probably Zia, c19th C, seated figure, relief carved legs and arms, head with broad nose, shallow round eyes possibly inlaid with mica, chest inlaid with irregular piece of turquoise, string necklace of early green turquoise beads with abalone pendant, smooth patina from handling **4,025.00**

10" h, c19th C, volcanic stone, possibly representing snake, eyes inlaid with old turquoise beds, smaller stone piece tied to back with buckskin, traces of red pigment **520.00**

Half leggings, 20" l, Plains, Sioux, c1890, hide, partially beaded with five-point star and diamond devices, one lane border, and boot straps on bottom, attached strap reads "From the collection of Richard A. Pohrt" **1,200.00**

Handbag, 8-3/4" l, Plateau, late 19th C, beaded cloth and hide, rect canvas form, beaded on both sides, bold simple geometric devices, different color backgrounds, edged at opening, red trade cloth and buckskin . . **210.00**

Jar, pottery, 8" h, Southwest, possibly Tesuque, bulbous form, black curvilinear devices, cream-colored slip, red bands painted on inside rim and below cream-colored slip **1,380.00**

Kachina, Southwest, polychrome carved wood and cloth

10-1/4" l, Hopi, first quarter 20th C, painted kilt, red and yellow body paint, large white case mask with protruding ears, snout, and Popeyes, black and red stepped devices connecting eyes and ears **2,070.00**

15" h, probably Zuni, c1940, cottonwood form, painted tablita, horsehair beard and hair, cloth clothing and sash, articulated arms **1,725.00**

Knife sheath, beaded hide

9" l without tab, Northern Plains, Cree, third quarter 19th C, tapered hide sheath with commercial leather liner, partially beaded on front in deep transparent red, off white, black, and white, unusual abstract floral beaded tabs hang from side and bottom, tin cone danglers and fringe details, bead loss **4,200.00**

9-1/2" l, Northern Plains, Cree, late 19th C, soft hide sheath beaded on front with polychrome floral pattern on top and polychrome geometric pattern on bottom **450.00**

16" l with fringe, Central Plains, Lakota, last quarter 19th C, rawhide-lined form beaded on one side with bold geometric devices using multicolored seed beads, tin cone danglers, quill wrapped carrying strap, fringed roll beaded drop from bottom, early trade knife with 1868 patent date . . . **3,760.00**

Leggings, man's

34" l, Northern Plains or Plateau, c1900, made from old faded trade blanket with red cloth panels at ankles, partially beaded in linear devices, red and green trade cloth sewn up sides **360.00**

36" l, Plains, possibly Ute or Jicarrilla Apache, c1900, beaded strips with polychrome and metallic seed

beads on white ground, long side fringe braided toward bottom, stains **1,880.00**

Leggings, woman's, 17" l, Central Plains, Arapaho, last quarter 19th C, hide, yellow and blue stained leggings beaded along bottom with stacked crosses and box and border devices using black, greasy blue, and white center red devices on white ground, roll beaded short flap along the side **1,200.00**

Mask, wood, painted

6-1/4" h, Inuit, northern Alaska, last half 19th C, hollow oval form, brow line in form of stylized whale fin, small round pierced eyes, pierced smiling mouth, traces of red pigment on upper lip, two small holes for attachment, minor wood loss **5,465.00**

10" l, Northwest, Iroquois, 20th C, hollow oval form, pierced eyes, large nose, pierced toothy grin, brown and red pigments . . **490.00**

14-1/2" l, Northwest Coast, early 20th C, hollow oval form crudely carved, pierced indented eyes, long nose, oval mouth, partially painted, black, blue, green, and red pigments **2,645.00**

Moccasins, pr, infant's, Woodlands, probably Micmac, mid-19th C, puckered tow soft hide, red cloth cuffs and vamps, beaded geometric and

Photograph, Standing Bear, Ponca Chief, Charles M. Bell, photographer, silver print, mounted on larger gray cardstock with Bell's Washington, DC blindstamp, **$825.** *Photo courtesy of Cowan Historic Americana Auctions.*

floral devices, multicolored small seed beads, silk ribbon ties **1,265.00**

Moccasins, pr, child's, 5-1/2" l, Northern Plains, possibly Crow, c1880, soft sole side-seamed, beaded on vamps and along seam, multicolored linear devices, medium blue ground **1,100.00**

Moccasins, man's, beaded hide

9-1/2" l, Central Plains, Lakota, c1900, hard sole cowhide forms beaded on front with large multicolored checkered diamond device on medium green ground, undecorated forked tongues **375.00**

9-1/2" l, Western Great Lakes, Ojibwa, late 19th C, soft sole forms partially beaded with multicolored floral devices, hide loss . . . **400.00**

10" l, Central Plains, Lakota, last quarter 19th C, beaded with hexagons and stepped pyramids in cobalt blue, greasy yellow, and white center red on white ground, apple green "buffalo tracks," beaded bifurcated tongues with tin cone danglers **4,700.00**

10" l, Central Plains, Lakota, late 19th C, hard sole forms with fully beaded uppers, white borders with multicolored stepped pyramids, light blue vamps, beaded bifurcated tongues with tin cone danglers, bead loss, old repairs **950.00**

Panel with 197 multi-colored Indian arrowheads and two bear claws, **$275.** *Photo courtesy of Joy Luke Auctions.*

10" l, Central Plains, Lakota, late 19th C, soft hide uppers beaded with simple geometric devices using three shades of blue and white center red, minor bead loss **885.00**

10" l, Central Plains, late 19th C, hard sole forms with fully beaded uppers, murky white borders with multicolored pyramids, medium blue vamps, pinked ankle edge, bead loss **950.00**

10" l, Southwest, Apache, c1900, hard sole form with soft uppers stained in two shades of ochre pigment, simple red and green cross beaded on vamp ... **650.00**

10-1/2" l, Eastern Plains, Dakota, c1860, hard sole buffalo hide forms partially beaded with bilateral floral devices of multicolored small seed beads, remnant silk ankle trim **1,800.00**

Moccasins, pr, woman's, 24" l, high-top, Southwest, Apache, first quarter 20th C, yellow stained tops and bottoms, rawhide soles with Cactus Kicker toes, beaded Maltese crosses on vamps, dark red, dark blue, and white seed beads **920.00**

Necklace, 26" l, Plains, late 19th C, stacked shell discs interspersed with large medium-blue trade beads strung on hide and cord, traces of red-orange pigment **265.00**

Olla, pottery, Southwest

10" h, San Ildefonso, c1900, indented base, globular body, painted red and black, cream-colored clip, abstract floral devices on body, neck with band of tapered triangular devices, surface loss to lower body, rim crack **4,025.00**

10-1/2" h, Acoma, late 19th C, high rounded sides, tapering neck and concave base, orange, red, and dark brown slip, cream-colored ground, four large Acoma parrots, foliate, and rainbow devices, repaired neck section.... **8,625.00**

Paint bag, 10-1/2" l, Plains, Cheyenne, c1870, tab top buffalo hide form beaded with "bow tie" and stripe pattern using white center red, greasy yellow, and dark blue on white ground, fringe at bottom, traces of red and yellow pigments............**3,100.00**

Parfleche cylinder, 21" l, Northern Plains, Crow, last quarter 19th C, lidded buffalo rawhide case with classic Crow geometric devices in yellow, green, dark blue, and red polychrome, wear **2,500.00**

Parfleche envelope, polychrome

19" l, Plains, c1900, front flaps painted with hourglass and diamond devices using green, red, and blue pigments **2,350.00**

24" l, Central Plains, possibly Lakota, third quarter 19th C, front flaps painted with gold geometric devices using red, yellow, and blue pigments, paint loss **3,900.00**

25" l, Plains or Plateau, late 19th C, front flaps painted with bordered hourglass devices using red, green, blue, and yellow pigments **900.00**

28-1/2" l, Plains or Plateau, possibly third quarter 19th C, buffalo rawhide, front flaps painted in bold geometric devices using green, red, yellow, and blue pigments, minor paint loss........ **3,300.00**

28-1/2" l, Plains or Plateau, last quarter 19th C, polychrome, front flaps painted with bold geometric devices using red, green, blue, and yellow pigments **1,880.00**

Pipe bag, beaded hide

18" l, Plains, Cheyenne, c1870, four-tab top edge beaded in white and white-center red seed beads, buckskin bag sinew sewn with three feather devices on each side, typical bar design pattern, white, dark bottle green, pumpkin, and Kiowa red, traces of yellow pigment on fringe and bag **6,900.00**

19" l, Central Plains, Lakota, late 19th C, buckskin bag roll beaded at top with three lanes of beadwork descending to lower panel beaded in multicolored geometric devices,

Rug, flatweave, red, black and white, diamond and lightning design, 78" x 57", $5,280. Photo courtesy of Joy Luke Auctions.

white ground, horse track design, multicolored quilled slats and restored fringe hang below the panel, further beaded and quill attachments, traces of yellow pigment **1,955.00**

31" l, Northern Plains, Cree, c1880, six-tab top edge beaded in pink, panel beaded on both sides with multicolored bilateral floral devices, white ground, fringe with dark bugle bead attachments on top **1,725.00**

35" l, Central Plains, Lakota, last quarter 19th C, yellow stained buckskin bag, row of beadwork at top, three rows of lazy-stitch beadwork descending to a lower beaded panel, both sides beaded with typical Lakota dark blue, white centered, and green designs on white ground, below beaded panel are quill wrapped rawhide slats and long yellow stained fringe, "C. E. Dallin" printed on upper part **3,220.00**

Pictorial bag, 11" x 8-1/4", Plateau, early 20th C, beaded cloth, partially beaded on front, man and woman in full attire, each holding up black tipped feather in their right hand, framed, damage to cloth bag, not examined out of frame................... **2,530.00**

Pipe, 20" l, Plains, late 19th C, file-branded ash stem, red pipestone elbow-type bowl **825.00**

Pipebag, hide

30" l, Northern Plains, Cree, last quarter 19th C, hide top with four tabs, central panel beaded on both sides with stepped diamond devices using multicolored glass and metal seed beads, minor bead loss................... **2,300.00**

38" l, Central Plains, Lakota, late 19th C, hide bag roll beaded at top with threes of beadwork descending to lower panel beaded on both sides with simple multicolored geometric devices on white ground, polychrome quilled slats and fringe at bottom **2,500.00**

Pipe tomahawk

18-1/2" l, Northeast, hand-forged head, possibly ash, stem pierced for smoking, four pierced holes along stem for attachments, missing gasket.......... **950.00**

22" l, Plains, tomahawk with hand-forged head, file-burned ash stem pierced for smoking, covered with thread sewn buckskin sleeve, printed on sleeve "War Hatchet, Sioux Indian - 1877, S.E. of Spring Lake - Dakota Terr. Gottschall Collection," head appears to have been polished, traces of red pigment on buckskin **885.00**

Pouch, beaded hide

4-1/2" l, Northern Plain, Crow, c1880, rect commercial hide, beaded on front in geometric devices, white-center red, dark and light blue, greasy yellow seed beads, tin cone danglers along bottom, orig tag "From the Crow Indian 'Alligator' Crow Agency Montana Ty April 27th 1888," collected on Crow Reservation **2,760.00**

5" l, Central Plains, probably Cheyenne, c1880, rect buffalo hide, beaded on front in typical Cheyenne pattern, white-center red, dark blue, and green, white ground, tin cones on flap and bottom, orig tag "Crow Indian Ration Ticket Case, from 'Shows A Fish' Crow Agency, Montana, April 9, 1889," collected on Crow Reservation **2,415.00**

6" l, Southern Plains, third quarter 19th C, "Strike-a-lite," trapezoid leather form, beaded stepped geometric devices in Kiowa red and blue on white ground, tin cone danglers hanging from flap and bottom, remains of old paper label on flap **3,100.00**

7-3/4" l, Plains, Ute, late 19th C, trapezoid form with pointed top, four triangular tabs off bottom, beaded on one side with multicolored glass seed beads in classic Ute-Crow geometric devices, beaded danglers from tabs **650.00**

11" l, Southwest, Apache, c1900, beaded hide, rect form, drawstring and fringe at bottom, partially beaded on both sides with geometric devices using multicolored seed beads. . . **230.00**

Powder horn, 8-1/2" l, 19th C, engraved with Hudson Bay seal and floating banner listing following trading posts: York, Moose, Cumberland House, Port Simpson, Ft. St. James, and Norway House; brass tacked rawhide strip at plug end, wood plug with ribbon dec. **4,460.00**

Rug, Navaho

3' 9" x 4' 8", Ganado, stepped motif of two interlocking diamonds, deep red, dark brown, and cream, red ground, cream and brown stepped borders, c1930, minor stains **1,610.00**

3' 11" x 6' 4", zigzag and broken lines, natural cream, light and dark brown, light brown ground, c1910 . . . . **1,840.00**

4' 2" x 5' 5", early Ganado area, finely hand-carded wool, black, white, tan, double dye red cross center, fret and geometric design . **700.00**

4' 6" x 7' 4", crystal regional weaving, spun and hand-carded wool, shaded gray/tan and natural white, minor wear, light stains, one end rebound **965.00**

Saddle blanket, Navaho, red and orange stripes, corner blocks centered by geometric stylized butterflies, 2' 6" x 2' 6" **150.00**

Scepter, 33" l, Northeast, 19th C, carved wood, tapered form, profusely carved spiral, linear, and geometric devices, knobbed end carved with myriad devices, including snake, turtle, heart, and human face, dark patina **425.00**

Shirt, man's

35" l, Great Lakes, Winnebago, c1900, cotton shirt with loom beaded strips on shoulders and bib, beaded tabs and yarn tassels, medium and dark blue glass seed beads on white ground, silk ribbon detailing, silk loss **2,235.00**

38" l, Northern Plains, Blackfoot, first quarter 20th C, muslin pullover form, painted with simple multicolored geometric and pictorial devices, including tipi, beaded hide strips with polychrome glass beads and faceted brass beads, both hide and cloth fringe, traces of red pigment on inner collar . . **3,525.00**

Shot pouch, 27" l, Western Great Lakes, possibly Cree, mid-19th C, red cloth strap, black cloth inlay, olive worsted tape binding, partially beaded with liner and connecting diamond devices, white seed beads, U-shaped pouch with central bilateral floral device, edge of beaded triangular silk ribbon appliqué, beads in three shades of blue, green, red, clear, and greasy yellow, blue cloth pouch backing has been replaced **9,775.00**

Skirt, Northern California, probably Yurok, 19th C, back skirt an entire deerskin folded laterally, dec with thin strips wrapped with three colored maiden hair fern fibers, fringe dec with small white clam shells, large abalone plaques, and glass grade beads, smaller front apron of long buckskin fringe wrapped and braided with vegetal fibers, trimmed white olivella shells, minor damage to buckskin **36,800.00**

Snow snake, 92" l, Northwest, Iroquois, late 19th C, wood and metal, long rounded form, flattened belly, pointed end with pewter cap **435.00**

Totem pole, Northwest Coast, carved wood

24" h, flat backed, bears and eagles, commercial paint details, first half 20th C **575.00**

31" h, openwork carved pole, frogs, birds, fish, and humans, whole cov with coat of commercial paint, "Sitka Alaska, July 1901" written on base, wood loss **2,415.00**

113", hollowed stem, raven, shaman eating frog, tribal chief eating frog, painted commercial pigments, collected in 1953, southeastern Alaska **5,750.00**

Vest

15" l, Central Plains, Lakota, late 19th C, child's, cloth and hide, beaded on front only in multicolored geometric devices on medium blue ground, bead loss, insect damage **950.00**

20" l, Central Plains, possibly Lakota, c1900, hide, fully beaded on front and back with abstract thunderbird-type devices using white center red, translucent light green, and white seed beads on medium blue background, printed cotton liner **1,880.00**

War club, Central Plains, probably Lakota, last quarter 19th C, rawhide wrapped wood handle stained dark blue, ax-shaped white quartz head, quilled horsehair adornment attached to handle, 29-1/2" h **420.00**

Watch case, 7" l, Northern Plains, Crow, c1880, beaded cloth and hide, teardrop form, beaded front with multicolored geometric devices, back cov in calico, orig tag "Watch case made by Crow Indian half breed Martha Rumpard, Crow Agency, Mont., ty 1888," collected from Crow Reservation **1,265.00**

INK BOTTLES

History: Ink was sold in glass or pottery bottles in the early 1700s in England. Retailers mixed their own formula and bottled it. The commercial production of ink did not begin in England until the late 18th century and in America until the early 19th century.

Initially, ink was supplied in often poorly manufactured pint or quart bottles from which smaller bottles could be filled. By the mid-19th century, when writing implements had been improved, emphasis was placed on making an "untippable" bottle. Shapes ranging from umbrellas to turtles were tried. Since ink bottles were usually displayed, shaped or molded bottles were popular.

The advent of the fountain pen relegated the ink bottle to the back drawer. Bottles lost their decorative design and became merely functional items.

Carter's, Cathedral, cobalt blue, emb lettering, orig cap, 3" d, 9" h . . . **250.00**
Cylindrical, 5-5/8" h, America, 1840-60, "Harrison's Columbia Ink," cobalt blue, applied flared mouth, pontil scar, 3" crack, mouth roughness, C #764
. . . . **140.00**
Figural, America, 1860-90
2" h, house, domed offset neck for, emb architectural features of front door and four windows, colorless, sheared mouth, smooth base, Carter's Ink, some remaining int. ink residue, C #614 . . . . . . **650.00**
2" h, locomotive, aquamarine, ground mouth, smooth base, C #715 . . . . **800.00**
2-5/8" h, house, 1-1/2-story cottage form, full label on reverse "Bank of Writing Fluid, Manuf by the Senate Ink Co Philadelphia," aquamarine, tooled sq collared mouth, smooth base, small area of label slightly faded, C# 682 . . . . **300.00**

Light green, applied lip, c1910, 2-1/2" h, $20.

Umbrella, rolled lip, smooth base, solid plum puce, $160. Photo courtesy of Pacific Glass Auctions.

Hexagonal, 9-7/8" h, America, 1900-20, "Carter," cathedral panels, colorless with pale yellow cast, machined mouth, smooth base, similar to C #820 . **700.00**
Inverted concial
2-3/8" h, Stoddard, NH, 1846-1860, deep yellow-olive, sheared mouth, pontil scar, pinhead flake on mouth edge, C #15 . . . . **170.00**
2-1/2" h, America, 1840-60, medium cobalt blue, tooled mouth, tubular pontil scar, C #23 . . . . **800.00**
Octagonal
G. H. Gilbert Co., West Brookfield, MA, orig label **150.00**
Harrison's Colombian Ink, light green
. . . . **60.00**
Laughlin's And Bushfield Wheeling Va., 2-7/8" h, aquamarine, inward rolled mouth, pontil scar . . . **300.00**
Sanford's, 2-1/4" h, 3-3/4" l, sterling silver stopper with flag and star dec
. . . . **125.00**
Sawyer's Crystal Blue Ink, 6-1/4" h
. . . . **10.00**
Umbrella, America, 1840-60
2-1/4" h, New England, 1840-60, octagonal, golden amber, sheared mouth, C #145 . . . . **160.00**
2-3/8" h, octagonal, sapphire blue, inward rolled mouth, pontil, scar, C #141 . . . . **700.00**
2-5/8" h, octagonal, lime green, labeled "Williams/Black/Empire/ Ink/New York," tooled mouth, smooth base, label 95 percent intact, C #173 . . . . **160.00**
2-5/8" h, octagonal, sapphire blue, inward rolled mouth, pontil, scar, C #129 . . . . **950.00**

INKWELLS

History: Most of the commonly found inkwells were produced in the United States or Europe between the early 1800s and the 1930s. The most popular materials were glass and pottery because these substances resisted the corrosive effects of ink.

Inkwells were a sign of the office or wealth of an individual. The common man tended to dip his ink directly from the bottle. The years between 1870 and 1920 represent the golden age of inkwells when elaborate designs were produced.

Additional Listings: See *Warman's Americana & Collectibles* for more examples.

Bronze and green slag glass, Pine Needle pattern, orig glass liner, dark patina, stamped "Tiffany Studios 30," 4" square, 3-3/4" h, $650. Photo courtesy of David Rago Auctions.

Brass
Embossed, double, two porcelain inserts, late 19th/early 20th C, 10-1/2" l, 6-1/2" w **150.00**
Engraved peaked cornice-form backplate cut with central trefoil and flowers, cabochon bloodstone surrounded by four cabochon red stones, rect base with engraved border, central cut glass well flanked by turned pen supports, Gothic Revival style, England, third quarter 19th C, 9-1/4 l, 5-7/8" h
. . . . **250.00**
Raised birds, cattails, flowers, sq base, ball feet, hinged lid with serpent finial, shell handles
. . . . **500.00**
Bronze
8" d, 5-1/2" h, central lidded baluster form inkwell, round dish raised on

Figural, seated camel, painted spelter, 8-1/2" l, 5-3/4" h, $225. Photo courtesy of Joy Luke Auctions.

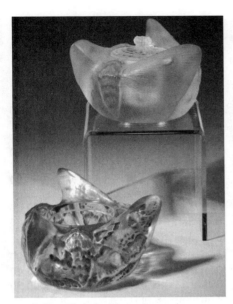

Lalique, Trois Papillons, clear and frosted glass, engraved "R. Lalique France," molded "R. LALIQUE," later version mark with ridged wings, together with an early version in clear and frosted glass with sepia patina, engraved "Lalique," c1912, lacking cover, 3-1/2" d, price for pair, $1,350. Photo courtesy of David Rago Auctions.

quadripartite leaf-form bronze base, dark green enamel ground, stylized foliate bands with gilt accents, faux jewelling, French, late 19th C **435.00**

12" l, cast, Victorian, figural, greyhound dog changed to fencepost, two orig glass wells with covers **815.00**

12-3/8" l, horse head within horseshoe to left, oblong pen tray, sq lidded inkwell with glass liner, traces of brown painted finish, Austrian, early 20th C **290.00**

Enameled, 8" l, 4-1/2" h, cast brass, rococo scrolls, cloisonné-like enamel, pale blue, dark blue, red, white, pale yellow, and green leaves, insert missing **80.00**

Glass, crystal, square, four molded rococo feet, 3-1/4" w, 3-1/2" h . . . **175.00**

Gilt metal, 14" l, bronze, French, rococo style, lion's head supporting pen rest above tray with two cov wells, dolphin feet. **460.00**

Paperweight, 6-1/4" h, 4-1/2" d, multicolored concentric millefiore, base with 1848 date canes, Whitefriars **175.00**

Pearlware, 5-1/2" h, gilt highlights, imp "By F. Bridges, Phrenologist," and "EM"

Majolica, quatrefoil, Renaissance style, glazed with brown and yellow, lilac interior, Georges Dreyfus, c1890, 7-1/2" d, $395. Photo courtesy of David Rago Auctions.

on base, England, 19th C, very minor chips, gilt wear **520.00**

Sterling silver, two bottles, matching pen tray, center sander, Victorian, hallmarked. **1,800.00**

Stoneware

Brushed cobalt blue on top, imp "C. Crolius.Manhattan-Wells, New York," 3-1/8" d, 1-5/8" h, few chips on base **3,200.00**

Incised oval stamp "C. Crolius Stone Ware Manufacturer Manhatten Wells, New York," flat cylindrical form, incised edges, upper one enhanced with cobalt blue slip, center well surrounded by three pen holders, 3-1/2" d, 1-1/4" h, three lower edge chips . . **2,990.00**

Wood, Matthew Bolton, Birmingham, c1795, rect, emb silver mounts, gadroon and shell edge, two silver mounted cut glass inkwells in gardrooned holders, four scroll legs, paw feet, 14" l, 10" w **1,725.00**

IRONS

History: Ironing devices have been used for many centuries, with the earliest references dating from 1100. Irons from the medieval, Renaissance, and early industrial eras can be found in Europe, but are rare. Fine engraved brass irons and hand-wrought irons predominated prior to 1850. After 1850, the iron underwent a series of rapid evolutionary changes.

Between 1850 and 1910, irons were heated in four ways: 1) a hot metal slug was inserted into the body, 2) a burning solid, e.g., coal or charcoal, was placed in the body, 3) a liquid or gas, e.g., alcohol, gasoline, or natural gas, was fed from an external tank and burned in the body, or 4) conduction heat, usually drawing heat from a stove top.

Electric irons are just beginning to find favor among iron collectors.

Additional Listings: See *Warman's Americana & Collectibles* for more examples.

Advisers: David and Sue Irons.

Charcoal

Cummings & Bless, tall chimney, 1852 . . . . **100.00**

Dragon chimney, highly detailed, German **550.00**

Fat Hungarian, brass, bulging sides **140.00**

Head latch, various heads, including lady, soldier, lion, man with top hat, Mercury **250.00**

Peerless, box, 1910, odd base . **190.00**

Swivel chimney, Oriental, 1920s **110.00**

The Improved Progress Iron, 1913, lift off latch. **150.00**

Children's

Athin's Patent, hot water, curved bottom 4-7/8" **300.00**

Dover Sad Iron, No. 912, 4" **40.00**

European, brass, ox tongue, 3-1/2" **175.00**

Goffering iron, all iron, barrel, 2" **150.00**

Kenrick Lace Iron, two pcs, 4" . **175.00**

Mexican Amazoc, highly engraved, 2-1/2" **250.00**

Star #7, wood grip, 2-3/4" **150.00**

Swan, all cast, 2-1/2" **140.00**

Tri-bump, all cast, 3-1/4" **40.00**

Flat iron

Bless, Drake, detachable **160.00**

Czechoslovakia, green, detachable handle **160.00**

Charcoal, German Griffin latch, IBI 60I 8-1/2" l, $160. Photos courtesy of Dave Irons.

Enterprise, boxed set of five, detachable handles......... **500.00**
Enterprise, "Star Iron," holes in handle **40.00**
Indicator, temperature indicator, 1878 .... **375.00**
Ober, #6, patent 1912, ribbed handle **60.00**
Sensible, detachable handle, No. 90 .... **120.00**
Simmons Special, detachable handle **90.00**
Simplex Sad Iron, twist latch .. **160.00**
Wapak, #5................... **30.00**
Weida's Patent 1870, flip-back handle **260.00**

Fluter, combination type
Hewitt, clip-on plate **300.00**
Little Giant, fluter at angle **500.00**
Monroe, brass plates inside ... **300.00**

Fluter, machine type
English, box frame, fine flutes . **350.00**
Mrs. Susan Knox, with picture, good paint...................... **450.00**
Star, American Machine, good paint **300.00**

Fluter, rocker type
Geneva Improved, brass plates **350.00**
Good Luck, L. L. Brill **250.00**
The Erie Fluter, clip-off handle. **300.00**

Fluter, roller type
American Machine, wood handle **125.00**
Clarks 1879, script on handle.. **275.00**
Sundry Mfg. Co., stirrup handle **350.00**

Goffering irons
Double barrel, cast base, all iron **650.00**

Queen Anne, brass, tripod base, single **350.00**
Single, paw feet, all iron **400.00**
"S" wire, round base, most common **75.00**

Liquid fuel, gasoline, or kerosene
Coleman 4A, beige, Canada... **450.00**
Coleman 615, black......... **175.00**
Diamond Akron Lamp Co...... **50.00**
Imperial Brass Co. **70.00**
Improved Easy, Foote Mfg Co.. **100.00**
Tilley, English, cream........ **150.00**

Liquid fuel, natural gas
Clifton, chimney, wire protector. **300.00**
Humphrey, General Specialty Co. **160.00**
Kenrick, gray speckled enamel. **200.00**
Modern Home Gas Iron, double pointed **160.00**

Mangle board
Horse handle, heavily carved, orig paint **1,000.00**
Turned handle, turned posts, no carving **100.00**

Miscellaneous
Book, Glissman, 1970, out of print **200.00**
Clock, "I Want U At Ironing Time," small **700.00**
Give-away iron, Enterprise, 1-1/8" **400.00**
Iron sole plate to attach bottom of iron **35.00**
Laundry stove, holds eight irons **500.00**
Magazine ad, full page ad showing electric iron................. **15.00**
Paperweight, "W. H. Lent Tailor Supplies" **300.00**

Pleater rack, New Victoria Pleater **35.00**
Toy mangle machine........ **150.00**

Slug irons
Belgium, round back, lift gate . **500.00**
Bless-Drake, salamander box iron **160.00**
European, ox tongue, brass, decorated sides **500.00**
French, hand made, top latch . **400.00**
Family Laundry Iron, combination, revolving **1,000.00**
Italian, hand made, small "S" post, 1700s..................... **500.00**
Swedish, Husquarna, box **125.00**

Special purpose
Acme Seam Iron, odd form ... **500.00**
Ball iron, tripod legs......... **200.00**
Billiard table iron, London.... **300.00**
Entrekins, swing back burnisher, 1873 .... **400.00**
Flower iron, two pcs, brass, large **150.00**
Fluting scissors............ **200.00**
French long-handled sleeve iron, flower dec **225.00**
French polisher, dimpled bottom **250.00**
Geneva, polisher, grid bottom . **130.00**
Hat, movable/adjustable edge . **160.00**
Hat, Tolliker, wood.......... **150.00**
Keystone polisher.......... **160.00**
Salter, English, round bottom .. **125.00**
Soap stone polisher, Hood's.. **450.00**
Star polisher **250.00**
Tie press, wood **45.00**
Wapak, sleeve iron **125.00**

IRONWARE

History: Iron, a metallic element that occurs abundantly in combined forms, has been known for centuries. Items made from iron range from the utilitarian to the decorative. Early hand-forged ironwares are of considerable interest to Americana collectors.

Additional Listings: Banks, Boot Jacks, Doorstops, Fireplace Equipment, Food Molds, Irons, Kitchen Collectibles, Lamps, and Tools.

Andirons, pr, 20" h, cast, faceted ball finials, knife blade, arched bases, penny feet, rusted surface **325.00**
Apple roaster, 34-1/4" l, wrought, hinged apple support, pierced heat end on slightly twisted projecting handle, late 18th C................. **1,650.00**
Baker's lamp, 4-1/4" h, 8-1/2" l, cast iron, attached pan, hinged lid, bottom marked "No. 2 B. L.," pitted ... **250.00**

Polisher, MAB COOKS, IBI 271(M), 5" l, $85.

Charcoal, Dutch brass, IBI 65, 8" l, $180.

Bill holder, Atlantic Coast Line, cast, c1915, 4" h **50.00**

Boot scraper, 11-1/2" l, 18-1/2" h, cast, Scottie Dog, figural side profile, America, early 20th C, minor surface rust **590.00**

Calipers, pr, wrought

18-1/2" l, double, two arms meeting at "Y"-shaped central piece, ring handle with old split **125.00**

18-1/2" l, ending in delicate ladies legs, stamped "WTI 1863" . **115.00**

Candlestick, 9-3/4" h, wrought, spiral iron stem, curled finger loop and tab, wooden push up, old, cone shaped wooden base with dark patina . . **160.00**

Christmas tree holder, painted green, holly decoration, 4" h, 7" square base, $60.

Cast, kettle, cast maker's name on lid "W. Resor & Co., Cincinnati," swing bale handle, 6-1/2" d base made to fit old cook stove, 8" h, old black repaint, old replaced finial, $70. Photo courtesy of Cowan's Historic Americana Auctions.

Carriage fenders, cast, shaped like horse leg, sgd "Fiske, New York," c1880, price for pr **4,800.00**

Cleaver, 11-1/2" l, 4-1/2" h, figural-shaped blade with eagle's head, handle terminating in brass boot, 20th C, stand, minor surface corrosion **490.00**

Compote, 10" w, 7" h, cast, flower form bowl, shaped and molded star base, America, late 19th C, old rust surface **200.00**

Cookie mold, 5-1/4" l, oval, bird on branch, cast iron **335.00**

Door knocker, 5-1/2" l, cast, fox head, ring hangs from mouth **85.00**

Embossing wheel, 4" l, 1-3/4" w, 9-1/4" h, cast iron and bronze, scrolled foliate motif on wheel edge, imp maker's marks for M. W. Baldwin, Philadelphia, handle missing **460.00**

Figure, 24-1/4" w, 39" h, cast, Lady Liberty, Mott Foundry, New York, c1850, holding goblet and torch with octagonal marble base, later white wood plinth **7,425.00**

Fireback, 21-1/2" w, 33" h, cast, late Regency-style, arch top flanked by dolphins, central polychrome scene of shepherd with his flock by fountain, beaded surround, scrolling leaf border **300.00**

Herb grinder, 16-1/2" l, 4-1/2" w, 4" h, cast, footed trough form, 6" d round disk-shaped crusher with wooden handle through center, late 18th/early 19th C **980.00**

Hitching post, 31" h, cast, jockey, yellow, red, green, black, and white painted detail, wired for lantern. **275.00**

Jousting helmet, 18" h, wrought, 12th C style, 19th C, cylindrical, tapering vertically at front, narrow eye slits, pierced circular and cruciform breaths **1,495.00**

Kitchen utensils, 16" l, 9" h hanging rack, wrought, step down crest with scrolled heart, cut out cross bar, three spatulas, two dippers, with tooling and initials **675.00**

Knife, folding, 8-1/4" l closed, 15-1/2" l open, hand-forged blade with a trigger locking mechanism pivots into iron sheath bound with carved wood handle, held with two iron bands and six pins, blade illegibly marked, late 18th/early 19th C, wear **150.00**

Lamp, floor, arrow-shaped finial on shaft, two sockets, scrolled wrought iron tripod feet, woven striped paneled shades, scattered corrosion, price for pr **815.00**

Letter sealer, 1" d, coat of arms, European, late 18th/early 19th C . **40.00**

Mirror, 22" h, cast, gilt, rococo scrolled acanthus frame, oval beveled mirror, Victorian **75.00**

Mold, 7-1/4" w, 8" d, 8" h, figural pumpkin, smiling man face, invented by John Czeszczicki, Ohio, 1930, used to grow pumpkins in human forms, surface corrosion, later stand . . **635.00**

Mortar and pestle, 10-1/2" d, 8-1/4" h, urn shape, cast iron, pitted **50.00**

Pipe tongs, 17-1/4" l, wrought iron, 18th C **1,150.00**

Rush light holder, 15-3/4" h, wrought, twisted detail on stem and arm of counterweight, high tripod feet riveted to disk, traces of black paint . . . **330.00**

Shelf brackets, pr, 5-1/2" h, swivel **20.00**

Oil heater, cast iron, Climax Mfg. Co. Chicago, Ill, 19" h, $150. Photo courtesy of Joy Luke Auctions.

Spittoon, cast iron, top hat, Standard Manuf Co., Pittsburgh, PA, painted black, glazed porcelain int. **415.00**

Sugar nippers, 10" l, tooled flower at pivot points **600.00**

Trivet, 7-3/4" d, round, marked "The Griswold Mfg. Co., Eire, PA, USA/8/Trivet/206". **35.00**

Umbrella stand, 30-3/4" h, cast, backplate formed as figure of Admiral Nelson, titled at base, stepped base with double shell-form removable drip pan **750.00**

Utensil rack, 10-3/4" l, wrought iron, scrolled crest, five hooks with acorn terminals, minor brazed repair . **770.00**

Wafer iron, 5-1/4" d, 24" l, imp with seal of U.S., c1800, minor imperfections **550.00**

Wall frame, 8-1/2" h, 6" d, cast iron, gilt eagle crest, elaborately dec frame, C-scrolls and foliate devices, 19th C **575.00**

IVORY

History: Ivory, a yellowish white organic material, comes from the teeth or tusks of animals and lends itself to carving. Many cultures have used it for centuries to make artistic and utilitarian items.

A cross section of elephant ivory will have a reticulated crisscross pattern. Hippopotamus teeth, walrus tusks, whale teeth, narwhal tusks, and boar tusks also are forms of ivory. Vegetable ivory, bone, stag horn, and plastic are ivory substitutes, which often confuse collectors. Vegetable ivory is a term used to describe the nut of a South American palm, which is often carved. Look for a grain that is circular and dull in this softer-than-bone material.

Note: Dealers and collectors should be familiar with The Endangered Species Act of 1973, amended in 1978, which limits the importation and sale of antique ivory and tortoiseshell items.

Box, 2-5/8" d, lid painted with profile busts of man and woman in 18th C dress, blue ground, gilt-metal mounts on lid and base, French, late 19th **450.00**

Bridge, 12" l, carved from hippopotamus tusk, various figures in palace setting **175.00**

Bust, carved, 6-1/4" h, woman, hoop earrings, elaborate headdress, back of head cov with scarf and netting, pierced carved crown with four figures, central kneeling figure holding flower bulb and beads, sgd. **275.00**

Cane

34" l, 4-1/2" l x 2" h tan elephant ivory handled carved as Aztec or Inca man, head wearing crown, narrow porcelain eyes, 1/4" silver thread woven collar, rosewood shaft, 1-1/4" horn ferrule, c1885 . . **515.00**

35" l, 4" l x 1-1/2" h "L" shaped elephant ivory handle carved three-toed Japanese mythological dragon twisted among rocks and foliage, inlaid mother-of-pearl eyes, sgd by Japanese maker, 1-1/4" silver collar initialed for orig owner, dec with "C" scrolls, dark bamboo shaft, 7/8" replaced brass ferrule, England, c1890. . . . . **1,680.00**

36" l, 2" w x 5" h elephant ivory handle carved as crouching gargoyle with horns and cloven hooves, glass eyes, sitting on stump, gazing skyward, holding pointed tail, tin gold ring collar, ebony shaft, oval gold eyelets, 3/4" brass ferrule, French, c1890 . . . . **1,250.00**

36" l, 5" l, 1-1/2" h hippo ivory handle carved as two setters sitting on stone wall, larger with full body stretched out, 2/3" silver collar marked "Sterling," hardwood shaft worked under finish to simulate snakewood, 1-1/4" white metal and iron ferrule, American, c1885 . . . . **1,460.00**

36" l, 5" l x 2" h elephant ivory handle carved as crocodile, menacing teeth protruding from upper jar, when lever under lower jar engaged, mouth swings open, eyes roll, 1-1/2" sterling collar with London 1897 hallmarks, figured snakewood shaft, 3/4" horn ferrule **3,500.00**

36-1/4" l, 5-1/4" l x 1-1/2" elephant ivory handle carved as cannon, 1/4" dec silver collar, black shaft,

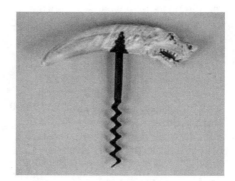

Cork screw, carved wolf head, glass eyes, red tongue and open mouth with large teeth, carved handle 4-1/4" h, **$290.** *Photo courtesy of James D. Julia, Inc.*

7/8" horn ferrule, English, c1890 . . . . **1,235.00**

36-1/3" l, 1-1/4" x 10" l elephant ivory handle carved as string of elephants, each one looking in different direction, perched on rock, sgd by Japanese maker, 3/4" dec gold-plated collar, cocobolo rosewood shaft, 7/8" brass ferrule, fashioned in England, c1895 . . . . **2,950.00**

37-1/3" l, 1-3/4" d x 1-3/4" h elephant ivory capstan handle carved as knob, relief carved coat of arms on top, highlighted by two early sailing ships, light tan hardwood shaft carved with 1/2" raised collar below handle, 1" brass and iron ferrule, English, c1880 . . . . **515.00**

Chess set

2-1/2" to 5" h, 16 crimson stained pieces, 15 natural pieces, detailed Chinese figures, lacquered case, gilt dec scenes and mother-of-pearl inlay, Oriental, 20th C. **1,100.00**

3" to 7" h natural and tea-stained pieces, each carved with Oriental figures standing on mystery ball bases, inlaid box with brass clasp **700.00**

3-1/2" to 7" h, each piece carved in form of Chinese figures, 16 natural color, 16 tea stained, fitted wood case with playing field, Oriental, 20th C. **920.00**

Cup, cov, foliate finial, oval body, carved frieze of putti with hound, mask and acanthus baluster stem, round foot, Continental, early 18th C. **1,200.00**

Fan, 11" l, sword form, anthemion-shaped fan, handle of fan with spiral reeding, kidskin case shaped as scabbard, ivory link chain and shield shaped belt clip with carved monogram, Continental, late 19th C **920.00**

Figure

Chinese sage carrying wooden staff, attached scroll and flowers, crane and child holding onto sage's robes, black inked beard and hair, 8-1/2" h, pierced wood base, fitted case, minor age cracks . . . **450.00**

Kwan Yin, Oriental woman holding roses, wearing bird headdress, 12" h, wooden base **440.00**

Laughing monk, carrying turtle, staff with palm frond, bat on head, dark yellow stain, sgd, 6-1/4" h . **200.00**

Figural group, parent with two small children, artist signed, 2-1/2" h, $170. Photo courtesy of Sanford Alderfer Auction Company.

Noh actor, Japan, Meiji period, 1868-1911, fan missing form one hand, 8-1/2" h **635.00**

Pekinese on Pillow, Continental, early 20th C, 1-5/8" w, 1-5/8" h
. . . .**300.00**

Poor Cleric, 6-1/2" h, standing male figure, tattered cloak, long crucifix, turned and carved ebonized wood socle, Continental, late 19th C
. . . .**450.00**

Shukei dancing, holding sword and fan, China, 19th C, minor loss, 7-1/2" h **230.00**

Jagging wheel, 19th C

5-3/4" l, pierced carved, whalebone, minute losses **2,875.00**

7-1/8" l, figural, unicorn, inlaid eyes and nostrils, minor losses **4,600.00**

Letter opener, 9-3/4" l, oblong blade carved to end with writhing dragon, Chinese, early 20th C **115.00**

Measure, 14-7/8" l, whalebone, ivory, and exotic wood, American shield inlay, inscribed "WH," 19th C, minor imperfections **195.00**

Miniature furniture, 4-1/2" h dressing table with two foliate pierced velvet-lined drawers, upright mirror, table with applied carved bottles, boxes, and basin, two miniature brushes and pen, glass dome, 5" l Regency-style scrolled settee with pierced outward scrolled arms, Continental, late 19th C **525.00**

Okimono, man giving grapes to child, Japanese, early 20th C **350.00**

Pickwick, 3-1/4" h, carved, 19th C, minor losses, repair **210.00**

Plaque, 3-3/8 x 2-1/8", rect carved ivory plaque, interior genre scene of man lighting pipe, framed, Continental
. . . .**345.00**

Puzzle ball, 14" h, carved and pierced with dragons and flowers, China **320.00**

Rolling pin, 19th C, minor insect damage, 13-5/8 l, exotic wood, baleen spacers, 19th C, cracks **225.00**

Seal, 3-7/8" l, intaglio, handle, 19th C, cracks **400.00**

Sewing bird, 4-1/8" l, four side-mounted spools, geometric and heart exotic wood inlay, 19th C, inlay loss and replacements **1,150.00**

Sewing egg, 2-1/2" l, walrus ivory, unscrews to reveal ivory spool, thimble, and needle case, 19th C **920.00**

Square, 10" l, whalebone and ivory inlaid walnut, diamond motif inlay, 19th C, cracks to ivory **1,095.00**

Stand, 7" h, pierced relief, pink and cream flowers, peony and lotus flowers, green stones **425.00**

Temple container, 23-1/2" h, pieced construction, overall carving, Greek key bands, relief carved dragons in six arched panels around body, in medallions at neck and foot, green jadite rings handing from mouths of mythical beasts as handles, each lid with armored warrior with horse, one woman with spear and bow case, other bearded man with spear and sword, round inset blue, green, red, and orange "gems," sgd, age cracks, minor edge damage, price for pr . . .**2,400.00**

Snuff box, painting on lid "Buy My Flowers," carved sides, gold paint, French, 2-1/4" d, $110. Photo courtesy of Sanford Alderfer Auction Company.

Tusk, 59" l, matched pair, full sized, polished satin finish, warm patina, fitted ivory end caps, 20th C **5,175.00**

Vase

9-3/4" h, narrow tapering cylindrical cup, carved with three high relief roundels with busts of maidens in floral wreaths, base of cup with grape carved knop, slender stem with single foliate and bead-flanked knop, fluted leaf and hexagonal foot, Continental, late 19th C, price for pr **1,000.00**

10-3/4" h, gourd shape, acanthus leaves around neck, two bands of dragons chasing pearls through clouds, carved in high relief, incised signature, few age cracks
. . . .**375.00**

Walking stick, 34-1/4" l, 1-1/3" d x 4-3/4" h elephant ivory handle, raised 2/3" basket-weave carving halfway down length, 1/3" plain silver collar, cherry-wood shaft, 1-1/3" white metal and iron ferrule, American, c1880
. . . .**400.00**

Wrist rest, 10-1/4" h, carved in high relief with numerous figures in palace garden, China, 19th C **1,265.00**

JADE

History: Jade is the generic name for two distinct minerals: nephrite and jadeite. Nephrite, an amphibole mineral from Central Asia that was used in pre-18th-century pieces, has a waxy surface and hues that range from white to an almost-black green. Jadeite, a pyroxene mineral found in Burma and used from 1700 to the present, has a glassy appearance and comes in various shades of white, green, yellow-brown, and violet.

Jade cannot be carved because of its hardness. Sawing and grinding with wet abrasives such as quartz, crushed garnets, and carborundum achieve shapes.

Prior to 1800, few items were signed or dated. Stylistic considerations are used to date pieces. The Ch'ien Lung period (1736-1795) is considered the golden age of jade.

Boulder, 13" h, finely carved interior of Guanyin figure, light green tones, polished amber colored ext., Oriental, 20th C. **815.00**

Box, 3-3/8" l, rect, silver mounted, early 20th C. **320.00**

Bowl, 5-1/2" d, highly translucent stone with lavender tone, deeply infused with apple green, well-formed foot ring, China, 19th C **2,650.00**

Brush pot, 4-1/4" h, scrolling cloud pattern, Chinese, 19th C **320.00**

Pair of phoenixes standing on curved rockery, carved Nephrite jade, polished finish, 28 pounds, 20th C, 12" h, $700. Photo courtesy of Jackson's International Auctioneers & Appraisers.

Candlesticks, pr, 12-7/8" h, dark green, carved low relief goose with out-spread wings, stands on tortoise, head supports three-tiered pricket, tripod bowl with int. carving, reticulated wood base with carved key scroll motifs and floral scrolls **550.00**

Cane, 33-1/2" l, 1-1/2" d jade ball handle, seven inlaid cabochon sapphires set in gold, 1/3" 18kt yg collar, French, c1900 . . . . **1,570.00**

Carving, 4" l, pair of crabs, celadon color, broad areas of russet **475.00**

Dish, 5-3/4" d, brownish-celadon, carved in Mughal style, open chrysanthemum flower, China, 19th C **475.00**

Figure

7" h, female immortal, garden setting, apple green nephrite jade, carved wood base, minor losses, Oriental, 20th C **115.00**

12" h, pair of phoenixes standing on curved rockery, polished finish, nephrite jade, Oriental, 20th C **690.00**

16" h, pair of phoenixes, mottled dark green, carved rosewood bases, Oriental, 20th C, price for pr **520.00**

16" h, three Chinese Gods, garden setting, white, lavender, and green colored jadeite, polished finish,

Fisherman, carved dark green Nephrite, 53 pounds, 20th C, 23" h, $200. Photo courtesy of Jackson's International Auctioneers & Appraisers.

fitted wood base, Oriental, 20th C **1,035.00**

18" h, wise man with scroll, white, lavender, and green, polish finish, Oriental, 20th C **1,495.00**

19" h, caparisoned form of Tang-style horse, mottled green and lavender jadeite, polished finish, carved and fitted wood base, Oriental, 20th C, repaired fissures **435.00**

21" l, three Chinese Gods, dark green mottled jadeite, polished finish, fitted wood base, Oriental, 20th C **460.00**

24" h, Chinese princess and royal attendants, garden setting, fitted wood base, Oriental, 20th C, some repairs **1,150.00**

Flute, 22" l, light and dark colored cylinders of celadon green tone, wooden frame, India, early 20th C **75.00**

Figural group, carved dark green mottled jadeite, three Chinese Gods, polished, fitted wood base, 100 pounds, 20th C, 21" l, $500. Photo courtesy of Jackson's International Auctioneers & Appraisers.

Inkstone, 3-5/8" l, oval, depression to one side, black and white mottling, incised rim band **200.00**

Letter opener, 10-3/4" l, carved interlocking C scrolls between keyfret bands handle, SS knife **250.00**

Libation cup, 5" l, celadon jade, incised dec, dragon head handles, Chinese, Qing dynasty, price for pr **425.00**

Palace figure, 76" h, carved herons, more than 200 pieces of dark green mottled jadeite feathers applied over wooden form, mahogany stained wooden plinth, 20th C, minor losses, price for pr **1,150.00**

Tang-style horse, carved mottled green and lavender jadeite, polished finish, carved and fitted wood base, repaired fissures, 40-1/2 pounds, 20th C, 19" h, $450. Photo courtesy of Jackson's International Auctioneers & Appraisers.

Pair of phoenixes standing on curved rockery, carved Nephrite jade, polished finish, 28 pounds, 20th C, 12" h, $700. Photo courtesy of Jackson's International Auctioneers & Appraisers.

Ring, 14k yellow gold, apple jade measures 11 x 16mm and is surrounded by 26 diamonds with eight diamonds on side, rosettes of a basket setting, ring size 7, **$1,100.**

Photo courtesy of Sanford Alderfer Auction Company.

Plaque, 5-1/2" x 8", spinach-green, carved and pierced lattice pattern, squirrel with grapes, China, 20th C, price for pr **300.00**

Snuff bottle, Grayish-white, mottled russet skin on one side, rose quartz stopper **550.00**

Urn, cov, 11" h, Buddhist figure, open work foliage, lavender and green jadeite, polished finish, Oriental, 20th C **1,100.00**

Green Nephrite beaded necklace with gold colored beads, 28" long, bracelet and matching earrings, **$85.** *Photo courtesy of Joy Luke Auctions.*

JEWEL BOXES

History: The evolution of jewelry was paralleled by the development of boxes in which to store it. Jewel-box design followed the fashion trends dictated by furniture styles. Many jewel boxes are lined.

2-1/4" x 1-3/4" x 3/4", Victorian, cameo carved shell, profile of man in classical dress framed by turquoise beads, 18kt yg box with glass bottom **1,300.00**

4-1/2" x 2-1/2", malachite, veneer, rect, raised feet, satin lining, Russian, 19th C **250.00**

4-5/8" h, 4-3/8" d, golden amber, inverted thumbprint, round, hinged, ormolu feet, sapphire blue serpent applied to lid, small enameled flowers and green leaves dec **235.00**

4-3/4" x 8-3/4", Russian Silver, rect, sky blue, deep red, and white enameled diapering patter, stylized flower heads, raised studded bands, swing handles on lid and sides, pale blue padded satin lining, four bun feet. **2,500.00**

5-1/8" w, 4" d, 4-3/8" h, Bohemian glass, white overlay cut to cranberry, oblong, gilt-metal hinge mount, cut with roundels and leaves, roundels enamel dec with floral bouquets, gilt details, late 19th C **1,035.00**

5-1/4" l, 2-5/8" d, 3-3/4" h, cranberry flashed glass, dome top box with scroll-engraved brass mounts, two round pendant handles, open C-scroll feet, Continental, late 19th C . . . **750.00**

6" h, 10" w, 6-3/4" d, engraved whalebone, top polychrome dec of elegant ladies and child flanked by birds among trees, sides with reserves of birds among foliage, top lists to reveal a removable tray, four cov compartments and door, dec with snakes, fish, and foliate devices, shaped bracket feet, minor imperfections. **5,660.00**

6-1/2" l, German Silver, heavily molded and bellied sides, winged dolphin form feet, early 19th C, 13 oz **850.00**

7" x 6-1/2", Wave Crest, puffy egg crate mold, hp lid, child with bow and arrow, satin finish, ftd, orig lining **1,200.00**

Bronze, cast, rectangular, panels of figural Egyptian motifs, cut-out bracket feet, 7-1/2" w, 6" d, 5-1/2" h, **$150.** *Photo courtesy of Sanford Alderfer Auction Company.*

7-1/4" l, 4" w, 4-1/4" h, silver plate, cov on all sides and domed lid with Art Nouveau flowers in relief, lock and bale handle, int. lined with red velvet, underside stamped "G. G. Lelykauf Nururnbert" **125.00**

8-1/8" l, 5-3/8" w, 2-7/8" h, mother-of-pearl and paper, rect box, mother-of-pearl plaques with floral etched banding on top and three sides, ormolu mounts cast with florals, husks, and beading throughout, sloped hinged lid set with painted paper floral spray under glass dome, four ball feet, faille-lined interior, French, Second Empire, c1870-80 . . . . **2,415.00**

9-1/2" h, 16" w, gilt bronze, elaborate Moorish design, semi precious stones, enamel dec **900.00**

9-3/8" l, 6-1/2" w, 3-1/4" h, bronze, pine needle design, copper finish, green and white slag glass panels, beading, wooden int. with two compartments, marked "Tiffany Studios New York" **1,650.00**

10" x 8" x 7", Art Nouveau, ormolu, raised figural and floral dec, plaque dated 1903 . . . . **245.00**

10" h, 11-1/2" w, 10-1/2" d, Victorian, painted and decoupage, lift top, pr of doors opening to small drawers, Chinese scenes on mustard yellow ground **815.00**

11-1/2" w, 9-5/8" d, 15-1/2" h, satinwood and inlay, molded top opening to fitted int., faux front drawer with shield shaped ivory escutcheon, over two glass fronted doors with ivory escutcheons, three drawers with turned ivory pulls, four pointed feet, English, mid-19th C **1,100.00**

12" h, 10" w, 10" d, painted papier-mâché, lit top, fitted int., two

Oriental-style jewelry chest, three drawers, black lacquer top, sides, and base, brass hardware, 17" h, **$85.** *Photo courtesy of Joy Luke Auctions.*

Silver gilt, Austrian, Renaissance style, elaborately encrusted with cabochon garnets, turquoise, miniature sculptures of knights at each corner, allover chased floral design shows remnants of white and blue enamel, two knight's heads on jeweled handle, 5" w, 3-1/2" d, 4" h, **$4,025.** *Photo courtesy of James D. Julia, Inc.*

doors enclosing small drawers, Victorian, mid-19th, minor restorations
.... **520.00**
13" x 5" x 4", sterling silver, repoussé sides, small petal-like beaded edges, fancy feet, red velvet lining, marked "Meriden".................. **160.00**

JEWELRY

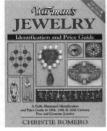

For more information, see this book.

History: Jewelry has been a part of every culture. It is a way of displaying wealth, power, or love of beauty. In the current antiques marketplace, it is easiest to find jewelry dating after 1830.

Jewelry items were treasured and handed down as heirlooms from generation to generation.
In the United States, antique jewelry is any jewelry at least 100 years old, a definition linked to U.S. Customs law. Pieces that do not meet the antique criteria but are at least 25 years old are called "period" or "heirloom/estate" jewelry.

The names of historical periods are commonly used when describing jewelry. Styles found in antique jewelry reflect several different design styles. These styles usually mirror what is found in the same period in other mediums, whether it is fine art, furniture, clothing, or silver. Each style has some distinctive characteristics that help to determine that what style it is. However, it is also important to remember that design styles may overlap as popular designs were copied and/or modified slightly from one designer and decade to another. Fashions often dictated what kind of jewelry was worn.

Georgian, 1714-1830. Fine jewelry from this period is very desirable, but few very good quality pieces have found their way to auction in the last few years. More frequently found are memorial pieces and

sentimental jewelry. Memorial pieces were made or worn to commemorate a loved one. Sentimental jewelry was often worn to express emotions that were not proper to express during those times. Often these sentimental jewelry pieces had flowers and other items, with each flower having a different sentiment attached to it. Diamonds were set open backed. Colored gemstones were set with closed-back settings lined with colored foil that enhanced their natural color. A popular motif was the bow, along with floral sprays and feathers. These designs tend to be rather stylized and flat. Paste (a high lead content glass) stones were popular and when set with foil backs they sparkled. Sadly, much jewelry from this period has been lost, as it was melted down to fund war efforts. During this time period, many folks would not wear expensive looking jewelry, as it was not wise to show one's wealth in such a manner. Gold was in short supply, so other metals were used to make fittings and chains.

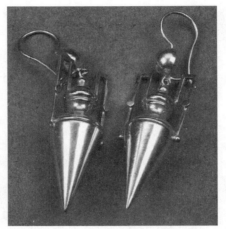

Earrings, Victorian, 15k yg, architectural design, **$250.** *Photo courtesy of Sloan's Auctioneers & Appraisers.*

Victorian, 1837-1901. The life of Queen Victoria set this whole period of design style. While Prince Albert lived, romantic themes in jewelry prevailed. One design element identified from the early part of the Victorian period is the snake, then thought of as a symbol of eternity or everlasting love. Victoria's engagement ring was a snake with a tail in its mouth. Snake necklaces, bracelets, and rings were also very popular. Floral designs of this period become more three-dimensional and truer in form to nature. The term "en tremblant," where the piece is designed to move with the motion of the wearer, reflects on the design as well as the French influence. Another popular symbol is a hand. Again, symbolic means were taken from whether the hand was clasped or open, holding flowers, or gemstones. Hair jewelry made from a loved one's hair was often given as a token of love. The fashion of long sleeved bodices with high necks caused throat pins to be popular. The practice of wearing ribbons around the neck and pinned with a brooch was also popular when necklines were lower. Earrings were not very popular in the early Victorian period because of the popular hairstyles. Bracelets were usually worn in multiples

and on both arms. When Prince Albert suddenly died in 1861, the gayety of English life subsided. Add to this the many widows created by the Civil War and one can understand why black mourning jewelry became such a fashion statement. Entirely black jewelry was popular, as was jewelry with black trim or backgrounds, such as black onyx. Positive influences of this period included interest in revivals of ancient cultures, such as Egypt. By this period, manufacturers were learning how to mass produce jewelry. By the end of the Victorian period, smaller and lighter pieces of jewelry became fashionable. Gold was still in short supply, but the newly developed electro-plating techniques allowed more gold colored jewelry to be made. Seed pearls were plentiful. Cameos and mosaics also became popular. Diamonds move from closed and foil settings to open-backed settings during this period. New cuttings shaped diamonds and other gemstones in ways that allowed more facets. The discovery of diamonds in South Africa helped lower prices in the 1880s, but they were always expensive. Other gemstones, like garnets, are found as both facet cut and cabochon. Natural stones like turquoise and agates were popular, too.

Lavaliere, Edwardian, heart-shape aquamarine suspends two collet-set old European-cut diamonds with pear-shape aquamarine terminal, three pearl accents, 14kt wg chain, **$1,410.** *Photo courtesy of Skinner's Auctioneers and Appraisers.*

Edwardian, 1890-1920. The Edwardian period also takes its name from an English Monarch, King Edward VII. This style emphasized the use of diamonds, pearls, and platinum in more monochromatic designs. The development of platinum led to strong, but lacy looking, filigree designs. Up until the Edwardian period, platinum used in jewelry making was usually plated with other metals as it was considered a lesser material. Diamond-cutting techniques continued to improve and new cuttings, such as marquise, baguette, and emerald cuts, became popular. Gemstones such as amethysts and peridots, blue sapphires, demantoid garnets, alexandrites, and rubies are also cut in these styles. Turquoise and opals are used as highlights. Jewelry for men was very popular in this period. The style is also known as Belle Époque.

Arts and Crafts, 1890-1920. This period of jewelry is dominated by hand made creations, often inspired by medieval and renaissance designs. Known for the high level of craftsmanship evident in metals, jewelry reflected the natural elements so loved in this period. Guilds of artisans banded together. Some jewelry was mass-produced, but the most highly

Brooch, Arts and Crafts, 14kt gold, oval openwork form depicting chased and engraved maple leaf and seeds within twig motif frame, 7.0 dwt., stamped Potter Studio, **$1,300.** *Photo courtesy of Skinner's Auctioneers and Appraisers.*

prized examples of this period are hand made and signed by their makers. The materials used reflect what was being used in other crafts: silver, copper, and some gold. Enamel highlights added colors. Cabochons, leaves, and naturally shaped pearls predominate the style.

Pin, Art Nouveau, attributed to Freys, figural bat, blue opalescent enamel work on spread wings, body is paved with approx 41 full-cut diamonds, one red stone eye, unmarked, 2-1/2" w, 1-1/4" h. Photo courtesy of James D. Julia, Inc.

Art Nouveau, 1895-1910. The free flowing designs associated with the Art Nouveau period are what are found in jewelry from that time. Borders and backgrounds undulate and often include vines, flowers, and leaves. Enamel decoration is one of the more distinctive elements of this style. Gemstones also

Pendant, Art Deco, rectangular, crystal plaque carved with an intaglio image of classical woman playing flute, platinum mount set with single-cut diamonds, engraved gallery, verso mirrored, suspended by platinum chain, $1,880. Photo courtesy of Skinner's Auctioneers and Appraisers.

enhanced the wide palette of colors available. Jewelry from this period is again mass-produced, but quickly went the way of fashion when clothing styles changed with the onset of the Art Deco period.

Art Deco, 1920-1935. The flappers and their love of straight lines dominate this period. When examining Art Deco jewelry, look for a skyscraper or fireworks motif, as both symbolize this striking period. French designers were the most influential. Many pieces from this period are large and were used as accents to the new lighter clothing styles. In 1924, Coco Chanel declared, "It does not matter if they are real, as long as they look like junk," setting the stage for an explosion of costume jewelry. Rhinestones, pastes, and cut glass became important parts of molded designs of silver or pot metal.

Retro-Modern 18kt yg cocktail ring, large emerald-cut aquamarine flanked three rows of 3.00 carats. Circular-cut diamonds, $2,200. Photo courtesy of Sloan's Auctioneers & Appraisers.

Beads, Post-War Modern, three strands of graduated faceted amethyst beads, Indian style adjustable clasp, $1,500. Photo courtesy of Sloan's Auctioneers & Appraisers.

Retro Modern, 1935-1945. A resurgence of romanticism overtook the design world at the start of this period. Colored gemstones were back, along with the now popular costume jewelry. The style embraces some aspects of former periods, such as the streamlined look of the 1920s, but also the softness and natural aspects of the Victorian period. Color spilled over to settings with bi-color, rose, and yellow gold being popular. Machine-made pieces incorporate bold designs and colors with most motifs rather massive.

Post-War Modern, 1945-1965. Designer jewelry is the most collected of this jewelry period. Names such as Harry Bertoia, Sam Kramer, and Ed Wiener are just a few of the top designers from this period. These designs were executed in various mediums, including brass, silver, Lucite, and plastics, as well as traditional materials. To be collectible, jewelry from this period should be signed or somehow identifiable. Designs tend to be sleek and innovative.

Notes: The value of a piece of old jewelry is derived from several criteria, including craftsmanship, scarcity, and the current value of precious metals and gemstones. Note that antique and period pieces should be set with stones that were cut in the manner in use at the time the piece was made. Antique jewelry is not comparable to contemporary pieces set with modern-cut stones and should not be appraised with the same standards. Nor should old-mine, old-European, or rose-cut stones be replaced with modern brilliant cuts.

The pieces listed here are antique or period and represent fine jewelry (i.e., made from gemstones and/or precious metals). The list contains no new reproduction pieces. Inexpensive and mass-produced costume jewelry is covered in *Warman's Americana & Collectibles.*

Bar pin
Art Deco

Diamond, center pear shape 0.45 ct diamond, flanked by four old European-cut diamonds set in an openwork mount with millegrain accents **1,325.00**
Platinum and diamond, set with 17 transitional-cut 2.55 cts diamonds, engraved geometric gallery
. . . . **1,725.00**
Ruby, collet-set oval 5.5 x 4.7 x 3.5 mm ruby, flanked by four old European-cut diamonds, four mine-cut diamonds, platinum topped 14kt yellow gold mount with millegrain accents **1,265.00**

Bar pin, Edwardian, set with 12 rose-cut diamonds, surmounted by three pearls of purple and ivory hue, silver and gold mount, French hallmark, $100. Photo courtesy of Skinner's Auctioneers and Appraisers.

Edwardian

14kt yg, centered by prong-set circular-cut ruby, flanked by flexible elements decorated with pearls and old European-cut diamonds, mounted with rings of rose-cut diamonds, pearl terminals, sgd "Tiffany & Co." **1,890.00**

Platinum, set with line of 13 old mine-cut 5.25 ct diamonds, framed by 28 demantoid garnets in scalloped design, millegrain accents............. **6,795.00**

Platinum, scrolling and floral openwork form centering old European-cut 0.20 ct diamond, further set with 22 old mine-cut diamonds, millegrain accents **535.00**

Etruscan Revival, 14kt gold, rose gold arched terminals, applied bead and wirework dec **260.00**

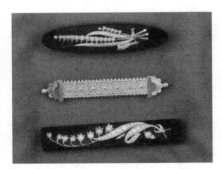

Bar pins, Victorian 14kt yg, one elongated oval, one rectangular onyx pin surmounted by gold and seed pearl lily of the valley motifs, third rectangle with applied bead and wiretwist decoration, slight areas of discoloration, **$400.** *Photo courtesy of Skinner's Auctioneers and Appraisers.*

Victorian, 14kt yg, center carnelian intaglio of three cherubs within wirework frame, applied floral, bead, and ropetwist motifs **420.00**

Bracelet

Art Deco

Diamond, 14kt white gold, 18 pierced filigree links each centered by box-set old European-cut diamond, approx. total 1.30 cts., 7" l.................. **1,300.00**

Paste, floral motif, multiple hinged plaques set with colorless pastes highlighted by geometric design of green and black stones, silver mount, French hallmarks, 7" l **1,175.00**

Bracelet, Art Deco, three rows of 3.9 mm pearls, platinum and diamond clasp, signed "Cartier," 8" l, **$2,115.** *Photo courtesy of Skinner's Auctioneers and Appraisers.*

Platinum, center line of 15 flexible box-set old European-cut diamonds, approx. total wt. 0.95 cts., expandable link bracelet, engraved gallery, dated "10/9/20," 6-3/4" l **885.00**

Platinum, center with two old mine cut diamonds, .40 ct and .55 ct, other 4.50 ct old mine, old European, and single cut diamonds, links apart from center alternate between diamonds and blue stones which are a combination of natural and synthetic sapphires, garnet, glass doublets **5,500.00**

Platinum, straight line, old European cut and single cut diamonds, 2 cts, calibre French cut sapphires **3,995.00**

Art Nouveau, 14kt yg, 10 openwork plaques in floral and scroll motif each centering collet-set sapphire, hallmark for Riker Bros., 7" l **4,350.00**

Bracelet, Post-War Modern, 14k yg, cuff, wave design, section of pave-set diamonds, weighing approx 5.50 carats, **$1,800.** *Photo courtesy of Sloan's Auctioneers & Appraisers.*

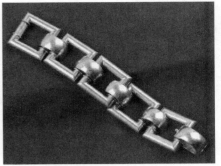

Bracelet, Post-War Modern, Art Moderne, bi-color 14kt gold, large openwork, square yellow gold links joined by domed rose gold links, 86.0 dwt, 9" l, **$1,880.** *Photo courtesy of Skinner's Auctioneers and Appraisers.*

Coin, 14kt yg, heavy curb link chain suspending 1892 U.S. five dollar coin in a wirework frame, 27.1 dwt., 6" l **325.00**

Edwardian, platinum, seven rows of alternating platinum and natural pearl links in mesh design, spaced by three platinum bars set with old European-cut diamonds and button pearls, similarly designed clasp, 6-3/4" l **3,550.00**

Etruscan Revival, bangle, 14kt gold, bead and wiretwist dec, 46.1 dwt, minor discoloration to gold, surface scratches, price for pr....... **2,530.00**

Jade, SS, four oval jade plaques pierced and carved with floral motifs, joined by woven foxtail chain bracelet, 7-1/4" l **175.00**

Retro Modern, double "tubogas"-style bracelet surmounted by bezel and bead-set old European-cut diamonds set in silver flowerheads, stems incorporating initials "H & L," 14kt yg, French hallmarks........... **425.00**

Victorian

Bangle, spiral design, surmounted by diagonal row of freshwater pearls, 18kt yg, hinged, French hallmarks, 16.0 dwt **650.00**

Bangle with locket, center medallion dec with gold floral and swag design on cobalt blue enamel ground set with pearls, center opens to reveal glass locket compartment, bracelet decorated with applied black tracery enamel motifs, 14kt yg, 45.5 dwt., locket probably not original, but is of the period............... **1,120.00**

Slide, 18kt yg, mesh design with adjustable oval slide engraved with scroll and fleur-de-lis motifs, edged with palmettes dec with black tracery enamel, foxtail fringe terminals, 137.8 dwt **1,200.00**

Brooch

Art Deco

Platinum and diamond, bow, openwork mount set throughout with 118 single and transitional-cut diamonds, millegrain accents, yellow gold pin stem **3,750.00**

Platinum and diamond, center row of five collet-set old European-cut diamonds, approx. total wt. 0.85 cts., numerous bead set diamonds within pierced navette-shape frame highlighted by four diamond trefoil motifs.............. **1,800.00**

Platinum and diamond, shaped rectangle, seven center collet-set old-European-cut diamonds, set throughout with old mine and European-cut diamonds in millegrain and pierced mount, approx total 5.60 cts **3,565.00**

Platinum, center sugarloaf moonstone, flanked by square-cut sapphires, edged with rect moonstones, all channel-set, oval moonstone terminals, wiretwist filigree accents, yellow gold pin stem, sgd "Tiffany & Co.," 3" l **24,150.00**

Brooch, Art Deco, white cultured pearl center measuring approx 6.50 mm., each side accented with modified rect-cut synthetic sapphire set in platinum mount enhanced with European-cut diamonds, $950. Photo courtesy of Sloan's Auctioneers & Appraisers.

Art Nouveau

Floral spray, white-cream translucent enamel lilies centered by cultured pearls, green enamel leaves, joined by gold coiled cord, 14kt polished gold stems **750.00**

Krementz & Co., light green enamel scrolling leaves centering heart-shape peridot, three old European-cut diamond accents, hallmark.............. **1,150.00**

Orchid, light greenish-yellow and purple openwork leaves, baroque pearl and old European-cut diamond highlights, retractable bail, 14kt gold.......... **1,265.00**

Pansy, yellow shading to purple enamel leaves edged by seed pearls, center old-European-cut diamond, retractable bail. **1,495.00**

Trout, basse-taille greenish-blue fading to pinkish-white iridescent translucent enamel....... **850.00**

Woman with flowing hair and dolphin with demantoid garnet eye amid waves within chased and engraved scallop shell, old mine-cut diamond moon, 14kt yg mount **385.00**

Arts and Crafts, 14kt yg, oval openwork form depicting chased and engraved maple leaf and seeds within twig motif frame, 7.0 dwt., stamped "Potter Studio"............. **1,300.00**

Edwardian

Amethyst, large oval faceted amethyst framed by pearls, 14kt gold mount, sgd Cartier, accompanied by copy of Cartier bill of sale............. **850.00**

Crescent, 14kt yg, 10 graduated faceted sapphires alternating with 11 pearls, 14kt yg mount .. **600.00**

Flower basket, 100 bead-set diamonds, (approx total 2.50 cts), platinum-topped gold mount, minor lead solder **4,025.00**

Openwork lattice set with seed pearls, framed by chased and engraved C-scroll, rocaille, and floral motifs, 14kt yg, 4.3 dwt. **500.00**

Platinum and diamond, 1.50 cts old mine-cut diamond, lacy filigree mount set throughout with rose and single-cut diamonds, millegrain accents, French assay mark **7,475.00**

Platinum, diamond, and sapphire circle, four diamonds spaced by four sapphires, filigree mount, millegrain accents, yellow gold pin stem **650.00**

Jugendstil, SS, shaped pendant set with two oval green agate, reverse stamped "MiG, TF, 900, depose" for Max Joseph Gradl, Theodor Fahrner **885.00**

Renaissance Revival, possibly Continental, openwork chased and engraved shield-form silver pendant with bird, scroll, floral, and foliate motifs

bezel-set with turquoise, mother-of-pearl, and faceted colored stones, one mother-of-pearl missing **425.00**

Brooch, Post-War Modern, 18K white gold, waving American flag accented with calibre-cut rubies, calibre-cut sapphires and round-cut diamonds, pole decorated with yellow gold twisted wire and American eagle, $700. Photo courtesy of Sloan's Auctioneers & Appraisers.

Retro Modern

Abstract ribbon motif, 14kt yg, set with eight oval cabochon rubies, 19 single-cut diamond accents, sgd "Reflections by Mauboussin" **1,410.00**

Pierced, 14kt bi-color gold, pink gold leaf supports flowerhead set with seven mixed-cut citrines... **470.00**

Ribbon motif set with 16 cabochon rubies and 48 old European and old mine-cut diamonds, four pearl accents, tri-color 18kt gold mount **950.00**

Victorian

Amethyst, chased and engraved floral and foliate frame, 14k yg mount **200.00**

Amethyst, oval faceted amethyst centered by bead-set cushion shape rose-cut diamond, 14kt yg mount with rose-cut diamond accents **385.00**

Amethyst, oval faceted amethyst framed by seed pearls, Birmingham hallmark, 14k yg mount **250.00**

Cameo, coral, oval, carved profile of classical woman, 14kt yg mount dec with mythical creatures **450.00**

Brooch, Victorian, shield-shape brooch surmounted by coral cameo carved with image of classical woman, grapeleaf motif, 15kt gold mount, $400. Photo courtesy of Skinner's Auctioneers and Appraisers.

Cameo, hardstone, profile of young woman with elaborate coiffure, seed pearl and 14kt yg wirework frame 385.00

Cameo, shell, shield shape, surmounted by coral cameo carved with classical woman with grapeleaf motif, 15kt yg mount 395.00

Coral, 14kt yg, coral branch with gold leaves and coral berries 775.00

Crescent, 21 oval-shaped rubies edged by old European-cut and mine-cut diamonds, silver-topped 14kt gold mount 2,300.00

Buckle

Art Nouveau, sterling silver, two repoussé plaques of female faces with flowing hair and flower blossoms, hallmark for William B. Kerr & Co. 300.00

Edwardian, rect openwork buckle edged with demantoid garnets spaced by old European-cut diamonds, silver-topped gold mount. 1,380.00

Cameo, Victorian, carved shell

Cupid and winged goddess, 14kt gold oval frame 425.00

Portrait bust of female in profile, 18kt gold and citrine frame with seed pearls, black enamel, and diamonds, chips to enamel. 1,850.00

Clip

Art Deco, Platinum and diamond, two old European-cut diamonds, 35 old European-cut diamonds 2,100.00

Retro, pave and circular-cut diamond set caps surmounted by similarly set swag, suspending spray of 18 square-cut rubies and eight tapered

baguette-cut ribbons, Austrian import assay marks, hallmark 4,715.00

Cuff links, pr

Art Deco, platinum, sq cut-corner design, set with horizontal line of single-cut diamonds and calibre-cut onyx 1,265.00

Art Nouveau, 14kt yg, double-sided oval link with female nude amid breaking wave, 10.1 dwt 500.00

Demi-Parure, Victorian, 14kt bi-color gold, brooch with engraved scroll design suspending loop set with seed pearls suspended within trapezoid, earrings ensuite, 5.8 dwt., $350. Photo courtesy of Skinner's Auctioneers and Appraisers.

Demi-Parure, brooch and earrings

Victorian

14kt, bi-color gold, brooch with engraved scroll design suspending loop set with seed pearls suspended within trapezoid, earrings ensuite, 5.8 dwt. . . . 335.00

14kt yg, C-scroll brooch, suspending an elliptical pendant within independent frame etched with trefoil designs, earrings ensuite 7.7 dwt. 500.00

18kt yg, cameo, hardstone, oval brooch with profile of classical woman wearing garland, suspending crescent-form pendant with three terminals, scrolling wirework, seed pearl and enamel accents, ear pendants ensuite, replaced ear pendant findings 1,525.00

18kt yg, oval rose gold brooch with applied yellow gold leaf and scroll motifs suspending flexible pendant of similar design with nine knife-edge bar terminals, accented throughout with seed pearls, hinged bangle bracelet with applied medallion of similar design, (missing one pearl),

earpendants ensuite, bracelet missing one pearl, boxed 3,000.00

18kt yg, shield shape pendant/brooch set with line of six oval faceted rubies and eight old mine-cut diamonds, black enamel accents, earrings ensuite, both with replaced findings 950.00

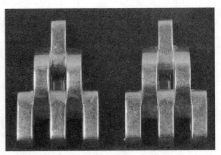

Dress clips, Retro-Modern, bi-color 14kt gold, triangular form consisting of domed links, signed WAB for Wordley, Allsopp & Bliss, 14.6 dwt., $750. Photo courtesy of Skinner's Auctioneers and Appraisers.

Earrings

Art Deco, platinum and diamond, calibre-cut emerald tops, centering collet-set diamond, suspending line of bead and collet-set single-cut diamonds, diamond and calibre-cut emerald oval terminals, 18kt white gold findings with Dutch hallmarks, emeralds abraded. 1,380.00

Retro, Ruby and diamond, pleated open discs accented by calibre-cut ruby and bead-set diamond arch, 14kt gold, one ruby missing 435.00

Victorian, Gold, engraved foliate tops suspending two gold balls 920.00

Earrings, Victorian, oval design, textured leaf suspending red glass cabochon set within onyx frame, $250. Photo courtesy of Sloan's Auctioneers & Appraisers.

Earrings, Victorian-style, early 1900s, 14k yg, screwback, center turquoise stone, blue and black enamel, seven tassels, $250. Photo courtesy of Sanford Alderfer Auction Company.

Jabot pin

Victorian, spiral handle accented with oval and prong-set amethysts and pearl, sgd "Mermod & Jaccai," 6" l
....................355.00

Lavaliere

Edwardian

Amethyst, 14kt gold, centered by oval amethyst within openwork scrolled frame surmounted by seed pearl trefoil, suspending similar drop, joined by trace link chain, 15" l.............450.00

Platinum, bow and foliate wreath set throughout with old mine, old European, rose, and single-cut diamonds, suspending two knife-edge bar pendants with old mine-cut diamond terminals weighing approx. 1.17 cts. and 1.00 cts. respectively, surmounted on 18kt yellow gold diamond motif with remains of blue and green guilloche enamel, major loss to enamel.............. 4,600.00

Platinum, heart-shape aquamarine suspends two collet-set old European-cut diamonds with pear-shape aquamarine terminal, three pearl accents, fine 14kt white gold ropetwist chain 1,410.00

Egyptian Revival, 14kt gold, centered by amethyst intaglio scarab within shaped lotus flower mount, baroque pearl drop terminal, stylized floral links, amethyst intaglio scarabs set at intervals, 16-1/2" l..........1,380.00

Locket

Art Nouveau, 18kt gold, portrait of a woman wearing diamond melee choker, 10.3 dwt.................1,380.00

Edwardian, enamel, circular, grayish-blue guilloche enamel,

surmounted by platinum and diamond openwork medallion 700.00

Etruscan Revival, oval 10kt locket with bead, seed pearl, and wiretwist dec, verso with hinged compartment, suspended from woven 14kg gold chain.....................450.00

Victorian, ovoid form surmounted by seed pearls, calibre-cut turquoise and rose-cut diamonds in fleur-de-lis and circle motif, 18kt yg, opens to glass compartment.............1,100.00

Lorgnette, Art Deco, hexagonal agate plaque both framed and surmounted by single-cut diamonds, millegrain accents, suspended by silvertone chain, $2,350. Photo courtesy of Skinner's Auctioneers and Appraisers.

Lorgnette

Art Nouveau, 14kt gold, repoussé iris handle, collet-set diamond highlight, verso monogrammed 990.00

Edwardian, 18kt gold, engraved dec handle and eye piece, handle set with three bands of rose-cut diamonds, French assay marks 750.00

Victorian, pale blue, ivory, pink and green enamel in floral design with old European-cut diamond highlight, 18kt yg...................1,410.00

Necklace

Art Deco, platinum, teardrop pendant, large, oval faceted citrine in center, 59 old European-cut diamonds, honeycomb pattern gallery, millegrain accents, paperclip link chain with two drops, sgd "M. & Co." for Marcus & Co., 17-1/2" l..................9,925.00

Art Moderne-style, c1970, Galalith

Geometric design of blue and black plastic links with ivorine highlights, signed "Guillemette l'Hoir, Paris," 23-3/4" l 300.00

Geometric design of black and white plastic links, signed "Guillemette l'Hoir, Paris," 18" l........325.00

Necklace, Art Nouveau, sterling silver, tri-partite abstract form pendant decorated en plein with blue and green enamel, suspended from baton-link chain, hallmarks for Chester, England, letter date for 1911, maker "C.H.," $350. Photo courtesy of Skinner's Auctioneers and Appraisers.

Art Nouveau, England, SS, tri-partite abstract form pendant decorated en plein with blue and green enamel, suspended from baton-link chain, hallmarks for Chester, letter date for 1911, maker "C.H." 325.00

Arts and Crafts, elliptical-shaped jade within conforming enamel scrolled links joined by trace link chains, similarly set pendant suspending three jade drops, 18kt gold, 18" l, sgd "Tiffany & Co.," some enamel loss 31,050.00

Necklace, Edwardian, 18kt white gold, negligee design featuring two diamond set drops surmounted by bead set diamond plaque suspending diamond pendulum, approx 0.75 cts., $800. Photo courtesy of Sloan's Auctioneers & Appraisers.

Edwardian

Festoon, 9kt gold, amethyst, graduating collet-set oval, round, and pear-shape amethysts joined by double trace link chain, 17" l
....................1,495.00

Fringe, 18kt yg, designed with wiretwist flowerhead links set with

Necklace, Post-War Modern, Art Moderne style, Galalith, 1970s, geometric design of black and white plastic links, signed Guillemette l'Hoir, Paris, 18" l, **$350**. Photo courtesy of Skinner's Auctioneers and Appraisers.

old European-cut diamonds and demantoid garnets, edged by freshwater pearls, bottom swag suspending 17 teardrop shape citrine drops in millegrained bezels, 14-1/4" l **6,500.00**

Etruscan Revival, Ivy leaf and berry motif, barrel clasp, 18kt yg, 15-3/8" l **2,850.00**

Jugendstil, SS, shaped pendant centered by oval green agate, suspended from silver paper clip chain, pendant stamped on reverse "TF" for Theodor Fahrner, 935, Depose, 21" l **1,530.00**

Necklace, Victorian, c1830, designed as graduating line of oval citrines within scrolled repousse borders alternating with single oval citrine links, front with similar decoration suspending three pear-shaped pendants, fitted case, **$3,000**. Photo courtesy of Sloan's Auctioneers & Appraisers.

Victorian

14kt gold and garnet, three floral engraved medallions surmounted by emerald-cut garnets set in ropetwist frames, reverse with plaited hair locket, suspended from 16-1/2" l snake chain **420.00**

18kt yg, 18 concave disks centering coral bead within gold wirework frames, joined by oval-shaped links, some replaced beads and links **1,650.00**

Pearl necklace, Edwardian

79 pearls graduating in size from approx. 3.7 x 3.6 mm to 5.0 x 4.8 mm, platinum-topped yellow gold barrel clasp set with rose-cut diamonds, 15-3/8" l, missing two stones, barrel clasp **650.00**

273 pearls measuring approx. 3.9 x 3.7 mm, platinum-topped yellow gold circular clasp set with cluster of 10 old European and single-cut diamonds, 41-1/2" l, plunger missing **600.00**

Pendant, Arts & Crafts, Jugendstil, sterling silver, shaped pendant set with two oval green agate, stamped on reverse MiG, TF, 900, depose for Max Joseph Gradl, Theodor Fahrner, **$900**. Photo courtesy of Skinner's Auctioneers and Appraisers.

Pendant
Art Deco

Diamond, pierced shield shape set with two marquise and 85 (approx total 5.50 cts) old European-cut and transitional-cut diamonds, seven calibre-cut synthetic emeralds, fleur-de-lis bail, platinum mouth with millegrain accents, one emerald missing **3,125.00**

Enamel and onyx, navette-shape silver, ivory and black enamel plaque, center sugarloaf onyx, marcasite highlights, black cord, French hallmarks, sgd "Batik" **875.00**

Platinum and diamond, shaped pendant centered by marquise and

Pendant, Art Nouveau, 14kt gold, oval opal framed by pink guilloche enamel lotus motif, two diamond accents, suspended by 14kt gold trace link chain, hallmark for Krementz & Co., crack to opal, **$750**. Photo courtesy of Skinner's Auctioneers and Appraisers.

circular-cut diamonds designed as flower, framed by single and circular-cut diamonds in pierced and millegrain platinum mount, approx. total wt. 4.00 cts., suspended from 14kt white gold curb link chain, 18-1/4" l, pendant fitting detachable **3,350.00**

Art Nouveau

Oval opal framed by pink guilloche enamel lotus motif, two diamond accents, suspended by 14kt yg trace link chain, hallmark for Krementz & Co., crack to opal **715.00**

Plique-a-jour enamel, lavender and green irid enamel flowers, green, pink, and white plique-a-jour enamel leaves, rose-cut diamonds and pearl accents, 18kt gold mount with later faux pearl chain **1,265.00**

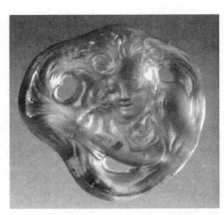

Pendant, Art Nouveau, Lalique, c1920, Ange et Colombe, clear and frosted glass with gilt backing, sepia patina, engraved "R. Lalique," 1-3/4" d, **$650**. Photo courtesy of David Rago Auctions.

Edwardian

Demantoid garnet and diamond, openwork, 6.6 x 6.6 x 4.6 mm garnet, rose and old mine-cut diamonds, suspending pear-shape rose-cut diamond drop, fine platinum chains accented by rose-cut diamond trefoils. **6,100.00**

Enamel and diamond, center neo-classical painted porcelain plaque framed by single-cut diamonds, verso with blue guillouche and white enamel dec, opens to reveal two powder compartments, diamond-set bail, platinum topped yellow gold **3,750.00**

Opal and diamond, oval-shaped opal set within navette-shape platinum mount, old European and single-cut diamonds, pierced gallery, millegrain accents, suspended from fine trace link chain **875.00**

Portrait, young boy within round 18kt gold frame, delicate independent platinum frame highlighted with rose-cut diamond foliage swag **700.00**

Renaissance Revival, shield form with Renaissance motifs, rose-cut diamonds, rubies, pearls and emerald, cobalt blue enamel highlights, silver-topped 18kt gold mount **. . 885.00**

Pin, Victorian, late 1880s, pin, octagonal, 14kt yg, minor damage to hair in compartment, bar pin, 10k yg, black onyx and pearls, each, $100. Photo courtesy of Sanford Alderfer Auction Company.

Victorian

Circular pendant edged by gold beads and decorated with black tracery enamel, suspending gold bead pendants, fancy double trace link chain, 14kt yg, 14.1 dwt., 23-1/2" l **385.00**

Pietra dura, rose branch, one open flower, two buds, inlaid in shades of pink, varying shades of green as leaves, 14kt rose gold bezel and bale **400.00**

Ring, Art Deco, 14k ornate wg, 14k yg top plate with black enamel and green accents, 12 x 16 mm sugarloaf style black onyx cabochon surrounded by 35 gray seed pearls, $300. Photo courtesy of Sanford Alderfer Auction Company.

Ring

Art Deco

Bezel-set with old European-cut 1.25 ct diamond and old mine-cut 1.36 ct diamond, framed by 32 old mine-cut diamonds, openwork platinum mount with millegrain accents, size 10-1/2 ..... **5,900.00**

Bypass, platinum, brownish-yellow old European-cut 0.90 ct diamond, transitional-cut 0.57 ct diamond, pierced, engraved, and diamond-set shank. **2,400.00**

Center 2.82 ct marquise-cut diamond, openwork foliate mount with single-cut diamond accents, engraved shank, partially obliterated date, possibly June 6, 1909, size 6, shank split. **18,800.00**

Center round star 12.6 x 12.7 mm ruby, shoulders set with 12 single-cut diamonds and six channel-set French-cut rubies, platinum mount. **2,600.00**

Cocktail, center full cut 1.19 ct diamond, 36 accent stones mixture of old European cut and single cut diamonds, diamond jacket with 26 single cut and old European cut diamonds **2,450.00**

Platinum, center sq cut synthetic ruby, gallery pierced in S-scroll motif, shoulders set with six old mine-cut diamonds, fully engraved shank, millegrain accents **1,200.00**

Platinum, designed with two bead-set old European-cut 0.60 ct diamonds, flanked by single and circular-cut diamonds, surrounded by calibre-cut emeralds within navette-shaped pierced platinum mount **825.00**

Ring, Edwardian, 14k pink gold, flower centering white pearl measuring approx 5.00 mm, surrounded by 0.75 cts old European-cut diamonds, $1,300. Photo courtesy of Sloan's Auctioneers & Appraisers.

Platinum, solitaire, bezel-set with full-cut 0.85 ct diamond, openwork geometric mount further enhanced with single-cut diamonds, millegrain accents, engraved shank................ **2,400.00**

Sapphire and diamond, center oval 7.1 x 5.4 x 5.6 mm sapphire, framed by circular-cut diamonds, pierced platinum mount, millegrain accents **1,265.00**

Sapphire and diamond, navette-shape, center circular cut diamond, three French-cut sapphires, highlighted by 18 single-cut diamonds, platinum mount **500.00**

Sapphire and diamond, three-stone, center (approx total 1.24 cts) old mine-cut diamond, flanked by pair of 5.2 x 4.5 x 3.4 mm oval sapphires, engraved foliate platinum mount **3,165.00**

Scarab, carved coral, three rose-cut diamonds, triangular onyx and rose-cut diamond shoulders, sgd "Koch" **2,185.00**

Art Nouveau, 18kt yg, shaped rectangular plaque etched with initials "HP" flanked by stylized flowers within

Ring, Edwardian, platinum on 14kt gold, 6 x 6 mm square-cut emerald, two old mine-cut diamonds, one stone is loose, 20 single cut diamonds, $800. Photo courtesy of Sanford Alderfer Auction Company.

Ring, Post-War Modern, large cat's eye chrysoberyl set within an 18kt yg mount. Signed De Vroomen, $450. Photo courtesy of Skinner's Auctioneers and Appraisers.

open and ribbed shank, inscribed "Vitaline a Hubert, 2 Janv. 1910," size 7-1/2 . . . . **355.00**

Edwardian, Princess, three (approx total 1.82 cts) old European-cut diamonds, framed by 16 bezel-set diamonds, platinum topped 14kt gold mount. **4,140.00**

Victorian, snake, tri-color gold engraved body, (approx total 0.45 cts) old European-cut diamond, stones missing from eyes **400.00**

Ring, Retro-Modern, 29.0 x 9.7 x 4.9 mm emerald-cut citrine, shoulders designed as openwork loop set with curved row of channel-set rubies, 14kt yg mount, $650. Photo courtesy of Skinner's Auctioneers and Appraisers.

Stickpin

Edwardian, nine bead-set old European-cut diamonds, set in platinum, centered by cultured pearl in floret design, 14kt gold shank . . **775.00**

Victorian, flowerhead design centering a round opal framed by 11 old mine-cut diamonds, 14kt yg setting **360.00**

Suite

Art Deco, gentleman's dress set, cuff links, four shirt studs, two collar studs, sq form with cut corners, diamond centers, platinum and 18kt yellow gold, Asprey fitted box **1,265.00**

Art Nouveau, brooch and earrings, 14kt gold, opaque light to dark pink enameled bleeding hearts, each bud accented with single-cut diamonds, translucent green enamel leaves, hallmark for Krementz & Co. . . **1,495.00**

Suite, Retro-Modern, c1940, 14kt yg, necklace with five abstract geometric form pendants interspersed with gold beads suspended from a snake link chain, earrings ensuite, 14-3/4" l, $450. Photo courtesy of Skinner's Auctioneers and Appraisers.

Retro Modern, stylized bow knot motif brooch centered by emerald-cut amethyst and circular-cut diamonds set in white gold, earrings set with faceted oval amethysts in stylized wing motif, both mounted in 14kt pink gold . **325.00**

Victorian, shield-shaped gold brooch set with oval amethyst, surmounted by rose-cut diamond bird, within bloomed floral frame highlighted by seven prong-set opals and suspending a mesh chain swag, together with similar ear pendants **600.00**

Watch chain, Victorian, 14kt yg, double foxtail chain supporting circular black tracery enamel decorated slides, suspending watch key and bloodstone fob, several bent links, 16-1/4" l, $450. Photo courtesy of Skinner's Auctioneers and Appraisers.

Watch chain and slide

Victorian, 14kt yg, fancy round link chain supporting engraved slide set with lozenge-shape cabochon amethyst, reverse with worn engraving, possibly "C.L. Hunter," 16.6 dwt, 24-1/2" l **500.00**

Watch fob

Victorian, 14kt gold, fleur-de-lis top suspending six trace link chains terminating in chased floral and vine motif, 3" l, 20 dwt **350.00**

Watch pin, Art Nouveau, profile of young woman with flowing hair encircled by enameled buds, foliage, and emerald-set blossom, 14kt yg mount, $1,775. Photo courtesy of Skinner's Auctioneers and Appraisers.

Watch pin, Art Nouveau

Foliate motif mount centering shaded green plique-a-jour enamel ground surmounted by budding lavender and green enamel anemones, freshwater pearl accent, 14k yg mount . . **1,300.00**

Four leaf clover, seed pearl and enamel dec, diamond highlights, 14kt yg mount **750.00**

Profile of young woman with flowing hair, encircled by enameled buds, foliage, and emerald-set blossom, 14kt yg mount **1,765.00**

Winged creature, diamond highlights, 14kg yg mount **600.00**

JUDAICA

History: Throughout history, Jews have expressed themselves artistically in both the religious and secular spheres. Most Jewish art objects were created as part of the concept of Hiddur Mitzva, i.e., adornment of implements used in performing rituals both in the synagogue and home.

For almost 2,000 years, since the destruction of the Jerusalem Temple in 70 A.D., Jews have lived in many lands. The widely differing environments gave traditional Jewish life and art a multifaceted character. Unlike Greek, Byzantine, or Roman art which have definite territorial and historical boundaries, Jewish art is found throughout Europe, the Middle East, North Africa, and other areas.

Ceremonial objects incorporated not only liturgical appurtenances, but also ethnographic artifacts such as amulets and ritual costumes. The style of each ceremonial object responded to the artistic and cultural milieu in which it was created. Although diverse stylistically, ceremonial objects, whether for Sabbath, holidays, or the life cycle, still possess a unity of purpose.

Notes: Judaica has been crafted in all media, though silver is the most collectible.

Diecut, woman dressed in blue, white bodice, red and white striped skirt, holding key, opening gate to family of immigrants, copyright 1909 by Hebrew Pub. Co., 3-1/4" w, 4" h, **$15.**

Amulet, 2-3/4" h, Italian, 18th/19th C, silver and silver filigree, irregular outline, inscribed "Shadai," with pendant chain and fitted leather box **520.00**

Breast plate, 14" h, Damascene, 20th C, cartouche form, surmounted by crown and dec with tablet, candleabrum, foliate motifs **550.00**

Candelabra, 15" h, brass, Polish, late 19/20th C, three-branch, lions and Star of David device supporting disks of candlesockets **365.00**

Candlesticks, pr, 4" d, 8-3/4" h, sterling silver, raised letters, one with "Shabbat," other with "Kadosh," slightly flaring bobeche, European hallmarks **300.00**

Ceremonial ring, 3-1/4" h, sterling silver, top applied with pavilion, side pierced with door and windows, three semi-precious stones, chased Hebrew words **425.00**

Chalice, 13" h, Continental silver, Herman Lang, Augsburg, 17th C, 29 oz **2,400.00**

Charity container, 3-3/4" h, silver, inverted-pear form, body engraved banding, and molding hinged lid with money slot and hasp, scroll handle, front inscribed "Zeduke für Arme kinder," German, late 19th/20th C **920.00**

Circumcision cup, 5" h, double, silver gilt, marked "Johanna Becker, Augsburg," 1855-57 .... **13,500.00**

Coffee pot, 10-1/2" h, silver, American, mid-19th C, maker illegible, overall foliate and scroll repousse dec, scrolled handle, spreading circular foot, inscribed "Presented by the --smouth Hebrew Congregation to Mr. Lewis Nathan, for his valuable services as Honorary Secretary, November 30th 5617-1856," small repair to cartouche **700.00**

Esther scroll, cased, 9" l, parcel-gilt and filigree, Continental, 19th C, applied jewels, hand-form thumb pc, nicely written ink on vellum scroll, fitted box **9,200.00**

Haggadah, Haggadah Shel Pesach, Offenbach, Zvi Hirsch Segal and his son Abraham, (1800), 40 leaves, 8vo, marbleized paper boards, new edition with German translation printed in Hebrew script beneath original woodblock illus, discoloration, shaken **815.00**

Hanukah lamp
4-5/8" h, bronze, Italian, 17th C, arched backplate with pierced geometric motifs, fronted by bank of oil fonts, old repair **665.00**

8" h, brass, Polish, late 19th C, cartouche-shaped backplate with servant lamp, crown, flower-filled basket, and deer, fronted by drip pan with candleholders, shaped feet **700.00**

9-1/4" h, brass, Bezalel, Jerusalem, early 20th C, U-form branches joined by horizontal candleholder, reeded support, Hebrew inscription to circular base, signed "Bezalel" **800.00**

9-1/2" h, silver, Russian/Polish, late 19th C, hallmarked, shaped backplate with lions, foliage, and candelabrum, servant lamp and oil jug, fronted by rect base with candleholders, cast feet ... **600.00**

9-1/2" h, silver, Russian-style, early 20th C, marked "sterling" and "84," shaped backplate with scrollwork and oil jug, servant lamp, temple columns, Decalogue, and

candelabrum, fronted by rect well with candleholders, paw feet **1,265.00**

12" h, brass, Moroccan, late 19th/20th C, backplate pierced and chased with Star of David device amidst foliage, sides similarly decorated, fronted with row of eight oil pans **1,100.00**

14-3/4" h, Damascene, 20th C, arched backplate with central servant lamp, with scrolling foliage, lions, and tablets, fronted by eight deep oil fonts **1,450.00**

Hanukah menorah, 11-1/2" h, silver plated, Polish, Warsaw, late 19th C, cartouche-shaped backplate with crown, palm trees, and lions, fronted by serpentine bank of candleholders, raised on cast feet, rosing **500.00**

Kiddush cup, Russia, silver, engraved decoration, hallmarked, c1888, 2-1/8" h, **$350.**

Kiddish cup, sterling silver
3" h, George III, double barrel form, Charles Aldridge, London, 1791-92, inscribed with the seven benedictions of wedlock, pr **7,200.00**

5-1/2" h, swirled fluted lower body, applied foliage at intervals, upper body chased with scrolls and foliage, circular foliate and beaded foot, 4 oz, 4 dwt **425.00**

6" h, American Coin, second half 19th C, dedicatory inscription "Presented to Mark L. Hirsch by Solomon Hirsch Feb. 23rd 1863" **550.00**

7" h, Wood & Hughes, late 19th C, contemporary enameling after Szyk **1,725.00**

Light bulb, 3-3/4" l, Star of David **100.00**

Lithographs, portfolio of six, The Mishna, A. Raymond Katz, orig woodcuts based on six principals, as compiled by Rabbi Judah Nasi, titled Seeds, (Zeraim), Festivals, (Mo'ed) Women (Noshim), Damages (Nezikim), Holy Objects (Kodashim), and Purity (Tohorot), each 13" x 10" image on heavy paper, titled numbered, and sgd in pencil, published by Arthur Rothman Fine Arts, NYC, 1964, hard cover folio, commentary by Charles Angoff. **575.00**

Menorah, 20" h, gilt bronze, after Salvador Dali, c1980, set on Jerusalem stone base **2,415.00**

Mezuzah, 5-1/2" h, 14k yg, after Ilha Schor, emb and cut-out with figure of Moses, "shin" finial **920.00**

Paperweight, 3" d, Star of David, millefiori, Whitefrairs, 1978, to commemorate 30th anniversary of Israel, orig box **395.00**

Passover plate, 15" l, pewter, 19th C, rim dec with figures amidst foliage, Hebrew text, center with lions, crown **775.00**

Passover table cloth, 76" x 56", linen, rect with shaped edges, white background, multicolored embroidered Passover implements, some staining **920.00**

Pendant, 14k yg, enameled, high priest breast plate motif, 12 step-cut multicolored synthetic stones, Retro, 1-1/2" l, 7.4 dwt **70.00**

Prayer book, miniature, *Seder U-Velechtekha Ba-derekh,* Feival Monk, Warsaw, 1884, Ashkenazi rite, gilt-stamped calf, faux jewel insets, 60 x 40 mm **490.00**

Rosewater bottle, 12" h, silver, South East Asian, late 19th/early 20th C, shaped as water bird swallowing fish swallowing acanthus bouquet, stepped pedestal base, emb and engraved dec, domed top pierced, approx 8 troy oz **225.00**

Sabbath candlesticks, pr, 12-1/2" h, silver plated, B.R. Henneberg, Warsaw, dated 1909, molded bobeche, baluster-form body, spreading circular foot on sq base, cast overall with foliage and Star of David, wear **500.00**

Sabbath hanging lamp, 16" h, Continental, 18th/19th C, brass, eight pointed star-form oval section, plain and turned stem, ratchet suspension hook for adjustable height **375.00**

Sabbath platter, 10-1/2" l, tin washed copper, marked "Israel Made,

Hakushut" orig sticker, die struck imprinted mark **150.00**

Shabbat candelabrum, 20" h, brass, Continental, early 20th C, five-light, supported by deer amidst branches, baluster turned support, domed circular foot, cast Hebrew inscription for Shabbat **500.00**

Spice box, silver, windmill form, 5-1/2" h, applied with floral baskets and birds, sq base, four scroll and foliate feet, 7 oz, 4 dwt **875.00**

Spice container, 7-1/4" l, German silver, articulated fish form, red glass eyes, mouth opens, scales with etched detail marked "835" and "Handarbeit" **700.00**

Spice tower

7-3/4" h, silver, second half 20th C, indistinctly marked, Nuremberg-type, steep roof, pendant flags, square body with door, spreading circular foot **650.00**

10-1/2" h, silver and silver-filigree, second half 20th C, indistinctly marked, typical German form, pendant flags, openwork base ending in four circular feet .**500.00**

12-1/4" h, German silver and silver filigree, American inscription, mid-19th C, illegibly marked, bird finial, tapered spire above stepped section with birds and pendant flags, central square spice section with hinged door, domed circular base on square foot, finely chased Greek-key and foliate details, inscribed in Yiddish "Von den Kindern und Enkeln aus Amerika Zur diamantenen Hochzeit," dated "17 January 1867," corresponding

Hebrew date, lacking several flags **995.00**

Torah breastplate, silver and silver filigree, Russian hallmarks, 20th C, cartouche-shape with crown finial, Decalogue, temple columns, festival plaques, etc. **900.00**

Torah crown, miniature, 5" h, silver-gilt filigree, Continental, probably Eastern Europe, early 19th C, unmarked, acorn finial, with bells, stepped form, inset paste stone details, cross support with apertures to base, lacking two stones **2,200.00**

Torah finials (Tik)

7-1/4" h, silver, North African, late 19th/20th C, unmarked, half-moon form, pointed finial, pendant bells, ribbed middle, flared base, overall chased foliate motifs, price for pr **300.00**

14" h, silver, Near Eastern, late 19th/20th C, unmarked, book-form, overall heavily repousse decoration of grape leaves and vines, fronted by temple columns, Decalogue, and candelabra, fitted with 11-1/2" h handwritten ink on parchment torah scroll ... **3,500.00**

Torah pointer (Yad)

8" l, silver, North African, early 20th C, unmarked, slender form, turned and leaf-tip dec, Hebrew text, terminating in pointed hand, suspension loop **350.00**

8-3/4" l, bone and turquoise mounted, North African, 20th C, turned and incised decoration, terminating in pointed hand **500.00**

Seder plate, master plate with indentations for six small dishes, designs tell story of Seder and other customs, marked "Royal Cauldron, Bone China, 17 crown 74, Made in England, Reg No. 889449, Illustrations by Erik Tunstall R.I.," original fitted box, **$200.**

2" l, silver mounted bone, possibly North Africa, 20th C, tapering form, carved detail and Hebrew lettering, terminating in silver hand, suspension loop and metal chain **950.00**

Traveling menorah, 3-1/2" x 2-1/2", sterling silver, book form, pierced flowers, animals, center anukah lamp, int. fitted with dividers to form eight oil receptacles, 11 oz, 6 dwt **1,200.00**

Watch, 2-1/2" d, Near Eastern, 19th C, silver-gilt, enamel, and rock crystal, six-sided star, floral enamel work, Hebrew numbers, rock crystal bezel and backplate, minor damage, enamel losses **2,415.00**

JUGTOWN POTTERY

History: In 1920, Jacques and Julianna Busbee left their cosmopolitan environs and returned to North Carolina to revive the state's dying pottery-making craft. Jugtown Pottery, a colorful and somewhat off-beat operation, was located in Moore County, miles away from any large city and accessible only "if mud permits."

Ben Owens, a talented young potter, turned the wares. Jacques Busbee did most of the designing and glazing. Julianna handled promotion.

Utilitarian and decorative items were produced. Although many colorful glazes were used, orange predominated. A Chinese blue glaze that ranged from light blue to deep turquoise was a prized glaze reserved for the very finest pieces.

Jacques Busbee died in 1947. Julianna, with the help of Owens, ran the pottery until 1958 when it was closed. After long legal battles, the pottery was reopened in 1960. It now is owned by Country Roads, Inc., a nonprofit organization. The pottery still is operating and using the old mark.

Bowl, 2" h, 4-1/4" d, Chinese blue glaze, imp mark, pr **425.00**

Candlesticks, pr, 3" h, Chinese Translation, Chinese blue and red, marked **125.00**

Charger, 15" d, orange glaze, marked, abrasion and flakes to surface .. **230.00**

Creamer, cov, 4-3/4" h, yellow ... **80.00**

Vase

3-3/4" h, 2-1/2" d, Chinese blue flambé glaze, imp mark.... **325.00**

4" h, 2-3/4" d, Chinese blue glaze, imp mark **275.00**

6-3/4" h, 6" d, ovoid, thick white semi-matte glaze dripping over brown clay body, imp mark. **450.00**

8-3/4" h, 6-1/2" d, stoneware, two small handles, top cov with matte

Charger, orange glaze, stamped "Jugtown Ware," surface abrasion and flakes, 15" d, $230. Photo courtesy of David Rago Auctions.

mustard glaze, bottom with clear coating, imp mark **850.00**

Vessel

7-1/4" h, 5" d, ovoid, white satin glaze, hairline to rim, stamped "Jugtown Ware" **300.00**

9" h, 6-1/4" d, four small handles, brown speckled luster glaze, red clay body, glaze flakes in making, imp mark **650.00**

Vessel, bulbous, two small handles, Chinese blue Crystalline mottled glaze, stamped "Jugtown Ware," 7-1/2" d, 9" h, $2,000. Photo courtesy of David Rago Auctions.

KPM

History: The "KPM" mark has been used separately and in conjunction with other symbols by many German porcelain manufacturers, among which are the Königliche Porzellan Manufactur in Meissen,

1720s; Königliche Porzellan Manufactur in Berlin, 1832-1847; and Krister Porzellan Manufactur in Waldenburg, mid-19th century.

Collectors now use the term KPM to refer to the high-quality porcelain produced in the Berlin area in the 18th and 19th centuries.

Figure, lady, standing with fruit basket, minor restoration, 8" h, $220. Photo courtesy of Sanford Alderfer Auction Company.

Cheese board, rose and leaf garland border, pierce for hanging, marked **48.00**

Cup and saucer, hunting scene, filigree, 19th C **65.00**

Dinner service, partial, basketweave molded rim, enamel painted sepia-toned floral sprays, 10 6-3/4" d side plates, nine 9-1/2" d dinner plates, eight 8-3/8" d salad plates, 12" l oval platter, 13-5/8" l oval platter, 8" oblong dish, late 19th/early 20th C, price for 30-pc set **520.00**

Figure, 8-1/2" h, 3-1/2" d, young man with cocked hat, long coat, trousers, and boots, young lady in Empire-style dress, fancy hat and fan, white ground, brown details, gold trim, round base, blue underglaze KPM mark, price for pr **350.00**

Perfume bottle, 3-5/8" l, rococo-cartouche form, sepia enamel

Match holders, bisque, young boys, one with rope, one with fishing net, one damaged at spyglass, 8" h, $60. Photo courtesy of Joy Luke Auctions.

dec of cherub in flight, floral bouquet, gilt detailing, gilt-metal and coral mounted stopper, late 19th C .. **230.00**

Plaque

6" d, German officer, round, painted with central rectangular portrait of gentleman in uniform, gilt frame with laurel and helmet, in gilt-metal surround, paper label identifying it as loan from the Fogg Art Museum, early 19th C
.... **4,320.00**

7-1/2" w, 10" h, First Snowfall, grandfather with two grandchildren standing in doorway, snowy foreground, 21" w, 18" h elaborate

Plaque, woman with lilacs, original gilt frame, artist signed Wagner, 5-1/2" w, 7-1/2" h porcelain, $4,760. Photo courtesy of Fontaine's Auction Gallery.

carved wood frame of scrolling acanthus, imp scepter mark and "KPM," artist std lower right "F. X. Thallmaier Munchen" ... **4,370.00**

9-3/4" l, 5-1/4" w, Aurora by Bierschneider, hp in very fine detail, beehive mark **3,500.00**

10" w, 12" h, Sistine Madonna, after Raphael, finely dec, period gilt frame, verso imp with scepter mark and "KPM"........... **1,955.00**

12-3/4" l, 7-7/8" w, Ruth, after painting by Bouguereau, late 19th C **2,300.00**

13-1/2" w, 17" h, Sistine Madonna after Raphael, oval porcelain, elaborately carved and gilt wood frame with scrolled acanthus and house, 24-1/2" w, 30" h glazed shadow box with red velvet lining, imp scepter mark and "KPM"
.... **4,025.00**

13-3/4" d, titled "Entflohen," two young beauties seated in windswept wood, diaphanous gowns, floral headbands, anthemion and quatrefoil border, irid teal ground, 22-1/4" d giltwood and gesso frame...... **10,925.00**

Punch bowl, cov, 12" d, 14-1/2" h, domed lid, Dionysian putto figural finial, enamel dec on one side with 18th C wigged gentleman at a drunken meeting of punch society, similar scene of gentleman at table to one side, vignette of couple outside village on other, floral bouquets and sprigs, imp basketweave rim, gilt edging, underglaze blue mark, late 19th C
.... **2,775.00**

Teapot, 6" h, oval, medallion with floral dec, gilt ground **95.00**

Vase, 8-1/2" h, baluster, two handles, hp multicolored florals, celery green ground **200.00**

KAUFFMANN, ANGELICA

History: Marie Angelique Catherine Kauffmann was a Swiss artist who lived from 1741 until 1807. Many artists who hand-decorated porcelain during the 19th century copied her paintings. The majority of the paintings are neoclassical in style.

Box, cov, 2-3/4" x 4-1/2", lilac, two maidens and child in woods on cov, brass hinges................. **70.00**

Cake plate, 10" d, ftd, classical scene, two maidens and cupid, beehive mark
.... **90.00**

Charger, Austrian porcelain, central panel decorated with figures, signed Kauffmann, 12" d, $100. Photo courtesy of Joy Luke Auctions.

Compote, 8" d, classical scene, beehive mark, sgd **85.00**

Cup and saucer, classical scene, heavy gold trim, ftd **90.00**

Demitasse set, 8" h demitasse pot, creamer, sugar, three cups and saucers, extra saucers, all with country scene, marked "Conaty, Germany," sgd "Kauffmann" on scene, price for 13-pc set **190.00**

Dresser tray, 11-1/2" x 7-1/2", cherub center, marked "Carlsbad, Austria"
.... **75.00**

Inkwell, pink luster, classical lady **85.00**

Pitcher, 8-1/2" h, garden scene, ladies, children, and flowers, sgd..... **100.00**

Plate, 8" d, cobalt blue border, reticulated rim, classical scene with two figures **65.00**

Portrait plate, portrait with cherubs, dark green and cream ground, gold trim, sgd "Carlsbad, Austria, Kauffmann," four-pc set **495.00**

Tobacco jar, classical ladies and cupid, green ground, SP top, pipe as finial..................... **415.00**

Vase, 10" h, baluster, small wing handles, cobalt blue ground, roundel with semi-nude painting, sgd "K," c1870, price for pr, damage to one handle **225.00**

KITCHEN COLLECTIBLES

History: The kitchen was the focal point in a family's environment until the 1960s. Many early kitchen utensils were handmade and prized by their owners. Next came a period of utilitarian products made of tin and other metals. When the housewife no longer wished to work in a sterile environment, enamel and plastic products added color, and their unique design served both aesthetic and functional purposes.

The advent of home electricity changed the type and style of kitchen products. Fads affected many items. High technology already has made inroads into the kitchen, and another revolution seems at hand.

For more information, see this book.

Additional Listings: Baskets, Brass, Butter Prints, Copper, Fruit Jars, Food Molds, Graniteware, Ironware, Tinware, and Woodenware. See *Warman's Americana & Collectibles* for more examples, including electrical appliances. See *Warman's Flea Market Price Guide* also.

Apple peeler, cast iron, Reading Hardware Co. **90.00**

Bean pot, cov, 6-1/2" h, Bristol glaze, handle, c1900. . . . . **25.00**

Broom holder, Little Polly Brooms, tin litho, image of little girl sweeping floor, 2-1/2" w, 6-1/4" h. **425.00**

Butter churn, 49" h, old blue paint, America, 19th C, minor imperfections **345.00**

Butter paddle
6-1/4" l, maple, unusual carved handle resembling bird with open beak, small rim chip **125.00**

Colander, stoneware, brown Albany glaze, handle, hand pierced holes, attributed to Midwest, c1870, 13" h, $250. Photo courtesy of Vicki and Bruce Waasdorp.

9-3/4" l, burl, dark patina, simple hooked handle **165.00**

Catalog
Manning-Bowman & Co., Meriden, CT, c1920, 34 pgs, gas stoves, chafing dishes, accessories, some recipes **40.00**
Sidney Shepard & Co., Buffalo, NY, c1924, 32 pgs, kitchen specialists, cuts of steam cereal cooker, egg poacher, roaster, perfection tins, etc. **45.00**

Cheese sieve, 10" d, 7" h, plus handle, hand-molded yellow clay, Albany glaze **320.00**

Colander, 13" h, stoneware, brown Albany glaze, handled, attributed to Midwest, c1870 . . . . **75.00**

Cookbook
Come Into The Kitchen Cook Book, Mary and Vincent Price, Straven Educational Press, 1969, dj . **12.00**
Cook It Outdoors, James Beard, 1941, 1st ed **7.00**
Mastering the Art of French Cooking, Julia Child, volumes one and two, Knopf, 1971-76, dj **25.00**
The Good Housekeeping Illustrated Book of Desserts, Step-by-Step Photographs, Hearst Books, 1991, 5th printing, dj **12.00**

Cookie mold
23-1/2" l, 5-1/4" w, people and rooster on one side, four animals and two birds on other, minor edge wear **125.00**
28" l, 3-3/8" w, carved woman at well, man and woman near potted plant, few worm holes **250.00**

Dough box, pine and turned poplar, PA, 19th C, rect removable top, tapering well, splayed ring-turned legs, ball feet, 38" w, 19-1/4" d, 29-1/2" h **425.00**

Egg beater, 10-1/2" l, Jacquette Scissor, marked "Jacquette, Phila, PA, Patented No. 3" **550.00**

Flatware, four 8-7/8" l knives and four forks, wooden handles, knife blades marked "J. Ward & Co., Riverside, Mass.," wear and some damage to orig box. **90.00**

Flour sifter, 14" h, 12" w, Tilden's Universal, wood, partial intact paper label. **335.00**

Food chopper, 7" w, wrought iron, scalloped edge blade, turned wood handle **270.00**

Griddle, cast iron, Griswold, No. 10 . . . . **70.00**

Kraut cutter, walnut, tombstone top, cutout for hanging, wrought steel double blades, old patina, American, 9-1/2" w, 27" l, $95. Photo courtesy of Cowan's Historic Americana Auctions.

Ice bucket, Frigidaire, frosted green glass. **35.00**

Kettle, cast iron, Griswold No. 4 . **85.00**

Kraut cutter, 25-5/8" l, 8" w, heart cutout, maple, mellow patina . . . **350.00**

Ladle, 15" l, wood, pothook handle **50.00**

Lemon squeezer, iron, glass insert, marked "Williams" **50.00**

Meat tenderizer, 9-1/2" h, stoneware, orig wood handle, marked "Pat'd Dec. 25, 1877" in relief on bottom, diamond point extensions with some use wear **90.00**

Nutmeg grater, 7" l, Champion, brass and wood **635.00**

Pantry box, cov, 11-1/2" d, 6-1/2" h, oak, bail handle **175.00**

Pastry board, wood, three sided **32.00**

Meat tenderizer, stoneware, original wooden handle, marked "Pat'd Dec 25, 1877" in relief on bottom, c1877, some damage to diamond point extensions from use, 9-1/2" h, $90. Photo courtesy of Vicki and Bruce Waasdorp.

Reamer, orange base, L-4, marked "Hand Painted, TT, Made in Japan," $65.

Pie crimper, 7" l, carved bone, unicorn with carved fish tail, ball-shaped hooves, front let glued, late replacement crimper, medium brown stain **220.00**

Pie safe, hanging, 31" w, 19" d, 31" h, mortised pine case, old thin red wash, door, sides, and back with punched tins with geometric circles and stars, white porcelain door pull, two int. shelves, edge damage **990.00**

Potato masher, 9" l, turned maple **40.00**

Pot scraper, Sharples Tubular Separator, tin litho, graphic advertising on both sides, 3-1/8" x 2-1/4" . . . **275.00**

Rack, 20" l, rect backplate with arched top, red and white enameled checkerboard pattern, narrow well, single rod suspending two strainer spoons **250.00**

Reamer
Grapefruit, green, US Glass, cone chips **575.00**
Orange, pink, Hazel Atlas . . . **195.00**

Orange, Sunkist, blocked pattern, white milk glass, Walker #331b **125.00**

Rolling pin
16-1/2" l, curly maple, dark color, good patina **275.00**
22" l, milk glass, cylindrical, turned wood handles, marked "Imperial Mfg., Co. July 25, 1921" **95.00**

Sausage stuffer, 17-1/2" l, turned wood plunger **30.00**

Skillet, cast iron, Griswold, No. 14 . . . . **165.00**

Spatula, 17-3/4" l, brass and wrought iron, polished **175.00**

Spice set, Griffiths, set of 16 glass jars with yellow tops, each with spice name, orig rack **160.00**

Stove, cast iron, chrome, nickel, colorful ceramic tile back **6,000.00**

Sugar shaker, Dutch boy and girl, Tipp City **22.00**

Syrup jug, 8" h, adv, clay inscribed "W. D. Streeter, Richland, NY," Albany glaze, c1890, tight hairline on side **35.00**

Taster, 7" l, brass and wrought iron, polished **150.00**

Tin
Donovan's Baking Powder, Mt. Morris, NY, 1 lb, paper label, 5-1/4" h, 3" d **475.00**
Egg-O Brand Baking Powder, paper label, 2-3/4" h, 1-1/4" d **110.00**
Kavanaugh's Tea, 1 lb, little girl on porch in dress, talking to doll, mother sipping tea in window, cardboard sides, tin top and bottom, 6" h, 4-1/2" w, 4-1/2" d **500.00**
Miller's Gold Medal Breakfast Cocoa, red and black, c1890, 2" h, 1-5/8" w, 1-1/8" d **250.00**

Salt, hanging, blue and white salt glazed stoneware, relief butterfly pattern, matching butterfly lid with chip and hairline, 6" d, 6" h, $100. Photo courtesy of Vicki and Bruce Waasdorp.

Opal Powdered Sugar, Hewitt & Sons, Des Moines, 8" h, 4-1/2" w, 3-1/4" d **180.00**
Parrot and Monkey Baking Powder, 4 oz, full, 3-1/4" h, 2-1/8" d . **375.00**
Sunshine-Oxford Fruit Cake, early 1900s, sq corners **20.00**
Towle's Log Cabin Brand Maple Syrup, cabin shaped, woman and girl in doorway, 4" h, 3-3/4" l, 2-1/2" d **110.00**

Sugar nips, wrought steel and brass, graceful engraved feather pattern, American, early 19th C, 10" l, $150. Photo courtesy of Cowan's Historic Americana Auctions.

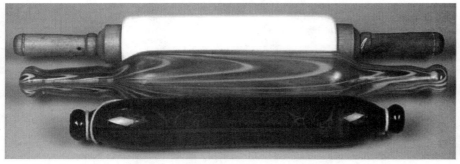

Rolling pins, top to bottom: molded white milk glass, turned wooden handles, glass marked "Imperial Mfg Co., Cambridge, Ohio, USA Pat July 26, 1921," 18-1/2" l; aqua glass, looped red and white interior ribbons, American, 19th C, snap pontil, 17-3/4" l; cobalt blue blown glass, gilt and enamel decoration of anchor and two masted schooner in scrollwork surround with "Remember Me," American, 19th C, snap pontil, 13-1/4" l, $465. Photo courtesy of Cowan's Historic Americana Auctions.

Sandwich server, Prelude pattern, clear glass, etched design, New Martinsville Glass, 1930-50, 13" d, $40.

Trivet, 12" l, lyre form, wrought iron frame and turned handle, brass top, replaced foot, stamped maker's mark **45.00**

Wafer iron, cast iron, octagonal, church with steeple and trees dec on one side, pinwheel with plants and star flowers on reverse, wrought iron handles **400.00**

KUTANI

History: Kutani originated in the mid-1600s in the Kaga province of Japan. Kutani comes in a variety of color patterns, one of the most popular being Ao Kutani, a green glaze with colors such as green, yellow, and purple enclosed in a black outline. Export wares made since the 1870s are enameled in a wide variety of colors and styles.

Beaker, 4-1/2" h, hp flowers and birds, red, orange, and gold, white ground, marked "Ao-Kutani" **95.00**

Biscuit jar, cov, Geisha Girl, c1890 . . . . **190.00**

Bowl, 6-3/8" d, gilt and bright enamel design, figural, animal, and floral reserves, kinrande ground, base inscribed "Kutani-sei," set of 10. **400.00**

Charger, 18-3/8" d, pomegranate tree, chrysanthemums, and two birds on int., birds and flowers between scrolling foliate bands, irregular floral and brocade border, 11-character inscription **600.00**

Chawan (tea bowl), 5" d, 3" h, sunflower design, orange and green, imp mark "RIJU" **100.00**

Chocolate pot, white ground, hp scenes of lake, three white cranes on shore, Mt. Fiji in distance, hills with wildflowers, white and pink

Vases, cylindrical, slightly tapering neck, fan-shaped handles, aka-e decoration of courtiers and pheasants, Japan, late 19th C, line to one, price for pair, 11" h, $500. Photo courtesy of Skinner's Auctioneers and Appraisers.

chrysanthemums, two white cranes with black tails, lid painted with wild flowers on cliff, crane, gold bamboo branch, gold knob, cream colored handle, wear to knob **95.00**

Creamer and sugar, summer scene, two court ladies, red, blue, gray, and gold, red handle, spout, and feet with gold overlay, c1910 . . . . **95.00**

Dessert service, country life dec, gold cloud borders, eight plates, two compotes, 20th C **435.00**

Figure

7" l, duck, gilt figure, purple, blue, green, and yellow feathers, Japan, late 19th C **1,100.00**

14" h, geisha with kitten, green, yellow, and brick red enamels, Japan, late 19th/early 20th C **600.00**

Jar, cov, 20-1/2" h, ovoid, fan-shaped reserves of warriors, molded ribbon tied tasseled ring handles, shippo-tsunagi ground, multicolored brocade patterned dome lid, pr **1,400.00**

Sake cup, 2-3/16" h, 1-1/8" w, crane in red center, gold lacquer trim **35.00**

Tea caddy, 6" h, bulbous, hexagonal, Nishikide diapering, figural raised gold reserves of children, red script mark **195.00**

Teapot, cov, 8" h, white, trees and flowers, gold trim, marked "Hand Painted Craftsman China, Kutani 391 Japan" **45.00**

Tray, 14" l, polychrome and gilt dec, figural scene, red, orange, and gold border **350.00**

Vases, paneled, Foo dog mounts, two handles. Chinese, late 19th C, 24-1/2" h. Photo courtesy of James D. Julia, Inc.

Vase

7-1/4" h, classic shape, white emb chrysanthemums on white ground, marked "Trade Mark Fujita Kutani, Made in Japan" **95.00**

10" h, double-gourd, red and gold roundels of auspicious animals on flowered ground, Japan, 19th C **300.00**

14" h, pear shape, Satsuma type dec of traveling scholar, Japan, late 19th/early 20th C **200.00**

LACE AND LINENS

History: Lace, lacy linens, embroidery, and hand-decorated textiles are different from any other antique. They are valued both as a handmade substance and as the thing the substance is made into. Thread is manipulated into stitches, stitches are assembled into lace, and lace is made into handkerchiefs, edgings, tablecloths, and bedspreads. Things eventually go out of style or are damaged or worn, and just as the diamonds and rubies are taken from old jewelry and placed into new settings, fine stitchery of embroidery and lace is saved and reused. Lace from a handkerchief is used to decorate a blouse, fragments of a bridal veil are made into a scarf; shreds of old lace are remounted onto fine net and used again as a veil.

At each stage in the cycle, different people become interested. Some see fragments as bits and pieces of a collage, and seek raw materials for accent pieces. Others use Victorian whites and turn-of-the-century embroidered linens to complement a life style. Collectors value and admire the stitches themselves, and when those stitches are remarkable enough, they will pay hundreds of dollars for fragments a few inches square.

Until the 1940s, lace collecting was a highly respected avocation of the wealthy. The prosperity of the New World was a magnet for insolvent European royalty, who carried suitcases of old Hapsburg, Bourbon, Stuart, and Romanov laces to suites at New York's Waldorf hotel for dealers to select from. Even Napoleon's bed hangings of handmade Alencon lace, designed for Josephine and finished for Marie Louise, found their way here. In 1932, *Fortune* magazine profiled socially prominent collectors and lace dealers. For the entire first half of this century, New York City's Needle and Bobbin Club provided a forum for showing off acquisitions.

Until 1940, upscale department stores offered antique lace and lacy linens. Dealers specializing in antique lace and lacy linens had prominent upscale shops, and offered repair, restoration, remodeling, and cleaning services along with the antique linens. In addition to collecting major pieces—intact jabots from the French Ancient Regime, Napoleonic-era Alencon, huge mid-Victorian lace shawls, Georgian bed hangings appliquéd with 17th-century needle lace—collectors assembled study collections of postcard-size samples of each known style of antique lace.

When styles changed round the 1940s and 1950s and the market for antique lace and linens crashed, some of the best collections did go to museums; others just went into hiding. With renewed interest in a gracious, romantic lifestyle, turn-of-the-century lacy cloths from the linen closets of the barons of the industrial revolution are coming out of hiding. Collectors and wise dealers know that many of the small study pieces of irreplaceable stitchery—fragments collectors will pay ten to hundreds of dollars for—still emerge in rummage and estate sales.

Very large banquet-sized lace tablecloths, especially those with napkins, continue to be especially popular. Appenzell, a white-on-white embroidered lacework of 19th century Switzerland, has become one of the hottest collector's items. Strong interest continues in patterned silk ribbons, all cotton lace yardage, and other lacy materials for heirloom sewing and fashion.

The market for antique lace definitely is changing. Interest is still rising for elaborate lace for home decorating and entertaining, and interest in fine-quality lace collars is increasing. Large lace shawls and veils, especially for bridal wear, continue to be in demand. Internet auctions and chat groups make it possible for a dealer in Wyoming to link up with a collector in Louisiana, and find a home for an interesting piece. Those interested in fine-quality lace are realizing they need to start buying at market prices instead of waiting for that lucky find that they alone recognize. Current market prices, although rising, still are usually far below what the pieces would have cost when new, or during the early 20th century heyday of lace collecting.

As prices rise, buyers more often want an accurate identification: what is it, where was it made, and how old is it? What makes it worth the price? Word spreads quickly over the Internet when it is obvious a dealer has mislabeled something, especially labeling something as handmade that is obviously machine made. Lace has long been a sideline for most dealers, and they did not bother to learn to identify it. As long as they could turn it over quickly for a small markup, they were satisfied. That is changing. More sophisticated buyers won't put up with that.

The basic techniques are bobbin lace, needle lace, crochet, tatting, knitting, knotting, and needle weaving. Identifying how a piece was made is the easy part, and there is no excuse for a dealer not being able to separate crochet from bobbin lace. Anyone can identify the technique after just a weekend workshop, or by comparing a piece to pictures in a good textbook. The technique, plus the quality of the design and condition, provides nearly all the information anyone needs to decide what a piece is worth.

After identifying the technique, many like to apply a name to the style (Duchesse bobbin lace, Point de Gaze needle lace, Irish crochet). This serves as a useful shorthand in talking about lace, but adds nothing to the value of the piece. This is often the confusing part. Unlike most antiques, there is no uniformity in labeling styles of lace. Names changed at different points in time, different names were used for similar products made in different countries, and foreign names often were translated differently. Any dealer should be expected to be able to explain why they chose to use any specific style name.

The Internet offers a unique access to a wide variety of kinds of lace and lacy linens. The small pictures available on the Internet, however, rarely show

enough detail to know just what you are buying. Insist on a return policy for any lace purchased sight unseen on the Internet. Even well intentioned dealers may miss details that significantly affect the value of lace. Handmade meshes cannot be positively identified without high-powered magnification. Repairs often go unnoticed and unreported. Color and texture make a great deal of difference in determining whether a piece of lace is attractive.

Whether purchasing fine quality collector's study samples, or boxes and bags of recyclable fragments for sewing, it is worth taking a close look at all the details. It is not uncommon to find good quality study samples that a collector will pay $10 to $100 for in the "rag bags."

Those who learn to recognize the artistry and value of old stitchery will not only enhance their lives with beauty, they may find a windfall.

Adviser: Elizabeth M. Kurella.

Bedspread

Crochet, double size, filet crochet grid-style design, scrolling leaves design **85.00**

Princess Lace (machine tapes appliquéd to machine net) scrolling flower and leaves design . . **350.00**

Bridal veil, Point De Gaze needle lace in rose and leaf design with scrolls and medallions in 12" edge border on 7' long teardrop shape veil **1,500.00**

Curtain panels, crewel embroidery in shades of blue, gold and green depicting stylized papyrus motif, natural linen ground, Arts & Crafts, each panel 30" w, 8', **$1,610**. Photo courtesy of David Rago Auctions.

Handkerchief, Gentle Sheppard, portrait of Alan Ramsay, six oval vignettes, framed, some deterioration, 23" w, 20" h, **$45**. Photo courtesy of James D. Julia, Inc.

Bridge set, linen, embroidered in red and black motifs of playing-card suits, matching napkins **85.00**

Collar, Duchesse bobbin lace, c1870, roses, daisies, and scrollwork design, 5" at center back, 32" l **125.00**

Curtains, hand-embroidered machine net, c1900, iris, roses, and filigree elaborate designs, 48" x 96", pr . **50.00**

Doily

Crochet, roses, raised petals, 8" d round **10.00**

Flemish bobbin lace, c1900, goldfish design in Petit de Paris ground, 10" d round, 3" deep lace **75.00**

Dresser scarf, drawnwork, Victorian, white geometric design, 28" x 48" **45.00**

Fragments of collector's lace

Gros Point de Venise, c1650, stylized scrolling floral design, motifs defined by raised and padded outlines dec with many styles of picots, 2" x 12" . . . **285.00**

Point de Venise a Reseau, stylized floral design, Alencon mesh background, no cordonnet, 3" x 6" fragment of edging **185.00**

Handkerchief

Linen

Edged with colored crochet scallop design, 12" sq **4.00**

Edged with half inch of white tatting, 12" sq **8.00**

Whitework, French, 1870s, edged with embroidery, drawnwork, and needle-lace inserts **95.00**

Napkin, cocktail, white, edge with single scallop of needle lace, 1" sq corner inserts of needle lace worked in stylized animal design, price for six-pc set **45.00**

Pillowcase

Linen, white, figural designs in needle-lace inserts, floral design in needle-lace edging, pr **125.00**

Maderia, white cotton, flower silhouetted in cutwork, embroidered with satin stitch, pr **15.00**

Pillow cover, linen, white, dec with inserts of needle lace, scrolling floral designs, embroidered in satin stitch, Cluny bobbin lace edging, 18" d round **125.00**

Pincushion, white satin, top cov with sq of white Italian drawn work in heavy linen, embroidered raised flower and tendril design, corners dec with whimsical knotted tassels, 4" sq, 1" deep **65.00**

Runner, Normandy work, patchwork of handmade Vaienciennes bobbin lace and other laces, mostly handmade, central motif of French embroidered whitework with birds and flowers, oval, 24" x 18" **145.00**

Tablecloth

Cotton, embroidered spring flowers design, tablecloth and six matching napkins, c1945 ...**75.00**

Crochet, round medallions design, 48" x 68" **75.00**

Cutwork, floral and scrollwork satin-stitch embroidery, needle-lace inserts, 8" deep border

Tablecloth, natural color linen, Richelieu, all handmade cutwork and embroidery, floral and scroll motif, early 20th C, 68" x 100", $595.

of filet in figural designs, Italian, c1900, 42" sq **175.00**

Filet, geometric design darned over knotted network, 48" x 72" . **125.00**

Linen, natural color, Richelieu, all handmade cutwork and embroidery, floral and scroll motif, early 20th C, 68" x 100" ... **575.00**

LALIQUE

History: René Lalique (1860-1945) first gained prominence as a jewelry designer. Around 1900, he began experimenting with molded-glass brooches and pendants, often embellishing them with semiprecious stones. By 1905, he was devoting himself exclusively to the manufacture of glass articles.

In 1908, Lalique began designing packaging for the French cosmetic houses. He also produced many objects, especially vases, bowls, and figurines, in the Art Nouveau and Art Deco styles. The full scope of Lalique's genius was seen at the 1925 Paris l'Exposition Internationale des Arts Décorative et Industriels Modernes.

Marks: The mark "R. LALIQUE FRANCE" in block letters is found on pressed articles, tableware, vases, paperweights, and automobile mascots. The script signature, with or without "France," is found on hand-blown objects. Occasionally, a design number is included. The word "France" in any form indicates a piece made after 1926.

The post-1945 mark is generally "Lalique France" without the "R," but there are exceptions.

For more information, see this book.

Reproduction Alert: The Lalique signature has often been forged; the most common fake includes an "R" with the post-1945 mark.

Animal, 3" h, toad, Gregoire, sitting, polished crystal, inscribed "Lalique France," 20th C, minor nicks to one leg **290.00**

Ashtray, 5-3/4" d, lion, molded gargoyle form rim, extended mane ridges, engraved script sgd **180.00**

Bonbon box, cov, 8-1/4" d, Boites Ronde Grande Libellulis, irid dragonfly, sgd "R. Lalique No. 51".....**1,295.00**

Ashtray, Dindon, c1925, opalescent glass, gray patina, engraved "R. Lalique. France," $460. Photos courtesy of David Rago Auctions.

Bookends, pr

4-1/4" w, 6-1/8" h, birds perched low with upraised tails and wings, press-molded, acid finished, polished colorless glass, paper label, bases inscribed "Lalique France," Shreve, Crump & Low Co. paper retailer's labels **175.00**

5-1/2" l, 3-1/8" w, 8-3/4" h, kneeling nude female figures, press-molded, acid finished, polished colorless glass, paper label, late 20th C **635.00**

Bowl

8" d, 3" h, Fleurons, press-molded opalescent, six wavy line swirl designs in relief, acid etched "R. LALIQUE FRANCE" on base, M 3314 ....**215.00**

18" l, 10" w, 7-3/8" h, leaf, two large press-molded and acid finished leaves, colorless glass, paper label, base inscribed "Lalique France" **490.00**

Cocktail glass, William, c1925, clear and frosted glass, blue enameled details, engraved "R. Lalique France," $980.

Buttons, pr, coiled serpent over red backing, sgd "Lalique," converted into earrings **435.00**

Car mascot, 7-7/8" and 8" h, Coq Nain, molded as roosters in crouched position, raised "R. LALIQUE FRANCE," M 1135, imperfections, pr **1,150.00**

Champagne flute, 8-1/8" h, cylindrical bowls etched with angel's wings, top of stem with molded angel face, etched "Lalique, France", 20th C, price for eight-pc set **750.00**

Coupe, 9-3/8" d, 3-1/4" h, shallow bowl, Vases No. 1, colorless, repeating polished urn-forms alternating frosted stylized bouquets, center molded "R. Lalique" **230.00**

Decanter set, 11" h decanter with donut stopper, Highlands, four matching glasses, #13301 and #1333412 . . . . **800.00**

Drawing, for jewelry design, drawn by Rene Lalique, c1898, ink and watercolor, BFK Rives parchment paper

   7-3/4" x 5-3/4", Pendentif Feuilles a Baies, swirl of leaves and berries, one berry with notation "Diamant" **5,350.00**

   10-1/2" x 8-1/4", Pendentif Figurine a Glycine, draped female figure within border of wisteria and jewels, numbered "8" in upper left **5,350.00**

Dressing table mirror, 12" l, 6-1/2" d, Narcisse Couche, frosted glass frame and handle, molded foliate motif centering male nude above handle, orig gray patina in recesses, inscribed "R. Lalique, France" top rim, mirror slightly stained **980.00**

Figure, 10-1/4" h, Two Dancers, sgd in script, c1960 . . . . **1,475.00**

Ice bucket, 8-7/8" h, cylindrical, press-molded dec of two nude dancing

Inkwell, Cernay, c1924, clear glass, green patina, molded "R. LALIQUE," $1,725.

Pendant, Guepes, c1920, deep amber glass, sepia patina, on black silk cord, engraved "Lalique," $860.

women with foliage background, acid finished and polished colorless glass, paper label, base inscribed "Lalique France," late 20th C **550.00**

Medallion, 1-3/8" d, Dana les Fleurs, 1924 model, frosted low relief of nude female under blossoms, made for Fioret perfume box, marked "R. Lalique/Fioret/Paris" **520.00**

Necklace, 40" l, Fueilles De Lierre, twenty opalescent green elements, orig

Statuette, Suzanne, c1925, opalescent glass with blue patina, molded "R. LALIQUE," engraved "R. Lalique France," $16,100.

Vase, Carmargue, 1942, clear and frosted glass, engraved "Lalique France," base with large polished area, $2,415.

golden silk cord, c1919, engraved "R. Lalique," M 558, No. 1505 . . . . **2,990.00**

Perfume bottle, 3-7/8" h, finial of roses, roses and column on bottle, peach patina, engraved "R. Lalique France," M 719 . . . . **575.00**

Perfume flacon

   3-3/4" h, Salamandres, colorless flattened oval, polished roundels surrounded by curving lizards, gray-green patina in recesses, motif repeated on stopper, base inscribed "L. Lalique, France" **1,495.00**

   5-1/2" h, Bouchon Mures, colorless barrel-shaped bottle, black ribbing, molded flawless matte black tiara stopper with berry clusters, molded "R. Lalique" on base **9,200.00**

Plate, 7-1/4" d, black crystal, Algues, sgd "Catalogue Number 10421," price for set of eight **2,500.00**

Vase, Domremy, c1926, opalescent glass, sepia patina, engraved "R. Lalique France no. 979," $1,725.

Powder box, cov, sepia wash, two ladies, arms entwined, fancy scrolls and flowers on cov, sepia washed garlands of flowers on base, sgd "Coty" and "Lalique Depose," c1915 . . **600.00**

Vase

5-1/2" d, 9-3/4" h, clear and frosted, ladies, garland of fruit and flowers, sgd "R. Lalique France" . **2,200.00**

9-1/2" h, Bacchantes, frieze of nude women, press-molded, acid finished, polished colorless glass, paper label, base inscribed "Lalique France," M 997 . . . **815.00**

LAMP SHADES

History: Lamp shades were made to diffuse the harsh light produced by early gas lighting fixtures. These early shades were made by popular Art Nouveau manufacturers including Durand, Quezal, Steuben, and Tiffany. Many shades are not marked.

For more information, see this book.

Aladdin

Cased, green **870.00**
Satin, white, dogwood dec . . . **65.00**

Artichoke, 10" d

Green **1,000.00**
White **800.00**

Cased art glass, 5-1/2" h, 2-1/4" d fitter rim, cased gold, opal glass ruffled bell shade, green pulled feather motif, gold irid luster, price for four-pc set . . **435.00**

Ceiling shade, 22" d, 9-1/2" deep, 5" opening, hipped O' Brien dome, leaded green glass segments arranged in

Gaslight, Nailsea, white loopings on sky blue ground, threaded surface, 2-3/8" d fitter rim, with chip, 5-1/4" w, 3-3/4" h, $195. Photo courtesy of Clarence and Betty Maier.

Leaded hanging dome, pink, white, tan, and green slag, $850. Photo courtesy of Sanford Alderfer Auction Company.

brickwork geometric progression, three orig int. bronze reinforcements, rim imp "Tiffany Studios, New York 1501"
. . . . **10,350.00**

Durand, 9-1/2" l, gold Egyptian crackle, blue and white overlay, bulbous, ruffed rim, sgd **225.00**

Fenton, 4" d, white opal hobnails, blue ground **90.00**

Fostoria, 5-1/2" d, Zipper pattern, green pulled dec, opal ground, gold lining **225.00**

Handel, 10" d, tam o'shanter, hand-painted green silhouette village scene with windmill and harbor, sgd "Handel 2862" **325.00**

Imperial, NuArt, marigold **65.00**

Leaded glass, 17-1/2" d, 3" d opening, narrow topped umbrella-shape, dropped apron, four bright red starburst blossoms with yellow disks on green stems, green slag background segments, conforming motif on apron, some restoration to inside leading
. . . . **635.00**

Loetz, 8-1/2" d, irid green oil spotting, ribbon work, white glass int., c1900
. . . . **250.00**

Lustre Art, 4-1/2" h, lily, opal, descent gold pulled feathers, sgd "Lustre Art"
. . . . **260.00**

Muller Freres, 6" h, frosted satin, white top, cobalt blue base, yellow highlights, three-pc set **400.00**

Pairpoint, 7" h, puffy, flower basket, reverse painted pink and yellow poppies and roses **425.00**

Quezal, 5-1/2" d, dark green, platinum feathers, gold lining **650.00**

Rubena, 7-1/4" d, 3-7/8" d fitter ring, cranberry shading to clear, frosted and clear etched flowers and leaves, ruffled
. . . . **460.00**

Leaded hanging shade, green and lavender slag glass panels, red glass diamond panels, beaded fringe, 21" d, one small panel cracked, $200. Photo courtesy of Joy Luke Auctions.

Steuben, Aurene, irid brown, platinum applied border **425.00**

Tartan, 6" h, 3-1/4" fitter ring, gaslight, bands of white, yellow, and pink, sgd "Tartan Rd. No. 46498," registered by "Henry Gething Richardson, Wordsley Flint Glass Works, near Stourbridge, Feb. 24, 1886" **285.00**

Tiffany, attributed to, 6" h, translucent glass, green tipped irid gold pulled feather dec, early 20th C **560.00**

LAMPS AND LIGHTING

History: Lighting devices have evolved from simple stone-age oil lamps to the popular electrified models of today. Aimé Argand patented the first oil lamp in 1784. Around 1850, kerosene became a popular lamp-burning fluid, replacing whale oil and other fluids. In 1879, Thomas A. Edison invented the electric light, causing fluid lamps to lose favor and creating a new field for lamp manufacturers. Companies like Tiffany and Handel became skillful at manufacturing electric lamps, and their decorators produced beautiful bases and shades.

Reproduction Alert.

Astral

11" h globe, 26" h overall, Cornelius & Co., gilt brass weighted base with Gothic detailing, applied prism ring with ovoid frosted etched glass globe with Greek key and floral designs, patent 1897, electrified, flakes on rim . . **775.00**
22-1/2" h, sq white marble base, ribbed then turned brass column, cut glass prisms, frosted shade with etched

Astral, frosted clear leaded glass shade with vintage copper wheel engraved design, 12 hanging three-part cut glass prisms, cast gilt bronze baluster form column with waist-length portrait of George Washington on each side, floral scrollwork surround, surmounted by spread-winged eagle, mounted on stepped white marble base with bronze acanthus scroll dividers, attributed to Sandwich, wear to gilt, electrified, 28" h, $975. Photo courtesy of Cowan's Historic Americana Auctions.

flowers and vintage dec, electrified **250.00**

24-5/8" h, grapevine etched colorless glass shade, gilt metal font, glass prisms, standard with Rococo bronze fittings, flared, ribbed, blue glass shaft with gilt highlights, white marble base, electrified, imperfections, America, 19th C **920.00**

Banquet, Classical Revival, English, early 20th C, silver plate and cut glass, electrified

21-3/8" h, Goldsmiths Company, bowl form cut glass oil font, fluted Corinthian column, tapered sq section loaded base with flower filled urns connected by swags **800.00**

21-1/2" h, Mappin & Webb, bowl form cut glass oil font, stop reeded fluted columns, stepped gadrooned base **825.00**

Boudoir

Aladdin, 14-1/2" h, 8" d, reverse painted bell shade, pine border, floral molded polychromed metal base **225.00**

American, early 20th C, 18-1/2" h, reverse painted conical shade with house, bridge, and tree-filled landscape, orange ground, metal base with raised foliate and geometric motif, raised "F. M." and partially visible marks on base **290.00**

Handel, 14" h, 7" d, gilt-finished spelter base, reverse painted etched glass

shade with umber harbor scene, orange sky, shade stamped "Handel 6450," Handel Lamps cloth tag on base, chips to patina **1,150.00**

Heintz Art Metal Shop, Buffalo, NY, 9-1/4" h, 8-1/2" d, bronze shade with cut-out Art Nouveau style flowers and foliage, in three sections, similar dec in silver overlay on round bronze base, paper label, two dents **1,265.00**

Obverse painted scenic, 13-1/2" h, closed top mushroom-cap glass shade with textured surface mounted on gilt metal handled lamp base, weighted foot, hand-painted silhouetted forested landscape scenes, rim marked "Patented April 29th, 1913" .. **1,150.00**

Pittsburgh Lamp, Brass & Co., 14" h, 7" d shade, reverse painted ribbed shade, winter landscape of black barren trees on snowy ground, blue shading to yellow and orange ground,

Chandelier, Arts and Crafts, brass, five Handel overlay shades, Meriden, CT, early 20th C, square domed ceiling mount above square shaft suspending five square hollow rods and shade mounts supporting hexagonal brass shades with stylized foliate overlay on striated caramel and white slag glass panels, leaves painted green against red ground, two shades retain a metal maker's tag signed "HANDEL," 43" drop, $3,525. Photo courtesy of Skinner Auctioneers and Appraisers.

metal base with raised foliage dec, raised "P.I.B. & Co." 2080" on base **635.00**

Chandelier

Arts & Crafts

18" h, 14-1/2" d, hammered bronze frame with pierced designs, suspending hammered bronze socket holders with four gold Aurene glass shades, c1910............ **1,380.00**

27" h, 32" d six panel, red brass, replaced mica panels, three-light cluster, orig dark patina, period chain and ceiling cap **2,300.00**

Empire-style, 31" l, 20th C, gilt metal and cut glass, six light, top with six outscrolled flat leaves hung with crystals, slender reeded standard with central cut glass orb, flat leaf ring supporting six short serpentine scrolled candle arms offset by pierced ribbon-tied laurel wreaths, strung throughout with crystal strands, end of standard with further crystals . **1,100.00**

French, 32" w, hand wrought iron frame supporting four arms with lavender mottled art glass shades, matching central planfonier, c1925...... **850.00**

Morreau, 20" h, 20" d, gilt and emb iron frame suspending four leaded glass domed shades, central matching spherical shade, frame emb "The Morreau Co."............. **1,100.00**

Muller Fres, 11" h, 21" d, ornate wrought iron frame finely dec with leafage supporting three scrolled arms, white, amethyst, and green mottled shades surrounding matching planfonier, sgd "Muller Fres," c1920 .... **2,450.00**

Desk

Handel, 14-1/4" h, 7-1/4" w, arched pivoting arm ending in pivoting blossom-shaped shade with orig opalescent bent glass panels and faux lead came, bronzed base, marked "HANDEL"............... **1,355.00**

Steuben, 20" h, 7" d, bronze, adjustable, irid hammered glass shade, orig patina, shade sgd "Steuben" **860.00**

Student, 23-1/2" h, brass frame and adjustable arm, white glass shade, early 20th C................ **260.00**

Tiffany, 13-1/2" h, 7" d swirl dec irid green ribbed dome Damascene shade cased to white, marked "L.C.T" on rim, swivel-socket bronze harp frame, rubbed cushion platform, five ball feet,

Desk, Tiffany, counterbalance, 7" green Favrile shade, base and shade signed, $10,640. Photo courtesy of Fontaine's Auction Gallery.

imp "Tiffany Studios New York 419" **3,740.00**

Early American

Betty lamp, 3-1/2" h wrought iron lamp, stamped "M," 4-1/4" h redware stand with incised wavy lines, minor rim chips **440.00**

Blown, colorless, 10" h, drop burners, pressed stepped base, chips on base, pr **385.00**

Cage lamp, 6" d, wrought iron, spherical, self righting gyroscope font, two repaired spout burners **500.00**

Candle holder, 19" h, wrought iron, hanging type, primitive twisted arms and conical socket **385.00**

Candle stand, 57-1/4" h, 24-1/2" w, wrought iron, double arms, brass candleholders and drip pans, attributed to PA, 18th C, pitting, losses to drip pans **8,100.00**

Dietz dainty, 12-1/2" h, brass, orig glass in doors, ring handles, slot for mounting bracket on either side, ruby glass inserts in backs, price for pr **225.00**

Fluid

American, 1860-80, 10-1/2" h, cut overlay, white cut to clear glass pear shaped font, cut oval, punty, and vesica slash cut designs, brass collar and brass standard, sq white marble base, base edges with small chips **300.00**

American, 1870, 9-7/8" h, cut overlay, ruby flashed, cut to clear font, cut trefoils, flowers, and punties, brass collar, ring-turned brass standard, sq stone base with green marbling, paint wear on base **415.00**

Grease, 23" h, wrought and cast iron, circular base, rooster finial, bale top fitted with long hanger, brass ring, old dark pitted surface **450.00**

Hour glass, 7" h, clear blown glass, pine and oak frame, whittled baluster posts, old brown finish, glued break in bottom plate **275.00**

Loom light, 14-3/4" h, wrought iron, candle socket, trammel **500.00**

Miner's lamp, 7-3/8" h, cast and wrought iron, chicken finial, replaced hanger **110.00**

Peg, 2" d, 4-1/2" l, overlay glass, pink cut to white cut to clear, frosted peg attached with clear wafer, brass collar **450.00**

Petticoat, 9" h, tin, round pan base, large ring handle applied to one side of column, small pick and chain attached to handle **260.00**

Rush light holder, 9-1/2" h, wrought iron, candle socket counter weight, tripod base, penny feet, tooled brass disk at base of stem, simple tooling **470.00**

Skater's lamp, 6-3/4" h, brass, clear glass globe marked "Perko Wonder Junior," polished, small splint in top of brass cap **160.00**

Splint holder, 9-1/2" h, wrought iron, candle socket counter weight, tripod base, diamond shaped feet ... **415.00**

Taper jack, 5" h, Sheffield silver on copper, old repairs **195.00**

Early, wrought iron grease lamp, four spouts, iron pedestal base, rivet construction, American, 14-3/4" h, $150. Photo courtesy of Cowan's Historic Americana Auctions.

Floor

Bradley and Hubbard, 56" h, 7" d, small domed leaded glass shade, green slag glass, gold key border, open framework adjustable standard, domed circular foot **400.00**

Faries Mfg. Co., Decatur, IL, 65-1/4" h, 12" d, bright chrome torchere, flaring trumpet shade, diecast mark ... **150.00**

Handel

57-1/2" h, 13" d Steuben shade with irid band, patina loss on base, some dents, unmarked .. **3,105.00**

61" h, 14" d, bronze, adjustable arm, four-sided shade with banded overlay, green and yellow slag glass panels, raised mark **1,840.00**

64" h, 24" d yellow and amber opalescent bent glass paneled shade with faux lead came, green diamond details, five-light, patinated copper columnar base, scrolling feet, marked "HANDEL" on base **9,780.00**

Tiffany/Aladdin, 50" h, 10" d spun bronze shade, reflective white int., marked "Tiffany Studios New York," adjustable bridge lamp base with Arabian Nights motif, orig dark bronze patina, elaborate platform base,

Floor, 58" h harp standard, 10" d Steuben shade with ribbon border, stepped circular base, $3,025. Photo courtesy of Fontaine's Auction Gallery.

stamped "Tiffany Studios New York 576" **2,990.00**

Unknown maker, Brass, 56-1/4" h, brass, hammered surfaces, electric sockets above oval rosettes, reeded columns, curved legs, quatrefoil bases, base stamped "L.C.T. NY 810," price for pr **750.00**

Hanging

American, 19th C, 18" h, patinated metal and cut glass, hall type, candle socket, Gothic arches, diamonds and flowerheads dec **1,380.00**

Arts and Crafts

17" drop, 22-1/2" d, four massive iron cross bars, hand hammered and bronzed surface, support chocolate slag glass shades with brass fleur-de-lis guards, electrified **950.00**

30" drop, 20-1/2" d brass and slag glass shade, linked metal chain suspending shade composed of eight panels of green, caramel, and white bent slag glass panels, dropped apron with emb and cut-out brass border overlay with Dutch windmills, trees, and cottages over band of multicolored slag glass, prisms below . . **920.00**

Handel, 10" d, hall type, spherical form, acid cut, translucent white, brown, vase and foliate dec, ornate orig hardware **4,200.00**

Morgan, John, and Sons, NY, attributed to, 39-1/2" h drop, 25-1/4" d, 11-1/2" h leaded shade, verdigris bronze leaves surrounding ceiling hook suspending four chains supporting six-socket domed shade, similar bronze

Fluid, overlay, red cut to white cut to clear font sets, black glass base with gold trim, small burst air bubble on edge of one quatrefoil, lamp has been electrified, but not drilled, 14-1/4" to top of collar, $1,560. Photo courtesy of James D. Julia, Inc.

Student, brass, double, two-ribbed green cased glass 10" d shades, electrified, 25-1/2" w, 21-1/2" h, $920. Photo courtesy of James D. Julia, Inc.

leaf dec, dropped apron, shade with striated green, amber, and white slag glass segments, round transparent purple "jewels" form grape-type clusters, few cracked segments **6,325.00**

Perzel, 40-1/4" d, chrome, metal, and glass **1,225.00**

Tiffany, 18" l, 15" d, attributed to Tiffany Glass and Decorating Co., late 19th C, square green and opalescent diamond-shaped glass jewels arranged as central pendant chandelier drop, twisted wire frame **2,990.00**

Unknown maker, 22" l, 9-3/4" d, cast iron, open work fixture with fleur-de-lys, three graduated levels of faceted prisms, electrified with reflective surface above light socket **315.00**

Novelty, 21" h, spelter, cast metal, bronzed patina, young man lighting pipe, glowing red filament bulb behind clasped hands, c1900 . . . .**635.00**

Piano

Handel, 17" l, gilt leaded lavender and opalescent yellow leaded shade suspended from bronze base, scrolled arm, unmarked, attributed to, c1915 . . . .**750.00**

Tiffany, 6-3/4" h, 19" l tripartite gold amber glass turtleback shade, framed in bronze, three center gold irid turtleback tiles, single-socket swiveling "dog leg" shaft, shade and weighted base imp "Tiffany Studios New York" **4,025.00**

Table

American, early 20th C

19-1/4" h, 15-1/2" d, 20 radiating caramel and white slag glass panels on domed shade, medial geometric green glass border, alternating green and caramel slag glass border, undulating dropped apron, two-socket fixture, ribbed trefoil base with brown/green patina, minor corrosion, some cracked segments **920.00**

24-3/4" h, 18" d reverse painted shade, hemispherical frosted glass shade, int. painted with trees and foliage silhouetted against yellow-orange shaded sky and water, two-socket bronze patinated cast metal base, raised scroll, foliate, and flower motif, base marked "A & R Co.," minor wear **920.00**

Arts & Crafts, 22" h, 18" d leaded glass shade of variegated caramel and green panels, bronzed base with hammered design **980.00**

Bigelow Kennard, Boston, 26" h, 18" d domed leaded shade, opalescent white segments in geometric progression border, brilliant green leaf forms repeating motif, edge imp "Bigelow Kennard Boston/Bigelow Studios," three

Table lamp, A. Hart, 20" h, 15" d leaded wisteria shade, multiple pieces of purple and blue glass, bell shaped shade, green leaves become denser toward open branch work on top, simple tree trunk base, shade signed "A. Hart 772," $6,160. Photo courtesy of Fontaine's Auction Gallery.

socket over Oriental-style bronze base cast with foo dog handles, Japonesque devices **2,875.00**

Boston Glass Works, early 20th C, 22" h, 18-1/2" d bent panel slag glass shade, floral and foliate overlay, bronze patina over six radiating striated caramel and white bent slag glass panels, two-socket fixture with similar illuminated base, minor patina wear, few dents **750.00**

Bradley & Hubbard, Meriden, CT, early 20th C

19-3/4" h, 15-1/4" d domed eight panel shade, graduating geometric tile and trefoil border overlay, striated yellow, green, and white slag glass, green trefoil painted frosted green glass border panels, four-arm spider on six-sided bronze column, hexagonal base with etched fleur-de-lis and foliage designs, raised "B & H" and "234" on base, imperfections . . **1,150.00**

28" h, 20" d leaded glass shade of variegated green radiating tiles, grape cluster and foliate border, three-light bronzed base with adjustable stem, base emb "Bradley & Hubbard" with triangle mark **2,650.00**

Duffner and Kimberly, New York, 26" h, 24-1/2" d dome leaded glass shade with tuck-under irregular rim, multicolored blossoms with yellow centers, green leaves, long stemmed flowers extending to top on segmented white background, three socket bronze lobed shaft with quatraform shaped base **7,435.00**

Durand, 29-1/2" h, brass, blue glass standard, opaque white and clear feather pattern **300.00**

Handel, Meriden, CT, early 20th

21" h, 16" d leaded glass shade with floral border, shades of green and pink, bronzed base emb "Handel," c1910 . . . . **1,725.00**

21-1/2" h, 14-3/8" h six panel bent glass shade, opalescent glass with green and mauve striations, floral and foliate overlay, red and green painted flowers and leaves, imp "Handel Lamps pat'd no. 979664," three-socket base with geometric scroll dec in relief, imp "Handel" mark, imperfections **1,265.00**

22-1/4" h, 18" d Teroma conical textured glass shade, painted green, light reflective opal white int., inscribed "Handel 5341 GR

Teroma" on rim, imp "Handel Pat'd No. 979684" on metal fitter rim, bronze patinated metal base fitted with fuel canister on ovoid standard, dec with raised band of Art Nouveau-style blossoms and leaves, four bracket feet, base electrified, patina wear, touch-ups **6,325.00**

22-3/4" h, 19-1/2" d grapevine overlay slag domed shade, geometric tile and grapevine border metal overlay, eight striated, green bent slag glass panels, conforming apron, metal "Handel" tag, two-socket ribbed, baluster-form bronze base, metal tag with emb "Handel" affixed to base, one cracked apron segment, joinery **1,955.00**

23" h, 18" d domed shade, multicolored leaded glass segments depicting baskets of fruit on ground of radiating caramel and white striated glass segments, narrow green rim border, metal "Handel" tag, three-socket baluster form metal base with bronze patination, raised "Handel" mark on base, couple cracked segments, minor patina wear **1,380.00**

23-5/8" h, 18-1/4" d conical frosted gray and textured glass shade, ext.

painted with landscape of trees, water, and mountains in distance, shades of blue, purple, rose, and teal, painted "Handel 6527" on int. rim, imp "Handel Pat'd No. 979664" on top of fitter rim, three-socket fixture, urn form base, dark brown patinated metal base with raised leaf blade and bud design, imp "Handel" on base, two shade pulls replaced **6,325.00**

25-1/2" h, 20-1/2" d 12-panel shade, mottled green progressively arranged geometric slag glass segments with border band of red glass segments, metal "Handel" tag, four-socket fixture, matte green glazed vegetal-form pottery base, metal "Handel" tag on metal plate under base, some cracked segments **5,750.00**

28" h, 22" d shade, leaded domed shade, pink and yellow striated glass flower segments arranged on entwining green leafy vine, graduating geometric amber and white striated tile background segments, imp "1933 I 25 Handel" on top shade opening, five-socket base with raised foliate motifs round base, dark brown and green patina, raised "Handel" mark on base **8,050.00**

Table lamp, Pairpoint, 20" h, 15" d reverse painted shade, black and white geese flying in formation over marshy lake, browns, yellows, and pale blues, base signed "Pairpoint, 0307" and "P" in diamond, **$3,360.** *Photo courtesy of Fontaine's Auction Gallery.*

Table lamp, Pairpoint, 22" h, 18" d reverse painted Temple shade, two temples by lake, blues, greens, and browns, cypress tree and cloudy skies, indented gourd shape base with copper finish, beaded foot, signed "The Pairpoint Corp'n," base signed "Pairpoint" and "P" within diamond, and D5058, **$2,240.** *Photo courtesy of Fontaine's Auction Gallery.*

Jefferson, 17" h, 12" d, reverse painted scenic shade with winter scene on textured satin shade, brass candlestick base, unsigned, c1915 .... **460.00**

La Verre Francais, 19" h, cased glass, frosted ext. over swirled orange, yellow, and cobalt blue, sgd on both shade and base, electrified, replaced shade holder **1,350.00**

MB Co., 20-1/2" h, paneled shade, conical base, openwork silverplate grape vine designs, five panels of green and white slag glass, cast leaf finial, engraved leaves on base, base marked "Made and Guaranteed by the MB Co. USA," electrified, five sockets **1,200.00**

Muller Frères, 19-1/4" h, 9-1/2" d round, paneled, etched colorless glass shade with rosette and geometric skyscraper influenced design, wrought iron base, shade sgd "Muller Frères Luneville," France, c1930, several minute rim nicks **1,100.00**

Pairpoint, 20-1/2" h, 11-1/2" d domed closed top mushroom-cap glass shade, Vienna, coralene yellow int., painted stylized olive green leaves and red berries, gold outline on ext., ball-decorated ring supported by four arms, quatraform base molded with

Table lamp, Pairpoint, 25" h, 18" d Windmill shade, shade and matching base painted with windmills, pale shades of blues, greens, and browns, **$5,320.** *Photo courtesy of Fontaine's Auction Gallery.*

Table lamp, Tiffany Studios, 30" h, 25" d Roman Helmet leaded glass shade, Roman Column bronze base with orig rich brown patina, vented cap and six fixtures, shade signed "TIFFANY STUDIOS/NEW YORK/1564," base impressed "TIFFANY STUDIOS/NEW YORK/529," **$28,700.** *Photo courtesy of David Rago Auctions.*

foliate devices, imp "Pairpoint Mfg Co., 3052" **2,070.00**

Pittsburgh Lamp, Brass and Glass Co., Pittsburgh, c1920, model no. 1595, 27" h, 17-3/4" d domed frosted and textured glass shade, interior painted with mountainous landscape, exterior painted with pine trees, paper manufacturer's label affixed to interior, three-socket patinated metal ribbed standard set into weighted metal base, scroll, shield, floral, and foliate motifs in relief, wear to patina **1,955.00**

Suess Ornamental Glass Co., Chicago, 23" h, 22" d leaded glass shade with stylized yellow, orange, green, and white slag flowers and leaves, brass-washed base, unmarked **5,350.00**

Tiffany Studios, 22-1/2" h, 16" d dome shade, layered and striated leaded glass segments designed as tulip blossoms and leaves, red, orange, amber, blue, and green, metal rim tag imp "Tiffany Studios New York 1456," three-socket bronze base with three pronged crutch supporting oval shaft, sq base with mottled brown and green patina, round disk on base imp "Tiffany Studios New York 444" **32,220.00**

Van Erp, Dirk, 17-1/2" h, 13" d, hammered copper classical base, four paneled mica shade with vented cap,

single socket, fine orig patina and mica, open box mark/San Francisco **9,200.00**

Williamson, Richard, & Co., Chicago, 25" h, 20" d peaked leaded glass dome, amber slag bordered by red tulips, pink and lavender-blue spring blossoms, green leaf stems, carved glass, mounted on four-socket integrated shaft with stylized tulip blossoms above leafy platform, imp "R. Williamson & Co./Washington & Jefferson Sts./Chicago, Ill," restored cap at top rim **3,220.00**

LANTERNS

History: A lantern is an enclosed, portable light source, hand carried or attached to a bracket or pole to illuminate an area. Many lanterns have a protected flame and can be used both indoors and outdoors. Light-producing materials used in early lanterns included candles, kerosene, whale oil, and coal oil, and, later, gasoline, natural gas, and batteries.

Barn, 5-1/4" w, 5-3/4" d, 8-3/4" h, mortised wood frame, four panes of glass, bentwood handle, tin cover over top vent, twisted wire latch, old patina, discolored glass in door, minor damage, make-do repaired split on top **825.00**

Candle

10-1/4" w, 9-3/4" l, 16-1/2" h, old red painted pine, rect, pierced top, bentwood handle, four sides with three rect glazed and pierced

Brass, cast, Arts & Crafts, faceted, rustic branch pattern, original white frosted seedy glass panels, original patina, original chains, replaced ceiling plate, unmarked, 7" w, 9-1/2" h, price for pair, **$630.** *Photo courtesy of David Rago Auctions.*

Garden, Bizen ware, stoneware, rustic form with floral piercings, Japan, 19th C, 10-1/2" h, $200. Photo courtesy of Skinner Auctioneers and Appraisers.

panels, door with leather hinges opening to candle socket, New England, 19th C, door appears to be replacement, imperfections **2,415.00**

15-3/4" h, tin, stamped "Parker's Patent, 1855, Proctersville, VT," glass panels on all four sides with wire protectors, peaked top with star cut-outs, large ring handle **525.00**

Dark room, 17" h, orig black paint, white striping, tin kerosene font and burner "Carbutt's Dry Plate lantern, PA April 25th 1882" label **75.00**

Folding, 10" h, tin, glass sides, emb "Stonebridge 1908" **75.00**

Globe, 17-1/2" h, fixed pear-shaped globe, pierced tin frame, ring handle,

Wagon, 16-1/2" h, tin, "Ham's Cold Blast," original flue, C.T. Ham Co., Rochester, NY, $95.

traces of black paint, America, mid-19th C.................. **215.00**

Hall, 26" h, glass and polychrome, gold painted flat leaf top suspending cut glass drops, joined by curved scrolls, suspending ovoid shade formed by five curved colorless glass panels in metal framework topped by ribbon tied laurel branches, accented with faceted bead trim, bead and glass prism trefoils, Italian, late 19th C **2,100.00**

Japanese, Patterson Bros., Lansing, MI, adv, panes with General U. S. Grant, puppies, young girl, and wilderness scene **195.00**

Jeweled, 11-1/2" h, sheet brass, punched designs radiating out from faceted blue, red, green, and pale gold glass jewels, bottom marked "NH Car Trimming Co. New Haven, Conn," ring hanger.................. **250.00**

Miner, 9-3/4" h, heavy duty iron and brass, threaded brass font and hasp, iron top with brass label "Thomas & Williams, Cambria Type…Aberdare," minor dents **115.00**

Nautical, 23" h, 11" d, masthead, copper and brass, oil fired, orig burner, label reads "Ellerman, Wilson Line, Hull," mid-19th C.......... **265.00**

Painted tin, 15-3/4" l, 12" d, 19-3/4" h, triangular black painted tin frame with glass panels, int. mirror paneled reflector, small tin kerosene lamp, glass chimney, America, late 19th C, seam separations **175.00**

Paul Revere Type, 16" h, punched tin, circular punching on door and body, cone top, round handle, light overall pitting.................... **275.00**

Railroad, Pennsylvania Railroad, 5" h red globe, marked "Keystone Lantern Co., Philadelphia," wire ring base **445.00**

Skater, 13-1/2" h, cast iron, lacy base, bulbous clear globe, pierced tin top and wire bail handle **245.00**

Wood, 9-1/2" h, pine, old black over red paint, four sides glass, candle access from top, socket pulled by wire bale handle **690.00**

LEEDS CHINA

History: The Leeds Pottery in Yorkshire, England, began production about 1758. Among its products was creamware that was competitive with that of Wedgwood. The original

factory closed in 1816, but various subsequent owners continued until 1880. They made exceptional cream-colored wares, either plain, salt glazed, or painted with colored enamels, and glazed and unglazed redware.

Marks: Early wares are unmarked. Later pieces are marked "Leeds Pottery," sometimes followed by "Hartley-Green and Co." or the letters "LP."

Reproduction Alert: Reproductions have the same marks as the antique pieces.

Bowl, 8-3/4" d, scalloped edge, green feathered edge.............. **440.00**

Charger, 14-3/8" d, yellow urn with double handles and brown swag design holds cobalt blue, brown, and yellow flowers, green foliage, blue line detail surrounding dec, scalloped blue father edge, in-the-making separation along inner edge, minor glaze flakes **1,870.00**

Chop plate, 11-1/4" d, blue and yellow brown polychrome flowers, green foliage, white ground, blue scalloped feather edge, wear, old chip beneath rim **825.00**

Creamer, yellow, brown, and green tulip, umber and green sprig design on sides, dark brown stripe on rim and applied handle, flakes on table ring **800.00**

Cup and saucer, handleless

Blue, yellow, green, and goldenrod floral design, underglaze blue brushed crescent mark.... **220.00**

Brown rim stripes, blue, green, shades of gold, and yellow floral swag, flakes, chips on saucer table ring, stains on cup **150.00**

Platter, hexagonal, blue feather edge, minor rim flake, 16-1/2" x 13", $80. Photo courtesy of Sanford Alderfer Auction Company.

Cup plate

4" d, round, green feathered edge
.... **150.00**

4-1/4" d, octagonal, green feathered
edge................. **200.00**

Dish, 5-3/4" l, leaf form, green feathered
edge, imp "Rogers"......... **225.00**

Egg cup, 2-3/4", creamware, reticulated
.... **150.00**

Miniature

Creamer and sugar, blue flower,
green and brown buds, tooled
handle on 2-3/4" h creamer, minor
flake on 2-1/2" h sugar **350.00**

Cup and saucer, handleless,
pearlware, gold flower, green and
brown leaves **275.00**

Teapot, cov, 4" h, yellow bands with
green, orange, blue, and brown
sprigs, flakes **450.00**

Mug, 5" h, multicolored polychrome
floral dec **250.00**

Pepper pot, 4-1/2" h, green feathered
edge, roughness, loss on rim and near
holes **200.00**

Plate

8" d, green feathered edge,
patterned design **225.00**

8-1/2" d, green feathered edge, imp
border design of acanthus leaves,
imp "Riley" **200.00**

10" d, green feathered edge, imp
"9," base chip........... **195.00**

Platter

11-1/2" x 11", oval, green feathered
edge, imp mark with crown, crack
in base **125.00**

17-1/4" x 14", oval, green feathered
edge, raised floral and foliage
design in wide border, imp "16,"
wear **600.00**

Platter, blue feathered edge, relief feather design, 17" x 14", $325. Photo courtesy of Sanford Alderfer Auction Co.

19" x 14-1/4", elongated octagonal
form, green feathered edge, rim
wear.................. **525.00**

Sauce boat, underplate, 7-1/2" l,
3-3/4" h sauce boat, 6-1/2" x 5-1/4"
underplate, green feathered edge,
small crack on base, minor edge
roughness.................. **335.00**

Teapot, blue and white leafy decoration, impressed "L. Wood" in bottom, c1820, 7-1/2" h, 11" w, $425.

Teapot, cov, creamware, 4-3/4" h,
intertwined ribbed handle, molded floral
ends and flower finial, polychrome
enameled rose **3,025.00**

Tureen, cov, 8-1/2" h, cov with pierced
rim, melon finial, enamel dec, feather
edge trim, floral sprays and wreaths,
urn designs, late 18th C, slight edge
nicks and enamel flaking **980.00**

Waste bowl, 4-1/4" d, 3" h, blue band,
green, gold, mustard, and black leaves,
minor flakes on table ring..... **110.00**

LEFTON CHINA

History: China, porcelain, and ceramic with that now familiar "Lefton" mark has been around since the early 1940s and is highly sought by collectors in the secondary marketplace today. George Zoltan Lefton, a Hungarian immigrant who arrived in the United States in 1939, founded the company. In the 1930s, he was a sportswear designer and manufacturer, but his hobby of collecting fine china and porcelain led him to a new business venture.

After the bombing of Pearl Harbor in 1941, Lefton aided a Japanese-American friend by helping him to protect his property from anti-Japanese groups. As a result, Lefton came in contact with and began marketing pieces from a Japanese factory owned by Kowa Toki KK. At this time, he embarked on a new career and began shaping a business that sprang from his passion for collecting fine china and porcelains. Though his funds were very limited, his vision was to develop a source from which to obtain fine porcelains by reviving the postwar Japanese ceramic industry, which dated back to antiquity. As a trailblazer, George Zoltan Lefton soon earned the reputation of "The China King."

Figurines and animals, plus many of the whimsical pieces such as the Bluebirds, Dainty Miss, Miss Priss, Angels, Cabbage Cutie, Elf Head, Mr. Toodles, and the Dutch Girl, are popular with collectors. Collectors eagerly acquire all types of dinnerware and tea-related items. As is true with any antique or collectibles, prices vary, depending on location, condition, and availability.

Marks: Until 1980, wares from the Japanese factory include a "KW."

Animal

5", squirrel, bisque **38.00**

8-1/2", tiger, black, white with gold
.... **65.00**

10", koala bear with club ... **180.00**

Bank, 7-1/4" h, Kewpie, orig foil label
"Lefton Exclusives, Japan," stamped
"145" **145.00**

Cake plate, 10" d, server, Hollyberry
.... **45.00**

Candy bowl, 7" d, pastel green,
pearlized bisque finish, fluted gold
edge, cherub dec, #837 ...... **240.00**

Cigarette set, Elegant Rose, five pcs
.... **200.00**

Coffee set, 8-1/2" h coffeepot, creamer,
cov sugar, 4" d coffee cups, 8" d
scalloped plates, green and white
background, deep pink roses, ornate
gilt trim, price for 13-pc set.... **200.00**

Compote, 8-3/16" d, 3" h, Americana
pattern, green mark "940"..... **125.00**

Bluebird pattern, creamer and sugar, $24 each, child's cup, $32, covered butter dish, $95. Photo courtesy of Walter Dworkin.

Cookie jar, cov

Holly, white, No. 6054.......**115.00**

Lady with scarf, 7-1/4" h, pastels,
marked "Geo. Z. Lefton, 1957, 040"
.... **325.00**

Santa Claus, No. 2097, 7-1/4" h
......................**115.00**

Cup and saucer

Christmas Cardinal......... **25.00**

Roses **45.00**

Demitasse cup and saucer, Rose
Heirloom **25.00**

Figure

Flamingo mother watching young, wings wide spread, marked "Lefton's, Occupied Japan" **165.00**

Rock A Bye Baby in the Treetop, 8" h **100.00**

Siamese Dancers, pr, 6-1/2" h **120.00**

Victorian lady, parasol with lace trim, violet blouse, pink lace trim, pink and white skirt with gold accent, #K8692, 8-3/8" h **135.00**

Head vase, 7" h, Kewpie, orig foil label "Lefton Exclusives, Japan," stamped "3631" **135.00**

Jam jar, Americana **65.00**

Miniature lamp, 3-5/8" d, 7-3/4" h, hp red flowers, green leaves, white ground, three gold dec feet, glass chimney with scalloped top, frosting on lower third, orig wick **15.00**

Mug

Hollyberry, 4" **10.00**

Poinsettia, white ground **15.00**

Planter

Angel, on cloud, with stones ..**40.00**

Calico Donkey, 5-1/2" **32.00**

Plate

9" d, Magnolia **28.00**

9-1/4" d, To A Wild Rose **28.00**

Salt and pepper shakers, pr

Fruit Basket, 2-3/4" **24.00**

Rustic Daisy, 6-3/4" **24.00**

Sugar, cov, Rose Chintz **175.00**

Tea cup and saucer, ftd, Elegant Rose **45.00**

Teapot

Festival **145.00**

Grape Line **85.00**

Honey Bee **125.00**

Wall plaque

Boy and Girl, oval, bisque, pr **120.00**

Santa's Room, Memories of Home, 6-1/2" **35.00**

LENOX CHINA

History: In 1889, Jonathan Cox and Walter Scott Lenox established The Ceramic Art Co. at Trenton, New Jersey. By 1906, Lenox formed his own company, Lenox, Inc. Using potters lured from Belleek, Lenox began making an American version of the famous Irish ware. The firm is still in business.

Marks: Older Lenox china has one of two marks: a green wreath or a palette. The palette mark appears on blanks supplied to amateurs who hand painted china as a hobby. The Lenox company currently uses a gold stamped mark.

Bouillon cup and saucer, Detroit Yacht Club, palette mark **85.00**

Chocolate set, cov chocolate pot, six cups and saucers, Golden Wheat pattern, cobalt blue ground, 13-pc set **275.00**

Coffee set, Rhodora pattern, 8-1/8" h coffeepot, creamer, sugar, 17-1/2" l platter **675.00**

Cream soup, Tuxedo, green mark **40.00**

Cup and saucer, Alden **25.00**

Dinner set, Cattail, 40 pcs, eight-pc place settings, c1959 ....**520.00**

Honey pot, 5" h, 6-1/4" d underplate, ivory beehive, gold bee and trim **85.00**

Jug, 4" h, hp, grapes and leaves, shaded brown ground, sgd "G. Morley" **250.00**

Figure, The Reader, done in Meissen style, lady in 18th C dress, book on her lap, green Lenox/USA stamp, 5" d, 5-1/2" h, **$525.**

Mug, 6-1/4" h, monk, smiling, holding up glass of whine, shaded brown ground, SS rim **160.00**

Perfume lamp, 9" h, figural, Marie Antoinette, bisque finish, dated 1929 ....**650.00**

Salt, 3" d, creamy ivory ground, molded seashells and coral, green wreath mark **35.00**

Shoe, white, bow trim **190.00**

Tea set, cov teapot, creamer, cov sugar, Hawthorne pattern, silver overlay **225.00**

Ten cups, 12 saucers, Monticello pattern, transfer printed, pre-1932, black stamps, **$325.**

Vase, ovoid vase, attributed to William Morley, pre-1932, large pink tea roses, green Lenox stamp, 8" d, 18-3/4" h, **$2,400.**

Urn, hand painted, decorated by one of Lenox's best artists, Sigmund Werkner, c1905, portrait of Empress Josephine, heavy floral and ribbon gilding on green ground, purple CAC/Lenox stamp, Josephine, and artist signature, possible restoration to handle, 8" d, 10" h, $975. Photos courtesy of David Rago Auctions.

Tea strainer, hp, small pink roses
. . . . **70.00**

Vase, 11-3/4" h, 4-1/2" d, corset shape, pink orchids dec by William Morley, green stamp mark, artist sgd . . **850.00**

Vase, ovoid vase, attributed to William Morley, pre-1932, large pink tea roses, green Lenox stamp, 8" d, 18-3/4" h, $2,400.

LIBBEY GLASS

1896–1906

History: Edward Libbey established the Libbey Glass Company in Toledo, Ohio, in 1888 after the New England Glass Works of W. L. Libbey and Son closed in East Cambridge, Massachusetts. The new Libbey company produced quality cut glass, which today is considered to belong to the brilliant period.

For more information, see this book.

In 1930, Libbey's interest in art-glass production was renewed, and A. Douglas Nash was employed as a designer in 1931.

The factory continues production today as Libbey Glass Co.

Art glass

Bell, 5-3/4" h, colorless, acid etched dec "1893 World's Fair," circular logo surrounded by acid-etched florals and banners, shoulder int. molded "1893 World's Columbian Xposition" (sic), twisted frosted handle with star at top, metal clapper **25.00**

Bud vase, 12" h, amberina, shape 3004, c1917, sgd in polished pontil
. . . . **1,400.00**

Compote, 10-1/2" w, 4" h, colorless, pink Nailsea-type loops, flaring top, sgd "Libbey" **595.00**

Cream pitcher, peachblow, made by Mount Washington Glass Company and sold by Libbey at 1893 Chicago World's Fair – The Columbian Exposition, minor loss to gold signature, 2-5/8" h, $585. Photo courtesy of Clarence and Betty Maier.

Amberina, compote, Inverted Thumbprint pattern, applied amber foot with acid etched insignia, 6-1/4" d, 4-1/4" h, $920. Photo courtesy of James D. Julia, Inc.

Creamer and sugar, 5-3/8" h creamer, 3-1/2" h, 4-3/4" d sugar, crystal, blue-green opaque dot trim, dark blue-green glass feet, polished pontil
. . . . **475.00**

Spooner, Maize, orig paint, slight rim roughness **65.00**

Vase, 4-1/4" h, ftd, red, vertical blue-gray dots form lines, swirled vertical ribs, unfinished pontil . . **775.00**

Cut glass

Banana boat, 13" x 7" x 7", scalloped pedestal base, 24-point hobstar, hobstar, cane, vesica, and fan motifs, sgd **1,500.00**

Bowl, 8" d, 4" h, three brilliant cut thistles surround bowl, flower in center, scalloped edge, etched "Libbey" label, price for pr. **400.00**

Candy dish, cov, 7", divided, clover shape, hobstar and prism, sgd. . **90.00**

Charger, 14" d, hobstar, cane, and wreath motifs, sgd. **300.00**

Miniature lamp, 2" sq base, 10-3/8" h, pinwheel design, sgd **425.00**

Tumble-up, star burst, hobstar, fern, and fan motifs, minor handle check
. . . . **725.00**

Vase
5" d, 10" h, sgd, c1910-20 . . **475.00**
18" h, No. 982, Senora pattern, cut glass, ftd, hexed vesicas, deep miter cuts, three 24-point hobstars at top between crossed miter cuts, small stars and trellises, clear knob and stem, scalloped foot cut with extended single star, Libbey over saber mark, c1896-1906, some flaws. **2,500.00**

Wine, Harvard pattern, faceted cut knob stems, sgd, 12-pc set . . . **350.00**

LIMOGES

History: Limoges porcelain has been produced in Limoges, France, for more than a century by numerous factories, in addition to the famed Haviland.

Marks: One of the most frequently encountered marks is "T. & V. Limoges," on the wares made by Tressman and Vought. Other identifiable Limoges marks are "A. L." (A. Lanternier), "J. P. L." (J. Pouyat, Limoges), "M. R." (M. Reddon), "Elite," and "Coronet."

Berry set, 9-1/2" d, master bowl, eight 8" serving bowls, hp, purple berries on ext. white blossoms on int., marked "T & V" 265.00

Bowl, 4-1/2" h, ftd, hp, wild roses and leaves, sgd "J. E. Dodge, 1892" . 85.00

Box, cov, 4-1/4" sq, cobalt blue and white ground, cupids on lid, pate-sur-pate dec 195.00

Cache pot, 7-1/2" w, 9" h, male and female pheasants on front, mountain scene on obverse, gold handles and four ball feet 225.00

Cake plate, 11-1/2" d, ivory ground, brushed gold scalloped rim, gold medallion, marked "Limoges T & V" 75.00

Candy dish, 6-1/2" d, ftd, two handles, silver overlay, white ground, c1920 . . . . 95.00

Chocolate pot, 13" h, purple violets and green leaves, cream-colored ground, gold handle, spout, and base, sgd "Kelly JPL/France" 350.00

Creamer and sugar, cov, 3-1/4" h, purple flowers, white ground, gold handle and trim 100.00

Cup and saucer, hp, roses, gold trim, artist sgd 75.00

Dessert plates, 8-1/4" d, Laviolette, gilt scalloped rim, printed green husk trim, center violet and grape sprays, retailed

Fish and game set, 13 pieces, 24" x 10" serving platter, 12 9" d plates, hand-painted decoration of fish in pond, game flying overhead, scalloped borders, gilt decoration, one plate repaired, $2,300. Photo courtesy of Sanford Alderfer Auction Company.

by Lewis Straus & Sons, New York, late 19th/early 20th C, price for 12-pc set 220.00

Dresser set, pink flowers, pastel blue, green, and yellow ground, large tray, cov powder, cov rouge, pin tray, talc jar, pr candlesticks, seven-pc set . . 425.00

Figure, 25" h, 13" w, three girls, arms entwined, holding basket of flowers, books, and purse, marked "C & V" and "L & L" 460.00

Hair receiver, blue flowers and white butterflies, ivory ground, gold trim, marked "JPL" 80.00

Lemonade pitcher, matching tray, water lily dec, sgd "Vignard Limoges" 350.00

Mortar and pestle, 3-1/4" x 2" mortar, 3-1/2" l pestle, hp flowers gold trim, deep rose ground, marked "GL, Halga, Decor Main, Paris, France, Limoges" 95.00

Mug, corn motif, sgd "T & V Limoges France" 65.00

Nappy, 6" d, curved gold handle, gold scalloped edges, soft pink blossoms, blue-green ground 35.00

Oyster plate, 9-1/4" d, molded, scalloped edge, gilt rim, enamel dec of poppy sprays, raised gilt detailing, marked "A. Lanternier & Co., Limoges," early 20th C, price for set of eight 1,500.00

Panel, 4-1/2" x 3-3/8", enameled, Christ with crown of thorns, framed . . . 250.00

Oyster plates, each with floral design and well painted blue, yellow, magenta, pink, or red-orange, gilt rims, marked "Limoges/A.K./France," 8 1/2" d, $950. Photo courtesy of Sanford Alderfer Auction Company.

Plate, white ground, gold border, center with two ladies in garden setting being serenaded by troubadour, marked "Triumph, Made in USA, Limoges, China D'or, Warranted 22 K Gold," $15.

Plate, white ground, gold border, center with two ladies in garden setting being serenaded by troubadour, marked "Triumph, Made in USA, Limoges, China D'or, Warranted 22 K Gold," $15 each.

Vase, bulbous, pink ground, floral garlands, gilt highlights and rim, distributed by Bailey, Banks, and Biddle, Philadelphia, loss to rim gilt, 4" h, $75. Photo courtesy of Sanford Alderfer Auction Co.

Pitcher, 6" h, 5-1/8" d, platinum handle, platinum mistletoe berries and leaves, gray and pink ground, Art Deco style, marked "J. P. Limoges, Pouyat" **155.00**

Plaque, 7-5/8" x 4-1/2", enameled, cavalier, after Meissonier, multicolored garb and banner, late 19th C .. **460.00**

Plate
8" d, transfer scene of peacocks and flowers, hp border **290.00**
9-1/2" d, Cavalier smoking pipe, marked "Coronet". **90.00**

Punch bowl, 14" d, hand painted grapes, marked "T& V Limoges France Depose," minor repairs **320.00**

Snuff box, cov, hp, wildflowers and gold tracery, pink ground, artist sgd, dated 1800 . . . . **200.00**

Tankard set, 14" h tankard, four mugs, hp, grape dec, gold and green ground, five-pc set **450.00**

Tea set, 9-1/2" h cov teapot, two 3" h cups, two 4-1/2" d saucers, 15" d tray, cream ground, floral dec, gold trim, red stamp "L. S. & S. Limoges France," green stamp "Limoges France" on two saucers, slight wear **500.00**

Vase, 15" h, hand painted, sgd "Florence Sladnick". **350.00**

LITHOPHANES

History: Lithophanes are highly translucent porcelain panels with impressed designs. The designs result from differences in the thickness of the plaque; thin parts transmit an abundance of light, while thicker parts represent shadows.

Lithophanes were first made by the Royal Berlin Porcelain Works in 1828. Other factories in Germany, France, and England later produced them. The majority of lithophanes on the market today were made between 1850 and 1900.

Candle shield, 9" h, panel with scene of two country boys playing with goat, castle in background **275.00**

Cup and saucer, gold, brown, and beige dragon dec, Geisha girl in base **75.00**

Fairy lamp, 9" h, three panels, lady leaning out of tower, rural romantic scenes **1,250.00**

Lamp, 20-3/4" h, colored umbrella style shade, four panels of outdoor Victorian scenes, bronze and slate standard, German **675.00**

Night lamp, 5-1/4" h, sq, four scenes, irid green porcelain base, gold trim, electrified **650.00**

Panel
PPM, 3-1/4" x 5-1/4", view of Paterson Falls **190.00**
PR Sickle, 4-1/4" x 5", scene of two women in doorway, dog, and two pigeons, sgd, #1320 . . . . . . **100.00**
Unmarked, 6" x 7-1/2", Madonna and Child **175.00**

Pitcher, puzzle type, Victorian scene, nude on bottom **175.00**

Stein, regimental, half liter **200.00**

Tea warmer, 5-7/8" h, one-pc cylindrical panel, four seasonal landscapes with children, copper frame, finger grip and molded base **250.00**

Gas lamp, four scenic removable panels, cube shape, pewter-colored metal holder, 4-1/2" x 5-1/2", $195. Photo courtesy of Woody Auctions.

Plaque, Suitor, imp "RPM, #22," c1860, 5-1/4" x 4-3/8", $175.

LIVERPOOL CHINA

History: Liverpool is the name given to products made at several potteries in Liverpool, England, between 1750 and 1840. Seth and James Pennington and Richard Chaffers were among the early potters who made tin-enameled earthenware.

By the 1780s, tin-glazed earthenware gave way to cream-colored wares decorated with cobalt blue, enameled colors, and blue or black transfers.

Bubbles and frequent clouding under the foot rims characterize the Liverpool glaze. By 1800, about 80 potteries were working in the town producing not only creamware, but soft paste, soapstone, and bone porcelain.

Reproduction Alert: Reproduction Liverpool pieces were documented as early as 1942. One example is a black transfer-decorated jug made in the 1930s. The jugs vary in height from 8-1/2 to 11 inches. On one side is "The Shipwright's Arms"; on the other, the ship Caroline flying the American flag; and under the spout, a wreath with the words "James Leech."

A transfer of the *Caroline* also was used on a Sunderland bowl about 1936 and reproduction mugs were made bearing the name "James Leech" and an eagle.

The reproduction pieces have a crackled glaze and often age cracks have been artificially produced. When compared with genuine pieces, reproductions are thicker and heavier and have weaker transfers, grayish color (not as crisp and black), ecru or gray body color instead of cream, and crazing that does not spiral upward.

Bowl, creamware

10-1/2" d, transfer printed and painted polychrome enamel dec, Hope with three-masted ship flying two American flags, six figural reserves on int., three transfer country scenes on ext., red enameled rim, repaired....**815.00**

10-7/8" d, black transfer printed and polychrome enamel dec, int. with British sailing ship, red, white, blue, gold, and green enamels above inscription "James and Sarah Venn Bridgewater, 1796," rim dec with military devices, outside with vignettes of "Poor Jack," and "Billy's Farewell," sea creatures and mermaids, imperfections...**560.00**

11-3/8" d, black transfer printed, polychrome enamel dec, int. with American sailing vessel *Apollo*, border of military devices, ext. with nautical themes, coat of arms, vignette of lovers holding heart, above inscription "J. & S. Appleton," green, yellow, red, white, and blue enamels, imperfections.........**5,875.00**

Cup and saucer, handleless, black transfer, bust of Washington and other

Jug, creamware, black transfer printed, obverse "Washington," oval design with medallion portrait on monument surmounted by wreath, birth and death dates below, flanked by eagle and grieving woman, upper ribbon inscribed "Washington in Glory," lower ribbon "America in Tears"; reverse transfer of American sailing vessel, American eagle beneath spout, imperfections, 10-1/4" h, $1,295. Photo courtesy of Skinner's Auctioneers and Appraisers.

gentleman on cup, "Washington, His Country's Father" on saucer, hairlines in cup **330.00**

Jug, creamware

7-1/4" h, 3-1/2" d, transfer printed, obverse with compass and verse, reverse with The Sailors Adieu, minor imperfections......**750.00**

8" h, black transfer printed and polychrome dec, obverse with American eagle holding banner in his beak inscribed "E. Pluribus Unum," sky with 16 stars bordered by semicircle of clouds; reverse with three-masted American sailing vessel dec in red, white, blue, green, and gold enamels, monogram in wreath beneath spout, imperfections.....**750.00**

8" h, black transfer printed, obverse American eagle surrounded by ring chain inscribed with names of 15 states, reverse with two-masted American sailing vessel, American eagle beneath spout, minor imperfections.........**2,465.00**

8" h, 4" d, transfer printed, obverse with The Sailor's Return, reverse with courting couple above verse "A Sailor's life's a pleasant life…" on other, motto reserve below spout "From Rocks & Sands and every ill…" imperfections..**550.00**

8-1/8" h, black transfer printed, obverse "O. Liberty thou Goddess!," poem in oval, bordered by wreath of olive leaves surrounded by entwined ribbon containing names of 15 states, reverse with stern view of sailing ship, American eagle beneath spout, imperfections....**1,100.00**

8-1/4" h, 4-1/2" d, transfer printed, obverse with eagle and shield, reverse with Independence with "as he tills your rich globe…" stanza, imperfections....**1,150.00**

8-5/8" h, 4-3/8" d, transfer printed and painted with polychrome enamels, obverse with Tom Truelove Going to Sea, reverse with three-masted ship with "Success to Trade" banner below, oval reserve of three figures by lake with "Peace to all Nations" below the spout, remnants of gilt lettering reading "John Frank" below that, imperfections.........**1,100.00**

8-3/4" h, black transfer printed and polychrome dec, obverse American Militia, oval scenic

reserve with militiaman with flag, ships, and armament, surrounded by inscription, reverse with American sailing vessel above banner inscribed "Success to Trade," American eagle with Jefferson quote, dated 1802 under spout, red, blue, green, and yellow enamels, yellow highlight around rim, minor imperfections .**3,525.00**

8-3/4" h, black transfer printed, "L. Insurgent and Constellation, Feb 10, 1799," depicting naval battle with American frigate on left, French frigate on right, inscription beneath each, reverse "Shipbuilding," oval wreath inscribed "Success to the Wooden Walls of America" beneath spout, imperfections.........**1,650.00**

8-3/4" h, black transfer printed, obverse "Shipbuilding," circular print with timber and logging operations above horizontal panel with verse, ship-building scene below, reverse with three-masted sailing vessel, American eagle beneath spout, imperfections **1,000.00**

8-3/4" h, 4-3/4" d, transfer printed, obverse with Commodore Prebels Squadron Attacking the City of Tripoli Aug. 3, 1804, reverse with Salem Shipyard scene and verse, eagle and shield below spout, imperfections **2,300.00**

8-3/4" h, 5-1/4" d, transfer print, obverse with Apotheosis of Washington, reverse with three-masted ship flying American flag, repaired...........**920.00**

9" h, black transfer printed, obverse with Tom Truelove Going to Sea, two lovers on shore, sailing ship in background, reverse with British three-masted sailing ship, three men in rowboat beneath spout, imperfections **700.00**

9" h, 4-3/4" d, transfer printed, obverse with Washington, Liberty, and Franklin viewing map of early 19th C US, reverse with three-masted ship painted with polychrome enamels, eagle and shield, standing figure of Hope below spout, imperfections.**990.00**

9-1/8" h, 5" d, transfer printed, obverse with Commodore Preble, reverse with Commodore Prebles Squadron Attacking the City of

Tripoli Aug. 3 1804, imperfections **2,185.00**

9-1/4" h, 4-5/8" d, transfer printed and painted with polychrome enamels, obverse with Hope, reverse with three-masted ship flying American flag, American eagle below spout with Jefferson quote, dated 1804, imperfections **3,740.00**

9-1/2" h, black transfer printed and painted, polychrome enamels, obverse "Boston Fusiliers," depicting officer in full uniform, holding Massachusetts flag within oval inscribed top "Aut Vincere Aut Mori," and at bottom "Success to the Independent Boston Fusiliers, Incorporated July 4th, 1787. America for ever," Masonic devices surmount design; reverse "Union," oval design with allegorical figures of Liberty, Justice, and Peace above inscription "United We Stand - Divided We Fall," above figures in oval, design surrounded by wreath with 16 stars, surmounted by American eagle, floral device beneath spout, 2" base chip, very minor discoloration and enamel losses, provenance includes small group of letters and accompanying material regarding legend that in 1790 a wealthy Boston Fusiliers officer ordered a limited number of these specially dec pitchers for each member of the company **11,165.00**

9-1/2" h, 4-1/2" d, transfer printed and painted with polychrome enamels, obverse with Boston Fusilier, reverse with "United We Stand, Divided We Fall," eagle and shield below spout, imperfections **17,250.00**

9-3/4" h, black transfer printed, obverse "By Virtue And Valour We Have Freed Our Country, Extended Our Commerce And Laid The Foundation Of A Great Empire" inscribed in a ribbon, depicting Continental soldier standing with his foot on head of British Lion, soldiers and sailing ship in background, scene surrounded by military devices; reverse with design of American warship, beneath the spout an oval cartouche with young boy and his rooster, base rim broken and repaired, two chips to spout, two

cracks to body, one to base of handle, transfers and glaze wear, small areas of discoloration **425.00**

10" h, 5" d, transfer printed and painted with polychrome enamels, obverse with Proscribed Patriots, reverse with "Success to America whose Militia...," eagle and shield with Jefferson quote dated 1802 below spout, repaired ... **3,220.00**

10" h, 5-1/4" d, transfer printed, obverse with Peace, Plenty, and Independence, reverse with three-masted ship, eagle and shield below spout, imperfections **920.00**

Jug, creamware, black transfer printed and painted, polychrome enamels, obverse "Boston Fusiliers," depicting officer in full uniform, holding Massachusetts flag within oval inscribed top "Aut Vincere Aut Mori," and bottom "Success to the Independent Boston Fusiliers, Incorporated July 4th, 1787. America for ever," Masonic devices surmount design; reverse "Union," oval design with allegorical figures of Liberty, Justice, and Peace above inscription "United We Stand – Divided We Fall," above figures in oval, design surrounded by wreath with 16 stars, surmounted by American eagle, floral device beneath spout, 2" base chip, very minor discoloration and enamel losses, provenance includes small group of letters and accompanying material regarding legend that in 1790 a wealthy Boston Fusiliers officer ordered a limited number of these specially decorated pitchers for each membossseder of the company, 9-1/2" h, $11,165. Photo courtesy of Skinner's Auctioneers and Appraisers.

10-1/4" h, black transfer printed, obverse "Washington," oval design with medallion portrait on monument surmounted by wreath, birth and death dates below, flanked by an eagle and grieving woman, upper ribbon is inscribed "Washington in Glory," lower ribbon "America in Tears"; reverse transfer of American sailing vessel, American eagle beneath spout, imperfections **1,295.00**

10-1/4" h, 4-7/8" d, transfer printed, obverse with Salem Shipyard and verse, revere with transfer printed with polychrome enamels of Boston Frigate, transfer "LW" in cartouche above eagle and shield, imperfections **4,890.00**

10-1/2" h, black transfer printed and polychrome, obverse "Washington," portrait surrounded by three female figures, Justice, Liberty, and Victory, cherub above, scrolling ribbon inscribed with names of 15 states and stars surround oval reserve, reverse with American three-masted sailing vessel dec in red, white, blue, yellow, and green enamels, monogram within wreath above American eagle beneath spout, traces of gilt and black highlights, minor imperfections **3,055.00**

10-1/2" h, black transfer printed, obverse with mortally wounded officer surrounded by his aides, successful sharpshooter waves his cap from background, reverse with British Man-of-War, beneath spout and rim dec with floral devices, imperfections **1,650.00**

Jug, Commodore Prebler Squadron attacking City of Tripoli, Aug. 3, 1805, 6-5/8" h, $675.

11-1/2" h, 5-3/4" d, transfer printed, obverse with three-masted ship, reverse with The Joiners Arms, eagle and shield below spout, repaired **865.00**

11-3/4" h, 6-5/8" d, transfer printed, obverse with ship *Massachusetts*, reverse with map of Newburyport Harbor with "Success to the Commerce of Newburyport" on other, gilt embellishments, circular reserve of Columbia, minor imperfections **14,950.00**

14-1/4" h, 6-1/4" d, transfer printed and painted with polychrome enamels, obverse with Hope on one side "Her lefs'ning boat u willing rows to land," reverse with three-masted ship flying American flag, below spout with transfer scenes around rim and base, motto reserve "From Rocks & Sans and ever ill May god preserve The Sailor still" below handle, gilt highlights, imperfections . **6,325.00**

Jug, pearlware, 6-1/4" h, black transfer printed, obverse with American eagle with ribbon in its beak, inscribed "E. Pluribus Unum," 15 scattered stars above it's head, reverse with vignette of embracing couple, fleet of sailing vessels below spout, rim dec with scattered blossoms, black enamel highlights on rim, shoulder, and handle edges, minor imperfections . . **1,120.00**

Jug and plate, 4-7/8" d, 8" h, creamware, jug transfer printed with Poor Jack on one side, "The Engagement between the Nymph 32 Guns 240 Men and the Cleopatra…" on other, garland and grape design below spout, plate with Poor Jack transfer dec **980.00**

Plate, 10" d, black transfer printed, 10 are dec with sailing vessels, one inscribed "Returning Hopes" with lady waiting for return of her lover's ship, minor imperfections, price for 11 pc set **1,570.00**

Sauce boat, 5-3/4" l, oval, paneled sides, underglaze blue floral dec, attributed to Pennington & Part, c1780 . . . . **460.00**

Tureen, cov, 12-1/4" d, 9-1/2" h, domed cov with oval handle, round base, black transfer dec on lid, int., and ext. depicting figure flanked by two coat-of-arm shields, two monograms "TF" and "BW" within oval, imperfections **1,100.00**

LOETZ

For more information, see this book.

History: Loetz is a type of iridescent art glass that was made in Austria by J. Loetz Witwe in the late 1890s. The Loetz factory at Klostermule produced items with fine cameos on cased glass, good quality glassware for others to decorate, as well as the iridescent glasswares more commonly associated with the Loetz name.

Marks: Some pieces are signed "Loetz," "Loetz, Austria," or "Austria."

Atomizer, 7" h, cameo, lemon yellow ground overlaid in blue, cameo cut leafy stemmed cockle shell flowers, sgd "Loetz" in cameo, c1910, no stopper **435.00**

Bowl, 3-5/8" x 6", 3-1/2" h, oblong, folded over and pinched rim, irid green threading on irid white body, etched label "Loetz Austria," minor frit specks on int. **250.00**

Candlestick, 15-1/2" h, irid finish, base chip **115.00**

Center bowl, 10" d, Onyx, dec . **395.00**

Compote, 10-5/8" d, 5-1/4" h, bright orange int., deep black ext., white flaring circular rim, three ball feet, c1920 . . . . **310.00**

Bowl, ruffled, pink oil spots, figural lily-of-the-valley holder, unsigned, 7", **$200.** *Photo courtesy of Woody Auctions.*

Cup, 3-3/4" d, round bowl, gold and polychrome irid, applied handle, incised "Loetz Austria" **290.00**

Inkwell, 3-1/2" h, amethyst, sq, irid, web design, bronze mouth **125.00**

Oil lamp, 19-1/2" h, 9-1/2" d, globular shade, bulbous base, all over irid oil-spot dec, orig brass fittings **3,000.00**

Pitcher, 6" h, irid green body, ground pontil, applied colorless handle, c1910 . . . . **100.00**

Rose bowl, 6-1/2" d, ruffled purple irid raindrop dec **265.00**

Sweetmeat jar, cov, 5" h, irid silver spider web dec, green ground, sgd **450.00**

Urn, 9-1/4" h, ovoid, irid, blue oil spot dec, inscribed "Loetz, Austria" **1,600.00**

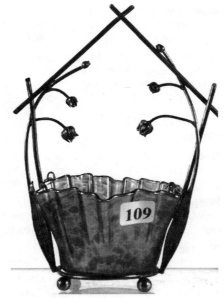

Sweetmeat jar, green base, maroon striping, sterling silver lid, square handle, signed "Loetz, Austria," 4-3/4" w, 5-1/4" h, **$200.**

Vase, octopus, brown glass with air trapped scrolls, gold enamel highlights, pink interior, 10" h, **$2,300.** *Photo courtesy of James D. Julia, Inc.*

Vase

2-3/4" h, amber shading to rose ground, green oil spot irid finish, irid blue horizontal leaves and trailings, c1910 . . . . **2,100.00**

3-3/4" h, gray ground, deep amethyst irid finish, blue oil spot dec, c1910 . . . . **865.00**

4" h, deep cobalt blue ground, irid patches of silvery blue dec, c1915 . . . . **435.00**

7-1/2" h, yellow ground, horizontal panels of undulating gold irid, c1910 . . . . **1,035.00**

8" h, amber irid ground, cranberry draped loops, overall gold oil spot finish **635.00**

8" h, textured green ground, overlaid in deep purple, wheel carved stemmed tulip, etched "L. A. Loetz AC68," c1900 . . . . **610.00**

10-1/2" h, 6" w, bulbous swirl, applied shell handles, Rainbow, white lining, gold trim, cased in crystal, pink, yellow, and blue irid surface, pr **675.00**

15-1/4" h, 8-1/2" d, Papillion, lustered gold, purple, and green . . . **750.00**

Wall sconce, three-light, brass, three bulbous opalescent shades with oil-spot pattern, green chain pattern, replaced brass parts, few minor nicks to top rim of one shade **690.00**

LUSTER WARE

History: Lustering on a piece of pottery creates a metallic, sometimes iridescent, appearance. Josiah Wedgwood experimented with the technique in the 1790s. Between 1805 and 1840, lustered earthenware pieces were created in England by makers such as Adams, Bailey and Batkin, Copeland and Garrett, Wedgwood, and Enoch Wood.

Luster decorations often were used in conjunction with enamels and transfers. Transfers used for luster decoration covered a wide range of public and domestic subjects. They frequently were accompanied by pious or sentimental doggerel, as well as phrases that reflected on the humors of everyday life.

Copper luster was created by the addition of a copper compound to the glaze. It was very popular in America during the 19th century, and collecting it became a fad from the 1920s to the 1950s. Today it has a limited market.

Using a gold mixture made pink luster. Silver luster pieces were first covered completely with a thin coating of a "steel luster" mixture, containing a small quantity of platinum oxide. An additional coating of platinum, worked in water, was then applied before firing.

Sunderland is a coarse type of cream-colored earthenware with a marbled or spotted pink luster decoration, which shades from pink to purple. A solution of gold compound applied to the white body developed the many shades of pink.

The development of electroplating in 1840 created a sharp decline in the demands for metal-surfaced earthenware.

Reproduction Alert: The market for copper luster has been softened by reproductions, especially creamers and the "polka" jug, which fool many new buyers. Reproductions are heavier in appearance and weight than the earlier pieces.

Canary, cup and saucer, black transfer print of women and children at piano, black rim, $265.

Canary

Child's mug, 1-3/4" h, "A Present for Charles," pink luster trim, minor wear **625.00**

Miniature, creamer, 2-3/4" h, red and green flowers, pink luster accents and rim, pinpoint flake **850.00**

Pitcher, 6-1/4" l, 6" h, baluster form, low neck and spout, sides printed with scenes titled "Attempt before the guard...," On Guard, Single Stick, Staffordshire, c1810 . . . . **220.00**

Copper

Goblet, 3" d, 3-3/4" h, mauve and green colored band with floral dec around mid section, c1850 . . . . **85.00**

Pitcher, 4" h, blue band with molded flower dec on both sides, copper luster bulbous base **50.00**

Planter, 4-1/4" d, 3-3/7" h, three ftd, kettle shape **25.00**

Tea cup and saucer, turquoise blue background, copper luster floral band **65.00**

Vase, 7-1/4" w, 6-1/2" h, two handles, stag scene **70.00**

Copper, pitcher, painted schoolhouses on light blue band, English, mid-19th C, minor scratches, 5-1/2" h, $95. Photo courtesy of Cowan's Historic Americana Auctions.

Pink

Child's mug, 2" h, pink luster band, reddish hunter and dogs transfer, green highlighted foliate transfer **85.00**

Creamer, 4-3/8" h, stylized flower band, pink luster highlights and rim, ftd **75.00**

Cup and saucer, magenta transfers, Faith, Hope, and Charity, applied green enamel highlights, pink luster line borders **60.00**

Figure, 4-1/2" h, dogs, white, luster gilt collar, cobalt blue base with gilt trim, Staffordshire, pr **620.00**

Pitcher, 5-3/4" h, emb ribs, eagle, and flowers in pink and purple luster **150.00**

Plate

7-3/4" d, green transfer of "Employ time well," emb floral border with polychrome enamel and luster trim **75.00**

9-3/4" d, painted flowers and leaves, pink, purple, and yellow, green and red overglaze **45.00**

Plaque, 9-3/8" l, 8-3/8" h, rect, "The Great Eastern Steam Ship," black transfer with polychrome, pink luster shaped border **450.00**

Posset cup and saucer, tray, 5" h, wide luster bands flanked by two red bands, 19th C **295.00**

Punch bowl, 10" d, black transfer print, "The Shipwright's Arms" on int., pink luster borders on ext., imperfections **120.00**

Teapot, 12" h, House pattern, Queen-Anne style, repaired finial on lid **285.00**

Toddy plate, 5-1/16" d, pink luster House pattern, emb floral sprigs border **45.00**

Waste bowl, 6" d, House pattern **125.00**

Silver, milk pitcher, black transfer printed Greek mythological characters, include Lepyrus, Cupid, and woman carving Lepyrus' name on tree on one side, luster painted borders and floral spray, reverse with peasant woman with wheelbarrow of market frits, being harassed by small dog, tugging at her skirt, C-shaped handle, tiny in-the-making glaze loss, 6-1/2" h, $345. Photo courtesy of Cowan's Historic Americana Auctions.

Silver

Coffee service, 7-3/8" h cov coffeepot, cov sugar bowl, six coffee cans and saucers, silver luster grape and leaves, rust enamel accents, yellow ground **450.00**

Creamer, 4" h, 5" w, ribbed loop base, incised band near top, shaped handle **85.00**

Cup and saucer, handleless, overall floral band on cup, scattered florals on saucer **45.00**

Figure, 11-7/8" l, standing lion, paw on globe, rect base, early 19th C, repaired **900.00**

Goblet, 4-3/8" h, silver luster grapes and vines, white ground, lustered foot **220.00**

Jug
5-1/2" h, blue printed hunting scene, border of flowers and leaves, luster ground, Staffordshire, c1815 . . . . **975.00**
6-1/2" h, shell detail, minor wear **100.00**

Pitcher, 5-1/2" h, squatty body, wide lip, overall silver luster, 19th C **95.00**

Spill vase, 4-1/8" h, gray marbleized applied vines and fruits, silver luster accents, white int., pr **95.00**

Teapot, 5-1/4" h, reeded detail . . **140.00**

Sunderland

Bowl, 8-1/4" d, polychrome highlighted black transfers of ship and verse, pink marble luster, mid-18th C **265.00**

Creamer, 5" h, "The Sailor's Tear," outlined in florals, verse with sailing ship and "May Peace and Plenty...," luster trim **275.00**

Jug, pearlware7" h, two oval reserves with black transfer printed portraits, "Captain Hull of the Constitution" and "Pike-be always ready to die for your country," imperfections **5,750.00**
8-3/4" h, God Speed the Plow, black and white printed transfer of farmer's coat of arms flanked by farmer and wife, surrounded by various symbols in agricultural setting, hand colored with polychrome enamels, reverse with inspirational verse, oval reserve beneath spout sgd "Mary Hayward Farmer Sandhurft Kent," embellished with pink luster and floral dec, imperfections . **1,150.00**
9-3/8" h, black transfer printed, pink luster and polychrome enamel dec, obverse British ship under full sail, verse in cartouche "May Peace and Plenty On Our Nation Smile and Trade with Commerce Bless the British Isle," reveres with verse in floral wreath "The Sailor's Tear," Mariner's Compass flanked by British ships under spout, imperfections **650.00**
9-3/8" h, black transfer printed, pink luster and polychrome enamel dec, obverse "The Sailor's Farewell," reverse with sailor's verse, panel under spout inscribed "George Henry Page Born Sept. 7th, 1800, Charlotte Page Born Feb," imperfections **3,290.00**

Sunderland, pitcher, pink ship and description, green and copper bands on top and handle, spout repaired, chipped, $350. Photo courtesy of Joy Luke Auctions.

10-1/8" h, black transfer printed, pink luster dec, obverse "A West View of the Iron Bridge over the Wear under the Patronage of R. Burdon Esq. M. P.," reverse with inspirational verse in floral wreath, pouring handle beneath spout and sailing vessel transfer, inscription "Auther Rutter 1840," minor imperfections **1,650.00**

Mug, 5" h, black transfer of compass on front, "The Sailor's Farewell" on reverse **160.00**

Mustard pot, 4" h, loop handle . **150.00**

Pitcher, 7-1/8" h, hex panels, black transfers of John Wesley on one side, verse on other, pink marble luster, c1850 . . . . **150.00**

Plaque, 8-1/2" l, 7-1/2" w, "Thou God Seeist Me," luster trim, Dixon mark **175.00**

Plate, 10" d, center transfer print of Pike and "Be always Ready to Die for your Country," pink luster and yellow banded border, c1820 . . . . **2,650.00**

Salt, master, Cloud pattern, ftd . . **50.00**

MAJOLICA

History: Majolica, an opaque, tin-glazed pottery, has been produced in many countries for centuries. It was named after the Spanish Island of Majorca, where figuline—a potter's clay—is found. Today, however, the term "majolica" denotes a type of pottery was made during the last half of the 19th century in Europe and America.

Majolica frequently depicts elements of nature: leaves, flowers, birds, and fish. Designs were painted on the soft-clay body using vitreous colors and fired under a clear lead glaze to impart the rich color and brilliance characteristic of majolica.

Victorian decorative art philosophy dictated that the primary function of design was to attract the eye; usefulness was secondary. Majolica was a welcome and colorful change from the familiar blue and white wares, creamwares, and white ironstone of the day.

Marks: Wedgwood, George Jones, Holdcraft, and Minton were a few of the English majolica manufacturers who marked their wares. Most of their pieces can be identified through the English Registry mark and/or the potter-designer's mark. Sarreguemines

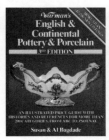

For more information, see these books.

in France and Villeroy and Boch in Baden, Germany, produced majolica that compared favorably with the finer English majolica. Most Continental pieces had an incised number on the base.

Although 600-plus American potteries produced majolica between 1850 and 1900, only a handful chose to identify their wares. Among these manufacturers were George Morely, Edwin Bennett, the Chesapeake Pottery Company, the New Milford-Wannoppee Pottery Company, and the firm of Griffen, Smith, and Hill. The others hoped their unmarked pieces would be taken for English examples.

Adviser: Mary D. Harris.

Note: Prices listed below are for pieces with good color and in mint condition. For less-than-perfect pieces, decrease value proportionately according to the degree of damage or restoration.

Reproduction Alert: Majolica-style pieces are a favorite of today's interior decorators. Many exact copies of period pieces are being manufactured. In addition, fantasy pieces incorporating late Victorian-era design motifs have entered the market and confused many novice collectors.

Modern majolica reproductions differ from period pieces in these ways: (1) modern reproductions tend to be lighter in weight than their Victorian ancestors; (2) the glaze on newer pieces may not be as rich or deeply colored as on period pieces; (3) new pieces usually have a plain white bottom, period pieces almost always have a colored or mottled bases; (4) a bisque finish either inside or on the bottom generally means the piece is new; and (5) if the design prevents the piece from being functional—e.g., a lip of a pitcher that does not allow proper pouring—it is a new piece made primarily for decorative purposes.

Some reproductions bear old marks. Period marks found on modern pieces include (a) "Etruscan Majolica" (the mark of Griffen, Smith and Hill) and (b) a British registry mark.

Basket

English, oblong, turquoise ground, pink flowers, pink interlaced double strap looking handles, 13" l. **500.00**

Rustic, brown and green, bark, 9" x 8" **325.00**

Bread tray

Corn, brown, yellow, and green, 11" x 13" **550.00**

Wheat, "Eat Thy Bread with Thankfulness," cobalt blue center, 13" x 11" **450.00**

Wild Rose, cobalt ground, pink flowers, 11" x 14" **375.00**

Butter pat

Cobalt blue ground, pink flowers in center **135.00**

Copeland pansy, yellow and cobalt blue **140.00**

Etruscan, maple leaf center, pink ground **125.00**

Etruscan, Pond Lily, pink, green, and yellow **100.00**

Ruffled leaf, brown, green, and yellow **95.00**

Cake stand

English, Pond Lily, lily top, three storks in relief on base, 9" d, 6" h **450.00**

George Jones, leaf on napkin, white ground, 9" w, 6" h **450.00**

Wedgwood, green leaf, green ground, 8" d, 2-1/2" h **125.00**

Candlestick, figural

Palmer Cox Brownie, 8-1/2" h **250.00**

Wardle, water lily form, all green **125.00**

Cheese keeper, cov

English, brown ground, green holly leaves, pink, white berries, 10" d, 7-1/2" d **675.00**

Wedgwood, white ground, colorful mums design, 8" d, 7" h . . . **350.00**

Compote

Basketweave turquoise ground, yellow center, maple leaf center, 9" w, 5" h **200.00**

Pineapple, yellow, green, 8" d, 4-1/2" h **275.00**

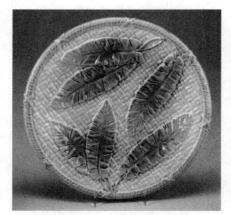

Bread plate, Victorian, probably English, c1880, naturalistically colored banana leaves, yellow rope border, cream-color basketweave ground, hairline crack, 12-1/4" d, **$150.** *Photo courtesy of David Rago Auctions.*

Cake plate, Maple leaf pattern, rustic stem, Etruscan, c1875, impressed monogram, 9-1/4" d, **$175.** *Photo courtesy of David Rago Auctions.*

Cup and saucer

English, Shell and Waves, red, yellow, fish handle **150.00**

Etruscan, Shell and Seaweed **225.00**

Minton, cobalt blue ground, green pond lily **1,500.00**

Humidor, cov, figural

Devil head, 6" h **85.00**

Frog, pink jacket, 7-1/2" h. . . **275.00**

Owl, 7-1/4" h **200.00**

Match striker, Continental

Boy playing mandolin. **125.00**

Elephant **250.00**

Parrot **275.00**

Mug

Art Nouveau, lady's head **50.00**

Etruscan, Pond Lily. **200.00**

Oyster plate, Minton, turquoise ground, seven wells **1,000.00**

Pitcher

English, Fern and Bamboo, brown ground, green leaves, 9" h**. 250.00**

Dessert plate, Daisy, Victorian, c1880, green, yellow, brown and white glazes, 8-1/2" d, **$100.** *Photo courtesy of David Rago Auctions.*

Dessert plate, Bird and Fan pattern, Wedgwood, dated 1879, pale blue ground, impressed marks, date code, 9" d, $175. Photo courtesy of David Rago Auctions.

Eureka, Bird and Fan, triangle shape, white ground, pink, blue, yellow, and gray, 7" h **275.00**

Figural, owl, brown and green, 7" h **225.00**

Sharkskin, floral and bow white ground, two bouquets of flowers, 7" h **225.00**

Wedgwood, Bird and Fan, white ground, 6" h **200.00**

Plate

Choisy Le Roi, bunny, 9" d . . . **250.00**

English, Fern and Floral, green, pink, and blue, 9" d **175.00**

French Salins, asparagus plate, with napkin, 9-1/2" d **175.00**

K & C St. Clement, fruit plate . . **75.00**

Leaf shape, red and green, 8-1/2" x 11" **175.00**

Fish plate, Argenta, Wedgwood, dated 1880, three fish and aquatic foliage in naturalistic color, impressed marks, date code, 8-1/4" d, $150. Photo courtesy of David Rago Auctions.

Dessert plate, Strawberries, George Jones, c1870, pale blue ground, painted design number 3363, 8" d, $350. Photo courtesy of David Rago Auctions.

Palm leaf and basketweave, cobalt blue, yellow, and green, 9" d **200.00**

Wanopee, lettuce leaf, 9" d . . **125.00**

Platter

Clover-leaf shape, fox, yellow ground, green ivy **350.00**

French Palissy Avesseau, many reptiles in relief **2,500.00**

Luneville, artichoke and asparagus platter, 11" x 14", blues, greens **250.00**

Strawberry and bows, 10" x 13" oval, basketweave ground **275.00**

Sardine box, cov, figural fish on top

Pineapple, yellow, green . . . **375.00**

Wedgwood, mottled brown, green **300.00**

Spittoon, Etruscan, Shell and Seaweed **600.00**

Pitcher, blossom design, Etruscan, c1875, cobalt blue ground, butterfly molded lip, imp full roundel and design number, 6-3/4" h, $175. Photo courtesy of David Rago Auctions.

Conservatory stool, French Choisy-Le-Roi, c1880, in Japanese taste, prunus blossoms panels, cobalt blue ground, yellow rope borders, 18" h, $1,400. Photo courtesy of David Rago Auctions.

Syrup, pewter top

Fish, cobalt blue, 7" h **350.00**

Etruscan, pink sunflower **750.00**

Pineapple, yellow, green, 6-1/2" h **225.00**

Teapot, cov

Etruscan, Bamboo, green, yellow, and brown, 6-1/2" h **225.00**

Etruscan, Bird and Bamboo, cobalt blue, rect shape **350.00**

MAPS

History: Maps provide one of the best ways to study the growth of a country or region. From the 16th to the early 20th century, maps were both informative and decorative. Engravers provided ornamental detailing, such as ornate calligraphy and scrolling, especially on bird's-eye views and city maps. Many maps were hand colored to enhance their beauty.

Maps generally were published as plates in books. Many of the maps available today are simply single sheets from cut-apart books.

In the last quarter of the 19th century, representatives from firms in Philadelphia, Chicago, and elsewhere traveled the United States preparing county atlases, often with a sheet for each township and each major city or town.

Notes: Although mass produced, county atlases are eagerly sought by collectors. Individual sheets sell for $45 to $95. The atlases themselves can usually be purchased in the $250 to $500 range. Individual sheets should be viewed solely as decorative and not as investment material.

A Map of North America, Edward Wells, London, 1700, double page, engraved, wide margins, 355 x 480 mm **635.00**

A Map of the British Empire in America, from the Head of Hudson's Bay to the Southern bounds of Georgia, London, c1750, engraved, folding, hand colored and in outline, wide margins, 265 x 325 mm **260.00**

Americae Nova Tabula, Willem Blaeu, Amsterdam, 1633, double page, engraved, wide margins, 365 x 465 mm
. . . .**2,990.00**

A New and Accurate Map of the World, John Overton, London, 1670, engraved, folding, double-hemispheric, margins trimmed, 390 x 515 mm
. . . .**8,625.00**

A New Map of Nova Scotia, Thomas Jeffreys, London, 1750, double page, engraved, very wide margins, all edges tissue-backed on verso, 325 x 415 mm
. . . . **220.00**

A Plan of the Town and Chart of the Harbour of Boston, London, February, 1775, engraved, folding, extracted from 1775 issue of *Gentleman's Magazine*, 290 x 350 mm **220.00**

Asia, Giovanni Botero, Rome, c1595, small double page, engraved, trimmed margins, 205 x 245 mm **300.00**

Bay of Seven Islands, J. F. Des Barries, London, 1779, double page, engraved, hand colored, lower margin trimmed, 765 x 545 mm **115.00**

British Dominions in America agreeable to the Treaty of 1763, Thomas Kitchin, Dury, London, 1777, double page, engraved, hand colored in outline, wide margins, 445 x 540 mm
. . . .**6,440.00**

Canada et Louisiane, George Louis Le Rouge, Paris, 1755, double page, engraved, wide margins, hand colored in outlined, 625 x 510 mm **375.00**

Capt James Lane Property, Bedford, MA, 1773, watercolor and ink on paper, shows distances, boundaries, and 223 acres, divided between sons James and Samuel in accordance with last will and testament, "Surveyed and divided by Stephen Davis, Surveyor of Lands," 12-3/4" x 30-1/2", laid down on muslin, creases and separations, tears, fading, staining **150.00**

City of Atlanta, Georgia, 1880s, hand colored, 14" x 11". **65.00**

Cruchley's New Plan of London, George Frederick Cruchley, London, 1836, engraved, 30-section map, hand colored, linen backed, orig board cover with publisher's label, 460 x 855 mm overall **175.00**

Custer's Battle-Field, Charles Becker, c1877, folding, lithographed, 420 x 475 mm. **220.00**

Eastern Hemisphere, Western Hemisphere, Anthony Finley, Philadelphia, 1826, from *Finley's New General Atlas,* engraved, hand colored, wide margins, 315 x 250 mm, pr. **60.00**

Haemisphaerium Stellatum Astrale Antiquum, Andres Cellarius, Amsterdam, 1660, double page, engraved celestial map, hand colored, wide margins, clear tear at vertical fold at lower margin just extending into image, 440 x 515 mm. **2,530.00**

Jamaica, John Thomson, Edinburgh, 1817, double page, engraved, two insets showing harbors of Bluefields and Kingston, wide margins, hand colored in outline, 440 x 630 mm. **320.00**

Map of Oregon and Upper California, John Charles Fremont, Washington, 1848, folding, lithographed, hand colored in outline, overall browning, 905 x 755 mm **2,185.00**

Map of the United States and Territories, Washington, 1866, litho, folding, hand colored in outline, some minor loss at folds, linen backed, 775 x 1,450 mm **550.00**

Marshfield, Massachusetts, litho on paper, John Ford Jr., Survenor, [sic] framed, 30" x 21-1/2" **345.00**

Minnesota & All of Unsettled Dakota Territory, Colton, 1855, hand colored, 17" x 14" **95.00**

Northern America, including Russian Alaska, entire British Possessions & Danish Iceland, Colton, 1857, hand colored, 17" x 14" **95.00**

Ohio, A J. Johnson, New York, with view of capitol building in corner, from "*New Illustrated Family Atlas of the World 1864,*" printed, hand colored, matted, unframed, 23" h, 29" w **75.00**

Canada, titled, "This Map of Upper and Lower Canada and United States Contiguous Contracted from the Manuscript survey of P.F. Tardieu is Respectfully Inscribed by the Publics Most Obedient Servant Thomas Kensells," ribbon banner above this title cartouche reads "To The Officers of The Army of the Citizens of The United States," hand colored and drawn, mounted in modern black finished wood frame, 16" x 20", $880. Photo courtesy of Cowan Historic Americana Auctions.

North America, hand colored, by Vaugondi, 1772, mounted, framed, some surface toning, 16" x 12-1/2", $495. Photo courtesy of Sanford Alderfer Auction Company.

Survey Map, Jericho, New York or Vermont, showing lands owned by Henry Allen, several homesteads in the area, pen and ink, hand colored, 1794, imperfections, 28-1/2" x 30". **575.00**

United States of America, W. and D. Lizars, London, c1810, engraved, folding, hand colored, margins trimmed, several folds closed at lower edge with archival tape, 395 x 460 mm
. . . . **260.00**

MARBLEHEAD POTTERY

History: This hand-thrown pottery was first made in 1905 as part of a therapeutic program introduced by Dr. J. Hall for the patients confined to a sanitarium located in Marblehead, Massachusetts. In 1916, production was removed from the hospital to another site. The factory continued under the directorship of Arthur E. Baggs until it closed in 1936.

Most pieces found today are glazed with a smooth, porous, even finish in a single color. The most desirable pieces have a conventional design in one or more subordinate colors.

Bulb bowl, 6" d, slate gray glaze, c1915 . . . . **160.00**

Centerpiece bowl, 3-3/4" h, 8-1/4" d, flaring, incised lotus leaf design on ext., dark blue matte glaze, imp sip mark
. . . . **425.00**

Chamberstick, 4" h, 4-1/2" d, bright yellow matte glaze, imp ship mark
. . . . **275.00**

Humidor, 5" h, 4-1/4" d, lightly modeled stylized dark blue flora, speckled sandy ground, rare large paper label, Arthur

Vase, curved rim, widening at base, mottled lavender semi-matte glaze, impressed mark, c1915-36, 6" h, $650. Photo courtesy of Skinner Auctioneers and Appraisers.

Baggs, marked "AEB and MHC/$5.00" **4,100.00**

Tile, 6" sq, cuerda seca, polychrome trees and house, matte gray ground, mounted in period frame, ship mark, remnant of paper label, restoration to Y-shaped crack **1,725.00**

Bulbous, speckled brown matte glaze, impressed ship mark, 4-1/4" d, 3-1/4" h, $375. Photo courtesy of David Rago Auctions.

Vessel, squat, smooth dark blue matte glaze, impressed ship mark, 4-1/4" d, 3-1/2" h, $475. Photo courtesy of David Rago Auctions.

Vase, ovoid, smooth matte lavender glaze, impressed ship mark, couple of minor burst bubbles, 3-1/4" d, 5-1/4" h, $375. Photo courtesy of David Rago Auctions.

Tile frieze, two 7-1/2" sq tiles, incised lake scene, matte yellow, browns, and greens, imp mark, paper label, orig price tag on each, orig frame retaining sticker marked "o. 2-64 tiles Poplars with Reflections, Dec by A. E. Baggs, Price $10.00," minor edge nicks, kiln pops, from estate of Dr. Hall, founder of Marblehead Pottery **21,850.00**

Trivet, 6" sq, stylized flowers, matte blue, green, yellow, and red, imp mark, paper label, remnant of price label, from estate of Dr. Hall, founder of Marblehead Pottery **865.00**

Vase

2-3/4" d, 4-1/4" h, cabinet, tapering, designed by Arthur Baggs, dec by Hannah Tutt, incised chevron pattern, two-tone mottled matte green glaze, imp ship mark, artist's cipher **5,350.00**

Vase, beaker shape, brown gooseberry leaves, indigo branches, dark blue ground, impressed ship mark, 5" d, 6" h, $1,955. Photo courtesy of David Rago Auctions.

Vase, barrel shape, blue and gray band of flying geese, speckled gray ground, remnant of impressed ship mark, drilled bottom, 6" d, 6-1/4" h, $4,025. Photo courtesy of David Rago Auctions.

3-3/4" d, 4-1/2" h, cylindrical, incised stylized holly branches, green leaves, red berries, dark blue matte ground, imp ship mark . . **6,275.00**

4" d, 8-3/4" h, cylindrical, carved band of stylized palm fronds, gunmetal under speckled matte green ground, ship mark. **5,350.00**

4-1/4" d, 6-1/4" h, geometric, lightly tooled, stylized light brown trees, matte speckled sand-colored ground, imp ship mark . . **4,750.00**

5" d, 6" h, beaker shape, brown gooseberry leaves, indigo branches, dark blue ground, imp ship mark **1,955.00**

6" h, curved rim, widening at base, mottled lavender semi-matte glaze, imp mark, c1915-36 . . . . . . **650.00**

6" d, 6-1/4" h, barrel shape, blue and gray band of flying geese, speckled gray ground, remnant of imp ship mark, drilled bottom **4,025.00**

8" d, 6-1/4" h, fan shape, matte blue glaze, imp mark, paper label **320.00**

Wall pocket, 5-1/4" w, 5" h, speckled gray ext., robin's egg blue int., unmarked **295.00**

MATCH SAFES

History: Pocket match safes are small containers used to safely carry matches in one's pocket. They were first used around the 1840s. Match safes can be found in various sizes and shapes, and were made from numerous materials such as sterling, nickel-plated brass, gold, brass, ivory, and vulcanite.

Some of the most interesting and sought after ones are figurals in the shapes of people, animals, and anything else imaginable. Match safes were also a very popular advertising means from 1895-1910, and were used by both large and small businesses.

Note: While not all match safes have a striking surface, this is one test, besides size, to distinguish a match safe from a calling card case or other small period boxes. Values are based on match safes being in excellent condition.

Adviser: George Sparacio.

Reproduction Alert: Reproduction, copycat, and fantasy match safes abound. Reproductions include Art Nouveau styles, figural/novelty shapes, nudes, and many others. Fantasy and fakes include Jack Daniel's and Coca-Cola.

A number of sterling reproduction match safes are marked "925" or "Sterling 925." Any match safe so marked requires careful inspection. Many period, American match safes have maker's marks, catalog numbers, 925/1000, or other markings. Period English safes have hallmarks. Beware of English reproduction match safes bearing the "DAB" marking. Always verify the date mark on English safes.

Check enameled safes closely. Today's technology allows for the economic faking of enamel motifs on old match safes. Carefully check condition of enameling for telltale clues.

A Midsummer Night's Dream, by Goldsmiths and Silversmiths Co., sterling, 1-5/8" x 1-3/8"....... **300.00**

Advertising, stamp combo, double lid, by August Goertz & Co., aluminum, 2-5/8" x 1-3/8" **85.00**

Agate, black, brown, white banded agate, brass trim, engine turned design, push button lid release, abrasive striker inside lid, 2-3/4" x 1" **75.00**

Anheuser Busch logo, red and blue enamel on G. Silver, 2-3/4" x 1-1/2" **350.00**

Aluminum, brite cut design, double lid, stamp combo, by August Goertz Co., patent #484,092, 2-5/8" x 1-3/8" **350.00**

Arabian man motif, by Aikin Lambert Co., sterling, 2-3/4" x 1-3/4".... **350.00**

Automobile, three passengers, floral edge design, by E & J Bass, sterling, 2-1/2" x 1-1/2" **450.00**

Baby, in blanket, figural brass face, marked "GESETLICH GESCHUTZT," (German for protected by patent), nickel plated brass, 1-1/4" x 1-1/2" **300.00**

Anheuser Busch logo, red and blue enameling on G. Silver, 2-3/4" x 1-1/2", $350. Photo courtesy of George Sparacio.

Baden Powell, wearing scout hat, figural, nickel-plated brass, 1-7/8" x 1-1/2" **350.00**

Bartholomay Beer, winged wheel logo, by Barstow & Williams, silver plated, 2-1/2" x 1-1/2" **100.00**

Biscuit, figural, adv for Huntley & Palmer, orig paint on brass, 2-1/8" d **125.00**

Black Cat Cigarettes, multicolored celluloid on top, trick, nickel plated brass, 2" x 2-1/2"............. **475.00**

Book shape, golf motif on one side, cricket motif on other, vulcanite, 2" x 1-1/2" **200.00**

Bowler Bros., Tadcaster Ale, multicolored celluloid wrap, plated brass ends, 2-3/4" x 1-1/2" **85.00**

Boxing glove, figural, sterling, 1-5/8" x 1-1/8" **800.00**

BPOE

Dropped forged elk head, enameled clock in antlers, glass eyes, by

Baby in blanket, figural, brass case, marked "GESETLICH GESCHUTZT" nickel-plated brass, 1-1/4" x 1-1/2", $300. Photo courtesy of George Sparacio.

Fairchild & Johnson, sterling, 2-1/4" x 1-7/8"............... **250.00**

Fob type, red, white, and blue enameled clock, by Simons Bros. & Co., sterling, 2-5/8" x 1-1/2" **275.00**

Bull, standing, figural, brass, 2-5/8" x 1-7/8"..................... **300.00**

Burgyus Company, steam shovel motif, black and white graphics, celluloid wrapped, plated brass ends, 2-1/2" x 1-1/2" **325.00**

Business card, by Sampson Mordon & Co., enameled on sterling, English hallmarks, 1-1/4" x 2-1/4"...... **500.00**

Channel Fleet at Blackpool, nickel plated, enameled lettering, 1-7/8" x 1-1/2"..................... **75.00**

Charlie's Aunt, Dec. 21st, 1895, by Walker & Hall, sterling, 1-3/4" x 1-3/8" **225.00**

Cherry tree motif, by Wallace, silver plate, 2-1/2" x 1-1/2" **150.00**

Cherubs, nine faces along edges, sgd "Unger Bros.," sterling, gold wash int., 2-1/2" x 1-3/4" **375.00**

Cigars, bunch of four, marked "Havana," nickel-plated brass, 2-3/4" x 1-1/2"..................... **225.00**

Clown, French type pierrot, figural, nickel plated brass, 2-1/2" x 1-1/2" **400.00**

Combination, coin and stamp holder, pick, propelling pencil, engraved dec, by Wm Neale, sterling, 2-1/2" x 1-1/2" **175.00**

Dog, figural, by Gorham Mfg Co., silver plated, 1" x 2-1/8" **300.00**

Drunken revelers, by Gorham Mfg Co., silver plated, 2-3/8" x 1-5/8".... **400.00**

Eagle head, figural, brass, glass eyes, 1-1/4" x 2-3/8" **200.00**

Elephant, figural

Reclining, Japanese, painted brass, 1-1/2" x 2-5/8" **475.00**

Standing, nickel-plated brass, ivory tusks, 2-1/8" x 1-5/8"...... **225.00**

Envelope, figural, enameled stamp, sterling, 2-1/4" x 1-1/4" **350.00**

Firemen's Fund, 1905, sterling emblem on brass, by Shreve & Co., 2-1/2" x 1-3/4" **375.00**

Flask, figural, top nickel-plated brass, bottom glass, 2-3/4" x 1-3/8" ... **150.00**

Gamewell Fire Alarm, insert type by Augusts Goertz Co., nickel plated brass, red painted design, 2-3/4" x 1-1/2"..................... **400.00**

Horse with rider, country motif, nickel plated brass, crimped edges, 2-7/8" x 1-1/4"..................... **40.00**

Hunter Baltimore Rye, multicolored graphics, celluloid wrapped, by Whitehead & Hoag, 2-3/4" x 1-1/20" **135.00**

Indian chief, sgd "Unger Bros.," sterling, 2-1/4" x 1-7/8" **1,100.00**

Jurogin, holding staff and scroll, Japanese, brass, 2-5/8" x 1-1/2". **500.00**

Kappa, figural, mythological Japanese figure, by Gorham Mfg Co., silver plated, 2-1/4" x 1-1/2" **400.00**

King George V, figural, nickel-plated brass, 2" x 1-5/8" **325.00**

Lady, in boat, by James E. Blake Co., sterlinE, 2-1/4" x 1-3/8" **85.00**

Lady, sitting on potty, painted design, cover marked "Guide," book shape, leather and brass, 1-5/8" x 1-1/4" **425.00**

Leonardt & Co., pen points, book shape, gold lacquered tin, 2-1/8" x 2-5/8" x 3/4" **85.00**

Lion, reposing position, figural, nickel plated brass, 1-3/8" x 3" **250.00**

Molassine, advertising, nude and pig, colored graphics, celluloid wrapped, 2-3/4" x 1-1/2" **135.00**

Molassine Livestock Food, steer on one side, multicolored celluloid wrapped, nickel-plated ends, 2-1/2" x 1-1/2" **85.00**

Mussel shell, fluted, figural, brass, 2" x 1-1/8" **100.00**

Mythological figure, Japanese, patinated brass, 2-5/8" x 1-1/2" . **500.00**

National Lead Co., advertising, multicolored logo, celluloid wrapped, 2-3/4" x 1-1/2" **115.00**

Oriental, lady holding lantern, working compass, brass, 2-1/2" x 1-1/4" **300.00**

Parker, double compartment, candle, patent 6/4/1867, unpainted tin, slip top, 2-3/4" x 1-1/4" **175.00**

Queen Victoria, In Memoriam, design outlined in gold gilt, book shape, vulcanite, 2" x 1-1/2" **75.00**

RCA, soft tone needles, striker on bottom, aluminum, 1-1/2" x 1-7/8" **50.00**

Red Man, fraternal, insert type, by August Goertz Co., nickel-plated brass, 2-3/4" x 1-1/2" **75.00**

Red Top Rye, orig white and red highlights, thermoplastic, 2-7/8" x 1-1/8" **115.00**

Sailboat motif, sterling, 2-1/2" x 1-5/8" **275.00**

Sorrento ware, inlaid with image of boy, wood, 2-7/8" x 1-3/8" **125.00**

St. Louis World's Fair, enameled official flag on lid, by August Goertz Co., nickel-plated brass, pillbox type, 1-5/8" x 2-1/2" **65.00**

Telescopic, image of semi-nude female, paper-board, 2-3/8" x 1-5/8" **250.00**

The Wave, nude in wave, by Unger Bros., sterling, 2-1/2" x 1-7/8" . . **175.00**

Toby dog, figural, nickel plated brass, 2-3/8" x 1" **325.00**

US Cartridge, advertising, by Reed and Barton, silver plated, 2-7/8" x 1-1/2" **265.00**

United Hatters, multicolored graphics, celluloid wrapped, by Whitehead & Hoag, 2-3/4" x 1-1/2" **100.00**

Venus Rising, by Wm Kerr, sterling, 2-3/4" x 1-5/8" **275.00**

Village motif, raised figures, made by the "lost wax process," cylindrical, brass, 2-5/8" x 1" **135.00**

Winged car, advertising Velocity Oil, by August Goertz Co., insert type,

nickel-plated brass, 2-3/4" x 1-1/2" **175.00**

Wishbone and cherubs, by Wm Kerr & Co., sterling, 2-5/8" x 1-1/2" **225.00**

McCoy Pottery

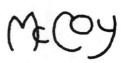

History: The J. W. McCoy Pottery Co. was established in Roseville, Ohio, in September 1899. The early McCoy company produced both stoneware and some art pottery lines, including Rosewood. In October 1911, three potteries merged, creating the Brush-McCoy Pottery Co. This firm continued to produce the original McCoy lines and added several new art lines. Much of the early pottery is not marked.

In 1910, Nelson McCoy and his father, J. W. McCoy, founded the Nelson McCoy Sanitary Stoneware Co. In 1925, the McCoy family sold their interest in the Brush-McCoy Pottery Co. and started to expand and improve the Nelson McCoy Co. The new company produced stoneware, earthenware specialties, and artware.

Marks: The Nelson McCoy Co. made most of the pottery marked "McCoy."

Reproduction Alert: Unfortunately, Nelson McCoy never registered his McCoy trademark, a fact discovered by Roger Jensen of Tennessee. As a result, Jensen began using the McCoy mark on a series of ceramic reproductions made in the early 1990s. While the marks on these recently made pieces copy the original, Jensen made objects that were never produced by the Nelson McCoy Co. The best-known example is the Red Riding Hood cookie jar, originally designed by Hull, and also made by Regal China.

The McCoy fakes are a perfect example of how a mark on a piece can be deceptive. A mark alone is not proof that a piece is period or old. Knowing the proper marks and what was made in respect to forms, shapes, and decorative motifs is critical in authenticating a pattern.

Additional Listings: See *Warman's Americana Collectibles* for more examples.

Bean pot, cov, Suburbia Ware, brown, blue lid **48.00**

Cookie jar, cov
    Aunt Jemima **275.00**
    Bobby Baker **95.00**
    Bugs Bunny, cylinder, 1971-72 . . . . **185.00**
    Cauliflower Mammy **900.00**
    Chairman of the Board, 10-1/2" h **795.00**
    Chef, "Cookies" on hat band . . **85.00**
    Clown, bust, c1943 . . . . **95.00**

Cherubs, nine faces along edges, signed "Unger Bros," sterling, gold wash int., 2-1/2" x 1-3/4", $375. Photo courtesy of George Sparacio.

Padlock, sterling silver, English, c1882, 1-3/4" h, $285.

Jardinière, green, brown, and gold, embossed lion's heads and columns, 5-3/4" d, 5-1/4" h, unmarked, $45.

Clown in Barrel, marked "McCoy USA," c1953-56, overall crazing 145.00
Davy Crocket, 10" h, c1956 . 325.00
Engine, black 175.00
Jack-O-Lantern, orange and green 600.00
Kangaroo with Joey, 12" h . 525.00
Kittens, basketweave base, 10-1/2" h 1,285.00
Little Red Riding Hood, 10-1/2" h 650.00
Panda, upside down, Avon label in heart logo on paw 150.00
Rooster, shades of brown, light tan head, green highlights 225.00
Squirrel 225.00
Touring Car, 6-1/2" h, marked "McCoy USA," c1962-64 . . 155.00

Low bowl and flower frog, polychrome squeezebag decoration, turtle on flower frog, swastikas on bowl, unmarked, tight hairline, small rim chip, 7" d, 2-3/4" h, $460. Photo courtesy of David Rago Auctions.

Creamer and sugar, Sunburst . . 120.00
Decanter set, Jupiter 60 Train, Central Pacific locomotive, c1969 . . . . . 350.00
Flower pot, saucer, hobnail and leaf 40.00
Hanging basket, Pine Cone Rustic 45.00
Jardinière, green, emb fern motif 65.00
Jardinière pedestal, 16-1/4" h, Onyx glaze, sgd "Cusick," c1909 . . . . 400.00
Lamp base, 14" h, cowboy boots, c1956 . . . . 150.00
Mug, corn 90.00
Pitcher, Hobnail, pastel blue, 48 oz 120.00
Planter
   8" h, three large pink chrysanthemums, marked "McCoy" 155.00
   12" l, Hunting Dog, No Fishing on sign 275.00
Spoon rest, 8" l, yellow, foliage, 1940s, overall crazing 145.00
Strawberry jar, 12" h, stoneware 150.00
Tankard pitcher, 8-1/2" h, Buccaneer, green 135.00
Tea set, cov teapot, open creamer and sugar, Pinecone, c1946 . . . . . . 350.00
Umbrella stand, 11" d, 22" h, maroon, rose, and yellow glaze, c1915 . . 795.00
Valet, eagle 75.00
Vase
   7-1/4" h, cornucopia, green . . 125.00
   9-1/2" h, swan, white, gold trim 350.00
   14-1/2" h, white ground, blue floral dec, marked "McCoy, USA" 235.00
Wall pocket
   Bellows 60.00
   Cuckoo Clock, brown, green, white, yellow bird 225.00
   Fan, blue 65.00
   Post Box, green 70.00
   Sunflower, blue 80.00

Vase, bulbous, flaring rim, jeweled, pastel squeezebag decoration, green base, marked "042," minute fleck on one drop, 5-1/2" d, 8-3/4" h, $575. Photo courtesy of David Rago Auctions.

Vase, yellow, swan and rushes, $35.

Woman in bonnet, bow, white, red trim 70.00
Window box, Pine Cone Rustic . 40.00

McKee Glass

c1852–1950   **1904–30s**

History: The McKee Glass Co. was established in 1843 in Pittsburgh, Pennsylvania. In 1852, it opened a factory to produce pattern glass. In 1888, the factory was relocated to Jeannette, Pennsylvania, and began to produce many types of glass kitchenwares, including several patterns of Depression glass. The factory continued until 1951, when it was sold to the Thatcher Manufacturing Co.

McKee named its colors Chalaine Blue, Custard, Seville Yellow, and Skokie Green. McKee glass may also be found with painted patterns, e.g., dots and ships. A few items were decaled. Many of the canisters and shakers were lettered in black to show the purpose for which they were intended.

For more information, see this book.

Animal dish cover, Lion, top only, white milk glass 25.00
Batter bowl, Skokie Green, spout, c1940 . . . . 55.00
Berry set, Hobnail with Fan pattern, blue, master berry and eight sauce dishes 170.00
Butter dish, cov, Ships, red dec on white 85.00

Child's butter dish, opaque blue, 5" w base, 3-3/4" h, **$55.**

Candleholder, 6-3/4" w, 5-1/2" h, Rock Crystal, clear, double light **65.00**
Candy dish, cov, Rock Crystal, red, 4-1/2" w, 10-1/2" h **400.00**
Canister, cov, 10 oz, custard **75.00**
Cereal canister, cov, custard, 48 oz **145.00**
Cheese and cracker set, Rock Crystal, red **170.00**
Creamer, Aztec, purple carnival **125.00**
Egg beater bowl, spout
    Ships, black dec on white **70.00**
    Skokie Green **50.00**
Flour shaker
    Custard **58.00**
    Seville Yellow **65.00**
Grill plate, custard, marked "McK" **25.00**
Kitchen bowl, 7" d, spout, Skokie Green **75.00**
Measuring cup, 4-cup, Seville Yellow **185.00**
Mixing bowls, nested set, Ships, red dec on white, 6", 7", 8", 9" **185.00**
Pepper shaker
    Roman Arch, black, "P" **40.00**
    Ships, red dec on white **35.00**

Children's dishes, custard, red trim, 10-piece set, **$90.**

Bottoms Up Tumbler, opalescent, Pat. No. 77726, 3-1/4" h, **$325.**

Pitcher, 8" h, Wild Rose and Bowknot, frosted, gilt dec **65.00**
Reamer, pointed top, Skokie Green **45.00**
Refrigerator dish, cov
    Custard, 4" x 9" **42.00**
    Ships, clear lid, 4" x 5" **34.00**
Ring box, cov, Seville Yellow . . . **20.00**
Salt shaker, 2-3/8" sq, 5" h, Skokie Green, orig label and top, inside rim chip **75.00**
Server, center handle, Rock Crystal, red **140.00**
Sugar bowl, Aztec, purple carnival **125.00**
Sugar shaker, 2-3/8" sq, 5" h, Skokie Green, orig label and top **115.00**
Tea canister, custard, 48 oz . . . **145.00**
Tom and Jerry punch bowl set, 11-1/2" d, 5" h punch bowl, eight 3-1/2" h mugs, white, black lettering and trim, three mugs with chips **125.00**
Tray, 13-1/2" l, 6-1/2" w, 2-1/2" h, Rock Crystal, red, rolled rim **150.00**
Tumbler, Bottoms Up, caramel, 3-1/8" h, 2-3/4" d **110.00**
Water cooler, 21" h, spigot, vaseline, two pcs **325.00**

MEDICAL AND PHARMACEUTICAL ITEMS

History: Modern medicine and medical instruments are well documented. Some instruments are virtually unchanged since their invention; others have changed drastically.

The concept of sterilization phased out decorative handles. Handles on early instruments, which were often carved, were made of materials such as

mother-of-pearl, ebony, and ivory. Today's sleek instruments are not as desirable to collectors.

Pharmaceutical items include those things commonly found in a drugstore and used to store or prepare medications.

Advertising, button
    Cloverine Salve Authorized Agent, celluloid, product described in detail, tiny white clover buds on green stems, blue, red, or white rim inscriptions **45.00**
    Dental Manufacturers Club, red on white celluloid, oval, early 1900s **12.00**
    Luden Cough Drops, black and white celluloid, center package of Luden's Menthol Cough Drops, two gold fabric 1-1/2" unmarked ribbons on back **2.00**
Advertising tin
    Dr. White's Cough Drops, tin litho, white ground, red lettering, 3-1/2" l, 2-1/4" w, 5/8" h, C-8+ **550.00**
    SilverTex Deluxe, Killian Mfg. Co., 2-1/8" l, 1-5/8" w, 1/4" h, white ground, black lettering, red center stripe **130.00**
Apothecary chest and bottles, English
    10-1/2" w, 8-5/8" d, 12-5/8" h, second half 19th C, mahogany, rect box, brass handles on side, hinged lid at top opening to int. fitted with four extant bottles, front with side opening hinged door, int. fitted with six extant bottles in compartments,

Apothecary mortar stand, oak, Mission-style, inset 10" d, 6" h white marble mortar, 13-1/2" square, 26" h, **$240.** *Photo courtesy of Cowan's Historic Americana Auctions.*

Apothecary bottles, colorless glass, 10-1/2" h and 7" h with twisted details and stoppers over straight cylindrical jar and pedestal base, 13-1/2" h, cylindrical, solid glass stopper, $615. Photo courtesy of Sanford Alderfer Auction Company.

two long drawers each fitted with four labeled medicine drawers, above two further medicine drawers flanking central drawer fitted with extant glass mortar and pestle, above two further drawers fitted with four glass mixing wells (seven extant), back of box with another side opening drawer enclosing eight further extant bottles............... **575.00**

13" w, 6-1/2" d, 8-3/8" h, Savory & Moore, London, third quarter 19th C, mahogany, rect box, flush brass handle on lid, and front drawer, int. lined with red velvet, fitted for 22 extant bottles, int. of lid bearing ivory makers' label and imp "Thompson London," drawer fitted for further bottles, eight included **815.00**

13-1/4" w, 8" d, 10" h, mahogany, hinged lid opening to velvet-lined interior, fitted with 17 colorless glass bottles, ceramic board, interior of lid with folio compartment, lower drawer fitted with compartments enclosing glass mortar and pestle, measure, two sterling spoons, and pan scale with weights, mid-19th C **700.00**

Bifocal spectacles, by McAllister, Philadelphia, silver frame, horseshoe-shaped lenses, sliding temples **375.00**

Book

Anatomy & Physiology, C. Gray, and D. Dimber, 1931, 8th ed., 629 pgs **25.00**

Diseases of the Blood, Roy R. Kracke, 1941, 2nd ed., 54 color plates, 46 illus, 692 pgs **25.00**

Harris' Principles and Practice of Dentistry, Ferdinand Gorges, D.D.S., Philadelphia, 1892, 10th ed., 1,222 pgs, ads and numerous illus **50.00**

Infectious Lung Diseases, Med Clinics of N. America, September 1978 .... **7.50**

Synopsis of Clinical Lab Methods, W. A. Bray, 1946, 93 illus, 20 color plates.................. **20.00**

Broadside

Dr Harding's Vegetable Medicines, top text reads "Dr. Harding's Vegetable Medicines; A Cure For Constipation, and Those Diseases...," text details various medicines, mid-19th C, some folds, light foxing, minor edge chipping, ink notation on bottom border, 18" x 9-3/4" **150.00**

Drs White & Oatman, top text reads "Stuttering or Stammering Permanently and Easily Cured!" text details accomplishments and details of cure, some folds, mid-19th C, 18" x 8-3/4".... **150.00**

Apothecary show globe, Whitall Tatum Co., ornate brass-plated cast iron holder, fancy brass plated cast iron bracket, original chain, some loss to plating, 21" h globe, $750. Photo courtesy of James D. Julia, Inc.

Dental cabinet, 55-3/4" h, 34" w, 12-1/8" h, mahogany, flat top surmounted at rear with long drop-front cabinet raised on stepped base, streamlined main cabinet fitted with tree banks of five stacked short drawers over two banks of two stacked short drawers, over three banks of assorted short drawers above central kneehole franked by two deep short drawers, molded colorless glass drawer pulls, some drawers with porcelain and white glass receptacles and liners, four sq tapering legs, old medium finish, America, early 20th C **1,035.00**

Dental chair, portable, 60" h extended, oak, adjustable height, back, and head rest, seat leather replaced, late 19th C **1,150.00**

Dental sterilizer, 11-3/4" x 7" x 8", paneled mahogany case, nickeled brass fittings, compartment with alcohol burner, steam boiler fitted in large zinc copper cavity, three removable wood slat racks, 19th C **230.00**

Electro-medical induction coil, 10" h, T. Hall, Boston, silvered coil and switches, mahogany base, pair of later handles **1,150.00**

Field surgeon's set, 10-1/2" w, Lentz & Sons, Philadelphia, all metal instruments, including Rust's pattern bone saw, Liston knife, trephine, bone forceps, etc., metal case with canvas

Advertising figure, OTC Medical Supports, "A Supporting Appliance for Every Condition Fitted Skillfully-Professionally," multicolored plaster pharmacist holding truss, lined carrying case, early 20th C, 19" w, 25" h, $115. Photo courtesy of James D. Julia, Inc.

cover case, both marked "2nd Reg. N.G.P." **350.00**

Forceps tooth key, 7-1/2" l, removable bolster/claw, hatched handles, W & H Hutchinson, Sheffield, England, mid-19th C, restorations **690.00**

Hour glass, 9-1/2" h, Tartanware, McDuff pattern, half hour **175.00**

Jar, orig stopper, 10-1/2" h, Duff's Colic & Diarrhea Remedy, cylindrical glass, recessed reverse painted on glass label, ground stopper matches pattern at base, some minor staining . . . **250.00**

Medicine chest, 13" w, 7-1/4" d, 11-3/4" h, mahogany and poplar, scrolled sides flank graduated shelves with round perforations above two small drawers, bottom of one inscribed "Grandmother Beal's Medicine Chest," New England, first half 19th C, old surface, minor staining and losses
. . . . **460.00**

Optician's trial set, 21" w, Brown, Philadelphia, retailer's label, oak case, partial set **175.00**

Optometrist's sample case, 20" w, mahogany, containing three trays of 20 spectacles each, chart in lid . . . **690.00**

Periodontal set, 16" l, 140 (out of 150) various scalers, fitted cream-colored painted wood case. **60.00**

Phrenological bust, 9-1/2" h, plaster, Fowler, Wells & Co., Boston, labeled cranium, label on back, damaged
. . . . **80.00**

Plugger, 8" l, Goodman & Shurtler's Patent, mechanical gold foil, sprung, hinged mallet on ebonite body, interchangeable head **460.00**

Scarificator, brass, 16 blades, sgd "Kolb," European, early 19th C. . **215.00**

Sign
C. F. Hussey Optometrist, zinc, double sided, polychrome and gilt dec, figural eyeglasses, name, and title in banner at base, late 19th C, 41" l, 12-1/2" h, imperfections
. . . . **2,550.00**

Dr. Trovillion, Skin Diseases and Skin Cancer, gold letters, black galvanized metal ground, double sided, 14" w, 18" h, worn dec **85.00**

Spittoon, brass, Rochester Stamping Co. **90.00**

Tooth extractor, 6-3/4" l, W. R. Goulding, New York, marked "Baker & Riley patented 1845," removable claw/ bolster, cross-hatched handles **1,380.00**

Tooth key
5" l, turned horn handle, cranked shaft, adjustable claw **150.00**

Optometrist cabinet, roll-top, display type, 25-1/2" w, 51" h, $200. Photo courtesy of Joy Luke Auctions.

5-1/2" l, turned wood handle, straight shaft, kidney-shaped bolster, removable claw **150.00**

5-3/4" l, wrought-iron handle, cranked and curved octagonal shaft, circular bolster, 10 interchangeable claws, possibly French, 19th C **635.00**

6-1/2" l, turned and hatched removable rosewood handle, turned cranked shaft, adjustable circular bolster and claw, early 19th C. **215.00**

7-1/2" l, turned ivory handle, turned shaft, adjustable claw **460.00**

Trepan, 10-1/4" l, burnished steel, sgd "Sir Henry a Paris," 18th C, arrowhead perforator, ivory pivot, ebony handle, five elevators **1,725.00**

Veterinary cabinet, 20" w, 10-1/4" d, 27-3/4" h, Humphrey's Remedies, tin front lists remedies, seven different unopened orig remedies in cabinet, some damage **400.00**

MEDICINE BOTTLES

History: The local apothecary and his book of formulas played a major role in early America. In 1796, the U.S. Patent Office issued the first patent for a medicine. At that time, anyone could apply for a medicinal patent and as long as the dosage was not poisonous, the patent was granted.

Patent medicines were advertised in newspapers and magazines and sold through the general store and at "medicine" shows. In 1907, the Pure Food and Drug Act, requiring an accurate description of contents on a medicine container's label, put an end to the patent medicine industry. Not all medicines were patented.

Most medicines were sold in distinctive bottles, often with the name of the medicine and location of manufacture in relief. Many early bottles were made in the glass-manufacturing area of southern New Jersey.

Later, companies in western Pennsylvania and Ohio manufactured bottles.

American Expectorant, America, 1840-60, octagonal, greenish aquamarine, outward rolled mouth, pontil scar, 5-7/8" h **425.00**

Booth & Sedgwick's London Cordial Gin, American, 1845-60, sq, beveled corners, deep blue green, applied sloping collared mouth with ring, iron pontil mark, 9-3/4" h **375.00**

Davis & Miller Druggist, Baltimore, attributed to Baltimore Glass Works, Baltimore, MD, 1845-60, cylindrical, brilliant sapphire blue, applied sq collared mouth, iron pontil, mark, 3" d, 7-1/2" h **1,800.00**

Dr. Chas T. Price-67 William St., New York, Cure for Fits, oval, tooled mouth, smooth base, c1880-95, clear, 8-1/2" h
. . . . **330.00**

Dr. Ham's Aromatic Invigorating Spirit, cylindrical, applied mouth, smooth base, c1875-85, orange-amber, 8-1/2" h **65.00**

Dr. Wilson's Horse Ointment, teal-blue, rolled lip, open pontil
. . . . **3,200.00**

Dysentery Syrup, Graefenberg & Co., New York, rect, beveled corners, paneled sides, applied sloping collared mouth, open pontil, c1845-55, aqua, 6" h **80.00**

E. A. Buckhout's Dutch Liniment, Prepared At Mechanicsville, Saratoga Co. NY, rect, beveled corners, figure of standing Dutch man, tooled mouth, pontil scar, 4-5/8" h **400.00**

Fountain Of Youth Hair Restorer, cobalt blue, tooled lip, attributed to Sacramento, 7-1/2" h, $1,050. Photo courtesy of Pacific Glass Auctions.

From the Laboratory of G. W. Merchant, Chemist, Lockport, N. Y., attributed to Lockport Glass Works, Lockport, NY, 1840-60, rect, chamfered corners, deep yellowish green, applied sloping collard mouth, tubular pontil scar, 5-1/2" h **500.00**

Gleet Seven-Days Gonorrhea, rect, tooled mouth, "M. B.W. Millville" on smooth base, c1890-1910, deep cobalt blue, 5" h, some stains **800.00**

Gogings Wild Cherry Tonic, sq, beveled corners, tooled mouth, smooth base, c1890-1900, medium amber, 8-3/4" h **90.00**

Houcks Vegetable Pancea, Goodlestville, Tenn, rect, beveled corners, applied double-collar mouth, smooth base, c1855-60, deep blue-aqua, 7-1/8" h **700.00**

Iceland Balsam for Pulmonary Consumption, Iceland Balsam, America, 1830-50, rect, beveled corners, emb on three sides, yellow olive, short applied sloping collared mouth, pontil scar, 6-1/2" h, professionally cleaned, light emb lettering **5,500.00**

I. Newport's Panacea Purifier of the Blood, Nerwich, VT, attributed to Stoddard Glasshouse, Stoddard, NH, 1846-60, cylindrical, indented emb panels, yellow olive, applied sloping collared mouth with ring, iron pontil ring, 7-3/8 h, small chip on sloping collar **1,900.00**

L. P. Dodge Rheumatic Liniment Newburg, America, 1840-60, rect, beveled corners, light golden amber, applied sloping collared mouth, pontil scar, 6" h, appears to have been cleaned................... **750.00**

Mother Putnam's Blackberry Cordial, Rheinstrom Bros. Proprietors, rect, paneled sides, applied mouth, tall ringed neck, smooth base, c1880-90, medium amber, 10-7/8" h **250.00**

Orcuff's Sure Rheumatic Cure, rect, paneled sides, tooled lip, smooth base, c1885-95, deep cobalt blue, 6-1/2" h **635.00**

Pearl's White Glycerine, rect, sunken panel, tooled mouth, smooth base, c1890-90, deep cobalt blue, 6-3/8" h **145.00**

Sanford's Extract of Hamamelis (Witch Hazel), rect, tooled mouth, smooth base, orig paper label SSanford's Radical Cure for Catarrh," c1870-80, deep cobalt blue, 7-5/8" h **175.00**

Shaker Family Pills, Dose 2 to 4, A. J. White, rect, paneled sides, sheared lip, smooth base, c1890-1900, medium amber, 2-1/4" h **95.00**

Swaim's Panacea, Philada, paneled cylinder, applied sloping double collar, open pontil, c1840-50, medium yellow-olive, 7-3/4" h......... **860.00**

Swift's Syphilitic Specific, flask form, applied mouth, smooth base, c1870-90, deep cobalt blue, 9-1/8" h, some roughness on orig strap edge .. **635.00**

Turner's Balsam, eight sided, aqua, 4-7/8" h.................... **65.00**

MERCURY GLASS

History: Mercury glass is a light-bodied, double-walled glass that was "silvered" by applying a solution of silver nitrate to the inside of the object through a hole in its base.

For more information, see this book.

F. Hale Thomas of London patented the method in 1849. In 1855, the New England Glass Co. filed a patent for the same type of process. Other American glassmakers soon followed. The glass reached the height of its popularity in the early 20th century.

Bowl, 8" d, small plug in bottom, some wear...................... **120.00**

Cake stand, 8" d, pedestal base, emb floral dec.................... **80.00**

Candlestick, 10-1/2" h **110.00**

Cologne bottle, 4-1/4" x 7-1/2", bulbous, flashed amber panel, cut neck, etched grapes and leaves, corked metal stopper, c1840 .. **160.00**

Creamer, 6-1/2" h, etched ferns, applied clear handle, attributed to Sandwich.................. **140.00**

Curtain tiebacks, 3-1/8" d, 4-1/2" l, etched grape design, price for pr **140.00**

Door knob set, 2-1/4" d **80.00**

Goblet, 5" d, gold, white lily of the valley dec **40.00**

Pitcher, 5-1/2" x 9-3/4" h, bulbous, panel cut neck, engraved lacy florals and leaves, applied clear handle, c1840 .... **225.00**

Salt, 3" x 3", price for pr **100.00**

Sugar bowl, cov, 4-1/4" x 6-1/4", low foot, enameled white foliage dec, knob finial...................... **65.00**

Owl Drug Co., Incorporated Valdez, Alaska, embossed owl, 13-sided reverse panel, slight interior stain, 5-1/8" h, **$550.** *Photo courtesy of Pacific Glass Auctions.*

Rowlers Rheumatism Medicine, applied top, smooth base, medium green, attributed to Pacific Glass Works, Sacramento, 7-3/4" h, **$220.** *Photo courtesy of Pacific Glass Auctions.*

Liqueur set, small decanter, six small liqueur glasses, hinged, lidded, egg-shape, coralene floral decoration, hinge broken, 12" h, **$225.** *Photo courtesy of Joy Luke Auctions.*

Vases, pair, frosted palm trees and flowers, paneled sides, gold luster interior, 10-1/4" h, **$145.**

Vase, 9-3/4" h, cylindrical, raised circular foot, everted rim, bright enameled yellow, orange, and blue floral sprays and insects, pr **225.00**

METTLACH

History: In 1809, Jean Francis Boch established a pottery at Mettlach in Germany's Moselle Valley. His father had started a pottery at Septfontaines in 1767. Nicholas Villeroy began his pottery career at Wallerfanger in 1789.

In 1841, these three factories merged. They pioneered underglaze printing on earthenware, using transfers from copper plates, and also were among the first companies to use coal-fired kilns. Other factories were developed at Dresden, Wadgassen, and Danischburg. Mettlach decorations include relief and etched designs, prints under the glaze, and cameos.

For more information, see this book.

Marks: The castle and Mercury emblems are the two chief marks, although secondary marks are known. The base of each piece also displays a shape mark and usually a decorator's mark.

Additional Listings: Villeroy & Boch.

Note: Prices in this listing are for print-under-glaze pieces, unless otherwise specified.

Coaster, 4-7/8" d, PUG, drinking scene, marked "Mettlach, Villeroy & Boch" **150.00**

Plaque, #2196, castle scene and boats, 17-1/2" d, **$490.** Photo courtesy of James D. Julia, Inc.

Jardinière, 5-1/2" h, 8-3/4" x 10", green ground, off-white cameo figures of Grecian men and women riding in carriage, sitting at table and drinking, base imp "#7000" and "#17" . . . **425.00**

Loving cup, 7-3/8" w, 6-3/4" h, three handles, musicians dec **185.00**

Plaque

#1044-1067, water wheel on side of building, sgd "F. Reiss," PUG, gold wear on edge, 17" d **495.00**

#1168, Cavalier, threading and glaze, sgd "Warth," chip on rear hanging rim, 16-1/2" d **465.00**

#2196, Stolzensels Castle on the Rhein, 17" d **1,100.00**

#2442, classical scene of Trojan warriors in ship, cameo, white high relief, blue-gray ground, artist sgd "J. Stahl," 18-1/4" d, some professional restoration . . **1,200.00**

#2443, classical scene of women and eight attendants, cameo, white

Stein, etched and glazed stoneware, half liter, #1998, cavalier holding trumpet, inlaid lid with castle, **$775.** Photo courtesy of Joy Luke Auctions.

Stein, etched and glazed stoneware, half liter, #2001B, books on medicine, inlaid lid, **$600.** Photo courtesy of Joy Luke Auctions.

high relief, blue-gray ground, artist sgd "J. Stahl," blue-gray ground, 18-1/4" d **1,550.00**

Stein

#1027, 1/2 liter, relief, beige, rust, green, inlaid lid, floral, and face **215.00**

#1526, transfer and enameled, Student Society, Amico Pectus Hosti Frontem, dated 1902, roster on either side of crest, pewter lid, slight discoloration to int. . . **465.00**

#1896, 1/4 liter, maiden on one side, cherub face on other, grape dec, pewter lift handle **350.00**

#2028, 1/2 liter, etched, men in Gasthaus, inlaid lid **550.00**

#2057, 1/2 liter, etched, festive dancing scene, inlaid lid . . . **325.00**

#2093, 1/2 liter, etched and glazed, suit of cards, inlaid lid **700.00**

Stein, etched and glazed stoneware, half liter, #2075, telegrapher, eagle, inlaid lid with train and beer stein, **$1,950.** Photo courtesy of Joy Luke Auctions.

#2100, 1/3 liter, etched, Germans meeting Romans, inlaid lid, H. Schlitt **495.00**

#2204, 1/2 liter, etched and relief, Prussian eagle, inlaid lid . . **780.00**

#2580, 1/2 liter, etched, Die Kannenburg, conical inlay lid, knight in castle **695.00**

#2950, 1/2 liter, cameo, Bavarian crest, pewter lid with relief crest **825.00**

#5001, 4.6 liter, faience type, coat of arms, pewter lid **850.00**

MILITARIA

For more information, see this book.

History: Wars have occurred throughout recorded history. Until the mid-19th century, soldiers often had to provide for their own needs, including supplying their own weapons. Even in the 20th century, a soldier's uniform and some of his gear are viewed as his personal property, even though issued by a military agency.

Conquering armed forces made a habit of acquiring souvenirs from their vanquished foes. They also brought their own uniforms and accessories home as badges of triumph and service.

Saving militaria may be one of the oldest collecting traditions. Militaria collectors tend to have their own special shows and view themselves outside the normal antiques channels. However, they haunt small indoor shows and flea markets in hopes of finding additional materials.

Reproduction Alert: Pay careful attention to Civil War and Nazi material.

Revolutionary War

Autograph, document sgd, promotion of First Lieutenant, by Benjamin Harrison, 1783, paper seal, 6" x 8" **650.00**

Map, seat of war in New England, 1775, printed by Sayer and Bennett, partially hand colored, troop movements, vignette of Charlestown in flames, 19-1/2" x 22-3/4" sight **10,350.00**

Muster roll, Capt. Job Whipples Company in the Massachusetts Bay Forcesses in the Service of the United States, Commanded by Col. Rufus Putnam, including all who have servd (sic) in said Regt. From Jany 1777 to Feb 21 1778," includes 67 men, rank, town, country, length of enlistment, and remarks, framed, 18" x 22", imperfections **1,100.00**

Print

Perry's Victory on Lake Erie, Perry in rowboat, eight sailors in midst of battle, steel engraving from painting by Thomas Birch, engraved by A. Lawson, published by William Smith, Philadelphia, Eastlake frame, 24" x 31" . . . **295.00**

Volunteer Refreshment Saloon Supported Gratuitously by the Citizens of Philadelphia, PA, large ext. view of saloon, three int. vignettes below, facsimile signatures of supporters, printed by Boell, published by B. S. Brown, Philadelphia, blind stamp, framed, 21" x 27-1/2" **425.00**

Washington's Dream, litho by Currier and Ives, NY, 1857, Washington, in uniform, sleeping in camp cabin, vignette dream of three women representing Liberty, Plenty, and Justice standing over America, stepping on crown of tyranny, framed, 25" x 19" **775.00**

War Bond, Commonwealth of Massachusetts Bay, June 1, 1777, vignette of Continental soldier with sword, holding document with "Independence" printed on it, 9" x 8" **200.00**

Pocket watch, key wound, orig key, inscribed "I Shelby 1802," watch movement by John J Wilmurt of NY, English silver case with paper label from GW Stewart, Lexington, KY watchmaker, hero Issac Shelby was first governor of KY **3,520.00**

Snuff box, cov, 2-7/8" d, gutta percha, round, relief scene of battle, ships, coastline, buildings, French inscription "Prise d'Yorck 1781 (Taking of Yorktown or Battle of Yorktown)" **750.00**

French and Indian War

Marching order, letter addressed to Captain Josiah Thatcher, Yarmouth, his Majesty's Service, Boston, June 24, 1761, ordering Thatcher to march troops to Springfield to be mustered, sgd by J. Hoar, some fold weakness, 8" x 6-1/4" **185.00**

Uniform button mold, 9" l, brass, American, 18th C, casts six round buttons with central raised letter "I" for infantry, one 25 mm, one 18 mm, four 14.5 mm, each with eyelet, wooden handles missing **625.00**

War of 1812

Broadside, Aug. 18, 1814, printed calvary orders for the 2nd Brigade 1st Visis, and 7th Reg 2nd Brig 1st Divis, Edmund Fitzgerland Lt. Col. 7th Reg & Cavalry, one sheet **375.00**

Cartridge box, leather, white cloth strap, very worn, missing plate . . **70.00**

Flag, 60-1/2" x 110", 13 stars, Naval, hand sewn **1,100.00**

Military drum, large eagle painted on sides, red, and blue stripes, one drum head, 22" h, 17" d **750.00**

Ship document, British, articles pertaining to private armed ship *Dart* and four carriage guns, six nine-pounders, four swivel guns lying in St. John, New Brunswick, designed to cruise against Americas, details prize division, chain of command, other shipboard administration, dated July 1813, right section includes signatures and ratings of 44 seamen and officers as crew, some staining, edge chipping, foxing, and fold splitting, Whatman 1808 watermark, 21" x 29" **500.00**

Civil War

Autograph album, GAR, 4-1/2" x 7", most pages signed at Milwaukee Reunion, Aug. 29, 1889, maroon velvet cover **110.00**

Badge

Delegate, G.A.R., Indiana, metal hanger bar, cello pendant joined by red, white, and blue striped ribbon, inscribed in gold, dark bronze luster hanger with IN state seal, view of "Entrance to Soldier's Home, Marion, Ind.," 36th annual encampment, May, 1915, ribbon worn **25.00**

Civil War, backpack, tarred cotton, large 14" x 13" pouch, 10" x 13" pouch, double leather closure straps, leather shoulder harness, brass and iron hooks and buckles, one strap marked "WM. BUTTE NY, August 13, 1864," tears, leather dry and crackled, $230. Photo courtesy of James D. Julia Auctions.

Civil War, broadside, "4th of July Celebration! Madison General Hospital," schedule of events such as reading of Declaration of Independence, signed at footer "Geo. E. Gresham, Sec'y Com. Of Arrangements," c1860, some tears, staining, evidence of previous mounting, now archival framed, 9-1/2" x 6-1/2", $100. Photo courtesy of Sanford Alderfer Auction Company.

G.A.R. 31st National Encampment-Buffalo, 1897, dark bronze luster finish, diecut link badge, official star symbol, eagles, flags, patriotic shield dated 1897 .... **35.00**

Belt and plate, black leather belt, brass loops, two-piece brass VA state plate, minor wear and splits **2,350.00**

Book

Down in Tennessee, 1861-1865, J. Gilmore, 1864, 282 pgs... **45.00**

Gettysburg to the Rapidan by General Meade's Chief of Staff, Andrew Humphreys, 1883, 243 pgs, maps **45.00**

The Gettysburg Campaign and the Campaigns of 1864 & 1965 in Virginia by A Lieutenant in Confederate Artillery, Stribling, 1905, illus, 308 pgs **45.00**

The Life of Stonewall Jackson, J. E. Cooke, 1863 .... **45.00**

Cane

35-3/4" l, carved wood, 1-1/2" w x 3" h oval wood knob, relief carved and polychromed shaft with American flag, 24 Union army corps badges, worn red, white, blue, and green polychrome, 1-3/4" brass ferrule, made for veteran, c1880 .... **350.00**

36" l, carved wood, carved fist at top, carved snake spiraling up shaft, engraved silver plaque "Made at camp A Hospital near South Mountain and presented to H. C. Gray by J. C. Barlow &Th's Blasand

of the 15th M.T. Feb 1863," loss on eyes **765.00**

Canteen, 7-5/8" d, bull's eye, orig woven cloth strap, pewter spout sgd "Hadden, Porter & Booth, Phila" **325.00**

Cartridge box, cross belt and eagle plate, "Calhoune New York" maker's stamp on inner flap, tin liners, oval U.S. plate. **900.00**

Confederate notes, group of $500, $10, and $5, from Richmond, matted and framed, 21-1/2" x 17" **275.00**

Coat, Confederate Officer's, double breasted, blue-gray wool, low collar, blue piping along front, 12 large VA and NC buttons marked "Scovill Mfg. Waterbury," three small buttons with same markings, two have black velvet coverings, Captain's bars on collar, buttons and insignia removed for previous cleaning, minor moth damage to ext. **39,600.00**

Fife, 17-1/2" l, rosewood, nickel silver ends, eight bands, orig dark finish, faint signature "W. Crosby, Boston" . **125.00**

Newspaper, *Cincinnati Gazette*, for year of 1863, fold lines and minor damage, group of 19 newspapers **150.00**

Photograph, painted ambrotype, ninth plate photo size, Confederate soldier, red haired, blue uniform, brass buttons,

Civil War, pocket watch, Confederate, gold hunter case, key wind, early wood fired locomotive engraved on cover with surrounding floral and arabesque pattern and engraving, back cover engraved "TGR TO S.W. RABB," inside back cover engraved "John Watt Rabb/Son Of John Glazier Rabb/Was Killed In The Battle Of Gaines/Mills, Va., June 30-1862, Wearing/This Watch, And Carrying The/Colors Of The 6th South Carolinas/Regiment," size 16, single spring-loaded cover, unmarked dial, watch is accompanied by invoices of sale and letter from Sumpter Military Antiques dated 1-31-96 and two packets of copies of archival muster rolls of the 6th Reg't So. Carolina Infantry giving more information about original owner, $4,255. Photo courtesy of James D. Julia, Inc.

wearing red and black bow tie, 8-3/4" x 6-7/8" carved split baluster frame with cornice moldings, shaped side pieces, painted in black and brown with gold highlights, wear **1,410.00**

Photograph, tintype, cased

Cavalryman, wearing shell jacket with gilt detail on collar and buttons, lightly tinted blue pants, holding cavalry saber, Colt pistol in belt, forage cap with "D2," sixth plate **770.00**

Confederate, checked shirt, butternut colored coat, CDV mount **110.00**

Infantryman, waist-up portrait, holding Hardee hat with feather, "K," and bugle insignia, wearing epaulettes, cartridge box, holding musket with bayonet, ninth plate **550.00**

Soldiers in front of tent, very worn quarter plate tintype, gutta-percha case with relief scene of officers standing at table, scrolled border, minor edge chips **470.00**

Pinback button

Battle of Gettysburg 1913 Anniversary, multicolored, blue lettering **25.00**

Col. W. C. Johnson, G.A.R., black and white photo, orange ground, black lettering for sponsor "Snellenburg Stores, Philadelphia, Pa.," and "G.A.R. Encampment 1899" **20.00**

Print, 19-3/4" x 27-1/2", chromolithograph on paper, The Battle of Gettysburg and Battle of Missionary Ridge, Kurz & Allison, publishers, identified in inscriptions in matrix, framed, minor damage to both, price for pr **470.00**

Quilt, 84-1/2" x 79", cotton, three central panels, upper with American eagle pieced of yellow and brown, holding red banner in beat, inscribed "The Union Forever," above white dotted blue field with 34 stars arranged in Great Star pattern, above white field containing symbolic broken chain and pieced letters "End of the War," quilted stars and ships on panels, flanked by 13 red and white stripes quilted alternately with guns and swords, backed with white cotton, edged in blue, made by Ladies Auxiliary group of mothers and sisters of boys serving in Union Army from Sandy Creek Co., NY, started in 1861, sent to Gen. Grant in April 1865, who returned it with a note of thanks and asking it be sold to raise funds for local charity, sold at auction at rally to Mr. P. M. Newton of Sandy Creek, then descended in family, imperfections.............**21,150.00**

Revolver, Remington, Major General Godfrey Weitzel's, new model police revolver, .36 caliber, 4-1/2" barrel, old brown finish, framed letter dated Jan. 12, 1931, accompanies revolver detailing career of owner, early holster **1,200.00**

Spurs, pr, 4" h, brass, Confederate, Leech & Rigdon style **115.00**

Sword, belt rig, non-commissioned officer, NCO sword by Ames Mfg, Chicopee MA, marked on blade, also marked "US, GWC, 1864," marked "GKC" on guard, leather scabbard, NCO sword belt ring, eagle buckle, plated wreath, frog for NCO sword and hangers, some leather deterioration to belt and scabbard........... **900.00**

Walking stick, 36-1/4" h, carved wood, dog's head finial with silver collar

Indian War, non-regulation staff captain's undress uniform sack coat, fatigue uniform coat manufactured by private tailor "John G. Haas, Lancaster, Pa.," black wool, dark green tape edge decoration at edges of fall-front collar and down breast, five-button front with Horstmann marked three-piece U.S. staff officer buttons, functional cuffs have three buttons, two large interior pockets. Original Captain of Staff shoulder strap rank insignias, original maker's label, $780. Photo courtesy of James D. Julia Auctions.

inscribed "Thos. Thompson Co. H 106 Reg. Pa. Vols. Evacuation of York Town 1862," natural branch carved with dog, squirrel, leafy vine, and reeded and geometric devices, wear **775.00**

Indian War
Bayonet, Model 1873, 3-1/2" w blade **80.00**

Belt buckle, Naval officer, brass, stamped "Horstman, Phila" **120.00**

Broadside, Ohio massacre, No. 4, 1791, printed in Boston, 1792, foxed, water stained, modern frame ...**900.00**

Spanish American War
Hat badge, infantry, brass, crossed krag rifles, 2" l................**55.00**

Cartridge box, U.S. Army **125.00**

Pinback button, "Remember the *Maine*," battleship scene, patent 1896 ....**25.00**

Spy glass, pocket, brass, Naval, round holder, brown leather grip, 16" l . **110.00**

World War I
American flag, 6-1/4" x 10-1/4" sight, cloth, eight stars and five stripes, made by Prisoner of War, "Arlon Belgium Dec 11th, 1918" written on mat, framed, some losses, discoloration.....**350.00**

Bayonet, British, MK II, No. 4, spike, scabbard **20.00**

Book, *Regimental History of the 316 Infantry*...................**25.00**

Buckle, U.S. Balloon Corps, emb hot air balloon...................**75.00**

WWI, medal, US Military Distinguished Service Cross #1867, wrapped brooch medal, identified by number to PFC Harry C. Dommet of the Medical Detachment of the 108th Machine Gun Battalion, 28th Division for his actions near Villet, France on September 5, 1918, $1,210. Photo courtesy of Sanford Alderfer Auction Company.

Compass, marked "Made in France" **45.00**

Dog tag stamping kit, orig wood box, complete **250.00**

Flare pistol, Model 1918, French **100.00**

Gun sling, soft leather, 1917, for 03 Springfield..................**17.50**

Helmet, German, Pattern, 1916, painted gray/green **80.00**

Overcoat, U.S. Army officers, Melton, olive drab, wool, double breasted, 10 bone buttons................**65.00**

Trench flashlight and note pad, German, black tin container, orig pad and pencil **65.00**

Tunic and trousers, gabardine, pinback, Air Corps and U.S. discs **75.00**

Watch fob, Federal Seal, U.S. officer **15.00**

World War II
Armband, Japan, military police, red lettering, white cotton **48.00**

Cane, 30-3/4" l, Civilian Conservation Corps, fully carved, U-shaped horse-head handle, one piece, carved low relief of trees, bathing beauty, alligator, name of carver's friends, "Middle Creek Camp F34 Co. 997," 1933, finish removed around later added date **125.00**

Cookbook, *Meat Reference Manual for Mess Sergeants and Cooks*, Prepared for the United States Army by the National Live Stock and Meat Board, March 1943, 36 pgs, soft cover . **18.00**

Flag, New Zealand PT boat, printed on blue cotton **55.00**

Flyers goggles, Japanese, boxed, gray fur lined cups, yellow lenses **35.00**

WWII, flag, Japanese, meatball-style flag with many signatures, some staining, $115. Photo courtesy of James D. Julia Auctions.

World War II, poster, United We Are Strong – United We Will Win, guns with allied flags, 1943, 40" x 28," **$75.** *Photo courtesy of Joy Luke Auctions.*

Gas mask, German, canister style, rubber mask, canvas straps, carrying container **80.00**
Helmet, Italian, steel, leather chip strap **100.00**
ID tag, U.S. Army, oval pattern, instruction envelope, chain **25.00**
Manual, 6-1/4" x 10", War Department, FM30-30, Military Intelligence, *Aircraft Recognition Pictorial Manual,* Bureau of Aeronautics, Washington, DC, 1943, 179 pgs, illus of US, Great Britain, German, Japanese, Italian, Russian, etc. plans **40.00**
Telescope, 14" l, Australian, MK 1, heavy leather case and carrying straps **45.00**

MILK GLASS

History: Opaque white glass attained its greatest popularity at the end of the 19th century. American glass manufacturers made opaque white tablewares as a substitute for costly European china and glass. Other opaque colors, e.g., blue and green, also were made. Production of milk-glass novelties came in with the Edwardian era.

The surge of popularity in milk glass subsided after World War I. However, milk glass continues to be made in the 20th century. Some modern products are reissues and reproductions of earlier forms. This presents a

significant problem for collectors, although it is partially obviated by patent dates or company markings on the originals and by the telltale signs of age.

Collectors favor milk glass from the pre-World War I era, especially animal-covered dishes. The most prolific manufacturers of these animal covers were Atterbury, Challinor-Taylor, Flaccus, and McKee.

Notes: There are many so-called "McKee" animal-covered dishes. Caution must be exercised in evaluating pieces because some authentic covers were not signed. Furthermore, many factories have made, and many still are making, split-rib bases with McKee-like animal covers or with different animal covers. The prices below are for authentic McKee pieces with either the cover or base signed.

Animal dish, cov
    Camel, Newbound **155.00**
    Cat on drum, Newbound . . . **195.00**
    Cat on hamper, green, V mark **115.00**
    Chick on sleigh, white **115.00**
    Cow, Newbound **160.00**
    Dewey, Newbound 80, chips on base **90.00**
    Dolphin **145.00**
    Duck, white, Newbound 63, top **145.00**
    Fish, flat, white, Newbound . **120.00**
    Kitten, ribbed base, Westmoreland, white **130.00**
    Lion, reclining, white, criss-cross base, similar to Newbound 57 . . . . **135.00**
    Robin on nest, med blue, Newbound 63 . . . . **165.00**
    Setter dog, blue, Newbound 64 . . . . **265.00**
    Swan, closed neck, white, Newbound 65 . . . . **120.00**
    Turkey, amethyst head, white body **220.00**
    Turkey, white head, dark amethyst body **170.00**

Animal-covered dish, rooster, Westmoreland, introduced 1948, **$85.** *Photo courtesy of R Rhoads Auctions.*

Animal dish, covered, chicken and eggs on nest, red glass eyes, 6-7/8" l, 6-1/2" h, **$85.**

Bowl, 8-1/4" d, Daisy, allover leaves and flower design, open scalloped edge (F165) **85.00**
Bust, 5-1/2" h, Admiral Dewey . . **300.00**
Butter dish, cov, 4-7/8" l, Roman Cross pattern, sq, ftd base curves outward toward top, cube-shape finial (F240) **75.00**
Candy container, cat in boot, goofus dec **80.00**
Calling card receiver, bird, wings extended over fanned tail, head resting on leaf, detailed feather pattern (F669) **150.00**
Centerpiece bowl, 13" l, 11" w, lattice edge, Westmoreland **125.00**
Child's mug, elephant handle . . . **60.00**
Compote, Atlas, lacy edge, blue **185.00**
Creamer and sugar, Trumpet Vine, fire painted dec, sgd "SV" **130.00**
Egg cup, cov, 4-1/4" h, bird, round, fluted, Atterbury (F130) **135.00**

Decanter, four oval medallions with paper scenes of girl and puppies, painted gold rose stoppers, one scene blank, 11" h, price for pair, **$60.** *Photo courtesy of Woody Auctions.*

Syrup, left: Bellflower, 5-1/2" h, right: Swan with heron, 5-1/2" h, each, $120. Photo courtesy of James D. Julia, Inc.

Hat, Stars and Stripes, black rim
.... **235.00**
Ink blotter, Scottie, chips to ear . **65.00**
Lamp, 11" h, Goddess of Liberty, bust, three stepped hexagonal bases, clear and frosted font, brass screw connector, patent date, Atterbury (F329) **300.00**
Match holder, smiling boy **170.00**
Milk pitcher, 8-3/4" h, Wild Iris, gilt trim, c1825.................... **125.00**
Mug, 3-1/4", Medallion, c1870... **50.00**
Plate
    Donkey **50.00**
    Easter, bunny, basket of eggs **35.00**
    Easter, gold hen and peeps, gold border, little orig paint...... **10.00**
    Fort Necessity, Indian chief, some orig paint, edge chip **30.00**
    Indian Chief, no paint **70.00**
    Rabbit center, horseshoe and clover border................. **145.00**
    Three dogs and squirrel **65.00**
Spooner, 5-1/8" h, monkey, scalloped top (F275) **125.00**
Sugar shaker, Forget-me-not, green, orig top **50.00**
Syrup, plain, hp red flowers, damage to pewter top **65.00**
Tumbler, Royal Oak, orig fired paint, green band **50.00**
Vanity box, cov, 7" l, 2" w, 2" h, hand painted enamel floral dec, gold trim, imp "16" on both lid and base.. **250.00**
Water pitcher, Guttate, gold trim
.... **175.00**

MILLEFIORI

History: Millefiori (thousand flowers) is an ornamental glass composed of bundles of colored glass rods fused together into canes. The canes were pulled to the desired length while still ductile, sliced, arranged in a pattern, and fused together again. The Egyptians developed this technique in the first century B.C. It was revived in the 1880s.

For more information, see this book.

Reproduction Alert: Many modern companies are making Millefiori items, such as

Barber bottle, orig top, red, white dec
.... **350.00**
Beads, 16" l, multicolored millefiori beads, blue glass bead spacers . **55.00**
Bowl, 8" d, tricorn, scalloped, folded sides, amethyst and silver deposit
.... **125.00**
Candy dish, 11-1/2" l, 9" w, light blue, various sized multicolored millefiori flowers, swirled shape, Murano, c1950
.... **85.00**
Creamer, 3" x 4-1/2", white and cobalt blue canes, yellow centers, satin finish
.... **110.00**
Cruet, bulbous, multicolored canes, applied camphor handle, matching stopper..................... **120.00**
Decanter, 12" h, deep black ground, allover multicolored flux and canes, including peachblow, and opal, enamel dec, Gundersen **1,450.00**
Demittase cup and saucer, red and white millefiori, angular applied pink handle, broken pontil scars, Italian
.... **275.00**

Vase, purple bands with white oval line, white band with red flowers, yellow centers, 5-1/2" h, $165.

Door knob, 2-1/2" d, paperweight, center cane dated 1852, New England Glass Co.................... **395.00**
Goblet, 7-1/2" h, multicolored canes, clear stem and base **150.00**
Lamp, 23" h, mushroom shaped shade and matching baluster base, deep cranberry and white sunburst rod millefiori, ring of cut glass prisms
.... **610.00**
Pitcher, 6-1/2" h, multicolored canes, applied candy cane handle ... **195.00**
Slipper, 5" l, camphor ruffle and heel
.... **125.00**
Sugar bowl, cov, 4" x 4-1/2", white canes, yellow centers, satin finish
.... **125.00**
Sugar shaker, bulbous, reds and yellows, orig top **275.00**
Syrup, pewter top, dark green, browns, blues, applied colorless handle **295.00**
Vase, 8-1/4" h, bulbous, cased, clear over emerald green, burnt orange int., scattered trailing millefiori dec, 8-1/4" h
.... **375.00**

MINIATURE LAMPS

History: Miniature oil and kerosene lamps, often called "night lamps," are diminutive replicas of larger lamps. Simple and utilitarian in design, miniature lamps found a place in the parlor (as "courting" lamps), hallway, children's rooms, and sickrooms.

Miniature lamps are found in many glass types, from amberina to satin glass. Miniature lamps measure 2-1/2 to 12 inches in height, with the principle parts being the base, collar, burner, chimney, and shade. In 1877, both L. J. Atwood and L. H. Olmsted patented burners for miniature lamps. Their burners made the lamps into a popular household accessory.

Note: The numbers given below refer to the figure numbers found in the Smith books.

For more information, see this book.

Reproduction Alert: Study a lamp carefully to make certain all parts are original; married pieces are common. Reproductions abound.

Amberina, 3-1/2" w, 9" h, pressed, deep red to yellow, several chips
.... **175.00**
Consolidated, 10-1/4" h, milk glass, raised thumbprints **295.00**

Left: Cosmos, original shade, clear, remnants of paint in flowers, $45; center: Drape variant, original frosted shade, $65; right: Bull's Eye, no shade, clear, $40. Photo courtesy of Joy Luke Auctions.

Fenton, Cranberry Coin Spot, 11" h, 4-1/2" d globe shade **600.00**
Figural
    Log Cabin, blue, handle . . **1,200.00**
    Santa Claus **2,750.00**
Libbey, cut glass, 10-3/4" h base, 2" sq base, sgd **425.00**
Milk glass
    Apple Blossom, light pink band around top of base and shade, white mid-section with floral dec, green band at base, nutmeg burner, 7-1/4" h **225.00**

Milk glass, shaded yellow background, pink roses, Smith SI-266, shade spider poorly fitting replacement, flake to inside of shade rim, 8-1/2" h, $230. Photo courtesy of James D. Julia, Inc.

Reverse swirl, honey colored, swirling from right to left and white opalescent swirl, Smith H-205, 8-1/4" h, $1,150. Photo courtesy of James D. Julia, Inc.

Drape pattern, pink and white, Smith #231-I **75.00**
Embossed design, hp flowers, green shading on base, nutmeg burner, 8-3/4" h **225.00**
Medallion, emb, Smith #211-I . **45.00**
Moon & Stars, L. G. Wright, white **295.00**
Plume pattern, pink ext., white int., gilt dec, nutmeg burner, 7-1/2" h **270.00**
Swan, Smith #327-II **250.00**
Opalescent, cranberry, Spanish Lace **750.00**
Pattern glass, Beaded Heart, clear, Smith #109-I **115.00**
Satin, Acanthus Leaf, red, 5" w, 9" h, c1890, replaced chimney **425.00**

Swirl, blue, married, Smith SI-299 mini lamp base is paired with SI-524 shade, several flakes to shade fitter rim, replaced spider, 7-3/4" h, $635. Photo courtesy of James D. Julia, Inc.

Satin, DQ, MOP, blue, shade with ruffled lip, eight petal shaped frosted feet, Smith H-117, 10-1/2" h, $665. Photo courtesy of James D. Julia, Inc.

Unknown maker, Grecian Key, emb clear glass base, acorn burner, red cased to white shade, patent date Nov. 14, 1911 in glass around collar . **135.00**

MINIATURE PAINTINGS

History: Prior to the advent of the photograph, miniature portraits and silhouettes were the principal way of preserving a person's image. Miniaturists were plentiful, and they often made more than one copy of a drawing. The extras were distributed to family and friends.

    Miniaturists worked in watercolors and oil and on surfaces such as paper, vellum, porcelain, and ivory. The miniature paintings were often inserted into jewelry or mounted inside or on the lids of snuff boxes. The artists often supplemented commission work by painting popular figures of the times and copying important works of art.

    After careful study, miniature paintings have been divided into schools, and numerous artists are now being researched. Many fine examples may be found in today's antiques marketplace.

1-1/8" sight, on ivory, oval, gentleman in powdered wig, early 18th C, oval 3-3/4" giltwood frame **450.00**
1-7/8" x 2-1/4", on ivory, Julia Clarke Brewster (1796-1826), attributed to John Brewster Jr., painted in the Columbia or Hampton, CT area, c1820, orig oval gilded copper locket case within orig red leather hinged case **4,600.00**
2" x 1-3/8", watercolor on ivory, gentleman, Anglo/American School, late 18th C, engraved gold pendant frame, reverse centered with en grisaille dec ivory oval medallion depicting dove with ribbon and two hearts suspended

Watercolor on ivory, allegorical painting of young woman in white classical Roman-style dress, blue and gold trim, red cap, laurel wreath in hair, holding rod, signed "J. A.," brass oval frame, 3-1/2" x 3", $375. Photo courtesy of Cowan's Historic Americana Auctions.

in it's beak above curved panel inscribed "one mind," surrounded by woven hair, glass cracked. **650.00**

2-5/8" x 1-7/8", watercolor and gilt on ivory, child wearing coral necklace, American School, 19th C, oval format, molded gilt frame, couple of cracks to edges of ivory, fading, laid down **420.00**

2-3/4" x 2-1/8", watercolor on ivory, George Washington, familiar pose, dark

Watercolor on ivory, George Washington, period frame, gilt paper mat, inked "Washington" on rear, 2-3/4" x 3-3/4" elephant ivory plaque, 4-5/8" x 5-3/4" frame, early 19th C, $1,130. Photo courtesy of Cowan's Historic Americana Auctions.

Watercolor on ivory, oval format, young girl in white empire waisted off-the-shoulder dress, unclear artist's signature, cast brass frame, 3-1/4" x 2-1/2", $350. Photo courtesy of Cowan's Historic Americana Auctions.

blue coat, white stock, unsigned, American School, an early oval thermoplastic frame with gilt liner, molded mark on the reverse "PATENTED AUG. 7. 1855," frame size 5-1/4" x 4-3/4" **500.00**

2-3/4" x 2-1/4", watercolor in ivory, military officer wearing a navy blue coat with crimson collar, white braid, and cross belt, silver breast plate, epaulettes, and buttons, unsigned, American School, oval format, ebonized wood frame. **1,100.00**

2-3/4" x 2-1/4" l, watercolor on ivory, young boy, sgd "Jared Sparks Handerson, Baltimore" in pencil on reverse, American School, 19th C, oval format. **620.00**

2-3/4" x 2-1/4", watercolor on ivory, young gentleman, black great coat, white waist coat, pleated shirt with stickpin and black neck cloth, unsigned, Anglo/American School, 19th C, gilt-metal frame, aperture containing lock of braided hair, fitted leather case **950.00**

3" x 2-1/2", watercolor on ivory, attributed to Frederick Buck, late 18th/early 19th C, young woman with curled hair, wearing coral necklace, oval format **825.00**

3" x 2-1/2", watercolor on ivory, Gustavis Tuckerman Jr., sgd and dated "Sacro

Fratelli 1847" lower right, inscribed on paper within opening on reverse "Gustavis Tuckerman (Jr.,) Born Edgbaston, England, May 15th 1824, Died New York, February 12, 1897," painted in Palermo, Italy, 1847 by Sacro Fratelli, oval engine-turned gilt-metal frame within rect papier-mâché frame inlaid with abalone floral dec . . **450.00**

3" x 2-1/2" d, watercolor on ivory, portrait of balding man, American School, 19th C. **415.00**

3-1/8" x 4-1/4" h, young brunette seated in lush interior, hair dressed with pearls, lace-trimmed gown and blue wrap, signed to left "J. Isabey," Continental, late 19th C, 6" x 4-7/8" gilt-metal frame **1,725.00**

3-1/4" x 2-1/2", watercolor on ivory, Napoleonic portrait, tortoiseshell and brass frame, oval format, signature obscured. **725.00**

3-1/4" x 2-1/2", watercolor on ivory, portrait of man in military uniform, pierced ivory frame, illegibly signed, surface scratching **400.00**

3-1/2" x 2-3/4", watercolor on ivory, gentleman wearing spectacles, sgd "M. B. Katze," brass framed, fitted in leatherette case. **200.00**

3-1/2" x 2-3/4", watercolor on ivory, identified as Elizabeth Maderia, 1934, sgd "E. B. Taylor," reverse with locket of hair, engraved name and date, oval brass frame, fitted in leatherette case **225.00**

Watercolor on ivory, man in Napoleonic uniform, signed "Isaberg/y/1812," frame with ormolu mounts, portrait 4" x 3-1/4", overall size 7-3/4" x 5-1/2", $750. Photo courtesy of Sanford Alderfer Auction Company.

Oil on paper, Continental School, 18th C, reverse inscribed "Jean Antonius Arlaud/1668-1748," oval mounted on blue velvet mat and rect giltwood frame, 3-5/8" w, $650. Photo courtesy of Sloan's Auctioneers & Appraisers.

3-1/2" x 2-3/4", watercolor on ivory, lady in burgundy, wearing lace bonnet, sgd "G. Harvey" lower right, hinged red leather case with ormolu mat . . . **725.00**

3-1/2" x 3-1/2", watercolor on ivory, young gentleman sitter identified on note as Johannes Josephus Kidder, Medford, Massachusetts, attending "Boy's school preparing for Harvard," seated on classical sofa having red upholstery, matching drapery and column in background, American School, early 19th C, framed in red leather case, heavy gilt liner, velvet int., minor abrasion to center background
.... **1,645.00**

4" x 3-1/4", watercolor and pencil on paper, lady in black, hair comb, reverse inscribed "painted May 12th 1834 by J Sears," oval eglomise mat, framed, scattered small abrasions, toning
.... **470.00**

4-1/8" x 3-1/2", watercolor on paper, lady in blue dress, white cap, brown ribbon, attributed to Edwin Plummer, Boston, c1841-46, oval eglomise mat, framed, laid down, small tear, minor toning, losses, repaint to mat . . **765.00**

4-1/2" x 3-1/2", ink and watercolor on paper, young lady, attributed to Rufus Porter, oval mat, framed, hinged at top, toning.................. **1,170.00**

4-3/4" x 3-5/8", watercolor on paper, woman wearing tortoiseshell comb, sitter identified on reverse as "Mrs. A. Saunders age 18 years," oval eglomise format, molded gilt frame, American School, c1840, toning, gilt loss on mat
.... **2,585.00**

5" x 4", watercolor on ivory, young girl, unsigned, American School, early 19th C, brass and ebonized wood frame
.... **500.00**

5-1/2" x 4-3/8", watercolor on paper, young man, unsigned American School, mid-19th C, backboard inscribed "J. Harrington," stamped brass and wood frame, oval format, minor fading **325.00**

5-3/4" x 4-3/4", pencil and watercolor on paper, Brigadier General James Miller, Peterboro, NH, American School, early 19th C, oval frame, toning, sold with accompanying note giving brief history of General's career **1,880.00**

5-3/4" x 4-3/4", watercolor on paper, gentleman, reverse identified as "1825, Eleazar Graves, father of Laura Graves Lincoln," unsigned, attributed to Rufus Porter, America, c1792-1884, grain painted frame, laid down, staining in margins, minor toning **445.00**

5-3/4" x 4-3/4", watercolor on paper, lady in elegant costume, attired in a brown and red dress with green trim and wearing a coral necklace and gold ear drops, American School, framed, minor foxing **2,000.00**

MINIATURES

History: There are three sizes of miniatures: dollhouse scale (ranging from 1/2 to 1 inch), sample size, and child's size. Since most early material is in museums or extremely expensive, the most common examples in the marketplace today are from the 20th century.

Many mediums were used for miniatures: silver, copper, tin, wood, glass, and ivory. Even books were printed in miniature. Price ranges are broad, influenced by scarcity and quality of workmanship.

The collecting of miniatures dates back to the 18th century. It remains one of the world's leading hobbies.

Child or doll size

Bed, 28-5/8" l, 16" w, 15-3/4" h, Arts & Crafts, rect headboard with two cartoon-like images of baby dolls, footboard with two sq-form cut-outs, imperfections **230.00**

Blanket chest

10-1/4" w, 6-1/4" d, 5-1/4" h, pine, nail construction, mustard ground, front panel with red and green landscape, red and white house with multiple windows, dark green trees, red and black tulips on sides, black flower with petals and red and green leave on lid, wire staple hinges, tin hasp, dec by Jacob Weber, Lancaster County, PA, underside with pencil inscription "Peter S. Clark's box," mane has been removed from front panel, but date of "1851" remains, feet missing......... **18,400.00**

11-5/8" l, 5" d, 4-1/4" h, carved wood, dark stained finish, hinged lid, two openwork spindled flowerheads on front section, chip-carved and stippled stylized floral dec on sides, Normandy, early 20th C
.... **300.00**

13" w, 7-1/2" d, 6-1/4" h, dovetailed case, old dark green paint, molded base and lid, int. till missing lid, hidden compartment in till, edge chips **495.00**

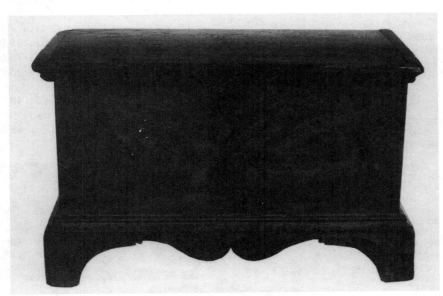

Blanket chest, Pennsylvania, decorated, reddish brown graining over yellow ground, pine, molded edge top, well-shaped bracket feet, 15-1/2" l, $5,610. Photo courtesy of Garth's Auctions, Inc.

Blanket chest, saleman's sample or child size, pine, lid with strap hinges, interior with till, ogee bracket feet, replaced molding and till lid, 22-3/4" w, 13" d, 16" h, $1,100. Photo courtesy of Sanford Alderfer Auction Company.

15" w, 8" d, 10" h, poplar, old black repaint, bracket feet with arched cut-outs on front and side aprons, applied beveled trim molding around lid, restorations to feet and hinge rail. **440.00**

Buffet, 9" w, 4-3/4" d, 13-3/4" h, carved wood, dark stained finish, two spindled shelves, lower section with two chip carved front doors, carved and stippled stylized floral dec on sides, Normandy, early 20th C **235.00**

Bookcase, hp, scalloped cornice over four open shelves, base with three drawers, Peter Hunt dec **1,650.00**

Chair, arm, 7" w, 5-3/4" d, 13-1/2" h, New England, mid-19th C, carved maple, ball, vase, and ring turnings on banister back, stiles ending in ball finials, finely turned arms, legs, and stretchers, orig upholstered seat **470.00**

Chair, side, 10-3/4" seat, 22" h, worn orig light green paint, black striping, gold stenciling, polychrome floral dec, pr **625.00**

Chest of drawers

9-3/8" l, 7-1/4" d, 7" h, carved mahogany and cherry, probably Massachusetts, c1825, top intricately carved with basket of flowers and leaves, fanciful border, mahogany veneered two short drawers over long drawer, ivory heart inlay, carved scrolled leaf motif on skirt, paw feet, names "H.M. Elliot and J.M. Ba--s" inscribed on backs and bottom of drawers, age crack **1,530.00**

13-3/8" l, 6-3/4" d, 11-1/8" h, painted pine, rect top, three drawers, shaped skirt, brass pulls, painted

Chair, child size, Victorian-type rose on back splat, needlepoint seat with dog motif, $125. Photo courtesy of Sanford Alderfer Auction Company.

brown, later floral and gilt embellishments, America, early 19th C, repair to rear leg, wear **250.00**

18" w, 8-1/8" d, 18-1/2" h, pine, old red wash, bracket feet, scalloped front apron, applied moldings around base and top, sq nail construction, turned wooden drawer pulls **675.00**

Mantel luster, 3-1/4" d, 7" h, mint green Bristol glass, hp mauve and pink flowers, blue forget-me-nots, green leaves, ruffled edge, remnants of gold trim, polished pontil, c1890, 2" l crystal prisms **275.00**

Rocker, Empire style, mahogany, vase-shaped splat, rush seat, scrolled arms, 22" h **225.00**

Settee, 7-5/8" l, 7-5/8" w, 4-1/4" h, carved wood, dark stained finish, serpentine back, openwork spindled

Chest of drawers, saleman's sample or child size, Empire-style, mahogany, five dovetailed drawers, double wood knobs, top drawer pencil signed "John Logan November 1930," 15" w, 7-1/2" d, 19-1/2" h, $550. Photo courtesy of James D. Julia, Inc.

flowerheads and chip-carved and stippled stylized floral dec, hinged lid, Normandy, early 20th C **145.00**

Settle bench, 24" l, 6-1/2" w, 6-1/2" h seat, PA, orig gold, copper, and silver fruit dec along crest and back slats, mustard yellow ground with areas of wear and touch-up, scrolled arms, plank seat with incised borders, eight turned legs, restoration **825.00**

Spiral staircase, 17-5/8" w, 8-5/8" d, 22-1/8" h, mahogany, dark rosewood grained finials, rect base with demilune cut out in center, late 19th C . . **1,500.00**

Table, drop leaf, Sheraton, walnut, pine secondary wood, leaves with decoratively cut corners, one dovetailed drawer, turned legs, old finish, minor edge damage, hinges replaced, age crack on top, 23-1/2" l, 12-1/2" w, 10-3/4" l leaves, 19" h **1,100.00**

Dollhouse accessories

Bird cage, brass, bird, stand, 7" h **65.00**

Carpet sweeper, gilt, Victorian . . **65.00**

Christmas tree, decorated. **50.00**

Coffeepot, brass. **25.00**

Cup and saucer, china, flower design, c1940 . . . . **10.00**

Decanter, two matching tumblers, Venetian, c1920. . . . . **35.00**

Fireplace, tin, Britannia metal fretwork, draped mantel, carved grate . . . **85.00**

Iron, 2" h, pot metal, white ground, multicolored dec **6.00**

Miniature lamp, 2-1/2" h, pot metal, white ground, multicolored dec. . . **7.50**

Radio, Strombecker, c1930 . . . . **35.00**

Refrigerator, Petite Princess . . . **75.00**

Silhouettes, Tynietoy, c1930, pr. **25.00**

Telephone, wall, oak, speaker and bell, German, c1890 . . . . **40.00**

Towel stand, golden oak, turned post **45.00**

Cradle, doll size, hand made, pine, slight play wear, $125. Photo courtesy of Sanford Alderfer Auction Company.

Umbrella stand, brass, ormolu, sq, emb palm fronds **60.00**
Urn, silver, handled, ornate **100.00**

Dollhouse furniture

Armoire, tin litho, purple and black **35.00**
Bathroom, wood, painted white, Strombecker **40.00**
Bedroom, Victorian style, metal, veneer finish, bed, nightstand, commode with faux marble tops, armoire and mirror, cradle, Biedermeier clock, metal washstand **675.00**
Bench, wood, rush seat **25.00**
Blanket chest, 7-1/8" l, 4-3/4" h, painted wood, six-board, wallpaper lined int., open till, replaced hinges, lock missing, America, 19th C **2,990.00**
Buffet set, stenciled, three shelves, column supports, Biedermeier, 6" h **400.00**
Chair, ormolu, ornate, 3" h, c1900, pr **75.00**
Cradle, cast iron, painted green, 2" l **40.00**
Desk, Chippendale style, slant front, drawers open **60.00**
Dining room, Edwardian style, dark red stain, extension table, chairs, marble top cupboard, grandfather clock, chandelier, candelabra, 5" h bisque shoulder head maid doll, table service for six, Gebruder Schneerass, Waltershausen, Thuringa, c1915 . . . . **1,400.00**
Hall rack, walnut, carved fretwork, arched mirror back shelves, umbrella holder **450.00**
Kitchen set, litho tin, Modern Kitchen, all parts and pieces, animals, and related items, orig box, Louis Marx **250.00**
Living room, Empire-style, sofa, fainting couch, two side chairs, upholstered tapestry, matching drapery **350.00**
Piano, grand, wood, eight keys, 5" h **35.00**
Rocker, painted tin, lithographed tin seated child holding doll, compartment under seat concealed candy storage, Meier, Germany, 3" l **275.00**
Sewing table, golden oak, drawer, c1880 . . . . **100.00**
Table, tin, painted brown, white top, floral design, 1-1/2" x 3/4" h, ornate **30.00**
Tea cart, Petite Princess **25.00**
Vanity, Biedermeier **90.00**

MINTON CHINA

History: In 1793, Thomas Minton joined other men to form a partnership and build a small pottery at Stoke-on-Trent, Staffordshire, England. Production began in 1798 with blueprinted earthenware, mostly in the Willow pattern. In 1798, cream-colored earthenware and bone china were introduced.

A wide range of styles and wares was produced. Minton introduced porcelain figures in 1826, Parian wares in 1846, encaustic tiles in the late 1840s, and Majolica wares in 1850. Many famous designers and artists in the English pottery industry worked for Minton.

In 1883, the modern company was formed and called Mintons Limited. The "s" was dropped in 1968. Minton still produces bone-china tablewares and some ornamental pieces.

Marks: Many early pieces are unmarked or have a Sevres-type marking. The "ermine" mark was used in the early 19th century. Date codes can be found on tableware and majolica. The mark used between 1873 and 1911 was a small globe with a crown on top and the word "Minton."

Bowl, 12" x 10", oval, Palissy style, minor base chip **3,080.00**
Centerpiece, 16" l, elongated parian vessel, molded scroll handles and feet, pierced rim, two brown reserves, white pate-sur-pate amorini, gilding, dec, attributed to Lawrence Birks, marked "Minton," retailer's marks of Thomas Goode & Co., Ltd., London, c1889 . . . . **1,400.00**
Compote, 10-1/2" l, majolica, figural, lobed oval dish and plinth, brown glaze

Oyster plate, six shell-form oyster wells, tortoise shell glaze, ground of naturalistically colored shells and seaweed, imp marks, date cipher for 1870, indistinct registry mark, 9" d, $695. Photo courtesy of David Rago Auctions.

on agate body, dish supported on backs of two cherubs holding laurel wreaths, center lovebirds, impressed mark, c1863 . . . . **2,415.00**
Dinner service, partial, Florentine pattern, 12 10-1/2" d dinner plates; 12 9" d luncheon plates; 12 2-3/8" h teacups; 11 saucers; 10 10-1/2" d soup plates; eight 8" d dessert plates; seven 2-5/8" h coffee cups; six 7" d side plates; five 4-5/8" bowls; three 13", 15", 17" l graduated serving platters; two 10-1/2" l cov serving dishes; two small oval dishes; two pickle dishes; two 5-5/8" d side plates; a sq cov serving dish; cov sugar; creamer; milk jug; sauce boat and undertray; 9-3/4" d serving bowl; open 12" l serving tureen; 15" l cov tureen, 108 pieces total, third quarter 19th C **2,185.00**

Dinner service, partial, hand-painted pink, turquoise, green and blue enamel birds and flowers, six place settings, additional place pieces, serving pieces, 92 pieces, some imperfections, $715. Photo courtesy of Sanford Alderfer Auction Company.

Tiles, set of 12 transfer-decorated in two patterns of the Aesthetic movement in browns and black on ivory, raised Minton Chinaworks mark, abrasion and chips, each 6" square, $435. Photo courtesy of David Rago Auctions.

Figure, 10-1/2" h, putti, yellow basket and grape vine, 1867, professional repair at rim of basket 2,750.00

Floor urn, 35" h, 18" d, majolica, Neo-Classical, turquoise, massive foliage handles 12,650.00

Garden set, 17-3/4" h, earthenware, barrel form, central pierced band of entwined rings between blue printed bands of flowers, scrolled vines, imp mark, 19th C, glaze wear, price for pr 1,100.00

Jardinière, 7" h, molded wooden plants, white vines, lilac int., majolica, matching stands, pr 475.00

Nut dish, 9-3/4" l, majolica, leaf molded dish with squirrel handle, imp mark, c1869, restored chips to ears 1,840.00

Oyster plate, majolica

Cobalt blue 1,650.00
Mottled 935.00
Turquoise 495.00

Oyster server, four tiers, majolica, green and brown, white wells, turquoise finial, rim damage to six wells, mechanical turning mechanism missing 3,575.00

Plaque, 11-1/2" sq, painted scene of Dutch man reading document by row of books, initials "HH" lower right, date mark for 1883, framed 290.00

Plate

9" d, hp, polychrome dec, garlands and swags on rims, marked "Mintons/England/Rd. No. 608547/73793/Pat. Apr 1st 1913," price for set of 12 . . . . 225.00

9-1/4" d, scalloped rim, gilt dec pierced border with florets within arch frames, center enameled dec with English castles in landscape, titled on reverse, artist sgd "J. E. Dean," printed and imp marks, c1910, six with hairlines and repairs, price for set of 12 . 575.00

Portrait plate, 9" d, Duchess de Berri Caroline, Princis Lambelle, Madame Mars, Madame Elizabeth, sgd "A.S.I.," names on reverse, price for set of four 350.00

Sweetmeat dish, 8" d, majolica, blue titmouse on branch, leaf-shaped dish, imp mark, 1888. . . . . 675.00

Tower pitcher, 12-1/2" h, majolica, castle molded body with relief of dancing villagers in medieval dress, imp marks, c1873, chips to cov thumb rest, spout rim. 1,035.00

Vase, 6-1/4" h, celadon green ground, five-spout, fan form, applied white floral relief, fish head feet, imp mark, c1855, foot rim chip 215.00

MOCHA

History: Mocha decoration usually is found on utilitarian creamware and stoneware pieces and was produced through a simple chemical action. A color pigment of brown, blue, green, or black was made acidic by an infusion of tobacco or hops. When the acidic colorant was applied in blobs to an alkaline ground, it reacted by spreading in feathery designs resembling sea plants. This type of decoration usually was supplemented with bands of light-colored slip.

Types of decoration vary greatly, from those done in a combination of motifs, such as Cat's Eye and Earthworm, to a plain pink mug decorated with green ribbed bands. Most forms of mocha are hollow, e.g., mugs, jugs, bowls, and shakers.

English potters made the vast majority of the pieces. Collectors group the wares into three chronological periods: 1780-1820, 1820-1840, and 1840-1880.

Reproduction Alert.

Beaker, pearlware

3" h, dark brown, medium brown, and ochre marble decoration on rust field, thin lines of medium brown at rim and base, England, early 19th C, rim chips and glaze wear. 2,475.00

3" h, rust, dark brown, medium brown, and white combed marble slip, England, early 19th C 2,820.00

Bowl, 7-3/8" d, 3-5/8" d, reeded green rim band above blue, rust, white, and brown slip marbling on mustard colored creamware ground, England, late 18th/early 19th C 4,115.00

Chamber pot, 8-3/4" d, two-tone blue bands, black stripes, black and white earthworm, leaf handle, some wear and edge flakes 125.00

Child's mug

2-1/2" h, pearlware, green glazed rouletted upper and lower bands flanking rust field with dark brown scroddled dots, with bisecting lines cut through slip to white body, applied handle, England, early 19th C, repaired 825.00

2-5/8" h, black banding with black and gray earthworm dec on green field, yellow glazed, extruded handle with foliate terminals, impressed partial maker's mark on bottom, England, early 19th C, chips to base edge, glaze wear to rim 2,990.00

Creamer, 5-1/4" h, black and white checkered band on shoulder medium blue glaze 215.00

Cup, 2-7/8" h, imp border above brown and white earthworm design, blue ground, 19th C, imperfections . 375.00

Ink sander, 3-1/4" h, pearlware, two rows of dark brown trailed slip "tendrils" on blue field, England, early 19th C, two small chips 1,175.00

Jug, 7-1/2" h, barrel-form, banded in blue and black, black, white, and blue earthworm dec on ocher field, handles with foliate terminals, England, c1840, 5/8" rim chip, associated crack, 1/2" chip on spout 1,880.00

Measure, 5", 6", and 6-1/4" h, tankard, blue, black and tan seaweed dec, one with applied white label "Imperial Pint," other with resist label "Quart," minor stains, wear, and crazing, three-pc set 440.00

Cann, yellow ware body, purple seaweed decoration on white band, blue band above, English, two tiny chips on table ring, 5" d, 4" h, $195. Photo courtesy of Cowan's Historic Americana Auctions.

Creamer, blue band, black stripes, wide pale green band with balloons in pink, black, and white, leaf molded handle, minor edge wear and hairlines, 5" h, $450. Photo courtesy of Garth's Auctions, Inc.

Milk pitcher, 4-5/8" h, dark bluish-gray band, black stripes, emb band with green and black seaweed, leaf handle, wear and painted over spout flake 440.00

Mug

3-1/2" h, pearlware, blue, dark brown, medium brown, and white combed marble slip on rust field, extruded handle, England, early 19th C, small crack, rim chips, discoloration **2,940.00**

3-1/2" h, 4-1/8" d, ftd, pink, blue, and black marbling, England, 19th C, five small hairlines on rim ..**360.00**

3-3/4" h, pearlware, banded in dark brown, white field, engine-turned geometric pattern of wavy lines

Mug, quart, pearlware, banded in dark brown and rust, two rows of blue, dark brown, rust, and white earthworm flanked by upper and lower white rouletted bands, extruded handle with foliate terminals, England, early 19th C, circular and spider cracks in the base, three rim chips, 6" h, $1,765. Photo courtesy of Skinner's Auctioneers and Appraisers.

flanked by tiny line of rick-rack, green glazed reeded band, extruded handle with green glazed foliate terminals, England, early 19th C, rim repair, minor edge nicks.................**2,350.00**

3-7/8" h, barrel-form, black mocha seaweed dec on ocher field between black and blue bands, extruded handles with foliate terminals, England, c1820, small chip on base edge......**1,410.00**

6" h, quart, banded in dark brown and rust, two rows of blue, dark brown, rust, and white earthworm flanked by upper and lower white rouletted bands, extruded handle with foliate terminals, England, early 19th C, circular and spider cracks in the base, three rim chips **1,765.00**

Mustard pot, cov

2-1/2" h, creamware, blue banded lid with blue reeded band, cylindrical body with matching banding, dark brown, rust, gray, and white earthworm pattern, extruded handle with foliate handles, creamware, England, early 19th C, chips to the lid, small crack to the body, discoloration......**1,300.00**

3-1/2" h, pearlware, lid with acorn finial, brown bands with dendritic seaweed on rust field, body decorated in the same manner, extruded handle with foliate terminals, England, early 19th C, finial repair, small rim and base chips.................**1,645.00**

3-1/2" h, pearlware, lid with ball finial banded in dark brown and rust, matching banding on the body, unusual band of rust and dark brown slip in finely trailed diamond pattern, extruded handle with foliate terminals, England, early 19th C, crack in the handle, minor glaze wear **2,585.00**

Pitcher, 7-3/4" h, three bands of dark brown seaweed on ochre ground, alternating with imp dark brown shell bands bordered with olive green stripes, upper and lower imp chevron bands on green ground, bordered with olive green stripes, applied handle, early 19th C, imperfections ...**3,750.00**

Salt, open, 2-1/2" d, pearlware, rounded form, medium blue rim band, vertical ribbed dark brown slip dec on white ground, England, early 19th C 590.00

Shaker

4-1/8" h, tan bands, brown stripes, black seaweed dec, chips . 220.00

4-7/8" h, blue band, black stripe, brown, black, and white earthworm dec, blue top, repair 330.00

Tea canister, 4" h, blue, black, and white band on shoulder, white fluted band on bottom, medium blue glaze 125.00

Teapot, 5-7/8" h, oval shape, medium blue, fluted band on bottom, black and white checkered band on top, acorn finial 500.00

Waste bowl, 4-3/4" d, amber band, black seaweed dec separated into five segments by squiggly lines, green molded lip band, stains and hairlines 275.00

MONT JOYE GLASS

For more information, see this book.

History: Mont Joye is a type of glass produced by Saint-Hilaire, Touvier, de Varreaux & Company at its glassworks in Pantin, France. Most pieces were lightly acid etched to give them a frosted appearance and were also decorated with enameled florals.

Jack in the pulpit vase, 14-1/2" h, amethyst shading to clear, enamel dec, gold sponged dec, polished pontil 995.00

Vase, green acid etched background, gilt cameo flowers, stems and leaves, base signed "Mont Joye," slight rim damage, 12-1/2" h, $400. Photo courtesy of James D. Julia, Inc.

Vase, amethyst shading to clear, ribbed, yellow and white flower decoration, unsigned, 13" h, $450. Photo courtesy of Joy Luke Auctions.

Pitcher, 10" h, amethyst, enameled flowers, aqua, blue, pink, and gold, sgd **350.00**

Rose bowl, 3-3/4" h, 4-1/4" d, pinched sides, acid etched, enameled purple violets, gold stems and dec . . . **295.00**

Vase

4" h, pink enameled poppy and gold leaves, frosted textured ground, marked **275.00**

6" w, 16" h, colorless body, enameled purple iris on one side, white iris on other, green leaves, gold trim **2,200.00**

8" h, gourd shape, acid cut back, enamel floral dec, gilt trim, four applied handles **1,150.00**

10" h, bulbous, narrow neck, clear to opalescent green, naturalistic thistle dec, gold highlights . **375.00**

12" h, rubena colored satin ground, enameled lily, c1890. . . . . . **550.00**

15-1/4" h, cameo, cut with flowering iris, enameled dec, sgd "Mont Joy" in gilt, c1900. . . . . **500.00**

Violet vase, 6" h, frosted etched surface, colorless glass, naturalistic enameled purple violet blossoms, gold highlights, base marked "Dimier Geneve". **260.00**

MOORCROFT

History: William Moorcroft was first employed as a potter by James Macintyre & Co., Ltd., of Burslem in 1897. He established the Moorcroft pottery in 1913.

The majority of the art pottery wares were hand thrown, resulting in a great variation among similarly styled pieces. Color and marks are keys to determining age.

Walker, William's son, continued the business upon his father's death and made wares in the same style.

Marks: The company initially used an impressed mark, "Moorcroft, Burslem"; a signature mark, "W. Moorcroft" followed. Modern pieces are marked simply "Moorcroft," with export pieces also marked "Made in England."

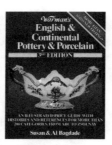

For more information, see this book.

Bowl, 3-5/8" d, pansy dec, pale green ground, imp maker's mark **150.00**

Box, cov, 4-3/4" l, 1-1/2" w, 1-3/4" h, pansy dec on lid, pale green ground, imp maker's mark, crazing **200.00**

Compote, 7-1/4" d, Lily motif, yellow and green ground **150.00**

Ginger jar, cov, 11-1/2" h, pomegranate dec **525.00**

Jar, cov, Cornflower, ivory ground, coat of arms of Kings College, Oxford, c1911 . . . . **1,450.00**

Lamp base, 6-1/4" d, 11-1/4" h, Anemone **920.00**

Loving cup, 6" d, 5-1/2" h, Pomegranate pattern, stamped mark, 1914-16, minor rim fleck. **1,150.00**

Pitcher, 6-1/4" h, Forget-Me-Not, c1902 . . . . **1,350.00**

Plate, 7-1/4" d, toadstool, blue ground, imp "Moorcroft Claremont". **600.00**

Vase

6-1/2" d, 15" h, Eventide pattern, ovoid, squeezebag green tall trees, cobalt blue ground, stamped "Moorcroft/Made in England" and signature, rim chip, 2" line **1,840.00**

7" h, Leaf & Berry, matte glaze, William's initials in blue . . **1,150.00**

Vase, Hibiscus, coral hibiscus, green ground, paper label "Moorcroft Potters to the Late Queen Mary," 1953-78, minor crazing, 4-1/4" h, $250. Photo courtesy of Skinner Auctioneers and Appraisers.

Bowl, Florian Ware, blue tones, 7-5/8" h, 2-1/2" h, $595.

8-3/8" h, swollen cylindrical, alternating bands of floral motifs and ovals, red and blue semi-gloss glaze, imp "Moorcroft, Made in England" **700.00**

10" h, Clematis, blue Walter initials, imp mark **1,050.00**

12" h, Orchid, flambé, sgd by William in blue, imp "Potter to HM The Queen". **4,350.00**

MORGANTOWN GLASS WORKS

History: The Morgantown Glass Works, Morgantown, West Virginia, was founded in 1899 and began production in 1901. Reorganized in 1903, it operated as the Economy Tumbler Company for 20 years until, in 1923, the word "Tumbler" was dropped from the corporate title. The firm was then known as The Economy Glass Company until reversion to its original name, Morgantown Glass Works, Inc., in 1929, the name it kept until its first closing in 1937. In 1939, the factory was reopened under the aegis of a guild of glassworkers and operated as the Morgantown Glassware Guild from that time until its final closing. Purchased by Fostoria in 1965, the factory operated as a subsidiary of the Moundsville-based parent company until 1971, when Fostoria opted to terminate production of glass at the Morgantown facility. Today, collectors use the generic term, "Morgantown Glass," to include all periods of production from 1901 to 1971.

Morgantown was a 1920s leader in the manufacture of colorful wares for table and ornamental use in American homes. The company pioneered the processes of iridization on glass, as well as gold and platinum encrustation of patterns. It enhanced Crystal offerings with contrasting handle and foot of India Black, Spanish Red (ruby), and Ritz Blue (cobalt blue), and other intense and pastel colors for which it is are famous. The company conceived the use of contrasting shades of fired enamel to add color to its etchings. It was the only American company to use a chromatic silk-screen printing process on glass, its two most famous and collectible designs being Queen Louise and Manchester Pheasant.

For more information, see this book.

The company is also known for ornamental "open stems" produced during the late 1920s. Open stems separate to form an open design midway between the bowl and foot, e.g., an open square, a "Y," or two diamond-shaped designs. Many of these open stems were purchased and decorated by Dorothy C. Thorpe in her California studio, and her signed open stems command high prices from today's collectors. Morgantown also produced figural stems for commercial clients such as Koscherak Brothers and Marks & Rosenfeld. Chanticleer (rooster) and Mai Tai (Polynesian bis) cocktails are two of the most popular figurals collected today.

Morgantown is best known for the diversity of design in its stemware patterns, as well as for its four patented optics: Festoon, Palm, Peacock, and Pineapple. These optics were used to embellish stems, jugs, bowls, liquor sets, guest sets, salvers, ivy and witch balls, vases, and smoking items.

Most glass collectors recognize two well-known lines of Morgantown Glass today: #758 Sunrise Medallion and #7643 Golf Ball Stem Line. When Economy introduced #758 in 1928, it was originally identified as "Nymph." By 1931, the Morgantown front office had renamed it Sunrise Medallion. Recent publications erred in labeling it "dancing girl." Upon careful study of the medallion, you can see the figure is poised on one tiptoe, musically saluting the dawn with her horn. The second well-known line, #7643 Golf Ball, was patented in 1928; production commenced immediately and continued until the company closed in 1971. More Golf Ball than any other Morgantown product is found on the market today.

Basket

Patrick, #19-4358, Ritz Blue, applied crystal twisted handle, mint leaf prunts, 5" d, 9-3/4" h **750.00**

Quilt, crystal, black/amethyst rope-twist handle, leaf form appliqués where handle joins basket, ground pontil . . . **1,100.00**

Trindle, #4357, amethyst, applied crystal twisted reed handle, c1930, 9" **725.00**

Berry jug, Palm Optic, #37, pink, 8-1/2" w, 9-1/8" h **235.00**

Bowl

Fantassia, Bristol Blue, #67, 5-1/2" d **95.00**

Janice, #4355, Ritz Blue, 13" d **475.00**

Woodsfield, Genova Line, 12-1/2" d, #12-1/2 . . . . **565.00**

Brandy snifter, Golf Ball, #7643, red, crystal base, 4" w, 6-1/4" h **130.00**

Candleholders, pr

Golf Ball, #7643, Torch Candle, single, Ritz Blue, 6" h **300.00**

Hamilton, #87, Evergreen, 5" h **65.00**

Modern, #80, Moss Green, 7-1/2" h **90.00**

Candy jar, cov

Mansfield, #200, burgundy matte, 12" h **200.00**

Rachael, crystal, Pandora cutting, 6" h **395.00**

Champagne

Golf Ball, #7643, Ritz blue, 5" . **55.00**

Lawton, #7860, Azure, Festoon Optic, 5 oz **50.00**

Ruby Red Filament Stem, 3" d base, price for pr **90.00**

Cocktail

Chanticleer, clear and smoke . **65.00**

Golf Ball, #7643, Stiegel Green, 3-1/2 oz **48.00**

Top Hat, Copen Blue, 5-1/4" h, 3-1/8" d **95.00**

Venus, #7577, Anna Rose, Palm Optic, 3 oz **40.00**

Cocktail set, Deco, black, 7-3/4" h pitcher with weighted base, five 3" w, 3" h cocktail glasses **65.00**

Compote, Reverse Twist, #7654, aquamarine, 6-1/2" d, 6-3/4" h . . **225.00**

Console bowl, El Mexicana, #12933, Seaweed, 10" d **425.00**

Cordial, 1-1/2 oz

Brilliant, #7617, Spanish Red **140.00**

Golf Ball, #7643, Pastels **65.00**

Mikado, crystal **30.00**

Finger bowl, Art Moderne, #7640, Faun etch, crystal and black, 4-1/2" d, ftd **150.00**

Goblet

Art Moderne, #7640, Faun etch, crystal and black, 7-3/4" h . **125.00**

Courtney, #7637, DC Thorpe satin open stem **195.00**

Golf Ball, #7643, Ritz blue . . . **60.00**

Laura, #7665, Nasreen etch, topaz **115.00**

Ivy ball, Kimball, Golf Ball, #7643, Ritz Blue (cobalt blue) on crystal stem and foot, 6-3/4" h, $120. Photo courtesy of Michael Krumme.

Paragon, #7624, ebony open stem, 10 oz **215.00**

Queen Louise, #7664, 3-1/2" d, 7-1/2" h **400.00**

Guest set, Trudy, #23, Bristol Blue, 6-3/8" h **145.00**

Ice tub, El Mexicana, #1933, Seaweed, 6" d **225.00**

Jug

Kaufmann, #6, Doric star sand blast, 54 oz **295.00**

Melon, #20069, Alabaster, Ritz Blue trim **1,450.00**

Measuring cup, 3-1/8" d, 2-7/8" h, adv "Your Credit is Good Pickerings, Furnishings, 10th & Penn, Pittsburgh," clear **315.00**

Oyster cup, 2-3/8" d, Sunrise Medallion, blue **190.00**

Pilsner, Floret, etch #796, Lando, 12 oz **65.00**

Plate

Anna Rose, #734 American Beauty etch, 7" d **65.00**

Carlton Madrid, topaz, 6" d . . . **35.00**

Country Ladies Violets, 1982, orig box and certificate, 9" d **40.00**

Goblet, Yale, Spanish Red bowl, crystal stem and foot, 9-1/2 oz, $145.

Vase, Electra, #35-1/2, Old Amethyst, Continental Line, applied clear twisted handles, 10" h, $1,400. Photo courtesy of Michael Krumme.

Sherbet

Crinkle, #1962, pink, 6 oz **30.00**
Golf Ball, #7643, Ritz blue . . . **50.00**
Sophisticate, #7646, Picardy etch,
5-1/2 oz **55.00**
Sherry, Golf Ball, #7643, Spanish Red
. . . . **43.00**
Tumbler, water, Belton, Primrose,
vaseline, pillar optic, 9 oz **135.00**

Vase

Catherine, #26, Azure, #758 Sunrise
Medallion etch, bud, 10" h . **265.00**
Daisy, #90, crystal, green and white
wash, 9-1/2" w **475.00**
Peacock Optic, tangerine, cylinder,
c1958, 60-1/2" h **35.00**
Raindrop pattern, red/orange, yellow
base, hobnail design on inside
graduating in size down to base,
4-1/2" d, 10" h **35.00**

Wine

Empress, #7680-1/2, Spanish Red,
3 oz. **90.00**
Mikado, 3 oz, price for set of nine
. . . . **225.00**

MOSER GLASS

History: Ludwig Moser (1833-1916) founded his
polishing and engraving
workshop in 1857 in
Karlsbad (Karlovy Vary),
Czechoslovakia. He
employed many famous
glass designers, e.g.,
Johann Hoffmann, Josef
Urban, and Rudolf Miller.
In 1900, Moser and his
sons, Rudolf and Gustav,
incorporated Ludwig
Moser & Söhne.

Moser art glass
included clear pieces with
inserted blobs of colored
glass, cut colored glass
with classical scenes,
cameo glass, and intaglio cut items. Many
inexpensive enameled pieces also were made.

In 1922, Leo and Richard Moser bought Meyr's
Neffe, their biggest Bohemian art glass rival. Moser
executed many pieces for the Wiener Werkstätte in the
1920s. The Moser glass factory continues to produce
new items.

*For more
information,
see this book.*

Basket, 5-1/2" h, green malachite,
molded cherubs dec, pr **800.00**
Bowl, 12-1/4" w, 3" h, cameo, cobalt
blue, 18 elephants, nine palm trees,
birds, large polished pontil, sgd in four
places, minor int. scratching . . **3,000.00**

*Cup and saucer, cobalt blue, brilliant
gold decorated background, 43 pink,
blue, and coral enamel daisy-type
flowers, raised gold stems and tendrils,
various shades of green on leaves with
painted veins, 2-3/4" h cup, 5-5/8" d
saucer, $395. Photo courtesy of
Clarence and Betty Maier.*

Cologne bottle, 7-1/2" h, 3-1/2" d,
amethyst shaded to clear, deep intaglio
cut flowers and leaves, orig stopper,
sgd **695.00**
Cup and saucer, amber, gold scrolls,
multicolored enameled flowers . **295.00**
Demitasse cup and saucer, amber
shading to white, enameled gilt flowers
. . . . **100.00**
Ewer, 10-3/4" h, cranberry, gilt surface,
applied acorns and clear jewels
. . . . **2,000.00**
Goblet, 8" h, cranberry, Rhine-style,
enameled oak leaves, applied acorns,
four-pc set **1,800.00**
Loving cup, 6-3/4" h, three colorless
handles, cranberry, gold enameled
dec, polished pontil, marked "2773"
. . . . **1275.00**
Perfume, 4-3/4" h, pink-lavender
alexandrite, faceted panels, matching
stopper, sgd in oval **275.00**

*Vase, applied
enamel
salamander
applied crystal
rigaree enameled
floral decoration,
top may be ground
down at points,
10-1/2" h, $460.
Photo courtesy of
James D. Julia,
Inc.*

Pitcher, 6-3/4" h, amberina, IVT, four
yellow, red, blue, and green applied
glass beaded bunches of grapes,
pinched in sides, three-dimensional
bird beneath spout, allover enamel and
gold leaves, vines, and tendrils
. . . . **3,200.00**
Portrait vase, 8-1/2" h, woman, gold
leaves, light wear **450.00**
Rose bowl, 3-1/2" h, cranberry ground,
enameled florals and butterfly, applied
acorns, c1900 . . . . **750.00**
Tankard, 12-1/4" h, emerald green
shading to colorless ground, finely dec
with silvered and gilt scrolled florals,
c1910 . . . . **450.00**
Tray, 7-1/4" w, cranberry, crackle, hand
enameled white and blue marsh scene
with egret, polished edges . . . **2,500.00**
Tumbler, 3-3/4" h, enameled dec,
c1910
Pale amber **50.00**
Pale blue. **50.00**
Urn, 15-3/4" h, cranberry, two gilt
handles, studded with green, blue,
clear, and red stones, highly enameled
surface, multicolored and gilt Moorish
dec **3,500.00**

Vase

7" h, paneled amber baluster body,
wide gold medial band of women
warriors, base inscribed "Made in
Czechoslovakia-Moser Karlsbad"
. . . . **550.00**
8" h, floriform, pink and green, foliate
dec, gilt trim **2,000.00**
9" h, cranberry, two gilt handles,
medallion with hp roses, sgd
. . . . **1,050.00**
10" h, heavy walled dark amethyst
faceted body, etched and gilded
medial scene of bear hunt,
spear-armed men and dogs
pursuing large bear **345.00**
12-1/4" h, cornucopia shape,
cranberry ground, allover blue,
orange, and green enameled ferns,
pedestal base, c1900 . . . **1,495.00**
15-3/4" h, green ground, enameled
dec, c1900. . . . . **150.00**

MOUNT WASHINGTON GLASS COMPANY

History: In 1837, Deming Jarves, founder of the
Boston and Sandwich Glass Company, established for
George D. Jarves, his son, the Mount Washington
Glass Company in Boston, Massachusetts. In the

For more information, see this book.

following years, the leadership and the name of the company changed several times as George Jarves formed different associations.

In the 1860s, the company was owned and operated by Timothy Howe and William L. Libbey. In 1869, Libbey bought a new factory in New Bedford, Massachusetts. The Mount Washington Glass Company began operating again there under its original name. Henry Libbey became associated with the company early in 1871. He resigned in 1874 during the Depression, and the glassworks was closed. William Libbey had resigned in 1872, when he went to work for the New England Glass Company.

The Mount Washington Glass Company opened again in the fall of 1874 under the presidency of A. H. Seabury and the management of Frederick S. Shirley. In 1894, the glassworks became a part of the Pairpoint Manufacturing Company.

Throughout its history, the Mount Washington Glass Company made different types of glass including pressed, blown, art, lava, Napoli, cameo, cut, Albertine, and Verona.

Additional Listings: Burmese, Crown Milano, Peachblow, and Royal Flemish.

Beverage set, satin, mother-of-pearl, yellow sea weed coralene dec, glossy finish, 9" h, bulbous water pitcher, three spout top, applied reeded shell handle, three matching 4" h tumblers, two blisters on pitcher, three-pc set **. 750.00**

Bonbon, 6-1/2" l, 4-3/4" w, 2-3/8" h at handle, Burmese, shiny finish, three applied lemon-yellow prunts, applied handle, re-fired heart-shaped rim **835.00**

Bowl, 4-1/2" d, 2-3/4" h, Rose amber, fuchsia, blue swirl bands, bell tone flint **295.00**

Box, 4-1/2" h, 6-1/2" d, opalware, mint green ground, deep pink roses, small red cornflowers, gold trim, blown-out floral and ribbon design, #3212/20 . . . . **1,750.00**

Collars and cuffs box, opalware, shaped as two collars with big bow in front, cov dec with orange and pink Oriental poppies, silver poppy-shaped finial with gold trim, base with poppies, white ground, gold trim, bright blue bow, white polka dots, buckle on back, sgd "Patent applied for April 10, 1894," #2390/128. . . . .**950.00**

Cracker jar, 8" h, opal glass, Egyptian motif, several camels at oasis, distant pyramid and mosque, sgd in lid with

Pairpoint Diamond P, #3910, corresponding #3910/530 on jar **2,760.00**

Cruet, 7" h, Burmese, shiny finish, butter-yellow body, applied handle, mushroom stopper, each of 30 ribs with hint of pink, color blush intensifies on neck and spout, Mt. Washington **1,250.00**

Flower holder, 5-1/4" d, 3-1/2" h, mushroom shape, white ground, blue dot and oak leaf dec **425.00**

Fruit bowl, 10" d, 7-1/2" h, Napoli, solid dark green ground painted on clear glass, outside dec with pale pink and white pond lilies, green and pink leaves and blossoms, int. dec with gold highlight traceries, silver-plated base with pond lily design, two applied loop handles, four buds form feet, base sgd "Pairpoint Mfg. Co. B4704" . . .**2,200.00**

Humidor, 5-1/2" h, 4-1/2" d top, hinged silver-plated metalwork rim and edge, blown-out rococo scroll pattern, brilliant blue Delft windmills, ships, and landscape, Pairpoint **950.00**

Jar, cov, 6" w, 5-1/2" h, peachblow, rim of jar and rim of lid cased in gold metal with raised leaves **400.00**

Jewel box, 4-1/2" d top, 5-1/4" d base, 3-1/4" h, opalware, Monk drinking glass of red wine on lid, solid shaded green background on cover and base, fancy gold-washed, silver-plated rim and hinge, orig satin lining, artist sgd "Schindler". **550.00**

Jug, 6" h, 4" w, satin, Polka Dot, deep peachblow pink, white air traps, DQ, unlined, applied frosted loop handle **475.00**

Lamp, parlor, four dec glass oval insert panels, orig dec white opalware ball shade with deep red carnations, sgd "Pairpoint" base, c1890. . . . . . .**1,750.00**

Syrup pitcher, Colonial Ware, Dresden floral decoration, 15 sprays of roses, pansies, daisies, and forget-me-nots, melon-ribbed body, fancy gold scrollwork on body, ornate pewter-like collar and lid, minimal wear, $950. Photo courtesy of Clarence and Betty Maier.

Temple jar, blue draping flowers, green leaves and vines, all highlighted with gold enamel, gold beads at lip, 8" h, $650. Photo courtesy of James D. Julia, Inc.

Lamp shade, 4-1/4" h, 5" d across top, 2" d fitter, rose amber, ruffled, fuschia shading to deep blue, DQ **575.00**

Miniature lamp, 17" h, 4-1/2" d shade, banquet style, milk glass, bright blue Delft dec of houses and trees, orig metal fittings, attributed to Frank Guba **795.00**

Mustard pot, 4-1/2" h, ribbed, bright yellow and pink background, painted white and magenta wild roses, orig silver-plated hardware **185.00**

Perfume bottle, 5-1/4" h, 3" d, opalware, dark green and brown glossy ground, red and yellow nasturtiums, green leaves, sprinkler top. **375.00**

Pickle castor, 11" h, opalescent stripes with light and dark pink, Pairpoint #604 frame **850.00**

Pitcher, 6" h, 3" w, satin, DQ, MOP, large frosted camphor shell loop handle **325.00**

Rose bowl, 5" d, satin, blue shading to white base **45.00**

Salt shaker, 2-1/4" h, tomato shape, opaque body, one green, one blue, raised enameled daisies **100.00**

Sugar shaker, 4-1/4" h, egg shape, white opaque body, holly leaves and raised enameled red berries dec **150.00**

Sweet meat, 5-1/2" d, opaque ground, pseudo Burmese enameling, gilt flowers and leaves, accented with jeweled cabochons, emb bail handle, sgd, lid #P4408, one jewel missing **815.00**

Toothpick holder, 2-1/2" h, Burmese, flared painted blue rim, mold-in ferns motif, scrolls at base, white blossoms with yellow dot centers. **1,085.00**

Tumbler, Burmese, shiny finish, thin satin body, soft color blushes from rim to center then shading to pastel yellow base, Mt. Washington. **375.00**

Vase, lily, amberina, 16 optic ribs, wafer base, 4-1/4" w, 10-1/4" h, **$565.** *Photo courtesy of Clarence and Betty Maier.*

Vase

2-3/4" h, Burmese, pink shading to yellow, three applied pale yellow feet **350.00**

6-1/2" h, Burmese, satin finish, 10 scallops with hint of yellow at edges, #52-1/2 S **500.00**

7-3/4" h, Burmese, satin finish, double gourd shape, finely drawn green and coral leafy tendrils, seven nosegays of blossoms, raised blue enamel forget-me-nots, each with pastel center with five coral dots, Mt. Washington, #147, c1885 . . . . **985.00**

8-3/4" h, Burmese, pink shading to pale yellow, colorful foliage dec in pointillism style, raised enameled berries **1,035.00**

10-1/4" h, stick, Burmese, yellow shading to pink, multicolored flowers dec, remnants of orig paper label **1,035.00**

11-1/4" h, gourd shape, 6" l flaring neck, satin, deep brown shading to gold, white lining, allover enameled seaweed design **550.00**

MULBERRY CHINA

History: Mulberry china was made primarily in the Staffordshire district of England between 1830 and 1860. The ware often has a flowing effect similar to flow blue. It is the color of crushed mulberries, a dark purple, sometimes with a gray tinge or bordering almost on black. The potteries that manufactured flow blue also made Mulberry china, and, in fact, frequently made some

For more information, see this book.

patterns in both types of wares. To date, there are no known reproductions.

Adviser: Ellen G. King.

Athens, Adams
Cup plate **65.00**
Plate, 9" d **80.00**
Posset cup, 12 panel **90.00**

Avon, Furnivals, teapot, cov, spout restored **450.00**

Beauties of China, Venables, teapot, cov **550.00**

Berry, Ridgways, plate, 10" d . . **145.00**

Blackberry Lustre, Mellor Venables, plate, 9" d **95.00**

Bryonia, Utzschneider
Cake/dessert plate, 14" d, pedestal base **375.00**
Compote, handles, 10" d **225.00**
Dessert/individual vegetable dish **30.00**

Demitasse cup and saucer . . **65.00**
Plate, 7-1/4" d **40.00**

Corean, Podmore Walker
Chamber pot **300.00**
Plate, 10" d **125.00**
Sauce tureen, cov, tray (no ladle) **450.00**
Teapot, cov, gothic, eight panels **350.00**

Cyprus, Davenport
Shaving mug, 3-1/2" **275.00**
Teacup and saucer, handleless **100.00**
Wash bowl and pitcher set, hairline in pitcher spout **625.00**

Eagle, Podmore Walker, vegetable tureen, cov, undertray **375.00**

Flora, Walker
Plate, 9" d **90.00**

Avon, Furnivals, teapot, cover, spout restored, **$450.** *Photos courtesy of Ellen G. King.*

Bryonia, Utzschneider, demitasse cup and saucer, **$65.**

Pelew, Challinor, gravy boat, **$145.**

Teacup and saucer, handleless
. . . .**80.00**

Jeddo, Adams
 Plate, 7-1/2" d **40.00**
 Teacup and saucer **75.00**
Lillium, Davenport, platter, 15" l.**275.00**
Loretta, Alcock, platter, 13-1/4" l **200.00**
Marble, Wedgwood, plate, 8-1/2" d
. . . .**45.00**
Medina, J F & Co., plate, 10-1/4" d
. . . .**65.00**
Nankin, Davenport
 Creamer. **75.00**
 Honey dish. **60.00**
 Plate, 9" d. **65.00**
Ning Po, Hall
 Creamer and sugar, set. **350.00**
 Cup plate. **75.00**
 Milk pitcher, restored spout . .**175.00**
 Plate, 7-1/2" d **40.00**
 Plate, 9-1/2" d **50.00**
 Plate, 10-1/2" d **60.00**
 Teapot, cov, lid restored **325.00**
Pelew, Challinor
 Gravy boat. **145.00**
 Tea set, cov teapot, creamer, cov
  sugar **900.00**
Rhone Scenery, Mayer
 Plate, 10" d. **70.00**

Strawberry, Walker, plate, 9" d, **$110.**

Vincennes, Alcock, wash bowl and pitcher set, **$900.**

Teacup and saucer, handleless
. . . .**50.00**
Scinde, Walker, soup tureen, cov
. . . .**2,000.00**
Seaweed, Ridgway, platter, 16" l
. . . .**375.00**
Strawberry, Walker, plate, 9" d . .**110.00**
Temple, Podmore WalkerPlate, 9" d
. . . .**80.00**
 Sauce tureen stand, on small foot
. . . .**60.00**
Tiger Lily, Furnivals, punch bowl,
pedestal, polychromed dec . . .**850.00**
Vincennes, Alcock
 Cup plate **85.00**
 Plate, 9-1/2" d **75.00**
 Relish dish, mitten shape . . .**250.00**
 Vegetable tureen, cov, 8-3/4"
. . . .**325.00**
 Wash bowl and pitcher set . .**900.00**
Washington vase, Podmore Walker
 Creamer **195.00**
 Pitcher, 8" h, octagonal. **325.00**
 Plate, 8-1/2" d **85.00**
 Platter, 17-3/4" l. **300.00**

MUSICAL INSTRUMENTS

History: From the first beat of the prehistoric drum to the very latest in electronic music makers, musical instruments have been popular modes of communication and relaxation.

The most popular antique instruments are violins, flutes, oboes, and other instruments associated with the classical music period of 1650 to 1900. Many of the modern instruments, such as trumpets, guitars, and drums, have value on the "used," rather than antiques market.

Collecting musical instruments is in its infancy. The field is growing very rapidly. Investors and speculators have played a role since the 1930s, especially in early string instruments.

Drum, metal, leather skin, rope binders and wood trims, Uncle Sam, c1914, scribbling on drumheads, puncture in bottom head, dent to side, 10-7/8" d, **$175.** *Photo courtesy of James D. Julia, Inc.*

Banjo
 Global, with case. **225.00**
 Korean, with case **90.00**
 Peerless, with case **60.00**
Cello, with bow and case **200.00**
Clarinet, with case
 Henry Bouche **675.00**
 Selmer **350.00**
Coronet, English, silver plated, stamped "F. Besson, Brevetee...," with case **320.00**
Drum set, Gretsch, three pcs, aqua sides. **600.00**
Fife, American, Meacham & Co., Albany, maple, brass fittings, case
. . . .**320.00**
Flute, American
 Gemeinhardt, with case **125.00**
 Haynes, William S., Co., Boston, 1911, Grenadilla, open G key
. . . .**1,100.00**
 Peloubet, C., five keys, rosewood, round key covers **550.00**
 Phaff, John, Philadelphia, 19th C, faintly stamped "J. Phaff...," eight keys, rosewood, silver fittings, period case. **1,265.00**
Flute, English
 Cubitt, W. D., & Son, London, 19th C, blackwood, open and nickel covered case, case **690.00**
 Monzani, London, 19th C, eight keys, head with turned reeding, silver fittings, round covered keys
. . . .**200.00**
 Rudall Carte & Co., London, silver, multiple stamps, hallmarks, case
. . . .**750.00**
 Wrede, H., London, c1840, four keys, stained boxwood, ivory fittings, silver round cover keys, case **320.00**

A valuable trumpet

Massachusetts was the home to American's first recorded maker of brass instruments. Elbridge G. Wright worked in Roxbury, MA, from 1839 to 1841, moved to Boston in 1841, and continued there until 1871. He also had a shop in Lowell, MA, from 1858 to 1859. The Metropolitan Museum added what could possibly be the earliest coronet/trumpet created by E. G. Wright in 1839 to its collection this past year when it purchased it for $31,050. The 15-1/2" l instrument has Vienna-valves, original silver maker's label reading "E. G. Wright, Maker, Boston," attached to the underside of the bell. The original walnut carrying case enhanced the value.

Guitar, archtop

D'Angelico, John, Model New York, irregular curl maple two-piece back, medium curl sides, medium grain with cross-bracing top, medium curl neck, bound peghead with inlaid pearl D'Angelico logo, bound ebony fingerboard with split-block pearl inlay, stamped internally "D'Angelico, New York, 1808," 21-7/16" l back, 18-1/2" w bottom bout, 1947 . . . . . **13,800.00**

Gibson Inc., Model Super 400, irregular curl maple two-piece maple back, medium curl sides, spruce top with medium grain, light medium curl neck, inlaid pearl Gibson logo peghead with split-diamond design, bound fingerboard with split-block pearl inlay, natural finish, labeled "Gibson Super Style 400, Number EA-5309 is hereby guaranteed, Gibson Inc., Kalamazoo, Michigan, USA," 21-7/8" l back, 17-13/16" w lower bout, c1939, with orig hard shell case and cover . . . **14,950.00**

Guitar, classical

Bazzolo, Thomas, three-piece rosewood back, similar sides, spruce top of fine grain fully bound, mahogany neck, ebony fingerboard, labeled "Thomas Bazzolo, Luthier #65C24, 1994, Lebanon, Connecticut, USA," and sgd, 18-15/16" l back, 14-1/8" w lower bout, with case **750.00**

Chica, Manuel de la, two-piece Brazilian rosewood back, labeled "Manuel De La Chica, Constructore, De, Violines Y

Guitarras, Placeta De La Silleria 8, Granada, Ano De 1966," 19-1/4" l back **1,725.00**

Martin, C. F., Style D-35, three-piece Indian rosewood back, similar sides, spruce top of fine to medium grain, mahogany neck with bound ebony fingerboard, inlaid pearl eyes, stamped internally "CF Martin & Co., Nazareth, PA, Made in USA, D-35," 1975 . . . . **1,475.00**

Fischesser, Leon, narrow curl two-piece back, similar ribs and scroll, fine grain top, red color varnish, labeled "Leon Fischesser Luthier D'Art, No. 47, 28 Faubuorg Poissonniere Paris L'Anno 1907," 14" l back, 356 mm, with case **2,760.00**

Guitar, flat top, Gibson, flat top, orig case **900.00**

Hawaiian guitar, National, New Yorker, with case **395.00**

Mandolin

Flat back, with case **175.00**
Gibson, F5, orig case . . . **29,000.00**
Washburn, melon base, with case **100.00**

Piano, Wetzels, c1810, French carved walnut, relief work of scrolled acanthus, 31 inlaid panels of engraved ivory depicting scenes from classical literature, two scenic carved panels depicting classical nudes at each end, 47 ivory keyed board supported by fully carved winged lion pedestals, period oval paper label inscribed "No. 800/31," sgd, dated in engraved ivory cartouches, "Wetzels Facteur de Pianos" and "Vitel Scupteur A Paris 1810," 48" l, 23" d, 41" d **3,220.00**

Piano, baby grand, Whitney, Chicago, manufactured by W. W. Kimball Co., walnut, matching bench, 53" l, $3,200. Photo courtesy of Joy Luke Auctions.

Recorder, Moeck **135.00**
Trumpet, valve type
Buescher **125.00**
Sears & Roebuck **115.00**
Ukulele
Aloha Royal, with case **90.00**
Hawaiian, three mele, Bares inscription, no strings **90.00**
Giamnini, baritone, with case . **95.00**
Kkamakall, with case **250.00**
Vibraphone **350.00**
Viola, no inscription, with orig case, orig bow **475.00**
Violin, **German**, D'Amore, faint curl on one-piece back, irregular curl ribs, later carved scroll of narrow curl, fine grain top, brown color varnish, unlabeled, c 1780, 13-3/8" l back, 339 mm, case, ivory mounted period bow . . . **4,150.00**

Piano, Wetzels, carved walnut and ivory inlay, relief work of scrolled acanthus, 31 inlaid panels of engraved ivory depicting scenes from classical literature, end panels with carved classical nudes, 47 ivory keyed board supported by fully carved winged lion pedestals, period oval paper label inscribed "No. 800/31," signed and dated in engraved ivory cartouches Wetzels Facteur de Pianos, and Vitel Scupteur A Paris 1810, 48" l, 23" w, 41" d, $3,220. Photo courtesy of Jackson's International Auctioneers & Appraisers.

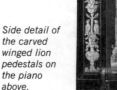

Side detail of the carved winged lion pedestals on the piano above.

Roller Organ, Mettez, carved wood case, painted screen panel on top of sailing vessel and cottages, cast metal handles mounted on either side, crank on left side, 10 tunes, play card, bell attachment, makers name marked on refinished case, 19th C, 26"d x 59" h, $980. Photo courtesy of James D. Julia, Inc.

Violin, Hungarian, medium curl two-piece back, similar ribs, medium curl scroll, fine grain top, red color varnish, labeled "Janos Spiegel, Budapest, 1907," 14-1/16" l back, 358 mm, with case **6,620.00**

Violin, Italian

Attributed to Andrea Postacchini, narrow curl one-piece back, irregular curl ribs, faint curl scroll, fine grain top, golden brown color varnish, labeled "Andreas Postacchini Amieie Filius Fecit Firmi Anno 1819, Opus 11?," 14" l back, 356 mm, with case, accompanied by bill of sale **17,250.00**

Bisiach, Leandro, strong medium curl two-piece back, strong narrow curl ribs and scroll, fine grain top, golden brown color varnish, labeled "Leandro Bisiach Da Milano, Fece L'Anno 1942," sgd, 14" l back, 356 mm, with case, undated numbered certificate **18,400.00**

Oddone, Carlo, strong medium curl one-piece back, similar ribs, narrow curl scroll, fine to medium curl grain top, orange color varnish, labeled "Carlo Giuseppe Oddone, 235 Fece Torino A 1930," stamped "C. Oddone, Torino" at lower rib and upper and lower interior blocks, sgd on int. of top, 14-1/16" l back, 357 mm **39,100.00**

Violin, Mittenwald, Klotz School, medium curl two-piece back, similar ribs and scroll, fine grain top, brown color varnish, unlabeled, c1780, 13-7/8" l back, 353 mm, with case **2,415.00**

Violin bow, gold mounted

Ouchard, Emile, round stick stamped "Emile Ouchard" at butt, ebony frog with Parisian eye, plain gold adjuster, 63 grams .. **4,025.00**

Seifert, Lothar, octagonal stick stamped "Lothar Seifert" at butt, ebony frog with Parisian eye, gold and ebony adjuster, 61 grams **1,265.00**

Unstamped, octagonal stick, later frog engraved "A. Vigneron A Paris 1886," 59 grams........ **1,485.00**

Violin bow, silver mounted

Hill, W. E., round stick stamped "W. E. Hill & Sons" at butt, ebony eye with Parisian eye, plain silver adjuster, 60 grams, baleen wrap **2,530.00**

Morizot, Louis, French, round stick stamped "L. Morizot" at butt, ebony frog with Parisian eye, plain silver adjuster, 60.5 grams **2,300.00**

Nurnberger, Albert, octagonal stick stamped "Albert Nurnberger" at butt, "Saxony" under plain ebony frog, silver and ebony adjuster, 61 grams............... **1,265.00**

Peccatte, Charles, round stick stamped "Peccatte" at butt, ebony frog with Parisian eye, plain silver adjuster, 60.5 grams, with certificate from Kenneth Warren & Son, Chicago **18,400.00**

Unstamped, French, Francois-Nicolas Voirin, c1860, round stick, ebony frog with pearl eye, later silver and ebony adjuster, 63 grams **4,890.00**

Weichold, Richard, octagonal stick stamped "R. Weichold A. Dresden" and "Imitation De Tourte" at butt, ebony frog with pearl eye, silver and ebony adjuster, 56 grams **1,265.00**

Violoncello, America, Settin, Joseph, strong narrow curl two-piece back, similar ribs and scroll, fine to medium grain top, golden brown color varnish, labeled "Joseph Settin Venetus, Fecit Anno Domani 1953," 29-7/16" l back, 748 mm **8,100.00**

Violoncello, child's, plain one-piece back, similar ribs and scroll, medium curl top, brown color varnish, possibly

Italian, 22-13/16" l back, 581 mm **3,795.00**

Violoncello, Czech, two-piece medium curl back, similar ribs and scroll similar, medium curl top, red color varnish, labeled "CAK Dvorni, A Armadni Dodvatel, Preniceska Tovarna Nastrouju Na Morave, Joseflidil V Brne Zelny Irh 11," 30-3/16" l back, 767 mm. **3,795.00**

Violoncello, English, James and Henry Banks, narrow curl two-piece back, medium curl ribs, faint curl scroll, fine to medium grain top, red color varnish, sgd internally on table, "James and Henry Banks, Salisbury," c1800, 28-34" l back, 729 mm **18,400.00**

Violoncello, French

Gand, Francois Eugene, one-piece narrow curl back, similar ribs and scroll, medium grain top, red color varnish, labeled "Gand, Luthier De La Muisque Du Roi, E Du Conservatoire De Musique, Rue Croix De Petits Champs No. 24, Paris, 1845, 113," 14-1/16" l back, 357 mm, with case **13,800.00**

Thibouville-Lamy, Jerome, narrow curl two-piece back, similar ribs, medium curl scroll, medium to wide grain top, orange color varnish, labeled "Jerome Thibouville-Lamy, 70 Rue Reaumur, Paris, 1938," 29-3/4" l back, 756 mm, with case **3,795.00**

Violoncello, German, irregular narrow curl two-piece back, similar ribs, narrow curl scroll, medium to wide grain top, orange color varnish, labeled "Erich Grunert, Penzberg Anno 1976," 29-3/4" l back, 756 mm, with case ... **1,150.00**

Violoncello bow, nickel plated, round stick stamped "L. Bausch, Leipzig," 81 grams **1,840.00**

Music Boxes

History: Music boxes, invented in Switzerland around 1825, encompass a broad array of forms, from small boxes to huge circus calliopes.

A cylinder box consists of a comb with teeth that vibrate when striking a pin in the cylinder. The music these boxes produce ranges from light tunes to opera and overtures.

The first disc music box was invented by Paul Lochmann of Leipzig, Germany, in 1886. It used an interchangeable steel disc with pierced holes bent to a point that hit the star-wheel as the disc revolved, and thus produced the tune. Discs were easily stamped out of metal, allowing a single music box to play an endless variety of tunes. Disc boxes reached the height of their popularity from 1890 to 1910, when the phonograph replaced them.

Music boxes also were incorporated in many items, e.g., clocks, sewing and jewelry boxes, steins, plates, toys, perfume bottles, and furniture.

Additional Listings: See *Warman's Americana & Collectibles* for more examples.

Black Forest, Carl Frei, hand cranked street organ, Waldkirch, Germany, $8,365. Photo courtesy of Auction Team Breker.

Bremond, 23" w, No. 2630, 13" cylinder with bird strikers, nine bells, plays eight airs, veneered and inlaid case **3,680.00**

Cellesta, 8-1/4" disc, single-comb ratchet-wind mechanism, walnut case with bone inlaid top and color print in lid, 16 discs **980.00**

Eight-Air, 15" w, 4-1/2" nickeled cylinder and tune indicator, grained case **375.00**

Lecoulture, D., 17" l, 8-1/4" cylinder, plays four airs, plain case **1,100.00**

Match striker, 9" h, gilt cast metal figure of man holding his chamber pot out window, strike-plate activating two-air movement playing "Dixie" and "La Marsille".................. **635.00**

Mermod Freres, 30" w, 13-1/2" cylinder, plays 12 airs, crank-wind motor, tune selector/indicator, grained case with veneered and inlaid front and lid, inner lid and divisions replaced **1,495.00**

Olympia, No. 6566, 20-1/2" upright disc, twin-comb mechanism, disengaged coin slide, manual control, two-piece mahogany cabinet, side disc storage, 32 discs, sounding boards replaced, 70" h **6,900.00**

Paillard, tune card
   23-1/2" l, No. 48375, 13" cylinder, plays 10 dance and other airs, tune indicator, tune card, grained case with inlaid lid........... **2,300.00**
   34" l, No. 32378, Excelsior Interchangeable, three 9-1/4" cylinders, plays eight airs each, double-spring motor, tune indicator

and zither attachment, grained case, torn tune card, veneered and inlaid front and lid, cylinder drawer in plinth **3,750.00**
   36" w, 17" cylinder, No. 41738/39235, plays eight operatic airs by Verdi, Chopin, Rosetti, and others, double-spring motor, tune selector and indicator, grained case with inlaid lid, fitted Aesthetic Movement ebonized table with incised gilt dec **5,750.00**

Polychon, No. 27498, 15-1/2" disc, twin comb movement, coin slide, walnut case with bobbin turned corner columns, paneled and inlaid top, monochrome print in lid, disc storage drawer in plinth, 36 zinc disks, 24" w **460.00**

Regina
   No. 13632, 15-1/2" disc, coin operated, twin-comb mechanism, coin slide, oak case with rope twist and egg and dart molding, instruction label, Murray, Sping & Co. Providence, RI, retailer's label, oak table with bobbin-turned legs, brass claw feet, 22 disks, 38" h **3,450.00**
   No. 14225, 15-1/2" disc, twin-comb mechanism, mahogany case with paneled lid, rope twist molding, stand with two pull-out shelves, disc storage compartment enclosed by double doors, 100 zinc discs, print replaced, 42-1/2" h **5,465.00**
   No. 55426, 15-1/2" disc, twin-comb movement, oak case with engaged corner columns, bone stringing,

Regina, 13372, disc player, sarcophagus top case with rope turned ornamentation, bun feet, conforming stand with shaped pedestal and scroll feet, 40 discs, $3,025. Photo courtesy of Sanford Alderfer Auction Company.

Swiss, 8-1/4" d brass cylinder, fruitwood and ebonized wood case with floral inlay on lid, Minor scratching on case, some tips of teeth broken, 16" w, 8-1/4" d, 5-1/2" h, $880. Photo courtesy of Sanford Alderfer Auction Company.

domed lid with monochrome print, 30 discs **5,175.00**
   No. 67095, 12-1/4" disc, single-comb movement, mahogany case with orig price tag, monochrome print, domed lid, 32 discs, main spring defective **2,100.00**

Singing bird
   3-3/4" w, blue enameled case, ivory beak, moving wings and perch, lid with Alpine scene and floral spray **2,645.00**
   4" w, silver plated, serpentine front and sides, cast with views of country scenes, leather traveling case, bird detached and featherless **815.00**
   11" h, brass, moving head, circular base **420.00**

Symphonion, 12" metal disc, double comb movement marked "Schutz-Marke Trademark, Made in

Swiss, eight-tunes, Geneva, Switzerland, cover faced with rosewood veneer inlaid with contrasting colored wood, original hand lettered paper label, 20" l, 8-3/8" d, 5- 1/2"h, $1,100. Photo courtesy of James D. Julia, Inc.

Victorian, mechanical landscape with boat on ocean, castle with turret and figure, watermill, and windmill, glass dome, wooden base, 18" d, 19" h, $3,400. Photo courtesy of Joy Luke Auctions.

Germany," fruitwood marquetry case, molded accents, Victorian brass hardware, includes 16 12" disks, 18" w, 15" d, 9-1/2" h, losses to combs
. . . . **1,450.00**
Unknown maker
5-3/8" w, 4" d, 6-5/8" h, morocco covered case formed as upright piano, plays march and air, hinged lid enclosing ivory and ebonized keys with starting latch, mirrored backplate, fitted with two glass perfume bottles, four-piece cut-steel manicure set, Continental, late 19th C **550.00**
8" l, automation, fabric covered cabbage, central white fur covered head of rabbit, glass eyes, plays one air as rabbit emerges from cabbage and moves ears, Continental, late 19th C **550.00**
21-1/2" w, 11" cylinder, six bells, plays eight airs, optional engine turned bells, veneered case
. . . . **1,380.00**
Unknown Swiss maker
16" l, 10-1/4" d, 8-1/2" h, 6-1/4" cylinder, plays eight airs, drum with five strikers, tune card, rect case inlaid to hinged lid with central cartouche of drum and pipes, line banding throughout, bracket feet, late 19th C **2,425.00**
24-5/8" l, 12-3/8" w, 10-1/4" h, 15" cylinder, plays 12 airs, engine-turned bells, tune card, rect case inlaid to hinged lid with central brass and mother-of-pearl cartouche, bracket feet, late 19th C
. . . . **2,645.00**

NAILSEA-TYPE GLASS

History: Nailsea-type glass is characterized by swirls and loopings, usually white, on a clear or colored ground. One of the first areas where this glass was made was Nailsea, England, 1788-1873, hence the name. Several glass houses, including American factories, made this type of glass.

For more information, see this book.

Bell, 11-3/4" h, white, rose loopings
. . . . **95.00**
Bottle, 8" h, gemel, flattened ovoid body, two necks, white casing, red, white, and blue loopings **400.00**
Candlestick, 10" h, colorless, white loopings, folded socket rim, hollow blown socket drawn out to a double knop, bulb shaped stem, two additional knops, inverted cone-shaped base, early 19th C **375.00**
Fairy lamp, 5-1/4" h, 6-1/4" d, frosted blue, opaque white loopings, colorless Clarke insert **695.00**
Flask
8-3/4" h, cobalt blue, England or eastern US, 19th C **215.00**
10-1/2" h, colorless, white and transparent pink marbrie and applied colorless rigaree, prunts, handles, England or eastern US, late 19th C, imperfections . **215.00**

Witch ball, colorless, white ribbon decoration in interlocking loops, open snapped pontil, early to mid 19th C, 7" d, $275. Photo courtesy of Cowan's Historic Americana Auctions.

10-7/8" h, ruby, applied colorless rigaree, England or eastern US, 19th C, very minor imperfections
. . . . **165.00**
12-1/2" h, colorless, white and transparent pink marbrie and applied colorless rigaree, prunts, handles, England or eastern US, late 19th C, imperfections . . **225.00**
Lamp, 11-1/2" h, colorless ground, pink and white loopings on font and ruffled shade, applied colorless feet, berry prunt. **2,500.00**
Pitcher, 6-1/2" h, 4" d, colorless ground, white loopings, ftd, solid applied base, triple ribbed solid handle with curled

Four fairy lamps, left to right, all with cranberry shade with white Nailsea loopings, slight differences in clear S. Clarke bases: 4-3/4" h, clear Clarke's Cricklite base, $175; 6" h, clear Clarke's Cricklite holder with metal base, $130; 4-1/2" h, clear Clarke Cricklite base, $225; 4-3/4" h, clear S. Clark's base, $200. Photo courtesy of Woody Auctions.

end, flaring formed mouth, attributed to South Jersey, c1840-60 . . . . . **1,200.00**
Rolling pin, 13-3/4" l, freeblown, rose and white loopings, colorless ground, ground mouth, smooth base, 1850-80 . . . . **220.00**
Tumbler, white ground, blue loopings **120.00**
Vase, 8" h, 5" d, cylindrical, flared mouth and base, colorless, white loopings, plain sheared rim, pontil, attributed to South Jersey **195.00**
Witch ball, 4-3/8" d, white ground, pink and blue loopings **450.00**

NANKING

History: Nanking is a type of Chinese porcelain made in Canton, China, from the early 1800s into the 20th century. It was made for export to America and England.

Four elements help distinguish Nanking from Canton, two similar types of ware. Nanking has a spear-and-post border, as opposed to the scalloped-line style of Canton. Second, in the water's edge or Willow pattern, Canton usually has no figures; Nanking includes a standing figure with open umbrella on the bridge. In addition, the blues tend to be darker on the Nanking ware. Finally, Nanking wares often are embellished with gold, Canton is not.

Green and orange variations of Nanking survive, although they are scarce.

Reproduction Alert: Copies of Nanking ware currently are being produced in China. They are of inferior quality and decorated in a lighter, rather than in the darker, blues.

Bowl, 10" d, shaped, 19th C . . . **880.00**
Candlesticks, pr, 9-1/2" h **775.00**
Cider jug, 10" h, gilt highlights, 19th C, pr **825.00**
Cup and saucer, handleless, 3-3/4" h cup, 5-3/4" d saucer, pagodas, man on bridge, c1780-1820 . . . . **235.00**

Platter, 11-1/2" x 14-1/2", **$345.**

Ewer, 11" h, small spout, blue and white, mid-19th C **300.00**
Pitcher, cov, 9-1/2" h, blue and white, Liverpool shape **550.00**
Plate, 9-1/2" d, water's edge scene, c1780-1800 . . . . **85.00**
Platter, 12-3/4" l, Chinese, 19th C, chips **415.00**
Rice bowl, 19th C **100.00**
Salad bowl, 10" h, 19th C . . . **1,200.00**
Soup bowl, 9-1/2" d, pagodas, man on bridge, islands, and horse, c1840-60 . . . . **240.00**
Soup tureen, cov, 11-3/4" h, 19th C, imperfections **475.00**
Teapot, 6-1/2" h, globular, diaper border above watery pagoda landscape reserve **155.00**

NAPKIN RINGS, FIGURAL

History: Gracious home dining during the Victorian era required a personal napkin ring for each household member. Figural napkin rings were first patented in 1869. During the remainder of the 19th century, most plating companies, including Cromwell, Eureka, Meriden, and Reed and Barton, manufactured figural rings, many copying and only slightly varying the designs of other companies.

Notes: Values are determined by the subject matter of the ring, the quality of the workmanship, and the condition.

Baby, seated, arms extended, Pairpoint #52, resilvered **650.00**
Bird, wings spread over nest of eggs **175.00**
Boy, sitting on bench, holding drumstick **200.00**
Brownie, climbing up side of ring, Palmer Cox **185.00**

Angel holding leash of crouched dog with padlock on collar, silver plated, marked "James Tufts Boston 1543," 4 3/4" w, 3-1/2" h, **$1,100.** *Photo courtesy of James D. Julia, Inc.*

Parrot, standing, holding hand chased napkin ring via rope around neck, base cast with berries, leaves, and flowers, silver plated, marked "Meriden #158," 4" w x 3-1/4" h, **$835.** *Photo courtesy of James D. Julia, Inc.*

Butterfly, perched on pair of fans **125.00**
Cat, glass eyes, ring on back . . **275.00**
Cherub, sitting cross-legged on base, candleholder and ring combination **195.00**
Chicken, nesting beside ring . . **150.00**
Child, crawling, ring on back . . **300.00**
Dog, sitting next to barrel-shaped ring, sgd "Tufts, #1531" **125.00**
Double eagle, marked "Meriden" **125.00**
Double rifles, Meriden B. #235 **850.00**
Dutch Boy, pulling on boots, resilvered **110.00**

Two putti supporting engraved napkin ring, engraved base, four ball feet, silver plated, marked "Wilcox Quadruple Plate, #01536, Meriden, Conn," 2-1/4" w, 3-1/4" h, **$250.** *Photo courtesy of Sanford Alderfer Auction Company.*

Vase with Egyptian motifs next to ring napkin holder, supported by turtle, footed rectangular base, silver plated, marked "Derby Co. Quadruple Plate, #342," 3-1/4" h, **$470.** *Photo courtesy of Sanford Alderfer Auction Company.*

Frog, holding drumstick, pushing drum-like ring **300.00**
Girl carrying basket, #734 . . . . **795.00**
Goat, pulling wheeled flower cart
. . . . **250.00**
Kate Greenaway, girl with muff on one side, dog on other, Derby #514, resilvered **875.00**
Owl, sitting on leafy base, owls perched on upper limbs **250.00**
Parrot, on wheels, Simpson, Hall, Miller & Co. **185.00**
Rabbit, sitting alertly next to ring
. . . . **175.00**
Ring on lotus flowers and pads, silverplate **100.00**
Sailor boy, anchor **220.00**
Schoolboy with books, feeding begging puppy **235.00**
Turtle, crawling, ornate ring on back
. . . . **300.00**

NASH GLASS

History: Nash glass is a type of art glass attributed to Arthur John Nash and his sons, Leslie H. and A. Douglas. Arthur John Nash, originally employed by Webb in Stourbridge, England, came to America and was employed in 1889 by Tiffany Furnaces at its Corona, Long Island, plant.

While managing the plant for Tiffany, Nash designed and produced

For more information, see this book.

Console bowl, Chintz, clear ground with pink and green chintz, signed 501/DD/Nash, 11-1/2" d, 3-1/2" h, **$200.** *Photo courtesy of David Rago Auctions.*

iridescent glass. In 1928, A. Douglas Nash purchased the facilities of Tiffany Furnaces. The A. Douglas Nash Corporation remained in operation until 1931.

Bowl, 7-3/4" x 2-1/2", Jewel pattern, gold phantom luster **285.00**
Candlestick, 4" h, Chintz , ruby and gray, sgd **450.00**
Compote, 7-1/2" d, 4-1/2" h, Chintz, transparent aquamarine, wide flat rim of red and gray-green controlled stripe dec, base inscribed "Nash RD89"
. . . . **865.00**
Cordial, 5-1/2" h, Chintz, green and blue **95.00**
Creamer and sugar, 5-3/8" h creamer, 3-1/2" h sugar, blue-green opaque dots, dark blue-green base, creamer with polished pontil, sugar with waffle pontil
. . . . **475.00**
Goblet, 6-3/4" h, feathered leaf motif, gilt dec, sgd **295.00**
Plate, 8" d, Chintz, green and blue
. . . . **195.00**

Vase, iridescent blue, marked "B526 Nash," 5-1/2" h, **$625.**

Sherbet, bluish-gold texture, ftd, sgd, #417 . . . . **275.00**
Vase
5-1/2" h, Chintz, pastel, transparent oval, internally striped with pastel orange alternating with yellow chintz dec **275.00**
9" h, Polka Dot, deep opaque red oval, molded with prominent 16 ribs, dec by spaced white opal dots, base inscribed "Nash GD154" **1,100.00**

NAUTICAL ITEMS

History: The seas have fascinated man since time began. The artifacts of sailors have been collected and treasured for years. Because of their environment, merchant and naval items, whether factory or hand-made, must be of quality construction and long lasting. Many of these items are aesthetically appealing as well.

Account book, *Bark Arab,* showing purchases and sales from October 1853 to December 1856, 96 pgs, folio, New Bedford or Hawaii, label reads "purchased of John Kehew at his Navigation Store in New Bedford," Kehew's label mounted on front paste down, two volumes **1,955.00**
Arrest warrant, document issued by Marshall of the District of Rhode Island, to arrest Edward Thurston and Nicholas Brown for stealing shares in the sloop *Liberty* valued at $8,000, dated July 18, 1797, some surface toning, 8" x 12-1/2"
. . . . **90.00**
Banner, 26" x 8-1/2", carved and polychrome painted pine, "Don't Give Up The Ship!," American eagle, attributed to John Hales Bellamy
. . . . **24,150.00**
Book
Allyn, Captain Gurdon L., *Old Sailor's Story, or a Short Account of the Life, Adventures, and Voyages, The,* Norwich, 1879, 111 pgs, 8vo, orig flexible cloth wrappers
. . . . **316.00**
Bligh, William, *Dangerous Voyage of Captain Bligh, in an Open Boat, over 1200 Leagues of the Ocean, in the Year 1789,* Dublin, 1818, five full-page woodcut engraved illus, 180 pgs, small 12mo **345.00**
Dexter, Elisha, *Narrative of the Loss of the William and Joseph, of Martha's Vineyard,* Boston, 1842, five wood engraved plates, 54 pgs, 8vo **1,370.00**

Boarding axe, belt hook on left side of shaft, marked only with two different size anchors on the left side, 5-1/4" blade, 10-3/4" l including spike, gray patina, light surface rust and pitting, shaft and upper attaching tang are broken at head repaired with poor glue repair, **$1,440.** *Photo courtesy of James D. Julia Auctions.*

Box, cov, 4-3/4" h, 12" l, 6-5/9" d, walnut, dovetailed, ropework handle, polyhedron carved terminals, attributed to New England sailor, early 19th C, one terminal missing **460.00**

Broadside, 415 x 335 mm, issued as circular to mariners at Table Bay, Robben Island, advising of berthing procedures, 1827 . . . . **345.00**

Cane

32-7/8" l, carved from single piece of tooth, 1-3/4" d x 2" h whale ivory handle, carved sailor's Turks-head knot, thin baleen spacer separates whalebone shaft, inlaid at top with four-pointed baleen fingers, white whalebone shaft, tapered with very slight natural bow, American, c1850 . . . . **2,800.00**

36-1/2" l, 1-3/4" d x 2/3" h flat brass handle, wide all metal black shaft fashioned with metal nubs all along length, when handle pulled off, hollow exposed to reveal watertight compartment to store nautical charts and documents, 3/4" brass ferrule, English, c1890 . . . . **450.00**

Canoe paddle, 60" l, painted deep red with black crescent moon and star, America, late 19th C, with stand **375.00**

Children's book

Adventures of Jack, or a Life on the Wave, The, Charles L. Newhall, Southbridge, 1859, 134 pgs, 12 mo **230.00**

On the Seas, a Book for Boys, Boston, c1875, plates, small 8vo **130.00**

Chronometer, 8-1/2" h, 8-1/4" w, 8-1/4" d, "M.F. Dent, 33 Cockspur St. Chronometer Maker to the Queen, London," late 19th C, gimbal mounted in brass fitted mahogany case, brass bezel, silver wash dial, eight days **5,175.00**

Clock, 10-1/2" h, brass, Seth Thomas, one-day lever-striking movement, circular case, domed bell mounted below on wooden backboard, late 19th C **520.00**

Compass, lifeboat, 8" sq, 7-1/4" h, boxed, 20th C **175.00**

Crew list, partly printed, two languages, *Jireh Swift,* lists 13 additional Hawaiian crew members, Lahaina, March 29, 1865 . . . . **2,000.00**

Diorama, 32-1/2" w, 23" h, black, red, and green sailing ship, white sails, lighthouse and other sailing ships painted into v background, gesso frame with old gold repaint. . . **1,450.00**

Figurehead, 30" h, carved, Nantucket Island origin, c1830 . . . . . . **12,000.00**

Fishing license, issued to sloop *Kial,* April 23, 1808, for cod fishing, issued in Newport, RI, some edge chipping, fold splitting, 16-1/2" x 10-1/2" **165.00**

Hourglass, 7" h, 19th C **550.00**

Inclinometer, 4-1/2" d, brass, cased, bubble type, Kelvin Bottomley & Baird Ltd. **65.00**

Indenture, document indenturing William McGraa to Isaac Fisher as apprentice mariner for four years, details duties, payment schedule, May 19, 1813, signed by all parties, some foxing, edge chipping, 1810 watermark, 16" x 13-1/2" **100.00**

Jewelry chest, 18-1/4" l, 12-1/2" d, 10-3/8" h, sailor-carved walnut and whalebone, America, 19th C, carved rosette, fan, lapped leaf, pendant, and other designs, front and side drawers, hinged lid opens to mirror which further opens to three oval frames with rope trim, box int. fitted with four compartments with carved lids, carved whalebone drawer and lid handles **2,350.00**

Log book, Ship *Geneva,* George M. Tucker, Master, sailed from Boston, March 4, 1852 towards Richmond, later to San Francisco, then to Calcutta, back to Boston where she docked at Central Wharf on Aug. 13, 1853, worn spine, cover. **1,150.00**

Masthead, 16" h, 9-1/2" d, copper and brass, oil fired, complete with burner, 360 degrees, late 19th C **200.00**

Membership certificate, 12-3/8" x 17-1/2", certifying "...That Capt. Green Walden was by a majority of votes regularly admitted a member of the Portland Marine Society at a meeting held the 17th day of September 1839...," certificate dec with reserves depicting various marine scenes, toning, foxing, framed **530.00**

Model, carved and painted wood

27" l, 23" h, two-masted fishing schooner, hull painted two shades of green, light blue details, metal fittings, minor breaks **355.00**

31" l, 19-1/2" h, three-masted square-rigged ship, metal fittings, black and white painted hull with light blue details, wooden stand, some breaks in rigging . . . **600.00**

31-1/2" l, 11-1/2" w, 21-1/2" h, three-masted clipper, carved wooden fittings, painted green and black, white trim, mounted into mahogany framed display case **400.00**

31-1/2" l, 22-3/8" h, three-masted ship *Corsair,* carved wood, ivory, and metal implements and fittings, hull painted green and black, red, yellow, and white details, mounted on wooden stand, some breaks **950.00**

111" l, 67" h, three-masted ship *Ocean Monarch,* carved wood and metal implements, hull painted black, blue and gilt details, some breaks in rigging **4,995.00**

Oar, 57-1/2" l, curly maple, well carved, thin broad end, good figure . . . **420.00**

Painting, 17-1/2" x 22-7/8", American Barque *Nellie Chapin* in Chinese Waters Signaling for a Pilot, unsigned, Chinese School, 19th C, oil on canvas, carved and painted Chinese Chippendale frame, puncture, minor retouch, prevalent craquelure **7,475.00**

Compass, gimmal mounted in wooden box, **$115.** *Photo courtesy of Joy Luke Auctions.*

Model of sailing ship, 61" l, 20" h, **$600.**
Photo courtesy of Joy Luke Auctions.

Protest certificate, document regarding Spanish seizure of American brig *Exchange* sailing from New Orleans to Charleston, six pgs, dated July 7, 1808, overall toning, 12-1/2" x 8" **90.00**

Quadrant, ebony, cased, marked "D Booth" and "New Zealand" **330.00**

Sailmaker's kit, 17" l, orig bag with various tools, ornate ropework ties, 19th C **350.00**

Sail maker's bench

77" l, 16" w, 15" h, long canvas cov bench, turned splayed legs, one end with compartments and pierced for tools, suspending two canvas pouches, two canvas sacks with sail maker's tools, America, 19th C **1,765.00**

78-1/2" l, 15-3/4" d, 15-1/2" h, ash and cedar, rect top, tacked canvas seat, compartmented, pierced, section centering circular canvas hanging bag, splayed ring-turned tapering legs, sold with sail maker's tools, New England, early 19th C **1,725.00**

Sailor's valentine, 9-5/8" octagonal segmented case, various exotic shells, "For My Love," 19th C, very minor losses **750.00**

Sea chest, child's, New England, early 19th C, green painted pine and poplar, hinged top, dovetail constructed box, applied chamfered base, becket handles, int. lined with mid-19th C newspaper "The Light Ship," minor imperfections **1,380.00**

Sea chest, painted, green, lid painted with flags and pennants centered by Union Jack, name "William Bevan" **2,760.00**

Ship anchor, 54" w, 106" h, cast, iron ring and chain, mounted on later iron brackets, corrosion.......... **825.00**

Ship bell, cast bronze

13" d, 13-1/2" h, weathered surface, raised "J. Warner & Sons, London, 1855"................ **1,175.00**

14" d, 16" h, verdigris surface, raised "1945" on shoulder, America **425.00**

14" d, 17" h, raised linear bands **560.00**

Ship billethead, carved wood, 19th C

24" l, 7-1/2" w, scrolled foliate design, painted black, green and gilt highlights, minor loss on scroll, cracks................. **715.00**

27-1/2" l, 5-1/2" w, and 23" l, 7-1/4" w, scrolled foliate design, weathered cracked surface, pr **4,995.00**

Ship builder's half model, America, 19th C

30" l, 6" h, alternating laminated mahogany and other wood, mounted on walnut panel. **1,995.00**

37-1/2" l, 5" h, pine and other woods, mounted on pine panel .. **1,300.00**

42" l, 10-5/8" h, natural finished pine, black and gilt trim, loose stempost **9,400.00**

Ship license

Issued by Governor and Company of the Merchants of Great Britain to ship *Harriet,* 247 tons, 10 guns, sgd by Governor of company, August 6, 1812, some edge chipping, fold splitting, 15" x 9-3/4" **35.00**

Issued for schooner *Trafalgar Nelson,* issued on the island of Montserrant, dated Nov. 17, 1813, some edge chipping, hinge weakness, minor foxing, 8" x 13" **35.00**

Issued for ship *Aurora*, 303 tons, armed with 14 guns, two swivel guns, 20 muskets, 20 pistols, 20 cutlasses, 20 pikes, Nov. 4, 1912, minor edge chipping, 12-1/2" x 8" **135.00**

Issued to the ship *Nancy* of Newfoundland, two guns weighing 222 tons, issued by High Admiral,

Plank (souvenir), piece from US Constitution, removed from ship during rebuilding of 1927, 4" x 2" x 1-7/8", **$60.**

Snuff box, silver, oval, scene of ship, launch, lighthouse, and sailor, marked "Pat'd Jan 24 1860 C. Parker," gilt wash interior, 3-1/4" l, **$225.** *Photo courtesy of Sanford Alderfer Auction Company.*

April 24, 1812, masthead scene of allegorical figures and chip, scallop cut top, minor soiling, 18" x 11-1/2" **450.00**

Ship model, 36" l, 7-1/2" h, *Sea Serpent,* executed by George Ranes, c1870, finely detailed, cabins, lifeboats, gear, carved and gilded serpent figurehead, mounted in 42" l, 10" w, 15-1/4" h mahogany and glass case **11,165.00**

Shipping circular, concerning marine papers lost, stolen, or taken by force on various ships, issued to port collector of Bristol, sgd by Clerk of Marine Records of the Treasury Dept, March 31, 1810, federal eagle watermark, some chipping, fold splitting, 15-1/2" x 9-1/2" **35.00**

Ship wheel, 48" d, various hardwoods, turned spokes, iron reinforced center hub **350.00**

Carved ivory, 19th C, **$115.**

Stern board, 7-3/4" h, 66" l, Hesperus, New England, 19th C, rect form, rounded ends, chamfered edges, chiseled carved letters flanked by star, painted white on black ground, imperfections **980.00**

Telescope, 32-3/4" l, silver plated, one draw, Troughton & Simms, London, mid-19th C, orig leather casing, inscription reads "Presented by the British Government, Captain Christopher Crowell, Master of the American Ship 'Highland Light' of Boston, in acknowledgment of his humanity and kindness to the Master and the Crew of the Barque 'Queen of Sheba' when he rescued from their waterlogged vessel, on the 16th, December 1861," damage to leather **980.00**

Walking stick, 35" l, wood, ivory knop, silver band on shaft engraved "U.S. Frigate Constitution 1797, J.L.S.," brass and iron tip, age cracks on ivory, wear **1,295.00**

NETSUKES

History: The traditional Japanese kimono has no pockets. Daily necessities, such as money and tobacco supplies, were carried in leather pouches, or inros, which hung from a cord with a netsuke toggle. The word netsuke comes from "ne"—to root—and "tsuke"—to fasten.

Netsukes originated in the 14th century and initially were favored by the middle class. By the mid-18th century, all levels of Japanese society used them. Some of the most famous artists, e.g., Shuzan and Yamada Hojitsu, worked in the netsuke form.

Netsukes average from 1 to 2 inches in length and are made from wood, ivory, bone, ceramics, metal, horn, nutshells, etc. The subject matter is broad based, but always portrayed in a lighthearted, humorous manner. A netsuke must have smooth edges and balance in order to hang correctly on the sash.

Reproduction Alert: Recent reproductions are on the market. Many are carved from African ivory.

Notes: Value depends on artist, region, material, and skill of craftsmanship. Western collectors favor katabori, pieces which represent an identifiable object.

Boxwood

Ashikaga and Tenaga seated **450.00**

Fisherman holding basket of fish, horn inlay, sgd "Akinide," Japan, 20th C **815.00**

Rice mixer, ivory inlaid eyes, teeth, and rice, carved by Tokoku, 19th C **5,750.00**

Seated figure, tortoise, sgd with "kakihan," 18th/19th C **435.00**

Shoki with demon, damage to sword **250.00**

Study of Oni holding Shoki's sword, blowing trumpet, 19th C, chip to one toe, 3" l **1,495.00**

Turtle and snake, c1800, 2-3/8" l **10,120.00**

Horn

Lotus leaf, stag horn, 19th C . **100.00**

Shishi form, pressed, 19th C . . **50.00**

Ivory

Bell with dragon, sgd "Komei," 19th C **260.00**

Bowing samurai, stained details, sgd "Meigyokusai" **425.00**

Eggplant, carved and colored **195.00**

Fish on bed of reeds, naturalistically carved, stained, slight gold highlights, Japan, 19th C . . **750.00**

Frogs with inlaid eyes, lotus plants, lightly colored details, 3-3/4" l **250.00**

Four children playing in tub . . **250.00**

Gama Sennin, 18th/19th C, 2-1/4" l, repair to foot **290.00**

Hoe Tei being carried in a bag by children, sgd "Tadayasu," Japan, 19th C **700.00**

Juojin, small child, sgd "Meigyokusai" **415.00**

Ivory, carved, man with pipe holding basket, leaning down toward an animal, some etched details, signed on feet, 2" h, $100. Photo courtesy of Sanford Alderfer Auction Company.

Ivory, carved, creature with popping eyes, $115.

Monkey arm wrestling with Oni demon on lotus pad, Japan, 19th C **700.00**

Okami playing with kitten and ball of string, 19th C **125.00**

Oni with drum, 19th C, 1-3/4" h **200.00**

Ono no komachi seated on gate post, old can hat, 19th C . . **350.00**

Parrot perched on branch, 19th C, 2-1/4" l **1,100.00**

Rooster, sgd "Chomei" **250.00**

Sennin holding staff, 18th/19th C, 3-1/4" l **250.00**

Skull with snake, 19th C **320.00**

Snail, 19th C **200.00**

Two sculptures working on dragon carp, cinnabar inlaid cartouche reading "Shizetomo," 19th C **350.00**

Ivory and wood, Oni demon in ivory, inside box with horn, coral, and gold inlay, sgd "Meigyokusai" **700.00**

Porcelain

Fruit and leaves, red, brown, and celadon, 19th C **60.00**

Carved ivory, ebony, and coral, mounted on carved ivory base of seashells and scrolling waves, 2" x 1-1/4", minor imperfections, $375. Photo courtesy of Sanford Alderfer Auction Co.

Hotei, marked "Masakazu," 19th C
.... **60.00**
Two puppies, 19th C **85.00**
Sandalwood, carved rustic retreat with pavilions, trees, mountains, and figures
.... **635.00**
Wood
Geisha, seated, wearing flowing robe, holding tray, carved by Toshikazu, 19th C **245.00**
Karasu tengu, seated figure with beaked and fanged face, holding cucumber, carved by Jugyoko, 19th C **825.00**
Noblewoman, wretched beggar form, dying by roadside, carved by Ichihyo, first half 19th C.... **300.00**
Persimmon, stippled skin and leaves, unsgd, 19th C **295.00**
Scribe, sitting, holding writing slip and brush, carved by Shinsai, 19th C **275.00**

NEWCOMB POTTERY

History: The Sophie Newcomb Memorial College, an adjunct of Tulane University in New Orleans, LA, was originated as a school to train local women in the decorative arts. While metalworking, painting, and embroidery were among the classes taught, the production of fine, handcrafted art pottery remains its most popular and collectible pursuit.

Pottery was made by the Newcomb women for nearly 50 years, with earlier work being the rarest and most valuable. This is characterized by shiny finishes and broad, flat-painted and modeled designs. More common, though still quite valuable, are the matte glaze pieces, often depicting bayou scenes and native flora. All bear the impressed NC mark.

Adviser: David Rago.

Bud vase, 9" h, 3-1/4" d, tapered, high glaze, carved yellow jonquils, tall green leaves, blue ground, by Anna Frances Simpson, 1908, marked "NC/Q/FS/CQ52/JM" **6,900.00**
Cabinet vase, 2" d, 4-1/2" h, by Anna F. Simpson, 1926, blue live oak and Spanish moss, gray ground, high glaze, marked "NC/JH/PP56/15/AFS"
.... **3,335.00**
Jardinière, 10" d, 8" h, yellow daffodils, blue-green leaves, ivory ground, by Harriet Joor, 1902, marked "NC/JM/R29/HJ," four lines to rim, shallow spider lines at base . **19,550.00**
Low bowl, 9-1/4" d, 3-1/4" h, carved pink irises, green leaves, medium blue

Inkwell, painted by G. R. Smith, c1902, pink thistles and green leaves, ivory ground, original liner, NC/GRS/U, glaze misses to pink centers, short and tight line to rim, reglued lid, 4" d, 2-3/4" h, $3,250. Photo courtesy of David Rago Auctions.

matte ground, by A. F. Simpson, 1923, marked "NC/NF31/313/JM" and artist's cipher, couple of short, tight lines to rim
.... **1,610.00**
Print, woodblock, 5-1/2" w, 6" h sight, by Mary F. Baker, young girl dec vase, monogrammed "MFB" lower left, matted, framed **2,070.00**
Trivet, 3-3/4" d, swirl of whit blossoms, waxy green ground, by Henrietta Bailey, 1912, marked "NC/HB/JM/FA28/B," orig paper label **1,840.00**
Vase
3-3/4" d, 4-3/4" h, transitional, bulbous, by Anna F. Simpson, 1914, white orchids, green leaves, pale blue ground, marked "NC/JM/126/GO33/AFS" . **1,840.00**

Loving cup, by Katherine Kopman, 1902, white clover blossoms, green leaves, pale blue and white glossy ground, NC/KK/E18/X, 1" rim chip, 5" d, 4" h, $7,500. Photo courtesy of David Rago Auctions.

Low bowl, by A.F. Simpson, 1923, carved pink irises and green leaves, medium blue matte ground, NC/NF31/313/JM/artist's cipher, short, tight lines to rim, 9-1/4" d, 3-1/4" h, $1,610. Photo courtesy of David Rago Auctions.

4" d, 8" h, ovoid, by Corrine Marie Chalaron, 1923, broad leaves alternating with yellow and white stylized blossoms, denim blue ground, marked "NC/JM/MZ61/82/CMC" . **4,315.00**
4-1/2" d, 4-1/2" h, bulbous, live oaks and Spanish moss, by Anna Frances Simpson, 1929, orig paper label, "NC/RY17/JH/29/AFS"
.... **2,875.00**
4-1/2" d, 5-1/2" h, bulbous, by Sadie Irvine, 1927, Espanol pattern, blue-green, pink, and white, dark denim blue ground, "NC/24/QH96/S" **4,025.00**
4-1/2" d, 6-1/2" h, carved matte, by Sadie Irvine, 1924, pink and red loquat fruit and leaves around undulating rim, marked "NC/SK/JM/I47/NP47," small chips

Plate, decorated by Henrietta Bailey, 1906, band of carved white and yellow flowers, blue and green ground. NC/JM/Q/HB/AY50, restoration to few small rim chips, 8 1/4" d, $4,750. Photo courtesy of David Rago Auctions.

Trivet, by Henrietta Bailey, 1912, swirl of white blossoms, waxy green ground. NC/HB/JM/FA28/B, paper label, 3-3/4" d, $1,840. Photo courtesy of David Rago Auctions.

to foot ring, short tight line to rim
. . . . **1,150.00**
5" d, 9" h, bulbous, by Anna F. Simpson, 1921, carved wreath of pink trumpet vines, green leaves, denim blue ground, marked "NC/JM/LS97/179/A.F.S." . **3,220.00**
5" d, 11-1/4" h, scenic, ovoid, crisply carved with full moon shining through oak trees and Spanish moss, blue and green matte glazes, by A. F. Simpson, 1930, marked "NC/SN43/131/JH/AFS," three small flat manuf chips to base
. . . . **16,100.00**
6-1/2" d, 8-1/4" h, transitional, by Sadie Irvine, 1914, tall pines cov in Spanish moss, marked "NC/SI/JM/184/B/GK11," remnant of paper label, minor chip on edge of foot ring **5,175.00**

Vase, carved by Henrietta Bailey, 1931, ovoid, tall pine trees in blues and greens, full moon, NC/HB/330/TA31, some glaze dripping, 4" d, 9-1/4" h, $4,000. Photo courtesy of David Rago Auctions.

Vase, scenic, carved by Sadie Irvine, 1919, palm trees, full moon, NC/SI/268/KJ 70, drilled bottom for lamp, 6-1/2" d, 10-3/4" h, $2,900. Photo courtesy of David Rago Auctions.

Vessel
5-1/4" d, 3-1/4" h, squatty, transitional, by Sadie Irvine, 1914, carved light blue bell flowers, green leaves, dark blue ground, marked "NC/GN47/JM/257/SI"
. . . . **2,300.00**
6-1/2" d, 4-1/2" h, matte, squatty, by Sadie Irvine, 1922, sharply carved pink Japanese iris, green stems, around undulating top conforming to shape of blossoms, purple and blue ground, marked "NC/SI/JM/213?MV17" . . **3,220.00**
7-1/2" d, 6" h, organically-shaped, by Marie De Hoa LeBlanc, c1905, three modeled ginkgo leaf handles, semi-matte olive green and gunmetal glaze, marked "NC/Q/JM/MHL," orig price tag
. . . . **5,175.00**

Vase, scenic, by A.F. Simpson, 1930, ovoid, carved full moon shining through oak trees and Spanish moss, blue and green matte glazes, NC/SN43/13 1/JH/AFS, three small flat manufacturing chips to base, 5" d, 11-1/4" h, $16,100. Photo courtesy of David Rago Auctions.

NILOAK POTTERY, MISSION WARE

History:
Niloak Pottery was made near Benton,
Arkansas. Charles Dean Hyten experimented with native clay, trying to preserve its natural colors. By 1911, he perfected Mission Ware, a marbleized pottery in which the cream and brown colors predominate. The company name is the word "kaolin" spelled backward.

After a devastating fire, the pottery was rebuilt and named Eagle Pottery. This factory included enough space to add a novelty pottery line in 1929. Hyten left the pottery in 1941, and in 1946 operations ceased.

Marks: The early pieces were marked "Niloak." Eagle Pottery products usually were marked "Hywood-Niloak" until 1934, when the "Hywood" was dropped from the mark.

Additional Listings: See *Warman's Americana & Collectibles* for more examples, especially the novelty pieces.

Note: Prices listed below are for Mission Ware pieces.

For more information, see this book.

Bowl, 4-1/2" d, marbleized swirls, blue, tan, and brown **65.00**
Candlesticks, pr, 8" h, marbleized swirls, blue, cream, terra cotta, and brown **250.00**
Console set, pr 8-1/2" h candlesticks, 10" d bowl, marbleized swirls, marked
. . . . **275.00**

Candlesticks, pair, Mission Ware, blue and gray marbleized clay, impressed mark, 8" h, $300. Photo courtesy of David Rago Auctions.

Punch bowl, Mission Ware, scroddled brown, tan and blue clays, corseted pedestal base, glazed interior, stamped "Niloak," foil label on bowl, incised "H.B. III," small chip to base, 13-1/2" d, 11" h, **$3,775.** *Photo courtesy of David Rago Auctions.*

Flower pot, ruffled rim, green matte glaze, c1930 . . . . **155.00**
Toothpick holder, marbleized swirls, tan and blue **100.00**
Urn, 4-1/2" h, marbleized swirls, brown and blue **45.00**
Vase
   3-1/4" h, early foil label, c1920-30
   . . . . **95.00**
   3-1/4" h, second art marks, c1930
   . . . . **85.00**
   4-1/2" h, second art mark, c1925
   . . . . **75.00**
   4-1/2" h, starved rock mark, c1925
   . . . . **95.00**
   6" h, applied twisted handles, Ozark Dawn glaze, c1930 . . . . **120.00**
   8-1/2" h, swirled colors, first art mark, c1910-24 . . . . **230.00**
   8-3/4" h, Ozark Dawn glaze, c1930
   . . . . **140.00**

Vase, Mission Ware, cylindrical, brown and terra cotta scroddled clay, stamped "Niloak," 10" h, **$375.** *Photo courtesy of David Rago Auctions.*

10-1/2" h, swollen baluster with broad rim, brown, rose, blue, and cream, second art mark . . . **500.00**

NIPPON CHINA, 1891-1921

History: Nippon, Japanese hand-painted porcelain, was made for export between 1891 and 1921. In 1891, when the McKinley Tariff Act proclaimed that all items of foreign manufacture be stamped with their country of origin, Japan chose to use "Nippon." In 1921, the United States decided the word "Nippon" no longer was acceptable and required all Japanese wares to be marked "Japan," ending the Nippon era.

Marks: There are more than 220 recorded Nippon backstamps or marks; the three most popular are the wreath, maple leaf, and rising sun. Wares with variations of all three marks are being reproduced today. A knowledgeable collector can easily spot the reproductions by the mark variances.

The majority of the marks are found in three different colors: green, blue, or magenta. Colors indicate the quality of the porcelain used: green for first-grade porcelain, blue for second-grade, and magenta for third-grade. Marks were applied by two methods: decal stickers under glaze and imprinting directly on the porcelain.

Reproduction Alert
Distinguishing old marks from new:

A common old mark consisted of a central wreath open at the top with the letter M in the center. "Hand Painted" flowed around the top of the wreath; "NIPPO Box N" around the bottom. The modern fake mark reverses the wreath (it is open at the bottom) and places an hourglass form, not an "M," in its middle.

An old leaf mark, approximately one-quarter inch wide, has "Hand" with "Painted" below to the left of the stem and "NIPPO Box N" beneath. The newer mark has the identical lettering, but the size is now one-half, rather than one-quarter, inch.

An old mark consisted of "Hand Painted" arched above a solid rising sun logo with "NIPPO Box N" in a straight line beneath. The modern fake mark has the same lettering pattern, but the central logo looks like a mound with a jagged line enclosing a blank space above it.

Basket
   7-1/4" h, rose dec, pale yellow ground, gilt accents, unmarked, flakes on base **265.00**
   8-1/2" h, orchid design, gilt and green ground, green maple leaf mark **295.00**

Tankard, rose floral decoration, gilt accents, blue maple leaf mark, 7" h, **$250.** *Photo courtesy of Sanford Alderfer Auction Company.*

Berry set, 10-1/4" d master bowl, four 5" d individual bowls, azalea dec, enameled and gilt floral borders, green M in wreath mark **90.00**
Bowl
   8-1/2" d, hp, sailing ships with palm tree and ruins, three handles, green wreath mark **150.00**
   9-1/2" d, ftd, grape dec, gilt borders, green M in wreath mark . . . **175.00**
   9-1/2" d, octagonal, lavender coastal scene, green and gilt borders, blue maple leaf mark **295.00**
Cake plate, 10-1/2" d, lavender coastal scene, green and gilt borders, blue maple leaf mark **195.00**
Cake set, 10-1/4" d cake plate, six 6-1/2" d serving plates, two handles, scenic dec with swans, floral borders with gilt accents, green M in wreath mark **330.00**
Chocolate pot
   7-1/2" h, hp, cottage and lake scene, green wreath mark **260.00**
   9-1/2" h, hp, etched gold panels, jewel trim, green wreath mark
   . . . . **175.00**
Condensed milk jar, cov, underplate, pink roses, green leaves, gilt accents, unmarked **295.00**
Doll, 18-1/2" h, bisque socket head, brown glass eyes, closed pouty mouth, human hair wig, jointed wood and composition body, marked "FY/Nippon/304" on back of head, tiny chips at neck opening, body repainted with some flaking at joints **875.00**

Ewer, 13-1/2" h, hp, three floral medallions outlined in gold, unmarked
.... **350.00**

Mayonnaise set, ftd bowl, matching underplate, ladle, delicate floral design, green M in wreath mark, blue mark on ladle...................... **80.00**

Nut dish, 7-1/4" d, blown-out design, three ftd, green M in wreath mark **55.00**

Plate

7-1/2" d, rose dec, raspberry and gilt border, blue maple leaf mark
.... **220.00**

9-3/4" d, floral dec, gilt borders, cobalt blue ground, blue maple leaf mark............... **350.00**

10" d, scalloped edge, rose dec, gilt dec, blue maple leaf mark . **250.00**

Punch set, bowl with double handles, claw foot base, six ftd cups, grape dec, green M in wreath mark....... **990.00**

Tankard, 13" h, hp, gold dec rim and base, applied scrolled handle, blue maple leaf mark, minor gold loss
.... **350.00**

Tea set, hp, powder blue background, swans dec, Paolownia flower mark
.... **325.00**

Tray, 8" l, 6-1/4" w, hp, scenic center, medallions of roses at ends, green wreath mark............... **150.00**

Urn

12" h, hp, landscape, bolted. **435.00**

17" h, hp, four scenic panels, gold and cobalt blue dec, green wreath mark, bolted.......... **1,100.00**

Vase

7" h, hp, moriage dec, four painted floral panels, two handles . . **430.00**

7-1/2" h, hp, four painted floral panels separated by gold enameled bands, green wreath mark, price for pr........ **350.00**

8" h, hp, coralene, florals with gold accents, marked "Patent applied for No. 38257," small professional repair to rim............. **575.00**

8-1/2" h, hp, moriage dec, magenta ground, unmarked........ **750.00**

8-1/2" h, hp, lake with swan, green wreath mark............. **400.00**

9" h, hp, basket weave body, red and white roses, blue M in wreath mark
.... **750.00**

9" h, hp, coralene, art deco lotus leaves and flowers, marked "KinRan U.S. Patent, Feb. 9, 1909" in magenta, minor beading loss
.... **660.00**

9-1/2" h, hp, landscape with trees and lake................ **290.00**

11" h, hp, black and gold silhouette trees, green maple leaf mark
.... **435.00**

11" h, hp, roses, gold outlines at top and base, two handles **320.00**

11-1/2" h, hp, yellow and gold roses, three gold handles with rings
.... **320.00**

12" h, hp, gold ferns, jeweled designs, magenta maple leaf mark
.... **400.00**

13" h, hp, studio dec, landscape, heavy etched gold floral dec and

striped band, green M in wreath mark.................. **485.00**

Whiskey jug, 8" h, hp, scenic, enameled border dec, blue maple leaf mark **460.00**

NORITAKE CHINA

History: Morimura Brothers founded Noritake China in 1904 in Nagoya, Japan. The company made high-quality chinaware for export to the United States and also produced a line of china blanks for hand painting. In 1910, the company perfected a technique for the production of high-quality dinnerware and introduced streamlined production.

During the 1920s, the Larkin Company of Buffalo, New York, was a prime distributor of Noritake China. Larkin offered Azalea, Briarcliff, Linden, Modjeska, Savory, Sheridan, and Tree in the Meadow patterns as part of its premium line.

The factory was heavily damaged during World War II, and production was reduced. Between 1946 and 1948, the company sold its china under the "Rose China" mark, since the quality of production did not match the earlier Noritake China. Expansion in 1948 brought about the resumption of quality production and the use of the Noritake name once again.

Marks: There are close to 100 different marks for Noritake, the careful study of which can determine the date of production. Most pieces are marked "Noritake" with a wreath, "M," "N," or "Nippon." The use of the letter N was registered in 1953.

Berry bowl, Roanne **12.00**

Bowl, 10" l, oval, Rosewin #6584 pattern..................... **30.00**

Cake set, 11" d cake plate, six 6-1/4" serving plates, desert scene with tent and man on camel, cobalt blue and gilt

Vase, two handles, flowers and gilding, 9" h, **$175.** Photo courtesy of Joy Luke Auctions.

Vase, Moriage, double handles, blue enamel, green ground, gilt accents, blue maple leaf mark, 6" h, **$600.** Photo courtesy of Sanford Alderfer Auction Company.

Chocolate pot, polychrome dec flowers, gilt accents, unmarked, 9" h, **$190.** Photo courtesy of Sanford Alderfer Auction Company.

border, marked "Noritake/Made in Japan/Hand Painted" **770.00**

Candlesticks, pr, 8-1/4" h, gold flowers and bird, blue luster ground, wreath with "M" mark **125.00**

Console set, 11-3/4" d bowl, pr 8" h candlesticks, amber pearl center, 1" black rim with gold floral dec, green mark **465.00**

Creamer and sugar, Art Deco, pink Japanese lanterns, cobalt blue ground, basket type handle on sugar, wreath with "M" mark **50.00**

Cup and saucer
Florola **24.00**
Roanne **18.00**

Demitasse cup and saucer, Tree in the Meadow **45.00**

Dinner set, floral motif, gold rimmed, 115-pc set **375.00**

Gravy boat, Tree in the Meadow . **50.00**

Hair receiver, 3-1/4" h, 3-1/2" w, Art Deco, geometric designs,, gold luster, wreath with "M" mark **50.00**

Inkwell, owl, figural **125.00**

Marmalade, underplate, 5-1/2" h, poppy dec, double handled jar . **185.00**

Napkin ring, Art Deco man and woman, wreath with "M" mark, pr . **60.00**

Place card holder, figural, bluebird with butterfly, gold luster, white stripes, wreath with "M" mark, pr **35.00**

Plate, two 8-1/2" d, seven 6-1/4" d, cranberry and pale blue rose motif dec, gilt borders, blue "RC Noritake Nippon Hand Painted" mark **175.00**

Punch bowl set, 12" h two-part punch bowl with three-ftd base, six 2-3/4" h cups
Cottage landscape at dusk, swans in pond dec, cobalt blue and gilt borders, opalescent melon int. **880.00**
Peacock design, cobalt blue and gilt borders, blue ground ext., melon

Vegetable dish, House by Lake pattern, oval, marked, 9-3/8" l, $48.

and blue interior, "M" in wreath mark **600.00**

Salt, 3" l, swan, white, orange luster, pr **25.00**

Salt and pepper shakers, pr, Tree in the Meadow, marked "Made in Japan" **35.00**

Soup bowl, Florola **15.00**

Tea tile, Tree in the Meadow, 5" w, green mark **35.00**

Vegetable bowl, cov, Magnificience, #9736. . . . . **350.00**

Waffle set, handled serving plate, sugar shaker, Art Deco flowers, wreath with "M" mark **50.00**

Wall pocket, butterfly, wreath with "M" mark. **75.00**

NORTH DAKOTA SCHOOL OF MINES

History: The North Dakota School of Mines was established in 1890. Earle J. Babcock, a chemistry instructor, was impressed with the high purity level of North Dakota potter's clay. In 1898, Babcock received funds to develop his finds. He tried to interest commercial potteries in the North Dakota clay, but had limited success.

In 1910, Babcock persuaded the school to establish a Ceramics Department. Margaret Cable, who studied under Charles Binns and Frederick H. Rhead, was appointed head. She remained until her retirement in 1949.

Decorative emphasis was placed on native themes, e.g., flowers and animals. Art Nouveau, Art Deco, and fairly plain pieces were made.

Marks: The pottery is marked with a cobalt blue underglaze circle of the words "University of North Dakota/Grand Forks, N.D./Made at School of Mines/N.D. Clay." Some early pieces are marked only "U.N.D." or "U.N.D./Grand Forks, N.D." Most pieces are numbered (they can be dated from University records) and signed by both the instructor and student. Cable-signed pieces are the most desirable.

Bowl, 7-1/2" d, 4-1/4" h, closed-in, incised birds of paradise and cornflowers, blue, ivory, and green, by L. Whiting, circular ink stamp, incised "L. Whiting," minor fleck at shoulder **1,725.00**

Cookie jar, 6-3/4" d, 10-1/2" h, Mammy, dark brown matte glaze, by Margaret Cable, circular ink stamp, incised "Aunt Susan/dht/M. Cable/118A," small nick inside lid rim **1,610.00**

Figure, 4-1/2" h, 3-1/4" w, Bentonite cowboy, brick-red, black, and gold glaze, incised "JJ/13/UND," Julia Mattson, 1913 . . . . **650.00**

Bowl, closed-in, by L. Whiting, incised birds of paradise and cornflowers in blue, ivory and green, circular ink stamp, incised "L. Whiting," minor fleck to shoulder, 7-1/2"d, 4-1/4" h, $1,725. Photo courtesy of David Rago Auctions.

Vase
3-1/2" d, 5-1/2" h, bulbous, polychrome painted band of pioneers and covered wagons, glossy brown ground, by Flora Huckfield, circular stamp mark/72/Huck, incised H? **1,850.00**
4-1/2" d, 5" h, bulbous, emb prairie roses, mottled green crystalline glaze, circular ink mark, incised "Steen-Huck-1100," Huckfield and Steen. **1,200.00**
5" d, 3" h, conical, by Flora Huckfield and student, glossy celadon and brown glaze, circular ink stamp, incised "Huck" and "Le Masurier/2371" **230.00**
5" d, 7-1/4" h, bulbous, emb cowboy scene, matte chocolate brown

Vase, bulbous, by M.C.M., shaded powder blue and pink semi-matte glaze, circular ink stamp/M.C.M. 6-1/4" d, 6-1/4" h, $200. Photo courtesy of David Rago Auctions.

Vase, bulbous, by Flora Huckfield, painted with band of pioneers and covered wagons in polychrome against glossy brown ground, circular stamp mark/72/Huck, incised H?, 3-1/2" d, 4-1/2" h, **$1,840.** *Photo courtesy of David Rago Auctions.*

glaze, circular ink stamp, sgd "Flora Huckfield," titled "N. D. Rodeo" **1,500.00**

5" h, 9" d, carved mocha brown narcissus, dark brown ground, ink stamp, incised "E. Cunningham/ 12/6/50," E. Cunningham, 1950 . . . . **1,000.00**

5-1/2" d, 7-1/2" h, bulbous, carved narcissus, brown and umber matte glaze, by Margaret Cable, stamped circular mark, incised "M. Cable/ 223" **1,840.00**

5-1/2" d, 8" h, carved daffodils, mahogany matte glaze, circular ink mark, incised "McCosh '48" **1,100.00**

5-1/2" d, 10" h, ovoid, carved sheaves of what, purple-brown matte glaze, ink stamped and incised "Huck 30/No. Dak. Wheat," F. Huckfield **1,300.00**

6-1/4" d, 4-3/4" h, sq tapering, repeating scenes of farmer and horse-drawn plough, green and brown matte glaze, circular ink mark, incised "The Plowman/Huck/ 119," F. Huckfield **1,200.00**

Vessel

3-1/2" h, 3-1/2" d, beaker shape, matte brown glaze, stamped and incised marks, c1915, small rim chip **115.00**

5" d, 3-1/2" h, squatty, carved band of cowboys under terra cotta and brown matte glaze, by Julia Mattson, stamped circular mark,

incised "Cowboy-54C/J Mattson" **980.00**

7" d, 6" h, spherical, Covered Wagon, carved frieze of wagons and oxen, sandy brown matte glaze, circular ink mark, incised "M. Cable" and title, by Margaret Cable **1,400.00**

WALLACE NUTTING

History: Wallace Nutting (1861-1941) was America's most famous photographer of the early 20th century. A retired minister, Nutting took more than 50,000 pictures, keeping 10,000 of his best and destroying the rest. His popular and best-selling scenes included "Exterior Scenes," apple blossoms, country lanes, orchards, calm streams, and rural American countrysides; "Interior Scenes," usually featuring a colonial woman working near a hearth; and "Foreign Scenes," typically thatch-roofed cottages. Those pictures that were least popular in his day have become the rarest and most-highly collectible today and are classified as "Miscellaneous Unusual Scenes." This category encompasses such things as animals, architecturals, children, florals, men, seascapes, and snow scenes.

Nutting sold literally millions of his hand-colored platinotype pictures between 1900 and his death in 1941. Starting first in Southbury, Connecticut, and later moving his business to Framingham, Massachusetts, the peak of Wallace Nutting's picture production was 1915 to 1925. During this period, Nutting employed nearly 200 people, including colorists, darkroom staff, salesmen, and assorted office personnel. Wallace Nutting pictures proved to be a huge commercial success and hardly an American household was without one by 1925.

While attempting to seek out the finest and best early-American furniture as props for his colonial Interior Scenes, Nutting became an expert in American antiques. He published nearly 20 books in his lifetime, including his 10-volume State Beautiful series and various other books on furniture, photography, clocks, and his autobiography. He also contributed many photographs published in magazines and books other than his own.

Nutting also became widely known for his reproduction furniture. His furniture shop produced literally hundreds of different furniture forms: clocks, stools, chairs, settles, settees, tables, stands, desks, mirrors, beds, chests of drawers, cabinet pieces, and treenware.

The overall synergy of the Wallace Nutting name, pictures, books, and furniture, has made anything "Wallace Nutting" quite collectible.

Marks: Wallace Nutting furniture is clearly marked with his distinctive paper label, glued directly onto the piece, or with a block or script signature brand, which was literally branded into his furniture.

Note: "Process Prints" are 1930s' machine-produced reprints of 12 of Nutting's most popular pictures. These have minimal value and can be detected by using a magnifying glass.

Adviser: Michael Ivankovich.

Books

American Windsors **85.00**
Cruise of the 800, The **95.00**
England Beautiful, 1st ed. **125.00**
Furniture of the Pilgrim Century, 1st ed. **140.00**
Furniture Treasury, Vol. I **125.00**
Furniture Treasury, Vol. II **140.00**
Furniture Treasury, Vol. III **115.00**
Ireland Beautiful, 1st ed. **45.00**
Pathways of the Puritans **85.00**
Social Life In Old New England . **75.00**
State Beautiful Series

Connecticut Beautiful, 1st ed. **75.00**
Maine Beautiful, 1st ed. **45.00**
Massachusetts Beautiful, 2nd ed. **45.00**
New Hampshire Beautiful, 1st ed. **75.00**
New York Beautiful, 1st ed. . . . **85.00**
Pennsylvania Beautiful, 1st ed. **48.00**
Vermont Beautiful, 2nd ed. **40.00**
Virginia Beautiful, 1st ed. **60.00**

Catalog, Wallace Nutting's Original Studio **1,100.00**

Furniture

Candle stand, #17, Windsor . . . **495.00**
Chair

#390, Ladderback, arm, script brand **300.00**
#408, Windsor, bowback, arm, block brand **825.00**
#440, Windsor, writing arm, Pennsylvania turnings, drawer beneath seat, block brand **2,145.00**
#464, Carver, arm, script brand **550.00**

Cupboard, #923, pine, scrolled **4,290.00**

High chair, liftable food tray, New England turnings, orig light maple finish, block branded signature **2,310.00**

Silhouette, Mary's Little Lamb, 5" x 7", $60.

Untitled, exterior, pond and trees, green trees reflect in calm blue pond, 7" x 9", $115. Photos courtesy of Michael Ivankovich Auctions.

Stool, #102, Windsor, script brand
. . . .**220.00**

Table
#619, crane bracket **685.00**
#628b, Pembroke, mahogany
. . . .**1,495.00**

Pictures
Among the Ferns, 14" x 17" **165.00**
An Elaborate Dinner, 14" x 17" . .**200.00**
An Old Tune Revived **1,265.00**
A Pennsylvania Stream. **770.00**
Better than Mowing, 16" x 20". . .**490.00**
Between the Games. **800.00**
Between the Spruces, 10" x 14" .**200.00**
By the Fireside, 9" x 13" **100.00**
California Hilltops, 11" x 14" **185.00**
Christmas Welcome Home. . .**1,100.00**
Colonial Days, Nantucket. . . .**1,128.00**
Dog-On-It, 7" x 11" **1,265.00**
Elizabeth Park Rose Garden .**1,210.00**
Elm Drapery, 15" x 22" **385.00**
Fleur-de-lis and Spirea, 13" x 16"
. . . .**685.00**
Four O' Clock, cows **1,295.00**
Gloucester Cloister, 16" x 20" .**1,100.00**
Going for the Doctor, children**1,100.00**

A Chair for John, girl sitting at fireside table writes letter while "John's" chair remains empty at opposite end of table, 11" x 14", $325.

Bee's Paradise, 11" x 17", $100.

Grandmother's Hollyhocks, 9" x 11"
. . . .**400.00**
Helping Mother, 14" x 17" **410.00**
Hepatica **1,595.00**
Her First Proposal **1,240.00**
Lockside Cottage **745.00**
Parting at the Gate, 10" x 14" . .**550.00**
Pennsylvania Arches, 14" x 17".**300.00**
Priscilla's Cottage, 14" x 17" . . .**360.00**
Rapid Transit, stagecoach scene
. . . .**1,540.00**
Reflected Aspirations **1,705.00**
Roses and Larkspur **1,210.00**
Russet and Gold, 16" x 20" **315.00**
Shadowy Orchard Curves, 11" x 14"
. . . .**85.00**
Stepping Stones to Bolton Abbey, 11" x 14" **330.00**
The Delaware Canal Turn, PA . .**365.00**
The Donjon Chenaceau, French Castle
. . . .**660.00**
The Isle in the Tiber. **1,100.00**
The Meeting Place, horse and cows
. . . .**2,420.00**
The Old Homestead **880.00**
To Meet the Rector **990.00**

A Dahlia Jar, 8" x 10", $350.

Hope, 9" x 11", $80.

Tranquillity Farm. **880.00**
Village Spires, 10" x 12" **125.00**
Watching for Papa, 13" x 16" . . .**420.00**
Wrencote **565.00**

Silhouettes
George and Martha Washington, 3" x 4"
. . . .**90.00**
Girl at Vanity Desk, 4" x 4" **85.00**
Girl by Garden Urn, 4" x 4". **75.00**
Girl by Spider Web, 5" x 4". **50.00**
Scenes. **40.00**

A Warm Spring Day, sheep grazing beside rippling blue pond, 15" x 22", $425.

Wallace Nutting-like Photographers

History: Although Wallace Nutting was widely recognized as the country's leading producer of hand-colored photographs during the early 20th century, he was by no means the only photographer selling this style of picture. Throughout the country, literally hundreds of regional photographers were selling hand-colored photographs from their home regions or travels. The subject matter of these photographers was comparable to Nutting's, including Interior, Exterior, Foreign, and Miscellaneous Unusual scenes.

Several photographers operated large businesses, and, although not as large or well known as Wallace Nutting, they sold a substantial volume of pictures which can still be readily found today. The vast majority of their work was photographed in their home regions and sold primarily to local residents or visiting tourists. It should come as little surprise that three of the major Wallace Nutting-like photographers—David Davidson, Fred Thompson, and the Sawyer Art Co.—each had ties to Wallace Nutting.

Hundreds of other smaller local and regional photographers attempted to market hand-colored pictures comparable to Wallace Nutting's during the period of 1900 to the 1930s. Although quite attractive, most were not as appealing to the general public as Wallace Nutting pictures. However, as the price of Wallace Nutting pictures has escalated, the work of these lesser-known Wallace Nutting-like photographers has become increasingly collectible.

A partial listing of some of these minor Wallace Nutting-like photographers includes: Babcock; J. C. Bicknell; Blair; Ralph Blood (Portland, Maine); Bragg; Brehmer; Brooks; Burrowes; Busch; Carlock; Pedro Cacciola; Croft; Currier; Depue Brothers; Derek; Dowly; Eddy; May Farini (hand-colored colonial lithographs); George Forest; Gandara; Gardner (Nantucket, Bermuda, Florida); Gibson; Gideon; Gunn; Bessie Pease Gutmann (hand-colored colonial lithographs); Edward Guy; Harris; C. Hazen; Knoffe; Haynes (Yellowstone Park); Margaret Hennesey; Hodges; Homer; Krabel; Kattleman; La Bushe; Lake; Lamson (Portland, Maine); M. Lightstrum; Machering; Rossiler Mackinae; Merrill; Meyers; William Moehring; Moran; Murrey; Lyman Nelson; J. Robinson Neville (New England); Patterson; Own Perry; Phelps; Phinney; Reynolds; F. Robbins; Royce; Frederick Scheetz (Philadelphia, Pennsylvania); Shelton, Standley (Colorado); Stott; Summers; Esther Svenson; Florence Thompson; Thomas Thompson; M. A. Trott; Sanford Tull; Underhill; Villar; Ward; Wilmot; Edith Wilson; and Wright.

Adviser: Michael Ivankovich.

Notes: The key determinants of value include the collectibility of the particular photographer, subject matter, condition, and size. Exterior Scenes are the most common.

Keep in mind that only the rarest pictures, in the best condition, will bring top prices. Discoloration and/or damage to the picture or matting can reduce value significantly.

David Davidson

Second to Nutting in overall production, Davidson worked primarily in the Rhode Island and southern Massachusetts areas. While a student at Brown University around 1900, Davidson learned the art of hand-colored photography from Wallace Nutting, who happened to be the minister at Davidson's church. After Nutting moved to Southbury in 1905, Davidson graduated from Brown and started a successful photography business in Providence, Rhode Island, which he operated until his death in 1967.

A Puritan Lady **80.00**
Berkshire Sunset **80.00**
Christmas Day **160.00**
Driving Home the Cows **120.00**

David Davidson, interior, Easter Bonnet, girl in long paisley dress samples bonnets while standing before hallway mirror, 5" x 7", $75. Photos courtesy of Michael Ivankovich Auctions.

Heart's Desire 30.00
Her House in Order 75.00
Neighbors 170.00
Old Ironsides 170.00
Plymouth Elm 20.00
Rosemary Club 40.00
Snowbound Brook 55.00
The Brook's Mirror 95.00
The Lamb's May Feast 130.00
The Seine Reel 190.00
Vanity 70.00

Sawyer

A father and son team, Charles H. Sawyer and Harold B. Sawyer, operated the very successful Sawyer Art Company from 1903 until the 1970s. Beginning in Maine, the Sawyer Art Company moved to Concord, New Hampshire, in 1920 to be closer to its primary market—New Hampshire's White Mountains. Charles H. Sawyer briefly worked for Nutting from 1902 to 1903 while living in southern Maine. Sawyer's production volume ranks third behind Wallace Nutting and David Davidson.

A February Morning 210.00
A New England Sugar Birth 300.00
At the Bend of the Road 35.00
Crystal Lake 65.00
Echo Lake, Franconia Notch 50.00
Indian Summer 35.00
Lake Morey 30.00
Lake Willoughby 50.00
Mt. Washington in October 55.00
Old Man of the Mountains 35.00
Original Dennison Plant 100.00

Sawyer, San Juan, Capistrano, colorful flower garden beside adobe San Juan Capistrano Spanish Mission, original backing paper, original Sawyer label, hand-written title still remains, 10" x 13", $235.

Silver Birches, Lake George 50.00
The Meadow Stream 80.00

Fred Thompson

Frederick H. Thompson and Frederick M. Thompson, another father and son team, operated the Thompson Art Company (TACO) from 1908 to 1923, working primarily in the Portland, Maine, area. We know that Thompson and Nutting had collaborated because Thompson widely marketed an interior scene he had taken in Nutting's Southbury home. The production volume of the Thompson Art Company ranks fourth behind Nutting, Davidson, and Sawyer.

Apple Tree Road 45.00
Blossom Dale 75.00
Brook in Winter 190.00
Calm of Fall 50.00
Fernbank 35.00
Fireside Fancy Work 140.00
High and Dry 45.00
Knitting for the Boys 160.00
Lombardy Poplar 100.00
Nature's Carpet 50.00
Neath the Blossoms 95.00
Portland Head 440.00
Six Master 100.00
The Gossips 80.00

Minor Wallace Nutting-Like Photographers

Generally speaking, prices for works by minor Wallace Nutting-like photographers would break down as follows: smaller pictures (5" x 7" to 10" x 12"), $10-$75; medium pictures (11" x 14" to 14" x 17"), $50-$200; larger pictures (larger than 14" x 17"), $75-$200+.

never happened. The entire collection remained in storage until it was rediscovered in 1972.

Today Ohr is recognized as one of the leaders in the American art-pottery movement. Some greedy individuals have taken the later unglazed pieces and covered them with poor-quality glazes in hopes of making them more valuable. These pieces do not have stilt marks on the bottom.

Marks: Much of Ohr's early work was signed with an impressed stamp including his name and location in block letters. His later work was often marked with the flowing script designation "G. E. Ohr."

Cup pitcher, pinched rim, rare amber volcanic glaze, stamped G.E. OHR/BILOXI, restored chip to rim and minor nick, 4-3/4" d, 2-1/2" h, $1,500.

Bank, 2" d, 4" h, acorn shape, lustered brown and mirror black glaze, int. rattle, stamped "G.E.OHR/Biloxi,Miss" **1,100.00**
Candleholder, 6-1/2" h, 4" d, organic, pinched ribbon handle, in-body twist, ribbed base, yellow, green, and raspberry matte mottled glaze, small chip to base, script mark **3,300.00**
Chalice, 3-1/4" d, 6" h, ovoid cup, flaring base, lustered black and umber glaze, script signature, restoration to cup **805.00**
Demitasse cup, 2-1/2" h, 3-3/4" d, ext. with rare green, cobalt blue, and raspberry marbleized glaze, int. with sponged cobalt and raspberry volcanic glaze, die-stamped "G. E. Ohr, Biloxi, Miss" **1,500.00**
Jar, cov, 4-1/4" h, 5" d, spherical, gunmetal and green glaze dripping over mottled raspberry ground, shallow storage abrasion, die-stamped "G.E. OHR, Biloxi, Miss" **1,500.00**
Mustache cup, 2-3/4" h, 4" d, hand built as a shirt cuff, ribbon handle, sponged blue glaze, die-stamped "GEO. E. OHR/BILOXI, MISS" **2,000.00**
Pitcher
4" h, 5-1/4" d, pinched and folded bisque, scroddled terra cotta and buff clays, script sgd, two large sanded rim chips **3,775.00**

Pitcher, ribbon handle, incised bird of paradise and framed landscape, mottled brown and amber glaze, handle incised HP, bottom stamped G.E. OHR, BILOXI, 7" d, 7-1/2" h, **$6,275.** Photos courtesy of David Rago Auctions.

7" h, 7-1/2" d, ribbon handle, incised bird of paradise, framed landscape, mottled brown and amber glaze, handle incised "HP," bottom stamped "G. E. OHR, BILOXI" **6,275.00**
Vase
2-3/4" d, 5-1/4" h, tapered, asymmetrically folded rim, gunmetal and yellow glaze ext., bright orange int., marked "G.E.OHR/Biloxi, miss," few minute rim flecks **4,875.00**
3" d, 8" h, bulbous, folded rim, top cov in speckled mahogany glaze, base in sponged green and amber, marked "G.E.OHR/Biloxi, Miss,"

Vase, gourd shape, closed-in rim, gunmetal glaze, script signature, small bruise to base, 3-3/4" d, 3-1/4" h, $1,200.

Charles Higgins, exterior, The Pine Road, Maine scene, country road running past tall green pine trees, 13" x 15", **$145.**

Baker, Florian A., Rushing Waters **50.00**
Farini, In Her Boudoir **30.00**
Gardiner, H. Marshall, The Rainbow Fleet, Nantucket **635.00**
Gutmann, Bessie Pease Gutmann
Lorelei **1,760.00**
The Great Love **1,155.00**
Haynes, Untitled Waterfalls **20.00**
Higgins, Charles A., A Colonial Stairway **65.00**
Payne, George S., Weekly Letter . **25.00**

OHR POTTERY

History: Ohr pottery was produced by George E. Ohr in Biloxi, Mississippi. There is a discrepancy as to when he actually established his pottery; some say 1878, but Ohr's autobiography indicates 1883. In 1884, Ohr exhibited 600 pieces of his work, suggesting that he had been a potter for some time.

Ohr's techniques included twisting, crushing, folding, denting, and crinkling thin-walled clay into odd, grotesque, and, sometimes, graceful forms. His later pieces were often left unglazed.

In 1906, Ohr closed the pottery and stored more than 6,000 pieces as a legacy to his family. He had hoped the U.S. government would purchase it, but that

For more information, see this book.

Vase, flaring, crumpled neck, deep in-body twist, squat base covered in gunmetal glaze, mirror black at top, stamped GEO. E. OHR, BILOXI, MISS, 4" d, 4-1/2" h, $6,900.

couple of small nicks to rim, touch-up to kiln kiss on shoulder 10,450.00

4" d, 3-1/4" h, cinched middle, folded rim, speckled brown and amber glaze, stamped "G. E. OHR/Biloxi, Miss" 3,220.00

4" d, 4-1/2" h, squat base, deep in-body twist, flaring crumpled neck, mirror black glaze on top, gunmetal glaze on base, stamped "GEO. E. OHR, BILOXI, MISS" 6,900.00

7" h, three-sectioned bottle form, glossy olive glaze, top and bottom sponged dark blue, center purple metallic glaze, die-stamped "G. E. OHR/Biloxi, Miss" 1,200.00

Vase, cinched middle and folded rim, speckled brown and amber glaze, stamped G.E. OHR/Biloxi, Miss, 4" d, 3-1/4" h, $3,220.

Vessel, squat, speckled brown and green glaze, stamped GEO E. OHR/BILOXI, MISS, repair to rim chip, 5-1/2"d, 3-1/2" h, **$1,100.**

8-1/2" h, bottle shape, brown, green, and amber speckled lustered glaze, restoration to tiny rim chip, die-stamped "G. E. OHR, Biloxi, Miss" 1,200.00

9-1/4" h, bottle shape, mottled raspberry, purple, cobalt blue, and green satin glaze, small abrasion ring around widest part from years of storage at production site, die-stamped "G. E. OHR/Biloxi, Miss" 2,500.00

Vessel

3" d, 4-1/2" h, collared rim, bulbous base, mottled dark brown and gunmetal glaze, incised "Biloxi" 2,300.00

4-1/2" d, 3" h, dimpled, squatty, floriform top, black-mirrored glaze sponged on amber ground, stamped "G. E. OHR/Biloxi, Miss" 4,025.00

4-1/2" d, 4" h, ftd, crimped rim, tapering base, aventurine glaze, imp "GEO.E.OHR/BILOXI, MISS," underglaze tear, short rim tear 4,660.00

OLD PARIS CHINA

History: Old Paris china is fine-quality porcelain made by various French factories located in and around Paris during the 18th and 19th centuries. Some pieces were marked, but most were not. In addition to its fine quality, this type of ware is characterized by beautiful decorations and gilding. Favored colors are dark maroon, deep cobalt blue, and a dark green.

Basket, reticulated, gold and white dec, c1825 . . . . 1,400.00

Cake stand, Honore style, green border, c1845 . . . . 220.00

Charger, 13-1/2" d, hp portrait of young girl with feathered hat and ringlet curls, artist sgd "P. Amaury" 150.00

Cup and saucer, 5-3/4" d saucer, ftd, floral dec 55.00

Figure, 18-3/4" h, Napoleon, standing, one arm tucked behind back, other tucked into shirt, full military dress, gilt dec, low sq base, inscribed "Roussel-Bardell," late 19th C. . . 700.00

Luncheon set, light blue ground banding, gilt and iron-red cartouche and monogram, 28 9-1/4" d plates, 18 8-1/4" d plates, 11 6-5/8" d plates, 12 sauce dishes, 11 soup plates, oval 12-1/2" l serving bowl, oval 17-1/2" l platter, two circular cov vegetable tureens, cov sauce tureen, cov oval 12-1/4" tureen with underplate, cov jam jar with attached dish, chips, gilt wear 1,610.00

Mantel vase, bell-like flowered handles, blue ground, paneled enamel portraits of lowers, gilt trim, minor flower damage, pr 350.00

Plate, 9-1/2" d, dec by Boyer Feuillet Studio, cobalt blue and gold cobblestone border, hp flower arrangement in center, some wear to gilt, price for pr 250.00

Tea set

5-3/4" h cov teapot, creamer, sugar, 8" d waste bowl, eight cups and saucers, gilt trim, floral design, enameled floral panels, 19th C, gilt wear, creamer handle broken 250.00

8-5/8" h cov teapot, 7-3/4" h cream pitcher, 5-1/2" cov sugar bowl, gilt ground, enamel dec floral bouquets and banding, 19th C, sugar cov damaged. 460.00

Tray, 11" sq, shaped sides, hp floral dec, gold trim 225.00

Vase, figural mask, some gilding, 11" h, $75. Photo courtesy of Joy Luke Auctions.

Vase, 7" w, 9" h, two nude women on sides, one draped with blue fabric, other with pink fabric, hp rose and peach flowers, wear to gilt trim
.... **2,195.00**

OLD SLEEPY EYE

History: Sleepy Eye, a Sioux Indian chief who reportedly had a droopy eye, gave his name to Sleepy Eye, Minnesota, and one of its leading flour mills. In the early 1900s, Old Sleepy Eye Flour offered four Flemish-gray heavy stoneware premiums decorated in cobalt blue: a straight-sided butter crock, curved salt bowl, stein, and vase. The premiums were made by Weir Pottery Company, later to become Monmouth Pottery Company, and finally to emerge as the present-day Western Stoneware Company of Monmouth, Illinois.

For more information, see this book.

Additional pottery and stoneware pieces also were issued. Forms included five sizes of pitchers (4, 5-1/2, 6-1/2, 8, and 9 inches), mugs, steins, sugar bowls, and tea tiles (hot plates). Most were cobalt blue on white, but other glaze hues, such as browns, golds, and greens, were used.

Old Sleepy Eye also issued many other items, including bakers' caps, lithographed barrel covers, beanies, fans, multicolored pillow tops, postcards, and trade cards. Regular production of Old Sleepy Eye stoneware ended in 1937.

In 1952, Western Stoneware Company made 22- and 40-ounce steins in chestnut brown glaze with a redesigned Indian's head. From 1961 to 1972, gift editions were made for the board of directors and others within the company. Beginning in 1973, Western Stoneware Company issued an annual limited edition stein for collectors.

Marks: The gift editions made in the 1960s and 1970s were dated and signed with a maple leaf mark. The annual limited edition steins are marked and dated.

Reproduction Alert: Blue-and-white pitchers, crazed, weighted, and often with a stamp or the word "Ironstone" are the most common reproductions. The stein and salt bowl also have been made. Many reproductions come from Taiwan.

A line of fantasy items, new items which never existed as Old Sleepy Eye originals, includes an advertising pocket mirror with miniature flour-barrel label, small glass plates, fruit jars, toothpick holders, glass and pottery miniature pitchers, and salt and pepper shakers. One mill item has been made: a sack marked as though it were old, but of a size that could not possibly hold the amount of flour indicated.

Advertising print, portrait medallion of American Indian, The Sleepy Eye Mills, Sleepyeye Minn. Sleepy Eye Cream, framed, 20" square, **$175.** *Photo courtesy of Joy Luke Auctions.*

Mill items

Advertising premium cards, 5-1/2" x 9", full-color Indian lore illus, Old Sleepy Eye Indian character trademark, 10-pc set **875.00**

Cookbook, Sleepy Eye Milling Co., loaf of bread shape, portrait of chief **150.00**

Label, 9-1/4" x 11-1/2" d, egg crate, Sleepy Eye Brand, A. J. Pietrus & Sons Co., Sleepy Eye, MN, red, blue, and yellow...................... **25.00**

Letter opener, bronze, Indian-head handle, marked "Sleepy Eye Milling Co., Sleepy Eye, MN" **750.00**

Pinback button, "Old Sleepy Eye for Me," bust portrait of chief **175.00**

Pottery and stoneware

Bowl, 4" h, ftd, Bristol glaze, relief profile of Indian on one side, floral design on other, imp "X" on bottom
.... **360.00**

Butter crock, blue and gray stoneware, hairline crack, 6-1/2" d, 4-3/4" h, **$195.** *Photo courtesy of Joy Luke Auctions.*

Stein, Bristol glazed stoneware, relief and blue accented Indian profile on one side, teepee and trees on reverse, relief and blue accented Indian profile handle, impressed "S" on bottom, 7-1/2" h, **$470.** *Photo courtesy of Vicki and Bruce Waasdorp.*

Butter crock, cov, 4-3/4" h, blue and gray salt glaze, relief and blue accented Indian profile on one side, trees and teepee on other side, imp "H" on bottom, surface rim chip.... **495.00**

Mug
  3-1/2" d, 4-3/4" h, marked "WS Co. Monmouth, III" **395.00**
  4-1/2" d, 4-1/2" h, attributed to Brush/McCoy **250.00**

Pitcher, 7-3/4" h, #4 .... **675.00**

Stein, 7-1/2" h, Bristol glaze, relief and blue accented Indian profile on one side, trees and teepee on other side
.... **470.00**

Tile, cobalt blue and white..... **950.00**

ONION MEISSEN

History: The blue onion or bulb pattern is of Chinese origin and depicts peaches and pomegranates, not onions. It was first made in the 18th century by Meissen, hence the name Onion Meissen.

Factories in Europe, Japan, and elsewhere copied the pattern. Many still have the pattern in production, including the Meissen factory in Germany.

Marks: Many pieces are marked with a company's logo; after 1891, the country of origin is indicated on imported pieces.

Note: Prices given are for pieces produced between 1870 and 1930. Early Meissen examples bring a high premium.

Ashtray, 5" d, blue crossed swords mark **75.00**

Bowl, 8-1/2" d, reticulated, blue crossed swords mark, 19th C .. **395.00**

Box, cov, 4-1/2" d, round, rose finial
.... **80.00**

Bread plate, 6-1/2" d **75.00**

Cake stand, 13-1/2" d, 4-1/2" h . **220.00**

Platter, Blue Onion pattern, oval, scalloped rim, well and tree, blue underglaze decoration of flowering branches, underglaze blue oval mark, 17" x 11-3/4", $135. Photo courtesy of Sanford Alderfer Auction Company.

Candlesticks, pr, 7" h **90.00**
Creamer and sugar, gold edge, c1900
. . . . **175.00**
Demitasse cup and saucer, c1890
. . . . **95.00**
Dish, 12" d, circular, divided . . . **175.00**
Fruit compote, 9" h, circular, openwork bowl, five oval floral medallions. **375.00**
Fruit knives, six-pc set **75.00**
Hot plate, handles **125.00**
Ladle, wooden handle **115.00**
Lamp, 22" h, oil, frosted glass globular form shade **475.00**
Plate, 10" d **100.00**
Platter
    12-1/4" d **175.00**
    13" x 10", crossed swords mark
    . . . . **295.00**
Pot de creme **65.00**
Serving dish, 9-1/4" w, 11" l, floral design on handle **200.00**
Tray, 17" l, cartouche shape, gilt edge
. . . . **425.00**
Vegetable dish, cov, 10" w, sq . **150.00**

OPALESCENT GLASS

History: Opalescent glass, a clear or colored glass with milky white decorations, looks fiery or opalescent when held to light. This effect was achieved by applying bone ash chemicals to designated areas while a piece was still hot and then refiring it at extremely high temperatures.

    There are three basic categories of opalescent glass: (1) blown (or mold blown) patterns, e.g., Daisy & Fern and Spanish Lace; (2) novelties, pressed glass patterns made in limited quantity

For more information, see this book.

and often in unusual shapes such as corn or a trough; and (3) traditional pattern (pressed) glass forms.
    Opalescent glass was produced in England in the 1870s. Northwood began the American production in 1897 at its Indiana, Pennsylvania, plant. Jefferson, National Glass, Hobbs, and Fenton soon followed.

Ewer, long neck, trefoil top, blue tinted, applied pink and clear blossom, green leafy branch forms looping handle, slightly ribbed, diamonds of pale opalescent blue at base gradually merge, 10-1/2" h, $375. Photo courtesy of Clarence and Betty Maier.

Blown
Basket
    6-3/4" h, cranberry, shading from translucent opalescent to deep rose, crystal handle **115.00**
    10-3/4" h, green, applied lime stemmed flower, applied feet, thorny twist handle **125.00**
Barber bottle, Raised Swirl, cranberry
. . . . **295.00**
Berry bowl, master, Chrysanthemum Base Swirl, blue, satin **95.00**
Biscuit jar, cov, Spanish Lace, vaseline
. . . . **275.00**
Bride's basket, Poinsettia, ruffled top
. . . . **275.00**
Butter dish, cov, Hobbs Hobnail, vaseline **250.00**
Celery vase, Seaweed, cranberry
. . . . **250.00**
Creamer
    Coin Dot, cranberry **190.00**
    Windows Swirl, cranberry . . . **500.00**
Cruet
    Chrysanthemum Base Swirl, white, satin **175.00**
    Ribbed Opal Lattice, white . . **135.00**
Finger bowl, Hobbs Hobnail, cranberry
. . . . **65.00**
Lamp, oil
    Inverted Thumbprint, white, amber fan base **145.00**
    Snowflake, cranberry **800.00**
Mustard, cov, Reverse Swirl, vaseline
. . . . **65.00**
Pickle castor, Daisy and Fern, blue, emb floral jar, DQ, resilvered frame
. . . . **650.00**

Pitcher
    Arabian Nights, white **450.00**
    Fern, blue **450.00**
    Hobbs Hobnail, cranberry . . **315.00**
    Seaweed, blue **525.00**
Rose bowl, 5" h, Double Diamond, pink opalescent, gold enameled flowers
. . . . **90.00**
Salt shaker, orig top
    Consolidated Criss-Cross, cranberry
    . . . . **85.00**
    Ribbed Opal Lattice, cranberry
    . . . . **95.00**
Spooner, Reverse Swirl, cranberry
. . . . **175.00**
Sugar, cov, Reverse Swirl, cranberry
. . . . **350.00**
Sugar shaker
    Coin Spot, cranberry **275.00**
    Ribbed Opal Lattice, cranberry
    . . . . **325.00**
Syrup, Coin Spot, cranberry . . . **175.00**
Tumbler
    Acanthus, blue **90.00**
    Christmas Snowflake, blue, ribbed
    . . . . **125.00**
    Maze, swirling, green **95.00**
    Reverse Swirl, cranberry **65.00**
Waste bowl, Hobbs Hobnail, vaseline
. . . . **75.00**

Novelties
Back bar bottle, 12-1/4" h, robin's egg blue ground, opalescent stripes swirled to the right **100.00**
Barber bottle, 8" h, sq, diamond pattern molded form, light cranberry, white vertical stripes **275.00**
Bowl, Winter Cabbage, white . . . **45.00**
Bushel basket, blue **75.00**
Chalice, Maple Leaf, vaseline . . **45.00**
Hat, Opal Swirl, white, blue edge **95.00**

Water set, 8-1/2" water pitcher, four matching tumblers, apricot opalescent, $200. Photo courtesy of Woody Auctions.

Vase, Acorn and Oak Leaf pattern, pale blue, acid etched to clear decoration, gilt ruffled rim, unsigned, 6" h, $165. Photo courtesy of Sanford Alderfer Auction Company.

Jack-in-the-pulpit vase, 6" h, green swirl, applied red flower, crystal stem 115.00

Pressed

Berry bowl, master, Tokyo, green 60.00

Butter dish, cov, Water Lily and Cattails, blue. 300.00

Card receiver, Fluted Scrolls, white 40.00

Cracker jar, cov, Wreath and Shell, vaseline 750.00

Creamer, Inverted Fan and Feather, blue. 125.00

Cruet, Stars and Stripes, cranberry 575.00

Jelly compote, Intaglio, blue. . . . 55.00

Salt and pepper shakers, pr, Jewel and Flower, canary yellow, orig tops 250.00

Pickle castor, Snowflake pattern, cranberry, Aurora silver plate holder, 12-1/2" h, $600. Photo courtesy of Woody Auctions.

Sauce, Drapery, dec, blue 35.00
Spooner, Swag with Brackets, blue 70.00
Toothpick holder, Ribbed Spiral, blue 90.00

Tumbler
Drapery, blue 90.00
Jeweled Heart, blue 85.00
Vase, Northwood Diamond Point, blue 75.00

OPALINE GLASS

For more information, see this book.

History: Opaline glass was a popular mid- to late-19th century European glass. The glass has a certain amount of translucency and often is found decorated with enamel designs and trimmed in gold.

Basket, 7-1/4" h, opaque white ground, applied amber stemmed pink flowers, amber twist handle 90.00

Bouquet holder, 7" h, blue opaline cornucopia-shaped gilt dec flower holders issuing from bronze stag heads, Belgian black marble base, English, Victorian, early 19th C, pr 725.00

Box, cov, 6" l, 4-3/4" d, 5" h, oblong, green, serpentine scrolled ends, gilt-metal mounts and escutcheon, Continental, mid-19th C. 920.00

Bride's basket, 12" d, 7-1/2" h, white opaline, cased in pink, overall colorful enameled dec, emb Middletown plated holder, applied fruit handles, Victorian, minor losses 525.00

Candelabra, Louis XV style, late 19th C
18-1/2" h, gilt bronze and blue opaline, scrolled candle arms and base, two-light 175.00
26-1/2" h, gilt metal and blue opaline, five-light 400.00

Chalice, white ground, Diamond Point pattern. 35.00

Dresser jar, 5-1/2" d, egg shape, blue ground, heavy gold dec 200.00

Ewer, 13-1/4" h, white ground, Diamond Point pattern 135.00

Jardinières, 5-1/4" h, gilt bronze and blue opaline, sq, Empire style, tasseled chains, paw feet, early 20th C, pr 1,610.00

Mantel lusters, 12-3/4" h, blue, gilt dec, slender faceted prisms, Victorian, c1880, damage, pr 250.00

Oil lamp, 24" h, dolphin-form stepped base, clear glass oil well, frosted glass shade, late 19th C, converted to electric, chips. 460.00

Oil lamp base, 22" h, blue, baluster turned standard on circular foot, 20th C, converted to electric, pr. 635.00

Perfume bottle, 4" h, baluster form, blue opaline bottle, gilt metal floral overlay, foot, and neck mounts, hinged lid set with shell cameo of young man in feathered cap, French, late 19th/early 20th C. 200.00

Salt, boat shaped, blue dec, white enamel garland and scrolling . . . 75.00

Vase
4-1/2" h, opaque white ground, applied amber stemmed acorn and red leaves 90.00
6-1/4" h, cased pink ground, colorful enameled flower spray 225.00
7-7/8" h, elongated neck, ftd bulbed form, enamel dec of three medallions of Etruscan figures connected with Greek key and scroll designs in rust, gold, and black, light link enameled ground, Neoclassical, possibly England, late 19th C, minor wear to enamel 575.00
8-1/8" h, bulbed rim, urn-form, enameled dec of Etruscan figures in beige, gold accent designs, stamped "Richardson's Strourbridge," England, c1845-50 . . . . 750.00
9-1/2" h, pink cased ground, enameled gold day lilies, three

Vases, pair, Fireglow, gilded banding, 13-3/4" h, $95. Photo courtesy of Joy Luke Auctions.

rolled over handled rim, Victorian
.... **125.00**
10" h, homogenized gray ground, enameled perched birds, 19th C, price for matched pr...... **175.00**

Water pitcher, 12-1/4" h, blue, high looped handle, bulbous, early 20th C
.... **240.00**

ORIENTALIA

History: Orientalia is a term applied to objects made in the Orient, an area which encompasses the Far East, Asia, China, and Japan. The diversity of cultures produced a variety of objects and styles.

Additional Listings: Canton, Celadon, Cloisonné, Fitzhugh, Nanking, Netsukes, Rose Medallion, Japanese Prints, and other related categories.

Album, fan paintings, 11 works by various artists including, Ch'en Fang Ting, Hsu Lin Lu (b1916), Shao Ping Chang, Wu Hsi Tsai (1799-1870), Kuo Shang Hsien (1796-1820), Fei Shih Po, Wu Hua Yuan (1893-1972), Wang I Ting, Yang I, Wang I Ting, Hou Pi I (2)
.... **600.00**

Altar table, 58-1/2" x 34-1/4" x 16", China, chi chi mu or chicken wing wood, archaic-style spandrels, beaded borders, 18th C **1,955.00**

Architectural element
Capitals, 22" l, carved wood, foo dogs, gold lacquered surface, China, 19th C, price for pr . **775.00**
Finial, 4-3/4" h, bronze, figural dragon, patina with azurite areas, Khmer, 13th C **850.00**

Bell, 19" h, bronze, lid surmounted by two kneeling figures, iron mount with two apsara figures, Burma, 19th C
.... **400.00**

Bottle, 11-1/2" d, porcelain, sq form, blue and white dec of Buddhist lion dogs, China, Transitional period, 1630-50 .... **2,850.00**

Box, cov, 4" h, iron, hexagonal form with mixed metal inlay, sgd "Seijo," Japan, 19th C **1,550.00**

Bowl
6-1/2" d, nephrite, white and pale green, incised and gilt character inscriptions with four character reign mark on base, Qing Dynasty, 20th C, price for pr...... **920.00**
7-1/2" d, porcelain, dark blue ext. with gilt dragons, clouds, and pearls, white int., China, Ch'ien Lung six-character seal mark, 1736-95 .... **600.00**

Brush pot, 4-3/4" h, rect, pale green glaze, Ch'ien Lung mark, 1736-1795
.... **900.00**

Buddha
13" h, hardwood figure, seated on lotus throne, numerous coatings of lacquer, China, 18th C **425.00**
17" h, Buddha Amida, lacquered wood, standing with his hands in "abeyance of fear" mudra, gold lacquered robes, eyes inlaid with crystal, Japan, 18th C... **1,350.00**

Buddhist bell, 14" d, Japan, hammered brass with a lacquered design of a dragon and thunder meanders, late 19th/early 20th C **450.00**

Cane, 37" h, 1-1/2" d, 4-3/4" h staghorn handle, carved Shishi standing on rocky prominence, black ink highlights, 1/18" rolled gold collar, figured rosewood shaft, 1" replaced brass ferrule, Japan, c1895 .... **1,100.00**

Charger, 23-1/2" d, Imari dec, tomato red, blue, green, orange, and gold, center scene of family with nine figures at table beneath tree **495.00**

Chest, 30-3/4" l, 16-1/4" w, 16-1/2" h, camphor wood, dovetailed case, bracket feet, lift-out interior tray with four cov compartments, additional compartment at either end, all with relief carved mums on top, geometric line detail on int. of lid, old replaced brass hinges and hasp, orig wrought iron handles on either end, old waxed finish
.... **350.00**

Chair, China
Elmwood, armchair, back splat carved with roundels of archaic dragons, 19th C, price for set of four **1,265.00**
Red lacquer, 17-1/2" w, 15" d, 34" h, 19th C, price for pr **1,050.00**

Cup, Chinese, porcelain, engraved dragons under egg yolk yellow color, six-character underglaze blue Kuang Hsu mark, 1874-1908, possibly of the period................... **200.00**

Brush pot, rectangular, pale green glaze, Ch'ien Lung mark (1736-1795) and of the period, 3-3/4" h, $900. Photo courtesy of Skinner Auctioneers and Appraisers.

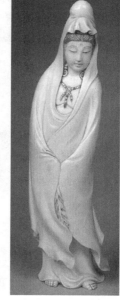

Figure, woman in hooded long flowing wrap, holding bamboo branch, wearing detailed necklace with inlaid jewels and MOP, carved elephant ivory, artist signed on base, some inset stones and MOP missing, $1,360. Photo courtesy of Cowan's Historic Americana Auctions.

Embroidery, on silk
17" x 13", crane by flowering tree, Japanese, Meiji period, 1867-1912
.... **320.00**
28" x 20", courtesan in elaborate costume holding pole with suspended basket of flowers, Chinese, 19th C **345.00**

Fan, folding, China, 19th C
Ivory, shaped stays with numerous figures in garden scenes, fan painted with harbor scene, other vignettes of idyllic village scenes, black lacquer box with gilt butterflies and flowers **490.00**
Wooden stays with black lacquer and gold dec, fan of paper dec with figures in silk and ivory, reverse magenta with three reserves of country scenes, gold and black lacquer case... **250.00**
Wooden stays with black lacquer and gold dec of figures in garden vignettes, fan of paper dec in silk and ivory, numerous figures, black and gold lacquered box, 10-1/2" l, very minor loss **230.00**

Fan, folding, Japan, 19th C
All ivory stays dec with shibayama inlay of gold lacquer and semi-precious inlay of birds and flowers, 11-1/2" l, orig box
.... **4,025.00**
Carved ivory stays with shibayama inlay, one side dec with landscape, other with children watching fireworks.............. **375.00**

Figures, carved ivory, set of six, a man with carp, man with staff, woman with lute, man with hammer, various coloring added, all are signed, 20th C, stepped stand, **$575.** *Photo courtesy of James D. Julia, Inc.*

Figure

5-1/2" h, seated goddess of mercy, Blanc de Chine, Te Hua ware, sgd with illegible mark within double-gourd, carved hardwood stand, ornate glass case, China, 19th C **920.00**

8" l, 7-1/4" h, rabbit, bronze, textured surface, sgd, Japan, Meiji period (1868-1911) **3,500.00**

11-1/2" h, carved ivory, wise man with book of Proverbs, carved wood plinth, early 20th C . . **520.00**

12" h, carved ivory, wise man with branch of fruit, young woman with cherry blossoms, etched details, incised chop marks on base, early 20th C **615.00**

12-3/4" h, Deity Khmer, bronze, standing image in dhoti, crown and various jewels, Khmer, possibly 13th C **775.00**

15" h, Deity, bronze, traces of polychrome remaining, China, Ming period (1368-1644) . . **875.00**

18" h, Buddhist Lions, San Tsai ware, glaze of mustard yellow, aubergine, and green, fitted hardwood stands, China, 19th C, price for pr **2,950.00**

40" h, Goddess, carved stone, gray schist image of Kuan Yin, China, 20th C **285.00**

Fish bowl, porcelain, blue and white, design of phoenix in garden, scrolling at mouth, Ming period, probably Chia Ching period, 1522-1566, hairline **1,175.00**

Foo Dog, 11" l, 10-1/2" h, carved wood, surface lacquered in red and gold, China, 19th C **600.00**

Garden seat

18" h, porcelain, hexagonal form, blue and white dec, China, 19th C **900.00**

20" h, porcelain, blue and white transfer decoration of a landscape, Japan, early 20th C **195.00**

Ginger jar, 8-1/2" h, China, blue and white mythical animals and floral prays, K'ang His mark on base, 19th C **250.00**

Incense burner, Japan

Porcelain, Hirado ware, basketweave design, underglaze blue floral sprays, late 19th C, 4-1/4" h **300.00**

Pottery, figure of elephant, urn on back, green, white, and purple enamel dec, 19th C, losses **520.00**

Hand scroll

65-1/2" x 3", ink on silk, landscapes, colophons by various members of the Wu family, Tao Kuang period, 1821-48 . . . . **400.00**

87" x 9", ink and colors on silk, titled "Sun Geese," various colophons dated Wan Li and Ch'ien Lung, 34 seals, including various imperial seals, late 19th C **500.00**

Hanging scroll

27" x 16-1/2", painting of two magpies in flowering prunus tree, sgd "Tsui Tzu Fan" for Tsui Shang Chih, 20th C **400.00**

42-1/2" x 22-1/4", ink and color on paper, map of the temples of Wu Tai Shan with a central figure of Manjushri, the Buddha of the future, China, Ching dynasty, probably 18th/19th C **950.00**

54" x 26", ink and color on paper pine and rocks, sgd, two artist's seals, Chen Hen Ko 1878-1923, slight toning and foxing . . . **450.00**

Guan, blue and white porcelain, painted as dragon chasing flaming pearl of wisdom Chinese, Yuan dynasty, 6" h, **$1,100.** *Photo courtesy of Sloan's Auctioneers & Appraisers.*

Image, gilt bronze

4" h, Lama, probably second Dalai Lama, one hand holding Kalasa, other holding jewel of bliss, Tibet, 16th C **2,350.00**

9-3/4" h, Maitreya, Buddha of Future, seated in princely attire, right hand raised in fearlessness, left hand setting wheel-of-law in motion, two nagakesvara stalks at either side with symbols of maitreya, blossom, and hamadalu bottle, figure is set on double-lotus throne, Tibet, 15th C **5,875.00**

Incense box, 2" x 2", Komei-style, iron inlaid with gold and silver, Japan, Meiji period (1868-1911) **600.00**

Incense burner

6-1/2" h, silver, China, 19th C, chalice form, claw feet, cover pierced and engraved with flowers, body engraved with flowers on punch-work ground, three illegible touch marks on the base, China, 19th C **470.00**

15" h, pottery, San Tsai glaze, impressed six-character K'ang Hsi mark on the base, China, 19th C **425.00**

16" h, bronze, inlay of silver and copper in the manner of Shih So, China, 19th C **775.00**

Jar, cov, baluster

26" h, blue ground with roses, surround reserves of flowers and butterflies, lotus finial, China, 20th C, hairline **950.00**

32" h, blue and white dec of Buddhist lion dogs on cloud strewn ground, lion-mask handles, lion finials, China, 19th C, minor loss **3,200.00**

Okimono, 3" l, ivory study of group of rats and lantern, horn inlay, 19th C **635.00**

Painting, oil on canvas, Chinese Export School, 19th Century, portrait of American clipper ship, gilt frame

The Almeda of Bath, Maine, 20" x 27", lined, "Shanghai China 1878, May 8," scattered retouch, craquelure **9,990.00**

The Charles B. Kenney of New York, handwritten inscription on the stretcher reads "Shanghai China 1878, May 8," 20" x 27", lined, scattered retouch, craquelure **9,400.00**

Palace Urn, 24" h, bronze, elaborately dec with scenes of birds, Foo dogs, foliage, large applied dragons, rich chocolate brown patina, Chinese, c1900, price for pr **750.00**

Panel, 23" x 16", rosewood, deep relief carving of two peacocks on flowering tree, Chinese, early 20th C **125.00**

Plaque, 8" x 6", bronze, relief dec of Kuan Yin surrounded by attending deities, extensive inscription on back, China, 19th C **135.00**

Saucer dish

5-3/4" d, porcelain, blue and white dec, int. with deer, tiger, and chih lung, borders of aquatic life, ext. with five flowers, Wan Li six-character mark, 1573-1619
. . . . **2,000.00**

6-1/2" d, yellow, white int., Tao Kuang mark and period, 1821-1848
. . . . **1,600.00**

Screen

41" x 27-1/2", two panels, mahogany frame, pierced fretwork across center, worn silk panels on top, small scroll missing from base
. . . . **55.00**

94" x 18", six panels, finely detailed Buddhist and Taoist figures, checkered silk border, black lacquered frame, Japanese, c1750, accompanied by "Certificate of Antiquity" dated 1971 addressed to US Customs by David Kidd and Y. Morimoto of "Three Dynasties," Ashiya City, Japan, minor losses **1,450.00**

Screen, carved rosewood, four panels, stile of each section carved in relief with scrolling blossoms and foliage, each panel carved in the round with rosettes, grape leaves, vines, and grape clusters, c1900, minor losses and repairs, 80" l, 72" h, $575. Photo courtesy of Jackson's International Auctioneers & Appraisers.

Portraits, pair, ornately costumed elderly man and woman seated on colorful thrones, silk ivory border, matching black and gold dec frames, David Bendann, Baltimore, label on back, some discoloration, 19" w, 40" h, $460. Photo courtesy of James D. Julia, Inc.

Sculpture

6" h, bronze, figure of Vishnu upheld by Garuda, slate green patina, Khmer, 11th C **500.00**

11" h, stone, head of Buddha, China, 19th C **575.00**

20" l, Asian Rhinoceros, bronze, sgd on the rear feet, Japan, late 19th C
. . . . **5,200.00**

39-1/2" h, Buddha, bronze, four-armed image of Shadakshari Lokeshvara seated on lotus throne, inlay of blue and red glass, Nepal, 20th C **550.00**

Shrine

7" h, black lacquer case, gilt standing image of Amida Buddha, Japan, 19th C **395.00**

27" h, black lacquer, gold lacquered figure of Kshitagarba, inlaid eyes, Japan, 18th/19th C **3,200.00**

86" h, lacquered, structured as temple building, triple roof; ornately carved with shishi, dragons, and flowers, surface lacquered in gold, red, brown, and black, engraved gilt copper metal mounts, Japan, Meiji period (1868-1911) . **1,250.00**

Stele of Buddha, 21" h, black chlorite, seated under royal canopy with hands in "earth witnessing" mudra, flanked by lotus leaves, surrounded by scenes from his life, Pala period, 12th C
. . . . **9,400.00**

Stupa, 6-1/2" h, bronze, four makala supports, stupa surmounted by four figures of Buddha, Nepal, 19th C
. . . . **550.00**

Tankard

4" h, porcelain, famille rose enamel landscape scene, China, 18th C
. . . . **360.00**

8" h, blue and white, scholar in garden scene, Continental silver mounts with Dutch export hallmarks, China, Transitional period, c1620 . . . . **3,985.00**

Table, side, teakwood, dark finish, high rect legs with relief edge moldings and scrolling with foliage, pierced aprons with dragons' heads, scrolled returns of raised paneled top match pierced apron, 20th C, 20-1/4" l, 16-3/4" d, 33-1/2" h **450.00**

Teapot, cov, porcelain, Batavia ware, brown glazed ground, enamel flowers and gilt, China, 18th C **270.00**

Vase

3" and 5-1/2" h, Yu-hu-chun shape, irid lemon yellow glaze, China, 18th C, boxed, price for matched pr
. . . . **300.00**

7" h, porcelain, high shouldered, wide neck form, camellia-leaf green glaze with iridescence, China, 18th C **250.00**

8-1/2" h, enameled silver, pear shaped with jump rings, enamel dec of phoenix in flowering trees, sgd "Peking, Pure Silver," maker's mark, China, dated 1916 in extensive inscription, minor loss to enamel, some dents, price for pr
. . . . **500.00**

8-1/2" h, studio pottery, ovoid form, four lug handles, top covered in blue-brown glaze, bottom engraved with Archaic-style horses and fish, sgd with an impressed seal on bottom, Japan, late 19th/early 20th C **395.00**

Tankard, blue and white, scholar in a garden scene, Continental silver mounts with Dutch export hallmarks, China, Transitional period, c1620, 8" h, $3,900. Photo courtesy of Skinner Auctioneers and Appraisers.

Tea set, Japanese, Moriage, porcelain, dragons decoration, $150. Photo courtesy of Joy Luke Auctions.

13" h, oxblood, glazed purple at mouth shading to deep red at base, ling chih handles, China, late 19th C, drilled and mounted as a lamp **450.00**

15" h, bronze, relief dec of waves with dragon in round holding glass pearl, sgd "great Japan sei don sai," Japan, Meiji period . **1,650.00**

20-1/2" h, Tsun-shape, Wu Tsai ware, birds and flowers dec, China, Transitional period, c1640 . . . . **2,000.00**

42" h, bronze, flared rim, paneled shoulder takers to base with flower petals, detailed peacock sits on flowering tree branch, peahen below, dark patina, peacock's crest missing **3,500.00**

Votive plaque, 7" d, gilt copper and bronze, a central image of the Buddha surrounded by the wheel of law, Japan, late 19th/early 20th C **250.00**

Water coupe, 5" d, porcelain, deep crushed-strawberry copper-red color, China, 18th C **275.00**

Wine ewer, 6-1/4" h, Hirado ware, form of Hoi tea, bag of wealth, underglaze

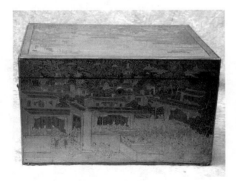

Tea chest, gold lacquer, teahouse scenes, foliate and floral borders, engraved pewter liner with ivory knob, English lock with hallmarks, cracking, touch-up, 13-1/2" w, 10-3/4" d, 7-1/4" h, $990. Photo courtesy of Sanford Alderfer Auction Company.

blue, yellow, pale green, tan, and black accents, 19th C, cover missing
. . . . **750.00**

ORIENTAL RUGS

History: Oriental rugs or carpets date back to 3,000 B.C., but it was in the 16th century that they became prevalent. The rugs originated in the regions of Central Asia, Iran (Persia), Caucasus, and Anatolia. Early rugs can be classified into basic categories: Iranian, Caucasian, Turkoman, Turkish, and Chinese. Later India, Pakistan, and Iraq produced rugs in the Oriental style.

The pattern name is derived from the tribe that produced the rug, e.g., Iran is the source for Hamadan, Herez, Sarouk, and Tabriz.

> **Reproduction Alert:** Beware! There are repainted rugs on the market.

Notes: When evaluating an Oriental rug, age, design, color, weave, knots per square inch, and condition determine the final value. Silk rugs and prayer rugs bring higher prices than other types.

Afshar, South Persia, second quarter 20th C, 6' 4" x 5', five stepped polygons and two vases of flowers in midnight blue, navy blue, sky blue, gold, brown, and blue-green on terra-cotta red field, three narrow floral borders of similar coloration, small areas of minor wear, brown corrosion. **1,035.00**

Agra, India, last quarter 19th C, 8' 6" x 6' 10", overall design of palmettes, rosettes, and flowering vines in rose, tan, light aubergine, ivory, olive, and blue-green on deep wine red field, wide blue-green border of similar design, small areas of wear, edges, and ends very slightly reduced and machine reovercast **8,625.00**

Anatolian Yastik, last quarter 19th C, 2' 8" x 1' 10", column of four hooked hexagonal medallions in navy blue, sky blue, red, gold, aubergine, apricot, and light blue-green, red spandrels, multicolored S-motif border, minor wear to center, slight moth damage. **1,725.00**

Armenian Karabagh, South Caucasus, dated 1911, 8' 10" x 3' 9", three lightning medallions each inset with quatrefoil floral motifs, navy blue, royal blue, dark red, rose, camel, aubergine, and blue-green on midnight blue field, navy blue rosette border, small replied areas, corner repairs **1,265.00**

Baluch, Northeast Persia, second half 19th C, prayer rug, eight columns of

meandering vines in midnight blue, red, brown, and aubergine on ivory field, borders of similar coloration, even wear, brown corrosion **600.00**

Bidjar, Northwest Persia, late 19th C, 8' x 4' 2", overall Herati design in red, royal blue, camel, plum, gold, and dark blue-green on midnight blue field, red spandrels, royal blue border, slight even wear to center, small corner gouge
. . . . **2,235.00**

Bordjalou Kazak, Southwest Caucasus, third quarter 19th C, prayer rug, 4' 6" x 3' 7", rect prayer cartouche inset with concentric gabled sq medallion in navy blue, ivory, and light blue-green on red field, ivory border, small rewoven and replied areas, end fraying **2,235.00**

Ersari Torba, West Turkestan, late 19th C, 6' x 1' 3", three elongated hexagons surrounded by geometric motifs in rust-red, ivory, gold, and royal blue on variegated midnight blue, dark brown field, multicolored border, small stain, very slight moth damage **825.00**

Hamadan, Persian, 3' 4" x 9' 7", runner, salmon and blue medallions . . . **395.00**

Heriz, Northwest Persia

10' 9" x 7' 9", late 19th C, overall design of palmettes, flowerheads, and deeply serrated leaves in red, rose, camel, abrashed sky blue, and light blue-green, abrashed midnight blue-black field, red border, small areas of wear, guard

Qashqai, Iran, late 20th C, browns, reds, greens, and blue on ivory field, 100" x 130", $920. Photo courtesy of Jackson's International Auctioneers & Appraisers.

stripe missing from both ends, fringes added **1,000.00**

20' x 10' 4", second quarter 20th C, large multi-gabled medallion surrounded by serrated leaves and flowering vines, midnight, royal, and ice blue, rose, gold, red-brown, and dark green on red field, large ivory spandrels, midnight blue turtle border, small areas of minor wear, some black corrosion **5,875.00**

Jaf Kurd, Northwest Persia, early 20th C, bagface, 2' 7" x 2' 7", diamond lattice of hooked diamonds in midnight and navy blue, red, gold, brown, rust, aubergine, and blue-green, aubergine border, slight brown corrosion . . **530.00**

Karabagh, South Caucasus, last quarter 19th C

6' 10" x 3' 8", three diamond medallions flanked by numerous small animal motifs in abrashed sky blue, red, rose, gold, camel, and blue-green, dark brown field, red border, brown corrosion, re-overcast, guard stripe partially missing from one end **1,000.00**

7' 10" x 4' 6", two large octagonal medallions inset with "cloudband" motifs in midnight and navy blue, ivory, red, gold, and blue-green on rust field, ivory border, small area of wear, area of flat stitch restoration **1,650.00**

Kazak, Southwest Caucasus, last quarter 19th C

Sarouk, North Persia, early to mid 20th C, blue, yellow, and green on red field, 122" x 171", $750. Photo courtesy of Jackson's International Auctioneers & Appraisers.

Sarouk, North Persia, early to mid 20th C, blue, yellow, and green on red field, 122" x 171", $750. Photo courtesy of Jackson's International Auctioneers & Appraisers.

8' 4" x 4', diamond lattice of concentric hooked diamonds in midnight and sky blue, red, rose, ivory, gold, brown, and blue-green, ivory border, areas of some wear, small repairs **715.00**

8' 6" x 4' 10", two and a half stepped diamond medallions flanked by six large stepped triangles in midnight and navy blue, ivory, orange-gold, and blue-green on terra-cotta red field, navy blue border, small areas of wear and creases, slight end fraying **1,530.00**

Konaghend, Northeast Caucasus, late 19th/early 20th C, 6' x 4' 3", characteristic arabesque lattice in ivory, red, rose, royal blue, gold, and blue-green on black field, ivory border, some black corrosion **1,295.00**

Kuba, Northeast Caucasus, late 19th/early 20th C, 4' 10" x 3' 6", three diamond medallions, each radiating four serrated motifs and four small diamonds in red, red-brown, navy blue, ivory, orange, and blue-green, abrashed midnight blue field, navy blue border, areas of minor wear, slight dye runs, black corrosion, some glue to back **1,000.00**

Kurd, Northwest Persia, early 20th C, 9' 5" x 3' 9", column of five turkoman-style octagonal turret guls in red, sky blue, gold, aubergine-brown, olive, and blue-green, midnight blue field, dark red border, end fraying **900.00**

Lenkoran, Southeast Caucasus, last quarter 19th C, 10' x 4' 4", three large calyx medallions separated by two large rect medallions in red, navy blue,

aubergine, ivory, apricot, light camel, and blue-green on dark brown field, ivory border, brown corrosion, even wear to center, creases **715.00**

Lesghi, Northeast Caucasus, last quarter 19th C, 4' 10" x 3' 9", column of four Lesghi stars in red, sky blue, ivory, tan-gold, and blue-green on navy blue field, two ivory borders, even wear, slight end fraying **1,300.00**

Luri, Southwest Persia, early 20th C, 7' x 4' 7", large gabled and serrated sq medallions flanked by six large rosettes in red, navy blue, apricot, gold, and dark blue-green on midnight blue field, ivory border, even center wear . **765.00**

Malayer, Northwest Persia, second quarter 20th C, 4' 10" x 3' 6", overall design of flowerheads and blossoming vines in red, ice blue, camel, and olive on abrashed royal blue field, ivory border, outer guard stripes partially missing from both ends **1,000.00**

Qashqai, Southwest Persia, late 19th/early 20th C, 6' 9" x 4', large hooked hexagonal medallion inset with blossoming angular vines in red, navy blue, ivory, gold, brown, and blue-green, midnight blue field, brown border, slight wear to center, minor moth damage, small repair . . **1,100.00**

Senneh, Northwest Persia, late 19th C, 5' 9" x 4' 3", diamond medallion and large matching spandrels with overall Herati design in sky blue, red, rose,

Heriz, Persian, early 20th C, Persian garden, reds, blues, and yellow on ivory ground, 89" x 123", $575. Photo courtesy of Jackson's International Auctioneers & Appraisers.

Kazak, Southwest Caucasus, late 19th C, staggered rows of stepped polygons in midnight and navy blue, ivory, gold, apricot, brown, and blue-green on red field, navy blue border, areas of minor wear, 6'6" x 3'8", $1,765. Photo courtesy of Skinner Auctioneers and Appraisers.

gold, and gray-brown on midnight blue field, slate blue border, even wear, slight moth damage, guard stripe missing from both ends **890.00**

Shahsavan Kelim, Northwest Persia, late 19th/early 20thC, cargo bag, two concentric stepped hexagons flanked by six small hexagons in navy blue, rust, ivory, gold, dark red-brown, and blue-green on red field, navy blue border, crease, very small hole . **385.00**

Shirvan, East Caucasus, late 19th C

5' 6" x 3' 10", prayer rug, serrated diamond lattice of flowering plants in midnight and navy blue, red, gold, and blue-green on ivory field, dark red border, creases, black corrosion, small repairs . . **1,645.00**

5' 10" x 3' 3", large keyhole medallion inset with four octagons in midnight and royal blue, ivory, gold, and blue-green on red field, ivory border, guard stripe partially missing from both ends, some moth damage, small repairs **1,425.00**

Soumak, Northeast Caucasus, late 19th C, 9' 4" x 8' 6", four elongated diamond medallions flanked by half medallions in midnight blue, black, rose, red, and tan on maroon-brown field, black border, areas of slight wear **2,475.00**

South Caucasian, last quarter 19th C, 9' 2" x 3", column of nine serrated palmette motifs in midnight and royal blue, red, rose, gold, camel, and red-brown, royal blue border, crease, slight end fraying **1,120.00**

Tekke, West Turkestan, late 19th/early 20th C, three columns of eight main carpet guls in midnight blue, deep apricot, ivory, and blue-green on rust-red field, border and elems of similar coloration, slight moth damage **835.00**

Yomud Chuval, West Turkestan, last quarter 19th C, 3' 4" x 2' 3", nine Chuval guls in midnight blue, red, ivory, and blue-green on dark aubergine field, ivory border, plain aubergine elem, small spots of slight wear, re-overcast **825.00**

OWENS POTTERY

History: J. B. Owens began making pottery in 1885 near Roseville, Ohio. In 1891, he built a plant in Zanesville and in 1897, began producing art pottery. After 1907, most of the firm's production centered on tiles.

Owens Pottery, employing many of the same artists and designs as its two cross-town rivals, Roseville and Weller, can appear very similar to that of its competitors, e.g., Utopian (brown glaze), Lotus (light glaze), and Aqua Verde (green glaze).

There were a few techniques used exclusively at Owens. These included Red Flame ware (slip decoration under a high red glaze) and Mission (over-glaze, slip decorations in mineral colors) depicting Spanish Missions. Other specialties included Opalesce (semi-gloss designs in lustered gold and orange) and Coralene (small beads affixed to the surface of the decorated vases).

Bud vase

6-1/4" h, 2-1/2" w, standard glaze, yellow roses, marked "#804," initials for Harry Robinson . **150.00**

9" h, molded body under metallic glaze, hairline to body **160.00**

Ewer, 10" h, brown high glaze, cherry design **200.00**

Jug, 8" w, 4-1/2" w, standard glaze, ear of corn dec, marked and sgd "Tot Steele" **230.00**

Lamp base, Utopian, classically shaped, painted yellow daffodils, unmarked, drilled, some glaze bubbles to back, hairline around neck, 5" d, 11-1/4" h, $300. Photo courtesy of David Rago Auctions.

Lamp base, 5" d, 11-1/4" h, classic shape, painted yellow daffodils, unmarked, drilled, some glaze bubbles on back **365.00**

Mug, 7-1/2" h, standard glaze, cherries, marked "#830," sgd "Henry R. Robinson," hairlines to int. **110.00**

Pitcher, 8-1/2" h, dark brown to green, orange and brown flowers, green leaves, marked "JBO" intertwined, artist sgd "HK," crack in handle **110.00**

Tankard

7" h, brown high glaze, Indian design, incised signature, restored **325.00**

Tankard, leathery green glaze with brown trim stamped OWENS 1228/XX, lines at base, repaired rim chip, 5" d, 6-1/2" h, $215. Photo courtesy of David Rago Auctions.

Vase, baluster, painted white chrysanthemums, shaded gray ground, stamped OWENS 1122/Artist's cipher?, firing line, several base chips, 5-3/4" d, 12-1/4" h, $350. Photo courtesy of David Rago Auctions.

12" h, brown glaze, artist sgd, imp mark 210.00

Vase

4" h, Lotus, bee flying above green blades of grass, ivory to blue ground, imp mark, artist initials
. . . . 400.00

4" h, 4" w, yellow chick surrounded by thinly painted grass, four feet, artist sgd 300.00

6-3/8" h, Utopian Ware, silver overlay, flared rim on tapered oviform, glossy glaze, cream and brown rose blossoms and leaves, shaded brown ground, silver overlay imp "Utopian J. B. Owens 923" and "Phee F.N. Silver Co.," crazing, scratches, nicks 290.00

7" h, fluted, Ida Steel, floral . . 625.00

7-1/2" h, high glaze, orange, white, and green grapes, vines, and leaves, pink to green ground, imp "Owens #1260" 300.00

8" h, Aqua Verdi, green matte, textured surface, incised geometrics, four handles around neck, unmarked 550.00

8" h, 8-1/2" w, ftd pillow, dark to light brown with yellow ground, Indian portrait, cream and red vest, blue in hair, imp mark, repaired top
. . . . 1,100.00

10" h, orange and yellow tulips, green leaves, brown ground, imp mark 250.00

10" h, 5" w, standard glaze, marked "Owens #010" 210.00

10-3/4" h, 5-3/4" d, sgraffito, orange and blue irises, dark brown ground,

Henri Deux, unmarked, pea-sized burst bubble on shoulder . . 650.00

11-3/4" h, ovoid, pierced rectangles on shoulder, panels of stylized swans in relief, matte green, imp "Owens 1025", c1905 . . . 1,495.00

12-1/2" h, pink poppy, green stems and leaves, pink, ivory, and light blue ground, artist initialed, imp mark 600.00

PADEN CITY GLASS

History: Paden City Glass Manufacturing Co. was founded in 1916 in Paden City, West Virginia. David Fisher, formerly of the New Martinsville Glass Manufacturing Co., operated the company until his death in 1933, at which time his son, Samuel, became president. A management decision in 1949 to expand Paden City's production by acquiring American Glass Company, an automated manufacturer of bottles, ashtrays, and novelties, strained the company's finances, forcing it to close permanently in 1951.

For more information, see this book.

Contrary to popular belief and previously incorrect printed references, the Paden City Glass Manufacturing Company had absolutely no connection with the Paden City Pottery Company, other than its identical locale.

Although Paden City glass is often lumped with mass-produced, machine-made wares into the Depression Glass category, Paden City's wares were, until 1948, all handmade. Its products are better classified as "Elegant Glass" of the era, as it ranks in quality with the wares produced by contemporaries such as Fostoria, New Martinsville, and Morgantown.

Paden City kept a low profile, never advertising in consumer magazines of the day. It never marked its glass in any way because a large portion of its business consisted of sales to decorating companies, mounters, and fitters. The firm also supplied bars, restaurants, and soda fountains with glassware, as evidenced by the wide range of tumblers, ice cream dishes, and institutional products available in several Paden City patterns.

Paden City's decorating shop also etched, cut, hand painted, and applied silver overlay and gold encrustation. However, not every decoration found on Paden City shapes will necessarily have come from the factory. Cupid, Peacock and Rose, and several other etchings depicting birds are among the most sought-after decorations. Pieces with these etchings are commanding higher and higher prices even though they were apparently made in greater quantities than some of the etchings that are less known, but are just as beautiful.

Paden City is noted for its colors: opal (opaque white), ebony, mulberry (amethyst), Cheriglo (delicate pink), yellow, dark green (forest), crystal, amber, blue,

and great quantities of ruby (red). The firm also produced transparent green in numerous shades, ranging from yellowish to a distinctive electric green that always alerts knowledgeable collectors to its Paden City origin.

Rising collector interest in Paden City glass has resulted in a sharp spike in prices on some patterns. Currently, pieces with Orchid or Cupid etch are bringing the highest prices. Several truly rare items in these etchings have recently topped the $1,000 mark. Advanced collectors seek out examples with unusual and/or undocumented etchings. Colored pieces, which sport an etching that is not usually found on that particular color, are especially sought after and bringing strong prices. In contrast, prices for common items with Peacock and Rose etch remain static, and the prices for dinnerware in ruby Penny Line and pink or green Party Line have inched up only slightly, due to its greater availability.

Adviser: Michael Krumme.

Color is crystal (clear) unless otherwise noted.

Box, covered, Line #411, Mrs. B, Ardith etch on cover, base unetched, one interior diagonal divider, black, 7-1/2" w diagonally, 4" h, $150. Photo courtesy of Michael Krumme.

Bowl, console

#215 Glades, three-footed, two sides turned up, ruby 50.00

#220 Largo, three-footed, gray cutting 25.00

#220 Largo, three-footed, Garden Magic etch 50.00

#300 Archaic, oval, Cupid etch, pink or green 250.00

#300 Archaic, oval, Peacock & Rose etch, pink 150.00

#300 Archaic, 11" d, Cupid etch, pink 200.00

#300 Archaic, oval, Peacock & Rose etch, one panel plain 230.00

#300 Archaic, oval, Peacock & Rose etch, light blue 475.00

#300 Archaic, 13" d, Cupid etch, pink 300.00

#412 Crow's Foot Square, Delilah Bird etch, cobalt 650.00

#412 Crow's Foot Square, opal **75.00**
#412 Crow's Foot Square, Orchid etch, pink. **118.00**
#412 Crow's Foot Square, Orchid etch, yellow **150.00**
#555, beaded edge, cutting . . **30.00**
#890 Crow's Foot Round, three-footed, cupped up, amber **50.00**
#890 Crow's Foot Round, three-footed, flat rim, ruby. . **150.00**
Unknown #, all-over Frost etch **140.00**

Bowl, nappy
#210 Regina, Black Forest etch, ebony **130.00**
#211 Spire, Eden Rose etch . . **38.00**
#701 Triumph, 6-1/2", Gothic Garden etch, amber **50.00**

Bowl, serving, two handles
#210 Regina, Black Forest etch, pink **75.00**
#220 Largo, 9-1/2", ruby or light blue **50.00**
#412 Crow's Foot Square, opal **75.00**
#440 Nerva, ruby **75.00**
#881 Gadroon, Irwin etch, ruby **145.00**

Bowl, vegetable, oval
#412 Crow's Foot Square, ruby **25.00**
#412 Crow's Foot Square, cobalt **40.00**

Cake salver, stemmed
#191 Party Line, high foot, green **85.00**
#210 Regina, Black Forest etch, ebony **75.00**
#300 Archaic, low, ftd, Cupid etch, pink **250.00**

Cottontail Bunny, crystal satin, 5" h, **$50.**
Photos courtesy of Michael Krumme.

#411 Mrs. B., Ardith, yellow . . **70.00**
#412 Crow's Foot Square, 4-1/2" tall, opal **100.00**
#890 Crow's Foot Round, cobalt **45.00**
#890 Crow's Foot Round, ruby **135.00**

Candy box, cov, flat
#211 Regina, Harvesters etch, amber **80.00**
#215 Glades, Spring Orchard etch **50.00**
#411 Mrs. B., Gothic Garden etch, pink. **225.00**
#412 Crow's Foot Square, square shape, ruby **80.00**
#412 Crow's Foot Square, Orchid etch, crystal **75.00**
#412 Crow's Foot Square, Orchid etch, ruby **250.00**
#412-1/2 Crow's Foot Square, cloverleaf shape, cobalt blue **125.00**
#412-1/2 Crow's Foot Square, cloverleaf shape, silver overlay, metal frame with kneeling nudes **115.00**
#440 Nerva, ruby **170.00**
#555 7" flat with teardrop finial, blue **25.00**
#555 heart-shaped, Utopia etch, crystal. **75.00**
#555 heart-shaped, Utopia etch, light blue. **175.00**

Candy dish, cov, footed
#191 Party Line, gold encrusted band etch, green **30.00**
#300 Archaic, Cupid etch, pink **440.00**
#555, Gazebo etch, light blue **75.00**
#555, Trumpet Flower etch. . **100.00**
#890 Crow's Foot Round, three-footed, Leeuwen etch. **50.00**
#890 Crow's Foot Round, three-footed, ruby, silver overlay . . **95.00**

Candleholders, pr
#191 Party Line, dome foot, early blue **25.00**
#300 Archaic, Ardith etch, mushroom style, green. . . . **150.00**
#411 Mrs. B., keyhole style, Ardith etch, ebony **95.00**
#412 Crow's Foot Square, keyhole style, ruby. **80.00**
#412 Crow's Foot Square, keyhole style, ruby, silver overlay . . . **50.00**
#412 Crow's Foot Square, keyhole style, Orchid etch, crystal . . **65.00**
#412 Crow's Foot Square, keyhole style, Orchid etch, ruby . . . **225.00**
#440 Nerva, double, ruby. . . **125.00**

Cheese and cracker set
#210 Regina, Black Forest etch, green. **145.00**
#215 Glades, Spring Orchard etch **45.00**
#220 Largo, cutting **40.00**
#220 Maya, dome lid, light blue **60.00**

Cigarette box and lid, #220 Largo, ruby **200.00**

Cocktail shaker
#215 Glades, Spring Orchard etch, gold encrusted etch **55.00**
#902, three-part with strainer, Rooster stopper **85.00**

Compote, footed
#191 Party Line, 6" h, green . . **15.00**
#210 Regina, Black Forest etch, pink **85.00**
#211 Spire, 7", Trumpet Flower etch **27.00**
#211 Maya, oval, light blue . . . **65.00**
#215 Glades, low foot, 11" cobalt **165.00**
#300 Archaic, pink **35.00**
#300 Archaic, Cupid etch, green **250.00**
#300 Archaic, Lela Bird etch. . **55.00**
#411 Mrs. B., 7-1/2" h, ebony . **20.00**
#411 Mrs. B., 7-1/2" w, 6" h, 10-1/2" l, Ardith etch, ebony. **80.00**
#411 Mrs. B, 10" w, 5" h, Gothic Garden etch, pink or yellow . **95.00**
#412 Crow's Foot Square, mulberry **35.00**
#412 Crow's Foot Square, opal **55.00**
#412 Crow's Foot Square, 9" w, 5" h, Delilah Bird etch **128.00**
#444 Nerva 9" wide **125.00**
#890 Crow's Foot Round, ruby **50.00**
#890 Crow's Food Round, 6-1/2", green. **50.00**
#890 Crow's Foot Round, 7", etched **40.00**
#895 Lucy, Oriental Garden etch, amber **115.00**

Cup and saucer, #211 Maya, ruby, **$30.**
Photo courtesy of Michael Krumme.

Creamer

#90 Chevalier, ruby **40.00**
#191 Party Line, Cheriglo **40.00**
#210 Regina, Harvesters etch,
   amber **85.00**
#220 Largo, Garden Magic etch
   . . . . **50.00**
#220 Largo, ruby **95.00**
#412 Crow's Foot Square, cobalt,
   silver overlay **80.00**
#412 Crow's Foot Square, Paden
   Pony etch **85.00**
#701 Triumph, Cupid etch, Cheriglo
   . . . . **300.00**
#701 Triumph, cutting, Cheriglo
   . . . . **45.00**
#701 Triumph, Nora Bird etch, green
   . . . . **45.00**
#777 Comet, light blue **90.00**
#881 Gadroon, Irwin etch, ruby
   . . . . **95.00**
#890 Crow's Foot Round, Forest
   Green **50.00**

Cream soup

#215 Glades, mulberry **15.00**
#220 Largo, ruby **20.00**
#412 Crow's Foot Square, cobalt
   . . . . **25.00**

Cruet, stopper, #210 Regina, yellow
. . . . **40.00**

Cup and saucer

#191 Party Line, pink **15.00**
#412 Crow's Foot Square, ruby **15.00**
#412 Crow's Foot Square cup,
   yellow, Delilah Bird **95.00**
#991 Penny Line, ruby **20.00**

Decanter

#69 Georgian, cobalt blue . . . **85.00**
#191 Party Line, cordial, pink **140.00**
#215 Glades, bottle shape, ruby
   . . . . **85.00**
#215-1/2 Glades, handle, tilt-style,
   cordial, gold encrusted Spring
   Orchard etch **50.00**
#215-1/2 Glades, handle, tilt-style,
   cordial, ruby **40.00**
#991 Penny Line, ruby **65.00**
Horseshoe shape, Spring Orchard
   etch, etched "Scotch" or "Rye"
   . . . . **40.00**

Epergne, three pieces, #888, Forest
Green **150.00**

Hat, 5-1/2", Trumpet Flower etch. **75.00**

Ice bucket, metal bail

#191 Party Line, green **40.00**
#902, Cupid etch, green **350.00**

Ice tub, tab handles

#210 Regina, Black Forest etch,
   black **250.00**
#210 Regina, green **25.00**

#300 Archaic, Cupid etch . . . **300.00**
#300 Archaic, Peacock & Rose etch
   . . . . **110.00**

Lamp, Emeraldglo candlelamp, brass
base, cut stars on chimney **70.00**

Mayonnaise comport

#221 Maya, ruby **42.00**
#300 Archaic, Cupid, green, with
   orig ladle **100.00**
#411 Mrs. B., Orchid etch, green
   . . . . **65.00**
#412 Crow's Foot Square, Delilah
   Bird etch, ruby **175.00**
#701 Triumph, Cupid etch variant,
   green **175.00**
#890 Crow's Foot Round, with orig
   liner **100.00**

Napkin holder, #210 Regina, green
. . . . **150.00**

Pitcher

#191 Party Line, Eden Rose etch,
   green **125.00**
#994 Penny Line, cobalt, orig label
   . . . . **700.00**

Plate

#221 Maya, 9" dinner **45.00**
#412 Crow's Foot Square, 8-1/2",
   Orchid etch, cobalt **150.00**
#890 Crow's Foot Round, 9" dinner,
   crystal **30.00**

Platter, oval

#412 Crow's Foot Square, cobalt
   . . . . **50.00**
#412 Crow's Foot Square, ruby
   . . . . **35.00**

Powder jar, cov

#191 Party Line, flat, Marie cut, pink
   . . . . **25.00**
#191 Party Line, ftd, green . . . **30.00**
Victory Vanity, military hat, amber
   . . . . **40.00**

Pitcher, Penny Line, #991, ruby, 8" h,
$175.

Victory Vanity, military hat, light blue
. . . . **50.00**

Samovar, three-piece, all glass, amber
. . . . **155.00**

Syrup pitcher, #180 with glass lid,
applied handle, gold encrusted band
etch **35.00**

Tray, center handle

#210 Regina, Black Forest etch,
   green or pink **75.00**
#215 Glades, Garden Magic etch
   . . . . **40.00**
#220 Largo, Garden Magic etch
   . . . . **50.00**
#220 Largo, ruby **55.00**
#300 Archaic, Cupid etch, crystal
   . . . . **125.00**
#300 Archaic, Cupid etch, cupped,
   green **200.00**
#300 Archaic, Peacock & Rose etch,
   pink **125.00**
#411 Mrs. B., Ardith etch, cupped,
   pink or ebony **85.00**
#411 Mrs. B., Cheriglo, etched and
   gold encrusted **45.00**
#411 Mrs. B., Gothic Garden etch,
   cupped, yellow **170.00**
#412 Crow's Foot Square, cobalt
   . . . . **50.00**
#412 Crow's Foot Square, ruby
   . . . . **40.00**
#412 Crow's Foot Square, Orchid
   etch, clear **75.00**
#412 Crow's Foot Square, Orchid
   etch, green **175.00**
#701 Triumph, Black Forest etch,
   green **120.00**
#881 Gadroon, Irwin etch, clear
   . . . . **45.00**
#881 Gadroon, Irwin etch, ruby
   . . . . **95.00**
#890 Crow's Foot Round, platinum
   Cupid & Venus etch, ruby . . **50.00**
#1504 swan-shaped handle,
   Gazebo etch **35.00**

Salt and pepper shakers, pair, Party Line,
#191, ruby, 3-1/4" h, **$75.**

Vase, Ardith etch with cherry blossoms, ebony (black), design highlighted with glass chalk for photo, 7-1/2" h, $150.

Tray, two handles

#210 Regina, Black Forest etch, pink **50.00**

#220 Largo, forest green **65.00**

#220 Largo, light blue **50.00**

#221 Maya, ruby **95.00**

#411 Mrs. B., Ardith Garden, ebony **65.00**

#881 Gadroon, Irwin etch, ruby **145.00**

#890 Crow's Foot Round, cobalt **40.00**

Tumblers and stemware

#154 Rena tumbler, 9 oz, green **15.00**

#191 Party Line, parfait, pink . . **20.00**

#191 Party Line whiskey, green . **6.00**

#210 Regina, tumbler, 3-1/2", Black Forest etch, green **55.00**

#210 Regina, tumbler, 5-1/2", Black Forest etch, green **55.00**

#215 Glades, water goblet, ruby **25.00**

#890 Crow's Foot Round, tumbler, cobalt **75.00**

#991 Penny Line, champagne, cobalt **10.00**

#991 Penny Line, cordial, ruby **20.00**

#991 Penny Line, whiskey (shot glass), mulberry **6.00**

#991 Penny Line, low sherbet, mulberry **6.00**

#994 Popeye & Olive, goblet, ruby **14.00**

Unknown #, 1-1/2 oz whiskey, Black Forest etch, pink **110.00**

Vases

#180 Butterfly & Zinna, Cheriglo **155.00**

#180 Rose Bouquet etch, green **270.00**

#182 elliptical, Daisy etch, Cheriglo **85.00**

#182 elliptical, Peacock and Rose etch, pink **200.00**

#182 elliptical, Utopia, ebony **170.00**

#182-1/2 small elliptical, Ardith etch, ebony **185.00**

#182-1/2 small elliptical, Oriental Garden etch **100.00**

#184 8" bulbous, Ardith etch, pink **185.00**

#184 8" bulbous, Gothic Garden etch, black **175.00**

#184 10" bulbous, Cupid silver dec, pink **250.00**

#184 10" bulbous, Daisy etch, pink or green **85.00**

#184 10" bulbous, floral etch, gold band **150.00**

#184 10" bulbous, Lela Bird etch, ebony **125.00**

#184 10" bulbous, Lela Bird etch, green **95.00**

#184 12" bulbous, Gothic Garden etch, ebony **200.00**

#184 12" bulbous, Lela Bird etch, ebony, gold encrustation . . **235.00**

#184 12" bulbous, Peacock & Rose etch, ruby **950.00**

#184 12" bulbous, Rose Bouquet etch, green **200.00**

#184 12" bulbous, Utopia etch, ebony **275.00**

#191 Party Line, 8" blown, hourglass shape, crimped top, pink or green **40.00**

#191 Party Line, fan, pink or green **35.00**

#210 Regina 7" squatty, Ardith etch, ebony **175.00**

#210 Regina 7" squatty, Orchid etch, ebony **225.00**

#210 Regina 9" cylinder, Black Forest etch, ebony **285.00**

#411 9" satin finish, silver overlay lilies and butterfly **90.00**

#412 Crow's Foot Square, 10" cupped rim, ruby **110.00**

#412 Crow's Foot Square, 12" cupped rim, cobalt **130.00**

#503 dome footed, fan, blue satin, Eden Rose etch **260.00**

#503 dome footed, fan, pink . . **35.00**

#994 Popeye & Olive, 7", cobalt **80.00**

Unknown #, 7-1/2", squat base, slender neck, Delilah Bird etch, ebony **365.00**

Unknown #, 7-1/2", squat base, slender neck, Orchid etch, ebony **400.00**

Water bottle, #191 Party Line, pink **60.00**

PAIRPOINT

History: The Pairpoint Manufacturing Co. was organized in 1880 as a silver-plating firm in New Bedford, Massachusetts. The company merged with Mount Washington Glass Co. in 1894 and became the Pairpoint Corporation. The new company produced specialty glass items, often accented with metal frames.

For more information, see this book.

Pairpoint Corp. was sold in 1938 and Robert Gunderson became manager. He operated it as the Gunderson Glass Works until his death in 1952. From 1952 until the plant closed in 1956, operations were maintained under the name Gunderson-Pairpoint. Robert Bryden reopened the glass manufacturing business in 1970, moving it back to the New Bedford area.

China

Box, cov, 5" l, 3-1/2" w, 2-1/2" h, raised gold rococo scrolls, reverse on lid with three Palmer Cox Brownies playing cards, Pairpoint-Limoges logo, numbered **750.00**

Chocolate pot, 10" h, cream ground, white floral dec, gold trim and scrolls, sgd "Pairpoint Limoges 2500 114" **675.00**

Gravy boat and underplate, fancy white china with scrolls, Dresden

Table lamp, 31-1/4" h, 18-3/4" d octagonal shade with basketweave and swag motifs inset with blue, purple and green puffed slag glass panels, base embossed with leaves, base stamped Pairpoint with "P" in diamond/C3066, $920. Photo courtesy of David Rago Auctions.

multicolored flowers, elaborate handle, Limoges, two pc **175.00**

Plate, 7-3/8" d, hp harbor scene, artist sgd "L. Tripp," fuchsia tinted rim, gold highlights, back sgd "Pairpoint Limoges" **550.00**

Lamp, table

Begonia, puffy, 24" h, 16" d reverse painted shade, Pairpoint tree trunk base painted white, chip on shade **38,500.00**

Candlestick type, 18" h, urn shaped tops, electric sockets, clear cut columns with diamond designs, octagonal base with fine leaf detail, relief cast signatures on bases "Quadruple Plate," price for pr . **550.00**

Landscape, 26" h, 19" d reverse painted circular shade, flared rim, buildings, figures, and river, sgd "M. Ano," three-light fluted vasiform base with cornucopia, flowers, and serpents, marked "Pairpoint, D3055, Made in U.S.A.," flakes on top rim, chip in shade **990.00**

Table lamp, 22" h, 10" d puffy azalea shade, more than 20 pink to pure white azaleas, each with yellow center, brown stamens, pale green leaves, dark green background, four-sided base with raised floral design, four delicate arms dec with vines, green patina, base signed "Pairpoint Mfg Co., 3049," and "P" in diamond, **$16,800.** *Photo courtesy of Fontaine's Auction Gallery.*

Orange Poppy, 21" h, 14" d, reverse painted mold blown puffy shade, silvered base, imp "Pairpoint 3085," shade damaged and repaired **1,500.00**

Papillon, puffy, 20-1/2" h, 14" d reverse painted shade, colorful butterflies, pink and red roses, stamped "The Pairpoint Corp," four-arm spider and silver metal base with reticulated designs, base imp "Pairpoint Mfg Co.," "P" in diamond, and "3086" **5,750.00**

Scenic reverse, 21" h, 15-1/2" d frosted and textured Copley shade, int. painted with pastoral scene of shepherd, sheep, rolling hills, trees, and distant ponds, naturalistic tones, sgd "H. Fisher," stamped "The Pairpoint Corp'n," turned mahogany baluster-form shaft with bands of brass trim, imp "Pairpoint C3087" on metal disk under base, few chips on fitter rim **1,880.00**

Seville, 21" h, 16" d, reverse painted Italian garden scene, gilt base, sgd "Pairpoint D2084," c1920 . . . . **3,335.00**

Metal

Lamp base

12" h, 8" d ring, patinated metal, quatrefoil wirework supporting shade ring, ribbed standard with applied foliate handles and feet, bronze patina on white metal, imp "Pairpoint Mfg Co.," "P" in diamond and "30031/2" on base, worn patina **400.00**

15" h, patinated metal, two-socket fixture, four-sided shaft and lobe base, bronze patina on white metal, imp "Pairpoint Mfg Co.," "P"

Pitcher, Alexandrite, blue shading to amber, applied amber handle and foot, rough pontil, 6-3/4" h, **$575.** *Photo courtesy of James D. Julia, Inc.*

in diamond, and "B3040" on base, patina wear **350.00**

Trophy, 7" d, 8-1/2" h, copper, two fancy handles, feather design, plaque inscribed "New Bedford Yacht Club Ocean Race won by Nutmeg for the fastest time, Aug. 5, 1909," base marked "Pairpoint Mfg Co.," "P" in diamond mark, numbered. **400.00**

Glass

Box, cov, 7-1/4" d, Russian pattern cut glass, silver mountings, sgd "Pairpoint" **410.00**

Candlesticks, pr, cobalt blue, controlled bubble sphere **450.00**

Compote, 12-1/8" d, 6-1/2" h, canary bowl and base, wide flared rim, copper wheel etched grape vine dec, colorless ball knop stem with air bubbles **350.00**

Console set, three-pc set, 12" d bowl, matching 3" h candlesticks, Tavern glass, bouquet of red, white, and green flowers. **575.00**

Cracker jar, cov, 6-3/4" h, 7-1/2" w, Mt. Washington opalware, pistachios green top and bottom, 3-1/2" w band of deep pink and red roses, green leaves, gold trim, fancy silver-plated cov, handle, and bail, cov sgd "Pairpoint -3912," base sgd "3912-268" **725.00**

Dish, fish shape, teal blue, controlled bubbles dec, late **275.00**

Perfume bottle, 6-3/4" h, amethyst, painted butterfly, teardrop stopper, "P" in diamond mark **375.00**

Pokal, cov, 14" h, Chrysopras, dark yellow-green, wheelcut grapes and leaves, finial wheelcut with eight-petaled flower **625.00**

Vase

5-1/2" h, 4-1/2" w, Tavern glass, bulbous, enameled floral dec of vase of flowers, base numbered **225.00**

14-1/2" h, flared colorless crystal trumpet form, bright -cut floral dec, gilt metal foliate molded weighted pedestal base, imp "Pairpoint C1509" **490.00**

PAPER EPHEMERA

History: Maurice Rickards, author of *Collecting Paper Ephemera*, suggests that ephemera are the "minor transient documents of everyday life," material destined for the wastebasket but never quite making it. This definition is more fitting than traditional dictionary definitions that emphasize time, e.g., "lasting a very short time." A driver's license, which is used for a year or longer, is as much a piece of ephemera as is a ticket to a sporting event or music concert. The transient nature of the object is the key.

Collecting ephemera has a long and distinguished history. Among the English pioneers were John Seldon (1584-1654), Samuel Pepys (1633-1703), and John Bagford (1650-1716). Large American collections can be found at historical societies and libraries across the country, and museums, e.g., Wadsworth Athenaeum, Hartford, CT, and the Museum of the City of New York.

When used by collectors, "ephemera" usually means paper objects, e.g., billheads and letterheads, bookplates, documents, labels, stocks and bonds, tickets, and valentines. However, more and more ephemera collectors are recognizing the transient nature of some three-dimensional material, e.g., advertising tins and pinback buttons. Today's specialized paper shows include dealers selling other types of ephemera in both two- and three-dimensional form.

Additional Listings: See Advertising Trade Cards, Catalogs, Comic Books, Photographs, and Sports Cards. Also see Calendars, Catalogs, Magazines, Newspapers, Photographs, Postcards, and Sheet Music in *Warman's Americana & Collectibles*.

Bookmarks

Advertising

Austin Young & Co., Biscuits, multicolored, 2" x 7" **5.00**
Bell Pianos, Art Nouveau woman, multicolored. **12.00**
Palmer Violets Bloom Perfume, gold trim **15.00**
Youth's Companion, 1902, multicolored, 2-3/4" x 6" **8.00**

Broadside, Brockton, Massachusetts, late 19th century, "AUCTION! BOOT & SHOE FACTORY. STABLE, WITH STOCK," framed, creases, 13-3/8" w, 19-1/4" h, **$60.** *Photo courtesy of Skinner Auctioneers and Appraisers.*

Calendar, 1934, An Enchanted Garden, Liberty Furniture Co., Peoria, Illinois, two ladies in garden, **$50.** *Photo courtesy of Joy Luke Auctions.*

Cross stitch on punched paper

Black Emancipation, black couple dancing, 1860s, 3-7/8" x 1-1/2"
. . . . **40.00**
In God We Trust **15.00**
Broadside, 19-1/4" x 13-3/8", "Auction! Book & Shoe Factory, Stable with Stock," Brockton, MA, late 19th C, framed, creases **60.00**

Calendars

1894, C. I. Hood, Lowell, Mass, complete pad, titled "Sweet Sixteen"
. . . . **140.00**
1886, Middlesex Fire Insurance, Concord, MA, 11" x 5-1/2" **100.00**
1899, C. I. Hood Co., Lowell, Mass, complete pad, titled "The American Girl" **115.00**
1901, Colgate, miniature, flower . **20.00**
1906, Hiawatha, multiple images of Indian scenes, monthly calendars placed throughout, metal band and grommet at top, metal band missing at bottom, 7-1/2" w, 36" h **125.00**
1909, Bank of Waupun, emb lady **32.00**
1916, Putnam Dyes **40.00**
1918, Jan/Feb/March, Swifts Premium, soldier saying good-bye to his love, "The Girl I Leave Behind," illus by Haskell Coffin, 15" x 8-1/4" **100.00**
1922, Warren National Bank, Norman Rockwell illus. **300.00**
1923, Winona, F. A. Rettke, Indian Princess on cliff overlooking body of water, full pad, 6-1/2" w, 21-1/2" l
. . . . **50.00**
1932, Betsy Ross sewing flag, George Washington looking on, full calendar pad, large size. **35.00**
1940, Columbian Rope **40.00**
1947, Petty, pin-up, 9" x 12" **155.00**
1948, Esquire, pin-up, 9" x 12" . **135.00**

Calendar, 1910, Ballistite and Empire Powders, N.C. Wyeth print, copyrighted 1909, 19" x 12-1/2" vertical image depicting two gentleman hunters, one carrying dbl bbl shotgun, other with pump shotgun, one holding two setters on leashes, farmer pointing ahead, farmstead in background, titled "OVER YONDER," green border, complete calendar pad, slight fading, 26" x 15", **$1,495.** *Photo courtesy of James D. Julia Auctions.*

Cigar box labels

Artoria, mounted and framed, 9-1/2" x 11-1/2" **28.00**
Chapman House, 10" x 6-1/2" . . . **12.00**
Dan O'Brien, 6-3/4" x 8-1/2" **15.00**
First Cabinet Cigars, 8" x 6" **12.00**
King Alfred, 8-1/2" x 9" **8.00**
Optimo, 8-1/2" x 6-1/2" **15.00**
Perfecto Garcia & Bros., Perfecto Garcia Senators, Tampa, FL, diecut, 3-1/2" x 5-1/4" **4.00**
Royal Hunter, 8-1/2" x 6-1/2" **15.00**

Coloring books

Annie Oakley, Whitman, 11" x 14", 1955, unused **20.00**
Blondie, Dell Publishing, 8-1/2" x 11", 1954, unused **24.00**
Dick Tracy, Saalfield, #2536, 8-1/4" x 11", © 1946. . . . . **30.00**
Donald Duck, Whitman, 7-1/2" x 8-1/2", 1946, unused **25.00**
Lone Ranger, Whitman, 8-1/2" x 11", Cheerios premium, 1956 . . . . **75.00**
Superman, Whitman, National Periodical Publications, © 1966, unused **25.00**

Documents

Appointment of administrator of estate, sgd by John Evans, Colonial Gov or PA, dated March 24, 1704, wax seal, some fold weakness, 9-1/2" x 15" **500.00**
Appointment of Gideon Mumford Deputy Postmaster at East Greenwich, RI, dated April 19, 1796, foxing, fold weakness, 12-1/2" x 7-1/2" **75.00**
Bill of Exchange, written for Robert Robson, London, March 2, 1796, in

Charleston, SC, two pgs, concerns exchange for 160 pounds sterling, 8-1/2" x 7" **50.00**

Legal deposition, concerning patent issues of William A Hopkins, for improvement to cooking stoves, Sept. 30, 1846, nine pgs, attached detailed drawings labeled "Exhibit A," some discoloration of blue paper, 12-1/2" x 7-1/2" **35.00**

Legal deposition, involving litigation between Horace Day and Charles Goodyear, Aug. 29, 1851, concerning Indian rubber fabric, attached map of eastern US printed on Indian rubber fabric, reverse marked "Exhibit A4," damaged cover sheet, some soiling to sheets, 13" x 8" **350.00**

Ship paper, issued by port of Charleston, SC, for brig *Mary*, March 10, 1812, 8" x 11" **80.00**

Greeting cards
Birthday
Blondie, Dagwood illus, full color, Hallmark, © 1939 .... **18.00**
Snow White and the Seven Dwarfs, c1938 .... **42.00**
Space Patrol Man, diecut, full color, transparent green helmet, orig envelope **25.00**

Christmas, 4-3/4" x 6-1/2" closed, glossy stiff paper, choice color pop-up scene of Borden's Elsie and family retrieving Christmas tree trimmings from attic, greeting "From Elsie, Elmer, Beulah, Beauregard and all of us at Borden's," full-color Christmas tree and gift package art on front, copyright 1940s **45.00**

Get Well, Amos n' Andy, black and white photo, Hall Bros., © 1951 .. **30.00**

Mother's Day, Cracker Jack, diecut puppy, full color, c1920 .... **18.00**

Hotel receipt with large graphic masthead featuring Lake George House and Steamer Minnehaha, dated July 28, 1859, 7" x 8-1/2", **$165.** *Photo courtesy of Sanford Alderfer Auction Company.*

Invitations and programs
Eddie Cantor, "How To Make A Quack-Quack," program on back, portrait on cov, printed, black and white, four-part fold-out ... **15.00**

Grand Masquerade Ball, Marion House Co., NY, 1901, gold trim .. **10.00**

Invitation and Program for Carnival in Honor of George Washington, Request at Opera House, 1893, multicolored cover **12.00**

Leap Year Party by Young Ladies, 1888, opens, dance program inside, printed black and white **10.00**

Richland Library Literary Society, Benefit Musical, opens, lists musical selections, poems to be read, black and white **5.00**

Sonja Henie Program, white cov, orig tissue cov, 1949 .... **12.00**

St. Patrick's Ball, Lusks Hall, Jacobs City, UT, 1878, red lettering, blue ground, emb, opens **15.00**

Menus
Banquet to the Western Michigan Press, Reed City, 1883, fold-over, Robison Engraving Co., 1882, printed, black and white **15.00**

Collation at Norombega Hall, Bangor, Wednesday, Oct. 18, 1871 to the President of the United States, the Governor-General of Canada...Upon the Formal Opening of the European & North America Railway, four pgs, decorative stick, 8" x 5-1/4" **95.00**

Francaise, Art Nouveau design, sgd "Mucha," dated 5 Janvier 1913, 5" x 9" **350.00**

Johnson Line **15.00**

Metropolitan Hotel, four pgs, c1974 .... **35.00**

SS City of Omaha, Christmas, 1940 .... **10.00**

United States Hotel, Saratoga Springs, NY, 1892, 7" x 10" **15.00**

Postcards
Advertising
Case Stem Tractor, salesroom, Columbus, OH **60.00**
Champagne Rommeriz & Greno, French wines **30.00**
Planters Peanuts at Times Square, 1940s scene, unused **20.00**
Scottish Bagpipes, Swift's Premium Oleomargarine, ©1914, Swift's **50.00**
Victoria Quay, Guiness Brewery, Dublin **40.00**

Postcard, artist signed Clarence Underwood, 1913, **$20.**

Artist signed
Cady, Harrison, Happy Jack Squirrel **300.00**
Feilig, Hank, Sinner Liqueur, Elves Frog **50.00**
Fisher, Harrison, Their New Love, couple with newborn, Charles Schribner Sons, NY, Reinthal and Newman Publisher, NY, glued to backing, framed **50.00**

Baseball, Palace of Fans Ballpark, Cincinnati, stamped "Sept. 18 1908" **125.00**

Scrapbooks, pair, early 19th C, containing hundreds of engravings, cut and removed from various late 18th and early 19th C publications and books, 57 original water color and pen and ink drawings by various acquaintances of scrap book creator, many of images accented by pen and ink type framing, 15-1/2" x 11", **$3,300.** *Photo courtesy of Sanford Alderfer Auction Company.*

Dog

Borzoi, sgd "W. Klett," published in Switzerland, unused **30.00**

Dachshunds, one in doghouse, second one in front, comical verse, unused **25.00**

Scottish Terriers, sgd "M. Gear," published by Valentine & Sons, Ltd., Dundee and London, unused **30.00**

Hold to light

A Merry Christmas to You, unused **125.00**

Angel, A Merry Christmas, 1907, Belgium, used **100.00**

Cat and Mouse, kissing couple, used **15.00**

Cinderella, 1900, Belgium, used **85.00**

Girl with Umbrella, used **30.00**

Happy New Year, 1910, windmill **85.00**

Kind Christmas Greetings, 1908, used **50.00**

US Treasury Building, Washington, DC, used **25.00**

Nazi

Humor, dated 1941 . . . . **15.00**

Portrait of Hitler, wearing formal attire **25.00**

Portrait of Hitler, wearing uniform, facsimile autograph, 3" x 5" . . **30.00**

Real photo

Bakery interior **85.00**

Fabric store interior **100.00**

Shoe Maker, factory scene, workers at machines **40.00**

Steam roller **40.00**

Terry Ironing, Miss Ellen Tracy (actress) ironing, J. Beagles & Co., London **35.00**

PAPERWEIGHTS

History: Although paperweights had their origin in ancient Egypt, it was in the mid-19th century that this art form reached its zenith. The finest paperweights were produced between 1834 and 1855 in France by the Clichy, Baccarat, and Saint Louis factories. Other

For more information, see this book.

weights made in England, Italy, and Bohemia during this period rarely match the quality of the French weights.

In the early 1850s, the New England Glass Co. in Cambridge, Massachusetts, and the Boston and Sandwich Glass Co. in Sandwich, Massachusetts, became the first American factories to make paperweights.

Popularity peaked during the classic period (1845-1855) and faded toward the end of the 19th century. Paperweight production was rediscovered nearly a century later in the mid-1900s. Baccarat, Saint Louis, Perthshire, and many studio craftsmen in the U.S. and Europe still make contemporary weights.

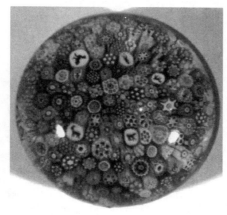

Baccarat, millefiori, dog, horse, goat, rooster, figure, and 1848 date canes, $3,500. Photo courtesy of Joy Luke Auctions.

Antique

Baccarat, France, 19th C, Double Garland, double trefoil garland of red and white canes centered by ring of blue canes, pink white and green cane, 3" d, 2" h, minor wear. **490.00**

Clichy, France, 19th C

Bottle, squat spherical body of colorless glass, dec internally with complex millefiori canes set concentrically on lace ground, 3-1/2" d, 3-1/2" h, stopper missing **2,185.00**

Chequer, complex millefiori canes centered by pink and green Clichy rose, all divided by white latticinio twists, 2-3/4" d, 2" h **1,265.00**

Millefiori, complex millefiori canes set in colorless crystal, 1-3/4" d, 1-3/8" h **375.00**

Mushroom, close concentric design, large central pink and green rose surrounded by pin, white, cobalt blue, and cadmium green complex millefiori, middle row of canes with 10 green and white roses alternating with pink pastry mold canes, pin and white stems, 2-3/4" d **6,600.00**

Swirled, alternating purple and white pinwheels emanating from white, green, and pink pastry mold cane, minor bubbles, 2-5/8" d . . **2,200.00**

Degenhart, John, window, red crystal cube with yellow and orange upright center lily, one to window, four side windows, bubble in center of flower's stamens, 3-3/16" x 2-1/4" x 2-1/4" **1,225.00**

Gillinder, orange turtle with moving appendages in hollow center, pale orange ground, molded dome, 3-1/16" d **500.00**

Millville, umbrella pedestal, red, white, green, blue, and yellow int., bubble in sphere center, 3-1/8" d, 3-3/8" h. **800.00**

New England Glass Co.

Crown, red, white, blue, and green twists interspersed with white latticinio emanating from a central pink, white, and green complex floret/cog cane, minor bubbles in glass, 2-3/4" d **2,400.00**

Pink flower, striated pink five-petal flowers, millefiori cane center, pink bud on deep green leafy stem, white latticinio bed, 2-1/4" d, 1-3/4" h, minor wear **690.00**

Pinchbeck, pastoral dancing scene, couple dancing before group of onlookers, 3-3/16" d **650.00**

Sandwich Glass Co.

Dahlia, c1870, red petaled flower, millefiori cane center, bright green leafy stem, highlighted by trapped bubble dec, white latticino ground, 2-1/2" d, 1-3/4" h **650.00**

Poinsettia, double, red flower with double tier of petals, green and white Lutz rose, green stem and leaves, bubbles between petals, 3" d **1,200.00**

St. Louis

Fruit basket, red and green ripening fruits, latticino base basket, central base cane, 3" d, 2-1/2" h. **1,150.00**

Lalique, Deux Aigles, c1914, deep amber glass, wheel-cut "R. Lalique," 3" h, $690. Photo courtesy of David Rago Auctions.

Queen Victoria, c1840, sulfide portrait sgd "Victoria" in blue at base, 3-1/2" d, 2-1/2" h, few small inclusions **750.00**

Val St. Lambert, patterned millefiori, four red, white, blue, pistachio, and turquoise complex canes circlets spaced around central pink, turquoise and cadmium green canes circlet, canes set on stripes of lace encircled by spiraling red and blue torsade, minor blocking crease, 3-1/2" d **950.00**

Whitefriars, close concentric millefiori, pink, blue, purple, green, white, and yellow cog canes, 1948 date cane, minor bubble in dome, 3-5/8" d. **900.00**

Modern

Ayotte, Rick, yellow finch, perched on branch, faceted, sgd and dated, limited edition, 1979 . . . . **750.00**

Baccarat, Gridel pelican cane surrounded by five concentric rings of yellow, pink, green, and white complex canes, pink canes contain 18 Gridel silhouette canes, lace ground, 1973 date cane, signature cane, sgd and dated, limited ed. of 350, 3-1/6" d
. . . . **850.00**

Banford, Bob

Cornflower, blue flower, yellow center, pink and white twisted torsade, "B" cane at stem, 3" d
. . . . **550.00**

Flower bouquet, five red-stemmed blossoms, "B" cane below, diamond cut recessed base, 3-1/4" d **475.00**

Kaziun, Charles, concentric millefiori, heart, turtle silhouette, shamrocks, six-pointed stars, and floret canes encircled by purple and white torsade, turquoise ground flecked with

St. Louis, 1971, signature cane, 3" d, $190. Photo courtesy of James D. Julia, Inc.

goldstone, K signature cane, 2-1/16" d **1,200.00**

Kesey, Sunshine, Sunstone, multicolored abstract design, millefiori against background of multicolored leaves, sgd **75.00**

Labino, free form, white, amber, and irid gold flower center, air bubbles, surrounded by green glass, sgd "Labino 1969," 2-1/2" d **210.00**

Orient and Flume, red butterfly with blue and white accents, brown and green vines, white millefiori blossoms over dark ground, 3-1/2" d, dated 1977, orig sticker and box **235.00**

Parabelle

Five rows of concentrically arranged canes around larger center rose cane, closely packed white millefiori ground, signature/date cane, 2-3/8" d **425.00**

Tightly packed multicolored millefiori canes, dark blue ground, attributed to Gary and Doris Scrutton, signature and date cane, orig paper label, 2-3/4" d **575.00**

Perthshire

Miniature bouquet, yellow flowers, pink buds, basket of deep blue canes, green and pink millefiori canes cut to form base, orig box and certificate, 2-1/2" d **160.00**

Star of David, white stardust canes form star, encircled by millefiori garland, cobalt blue ground, 2-1/2" d, orig box **125.00**

Rosenfeld, Ken

Magnum red, purple, and white blossoms and buds, transparent blue ground, R signature cane,

Paul Ysart, dahlia, purple flower, circle of red and white canes, cobalt blue carpet, original paper label, signed "PY," $375.

Zimmerman, free blown bubbles, crystal, signed, $45.

inscribed "Ken Rosenfeld, '93, 9/25," 2-3/4" h, 3-1/2" d . . . **435.00**

Monarch butterfly, leafy stem, red blossom with three buds, R signature cane, inscribed "KR 2001," 1-7/8" h, 2-5/8" h . . . **350.00**

Salazar, David, compound floral, lavender six-petal poinsettia star blossom, three-leaf stem over green and red wreath, white ground, inscribed "David Salazar/111405/Lundberg Studios 1991," 3-1/4" d **225.00**

Stankard, Paul

Flowering Seed Pod with Insects and Berries, red berries, white and yellow flowers, ants, bee, figural roots, word canes "Seeds" and "Fertile," inscribed "Paul J Stankard 2000 M5," 2-1/2" h, 3-1/4" h **3,220.00**

Morning Glory, bee on hive in center of two blue morning glories, three orange berries, two yellow flowers, sandy ground, root figure and word canes "Moist" and "Fertile" beneath, inscribed "Paul J. Stankard V32 '97," 2-3/8" h, 3-1/4" d **2,875.00**

Tarsitano, Debbie

Orange and purple bird of paradise flower on stalk, striped green leaves, star cut ground, DT signature cane, 2-15/16" d. **550.00**

Pansy, two central blue and yellow pansies flanked by three rose-pink blossoms, three yellow blossoms, green leafy stems, signature cane
. . . . **475.00**

Trabucco, Victor, Buffalo, NY, magnum pansy, purple pansy blossom and bud, leaf stem, white lace cushion, inscribed

"Trabucco 1998," 2-1/2" h, 3-1/2" d **635.00**

Whitefrairs, Star of David, five rows of tightly packed blue and white millefiori canes, 3" d **395.00**

Whittemore, Francis, two green and brown acorns on branch with three brown and yellow oak leaves, translucent cobalt blue ground, circular top facet five oval punties on sides, 20-3/8" d **300.00**

Ysart, Paul, green fish, yellow eye, yellow and white jasper ground encircled by pink, green, and white complex cane garland, PY signature cane **550.00**

PAPIER-MÂCHÉ

History: Papier-mâché is a mixture of wood pulp, glue, resin, and fine sand, which is subjected to great pressure and then dried. The finished product is tough, durable, and heat resistant. Various finishing treatments are used, such as enameling, japanning, lacquering, mother-of-pearl inlaying, and painting.

During the Victorian era, papier-mâché articles such as boxes, trays, and tables were in high fashion. Banks, candy containers, masks, toys, and other children's articles were also made of papier-mâché.

Candy container, 5-1/2" h, turkey, polychrome dec **45.00**

Cat, 4" h, black, Halloween type, head only......................**350.00**

Figure, Uncle Sam, striped pants, blue coat, red vest, blue hat with stars on band, blue base, Unger Doll & Toy Co, c1890-93, 12" h, $350. Photo courtesy of James D. Julia, Inc.

Fan, 15-1/2" l, demilune, scalloped border, turned wooden handle, one side painted with variety of ferns on ochre ground, black japanning on other side, Victorian, late 19th C, price for pr **250.00**

Milliner's model, attributed to France, early 19th C

14-1/2" h, painted hair and facial features, green bodice, wear, paint losses **235.00**

14-3/4" h, green, yellow, and white striped cap, name "Delphine" painted in script in oval on base, crack, some repaint **1,645.00**

15" h, lithographed paper eyes, mouth, and bodice, figure separated in half, wear....**765.00**

15-1/2" h, painted hair and facial features, lithographed paper bodice, wear, paint losses, cracks **235.00**

16" h, applied lithographed paper eyebrows, eyes, and mouth, wear **1,000.00**

Nodder, 9-3/4" h, Easter Rabbit, oval cardboard base, orig polychrome paint **65.00**

Notebook, 11-1/2" x 9-1/2", black lacquered ground, dec with floral arrangement, mother-of-pearl vines, hand painted accents, int. with notebook with some sketches, blank pages **295.00**

Pip-squeak, 4-1/4" h, rooster, orig paint, yellow, orange, and black, recovered wooden bellows, faint squeak...**85.00**

Plate, 12" d, painted cat, marked "Patented August 8, 1880" **35.00**

Roly poly, 4-1/8" h, clown, orig white and blue polychrome paint, green ribbon around neck...........**65.00**

Snuffbox, 3-7/8" d, round, lid painted with interior genre scene of family with baby, interior lid painted with title "Die

Snuffbox, English, lid with painting of sailing ships, one flying the Union Jack, 2-1/2" l, $330. Photo courtesy of Sanford Alderfer Auction Company.

Snuffbox, lined with copper, painting on lid depicts man with pipe and glass snuff bottle, possibly Samuel Johnson (1780), minor loss, 4" d, $325. Photo courtesy of Sanford Alderfer Auction Company.

Tanzpuppen," painted mark "StabwassersFabrik in Braunschweig," German, late 19th/early 20th C .**460.00**

Table, tilt-top, 24" h, hinged 20" d top painted with Continental city view, pedestal painted as stone tower, circular base with maritime scene, Victorian, stamped "J & B/Patent" for Jennens and Bethridge, Birmingham, England **7,475.00**

Tray, 12" d, Victorian, English, mid-19th C, round, black ground, large central scene of Master of Hounds seated on bobtail bay in wooded setting, house in background, gold scroll painted rim **980.00**

Tray and stand, English

18-1/4" l, 14-1/8" w, rect, black ground, large central scene of white haired gentleman on bobtail chestnut, five hunting dogs in open field, border gold painted with egg and dart design, 7-3/4" w, 4-1/4" d, 9" h mahogany stand ...**1,100.00**

30" l, 24" w tray, 11-1/4" w, oval, black ground, large central scene with two scarlet-coated huntsmen, one standing, other seated on bobtail chestnut with black foal on a hill, border with gilt transfer printed guilloche border, Mark Knowles & Son maker, English Registry mark for 1864, burl hardwood 6-1/4" d, 18-3/4" h stand **1,250.00**

PARIAN WARE

History: Parian ware is a creamy white, translucent porcelain that resembles marble. It originated in England in 1842 and was first called "statuary porcelain." Minton and Copeland have been credited with its development; Wedgwood also made it. In America, parian ware objects were manufactured by Christopher Fenton in Bennington, Vermont.

At first, parian ware was used only for figures and figural groups. By the 1850s, it became so popular that a vast range of items was manufactured.

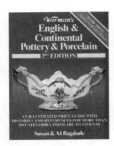

For more information, see this book.

Bust

9" h, Martha Washington, England, 19th C, very minor chips, firing blemishes **225.00**

10" h, Ulysses S. Grant, civilian dress, inscribed on back "Broome, Sculpt. 1876," and "Ott and Brewer Manufacturers, Trenton, New Jersey" **2,750.00**

12-3/4" h, Shakespeare, raised circular base, Robinson and Ledbetter mark, c1875, minor chip to hair **725.00**

15-1/2" h, Abraham Lincoln, raised circular base, English, c1860 . . . . **295.00**

Creamer, 5" h, Tulip pattern, relief dec **100.00**

Bust, Lord Zetland, modeled wearing numerous medals, mounted atop waisted circular socle, incised Registered 11th December 1868, impressed Wedgwood factory mark, Edge (scultor) and Proof, hairline to body, 20" h, $1,400. Photo courtesy of Skinner Auctioneers and Appraisers.

Spill holder, detailed face of young woman, long hair, tree trunks with spreading leaves on sides which spread to form crown, 5-3/8" h, $75.

Doll

18-1/2" h, Countess Dagmar, shoulder head, café au lait molded hair with side-swept wings to comb and curls in back, curls on forehead held by molded band, blue painted eyes, pierced ears, cloth body, brown leather arms, blue plaid wool dress, orig underwear, blue leather shoes, c1870 . . . . **250.00**

20" h, lady, bisque shoulder head, very pale coloring, center part blond hairstyle, 10 vertical curls, painted features, blue eyes, closed mouth, three sew holes, cloth body, kid arms, separate fingers, red cotton print jumper, white blouse with tucking and lace trim, leather slippers, Germany, c1870 . . **350.00**

Figure

11" h, Grecian goddess riding in carriage, pulled by five putti, c1890 . . . . **450.00**

11-3/4" h, Farmer, modeled seated on rocky freeform base, holding bagpipes, imp Copeland mark, c1875, pipes and fingers restored, small chips to sheaf of wheat **175.00**

15" h, Canova, imp title on circular base, imp Minton marks, c1863, chips to floral garland **750.00**

Urn, elaborately decorated with applied garlands of flowers, double handles, possibly American, unmarked, 5-1/4" d, 12-1/2" h, $850. Photo courtesy of David Rago Auctions.

Plaque, 6" d, relief, angels, brass frames, orig German labels, Boston retailers label, pr **275.00**

Sculpture, nude riding back of lion, early registry marks, c1860 . . . . **895.00**

Urn, cov, 20" h, classical shape, allegorical scene in low relief, three Graces, temples, revelers, and centaur, fish scale pattern on pedestal base, double scrolled handles, fruit finial, base marked with crown with ribbon and "FB" **250.00**

Vase, 10" h, applied white monkey type figures, grape clusters at shoulders, blue ground, c1850, pr **265.00**

PATE-DE-VERRE

History: The term "pate-de-verre" can be translated simply as "glass paste." It is manufactured by grinding lead glass into a powder or crystal form, making it into a paste by adding a two percent or three percent solution of sodium silicate, molding, firing, and carving. The Egyptians discovered the process as early as 1500 B.C.

In the late 19th century, the process was rediscovered by a group of

For more information, see this book.

French glassmakers. Almaric Walter, Henri Cros, Georges Despret, and the Daum brothers were leading manufacturers.

Contemporary sculptors are creating a second renaissance, led by the technical research of Jacques Daum.

Bookends, pr, 6-1/2" h, Buddha, yellow amber pressed molded design, seated in lotus position, inscribed "A Walter Nancy" **2,450.00**

Bowl, 3-3/8" h, squatty form, mottled brown translucent glass, inscribed "Daum (cross) Nancy" on side" . **300.00**

Center bowl, 10-3/8" d, 3-3/4" h, blue, purple, and green press molded design, seven exotic long-legged birds, central multi-pearl blossom, repeating design on ext., raised pedestal foot, sgd "G. Argy-Rousseau" **6,750.00**

Clock, 4-1/2" sq, stars within pentagon and tapered sheaves motif, orange and black, molded sgd "G. Argy-Rousseau," clock by J. E. Caldwell **2,750.00**

Dagger, 12" l, frosted blade, relief design, green horse head handle, script sgd "Nancy France" . . . **1,200.00**

Dish, Leaf-shaped dish, modeled frog, purple, green, and yellow, etched "Daum/France," 6-1/4" l, $2,900. Photo courtesy of David Rago Auctions.

Jewelry

Earrings, pr, 2-3/4" l, teardrop for, molded violet and rose shaded tulip blossom, suspended from rose colored swirl molded circle **2,200.00**

Pendant, 2-1/4" d, round plaque, low relief molded rose blossom and branch, shaded rose, brown, and frosted glass, molded "G.A.R.," (G. Argy-Rousseau), c1925 **700.00**

Paperweight, 3/4" w, 1-1/4" h, large beetle, green leaves, mottled blue ground, intaglio "AW" mark . . **6,800.00**

Sculpture, 9-5/8" l, crab in sea grasses, lemon yellow, chocolate brown, pale mauve, and sea green, sgd "A.

Walter/Nancy" and "Berge/SC" **8,500.00**

Tray, 6" x 8", apple green, figural green and yellow duck with orange beak at one end, sgd "Walter, Nancy" . . **950.00**

Vase, 5-1/2" h, press molded and carved, mottled amethyst and frost ground, three black and green crabs, red eyes, naturalistic seaweed at rim, center imp "G. Argy-Rousseau," base imp "France" **5,500.00**

Veilleuse, 8-1/2" h, Gabriel Argy-Rousseau, press molded oval lamp shade, frosted mottled gray glass, elaborate purple arches with three teardrop-shaped windows of yellow, center teal-green stylized blossoms on black swirling stems, imp "G. Arty-Rousseau" at lower edge, wrought iron frame, three ball feet centering internal lamp socket, conforming iron cover **6,900.00**

PATE-SUR-PATE

History: Pate-sur-pate, paste-on-paste, is a 19th-century porcelain-decorating method featuring relief designs achieved by painting layers of thin pottery paste one on top of the other.

About 1880, Marc Solon and other Sevres artists, inspired by a Chinese celadon vase in the Ceramic Museum at Sevres, experimented with this process. Solon emigrated to England at the outbreak of the Franco-Prussian War and worked at Minton, where he perfected pate-sur-pate.

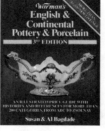

For more information, see this book.

Box, cov, 5-3/4" d, round, white female portrait, blue ground, Limoges, France, late 19th C **690.00**

Bud vase, 4-3/8" h, gourd shape, irid mother-of-pearl ground, raised gilt foliate framed cartouche, central pale mauve roundel featuring white painted female figure blowing bubbles, Germany, 20th C **290.00**

Centerpiece, 16" l, elongated parian vessel, molded scroll handles and feet, pierced rim, two brown reserves, white pate-sur-pate amorini, gilding, dec attributed to Lawrence Birks, marked "Minton," retailer's mark of Thomas Goode & Co., Ltd., London, c1889 . . . . **1,400.00**

Dresser jar, 3-3/4" d, ovoid, cobalt blue ground, lid with pate-sure-pate profile

Canteen, black background, white figures of three naked children playing in a garden, one gently holds bird while others look on, sides decorated with stylistic flowers and leaves, gold enamel ring of flowers on back, four short legs with gold enamel trim, signed on bottom "MINTON" in a globe, 6" h, $1,785. Photo courtesy of James D. Julia, Inc.

bust of classical woman, gilt banding, Meissen, Germany, early 20th C **1,955.00**

Lamp base, 10-1/4" h, Chinoiserie-style, black ground moon flask with pate-sur-pate and blue-printed dec of village scenes, mounted on gilt-metal beaded and scroll ftd base, 20th C, price for pr **490.00**

Medallion, 2-3/8" x 3-3/8", oval, blue ground, white relief cherub figure, unidentified factory mark on reverse, France, 19th C, edge ground . . . **320.00**

Plaque

5-1/4" x 11-1/4", Victoria Ware, Wedgwood, rust ground, gilt florets, applied white figure of Adam, imp mark, c1880, rim chip, framed **2,200.00**

7-5/8" d, one with maiden and cupid spinning web, other with maiden seated on bench with whip in one hand, sunflowers stalked with humanistic snail on other, artist sgd "Louis Solin," both marked on back, framed, pr **2,500.00**

11" x 16", mottled blue-gray ground, colored slips of partially clad female holding lantern, putti figure lights torch, titled "La Nouvelle Psyche," unsgd, attributed to Louis Solon **27,600.00**

15" l, demi-lune shape, green ground, white slip, central figure of Venus holding mirror in each hand,

Urn, double handles, reticulated detailing, pale yellow and blue ground, hand-painted iris decoration, central pate-sur-pate panel in white on pink of winged angel with scepter, Austrian, c1893-1907, signed "LCF," mounted on conforming paint decorated lamp base, urn lid as finial, 14" h urn, 36-1/2" overall height, **$1,210.** *Photo courtesy of Sanford Alderfer Auction Company.*

fending off two groups of putti with their reflections, artist sgd Louis Solin, rosewood frame . . . **9,200.00**

Plate, 9-1/8" d, deep brown ground, gilt trim, white dec of nude child behind net supported by two small trees, artist monogram sgd "Henry Saunders," printed and imp Moore Brothers factory marks, c1885 . . . . **750.00**

Tile, 7" l, 5" w, sword wielding warrior on horseback, cobalt blue ground, sgd "Limoges France" in gold script, mounted in antique frame **220.00**

Urn, 8" h, double handles, pedestal base, portrait medallion, pale green ground, ivory trim, gilt accents . **250.00**

Vase

6-1/2" h, cov, two handles, deep teal blue ground, gilt framed gray ground panel with white slip dec of reclining maiden, artist sgd Albione Birks, printed Minton factory marks, c1900, shallow restored chip on cov **1,840.00**

7-1/4" h, 5-3/4" w, white flowers, green ground, gold serpent skin twisted handles, gold trim, pr **1,100.00**

13-3/4" h, cov, dark brown ground, white slip of partially draped female figure holding flowering branch, shaped tripod base, gilt dec at rim, artist sgd Louis Solon, printed and imp marks, 1898, rim cover damage, minor gilt wear . **2,300.00**

16-1/2" h, cov, deep green ground, circular panels dec in white slip, Psyche being carried heavenward by Mercury, maiden figures applied to shoulder, gilt trim, artist sgd Frederick Schenck, dated 1880, imp George Jones factory marks, cov damaged, hairlines to figures, light gilt wear **3,565.00**

PATTERN GLASS

History: Pattern glass is clear or colored glass pressed into one of hundreds of patterns. Deming Jarves of the Boston and Sandwich Glass Co. invented one of the first successful pressing machines in 1828. By the 1860s, glass-pressing machinery had been improved, and mass production of good-quality matched tableware sets began. The idea of a matched glassware table service (including goblets, tumblers, creamers, sugars, compotes, cruets, etc.) quickly caught on in America. Many pattern glass table services had numerous accessory pieces such as banana stands, molasses cans, and water bottles.

Early pattern glass (flint) was made with a lead formula, giving many items a ringing sound when tapped. Lead became too valuable to be used in glass manufacturing during the Civil War, and in 1864, Hobbs, Brockunier & Co., West Virginia, developed a soda lime (non-flint) formula. Pattern glass also was produced in transparent colors, milk glass, opalescent glass, slag glass, and custard glass.

The hundreds of companies that produced pattern glass experienced periods of development, expansions, personnel problems, material and supply demands, fires, and mergers. In 1899, the National Glass Co. was formed as a combine of 19 glass companies in Pennsylvania, Ohio, Indiana, West

For more information, see these books.

Virginia, and Maryland. U.S. Glass, another consortium, was founded in 1891. These combines resulted from attempts to save small companies by pooling talents, resources, and patterns. Because of this pooling, the same pattern often can be attributed to several companies.

U.S. Glass created the States series by using state names for various patterns, several of which were new issues while others were former patterns renamed. Other glass companies named their patterns after states also, but not all 50 states have patterns named after them. For this edition of *Warman's*, the States series and other states have been used as an example of the current pattern-glass market.

Reproduction Alert: Pattern glass has been widely reproduced. Items in the listing marked with an * are those for which reproductions are known to exist. Care should be exercised when purchasing such pieces.

Additional Listings: Bread Plates, Children's Toy Dishes, Cruets, Custard Glass, Milk Glass, Sugar Shakers, Toothpicks, and specific companies.

Advisers: John and Alice Ahlfeld.

Abbreviations:

ah	applied handle
GUTDODB	Give Us This Day Our Daily Bread
hs	high standard
ind	individual
ls	low standard
os	original stopper

ACORN

Acorn Band, Acorn Band and Loops, Paneled Acorn Band, Beaded Acorn

Acorn and the variant patterns were made in flint and non-flint, 1860s-70s. There are additional acorn variant patterns, but they were not made in table sets. Prices for all the acorn variants are similar.

Reproductions: The Acorn goblet is reported to be reproduced in blue. Originally it was only made in clear.

ACORN (cont.)

Items	Flint	Non-Flint
Bowl		
cov.	—	60.00
open	—	42.00
Butter dish, cov	65.00	—
Celery	60.00	—
Compote		
cov.	225.00	90.00
open	90.00	72.00
Creamer	55.00	42.00

Items	Flint	Non-Flint
Egg cup	30.00	18.00
Goblet φ	48.00	30.00
Pitcher, water, ah	180.00	90.00
Sauce, flat	—	9.00
Spooner	48.00	36.00
Sugar bowl, cov	90.00	60.00
Sugar, open, buttermilk type	42.00	24.00

BEADED ACORN MEDALLION

Beaded Acorn

Manufactured by Boston Silver Glass Company, East Cambridge, MA, c1869. Shards have been found at the site of the Boston and Sandwich Glass Company, Sandwich, MA. Made non-flint, clear only. The pattern is one with heavy stippling, applied handles are typical and an interesting finial in the shape of an acorn.

Items	Clear
Butter dish, cov, acorn finial	66.00
Champagne	66.00
Compote	
cov, hs, 8" d	72.00
cov, ls, 9" d	60.00
Creamer, ah	48.00

Items	Clear
Egg cup	30.00
Fruit bowl	55.00
Goblet	36.00
Honey dish, 3-1/2" d	18.00
Lamp, brass trim, orig burner and chimney	118.00
Pitcher, water, ah, bulbous	130.00

Items	Clear
Plate, 6" d	36.00
Relish	18.00
Salt, master	36.00
Sauce, flat, 4" d	15.00
Spooner	30.00
Sugar bowl, cov	55.00
Wine	55.00

CARDINAL

Blue Jay, Cardinal Bird

Manufacture attributed to Ohio Flint Glass Company, Lancaster, OH, c1875. Shards have been found at Burlington Glass Works, Hamilton, Ontario, Canada. Made in non-flint, clear. There were two butter dishes made. One in the regular pattern and one with three birds on the base, labeled in script "Red Bird, Pewit, and Titmouse." The latter is less common.

Reproductions: Reproduction goblets have been made by Summit Art Glass Company, Akron, OH. These goblets can be found in blue, clear, and green.

Item	Clear
Berry bowl	65.00
Butter dish, cov	
regular	65.00
three birds	124.00
Cake stand, hs	90.00

Item	Clear
Creamer φ	48.00
Goblet φ	42.00
Honey dish	
cov	55.00
open	24.00
Pitcher, water	180.00

Item	Clear
Sauce	
flat, 4" d or 4-1/2" d	12.00
ftd, 5-1/2" d	24.00
Spooner	48.00
Sugar bowl, cov	72.00

ESTHER
Tooth and Claw

Manufactured by Riverside Glass Works, Wellsburg, WV, c1896. Made in non-flint, amber stained, clear, green, and ruby stained. Some green pieces have gold trim. Stained pieces may be etched or have enamel decoration.

Items	Clear	Green	Ruby Stained
Bowl, 8" w	30.00	60.00	72.00
Butter dish, cov	65.00	120.00	180.00
Cake stand, hs, 10-1/2" d	72.00	95.00	115.00
Castor set, four bottles	85.00	—	—
Celery vase	48.00	110.00	85.00
Cheese dish, cov	85.00	142.00	130.00
Compote, open, 6" d	30.00	55.00	55.00
Creamer			
individual	55.00	85.00	75.00
table size	60.00	80.00	95.00
Cruet, os	55.00	255.00	265.00
Goblet	55.00	85.00	75.00
Jelly compote, hs	36.00	75.00	85.00
Pickle dish	18.00	60.00	48.00
Pitcher, water	65.00	165.00	300.00
Plate, 10" d	30.00	72.00	72.00
Relish tray	24.00	30.00	30.00
Salt shaker	24.00	42.00	48.00
Sauce, flat, 4" d	12.00	18.00	24.00
Sugar bowl, cov	55.00	85.00	120.00
Syrup, orig top	65.00	240.00	190.00
Toothpick holder	55.00	85.00	120.00
Tumbler	30.00	36.00	55.00
Vase	30.00	55.00	55.00
Wine	42.00	55.00	55.00

FROSTED CIRCLE
Clear Circle, Horn of Plenty, US Glass Pattern Line No. 15,007

Manufactured by Bryce Brothers, Pittsburgh, PA, c1885. Reissued by United States Glass Company, Pittsburgh, PA, in the late 1890s. Made in non-flint, clear with either a clear circle or frosted circle.

Reproductions: The goblet has been reproduced.

Items	Clear Circle	Frosted Circle
Bowl		
cov, 7" d or 8" d	30.00	36.00
open, 5" d, 6" d or 7" d	12.00	18.00
Butter dish		
cov	55.00	65.00
open	55.00	55.00
Cake stand, hs, 9" d	42.00	48.00
Celery vase	36.00	42.00
Champagne	42.00	55.00
Compote		
cov, hs, 7" d	42.00	55.00
open, hs, 5" d or 6" d	18.00	24.00
open, hs, 10" d	55.00	55.00
Creamer	42.00	55.00
Cruet, os	55.00	65.00
Cup and saucer	30.00	48.00
Goblet φ	42.00	55.00
Juice tumbler	18.00	36.00
Pickle dish, oblong	12.00	24.00
Pitcher, water	55.00	95.00
Plate, 7" d	42.00	60.00
Punch cup	18.00	24.00
Salt shaker	30.00	36.00
Spooner, ftd, scalloped	36.00	42.00
Sugar bowl, cov	55.00	72.00
Sugar shaker	48.00	72.00
Syrup, orig top	115.00	65.00
Tumbler	30.00	42.00
Wine	42.00	55.00

GRAPE BAND

Ashburton with Grape Band, Early Grape Band, Grape Vine

Manufactured by Bryce, Walker and Company, Pittsburgh, PA, in the late 1850s in flint. Non-flint was made in 1869. Made in flint, non-flint, clear.

Reproductions: Only the goblet has been reproduced in this pattern.

Items	Flint	Non-Flint	Items	Flint	Non-Flint
Butter dish, cov	75.00	60.00	Pitcher, water	—	85.00
Compote, cov			Plate, 6" d	—	24.00
hs	—	60.00	Salt		
ls	—	55.00	individual	—	24.00
Compote, open, hs	—	30.00	master, ftd	—	36.00
Cordial	65.00	—	Spooner	—	36.00
Creamer, ah	—	60.00	Sugar bowl, cov	—	55.00
Egg cup	—	24.00	Tumbler	42.00	24.00
Goblet φ	48.00	30.00	Wine	42.00	30.00
Pickle dish, scoop shape	—	18.00			

HONEYCOMB

Manufactured by numerous firms, including Bakewell Pears & Company, Pittsburgh, PA; Bellaire Goblet Company, Bellaire, OH; Doyle & Company, Pittsburgh, PA; Boston Silver and Glass Company, East Cambridge, MA; Gillinder & Sons, Philadelphia, PA; Grierson & Company, Pittsburgh, PA; New England Glass Company, East Cambridge, MA, O'Hara Glass Company, Pittsburgh, and United States Glass Company, Pittsburgh, PA, c1850-1900, resulting in minor pattern variations. Made in flint, non-flint, clear. Found with copper wheel engraving. Rare in color.

Reproductions: There are many reproduction pieces of Honeycomb. Fenton Art Glass Company, Williamstown, WV, created copies as early as 1930 in amber, black, clear, green, moonstone, pink, royal blue, ruby, and topaz. The Jeannette Glass Company, Jeannette, PA, c1928, made other pieces, including forms not originally created, in carnival glass, green, and pink. Viking Glass Company, New Martinsville, WV, also created new forms in 1972. They made reproductions in amber, blue, brown, green, and ruby.

Items	Flint	Non-Flint	Items	Flint	Non-Flint
Ale glass	60.00	30.00	Decanter, bar lip		
Barber bottle	55.00	30.00	pint	65.00	24.00
Beer mug	30.00	18.00	qt	90.00	—
Bowl			Decanter, os		
cov, collared, Brittania or tin lid, 8" d	80.00	—	pint φ	72.00	90.00
cov, flat, 5-1/2" d or 6" d	65.00	—	qt φ	85.00	80.00
cov, pat'd 1869, acorn finial, 7-1/4" d	120.00	55.00	Dish, oval, 7" l or 8" l	24.00	12.00
open, collared, deep, 8" d or 9" d	55.00	—	Egg cup, ftd, flared or straight-sided	24.00	18.00
open, collared, saucer, 9" d or 10" d	—	48.00	Finger bowl φ	55.00	—
Butter dish, cov φ	80.00	55.00	Goblet φ	30.00	18.00
Cake stand, hs, 11-1/4" d	65.00	42.00	Honey dish, cov, 3" d or 3-1/2" d	18.00	30.00
Candlestick	160.00	—	Lamp		
Castor bottle	30.00	110.00	all glass	—	105.00
Celery vase, pedestal			marble base	—	110.00
scalloped rim	55.00	24.00	Lemonade mug, ftd, ah φ	48.00	24.00
sawtooth rim	60.00	30.00	Mug, half pint	30.00	18.00
Champagne	60.00	30.00	Pepper sauce bottle	36.00	—
Claret φ	42.00	42.00	Pickle jar, cov	110.00	80.00
Compote			Pitcher		
cov, hs, deep bowl, 8" d or 9" d	115.00	65.00	milk, ah or ph, qt	105.00	80.00
cov, hs, 6-1/2"d, 8-1/2" h	120.00	60.00	water, 1/2 gal, dated handle "Pat. 1865"	180.00	72.00
open, hs, deep bowl, 10" d	55.00	42.00	water, 1/2 gal, plain handle φ	120.00	90.00
open, hs, saucer bowl, 8" d	48.00	36.00	Plate, 6" d or 7" d φ	—	18.00
open, ls, deep bowl, 8" d or 9" d	48.00	36.00	Pomade jar, cov	60.00	24.00
open, ls, saucer bowl, 6" d or 7" d	42.00	30.00	Pony mug	36.00	—
Cordial, 3-1/2" h φ	42.00	30.00	Relish dish	36.00	24.00
Creamer, ah or ph φ	42.00	24.00	Salt		
Custard cup, ftd, ah	80.00	—	individual, oblong or round	18.00	12.00

HONEYCOMB (cont.)

Items	Flint	Non-Flint
master, cov, ftd	80.00	—
master, open, flat	42.00	36.00
Salt shaker, orig top φ	—	42.00
Sauce, flat, 4" d	15.00	7.50
Spill holder	42.00	24.00
Spooner	80.00	42.00
String holder, two sizes	130.00	—
Sugar bowl, cov		
frosted rosebud finial	—	60.00
regular	90.00	55.00

Items	Flint	Non-Flint
Syrup, orig top		
half pint	240.00	—
pint	270.00	120.00
three pint	260.00	—
qt	290.00	—
Tumble-up	112.00	—
Tumbler		
bar	42.00	—
flat φ	48.00	12.50
ftd φ	55.00	18.00
Vase, 7-1/2" h	55.00	—
Whiskey, handled φ	130.00	—
Wine φ	42.00	18.00

INVERTED STRAWBERRY

Manufactured by Cambridge Glass Company, Cambridge, OH, c1908. Made in non-flint, clear, and ruby stained. Ruby stained also found with souvenir inscriptions. No toothpick holder was originally made.

Reproductions: This pattern has been reproduced in amethyst, carnival glass, and green by Guersney Glass Company, Cambridge, OH.

Items	Clear	Ruby Stained
Basket, ah φ	80.00	—
Bowl, 9" d	30.00	—
Butter dish, cov	80.00	—
Celery tray, handled	36.00	—
Compote, open, hs, 5" d	310.00	—
Creamer φ	30.00	—
Cruet, os φ	55.00	—
Goblet	30.00	—
Mug	24.00	36.00
Nappy φ	18.00	—
Pitcher, water φ	55.00	—

Items	Clear	Ruby Stained
Plate, 10" d φ	30.00	48.00
Punch cup	15.00	—
Relish tray, 7" φ	15.00	—
Rose bowl	36.00	—
Salt, individual	24.00	—
Sauce, flat, 4" d	110.00	—
Spooner	30.00	—
Sugar bowl, cov φ	55.00	—
Toothpick holder φ	30.00	—
Tumbler φ	36.00	55.00

JERSEY SWIRL

Swirl, Swirl and Diamonds, Windsor Swirl, Windsor

Manufactured by Windsor Glass Company, Pittsburgh, PA, c1887. Made in non-flint, amber, blue, canary-yellow, and clear.

Reproductions: Heavily reproduced in color by L. G. Wright Company, New Martinsville, WV, from 1968 to 1974. The clear goblet is also reproduced.

Items	Amber	Blue	Canary	Clear
Bowl, 9-1/4" d	65.00	65.00	55.00	42.00
Butter dish, cov	65.00	65.00	60.00	48.00
Cake stand, hs, 9" d	90.00	85.00	55.00	36.00
Celery vase	45.00	45.00	42.00	36.00
Compote, hs, 8" d	60.00	60.00	55.00	42.00
Creamer	55.00	55.00	48.00	36.00
Cruet, os	—	—	—	30.00
Goblet, buttermilk	48.00	48.00	42.00	36.00
Goblet, water φ	48.00	48.00	42.00	36.00
Marmalade jar	—	—	—	60.00
Pickle castor, silver plate frame and lid	—	—	—	130.00
Pitcher, water	60.00	60.00	55.00	42.00

JERSEY SWIRL (cont.)

Items	Amber	Blue	Canary	Clear
Plate, round, 8" d	36.00	36.00	30.00	24.00
Salt, individual ɸ	24.00	24.00	110.00	18.00
Sauce, flat, 4-1/2" d ɸ	24.00	24.00	18.00	12.00
Spooner	36.00	36.00	30.00	24.00
Sugar bowl, cov	48.00	48.00	42.00	36.00
Tumbler	36.00	36.00	30.00	24.00
Wine ɸ	60.00	60.00	48.00	18.00

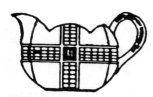

KLONDIKE

Amberette, English Hobnail Cross, Frosted Amberette

Manufacturing attributed to A. J. Beatty and Company, Tiffin, OH, c1885. It was also made by Hobbs, Brockunier & Company, Wheeling, WV, and Daizell, Gilmore and Leighton Company, Brilliant, OH, c1880. Created to commemorate the Alaskan Gold Rush. The frosted panels depict snow; the amber bands depict the gold. Made in non-flint, clear, and frosted, with amber stained bands. Found with or without scrolls, depending on the maker. Prices are listed for frosted; clear prices would be approximately 20 percent of those shown.

Items	Frosted Amber Stain
Berry bowl, sq, 8" w	240.00
Bowl, sq, 9" w	270.00
Butter dish, cov	360.00
Cake stand, hs, sq, 8" w	460.00
Celery tray	240.00
Condiment set	1,200.00
Creamer	260.00

Items	Frosted Amber Stain
Cruet, os	460.00
Custard cup	130.00
Goblet	480.00
Pitcher, water	660.00
Punch cup	120.00
Salt shaker, single	120.00
Sauce	
flat	90.00
ftd	95.00

Items	Frosted Amber Stain
Spooner	190.00
Sugar bowl, cov	260.00
Syrup, pewter lid	660.00
Toothpick holder	360.00
Tray, 5-1/2" sq	240.00
Vase, 8" h	270.00
Wine	480.00

LIBERTY BELL

Centennial

Manufactured by Gillinder and Company, Philadelphia, c1875. James C. Gillinder registered his design patent on September 28, 1875. The pattern was made at the Gillinder factory located on the grounds of the Centennial Philadelphia Exhibition of 1876. Made in clear. Some items made in milk glass. A milk glass bread plate, 13-3/8" x 9-1/2", is known and shows John Hancock's signature (valued at $360).

Reproductions: Reproductions bear the year "1876" and "200 Years" instead of the original inscriptions. The American Historical Replica Company, Grand Rapids, MI, issued reproductions for the American Bicentennial. The company modified the design to include "1776-1976," and phrases such as "Declaration of Independence," etc. Their reproductions are clearly embossed "A. H.B. C. Grand Rapids, MI."

Items	Clear
Bowl, 8", ftd	120.00
Bread plate, 13-3/8" x 9-1/2", clear, no signatures ɸ	100.00
Butter dish, cov	155.00
Celery vase, pedestal	100.00
Child's butter dish, cov	180.00
Child's creamer, ph	90.00
Child's mug, 2" h	240.00
Child's spooner	240.00
Child's sugar bowl, cov	180.00

Items	Clear
Compote, open, 6" d	90.00
Creamer	
applied handle	115.00
reed handle	120.00
Goblet	48.00
Mug, snake handle	440.00
Pickle	55.00
Pitcher, water, ah	960.00
Plate	
6" d, dated	90.00
10" d	95.00

Items	Clear
Platter, 13" x 8"	75.00
Relish, oval	72.00
Salt shaker	115.00
Sauce	
flat, 4-1/2" d	24.00
ftd, 4-1/2" d	24.00
Spooner, pedestal	72.00
Sugar bowl, cov, pedestal	110.00

MINERVA
Roman Medallion

Manufactured by Boston and Sandwich Glass Company, Sandwich, MA, c1870, as well as other American companies. Shards have been found at Burlington Glass Works, Hamilton, Ontario, Canada. Made in non-flint, clear.

Items	Clear
Bowl	
ftd, 8" d	42.00
rect, 8" l	36.00
Bread plate	75.00
Butter dish, cov	90.00
Cake stand	
hs, 8" d	180.00
hs, 13" d	155.00
Champagne	100.00
Compote	
cov, hs, 7" d	135.00

Items	Clear
cov, ls, 8" d	130.00
open, hs, 10-1/2" d	115.00
Creamer	55.00
Goblet	110.00
Honey dish, 3-1/2" d	12.00
Marmalade jar, cov	180.00
Pickle dish	30.00
Pitcher, milk, qt	190.00
Pitcher, water, 1/2	200.00

Items	Clear
Plate	
8" d	65.00
20" d, handle	72.00
Platter, oval, 13" l	75.00
Sauce	
flat, 4-1/4" d or 4-1/2" d	18.50
ftd, 4-1/4" d or 4-1/2" d	24.00
Spooner	48.00
Sugar bowl, cov	75.00
Waste bowl	60.00

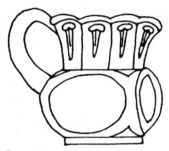

NAIL
Recessed Pillar-Red Top, Recessed Pillar-Thumbprint Band, US Glass Pattern Line No. 15,002

Manufactured by Ripley and Company, Pittsburgh, PA, c1892. Reissued by United States Glass Company, Pittsburgh, PA. Made in non-flint, clear and clear with ruby stain. Pieces can be found plain or with copper wheel engraving.

Items	Clear	Ruby Stained
Berry bowl	30.00	55.00
Butter dish, cov	55.00	115.00
Celery vase	75.00	130.00
Claret	42.00	—
Compote, cov, hs, 8"d	55.00	95.00
Creamer	36.00	72.00
Cruet, os	72.00	260.00
Finger bowl	36.00	—
Goblet	42.00	75.00
Jelly compote, open, hs	24.00	48.00
Mustard, cov	60.00	115.00
Pitcher, water	90.00	230.00

Items	Clear	Ruby Stained
Sauce		
flat	18.00	36.00
ftd	18.00	36.00
Spooner	30.00	36.00
Sugar bowl, cov	48.00	95.00
Sugar shaker, orig top	120.00	190.00
Syrup, orig top	90.00	130.00
Tumbler	24.00	48.00
Vase, 7" h	18.00	—
Waste bowl	36.00	—
Water tray	55.00	—
Wine	42.00	85.00

ONE HUNDRED ONE
Beaded 101

Manufactured by Bellaire Goblet Company, Findlay, OH, in the late 1880s. Shards have been found at the site of the Burlington Glass Works, Hamilton, Ontario, Canada. Made in non-flint, clear.

Reproductions: Only the goblet has been reproduced in this pattern. It has been reproduced in clear and colors.

ONE HUNDRED ONE (cont.)

Items	Clear	Items	Clear	Items	Clear
Bread plate, 101 border, Farm implement center, 11" l	.90.00	Goblet φ	60.00	Relish tray	.35.00
Butter dish, cov	.48.00	Lamp, oil		Salt shaker, orig top	.18.00
Cake stand, hs, 9" d	.75.00	hand	95.00	Sauce	
Celery vase	.60.00	table	120.00	flat, 4" d	.12.00
Compote		Pickle	35.00	ftd, 4" d	.18.00
cov, hs, 8" d	.72.00	Pitcher, water, ah	130.00	Spooner	.30.00
cov, ls	.72.00	Plate		Sugar bowl, cov	.55.00
Creamer	.55.00	6" d	18.00	Vase	.30.00
		9" d	35.00	Wine	.72.00

PRINCESS FEATHER

Lacy Medallion, Princes' Feather, Rochelle

Manufactured by Bakewell, Pears and Company, Pittsburgh, PA, in the 1860s and 1870s. Later made by United States Glass Company, Pittsburgh, PA, after 1891. Shards have been identified at Boston and Sandwich Glass Company, Sandwich, MA, the Burlington Glass Works, Hamilton, Ontario, Canada, and the Diamond Glass Company, Ltd., Montreal, Quebec, Canada. Made in flint and non-flint, clear. Also made in milk glass. A rare blue opaque tumbler has been reported.

Items	Clear	Items	Clear	Items	Clear
Bowl, cov, pedestal, 7" d	.60.00	ls, 8" d	48.00	Plate, 8" d	.48.00
Bowl		open, ls, 8" d	42.00	Relish	.35.00
flat, 6" d	.30.00	Creamer, ah	65.00	Salt, master, open, ftd	.35.00
oval, 7" l	.35.00	Dish, oval	35.00	Sauce	
Butter dish, cov	.60.00	Egg cup	48.00	flat, 4" d	.10.00
Cake plate, handles, 9" d	.42.00	Goblet	55.00	ftd, 4" d	.12.00
Cheese dish	.55.00	Honey dish, flat, 3" d	12.00	Spooner	.36.00
Compote, cov		Pitcher		Sugar bowl, cov	.65.00
hs, 7" d	.60.00	milk	85.00	Sugar, open	.30.00
		water	90.00	Wine	.55.00

QUESTION MARK

Oval Loop

Manufactured by Richards & Hartley Glass Company, Pittsburgh, PA, in 1888 and later by U.S. Glass Company, Pittsburgh, PA, in 1892. An 1888 catalog lists 32 pieces. Made in non-flint, clear. Scarce in ruby stained.

Items	Clear	Items	Clear	Items	Clear
Bowl		open, hs, 8" d	36.00	water, tankard, 1/2 gal	.65.00
collared, round, 7" d	.30.00	Cordial	35.00	Salt shaker	.18.00
oblong, 5" l	.18.00	Creamer	36.00	Sauce	
oblong, 10" l	.30.00	Goblet	30.00	collared, 4" d	.12.00
Bread tray	.36.00	Nappy, ftd	35.00	ftd, 4" d	.12.00
Butter dish, cov	.36.00	Pickle jar, cov	55.00	Spooner	.35.00
Candlestick, chamber, finger loop	.55.00	Pitcher		Sugar bowl, cov	.30.00
Celery vase	.210.00	milk, bulbous, qt	48.00	Sugar shaker	.42.00
Compote		milk, tankard, qt	55.00	Tumbler	.35.00
cov, hs, 7" d	.60.00	water, bulbous, 1/2 gal	60.00	Wine	.35.00

ROMAN KEY

Frosted Roman Key, Grecian Border, Plain Roman Key

Manufactured by Union Glass Company, Somerville, MA, c1860, and by others in several variants. Made in flint, frosted and in clear, but not as popular. Sometimes erroneously called "Greek Key."

Items	Clear	Frosted
Bowl, cable rim, 9-1/2" d	42.00	60.00
Butter dish, cov	48.00	95.00
Castor set	120.00	130.00
Celery vase, ftd	48.00	95.00
Champagne	48.00	100.00
Compote		
open, hs, cable rim, 9" d	40.00	75.00
open, ls, cable rim, 7" d	40.00	75.00
Creamer, ah, ftd	115.00	118.00
Custard cup	18.00	36.00
Decanter, os		
pint	—	160.00
qt	—	175.00
Egg cup	30.00	55.00

Items	Clear	Frosted
Goblet	30.00	60.00
Lamp, oil, orig burner and chimney	—	160.00
Mustard jar, cov	—	55.00
Pickle dish	—	55.00
Pitcher		
milk, qt	—	230.00
water, 1/2 gal	—	230.00
Plate, 6" d	—	42.00
Preserve dish	—	55.00
Relish dish, oval, cable rim	—	35.00
Salt, master, ftd	30.00	55.00
Sauce, flat, 4" d	12.00	110.00
Spooner, pedestal	30.00	55.00
Sugar bowl, cov	55.00	100.00
Tumbler, bar, flat or ftd	30.00	55.00

SCALLOPED DIAMOND POINT

Late Diamond Point Band, Panel with Diamond Point, Diamond Point with Flute

Manufactured by Central Glass Company, Wheeling, WV. Also made by United States Glass Company, Pittsburgh, PA, after 1891. Made in non-flint, clear. A wine ($90) is known in electric blue and in amber ($60).

Items	Clear
Bowl, oval, 9" l	24.00
Butter dish, cov	65.00
Cake stand, hs, 8" d	36.00
Cheese dish, cov, 8" d	60.00
Compote	
cov, hs, 8" d	90.00

Items	Clear
open, hs, 7" d	48.00
Creamer	60.00
Goblet	36.00
Jelly compote, cov, 5" d	45.00
Mustard jar, cov	36.00
Pickle dish, oval	24.00

Items	Clear
Pickle jar, cov	55.00
Plate, 9" d	24.00
Sauce, ftd, 4" d	12.00
Spooner	30.00
Sugar bowl, cov	48.00
Wine	45.00

TREE OF LIFE

Portland's

Manufactured by Portland Glass Company, Portland, ME, c1870. Made in flint, and non-flint, in amber, clear, dark blue, green, light blue, purple, and, yellow. Color is rare. A blue finger bowl in a silver plated holder is valued at $190.

Reproductions: Reproductions of Tree of Life were made by L. G. Wright Glass Company, New Martinsville, WV, 1968. Colors of these reproductions include amber, blue, and clear.

TREE OF LIFE (cont.)

Items	Non-Flint
Bowl, berry, oval	36.00
Butter dish, cov	65.00
Celery vase, SP frame	65.00
Cologne bottle, os	55.00
Champagne	65.00
Compote	
open, hs, 8-1/2" d	130.00
open, ls, 10" d	60.00
Creamer	
applied handle	85.00
molded handle	60.00
Creamer, SP holder	90.00
Egg cup	36.00

Items	Non-Flint
Epergne, sgd "P.G. Company Patd"	130.00
Finger bowl, underplate	72.00
Fruit dish, SP holder	110.00
Goblet	
clear shield on side	60.00
plain φ	45.00
regular, sgd "P.G. Flint"	75.00
Ice cream tray	60.00
Lemonade	60.00
Pitcher	
milk, applied handle	115.00
milk, molded handle	75.00
water, applied handle	115.00
water, molded handle	75.00

Items	Non-Flint
Plate, 6" d	30.00
Sauce	
flat, 3-3/4" d φ	15.00
leaf shape	18.00
Spooner	45.00
Sugar bowl	
cov	85.00
SP holder	90.00
Toothpick holder, ftd, scalloped	60.00
Tumbler, ftd	48.00
Vase	60.00
Water tray	110.00
Wine φ	65.00

VALENTINE

Non-flint pattern made by United States Glass Company, Pittsburgh, PA, 1891-95. Made in non-flint, clear.

Reproductions: Degenhart Glass Company, Cambridge, OH, created reproduction toothpick holders from new molds in many colors, including clear and opalescent shades. They are usually signed with the Degenhart logo.

Items	Clear
Berry bowl	110.00
Butter dish, cov	110.00
Cologne bottle, os	110.00

Items	Clear
Creamer, 4-1/2" h	110.00
Goblet	135.00
Pitcher, water	250.00
Sauce, flat, 4-1/2" d	30.00

Items	Clear
Spooner	75.00
Sugar bowl, cov	135.00
Toothpick holder φ	110.00
Tumbler	110.00

WEDDING RING

Double Wedding Ring

Original manufacturer unknown. Flint production is dated to c1860 while non-flint production dates to c1870. Made in flint, clear only.

Reproductions: The toothpick holder, frequently seen in muddy purple, was not originally made. It has now been reproduced in various colors. Dalzell/Viking Glass Company, New Martinsville, WV, c1989, has issued several flat pieces in colors and clear that were not produced earlier, including a sherbet and toothpick holder.

Items	Flint
Butter dish, cov	125.00
Celery vase	115.00
Champagne	120.00
Cordial	110.00
Creamer	110.00
Decanter, bar lip	135.00

Items	Flint
Decanter, os	135.00
Goblet, faceted knob stem	90.00
Goblet, plain stem φ	90.00
Lamp, oil, finger, orig burner and chimney, 5" h	110.00
Pitcher, water	250.00

Items	Flint
Relish	85.00
Sauce, flat	42.00
Spooner	115.00
Sugar bowl, cov φ	125.00
Syrup, ah, orig top	125.00
Tumbler, flat	110.00
Wine φ	135.00

ZIPPER

Cobb, Late Sawtooth

Manufactured by Richards & Hartley Glass Company, Tarentum, PA, c1888. Made in non-flint, clear. Rare pieces are known in amber and possibly other colors.

Items	Clear
Bowl, 7" d	25.00
Butter dish, cov	55.00
Celery vase	35.00
Cheese dish, cov	80.00
Compote, cov	
hs, 8" d	65.00
ls, 8"d	55.00
open, hs	42.00

Items	Clear
Creamer, ph	
high foot	45.00
low foot	42.00
Cruet, os	65.00
Dish, 9-3/4" l, 6" w	30.00
Goblet	30.00
Marmalade jar, cov	55.00
Pitcher	
milk, ph, qt	45.00
water, ph, 1/2 gal	55.00

Items	Clear
Relish, 10" l	25.00
Salt, individual	8.00
Sauce	
flat	10.00
ftd	20.00
Spooner	35.00
Sugar bowl, cov	45.00
Tumbler	30.00

PAUL REVERE POTTERY

History: Paul Revere Pottery, Boston, Massachusetts, was an outgrowth of a club known as The Saturday Evening Girls. The S.E.G. was composed of young female immigrants who met on Saturday nights to read and participate in craft projects, such as ceramics.

Regular pottery production began in 1908, and the name "Paul Revere" was adopted because the pottery was located near the Old North Church. In 1915, the firm moved to Brighton, Massachusetts. Known as the "Bowl Shop," the pottery grew steadily. In spite of popular acceptance and technical advancements, the pottery required continual subsidies. It finally closed in January 1942.

Items produced range from plain and decorated vases to tablewares to illustrated tiles. Many decorated wares were incised and glazed either in an Art Nouveau matte finish or an occasional high glaze.

Marks: In addition to an impressed mark, paper "Bowl Shop" labels were used prior to 1915. Pieces also can be found with a date and "P.R.P." or "S.E.G." painted on the base.

Bookends, pr, 4" h, 5" w, night scene of owls, 1921, ink marked "S.E.G./11-21," flat chip to one base **1,300.00**

Bowl

4-1/4" d, 2-1/4" h, yellow and black band of walking ducks, marked "S.E.G. 6-21, B.L" **520.00**

5-1/4" d, tree bands with black outline scene, blue sky, green trees, marked "S.E.G. 4/15, I.G." **275.00**

Bookends, pair, each painted with different snowy landscape of trees and clouds in dead-matte glaze, slate-gray ground, paper labels/EM/6/26, 1926, few minor shallow edge flakes, 4" x 5-1/4" x 2-1/2", $1,050. Photo courtesy of David Rago Auctions.

Cake set, Tree pattern, black outline scene, blue sky, green trees, 10" d cake plate, six 8-1/2" d serving plates, each marked "J.G., S.E.G.," three dated 7/15, three dated 1/4/15, one dated 3/15, price for seven-pc set **1,840.00**

Child's breakfast set, 3-1/2" h mug, 5-5/8" d bowl, and 7-3/4" d plate, dec with running rabbits, white, green, and blue, monogrammed "David His Mug," "His Bowl," "His Plate," potter's mark, two chips on mug **1,380.00**

Dessert plate

7-3/8" d, experimental speckled glaze, light gray and green, marked "S.E.G. 5310.09," unglazed base, c1909 .... **265.00**

7-5/8" d, stylized border, crackled black and sea green glaze, edge chip, crazing **195.00**

Humidor, cov, 6-1/4" h, 5-3/4" d, spherical, blue matte glaze, pink int., minute int. rim nick, sgd in slip "P.R.P. 3/36" **400.00**

Lamp base, 18-3/4" h, ovoid, yellow glaze, reticulated wooden base, unmarked **230.00**

Luncheon plate

7-5/8" d, borders dec with incised lotus blossoms in white on blue ground, green-blue center, marked "S.E.G. 6-14," artist's initials S.G.,

Mug and dish, bunny on grassy ground, blue sky, outlined with blue and black band, cream-colored ground, both painted "P.R.P. 1-39," and artist initials "R.C.," on 3-4/8" h mug, 7-1/2" d dish, $1,200. Photo courtesy of Skinner Auctioneers and Appraisers.

c1914, one cracked, price for three plates **1,100.00**

7-5/8" d, incised geese in mottled green on speckled blue ground, painted "S.E.G. 6-13," artist's initials "I.G.," c1913 . . . . . . **490.00**

Pitcher

6-3/4" h, ovoid, applied handle, charcoal gray glaze, partial imp potter's mark, painted "4 26," artist's initials L.S., c1926, three rim chips **70.00**

7-1/8" h, ovoid, applied handle, green glaze, painted "J.M.D. June 17, 1920 S.E.G. 5-20," by Josephine M. Davis, handle repaired **115.00**

Pitcher, white, green, and blue Greek key border design, painted "S.E.G.," artist's initials on base, 4-1/4" h, $800. Photo courtesy of Skinner Auctioneers and Appraisers.

Plate

6-1/2" d, incised white mice, celadon and brown band, ink mark "Dorothy Hopkins/Her Plate," 1911 . **1,300.00**

8" d, cuerda seca dec, white and blue geese and water lilies, green matte ground, marked "S.E.G./6-17/AM" **1,380.00**

Ring tray, 4" d, circular, blue-gray and green band of trees, blue-gray ground, marked "S.E.G./J.G." **275.00**

Teapot, 4-1/2" h, 9" d, brown and white wavy band of sailboats, yellow sky, 1918, restored **700.00**

Tile, 3-3/4" sq, Washington Street, blue, white, green, and brown, marked "H.S. S4 9/1/10," edge chips **420.00**

Trivet

4-1/4" d, medallion of house against setting sun, blue-gray ground, 1924, imp P.R.P. mark **425.00**

5-1/2" d, medallion of poplar trees in landscape, blue-green ground, 1925, imp P.R.P. mark **600.00**

Vase

4-1/4" h, 3" d, bottle shape, glossy orange and matte brown glaze, ink P.R.P. mark **225.00**

7" h, 5-1/4" d, baluster shape, band of orange lotus blossoms, frothy green ground, green base, imp P. R. mark **1,300.00**

10-1/2" h, 5-3/4" h, satin green glaze, ink "S.E.G." mark **250.00**

PEACHBLOW

History: Peachblow, an art glass which derives its name from a fine Chinese glazed porcelain, resembles a peach or crushed strawberries in color. Three American glass manufacturers and two English firms produced peachblow glass in the late 1880s. A fourth American company resumed the process in the 1950s. The glass from each firm has its own identifying characteristics.

Hobbs, Brockunier & Co., Wheeling peachblow: Opalescent glass, plated or cased with a transparent amber glass; shading from yellow at the base to a deep red at top; glossy or satin finish.

Mt. Washington "Peach Blow": A homogeneous glass, shading from a pale gray-blue to a soft rose color; some pieces enhanced with glass appliqués, enameling, and gilding.

New England Glass Works, New England peachblow (advertised as Wild Rose, but called

For more information, see this book.

Peach Blow at the plant): Translucent, shading from rose to white; acid or glossy finish; some pieces enameled and gilded.

Thomas Webb & Sons and Stevens and Williams (English firms): Peachblow-style cased art glass, shading from yellow to red; some pieces with cameo-type relief designs.

Gunderson Glass Co.: Produced peachblow-type art glass to order during the 1950s; shades from an opaque faint tint of pink, which is almost white, to a deep rose.

Marks: Pieces made in England are marked "Peach Blow" or "Peach Bloom."

Gundersen

Bottle, 2-1/2" d, 6" h, shaded pink to white **110.00**

Cruet, 8" h, 3-1/2" w, matte finish, ribbed shell handle, matching stopper with good color **875.00**

Cup and saucer **275.00**

Decanter, 10" h, 5" w, Pilgrim Canteen form, acid finish, deep raspberry to white, applied peachblow ribbed handle, deep raspberry stopper **950.00**

Goblet, 7-1/4" h, 4" d top, glossy finish, deep color, applied Burmese glass base **285.00**

Jug, 4-1/2" h, 4" w, bulbous, applied loop handle, acid finish **450.00**

Pitcher, 5-1/2" h, Hobnail, matte finish, white with hint of pink on int., orig label **550.00**

Plate, 8" d, luncheon, deep raspberry to pale pink, matte finish **375.00**

Punch cup, acid finish **275.00**

Tumbler, 3-3/4" h, matte finish . . **275.00**

Morgan vase, Hobbs, Brockunier & Co., satin finish, deep blush at neck and shoulders gradually changes to buttery-cream lower half, satin Griffin holder with minor chips, 2" h holder, 8" h vase, $1,750. Photo courtesy of Clarence and Betty Maier.

Urn, 8-1/2" h, 4-1/2" w, two applied "M" handles, sq cut base, matte finish **550.00**

Vase
  5" h, 6" w, ruffled top, pinched-in base **525.00**
  9" h, 3-1/4" w, Tappan, acid finish **425.00**

Wine glass, 5" h, glossy finish . **175.00**

Harrach

Vase
  8" h, pink shading to rose glossy cased ground, enameled gold trailing vine, propeller mark **250.00**
  12-1/4" h, stick, pink shading to deep rose cased ground, enameled flowers, propeller mark **300.00**

Mount Washington

Bowl, 3" x 4", shading from deep rose to bluish-white, MOP satin int... **150.00**

Bride's basket, shades of pink, replated Meriden frame **650.00**

Low bowl, 5" d, 2-12" h, deep rose shading to amber, cased in powder blue, gold enameled trailings .. **365.00**

Milk pitcher, 7" w handle to spout, 5-3/4" h, thin walls, gray handle **3,950.00**

Vase, 8-1/4" h, lily form, satin finish **1,850.00**

New England

Celery vase, 7" h, 4" w, sq top, deep raspberry with purple highlights shading to white **785.00**

Cruet, 6-3/4" h, 4" d at base, petticoat form, applied white handle and stopper, three lip top, acid finish **1,950.00**

Pear, 4-1/2" h, translucent, shading from white to pink **100.00**

Pitcher, 6-3/4" h, 7-1/2" w, 3-1/4" w at top, bulbous, sq top, applied frosted handle, 10 rows of hobs, Sandwich **550.00**

Spooner, sq top, acid finish. ... **825.00**

Tumbler, 3-3/4" h, shiny finish, deep color upper third, middle fading to creamy white bottom, thin walls . **445.00**

Vase
  3-1/4" h, 2-1/2" d, bulbous bottom, ring around neck, flaring top, matte finish **550.00**
  5-1/2" h, satin finish, bulbous. **485.00**
  7-3/4" h, lily, glossy, shading from near white to dark pink rim . **875.00**
  10-1/2" h, 5" w at base, bulbous gourd shape, deep raspberry with fuchsia highlights to white, coloring extends two-thirds way down, four dimpled sides **1,450.00**

Webb

Cologne, 5" h, bulbous, raised gold floral branches, silver hallmarked dome top **900.00**

Creamer, satin finish, coralene dec, rolled rim, flat base.......... **650.00**

Finger bowl, 4-1/2" d, cased... **195.00**

Vase
  5" h, glossy cased ground, enameled gold leafy vines . **100.00**
  8-1/2" h, glossy cased rose shading to pink, flat-sided, enameled gold ferns and flowers, four applied amber feet.............. **690.00**
  10" h, cased deep crimson to pink, cascading green leafy branch, gold highlights......... **1,265.00**

10-1/2" h, glossy cased ground, dec with gold and gray cascading vine, insert **225.00**

Wheeling

Cruet, 6-3/4" h, Hobbs, Brockunier & Co., teardrop shape, mahogany spout, neck, and shoulder changes to butter yellow, amber applied handle and faceted stopper............ **1,085.00**

Ewer, 6-3/4" h, 4" w, glossy finish, duck bill top, applied amber loop handle **3,500.00**

Morgan vase, 8" h, shiny finish, mahogany neck and shoulder, butterscotch on one side, other side with darker butterscotch with red overtones.................. **585.00**

Morgan vase with stand, 10" h, Hobbs, Brockunier & Co., satin finish, deep blush at neck and shoulders shades to buttery cream, satin Griffin holder with small flake....... **1,750.00**

Mustard, SP cov and handle .. **475.00**

Pear, hollow blown, 4-3/4" w, 3" w base, matte finish, bright red and yellow, white lining, very tip of stem gone ... **900.00**

Punch cup, 2-1/2" h, Hobbs, Brockunier................. **535.00**

Tumbler, shiny finish, deep colored upper third shades to creamy base **385.00**

Vase
  9-1/4" h, ball shaped body, 5" slender neck, shape #11 .. **735.00**
  11-1/2" h, creamy int., enameled dogwood branches **750.00**

Vase, Mt. Washington, shape #148, satin finish, c1885, pale pink color shading to pale blue-gray base, 8-1/2" h, $1,975. Photo courtesy of Clarence and Betty Maier.

Vase, Webb, frilly ruffled top, gold and silver butterfly hovering over gold and silver branch and prunus blossoms, smaller branch on reverse, knurled amber handles, signed "10," 4-1/2" h, $485. Photo courtesy of Clarence and Betty Maier.

Left: pitcher, Wheeling, handle, 9-1/2" h, $475; right: vase, Webb, gold enamel dragonfly and branch decoration, 11" h, $350. Photo courtesy of Woody Auctions.

PEKING GLASS

History: Peking glass is a type of cameo glass of Chinese origin. Its production began in the 1700s and continued well into the 19th century. The background color of Peking glass may be a delicate shade of yellow, green, or white. One style of white background is so transparent that it often is referred to as the "snowflake" ground. The overlay colors include a rich garnet red, deep blue, and emerald green.

Bowl, green overlay, white ground, carved prunus branches, flowers, and butterfly, late Ching dynasty **375.00**

Cup, 2-1/2" h, deep form, gently flaring rim, ring foot, continual band of overlapping dragons, cloud collar border, lappet border, red overlay, Snowflake **2,185.00**

Cup, footed, Ch'ien Lung period (1736-95), carved opaque pale lemon yellow, two dragons form handle, geometric symbols, Chinese seal-type characters on sides, 3" d, 2-1/4" h, $750. Photo courtesy of Cowan's Historic Americana Auctions.

Vase, cameo green carved to white, scene of man riding tiger, next to tree-lined mountain stream, Mei-Ping, some wear on base, 10-1/4" h, $350. Photo courtesy of Cowan's Historic Americana Auctions.

Snuff bottle, flattened ovoid, enameled birds perched on flowering tree, marked "Ku Yueh Hsuan Ancient Moon Terrace," Chinese, Qianlong, $550. Photo courtesy of Sloan's Auctioneers & Appraisers.

Dish, 11-3/4" l, flattened round form, bright yellow, 19th C **850.00**

Ginger jar, cov, 9-1/4" h, three different scenes on white grounds, coral-colored ground **750.00**

Snuff bottle, green over white, floral design, attached spoon, carved ivory top **400.00**

Vase

7" h, high shouldered form, ducks swimming among tall lotus plants, green overlay, white ground, pr **500.00**

8-3/4" h, carved green over white lotus design, small rim chip **900.00**

9-1/4" h, ovoid, opaque raised yellow flowers, translucent yellow ground, 19th C **525.00**

10-1/2" h, turquoise blue, interior painted landscape, China, early 20th C **450.00**

Vase, China, early 20th C, turquoise blue, an interior painted landscape, 10-1/2" h, $500. Photo courtesy of Skinner Auctioneers and Appraisers.

PERFUME, COLOGNE, AND SCENT BOTTLES

History: The second half of the 19th century was the golden age for decorative bottles made to hold scents. These bottles were made in a variety of shapes and sizes.

An atomizer is a perfume bottle with a spray mechanism. Cologne bottles usually are larger and have stoppers that also may be used as applicators. A perfume bottle has a stopper that often is elongated and designed to be an applicator.

Scent bottles are small bottles used to hold a scent or smelling salts. A vinaigrette is an ornamental box or bottle that has a perforated top and is used to hold aromatic vinegar or smelling salts. Fashionable women of the late 18th and 19th centuries carried them in purses or slipped them into gloves in case of a sudden fainting spell.

Atomizer

Cambridge, 6-1/4" h, stippled gold, opaque jade, orig silk lined box. **140.00**

Cameo, Gallé, 8" h, lavender flowers and foliage, shaded yellow and frosted ground **1,250.00**

Moser, 4-1/2" h, sapphire blue, gold florals, leaves, and swirls, melon ribbed body, orig gold top and bulb ... **275.00**

Cologne

Art glass, 11" h, transparent green bottle, delicate floral design, colorless pedestal foot, faceted teardrop stopper **175.00**

Baccarat, 5-7/8" h, colorless, panel cut, matching stopper **75.00**

Cut glass, 7" h, cranberry cut to colorless, cane cut, matching stopper **250.00**

Paperweight, 7" h, 5" d, , double overlay, crimson red over white over colorless squatty bottle, five oval facet windows reveal concentric millefiore cane int., matching stopper **460.00**

Vaseline, 4-1/2" h, vaseline, attributed to New England Glass Co., flint, orig stopper **225.00**

Perfume

Enamel, Continental

2-1/8" l, tapered colorless glass bottle encl in rect enamel case with hinged lid, pink ground, green

Iridescent gold/green perfume bottle with atomizer, $275. Photo courtesy of Joy Luke Auctions.

ground roundels with white birds and flowers, crenellated surrounds, late 18th/early 19th C **115.00**

3-1/4" l, pear shape, silvered metal lid with bale, green ground, two central cartouches of courting couples, late 18th/early 19th C
. . . . **215.00**

Glass

3-7/8" l, Continental, early 19th C, latticino, tapered ovoid, clear, white, and yellow strands, ext. of bottle with horizontal ribbing, silver gilt floral engraved hinged lid, enclosing glass stopper . . . **425.00**

4" h, French, late 19th/early 20th C, baluster form, blue opaline bottle, gilt metal floral overlay, foot, and neck mounts, hinged lid set with shell cameo of young man in feathered cap **200.00**

4-3/4" h, cameo, opaque glass body, acid etched cobalt blue leaf design
. . . . **165.00**

4-3/4" l, cut glass, colorless, pistol-form, etched silver-gilt mounts, short chain, spring-action trigger opens lid set with maker's medallion, French, late 19th/early 20th C **1,380.00**

5-1/4" h, French, late 19th C, double, ruby glass, tapered cylindrical body with floral and garter engraved silver mounts, one end with round hinged lid opening to glass stopper, other end with round lid hinged silver mount at center, opening to vinaigrette grille, ends mounted with link chain . . . **575.00**

Glass and silver, Victorian, London, 1885, fish-form flask, 6-1/4" l, green and metallic flecked blown glass body, gilt over enamel detailing of scales and

eyes, engraved silver tail, retailed by W.Thornill & Co., fitted velvet lined case
. . . . **1,500.00**

Porcelain

2-1/2" l, Continental, late 19th C, underglaze blue crossed swords mark, leg-form, garter and pale blue shoe, flat metal lid **230.00**

2-1/2" l, Meissen, Germany, late 19th C, courting couple, ivy covered tree trunk, enamel and gilt detailing, orig stopper **635.00**

3-1/4" l, Continental, late 18th/19th C, swaddled infant shape, enamel detailing, silvertone domed lid, tapered base **325.00**

3-1/2" l, Brenner & Liebmann, Eduard Liebmann Porcelain Factory, Germany, late 19th C, oblong, Blue Onion style underglaze dec, red overpainted detailing, silver gilt neck and stopper mount **290.00**

Silver gilt, 1-3/4" l, shield shaped, collet-set heart-shaped opal applied to front, surrounded by applied ropetwist, green and yellow enamel dec, back engraved with leafy scrolls, conical screw-in stopper, Hungarian, 20th C
. . . . **115.00**

Silver plate, Victorian, London, 1885, 2-3/4" l, bud shape, engraved rim, all over repoussé reeding, glass int.
. . . . **190.00**

Sterling silver

2-3/4" l, Victorian, London, 1885, bud shape, engraved rim, body with all

Lalique, La Violette, perfume bottle for Gabilla, c1925, clear glass with violet enamel, molded "LALIQUE," $3,500. Photo courtesy of David Rago Auctions.

over repoussé reeding, glass int.
. . . . **175.00**

3-1/4" l, Birmingham, England, 1897, hinged heart-shaped case, domed lid, emb angel dec, gilt int. with heart-shaped green glass bottle, monogrammed, 2 troy oz . . **230.00**

Sterling silver and champleve enamel, Gorham, everted oblong flask with diapered champleve centered by stars on cobalt blue enamel ground, small silver screw-in lid, late 19th/early 20th C **290.00**

Scent

2-1/2" h, amethyst, teardrop shape, emb sunburst design **225.00**

3" h, agate, flattened globe form, silver hinged rim and screw cap, marked "Black, Starr, & Frost" **260.00**

3" h, porcelain, egg shape, Germany or Russia, late 19th C, dec with scene of pedestrians in front of building and monument, gilt border, reserves of gilt foliate scrolls, corn and brass stopper
. . . . **1,955.00**

4" d, satin glass, bridal white, 24 white vertical stripes, 12 silk ribbons alternating with 12 muted satin ribbons, sterling silver flip top cap, collar stamped "CS, FS, STd, SILr," engraved name **400.00**

3-5/8" l, silver, Japanese, late 19th/early 20th C, tear shape, molded dragon dec on stippled ground, attached silver chains, approx 1 troy oz **450.00**

Lalique, Perles, c1926, opalescent glass, molded "R. LALIQUE," $750. Photo courtesy of David Rago Auctions.

3-3/4" h, ivory, figural, woman holding basket of flowers in one hand, fan in other, polychrome dec, Japan . . . **90.00**

4-1/8" h, blown, colorless, cranberry and white stripes, white and gold metallic twist **95.00**

Set

Perfume and etui, 3-3/4" l, France, late 18th/early 19th C, enameled pear shape, white ground, enamel dec with floral sprays, opening at center to storage box base, lid mounted with bird-form perfume stopper **490.00**

Perfume and vinaigrette, 3-1/2" l, paneled cylindrical segmented clear glass bottle, mounted on one end with engine turned gold lid, with lappet neck, top set with central seed pearl surrounded by band of calibre cut turquoises, other end of bottle set with flat monogrammed lid with lappet band, opening to grille for vinaigrette, fitted Tiffany & Co. red morocco case, third quarter 18th C **1,840.00**

Perfume bottles, three 3-3/8" h square bottles mounted with gilt-metal quatrefoil neck bands, gilt-metal rope twist-edged lids set with painted miniatures on ivory under glass, each depicting European city scene, enclosed in 6" l, 2-3/4" w, 3-3/8" h leather carrying case, mounted with mother-of-pearl bands accented by gilt metal flowerheads, Continental, late 19th C **575.00**

Vinaigrette

Cranberry glass, 2-1/4" x 1", rect, allover cutting, enameled tiny pink roses, green leaves, gold dec, hinged lid, stopper, finger chain **185.00**

Paperweight perfume bottle with internal orange flowers, 5-1/2" h, $65. Photo courtesy of Joy Luke Auctions.

Cut glass, 3-7/8" l, cobalt blue, yellow flashing, sterling silver overlay, emb sterling silver cap **125.00**

English, silver

7/8" l, tooled purse shape, gilded int., John Turner, Birmingham hallmarks, 1792 . . . . **250.00**

1" w, 1-1/2" l, marker's mark "JT," Birmingham, c1845, rect, foliate engraved lid, base with molded scroll rims, gilt interior with pierced and engraved dec, approx 1 troy oz **290.00**

1-1/4" l, tooled purse shape, gilded int., S. Pemberton, Birmingham hallmarks, 1790 . . . . **220.00**

European, silver, late 19th/early 20th C, 3" shaped as three squashes on vine, engine-turned textured dec, threaded bases, largest with pierced grate to interior, 1 troy oz **350.00**

Victorian, late 19th C, staghorn, 2-1/2" l rough-textured horn mounted with thistle-cast lid, quatrefoil neck band, horn with guilloche strapping, short link chain **350.00**

PETERS AND REED POTTERY

History: J. D. Peters and Adam Reed founded their pottery company in South Zanesville, Ohio, in 1900. Common flowerpots, jardinieres, and cooking wares comprised the majority of their early output. Occasionally, art pottery was attempted, but it was not until 1912 that their Moss Aztec line was introduced and widely accepted. Other art wares include Chromal, Landsun, Montene, Pereco, and Persian.

Peters retired in 1921 and Reed changed the name of the firm to Zane Pottery Company.

Marks: Marked pieces of Peters and Reed Pottery are unknown.

Jardiniere, Moss Aztec, c1925, unmarked, few small chips to decoration, 9" x 9-1/2" d, 9" h, $175. Photo courtesy of David Rago Auctions.

Vase, Moss Aztec, corseted, stylized flowers and leaves, unmarked, 4-1/4" d, 10-1/2" h, $200. Photo courtesy of David Rago Auctions.

Bowl, 9" d, 3-1/4" h, closed-in rim, round tapering bowl, raised budding branches and berries in relief, matte green glaze, couple of chips on branch **175.00**

Doorstop, cat, yellow **375.00**

Ewer, 11" h, orange and yellow raised grapes dec, brown ground **50.00**

Jardinière, 9-1/2" d, 9" h, Moss Aztec, c1925, unmarked, few small chips to dec **200.00**

Mug, blended glaze **40.00**

Pitcher, 4" h, green and yellow raised fern leaves, gloss dark brown ground **65.00**

Vase

4-1/4" d, 10-1/2" h, Moss Aztec, corseted, stylized flowers and leaves, unmarked **230.00**

10-1/2" h, squatty base, one in yellow, blue, and black dripping glaze, other in orange, yellow and black dripping glaze, unmarked, price for pr **225.00**

Vessel, 5-1/4" h, Sprig Dawn, unmarked **95.00**

PEWTER

History: Pewter is a metal alloy consisting mostly of tin with small amounts of lead, copper, antimony, and bismuth added to make the shaping of products easier and to increase the hardness of the material. The metal can be cast, formed around a mold, spun, easily cut, and soldered to form a wide variety of utilitarian articles.

Pewter was known to the ancient Chinese, Egyptians, and Romans. England was the primary source of pewter for the American colonies for nearly

150 years until the American Revolution ended the embargo on raw tin, allowing the small American pewter industry to flourish until the Civil War.

Note: The listings concentrate on the American and English pewter forms most often encountered by the collector.

Baptismal bowl, 9" d, Boardman, Hartford, CT, stamped "BX," marked "Jacobs," 19th C **950.00**

Basin, 9" d, Parks Boyd, Philadelphia, PA, c1771-1819, touch mark on center int. **550.00**

Beaker

4-3/8" h, unidentified maker, faint touch mark under mid-bands, flaring lip, minor dents **60.00**

5-1/8" h, Thomas D. and Sherman Boardman, Hartford, CT, marked "Laughlin," c1810-30 . . . . . **650.00**

Bud vase, 5" d, 10-1/2" h, Secessionist style, orig green glass insert, peacock feather emb, stamped "WMF" . . **865.00**

Butter plate, 6" d, American, unmarked **70.00**

Candlesticks, attributed to Horman, Cincinnati, one 8", other 10" h, $245. Photo courtesy of Cowan's Historic Americana Auctions.

Candlesticks, pr

8-3/4" h, marked "Jacobs," 1822-71 . . . . **950.00**

9-3/4" h, unmarked American, attributed to CT, with bobeches **275.00**

Charger

12-1/2" d, faint angel touch on back, engraved "C. K." along rim, tooled rim around edge, knife marks, minor dents **200.00**

13-1/4" d, touchmarks for Thomas Danford II, knife scratches and areas of pitting **660.00**

Coffeepot, cov

7" h, Israel Trask, Beverly, MA, lighthouse, bright cut engraving **350.00**

11-1/4" h, Boardman & Hart, Hartford, CT, second quarter 19th C, double belly form, dec with bands of incised line, footed base, minor imperfections **435.00**

13-1/2" h, Reed and Barton, marked "Leonard Reed & Barton 3500" **250.00**

Communion chalice, 6-1/4" h, unmarked American, handles removed, pr **200.00**

Creamer, 5-7/8" h, unmarked American, teapot shape **250.00**

Coffeepot, floral finial, original black paint on handle, marked "Sellew," Cincinnati, minor oxidation, wear to paint, 11" h, $250. Photo courtesy of Cowan's Historic Americana Auctions.

Deep dish

8-5/8" d, John Brunstrom, two touch marks on reverse **295.00**

11" d, Samuel Kilbourn, Baltimore, Maryland, 1814-30, impressed maker's touchmark on the reverse, minor dents **650.00**

13" d, B. Barns, Philadelphia, PA, two touch marks on reverse, eagle with "B. BARNS" in banner and "B BARNS/PHILADA" in rect . . **500.00**

13" d, Thomas Danforth, III, Philadelphia, PA 1717-1818, reverse with eagle touch mark and "T.D.", separate "T. DANFORTH/ PHILDA" touch mark **475.00**

Flagon

12-1/2" h, attributed to Israel Trask, Beverly, MA, 1807-56, minor dents **300.00**

14" h, Thomas D. and Sherman Boardman, Hartford, CT, marked "Laughlin," 1810-30 . . . . . **3,750.00**

Inkwell, 1-3/4" h, small circular lid, four quill holes surrounding wide flat circular base, replaced glass receptacle, 19th C **225.00**

Ladle, 13" l, plain pointed handle, touch mark "WH" in oval, 19th C **65.00**

Whale oil lamp, unmarked, egg/acorn shaped font, double burner, stepped round base, 9" h, $225. Photo courtesy of James D. Julia, Inc.

Lamp

5-3/4" h plus brass and tin whale oil burner, Putnam touch, James Putnam, Madison, MA, some splits in rim of base **315.00**

7" h plus fluid burner, unmarked American, attributed to Meriden, reeded detail on base, ear handle, light pitting **110.00**

8-1/2" h plus burner, Yale and Curtis, NY 1 touch, matching fluid burner missing, snuffers and one brass tube loose **190.00**

Measure

2-3/8" to 8" h, assembled set, bellied, English, minor damage . . . **550.00**

5-3/4" h, John Warne, English, brass rim, battered, old repair, quart **100.00**

Mug, quart

4" h, Thomas Danforth Boardman, Hartford, CT, tankard, partial "T.D.B." touch, some battering, soldered repairs **500.00**

5-7/8" h, Samuel Hamlin, Hartford, Middletown, CT, and Providence RI, dent at base **625.00**

Pitcher

6" h, Freeman Porter, Westbrook, ME, two quart **225.00**

6-1/2" h, Continental, swirl design, hinged lid, angel touch **85.00**

Plate, double marked "G. Lightner, Baltimore, Md," minor bends, short split in shoulder, shallow knife scratches, 8-1/2" h, $275. Photo courtesy of Cowan's Historic Americana Auctions.

Plate

7-3/4" d, Thomas Danforth III, Philadelphia, 1717-1818, reverse with eagle touch mark and "T. D.," separate 'T. DANFORTH/PHILDA" touch mark **350.00**

7-7/8" d, Joseph Danforth lion touch, minor wear **330.00**

8-3/8" d, David Melville, Newport, RI, 1776-94, marked on base, knife marks, minor pitting **500.00**

8-3/4" d, John Dolbeare, rim stamped "ABB" and "B/RE," reverse with three touches . . **80.00**

8-7/8" d, Thomas Danforth III, Philadelphia, 1717-1818, reverse with eagle touch mark and "T. D.," separate 'T. DANFORTH/PHILDA" touch mark **275.00**

Platter, 28-3/4" l, Townsend and Compton, London, pierced insert, marked "Cotterell" **2,400.00**

Porringer

3-7/8" d, cast handle, marked "TD & SB" touch (Thomas Danford Boardman, et al, Hartford) . . **220.00**

5-3/8" d, Boardman & Hart, Hartford, CT, second quarter 19th C, Boardman-style handle engraved with "RNE" and anchors, reverse

Porringers, pair, attributed to Richard Lee, handle has Lee configuration, unsigned, minor dents, 5" d, $575. Photo courtesy of James D. Julia, Inc.

with lion touchmark flanked by "TD," minor imperfections . **490.00**

5-1/4" d, 7-1/8" l, Westtown School, PA, form, possibly by Elisha Kirk, York, PA, plain tab handle with hole for hanging **775.00**

Soup plate, 8-7/8" d, unmarked Continental, angel touch **75.00**

Sugar bowl, 6" h, Ashril Griswold, Meriden, CT, eagle touch **490.00**

Syrup pitcher, 4-1/2" h, hinged lid, unmarked, American **220.00**

Tankard, spout shaped like eagle's head, wings coming off body, unmarked, 13-1/2" h, $225. Photo courtesy of Woody Auctions.

Tablespoon, rattail handle, heart on back of bowl, marked "L. B.," (Luther Boardman, MA and CT). set of six **330.00**

Tea box, 5-1/2" l, 5" h, oblong, leaf dec handle top, four bun feet, marked "Littlejohn," two feet bent **150.00**

Teapot

6-3/4" h, Roswell Gleason, Dorchester, MA, eagle touch **495.00**

6-3/4" h, Ashbil Griswold, Meriden, CT, eagle touch, some battering and repairs **200.00**

Snuffbox, presentation type, dated 1785, illegible mark on inside of lid, broken hinge, 2-3/4" l, $80. Photo courtesy of Sanford Alderfer Auction Company.

7" h, Eben Smith, Beverly, MA, 1813-56, minor pitting and scratches **375.00**

7-3/4" h, Smith & Co touch, (Albany, NY,) some battering and damage **175.00**

Tobacco box, 4-3/8" h, Thomas Stanford, cast eagle feet, engraved label with scroll work "Thomas Stanford, Gospel Hill, 1838," wear, final and one foot soldered **125.00**

Tumbler, 2-3/4" h, Thomas Danforth Boardman, Hartford, CT, partial eagle touch **175.00**

Warming platter, 19" l, hot water type, tree and well, marked "Dixon & Sons," English, repairs **250.00**

PHOENIX GLASS

History: Phoenix Glass Company, Beaver, Pennsylvania, was established in 1880. Known primarily for commercial glassware, the firm also produced a molded, sculptured, cameo-type line from the 1930s until the 1950s.

Ashtray, Phlox, large, white, frosted **80.00**

Bowl, 14" d, nude diving girl, white **495.00**

Creamer and sugar, Catalonia, light green **45.00**

Lamp shade, ceiling type, 12" d, pale pink, emb floral dec **115.00**

Umbrella stand, 18" h, Thistle, pearlized blue ground **450.00**

For more information, see this book

Vase, bulbous, molded lovebirds, opalescent pink, 9-1/4" d, 10-1/4" h, $365. Photo courtesy of David Rago Auctions.

Vase, pillow shape, three geese in relief on each side, brown ground, several tiny lip chips, 11" w, 9" h, $135. Photo courtesy of James D. Julia, Inc.

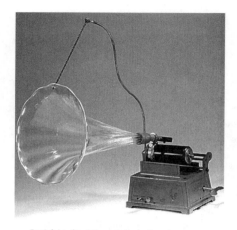

Pathé Le Gaulois, original glass horn, 1900-1903, $5,230. Photo courtesy of Auction Team Breker.

Vase

4-3/4" d, 4-3/4" h, Jewel, brown over milk glass **200.00**

6" w, 7" h, white ferns, blue ground **130.00**

6-1/2" w at top, 3-1/2" d base, 7-1/2" h, blue, white floral dec, orig sticker, two chips on inside rim **190.00**

8" h, Daisy, pearlized daisies, light green ground, orig label . . . **360.00**

8-1/8" d, 11-3/4" h, Nude Scarf Dancers, light brown ground, cream figures, orig label . . **650.00**

10-3/4" h, Dogwood, green and white **600.00**

11" h, Wild rose, blown out, pearlized dec, dark rose ground, orig label **275.00**

14" h, Philodendron, blue, ormolu mounts **400.00**

Vase, green cameo floral and leaves decoration, feather type design at rim, white ground, 9-1/2" h, $210. Photo courtesy of James D. Julia, Inc.

PHONOGRAPHS

History: Early phonographs were commonly called "talking machines." Thomas A. Edison invented the first successful phonograph in 1877; other manufacturers followed with their variations.

Adviser: Lewis S. Walters.

Columbia

Grafonola, A. M. Graphophone Co., Bridgeport, CT, hardwood case, horizontal louvers in front . . **600.00**

HG cylinder player **2,400.00**

BQ cylinder player **1,200.00**

Decca, Junior, portable, leather case and handle **150.00**

Grobes Luxus-Trichter Grammophon, Maestrophone, giant brass horn, $4,700. Photo courtesy of Auction Team Breker.

Edison

Amberola 30 . . . . **400.00**

Army-Navy, WWI **1,200.00**

Diamond Disc VV-19, William and Mary **500.00**

Excelsior, coin op **2,500.00**

Fireside, with original horn . . **900.00**

Gem, maroon, 2- to 4-minute reproducer **1,700.00**

Opera, has moving mandrel and fixed reproducer **2,500.00**

Standard, Model A, oak case with metal horn **550.00**

Triumph, with cygnet horn, mahogany case **2,500.00**

Graphone

12.5 oak case, metal horn, retailer's mark, cylinder **450.00**

15.0 oak case with columns on corners, nickel-plated platform, metal horn, stenciled cast-iron parts **725.00**

Home Grand, oak case, nickel-plated works, #6 spring motor **1,300.00**

Harvard, trumpet style horn . . . **300.00**

Kalamazoo, Duplex, reproducer, original horns with decals, pat. date 1904 . . . . **3,300.00**

Odeon Talking Machine Co., table model, crank wind, brass horn, straight tone arm **500.00**

RCA-Victor, "45" Bakelite Record Player **65.00**

Silvertone (Sears), two reproducers **500.00**

Sonora, Gothic Deluxe, walnut case, triple spring, gold-plated parts, automatic stop and storage . . . **400.00**

Edison, oak case, domed top, old varnished finish, original horn and crank, sold with 60 cylinders, needs new belt, 12-1/4" x 16" x 8-3/4", $415. Photo courtesy of Garth's Auctions, Inc.

Talk-O-Phone, Brooke, table model, oak case rope decorations, steel horn **200.00**

Victor

Credenza, crank **1,100.00**
Monarch, table model, corner columns, brass bell horn. **1,500.00**
School House **2,500.00**
Victor I, mahogany case, corner columns, bell horn. **1,500.00**
Victor II, oak case, smooth oak horn **5,500.00**
Victor III, papier-mâché horn **1,400.00**
Victor V, oak case, corner columns, no horn **1,500.00**
Victor VI, oak case, no horn **4,000.00**

PHOTOGRAPHS

History: A vintage print is a positive image developed from the original negative by the photographer or under the photographer's supervision at the time the negative is made. A non-vintage print is a print made from an original negative at a later date. It is quite common for a photographer to make prints from the same negative over several decades. Changes between the original and subsequent prints usually can be identified. Limited edition prints must be clearly labeled.

Album

"A Souvenir of the Harriman Alaska Expedition, volumes I and II,"" 251 photographs, more than 100 by Edward Curtin, additional images by Edward H. Harriman, C. Hart Merriam, G. K. Gilbert, D. G. Inverarity, and others, silver prints, various sizes to 6" x 7-1/2", several with handwritten credit and date in negative, others with copyright, album disbound and defective, title pages and map laid in, prints generally in excellent condition, 1899, pr **21,850.00**
"Kodak," 104 photographs of Eastern and Midwestern U. S. by Wm Hoblitzell, prints document his train ride across country from MD to Missoula, MT, unposed glimpses of trains and local stations, Missoulan bicyclists and Native-Americans on horseback, handwritten captions and/or dates on mount rectos, mounted four per page recto and verso, oblong 4to, gilt-lettered morocco, spine and edges worn, pgs loose, photographer's handstamp on front and rear pastdowns, ties missing, 1890-91 . . . . **575.00**

Albumen print

Lincoln, Abraham **1,550.00**
View of the Oswego Harbor, arched top, 13" x 16-1/2", title, photographer, and date printed on label affixed below image, 1869 . . . . **1,380.00**

Ambrotype, William Gannaway

Brownlow, known as Parson Brownlow, the fightin' preacher, half plate **3,190.00**

Cabinet card

Early, Gen. Jabal A., sgd, 6-1/4" x 4-1/4" **1,840.00**

Albumin, titled on printed mount "The President and General McClellan on the Battle-field of Antietam," Lincoln with General McClellan in tent, image titled in mount with date of October 4, 1862 and credit given to Gardner as photographer and Brady as publisher, 9" x 7" albumin, mounted to 14" x 16.5" heavy stock, $6,600. Photo courtesy of Sanford Alderfer Auction Company.

Garfield, J.A., sgd, 6-1/2" x 4-1/4" **1,495.00**
Lincoln, Abraham, lengthy inscription to Lucy Speed, 6-1/2" x 4-1/4". **1,840.00**
Sitting Bull, D. F. Barry, titled, copyrighted, dated, and Barry's imprint on recto, Bismarck D. T. imprint on mount verso, 1885, 7" x 5" **1,495.00**
Wilde, Oscar, age 32, Alfred Ellis & Wallery imprint on mounts recto and verso, period German inscription handwritten on mount verso, 1892, 5" x 4" **1,100.00**

CDV, carte de visite

Davis, Jefferson, President of Confederacy **80.00**
Lee, Robert E., sgd, large bold signature, 3-3/4" x 2-1/2". **4,025.00**
Lincoln, Abraham, taken by Matthew Brady, 1864. . . . . **1,045.00**
Mrs. Lincoln, portrait with spirit of Abe behind her, Wm Mumler's Boston imprint on mount verso, c1869 . . . . **1,725.00**

Daguerreotype

Afro-American woman, seated, keeps-up in chair, patterned dress, white apron and head wrap, sixth-plate image, unknown photographer, orig seal, slight tarnishing at ends of matte

CDV, unknown Union Colonel, seated portrait, wearing military frock, colonel's eagles on shoulders of coat, c1860, both Brady & Co. backmark and Brady with Washington location beneath image on obverse, card exhibits minor corner bumps and slight spotting to image, $175. Photo courtesy of Sanford Alderfer Auction Company.

opening, full leatherette case, c1850 . . . . **4,775.00**

Sell, John Todhunter, seated young child, tinted, sixth plate by M. A. Root, Philadelphia, stamped on matt, orig seal, some discoloration to mat, damaged leatherette case, c1840 . . . . **475.00**

Store front, four-story brick building, signage on building, crates pilled in front, man with top hat, unknown photographer, quarter-plate, image not sealed, plate marked "Chapman," leatherette case with some damage, c1850 . . . **4,775.00**

Unknown gentleman, sixth-plate image by Robert Cornelius, orig brass Cornelius frame with repeating diamond pattern, orig seal, affixed yellow paper label on reverse "Daguerreotype Miniatures by R. Cornelius, Eighth Street, above Chestnut, Philadelphia," minor oxidation to image, slight mineral deposits on glass, c1840 . . . . **13,200.00**

Unknown gentleman, seated, sixth-plate image by W & F Langenheim, Philadelphia Exchange, re-sealed image, verdigris on mat, heavy tarnish halo at mat opening, leatherette case with photographer's name on pad, c1840 . . . . **425.00**

Unknown woman, seated, dark taffeta dress, quarter-plate image by unknown photographer, image resealed, paper matte, leatherette case with hinge separation, c1840 . . . . **395.00**

Unknown woman, seated, sixth-plate image by W & F Langenheim, Philadelphia Exchange, re-sealed image, verdigris on mat, heavy tarnish halo at mat opening, leatherette case with photographer's name on pad, c1840 . . . . **425.00**

Unknown woman, well dressed in dark taffeta dress, lace collar and cuffs, leather gloves, portrait brooch at neck, slight tint on cheeks, by Collins, 3rd & Chestnut St., Philadelphia, half-plate, orig seal, Collins paper label, full leatherette case, c1840-50. **450.00**

Magic lantern slides, group of 320 photographic images from 1920s and 1930s, Atlantic City views and events, yachting, fireboats, Mohonk (NY), Duluth (MN), etc. housed in four individual carrying cases, several slides cracked **230.00**

Photograph

Aspens, New Mexico, 1958, by Ansel Adams, sgd "Ansel Adams" in ink on mount, identified on label from Boston gallery on reverse, 19-1/2" x 15-1/2", framed. **6,325.00**

Portrait of Albert Einstein, c1938, by Lotte Jacobi, sgd "Lotte Jacobi" in pencil lower right, 9-3/4" x 7", framed **1,265.00**

Portrait of Marc Chagall and His Daughter in His Studio, by Lotte Jacobi, sgd "Lotte Jacobi" in pencil lower right, 6-3/4" x 5-1/2", framed **300.00**

Postcard, real photo, Thomas A. Edison, sgd, Pach Bros, 1904, 5-1/4" x 3-1/4" **3,220.00**

Silver print, Chief Hairy Chin, dressed as Uncle Sam, photographer's (D. F. Barry) blindstamp on recto, 1889, printed c1900, 6-1/4" x 4" **825.00**

Tintype

Family, identified on mat "Marshall Kimpton," man wearing military coat, wife wearing elaborate hat, huge bow, daughter stands behind, ninth plate, cased, minor bends, case hinge has old taped repair **150.00**

Unidentified Union soldier with rifle and bayonet, 1/6th plate . . . **360.00**

PIANO BABIES

History: In the late 1900s, a well decorated home had a parlor equipped with a piano, which usually was covered by a lovely shawl. To hold the shawl in place, piano babies were used. Piano babies are figures of babies, usually made of unglazed bisque. These "Piano Babies" range in size from three inches to more than 20 inches. They were made in a variety of poses—sitting up, crawling, lying on their tummies, and lying on their backs.

Most piano babies were produced in Germany and France. There were more than 15 factories in Germany that produced this type of bisqueware. Among them, Hertwig and Co., Julius Heubach, Royal Rudolstadt, Simon and Halbig, Kling and Co, and Gerbruder Heubach, were the most prolific. Many of these manufacturers also made dolls and carried the artistry required for fine doll making to their piano baby creations.

Many of the piano babies found today were manufactured by the Heubach Brothers (1820-1945) in Germany, whose rising sun mark is well known. However, many pieces left factories with no mark. The Heubach factory is well known also for creating the same baby but in different sizes. The Heubach babies are well known for their realistic facial features, as well as their attention to minute details, such as intaglio eyes, small teeth looking out from lips, blonde hair, blue eyes, etc.

Adviser: Jerry Rosen.

3-1/8", baby crawling on the floor, holding small cat, beaded dec. **150.00**

3-1/4" h, baby with curl, sitting upright, hands on legs, white gown, blue intaglio eyes, pink cheeks, blue trim, unmarked **135.00**

3-1/2" h, seated boy, raising hands above head, white nightgown, pink trim, Heubach **225.00**

4" l, lying on back, left foot in air, white gown, blue trim, Heubach **200.00**

4" h, seated, holding rattle, yellow floral trimmed nightgown with large bows and gold beading **250.00**

4", sitting baby, bottle in hands, white gown, gold beaded trim **200.00**

4-1/2" h, Baby Stuart, lying on back with detailed hobnail bonnet, playing with toes **250.00**

4-1/2" h, girl sitting on swing, pink and blue dress with large floppy hat, holes through hands and string enabling her to swing from a shelf **250.00**

5", baby, lying on stomach, crawling, one leg in air, dressed in baby dress with blue ribbon on back, marked "Heubach" **250.00**

5", boy, lying on back, one foot in air, one arm raised **300.00**

5-1/2", crawling baby, one arm and right foot up, white gown, "9467" incised on bottom **125.00**

5-1/2", seated girl, arms crossed and resting in lap, wearing flowing nightgown and huge floppy hat, Heubach **300.00**

6" h, baby, all bisque, molded clothes, painted features, light brown hair, blue

Pair of bisque children, both holding teddy bears, wearing pink hats, blue and white ruffled collars, yellow dresses with gold dot floral decorated, white socks with blue trim, **$1,495 for pair.**

intaglio eyes, legs crossed at ankles, arms and hands positioned up and away from body, Heubach, marked with circular rising sun with H superimposed over C **450.00**
6-1/2" l, 13" h, boy, lying on tummy, stretched out, yellow gown with blue trim, blond hair, blue eyes, marked "5032 Germany" with crown and "R" in red, Meissen **650.00**
6-3/4" h, baby, sitting upright with hands out as if she is catching ball, blue intaglio eyes, pale green dress with brown and maroon design transfers, tiny white beads line collar **255.00**
7", baby, lying down, one leg in air, other holding plate of cookies, "7 – 3988" incised on bottom, price for pr **150.00**
7" l, 3-3/4" h, girl with rosy cheeks and bonnet, lying on tummy, holding doll in hand, feet up **150.00**
7-1/2" h, baby, all bisque, molded clothes, painted features, light brown hair, blue intaglio eyes, legs crossed at ankles, arms and hands positioned up and away from body, Heubach, marked with circular rising sun with H superimposed over C **650.00**
7-1/2", baby lying on back, hands touching toes of lifted leg, red mark "23/111" on underside **150.00**
7-1/2" h, Victorian, bisque baby in straw trunk, soft pink and white gown, blue and white socks, floral decoration on trunk, marked "cabin baggage" on front, unmarked **250.00**
7-3/4" h, baby with curl, sitting upright, hands on legs, white gown, blue intaglio eyes, pink cheeks, blue trim, Heubach **400.00**
8", baby, lying on stomach, crawling, one leg in air, dressed in baby dress with blue ribbon on back, marked "Heubach" **650.00**
8-1/4" w, 4-1/4" h, German bisque, crawling baby and toy bear, wearing nightcap, marked "Germany" . . . **800.00**
9-1/2" h, girl with floppy hat, finger pointed to mouth, no marking . . **250.00**
9-1/2" l, 5-1/2" h, baby lying down, white gown, pink bow on shoulder, beading around collar, bottom incised "23/109" on bottom **255.00**
10" h, girl, molded blond curls, intaglio blue eyes, rosy cheeks, smiling mouth with tiny teeth, dressed in period gown with blue ribbons on each side of dress yoke, standing in front of chair, incised Heubach sunburst **500.00**

PICKARD CHINA

History: The Pickard China Company was founded by Wilder Pickard in Chicago, Illinois, in 1897. Originally the company imported European china blanks, principally from the Havilands at Limoges, which were then hand painted. The firm presently is located in Antioch, Illinois.

For more information, see this book.

Bowl
6" d, Autumn Blackberries, sgd "O. Goess" (Otto Goess), 1905-10 mark **200.00**
8-1/2" d, shallow, fish dec, sgd "Motzfeldt" (Andrew Motzfeldt), 1903-05 mark **500.00**
9-1/2" d, 4-1/2" h, ftd, strawberries, white blossoms, and gooseberries dec, sgd "E. Challinor" (Edward Challinor), 1905-10 mark . . **300.00**
10" d, red and white tulips, gold dec, Limoges blank **230.00**

Cabinet plate
8-1/2" d, heavy gold enameled border, Limoges blank **175.00**
9" d, lilies, gold background, artist sgd "Yeschek" **100.00**

Celery set, two-handled oval dish, five matching salts, allover gold dec, 1925-30 mark **125.00**
Chocolate pot, white poppies, gilded band, sgd "Menges" (Edward Mentges), 1905-10 mark **350.00**

Claret set, claret jug, five tumblers, 11-1/2" d tray, Deserted Garden pattern, sgd "J. Nessy" (John Nessy), 1912-18 mark **2,600.00**

Coffee set
Aura Argenta Linear, coffee pot, creamer, sugar, six demitasse cups and saucers, two salt shakers, sgd "Hess" (Robert Hessler), 1910-12 marks **1,300.00**
Modern Conventional pattern, coffee pot sgd "Hessler" (Robert Hessler), 1910-12 mark, eight cups and saucers sgd "Hess & RH" (Robert Hessler), 1912-18 mark. . **1,450.00**

Creamer, 5-1/4" h, Tulip Conventional, sgd "Tomash" (Rudolph Tomascheko), 1903-05 mark **400.00**

Creamer and sugar
Deserted Garden pattern, sgd "J. Nessy" (John Nessy), 1912-18 mark **200.00**
White Poppies & Daisy, sgd, 1912-18 mark **250.00**

Demitasse cup and saucer
Gold Tracery Rose & Daisy pattern, green band, 1925-30 mark . . **40.00**
Poppy pattern, sgd "LOH" (John Loh), 1910-12, price for pr . **325.00**

Lemonade pitcher
Encrusted Honeysuckle pattern, 1919-22 mark **100.00**
Schoner Lemon pattern, sgd "Schoner" (Otto Schoner), 1903-05 mark **1,700.00**

Match holder, Rose & Daisy pattern, allover gold, 1925-30 . . . . **40.00**
Pin dish, violets dec **40.00**

Lemonade pitcher, Lilum Ornatum, white lilies, signed Beulet, 1910-1912 mark, 8" h, **$600.** *Photo courtesy of Joy Luke Auctions.*

Plate, grapes and leaves, etched gilded border, signed Coufall, 1903-1905 mark, 8-1/2" d, **$195.** *Photo courtesy of Joy Luke Auctions.*

Tea set, Metallic Grape pattern, all signed Hessler, 1905-1910 mark, **$750.** *Photo courtesy of Joy Luke Auctions.*

Plate

8-1/4" d, gooseberries dec, sgd "P. G." (Paul Gasper), 1912-18 mark **45.00**

8-1/2" d, blackberries and leaves, sgd "Beitler" (Joseph Beitler), 1903-15 . . . . **90.00**

8-1/2" d, Calla Lily pattern, sgd "Marker" (Curtis H. Marker), 1905-10 mark **225.00**

8-1/2" d, Gibson Narcissus pattern, sgd "E. Gibson" (Edward Gibson), 1903-05 mark **300.00**

8-1/2" d, Lilium Ornatum pattern, sgd "Beulet" (F. Beulet), 1910-12 mark **100.00**

8-3/4" d, Florida Moonlight, sgd "E. Challinor" (Edward Challinor), 1912-18 mark **2,300.00**

8-3/4" d, orange flowers, sgd "James" (Florence James), 1905-10 mark **100.00**

9" d, Yeschek Currants in Gold pattern, sgd "Blaha" (Joseph Blaha), 1905-10 mark **110.00**

Tankard, 16" h, hexagonal, Chrysanthemums, Lustre & Matte Red pattern, sgd "Rean" (Maxwell Rean Klipphahn), 1905-10 mark **950.00**

Tea set, cov teapot, creamer, cov sugar, Carnation Garden pattern, each sgd "Yeschek" (Joseph T. Yeschek), 1903-05 marks **2,600.00**

Vase

8" h, Golden Pheasant pattern, sgd "E. Challinor" (Edward Challinor), 1919-22 mark **500.00**

8-1/4" h, scenic, sgd "E. Challinor" (Edward Challinor), 1912-18 mark **425.00**

11" h, Calla Lily pattern, sgd "Marker" (Curtis H. Marker), 1905-10 mark **550.00**

13-3/4" h, two handles, scenic, birch trees, gilding, sgd "E. Challinor" (Edward Challinor), 1912-18 mark **1,900.00**

PICKLE CASTORS

For more information, see this book.

History: A pickle castor is a table accessory used to serve pickles. It generally consists of a silver-plated frame fitted with a glass insert, matching silver-plated lid, and matching tongs. Pickle castors were very popular during the Victorian era. Inserts are found in pattern glass and colored art glass.

Amberina, melon ribbed IVT insert, SP lid, ftd frame, lid, tongs, c1875-95 . . . . **700.00**

Amber, coin spot insert, E.G. Webster Bros. Quadruple plate frame with tongs, replaced old silver plate lid, 10-1/2" h, **$410.** *Photo courtesy of James D. Julia, Inc.*

Double, clear pressed glass inserts, Aurora silver-plated holder, 11" x 7", **$250.** *Photo courtesy of Woody Auctions.*

Colorless, 11-3/4" h, acid etched insert, floral dec with bird medallion, octagonal SP frame, marked "Meriden Co. 182" **200.00**

Cranberry, IVT insert, enameled blue and white florals, green leaves, shelf on frame dec with peacocks and other birds **325.00**

Double, vaseline, pickle leaves and pieces, resilvered frame **800.00**

Mt. Washington, 11" h, 6" d, decorated satin glass insert, blue enamel and painted yellow roses, green leaves, orange and yellow blossoms, silver-plated Rogers stand and tongs **875.00**

Opalescent, Daisy & Fern, blue, emb DQ floral jar, resilvered frame . . **450.00**

Pink, shiny pink Florette pattern insert, white int., bowed out frame **325.00**

PIGEON BLOOD GLASS

History: Pigeon blood refers to the deep orange-red-colored glassware produced around the turn of the century. Do not

For more information, see this book

Pickle castor, Inverted Thumbprint pattern insert, unmarked silver-plated frame with tongs, minor denting, 9-1/2" h, $575. Photo courtesy of James D. Julia, Inc.

confuse it with the many other red glasswares of that period. Pigeon blood has a very definite orange glow.

Berry bowl, master, Torquay ... **195.00**
Butter dish, cov, Torquay **595.00**
Celery vase, Torquay **200.00**
Condiment set, Torquay **1,150.00**
Cracker jar, cov, Quilted Phlox, Consolidated Glass Co, resilvered hardware **325.00**
Creamer, Venecia, enameled dec **125.00**
Cruet, Torquay **900.00**
Decanter, 9-1/2" h, orig stopper. **175.00**
Hand cooler, 5" l, cut panels, two compartments, SS fittings **145.00**
Pickle castor, cov, Torquay **895.00**
Pitcher, 9-1/2" h, Bulging Loops, applied clear handle, ground pontil **225.00**
Salt and pepper shakers, pr, Bulging Loops, orig top **150.00**
Spooner, Torquay **125.00**
Syrup pitcher, squatty, Torquay. **450.00**
Sweetmeat, Torquay **125.00**
Tobacco jar, cov, Torquay **450.00**
Tumbler, 3-1/4" h, alternating panel and rib **85.00**
Water carafe, Torquay **395.00**

PINK SLAG

History: True pink slag is found only in the molded Inverted Fan and Feather pattern. Quality pieces shade from pink at the top to white at the bottom.

For more information, see this book

Berry bowl, 10" d **750.00**
Creamer **465.00**
Cruet, 6-1/2" h, orig stopper .. **1,300.00**
Jelly compote, 5" h, 4-1/2" d, scalloped top **375.00**
Marmalade jar, cov **875.00**
Pitcher, water **775.00**
Punch cup, 2-1/2" h, ftd **275.00**
Salt shaker **300.00**
Sauce dish, 4-1/4" d, 2-1/2" h, ball feet **225.00**
Spooner **350.00**
Sugar bowl, cov **550.00**
Toothpick holder **825.00**
Tumbler, 4-1/2" h **475.00**

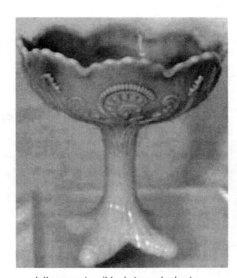

Jelly compote, ribbed stem, shades to off-white at foot, 5" h, $600. Photo courtesy of Clarence and Betty Maier.

PIPES

History: Pipe making can be traced as far back as 1575. Pipes were made of almost all types of natural and manmade materials, including amber, base metals, clay, cloisonné, glass, horn, ivory, jade, meerschaum, parian, porcelain, pottery, precious metals, precious stones, semiprecious stones, and assorted woods. Some of these materials retain smoke and some do not. Chronologically, the four most popular materials and their generally accepted introduction dates are: clay, c1575; wood, c1700; porcelain, c1710; and meerschaum, c1725.

Pipe styles reflect nationalities all around the world, wherever tobacco smoking is custom or habit. Pipes represent a broad range of themes and messages, e.g., figurals, important personages, commemoration of historical events, mythological characters, erotic and pornographic subjects, the bucolic, the bizarre, the grotesque, and the graceful.

Pipe collecting began in the mid-1880s; William Bragge, F.S.A., Birmingham, England, was an early collector. Although firmly established through the efforts of freelance writers, auction houses, and museums, but not the tobacco industry, the collecting of antique pipes is an amorphous, maligned, and misunderstood hobby. It is amorphous because there are no defined collecting bounds, maligned because it is perceived as an extension of pipe smoking, and now misunderstood because smoking has become socially unacceptable—even though many pipe collectors are avid non-smokers.

Burl, 3-1/2" w, 7-1/4" h, carved tiered archways and staircase, animal and human faces, traces of old dark paint, America, late 19th/early 20th C, minor repair **115.00**
Clay, 6-5/8" l, red clay, 18 incised presentation signatures, unglazed, chips **55.00**
Glass, large ovoid bowl, long shaped stem, red and ivory dec **90.00**
Meerschaum
> 3-1/2" l, two carved dogs on top, cracked amber mouthpiece, orig leather case with velvet and satin lining **125.00**
> 4-3/4" l, 2" h, horses and barking dog, orig case **345.00**

Figural, lion's head, eagle's claw, woman, flora, dog, horse, deer, fox, lady in chair, price for 10, $275. Photo courtesy of Woody Auctions.

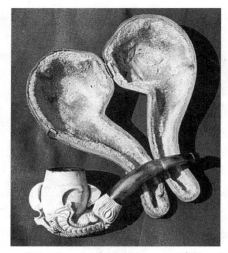

Meerschaum, original leather case, **$90.**

6-1/2" l, 1-1/2" h, face of black boy, carved elephant on stem, marked "Made in Tranzania" **165.00**

Porcelain

12" l, floral, relief dec **125.00**

19" l, drunken man lying under barrel, small porcelain animal on bowl lid **280.00**

29" l, hunter, sleeping **135.00**

Regimental, 41" l, porcelain bowl, 112 Infantry, Sohlettstadt 1888, named to Res. Huck., two scenes, helmet cover, new spike and hairline in bowl, minor repair on flexible cord **225.00**

Wood, carved

7-1/2" l, hand carved bears crawling on stump, 3-5/8" l celluloid stem **250.00**

8-1/4" l, bearded man's head above deer's head, stem with carved dog's head, America, 19th C, stand **700.00**

POCKETKNIVES

History: Alcas, Case, Colonial, Ka-Bar, Queen, and Schrade are the best of the modern pocketknife manufacturers, with top positions enjoyed by Case and Ka-Bar. Knives by Remington and Winchester, firms no longer in production, are eagerly

Notes: Form is a critical collecting element. The most desirable forms are folding hunters (one or two blades), trappers, peanuts, Barlows, elephant toes, canoes, Texas toothpicks, Coke bottles, gun stocks, and Daddy Barlows. The decorative aspect also heavily influences prices.

Case

Case uses a numbering code for its knives. The first number (1-9) is the handle material; the second number (1-5) designates the number of blades; the third

and fourth numbers (0-99) the knife pattern, stage (5), pearl (8 or 9) and bone (6) are the most sought handle materials. The most desirable patterns are 5165—folding hunters, 6185—doctors, 6445, scout, muskrat—marked muskrat with no number, and 6254—trappers. In the Case XX series, a symbol and dot code are used to designate a year.

Advertising, wood body, single tin covered blade, recast marked "Case Bros.," simulated pick bone handles, silver painted bolsters and blade, handles painted brown, two screw eyes, hanger chain, 39" l blade, 86-1/2" l, **$750.** *Photo courtesy of James D. Julia Auctions.*

3254, yellow composition, 4-1/8", stamped "XX," 1940-65 .... **150.00**

5265, stag, 5-1/4", saber ground, stamped "USA," 1965-70 ...... **100.00**

6265, 5-1/4", flat blade, stamped "Tested XX," green bone, 1920-40 .... **300.00**

8271, genuine pearl, 3-1/4", long pull, stamped "XX," 1940-65 .... **450.00**

9265, imitation pearl, 5-1/4", flat blade, stamped "Tested XX," 1920-40 . **450.00**

420657, white composition, 3-3/8", "Office Knife" marked on handle, 1940-56 .... **100.00**

Ka-Bar (Union Cut. Co., Olean, NY)

The company was founded by Wallace Brown at Tidiote, PA, in 1892. It was relocated to Orlean, NY, in 1912. The products have many stampings, including Union (inside shield); UOR co., Tidoute (variations); Union Cutlery Co. Olean, NY; Aklcut Olean, NY; Kenwell, Olean, NY, and Ka-Bar. The larger knives with a profile of a dog's head on the handle are the most desirable. Pattern numbers rarely appear on a knife prior to the 1940s.

6191L **600.00**

31187, two blades **185.00**

61161, light celluloid handle.... **130.00**

61187, Daddy Barlow **175.00**

Keen Kutter (Simons Hardware, St. Louis, MO)

K1881, Barlow **85.00**

K1920 .... **300.00**

6354, Scout **125.00**

Figural, English, lying dog, **$90.**

Remington

R293, Field and Stream Bullet, bone, long pull **1,800.00**

R953, toothpick, bone **250.00**

R3273, Cattle, brown bone, equal end **275.00**

Winchester

2337, Senator, 3-1/4", pearl **125.00**

2703, Barlow, 3-1/2", brown bone **160.00**

3944, Whittler, 3-1/4", bone **225.00**

POISON BOTTLES

History: The design of poison bottles was meant to serve as a warning in order to prevent accidental intake or misuse of their poisonous contents. Their unique details were especially helpful in the dark. Poison bottles generally were made of colored glass, embossed with "Poison" or a skull and crossbones, and sometimes were coffin-shaped.

John H. B. Howell of Newton, New Jersey, designed the first safety closure in 1866. The idea did not become popular until the 1930s, when bottle designs became simpler and the user had to read the label to identify the contents.

Bowker's Pyrox Poison, colorless **30.00**

Coffin, 3-1/2" h, cobalt blue, emb, 1890 .... **100.00**

Cylindrical, crosshatch dec, cobalt blue, flared mouth with stopper, smooth base, 6-1/4" h **250.00**

Diamond Antiseptics, 10-3/4" h, triangular shape, golden amber, emb **385.00**

Figural, skull, America, 1880-1900, cobalt blue, tooled mouth, smooth base, 2-7/8" h **500.00**

Imperial Fluid Co. Poison, one gallon, colorless **95.00**

Owl Drug Co., three-sided, embossed owl, cobalt blue, 9-3/4" h, $650. Photo courtesy of Pacific Glass Auctions.

Norwich Coffin, 3-3/8" h, amber, emb, tooled lip **95.00**
Owl Drug Co., 3-3/8" h, cobalt blue, owl sitting on mortar **70.00**
Plumber Drug Co., 7-1/2" h, cobalt blue, lattice and diamond pattern **90.00**
Poison, 3-1/2" h, hexagonal, ribbed, cobalt blue **20.00**
Tinct Iodine, 3" h, amber, skull and crossbones **45.00**

POLITICAL ITEMS

History: Since 1800, the American presidency has been a contest between two or more candidates. Initially, souvenirs were issued to celebrate victories. Items issued during a campaign to show support for a candidate were actively being distributed in the William Henry Harrison election of 1840.

There is a wide variety of campaign items—buttons, bandannas, tokens, pins, etc. The only limiting factor has been the promoter's imagination. The advent of television campaigning has reduced the quantity of individual items, and modern campaigns do not seem to have the variety of materials that were issued earlier.

Additional Listings: See *Warman's Americana & Collectibles* for more examples.

Adviser: Theodore L. Hake.

Ashtray, 3-1/2" sq, smoked glass, "Thanks To A Key Leader," facsimile signature "Dick Nixon," 1960 . . . **15.00**

Badge
1-3/16", Wilson, diecut white metal, name on bar at top, portrait on six-pointed star below, stickpin **65.00**
1-1/2" x 5", DNC Page, 1984, black and brass luster medals, red, white, and blue fabric ribbon, 1-1/2" d bar pin medal with raised image of Golden Gate bridge and DNC logo **15.00**
4", Ike, red, white, and blue fabric covering bar pin at top, tiny brass flag accent suspended below, 2" clear plastic disk with name "Ike" printed in gold lettering on reverse **30.00**

Bank
3" h, 3" d, New Deal Bank, Chein, coin slot on solid red painted top, red, white, and blue stars and stripes, eagles, center red band, c1930s **85.00**
5" h, cast iron, 3-D bust of T Roosevelt, inscribed "Teddy," gold paint, silver eyeglasses, small red accent on his Spanish-American

Badge, William McKinley, 1896-1900 $75.

Button, glossy cello, bluetone photo on white beneath words "I Like" in blue lettering, "Ike" in white lettering, rim curl names maker Bastian Bros. Co., 3-1/2" d, $45.

War hat, 75 percent orig paint remains, c1898-1904 . . . . . **195.00**
Bar pin
3/4" l, Hoover, brass lettering, whit enamel dec **5.00**
1-1/2" l, Theodore Roosevelt, sterling silver, lettering on stippled background **35.00**
Booklet, 9" x 12", "Our Patriotic President, His Life in Pictures," Theodore Roosevelt, Columbia Press, 1904, bright red and blue on tan cover with large black and white photo, anecdotes, sayings, principles, biography, and photos **25.00**
Brass shell
1-1/8", Blaine and Logan, single sheet of cardboard with photos surmounted by pair of six-sided panels accented by emb stars **275.00**
1-1/8", Benjamin Harrison, from 1888, Our Next President, eagle atop horseshoe surrounding cardboard photo **165.00**
Bust, 7" h, hollow cast metal, Wm McKinley, black patina, reverse stamped "G. B. Haines & Co., Chicago" **70.00**
Button
7/8", Teddy Roosevelt, brown and white Progessive Party, 1916 **75.00**
1" d, Aldai Likes Me, red, white and blue litho **20.00**
1-1/4", For President Harry S. Truman, black on cream **60.00**
1-1/2", No Roosevelt Dynasty, blue on cream **15.00**
1-3/4", All The Way With Kennedy For President, slogan in blue, white

Jugate, Hoover, black and white oval photos below brown eagle, red, white, and blue background, 1-1/4" d, $600. Photo courtesy of Hake's Americana & Collectibles.

background, name in bright red **75.00**

3-1/2", Re-elect LBJ sepia toned photo in center, white background, red "Re-elect" at top, blue "Johnson For President" at bottom **25.00**

3-1/2", Willkie Our Next President, black and white, some scratches **20.00**

6", Humphrey Delegate, red, white, and blue, 6" neck cord attached to black cardboard easel back **20.00**

Coin, 1-1/8" US one-cent coin, Liberty head on front, date 1838, front stamped "Vote the Land Free," issued in 1848 for Martin Van Buren, reverse lightly struck **135.00**

Electoral ticket, 1856, 10-1/2" x 18" linen-like fabric, black printed text, cream-colored ground, top reads "National American Fillimore and Donelson Ticket," various elector names, some as-made flaws, archival tape repair **200.00**

Ferrotype, Stephan A. Douglas 1860, rim hole, brass lustered rim **275.00**

Flicker

2-1/2", Stevenson, Tucker, and 1956 Indiana governor candidate . **40.00**

3" d, red tin litho frame holds full color cardboard photo of John F. Kennedy by Fabian Bachrach, suspended below is 5" gold on blue ribbon "I Was At The Inauguration of President Kennedy," date and city, mounted above text is 1-1/4" w full-color

flicker which alternates between White House and US Capitol. **35.00**

Jugate

1-1/4", Parker and Davis 1904, real photos, eagle design at top . **75.00**

1-3/4", JFK and LBJ, 1961, The New Frontier Inauguration, black and white photos against top panel in white, lower panel in light blue, red text, four gold stars **75.00**

2-1/4", Reagan and Baker, bluetone photos, blue text, white background, bright red date and slogan "The Balanced Team For The Eighties" **20.00**

3", Carter and Birch Bayh, 1976, bluetone photos and text, red stars, white background, "Bayh-Centennial" at top, names below **15.00**

3-1/2", Nixon, black and white photos outlined in gold against red, white, and blue background, for 1960 PA campaign **20.00**

3-1/2", Truman and Barkley, celluloid, sepia photos against cream background, names in red, red, white, and blue flag **325.00**

Lapel stud, 7/8" d, McKinley, black and white photo, 1896 . . . . **24.00**

Letter opener, 9" l, brass, Roosevelt, die-cut and raised FDR image handle, 1930s **45.00**

Mechanical card, 3-1/4" x 5", large tab below, hand colored and black and white image of Van Buren frowning as he holds a cup with initials WHH (William Henry Harrison), cut-out panel below is text "An Ugly Mug of Log-Cabin Hard Cider," when tab is pushed upward Van Buren's frown changes to smiling grin and he holds fancier cup bearing his initials and slogan "A Beautiful Goblet of White-House Champagne," c1840, slight moisture damage **195.00**

Medalet

Grant Memorial, brass hanger with eagle perched on crossed cannons, cannonballs below, white metal, portrait name, reverse with wreath surrounding dates of birth and 1885 death, some fading to silver luster **18.00**

W. H. Harrison, 1-1/8" d, copper, portrait name and date of birth, log cabin and slogan "The People's Choice The Hero Of Tippecanoe" on back, silver finish worn off **35.00**

Lincoln, 1860, 1" d, bright luster, spread-wing eagle with slogan "Success to Republican Principles" on one side, other "Millions for Freedom Not One Cent For Slavery" **75.00**

Paint book, "Young America Paint Book and Little Stories of Our Presidents," issued by Playtime Publishing Corp, 1934, set of four, each 9" x 12", stiff cardboard covers, thin paper interior sheets, spine edge of each neatly punched so they could be combined by a cord **50.00**

Photograph

1" x 1-3/8", Garfield, cardboard, emb brass frame with bright luster, 1880 . . . . **225.00**

7-1/2" x 9-1/2" oval, 1903, browntone photo, "President Roosevelt and Family," orig owner's name inked on reverse, four raised ornamental designs on frame, slight damage to frame **35.00**

Plate, 7" d, milk glass, green and brown accent paint, center bear holds open book, left bear smokes pipe, right bear wearing pince-nez glasses, c1904, 50 percent paint loss **70.00**

Magazine, published by New York Times for September 9, 1920, 24 pages printed in sepia, briefly captioned photos related to news, entertainment and human interest events, front cover has large oval photo portrait of Governor James M. Cox, of Ohio, Democratic candidate for President. 11" x 16", $60. Photos courtesy of Hake's Americana & Collectibles.

Plate, white china, sepia tone portrait of William H. Taft above campaign motto in small type, outer rim trimmed by thin gold accent line, underside has signature stamp for "Carollton China," 8-3/4" d, $25.

Postcard, 3-1/2" x 5-1/2", bright red, white, and blue flag design, emb white oval frame at center surrounding browntone image of Teddy Roosevelt, musical notes above "Yankee Doodle" and slogan "Glory to the Union," printed in Germany, undivided back **35.00**

Puzzle, 3-1/2" x 5" x 1", red, white, and blue paper covered cardboard box, red and blue puzzle parts inside, 3" x 5" red and white paper giving address of puzzle solution, c1933, FDR. **60.00**

Ribbon, 1-5/8" x 3-5/8", black on white silk, Garfield portrait, text for "Garfield Barbeque Oct. 21, 1880, Sacramento, Cal". **125.00**

FDR and Wallace, "For Freedom and Humanity," 1940, blue ground, gold lettering, 1-7/8" x 5" l, $35.

Stickpin

7/8" d, narrow brass rim holding ferrotype with large image of beardless Lincoln, 1860, brass stickpin removed, replaced by 1" silver luster straight pin . . . **700.00**

1-1/16" tall emb brass frame, bright luster, cardboard photo of Tilden and Hendricks, 1876, 1-1/4" l stickpin. **400.00**

Tie tack, 1" black luster frame with alternating black and white flicker images of Nixon and Lodge, needle post and brass clutch on back . . **15.00**

Trade card

2-3/4" x 4-1/2", browntone illus of Grant on cream, black text for "Welcome Soap," c1870 . . . **22.00**

3" x 4", Garfield and Arthur, black images, off-white paper, reverse with text promoting cigar and mineral water sales, Kansas City, Missouri, store **20.00**

Window decal, 2-3/4" x 3", dark blue decal on pale blue sheet, button like design "Forward with President Truman "No Retreat," direction text on edge **45.00**

Portrait Ware

History: Plates, vases, and other articles with portraits on them were popular in the second half of the 19th century. Although male subjects, such as Napoleon or Louis XVI, were used, the ware usually depicts a beautiful, and often unidentified, woman.

A large number of English and Continental china manufacturers made portrait ware. Because most was hand painted, an artist's signature often is found.

Bud vases, 4-1/8" h, baluster, green ground, central portrait roundel of bust of lady in mediaeval dress, over enameled gilt floral surround, back with gilt over enameled floral spray, French, early 20th C, price for pr **1,300.00**

Charger, 14" d, Marie Antoinette, sgd "Johner," dark green border, gilt scrolled and leaf dec, blue Austrian beehive mark. **275.00**

Dresser box, cov, 4" l, 3-1/4" w, 1-1/2" h, brass heart-shaped box, inlaid lid with hp portrait on ivory of women in formal dress, Florentine designs on box, portrait sgd "Brun" **350.00**

Medallion, 3-1/2" d, Le Pensee, sgd "Wagner," jeweled gilt bronze frame **975.00**

Plaque

2-1/4" l, brunette beauty with diaphanous drape, German, late

19th/early 20th C, 9-5/8" x 9-1/8" ebonized giltwood shadowbox frame. **375.00**

6" x 4", woman in white gown, pink drape, outstretched hand with flowers, gilt bronze frame, putti and garlands, minor scratches . **725.00**

Plate

8" d, young woman in blue dress, titled "Rose," blue beehive Germany mark **375.00**

9-1/4" d, Empress Louise, central printed portrait, indistinctly titled and signed "L. Dgt," in gilt surround, paneled rim with scrolls, urns, and griffins, possibly Hutschenreuther, Bavaria, late 19th/early 20th C. **115.00**

9-1/2" d, dark haired mother and child, deep olive green border, gold tracery, marked "Royal Vienna" **95.00**

9-1/2" d, Nach dem Ball, sgd "Wagner," borders of Roman key, green garlands, red berries, white ground. **785.00**

9-1/2" d, Napoleon I, sgd "Wagner," cobalt blue and pale blue band, cornucopia and urn ornamentation, inscribed "Made for Mrs. John Doyle" verso, minor gilt loss **970.00**

9-3/4" d, octagonal shape, hp portrait of Psyche, blue Vienna beehive mark **490.00**

Plate, Wiener Frowen Schonhert, woman with fan and pearl necklace, surrounded by banded gilt decoration, rim decorated with gilt, blue enamel on cranberry ground, signed "H. Roldas," Austrian beehive mark, 9-1/2" d, gilt loss, $400. Photo courtesy of Sanford Alderfer Auction Co.

10" h, young woman with wreath of flowers in hair, marked "Royal Munich" **115.00**

12" d, young woman, gilt bronze-colored border, mounted in 15" x 17" walnut frame, German **300.00**

Soup bowl, 9-1/2" d, Rinaldo & Armida, lovers in garden, soldiers looking on, paneled border, sections of animals and floral dec, pink and violet grounds, blue Austria beehive mark, gilt loss **275.00**

Tray, 9-1/2" sq, Napolean I, standing, looking left, left hand behind back exposing dress sword and medals, background of fine furniture and papers, gilt garland border, dark blue-green ground, fitted frame, sgd "Reseh," marked "Vienna, FD, Austria" **1,320.00**

Urn, cov, 15-1/2" h, double handles, "Mme de Montesson," central portrait of French woman wearing white wig, floral designs, reverse with floral dec, marked "2912, S-2," illegible ring mark, restored lid **275.00**

Vase

4-3/4" h, bulbous, titled "Ariadne," sgd "Wagner," maroon ground, gilt floral dec, Austrian beehive mark **850.00**

5-3/4" h, gold enamel framed portrait of Ruth, violet luster ground, blue beehive mark with "Germany" in script **435.00**

6-1/2" h, young beauty with basket of flowers in garden setting, artist sgd "Garnet," base imp "Made in

Vase, squatty, two ring handles, portrait of woman and floral decoration, gilt decoration, blue maple leaf Nippon mark, 5-1/2" h, $330. Photo courtesy of Sanford Alderfer Auction Company.

France," enamel on bronze, c1900 . . . . **500.00**

7" h, young beauty in red dress, red roses in hair, finely enameled on bronze, tinted silver foil cartouche against translucent emerald green ground, French, c1900 . . . . **865.00**

7-1/2" h, finely dec portrait of young man, natural colors, enameled bronze, tinted silver foil under sparkling crystal glaze, unmarked, attributed to Limoges, early 20th C **750.00**

8" h, hp portrait of young girl framed in gold enamel, violet luster ground, German, unmarked **375.00**

8-1/2" h, Clementine, sgd "N. Kiesel," Art Nouveau form, green-brown mirrored ground, heavily gilt acanthus leaves and vines, bearing mark of Richard Klemm **1,690.00**

9" h, portrait of woman with conch shell to ear and flower, Art Nouveau form, blue ground fading to violet, gilt dec, enamel jewelling, mark of Erdmann Schlegelmilch, early 1900s, loss to jewels, wear to background **485.00**

12" h, woman holding yellow roses, opalescent ground in shades of green and purple, gilt floral design, Dresden, wear to gilding . **1,570.00**

13-1/8" h, French, Aesthetic Movement, third quarter 19th C, earthenware, portraits of ladies in exotic costumes, one sgd lower right "Leonard" in gilt border, reverse painted with landscape scenes, sides with royal blue stars outlined in gold on cobalt blue ground, two short gilt handles, ovoid foot, price for pr . . . **2,300.00**

POSTERS

History: Posters were a critical and extremely effective method of mass communication, especially in the period before 1920. Enormous quantities were produced, helped in part by the propaganda role posters played in World War I.

Print runs of two million were not unknown. Posters were not meant to be saved; they usually were destroyed once they had served their purpose. The paradox of high production and low survival is one of the fascinating aspects of poster history.

The posters of the late 19th and early 20th centuries represent the pinnacle of American lithography. The advertising posters of firms such as Strobridge or Courier are true classics. Philadelphia was one center for the poster industry.

Europeans pioneered posters with high artistic and aesthetic content, and poster art still plays a key role in Europe. Many major artists of the 20th century designed posters.

Adviser: George Theofiles.

Advertising

Clarenbach & Herder Ice Skate Manufacturers, Philadelphia, PA, large scene of ice skaters on Schuylkill River, Waterworks in background, mid-19th C, later archival backing, 17-1/4" x 23" **675.00**

Do It Electrically, "Comfort, Convenience, Efficiency in the Home…Save Fuel, Food, Time, Money -By Wire," image of angel holding electric motor, period electrical appliances, full color, blue background, expert restoration to edges,c1915, 27" x 35" **600.00**

Ferry's Seeds, full-color image of pretty young lass amid towering hollyhocks, light fold lines, restoration to edges, thin tears, 1925, 21" x 28" **325.00**

Fire! Fire! Fire!, "Chicago Lost But J. Dearman of Knoxville, Penna. Continues to Roll Up, Bundle Up, and Box Up As Many Goods As Ever!" red and black, some replacement to border, Oct. 15, 1871, 22" x 27" **225.00**

Hogan & Thompson, Philadelphia, PA, publishers, manufacturers, and wholesale dealers of books and commercial stationery, black graphics show variety of merchandise, white ground, early to mid-19th C, trimmed to borders, 9-1/4" x 11-1/4" **125.00**

Longacre & Co., Philadelphia, PA, engraver, black graphics of their work, white ground, c1876, 11" x 10-1/2" **115.00**

Earliest racing poster

The earliest known American auto-racing poster sold at an Cohasco, Inc. auction in June 2002 for $4,400. The 9-1/2" x 12" broad++sheet from the 1897 fair in Pittsfield, Massachusetts, showed Duryea Motor Wagon and other attractions, such as balloon rides, bicycle races, and livestock, culinary, and ladies' exhibits. Printed on both sides, the reverse was autographed by J. Frank Duryea. The inscription, in blue ink, reads, "My first design for the Duryea Motor Wagon Co., 1895-96. The 3rd Duryea from standpoint of design."

Richfield Gasoline, race driver in car, c1930, 39" x 53" **1,100.00**

Royal Portable Typewriter, dark green detailed manual portable typewriter against leafed red and green ground, c1940, 24" x 36" **285.00**

Waterman's Ideal Fountain Pen, paper, Uncle Sam at Treaty of Portsmouth, early 1900s, 41-1/2" x 19-1/2" **950.00**

Circus Shows, and Acts

Barnum and Bailey Circus, Strobridge Litho, Co., "Jockey Races," 1908, 19" x 28" **900.00**

Downey Bros. Big 3 Ring Circus, "Leaps-Revival of that Astounding and Sensational exhibition," group of elephants, camels, and horses in line, aerial artist leaping overhead, audience background, c1925, 41" x 27" . . **125.00**

Hollywood Peep Show, burlesque strip revue, c1950, 27" x 41" **150.00**

Hot From Harlem, black burlesque show, color, Anon, c1947, 22" x 28" **250.00**

Ringling Bros. Barnum & Bailey Liberty Bandwagon, color litho, ornate wagon with Merue Evans portrait, 1943, 30" x 19" **225.00**

Tim McCoy's Wild West, circle of riders around red circle, on canvas, 1938, 54" x 41" **900.00**

Magic

Buddha and Heartstone, Polish magician performing tricks, English and Polish text, c1914, 14" x 26" **100.00**

Carter the Great-A Baffling Chinese Mystery—The Elongated Maiden, Otis Litho, "A pretty Chinese girl tied to a torture rack without seeming discomfort..," life-sized Chinese nobleman looking down on vignettes of complicated rack, stretched maiden, banshees, imps, devils, in color, c1920, 41" x 81" **650.00**

Friedlander Stock Magic, Adolph Friedlander #6966, smiling devil holds card-like vignettes of magic acts in one hand, wand in other, yellow ground, c1919, 14" x 19" **150.00**

Kar-Mi Swallows a Loaded gun Barrel, National, "Shoots a cracker from a man's head," Kar-Mi with gun in mouth blasts away at blindfolded assistant, crowd of turbaned Indians, 1914, 42" x 28" **350.00**

Movie

"African Queen," French release of classic Bogart and Hepburn film, color

portraits of both above steamy jungle setting, c1960, 22" x 31" **150.00**

"Amazing Transparent Man," Miller Consolidated, D. Kennedy, Marguerite Chapman, sci-fi silhouette against blue, 1959, 27" x 41" **125.00**

"Anatomy of a Murder," Columbia, Saul Bass design, 1959, 27" x 41" **125.00**

"Atlantic City," Republic, Constance Moore, Jerry Colonna in drag, by James Montgomery Flagg, 1941, 14" x 36" **200.00**

"Blondie in the Dough," Columbia Pictures, Penny Singleton, Chick Young's Blondie cartoon film, full color, 1947, 27" x 41" **95.00**

"Bad Boy," James Dunn and Louise Fazenda, Fox, 1934, 27" x 41" . . **150.00**

"Double Danger," Preston Foster and Whitney Bourne, RKO, 1938, 27" x 41" **110.00**

"Dr. No," United Artist, Sean Connery, Ursula Andress, 1962, 27" x 41" **325.00**

"Goodbye Mr. Chips," Robert Donat and Greer Garson, MGM, 1939, 27" x 41" **450.00**

"I'll Be Seeing You," Ginger Rogers, Joseph Cotton, and Shirley Temple, United Artists 1945, 27" x 41" . . **150.00**

"Love Takes Flight," Bruce Cabot and Beatrice Roberts, Grand National, 1937, 22" x 28" **135.00**

"Mule Train," Columbia Pictures, Gene Autry, Champion, full-color portraits, 1950, 27" x 41" **150.00**

"New York, New York," United Artists, Robert Diniro, Liza Minnelli, 1977 **35.00**

"Smoldering Fires," Pauline Frederick and Laura La Plante, Universal, 1925, 14" x 22" **125.00**

Campaign, Bryan and Sewell, 1896, full-color chromolithograph, oval black and white bust portraits of candidates, spread winged bald eagle sitting atop U.S. shield and arrows, and "Free Silver Sixteen to One" above laurel wreath and ribbon banner with "'Democratic Nominees" and "1896" below, light blue background, red band across center, 20-1/4" x 26-1/4" poster, mounted on acid free backing and framed, light even toning, $3,100. Photo courtesy of Cowan Historic Americana Auctions.

Political and patriotic

America Lets Us Worship As We Wish—Attend The Church Of Your Choice, for American Legion sponsored "Americanism Appreciation Month," full-color image of praying Uncle Sam, family at dinner table behind him, c1945, 20" x 26" **275.00**

Bridge of Peace, Venette Willard Shearer, anti-war poster from American Friends Service Committee, National

WWI, stone litho, "Join the Air Service and Serve in France," colorful illustrations by Paul Verrees, c1917, Air Force biplane in skies over France, Ketterlinus Litho, Philadelphia, professionally linen mounted, margins appear trimmed after mounting, 25" w, 36-3/4" h, $520. Photo courtesy of James D. Julia, Inc.

Council to Prevent War, in color, children of all nations play beneath text of song of peace, c1936, 16" x 22" **125.00**

Confidence, large color portrait of Roosevelt over yacht at sea, "Election Day was our salvation/Franklin Roosevelt is the man/Our ship will reach her destination/Under his command...Bring this depression to an end...," c1933, 18" x 25" **250.00**

Extra Post. Democratic Salt River Excursion, Incidents of the Annual Voyage to the Old Stamping Ground, Philadelphia, Tuesday, Oct. 10, 1871, comic details of Philadelphia political events, text and 9 vignettes, published by Philadelphia Post, later archival backing, 17-3/4" x 14-1/2" **200.00**

United Nations Day, blue and white U.N. banner waves over airbrushed stylized brown and yellow globe, minor edge crumple, 1947, 22" x 23" . **250.00**

Theater

Bringing Up Father, McManus, "Jiggs, Maggie, Dinty Moore-George McManus's cartoon comedy with music," early newspaper cartoon characters against New York skyline, c1915, 41" x 81".............. **425.00**

Claudine Clerice Fr, Collette Willy opera, full color, French, 1910, 26" x 35" **275.00**

Dangers of a Great City, National show Print, Chicago, play by Oliver North, men fighting in an office, gleaming stock ticker, "Give me the papers or I'll...," c1900, 21" x 28" **150.00**

No No Nanette, Tony Gibbons, Theatre Mogador, Paris, European production of American musical, c1925, 15" x 22" **375.00**

Transportation

Air France—North Africa, Villemot, stylized imagery of mosques and minarets, lavenders, yellow, and blues against sky blue background, plane and Pegasus logo, c1950, 24" x 39" **225.00**

Motorlobene-Fano, Alfred Olsen, Danish auto race, car raising cloud of dust, 1922, 24" x 35" **1,250.00**

Royal Mail Atlantis, Padden, tourists in Royal mail motor launch approaching harbor village, mountains in background, c1923, 25" x 38" .. **675.00**

SS France, Bob Peak, launching of French ocean liner, champagne and confection in front of huge, night-lit bow of ship, 1961, 30" x 46" **450.00**

SS Michelangelo and **SS Raffaello**, Astor, detailed cutaway of Italian ocean liners, designed for use in travel office, printed on plasticized stock, metal frame, 1964, 54" x 22".........**300.00**

Travel

Arizona—Fly TWA, Austin Briggs, full-color western lass in 1950s style, c1955, 25" x 40" **300.00**

Boston—New Haven Railroad, Nason, full color, stylized montage of Historic Boston by day and night, faint folio folds, c1938, 28" x 42" **275.00**

Come to Ulster, Norman Wilkinson, sailboats and fishermen in front of lighthouse, full color, c1935, 50" x 40" **450.00**

Hawaii—United Air Lines, Feher, stylized wahini, island behind her, full color, c1948, 25" x 40" **650.00**

Palace Hotel Wengen, Klara Borter, hotel in foothills of Alps, 1928, 27" x 40" **800.00**

Paris, Paul Colin, doves floating above stylized Eiffel tower and Arc de Triumph, 1946, 24" x 39" **600.00**

World War I

Call to Duty—Join the Army for Home and Country, Cammilli, recruiting image

WWI, stone litho, "Boys and Girls! You can help your Uncle Sam win the war. Save your quarters. Buy War Savings Stamps," full color, issued by the U. S. Government with Torch of Liberty seal, James Montgomery Flagg artist, c1917, overall light browning of paper, 20" w, 30" h, **$700**. *Photo courtesy of James D. Julia, Inc.*

of Army bugler in front of unfurled banner, 1917, 30" x 40" **325.00**

Clear the Way!, Howard Chandler Christy, Columbia points the way for Naval gun crew, c1918, 20" x 30" **250.00**

Follow the Flag—Enlist in the Navy, James Daugherty, sailor plants flag on shore, 1917, 27" x 41" **450.00**

Treat 'Em Rough—Jon The Tanks, A. Hutaf, window card, electric blue-black cat leaping over tanks in fiery battle, white border, c1917, 14" x 22".. **900.00**

You Wireless Fans—Help The Navy Get A Hun Submarine—A Thousand Radio Men Wanted, C. B. Falls, wireless operator reaching up to grab lightening bolt, starry night background, blue, green, red, and white, 1918, 27" x 44" **550.00**

Will You Supply Eyes For The Navy? Gordon Grant, "Navy Ships Need Binoculars and Spy-Glasses...Tag Each Article with Your Name and Address, Mail to Hon. Franklin D. Roosevelt, Asst. Sec'y of Navy,..." image of Naval captain ready with blindfold on stormy deck, gun crew at ready behind him, 1918, 21" x 29".............. **625.00**

POT LIDS

History: Pot lids are the lids from pots or small containers which originally held ointments, pomades, or soap. Although some collectors want both the pot and its lid, lids alone are more often collected. The lids frequently are decorated with multicolored underglaze transfers of rural and domestic scenes, portraits, florals, and landmarks.

The majority of the containers with lids were made between 1845 and 1920 by F. & R. Pratt, Fenton, Staffordshire, England. In 1920, F. & R. Pratt merged with Cauldon Ltd. The firm reissued several lids, using the original copper engraving plates. They were used for decoration and never served as actual lids. Reissues by Kirkhams Pottery, England, generally have two holes for hanging. Cauldon, Coalport, and Wedgwood were other firms making reissues.

For more information, see this book.

Marks: Kirkhams Pottery reissues are often marked as such.

Note: Sizes given are for actual pot lids; size of any framing not included.

Arctic Expedition, T. J. & J. Mayer, multicolored, 3" d, rim chip **320.00**

Fishing scene, marked "Strasburg," multicolored transfer, **$125.**

Burgess's Genuine Anchovy Paste, white glaze, brown and black transfer, 3-1/4" d, shallow chips on reverse **50.00**

Cold Cream, white glaze, brown and black transfer, 2-1/2" d **40.00**

Dr. Hassall's Hair Restorer, 1-3/4" d **250.00**

Dublin Industrial Exhibition, multicolored, 3-3/4" d **65.00**

Embarking For The East, Pratt, multicolored, 4-1/8" d, orig jar . . **125.00**

Golden Eye Ointment, white glaze, brown and black transfer, 1-3/4" d **50.00**

Hazard, Hazard & Co., Violet Cold Cream, 1150 Broadway New York, white glaze, brown transfer, 2-3/4" d . . **210.00**

Morris's Imperial Eye Ointment **200.00**

Mrs. Ellen Hale's Celebrated Heal All Ointment, black on white, 4" d . **350.00**

Persuasion, multicolored, 4-1/8" d **160.00**

The Sportsman, multicolored, 4-1/8" d, **$90.**

Queen Victoria on Balcony, T. J. & J. Mayer, large **275.00**

Roussels's Premium Shaving Cream Philadelphia, white glaze, gray transfer, 3" d, minor age line in rim of lid, orig base **220.00**

Tam O' Sahnger and Souter Johnny, 4" d, framed **275.00**

View of Windsor Castle, Pratt, 6-1/2" d **170.00**

Walmer Castle, Kent, Tatnell & Son, 4-1/2" d **215.00**

PRATT WARE

PRATT

PRATT FENTON

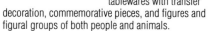

For more information, see this book.

History: The earliest Pratt earthenware was made in the late 18th century by William Pratt, Lane Delph, Staffordshire, England. From 1810 to 1818, Felix and Robert Pratt, William's sons, ran their own firm, F. & R. Pratt, in Fenton in the Staffordshire district. Potters in Yorkshire, Liverpool, Sunderland, Tyneside, and Scotland copied the products.

The wares consisted of relief-molded jugs, commercial pots and tablewares with transfer decoration, commemorative pieces, and figures and figural groups of both people and animals.

Marks: Much of the early ware is unmarked. The mid-19th century wares bear several different marks in conjunction with the name Pratt, including "& Co."

Bank, 5" h, figural, underglaze enamel dec center chimney house, male and female figure to either side, Yorkshire, 19th C, damage to chimney and backside of roof **275.00**

Cradle, pearlware

4" l, underglaze polychrome enamels, one molded with baby sleeping, c1800, repairs to hood and side of body **100.00**

5-1/4" l, cradle, underglaze polychrome enamel, c1800, restored chip **100.00**

7-3/4" l, underglaze polychrome enamels, oval form molded as hooded cradle with sleeping child, c1800, restored to lower body and under base, chip and hairline to hood **600.00**

Creamer, 5-1/4" h, cow and milkmaid, yellow and black sponged cow, underglaze enamels, translucent green

Teapot and cream jug, pearlware, underglaze polychrome enamels on oval forms molded with ribbed bodies and central medallions of classical reliefs, 6" h covered teapot with swan finial, slight flake and line to cover, chip to spout, restored at body below handle and rim chips, 4-1/2" h cream jug with rim chip, **$650.** *Photo courtesy of Skinner Auctioneers and Appraisers.*

stepped rect base, horns chipped **450.00**

Cup plate, 3-1/8" d, Dalmatian, white, black spots **95.00**

Figure, pearlware

8-1/2" h, Autumn, underglaze polychrome enamels, c1800 . . . . **125.00**

8-1/2" h, Winter, underglaze polychrome enamels, c1800, missing plinth base **95.00**

9" h, Summer, underglaze polychrome enamels, c1800, chip on plinth base **115.00**

Flask, 4-1/8" l, pearlware, shell-form, underglaze polychrome enamels, c1800, slight glaze blemishes . . **765.00**

Jar, 7-3/4" h, molded oval panels of peacocks in landscapes, blue, brown, green, and ochre, lower section with vertical leaves, band of foliage on rim, c1790 . . . . **620.00**

Toby jug, Martha Gun, underglaze polychrome on seated female figure modeled holding bottle and cup, restored chip to hat brim, 8-3/4" h, **$1,100.** *Photo courtesy of Skinner Auctioneers and Appraisers.*

Jug, 8" h, molded leaves at neck and base, raised and polychrome painted hunting scene on colored ground, c1800 . . . . **750.00**

Mug, 4" h, colorful tavern scene transfer **95.00**

Mustard jar, cov, dark blue hunt scene, tan ground **75.00**

Pitcher

5-5/8" h, molded figures on sides, leaves at rim and base, one side with Toby Philpots, other with classical warrior, green, gold, dark brown, and cobalt blue, flakes on base and handle, short hairline on spout **675.00**

6-1/8" h, molded hunt scene with riders and dogs chasing rabbit, cobalt blue, dark brown, green, and gold, molded oak leaves and acorns at rim and shoulder, leaves on base, blue feather edge spout and handle **935.00**

Plaque, 6-1/4" x 7-1/4", Louis XVI portrait, oval form, beaded border, polychrome enamels, c1793, rim nicks, glaze wear **900.00**

Plate, 9" d, Haddon Hall, classical figure border **120.00**

Tea caddy, 6-1/4" h, rect, raised figural panels front and back, fluted and yellow trimmed lid, blue, yellow, orange, and green dec **350.00**

PRINTS

History: Prints serve many purposes. They can be a reproduction of an artist's paintings, drawings, or designs, but often are an original art form. Finally, prints can be developed for mass appeal rather than primarily for aesthetic fulfillment. Much of the production of Currier & Ives fits this latter category. Currier & Ives concentrated on genre, urban, patriotic, and nostalgic scenes.

Additional Listings: See Wallace Nutting.

Arms, John Taylor, *Rodez/The Tower of Notre Dame*, etching on paper, edition of 120 plus six trial proofs, sgd and dated "John Taylor Arms-1927" in pencil lower right, inscribed "Arms 1926" and "Rodez 1926" in the plate, 11-7/8" x 4-7/8", framed **230.00**

Atkins & Nightingale, publisher, J. Cartwright, engraver, *Georgetown and Federal City, or City of Washington*, 1801, etching with aquatint and hand coloring on paper, 16" x 23-1/4", framed, few minor scattered stains, light toning **17,625.00**

Reproduction Alert: The reproduction of Maxfield Parrish prints is a continuing process. New reproductions look new, i.e., their surfaces are shiny and the paper crisp and often pure white. The color on older prints develops a mellowing patina. The paper often develops a light brown to dark brown tone, especially if it is acid based or was placed against wooden boards in the back of a frame.

Size is one of the keys to spotting later reproductions. Learn the correct size for the earliest forms. Be alert to earlier examples that have been trimmed to fit into a frame. Check the dimensions before buying any print.

Carefully examine the edges within the print. Any fuzziness indicates a later copy. Also look at the print through a magnifying glass. If the colors separate into dots, this indicates a later version.

Apply the same principles described above for authenticating all prints, especially those attributed to Currier & Ives. Remember, many prints were copied soon after their period introduction. As a result, reproductions can have many of the same aging characteristics as period prints.

Baille, James, publisher, colored lithograph

The Marriage, 1849, 12" x 8-1/2", period frame **115.00**

The Young Bride, 1848, 17" x 13", period frame **75.00**

Benson, Frank Weston, *Geese Alighting*, drypoint on paper, 1916, second of two published states, sgd "Frank W. Benson" in pencil lower left, dated in the plate lower left, numbered "44" in pencil lower right, 9-3/4" x 8" plate size, framed **1,035.00**

Benton, Thomas Hart

New England Farm, lithograph on paper, sgd in pencil lower right

James Audubon, The Birds of America by R. Havell, Cow Bunting, No. 20, plate 99, 1830, 19" w, 12" h image, 25-3/4" w, 18-1/4" h new frame with large white mat, **$250.** *Photo courtesy of James D. Julia, Inc.*

"Thomas H. Benton," edition of 300, commission and circulated by Friends of Art of Kansas State Univ, Manhattan, Kansas, c1951, 13-15/16" x 9" **1,100.00**

Youth Music, lithograph on paper, sgd in pencil lower right "Benton," 16-1/2" x 20-1/2" **3,450.00**

Boydell, John, publisher, image by Benjamin West, engraved by John Hall, *William Penn's Treaty with the Indians, When He Founded the Province of Pennsylvania in North America in 1681*, hand colored engraving, c1775, 18-1/2" x 23-1/2", minor repairs to border **1,450.00**

Chagall, Marc, *The Cello*, color litho on wove paper, sgd "Marc Chagall" in pencil lower right, numbered "38/50" in pencil ll., 13-1/2" x 9-3/4", framed **5,750.00**

Currier, Nathaniel, publisher, after Arthur Fitzwilliam Tait, *The Cares of a Family 1856*, lithograph with hand coloring heightened by gum Arabic on paper, identified in inscription in the matrix, Conningham, 814, 22" x 28", matted, unframed **2,990.00**

Currier, Nathaniel, publisher, Frances Flora Palmer, lithographer, lithograph with hand coloring on paper, identified in inscription in matrix

American Farm Series No. One, 1853, Conningham 134, 21-3/8" x 28-1/4", framed **2,185.00**

James Baillie, The Young Bride, 1848, period frame, 17" x 13" overall, **$125.** *Photo courtesy of Sanford Alderfer Auction Company.*

American Farm Series No. Two, 1953, Conningham 135, 22" x 29-1/8", matted, unframed, toning, hinged to mat **2,990.00**

American Farm Series No. Three, 1853, Conningham 133, 20-3/4" x 27-3/4", matted, unframed **2,415.00**

American Farm Series No. Four, 1853, Conningham 136, 20-1/8" x 26-3/4", label from Kennedy & Co., New York, framed **5,465.00**

American Forest Scene, Maple Sugaring, 1856, Conningham 157, 24-7/8" x 32-5/8", label from Old Print Shop, NY on reverse, framed **19,550.00**

American Winter Scene, Morning, 1854, Conningham 208, 21-1/4" x 28", framed **19,550.00**

American Winter Scene, Evening, 1854, Conningham 207, 20-3/4" x 27", unframed **8,625.00**

The American Clipper Ship, Witch of the Wave, undated, Conningham 115, 13" x 16-1/2", framed, overall toning, scattered staining, fox marks, creases throughout **865.00**

Currier, Nathaniel, publisher, Louis Maurer, lithographer, lithograph with hand coloring on paper, identified in inscription in matrix

American Winter Sports, Deer Shooting On the Shattagee, 1855, Conningham 209, 22-1/2" x 29-5/8", framed **5,175.00**

Arguing the Point, 1855, Conningam 265, 21-3/4" x 27-1/2", matted, unframed **3,335.00**

Currier and Ives, publishers, after Arthur Fitzwilliam Tait, lithograph with hand coloring, heightened with gum Arabic on paper, identified in matrix

American Frontier Life, The Hunter's Stratagem, 1862, Conningham 158, 22-1/8" x 30-1/2", framed **4,315.00**

American Hunting Scenes, A Good Chance, 1863, Conningham, 174, 24-1/2" x 32-5/8", framed, label from Old Print Shop, NY on reverse **6,990.00**

American Hunting Scenes, An Early Start, 1863, Conningham 173, 23-5/8" x 31-1/2", framed. **8,625.00**

Brook Trout Fishing, An Anxious Moment, 1862, Conningham 703, 22-1/2" x 31", framed, Old Print Shop, NY label on reverse **14,950.00**

N. Currier, painted by A. Fl Tait, titled A Check—Keep Your Distance, plainsman shooting at four pursuing native American warriors as another plainsman escapes with pack animals, 1853, framed, foxing, partial center burn line, waterstains at border, 19" x 24", $1,875. Photo courtesy of Sanford Alderfer Auction Company.

Currier and Ives, publishers, after G. H. Durrie, lithograph with hand coloring, heightened with gum Arabic on paper, Winter Mourning-Feeding the Chickens, 1863, Conningham 6741, identified in inscriptions in the matrix, hinged to mat, label of Old Print Shop NY on reverse **5,230.00**

Currier and Ives, publisher, Louis Maurer, lithographer, lithograph with hand coloring, heightened with gum Arabic on paper, identified in inscription in the matrix, Camping Out, Some of the Right Sort, 1856, Conningham 777, 23" x 31", framed, Old Print Shop, NY label on reverse **2,185.00**

Endicott & Co, Hambletonian, 1865, identified within matrix, chromolithograph on paper, 20-1/2" x 26", framed **230.00**

Gearhart, Frances Hammel, color woodcut on paper, sgd "Frances H. Gearhart" in pencil lower right, titled or numbered in pencil lower left, identified on label on mat

A Tatoosh Vista, 10-1/4" x 7-1/2" image size, 1/2" or more margins, matted **1,495.00**

Geraniums, 8" x 4-1/4" image size, 1/4" or more margins, matted **575.00**

Hall, Edith Emma Dorothea, Still Life/Vegetables, color woodcut on paper, sgd and dated "Emma Hall '54" in pencil lower right, 9-1/4" x 7-1/2", matted **115.00**

Hundertwasser, Friedensreich, Pacific Steamer, color woodcut on paper, 1986, dated, numbered and inscribed "989/999 ©…868A Auckland 3 March 1986" in ink lower left, sgd with various chops lower right, 20-1/2" x 15-3/4" image size, framed, deckled edges **2,875.00**

Hyde, Helen, Moon Bridge at Kameido, color woodcut on paper, sgd "Helen Hyde" in pencil lower right, monogram and clover seals lower left, numbered "67" in pencil lower left, inscribed "Copyright, 1914, by Helen Hyde" in the block lower left, 13-1/4" x 8-7/8", framed **460.00**

Icart, oval, hand colored, sleeping woman, blond hair, light green dress, brown and white dog at foot of bed, imp windmill mark at lower margin with signature, glued to matting, 23-1/2" x 27-1/4" **1,320.00**

Kellogg, The Farmer's Pet, girl in pink dress, holding yellow, blue, and red rooster, light stains, margin damage, 12-1/4" w, 16" h, period paint dec frame **415.00**

Kent, Rockwell

Diver, wood engraving on paper, 1931, edition of 150, sgd "Rockwell Kent" in pencil lower right, 7-3/4" x 5-1/4" image size, framed, 3/8" margins or more **1,120.00**

Resting, lithograph on paper, 1929, edition of 100, sgd "Rockwell Kent" in pencil lower right, 9-5/8" x 5-7/8" image size, framed, 3/8" margins or more **1,175.00**

Kitaj, R. B.

Head Reclined, lithograph in brick red on wove paper, edition of 30, sgd and numbered "Kitaj 25/30" in pencil lower left, 6-1/8" x 6" image size, unmatted, unframed, wide margins with deckled edges **235.00**

Monuments, soft ground etching on cream and white paper, edition of 50, sgd and numbered "Kitaj 2/50"

Louis Icart, two ladies with kitten, signed in plate, 28-1/2" x 33-1/2", $350. Photo courtesy of Joy Luke Auctions.

in pencil lower left, with watermarks "AUVERGNE..." and "326... RICHARD BAS," 15-1/4" x 21-3/4" plate size, unmatted, unframed, deckled edges, subtle handling marks and creases **300.00**

Knight, Dame Laura Knight, *Gilding the Lily*, etching and aquatint on paper, edition of 35, sgd "Laura Knight" in pencil lower right, 11-1/2" x 7-1/2" plate size, framed, margins over 1" . . **750.00**

Kuniyoshi Yasuo, *Burlesque Queen*, lithograph on paper, 1936, edition of 100, sgd in matrix, inscribed "100 prints" in pencil lower left, stamp from American Artists School, New York, on reverse, 11-5/8" x 9-1/2" image size, unmatted, unframed, margins 1" or more, unobtrusive soiling and toning, cellophane tape on reverse at upper edge with resultant staining to face, pinholes to corners **1,175.00**

Leighton, Clare, *The Lovers*, woodcut on paper, 1940, edition of 30, sgd "Clare Leighton" in pencil lower right, numbered and titled "26/30..." in pencil lower left, 7" x 4-7/8" image size, matted, unframed, margins over 1", scattered foxing, annotations to margins **325.00**

Lindenmuth, Tod, *Low Tide*, color woodcut on paper, sgd "Tod Lindenmuth" in pencil lower right, titled in pencil lower left, 15" x 14" image size, framed **1,600.00**

Lindner, Richard, *Man's Best Friend*, color lithograph on paper, c1970, edition of 250, sgd "R. Lindner" in pencil lower right, numbered "31/250" in pencil lower left on Arches cream paper with watermark, 27-3/4" x 21-1/2" sheet size, unmatted, unframed, minor handling marks, nicks, creases . **530.00**

Marin, John, *La Cathedral de Meaux*, 1907, etching on Arches wove paper with watermark, sgd "...de J. Marin" in pencil lower center, sgd and dated within the plate, 8-1/2" x 6-1/8" plate size, matted, deckled edges on two sides **350.00**

Marsh, Reginald, *Old Paris Night Street with Two Girls*, litho on chine collé, sgd "Reginald Marsh" in pencil lower right, sgd and dated within the matrix, inscribed "30 proofs" in pencil lower left, 12-3/4" x 8-7/8" image size, framed **1,150.00**

Matisse, Henri, lithograph on paper
Danseuse au Fauteuil en Boi, from *DIX DANSEUSE*, 1927, total edition of 150, sgd and numbered "3/15

Henri-Matisse" in pencil lower right, 18" x 10-1/2" image size, framed, approx 1" margins, toning, subtle rippling and soiling **10,575.00**

Danseuse au Divan Pliee en deux from DIX DANSEUSES, 1927, total edition of 150, sgd and numbered "51/130 Henri-Matisse" in pencil lower right, label from Goodspeed's Book Shop, Boston, on reverse, 18" x 11" image size, framed, deckled edges to three sides, mat staining, subtle soiling, masking tape to upper edge on reverse **14,100.00**

Milton, Peter, *Light Sweet Crude*, etching and aquatint, 1996, edition of 175, sgd and dated "PMilton 96" in pencil lower right, numbered "71/175" in pencil lower left, titled in pencil lower center, on Somerset cream wove paper with watermark, 18-3/8" x 15-1/4" plate size, unmatted, unframed, margins over 2" with deckled edges, subtle foxing and/or staining **235.00**

Motherwell, Robert, *Plate Four from The Basque Suite*, screenprint, 1970, edition of 150 plus proofs, published by Marlborough Graphics, Inc., initialed and numbered "RM 114/150" in pencil lower right, signed within matrix, artist's drystamp lower right, printed in black, red, and orange on paper, sheet size 40-1/2" x 28", framed, deckled edges **1,410.00**

Newell, J. P., lithographer and publisher, *Newport, R.I.*, identified in inscription in matrix, lithograph with hand-coloring on paper, framed, tear to margin upper right, toning, stains, foxing **1,175.00**

Picasso, Pablo
Deux Femmes Nues, etching on paper, 1930, edition of 125, sgd and numbered "34/125 Picasso..." in ink beneath image, label from Goodspeed's Book Shop, Boston, on reverse, 12-1/4" x 8-7/8" plate size, framed, scattered pale foxing **5,875.00**

La Guitare Sur la Table, etching with drypoint on paper, 1922, reprinted 1961, total edition of 70, stamped signature "Picasso" lower right, numbered "29/50" in pencil lower left, 3-1/8" x 4-3/4" plate size, framed **1,100.00**

Prior, Scott, *Provincetown Rooftops*, etching on heavy wove paper, 1971, sgd and dated "Scott Prior 1971" in pencil lower right, titled in pencil lower

J. H. King, We've Made a Monkey Out of You! Copyright 1943, 20" x 15", **$190.** *Photo courtesy of James D. Julia, Inc.*

center, inscribed "Artist's Proof" in pencil lower left, 8-7/8" x 11-3/4" plate size, matted, unframed, wide margins, minor staining **230.00**

Ramos, Mel, *Phantom Lady*, color screenprint on paper, 1963, sgd "Mel Ramos" in pencil lower right, numbered "HC 9/20" in pencil lower left , copyright, printer and publisher noted within matrix, 37" x 30" sheet/image size, unmatted, unframed, minor handling marks and creases . . . **420.00**

Ripley, Aiden Lassell, *Grouse on Pine Bough*, drypoint on paper, c1941, sgd "A Lassell Ripley" in pencil lower right, titled in pencil lower left, 8-3/4" x 11-7/8" plate size, framed, unobtrusive mat toning **1,100.00**

Roth, Ernest David, *Florentine Roofs*, Florentine, etching on laid paper with "G" watermark, sgd and dated "Ernest D. Roth 1912" in pencil lower center, titled dated and inscribed "Trial Proof" in pencil lower left, 10-1/2" x 10-3/8", matted, soiling, breaks to hinges **315.00**

Sachse, *View of Washington City*, Capitol building in foreground, Washington monument in back, colored lithograph, marked "Lith. & Print by E. Sacshe & Co., Baltimore, MD," stains and edge tears, 36" w, 28" h . . . **700.00**

Sloan, John, *Washington Arch*, etching on paper, sgd "John Sloan" in pencil lower right, sgd and dated within the plate lower right, titled in pencil lower left, 7-3/4" x 4-3/4", framed . . . **1,265.00**

Soyer, Raphael, *Bust of a Girl*, lithograph in black, red and blue on paper, edition of 300, sgd "Raphael Soyer" in pencil lower right, numbered "86/300" in pencil lower left, image size 18-3/8" x 13-5/8", framed, over 1" margins................**210.00**

Spence, R. S., publisher, printed by Wm Robertson, NY, *American Hunting Scene,* four gentlemen with guns, dogs, and boat hunting waterfowl, hand colored lithograph, 22" x 28", framed, some foxing and waterstains at borders **330.00**

Sterner, Albert Edward, *The Reveil,* etching with drypoint on wove paper with watermark, sgd "Albert Sterner" in pencil lower right, numbered "Ed. 250" in pencil lower left, annotated within lower margin, 8-7/8" x 7" plate size, matted **325.00**

Prang & Mayer, publishers, J. F.A. Cole, delineator and lithographer, *New Bedford, Massachusetts,* identified in inscriptions in the matrix, hand coloring, 16" x 32" image size, framed, repaired tears and punctures, scattered fox marks, staining, light toning **865.00**

Vogt, C H., *View of the City of New Bedford, Massachusetts*, 1876, identified in inscriptions in the matrix, 22" x 33" image size, framed, tear at left margin, scattered fox marks, overall toning **525.00**

Walker, George H. and Co., publisher, Joe L. Jones, lithographer, *Deacon Jones' One Hoss Shay, No. 2,* lithograph in blue and black, hand coloring, on paper, identified in inscriptions in matrix, 22-1/2" x 29-5/8" **490.00**

Welliver, Neil G., *Shadow from Zeke's,* color screen print on paper, sgd "Welliver" in pencil lower right, numbered "116/144" lower left, identified on label on reverse, 36" x 36-1/4", framed.............**920.00**

Wengenroth, Stow, *Great Horned Owl,* litho on paper, 1960, sgd "Stow Wengenroth" in pencil lower right,

Grant Wood, Seed Time & Harvest, signed, 1937, $325.

numbered "Ed./50" in pencil lower left, titled and annotated lower left, 15-1/4" x 11-3/4", matted, deckled edges on two sides, mat and other toning. **575.00**

Whistler, James Abbott McNeill

Billingstate, c1859, etching with drypoint on paper, sgd and identified within the plate, 6" x 9" plate size, framed, rippling, minor creases..............**1,035.00**

Fumette, c1858, etching on paper, sgd and identified within the plate, identified on label from Frederick Keppel, NY, on reverse, 6-1/2" x 4-1/4", framed, rippling...**1,495.00**

Wood, Grant, published by Associated American Artists

Tree Planting Group, litho on paper, sgd "Grant Wood-1937" in pencil lower right, 8-3/8" x 10-7/8", matted **4,025.00**

Vegetables, 1938, litho with hand coloring on paper, sgd "Grant Wood" in pencil lower right, identified on label from AAA on reverse, 7" x 9-1/2", framed **550.00**

PRINTS, JAPANESE

History: Buying Japanese woodblock prints requires attention to detail and abundant knowledge of the subject. The quality of the impression (good, moderate, or weak), the color, and condition are critical. Various states and strikes of the same print cause prices to fluctuate. Knowing the proper publisher's and censor's seals is helpful in identifying an original print.

Most prints were copied and issued in popular versions. These represent the vast majority of the prints found in the marketplace today. These popular versions should be viewed solely as decorative since they have little monetary value.

A novice buyer should seek expert advice before buying. Talk with a specialized dealer, museum curator, or auction division head.

The following terms are used to describe sizes: chuban, 7-1/2 x 10 inches; hosoban, 6 x 12 inches; and oban, 10 x 15 inches. Tat-e is a vertical print; yoko-e a horizontal one.

Note: The listings below include the large amount of detail necessary to determine value. Condition and impression are good unless indicated otherwise.

Album, Toyokuni III, Kuniyoshi, Hiroshige, mostly from series *Ogura Imitations of the One Hundred Poets* and *Keniyshi Genji* **2,645.00**

Chikanobu, framed triptych of women by lake, c1890, good impression, somewhat faded **125.00**

Eishi, four courtesans in elaborate kimonos, 1790s, framed, good impression, somewhat faded ..**345.00**

Eisan, courtesan with water view in background, fair impression, faded **245.00**

Goyo, *Portrait of a Beauty,* Dai-oban, excellent impression, toned and matted to within image **1,100.00**

Harunobu, pillar print of woman carrying bucket, framed, very good impression, horizontal creases and tears **345.00**

Hasui

A Farmer with Wagon in View of Tall Pines and Mt. Fuji, fine color, impression, and condition..**650.00**

Cryptomeria Avenue to Nikko, excellent impression, color, and condition, framed **500.00**

Mt. Fuji from Miho-No-Matsubara, excellent impression, stained and creased...............**590.00**

Nezu Shrine in Snow, excellent impression, color, and condition, framed.................**775.00**

Rainy Season at Ryoshimachi, Shinagawa, excellent impression, color, and condition, framed **775.00**

Hiroshige

Ferry at Kawaguchi and Zenkoji, from *One Hundred Famous Views of Edo,* c1856-59, fine impression, color, and condition, seals partially trimmed................**600.00**

Mitsuke, from *53 Famous Views of the Tokaido,* good impression and color, trimmed, framed **200.00**

Hausi, winter snow scene, 10-1/4" w, 15-1/2" h, $200.

Tajeo Takei, Still Life, 1953, color woodcut on paper, signed and dated lower right, shadow-box frame, 11-1/2" x 16-1/2", $140. Photo courtesy of Cowan's Historic Americana Auctions.

Morning at Nihon-Bashi, from *53 Stations of the Tokaido,* c1833-34, good impression, fair condition, stained and rubbed **5,000.00**
Utsu Mountain, from *53 Stations of the Tokaido,* c1833-34, good color, seal partially trimmed, backed and slightly rubbed and soiled . **500.00**
Hiroshige II, *Mimeguiri Embankment and the Sumida River,* from *Toto Meisho,* 1862, good impression, fine color. **350.00**
Hiroshi Yoshida
Fuji san from Yamanka, good impression, juzuri seal, good color, slight soil to margins. **375.00**
Market of Mukden, people in market place before temple gate, good impression, juzuri seal, framed **525.00**
Hokusai, *Flower Arrangement,* surimono, early 19th C, good impression and color, some toning and rubbing **245.00**
Jacoulet, *Joaquina et su Mere,* young woman and mother, good impression, faded, framed **290.00**
Junichiro Sekino, portrait of actor Kichiemon, "il ne etat," printed signature and seal lower right within the image, pencil sgd, 13/50 in lower margin, 22" x 18"**920.00**
Kawamishi, *The Water Lily Season,* sgd and titled in pencil, dated, numbered, framed**425.00**
Kiyonaga, Torri
Children Reading, Writing, and Decorating a Bamboo Spray, c1785, good impression, fair condition, much fading, stains, and abrasions, framed**490.00**
Two women wearing kimonos by side of stream, wooden garden trellis in background, red, green, brown, and black, old wooden mat

and frame, c1800, 16-1/4" w, 19-3/4" h, split to mat. **110.00**
Kiyotomo, *A Samurai with a Courtesan,* c1740, hosoban, with hand-coloring (tan-e), toning, creases, holes, and abrasions **230.00**
Koryusai, pair of prints, *Young Samurai with Letter Calling on a Lady,* c1780 or later, good impression, fair color and condition, faded with stains and creases; and *A Courtesan with a Playful Monkey,* c1780 or later, good impression and color, slight staining **2,750.00**
Kunihiro, *Viewing a Waterfall,* c1860, good impression and color, stains, and matted and framed to image . . . **190.00**
Kunisada, courtesan and two kamuro, landscape in background, printed in blue, c1830, good impression and color **215.00**
Kuniyoshi
A Courtesan in Elegant Kimono Holding a Pipe, excellent impression and color with visible wood grain, slight staining and holes **190.00**
Ladies Feeding Carp from a Pleasure Boat, triptych, c1840, excellent impression, color, and condition, with some fading of the blue **950.00**
Okiie Hashimoto, *Village in the Evening,* sgd in pencil in margin, dated, Hashi seal, good impression, framed, 17" x 21-1/2" **250.00**
Sekino, *Bridge in Snow,* sgd in image, seal, good impression, 18" x 12-1/2" **200.00**
Shigenobu, surimono of courtesan in an interior, make-up table and mirror to left, fine impression and color . . **634.00**
Toyokuni, perspective print of busy shopping area and temple grounds, 1790s, framed, good impression, faded **260.00**

Yoshida Hiroshi, Rapids, 1928, color woodcut, signed in brush in Japanese, pencil signed in roman script Hiroshi Yoshida, jizuri seal, $3,300. Photo courtesy of Sloan's Auctioneers & Appraisers.

Toyokuni II, *Two Courtesans,* c1800, good impression, faded, trimmed, small hole, stains, and creases **150.00**
Toyokuni III, Pentaptcyh of people in boat feeding goldfish, iris garden, framed, very good impression, missing leaf, somewhat faded **230.00**
Utamaro, *Woman Washing Her Hair,* good impression, stained, rubbed, and faded, framed **725.00**
Utamaro II, three women in an interior, c1811, good impression, faded, soiled **175.00**
Yoshida Hiroshi, *Daibutsu Temple Gate,* signed in pencil, with Jizuri seal, excellent impression and color . **490.00**

PURPLE SLAG (MARBLE GLASS)

History: Challinor, Taylor & Co., Tarantum, Pennsylvania, c1870s-1880s, was the largest producer of purple

Staffordshire, embossed alphabet on rims, polychrome printed transfer decoration, pearlware bodies, 5-1/4" d plate impressed "Meakin," 5-1/2" d plate unmarked, with staining and hairline, $195. Photo courtesy of Cowan's Historic Americana Auctions.

slag in the United States. Since the quality of pieces varies considerably, there is no doubt other American firms made it as well.

Purple slag also was made in England. English pieces are marked with British Registry marks.

Other slag colors, such as blue, green, and orange, were used, but examples are rare.

> **Reproduction Alert:** Purple slag has been heavily reproduced over the years and still is reproduced at present.

Animal
Bunny, Fenton, purple, 3" l, 2" w, 3-1/2" h **115.00**
Swan, Imperial, deep purple, 9-5/8" l, 5-1/4" w, 5-1/8" h **125.00**
Bowl, 9" d, Rose, caramel slag, Imperial IG mark **50.00**
Cake stand, Flute, purple **75.00**
Compote, cov, Eagle, Imperial, orig sticker, dark purple, 6-1/4" l, 5-1/4" d, 8-3/4" h **150.00**
Creamer, Flower and Panel, purple **85.00**
Goblet, Flute, purple **40.00**
Jar, cov, figural, owl, glossy, green slag, Imperial IG mark **60.00**
Match holder, Daisy and Button, green **30.00**
Miniature lamp, Imperial, orig sticker, white shade, purple and white swirled base, 4-1/2" w, 8" h **225.00**
Mug, rabbit, purple **65.00**
Pickle castor, 12" h, emb pickles and leaves on dark purple insert, resilvered frame, marked "Tufts #2361" . **1,100.00**
Pitcher, Windmill, glossy, purple slag, Imperial IG mark **45.00**
Pate, 10-1/2"d, closed lattice edge, purple **75.00**
Platter, oval, notched rim, wildflowers dec, purple, nick **20.00**
Spooner, Majestic, dark purple, 3-3/4" w, 5-1/2" h **125.00**
Sugar bowl, cov, Flute, purple . . **190.00**

Shoe, 5" l, 2" h, **$150.**

Fluted Rib pattern, Challinor, celery vase, 8-1/4" h, 4-1/4" d, **$95.**

Toothpick holder, Scroll and Acanthus, Northwood, blue and purple, 1902 . . . . **165.00**

PUZZLES

History: The jigsaw puzzle originated in the mid-18th century in Europe. John Spilsbury, a London map maker, was selling dissected-map jigsaw puzzles by the early 1760s. The first jigsaw puzzles in America were English and European imports aimed primarily at children.

Prior to the Civil War, several manufacturers, e.g., Samuel L. Hill, W. and S. B. Ives, and McLoughlin Brothers, included puzzles in their lines. However, it was the post-Civil War period that saw the jigsaw puzzle gain a strong foothold among the children of America.

In the late 1890s, puzzles designed specifically for adults first appeared. Both forms—adult and child—have existed side by side ever since.

Prior to the mid-1920s, the vast majority of jigsaw puzzles were cut out of wood for the adult market and composition material for the children's market. In the 1920s, the die-cut, cardboard jigsaw puzzle evolved and was the dominant medium in the 1930s.

Interest in jigsaw puzzles has cycled between peaks and valleys several times since 1933. Mini-revivals occurred during World War II and in the mid-1960s, when Springbok entered the American market. Internet auction sites are impacting the pricing of puzzles, raising some (Pars, Pastimes, U-Nits, figure pieces), but holding the line or even reducing others (Straus, Victory, strip cut). As with all auctions, final prices tend to vary depending upon the time of year and the activity of at least two interested bidders.

Adviser: Bob Armstrong.

Note: Prices listed here are for puzzles that are complete or restored, and in good condition. Most puzzles found in attics do not meet these standards. If evaluating an old puzzle, a discount of 50 percent should be calculated for moderate damage (one to two missing pieces, three to four broken knobs), with greater discounts for major damage or missing original box.

Wood and/or hand cut, pre-1900
Chamberlain, Mrs. Alice J., The Temple of Knowledge, c1890, solid wood, 11-1/2" x 18", 78 pcs, two-sided, orig box **80.00**
Milton Bradley, United States, Flags of Nations, c1890, pressboard, 20" x 14", 64 pcs, two-sided, orig box **35.00**

Wood and/or hand cut, pre-1930
Ayer, Isabel, Picture Puzzle Exchange, Fox Hunt at Mt Vernon, The Meet, 1910s, plywood, 16" x 9-1/4", 261 pcs, orig box **110.00**
Bates, Harriet, Picture Puzzle Exchange, The Birth of Old Glory, 1920s, plywood, 13-3/4" x 9-1/4", 213 pcs, orig box **80.00**
Keyes Puzzles, House of Seven Gables, c1910-20, plywood, 19-1/2" x 16", 548 pcs, one figural pc and "k" signature pc, orig box **195.00**
McDougall, E., Anglican Jigsaw, The Nosegay, C. E. Brock artist, English, c1910-20, plywood, 17-1/2" x 16-1/2", 300 pcs, cloth bag **130.00**
Pastime Puzzles, Parker Brothers, plywood
Evening on Grand Canal, Venice, #2, c1930, 9-3/4" x 10", 150 pcs, 20 figural pcs, orig box **60.00**
Good Old Times, Fishing, #17, 1910, 7-1/2" x 11", 163 pcs, 14 figural pcs, orig box **80.00**
Point of View, 1920s, W. M. Thompson artist, 19-3/4" x 15-3/4", 481 pcs, 43 figural pcs, replaced box **175.00**
Sunset, #7, c1928, 7" x 9", 126 pcs, 12 figural pcs, orig box **55.00**

Unknown
The Bridal Party, 1920s, pressboard, 10-3/4" x 13-3/4", 155 pcs, orig box **30.00**
The Father's Return, c1909, solid wood, 7" x 10", 102 pcs, replaced box **45.00**
Untitled, Mamie reading palm of Belle, c1910, solid wood, 8-1/4" x 10", 70 pcs, replaced box . . . **30.00**
Untitled, Washington leading troops, c1909, solid wood, 15-1/2" x 10-1/2", 175 pcs, replaced box **65.00**

Wood and/or hand cut, 1930s-40s, plywood
Allen, P. J., Sparetime, Washington Displaying New American Flag, Percy Moran artist, 11-3/4" x 9", 194 pcs, orig box **40.00**

Bryant, W. E., Land of the Midnight Sun, 12" x 10", 160 pcs, one figural pc, "B" signature pc, orig box, mail lending library. **50.00**

Chad Valley, Cunard Line, Queen Mary in Trafalgar Square, W. McDowell artist, 1936, 11-1/2" x 16", 300 pcs, replaced box, English style cut **65.00**

Crosby, A. T., A Puzzler Picture, Le Petit Jean, 12" x 15", 324 pcs, seven figural pcs, orig box. **80.00**

Dodge, Don R., Old Ironsides, 16" x 20", 550 pcs, one replaced, orig box **125.00**

Hayes, J. M., Lending Library, By Gone Days, George Maroniez artist, 14" x 10-1/2", 327 pcs, four replaced, orig box. **75.00**

Hoadley House, Game of Chess, Pickwick, 17-3/4" x 13-3/4", 365 pcs, four replaced, replaced box **75.00**

Huvanco, Deluxe 9, Between Two Fires, 11-3/4" x 9-1/2", 200 pcs, orig box **50.00**

Jewel Puzzle, Lending Library, Beautiful Home by Wayside, 14" x 9-1/2", 252 pcs, eight figural pcs, two replaced, orig box. **65.00**

Jig Saw Puzzle, Golden Peaks, 15-3/4" x 20-3/4", 600 pcs, two replaced, orig box. **120.00**

Jones, A. V. N., Delta

Out of the Mist, 17-1/4" x 11-1/4", 400 pcs, orig box **70.00**

The Shipsail Yarder, Duncan Gleason artist, 22-3/4" x 17", 800 pcs, orig box **120.00**

Madmar, Interlox

Poppies and Larkspur, 19" x 23", 1,000 pcs, two replaced, orig box **200.00**

Tally-Ho, 11-1/2" x 14-3/4", 300 pcs, two replaced, orig box **75.00**

Merritt, R. H., Delta, Sunset in Nevada, 16" x 12", 465 pcs, orig box. . . . **150.00**

Milton Bradley, Premier, Kidnapped (bear), 12" x 9", 200 pcs, eight figural pcs, orig box **50.00**

Par Puzzles, Ltd., New York, NY, Pivot Point, Par 5:20, 15-1/2" x 24-1/2", 750 pcs, 23 figural pcs, orig box . . . **500.00**

Pastime Puzzles, Parker Brothers

Perfection, 1930s, 6-1/2" x 8-1/2", 88 pcs, eight figural pcs, replaced box **140.00**

Right Not Might, Lincoln, c1931, 11-3/4" x 9", 185 pcs, 18 figural pcs, orig box **85.00**

Russian Ballet Dancer, #142, c1931, 7-1/2" x 9-1/4", 105 pcs, 11 figural pcs, orig box. **50.00**

The Fisherman, c1938, 22-1/4" x 18-1/4", 613 pcs, 72 figural pcs, orig box **290.00**

Penelope, Le Petit Frere, 17-1/2" x 22", 1,000 pcs, 10 replaced, orig box **160.00**

Plantations, Rent-A-Puzzle, Roses Remind Me of You, 12" x 16", 350 pcs, orig box **75.00**

Sexton, Eugene, Lending Library, Painting the Vase, Goddard artist, 16" x 21-3/4", orig box. **150.00**

Straus, Joseph

Covered Wagon, F. G. Sayers artist, 20" x 16", 500 pcs, orig box . **60.00**

Murmring Waters, T. S. Barber artist, 19-3/4" x 15-3/4", 500 pcs, one pc replaced, orig box. **60.00**

Thayer, W. H., Lending Library, Fragrance Sweetest in Dewey Morn, Kent Dhu artist, 19-3/4" x 15-3/4", 580 pcs, orig box **120.00**

Tuck, Zag-Zaw

A Welcome Rest, Drummond artist, 8-1/4" x 12", 165 pcs, 19 figural pcs, orig box. **50.00**

Oliver Twist Asks for More, Harold Copping artist, 6" x 8-1/4", 96 pcs, 10 figural pcs, orig box. **50.00**

Unknown

A Canadian Landscape, R. Atkinson Fox artist, 19-3/4" x 13", 419 pcs, replaced box. **120.00**

Dutch Flower Market, Van Freeland artist, 9" x 12", orig box **55.00**

Dissected map of the United States, Milton Bradley Co., Springfield, MA, c1890, full color litho on paper, mounted on wood, orig box, 9-3/4" x 14-1/4", $115. Photo courtesy of James D. Julia, Inc.

Little House with Red Roof, Marguerite Kumm artist, 6-3/4" x 8-1/2", 77 pcs, replaced box **20.00**

Paradise, 10" x 13", 260 pcs, two replaced, orig box **35.00**

Sunrise above the Clouds, Fran Dmitri artist, 14-3/4" x 10", 258 pcs, orig box **100.00**

Sunset in the Desert, 16" x 11-3/4", 419 pcs, orig box **135.00**

Untitled, Colonial women sewing circle, Percy Moran artist, 15" x 11", 400 pcs, four replaced, replaced box **85.00**

Wood and/or hand cut, post 1950, plywood

Barbour, R. H.

Fast Water, 19" x 12", 277 pcs, trick edges, orig box **40.00**

Ice Boat Racing on the Hudson, Currier & Ives, 13-1/4" x 10", 151 pcs, orig box **35.00**

Browning, James, U-Nit, Young Traffic Officer, H. Hintermeister artist, plywood with mahogany back, 15-1/2" x 19-1/2", 500 pcs, 53 figural pcs, orig box **200.00**

Chesley, Roland, Buckfield, Maine

Monterey Peninsula, California, 17" x 17-1/2", 569 pcs, orig box . **100.00**

Snowscape Lancaster, NH, 16-1/2" x 13-1/2", 362 pcs, orig box . . **70.00**

Hayter, VictoryThe Conference, Dovaston artist, 23-1/2" x 17-1/4", 800 pcs, one replaced pc, orig box **100.00**

Mountain Stream, 38" x 25", 1,500 pcs, 88 figural pcs, orig box **250.00**

McGregor, Jim's Jig Saw Puzzles, Playmates, 10-3/4" x 17", 372 pcs, one replaced pc, replaced box **50.00**

Par Puzzles, Ltd., New York, NY, Never Too Hurried, Par 1:25, 13-1/2" x 9-1/2", 275 pcs, four figural pcs, orig box **300.00**

Pastime Puzzles, Parker Brothers, Open Air Market, #753, 1950s, 30-1/2" x 23", 1001 pcs, 125 figural pcs, orig box **450.00**

Russell, Charles, Auburn, Mass, Ocean Resort in Italy, 15-1/2" x 11", 369 pcs, 46 figural pcs, well cut with false edges, orig box. **125.00**

Spear, Hayter, Vict Gold Box, Peaceful Moments, 29-1/4" x 19-1/2", 1,000 pcs, one replaced, 52 figural pcs, orig box **135.00**

Stanfield, Master Craftsman, Ladyship's Favorite, 28" x 22", 1,000 pcs, orig box **95.00**

Straus, Joseph

Coming Through, 12" x 16", 300 pcs, orig box **35.00**

Le Moulin De La Giaette, Auguste Renoir artist, 23-3/4" x 17-3/4", 750 pcs, one replaced pc, orig box **100.00**

Mt. Hood and Lost Lake, 24" x 18", 750 pcs, orig box **75.00**

White, Sara, When Teacher's Back is Turned, 23-1/2" x 17-3/4", 925 pcs, seven figurals, interactive, orig box **325.00**

QUEZAL

Warman's
GLASS
A Value & Identification Guide
4TH EDITION

Edited by Ellen T. Schroy

For more information, see this book.

Quezal

History: The Quezal Art Glass Decorating Company, named for the quetzal—a bird with brilliantly colored feathers—was organized in 1901 in Brooklyn, New York, by Martin Bach and Thomas Johnson, two disgruntled Tiffany workers. They soon hired Percy Britton and William Wiedebine, two more Tiffany employees.

The first products, which are unmarked, were exact Tiffany imitations. Quezal pieces differ from Tiffany pieces in that they are more defined and the decorations are more visible and brighter. No new techniques were developed by Quezal.

Johnson left in 1905. T. Conrad Vahlsing, Bach's son-in-law, joined the firm in 1918, but left with Paul Frank in 1920 to form Lustre Art Glass Company, which copied Quezal pieces. Martin Bach died in 1924 and by 1925, Quezal had ceased operations.

Marks: The "Quezal" trademark was first used in 1902 and placed on the base of vases and bowls and the rims of shades. The acid-etched or engraved letters vary in size and may be found in amber, black, or gold. A printed label that includes an illustration of a quetzal was used briefly in 1907.

Bowl, 9-1/2" d, irid gold Calcite ground, stretch rim, pedestal foot, sgd "Quezal" **800.00**

Cabinet vase, 1-3/4" h, 4-1/4" dec, squatty, 16 ribs, undulating flared rim, irid blue-gold, strong red highlights, polished pontil marked "Quezal D685" **550.00**

Candlesticks, pr, 7-3/4" h, irid blue, sgd **575.00**

Shade, gold iridescent, ruffled rim, signed "QUEZAL," 2-1/4" d fitter, 6-1/2" h, $150. Photo courtesy of James D. Julia, Inc.

Ceiling lamp shade, 13-3/4" d, 21-1/2" l drop, radiating irid gold and green leaf dec, domed irid ivory glass shade supported by brass ring suspended from three ball chains, two-socket fixture, shade inscribed "Quezal," Brooklyn, NY, early 20th C. **6,325.00**

Chandelier, gilt metal

14" h, four elaborated scroll arms, closed teardrop gold, green, and opal shades, inscribed "Quezal" at collet rim, very minor roughness at rim edge **2,000.00**

16" h, three shouldered flared opal shades, rib molded design, gold

Chandelier, five ruffled shades in pulled-feather design, signed, $2,100. Photo courtesy of James D. Julia.

irid int., collet rim inscribed "Quezal," classic shaped socket, wheel with chain drop **450.00**

Cologne bottle, 7-1/2" h, irid gold ground, Art Deco design, sgd "Q" and "Melba" **250.00**

Lamp, desk, 14-1/2" h, irid gold shade with green and white pulled feather dec, inscribed "Quezal" at rim, gilt metal adjustable crook-neck lamp **575.00**

Lamp shade

4-3/4" h, 2" fitter ring, pulled feather design, gold feathers bordered by green band, opalescent white edge, ruffled top edge, sgd "Quezal" **150.00**

5-3/8" h, King Tut, dome shape, gold irid design, sgd "Quezal," minor scratches **690.00**

8" h, cylindrical, ruffled flared rim, irid gold, green, and polychromatic glass, sgd "Quezal" **3,450.00**

Salt, open, 2-1/2" w, 1-1/4" h, irid, sgd **375.00**

Toothpick holder, 2-1/4" h, melon ribbed, pinched sides, irid blue, green, purple and gold, sgd **200.00**

Vase

7-1/4" h, bottle shape, irid gold shades to bluish-red at rim, sgd "Quezal" in polished pontil, small scratch on side **965.00**

4-1/2" d, 7-3/8" h, flared rim, irid gold, blue-green coiled dec, polished pontil marked "Quezal" **2,500.00**

8-1/4" h, three pulled and folded loop handles, irid gold, strong red and blue highlights, polished pontil, unsigned **1,350.00**

12-5/8" h, flared rim, urn form, bulbed base, irid gold swirl pattern, crack at base **290.00**

Whiskey taster, 2-3/4" h, oval, irid gold, four pinched dimples, sgd "Quezal" on base **200.00**

QUILTS

History: Quilts have been passed down as family heirlooms for many generations. Each one is unique. The same pattern may have hundreds of variations in both color and design.

The advent of the sewing machine increased, not decreased, the number of quilts made. Quilts are still being sewn today.

Notes: The key considerations for price are age, condition, aesthetic appeal, and design. Prices are now level, although the very finest examples continue to bring record prices.

Appliqué, Bellflowers, red flowers, central panel with eagle, 95" x 80", $300. Photo courtesy of Joy Luke Auctions.

Appliqué

Eagle, red, green, and gold eagles, bordered nine block pattern, white ground, quilted in conforming eagle and geometric pattern, Missouri, 20th C, 83" x 77" **2,350.00**

Fish, stuffed fish designs between green and red floral panels, floral vining around edges, stains, light overall fading, 82" x 90"............ **550.00**

Flower Basket, red, green, and yellow calico, white ground, toning, minor staining, fabric wear, 77-1/2" x 67" **885.00**

Grape vines, green and purple vines meandering between quilted stuffed grapes, hand quilted following pattern, minor stains, 66" x 82" **800.00**

Nine blocks, each with large red flower, pink and yellow center, blue leaves and vines, red buds, border of blue quarter boons and red stars, white quilted ground, signed with embroidery "Polly Matthias (heart) Lug March 1837," 84" x 84" **1,750.00**

Oak leaf, red and green printed fabric vine border, white ground, late 19th C, 72" x 88", minor stains, marker lines **300.00**

Rose of Sharon, pieced scalloped border, red, green, pink, and yellow calico, white ground and backing, red binding, conforming floral pattern quilting, attributed to PA, c1840, 88" x 90" **1,530.00**

Rose Wreath Variant, red and green roses and leaves, meandering vine border, white ground, red banding, America, mid-19th C, fading, minor staining, 79" x 68" **500.00**

Tree of Life, Brodene Perse, 19th C, staining, 112" x 114" **4,600.00**

Appliqué, Rose of Sharon pattern, worked in red, green, and antimony cotton fabrics, swag border, white ground, quilted in grid and conforming swag patterns, Ohio, late 19th C, 84" x 65", $1,100. Photo courtesy of Skinner Auctioneers and Appraisers

Appliqué and pieced

Album, red plaid separates squares with appliquéd polychrome prints, most are floral, some have deer or birds, two have Eastern scenes with camels and elephants, inked signatures, dates in the 1850s, stains, 64" sq **1,870.00**

Nine floral medallions, red, yellow, and green, red and green sawtooth edging, hand quilted, feathering between medallions, scroll work along border, stains, 82" x 83" **1,430.00**

Tulips, pink, purple, and orange, green leaves and borders, hand quilted with flowers, feathering, and diamonds, dark black and blue pencil lines, light green edging, 70" x 82" **770.00**

Calamanco, panels of glazed indigo and dark olive green worsted fabric, quilted in scrolling feather and grapevine patterns, backed with brown woven tabby fabric, New England, c1800, 82" x 83", very minor losses **2,115.00**

Appliqué, Dogwood pattern, pink appliqué dogwood flowers, brown branches, green leaves, 93" x 76", $200. Photo courtesy of Joy Luke Auctions.

Chintz

Printed overall design of exotic birds drinking from urns hanging from trees, brown on white, printed gold, blue, green, and reddish-brown, brown floral baking, light stains, 94" x 116" **1,450.00**

Crazy

Pieced, many embroideries, including chenille goldenrod, owl at center of pin-wheeled fabrics, 1891.... **4,500.00**

Pieced velvet, black, burgundy, purple, red, gold, gray, green, and brown solid and printed shaped patches, arranged in 16 squares, colorful velvet border, late 19th C, 72" x 74" **885.00**

Hawaiian, pieced, nine pineapple
medallions, meandering floral vines, green and orange, white ground, quilted floral rosettes in corners, 64" sq **600.00**

Pieced

Bow Tie, dark maroon and floral chintz squares alternating with multicolored bow tie squares, brown border with yellow stars, hand stitched, stains, 92" x 96" **1,320.00**

Bow Tie, small green and red triangles, red zig zag border with green sawtooth edging, hand stitched four petal flower quilting, red edging, slight wear and facing, 74" sq **1,575.00**

Broken Star, orange, yellow, green, red, brown, blue, and white printed calico patches, red and white calico Flying Geese border, PA, 19th C, 80" x 76" **460.00**

Cathedral, multicolored diamonds within white circles, hand stitching, 90-1/4" x 105" **425.00**

Chinese Lanterns, green, red, blue, yellow, and white printed calico and solid patches, blue and white ground, red border, diamond and rope quilting, PA, late 19th C, minor staining, 82" x 84" **1,495.00**

Courthouse Steps, various silk colors, black border, highlighted by decorative embroidery, late 19th C, minor wear, 20" x 26-1/2" **260.00**

Diamond Nine Patch and Block, shades of pink, green, red, blue, and brown, alternating yellow blocks and brown border, backed with brown and white printed striped fabric, quilted in diagonal lines design, 90" x 92", two areas of staining, two small areas of wear on back.............. **355.00**

Flower Basket in Diamond design, red, yellow, pink, and red calico, 20th C, 89" x 87", 1" tear **450.00**

Four petal flowers in two shades of light yellow and pale green, white ground, border of arches with buds, hand stitched, princess feather medallions, fancy scrolls, and interlacing lines quilting, scalloped edge, light stains, 84" sq **495.00**

Irish Chain, pink, green, and peach calico, straight green and pink borders, brown calico backing, embroidered with red "B" in lower left hand corner, 6' 10" x 6' 11", very minor staining . **225.00**

Log Cabin

Black, purple, gray, blue, brown, ivory, red, and green, striped flannel backing, Mennonite, 71" x 84" **350.00**

Made from jockey silks, red, blue, yellow, orange, purple, brown, and black, yarn tied to brown silk back, found in KY, 91" x 100" **715.00**

Moon and Stars, pieced wool, 49 full and three-quarter circles composed of four pie-shaped wedges, shades or rust and green, tan twill binding, woven wool backing, 83" x 96", fading, stains, small holes **770.00**

Nine Patch, various colors, red grid, hand and machine stitched, backed and bound with red and white printed fabric, late 19th/early 20th C, minor fading, 79" x 71" **230.00**

Nine Patch variant

Chintz squares edged with triangles, floral printed border, hand stitched, diamond and floral quilting, orig pencil marks, some stains, 82" x 83" **1,540.00**

Multicolored squares alternating with off-white, arranged diagonally in block and surrounded by red grid, sawtooth border, backed with

Pieced, Triple Sunflower pattern, multicolored triple starflowers, green stems, and leaves, 91" x 76", **$175.** *Photo courtesy of Joy Luke Auctions.*

Pieced, Double X pattern, green, pink, red, and yellow cotton calico fabrics, multicolored patchwork blocks bordered by pink zig-zag design, three narrow yellow and red borders, wide pink border, stripes of calico fabric backing, late 19th C, 84" x 73", **$330.** *Photo courtesy of Sanford Alderfer Auction Co.*

white, red binding, minor imperfections, 81-1/2" x 75" **460.00**

Philadelphia Pavements, blue, red, orange, and white square printed and solid patches, orange and red banded borders with feather and floral fine quilting, PA, late 19th/early 20th C, 84" x 80" **825.00**

Pineapple corner elements with birds, central medallion, golden yellow on red, white green borders, burnt orange calico backing, hand stitched, 92" sq **725.00**

Pineapple Log Cabin, pieced calico, border of four bands, two yellow, green, and pink, backed with brown figured print, bound with green, Mennonite, Washington, PA, c1880, 96" x 84" **1,175.00**

Schoolhouse, red, orange, yellow, and tan buildings machine-stitched on white ground, several interesting quilting patterns, scallops, and zigzags on roofs, stars and geometric shapes in gable ends, birds and leaves on sashing, Midwest, late 19th C, 75-1/2" x 73-1/2" **1,060.00**

Serrated Square, corresponding border, pink and green calico, shell and diamond quilting, 82" x 84" **320.00**

Spider Web, pink, red, blue, purple green, peach, and brown printed calico patches, wide purple calico border, diagonal line quilting, Mennonite, PA, late 19th C, some staining, 82" x 80" **825.00**

Star of Bethlehem, purple, green, red, blue, and pink calico, white ground, early 20th C, toning, minor staining, fabric wear, 82" x 73-1/2" **650.00**

Stars, 30 red stars, white cotton ground, divided by feather wreath

quilting, pencil marks, some stains, 83-1/2" x 72-1/2" **690.00**

Sunburst in squares, burgundy alternating with green and dark blue-gray, burgundy flannel gathered bordered, plaid backing, yellow and white stitching, Mennonite, 52" x 84" **200.00**

Tulip medallions and potted tulips, red, green, and goldenrod calico, white ground, zigzags, tulips, stars, and circles border, hand quilted with tulips hearts, stars, and moons, 88" sq **800.00**

Windmill, yellow, red, green, and blue printed calico patches, wide red calico with swag quilting, PA, late 19th C, 86" x 76" **690.00**

QUIMPER

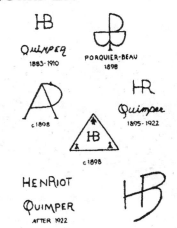

History: Quimper faience, dating back to the 17th century, is named for Quimper, a French town where numerous potteries were located. Several mergers resulted in the evolution of two major houses—the Jules Henriot and Hubaudière-Bousquet factories.

The peasant design first appeared in the 1860s, and many variations exist. Florals and geometrics, equally popular, also were produced in large quantities. During the 1920s, the Hubaudière-Bousquet factory introduced the Odetta line, which utilized a stone body and Art Deco decorations.

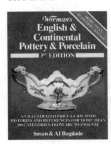

For more information, see this book.

The two major houses merged in 1968, the products retaining the individual characteristics and marks of the originals. The concern suffered from labor problems in the 1980s and was purchased by an American group.

Marks: The "HR" and "HR Quimper" marks are found on Henriot pieces prior to 1922. The "Henriot Quimper" mark was used after 1922. The "HB" mark covers a long time span. Numbers or dots and dashes were added for inventory purposes and are found on later pieces. Most marks are in blue or black. Pieces ordered by department stores, such as Macy's and Carson Pirie Scott, carry the store mark along with the factory mark, making them less desirable to collectors. A comprehensive list of marks is found in Bondhus book.

Advisers: Susan and Al Bagdade.

Additional Terms:

A la touche border decor—single brush stroke to create floral

Breton Broderie decor—stylized blue and gold pattern inspired by a popular embroidery pattern often used on Breton costumes, dates from the Art Deco era.

Croisille—criss-cross pattern

Decor Riche border—acanthus leaves in two colors

Fleur de lys—the symbol of France

Ivoire Corbeille pattern—red dots circled in sponged blue with red touches forming half a floral blossom, all over a tan ground

Quintal—five-fingered vase.

Bowl, covered, Ivoire Corbeille, black hat, cobalt blue jacket with orange stripes, chains of blue or green sponged circlets with red centers, red half flowerheads, blue sponged handles and knob, ivory ground, marked "HenRiot Quimper," 9-3/4" handle to handle, $325. Photos courtesy of Allen and Susan Bagdade.

Bell, 4-1/2" h, female peasant holding bouquet, four blue dots and foliage, red and green dashes, blue dot florals with yellow centers on reverse, olive green collar with yellow, red, and blue circles and dashes, blue handle, marked "HenRiot Quimper France" **125.00**

Biberon, 4-1/4" h, red, blue, and green flower band, blue sponged handle and rim, blue striped base, marked "HB Quimper" under handle....... **235.00**

Bookends, pr, 5-1/2" h, Modern Movement, standing figural child with cobalt blue dress, white cap, red striped yellow or red striped pink apron, leaning on brown wall, brown base, marked "HenRiot Quimper J. E. Sevellec," price for pr **450.00**

Inkstand, crest of Brittany on backplate, dark blue acanthus borders, yellow outlined shells and swirls, blue dotted feet, marked "HenRiot Quimper," 7-1/4" w, 6-1/2" h, $750.

Bowl, 6" d, peasant woman wearing olive green blouse, blue skirt, red apron, typical florals at sides, yellow inner band, border band of red and blue single stroke flowers, green foliage, blue outlined indented rim, marked "HenRiot Quimper" **80.00**

Bowl, cov

9" handle to handle, band of single stroke red and green florals on bowl, female peasant wearing yellow vest, olive blouse, blue apron, red skirt, holding flowers, vertical florals and border band of single stroke florals, yellow and blue lined rim, blue knob, blue dash and yellow outlined scroll handles, marked "HenRiot Quimper, France" **195.00**

9-3/4" handle to handle, Ivoire Corbeille, black hat, cobalt blue jacket with orange stripes, chains of blue or green sponged circlets with red centers, red half flowerheads, blue sponged handles and knob, ivory ground, marked "HenRiot Quimper". **325.00**

Box, cov, 2-3/4" l, 2" w, rect, seated peasant lady holding basket on cov, orange outlined blue acanthus borders, marked "HB Quimper" **220.00**

Butter tub, cov, attached underplate, 6" l, 4" h, oval, vertical fluting, band of red, blue, yellow, and green florals on body, female peasant on cov, pierced ear handles, blue shell knob, blue lined rims, marked "HenRiot Quimper France 101" **200.00**

Chamberstick, 6-1/4" l, 3-1/4" h, leaf shaped base, male peasant flanked by

green, red, and yellow-centered blue dot flowers, blue streaked rim, blue cross-hatched panels alternating with floral panels on nozzle, blue dash ring handle, marked "HenRiot Quimper France" **195.00**

Charger, 12-1/4" d, center painted female peasant reclining on rocks in meadow, Breton Broderie border of light blue enamel dots and orange enamel chevrons on blue-black ground, marked "HB Quimper" on front . **450.00**

Cider jug, cov, 7" h, male peasant on front under spout, blue sponged trees and vertical rushes, scattered four blue dot designs, single stroke florals, blue sponged overhead handle, spout, and knob, marked "HB Quimper" under spout **210.00**

Cheese dish, cov, 10-1/2" l, painted seated female peasant, egg basket on lap on cover, scattered florals, brown bagpipe horns and mouthpiece, blue acanthus border, scattered florals on base, molded pink ribbons and brown bagpipe pipes, blue "HenRiot Quimper" mark **475.00**

Cup and saucer

Male peasant on cup, green and red horizontal single stroke foliage, yellow-centered blue dot flowers, scattered four blue dot designs, blue banded rim, green sponged handle, marked "HR Quimper" **85.00**

Trefoil shape, scattered yellow-centered-blue flowers, green foliage, four blue dot designs, marked "HB" **100.00**

Figure

5-1/2" h, standing Breton youth, yellow edged cobalt blue jacket, green vest, orange trousers, circular green base with "Yann" in rect, blue "HenRiot Quimper 144" mark **175.00**

Fish platter, male peasant, blue jacket, orange pants, female peasant in blue dress, maroon apron, pale blue, red, and yellow florals, red and orange outlined rim, pierced for hanging, "HenRiot Quimper" mark, 19" l, 1,100.

Plate, left: male peasant, right: female peasant, blue and pale green costumes, red, blue, yellow, and green vertical florals, light green and red single stroke designs on border, blue outlined shaped rim, "HR Quimper" on front, 9-1/2" d, price for pair, $300. All Quimper photos courtesy of Susan and Al Bagdade.

8-1/2" h, dancing Breton couple, male wearing black jacket, blue trousers, female with black dress, blue apron, white coif, yellow Breton embroidery on dress, white circular base, "Micheau-Vernez," marked "HenRiot Quimper". **275.00**

9" h, standing child, holding cloth, overall white glaze, Berthe Savgny, marked "HB Quimper" **900.00**

Fish plate, 10" l, fish shape, yellow face, blue and red striped tail, frontal of male peasant, arms folded in center, demilune flowers at side, four blue dots and ermine tail trim, yellow lined margins, brown "HR Quimper" mark
. . . . **300.00**

Holy water font, 3-1/4" w, 4" h, relief molded bust of Mary and baby, red, yellow, and blue halos, yellow cross with red chevrons on top with hole, relief molded green, blue, and red florals on rip and cup, marked "Henriot Quimper"
. . . . **375.00**

Inkstand, 7-1/4" w, 6-1/2" h crest of Brittany on backplate, dark blue acanthus borders, yellow outlined shells and swirls, blue dotted feet, marked "HenRiot Quimper" **750.00**

Inkwell, 3-3/4" sq, spread base, male peasant blowing horn on front panel, small red and green floral sprays, blue croiselle edges, four pen holes, marked "HR Quimper" **450.00**

Jug, 11" h, painted Breton couple near fence on front, crest of Brittany on border, painted cornflowers on reverse, crest of Quimper on border, blue sponged handle, Porquier-Beau
. . . . **2,530.00**

Knife rest, 3-1/2" l, triangle shape, male or female peasant and foliage, blue dash edges, blue sponged ends,

marked "HenRiot Quimper France" on front, price for pr **90.00**

Menu, 3-1/4" w, 5" h, rect, frontal view of female peasant holding basket of produce, crowned crest of Quimper in corner, blue "Menu" at top, blue outlined shaped rim, sponged bracket feet, marked "HR Qumiper". . . . **300.00**

Oyster plate, 8-1/2" d, center well with blue shaded fleur-de-lys and inner band of small red hanging flowers, six blue outlined wells, two with male or female peasant, four with vertical red and green florals, four blue dot designs, orange and yellow shell designs between wells, marked "HR Quimper"
. . . . **700.00**

Pitcher

8-1/2" h, 9" w, double spout, overhead handle, stoneware, brown and blue enamel triangles around middle, lines, charcoal, white, and brown deigns around body and handles, Odetta. **550.00**

9-1/4" h, ftd, blue pear shaped geometrics, purple lines and accents, blue lined rim, center, and base, marked "HB Quimper"
. . . . **135.00**

Plate

5-5/8" d, large green centered red petaled daisy, yellow-centered blue dot flowers, scattered four blue dot designs, blue and yellow banded border, marked "HenRiot Quimper France". **65.00**

8-3/4" d, center large strutting peacock and half daisy, single stroke band of concentric circles on border, blue "HB" mark on front
. . . . **195.00**

9-3/8" d, center crowing rooster, red and green single stroke floral and yellow-centered blue dot florals in center, border band of single stroke red, green, and blue florals and foliate, marked "HB Quimper"
. . . . **195.00**

9-1/2" d, female peasant, hand on hip, holding yellow jug on shoulder, or male peasant blowing horn, flanked by red and green florals, yellow-centered blue dot flowers, border band of same designs, blue lined indented rim, marked "HR Quimper" on front, price for pr
. . . . **350.00**

9-5/8" d, female peasant wearing olive blouse, blue skirt, yellow apron, typical foliate at sides, blue and yellow banded border, c1920,

marked "HenRiot Quimper France"
. . . . **65.00**

Platter, 13" l, 10" w, rect, cut corners, blue painted stylized basket, center large red and blue daisies, scattered red, blue, yellow, and green foliate, band of red, yellow, and green single stroke florals on border, black ermine tails on corners, rim chip **150.00**

Porringer, 4-3/4" handle to handle, standing female peasant wearing red blouse, blue skirt, yellow apron, vertical red, blue, and green foliage, yellow and blue striped border, blue sponged tab handles, marked "HenRiot Quimper France 77" **80.00**

Salt, 3-3/8" w, 2" h, figural, double swans, blue wings, blue dotted breasts and heads, yellow bills, orange outlined blue dash center loop handle, female peasant on one int., floral sprig on other, marked "HenRiot Quimper France"
. . . . **50.00**

Snuff bottle

2-1/2" h, book shape, female peasant holding bouquet on front, yellow and gold fleur-de-lys on reverse, blue binding with "Souvenir," orig stopper, unmarked
. . . . **325.00**

3-1/4" l, oval doughnut shape, red and green band of geometrics in blue borders on front, "Souvenir de Bretagne" on reverse **350.00**

Vase, figural bagpipe, male peasant blowing horn on front, blue basket of half red daisy and garden flowers on reverse, molded green, blue, and yellow leaf forms on edge, brown pipe handle, blue molded bow at top, marked "HR Quimper" on reverse, 6" h, $300.

Soup plate, 9-5/8" d, peasant man playing horn, another playing bagpipe in meadow, scattered multicolored hanging local flower sprigs on border, rim with band of blue circles, orange and blue lines, marked "HenRiot Quimper" **350.00**

Tray, 11-1/2" handle to handle, busts of male and female Bretons on cream ground in center, Breton Broderie border of ochre enameled chevrons on cobalt blue ground, marked "HB Quimper" **125.00**

Trinket box, 4-1/4" w, shield shape, seated male peasant blowing horn on cov, dark blue on light blue acanthus borders, orange lined rims, marked "HenRiot Quimper" **395.00**

Tureen, cov, 14-1/2" handle to handle, base with male peasant seated on yellow rock holding pipe, female seated on rock on cov, red and green single stroke florals and yellow centered blue sponged stylized flowers, blue dash handles, arched knob with four blue dots, Adolphe Porquier **550.00**

Vase

5-1/2" h, moon flask shape, reclining Breton youth with scythe at side, pink, and yellow mallow flowers on reverse, green acanthus side borders, blue interlaced "PB" mark **1,800.00**

6" h, figural bagpipe, male peasant blowing horn on front, blue basket of half red daisy and garden flowers on reverse, molded green, blue, and yellow leaf forms on edge, brown pipe handle, blue molded bow at top, marked "HR Quimper" on reverse **300.00**

10" h, figural fleur-de-lys, walking Breton youth on petal, reverse with single stroke bouquet of red daisy and bluets, blue or yellow painted sides, crest of Brittany on base front and back, marked "HR Quimper" on front **675.00**

Wall pocket, figural

4" w, 4-1/2" l, open envelope, male or female peasant on front, four blue dot designs, red, green, and blue single stroke flowers, blue and yellow outlined borders, blue dashes around hanging hole, marked "HR Quimper," price for pr **575.00**

9-1/2" w, 13" l, open umbrella, male and female peasant with floral sprays, orange outlined blue acanthus border, brown umbrella

handle with tied cord, marked "HenRiot Quimper 141". . . . **475.00**

RADIOS

History: The radio was invented more than 100 years ago. Marconi was the first to assemble and employ the transmission and reception instruments that permitted the sending of electric messages without the use of direct connections. Between 1905 and the end of World War I, many technical advances affected the "wireless," including the invention of the vacuum tube by DeForest. Technology continued its progress, and radios filled the entertainment needs of the average family in the 1920s.

Changes in design, style, and technology brought the radio from the black boxes of the 1920s to the stylish furniture pieces and console models of the 1930s and 1940s, to midget models of the 1950s, and finally to the high-tech radios of the 1980s.

Additional Listings: See *Warman's Americana & Collectibles* for more examples.

Adviser: Lewis S. Walters.

Admiral

Portable, #33-35-37 . . . .**30.00**
Portable, #909, All World **85.00**
Y-2127, Imperial 8, c1959 . . . .**45.00**

Air King, tombstone, Art Deco **2,200.00**

Arvin

Mightymite #40 . . . .**75.00**
Rhythm Baby #417 . . . .**225.00**
Hoppy with lariatenna **585.00**
Table, #444 . . . .**80.00**
Table, #522A **75.00**
Tombstone, #617 Rhythm Maid **250.00**

Atwater Kent

Breadboard style, Model 9A **1,200.00**
Breadboard style, Model 10, with orig tags **1,200.00**
Breadboard style, Model 12 . . . . **1,250.00**
Cathedral, 80, c1931 . . . .**375.00**
Table, #55 Keil **225.00**
Tombstone, #854 . . . .**155.00**
Type R Horn **200.00**

Bulova, clock radio#100 . . . .**30.00**
#120 . . . .**30.00**

Atwater Kent Type TA, 1924, **$1,465.**
Photo courtesy of Auction Team Breker.

Colonial "New World Radio" . **1,000.00**
Columbia, table radio, oak **125.00**
Crosley

ACE V **170.00**
Bandbox, #600, 1927 . . . . **80.00**
Dashboard **100.00**
Gemchest, #609 . . . . **350.00**
Litfella, 1N, cathedral **175.00**
Pup, with box **575.00**
Sheraton, cathedral **290.00**
Showbox, #706 . . . . **100.00**
Super Buddy Boy **125.00**
#4-28 battery operated **130.00**
#10-135 . . . . **55.00**

Dumont, RA346, table, scrollwork, 1938 . . . .**110.00**

Emerson

AU-190 Catalin Tombstone. **1,200.00**
BT-245 . . . .**1,100.00**
Patriot **700.00**
Porcelain Dealer Sign **150.00**
#274 brown Bakelite **165.00**
#400 Aristocrat **525.00**
#409 Mickey **1,500.00**
#411 Snow White **1,200.00**
#570 Memento **100.00**
#640 Portable **50.00**
#888 Vanguard **80.00**

Fada

#43 . . . . **275.00**
#53 . . . . **750.00**
#60W **75.00**
#115 bullet shape **750.00**
#252 . . . . **575.00**
#625 rounded end, slide rule dial **700.00**
#1000 red/orange bullet **750.00**
#L56 Maroon and White . . . **1,750.00**

Federal

#58DX **750.00**
#110 . . . . **700.00**

General Electric

#81, c1934 . . . . **200.00**
#400, 410, 411, 414 . . . . **30.00**
#515, 517 clock radio **25.00**

Early German radio, c1926, **$1,960.**
Photo courtesy of Auction Team Breker.

K-126 . . . . **150.00**
Tombstone **250.00**

Grebe

CR-8 . . . . **700.00**
CR-9 . . . . **500.00**
CR-12 . . . . **700.00**
MU-1 . . . . **250.00**
Service Manual **50.00**

Halicrafters

TW-600 . . . . **100.00**
TW-200 . . . . **125.00**

Majestic

Charlie McCarthy **1,000.00**
#59, wooden Tombstone **375.00**
#381 . . . . **225.00**
Treasure Chest **125.00**

Metrodyne Super 7, 1925 . . . **220.00**

Motorola

#68X11Q Art Deco **75.00**
Jet Plane **55.00**
Jewel Box **80.00**
M logo **25.00**
Pixie **45.00**
Ranger, portable **60.00**
Table, plastic **35.00**

Olympic, radio with phonograph . **60.00**

Paragon

DA, two table **775.00**
RD, five table **775.00**

Philco

T-7, 126 transistor **65.00**
T1000 clock radio **80.00**
#17, 20, 38 Cathedral **250.00**
#20 Cathedral **250.00**
#37, 62 table, two tone **100.00**
#40, 180 console wood **150.00**
#46, 132 table **35.00**
#52, 544 Transitone **40.00**
#49, 501 Boomerang **475.00**
#60, Cathedral **125.00**
#551, 1928 . . . . **175.00**

Radiobar, with glasses and decanters
. . . . **1,000.00**

Radio Corporation of America–RCA

LaSiesta **550.00**
Radiola
#17 . . . . **120.00**
#18, with speaker **125.00**
#20 . . . . **165.00**
#28 console **200.00**
#33 . . . . **60.00**
#6X7 table, plastic **25.00**
8BT-7LE portable **35.00**
40X56 World's Fair **1,000.00**

Silvertone-Sears

#1 table **75.00**
#1582 Cathedral, wood **225.00**
#1955 Tombstone **135.00**
#9205 plastic transistor **45.00**
Clock radio, plastic **15.00**

Tombstone, 1934, walnut, front round airplane dial, upper grill cloth, Art Deco cut outs, four knobs, AC, **$120.**

Sony, transistor

TFM-151, 1960 . . . . **50.00**
TR-63, 1958 . . . . **145.00**

Sparton

#506 Blue Bird, Art Deco . . **3,300.00**
#5218 . . . . **95.00**

Stewart-Warner, table, slant . . . **175.00**
Stromberg Carlson, # 636A console
. . . . **125.00**

Westinghouse, Model WR-602 . **50.00**

Zenith

#500 transistor, owl eye **75.00**
#500D transistor **55.00**
#750L transistor, leather case **40.00**
Trans-Oceanic **90.00**
Zephyr, multiband **95.00**

RAILROAD ITEMS

History: Railroad collectors have existed for decades. The merger of the rail systems and the end of passenger service made many objects available to private collectors. The Pennsylvania Railroad sold its archives at public sale.

Notes: Railroad enthusiasts have organized into regional and local clubs. Join one if you're interested in this collectible field; your local hobby store can probably point you to the right person. The best pieces pass between collectors and rarely enter the general market.

Ashtray, Soo Line, ceramic, track and car design border, "Denver Wright Co." backstamp, 7" d **25.00**
Badge pendant, gold luster finish thin metal rim holding color celluloid, showing steam engine during night run, lower center with red, white, and blue logo for Brotherhood of Locomotive Engineers, early 1900s **20.00**

Book

From San Francisco to Salt Lake City Along the Western Pacific Railroad, c1920, orig mailer **60.00**
Katy Railroad and the Last Frontier, The, V. V. Masterson, Univ. of Oklahoma, Norman, 1952, 1st ed., 328 pgs, illus, maps, index . . **55.00**
1900 Chicago Rock Island & Pacific History, Biographical Publishing Co., 756 pages, CRIP and representative employees, beautiful tooled and gilt engine dec cover, gilt edges, center signatures are loose **260.00**

Brake gauge, Westinghouse, brass, two dial indicators, 140 lbs, 6-1/2" d
. . . . **35.00**

Broadside, Chicago, Rock Island & Pacific, c1870, full-color lithograph, int. of dining and restaurant cars on Rock Island route, black waiters, verso with hand-written family tree in black and red ink describing 76 generations of the Fowler family beginning with William Fowler (1637-1660), first magistrate of New Haven, CT, Cameron, Amberg & Co. Railroad Printers, Lake St. Chicago, glazed front and back, minor losses, 14" x 22" **4,255.00**

Builders plate

Corps of Engineers U.S. Army 45-ton Diesel Electric Locomotive Manufactured by Vulcan Iron Works, cast bronze, dated 1941, 11" x 6" **85.00**
Fairbanks-Morse, stainless steel, etched letters on enamel ground, 1955, serial #166-972, 17" x 8"
. . . . **115.00**

Calendar

Missouri Pacific Lines, Route of the Eagles, Engine #7003, color litho on tin, removable date cards, 19" x 13" **75.00**
New York Central, 1922, illustration depicting travel in 1830 and 1920,

Cabinet card, The Shenandoah Valley Excursion of 1885, price for group of 17 cards, **$1,155.** *Photo courtesy of Jackson's Auctioneers & Appraisers.*

timetables for various lines in margins, some minor losses, period oak frame, 18" x 30" **265.00**

Soo Line, 1930, illus, Lake Louise Alberta by R. Atkinson Fox, later oak frame and mat, overall 34" x 29" **230.00**

Calendar plate, Pennsylvania Lines, 1949, after a painting by Grif Teller, framed, 30" x 23" **35.00**

Cap

Agent, Soo Line, pill box style, embroidered "Agent" and "Soo Line," labeled "Marshall Field & Co. Chicago," size 7" **50.00**

Brakeman's, open-weave crown, missing name plate, labeled "A. G. Meier & Co. Chicago," size 6-3/4" **35.00**

Railroad Conductors, labeled "A.G. Meier & CO. Chicago," size 7-1/4" **95.00**

Chimes, dining car, wood case, four tone bars, orig striker, 10-1/2" l . **150.00**

China, chocolate pot, Pullman Porcelain, green glaze, gilt pin striping & "Pullman" lettering, Hall China back stamp, 6" h.................. **345.00**

Crimper, railroad seal, nickel plate, dies marked "CNS & M. R. R. Co.," handle emb "Porter Safety Seal Co.," 7" l **115.00**

Cuspidor

Missouri Pacific Railroad, white porcelain on metal, black "MOPAC" lettering, minor loss, 7-1/2" d **150.00**

Texas & Pacific Railroad, white porcelain on metal, blue lettering, minor loss, 8" d.......... **260.00**

Date stamp, Atlantic Coast Line Railroad, c1940, Defiance Stamp Co., 4" h......................... **35.00**

Depot clock, electric, patent date 1908, oak case, hinged face, marked "Property of the Ball RR Time Service St. Paul, Minn," 21" sq **210.00**

Depot sign, Rock Island System, reverse painted and mother of pearl, c1890, Chicago, Rock Island & Pacific 4-4-0 locomotive #476 pulling 11 cars, against tree-lined Midwest route, orig oak ogee frame with gilt liner, overall 50" x 22"................... **23,000.00**

Directory, *Soo Line Shippers Directory, Vol. III*, 1918-19, soft cover, 644 pgs, gilt, ads, illus, two-pg Soo Line map, four color maps of MI, MN, ND, WI **60.00**

Fire bucket, Missouri, Kansas & Texas Railroad, orig red paint, stenciled "Fire," emb "MK&T," 12" h............ **60.00**

Flare and flag box, Gulf Mobile & Ohio, tin, stenciled letters, contains flag and fuses, 30" l **20.00**

Hat

Chicago & Illinois Valley, celluloid name tag with "#1," size 7" .. **60.00**

Soo Line, brakeman's, open weave crown, silver nameplate, labeled "Carlson & Co. Chicago," size 7-1/4".................. **185.00**

Hollowware

Coffee pot, silver plate, "Dixie" engraved on front, ornate emb handle and lid, insulated zinc lining, copper bottom, 19th C, lid detached, some damage and losses, 11" h **60.00**

Coffee pot, silver plate, Chicago & Eastern Illinois, 10-oz size, marked "Reed & Barton 086-H, C&E.I.RY.CO" on base, 7" h **265.00**

Coffee server, silvered, Nashville, Chattanooga & St. Louis, applied emb "N.C.& St. L" logo on front, gooseneck spout, long wood handle, backstamped "Reed & Barton 482-32 oz, N.C. & St. L" **520.00**

Sauce tureen, silvered, Chicago Great Western Railway, two handles, lid. backstamped "C.G.W.R.R.–Reed & Barton," 8" l **125.00**

Sugar bowl, silvered, New York Central, imp "NYC" on hinged lid, 3-3/4" h **50.00**

Tea pot, silvered, Missouri Pacific & Iron Mountain, 10-oz size, front

Conductor's hat, Milwaukee RR, Carlson & Co., Chicago, IL, **$45.**

engraved "M.P.I.Mt.RY," backstamped "Missouri Pacific & Iron Mountain R. Wallace 03295," 4-1/2" h................ **230.00**

Illustration, Great Northern Railway, orig illus for cover of travel brochure, scenic marvel of America, Glacier National Park, c1920, full-color gouache on paper, detailed study, 9-1/2" x 14", 1/2" margins **315.00**

Jug, Baltimore & Ohio, stoneware, brown cone top, one gal, 11-1/2" **210.00**

Kerosene can, Chicago & Northwestern, one gal, oxidized finish, emb "C&NRR," 13" h.......... **25.00**

Lantern

5" h, PRR, etched red globe and dome, marked "Keystone Lantern Co., Phila, PA, USA," wire ring bail **445.00**

11" h, fixed globe, pierced tin frame, wire handle, globe engraved "E.R.R.," traces of black paint, dent, corrosion.......... **415.00**

13" h, Boston & Worchester, emb "B&W RR," fixed globe.... **665.00**

Lantern globe, clear, emb letters, by CNS, 5-1/2" h

Burlington Route........... **70.00**

Long Island RR............ **70.00**

Pennsylvania RR, logo **60.00**

Pere Marquette............ **90.00**

Pittsburgh & Lake Erie RR ... **60.00**

Letter opener, Southern Pacific, orig case, 7-3/4" l **30.00**

Locomotive nose plate, Frisco, black, heavy 1/8" stainless steel, 28" l **1,150.00**

Map

Chicago, Iowa, and Nebraska Railroad, color litho, published by J. Sage & Sons, Buffalo, NY, 1859, some discoloration and losses, mounted on linen, 26" x 23" **450.00**

Soo Line, Minneapolis, St. Paul, and Sault Ste. Marie RY, printed by Matthews, Northrup & Co. Buffalo, NY, c1890, 39" x 16"...... **130.00**

Williams Telegraph and Railroad Map of the New England States, dated 1852, by Alexander Williams, published by Redding & Co. Boston, printed table of construction costs for area railroads, hand-colored state borders, separated folds with later linen backing, some toning, 32" x 30" **60.00**

Name plate, Soo Line, cast aluminum, mounted on walnut back board, 24" l **95.00**

Operation manual, 4-1/2" x 7", New York Air Brake Co., 1909 ....**5.00**

Paperweight, Adlake Centennial, 1857-1957, extruded aluminum, 5" l **40.00**

Photo

Chicago, Rock Island & Pacific, Rocky Mountains, c1910, orig frame, 7" mat, 53" x 23" **920.00**

Denver & Rio Grande Railroad Depot, Canyon of the Rio Las Animas, Colo, hand colored black and white print, printed logo and title, "Copyright 1900 by Detroit Photographic Co.," orig oak frame, stains in margin, overall 33-1/2" x 27-1/2" **2,645.00**

Machinist Apprentices of the Chicago & Alton R.R., dated Sept. 5th 1908, depicting 34 apprentices posed on C & A R.R. locomotive #605, Stafford B. Cable photo, Bloomington, IL, orig frame and mat, 17" x 11" image size ..**490.00**

Soo Line, Lake Louise early 20th C, hand-colored black and white print, orig titled mat with Soo Line logo, orig oak frame, overall 25" x 21" **50.00**

Pinback button

Chesapeake & Ohio Railway Veteran Employees Assn, 21st annual meeting, Cincinnati Zoo, June 26, 1937 ....**20.00**

Division 241, American Assn of Street & Electric Railway Employees of America, purple and pink membership button **20.00**

Reading Lines, red image, white logo, green rim, c1930s **20.00**

Framed advertising print, winter landscape with steam locomotive engine, When Winter Comes, Twentieth Century Limited of the New York Central Lines, 24" x 28-1/2" overall, **$225.** *Photo courtesy of Joy Luke Auctions.*

Refrigerator Dairy Line Express, Merchants Dispatch Transportation Co., black and white photo of car, thin blue and red stripes, early 1900s **20.00**

Poster, Howard Chandler Christy Rail Safety Poster, colorful, Assoc. of American Railroads, 1936, some smudges, 14" x 22" **345.00**

Print, Union Pacific Railroad, c1910, "The Mail and Express" crossing the famous Dale Creek embankment, black and white heliotype, printed title and logos in margin, orig oak frame, brass plaque, minor stains in margin, 31-1/2" x 27-1/2"..................**1,265.00**

Steam whistle, brass

3" d, 8" h, single chime, lever control **200.00**

5-1/2" d, 12" h, triple chime, manufactured by Crosby Steam, Gage & Valve Company, Boston, Pat. Jan. 30, 1877 ......**720.00**

Step ladder, ST.L.K& N-W Railroad, folding, wooden, four steps, stenciled "St.L.K&N-W" and "Mail Car 103" **270.00**

Step stool, Denver & Rio Grande Western RR, rubber no-skid top, 9" h **260.00**

Switch plate, iron, emb "US&S CO," patented 1914, attached brass impedance plate, 16-1/2" x 12-1/2" **35.00**

Ticket cabinet, Soo Line, c1914, oak, locking tambour slant front, divided compartments for tickets, timetables, one drawer, stenciled "M.ST.P. & S.S.M.RY" on back, 21" x 35" x 16" **460.00**

Ticket window, 28" x 33-1/2", Baltimore & Ohio, clear emb glass, B&O logo on diamond point textured field, later walnut frame **600.00**

Timetable, 4" x 8-1/2"

Atlantic Coast, 1954 ....**2.50**

Delaware & Hudson, 1951 ....**2.50**

Lehigh Valley, 1951...........**3.50**

New York Central, 1946 ......**2.50**

New York-New Haven & Hartford, 1954 ....**3.50**

Rutland, 1941 ....**2.00**

Santa Fe, 1959 ....**2.50**

Seaboard, 1924-25..........**5.00**

Southern Pacific, 1912 ....**4.00**

Tobacco tin, Fast Mail Tobacco, Bagley & Co., tin litho, flat pocket type, detailed image of early train, some darkening to gold highlights, 3-5/8" l, 2-3/8" w, 5/8" h **1,000.00**

Tray, Soo Line, Montana Success, map of Soo Line Route, tin litho, 10-1/2" x 15" **200.00**

Wax sealer

American Exchange Co., El Paso, Ill, brass die with wood handle, 3" l **150.00**

Illinois Central Railroad, Agent-Minonk, brass die, wood handle, 4" l **375.00**

S.W. & B.V. RR, Agent-Bryan, Texas, one-piece brass die and handle, 2-1/2" l.................**550.00**

Toledo, Peoria & Western, Agent-El Paso, Ill, brass die, wood handle, 4" l....................**525.00**

RAZORS

History: Razors date back several thousand years. Early man used sharpened stones; the Egyptians, Greeks, and Romans had metal razors.

Razors made prior to 1800 generally were crudely stamped "Warranted" or "Cast Steel," with the maker's mark on the tang. Until 1870, razors were handmade and almost all razors for the American market were manufactured in Sheffield, England. Most blades were wedge shaped; many were etched with slogans or scenes. Handles were made of natural materials: horn, tortoiseshell, bone, ivory, stag, silver, or pearl.

After 1870, razors were machine made with hollow ground blades and synthetic handle materials. Razors of this period usually were manufactured in Germany (Solingen) or in American cutlery factories. Hundreds of molded-celluloid handle patterns were produced.

Cutlery firms produced boxed sets of two, four, and seven razors. Complete and undamaged sets are very desirable. The most popular ones are the seven-day sets in which each razor is etched with a day of the week.

Additional Listings: See *Warman's Americana & Collectibles* for more examples.

Notes: The fancier the handle or more intricately etched the blade, the higher the price. Rarest handle materials are pearl, stag, sterling silver, pressed horn, and carved ivory. Rarest blades are those with scenes etched across the entire front. Value is increased by the presence of certain manufacturers' names, e.g., H. Boker, Case, M. Price, Joseph Rogers, Simmons Hardware, Will & Finck, Winchester, and George Wostenholm.

F. J. Elwell, Rockdale, NY, 1900, images of political figures, **$250.**

Safety, Wilkinson Sword Co., seven day, 5" l, 2-1/4" d, 1-5/8" h, $165.

American blades

Case Bros., Tested XX, Little Valley, NY, hollow point, slick black handles, MOP inlaid tang **400.00**

Cattaraugus Cutlery Co., Little Valley, NY, sq point, blue handles with white liners **35.00**

Kane Cutlery Co., Kane, PA, hollow point, cream and rust twisted rope handles, c1884 . . . . **45.00**

Southington Cutlery Co., Southington, CT, Crescent Safety Razor, razor in orig 1-1/4" x 2-1/8" x 1/2" tin **1,050.00**

Standard Knife Co., Little Valley, NY, arc mark, round point, yellow mottled handles with beaded borders, 1901-03 . . . . **150.00**

Union Cutlery Co., Olean, NY, AJ Case Shoo-Fly, tiger-eye handle, c1912 . . . . **125.00**

English blades, Sheffield

George Wostenholme, etched adv on blade, emb ivory handle **40.00**

Joseph Rodgers & Sons, wedge blade, stag handle with inlaid rect escutcheon plate **125.00**

Ideal Safety Razor, patented Sept. 21, 1868, June 12, 1900, and March 5, 1906, leather like case, 9-1/2" l, $20.

German blades

Cosmos Mfg. Co., hollow ground blade, ivory handle, raised nude picking purple grapes, green leaves **125.00**

F. A. Koch & Co., ivory handle, colored scene with deer, branches, and oak leaves **50.00**

Imperial Razor, blade etched with U.S. Battleship Oregon scene, dark blue celluloid handle **45.00**

Wadsworth Razor Co., semi-wedge blade, carved bone handle, c1870 . . . . **60.00**

Sets of razors

Crown & Sword, seven-day set, blades etched "The Crown & Sword Razor Extra Hollow Ground," black handles with raised "Crown and Sword," homemade wood case with felt lining, emb "RAZORS," plaque on top . . **85.00**

G. W. Ruff's Peerless, two, hollow ground blade, ivory handles, leather over wood case with "Gentlemen's Companion Containing 2 Razors Special Hollow Ground," red lining **70.00**

Wilkinson Sword, seven days, safety, 5" l, 2-1/2" d, 1-5/8" h orig box . . **125.00**

RECORDS

History: With the advent of the more sophisticated recording materials, such as 33-1/3 RPM long-playing records, 8-track tapes, cassettes, and compact discs, earlier phonograph records became collectors' items. Most have little value. The higher-priced items are rare (limited-production) recordings. Condition is critical.

All records start with a master tape of an artist's or groups' performance. To make a record, mastering agent would play the master tape and feed the sound to a cutting lathe which electronically transcribes the music into the grooves of a circular black lacquer disc, known as an acetate. The acetate was the played to determine if the sound quality was correct, to listen for defects or timing errors, order of presentation, etc. The finished acetate was then sprayed with a metal film. Once the film dries, the acetate is peeled away, creating a new "master" with a raised groove pattern. Another metallic compound was sprayed on the new "master" and after this compound was removed, a "mother" disc is created. The "mother" disc is then coated with another metallic compound, and when that is removed, a "stamper" is made. Pertinent production information is often written on the stamper before it is pressed in the production process. Each two-sided record has two stampers, one for each side.

The material used for early 45s and LPs was polyvinyl chloride (PVC), and commonly called "vinyl." To make a record, hot PVC is pressed between the stampers using a compression molding process. Excess vinyl that is trimmed away after the pressing

process is recycled. When this re-cycled material is reused, it may result in a record that looks grainy or pockmarked. Each stamper was good for about 1,000 pressings, then the whole process began again. Vinyl is still used for LPs, but polystyrene is now used for 45s. The production process for polystyrene is slightly different in that the base material is more liquid. Application of labels can be made directly to the polystyrene record, eliminating the label stamping process used with vinyl. To tell the difference between vinyl and styrene records, consider the following points:

For more information, see this book.

- Vinyl records are thicker and heavier.
- 7-inch vinyl 45s won't bend
- A label of one color with information "engraved" or spray painted in the center indicates a styrene record.

As with many types of antiques, a grading scale has been developed.

Mint (M): Perfect condition, no flaws, scratches, or scuffs in the grooves. The cardboard jacket will be crisp.

Near Mint (NM) or Mint-Minus (M-): The record will be close to perfect, with no marks in the grooves. The label will be clean, not marked, or scuffed. There will be no ring wear on the record or album cover.

Very Good Plus (VG+): Used for a record that has been played, but well taken care of. Slight scuffle or warps to the grooves is acceptable as long as it does not affect the sound. A faint ring wear discoloration is acceptable. The jacket may appear slightly worn, especially on the edges.

Very Good (VG): Used to describe a record that has some pronounced defects, as does the cover. The record will still play well. This usually is the lowest grade acceptable to a serious collector. Most records listed in price guides are of this grade.

Good (G): This category of record will be playable, but probably will have loss to the sound quality. Careful inspection of a styrene record in this condition may allow the viewer to see white in the grooves. The cover might be marked or torn.

Poor or Fair (P, F): Record is damaged, may be difficult to play. The cover will be damaged condition, usually marked, dirty, or torn.

Additional Listings: See *Warman's Americana & Collectibles* for more examples.

Note: Most records, especially popular recordings, have a value of less than $3 per disc. The records listed here are classic recordings of their type and are in demand by collectors.

Blues

Holiday, Billie, An Evening with Billie Holiday, Clef MGC-144, 10" LP, 1953 . . . . **45.00**

Hooker, John Lee, High Priced Woman, Union Station Blues, 45, Chess 1505, 1952 . . . . **250.00**

Hopkins, Lightnin', Sinner's Prayer, Angel Child, 45, Bluesville 822, 1962 . . . .**5.00**

King, B. B., B. B. King Wails, Crown CLP-8115, LP, black label, mono, silver Crown, 1959 . . . .**25.00**

Muddy Waters, Muddy Waters Sings Big Bill, Chess LP-1444, LP, 1960, DJ white label promo **250.00**

Children's

Archies, The, Sugar Sugar, Melody Hill, Calender 63-1008, 1969, 45 . . . . . .**2.50**

Banana Splits, The, Tra-La-La Song, Toy Piano Medley, Decca 32429, 45, 1968, picture sleeve **9.25**

Dumbo, Disneyland, record and book, 1968, some wear **7.60**

Higitus Figitus, Walt Disney Productions, Little Golden Record, 1938 . . . .**8.00**

Star Wars, 24-page read-along book, 33-1/3 rpm record, Buena Vista . . .**5.00**

Strawberry Shortcake, 1980, LP **20.00**

Night Before Christmas, The, Golden Record, R33, 78 RPM, as told by Peter Donald, full orchestra directed by Mitchell Miller, c1950, some scratches and wear **5.00**

Country, LP

Campbell, Glen, Gentle on My Mind, Capitol, ST 2809, black label with rainbow border **12.00**

Cline, Patsy, Crazy, Who Can I Count On, Decca 31317, 1961, 45 . . . . . .**3.00**

Danny Davis & Nashville Brass, Movin' On, RCA, LSP 4232, orange label, 1969 . . . .**8.00**

Dudley, Dave, Six Days on the Road, Golden Ring 110, LP, 1963 . . . . . .**12.50**

Elvis Presley's "Love Me Tender" on an RCA label design that lasted until 1965, VG, $7.50.

In the Wee Small Hours by Frank Sinatra was released as a series of EPs, on two 10-inch LPs, and on a single 12-inch LP. This VG price of $25 is for the 10-inch LP.

Lewis, Jerry Lee, All Country, 1969 . . . .**10.00**

Miller, Roger, SMASH Mercury, SRS 67123, red label **12.00**

Reeves, Jim, The Intimate Jim Reeves, RCA Victor, LSP-2216, black label with dog at top **22.00**

Statler Brothers, The Big Hits, Columbia, CS 9519, red label . . .**18.00**

Twain, Shania, Whose Bed Have Your Boots Been Under? Any Man of Mine, Mercury 856 488-7, 1995, 45 . . . .**2.50**

Wells, Kitty, Country Music Time, Decca DL 74554, black label with rainbow band through center **8.00**

Williams, Hank, Reflections of Those Who Loved Him, MGM-Pro-912, 3 LPs, promotional box set, 1975 . . . . . .**60.00**

Wynette, Tammy, Your Good Girl's Gonna Go Bad, Epic LN 26305, LP, stereo, 1967 . . . .**5.00**

Jazz, 45s

Davis, Miles, Birth of the Cool, Capitol T-762, mono, 1956 . . . .**37.50**

Ellington, Duke, Ellington at Newport '56, Columbia CL-934, 1957, red-black label **10.00**

Fitzgerald, Ella, Ella Fitzgerald Sings the George and Ira Gershwin Song Book, Verve MGV-4029-5, 5 LPs, mono, 1959 . . . .**125.00**

Mingus, Charles, The Jazz Experiment of Charles Mingus, Bethlehem BCP-55, 1956 . . . .**25.00**

Moody, James, Moody's Mood for Love, Cadet LP-613, reissue, 1966 . . . .**3.75**

Rollins, Sonny, A Night at the Village Vanguard, 1958, Blue Note BLP-1581, 63rd St. address on label **20.00**

Lounge, LP

Ames, Ed, My Cup Runneth Over, RCA LPM-3774, mono, 1967 . . . .**2.50**

Astaire, Fred, Another Evening with Fred Astaire, Chrysler 1088 . . . . .**12.00**

Teresa Brewer's Greatest Hits, Phillips, PHS 600-062, black label with rainbow band through center, 1960s **16.00**

Como, Perry, Merry Christmas Music, Pickwick, Camden, CAS-660, black label with rainbow letter "P" in center, 1961 . . . .**10.00**

Ray Conniff & Johnny Mathis, Something Special, four-album boxed set, Columbia Special Products, C4 10303, red labels **18.00**

Crosby, Bing, Jerome Kern Songs, Decca, 5001 . . . .**20.00**

Denny, Martin, Hawaii Tattoo, Liberty LST-7394 . . . .**10.00**

Day, Doris, Wonderful Day, Columbia Records XTV 82022, 1960s **8.00**

Fountain, Pete, Those Were The Days, Coral, CRL 757505, black label with multicolored band through center **15.00**

Jones, Tom, Tom, Parrot, XPAS 71037, black label with green and yellow parrot **18.00**

Lee, Brenda, 10 Golden Years, Decca, DL 74757, black label with rainbow band through center **22.00**

Mills Brothers, The, Fortuosity, Dot, DLP 25809, black label, c1959 . .**12.00**

Sinatra, Frank, Cycles, Reprise, 1027, gold/orange label with picture of Frank **8.00**

Torme, Mel, California Suite, Capital P-200 . . . .**30.00**

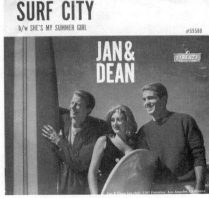

The picture sleeve for the Jan Berry/Brian Wilson collaboration of "Surf City," VG, $10.

Williams, Andy, Honey, Columbia, CS 9662, red label **8.00**

Rock
Animals, The, The Best of the Animals, MGM E-4324, 1966, yellow label promo **20.00**

Asylum Choir, Asylum Choir II, Shelber, SW-8910, LP, orig insert **10.00**

Beatles
Can't Buy Me Love, You Can't Do That, Capitol 4140, 1964, picture sleeve **200.00**
Help, I'm Down, Capitol 5476, 1965, with "A Subsidiary of Capitol" in white along perimeter **25.00**
I Wanna Hold Your Hand, Capitol 5112, 1964 . . . . **10.00**
Old Brown Shoe, Apple EPEM-10540, Mexican pcs, 45 rpm **18.00**

Bowie, David, Man Who Sang, Mercury SR-61325, LP **18.00**

Golden Earring, Greatest Hits, Polydor 236228, Dutch imp, LP **10.00**

Lennon, John, Roots, Adam Vii-A-80180, orig, LP **200.00**

Liverpool Five, Out of Sight, RCA LSP-33682, German imp, LP **8.00**

Lulu, To Sir with Love, Epic LN 24339, LP, mono, 1967 . . . . **6.25**

Presley, Elvis, 45
Bring It Back, Pieces of My Life, RCA Victor PB-10401, 1975, orange label **50.00**
Elvis Presley, RCA Victor, LPM-1254, mono, "Long Play" on label, "Elvis" in pale pink, 1956 . . . . **125.00**
If You Talk In Your Sleep, Help Me, RCA Victor, APBO-0280, 1974, picture sleeve **7.00**
Moody Blue, RCA AFL1-2428, 1977, black vinyl **50.00**
That's All Right, Blue Moon of Kentucky, Sun 209, 1954 . . **750.00**

The Hollies, Here I Go Again, Imperial LP-9265, 1964, black label with stars **25.00**

REDWARE

History: The availability of clay, the same used to make bricks and roof tiles, accounted for the great production of red earthenware pottery in the American colonies. Redware pieces are mainly utilitarian—bowls, crocks, jugs, etc.

Lead-glazed redware retained its reddish color, but a variety of colored glazes were obtained by the addition of metals to the basic glaze. Streaks and mottled splotches in redware items resulted from impurities in the clay and/or uneven firing temperatures.

Slipware is the term used to describe redwares decorated by the application of slip, a semi-liquid paste made of clay. Slipwares were made in England, Germany, and elsewhere in Europe for decades before becoming popular in the Pennsylvania German region and other areas in colonial America.

Bank, 6-1/2" w, 4" d, 4-1/2" h, Empire chest of drawers form, attributed to Philadelphia, PA, area, loss to feet, roughness on edges **225.00**

Bottle, 5-3/4" h, pinched sides and tooling, green glaze, brown flecks, green striping, incised label, "Made by I. S. Stahl, 11-1-1939" **70.00**

Bowl, 4-1/4" d, 2-1/8" h, cream, dark green and brown running glaze, two round applied handle buttons on each side, Shenandoah, crazing and minor glaze flakes **550.00**

Bowl with spout, 6" d, 3-3/4" h, tea-cup shape, applied ribbed handle on side, incised line, brown mottled glaze **220.00**

Canning jar, 4-1/2" d, 6-1/4" h, mottled dark brown stripes, incised line around middle, bottom inscribed "Medinger," attributed to Jacob Medinger, c1880-1900, Montgomery County, PA **495.00**

Charger, 12" d, slipware dec, yellow squiggle work, brown ground . . . **990.00**

Chicken feeder, 7" h, one quart, red and brown mottled applied glaze, c1850 . . . . **750.00**

Cooler, 18" h, ovoid, glaze flaking, mounted as lamp **75.00**

Creamer, 4-1/2" h, burnt orange glaze, running light green highlights, glazed over separation at handle, rim flakes **200.00**

Cup, handled, pouring lip, incised banding decoration in green glaze with dark blue-green spots, marked "Made by R.R. Stahl, 10/14/48," glaze flake, 4" d, 2" h, **$365.** *Photo courtesy of Sanford Alderfer Auction Company.*

Chicken feeder, red and brown mottled applied glaze, one quart, c1850, minor surface use wear, 7" h, **$750.** *Photo courtesy of Vicki and Bruce Waasdorp.*

Crock, 4-3/8" h, ovoid, thick rim, two rope twist applied handles, pumpkin-orange, dark brown slightly metallic splotches, minor crazing, int. glaze flake **660.00**

Cup, 3-3/4" h, flared lip, applied handle, clear glaze with mottled amber, minor wear and glaze flakes **90.00**

Cuspidor, 8" x 4-1/4", tooled bands, brown and green running glaze, brown dashes, some wear and edge chips **265.00**

Dish, 4" d, 4-3/4" l, hand modeled as goose, few incised feathers, pinched scalloped rim, black running glaze with faint green tinge, minor edge damage to tail **1,115.00**

Figure, 3-1/2" h, seated cat, molded with white glaze, brown sponging, green daubs, hairlines, edge damage **220.00**

Jug, ovoid form, applied handle, mottled green and brown glaze, imperfections, 10-1/2" h, **$935.** *Photo courtesy of Sanford Alderfer Auction Company.*

Loaf dish, yellow slip decoration, borders of triple wavy lines and central "S" designs, minor rim chipping, 9-1/2" x 13-1/2", $935. Photo courtesy of Sanford Alderfer Auction Company.

Flower pot, attached saucer base, 5-1/2" d, 5" h, imp "John W. Bell Waynesboro," Rockingham type brown mottled glaze **880.00**

Food mold, miniature, 4-1/4" d, 1-1/2" h, raised beaded edge, black mottling around rim. **295.00**

Grease lamp, 4-1/2" h, single pinch spout, strap handle, and saucer base, dark Albany glaze, black grease stains **725.00**

Harvest jug, 11" h, mottled brown and mustard alkaline glaze **90.00**

Jar, 13-1/4" h, tall, round, tapered shoulder, incised line, black sponged dec, glaze flakes **250.00**

Jug, 7" h, bulbous, applied handle, wheel thrown, dark brown slip . . **110.00**

Loaf dish, 13-1/2" l, 8-1/2" w, glazed, three wavy, looped, and straight line dec, coggled edge, chips, hairline **720.00**

Milk bowl, 9" d, white slip dec, greenish-amber glaze, surface chips **250.00**

Turk mold, green mottled alkaline glaze, relief oak leaf interior, minor glaze flake, 9" d, 3-1/2" h, $80. Photo courtesy of Vicki and Bruce Waasdorp.

Pie plate, coggled rim

8" d, yellow slip dec of wavy lines and flourishes, shallow rim flakes **990.00**

9-7/8" d, yellow and green slip dec of double loops and wavy lines **7,590.00**

10" d, yellow slip dec of three wavy lines, flag-like shapes, rim flake, minor stains **1,045.00**

10-3/4" d, yellow slip dec, three sets of wavy lines, few edge flakes **615.00**

11-1/4" d, yellow slip dec, three sets of wavy lines. **935.00**

Pitcher, 8-1/2" h, turned baluster form, loop side handle **125.00**

Plate

11" d, slip dec of five spotches, coggled edge, minor flake . **550.00**

11" d, slip monogram and wavy lines dec, coggled edge, loss to slip dec, minor rim flakes **200.00**

Storage jar, 7-1/2" h, dark brown mottled glaze, c1850, minor surface wear. **50.00**

RED WING POTTERY

History: The Red Wing pottery category includes several potteries from Red Wing, Minnesota. In 1868, David Hallem started Red Wing Stoneware Co., the first pottery with stoneware as its primary product. The Minnesota Stoneware Co. started in 1883. The North Star Stoneware Co. was in business from 1892 to 1896.

The Red Wing Stoneware Co. and the Minnesota Stoneware Co. merged in 1892. The new company, the Red Wing Union Stoneware Co., made stoneware until 1920 when it introduced a pottery line that it continued until the 1940s. In 1936, the name was changed to Red Wing Potteries, Inc. During the 1930s, this firm introduced several popular patterns of hand-painted dinnerware, which were distributed through department stores, mail-order catalogs, and gift-stamp centers. Dinnerware production declined in the 1950s and was replaced with hotel and restaurant china in the early 1960s. The plant closed in 1967.

Marks: Red Wing Stoneware Co. was the first firm to mark pieces with a red wing stamped under the glaze. The North Star Stoneware Co. used a raised star and the words "Red Wing" as its mark.

Bean pot, cov, stoneware, adv . . **85.00**

Beater jar, stoneware, half gallon, "Stanhope, Ia" adv **95.00**

Bookends, pr, fan and scroll, green **20.00**

Bowl, stoneware, 7" d, blue, rust, and cream sponging **75.00**

Crock, 15 gallons, lily decoration, $5,250. Photo courtesy of Seeck Auctions.

Butter crock, 20#, large wing, tight hairline **550.00**

Buttermilk feeder, stoneware . . . **75.00**

Casserole, cov, 8" d, sponge band, chip on handle **165.00**

Cookie jar, cov

French Chef, blue glaze **250.00**

Grapes, yellow, marked "Red Wing USA," 10" h **85.00**

Rooster, green glaze, #249, 9-1/4" l **150.00**

Creamer and sugar, #1376 . . . . . **20.00**

Crock, stoneware, one gallon, large wing **400.00**

Figure

Cowboy, rust **175.00**

Cowgirl, #B1414, white **175.00**

Jug, five gallon, shoulder, large wing, "California White Wine" stencil. . **135.00**

Vase, ovoid, raised rim, relief decorated with lions and foliage, sage green and blue semi-glossy glaze, partial circular stamp, 7-5/8" h, $200. Photo courtesy of Skinner Auctioneers and Appraisers.

Vase, tapered cylinder, straight neck, relief floral design, red matte glaze, stamped "Red Wing/Union/ Stoneware/Co./ Red Wing/Minn," 8-1/4" h, $75.

Mason jar, 7" h, stoneware, screw top metal lid, marked "Stone Mason Fruit Jar, Union Stoneware Co., Red Wing, Minn" **330.00**

Mixing bowl, 7" d, stoneware, "Cap," blue sponge dec, white ground **100.00**

Pitcher, 9" h, stoneware, brown glazed grape dec, rick-rack border, waffle ground, "Red Wing North Star Stoneware" mark **90.00**

Planter

Canoe **25.00**

Puppy **20.00**

Salt and pepper shakers, pr, Town and Country, dark green **65.00**

Teapot, cov, yellow rooster, gold trim
. . . . **65.00**

Vase

6-1/2" h, bulbous, leaf design, molded ring handles, shiny jade green glaze, marked "Red Wing Art Pottery" **80.00**

8" h, #1103 . . . . **35.00**

11-1/2" h, handles, #1376 . . . . **45.00**

Water cooler, six gallons, small wing, no lid **385.00**

RELIGIOUS ITEMS

History: Objects used in worship or as expressions of man's belief in a superhuman power are collected by many people for many reasons.

This category includes icons, since they are religious mementos, usually paintings with a brass encasement. Collecting icons dates from the earliest period of Christianity. Most antique icons in today's market were made in the late 19th century.

Reproduction Alert: Icons are frequently reproduced.

Altar, 16" w, 31" h, intricately carved wood, each figure polychromed, resurrected Christ in center flanked by Virgin on left and Apostle John on right, God the Father at top center, carved tabernacle atop altar rotates to reveal monstrance, crucifix, or covered ciborium, German or Spanish, 18th C, slight scattered loss to paint . **2,875.00**

Altar cross, 18" h, bronze cross, crucified Christ below two angels of the Lord, beneath a hollow crystal receptacle containing fine ashes, French, 19th C **400.00**

Altar Gospel, 17" x 12", velvet-wrapped cov set with repousse silver Resurrection scene, surrounded by four Evangelists, embellished with cloisonné enamel medallions, verso set with silver plaques including one of cross, Ignati Sazikov, Moscow, c1890 . . . . **4,600.00**

Altar shrine, circumference 80", 41" h, Gothic-style wood, ext. with applied cherub heads and four side-mounted votive stands, int. rotates to reveal shine, when closed it exhibits a carved-in relief Eucharistic Lamp beneath grapes and wheat, 19th C
. . . . **935.00**

Angel, wood, fully carved in the round

18-5/8" w, 15-5/8" l, gessoed, young standing figure, wings outstretched, face set with glass eyes, painted and gilded finish, Continental, mid-19th C . . . **490.00**

Angel, Italian, polychrome and gilt carved in the round wood, 41" h, $3,000. Photo courtesy of Jackson's International Auctioneers & Appraisers.

20-1/2" w, 27" h, polychrome and gold leaf, outstretched wings, kneeling in prayer, suspending device on back, Continental, 19th C **1,900.00**

41" h, polychrome and gold leaf, outstretched wings, Italian, 18th C **3,000.00**

Bible, 3-3/8" w, 4-1/8" h, German, late 19th/early 20th C, .800 silver cover with emb openwork genre scenes within scroll border, 1882 text, approx 4 troy oz. **290.00**

Bible cover, 10-1/2" x 7-1/2", vellum cover, front overlaid with massive gilded bronze and silvered plaque with champlevé enamel, depicting crucifixion with the four Evangelists, back cover with gilded bronze Romanesque-style angel and polished stone feet held in gilded and enamel frames, spine imp "Santa Biblia," matching bronze clasps **1,100.00**

Book

Betsy Ross, Quaker Rebel, Edwin Satterthwaite Parry, 1932, anniversary edition, John C. Winston Co. **10.00**

The Will to Believe, Marcus Bach, Prentice Hall, 1956, 3rd printing, sgd by author, dj **10.00**

Buddha

21" h, Thai, 19th C, gilt bronze, hands clasped in prayer, stepped base **2,300.00**

22-1/2" h, Nepal, 19th C, carved white marble, seated on lotus throne, hands in Bhumi Sparsa and Dhyana Mudras, some losses
. . . . **950.00**

33" h, Japan, 19th C, carved and gilt wood, standing on lotus throne, scrolled clouds backed by aureole, some losses **3,450.00**

Candlesticks, pr, 25" h, gilt bronze, pricket, ftd bases with open fretwork, enamel medallions inscribed "S. J.," building tools, flowers, and cabochons, French, 19th C **980.00**

Chalice, 12-3/4" h, silver, engraved cup with Diesis, four Evangelists engraved on base, Russian, 19th C **1,035.00**

Chalice and paten

8-1/4" h, silver gilt, French Gothic style, repousse and finely chased node, stem, and base, cup resting on pierced basket of floral forms, hallmarks, 19th C **1,150.00**

8-1/2" h, silver, rim of base finely sculpted with band of shamrocks, base set with three finely engraved medallions depicting Christ, the Virgin, and St. Joseph, gilt stippled backgrounds, engraved in Latin, hallmarked with French touchmarks, French, 19th C **1,265.00**

Ciborium, 11-1/4" h, silver gilt, large domed bases repoussed with figures representing Faith, Hope, and Charity, central node with wheat, grapes, and reeds, bowl with finely pierced basket with repousse medallions depicting face of Christ, Virgin, and St. Joseph, heavily repoussed domed lid, cross finial, French, 19th C **1,610.00**

Communion set, bishop's or cardinal's, 13-3/4" h chalice with chased base and three circular reserves of the Passion, separated by winged cherubs, oversized central node with wheat and grapes between three oval medallions depicting Christ, Virgin, and Apostle St. John, flared cup resting on intricate pierced basket with winged cherubs, three roundels sculpted with additional scenes from the Passion, 7-1/2" d paten with miniature sculpted depiction of Last Supper, edges engraved with implements of the Passion, 11-1/2" h cruet tray dec with repousse grapes and cattails, wine cruet chased with grapes, grape finial on lid, water cruet chased with cattails, sea shell finial on lid, gilded silver, ornately dec, A. Renaud, Paris, c1890, each pc clearly

marked, custom fitted silk-lined wood case **9,200.00**

Creche figure, 15-3/4" to 17-3/8" h, carved wood, two young women, old woman, painted detailing, glass eyes, excelsior bodies, and silken garb, mounted to turned wooden socles, young figures with fragmentary labels to bases concerning sale of the figures taken from suppressed Italian convents to benefit Catholic Church, price for three figures **2,415.00**

Cruet communion set, 10-1/4" w, 6-1/2" h, gilt bronze, matching engraved glass cruets in ornate holders, filigree and champleve enamel, similarly dec tray, French, 19th C **615.00**

Figure

11" w, 18" h, Virgin, carved wood, good old patina, minor worming, minor losses, Spanish, 17th/18th C **1,725.00**

13" h, Deity, carved sandalwood, rosewood plinth, India, 20th C **175.00**

27" h, Virgin and Child, French Gothic style, 19th C **1,100.00**

33" h, Madonna and Child, gilt and painted carved wood, Christ child delivering blessing, Italian, c1880 .... **1,610.00**

Folio, 14-3/4" x 25", leather bound, front with painted image of Madonna and Child after 14th C Sienses artist Lipp

Madonna and Child, Italian, gilt and painted carved in the round wood, c1800, 33" h, **$1,610.** *Photo courtesy of Jackson's International Auctioneers & Appraisers.*

Mimi, tooled gilt embossing, reverse with gilt embossing and six polychromed Heraldic shields, int. with finely woven cardinal red cloth, Italian, 19th C **435.00**

Gospel stand, 14" x 14-1/2", gilt bronze, four massive figural winged griffin feet, front and sides with elaborate fret work, embellished with Austrian crystals, 19th C **435.00**

Holy water font

6-1/4" w, 8-1/2" h, gilded bronze, figural, guardian angel, French, 19th C **1,265.00**

20" h, sculpted bronze figure of Guardian Angel filling font comprised of bank of clouds supported by winged cherubs, entire figure set on carved and beveled slab of alabaster, mounted to bronze back with suspension loop, French, 19th C **1,380.00**

Icon, 25-1/4" w, 32" h, patron Saint of Lima, St. Rose, painted over gesso on board, elaborate carved frame with arched inner linen, openwork foliage in gold, silver, and red, relief carved birds and grapes, small cobalt glass dec, early 20th C **650.00**

Monstrance, gilded bronze, figural

22" h, central exposition window encircled within ornate framework displaying rays, set with paste

Communion table, oak, English, 1680-1720, four-board top with breadboard ends, on stretcher base, bold reeded and fluted urn shaped turnings, six legs, 11' 5" l, 34" w, 32" h, **$3,300.** *Photo courtesy of Sanford Alderfer Auction Company.*

Virgin and child, French Gothic-style, carved wood, 19th C, 27" h, $1,100. Photo courtesy of Jackson's International Auctioneers & Appraisers.

stones, cross finial, central node and ornate base set with faux gemstones, three scroll feet, French, 19th C **1,035.00**

26-1/2" h, ornate ftd base supporting altar form, massive stem with grape dec node embellished with cherubs, central exposition window with brilliant sunburst, supported by bundle of wheat, surrounded by angels, French, 19th C . . . **1,035.00**

Painting

20" x 26-1/4", The Madonna and Child of Passau, Austrian School, c1800, oil on canvas, laid down, unsigned **350.00**

34" x 27", The Virgin and Child, Continental School, c1750, oil on wood panel, unsigned . . . **1,610.00**

36-1/2" x 25", St. Francis of Assisi, Italian School, c1700, oil on copper, unsigned **920.00**

40" x 29", The Flight Into Egypt, Franz Wagner, sgd lower right, oil on canvas **2,760.00**

55" x 44", The Madonna of the Harpies, after Andrea Del Sarto, oil on canvas, unsigned **2,185.00**

Plaque, 32" x 26", cast composition relief plaque of Madonna and Child, 58-1/2" x 43" polychrome and gilt carved wood frame, arched top, fluted columns, gild dec, inscribed "Ave Maria" in gold leaf, Italian, 19th C **2,530.00**

Reliquary

8" w, 7-1/2" h, gilt bronze, eye-shaped, displaying relics on both sides and stored below with documents, 19th C **1,150.00**

12" w, 13-3/4" h, bronze, casket-style, velvet pillows for relics, old document under pillows, 19th C **750.00**

14-1/2" h, gilt bronze, cross form, with relic of the True Cross, 19th C **2,415.00**

18-1/4" h, gilt bronze, exposition window containing reliquary with 11 individual relics, 19th C . **920.00**

20" h, gilt bronze, arched exposition window containing sealed oval reliquary with relics, verso with wax seal, 19th C **1,035.00**

20" w, 40" h, Baroque, wood carved in round, polychrome, gilt trim, Bishop Saint, deeply carved wavy beard, curly hair, high relief modeled clothing with faux embroidered elements, orig base with oval reliquary compartment, probably French, 18th C, very minor losses, minor worming **4,140.00**

Retablo, gessoed wood panel, polychrome, New Mexico, 19th C

9-1/2" x 7-1/4", Arroyo Hondo or José Aragón, San José, verso with hand written label relating work to N Mexican church **4,600.00**

Virgin, South German, polychrome and carved in the round wood, 19th C, 24-1/2" h, $1,150. Photo courtesy of Jackson's International Auctioneers & Appraisers.

12" x 7-1/4", School of Lagune Santero, Santa Gertrudis la Magna, losses **2,875.00**

12-1/4" x 8-1/2", Arroyo Hondo painter, San Francisco de Asís **6,440.00**

Sanctuary lamp, 39" l, cast bronze body, dark brown patina, three cast and hand finished cherub chain support strung with cast flat chain links, 15th/16th C **1,035.00**

Santos, Philippine, carved and painted wood

13" h, carved winged angel playing lute **200.00**

14" h, The Christ Child **120.00**

19" h, Mary **150.00**

21" h, Nun Saint, carved and painted, glass eyes, fragmentary base, mounted at back with modern wall bracket, possibly Northern European **250.00**

Santos Shrine, two pcs, top with two front doors revealing fitted int., conforming base with two cupboard doors, sides also have doors, inlaid panels, 40" w, 17" d, 60-1/2" h . . **200.00**

Shrine, 14" h, India, 19th C, Pala-style, probably to Manjushri, bronze, three sections, green patina, mounted on museum style display **865.00**

Shrine niche, 15" x 19" x 47" h, gilt bronze, French, 19th C **750.00**

Torcher, 22-1/2" h, fully carved wood, polychrome dec, angel with cornucopia, hand wrought pricket, Italian Baroque, c1700, price for pr **1,265.00**

Triptych wings, pr, each 14-1/2" w, 40-1/2" h, The Risen Christ visiting his Mother (obverse) and St. John the Baptist and St. Catherine of Alexandria with Donors (reverse), oil and tempera on wood panels, Antwerp School, c1520 . . . . **8,625.00**

REVERSE PAINTING ON GLASS

History: The earliest examples of reverse painting on glass were produced in 13th-century Italy. By the 17th century, the technique had spread to central and eastern Europe. It spread westward as the center of the glassmaking industry moved to Germany in the late 17th century.

The Alsace and Black Forest regions developed a unique portraiture style. The half and three-quarter portraits often were titled below the portrait. Women tend to have generic names, while most males are likenesses of famous men.

The English used a mezzotint, rather than free-style, method to create their reverse paintings. Landscapes and allegorical figures were popular. The Chinese began working in the medium in the 17th century, eventually favoring marine and patriotic scenes.

Most American reverse painting was done by folk artists and is unsigned. Portraits, patriotic and mourning scenes, floral compositions, landscapes, and buildings are the favorite subjects. Known American artists include Benjamin Greenleaf, A. Cranfield, and Rowley Jacobs.

In the late 19th century, commercially produced reverse paintings, often decorated with mother-of-pearl, became popular. Themes included the Statue of Liberty, the capitol in Washington, D.C., and various world's fairs and expositions.

Today craftsmen are reviving this art, using some vintage-looking designs, but usually with brighter colors than their antique counterparts.

Portraits

Geisha, holding paint brush, red robe, black and gold trim, gold hair ornaments, partially screened, much hand painting, 15-1/4" w, 21-1/2" h, minor flaking at top, black wooden frame with minor damage on back
. . . . **175.00**

Lincoln, Abraham, framed, 21-1/2" h, 18" w **425.00**

Rosinia, polychrome, dark green ground, orig frame, 9-1/8" h, 6-1/2" w
. . . . **450.00**

Young well-dressed lady, inscription "This box belonged to Lydia A Dowell, daughter of Richard and Barbara Dowell, She died in 1834 in the 13th year of her age," 5-1/2" x 7-1/4", probably lid to dresser box, **$110.** *Photo courtesy of Cowan's Historic Americana Auctions.*

Royal Couple, unsigned, Chinese Export School, 19th C, period Chinese frames, 15-1/2" w, 21-1/2" h, portrait of gentleman cracked lower left, price for pr **3,450.00**

Van Buren, Martin, marked "M. V. Buren," northern Europe, c1840, for American market, period frame, 7-3/4" w, 9-3/4" h **750.00**

Washington, George, silhouette, intricately painted border maple veneer frame, gilded liner with minor damage, 12-3/4" h, 11" w **250.00**

Scenes

Country house in winter, gold painted frame, 10-1/2" h, 12-1/2" w **75.00**

Perry's Lake Erie Victory, Sept. 10, 1813, naval battle scene, multicolored, 7" x 9" **250.00**

Roundel, 2" d reverse painted roundel with scene of Continental buildings and figures, beaded gilt metal surrounds, set in 13-1/4" h diamond-shaped giltwood shadowbox frames, early 20th C, price for pr **100.00**

Ship, *Ohio*, side wheeler steamship, poplar frame, 10-1/2" h, 12-1/2" w
. . . . **175.00**

Statue of Liberty, mica accents, oval frame **175.00**

RING TREES

History: A ring tree is a small, generally saucer-shaped object made of glass, porcelain, metal, or wood with a center post in the shape of a hand, branches, or cylinder. It is a convenient object for holding finger rings.

Nippon, round, handstand, scenic, boat, green M in wreath mark, 3-1/2" d, **$145.** *Photo courtesy of Sanford Alderfer Auction Company.*

Sterling silver, saucer base, repousse, three wire extensions, marked "RW & S," 3" d, base, 2" h, **$165.**

Glass

Black, 3-7/8" d, 4" h, all over dec on saucer and post, lacy gold vines and green enamel leaves, light blue, white, orange, and cream flowers **95.00**

Bristol, 3" h, 3-1/4" d, turquoise blue, lacy yellow leaves and large gold leaves dec **85.00**

Cameo, 3-1/4" h, 4" d, acid cut, red flowers, leaves, and stems, leaf ground, St. Louis **160.00**

Cranberry, 3-1/4" h, 3-1/2" d, hp, multicolored flowers, gold leaves
. . . . **115.00**

Opalescent, 2-1/2" h, 3-1/2" d, vaseline, striped **75.00**

Waterford, crystal **45.00**

Porcelain

Austria, hp pink and green floral dec, gold trim, marked "M. Z. Austria". **70.00**

Limoges, multicolored blossoms, white ground, marked "T. & V. Limoges" **40.00**

Minton, 3" h, pastel flowers, gold trim, marked "Minton England" **45.00**

Nippon, gold hand, rim dec **35.00**

Noritake, 3-1/2" d, 3" h, white hand, painted blue and pink flowers . . . **35.00**

Royal Worcester, 2-3/4" h, 4-1/2" l, oval dish, three-pronged holder, hp pink and yellow flowers, beige ground, c1898
. . . . **150.00**

R. S. Germany, 2-3/4" h, 5-1/2" l, hp, pink flowers, green leaves, told tree, sgd "E. Wolff" **50.00**

Wedgwood, 2-3/4" h, jasperware, center post, white cameos of classical ladies, floral border, blue ground, marked **150.00**

Silver

Tiffany & Co., angel shape **450.00**

Wilcox, open hand, saucer base, engraved edge, sgd **60.00**

ROCK 'N' ROLL

History: Rock music can be traced back to early rhythm and blues. It progressed until it reached its golden age in the 1950s and 1960s. Most of the memorabilia issued during that period focused on individual singers and groups. The largest quantity of collectible material is connected to Elvis Presley and The Beatles.

In the 1980s, two areas—clothing and guitars—associated with key rock 'n' roll personalities received special collector attention. Sotheby's and Christie's East regularly feature rock 'n' roll memorabilia as part of their collectibles sales. At the moment, the market is highly speculative and driven by nostalgia.

It is important to identify memorabilia issued during the lifetime of an artist or performing group, as opposed to material issued after they died or disbanded. Objects of the latter type are identified as "fantasy" items and will never achieve the same degree of collectibility as period counterparts.

> ◆—◆—◆
> **Reproduction Alert:** Records, picture sleeves, and album jackets, especially for The Beatles, have been counterfeited. When compared to the original, sound may be inferior, as may be the printing on labels and picture jackets. Many pieces of memorabilia also have been reproduced, often with some change in size, color, and design.
> ◆—◆—◆

Additional Listings: See The Beatles, Elvis Presley, and Rock 'n' Roll in *Warman's Americana & Collectibles* and *Warman's Flea Market Price Guide*.

Autograph, photo

Chuck Berry	**75.00**
Michael Jackson	**195.00**
Mick Jagger	**135.00**
Madonna	**195.00**
Paul McCartney	**275.00**

Backstage pass, cloth

Aerosmith, Pump Tour '89, afternoon **10.00**
Bon Jovi, NJ Guest **7.00**
KISS, 10th anniversary, after show, unused **7.00**
Cyndi Lauper, Crew '86-87 .... **6.00**
Rolling Stones, American Tour '81 .... **15.00**

Book

Beatlebook of Recorded Hits, No. 2, copyright 1964, pullout photo section, official fan club membership application form, slight wear to cover **95.00**
Elvis Presley, 1994, 240 pgs.. **24.00**

Bubble gum cards, complete set, issued by Boxcar Enterprises, 1978 .... **135.00**

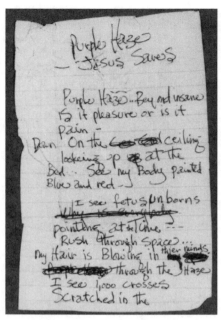

Signed document, Jimi Hendrix, hand-written lyrics, "Purple Haze," $18,000.

Counter display, Rolling Stones, "Made In The Shade," 1976, 21" x 19", 3-D cardboard, bowed diecut, with four previous LP covers at left and "Rolling Stones & Tongue" logo on silver at top right **250.00**
Divider card, Yardbirds, LP bin type, Epic, 1988, 12" x 14" plastic, purple names and logos emb at top ... **200.00**
Drumsticks

Alice in Chains............ **25.00**

Drawing, Psychedelic, Jimi Hendrix, 1969, $6,875.

Pinback button, Elvis Presley National Fan Club Member, black and white, c1956, 15/16" d, $175. Photo courtesy of Hake's Americana & Collectibles.

Black Crows, concerned used, logo **20.00**
Randy Castillo, Ozzy Osbourne **35.00**
Iron Maiden, 1985 .... **50.00**

Flyer, concert, Aerosmith, 1988, 8" x 6", two sided, Whitesnake and Def Leppard on back............. **45.00**
Label sticker, Deep Purple, promo LP label made for Come Taste The Band **25.00**
Magazine, *Life*, Oct. 24, 1968, Beatles on cover, feature article........ **40.00**
Menu, Elvis Presley, Las Vegas Hilton Hotel, 8-1/2" x 11" **1,000.00**
Merchandising kit, Queen, Night At the Opera, Elektra, 1985, 24" x 24" cardboard and tin paper poster with LP cover, two 15" x 24" two-sided thin cardboard "Hanging Arrow" displays, two 9" x 10" oval posters with LP cover art **200.00**
Pennant, 29-1/2" l, We Love Lil Richard, felt, white, red design and border, orig 30" l wood stick, 1950s **50.00**
Plaque, Bon Jovi, Anytime, Anywhere, with unused tickets from Belgium, Italy, and Istanbul, gold CD, only 45 produced.................. **250.00**
Portrait, Elvis Presley, by Ivan Jesse Curtain, wooden frame, 1960s . **125.00**
Postcard, Beatles, wearing gray suits, made in Germany **35.00**
Press kit, KISS, Casablanca, 1976, custom folder, three-page bio, one-page press clipping, five 8" x 10" black and white photos, orig mailing envelope with no writing or postage **500.00**

Record award

Beatles, "20 Greatest Hits," orig RIAA Gold strip plate award, gold wood frame **795.00**

Billy Joel, "Songs from the Attic," RIAA Platinum Strip plate, orig silver wood frame **450.00**

Eagles, "The Long Run," RIAA Platinum for four million sales **600.00**

Hootie & the Blowfish, "Fairweather Johnson," RIAA Gold LP . . . **600.00**

Scarf, Beatles, glossy fabric, half corner design, marked "The Beatles/ Copyright by Ramat & Co., Ltd./ London, ECI," 25" sq, c1964 . . . **160.00**

Ticket

Aerosmith, Pacific, 1989 . . . . . . **5.00**

Elvis, 9/88 . . . . **75.00**

Yardbirds/Doors, 1967 . . . . **50.00**

Tour book

Depeche Mode, Devotional Tour 1993/94 . . . . **10.00**

KISS, 10th anniversary, Vinnie V in makeup **125.00**

T-shirt

Bob Dylan, XL, True Confession, worn **10.00**

Bon Jovi, L, Slippery When…, never worn **25.00**

Deep Purple, L, Perfect Str…'85, never worn **25.00**

Rolling Stones, XL, Steel Wheels, never worn **20.00**

Wallet, Beatles, red and white, imprinted autographs and photo on front, clasp missing **95.00**

ROOKWOOD POTTERY

History: Mrs. Marie Longworth Nicholas Storer, Cincinnati, Ohio, founded Rookwood Pottery in 1880. The name of this outstanding American art pottery came from her family estate, "Rookwood," named for the rooks (crows) that inhabited the wooded grounds.

Though the Rookwood pottery filed for bankruptcy in 1941, it was soon reorganized under new management. Efforts at maintaining the pottery proved futile, and it was sold in 1956 and again in 1959. The pottery was moved to Starkville, Mississippi, in conjunction with the Herschede Clock Co. It finally ceased operating in 1967.

Rookwood wares changed with the times. The variety is endless, in part because of the creativity of the many talented artists responsible for great variations in glazes and designs.

Marks: There are five elements to the Rookwood marking system—the clay or body mark, the size mark, the decorator mark, the date mark, and the factory mark. The best way to date Rookwood art pottery is from factory marks.

From 1880 to 1882, the factory mark was the name "Rookwood" incised or painted on the base. Between 1881 and 1886, the firm name, address, and year appeared in an oval frame. Beginning in 1886, the impressed "RP" monogram appeared and a flame mark was added for each year until 1900. After 1900, a Roman numeral, indicating the last two digits of the year of production, was added at the bottom of the "RP" flame mark. This last mark is the one most often seen on Rookwood pieces in the antiques marketplace.

Architectural tile, 17-1/2" sq, cuenca, tree landscape, blue, green, and tan matte glazes, mounted in Arts & Crafts frame, imp "Rookwood Faience" **3,450.00**

Bookend, 6-1/4" w, 5-3/4" h, elephant, semi-matte ivory glaze, production, 1920, flame mark/XX/244C, firing line to back, X'd for glaze drip **145.00**

Bowl, 6-1/2" d, Ombroso, carved and inlaid poppy pod dec around top, dec by Charles Todd, 1915 . . . . . . **2,200.00**

Cabinet jug, 3-1/2" d, 4-1/2" h, by N. J. Hirschfeld, dec in Limoges-style, bamboo and butterfly, shaded brown, ivory, and blue-green ground, gilded details, stamped "Rookwood 1883 G 61," artist's cipher **410.00**

Cabinet vase, 3" d, 3" h, Tiger Eye, flame mark obscured by glaze, two very minor grinding base chips **350.00**

Plaque, Standard glaze, by Grace Young, 1902, "Study Head after Rembrandt," 9" x 7", mounted in period but not necessarily original gilded frame, flame mark/II/Study head after Rembrandt/GY, minute, glazed-over clay blemish to nose, **$3,750.** *Photos courtesy of David Rago Auctions.*

Vase, Iris Glaze, by Caroline Steinle, 1906, ovoid, painted indigo iris, green leaves, shaded blue-green, ivory, and yellow ground, flame mark/VI/904E/artist's cipher, overall crazing, 3" d, 6-3/4" h, $1,610.

Chamberstick, 3" h, Standard Glaze, painted by Jeannette Swing, yellow violets, flame mark, artist's cipher, 1894 . . . . **350.00**

Charger, 12-1/2" d, mauve and ochre galleon center, light blue splashed border, John Wareham, dated 1905 . . . . **1,500.00**

Chocolate pot, 10" h, standard glaze, oak leaves and across dec, shape #722, Lenore Ashbury, 1904 . . . **700.00**

Ewer, 4" d, 5-1/2" h, by Josephine E. Zettel, 1891, standard glaze, orchids on shaded ground, Gorham silver floral overlay, flame mark/509/W/artist's cipher, Gorham stamp on overlay **2,300.00**

Figure, 7-1/2" d, 8" h, woman's head, matte white glaze, 1924, flame mark/XXIV/2026 . . . . **365.00**

Floor vase, 17-3/4" h, matte glaze, scene of grapevine and fruit by Charles Stewart Todd, flowing deep purple and blue glaze, imp logo, date, artist initials, shape no. 139B and wheel ground "X," c1915 . . . . **3,335.00**

Flower boat, 16" l, standard glaze, pansies dec, shape #3745, Matt A. Daly, 1890 . . . . **900.00**

Flower frog, #2251, 1915 . . . . . **325.00**

Humidor, cov, 6" h, round, Standard Glaze, portrait of American Indian, Pueblo Man, painted by Grace Young, dated 1901 . . . . **3,750.00**

Jug, 3-1/2" d, 5-1/4" h, by Albert Humphrys, 1882, Limoges style, geese flying over bamboo thicket, stamped "ROOKWOOD 1882 A.H." with anchor **490.00**

Mug, 5" d, 5-1/2" h, emb owl on oak branch, matte green glaze, 1906, flame

mark/VI/X, X'd for small glaze blister on owl's toe, peppering **230.00**

Paperweight, 3-1/2" d, elephant, 1928 . . . . **250.00**

Pitcher

3-3/4" h, Standard Glaze Light, squatty, leaf handle, painted by Constance Baker, daisies dec, flame mark and "CAB," c1890 . . . . **265.00**

7-1/2" d, 6-1/2" h, oviform, incised palm leaves, gold and blue highlights, imp "Rookwood, 1883, small kiln, 'Y' 13". **230.00**

Planter, 8-3/4" h, 8-1/2" d, incised stylized leaves, frothy brown-green matte glaze, c12910, flame mark/XI/180C. **500.00**

Plaque, scenic vellum

7-1/2" x 3-1/2", Ombroso, pr of Rooks flanking bowl and reverse RP symbol, 1915, minor edge flakes **6,000.00**

9-1/2" x 11-1/2", The Morning Hour, Venetian sailboats, painted by Carl Schmidt **6,500.00**

10-3/8" w, 13-5/8" h, End of the Woods, view of trees and distant view, soft greens, blues, and pink, sgd "FR," flame mark and date on reverse, dec by Frederick Rothenbusch, 1920, orig wood frame **6,900.00**

11-1/2" x 9", winter scene, frozen lake at twilight, painted by Elizabeth F. McDermott, 1910 . . . . **7,500.00**

12" x 9-1/2", meadow and trees, painted by L. Asbury, 1922, orig frame **7,000.00**

12" sq, shade trees in foreground, lake and mountain in background, Arts & Crafts oak frame. . **2,500.00**

14-1/4" w, 8-3/4" h, Penacock Lane, Concord, NH, view of lake through trees, sgd "ED," Rookwood flame mark and date on reverse, dec by Ed Diers, Cincinnati, OH, 1916, framed, crazing. **8,625.00**

14-1/2" x 9-1/2", lake bordered by shade trees and mountain, painted by Ed Diers, 1919, orig frame **10,000.00**

Teapot, cov, 11", Turkish, frog fishing with pole and bobber on riverbank, painting attributed to Maria Longworth Nichols, dated 1833. . . . . **1,500.00**

Vase

2-3/4" d, 6-1/4" h, Wax Matte, by Margaret Helen McDonald, 1935, fine yellow glaze, white snowdrops, uncrazed, flame mark/XXXV/S/MHM **980.00**

3" d, 7-1/2" h, scenic vellum, by Carl Schmidt, 1922, marine, shaded pink to blue ground, flame mark/XXII/904E/V/artist's cipher, light overall crazing. **2,415.00**

3-1/4" d, 6-1/4" h, Wax Matte, by Caroline Steinle, 1918, band of cherry blossoms, semi-matte green glaze, flame mark/XVIII/924/CS **750.00**

3-1/4" d, 7" h, scenic vellum, by Edward Diers, 1921, landscape vista of tall trees, flame mark/XXI/2102/V/ED, uncrazed **2,070.00**

3-1/4" d, 7-3/4" h, Vellum, by Mary Grace Denzler, 1915, band of Art Deco roses around rim, flame mark XV/2032E/V/MGD, some peppering around rim **980.00**

3-1/2" d, 8-1/2" h, scenic vellum, by Carl Schmidt, tapering, white and lavender lady slipper orchids, green leaves, shaded pink to green ground, flame mark/V/960D/V/CS, fine crazing **4,025.00**

4" d, 9-1/2" h, Vellum, by Lenor Asbury, 1913, pink and white apple blossoms, shaded teal, ivory, and pink ground, flame mark/XII/2060D/V/L.A., fine overall crazing . **815.00**

4-1/2" d, 6-1/2" h, Standard Glaze, by A. M. Valentien, 1891, oak leaves and acorns, light glaze, flame mark/346B/W/A.M.V **750.00**

4-1/2" d, 7" h, Standard Glaze, by C. F. Bonsall, 1903, two handles, auburn maple leaves, flame mark/III/604D/C.F.B. **575.00**

4-1/2" d, 7" h, Vellum, by Ed Diers, 1911, pink roses, shaded celadon, teal, and pink ground, flame mark/XI/136E/V/ED, fine overall crazing **575.00**

4-1/2" d, 9-1/2" h, Wax Matte, by Janet Harris, 1929, shouldered, mauve and white daffodils and leaves, orchid matte ground, flame mark/XXIX/1920/JH **1,150.00**

4-3/4" d, 9" h, Standard Glaze, by Kataro Shirayamadani, 1900, floating draped skeleton bearing lamp, silver-washed copper overlaid rim and handle emb with half moon, wind-swept clouds, and incense from skeleton's burner,

Vase, Banded Scenic Vellum, by Ed Diers, 1916, tall, dark elm trees, blue sky with white clouds, flame mark/XVI/ED /892C/V, uncrazed, 4-3/4" d, 9-1/4" h, $3,450.

Vase, Scenic Vellum, by E.T. Hurley, 1916, ovoid, cluster of birch trees, shaded pink and blue sky with distant mountains, flame mark XVI/V/932CC/ ETH, uncrazed, 4-1/2" d, 11" h, $3,775.

Vase, Jewel Porcelain, by Sara Sax, 1922, flaring, tapered shoulder, French Red hibiscus, green foliage, black ground, impressed flame mark/XXII/ 1848/artist cipher, 6-3/4" d, 6" h, $2,500.

flame mark/564D/artist's cipher, tight line to base goes on inch up side, short tight lines below metal rim **3,450.00**

5" h, Standard Glaze, red poppies, green leaves, dec by Mary Luella Perkins, c1896. . . . . **350.00**

5" d, 6-1/4" h, Squeezebag, by Jens Jensen, 1928, brown and blue-gray stylized leaves, yellow ground, flame mark/XXVII/1781/artist cipher **1,150.00**

6" h, Vellum Glaze, snowberries, dec by Olga Geneva Reed, 1912, overall crazing. **460.00**

6" d, 9-1/2" h, Wax Matte, by Jens Jensen, 1929, stylized yellow, red, and purple flowers, pink ground, flame mark/XXIX/2303/artist's cipher **1,610.00**

7-3/8" h, artist sgd with initials for W. E. Hentschel, dated 1915, olive brown matte glaze above emb green, blue, and light gray flowers **1,775.00**

8" h, Standard Glaze, silver overlay of wild roses, poppies, and lily-of-the-valleys, painted nasturtiums, L. N. Lincoln, c1895 . . . . **5,750.00**

9-1/2" h, Later Tiger Eye, Empire Green, carved sea horse dec, by E. T. Hurley, 1923. . . . . **3,500.00**

10" h, black iris glaze, cherry blossom branches overlaid with black tree branches, colorful blue to green to peach background, by

Vase, Vellum, by Sara Sax, 1904, bulbous, large pale peony blossoms with yellow centers covered in green glaze, flame mark/IV/902C/V/artist cipher, glaze drip at rim and back, 1/2" tight rim line, 6-1/2" d, 9-1/2" h, **$2,900.** *Photo courtesy of David Rago Auctions.*

Kataro Shiriyamidani, c1906 . . . . **7,500.00**

13" h, purple and white hydrangeas, painted by Lenore Asbury, 1924 . . . . **8,500.00**

Vessel

5-1/2" w, 4" h, carved matte, squatty, by William Hentschel, 1910, Glasgow roses, burgundy and teal blue glaze, flame mark/X/1110/WEH **815.00**

9" w, 6-1/2" h, vellum, by Lenore Ashbury, 1920, squatty, golden dandelions, green leaves, blue and mauve ground, flame mark/XX/1375/V/L.A. **1,380.00**

ROSE BOWLS

History: A rose bowl is a decorative open bowl with a crimped, pinched, or petal top which turns in at the top, but does not then turn up or back out again. Rose bowls held fragrant rose petals or potpourri, which served as an air freshener in the late Victorian period. Practically every glass manufacturer made rose bowls in virtually every glass type, pattern, and style, including fine art glass.

For more information, see this book.

Reproduction Alert: Rose bowls have been widely reproduced. Be especially careful of Italian copies of satin, Mother of Pearl satin, peachblow, and Burmese, and recent Czechoslovakian ones with applied flowers.

2" h, 2-1/4" w, Bohemian, transparent amethyst with enameled flowers, polished bottom, six crimps . . . **225.00**

2-1/8" h, 2-3/4" w, Stevens & Williams, jeweled, cranberry red, threaded in "zipper" pattern, 12 tiny crimps, engraved registry number Rd 55693 on polished bottom. **180.00**

2-3/4" d, satin, baby blue, mother-of-pearl, ground pontil, attributed to Webb. **385.00**

3" h, Burmese, pale yellow shading to light pink **125.00**

3" h, inverted trefoil rim of opalescent glass, acid-etched surface, etched thistle sprigs, gilt highlights, painted gilt "Daum (cross) Nancy" on base, gilt wear. **290.00**

Cut glass, hobstars, zipper cut rim and feathered fans, minor roughness, 6-1/2" w, 6-1/4" h, **$230.** *Photo courtesy of James D. Julia, Inc.*

3" h, 3" w, millefiore, glossy white opaque background with individual millefiore scattered throughout the glass, nine uneven crimps, semi-ground bottom, c1960. . . . . **45.00**

3" h, 3-1/2" w, satin, shaded pink to white, soft white interior, undecorated, eight crimps, ground pontil **55.00**

3-1/4" h, Burmese, salmon shading to pale yellow, amethyst flower leafy stem, Webb **260.00**

3-1/4" h, 3-1/2" w, Fenton, Beaded Melon, white with yellow interior, eight crimps, collar base. **45.00**

3-1/2" h, Moser, cranberry, enameled florals and butterfly, applied acorns, c1900 . . . . **750.00**

3-1/2" h, satin, cased pink, Herringbone pattern, mother-of-pearl **75.00**

3-7/8" h, 3-3/4" w, satin, apricot, soft white interior, enameled with purple and white violets, gold foliage and

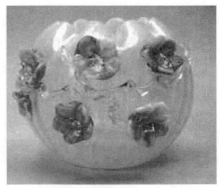

Opalescent, green, ribbed, applied pink flowers and clear glass stems, chips to four petals, 6" d, 5" h, **$65.** *Photo courtesy of James D. Julia, Inc.*

Stevens & Williams, Jewell glass, Zipper pattern, light sapphire blue, six box pleats, polished pontil, Rd. #55693, 4" h, 5" w, $125. Photo courtesy of Johanna Billings.

scrollwork, eight crimps, ground pontil
.... **175.00**

3-3/4" h, 4" d, mother-of-pearl satin, rainbow, Diamond Quilted pattern, ground pontil **1,100.00**

4" h, topaz, enameled figure of man drinking, Bohemian, c1900 .... **115.00**

4" h, 4" w, Dugan, Japanese line, light yellowish green, three crimps, three indentations on side, decorated with vertical rows of frit, collar base, c1907
.... **45.00**

4-1/2" h, amberina, applied amber petal feet, Lutz-type, price for pr **300.00**

4-3/4" h, 5-3/4" w, Consolidated Lamp & Glass Co., c1894, embossed Shell & Seaweed pattern, shaded purple to lavender, white interior, eight crimps, rough pontil **125.00**

7-1/4" h, 5" d, Rubena verde shading from chartreuse to rose, gold enameled highlights, jack-in-the-pulpit top **375.00**

ROSE CANTON, ROSE MANDARIN, AND ROSE MEDALLION

History: The pink rose color has given its name to three related groups of Chinese export porcelain: Rose Mandarin, Rose Medallion, and Rose Canton.

Rose Mandarin, produced from the late 18th century to approximately 1840, derives its name from the Mandarin figure(s) found in garden scenes with women and children. The women often have gold decorations in their hair. Polychrome enamels and birds separate the scenes.

Rose Medallion, which originated in the early 19th century and was made through the early 20th century, has alternating panels of figures and birds and flowers. The elements are four in number, separated evenly around the center medallion. Peonies and foliage fill voids.

Rose Canton, introduced somewhat later than Rose Mandarin and produced through the first half of the 19th century, is similar to Rose Medallion except the figural panels are replaced by flowers. People are present only if the medallion partitions are absent. Some patterns have been named, e.g., Butterfly and Cabbage and Rooster. Rose Canton actually is a catchall term for any pink enamelware not fitting into the first two groups.

> **Reproduction Alert:** Rose Medallion is still made, although the quality does not match the earlier examples.

Rose Canton

Brush pot, 4-1/2" h, scenic, ladies, reticulated, gilt trim........... **275.00**
Charger, 13" d, floral panels, 19th C
.... **215.00**
Platter, 16-1/2" l, 19th C, enamel and gilt wear **200.00**
Puzzle teapot, 6" h, Cadogan, painted birds and foliage, light blue ground, late 19th C, minor chips **150.00**
Umbrella jar, 24-1/4" h, 19th C, minor chips....................... **805.00**
Urn, cov, 19-1/4" h, minor chips, cracks, gilt wear, pr.............. **2,990.00**
Vase, 14" h, 19th C, chips, minor cracks, pr **1,265.00**

Rose Mandarin

Bowl, 9-1/2" d, scalloped edge . **300.00**
Charger, 13-1/2" d, Mandarin scenes, pink, green, blue, and orange, rim flake
.... **120.00**
Creamer, 3-5/8" h, three feet, plain handle..................... **50.00**

Rose Mandarin, platter, 15" l, 12" w, $200. Photo courtesy of Sanford Alderfer Auction Company.

Cup and saucer, scalloped edge rim, chips, price for pr **60.00**
Dish, 8" x 11", kidney shaped, celadon
   Dining scene, One Hundred
    Antiques border, minor glaze wear
    .... **250.00**
   Warriors, butterfly and floral border,
    minor glaze wear **300.00**
Mug, 4-3/8" h, rim chip **150.00**
Plate, 8-1/2" d, varying scenes with couples seated on porch, gold trim in their hair, worn gilt rims, center rings, minor flakes, one with short hairline, price for set of seven......... **295.00**
Platter, 16-1/4" l, chip **250.00**
Rice bowl, 4-5/8" d, scalloped rim, four-pc set.................**110.00**
Sauce boat, 8-1/4" l, intertwined handle
.................**110.00**
Serving dish, 9-7/8" d, 19th C, minor chips, enamel wear.......... **460.00**
Soup plate, 9-3/4" d, three with chips, six-pc set................... **55.00**
Sugar bowl, cov, 4-7/8" h, intertwined handles, fruit finial, minor enamel flaking **50.00**
Teapot, cov, 8-1/2" h, domed lid
.... **660.00**
Tureen, 13-3/4" l, 11-1/4" h, gilded handles and final........... **1,100.00**
Umbrella stand, 24" h, wrapped bamboo form, 19th C, star cracks, gilt and enamel wear........... **1,495.00**
Vase, 10" h, beaker, figural cartouche, chicken skin ground, Qianlong, c1775, price for pr................ **1,900.00**
Vegetable dish, cov, 11-1/2" d, almond shaped, fruit finial, minor flakes **200.00**

Rose Medallion

Basket and undertray, 9-3/4" l, 7-1/4" w, 3-3/4" h, two handles, reticulated, China, 19th C, chips
.... **325.00**
Bowl, 9" x 10-1/4", 4" h, reticulated high sides, flared rim, Mandarin scenes, red, blue, pink, and yellow, orange peel glaze, tiny rim flakes **450.00**
Charger
   10-1/2" d, celadon, court scene
    within shaped One Hundred
    Antiques border, textured ground,
    gilt wear to rim **275.00**
   13" d, celadon, court scene
    bordered with animals and floral
    trophies, textured ground, minor
    gilt wear **355.00**
   15" d **225.00**
Dish, 9-1/4" d, scalloped rim, 19th C
.... **275.00**

Rose Medallion 18" d charger, 9-3/4" w lidded tureen, **$295.** *Photo courtesy of Joy Luke Auctions.*

Platter

8-1/2" x 11", 19th C, minor glaze wear. **175.00**

9" x 12", oval, Mandarian scene, orange peel glaze ext. **275.00**

Punch bowl

15-3/4" d, 6-1/4" h, ftd, multiple mandarin scenes, shades of pink, light green, and blue, gilt ground between scenes, crow's foot in base **685.00**

24" d, hp scenes, four with birds, fruits, clouds, and flowers, alternating with panels of village scenes, gilt rim and highlights **3,680.00**

Serving dish, 10-3/4" l, 9-1/4" w, 1-3/4" h, oval, shaped rim, celadon, mid-19th C **400.00**

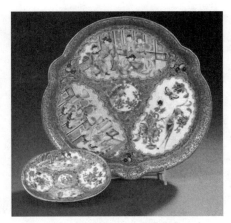

Rose Medallion, 11" tray, trefoil, figural and floral decoration, sold with small soap dish undertray, Chinese, Qing dynasty, **$350.** *Photo courtesy of Sloan's Auctioneers & Appraisers.*

Game plates, hand-painted fish and underwater life scenes, white ground, molded design on border and gilt rim, artist signed, marked "Rosenthal," minor gilt wear, 10" d, **$550.** *Photo courtesy of Sanford Alderfer Auction Company.*

Soup bowl, 8-1/4" d, Mandarin scene, gilding **110.00**

Spoon and spoon rest, 5-1/2" l, figural dec on bowl, rose dec on handle, matching 5" l spoon rest with conforming dec, set of six, one with chip and crack **300.00**

Teapot, 8" h, domed cov, squatty, gilt floral embellishments on handle and spout **765.00**

Tray, 9-1/8" sq, landscapes alternating with birds and flowers, hillside fort with multiple flakes, pagodas, fishing boats, orange peel glaze ext. **250.00**

Vase

10" h, baluster form, applied foo dog handles, kylins at shoulder, rim glaze chips, pr **400.00**

15-1/4" h, Ku-form, late 19th C, minor glaze wear **715.00**

17-1/4" h, gilt dragons, foo dogs, 19th C, minor wear **1,120.00**

Vegetable dish, cov, 9-1/2" l, 9" w, 5-1/2" h, celadon, pinecone knop, mid-19th C, imperfection. **450.00**

Wall cone, 13-1/2" h, 19th C . . . **865.00**

ROSENTHAL

History:
Rosenthal Porcelain Manufactory began operating at Selb, Bavaria, in 1880. Specialties were tablewares and figurines. The firm is still in operation.

Box, cov, Studio Line, sgd "Peynet" **175.00**

Cake plate, 12" w, grape dec, scalloped ruffled edge, ruffled handles **75.00**

Candlestick, 9-1/2" h, Art Deco woman holding candlestick **275.00**

Chocolate set, San Souci pattern, six cups and saucers, cov pot, creamer and sugar, marked "Selb Bavaria," c1880, 15-pc set **425.00**

Creamer and sugar, pate-sur-pate type blue cherries dec **115.00**

Cup and saucer, San Souci pattern, white **20.00**

Demitasse cup and saucer, Marie pattern **25.00**

Design page, 6" w, 9-1/2" h, hand rendered, each page showing transfer printed and hand-tinted designs, most numbered or named, some on graph paper, 10 pages **230.00**

Figure

6" h, clown **225.00**

10-1/2" h, Fairy Queen, sgd "L. Friedrich-Granau" **325.00**

Plaque, 9" x 7-1/2", titled "Die Falknerin," sgd "Hans Makart" **1,100.00**

Plate, 10" d, girl and lamb dec, multicolored **40.00**

Portrait plate, 9-7/8" d, bust portrait of lady, pale yellow and white ground, faux green, turquoise, blue, and red hardstone jewels **350.00**

Vase

7" h, modeled owls on branch **165.00**

11" h, hp, multicolored roses . **125.00**

ROSEVILLE POTTERY

History: In the late 1880s, a group of investors purchased the J. B. Owens Pottery in Roseville, Ohio, and made utilitarian stoneware items. In 1892, the firm was incorporated and joined by George F. Young, who became general manager. Four generations of Youngs controlled Roseville until the early 1950s.

A series of acquisitions began: Midland Pottery of Roseville in 1898, Clark Stoneware Plant in Zanesville (formerly used by Peters and Reed), and Muskingum Stoneware (Mosaic Tile Company) in Zanesville. In 1898, the offices also moved from Roseville to Zanesville.

In 1900, Roseville introduced Rozane, an art pottery. Rozane became a trade name to cover a large series of lines. The art lines were made in limited amounts after 1919.

The success of Roseville depended on its commercial lines, first developed by John J. Herald and Frederick Rhead in the first decades of the 1900s. In 1918, Frank Ferrell became art director and developed more than 80 lines of pottery. The economic depression of the 1930s brought more lines, including Pine Cone.

In the 1940s, a series of high-gloss glazes were tried in an attempt to revive certain lines. In 1952, Raymor dinnerware was produced. None of these changes brought economic success and in November 1954, Roseville was bought by the Mosaic Tile Company.

Basket

Blackberry, unmarked, 6" d, 7-1/2" h, very small nick to one berry 1,355.00

Foxglove, white and pink foxglove blossoms, green ground, marked "Roseville U.S.A. 375-12," c1942, 12" h 200.00

Gardenia, green, raised mark, No. 618-15" 490.00

Jonquil, pillow, unmarked, 10-1/2" d, 7-1/2" h 750.00

Mock Orange, No. 908-6, white blossoms, green leaves, rose ground, 6" h 200.00

Poppy, green, raised mark, No. 347-10" 350.00

Thorn Apple, conical, brown, imp mark, No. 342-10" 415.00

Basket, Columbine, blue, raised 368-12" mark, **$290.** *Photos courtesy of David Rago Auctions.*

Bookends, pair, Dawn, impressed mark, 5-1/4" x 4-1/4" x 4-1/2", **$500.**

Vista, unmarked, 4-3/4" d, 6-3/4" h 575.00

Basket planter

Apple Blossom, green, asymmetrical rim, raised mark, No. 311-12" 490.00

Iris, spherical, pink, imp mark, No. 354-8" 365.00

Bookends, pr

Dawn, pink, imp mark, 4-1/4" w, 4-1/2" d, 5-1/4" h 500.00

Iris, book shape, blue, raised mark, No. 5, 5-1/4" w, 5-1/4" h 290.00

Water Lily, model no. 14, molded open book form, water lily blossoms in relief, walnut brown glaze, raised "Roseville U.S.A." mark, 4-3/4" l, 5-1/4" d, 5-1/2" h, repair 200.00

Bowl

Ferella, rose colored, open work at rim and base, 8" x 6-1/2" . . . 900.00

Futura, 12-1/2" d, 3-3/4" h, flaring, flower frog, mottled blue, green, and orange glaze, unmarked 490.00

Rosecraft Panel, rolled rim, orange floral dec, brown ground, c1920, 8" d, 2-3/8" h 140.00

Bud vase

Orange blossoms, green ground, model no. 870, double reservoir,

Bud vase, Vintage, double, RV ink stamp, 4" x 8", **$225.**

c1940, raised "Roseville U.S.A." mark, 6-1/4" h 100.00

Pine Cone, blue, raised mark, 5" d, 7-1/2" h, minute flake on base 400.00

Candlesticks, pr

Blackberry, gold foil label, 4" d, 4-1/2" h 690.00

Moderne, ivory, triple, incised mark, No. 1112, 5-1/4" d, 6-1/4" h 490.00

Sunflower, black paper label, 3-3/4" d, 4-1/4" h 800.00

Wisteria, brown, unmarked, 4-3/4" d, 4-3/4" h 460.00

Coffee set, cov coffeepot, cov teapot, creamer, cov sugar, Mock Orange, green, raised marks, 10-3/4" h coffeepot, minor spider lines to spout 490.00

Compote, Donatello, 7-1/2" d . . 150.00

Console bowl

Cremona, oval, pink, unmarked, 11" d, 2-1/4" h 95.00

Ferella, ovoid, brown, black paper label, 13" l, 5-3/4" h 815.00

Moderne, semi-matte ivory glaze, incised mark, No. 301-10" . 230.00

Console set

Fuchsia, brown, imp marks, No. 1133-5 and No. 350-8" 490.00

Iris, pink, No. 360-10" oval centerbowl, pair of No. 1135-4-1/2" candlesticks, imp marks . . 375.00

Candlesticks, pair, Morning Glory, green, foil label, minor bruise to base of one, 5" x 4-1/4", **$475.**

Center bowl, Jonquil, flaring, attached flower frog, black paper label, 10 1/2" d, **$950.**

Thorn Apple, pink, low center bowl No. 307-6", pair of No. 1111 candlesticks, imp marks **. . . 290.00**

Cookie jar, cov

Clematis, No. 3-8, green ground **. 550.00**

Freesia, No. 4-8, blue ground **. 550.00**

Magnolia, No. 2-8, tan ground **. 450.00**

Water Lily, No. 1-8, gold shading to brown ground **. 555.00**

Zephr Lily, No. 5-8, blue ground **. 360.00**

Cornucopia vase

Pine Cone **. 140.00**

White Rose **. 95.00**

Ewer

Apple Blossom, green, raised mark, NO. 318-15, minute fleck to body **. 630.00**

Carnelian I, pink and gray glaze, RV ink mark, 7" d, 12-1/4" h **. . . 345.00**

Console set, Topeo, blue, silver foil label on 12-3/4" d x 4-1/4" h bowl, pair 4" h candlesticks, **$600.**

Cookie jar, Freesia, blue, raised 4-8" mark, 1/2" bruise to rim and lid, small glaze nicks to high points, **$400.**

Freesia, green, raised mark, No. 21-15", two base chips **. . . . 290.00**

Gardenia, brown, raised mark, No. 618-15" **. 490.00**

Mock Orange, No. 918-16, white blossoms, green leaves, pink ground, 16" h **. 310.00**

Pine Cone, brown, raised mark, No. 909-10" **. 690.00**

Floor vase

Fuchsia, brown, raised mark, No. 905-18" **. 750.00**

Pine Cone, brown, incised mark, No. 913-18", repair to rim and base **. 815.00**

Vista, bulbous, 18" h, unmarked, several bruises and chips **. 860.00**

Water Lily, green, raised mark, No.85-18" **. 630.00**

Flower pot and underplate, Iris, blue, raised marks, No. 648-5", 1" bruise to rim **. 365.00**

Hanging basket, Mock Orange, white blossoms, green leaves **. 375.00**

Flowerpot and underplate, Cosmos, blue, raised 650-5" mark, **$200.**

Hanging basket, Iris, blue, two handles, unmarked, some abrasion (shown upside down in photo), 5-1/4" x 8-1/2", **$300.**

Jardinière

Bleeding Heart, blue, 651-10", raised mark, two tight rim lines **. . . 460.00**

Fuchsia, bulbous, blue, imp mark, No. 645-8" **. 350.00**

Jonquil, spherical, unmarked, 9" d, 6" h, small stilt-pull chips **. 2,300.00**

Mostique, unmarked, 8-3/4" d, 7-1/2" h **. 230.00**

Jardinière on stand

Freesia, no. 669, Delftware blue glaze, creamy yellow and white blossoms, raised "Roseville U.S.A." mark, stand marked "U.S.A.," c1945 **. 500.00**

Freesia, no. 669-8, molded florals, blue ground, base emb "Roseville, USA, 669-8, c1935 **. 865.00**

Moss, green **. 3,250.00**

Mostique **. 900.00**

Lamp base, Pine Cone, brown, unmarked, 7-3/4" d, 10-1/4" h, small base chips **. 1,955.00**

Low bowl

Blackberry, unmarked, 7-3/4" d, 3-1/4" h, minor glaze bubbles **. 345.00**

Sunflower, low shoulder, unmarked, 7-1/4" d, 4" h, burst bubble on one leaf **. 535.00**

Mug, Pine Cone, blue, imp mark, No. 960-4", price for pr **. 700.00**

Pitcher

Fuchsia, brown, imp mark, 8-1/2" d, 8" h, peppering to body **. . . 400.00**

Pine Cone, no. 415, green glaze, brown, and cream tones, raised "Roseville, U.S.A." mark, c1931, 9-1/4" h **. 750.00**

Rozane Olympic, Ulysees at the Table of Circe, signed and titled, 8-1/2" d, 7" h, restoration to 5" spider lines **. 1,495.00**

Planter, Sunflower, four-sided, unmarked, 11" l, 3-3/4" h, $1,200.

White Rose, pink, raised mark, No. 1324, 8" d, 7" h, glaze drip around rim **275.00**

Planter

Blackberry, faceted, unmarked, 9-3/4" d, 3-1/2" h **435.00**

Florentine, brown, rect, 11-1/4" l, 5-1/4" h, few base chips . . . **290.00**

Morning Glory, oblong, green, unmarked, 11" l, 4-3/4" h . . **520.00**

Pine Cone, coupe shape, blue, imp mark, No. 124, 5" h **350.00**

Primrose, bulbous, pink, incised mark, No. 634-6", flecks to flowers and one handle **85.00**

Sunflower, four-sided, unmarked, 11" l, 3-3/4" h **1,200.00**

Planter bookends, pr, Columbine, blue, raised mark, 5" w, 5" d, 5-1/4" h **260.00**

Sand jar, Primrose, blue, 15-3/4" h, base chip and hairline **575.00**

Teapot, cov, Rozanne Della Robbia, hearts, cups, saucers, and Japanese fans dec, brown and celadon, Rozane Ware wafer, small lid nicks, 1" clay burst at rim **1,355.00**

Tea set, cov teapot, creamer, cov sugar

Freesia, blue, raised marks . **415.00**

Peony, yellow, raised marks . **415.00**

Snowberry, blue, raised marks **750.00**

Sconces, pair, Burmese, green, raised 80-B marks, 8" h, $200.

Snowberry, pink, raised marks, clay burst on creamer handle in firing **365.00**

White Rose, pink raised marks **490.00**

Wincraft, brown, raised marks, minor flaws **200.00**

Zephyr Lily, brown, raised marks, small burst bubble **435.00**

Umbrella stand, Pine Cone, brown, raised mark, No. 777-20", minor scaling area at handle, 1" rim bruise . **2,070.00**

Urn

Baneda, bulbous, pink, black foil label, 7-3/4" d, 10-1/2" h . **1,355.00**

Carnelian I, pink and gray glaze, RV ink mark, 8-1/4" d, 9-1/2" h . **375.00**

Iris, bulbous, pink, imp mark, No. 928-12" **460.00**

Moss, bulbous, buttressed base, incised mark, restorations to base and rim **200.00**

Pine Cone, blue, imp mark, No. 912-15", restoration to rim chip **2,185.00**

Teasel, flaring, blue, imp mark, No. 888-12" **435.00**

Thorn Apple, ftd, pink, imp mark, No. 822-10" **290.00**

Vase

Baneda, incised dec, 9" h . **1,000.00**

Cherry Blossom, 15-1/2" h, bruised foot **1,300.00**

Chloron, raised grape dec, green matte glaze, 8-1/2" h **1,200.00**

Cremo, red and green squeeze bag swirl dec, 6" h, repair to lip **2,000.00**

Falline, peapod-like beige, green, and yellow dec, shading to mottled blue at base, double handles, 9" h **1,600.00**

Freesia, slender neck on bulbous base, two low handles, purple

Vase, Futura, flaring pillow, fir tree pattern in mottled orange, blue and green matte glazes, unmarked, 6-1/4" x 9", $400.

freesia on stem in relief, shaded green ground, raised "Roseville U.S.A." 195-7" mark, 7-1/8" h **115.00**

Freesia, two handles, blue, 8-1/2" h **175.00**

Futura, balloon type, sq sloping base, 7" h **950.00**

Futura, conical form, three stepped rect devices on sides, round disk base, semi-gloss terra cotta, blue, and green glazes, c1928, unmarked, 8" h **575.00**

Futura, stacked rings form, blue-green high glaze, 10" h **2,400.00**

Futura, stepped rim on sq form tapering at base, raised geometric pattern, green and blue-gray, soft green ground, paper label on base, c1928, 6-1/4" h, glaze miss **520.00**

Morning Glory, pear shape, white, foil label, 7" d, 10-1/4" h, base grinding chips **495.00**

Rosecraft Panel, No. 293-8," bulbous, round shoulder, orange vines, leaves, and fruit dec, brown ground, c1920, 8" h **360.00**

Rozane Aztec, bulbous shoulder, tapering body, white, yellow, and blue stylized flowers and swags, blue-gray ground, unmarked, 4-1/2" d, 11" h, burst bubbles, couple of minor nicks **435.00**

Rozane Royal Dark, tapering, by Hester Pillsbury, painted yellow

Vase, Morning Glory, flaring, green, unmarked, restoration to flat chip under foot ring, 10" d, 14-3/4" h, $2,000.

Vase, Rozane, tear shape, Royal Dark, Turkish man in profile painted by H. Dunlavy, Rozane wafer and artist's signature, opposing tight lines to rim, 5" d, 8" h, $920.

wild roses, Roxane Ware wafer, 7" d, 8-3/4" h **475.00**

Rozane Woodland, corseted, enamel dec, white blossoms, green leaves, Rozane Ware/Woodland wafer, 3" d, 10" h **575.00**

Sunflower, double handles, 9" h **1,300.00**

Velmoss, flaring, broad leaves dec, unmarked, 5" d, 11-1/2" h, four rim chips **435.00**

Vista, bulbous, unmarked, 7-1/2" d, 17-1/2" h **1,890.00**

Wisteria, blue, 10" h **2,000.00**

Vessel

Baneda, bulbous, collared rim, green, black paper label, 5" l, 9-1/2" h **1,600.00**

Chloron, tapering, two handles, scalloped rim, body emb with cherries, stamped "Chloron/T.R.P. Co.," 7" d, 6-1/2" h **1,380.00**

Jonquil, squatty, pinched and scalloped rim, unmarked, 7" l, 5" h **495.00**

Savona, covered, yellow, black paper label, 8" l, 4" h **980.00**

Wall pocket, Pine Cone, double, blue, silver foil label, 8-3/4" x 4-1/2", $500.

Wall pocket, Panel, green, ink mark. 9" x 5", $300.

White Rose, spherical, blue, raised mark, NO. 388-7", 1" firing bruise to inner rim **230.00**

Wall pocket

Blackberry, flaring, unmarked, 7-3/4" l **1,610.00**

Cosmos, double, blue, unmarked, silver foil label **630.00**

Earlham, unmarked, 6-1/2" l . **920.00**

Foxglove, pink, unmarked, 8-1/2" l **460.00**

Moss, bucket, pink, unmarked, 10" l, 1/2" chip, small edge nick . **520.00**

Pine Cone, triple, blue, raised mark, 9" l **1,725.00**

Savona, blue, unmarked, 8-1/4" l **630.00**

Silhouette, pink, ivy leaves, raised mark No. 766-8" **290.00**

Wall shelf

Iris, blue, imp mark, No. 2, minute and shallow bruise to one side **5,175.00**

Pine Cone, green, unmarked, 5" w, 8" h **490.00**

ROYAL BAYREUTH

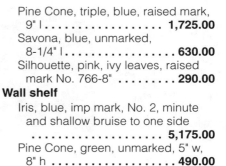

History: In 1794, the Royal Bayreuth factory was founded in Tettau, Bavaria. Royal Bayreuth introduced its figural patterns in 1885. Designs of animals, people, fruits, and vegetables decorated a wide array of tablewares and inexpensive souvenir items.

Tapestry wares, in rose and other patterns, were made in the late 19th century. The surface of the piece feels and looks like woven cloth. Tapestry ware was made by covering the porcelain with a piece of fabric tightly stretched over the surface, decorating the fabric, glazing the piece, and firing.

Top row, from left: Chamberstick with shield, scene of woman in hat with fan, 7-1/2" h, $175; pitcher, scene of woman with basket of flowers, 4-1/2" h, $100; bottom row, from left: ashtray, belt strap as handle, dogs hunting stag, 5-1/2", repaired, $80; toothpick holder, three handles, woman looking out, 3" h, $90. Photo courtesy of Woody Auctions.

Royal Bayreuth still manufactures dinnerware. It has not maintained production of earlier wares, particularly the figural items. Since thorough records are unavailable, it is difficult to verify the chronology of production.

For more information, see this book.

Marks: The Royal Bayreuth crest used to mark the wares varied in design and color.

Ashtray, elk **225.00**
Bell, Musicians scene, man playing cello and mandolin **300.00**
Candleholder, basset hound, dark body, unmarked **400.00**
Creamer
> Apple **195.00**
> Bird of Paradise **225.00**
> Cat, black and orange **200.00**
> Crow, brown bill **200.00**
> Duck **200.00**
> Eagle **300.00**
> Frog, green **225.00**
> Lamplighter, green **250.00**
> Pear **295.00**
> Robin **195.00**
> Water Buffalo, black and orange **225.00**

Cup and saucer, yellow and gold, purple and red flowers, green leaves, white ground, green mark **80.00**
Hatpin holder, courting couple, cutout base with gold dec, blue mark . **400.00**
Milk pitcher
> Butterfly **1,200.00**
> Owl **550.00**

Miniature, pitcher, portrait **95.00**
Plate, 6-1/4" d, musicians **65.00**
Ring box, cov, pheasant scene, glossy finish **85.00**
Salt and pepper shakers, pr, Elk **165.00**
Vase, 3-1/2" h, peasant ladies and sheep scene, silver rim, three handles, blue mark **60.00**

Dresser box, covered, tapestry, chrysanthemums decoration, 4-3/4" x 4", $325; rose tapestry creamer, 3-1/4" h, $150. Photo courtesy of Joy Luke Auctions.

Bowl, molded with four portraits, central panel decorated with flowers, pearlized finish, 10-1/2" d, $250. Photo courtesy of Joy Luke Auctions.

Patterns
Conch Shell
> Creamer, green, lobster handles **125.00**
> Match holder, hanging **225.00**
> Sugar, cov, small flake **85.00**

Corinthian
> Creamer and sugar, classical figures, black ground **85.00**
> Pitcher, 12" h, red ground, pinched spout **225.00**
> Vase, 8-1/2" h, conical, black, blue mark **225.00**

Devil and Cards
> Ashtray **650.00**
> Creamer, 3-3/4" h **195.00**
> Mug, large **295.00**
> Salt, master **325.00**

Lobster
> Ashtray, claw **145.00**
> Celery tray, 12-1/2" l, figural, blue mark **245.00**
> Pitcher, 7-3/4" h, figural, orange-red, green handle **175.00**
> Salt and pepper shakers, pr . **150.00**

Mustard pot, covered, Lobster pattern, $150; 4" h, pair leaf-shaped dishes decorated with tomatoes, 5-1/2" d, $120.

Pitcher, tapestry, grazing mountain sheep, gold trim, marked, 5" h, $285.

Nursery Rhyme
> Bell, Jack and the Beanstalk **425.00**
> Planter, Jack and the Beanstalk, round, orig liner **225.00**
> Plate, Little Jack Horner **125.00**
> Plate, Little Miss Muffet **100.00**

Snow Babies
> Bowl, 6" d **325.00**
> Creamer, gold trim **110.00**
> Jewelry box, cov **275.00**
> Milk pitcher, corset shape . . **185.00**
> Tea tile, 6" sq, blue mark . . . **100.00**

Sunbonnet Babies
> Bell, babies sewing, unmarked **425.00**
> Cake plate, 10-1/4" d, babies washing **400.00**
> Cup and saucer, babies fishing **225.00**
> Dish, 8" d, babies ironing, ruffled edge, blue mark **175.00**
> Mustard pot, cov, babies sweeping, blue mark **395.00**
> Nappy, Sunbonnet Babies, Wash Day, blue mark, 6" l **230.00**
> Plate, Sunbonnet Girls, pair, one washing, other sweeping . . **290.00**

Tomato
> Creamer and sugar, blue mark **190.00**
> Milk pitcher **165.00**
> Mustard, cov **125.00**
> Salt and pepper shakers, pr . . **85.00**

Rose tapestry
Basket, 5" h, reticulated **400.00**
Bell, American Beauty Rose, pink, 3" h **500.00**
Boot **550.00**
Bowl, 10-1/2" d, pink and yellow roses **675.00**

Cache pot, 2-3/4" h, 3-12/4" d, ruffled top, gold handles **200.00**
Creamer **250.00**
Dresser tray **395.00**
Hairpin box, pink and white . . . **245.00**
Nut dish, 3-1/4" d, 1-3/4" h, three-color roses, gold feet, green mark . . **175.00**
Pin tray, three-color roses **195.00**
Plate, 6" d, three-color roses, blue mark
. . . . **150.00**
Salt and pepper shakers, pr, pink roses **375.00**
Shoe, roses and figures dec . . . **550.00**

Tapestry, miscellaneous

Bowl, 9-1/2" d, scenic, wheat, girl, and chickens **395.00**
Box, 3-3/4" l, 2" w, courting couple, multicolored, blue mark **245.00**
Charger, 13" d, scenic, boy and donkeys **300.00**
Dresser tray, goose girl **495.00**
Hatpin holder, swimming swans and sunset, saucer base, blue mark . **250.00**
Tumbler, 4" h, barrel shape, gazebo, deer standing in stream, blue mark
. . . . **200.00**

ROYAL BONN

History:
In 1836, Franz Anton Mehlem founded a Rhineland factory that produced earthenware and porcelain, including household, decorative, technical, and sanitary items.

The firm reproduced Hochst figures between 1887 and 1903. These figures, in both porcelain and earthenware, were made from the original molds from the defunct Prince-Electoral Mayence Manufactory in Hochst. The factory was purchased by Villeroy and Boch in 1921 and closed in 1931.

Marks:
In 1890, the word "Royal" was added to the mark. All items made after 1890 include the "Royal Bonn" mark.

Cake plate, 10-1/4" d, dark blue floral transfer **35.00**
Cheese dish, cov, multicolored floral dec, cream ground, gold trim **90.00**
Cup and saucer, relief luster bands, marked **40.00**

*Mantel clock, Rainbow, green floral decoration, gold highlights, 11" x 12-1/2", **$450**. Photo courtesy of Woody Auctions.*

Ewer, 10-1/8" h, red and pink flowers, raised gold, fancy handle **75.00**
Plate, 8-1/2" d, red and white roses, green leaves, earthtone ground, crazing, c1900 . . . . **20.00**
Portrait vase, 8-1/4" h, central female portrait, floral landscape, printed mark, c1900 . . . . **575.00**
Tea tile, 7" d, hp, pink, yellow, and purple pansies, white ground, green border, marked "Bonn-Rhein" . . . **35.00**
Urn, cov, 13" h, hp, multicolored flowers, green, and yellow ground, two gold handles, artist sgd **120.00**

*Vases, left: double gourd with Art Nouveau design in shades of green, pink, purple, blue and brown, high gloss, painted "Royal-Bonn Old-Duton," crazing, 11" h, **$350**; right: squatty, narrow rim, pink poppies, green foliage, shaded brown ground, high gloss, painted "Royal-Bonn Old Butch," 3-3/4" h, **$200**. Photo courtesy of Skinner Auctioneers and Appraisers.*

Vase
18-3/4" h, blue ground, gilt and enameled floral designs, scrolled handles, printed and imp marks, late 19th C **400.00**
20" h, 5" d, hp multicolored floral spray with raised gold dec, link handles, ftd **240.00**

ROYAL COPENHAGEN

History:
Franz Mueller established a porcelain factory at Copenhagen in 1775. When bankruptcy threatened in 1779, the Danish king acquired ownership, appointing Mueller manager and selecting the name "Royal Copenhagen." The crown sold its interest in 1867; the company remains privately owned today.

Blue Fluted, Royal Copenhagen's most famous pattern, was created in 1780. It is of Chinese origin and comes in three styles: smooth edge, closed lace edge, and perforated lace edge (full lace). Many other factories copied it.

Flora Danica, named for a famous botanical work, was introduced in 1789 and remained exclusive to Royal Copenhagen. It is identified by its freehand illustrations of plants and its hand-cut edges and perforations.

Marks:
Royal Copenhagen porcelain is marked with three wavy lines, which signify ancient waterways, and a crown, added in 1889. Stoneware does not have the crown mark.

Bowl, reticulated blue and white
Round **125.00**
Shell shaped **150.00**
Butter pat, Symphony pattern, six-pc set **35.00**
Candlesticks, pr, 9" h, blue floral design, white ground, bisque lion heads, floral garlands **160.00**
Cream soup, #1812 . . . . **75.00**
Cup and saucer, 2-1/2" h cylindrical cup with angular handle, 5-1/2" d saucer with molded and gilded rim, hp floral specimen, 20th C **575.00**
Dish, reticulated blue and white
. . . . **175.00**
Figure
5-3/4" h, young, native dress, kneeling and holding floral garland, No. 21413, No. 12414, pr . . **550.00**

Dinner plate, Flora Danica pattern, reticulated rim, gilt detailing, hand-painted center floral specimen, reverse titled "Ribes rubrum L.," 20th C, 10-3/4" d, $775. Photo courtesy of Skinner Auctioneers and Appraisers.

6-3/4" h, girl knitting, No. 1314
.... **350.00**
7-1/2" h, 11" l, dachshund, blue wave mark **375.00**
15-1/4" h, Nymph with Satyr, timid satyr kneeling at feet of nude female nymph, on naturalistic ovoid base, 20th C........... **1,100.00**
Fish plate, 10" d, different fish swimming among marine plants, molded and gilt border, light green highlights, gilt dentil edge, crown circular mark, 10-pc set...... **8,250.00**
Inkwell, Blue Fluted pattern, matching tray..................... **150.00**
Pickle tray, 9" l, Half Lace pattern, blue triple wave mark **70.00**

Figure, Little Mermaid, 8-1/2" h, $100. Photo courtesy of Joy Luke Auctions.

Plates, two 7-5/8" d, six 10" d, each with gilt serrated rim and central hp floral specimen, price for eight-pc set
.... **2,990.00**
Platter, 14-1/2" l, #1556 .... **140.00**
Salad bowl, 9-7/8" d, Flora Danica, botanical specimen, molded gilt border, dentil edge, pink highlights, blue triple wave and green crown mark ... **825.00**
Soup tureen, cov, stand, 14-1/2" l, Flora Danica, oval, enamel painted botanical specimens, twin handles, finial, factory marks, botanical identification, modern
.... **5,750.00**
Tray, 10" l, Blue Fluted pattern... **65.00**
Vase, 7" h, sage green and gray crackled glaze **150.00**

ROYAL DOULTON

ROYAL
DOULTON
FLAMBE

History: Doulton pottery began in 1815 under the direction of John Doulton at the Doulton & Watts pottery in Lambeth, England. Early output was limited to salt-glazed industrial stoneware. After John Watts retired in 1854, the firm became Doulton and Company, and production was expanded to include hand-decorated stoneware such as figurines, vases, dinnerware, and flasks.

In 1878, John's son, Sir Henry Doulton, purchased Pinder Bourne & Co. in Burslem. The companies became Doulton & Co., Ltd. in 1882. Decorated porcelain was added to Doulton's earthenware production in 1884.

Most Doulton figurines were produced at the Burslem plants, where they were made continuously from 1890 until 1978. After a short interruption, a new line of Doulton figurines was introduced in 1979.

Dickens ware, in earthenware and porcelain, was introduced in 1908. The pieces were decorated with characters from Dickens's novels. Most of the line was withdrawn in the 1940s, except for plates, which continued to be made until 1974.

Character jugs, a 20th-century revival of early Toby models, were designed by Charles J. Noke for Doulton in the 1930s. Character jugs are limited to bust portraits, while Royal Doulton toby jugs are full figured. The character jugs come in four sizes and feature fictional characters from Dickens, Shakespeare, and other English and American novelists, as well as historical heroes. Marks on both character and toby jugs must be carefully identified to determine dates and values.

Doulton's Rouge Flambé (Veined Sung) is a high-glazed, strong-colored ware noted primarily for the fine

Warman's
English & Continental Pottery & Porcelain
3RD EDITION

AN ILLUSTRATED PRICE GUIDE WITH HISTORIES AND REFERENCES FOR MORE THAN 200 CATEGORIES, FROM ABC TO ZSOLNAY

Susan & Al Bagdade

For more information, see this book.

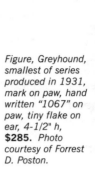

Figure, Greyhound, smallest of series produced in 1931, mark on paw, hand written "1067" on paw, tiny flake on ear, 4-1/2" h, $285. Photo courtesy of Forrest D. Poston.

modeling and exquisite colorings, especially in the animal items. The process used to produce the vibrant colors is a Doulton secret.

Production of stoneware at Lambeth ceased in 1956; production of porcelain continues today at Burslem.

Marks: Beginning in 1872, the "Royal Doulton" mark was used on all types of wares produced by the company.

Beginning in 1913, an "HN" number was assigned to each new Doulton figurine design. The "HN" numbers, which referred originally to Harry Nixon, a Doulton artist, were chronological until 1940, after which blocks of numbers were assigned to each modeler. From 1928 until 1954, a small number was placed to the right of the crown mark; this number added to 1927 gives the year of manufacture.

Animal

Alsatian, HN117 .... **175.00**
Bull terrier, K14........... **325.00**
Dalmatian, HN114 .... **250.00**
English bulldog, HN1074 ... **175.00**
French poodle, HN2631.... **150.00**
Irish setter, HN1055 .... **150.00**
Salmon, 12" h, flambé, printed mark
.... **435.00**
Scottish terrier, K18 .... **165.00**
Tiger, 14" l, flambé, printed mark
.... **375.00**
Bowl, 9" l, 7-1/2" w, rect, farm scene, 1932 mark.................. **115.00**
Candlesticks, pr, 6-1/2" h, Walton Ware, Battle of Hastings, cream color earthenware ground, stamped mark, c1910, small base chip on one. **290.00**
Chamberstick, 2" h, Walton Ware, fishermen dec, ivory earthenware ground, stamped mark, c1910, one of pair damaged **400.00**
Character jug, large
Cardinal **150.00**

Poacher, D6781 . . . . **350.00**
Character jug, miniature
Blacksmith **50.00**
Pickwick **65.00**
Character jug, small
Pearly King **35.00**
Toby Philpots **85.00**
Charger, 12-5/8" d, hp, allover incised leaf, berry, and vine border, central fruits and leaves, attributed to Frank Bragwyn, printed mark, c1930 . . **245.00**
Clock case, King's are, night watchman, c1905 . . . . **450.00**
Cracker jar
5" d, 6" h, Burslem, flowers, silver plated lid **115.00**
5" d, 6" h, white sharkskin, gold and black floral trim, silvered lid, bail handle, and collar, Slater's Patent **120.00**
Cuspidor, 7" h, Isaac Walton ware, polychrome dec, transfer printed, fisherman on ext., verses on int. lip, printed mark **325.00**
Dinner plate, Walton Are, fisherman dec, ivory earthenware ground, stamped mark, c1910, price for seven-pc set **750.00**
Figure
Carolyn, HN 2112, 7¹/₄" h, 3-1/2" d **335.00**
Fair Lady, coral pink, HN2835 . . . . **225.00**
Lady Charmain, HN1949 . . . . **225.00**
King Charles I, dark brown gloves, black flora at boots, imp date 1919 . . . . **1,312.00**
Nicola, HN2839 . . . . **350.00**
Orange Lady, HN1758 . . . . . . **245.00**

Queen Mother's 80th Birthday, HN464, 1980 . . . . **750.00**
Priscilla, pantaloons showing beneath crinoline, HN1380, 1920-40 . . . . **288.00**
Sandra, HN2275 . . . . **200.00**
The Leisure Hour, HN2055 . . **400.00**
Victorian Lady, HN1208, 1926-38 . . . . **355.00**
Fish plate, 9" d, swimming fish centers, pale yellow ground, gold bands and rims, sgd "J. Hallmark," 10-pc set **700.00**
Flask, 8" h, sharkskin ground, floral and fruit dec, rosette mark with Doulton Burslem under crown, over US patent **150.00**
Humidor, 7-1/2" h, Walton Ware, Battle of Hastings, cream color earthenware ground, stamped mark, c1910 . **365.00**
Inkstand, 3" h, stoneware, tapered cylindrical form molded with floral sprays, blue, ochre, and brown glazes, silver mounts, Doulton Lambeth, hallmarked London, 1901 . . . . . **215.00**
Jardinière, 4-1/2" h, Walton Ware, Battle of Hastings, cream color earthenware ground, stamped mark, c1910 . . . . **350.00**
Jug, 10-1/2" h, Regency Coach, limited edition, printed marks, 20th C . . **930.00**
Loving cup
9-3/4" h, Three Musketeers, limited edition, sgd "Noke, H. Fenton," orig certificate, 20th C **920.00**
10-1/4" d, King George V and Queen Mary, 25-year reign anniversary, c1935 . . . . **750.00**
Milk pitcher, 7" h, sharkskin ground, cobalt blue flowers trimmed in gold, US patent **150.00**

Toby mug, Santa, **$195.**

Mug
4" h, gladiator, #D6553 . . . . . **300.00**
8-1/4" h, St. John Falstaff **125.00**
Pitcher
6" h, The Gleaners, Old English scenes series **130.00**
7-1/2" h, motto, Be always as merry as you ever can" **95.00**
12-1/2" h, Walton Ware, fishermen dec, ivory earthenware ground, stamped mark, c1910, price for pr, one with bruise and restoration **400.00**
Plate, 8-1/2" d, English Garden series **115.00**
Platter, 9" l, 7-1/2" w, Dr Johnson at Bootham Bar-York, registered in Australia **120.00**
Service plate, 10-5/8" d, cream-colored ground, interior band of gilt anthemia, rim with gilt scrollwork over cream-colored ground, apple green reserves, gilt-shaped rim, mold date mark 1910, price for 18-pc set **5,465.00**

Dinner plate, set of 12, cobalt blue rim with raised gilt decoration, printed, impressed, and enameled marks, 10" d, **$1,100.** *Photo courtesy of Sloan's Auctioneers & Appraisers.*

Gibson girl plate, Miss Babbles, The Authoress Calls & Reads Aloud, 10-1/2" d, **$75.**

Vase, tapering, stylized fruit and leaves in yellow and green on shaded blue ground, stamped mark, 4" rim crack, 4" d, 7-1/2" h, **$290.** *Photo courtesy of David Rago Auctions.*

Spirits barrel, 7" l, King's Ware, double, silver trim rings and cov, oak stand, c1909.....................**1,200.00**

Sweet meat, 5" d, 3-1/2" h, sharkskin ground, applied flowers, silvered lid and handle, rosette mark artist sgd "Eleanor Tosen".............**125.00**

Tankard, 9-1/2" h, hinged pewter lid, incised frieze of herons among reeds, blue slip enamel, imp mark, sgd, c1875 ....**1,600.00**

Teacup and saucer, cobalt blue, heavy gold dec **120.00**

Tea set, Walton Ware, cov teapot with underplate, creamer, sugar bowl, Battle of Hastings, cream-colored earthenware ground, stamped mark, chip on spout, hairline on sugar lid **365.00**

Tobacco jar, 8" h, incised frieze of cattle, goats, and donkeys, imp mark, sgd, worn SP rim, handle and cover, dated 1880 ....**995.00**

Toby jug
Beefeater, #D6206, 6" h **85.00**
Winston Churchill, #8360 ....**95.00**

Toothpick holder, Walton Ware, Battle of Hastings, cream-color earthenware ground, stamped mark, c1910, set of six **535.00**

Umbrella stand, 23-1/2" h, stoneware, enamel dec, applied floral medallions within diamond formed panels, framed by button motifs, imp mark, glaze crazing, c1910.............**550.00**

Vase
4-1/2" d, 8-1/4" h, hand painted by Margaret Walker, Art Nouveau-style winged fairies, purple ground, stamped "Doulton/Lambeth/ England," marked "MW/A113," price for pr **1,495.00**

Vase, mid-scenic band showing mother and two children in classical setting, decorative upper and bottom borders, artist signed "J. P. Hewitt," black Doulton Burslem mark, 10-1/2" h, $1,380. Photo courtesy of James D. Julia, Inc.

16" h, stoneware, rough brown lace ground dec, floral sprays, Slaters patent "Chine"..........**375.00**

ROYAL DUX

History: Royal Dux porcelain was made in Dux, Bohemia (now the Czech Republic), by E. Eichler at the Duxer Porzellan-Manufaktur, established in 1860. Many items were exported to the United States. By the turn of the century, Royal Dux figurines, vases, and accessories, especially those featuring Art-Nouveau designs, were captivating consumers.

Marks: A raised triangle with an acorn and the letter "E" plus "Dux, Bohemia" was used as a mark between 1900 and 1914.

Bowl, 17-1/2" l, modeled as female tending a fishing net, oval shell-form bowl, imp mark, early 20th C ...**490.00**

Bust, 14" h, female portrait, raised leaves and berries on base, Czechoslovakia, early 20th C, unmarked, chips............**290.00**

Compote, figural, 14-1/2" l, modeled as female atop shell-form bowl, another figure within the wave modeled freeform base, imp mark, early 20th C...**750.00**

Figure
10" h, young girl holding cat, raised pink triangle mark "Royal Dux Bohemia #421" **1,150.00**
15" x 9-1/2" x 4-1/2", flamenco dancer, cobalt blue and white glaze, gold trim, pink triangle mark, stamped, numbered **1,250.00**
18" x 11" x 6", Pierrrot serenading lover, perched on harvest moon, pre-war "E" mark, price for facing pair **3,500.00**
21" x 11", mother and child, roses, partial pink triangle mark.**2,250.00**

Figure, dog, pink triangle mark, 11-3/4" l, $290.

Figure, man on camel, boy with baskets, bisque, 18" h, $250. Photo courtesy of Joy Luke Auctions.

Floor vase, 36-1/2" h, 37-1/4" h, date palm tree form, Middle Eastern woman and water urn on one, her suitor playing lute on other, matte finish flesh toned skin, cobalt blue clothing against white, gilt rims and highlights, ink labels "Royal Dux Bohemia" with acorn in triangle, glued unstable repairs to man, price for pr...............**5,225.00**

Tazza, 19-1/2" h, figural, putti and classically draped woman supporting shell, price for pr, one with hairline in base **880.00**

Vase
11" h, Grecian, "E" mark....**595.00**
19-1/4" h, bisque, Art Nouveau-style female to one side of leaf and floral molded body, imp mark, early 20th C.................**290.00**

ROYAL FLEMISH

History: Royal Flemish was produced by the Mount Washington Glass Co., New Bedford, Massachusetts. Albert Steffin patented the process in 1894.

Royal Flemish is a frosted transparent glass with heavy raised gold enamel lines. These lines form sections—often colored in russet tones—giving the appearance of stained-glass windows with elaborate floral or coin medallions.

For more information, see this book

Vase, globular, Roman heads in medallions, signed, original paper label, 6" d, $6,500.

Advisers: Clarence and Betty Maier.

Biscuit jar, cov, 8" h, ovoid, large Roman coins on stained panels, divided by heavy gold lines, ornate SP cov, rim, and bail handle, orig paper label "Mt. W. G. Co. Royal Flemish" **1,750.00**

Box, cov, 5-1/2" d, 3-3/4" h, swirled border, gold outlined swirls, gold tracery blossoms, enameled blossom with jeweled center on lid **1,500.00**

Ewer, 10-1/2" h, 9" w, 5" d, circular semi-transparent panel on front with youth thrusting spear into chest of winged creature, reverse panel shows mythical fish created with tail changed into stylized florals, raised gold dec, outlines, and scrolls, rust, purple, and gold curlicues, twisted rope handle with

Ewer, sepia-colored body with cerise-colored shoulder, eight vertical panels framed in heavy raised gold, four tinted pale mauve, alternating with four smoky-gray panels, raised gold tendril laden with multi-petaled blossoms of encrusted gold and tinted autumn leaves, 16 sky-blue circular medallions, each with frosted clear-glass stylized cross and framed in raised gold. Raised gold stylized floral dec on cerise spout and diminutive frosted clear-glass handle, slight loss of gold on rim and raised lines, 5-1/2" d, 12" h, $8,500. Photo courtesy of Clarence and Betty Maier.

brushed gold encircles neck, hp minute gold florals on neck, burnished gold stripes on rim spout and panels **4,950.00**

Jar, 8" h, classical Roman coin medallion dec, simulated stained glass panels, SP rim, bail, and cov, paper label "Mt. W. G. Co. Royal Flemish" **1,650.00**

Vase, 6" d, 6-1/2" h, stylized scrolls of pastel violet sweep down two tiny handles and across body, realistically tinged sprays of violets randomly strewn around frosted clear glass body, gold lines define violet nosegays and frame scrolls, gold accents daubed here and there, sgd with Royal Flemish logo and "0583" **2,200.00**

ROYAL VIENNA

1749 - 1864

History: Production of hard-paste porcelain in Vienna began in 1720 with Claude Innocentius du Paquier, a runaway employee from the Meissen factory. In 1744, Empress Maria Theresa brought the factory under royal patronage; subsequently, the ware became known as Royal Vienna. The firm went through many administrative changes until it closed in 1864, but the quality of its workmanship was always maintained.

Marks: Several other Austrian and German firms copied the Royal Vienna products, including the use of the "Beehive" mark. Many of the pieces on today's market are from these firms.

Cabinet vase, 3-1/2" h, children of four seasons, blue beehive mark . . . **350.00**
Chocolate pot, cov, 10" h, large reserve with artist dec vase, woman

Portrait plate, Ayesta, gypsy in green dress, red hat, gold and blue enameling on rim, blue beehive mark, 9-1/2", $700. Photo courtesy of James D. Julia, Inc.

looking on, cream ground, gilt handles and trim, Knoeller **350.00**
Cup and saucer, 2-3/4" h, cobalt blue, gold enamel dec, blue beehive mark, titled "Sommer" **200.00**
Ferner, 7-3/4" w, 4" h, portrait of lady one side, portrait of different lady on other, burgundy, green , and gold, beaded, scalloped edges, ftd, marked "Royal Vienna, Austria," artist sgd **425.00**

Portrait plate
9-1/2" d, dark haired mother and child, deep olive green border, gold tracery, marked "Royal Vienna" **195.00**
9-1/2" d, hp, cobalt blue border, gold enamel dec, titled "Amicitia," gold beehive and "Royal Vienna" mark **290.00**
9-1/2" d, hp, young woman, titled "Andacht," beehive mark . . **750.00**
Portrait vase, 8" h, Art Nouveau cylindrical form, portrait of auburn-haired woman with blue cap, marked "Royal Crown Germany" **200.00**
Snuffbox, 3" w, 2-1/2" d, 2-1/8" h, quatrefoil, landscape on lid, floral dec sides, blue beehive mark **250.00**
Stein, quarter liter, hp, copy of early Meissen Chinese scene, elaborate battle surmounted by gold border, four flowers painted in rear, similar scene of harbor of top of lid, floral design painted on underside of lid, eagle thumb lift, beehive mark **2,310.00**
Urn, cov, 11-1/2" h, hp, elaborate scene of man, women, and cherub, cobalt blue ground, gold trim, beehive mark **1,200.00**
Vase, 10-1/2" h, facing female portrait medallions, banded ground of medium green, pale green, and pink, gilt filigree, floral panels, blue beehive mark, gilt wear, price for pr **2,100.00**

ROYAL WORCESTER

c 1876-1891   1891

History: In 1751, the Worcester Porcelain Company, led by Dr. John Wall and William Davis, acquired the Bristol pottery of Benjamin Lund and moved it to

Worcester. The first wares were painted blue under the glaze; soon thereafter decorating was accomplished by painting on the glaze in enamel colors. Among the most-famous 18th-century decorators were James Giles and Jefferys Hamet O'Neale. Transfer-print decoration was developed by the 1760s.

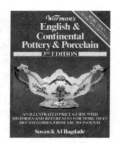

For more information, see this book.

A series of partnerships took place after Davis' death in 1783: Flight (1783-1793); Flight & Barr (1793-1807); Barr, Flight, & Barr (1807-1813); and Flight, Barr, & Barr (1813-1840). In 1840, the factory was moved to Chamberlain & Co. in Diglis. Decorative wares were discontinued. In 1852, W. H. Kerr and R. W. Binns formed a new company and revived the production of ornamental wares.

In 1862, the firm became the Royal Worcester Porcelain Co. Among the key modelers of the late 19th century were James Hadley, his three sons, and George Owen, an expert with pierced clay pieces. Royal Worcester absorbed the Grainger factory in 1889 and the James Hadley factory in 1905. Modern designers include Dorothy Doughty and Doris Lindner.

Basket, 8-1/2" d, flaring pierced sides mounted with floral heads, pine cone and floral cluster int., blue and white transfer dec, first period, mid-18th C **550.00**

Biscuit jar, cov, 7-1/4" h, fluted body, raised spear head borders surrounding enamel floral design **550.00**

Bowl, 10" d, scalloped border, shell molded boy, fruit and floral spray, blue and white transfer dec, first period, mid-18th C **320.00**

Butter tub, cov, 4-1/4" d, 3-1/4" h, cylindrical, fully sculpted finial, painted

floral sprays below geometric borders, first period, c1765 .... **450.00**

Centerpiece, 6-1/4" h, oval, ftd, Royal Lily pattern, first period, c1800, repaired **125.00**

Dish, 8" l, leaf form, molded body, underglaze blue floral sprays, branch handle, first period, c1765 .... **500.00**

Ewer, 9" h, pale pink powder horn shape, gold stag horn handle, minor chip **150.00**

Figure
6-1/2" h, Welsh girl, shot enamel porcelain, sgd "Hadley," late-19th C **690.00**
7-3/4" h and 8-1/4" h, lady and gentleman, George III costumes, sgd "Hadley," pr **1,100.00**
8-3/4" h, Cairo water carrier, 1895 .... **635.00**

Fish plates, 9-1/4" d, bone china, hp fish, gilt lattice and foliage border, sgd "Harry Ayrton," printed marks, c1930, 13-pc set **2,300.00**

Fruit cooler, 6-1/4" h, cylindrical, Royal Lily pattern, stylized floral reserve, stepped circular foot, first period, c1800 .... **225.00**

Lamp base, 13-3/4" h, baluster vase form, slender gilt neck, two short Moorish-style gilt handles, hand-painted scene of gilt shipwreck on shore by lighthouse, reverse with small scenic roundel, gilt guilloche foot, electrified **325.00**

Mustard pot, 4" h, cylindrical, blue and white transfer, floral clusters, floral finial, first period, mid-18th C **325.00**

Pitcher
5-3/4" h, cream, gold enamel dec **150.00**

Figures, titled "Crabapple & Butterfly," by Dorothy Doughty, each 9" w, 9-1/2" h, **$230.** *Photo courtesy of James D. Julia, Inc.*

5-3/4" h, Indian elephant head handle **175.00**
5-3/4" h, tri-corner shape, blue and white overlapping circles, gold enameled pouring lip, c1860 .... **260.00**
6" h, 5" d, floral dec, gold handle **230.00**

Plate
7" w, octagonal, landscape fan form reserves, cobalt blue ground, first period, 18th C, pr **350.00**
7-3/4" d, Blind Earl pattern, raised rose spray, polychrome floral sprays, scalloped border, first period, mid-18th C **1,100.00**

Sauce boat, 4-1/4" h, geometric band above foliate molded body, painted floral sprays, oval foot, first period, c1765, pr **275.00**

Sweetmeat jar, 6" d, molded swirl base, thistles dec, silverplate lid, bail, and

Ewer, handle, gold stippled background, colorful fern motif, 13-1/2" h, **$175.** *Photo courtesy of Woody Auctions.*

Figure, gold finch, model #2667, tree trunk-shaped base with hand-painted thistle decoration, marked, c1951, 6-1/8" h, **$145.** *Photo courtesy of Forrest G. Poston.*

Vases, pair, squared form, circular necks, applied lion mask and ring handles, footed base, full length carved decoration of Chinese-style work scenes on one side, carved oval cartouche of Chinese men working on other side, chips on one foot, 11" h, **$1,540.** *Photo courtesy of Sanford Alderfer Auction Company.*

handle, marked "RW" with crown
............................**200.00**
Tankard, 6" h, cylindrical, blue and white transfer dec of parrot among fruit, first period, mid-18th C........**325.00**
Teabowl and saucer, painted chinoisiere vignette, blue border, first period, c1865..............**185.00**
Teapot, cov, 6-1/2" h, globular form body, fully sculpted blossom finial, domed top, painted floral sprays, first period, c1765..............**375.00**
Urn, cov, 11-1/2" h, pierced dome top, globular body, painted floral sprays, basketweave molded base, early 20th C....................**195.00**
Vase, 16" h, gold dragon handles, aesthetic movement scene, drilled for lamp **415.00**

ROYCROFT

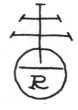

History: Elbert Hubbard founded the Roycrofters in East Aurora, New York, at the turn of the century. Considered a genius in his day, he was an author, lecturer, manufacturer, salesman, and philosopher.

Hubbard established a campus that included a printing plant where he published *The Philistine, The Fra,* and *The Roycrofter.* His most-famous book was *A Message to Garcia,* published in 1899. His "community" also included a furniture manufacturing plant, a metal shop, and a leather shop.

Ali Baba bench, 42-1/2" l, 11" w, 20" h, half-log top, flaring plank legs, keyed through tenon stretcher, carved orb and cross mark, minor loss to bark, orig finish....................**16,500.00**
Bookcase, slab sides with keyed tenon construction, plate rail top, orig iron hardware, orb mark, refinished, 46" w, 16" d, 71" h...............**9,775.00**
Bookends, pr, 4-1/8" w, 3-1/4" d, 5-1/4" h, model no. 309, hammered copper, rect, riveted center band

Bookends, pair, brass-washed hammered copper, embossed rope and ship medallion, orb and cross mark, minor wear to original patina, 5" x 5-1/2", **$225.** *Photo courtesy of David Rago Auctions.*

suspending ring, dark brown patina, imp Roycroft orb, minor wear .. **225.00**
Book, *Elbert Hubbard's Scrapbook,* emb leather cov, orig glassine dust jacket, fitted box, c1923, 228 pgs, 7" x 10" **90.00**
Bowl, 10-1/4" d, 4-1/8" h, hammered copper, rolled rim, shouldered bowl, three point feet, red patina, imp mark, traces of brass wash........**450.00**
Candle lamp, blue art glass, baluster form, flaring foot, stamped "Roycroft," electrified.................**175.00**
Candle sconce, 3-1/2" w, 10" h, hammered copper, riveted strap holder, imp backplate, orig dark brown patina, orb and cross mark, few scratches, price for pr.................**630.00**
Candlestick, 3-1/4" d, 7-3/4" h, hammered copper, Princess style, double stems, faceted bases, stamped orb and cross mark, orig patina, price for pr **980.00**
Chamberstick, 1-1/2" d, 3" h, hammered copper, stamped orb and cross mark, normal wear to orig patina, price for pr.................**460.00**
Chandelier, from Roycroft Inn, 14-1/2" w, 10-3/4" h, copper, triangular strap support base with cut-out hearts and three pendant fixtures, each with enameled amber glass shade dec in stylized floral motif, triangular ceiling plate, hanging chains, orb and cross mark.....................**1,955.00**
Desk lamp, 14-3/4" h, 7" d Steuben blown glass lustered glass shade, hammered copper, shaft of four curled and riveted bands, stamped orb and cross mark...............**5,750.00**
Desk set, hammered copper, paper knife, pen tray, stationery holding, perpetual desk calendar, pr of bookends, flower holder, match holder with nested ashtray, c1915 ....**550.00**

Bowls, pair, hammered copper, crimped rims, orb and cross marks, 4-1/4" d, 2-1/2" h, **$350.** *Photo courtesy of David Rago Auctions.*

Desk blotter, hammered copper, oversized, two riveted corners, two pentrays flanking an inkwell, orb and cross mark, original patina, missing inkwell liner, new green leather blotter, 18-1/2" x 28", **$2,760.** *Photo courtesy of David Rago Auctions.*

Frame, 15" w, 20-1/2" h, orig print, orig finish......................**450.00**
Goody box, 23" l, 13" d, 10" h, mahogany, wrought cooper strap hardware, monogrammed "H," orig finish, carved orb and cross on top
.........................**630.00**
Humidor, 4-3/4" w, 5-3/4" h, hammered copper, covered in brass wash, Trillium pattern, stamped orb and cross mark, minor wear to patina..........**690.00**
Lamp base, 7" d, 20" h, hammered copper, tall tapering form, flaring base, riveted bands, articulated handles, three-light fixture, orb and cross mark
.......................**2,760.00**
Letter holder/perpetual calendar, 3-1/2" x 4-3/4" x 2-1/4", copper, acid-etched border, orb and cross mark with "Roycroft," normal wear to patina
.........................**150.00**
Mirror, 23-1/2" w, 41-1/2" h, rect, beveled, orig medium finish, lap joint construction, unmarked **1,265.00**

Footstool, mahogany, original tacked-on cordovan leather seat, carved orb and cross mark, refinished, filled-in tack holes, 10" x 15-1/4" x 9-3/4", **$800.** *Photo courtesy of David Rago Auctions.*

Pedestal, oak, square form with stepped base, signed with orb and cross at side, original finish, c1907, minor wear, joint separation, 15" square, 39-1/8" h, $4,200. Photo courtesy of Skinner Auctioneers and Appraisers.

Nut set, hammered copper, ftd bowl, spoon, six plates, six picks, all but picks marked with orb and cross, orig patina, price for 14-pc set **4,890.00**

Plaque, motto, 5-1/4" h, 9-1/4" l, carved oak, "Be Yourself," orig dark finish, carved orb and cross mark . . . **3,400.00**

Sconce, 7-1/4" l, 5" w, 7" h, copper, from Roycroft Inn, spiral mount on shaped base, pressed glass shades, one replaced shade, price for pr . . . **690.00**

Tray, 17" d, octagonal, hammered copper, two handles, orb and cross mark, cleaned patina, slight bend to one edge **290.00**

Vase, 10-1/4" h, model no. 212, copper, tall cylindrical form, rim border of stylized dogwood flowers within diamonds, brass wash with green accents around rim, imp "Roycroft" orb on base, allover wear to brass wash **460.00**

Fine ROYCROFT hammered copper cylindrical vase, with tooled quatrofoils on tall stems, excellent original dark patina, orb and cross mark, 10" x 3-1/4", $2,185. Photo courtesy of David Rago Auctions.

RUBENA GLASS

History: Rubena crystal is a transparent blown glass which shades from clear to red. It also is found as the background for frosted and overshot glass. It was made in the late 1800s by several glass companies, including Northwood, and Hobbs, Brockunier & Co. of Wheeling, West Virginia.

Rubena was used for several patterns of pattern glass including Royal Ivy and Royal Oak.

For more information, see this book.

Bowl, 4-1/2" d, Daisy and Scroll . **65.00**
Butter dish, cov, Royal Oak, fluted
. . . . **250.00**
Compote, 14" h, 9" d, rubena overshot bowl, white metal bronze finished figural standard **170.00**
Cracker jar, cov
   Aurora, inverted rib, Northwood
   . . . . **325.00**
   Cut fan and strawberry design, fancy sterling silver cov, 7" h, 6" w
   . . . . **1,150.00**
Creamer and sugar bowl, cov, Royal Ivy **250.00**
Decanter, 9" h, bulbous body, narrow neck, applied clear handle. **170.00**
Finger bowl, Royal Ivy **65.00**
Pickle castor, enameled daisy dec, ornate sgd frame with two handles, pickle fork in front **245.00**
Salt shaker, Coquette **150.00**
Sauce dish, Royal Ivy **35.00**
Sugar shaker, Royal Ivy **250.00**
Toothpick holder, Optic **150.00**

Water pitcher, Inverted Thumbprint pattern, fuchsia coloring, square top spout, applied rope handle, ground pontil, 7" h, $175. Photo courtesy of James D. Julia, Inc.

Tumbler, Medallion Sprig **100.00**
Tumble-Up, tumbler and carafe, Baccarat Swirl **175.00**
Vase
   8-1/2" h, opalescent green to pink ground, applied pink flower, c1900
   . . . . **175.00**
   9-3/4" h, raised gilt spider mum dec, polished pontil, Victorian . . **150.00**
   12" h, satin body, gilt florals, French
   . . . . **150.00**
Water pitcher
   Opal Swirl, Northwood **275.00**
   Royal Ivy, frosted **295.00**

RUBENA VERDE GLASS

History: Rubena Verde, a transparent glass that shades from red in the upper section to yellow-green in the lower, was made by Hobbs, Brockunier & Co., Wheeling, West Virginia, in the late 1880s. It often is found in the Inverted Thumbprint (IVT) pattern, called "Polka Dot" by Hobbs.

For more information, see this book.

Basket, 11-1/4" h, opalescent Rubena verde, applied lime stepped flower feet, thorny twist handle, Victorian . . **425.00**
Bowl, 9-1/2" d, IVT, ruffled **175.00**
Bride's basket, 10-1/2" d, 12-1/2" h, sculptured vaseline shading to pink, yellow and green enameled flowers, Benedict silver plated holder . . **460.00**
Butter dish, cov, Daisy and Button
. . . . **250.00**
Celery vase, 6-1/4" h, IVT **225.00**
Creamer and sugar bowl, cov, Hobnail, bulbous, applied handle
. . . . **550.00**

Cruet, teepee shape, flashed ruby-red trefoil spout, vaseline handle and faceted stopper, Hobbs, Brockunier & Co., 7" h, $550. Photo courtesy of Clarence and Betty Maier.

Cruet, 7" h, IVT, teepee shape, trefoil spout, vaseline handle and faceted stopper, Hobbs, Brockunier **550.00**
Finger bowl, IVT **95.00**
Jack-in-the-pulpit vase, 7-1/2" h, vaseline shading to rose opalescent swirl body, applied white flower on lime stem, six applied feet **200.00**
Pickle castor, Hobb's Hobnail, SP frame, cov, and tongs **500.00**
Pitcher, 7" h, Coin Spot pattern, polished pontil, Victorian **350.00**
Salt and pepper shakers, pr, IVT
. . . . **210.00**
Tumbler, IVT **125.00**
Vase, 9-1/4" h, paneled body, enameled daises dec **85.00**
Water pitcher, Hobb's Hobnail . **395.00**

RUSSIAN ITEMS

ВРАТЬЕВЪ
Baterin's factory
1812-1820

КорНИЛОВЫХЪ
Korniloff's factory
c1835

History:
During the late 19th and early 20th centuries, craftsmen skilled in lacquer, silver, and enamel wares worked in Russia. During the Czarist era (1880-1917), Fabergé, known for his exquisite enamel pieces, led a group of master craftsmen located primarily in Moscow. Fabergé also had an establishment in St. Petersburg and enjoyed the patronage of the Russian Imperial family and royalty and nobility throughout Europe.

Almost all enameling was done on silver. The artist and the government assayer sign pieces.

The Russian Revolution in 1917 brought an abrupt end to the century of Russian craftsmanship. The modern Soviet government has exported some inferior enamel and lacquer work, usually lacking in artistic merit. Modern pieces are not collectible.

Rare icons
A rare set of feast day icons was sold by Jackson's International Auctioneers & Appraisers, in June 2002. The Palekh School, c1890, executed the set of 14 icons. Each 10-1/2" x 12-1/4" icon was masterfully painted by the same hand and executed in the traditional "Old Style." Each was executed on gold leaf ground with gilt title inscriptions along the upper margin. Feast day sets like this were usually commissioned for the iconostatis of a small church or private chapel of a wealthy person. The iconostais is a large framework inset with rows of icons, forming a solid screen between the congregation and the altar in Russian churches. Each icon was in a fine state of preservation with colors bright and vibrant. The set sold for $20,700.

Group of silver and shaded enamel, top: set of four silver-gilt and cloisonné enamel cups, Antip Kuzmichev, Moscow, dated 1895, marked "Made for Tiffany & Co.," 3" w, 2-1/4" h, $4,025; bottom left: Kovsh, Vasiliy Agafonov, Moscow, 1896, 4" l, $865; bottom right: Kovsh, Moscow, after 1908, Cyrillic maker's mark EC, 4" l, $900. Photos courtesy of Jackson's International Auctioneers & Appraisers.

Enamels

Blood cup, 4" h, transfer dec with Imperial double headed eagle and Cypher of the Tsar Nicholas II above date 1896 . . . . **690.00**
Cane, 35" l, 4-1/2" l x 3-1/4" tau handle dec with champleve style raised enamel, light blue, dark blue, green, white, and red, worn Russian hallmarks, heavy ebony shaft, 7/8" replaced brass ferrule, c1900 . . . . **2,350.00**
Cane handle, 2-1/4" l, attributed to Faberge, c1890, nephrite and gold, carved sphere set with 10 cabochons held with gold collars, resting on gold

Cross, Palekh or Mistera, 19th C, recessed edges, painted in classic 16th style, 19th C, 22" w, 47" h, $4,600.

column, band of acanthus at top and bottom, mounted with three fleur-de-lis, marked with gold standard "56"
. . . . **2,300.00**
Cigarette case, 3-1/2" l, 2-1/4" w, 84 standard, silver gilt, robin's egg blue enamel, feathered guillouche ground, opaque white enamel borders, diamond chips on clasp, gilt in., Ivan Britzin, St. Petersburg, 1908-17, small losses and chips to enamel **1,200.00**
Coffee spoon, blue dot border in bowl, stylized polychrome enamel foliage, gilt stippled ground, twisted gilt stem, crown finial, G Tokmakov, c1890
. . . . **300.00**
Cup, 3" w, 2-1/4" h, silver-gilt and cloisonné enamel, Antip Kuzmichev, Moscow, dated 1895, marked "Made for Tiffany & Co.," price for set of four
. . . . **4,025.00**
Egg, silver gilt and shaded enamel ware, two-pc construction, cabochon stone, maker's mark obliterated, 20th C, 3" h, ftd **700.00**
Kovsh
3" h, silver, shaded enamel on moss green field, Pan Slavic style, hallmarked Moscow, 1907, Cyrillic "Faberge" under Imperial Warrant
. . . . **2,875.00**
4" l, silver and shaded enamel, Vasiliy Agafonov, Moscow, 1896
. . . . **865.00**
Matchbox holder, 2-1/4" l, silver gilt and cloisonné, hallmarked Moscow, c1900, indistinguishable makers mark
. . . . **350.00**
Napkin ring, 1-3/4" x 1" x 1-1/2", enameled green, blue, pink, brown,

Tray, painted and lacquered metal, Lukutin, 19th C, Troika scene, verso signed in Cyrillic beneath Imperial warrant, 13-1/2" l, 10-1/2" h, $700.

white, light blue and maroon, Maria Semenova, Moscow, c1890 . . . **700.00**

Picture, 7-3/4" x 6-3/4", enamel dec, Holy Bishop Tikhon of Voronezh, orig copper frame, chased feather lined inner border, Rostov, c1880. . . . . **750.00**

Spoon

7-1/4" l, silver-gilt and shaded enamel, back with colorful plumed bird on stippled ground, beaded border, Dmitri Nicholiaev, Moscow, c1900 . . . . **865.00**

7-1/2" d, round bowl, twisted handle ending in crown finial with enamel accents, obverse of bowl dec with hp portrait of woman surrounded by band of blue and green plique-a-jour in geometric design, illegible mark **1,760.00**

Sugar shovel, 4-3/4" l, silver gilt and enamel, Antip Kuzmichev, Moscow, 1899. . . . . **500.00**

Sugar tongs, 5-1/4" l, silver gilt and cloisonné enamel, Moscow, 1899, indistinguishable makers mark . **250.00**

Vase, 11-1/2" h, champleve enamel, central cartouche on both sides, one with stylized double headed eagle, other side with roosters, Slavonic inscription at base rim, hallmarked Moscow, dated 1874, Cyrillic "P. Ovchinnikov" under Imperial Warrant **5,750.00**

Icon

7" x 9", The Lord Almighty, c1900, carried in wedding ceremony by groom, John 13:34 text, entire image overlaid with finely crafted four-piece riza with champleve enamel Gospel text, riza marked "Moscow," Cyrillic makers mark "I.T." for Ivan Tarabrov (1893-1913) **1,495.00**

Figural group, couple being driven in Troika, bronze, deep brown patina, signed on base in Cyrillic, "Tratchev" and "Voerfiel Foundry, St. Petersburg," 1831-1905, 12-1/4" l, 7" w, 7-1/2" h, $2,875.

Figural group, bronze, mounted Imperial soldier, c1890, indistinguishably signed in Cyrillic on base, dark brown patina, 38-1/2" w, 16-1/2" h, $2,300.

9-1/2" x 11-1/2", Korsun Mother of God, 17th C, personal icon of Tenderness variant. **2,300.00**

9-3/4" x 12-1/4", Saint John the Forerunner, c1550, John depicted turned toward Christ in prayer, green camel hair shirt, raw sienna colored chiton, white highlighting, left border with remnants of four successfully removed layers of over painting **6,625.00**

9-3/4" x 12-1/4", The Appearance of the Mother of God to Venerable Sergiy of Rodonezh, c1625, Mother of God with Saints Peter and Apostle John the Venerable Sergiy, his disciple Micah, double kovcheg **4,255.00**

11" x 12-1/4", The Vladimir Mother of God, 17th C, double kovcheg panel, Virgin and Child in cheek-to-cheek embrace, overall highlighted with cryospgraphy **3,220.00**

11" x 12-1/2", Saints Florus and Laurus, c1650, saints beside Archangel Michael who holds reins of two horses, below are three riders chasing herd of horses, borders with St. Piasiy and probably St. Makarity, double kovcheg **2,415.00**

11" x 13", The Shu-Smolensk Odigitria Mother of God, c1800, entire image overlaid with riza sewn with profusion of mother-of-pearl beards, orig pained surface intact **2,760.00**

11-1/4" x 13", The Smolensk Mother of God, 18th C, entire image overlaid with ornate silver-gilt and repousse riza, gilded silver and repousse halo attached, orig varnish **3,220.00**

12" x 14", The Resurrection, 19th C, Christ depicted atop fallen gates of

Hades, reaches down and grasps hand of Adam who emerges from stone sarcophagus, Eve also emerges from her tomb, background with Old Testament righteous men and women held in captivity and freed by Christ, names inscribed on their haloes: King David, King Solomon, Daniel, Moses, Abraham, Issac, and Jacob, votive lamp scar on lower margin **900.00**

Metal

Bonbonniere, 3-3/8" d, 2-3/16" h, orchid guillouche enamel on silver, cylindrical, cast silver bas-relief applied dec on cov and back, applied relief, monogram of Nicholas II set with precious stones, Henrik Wigstrom, workmaster, St. Petersburg, 1908-17, slight damage **4,225.00**

Bust, 10" h, Tsar Alexander Mikhailovich, Cyrillic foundry mark "F. Shopeen," dated 1867, bronze **1,250.00**

Cross, 47" x 22", Palekh or Mstera, 19th C, recessed edges (kovcheg), painted in classic 16th C style, top with Holy Napkin and Angels, center crossbeam with Mary and Apostle John, center with crucified Christ with implements of the passion, base with skull of Adam. **4,600.00**

Samovar

14" h, cylindrical, orig bowl and undertray, 19th C **400.00**

17-1/2" h, cylindrical, paneled body, 19th C. **375.00**

22" h, cylindrical, front and rim stamped with profusion of awards, Kvana Kaprzina, Tula, c1905 . . . . **575.00**

Sculpture, bronze

12-1/4" l, 7" w, 7-1/2" h, couple being driven in troika, deep brown patina,

Tray, painted and lacquered metal, Lukutin, 19th C, Troika scene, verso signed in Cyrillic beneath Imperial warrant, 13-1/2" l, 10-1/2" h, $700.

Icon, Saint Nicholas, c1880, kiot with carved and gold leaf inner frame of scrolling foliage and grapes surrounding colorfully painted icon, executed on gold leaf ground, storage drawer for candles, 3'5" x 3'3", **$5,175.**

sgd in base in Cyrillic "Gratchev" (Vasilil Iakovelvich Gratchev, 1831-1905) and "Voerffel Foundry-St Petersburg".. **2,875.00**
18-1/2" x 16-1/2" h, mounted Imperial soldier, dark brown patina, c1890, indistinguishably signed in Cyrillic on base **2,300.00**

Tray, 13-1/2" x 10-1/2", painted and lacquered metal, troika scene, verso sgd in Cyrillic "Lukutin," beneath Imperial Warrant, 19th C. **690.00**

Miscellaneous

Box, 6-1/2" x 4-1/2", lacquer and transfer printed papier-mache, colorful

foil backed transfer images of famous Russian scenes on lid, lock and key, c1890, price for pr **460.00**

Card case, 3-1/2" l, nephrite and gold, cabochon thumbpush, hallmarked St Petersburg 1908, standard 56, makers mark "A. A." **4,890.00**

Charger, 15" d, carved in Pan Slavic style, borders carved relief inscription "To Her Imperial Highness Princess Yevheniya Maximiliyanova of Oldenburg," center with Imperial Russian coat of arms and Princess's coat of arms, relief carved "Housewarming from th Chertkov and Sverbeyev families 1887," verso with makers plaque in Cyrillic "F. Schilling, Moscow" **850.00**

Photo album, 13" x 10-1/2", painted lacquer and leather bound, cov painted with scene of villages heading to market in distant city, int. with Moscow retailer's mark, attributed to Lukutin Factory, Moscow, c1880, unused **1,380.00**

Stool, 13-1/2" w, 9-1/4" d, 8-7/8" h, paint dec, geometric strapwork dec on top, turned tapered legs, early 20th C **125.00**

Porcelain

Cabinet plate, 9" d, cobalt blue, green, and red central rosette, gilt ground **275.00**

Icon, Saint Seraphim of Sarov, c1903, walking through wilderness, prayer rope in left hand, entire image overlaid with finely engraved silver-gilt riza, applied cloisonné halo and corners, titled engraved at center "The Holy Venerable Seraphim of Sarov Wonderworker," hallmarked Moscow, Cyrillic maker's mark "S.G.," for Gergiy Gupkin, hand-carved custom fitted kiot, 23" x 18", **$2,800.**

Icon, Saints Peter and Paul, c1890, borders ornately inscribed and colorfully decorated against gold leaf ground, icon set on hand-carved costume fitted kiot, 23" x 16-1/2", **$3,115.**

Cup and saucer, 4-1/2" h, blue glazed, honoring coronation of Nicholas II, 1878, M. S. Kuznetsov **250.00**

Dessert plate, floral rim, magenta ground, Islamic script, printed mark, I. E. Kuznetsov, 19th C, set of six . **265.00**

Egg, 4-1/2" l, floral and foliate polychrome dec, gilt highlights . . **50.00**

Plate, 8-3/4" d, two soldiers, verso with underglaze Cyrillic P.S. beneath crown mark **750.00**

Portrait plate, 8" d, Empress Elizabeth, Safronov, early 19th C, hairline . . **315.00**

Tankard, 8" h, figural, Turk's head, marked "F. Gardner, Moscow," 19th C, restored **1,210.00**

Tea service

13 pcs, 9" w x 5" h cov teapot, creamer, sugar, four cov cups, four saucers, two open cups, Kornilov Bros, c1910 . . . . **2,415.00**

31 pcs, 8" w x 7-1/2" h cov teapot, creamer, sugar, cake stand, compote, berry bowl, six each cake plates, cups, saucers, and sauce dishes, Gardner, Moscow, c1918 . . . . **2,760.00**

Vase, 8" h, one green with medallion of Olga, other puce with medallion of Vladimir, allover gilt foliate dec, Gardner, 19th C, drilled, price for pr **250.00**

Silver

Box, 2-3/4" d, 2-1/8" h, cylindrical, enameled blue, green, white, and coral, star design on lid, panels of bird and

Icon, New Testament Trinity, Eliya Yakovlev, 1843, lower right corner signed: "This Holy Image was Painted on the 15th day of May by Iconographer Eliya Yakovlev, St. Petersburg," 23" x 28", **$2,875.**

Icon, The Last Supper, 19th C, names of Apostles engraved in their haloes, lower margin signed in Cyrillic "M. Gololobov," 14" d, $2,800.

scroll designs on sides, gilt int., marked "?84" and double-headed bird, crazing in white enamel band on lid. . . . **600.00**

Cordial set, 7-3/4" h, maker's mark "BC," early 20th C, stoppered ewer, six footed cordials, circular tray, engraved foliates and stylized houses, approx 15 troy oz **260.00**

Figural group, 8" d, 9" h, silver, mounted officer, saddle blanket embroidered with cipher of Tsar Nicholas II, polished granite base, Cyrillic makers mark "A.L.," hallmarked Moscow, c1908 . . . . **4,600.00**

Punch ladle, 10" l, silver, bowl, stem, and handle finely enameled with scrolling foliage, red cabochon set in handle, Feodor Rückert, Moscow, c1899. . . . . **2,550.00**

Shashka, 36" l, silver gilt and niello, Georgian, 20th C **690.00**

Tabernacle, 23" h, silver gilt, multiple piece, hallmarked Moscow, dated 1893, Cyrillic maker's mark "I.A." **3,300.00**

Teaspoon, 5" l, silver-gilt and niello, twist handles with finial, monogrammed, Moscow, 1881, Cyrillic makers mark "S.D.S.," set of 12 **300.00**

SALT AND PEPPER SHAKERS

History: Collecting salt and pepper shakers, whether late 19th-century glass forms or the contemporary figural and souvenir types, is

For more information, see this book.

becoming more and more popular. The supply and variety is practically unlimited; the price for most sets is within the budget of cost-conscious collectors. In addition, their size offers an opportunity to display a large collection in a relatively small space.

Specialty collections can be by type, form, or maker. Great glass artisans, such as Joseph Locke and Nicholas Kopp, designed salt and pepper shakers in the normal course of their work.

Additional Listings: See *Warman's Americana & Collectibles* and *Warman's Flea Market* for more examples.

Art glass (priced individually)
Burmese, 4" h, branches and leaves dec, metal top, Mt. Washington . . **85.00**

Cranberry, Inverted Thumbprint, sphere **175.00**

Fig, enameled pansy dec, satin, orig prong top, Mt. Washington **120.00**

Hobnail, sapphire blue, Hobbs, Brockunier & Co., one orig metal top, 2-3/4" h **95.00**

Scrollware, blue scrolling **170.00**

Wave Crest, Erie Twist body, hp flowers, 2-1/2" h **185.00**

Figural and souvenir types
(priced by set)

Black cat, mother and baby, nodders, yellow and red collars, marked "Patent TN" and "Made in Japan," 4" h. . **425.00**

Bride and groom, pigs, nodders, marked "Made in Japan," c1950 **325.00**

Cardinal Tuck, holding book, marked "Goebel, W. Germany" bee inside V mark, paper label **325.00**

Christmas, barrel shape, amethyst **165.00**

Ducks, 2-1/2" h, sitting, glass, clear bodies, blue heads, sgd "Czechoslovakia" **45.00**

Egg shape, opaque white body, holly dec, 23 red raised enameled berries, Mt. Washington **175.00**

Opaque white ground, yellow and orange flowers, green leaves, St. Paul in gold letters, egg shape, original tops, 2" h, pair, $215.

Mammy and broom, orig "Norcrest Fine China Japan" foil labels, numbered H424, 4-1/4" h **395.00**

Strawberries, flashed amberina glass strawberry-shaped shakers, white metal leaf caps, suspended from emb white metal fancy holder, 2-3/4" h strawberries, 5" h stand, sgd "Japan," c1921-41 . . . . **285.00**

Opalescent glass
(priced individually)
Argonaut Shell, blue **65.00**

Fluted Scrolls, vaseline **65.00**

Seaweed, Hobbs, cranberry. . . . **60.00**

Windows, Hobbs, blue, pewter top **55.00**

Opaque glass (priced individually)
Bulge Bottom, blue **25.00**

Cathedral Panel, white. **20.00**

Creased Bale, pink. **20.00**

Fleur de Lis Scrolling, custard . **20.00**

Heart, blue **25.00**

Leaf Clover, blue **20.00**

Little Shrimp, white **20.00**

Swirl Wide Diagonal, white **20.00**

Torch Wreath, white. **20.00**

Opaque glass, Muranese pattern, New Martinsville, white, embossed scroll design, 3-1/2" h, $60.

Pattern glass, Daisy & Cube, light blue, original top, $30.

Pattern glass (priced individually)
Actress, pewter top 45.00
Beautiful Lady, colorless, 1905. . 25.00
Block and Fan, colorless, 1891. . 20.00
Franesware, Hobbs, Brockunier Co.,
c1880, hobnail, frosted, amber stained
. . . . 45.00
Lobe, squatty 120.00
Tulip 100.00
Twelve Panel, scrolled pink. . . . 130.00

SALT-GLAZED WARES

History: Salt-glazed wares have a distinctive pitted surface texture made by throwing salt into the hot kiln during the final firing process. The salt vapors produce sodium oxide and hydrochloric acid, which react on the glaze.

Many Staffordshire potters produced large quantities of this type of ware during the 18th and 19th centuries. A relatively small amount was produced in the United States. Salt-glazed wares still are made today.

For more information, see this book.

Bottle, 7-1/2" h, flat form, Albany glaze int., c1810 . . . . 210.00

Miniature jug, brown and white salt glaze, blue stencil on front "Wallace & Gregory Bros., Pure Vinegars, Paducah KY," 2-3/4" h, some age crazing, $70. Photo courtesy of Vicki and Bruce Waasdorp.

Bowl, 11-1/2" l, oval, matching undertray, reticulated, edge wear and hairlines 1,320.00
Canister, 7-1/4" h, one gallon, relief oak leaf design, blue and navy blue accents, orig matching lid and bale handle, relief diamond pattern all around 220.00
Canteen, 7-1/2" h, relief and blue accented tavern scene on front, relief and blue accented leaf design around rim, orig bale handle 495.00
Cheese jar, 4-1/2" h, blue accent bands, diamond point design, imp and blue accented "Bayle's Cheeses St. Louis, MO," nicely fitted replacement wooden lid, int. surface chip on back 110.00
Cream pitcher, 6-1/4" h, relief daffodil dec on front and back, heavy blue accents at floral designs and on handle 110.00
Custard dish, 2" h, three blue accent bands 35.00
Dish, 9" d, circular, scroll and latticino dec 325.00
Figure, 4-1/2" l, 3-1/4" h, seated ram, molded stoneware, blue accents at eyes and end of protruding horns, attributed to mold maker George Hehr, Red Wing Stoneware Co., c1896, piece broken off one horn, museum inventory code number inked on bottom . 825.00
Humidor, cov, 6-1/2" h, matching lid, relief and blue accented hunting dog on front, blue accent band at rim, overall diamond relief pattern 250.00
Miniature
Dish, 4" d, 1-1/4" h, blue and white, diffused blue banded pattern, two hairlines 15.00
Jug, 2-3/4" h, brown and white, adv "Wallace & Gregory Bros., Pure Vinegars, Paducah, KY," some age crazing to glaze 70.00
Mug
4" h, bulbous, two blue accent bands, imp and blue accented "Granby CT 1896," blue accents at handle, Albany glaze int., short hairline extending from rim. 440.00
5-1/2" h, blue accents at handle, blue bands top and bottom, imp and blue accented "The Indian King/Haddonfield, NJ, 1850-1910," imp Indian profile in circle below name, base imp "C. W. & Bro.," surface chip, short rim hairline 360.00
6-1/2" h, hinged pewter lid, two blue incised accent bands, Albany

Match safe, incised "Matches" on front, three blue accent bands, rim chip, stained from use, 5" h, $385. Photo courtesy of Vicki and Bruce Waasdorp.

glaze int., attributed to New York state, c1840 . . . . 210.00
Mustard pot, 4" h, relief and blue accented grape vine design on front, blue accent band at rim and knob of orig lid, turned wooden spoon . . 220.00
Pilsner glass, 7" h, imp and blue accented tooled lines top and bottom, center imp "Crystal Springs Lager" 330.00
Pitcher
8-1/2" h, blue and white, salt glaze, stenciled Dutch Boy and Girl scene on front and back 275.00
9" h, applied and blue accented female figure designs on each side, relief and blue accented banner incised "1889," blue accent and tooled relief designs top and

Pitcher, relief bark design, relief and blue accented male portrait on one side, leafy rose on other, mold mark #9, 8" h, age spider, $70. Photo courtesy of Vicki and Bruce Waasdorp.

bottom, attributed to Whites
. . . . **330.00**
9" h, relief and imp tooled design, four lines of cobalt accents, Whites, clay separation at handle occurred in making, professional restoration to surface chip at rim **110.00**

Plate, shaped reticulated rim, 8-1/4" d, emb border **600.00**

Platter, 16-3/4" d, molded diaper-work panels, scalloped rim, 18th C . . **250.00**

Salt, helmet shape, latticino star and lion, bird and shell dec, claw feet, c18th C **880.00**

Sauce boat, 3-1/8" l, oval, relief-molded diaper, ozier, and scrolling panels, loop handle **425.00**

Stein, 8" h, orig pewter lid, relief a d blue accented Longfellow on one side, framed German verse on opposite, blue accents on designs and handle, minor glaze flakes at base **110.00**

Syrup pitcher, 6-1/2" h, cylinder shape, relief and blue accented grape-vine design **90.00**

Tea caddy, 4-1/4" h, pear shape, latticino dec, knob finial, 18th C **375.00**

Teapot, cov, 7" h, ball shape, raised branch dec, bird finial on lid, 18th C
. . . . **2,850.00**

Tray, 7-3/4" l, oval, latticino dec, scalloped rim. **350.00**

SALTS, OPEN

History: When salt was first mined, the supply was limited and expensive. The necessity for a receptacle in which to serve the salt resulted in the first open salt, a crude, hand-carved, wooden trencher.

For more information, see this book.

As time passed, salt receptacles were refined in style and materials. In the 1500s, both master and individual salts existed. By the 1700s, firms such as Meissen, Waterford, and Wedgwood were making glass, china, and porcelain salts. Leading glass manufacturers in the 1800s included Libbey, Mount Washington, New England, Smith Bros., Vallerysthal, Wave Crest, and Webb. Many outstanding silversmiths in England, France, and Germany also produced this form.

Open salts were the only means of serving salt until the appearance of the shaker in the late 1800s. The ease of procuring salt from a shaker greatly reduced the use of and need for the open salts.

Note: The numbers in parentheses refer to plate numbers in the Smiths' books.

Pearlware, rounded form, medium blue rim band, vertical ribbed dark brown slip dec on white ground, England, early 19th C, 2-1/2" d, **$590.** *Photo courtesy of Skinner Auctioneers and Appraisers.*

Condiment sets with open salts

German silver, two castors, two salts, two salt spoons, Renaissance style with swan supports, c1900, marked ".800 fine" **800.00**

Limoges, double salt and mustard, sgd "J. M. Limoges" (388). **80.00**

Metal, coolie pulling rickshaw, salt, pepper, and mustard, blown glass liners, Oriental (461) **360.00**

Quimper, double salt and mustard, white, blue, and green floral dec, sgd "Quimper" (388) **120.00**

Early American glass

2-5/8" l, colorless, variant, Neal MN3, chips. **315.00**

3" h, cobalt blue, paneled with diamond foot **125.00**

3" l, colorless, lacy, eagle, Neal EE1, chips. **200.00**

3-1/8" l, fiery opalescent, 3-1/8" l, Neal BS2, chips **275.00**

3-1/4" l, fiery opalescent, eagles, Neal EE3b, chips **500.00**

Individual, china, white ground, blue butterfly and floral decoration, red character mark and "China" on base, #599, 2-1/4" w, 2" h, **$12.**

3-3/8" h, cobalt blue, facet cut, fan rim, sq foot, edges ground. **125.00**

3-5/8" l, sapphire blue, Neal BT 2, very minor flakes **1,075.00**

Figurals

Basket, 3" h, 2-3/4" d, coral colored glass, SP basket frame, salt with cut polished facets **55.00**

Boat, lacy, colorless, New England, Neal BT-9, slight rim roughness **160.00**

Bucket, 2-1/2" d, 1-5/8" h, Bristol glass, turquoise, white, green, and brown enameled bird, butterfly and trees, SP rim and handle **75.00**

Sea horse, Belleek, brilliant turquoise, white base, supports shell salt, first black mark (458) **350.00**

Individual

Cambridge, Decagon pattern, amber (468) **42.00**

Cameo, Daum Nancy, 1-3/8" h, cameo glass, bucket form, two upright handles, frosted colorless ground, cameo etched and enameled black tree lined shore, distant ruins, gilt rim, sgd "Daum (cross) Nancy" in gilt on base, small rim chips **575.00**

Cut glass, 2" d, 1-1/2" h, cut ruby ovals, allover dainty white enameled scrolls, clear ground, gold trim, scalloped top
. . . . **60.00**

German silver, dolphin feet, 1890-1910 (353) **100.00**

Moser, cobalt blue, pedestal, gold bands, applied flowers sgd (380)
. . . . **75.00**

Mount Washington, blue Johnny Jump-ups, cream ground, raised gold dots on rim **135.00**

Pattern glass

Fine Rib, flint. **35.00**
Hawaiian Lei, (477). **35.00**
Pineapple and Fan **25.00**
Three Face **40.00**

Individual, china, orange basketweave ground, red, and purple flowers, green leaves, marked "Marotomo Ware, Made in Japan," #472, 3" d, **$10.**

Individual, milk glass, pedestal base, #582, 2-5/8" d, 2" h, **$15.**

Purple slag, 3" d, 1-1/4" h, emb shell pattern **50.00**
Royal Bayreuth, lobster claw (87) **80.00**
Russian, 1-1/4" h, 1-3/4" d, colorless glass liner, gold finished metal, red and white enamel scallop design, Russian hallmarks, c1940 . . . .**110.00**
Sterling silver, Georg Jensen, Denmark, porringer (238) **200.00**

Intaglios
Niagara Falls, scene (368) **75.00**
Tree, six intaglios, Venus and Cupid (423) **115.00**

Masters
Coin silver, made by Gorham for retailer Seth E. Brown, Boston, ftd, gold washed int., monogrammed, pair in fitted case, two coin silver spoons by Jones, Ball & Poor, pr, approx 4 troy oz **375.00**
Cranberry, 3" d, 1-3/4" h, emb ribs, applied crystal ruffed rim, SP holder with emb lions heads **160.00**
Cut glass, 2" d, 2" h, green cut to clear, SP holder **115.00**
Green, light, dark green ruffled top, open pontil (449) **90.00**
Mocha, seaweed band, yellow ware ground, 2" h **250.00**

Individual, vaseline glass, carriage shape, #573, 3-1/2" l, 1-7/8" h, **$45.**

Master, sterling silver, Faberge, Moscow, c1896-1908, three ball feet, engraved EG monogram, 1-3/4" w, **$900.** *Photo courtesy of Sloan's Auctioneers & Appraisers.*

Pattern glass
Barberry, pedestal **40.00**
Basketweave, sleigh (397) . .**100.00**
Diamond Point, cov **75.00**
Portland, branches handle . . .**110.00**
Snail, ruby stained **75.00**
Sunflower, pedestal **40.00**

Pearlware
2-1/2" d, rounded form, medium blue rim band, vertical ribbed dark brown slip dec on white ground, England, early 19th C. **590.00**
2-3/4" d, rounded form, dark brown banding, dark brown dendritic dec on rust field, narrow green glazed reeded band, early 19th C, cracked, rim chip **590.00**
Pewter, pedestal, cobalt blue liner (349) **65.00**
Sterling silver, 1-3/4" h, Stieff Co., early 20th C, chased and emb allover floral pattern, applied floral rim, three scrolled shell feet, pr, 6 troy oz **260.00**
Vaseline, 3" d, 2-1/4" h, applied crystal trim around middle, SP stand . .**125.00**

Sterling silver, set of 12, porringer shape, by Towle Silversmiths, gold washed interiors, small pierced handle, retailed by Bigelow Kannard & Co., **$175.** *Photo courtesy of James D. Julia, Inc.*

SAMPLERS

History: Samplers served many purposes. For a young child, they were a practice exercise and permanent reminder of stitches and patterns. For a young woman, they were a means to demonstrate skills in a "gentle" art and a way to record family genealogy. For the mature woman, they were a useful occupation and method of creating gifts or remembrances, e.g., mourning pieces.

Schools for young ladies of the early 19th century prided themselves on the needlework skills they taught. The Westtown School in Chester County, Pennsylvania, and the Young Ladies Seminary in Bethlehem, Pennsylvania, were two institutions. These schools changed their teaching as styles changed. Berlin work was introduced by the mid-19th century.

Examples of samplers date back to the 1700s. The earliest ones were long and narrow, usually done only with the alphabet and numerals. Later examples were square. At the end of the 19th century, the shape tended to be rectangular.

The same motifs were used throughout the country. The name of the person who stitched the piece is a key factor in determining the region.

1797, Sarah McPherson, Chester County, PA, numerous symbols, birds, alphabets, trees, and pineapple topped baskets **16,500.00**
1799, Lydia Wood's sample Anno Domini 1799, stylized floral upper border above two alphabet panels over panel of flowering shrubs and birds, black, green, and pink silk threads, unframed, 15-1/4" x 10-1/2", fading, toning **715.00**
1801, Sally Clark, Aged 8 Years 1801, inspirational verse flanked by stylized vases of flowers, upper borders above birds on branches, landscape with thatched roof cottages, framed, 21" x 17", faded **890.00**

1843, Margaret Ann McCoy, from "Miss Decker's School," dated January 12, 1843, rose border surrounds alphabet and numbers, over verse "First at ? Shrine devoutly bend/And early make her guardian God thy friend/She'll safely guide thee through the snares of youth/And fix thy weaving steps in paths of truth", peacock in landscape, minor losses, 15" x 17", **$615.** *Photo courtesy of Sanford Alderfer Auction Company.*

1866, Aeta Frazer, May 31, small embroidered sampler with alphabet and numbers, 7" x 11-1/2", $120. Photo courtesy of Joy Luke Auctions.

1804, Elizabeth Willits, each corner with different flower in soft pale blue, ivory, and gold, central vining wreath with tulip drop encircles verse, numbers, and "Maidencreek, Elizabeth Willits 1804" all done in dark brown, loosely woven linen ground, modern frame, 13-1/4" x 14", minor stains **2,970.00**

1805, Adam and Eve, England, "Jane Harrison Vinnis is my name and with My Needle I did work the same that all the World may plainly see what care my Parents took of me, Finished at Mis Tucker Northfleet in Kent November the sixth one thousand eight hundred and five and in the twelve year of my age," floral symbols enclosed in panel above Adam, Eve, the tree, entwined serpent, flanked by various religious, animal, and floral devices, surrounded by stylized floral border, gray blue ground, framed, 15" x 19", imperfections **1,880.00**

1808, Abigail A Jenney, Plainfield, New Hampshire, three alphabets, trees, various devices, upper and lower borders, silk threads on linen ground, shades of green, yellow, and brown, 4-3/4" x 3-3/4" sight size, 6-3/4" x 5-3/4" frame **2,585.00**

1809, Elizabeth H. Kay's Work, 1809, PA, family register surrounded by foliate, bird, and geometric motifs, inspirational verses, lower panel of various animals among trees, meandering and geometric floral borders, framed, 21-5/8" x 22-3/4", toning, scattered staining, fading **3,750.00**

1809, Mary Chandler, silk threads on linen, Adam and Eve scene, snake coiled apple tree, stylized potted florals, woman tending sheep, man with dog, winged cherubs, various animals, stitched inscription "Honesty-Convince the world that you are just and true, be just in all you say and do, whatever be your birth you're sure to do a man of the first magnitude to me, Mary Chandler,

Sept 16, 1809," framed, 12" x 16-1/2", some losses **1,035.00**

1809, Waterford Township School Elizabeth Homer Kay's Work Wrought in the Year 1809, PA, alphabets above inspirational verses, geometric floral borders, framed, 17" x 16-1/4", minor toning, staining **2,990.00**

1810, Anne Armstrong, Aged 11 Years Clones 1810, geometric bands in red, pink, green, blue, brown, purple, and yellow, row of trees, alphabets, and vowels, linen ground, verse by "C. Quigley," minor stitch loss, framed, 19" w, 18-1/4" h **1,265.00**

1810, Frances Croll 1810, England or America, basket of flowers over alphabet panels above pious verse, surrounded by floral dec banner, worked in shades of red, blue, green, yellow, and blue threads, framed, 16-3/8" x 12-3/4", fading, scattered staining **825.00**

1819, Mary Houden, New England, "Mary Houden mark and finished this in the 13 year her age in the year of our Lord 1819," worked in a square flanked by Federal houses, inspirational verse, surmounted with bands of various foliate and floral devices alternating with alphabets, worked in black, brown, green, yellow, and white threads on linen ground, matted and framed, staining and toning, 21-1/2" x 16" **950.00**

1822, Jane Collins born July the 26 1822 aged 10 years, worked in black,

1849, Sarah Wilshaw, needlepoint, colorful little girl with her dog, seated in garden with poem above that reads "Our days are as the grass, Or like the morning flower; If one sharp blast sweep oer the field, It withers in an hour," colorful chain of flowers border, flame mahogany ogee frame, gold leaf liner, 12-1/2" x 14", $350. Photo courtesy of Cowan's Historic Americana Auctions.

blue, and red threads, 16-1/2" x 7-1/4", thread losses, scattered staining, toning, and fading **475.00**

1823, Massachusetts, 1823, "Wrought by Mary B Kimme--- of Bolton 1823 (?) Aged 12 Years," verse and alphabets, house and floral symbols below, right-hand side appears to be unfinished, unframed, small areas of thread losses, some fabric loss to the linen ground, minor fading, 17-1/4" x 17-1/2" **890.00**

1840, Isabella Lunds work Aged 16 AD 1840, inspirational verse, attached buildings, trees, vines, floral and animal devices surrounded by stylized floral border, 26-3/4" x 32-1/4", toning and fading **2,470.00**

1841, H. S. Chrismanis Sampler, cross stitch, birds, tulips, hearts, crown, and deer, block of script alphabets, verse, and name, blue, dark green, brown, and tan, loosely woven linen ground, shadow box frame with gilt liner, 20" w, 21" h, some stains **600.00**

1850, Mary Jane Flint, aged 11 years, April 19, 1850, five alphabet panels, pictorial scene, Federal buildings, trees, bird and inspirational verse, framed, 22-1/2" x 19-1/2", fading, toning, staining **1,175.00**

1917, member of Huetterite, Mennonite commune in SD, symbols and graphic art, flora, fauna, German passage, 29-1/2" x 34-1/2", two large holes **2,530.00**

Late 18th C, Cynthia Taft, Uxbridge, MA, pink and green floral vine encloses verse worked in pink linen above pictorial lower half with garden, trees, flowers, birds, and grass, pink, green, and red hues, good coloration and condition, reframed, minor imperfections, 10-5/8" w, 12" h, $4,115. Photo courtesy of Skinner Auctioneers and Appraisers.

Late 18th C, Cynthia Taft, Uxbridge, Massachusetts, pink and green floral vine encloses verse worked in pink linen above pictorial lower half with garden, trees, flowers, birds, and grass, pink, green, and red hues, good coloration and condition, reframed, minor imperfections, 10-5/8" w, 12" h
. . . . **4,115.00**

Undated

Elizabeth Dogell Aged 12, late 18th C, silk threads on linen, conical pine trees, stylized potted florals, birds, and butterflies within oval floral border with Lord's Prayer, sgd in silk, bird's eye maple period frame, 20" x 21-1/2", later cotton backing **650.00**

Mary Ann Isaccs Sampler finished in the year AD 18, flowers, foliage, insects, tulips, oak leaves, acorns, butterfly, and dragonfly, 26" x 16-1/2", staining, losses . . . **925.00**

SANDWICH GLASS

For more information, see this book.

History: In 1818, Deming Jarves was listed in the Boston Directory as a glass factor. That same year, he was appointed general manager of the newly formed New England Glass Company. In 1824, Jarves toured the glassmaking factories in Pittsburgh, left New England Glass Company, and founded a glass factory in Sandwich.

Originally called the Sandwich Manufacturing Company, it was incorporated in April 1826 as the Boston & Sandwich Glass Company. From 1826 to 1858, Jarves served as general manager. The Boston & Sandwich Glass Company produced a wide variety of wares in differing levels of quality. The factory used the free-blown, blown three mold, and pressed glass manufacturing techniques. Both clear and colored glass were used.

Competition in the American glass industry in the mid-1850s resulted in lower-quality products. Jarves left the Boston & Sandwich company in 1858, founded the Cape Cod Glass Company, and tried to duplicate the high quality of the earlier glass. Meanwhile, at the Boston & Sandwich Glass Company, emphasis was placed on mass production. The development of a lime glass (non-flint) led to lower costs for pressed glass. Some free-blown and blown-and-molded pieces, mostly in color, were made. Most of this Victorian-era glass was enameled, painted, or acid etched.

By the 1880s, the Boston & Sandwich Glass Company was operating at a loss. Labor difficulties finally resulted in the closing of the factory on January 1, 1888.

Candlesticks, pair, flint, amber, hexagonal form, 7-1/2" h, **$400.** *Photo courtesy of Cowan's Historic Americana Auctions.*

Bowl, Gothic paneled arches, hexagonal, clambroth **150.00**

Butter dish, cov, colorless, flint, Gothic pattern **225.00**

Candlesticks, pr

8-3/8" h, translucent blue socket, hexagonal clambroth shaft, stepped base, c1840-60, chips on base **765.00**

9-1/4" h, turquoise petal sockets, clambroth columnar standards, sq bases, c1850-65, small chips to underside of petals and base corners **1,175.00**

9-3/4" h, canary, petal sockets, dolphin standards, double-step sq

Decanters, matching stopper, sunburst and waffle design, other scrolls and ribs design, both 9" h, **$250.** *Photo courtesy of James D. Julia, Inc.*

Miniatures, pair 2" h vaseline candlesticks, 1" clear chamber stick, **$550.** *Photo courtesy of James D. Julia, Inc.*

bases, c1845-70, minor roughness at underside of one petal and base edge **825.00**

Champagne, Sandwich Star . . . **850.00**

Compote, 10-1/2" w, 4-3/4" h, cranberry overlay, oval cuts, enameled birds and flowers on inner surface, c1890 . . . . **495.00**

Creamer and sugar, colorless, flint, Gothic pattern **175.00**

Cup plate, lacy, blue, ship **125.00**

Decanter, 6-3/4" h, cobalt blue, ribbed, tam o'shanter stopper **195.00**

Dish, 9-1/4" d, lacy, beehive, scalloped, octagonal sides, flakes, roughness
. . . . **115.00**

Fluid lamp

9-1/2" h, mottled blue, Star and Punty pattern font, hexagonal standard and base, brass fitting, 1840-65, very minor base chips, price for pr **7,050.00**

10-3/4" h, clambroth, Star and Punty pattern font, hexagonal base, brass collar, c1840-65, small chips to one oval. **1,000.00**

Goblet, colorless, flint, Gothic pattern, 12-pc set **650.00**

Inkwell, 2-9/16", cylindrical-domed form, colorless, pink and white stripes, sheared mouth, applied pewter collar and cap, smooth base **2,300.00**

Paperweight, 3-1/2" w, 1-1/4" h, colorless and frosted, portraits of Queen Victoria and Prince Consort, 1851 . . . . **220.00**

Pitcher, 10" h

Amberina Verde, fluted top . . **525.00**

Electric Blue, enameled floral dec, fluted top, threaded handle **425.00**

Plate, 6" d, lacy, Shell pattern . . **175.00**

Pomade, cov, figural, bear, imp retailer's name, 3-3/4" h, clambroth, imp "F. B. Strouse, N.Y.," chips **525.00**

Salt, open

1-1/2" x 2-3/4" x 2", Mount Vernon pattern, cobalt blue, c1825-60 .... **350.00**

1-1/2" x 3" x 2", Stag's Horn, cobalt blue, c1825-60 .... **375.00**

Spooner, colorless, flint, Gothic pattern **85.00**

Sugar, cov, translucent blue, Lacy Gothic pattern **1,300.00**

Toddy, 5-3/8" d, brilliant dark amethyst, lacy, Roman Rosette, edge chips **330.00**

Undertray, Heart, lacy, flint **400.00**

Vase

9-1/4" h, amethyst, Three Printie Block pattern, trumpet shape, gauffered rim, triple ring turned connector, pressed colorless base, hairlines to base **2,900.00**

11-1/4" h, trumpet, brilliant cobalt blue, ruffled rim, panel and arch bowl, hexagonal waterfall base, small flakes on base **1,650.00**

Whiskey taster, cobalt blue, nine panels **175.00**

SARREGUEMINES CHINA

History: Sarreguemines ware is a faience porcelain, i.e., tin-glazed earthenware. The factory that made it was established in Lorraine, France, in 1770, under the supervision of Utzschneider

and Fabry. The factory was regarded as one of the three most prominent manufacturers of French faience. Most of the wares found today were made in the 19th century.

Jug, modeled as head of bewigged 18th C gentleman, majolica, c1900, printed mark, 6-1/2" h, **$350.** *Photo courtesy of David Rago Auctions.*

Marks: Later wares are impressed "Sarreguemines" and "Germany" as a result of changes in international boundaries.

Basket, 9" h, quilted, green, heavy leopard skin crystallization **250.00**

Centerpiece, 14-3/4" h, 14-3/4" d, bowl with pierced ringlets to sides, supported by center stem flanked by sea nymphs either side, mounted atop circular base on four scrolled feet, polychrome dec, imp marks, chips, restorations, c1875 .... **900.00**

Cup and saucer, Orange, majolica, crack to one cup, nicks, set of four **200.00**

Dinnerware service, white china, multicolored scenes, six luncheon plates, six bread and butter plates, six demitasse cups, six porringers, two platters, divided dish **150.00**

Face jug, majolica

Suspicious Eyes, #3320 .... **550.00**

Upward Eyes, #3257 ...... **500.00**

Garniture, Art Nouveau faience, 10-3/4" h pr of vases, shouldered trumpet form, shaped oval centerpiece bowl, each with wide gilt band of foliage within diamond borders centered by decorative medallion, verte ground **350.00**

Humidor, man with top hat, majolica **195.00**

Plate, 7-1/2" d, dec with music and characters from French children's songs, 12-pc set **375.00**

Tankard, cov, 11" h, stoneware, continuous country scene of dancing and celebrating villagers, branch handle, pewter lid with porcelain

Oyster plate, majolica, six shell-form oyster wells, glazed in pastel colors, printed mark, c1920, 9-1/2" d, **$125.** *Photo courtesy of David Rago Auctions.*

Oyster plate, majolica, six shell-form oyster wells, center well, golds and browns, green seaweed decoration, printed mark, 9-1/2" d, **$150.**

medallion and painted polychrome coat of arms, dated 1869 .... **325.00**

Urn, 31-1/4" h, gilt metal mounted majolica, baluster form, cobalt blue glazed, mounted with the figure of a crowned lion holding sword, lion and mask handled sides, pierced foliate rim, raised on four scrolling foliate cast feet, imp "Majolica Sarreguemines," second half 19th C **1,800.00**

SATIN GLASS

History: Satin glass, produced in the late 19th century, is an opaque art glass with a velvety matte (satin) finish achieved through treatment with hydrofluoric acid. A large majority of the pieces were cased or had a white lining.

For more information, see this book.

While working at the Phoenix Glass Company, Beaver, Pennsylvania, Joseph Webb perfected mother-of-pearl (MOP) satin glass in 1885. Similar to plain satin glass in respect to casing, MOP satin glass has a distinctive surface finish and an integral or indented design, the most well known being diamond quilted (DQ).

The most common colors are yellow, rose, or blue. Rainbow coloring is considered choice.

Additional Listings: Cruets, Fairy Lamps, Miniature Lamps, and Rose Bowls.

Bowl

4-1/2" h, 2-3/4" h, MOP, cased, blue shading to white, white int., Coinspot pattern, faint flowering branch dec **70.00**

8-1/2" d, 4" h, MOP, red, Thumbprint pattern, ruffled rim trimmed in blue **300.00**

Bride's basket, 15-1/2" h, deep rose, enamel swan and floral dec, heavy bronze holder with birds perched at top **450.00**

Celery vase, 5" h, MOP, cased blue, Herringbone pattern, waisted squared body **200.00**

Creamer and sugar bowl, 4-1/2" d, 4-1/2" h, MOP, cased pink, DQ, tightly crimped rim, ground pontil **350.00**

Cup and saucer, Raindrop MOP, pink to white, 3" h cup, 5" d saucer . . **385.00**

Epergne, 13-3/4" h, 10" d, pink and white, hobnail bowl, resilvered base and lily vase holder **395.00**

Ewer, 9-1/2" h, cased blue ground, enameled bird, coralene trailing branch with leaves **70.00**

Finger bowl and underplate, 6-1/2" h, 3" d, MOP, cased deep crimson shading to peach, DQ **980.00**

Lamp, 22" h, white satin body, matching font with air-trapped Flower and Acorn design, enameled Japanese cherry blossoms, bronze ftd base with lions' heads, burner marked "Hinks & Sons Patent" and "Sherwoods Limited," retailer's soldered tag "T. R. Grimes, New Broad St., London," some flakes under font lip **1,260.00**

Pink satin glass dresser set: powder jar, covered, cosmetic jar, covered, perfume bottle, with figural crown stopper, gold trim, wear to gold, **$175.** *Photo courtesy of Joy Luke Auctions.*

Mustard pot, 2-1/2" h, bright yellow, gold prunus dec, SP top, Webb **450.00**

Rose bowl

3-1/2" d, 3-1/2" h, mother-of-pearl, pink, Herringbone pattern . . **70.00**

4" d, 3-3/4" h, mother-of-pearl, rainbow, DQ, ground pontil **1,100.00**

Salt shaker, 3-1/4" h, rose shaded to white, MOP, DQ, tapered barrel, orig two-pc lid **550.00**

Sugar shaker, 6-1/4" h, blue, Raindrop, MOP, SP top **425.00**

Tumbler, 3-1/2" h, Rainbow, DQ, enameled floral dec, pr **375.00**

Vase

4-1/4" h, MOP, cased rose, white int., Herringbone pattern **70.00**

Water pitcher, Coin Spot, red shading to white, ruffled top, applied frosted reeded handle, 8-1/2" h, **$350.** *Photo courtesy of James D. Julia, Inc.*

5" h, MOP, cased yellow, Fleur de Lis pattern, multicolored insect and foliage in pointillism style . . **525.00**

5-3/4" h, glossy green ground, cased in blue, applied amber stems with pink and white flowers **90.00**

7" h, MOP, cased blue, DQ, two applied and enameled leafy stems, English patent numbers . . . **490.00**

7-1/2" h, shading cream to pink, amber enamel child in tree dec, English, 19th C **260.00**

9" h, stick, MOP, cased yellow shading to caramel, Coinspot pattern, ground pontil **150.00**

9-1/4" h, MOP, cased blue glass, DQ, multicolored coralene butterfly surrounded by flowering branches, ground pontil **435.00**

9-1/4" h, MOP, cased rose shading to pale pink, Herringbone pattern, price for pr **500.00**

9-1/2" h, MOP, cased yellow, DQ, two satin glass thorny handles . **300.00**

9-3/4" h, green ground, applied amber stem with bright red

Left, ewer, Zig-zag pattern, blue, frosted handle, 8" h, **$90;** *right: rose bowl, blue, yellow floral decoration, 5-1/2" d,* **$100;** *center: vase, cut-velvet satin, teardrop shape, blue, 6-1/2" h,* **$75.** *Photo courtesy of Woody Auctions.*

Tumbler, Rainbow, bands of blue, pink, and yellow swirl over molded-in tufts, lace-like narrow band of bright raised gold enamel encircles rim, 3-7/8" h, **$500.** *Photo courtesy of Clarence and Betty Maier.*

cherries, reverse with pink flowers, four amber feet, Victorian . . **300.00**
Water pitcher, 8-1/2" h, MOP, cased, shading from rose to pink, Coinspot pattern, applied reeded handle, ground pontil **425.00**

SATSUMA

History: Satsuma, named for a war lord who brought skilled Korean potters to Japan in the early 1600s, is a hand-crafted Japanese faience (tin-glazed) pottery. It is finely crackled, has a cream, yellow-cream, or gray-cream color, and is decorated with raised enamels in floral, geometric, and figural motifs.

Figural satsuma was made specifically for export in the 19th century. Later satsuma, referred to as satsuma-style ware, is a Japanese porcelain also hand decorated in raised enamels. From 1912 to the present, satsuma-style ware has been mass produced. Much of the ware on today's market is of this later period.

Bowl
4-3/4" d, design of women and children viewing cherry blossoms, sgd, early 20th C **250.00**
5" d, figures in reserves with butterflies and brocade patterns, late 19th C **500.00**
9-1/2" d, 4-1/2", molded as three chrysanthemum flowers in lavender, orange, and yellow with gilt, mille fleur int., marked "Kinkozan" in gold and imp seal, Meiji period, 1868-1911 . . **4,500.00**
Cache pot, 6-1/2" h, figural and landscape scene **120.00**
Censor
3-1/2" h, ovoid, three cabriole legs, two shaped handles rising from

Bowl, design of women and children viewing cherry blossoms, early 20th C, signed, 4-3/4" d, $250. Photo courtesy of Skinner Auctioneers and Appraisers.

Pair of miniature vases, three sages on one side, priestess surrounded by four sages on other, gilt dragon handles, red and gold royal mark on base, 3-3/4" h, $165. Photo courtesy of Cowan's Historic Americana Auctions.

shoulder, lid with large shishi seated on top, continual river landscape scene, patterned lappet border above, key fret border below, base sealed "Yabu Meizan," minor loss to one ear on shishi **2,990.00**
10-1/4" h, tapering rect form, lobed base, two squared handles, pierced domed lid, allover dec or Arhats, Meiji period **635.00**
Cup and saucer, bird and floral motif, cobalt blue border, Kinkozan, Japanese **115.00**
Dish, fan shape, pottery, Japan, 20th C **850.00**
Incense burner, 5" d, two reserves, one with sparrows and flowers, other of Mijo shrine, borders of brocade patterns, butterflies caught in net, and hanging jewels, sgd "Kinkozan," Meiji period, 1868-1911 . . . . **5,500.00**
Jar, cov, 4" d, 6" h, two cartouche panels, one of Samurai, other with birds, insects, and flowers, one side ring missing **230.00**
Koro, pierced lid, 3" h, hexagonal, six bracket feet, each side with flowers blooming behind garden fences, domed lid, sgd with Shimazu mon **2,185.00**
Miniature cup, 2" d, interior painted with Bishamon and Hoi tei, ext. with dancing children, mille fleur borders, sgd with paulownia crest in gold, Japan, Meiji period, 1868-1911 . **980.00**
Saki bottle, 6" h, two cartouches of Samurai, 19th C **115.00**
Seal paste box, 5" d, cobalt blue, gilt trim, reserve of children flying kites, sgd

Vase, ovoid, earthenware, ribbed body, Immortals and geisha decoration, Japanese, Meiji period, 10" h, $600. Photo courtesy of Sloan's Auctioneers & Appraisers.

"Kozan," Japan, Meiji period, 1868-1911, minor int. chip **320.00**
Tea bowl, 4-3/4" d, dec with butterflies, powdered gold ground, sgd "Kinkozan," Japan, Meiji period, 1868-1911 . . . . **350.00**
Tea cup and saucer, 1-3/4" h cup, . 4-3/4" d saucer, colorful groups of flowerheads with scrolling gilt vines, minor gilt wear, sgd "Yabu Meizan" **900.00**
Tea set, 6-1/2" h teapot, creamer, sugar, six cups and saucers, 6 7-1/4" d plates, paneled designs of courtesans in courtyard settings, c1900 . . . . . **290.00**
Tray, 11-1/2" d, rounded form with indented edge, design of scrolls of birds, flowers, and women, cobalt ground with gold bamboo, sgd with imp seal "Kinkozan," Japan, Meiji period, 1868-1911 . . . . **1,650.00**
Urn, 37-1/2" h, dragon handles, geishas in landscape **295.00**
Vase
6-1/4" h, mille fleur borders enclosing view of Fuji and pavilions in landscape, sgd "Unzan" in gold, Japan, Meiji period, 1868-1911 . . . . **2,645.00**
7" h, form of shishi carrying vase on it's back, "100 Rakan" pattern, sgd on underside, Japan, Meiji period, 1868-1911 . . . . **350.00**

Vessel, decorated with allover florals, saucer form on three feet, signed on underside, lid broken, 1-1/2" d top opening, 5" d base, 2" h, **$210.** *Photo courtesy of Sanford Alderfer Auction Company.*

9-1/2" h, tied back form, ornate brocade patterns, floral reserve, Japan, Meiji period, 1868-1911, chip **635.00**

16" h, reserves of people in garden vignettes, cobalt blue ground, gilt trim, sgd "Kinkozan," Japan, Meiji period, 1868-1911, drilled for lamp **1,495.00**

18-1/2" h, drum-shaped body with trumpet mouth and foot, molded dec of various birds and flowering cherry branches, Japan, Meiji period, 1868-1911, minor loss **950.00**

25" h, globular, tall cannon-mouthed neck flanked by two gate posts with entwined dragons, one side with sun goddess and various Buddhist divinities, other side with woman in garden scene, neck dec with Tokugawa mons and various brocade patterns, sgd "Kinkozan" in brown-colored seal characters within sq on base, Japan, Meiji period, 1868-1911, minor rubbing to gilt, small repair to dragon on one side. **6,900.00**

SCALES

History: Prior to 1900, the simple balance scale was commonly used for measuring weights. Since then, scales have become more sophisticated in design and more accurate. There are a wide variety of styles and types, including beam, platform, postal, and pharmaceutical.

4-1/2" h, 6-3/4" l, postal, S. Mordan & Co., England, 19th C, plates with blue and white Wedgwood jasper neoclassical roundels in ropetwist surround, rect base with three weights **350.00**

5-1/2" w, pocket balance, steel, silvered pans, silver mounted shagreen case, engraved plaque, velvet-lined interior, two fitted circular weights and various others, 18th C **575.00**

6" x 14" x 10", store, Hanson Weightmaster, cast iron, gold case with ground, black lettering and indicator **45.00**

7-3/4" h, postal, candlestick-style, gilt metal, British, 1840s, for American market, circular pan with scrolled foliate borders, red enameled stem, trellis work and C-scrolls, rate table with eagle dec, circular foot modeled in high relief with locomotive, steam clipper and farm implements interspersed with cornucopia **275.00**

9" l, Allender's Gold Scale, I. Wilson, New London, CT, cast brass rocker balance, slots and platforms for $1, 2-1/2, 5, 10, and 20, additional weight and instructions in shaped paper box, mid-19th C. **490.00**

11" l, Chonodrometer (grain scale), brass, Fairbanks, arm graduated for "lbs per bush," "lb & oz," and "% of lb," sliding weight, bucket, and suspension ring **350.00**

14" l, balance, cast iron, orig red paint with black and yellow trim, nickel plated brass pans, marked "Henry Troemner, Phila. No. 5B, Baker's". **120.00**

15-1/4" h, 17-1/2" w, merchant's type, "Computing Scale Co., Dayton, Ohio" **225.00**

Small brass shop counter scale with wooden stand & drawer, **$175.** *Photo courtesy of Joy Luke Auctions.*

Planter's Peanut, exact duplicate of Mr. Peanut mounted to old Hamilton scale mechanism, c1960, 44" h, **$3,165.** *Photo courtesy of James D. Julia, Inc.*

18" w, analytical beam balance, lacquered brass fittings, glazed mahogany case, set of weights . **175.00**

19-1/2" l, 15-3/4" h, apothecary, walnut, fitted ivory dec **250.00**

23" l, counter top, Toledo Scale Co., c1920, Style 621D, slight weight for 1-51 lbs, glazed display and pouring pan, repainted **175.00**

26" h, balance, J. L. Brown & Co., 83 Fulton St., New York, circular pans, baluster turned cast iron stand . **690.00**

63" h, platform, Peerless Junior, Peerless Weighing Machine Co., porcelainized steel, tiled platform, gold lettering **350.00**

SCHLEGELMILCH PORCELAINS

History: Erdmann Schlegelmilch founded his porcelain factory in Suhl in the Thuringia region in 1861. Reinhold, his brother, established a porcelain factory at Tillowitz in Upper Silesia in 1869. In the 1860s, Prussia controlled Thuringia and Upper Silesia, both rich in the natural ingredients needed for porcelain.

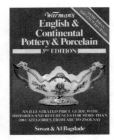

For more information, see this book.

By the late 19th century, an active export business was conducted with the United States and Canada due to a large supply of porcelain at reasonable costs achieved through industrialization and cheap labor.

The Suhl factory ceased production in 1920, unable to recover from the effects of World War I. The Tillowitz plant, located in an area of changing international boundaries, finally came under Polish socialist government control in 1956.

Marks: Both brothers marked their pieces with the "RSP" mark, a designation honoring Rudolph Schlegelmilch, their father. More than 30 mark variations have been discovered.

Reproduction Alert: Many "fake" Schlegelmilch pieces are appearing on the market. These reproductions have new decal marks, transfers, or recently hand-painted animals on old, authentic R. S. Prussia pieces.

Reproduction Alert: Dorothy Hammond in her 1979 book, *Confusing Collectibles*, illustrates an R. S. Prussia decal that was available from a china-decorating supply company for $14 a sheet. This was the first of several fake R. S. Prussia reproduction marks that have caused confusion among collectors. Acquaint yourself with some of the subtle distinctions between fake and authentic marks as described in the following.

The period mark consists of a wreath that is open at the top. A five-pointed star sits in the opening. An "R" and an "S" flank a wreath twig in the center. The word "Prussia" is located beneath. In the period mark, the leg of the letter "P" extends down past the letter "r." In the reproduction mark, it does not. In the period mark, the letter "I" is dotted. It is dotted in some fake marks, but not in others.

The "R" and the "S" in the period mark are in a serif face and uniform in width. One fake mark uses a lettering style that utilizes a thin/thick letter body. The period mark has a period after the word "Prussia." Some fake marks fail to include it. Several fake marks do not include the word "Prussia" at all.

The period mark has a fine center line within each leaf of the wreath. Several fake marks do not.

R. S. Germany

Biscuit jar, cov, 6" h, loop handles, roses dec, satin finish, gold knob **95.00**

Bonbon dish, 7-3/4" l, 4-1/2" w, pink carnations, gold dec, silver-gray ground, looped inside handle ... **40.00**

Bread plate, iris variant edge mold, blue and white, gold outlined petals and rim, multicolored center flowers, steeple mark **115.00**

Bride's bowl, floral center, ornate ftd stand **95.00**

Cake plate, deep yellow, two parrots on hanging leaf vine, open handles, green mark **235.00**

Celery tray, 11" l, 5-3/4" w, lily dec, gold rim, open handles, blue label ... **120.00**

Chocolate pot, white rose florals, blue mark **95.00**

Cup and saucer, plain mold, swan, blue water, mountain and brown castle background, RM **225.00**

Demitasse cup and saucer, 3" h, pink roses, gold-stenciled dec, satin finish, blue mark **90.00**

Dessert plate, 6-1/2" d, yellow and cream roses, green and rich brown shaded ground, six-pc set **135.00**

Hatpin holder, floral dec **95.00**

Lemon plate, cutout handle shaped as colorful parrot, white ground, gold trim, artist sgd "B. Hunter" **60.00**

Napkin ring, green, pink roses, white snowballs **55.00**

Nut bowl, 5-1/4" d, 2-3/4" h, cream, yellow, roses, green scalloped edge **65.00**

Pitcher, 5-3/4" h, light blue, chrysanthemums, pink roses, gold trim **85.00**

R. S. Germany

Plate, 9-3/4" d, white flowers, gold leaves, gilded edge, green ground, marked "RS Germany" in dark green, script sgd "Reinhold Schlegelmilch/ Tillowitz/Germany" in red **45.00**

Powder box, cov, green poppies, green mark **50.00**

Punch bowl, 17-1/4" d, 8" h, mahogany shading to pink, polychrome enameled flowers with gilt, imp fleur-de-lis mark with "J. S. Germany" **275.00**

Sauce dish, underplate, green, yellow roses, blue mark **45.00**

Tea tile, peach and tan, greenish white snowballs, RM over faint blue mark **165.00**

Vase, 6" h, crystalline glaze, orange and white................... **45.00**

R. S. Poland

Berry bowl, 4-1/2" sq, white and pale orange floral design, green leaves, small orange-gold border flowers, marked **45.00**

Creamer, soft green, chain of violets, applied fleur-de-lis feet, RM **110.00**

Dresser set, glossy, pink roses, pr 6-1/4" h candlesticks, 5" h hatpin holder, 13" x 9" tray **425.00**

Flower holder, pheasants, brass frog insert **675.00**

Vase

8-1/2" h, 4-3/4" d, large white and tan roses, shaded brown and green ground **195.00**

12" h, 6-1/4" d, white poppies, cream shaded to brown ground, pr **750.00**

E. S. Germany, double-handled urn mounted on conforming porcelain squared pillar, pale green to light yellow body, hand-painted gilt accents, oval portrait panels of women, marked "Prov. Saxe E.S. Germany," wear, chip on base of urn, 17-1/2" total height, $275. Photo courtesy of Sanford Alderfer Auction Company.

R.S. Prussia covered biscuit jar, decorated with pink flowers; R.S. Prussia bowl decorated with pink flowers, daisies and stream, molded scalloped rim, damaged at rim, 11" d, $200. Photo courtesy of Joy Luke Auctions.

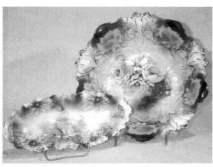

R.S. Prussia bowl decorated with pink and yellow roses, molded iris border, 10-1/2" d, matching two-handled dish with molded poppy border, 9-1/4" l, **$250.** Photo courtesy of Joy Luke Auctions.

R. S. Prussia

Bowl, cov, delicate handles, white ground, pink roses, gold tracery 190.00

Bowl

10-1/2" d, carnation mold, white, peach shading, Tiffany carnations, pink roses dec, satin finish, RM 595.00

11" d, white satin finish, swans, red mark 350.00

Butter dish, cov, porcelain insert, cream and gold shading, pink roses, raised enamel, RM 715.00

Cake set, 9-1/2" d plate, six 7" d plates, carnation mold, pale greens, Tiffany carnations, pink and white rose dec, RM 995.00

Celery tray, 9" l, gold and lavender, roses, bar mark.............350.00

Chocolate pot, cov, green and yellow luster, pink flowers 325.00

Creamer, floral 225.00

R. S. Prussia, plate, three swimming swans decoration, 9" d, **$250.** Photo courtesy of Joy Luke Auctions.

R. S. Prussia, dresser tray, pink and apricot roses, white daisies, two handles, 7-1/2" w, 11-1/2" l, **$100.** Photo courtesy of Joy Luke Auctions.

Demitasse cup and saucer, dainty flowers...................100.00

Ferner, 7" d, mold 876, florals on purple and green ground, unsgd.....165.00

Hair receiver, green lilies of the valley, white ground, RM 95.00

Milk pitcher, 5" h, Morning Glory mold, pink carnations dec..........200.00

Mustard pot, white, light blue and multicolored tiny roses 150.00

Plate, 11" d, Carnation mold, white, peach shading, Tiffany carnations, satin finish, slight wear to gilt.......250.00

Portrait vase, 9" h, double handles, mottled pink and blue ground, gilt flowers, portrait medallion of young lady with falling snow, red mark, wear 2,235.00

Spoon holder, 14" l, pink and white roses 200.00

Syrup, cov, underplate, green and yellow luster, pink flowers 125.00

Tankard, 11" h, Carnation mold, white, allover pink poppies, Tiffany carnations, satin finish, RM 1,100.00

Toothpick holder, green shadows, pink and white roses, jeweled, six feet, RM 250.00

Vase, 4-3/8" h, 2-5/8" d, Pheasant scene, handle, Mold 918......500.00

R. S. Suhl

Coffee set, 9" h, coffeepot, creamer, sugar, six cups and saucers, figural scenes dec, some marked "Angelica Kauffmann" 1,750.00

Pin tray, 4-1/2" d, round, Nightwatch 375.00

Plate, 6-3/4" d, cherubs dec....90.00

Powder dish, cov, Nightwatch, green shading 425.00

Vase, 8" h, four pheasants, green mark 275.00

R. S. Tillowitz

Bowl, 7-3/4" d, slanted sides, open handles, four leaf-shaped feet, matte finish, pale green ground, roses and violets, gold flowered rim, marked 125.00

Creamer and sugar, soft yellow and salmon roses 65.00

Plate, 6-1/2" d, mixed floral spray, gold beading, emb rim, brown wing mark 120.00

Relish tray, 8" l, oval, hp, shaded green, white roses, green leaves, center handle, blue mark 45.00

Tea set, stacking teapot, creamer, and sugar, yellow, rust, and blue flowers, gold trim, ivory ground, marked "Royal Silesia," green mark in wreath ...95.00

Vase, 10" h, pheasants, brown and yellow, two curved handles 125.00

SCHNEIDER GLASS

History: Brothers Ernest and Charles Schneider founded a glassworks at Epiney-sur-Seine, France, in 1913. Charles, the artistic designer, previously had worked for Daum and Gallé. Robert, son of Charles, assumed art direction in 1948. Schneider moved to Loris in 1962.

Although Schneider made tablewares, stained glass, and lighting fixtures, its best-known product is art glass that exhibits simplicity of design and often has bubbles and streaking in larger pieces. Other styles include cameo-cut and hydrofluoric-acid-etched designs.

For more information, see this book.

Marks: Schneider glass was signed with a variety of script and block signatures, "Le Verre Francais," or "Charder."

Bowl, 14" d, shallow, flared rim, pink, frosted ext. design of lines and circles, ftd base, etched "Schneider" on side of base, scratches to base.......285.00

Compote, 8" d, 3-7/8" h, shallow round bowl, pedestal base, mottled rose pink translucent glass with internal bubbles, shading to dark purple, polished pontil, acid etched "Schneider" on base, light edge wear, minor scratches....300.00

Ewer, 10-3/4" h, elongated spout, mottled purples, pink, yellow, and orange splashes, applied purple handle, bulbed disk foot, acid stamp "France" on base, c1925 ......450.00

Compote, purple and orange, circular flaring top, pedestal base, four applied loop handles, c1925, vase mark, 11-1/4" d, $900. Photo courtesy of Sloan's Auctioneers & Appraisers.

Finger bowl and underplate, 4-1/2" d bowl, 7-1/4" d underplate, mottled red, burnt umber and clear, stamped mark
.... **350.00**

Tazza, 7-5/8" h, shallow white bowl rising to mottled amethyst and blue inverted rim, amethyst double-bulbed stem, disk foot, sgd "Schneider," c1920
.... **865.00**

Vase

3-7/8" h, pale pink squatty body, flared rim, etched textured surface, stylized rays and arched devices, etched "Schneider" on lower side
.... **175.00**

Pitcher, Art Deco, ovoid, carved with stylized orange and violet flowers, shaded matte ground, applied handle and foot of violet glass, etched "Le Verre Francais," 5" d, 10" h, $1,250. Photo courtesy of David Rago Auctions.

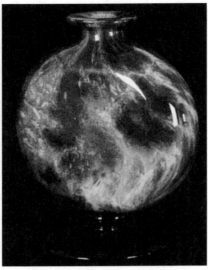

Vase, mottled and swirled brown, orange, amber, and yellow, signed, 10" h, $1,290. Photo courtesy of Fontaine's Auction Gallery.

8" h, cylindrical, mottled brown cameo-etched stylized flowers and foliage, mottled orange ground, pedestal foot, sgd "Charder, Le Verre Francais," c1928, imperfections **700.00**

12" h, gray ground, internal mottling, sgd "Schneider," c1925 ... **950.00**

14" h, tapering cylindrical, baluster neck, orange overlay, five clusters of pendant grapes, geometric pattern cut foot over yellow mottled ground, inset cane at base
.... **650.00**

17-3/4" h, tapered form, incurvate rim, shaded orange overlaid in mottled brown, cameo-etched and cut cascading fruit and leaves, pedestal foot inscribed "Le Verre Francais," polished pontil
.... **1,265.00**

SCIENTIFIC INSTRUMENTS

History: Chemists, doctors, geologists, navigators, and surveyors used precision instruments as tools of their trade. Such objects were well designed and beautifully crafted. They are primarily made of brass; fancy hardwood cases also are common.

The 1990s have seen a keen interest in scientific instruments, both in the auction market and at antique shows. The number of collectors of these mechanical wonders is increasing as more and more interesting examples are being offered.

Barograph, 12" w case, Wilson, Warden & Co., London, No. 4707/44, lacquered brass mechanism, clockwork motor, glazed mahogany case . **215.00**

Cane, gadget type

34" l, field microscope, 1-3/4" d x 2/3" h flat mushroom-shaped walnut handle, silver diamond inlaid initialed "N" for orig owner, handle removes to reveal green felt-lined compartment that holds small brass microscope, mirror base for reflecting light, two small dissecting knife with ivory handle and pr brass tweezers stored inside, 1/2" lined brass dec collar, walnut shaft, 1" white metal ferrule, American, c1850 .... **2,580.00**

36" l, spyglass, 2-1/8" l x 2-1/3" h brass handle, tortoiseshell dec, ebony eyepiece, moveable single drawer adjusts lens for focus, black enameled hardwood shaft, 1" brass ferrule, English, c1890 ... **1,365.00**

Circumferentor, 5-1/4" h, 9" d outside dia., 4-1/8" compass in center, attached to rotating sight vane/vernier arm, inset vial, silvered dial and outer ring, engraved with eight-point star, two outer fixed sight vanes, brass, marked "Dollond London," c1825 .... **1,955.00**

Educational globe, Holbrook's Apparatus Mfg Co., Westerfield, CT, c1860, 3", hinged sphere, colored gores on ext., world maps on int. of Western and Eastern hemispheres, varnish wear, interior lifting ... **2,100.00**

Microscope, compound monocular

12" h, 8-1/2" l, 1-1/8" d, tube with one obj, fine focus on arm, rect stage, five-hole diaphragm, double mirror on rotating arm, extra eyepiece,

Binocular microscope, C. Collins, London, c1875, $1,325. Photo courtesy of Auction Team Breker.

orig case, japanned and lacquered brass, sgd "Wm. H. Armstrong & Co., Indianapolis, Ind.," #11737, c1893 .... **635.00**

13-1/4" h, 9" l, 1-1/2" d single nosepiece tube with 3-1/2" d stage, condenser and double mirror revolve on arms centered on stage, against graduated vertical circular silvered dial, four obj. and three eyepieces, lacquered brass, case, marked "14668, Pat. Oct 13, 1885" **1,840.00**

15-1/2" h, 10-1/2" l, 1-1/4" d tube with single nosepiece, fine focus on front of tube, 4-1/2" d stage, two sub-stage condenses, double mirror, detachable parabolic mirror, extra 8" l, 1-1/8" d draw tube, detachable stand condenser lens with "B" holder, prism eyepiece, two obj., two eyepieces, lacquered brass, orig case, marked "Tolles Boston, 272," c1875 .... **2,275.00**

Octant, 10-7/8", Riggs & Bro., Philadelphia, ebony, ivory inlaid signature panel, scale with brass trim **550.00**

Palmer's computing scale, 8-1/2" d computing wheel on 11-1/4" sq outer scale, instructions on reverse, one fixed and one rotating logarithmic scale, values and gauge points numbered and noted, red, yellow, gold, and black, marked "Aaron Palmer, 1843 patent" **550.00**

Patent revolving interest table, 7-3/4" sq, C. M. Riley, Cincinnati, Ohio, twin revolving discs for calculating interest on prices, card folder with marbled cover, inscribed "1839 Cost $1.00" **575.00**

Recording device, 9" d, sgd "La Ledoise, Lede," circular nickeled case,

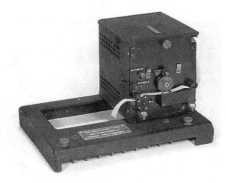

Printer of Engima cipher machine, $32,000. Photo courtesy of Auction Team Breker.

Replica of first mechanical calculator, by Blaise Pascal, Paris, 1652, $11,500. Photo courtesy of Auction Team Breker.

twin recording dish, fitted mahogany case...................... **150.00**

Refractometer, 13" h, Zeiss, No. 4255, arc, vernier, and rack-and-pinion adjustment, mahogany case... **260.00**

Sextant, nautical, 8-3/4" h, brass, black paint, two eye pieces, seven colored lenses, wooden handle, engraved "N. Beck Pedersen, Arendal," minor wear **495.00**

Sketching case, 10-1/2" l, 7" w, 4-1/2" x 6-1/8" plotting surface, 5" d graduated plotting scale, 2" l rotating trough compass, two paper rollers, varnished hardwood and lacquered brass, marked "W. & L. E. Gurley, Troy, N.Y., patented Sept 28, 1897" **750.00**

Solar time piece, 23" h, Timby's, by L. H. Whiting, Saratoga Springs, New York, No. 236, 6" terrestrial globe by Gilman Joslin, Boston, 1860, 24-hour ring divided 1-12-1-12, single train movement, upright architectural walnut case, torn instruction sheet in transit case, lacking finial.......... **4,890.00**

Spectrascope, 9" h, by Heele, Berlin, lacquered brass body tubes, cast iron stand **245.00**

Telescope

5-7/8" l open, 1-3/4" d, brass mounts, shagreen, embossed scrolling foliage on leather draw, E. Nairne, London, first quarter 19th C **550.00**

20-1/4" l, brass and leather, one draw, engraved "G. Young & Co. London Day & Night," England, 19th C, replaced leather .. **400.00**

Terrestrial globe

18-1/2" h, Hammond, 9", brass meridian circle, printed horizon ring, oxidized brass tripod stand **320.00**

29" h, Leipzig, by Pavel Rath and Professor A. Krause, 13" d, Empire-style ebonized stand with gilt Greek key border, early 20th C **750.00**

SCRIMSHAW

History: Norman Flayderman defined scrimshaw as "the art of carving or otherwise fashioning useful or decorative articles as practiced primarily by whalemen, sailors, or others associated with nautical pursuits." Many collectors expand this to include the work of Eskimos and French POWs from the War of 1812.

Reproduction Alert: The biggest problem in the field is fakes, although there are some clues to spotting them. A very hot needle will penetrate the common plastics used in reproductions but not the authentic material. Ivory will not generate static electricity when rubbed, plastic will. Patina is not a good indicator; it has been faked by applying tea or tobacco juice, burying in raw rabbit hide, and in other ingenious ways. Usually the depth of cutting in an old design will not be consistent since the ship rocked and tools dulled; however, skilled forgers have even copied this characteristic.

Box, 2-1/4" d, 2" h, circular, engraved and stained, whaling scene, large whale surrounded by compass positions, late 19th C **225.00**

Busk

12-3/8" l, bone, scratch carved eagle, pinwheels, vining foliage, compass stars, and heart at top, black coloring with red in eagle's shield and one flower, small chip at top.................... **550.00**

Corset busk, engraved whale bone, complex geometric designs of pinwheel, potted flower, steepled church flying American flag, tree of life, island with palm trees, American, old patina, tight interior age line, 1-1/2" w, 14" l, $965. Photo courtesy of Cowan's Historic Americana Auctions.

13-7/8" l, wood, dec with eagle, shield, lovebirds, and ship under sail, heart and foliate devices, inscribed "GC & EW," dated 1840 .... **345.00**

Cribbage board, carved walrus tusk, late 19th C

11" l, carved in relief with Northwest fish and sea life, polychrome dec **360.00**

23" l, carved on both sides, obverse, board in floral dec panel flanked by scenes of Northwest animals and fish, reverse with scenes of life in Northwest region, minor age splits **475.00**

Domino box, 6-7/8" l, bone and wood, shoe form, pierced carved slide top with star and heart dec, domino playing pcs, Prisoner of War, 19th C, cracks, minor insect damage........ **520.00**

Game box, 5-3/4" x 6-1/2", bone, pierced carved box with geometric dec, three slide tops, compartmented int., backgammon and other playing pcs, traces of paint dec, Prisoner of War, 19th C, repair, warping to tops, very minor loses **690.00**

Jagging wheel, 7-1/4" l, dec with building flying American flag, berried vines, 19th C, very minor losses **520.00**

Obelisk, 13-3/8" h, inlaid mahogany, inlaid with various exotic woods, abalone and ivory in geometric and star motifs, 19th C, minor losses, minute cracks **815.00**

Paperweight, 3-1/8" l, carved block, inked caribou, salmon, and insect motifs, Intuit **325.00**

Salt horn, 5-1/2" l, engraved "John Snow March...1780 by S. H.," crosshatched borders enclosing reserve of ship, geometric, and foliate devices, insect damage **460.00**

Powder horn, engraved "HCNRV + RRWN, SALVACC, RISH HARBOR 1807," butt carved in half-round and sealed with black, tar-like substance, 16" l on the curve, old replacement leather thong, $375. Photo courtesy of James D. Julia Auctions.

Seam rubber, 4" l, whalebone, geometric designs on handle, traces of orig paint, 19th C **850.00**

Snuff box, 5" l, horn, architectural and marine motifs, dated "AD 1853" and "William Sandilands Plumber," English **950.00**

Swift, 16" h, all whale bone and ivory, copper pegs, yarn ties, nicely turned detail, pincushion socket on top, age cracks, minor edge damage, possible replaced section............ **900.00**

Walrus tusk

17-3/4" h, reserves of animals, courting couples, ships under sail, memorials, sailors and armaments, later engraved brass presentation caps, "Presented by George M. Chase to Ike B. Dunlap Jan. 25th 1908," cracks, one restored, pr **2,530.00**

18-7/8" l, walrus, dec with two eagles, lady, Indian, and vulture, age cracks, 19th C **1,840.00**

Watch hutch, 11-7/8" h, bone, pierce carved floral and figural dec, brass backing, polychrome foliate highlights, Prisoner of War, 19th C, custom-made case, minor cracks, losses, repairs **750.00**

Whale's tooth, 19th C

4-3/8" l, dec with ship, woman resting on anchor holding flag, two

Rum horn, American, Federal period, 5" w rum keg fashioned from cow horn, 4" flat walnut plugs in each end, held in place by small iron tacks, wood stopper at top with two iron staples on each side of spout, spout section is decorated with four concentric inscribed circles, each end engraved with single line and scalloped edge dec, both sides have scrimshaw five-point stars, shading and set within single line circle, one side with star flanked by initials "W" and "T," other has date "1808" inscribed above, scrimshaw sawtooth design on bottom, $1,035. Photo courtesy of James D. Julia Auctions.

potted plants, chips, minor cracks, 19th C................. **690.00**

5-1/2" h, finely engraved, sailing ship *Ceres* and light house on one side, large eagle with shield, barrels, and banner marked "E. Pluribus Unum" over detailed panel of women holding anchor on other side, sgd "E. M. Chandler," good patina............... **10,725.00**

6-1/4" l, portrait of gentleman and lighthouse, Lady Liberty holding globe and shield surmounted by vines, billowing flag, and angel on reverse, red and black decoration, inscribed "Warren," 19th C **2,350.00**

6-5/8" h, historic landmarks, dec on both sides, very minor cracks and chips **865.00**

6-7/8" h, various ships under sail and young lady, cracks...... **1,380.00**

Whimsey, 5-3/4" h, carved bone, French soldier sharpening his sword on grinding wheel, Prisoner of War, 19th C, minor paint wear **4,715.00**

SEVRES

History: The principal patron of the French porcelain industry in early 18th-century France was Jeanne Antoinette Poisson, Marquise de Pompadour. She supported the Vincennes factory of Gilles and Robert Dubois and their successors in their attempt to make soft-paste porcelain in the 1740s. In 1753, she moved the porcelain operations to Sevres, near her home, Chateau de Bellevue.

The Sevres soft-paste formula used sand from Fontainebleau, salt, saltpeter, soda of alicante, powdered alabaster, clay, and soap. Many famous colors were developed, including a cobalt blue. Such famous decorators as Watteau, La Tour, and Boucher painted the wonderful scenic designs on the ware. In the 18th century, Sevres porcelain was the world's foremost diplomatic gift.

For more information, see this book.

In 1769, kaolin was discovered in France, and a hard-paste formula was developed. The baroque gave way to rococo, a style favored by Jeanne du Barry, Louis XV's next mistress. Louis XVI took little interest in Sevres, and many factories began to turn out counterfeits. In 1876, the factory was moved to St. Cloud and was eventually nationalized.

Marks: Louis XV allowed the firm to use the "double L" in its marks.

Reproduction Alert.

Box, cov

2-1/2" l, 1-1/4" w, 1-1/2" h, oval, cobalt blue ground, panels of putti dec, sgd "JB," chip on base **425.00**

7" l, 4-1/2" w, 3-1/4" h, oval, hp, hinged lid, opalescent cranberry ground, gilt roses and scrolls, lid with painted scene of woman and putti, sgd "E. Carelle," int. dec with polychrome floral panels . . . **650.00**

Bud vase, 6" h, gilt ground, enamel Art Nouveau stylized leaf and flower design, printed mark **635.00**

Bust, 13" h, Marie Antoinette, bisque bust, gilt highlights, cobalt blue ground, molded porcelain socle with central garland and monogram, 19th C . **650.00**

Café au lait cup and saucer, 6" h, ftd cup, cobalt blue enameled ground, gilt eagle roundel and torcheres, corresponding molded saucer, early 20th C **200.00**

Candelabra, pr, 30" h, porcelain urn, figure in landscape, fruit-filled cartouches, blue ground, candle nozzles and flowers, two handles cast with putti and floral dec, bronze mounts, worn gilt trim **5,250.00**

Centerpiece, 20-1/4" h, four youths in procession, each supporting basket, mounted on freeform base, white biscuit, imp mark, early 20th C . . **320.00**

Clock and garniture, painted porcelain and ormolu, 21" h Louis XVI-style clock, two-train half-strike movement, dial enamel dec with swags, shaped case, front painted with scene of Cupid and Venus, lower left sgd "Petit," pair of 21" h associated five-light candelabra, rocaille scrolled candle arms, central nozzle with rocaille finial, baluster stem, shaped foot painted to front with Cupid, early 20th C **2,990.00**

Cup and saucer

Cylindrical 2-7/8" h cup, central painted roundel of courting couple

Plate, painted in pate-sur-pate, profile of druid's head, sickle behind, enamel painted border of white and green mistletoe, green ground, gilded pattern, brown Sevres stamp mark, 1911, also monogrammed "H.B.," 8-1/2" d, $2,070. Photo courtesy of David Rago Auctions.

by river, jeweled surround, rim with gilded and jeweled garland and lappet design, saucer with matching border, central scene of two maidens, late 19th C . **1,495.00**

Cylindrical 3" h cup, cobalt blue ground, painted roundel depicting an 18th century couple playing with dog, gilt tooled surround, saucer with floral painted center, blue border with floral cartouches, late 19th C **815.00**

Display tray, 14-5/8" h, round, short gilt handles, cobalt blue rim with rocaille scrolls, center painted with scene of courting couple, sgd E. Roy, early 20th C **400.00**

Sevres-type, pair of urns, ivory ground, oval cartouche of courting scenes, gilt accent decoration, ormolu mounts, 18" h, $450. Photo courtesy of Sanford Alderfer Auction Company.

Figure, 8-1/2" h, pair in Elizabethian dress, royal blue ground, gold accents, early **640.00**

Ginger jar, 12" h, blue flambé, ormolu mounts, pr **2,000.00**

Lamp base, electrified, 28" h, cov urn, pink ground, body painted with central cartouche depicting old woman teaching a little girl to dance, lower right sgd "F. Yogt" in gilt surround, further allover gilt rococo scrollwork, late 19th C **5,175.00**

Patch box, cov, 3-1/4" l, shaped ovoid, green ground, hinged lid with hand painted scene of Napoleon on horseback, sgd lower right "Morin" **250.00**

Plaque, 10-1/2" l, 9-5/8" w oval format, Marie Antoniette, mauve gown, blue celeste border with gilt scrollwork, 10-3/4" x 13-5/8" giltwood and crème painted frame, late 19th C **550.00**

Portrait plate, 9" d, Lobelia portrait, surrounded by wreath, cobalt blue band border with gilt dec including Napoleonic crest and crowns, mounted in shadow box frame, gilt loss . . **150.00**

Tazza, 11-1/2" d, blue flambé, ormolu mounts **350.00**

Tray, 18-1/2" x 13", six-sided oblong form, French allegorical park scene, ladies with parasols, Florentine gilt border, sgd "Bertien" **525.00**

Vase, covered, gilt metal mounts, white ground, one side has musical instruments with flowers, other side with cherubs and flowers, two rams head ormolu handles, decorated ormolu base, blue Sevres mark and "France" on cover, finial missing, mounts loose, 13" h, $575. Photo courtesy of James D. Julia, Inc.

Urn

13" h, artist sgd scene of young lovers, bronze mounts, c1900 .... **460.00**

19" h, allegorical painting, sgd "E. Grisard," bronze satyr heads on body, 19th C **1,950.00**

Vase, 11" h, pink ground, oval cartouches with figural landscapes and ornaments, metal mount, pr .. **1,380.00**

Wine cooler, 10-1/4" h, Louis XVI style, circular tapering form, top section with gilded ram's heads over reeded band, base dec with ribboned garlands and entwined laurel, multicolored, white ground **2,300.00**

SEWING ITEMS

History: As recently as 50 years ago, a wide variety of sewing items were found in almost every home in America. Women of every economic and social status were skilled in sewing and dressmaking.

Iron or brass sewing birds, one of the interesting convenience items that developed, was used to hold cloth (in the bird's beak) while sewing. They could be attached to a table or shelf with a screw-type fixture. Later models included a pincushion.

Additional Listings: *Warman's Americana & Collectibles* for more examples.

Bodkins, whalebone and ivory, sealing wax inlaid scribe lines, 19th C, minor losses, nine-pc set **400.00**

Book, *Fleisher's Knitting & Crocheting Manual*, S. B. & B. W. Fleisher, Inc., Philadelphia, PA, 1924, 112 pgs, 7" x 9-1/2", 21st edition **15.00**

Catalog, E. Butterick & Co., New York, NY, 1878, 32 pgs, 7-1/2" x 10", Catalog for Fall of Women's Clothing Patterns **38.00**

Folder, 8-3/4" x 14-1/4", Wm. R. Moore Dry Goods Co., Memphis, TN, three pgs, c1937, heavy weight, "Guaranteed Fast Color No. 10 Batfast Suitings," 10 tipped-in blue Batfast Suiting swatches, 19-1/4" x 2" colored swatches tipped in **28.00**

Etui, 3-1/2" l, tapered ovoid agate case, ormolu mounts, hinged lid, fitted interior with scissors, knife, pen, ruler, needle, pincers, and spoon, Continental, late 18th/early 19th C **700.00**

Hand book, Davis Sewing Machine Co., Watertown, NY, *Centennial Hand Book Presented at the Great Exhibition*, 12 pgs, directions to get around at Exhibition, info. on sewing machine, cabinets, etc. **65.00**

Instruction book, *Singer Sewing Machines No. 99*, c1910, 32 pgs, 3-1/2" x 5-1/4" **16.00**

Magazine, *Home Needlework Magazine*, Florence Publishing Co., Florence, MA, 176 pgs, 1899, Vol. 1, No. 2, April **20.00**

Needle book, Rocket Gold Tipped Needles, cov illus of man and woman riding needle shaped like rocket, nighttime sky background, marked "Made in Japan," 1940s **10.00**

Needle case, tri-color 18kt gold, chase and engraved geometric and floral motifs, European hallmark **320.00**

Pin cushion

Half Doll, cotton skirt, marked "Germany," c1920 .... **40.00**

Velvet, blue and cream velvet pin cushion with elaborate beaded dec on top, white beaded loops on each of four sides, mounted on clear glass pedestal base.. **195.00**

Sewing box

5-1/2" w, 3-1/2" d, 3-1/4" h, inlaid hearts, arrows, diamonds, and circles, one dovetailed drawer, turned pull, worn pin cushion top, minor edge damage at corner **275.00**

Flax wheel, oak, appears to have all of its attachments, 37" h to top of wheel, **$175.** *Photo courtesy of James D. Julia, Inc.*

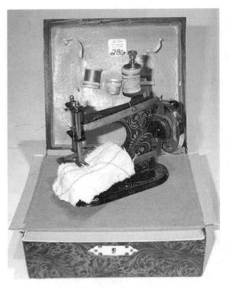

Sewing machine, toy, tin, threads and needles in wooden box, **$275.** *Photo courtesy of Joy Luke Auctions.*

12-1/4" w, 7-1/4" d, 5-5/8" h, mahogany inlaid, hinged lid, center inlaid oval reserve with shell motif, ext. with inlaid borders and corners, int. lid centered with diamond motif, lift-out tray with several compartments, America, 19th C, minor imperfections **998.00**

17-1/4" l, 11-1/2" w, 5-3/4" h, lacquered, ext. dec with Chinoiserie scenic panels surrounded by mosaic patterns, Greek key border, brass bail handles on each side, int. with mirrored lid, fitted compartments, single fitted drawer, Chinese Export, 19th C, minor wear and crackling **470.00**

Sewing chest, connected diamonds and floral borders in ivory, stone, and steel micro mosaic inlay, numerous fitted compartments and inlay lids on int., Indian, early 19th C, minor losses **700.00**

Sewing machine, child's, Betsy Ross, green metal machine, leather-looking case, 1949 .... **95.00**

Spinning wheel

34-1/2" h, upright, hardwoods, turned posts, iron fly wheel, ivory and ebonized wood details, old mellow refinishing, treadle with dec carving, old repair to cord belt **450.00**

Tape measure, chariot and rider, celluloid made to imitate bronze, 1-3/4" h, $225. Photo courtesy of Julie Robinson.

35" h, upright, hardwoods, turned posts, wood and wire fly wheel, small turned ivory pegs alternating with wheel spokes, traces of black paint on wheel, base, and legs, German, worm holes, some edge damage, one finial glued, two spokes damaged **295.00**

38" h, upright, cherry, mellow refinishing, small ivory buttons, turned legs, tripod base, 9-1/2" d wheel, single flyer **350.00**

Stand, 12-3/4" h, carved and turned walnut, the round, four-tiered, graduated stand, pin cushion mounted on top, two rotating discs, each having six ivory spool holders, four ivory ball feet, New England, mid-19th C . **300.00**

Tape loom, 39-1/2" h, standing, floor type, turned wormy maple post, oak step down, cross bar base, loom pegged into post, replacements to loom and base **150.00**

Tape measure, advertising

General Electric Refrigerator, black and white beehive-style refrigerator on dark blue background, light blue rim, black and white name and text for local distributor on back **20.00**

Kiwanis Club, blue and white celluloid canister printed on both sides, one side with international emblem, "We Build" on reverse **15.00**

Lydia E. Pinkham, pale brown and white celluloid canister, sepia portrait of Lydia on one side, reverse with Vegetable Compound Blood Medicine tonics line . . **25.00**

Parisian Novelty Co., celluloid canister printed in blue, white ground, both sides with text promoting celluloid novelties **35.00**

Pillsbury's Family of Foods, celluloid canister, red, white, and blue flour sack printed on white, blue rim **25.00**

Tape measure, figural, owl, metal, German **45.00**

Thimble, brass, fancy band design **15.00**

Thimble holder, 5-3/4" h, fisherman holding large rod, beautifully detailed large fish on ground, bucket by fish, post in front of fisherman, rect base, marked "Miller Silver Co. Silver Plate" **350.00**

Thread cabinet

Clarks, white lettering, four drawers, some damage to case **100.00**

Dexter Fine Yarn, oak, four drawers, 18-3/4" h, 18-5/8" w, 16" d . **650.00**

Merrick's Spool Cotton, oak, cylindrical, curved glass, 18" d, 22" h **725.00**

Willimantic, four drawers, ornate Eastlake style case, 14-1/4" h **550.00**

Yarn or cord winder, 28" w, 16-1/4" d, 29-1/2" h, enameled steel and brass works, mahogany platform base, turned feet, signature plate "Goodbrand & Co. Ltd., Makers, Staleybridge" **550.00**

SHAKER

History: The Shakers, so named because of a dance they used in worship, are one of the oldest communal organizations in the United States. Mother Ann Lee, who emigrated from England and established the first Shaker community near Albany, New York, in 1784, founded this religious group. The Shakers reached their peak in 1850, when there were 6,000 members.

Shakers lived celibate and self-sufficient lives. Their philosophy stressed cleanliness, order, simplicity, and economy. Highly inventive and motivated, the Shakers created many utilitarian household forms and objects. Their furniture reflected a striving for quality and purity in design.

In the early 19th century, the Shakers produced many items for commercial purposes. Chairmaking and the packaged herb and seed business thrived. In every endeavor and enterprise, the members followed Mother Ann's advice: "Put your hands to work and give your heart to God."

Apothecary cabinet, 66" x 14", stained wood, rect, front fitted with 12 small drawers, molded white glazed porcelain handles, identification labels, drawer sides inscribed with various content titles, New England, 19th C **450.00**

Basket, 12" x 12" x 4-3/8" h, finely woven splint, sq shape, two delicate bentwood handles, minor damage, traces of old red stain **360.00**

Blanket chest, 40-1/2" w, 18-1/2" d, 36" h, New Lebanon, NY, 1830-40, hinged rect breadboard lift top, nail construction well, two long scratch beaded drawers, tapering cut-out feet, allover later grain paint to simulate exotic wood, old replaced pulls, surface imperfections **1,265.00**

Bonnet, dark brown palm and straw, black ribbons, 9" flounce, KY . . **395.00**

Book, *How the Shakers Cook & the Noted Cooks of the Country, Feature the Chefs and Their Cooking Recipes*, A. J. White, New York, NY, 1889, 50 pgs, 3-3/8" x 6-1/8", bust of men illus, dusted, chips **15.00**

Bottle, 9" h, aqua, emb "Shaker Pickles," base labeled "Portland, Maine, E.D.P. & Co." **90.00**

Box, cov, bentwood

5-1/2" w, 3-1/2" d, 2-1/8" h, finger construction, two fingers on base, one finger on lid, copper tacks, old green repaint, some wear on lid **850.00**

6-1/8" w, 4" w, 2" h, finger construction, two fingers on base, one finger on lid, brass tacks, old green (black) repaint over traces of earlier green, minor wear . . **690.00**

Butter churn, old red paint, strap hinges, $380.

7-1/2" w, 5-1/8" d, 2-1/2" h, finger construction, two fingers on base, one finger on lid, copper tacks, reddish stain **320.00**

9-1/2" w, 7" d, 3-3/4" h, finger construction, two fingers on base, one finger on lid, copper tacks, old blue paint, some wear . . . **1,400.00**

12" w, 8-3/8" d, 4-3/4" h, oval, Harvard lap, copper tacks, mellow natural finish, remnants of paper label on one end **440.00**

Box, cov, domed lid, 25-1/2" w, 15-1/2" d, 15-1/4" h, attributed to Hancock community, pine, divided interior, dovetailed drawer, compartment at both ends of lid with sliding covers, old age splits in lid, refinished **550.00**

Carrier

9-1/4" l, 6-3/4" w, 8" h, oval, maple, three lapped fingers, swing handle, copper tacks, number "5" impressed on base, clear lacquer finish **425.00**

12-1/2" d, 1" h base, 6" h handle, round, single stapled finger, bentwood handle, some red stain remains, copy of old Currier & Ives hunting print in center, minor splits **250.00**

Chair, dining, 17" h seat, 25" h back, attributed to Canterbury, NH, c1835, birch and pine, concave rect back rail above turned stiles, four spindles, shaped seat, splayed turned tapering legs joined by stretchers, old red stain, missing right side stretcher **825.00**

Chair, side, maple and hickory, old brick red paint, pegged construction, back with three arched slats, high turned finials, turned and tapered posts with eight rungs each, old striped tape seats, minor variations in turnings, old pieced restoration to one leg, 16" h seat, 37-1/4" h, price for set of four **700.00**

Chest of drawers, 63" w, 17-1/2" d, 39-1/2" h, pine, eight graduated dovetailed drawers arranged in two banks of four, turned pulls, six high feet with semi-curved cut-outs, old mellow refinish, replaced back boards, some pulls replaced **14,300.00**

Child's rocker, Mount Lebanon, NY

8-1/2" h seat, 25" h back, No. 0, imp "0" on reverse of top slat, decal on a rocker, cherry, arms, old gold velvet seat, orig varnished surface **1,955.00**

Bench, pine, scrub top with traces of red paint, half moon cut out ends, 27" w x 15" d, 23" h, **$690.** *Photo courtesy of James D. Julia, Inc.*

12" h seat, 28" h back, No. 1, imp "#1" on top slat, "Shaker's Mt. Lebanon" label on bottom slat, orig dark finish, woven paper rush seat, tapering rear posts with turned finials **495.00**

Cloak

Adult's, pink wool, labeled "The Dorothy Shakers, East Canterbury, New Hampshire," c1880-1920 . . . . **1,195.00**

Child's, red wool, labeled "The Dorothy Shakers, East Canterbury, New Hampshire," c1880-1920 . . . . **1,195.00**

Infant's, white wool, pink silk lining, c1880-1920, shattering to lining **595.00**

Dough scraper, 4-1/2" l, wrought iron **40.00**

Flax wheel, 33-1/2" h, various hardwoods, old dark brown finish, stamped "SR. AL," (Deacon Samuel Ring of Alfred, Maine 1784-1848), two pieces of distaff replaced **330.00**

Grain measure, 7-1/2" d, bentwood, stencil label "Shaker Society, Sabbathday Lake, Me," minor edge damage **160.00**

Hanger, 24" w, bentwood, chestnut **65.00**

Oxen muzzle, 14" d, 14-1/2" h, woven splint, New England, mid-19th C, price for pr **2,875.00**

Recipe book, Laura Sarle, Canterbury, Shaker Village, New Hampshire, 1883-87, inscribed by author, recipes, brief autobiography, short play, housekeeping records, knitting instructions, pen and ink on paper, mottled orange cardboard cover with black binding, wear to cover, few random annotations by later hand **5,520.00**

Pantry box, maple and pine, three-finger construction, copper tacks, old pencil inscription on interior of lid with prices, unsigned, old refinishing, 8-1/4" l, 5-1/2" w, **$340.** *Photo courtesy of Cowan's Historic Americana Auctions.*

Rocker, production

No. 5, 17-3/4" h seat, 36" h, Mount Lebanon, NY, c1880, maple, turned stiles with acorn finials joining curved arms, flanking three arched slats over trapezoidal seat, turned legs, joined by double turned stretchers on rockers, vestiges of old stain, top slat stamped "5," imperfections **1,060.00**

No. 6, 16-3/4" h seat, 41" h, Mount Lebanon, NY, late 19th/early 20th C, maple, turned stiles with acorn-form finials, flanking single arched slat, tape back rest joining shaped arms with pommels, tape seat, turned legs joined by double stretchers on rockers, stamped "6" on back of slat, old dark stain, minor surface imperfections **775.00**

Sewing box, cov, 15" l, 11-1/4" w, 11" h including upright handle, oval, pine lid with maple sides and lid rim, swing handle, five lapped fingers, int. lined with light blue padded silk, repair, wear **1,880.00**

Sewing carrier, relined **275.00**

Storage box, cov, 5-1/2" x 10-1/2" x 7-1/2", four-finger lapped box, bittersweet wash, paper label attached to lid int., inscribed "Jennet Angus, Watervliet, 1832" **7,050.00**

Table, 34-3/4" x 35-1/2" x 28", maple, drop leaf, rect top, hinged rect leaves, single drawer, sq tapering legs, first half 19th C **6,500.00**

Table swift, 29-3/4" d extended, 25" h, maple, 19th C **230.00**

Wash tub, 24" d, 16-1/2" h, New England, late 19th C, stave and lap fingered hoop construction, two handles, old red paint, imperfections **460.00**

SHAVING MUGS

c1908

History: Shaving mugs, which hold the soap, brush, and hot water used to prepare a beard for shaving, come in a variety of materials including tin, silver, glass, and pottery. One style, which has separate compartments for water and soap, is the scuttle, so called because of its coal-scuttle shape.

Personalized shaving mugs were made exclusively for use in barbershops in the United Sates. They began being produced shortly after the Civil War and continued to be made into the 1930s.

Unlike shaving mugs that were used at home, these mugs were personalized with the owner's name, usually in gilt. The mug was kept in a rack at the barbershop, and it was used only when the owner came in for a shave. This was done for hygienic purposes, to keep from spreading a type of eczema known as barber's itch.

The mugs were usually made on European porcelain blanks that often contained the mark of "Germany," "France," or "Austria" on the bottom. In later years, a few were made on American-made semi-vitreous blanks. Decorators who worked for major barber supply houses did the artwork on mugs. Occasionally the mark of the barber supply house is also stamped on the bottom of the mug.

After a short time, the mugs became more decorative, including hand-painted floral decorations, as well as birds, butterflies, and a wide variety of nature scenes, etc. These are classified today as "decorative" mugs.

Another category, "fraternal mugs," soon developed. These included the emblem of an organization the owner belonged to, along with his name emblazoned in gold above or below the illustration.

"Occupational mugs" were also very popular. These are mugs that contained a painting of something that illustrated the owner's occupation, such as a butcher, a bartender, or a plumber. The illustration might be a man working at his job, or perhaps the tools of his trade, or a product he made or sold.

Of all these mugs, occupationals are the most prized. Their worth is determined by several factors: rarity (some occupations are rarer than others), size of mug, and size of illustration (the bigger the better), quality of artwork, and condition—although rare mugs with cracks or chips can still be valuable if the damage does not affect the artwork on the mug. Generally speaking, a mug showing a man at work at his job is usually valued higher than that same occupation illustrated with only the tools or finished product.

The invention of the safety razor by King C. Gillette, issued to three

For more information, see this book.

and one-half million servicemen during World War I, brought about changes in personal grooming—men began to shave on their own, rather than visiting the barber shop to be shaved. As a result, the need for personalized shaving mugs declined.

Note: Prices shown are for typical mugs that have no damage and show only moderate wear on the gilt name and decoration.

Fraternal

B.P.O.E., Elks, double emblem, Dr. title
. . . . **300.00**
F.O.E., Fraternal Order of Eagles, eagle holding F.O.E. plaque **260.00**
IB of PM, International Brotherhood of Paper Makers, papermaking machine, clasped hands. **275.00**
I.O.M., International Order of Mechanics, ark ladder. **270.00**
Loyal Knights of America, eagle, flags, six-pointed star **275.00**
Loyal Order of the Moose, gold circle with gray moose head, purple and green floral dec, gilt rim and base, marked "Germany" **220.00**
United Mine Workers, clasped hands emblem flanked by crossed picks and shovels, floral dec, rose garland around top, marked "Germany" **125.00**

Occupational

Baker, detailed hand-painted image of two bakers working at brick oven, automated mixing, kneading, etc. machinery, image worn, name and gold trim very worn, chip on back, 3-7/8" d, 4" h. **170.00**
Electrician, hand-painted image of electrician wiring inside of electrical box, T & V Limoges, France, wear to gold lettering and trim, 3-5/8" d, 3-5/8" h
. . . . **2,500.00**

Indian, hand painted, base marked "Daddy from Junior, Xmas, 1915," green mark "Hutschenreuther Selb Bavaria," $200.

Fabric store, colorful hp shop int., owner waiting on well-dressed woman, gold trim and name, 3-5/8" x 4-1/2"
. . . . **700.00**
General store, pork, flour, and whiskey barrels, Limoges, 4" x 4-3/4" . . . **650.00**
Hotel clerk, clerk at desk, guest signing register **375.00**
House painter, detailed hand-painted image of man painting side of building, marked "Fred Dole" on bottom, light crack mark around top of handle, wear to gold lettering and trim, 3-1/2" d, 3-1/2" h. **350.00**
Magician, detailed hand-painted image of man in suit holding top hat while flying through cloud-filled moon-lit sky, light wear to gold lettering and trim, 3-7/8" d, 3-7/8" h. **275.00**
Mover, detailed hand-painted image of two men in moving van, gold name and trim, Royal China Int'l, 3-7/8" d, 3-5/8"
. . . . **1,400.00**

Right: Florist, hanging wicker flower arrangement, bold red drapery surround, gilt "S. K. Ellis" below, minor wear to gilt edging, unmarked, $90; center: fabric salesman, painted interior of fabric shop with Victorian woman seated at counter while male salesman shows her bolt of fabric, shelving of bolts and gild scrollwork at ends, name "W. A. Bowermaster" in gilt, Vienna mark on base, minor wear to gilt edging, $850; right: Mason, black and brown painted crossed mason's trowel and hammer, gilt laurel wreath surrounds "C. G. Bertholet," minor wear to gilt edging, $275. Photo courtesy of Cowan's Historic Americana Auctions.

Bartender, gold trim, **$295.**

Photographer, detailed hand-colored image of portrait photographer, marked "Webb Bros" in gold, wear to gold lettering and trim, 3-5/8" d, 3-1/2" h **700.00**

Railroad, detailed hand-painted image of two railway workers on hand car, wear to gold lettering and trim, 3-1/2" d, 3-5/8" h **650.00**

Shoemaker, hp, scene of shoemaker in shop, gilt foot and swags around name **225.00**

Trolley repair wagon, horse drawn, scaffolding................ **1,250.00**

Tugboat, boat in water, crew and captain.................... **750.00**

Writer, black desk inkwell with sander, pen, and brass handle **350.00**

Other

Bicycle racer, pink and yellow flowers, gilt banner with "Bicycle Racers Madison Square Garden," trophy with inscription **550.00**

Coronation of H M King Edward VII, 18th May 1937, British seal with monarch, flags on reverse, scuttle **40.00**

Drape and flowers, purple drape, pot of flowers, gold name **85.00**

Fish shape, scuttle, green and brown **75.00**

Horses in storm, white and black horses, copied from painting... **100.00**

Skull, white, gray, black, and cream, scuttle, marked "Bavaria" **135.00**

SHAWNEE POTTERY

History: The Shawnee Pottery Co. was founded in 1937 in Zanesville, Ohio. The company acquired a 650,000-square-foot plant that had previously housed the American Encaustic Tiling Company. Shawnee produced as many as 100,000 pieces of pottery a day until 1961, when the plant closed.

Shawnee limited its production to kitchenware, decorative art pottery, and dinnerware. Distribution was primarily through jobbers and chain stores.

Marks: Shawnee can be marked "Shawnee," "Shawnee U.S.A.," "USA #——," "Kenwood," or with character names, e.g., "Pat. Smiley" and "Pat. Winnie."

Creamer, Smiley Pig, 1940s, marked, **$165.** *Photo courtesy of L & J Antiques & Collectibles.*

Bank, bulldog............... **50.00**
Basket, 9" l, 5-1/2" h at handle, turquoise glaze, relief flowers and leaves, USA 688.............. **45.00**
Batter pitcher, Fern........... **65.00**
Casserole, cov, Corn Queen, large **40.00**
Cookie jar, cov
  Cinderella, unmarked **125.00**
  Cottage, marked "USA 6," 7" h **900.00**
  Drum major, marked "USA 10," 10" h **295.00**
  Jo-Jo the Clown, marked "Shawnee USA, 12," 9" h **300.00**
  Little Chef................. **75.00**
  Muggsy Dog, blue bow, gold trim and decals, marked "Patented Muggsy U.S.A.," 11-3/4" h.. **900.00**
  Owl..................... **110.00**
Creamer
  Elephant................. **25.00**
  Puss n' Boots, green and yellow **65.00**
  Smiley Pig, clover bud...... **165.00**
Figure
  Gazelle................... **45.00**
  Puppy **50.00**
  Squirrel **30.00**
  Rabbit **40.00**

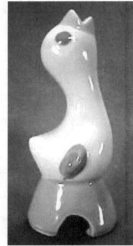

Pie bird, white bird, pink and green accents, made for Pillsbury, late 1940s or early 1950s, 5-1/2" h, **$90.** *Photo courtesy of L & J Antiques & Collectibles.*

Fruit bowl, Corn Queen **25.00**
Mug, Corn King.............. **35.00**
Paperweight, Muggsy **65.00**
Pitcher
  Bo Peep, blue bonnet, yellow dress **125.00**
  Chanticleer............... **75.00**
Planter
  Canopy bed, #734 .... **95.00**
  Gazelle **25.00**
  Horse with hat and cart **20.00**
  Locomotive, black **60.00**
  Mouse and cheese, pink and yellow **25.00**
  Rocking horse, blue **30.00**
  Wheelbarrow **20.00**
Salt and pepper shakers, pr
  Chanticleer, large, orig label . **45.00**
  Dutch Boy and Girl, large.... **55.00**
  Milk cans **30.00**
  Mugsey, small............. **65.00**
  Puss n' Boots, small **30.00**
  Smiley, small............. **30.00**
  Watering cans............. **27.50**
Teapot
  Granny Ann, peach apron .. **125.00**

Plate, King Corn, marked "Shawnee USA Oven-Proof," 10" d, **$50.** *Photo courtesy of L & J Antiques & Collectibles.*

Horseshoe, blue **65.00**
Tom Tom, blue, red, and yellow
. . . . **175.00**
Utility jar, Corn King **50.00**
Wall pocket
  Bird House. **25.00**
  Fern **35.00**

SILHOUETTES

History: Silhouettes (shades) are shadow profiles produced by hollow cutting, mechanical tracing, or painting. They were popular in the 18th and 19th centuries.

The name came from Etienne de Silhouette, a French Minister of Finance, who cut "shades" as a pastime. In America, the Peale family was well known for the silhouettes they made.

Silhouette portraiture lost popularity with the introduction of the daguerreotype prior to the Civil War. In the 1920s and 1930s, a brief revival occurred when tourists to Atlantic City and Paris had their profiles cut as souvenirs.

Marks: An impressed stamp marked "PEALE" or "Peale Museum" identifies pieces made by the Peale family.

3-1/2" h, 2-1/2" w, woman, hair up in bun, green dress with large ruffled sleeves, lace collar, gold pin, antique black molded frame **600.00**

Painted, Daniel Kemper, Revolutionary Wary clothier, 12" x 8" ink silhouette on heavy red textured cardstock, titled in ink "Col. Daniel Kemper. Aug 28-1749-Aug 6 1847 New Brunswick N.J. Bishop Jackson Kemper father," bird's eye maple frame, **$475.** *Photo courtesy of Cowan Historic Americana Auctions.*

4" h, 4" w, gentleman, reverse painted glass with dec oval in gold surrounded by black, gold highlights, antique black molded frame, pencil inscription on back "Parker Emerson," some damage to reverse painting. **90.00**
5-1/4" h, 3-3/4" w, cut-out portrait of matronly woman wearing bonnet, penciled eyelash, reeded frame with black paint and punched brass rosettes, minor edge damage to frame **220.00**
5-1/2" h, 4-1/2" w, hollow cut, gentleman, stenciled frock coat, eglomise glass mat with yellow painted designs, black velvet backing, black painted frame with traces of yellow on outer edge. **475.00**
5-3/4" h, 4-3/8" w, hollow cut, portrait of boy under leafy branch, very faint name underneath, worn gilt frame, fold lines with minor damage **85.00**
5-3/4" h, 4-7/8" w, hollow cut, bust, lady with ornate hat, back marked "Mrs. Norman" and "Mrs. Norman, Henley on Thames," black lacquered case with gilded fittings, wear and stain. . **200.00**
6" h, 5-1/4" w, hollow cut, man and woman, man with high collar, woman with hair comb, black cloth backing, molded gold frame, some foxing of paper, price for pair. **440.00**
6-1/4" h, 5" w, gentleman, hollow cut, old label "G. Saufer, Passe-Portouts, Philadelphia," framed, tears and repair **90.00**
6-3/8" h, 5-3/8" w, young woman, hollow cut, cut detail at collar, pencil inscription "Sarah Sage," stains **200.00**
6-1/2" h, 10" w, man and woman, hollow cut, ink and watercolor details, framed together, sgd "Doyle," eglomise glass mat with two ovals, gilded frame **425.00**
6-5/8" h, 5-1/2" w, man and wife, hollow cut, ink details, rosewood veneer frames, pr **580.00**
7-1/2" x 10-1/4", Emily and Rosa, two girls playing, hand painted detailing, 1838. . . . . **600.00**
7-5/8" h, 9-1/2" w, boy and girl, full length, standing facing each other, hollow cut, gilt detail, bird's eye veneer ogee frame **725.00**
8" h, 7" w, husband, wife, baby on knee, grandparents, two children, hollow cut, watercolor and pencil details, black cloth backing, paper professionally cleaned, orig bird's eye maple frames, turned dark wood buttons on corner blocks, five-pc set. **9,975.00**

8-1/2" x 7-1/2", girl with flower basket, jumping dog, titled "Miss Montague" **250.00**
9-3/4" x 7", full length, young gentleman, Augt. Edouart, fecit Saratoga Springs, Aug. 1844, sgd and dated lower left, cut and laid down on lithographed background, matted and framed, tears, minor stain, toning **520.00**
10" x 9-3/8", Mrs. Rosanna Lamb, full length, sgd and dated "Aug.st Edouart fecit 1842 Boston U.S.," cut-out paper figure laid down on paper, graphite, ink, and watercolor genre scene in background, sitter identified in note affixed to reverse, framed, toning, staining. **450.00**
14-3/4" x 33-1/2", Thomas Lamb family, Boston, MA, 1842, Mr. And Mrs. Lamb in single images, four children, Emily, William Eliot, Charles Duncan, Margy Eliot, 17th Jan'ry 1842, in group, one of Mrs. Lamb's brother, Frank Eliot, images framed in manner to reveal signatures on reverse, by August Edouart, gallery labels of Arthur Vernay, NY, matted, eglomise liner and gilt frame . **1,250.00**

SILVER

History: The natural beauty of silver lends itself to the designs of artists and craftsmen. It has been mined and worked into an endless variety of useful and decorative items. Pure silver is too soft to be fashioned into strong, durable, and serviceable utensils. Therefore, a way was found to give silver the required degree of hardness by adding alloys of copper and nickel.

Silversmithing in America goes back to the early 17th century in Boston and New York and the early 18th century in Philadelphia. Boston artisans were influenced by the English styles, New Yorkers by the Dutch.

Additional Listings: See Silver Flatware in *Warman's Americana & Collectibles* for more examples.

American, 1790-1840
Mostly coin

Coin silver is slightly less pure than sterling silver. Coin silver has 900 parts silver to 100 parts alloy. Sterling silver has 925 parts silver. American silversmiths followed the coin standards. Coin silver is also called Pure Coin, Dollar, Standard, or Premium.

Beaker, 3" h, 3" d, top and bottom molded rims, engraved, minor dents, Anthony Rasch, Philadelphia, 1807, 4 troy oz **490.00**
Cake server, 9-1/8" l, George C. Shreve, late 19th C, mark partially rubbed, shaped blade engraved with

American, bowl by Theodore B. Starr, New York, c1916, hammered, engraved presentation in scrolled cruciform, impressed marks on base, small dent, 20 troy oz, 7-1/2" d, 4" h, **$375.** *Photo courtesy of Skinner Auctioneers and Appraisers.*

harbor scene within foliate cartouche, unfurling flag, engine-turned ground, fitted case, 3 troy oz **200.00**

Coffee spoon, John David Jr., Philadelphia, PA, 1795-99, made for Cooch family, monogrammed, one with damage, dents, wear, 5-1/4" l, price for set of eight, 4 troy oz **1,035.00**

Creamer, 6" h, ewer form, beaded detailing, marked "RH" **2,750.00**

Cup, 2-1/2" h, scroll handle, geometric banding at top and bottom, engraved sun motif, inscribed "Awarded by the S.C.A.S. (Southern Central Agriculture Society) & Mechanical Ins of Georgia, Oct 19th, 1852, for the best half dozen pair of Brogan Shoes, marked "Pure Silver Coin, J. E. Caldwell & Co., Phila" **1,320.00**

American, candlesticks, pair by Gorham, Greek key design around base, mounted on square black and white veined Italian marble bases, 7-3/4" h, **$325.** *Photo courtesy of Cowan's Historic Americana Auctions.*

Dessert spoon, William Hollingshead, Philadelphia, PA, 1754-85, marked "WH" in shaped stamp, twice on each handle, engraved "KIS," wear to bowls, imperfections, price for set of five, 9 troy oz **490.00**

Ewer, 12" h, ftd, repoussé vintage dec, vine form handle extending round shoulder and around base of both pieces, engraved, minor dents, William F. Ladd, New York City, 1828-45 . . . . **1,200.00**

Ewer and tray, 9-1/4" h ewer, 11-1/4" d tray, Jones, Ball & Poor, Boston, c1845, bulbous ewer with molded rim, neck band, body vertically reeded, stepped circular foot, circular tray with molded rim, face with engraved foliates, modified, both monogrammed . . **550.00**

Forks, 7-3/4" l, stem with applied medallion profile roundel of young woman, engraved details, 11 troy oz, eight-pc set **690.00**

Goblet, 6-1/2" h and 6-3/4" h, Simon Chaudron, Philadelphia, PA, 1812-15, marked "Chaundron" in banner, floriform, raised flutes at base of bowls, applied foliate band on bases, price for pr, 16 troy oz **3,750.00**

Jug, 7" h, J. B. Jones & Co. makers, 2nd quarter 19th C, inverted pear-shaped body, scroll handle and stepped neck, round stepped foot, name engraved under spout, 12 troy oz **700.00**

Knives, 8-1/8" l, third quarter 19th C, medallion profile roundel to end of handle, engraved handle and blade, monogrammed on reverse, 14 troy oz, nine-pc set **920.00**

Mug, 4" h, John L. Westervelt, Newburgh, NY maker, mid-19th C, cylindrical, fine beading to foot and rim, scroll handle, central cartouche

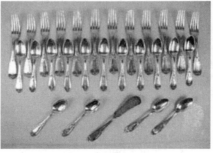

Coin silver, flatware by N. Harding & Co., 12 7-1/2" forks, 15 6" teaspoons and 7-1/2" master butter, monogrammed, 35 troy oz, **$495.** *Photo courtesy of James D. Julia, Inc.*

engraved with name and dated 1863, engraved Greek key border, allover engine turned ground, 6 troy oz **200.00**

Pitcher, 8" h, mid-19th C, bulbous, molded rim above engraved band, body with allover repoussé strawberries and vines, weighted circular foot with emb dec, inscription on front and foot . **290.00**

Salt, 1-1/2" x 3-1/2", oval form, four hoofed feet, repoussé floral and wreath dec at knees, gold wash bowls, minor dents, Ball, Black & Co., New York City, 1851-76, 7 troy oz, pr **290.00**

Snuff box, stamped "PP," flattened ovoid form, bottom inscribed "I trust this triffle in thy mind will favor find, 1791," imperfections, 1-1/2" x 3-1/2" x 2-5/8", 2 troy oz **1,100.00**

Soup ladle, Simon Chaudron, Philadelphia, PA, 1812-15, marked "Chaundron" in banner, English crest dec, 14-1/2" l, 10 troy oz **920.00**

Sugar bowl, cov, 8" h, Gorham, mid-19th C, squat baluster, stepped foot, wide band of engine-turning, one plain and one engraved cartouche, two serpentine handles, domed lid with flower form finial, 17 troy oz, minor dents **175.00**

American, hot water urn, Gorham, cupid finial, putti handle, twin square "C" handles with satyr masks, four raised bust medallions on rim, four flaring feet, original burner, 18-1/4" h, 105 troy oz, **$7,850.**

Tablespoon, 8" l, front tips, back engraved, bowl with emb scallop shell below short drop handle, minor dents, wear, Samuel Edwards, Boston, 1705-62, 2 troy oz **635.00**

Tea service, unmarked, 19th C, 9-1/2" h teapot with hinged lid, creamer, cov sugar, lids with floriform knob finials attached to circle of ribbing, above round form bowl with shaped shoulders having vertical ribbing on lower half of body, raised on round stepped bases, four ball feet, applied tooled banding at neck, shoulder, and base, foliate devices attached to hollow strap handles and spout, 60 troy oz . . **885.00**

American, 1840-1920
Mostly sterling

There are two possible sources for the origin of the word *sterling*. The first is that it is a corruption of the name Easterling. Easterlings were German silversmiths who came to England in the Middle Ages. The second is that it is named for the sterling (little star) used to mark much of the early English silver.

Sterling is 92.5 percent per silver. Copper comprises most of the remaining alloy. American manufacturers began to switch to the sterling standard about the time of the Civil War.

Basket, 9" d, 3" h, Whiting Mfg Co., late 19th C, reticulated, sides with scrolls and diapering, scroll rim, three scroll feet, fluted base, monogrammed, 11 troy oz **460.00**

Bowl, 10-7/8" d, 4-1/2" h, International Silver, early 20th C, fluted bowl, vitruvian scroll band at top, domed base with low concave foot, 28 troy oz **600.00**

Bread plate, 6-1/2" d, Reed & Barton, banded dec, monogrammed, marked "Sterling 700," set of 12, 50 troy oz **450.00**

Coin silver, America, 19th C, tea service, 11-1/2" w, 9-1/2" h teapot with hinged lid, creamer, covered sugar bowl, floriform knob finials attached to circle of ribbing, vertical ribbing, raised on round stepped bases and four ball feet, applied tooled banding at neck, shoulder, and base, foliate devices attached to hollow strap handles and spout, 60 troy oz, $885. Photo courtesy of Skinner Auctioneers and Appraisers.

Butter chip, 3" d, Gorham, gadrooned border, engraved dragon with crown, monogram for Henredon Family, price for eight-pc set **150.00**

Castor, S. Kirk & Sons, Baltimore, Egyptian Revival, 1861-1868, 5-3/4" h, urn form, domed lid with repoussé leaves, bud form finial, body with three cast loop handles, allover repoussé foliates, three cast sphinx feet, monogram, 4 troy oz **690.00**

Center bowl, 14-1/2" d, Frank W Smith Silver Co., Inc., late 19th C, retailed by Bigelow, Kennard & Co., ovoid, engraved with quilted style pattern, edges reticulated with engraved leafy scrolls, edge with wide cast border of rocaille shells and C-scrolls, monogrammed center, 31 troy oz **1,840.00**

Challis, 7" h, 3-1/2" d at rim, presentation, engraved "Award by the G & A.A. Society to W. F. Fannin for the best collection of Southern made Plows, Oct 1852," inscription flanked by repousse wheat sheaves, reverse side with repousse plow **1,650.00**

Coffee set, nesting, 7" h, Lebkuecher and Co., Newark, NY, 1896-1909, single serving, three-part set, cov sugar, creamer, pot, two angled wood handles, cylindrical form, bulbous base, flared circular foot, imp maker's mark "Sterling, 02741 5 12 oz," 12 troy oz, repair to handle **375.00**

Compote, 8-3/4" d, 4-1/2" h, Bigelow, Kennard & Co., late 19th C, Etruscan-style, bowl with central

American, pitcher by International Silver Co., Lord Saybrook pattern, baluster, leaf-capped scroll handle, 26 oz. two dwt, 8-3/4" h, $250. Photo courtesy of Sloan's Auctioneers & Appraisers.

roundel of classical man holding grapes, seated woman with baby, dog, beaded surround, engraved anthemion and flowerheads, short stem with single rib to center, trumpet foot, plain flattened loop handles, applied Greek key rim, 22 troy oz **700.00**

Dish, 8" l, Howard & Co., quatrefoil form, filigree sides in fleur-de-pattern, applied ornamentation on rim of "C" and "S" scrolls and shells, marked "Howard & Co., New York, Sterling, 1903," 15 troy oz **300.00**

Dresser set, International Silver Co., Meriden, CT, early 20th C, cut glass powder jar, hair receiver, three dresser jars, all with sterling lids, pair of cut glass perfume bottles with silver mounted stoppers, hair brush, two clothes brushes, mirror, nail buffer, shoehorn, and nail file, all with engraved and banded rims, monograms **920.00**

Fish knives, Gorham, Providence, Aesthetic Movement, late 19th C, blades with ornate monograms and bright cut foliates, mixed metal Japanese-style Kozuka handles with molded dec, price for set of 12 . . . . **2,300.00**

Flatware service, Queen Anne pattern, J. E. Caldwell, service for 12, monogrammed, 84 pcs total, sold with orig invoice from J. E. Caldwell, Jewelers and Silversmiths, Phila, 98 troy oz **1,320.00**

Fruit bowl, 12-1/2" d, Dominick & Haff, late 19th/early 20th C, retailed by Shreve, Crump & Low, fluted int., wide reticulated edge with realistically modeled chrysanthemums and daisies, 21 troy oz **1,150.00**

Ice cream slice, 10" l, George W. Shiebler & Co., late 19th C, hammered finish, handle with Roman style male medallion on end, engraved bands of classical style designs, gold washed blade with further classical style engraving, medallion to lower right,

American, punch ladle by Watson Silver Co., Magnolia, monogrammed, 8 troy oz, 12" l, $250. Photo courtesy of James D. Julia, Inc.

American, serving bowl by Shreve, Crump & Low Co., oval, fancy scroll and shell design border with piercing, four applied scroll feet, 27 troy oz, 16" x 8-1/2", **$575**. Photo courtesy of James D. Julia, Inc.

central horizontal band of further small medallions, monogrammed on back of handle, 6 troy oz **4,025.00**

Jug, Lewis E. Jenks, Boston, c1875, 10" h, vasiform, shaped lid with cast bird finial, lid and body with allover repoussé foliates, central monogrammed cartouche, spreading circular foot, 17 troy oz **635.00**

Kettle-on-stand, 13" h, bombe repoussé allover with flowers and leaves on fine stippled ground, hinged cover with similar dec, floral finial, fixed handle, circular base with conforming dec on four paw feet issuing from foliage, marked "S. Kirk & So., #101," c1903-24, burner marked "JI sterling silver," 56 oz **2,500.00**

Mustard pot, 4-1/2" d, S. Kirk & Son, Baltimore, mid 19th C, vegetal finial, glass liner, 7 troy oz **150.00**

Perfume flask, Dominick & Haff, 9" l, tapered cylindrical, floral chased and emb at lid, neck, and base, wide band of horizontal fluting at center, monogrammed, 5 troy oz **490.00**

Platter, Dominick & Haff, oval, border repoussé with flowers and leaves on fine matted ground, monogrammed, 16 oz **475.00**

Punch bowl and ladle, 14-3/4" d, 8-3/4" h, Gorham, bowl dated 1908, squat ovoid bowl, shaped edge, waterlilies dec, gold-washed int., domed foot, applied water lily dec, engraved with double monogram, names engraved on underside, 15" l ladle with fruiting berry vines, also monogrammed and dated, 92 troy oz **5,175.00**

Punch ladle, 9-1/2" l, terminal applied with scrolling foliage, monogrammed **100.00**

Roast platter, 20-5/8" l, 14-1/8" w, Gorham, early 20th C, Greek key border **750.00**

American, tea set by Gorham, teapot on warming stand, coffeepot, creamer, covered sugar, and waste bowl, **$2,500**. Photo courtesy of Joy Luke Auctions.

Salad serving set, spoon and fork, 9" l, Chambord pattern, Reed & Barton, monogrammed, 5 oz, 6 dwt **200.00**

Salt, open, 3-1/4" l, 1-3/4" h, Black, Starr & Frost, late 19th C, Classical Revival style, ovoid body, hoof feet terminating in lion's heads, red glass liner, 8 troy oz, four-pc set **450.00**

Salver, 7-1/4" x 7-1/8", Theodore B. Starr, late 19th C, sq, shaped edge reticulated with scrolls offset with small rocaille shells, pr, 14 troy oz **385.00**

Sauce ladle, Wood & Hughes, New York, second half 19th C, 6-3/4" l, scalloped bowl, beaded handle with

American, syrup jug by Shaw, Boston, MA, 20th C, hinged lid, impressed "Shaw" with hearts, "STERLING," 6 troy oz., 5-1/4" h, **$1,325**. Photo courtesy of Skinner Auctioneers and Appraisers.

portrait medallion of classical warrior, monogrammed on reverse, 1 troy oz **320.00**

Serving dish, cov, Thomas Kirkpatrick, NY, third quarter 19th C, 8-7/8" w, 11-5/8" l, oval, domed lid with beaded band, cast stag finial, emb key pattern and beading on underside of rim, base with similar dec, some loses, 59 troy oz **1,035.00**

Tazza, 7-1/8" d, 2-1/2" h, Howard & Co., dated 1898, vessel with wide reticulated band and applied scroll rim, center monogram, applied scroll base, reticulated foot, pr, 19 troy oz . . **700.00**

Tea and coffee service, S. Kirk & Son, Baltimore, 1880-90, teapot, coffeepot, creamer, cov sugar, waste bowl, kettle on stand, raised repoussé lids with foliage finials, angular handles with ram head mounts, bodies with allover repoussé foliates on stippled ground, knopped stems and circular bases, kettle with cast Asian figure finial and four foliate legs with rose knees, monogrammed, 163 troy oz . . **7,475.00**

Teapot, cov, 9" h, attributed to William Williams, London, 1742, George II, Rococo-style, domed lid with pineapple finial, body with allover repoussé foliates and scrolls, engraved crest on each side, bone scroll handle, molded circular foot, 23 troy oz **2,300.00**

Tea service

Ball, Black & Co., third quarter 19th C, tapered ovoid teapot, cov sugar, helmet-shaped open creamer, each with applied profile medallion and anthemion engraving, pendant handles, monogrammed, 36 troy oz **2,185.00**

Gorham, made for Blanche M. Halle, Cleveland, OH, each pc stamped with her name, panels separated by ribs, dec with repoussé and chased trumpet urns of fruit, lids with carved ivory pineapple finials, 10-1/2" h teapot, 11-1/2" h coffeepot, creamer, cov double handled sugar, waste bowl, 18-1/2" x 30" tray, 276 troy oz . . . **4,675.00**

Gorham, Plymouth pattern, coffeepot, teapot, creamer, cov sugar, waste bowl, monogrammed, 55 troy oz, some dents to sugar lid **875.00**

Shreve, Stanwood & Co., 1860, 16" h hot water urn on stand, creamer, cov sugar, open sugar, and 9" h teapot, ovoid, beaded detailing, lids with swan finials, domed stepped foot, urn with presentation inscription on side, burner and one sugar lid missing, 35 troy oz **2,185.00**

Tea tray, Gorham, Providence, 1912, 17-7/8" w, 25-3/4" l, shaped molded rim, beaded band, pierced handles, monogrammed, 114 troy oz . . **1,725.00**

Tete-a-tete, Gorham, Providence, 1880, 4" h teapot, creamer, open sugar, cone shape, ball finial, reeded handles, banded necks, gilt interiors, monogrammed, 16 troy oz **320.00**

Travel clock, 3-5/8" l, 3-1/8" w, Wm Kerr & Co., late 19th C, plain rect case with rounded corners, eight-day movement, oct goldtone engine-turned face, black Roman numerals, silver surround with engine turning, engraved scrolls and floral sprays, monogrammed cover **200.00**

American, tea strainer by Mary Winlock, Boston, MA, 1901-27, flared edge and pierced handle dec with enameled vine of iris blossoms in shades of purple, green, yellow, and brown, impressed "M. P. W.," "STERLING," wear to silver, two troy oz., 5-1/2" l, $1,500. Photo courtesy of Skinner Auctioneers and Appraisers.

American, tea set, Reed and Barton, 11" h teapot, cream pitcher, open sugar, 16" x 10" tray, baluster shape, scroll work cartouches flanked by repoussé floral decoration, applied double scroll handles, $825. Photo courtesy of Alderfer Auction Company, Inc.

Tray, Reed & Barton, Taunton, MA, late 19th/early 20th C, 10-1/4" w, 14-1/4" l, rect, shaped molded rim with openwork and engraved band, monogrammed center, 24 troy oz **350.00**

Trophy pitcher, Whiting, New York, Harvard University, c1892, cylindrical, inverted rim, waisted body with inscription on front, circular base with molded scroll dec, 33 troy oz . **1,380.00**

Vase
15-3/4" h, J. E. Caldwell & Co., late 19th/early 20th C, tapered baluster form with engraved laurel wreath on each side, one with monogram, everted rim with engraved band of lines and circles, trumpet foot with similarly engraved band, 34 troy oz **750.00**
20-1/2" h, Gorham, flared draped rim, scalloped edge, bulbous base, pedestal foot, engraved scroll, foliage, and floral urn designs, figural accents, monogrammed central cartouche, marked "1083L, Sterling", 99 troy oz **3,850.00**

Water pitcher
Dominick & Haff, New York, 20th C, 9" h, vasiform, molded rim, "S" scroll handle, molded base, 22 troy oz **375.00**
Gorham, Providence, 1885, 9-1/4" h, paneled vasiform, rim and base with beaded bands, handle with cast acanthus dec, octagonal molded base, monogrammed, 26 troy oz **635.00**
International Silver Co., Meriden, CT, early 20th C, 6-3/4" h, bulbous, molded rim, "C" scroll handle, monogram, 13 troy oz **250.00**

Arts & Crafts

Hand-crafted silver from the Arts & Crafts period is one of the most sought after types of silver. Wonderful examples can be found, usually with a hammered finish, and proudly displaying maker's marks, etc. Because much research has been done, collectors know individual makers in the various studios and shops.

Most pieces have impressed marks. Because the Arts & Crafts movement was international, guilds were located in the United States, Great Britain, Germany, and Austria, creating many forms.

Bowl
7-1/8" d, 1-7/8" h, Kalo Shops, hammered finish, floriform, five petal-like panels, rolled rim, imp "Hand Wrought At The Kalo Shops Chicago and New York, Sterling, 18" **400.00**
8-1/4" d, 3-1/8" h, Arthur Stone, executed by Herbert A. Taylor, 1910-38, circular form, central tooled flower, dot, and engraved line border, circular stepped foot, makers mark "Stone, Sterling," and "T," 18 troy oz, scratches and spotting **1,150.00**
9-1/2" d, 3" h, J. O. R. Randall, hammered, floriform, stamped "J.O.R. Randall/Sterling/ Hand-wrought" **500.00**

Brush and mirror, attributed to Whiting Manuf Co, NY, early 20th C, hammered surface with emb flower, scroll, and bead design, imp maker's marks and "Sterling 1250," 11 troy oz **490.00**

Candy dish, 5-1/2" d, 5-3/4" h, Kalo Shop, hammered finish, trumpet base, stamped "Kalo Shops/Park Ridge Ills/Serling" **900.00**

Arts & Crafts, bowl by Whiting, fluted, marked "Whiting Mfg Co.," date letter for 1908, very slight dents in base, 10-1/2" d, 2-1/2" h, $125. Photo courtesy of Cowan's Historic Americana Auctions.

Demitasse spoon, Liberty, set of six, orig leather case, spoons hallmarked, cast stamped "Liberty" **200.00**

Ladle, 8-1/8" h, Kalo Shop, Chicago, hammered finish, notched handle, entwined raised "KP" monogram, imp "Sterling Kalo 8597" **260.00**

Martini pitcher, 9-1/2" h, 7" d, LeBolt, hammered finish, strainer spout, angular handle, die-stamped mark and "LeBolt/Hand Beaten/Sterling 801" **600.00**

Martini spoon, 13-1/2" h, Kalo Shop, Chicago, hammered finish, stamped "Sterling Kalo 243" **200.00**

Pitcher, 9" h, 6-1/2" d, Kalo, hammered, sterling, ovoid, stamped "Kalo Sterling/Chicago/New York" . . **2,415.00**

Plate, 9-3/4" d, Handicraft Shop, Boston, style of Mary Knight, circular, pinched and emb scrolling floral and leaf design around extended and rolled rim, imp Handicraft Shop mark, "Sterling, 1904" **435.00**

Salt and pepper shakers, pr, Stone Associates, c1937, flattened baluster form, initials engraved on side, imp "Stone" with lower case "h" in shield, "Sterling" and "H" on base, 8 troy oz **460.00**

Serving spoon, 9" l, Th. Marthinsen, Norway, hammered finish bowl, squirrel and acorn motif handle, imp marks, "830S" **375.00**

Smoke set, Kalo, 10" x 19" rect tray with hammered surface, applied

Arts & Crafts, pitcher, Kalo, hammered sterling silver, embossed sections, monogrammed, stamped mark, 10-1/2" x 8", $2,600. Photo courtesy of David Rago Auctions, Inc.

monograms, five fitted sections, six 2-1/2" d matching ash trays, five 1-3/4" x 1-1/4" match box holders with monograms, marked "Sterling Hand Wrought At The Kalo Shop X221," 63 troy oz **1,550.00**

Tea set, Arthur Stone, Gardner, MA, c1918, teapot, creamer, cov sugar, waste bowl, ivory finials and insulators, leaf detail on spout, bulbous body, initialed "H" for Arthur L. Hartwell, Master Craftsman, engraved with presentees initials and date, 44 troy oz **3,000.00**

Continental

Generations have enjoyed silver created by Continental silversmiths. Expect to find well-executed forms with interesting elements. Most Continental silver is well marked.

Austria-Hungary

Beaker, 3-1/4" h, late 19th C, base with thin beaded rim, engraved with diapering centered by flowerheads with central cartouche with coat of arms **175.00**

Candlesticks, pr, 12-1/2" h, Rococo-style, late 19th C, paneled baluster stem and socket, scrolled weighted base, removable bobeche, lacquered **690.00**

Casket, mid/late 19th C, 3-3/8" w, 5-1/4" l, rect, lid with cast pear form finial, molded rim and foot, waisted body with silver mount on lock, 14 troy oz **575.00**

Continental

Asparagus server, 11-1/4" l, late 19th C, reticulated handles topped by crowned lion's head, flowerheads

Continental, Denmark, two spoons by Georg Jensen, 1915-30, 5-1/2" l blossom patterned jelly spoon with pierced and hammered bowl, hallmarked and Gl830S in circle of dots and artist's initials KA, possibly Knud Andersen; 4-1/2" l short handle spoon, 1933-44, in blossom pattern, allover hammered bowl with "GJ" in a box, two troy oz, $375. Photo courtesy of Skinner Auctioneers and Appraisers.

and scrolls, standing figure, ending in cherub face above floral basket flanked by cherub herms over reticulation, blades reticulated with C-scrolls and engraved with flowers and further scrolls, monogrammed, 9 troy oz . . **230.00**

Box, cov, 7-1/2" d, 2-3/4" h, late 19th/early 20th C, squatty ovoid, repoussé foliate and scroll banding, hinged lid with floral roundel, 14 troy oz **345.00**

Candelabra, 21-1/2" h, three-light, shaped sq lobed foot with scroll and floral rim rising to fluted stem applied with similar dec, two scrolling foliate branches, central fixed sconce, detachable bobeches, convertible to candlestick, engraved with monogram below crown, weighted base **900.00**

Condiment jar, 4-3/4" h, late 19th/early 20th C, formed as sedan chair, stamped with scrolls and cartouches of dancing couples, hinged lid with quadripartite finial, cobalt blue glass liner, restorations, 5 troy oz **375.00**

Creamer, 5-1/2" l, 4-1/4" h, figural, horned cow, fly hinged lid, 19th C **800.00**

Danish

Child's fork and spoon, 5-7/8" l, each with tapering handle, openwork finials formed as soldier fleeing peasant woman, 2 troy oz . . **65.00**

Compote, round bowl over round stepped standard, base imp "Denmark 300" at bowl center, 6-5/8" d, 5-3/8" h, price for pr **290.00**

Serving spoon, double leaf and berry design on handle, tapered shaft, rounded hammered bowl, 10-1/2" l, 4 troy oz **80.00**

Tea and coffee service, Georg Jensen, Johan Rohde, c1915, 45C pattern teapot, 10-1/2" h coffeepot, creamer, cov sugar, 45D pattern milk jug, 45 pattern tea strainer and stand, domed tops with ball finials, reeded handles with beaded terminals, reeded bases, 96 troy oz **13,800.00**

Water pitcher, 9-3/4" h, 20th C, tapered egg-shaped body, flared stem with beading to top, stepped foot, spout with curved reeding to underside, wooden handle with

stylized floral terminal to top
. . . .**750.00**

Wine coaster, F. Hingelberg, 20th C, 4-3/4" d, molded rim, twisted wire sides, composition base, price for pr **490.00**

Dutch

Bowl, 14-1/4" l, 3" h, 19th C, .833 fine, Dutch export mark, repoussé, lobed, reserves with chased and emb country scenes, two pierced handles with putto to top, central flowers flanked by putto riding dolphins, 15 troy oz **460.00**

Box, late 19th C, .833 silver, 2-5/8" w, 5-1/2" l, rect, shaped lid with engraved nativity scene within foliates, base with two biblical scenes, banded sides with engraved foliates, 8 troy oz.**960.00**

Chatelaine, c1890, 12-1/8" l, cast brooch with scene of putti with goddess, medallion mounted chains supporting two boxes, cylindrical container, pair of scissors, stylized crown, 9 troy oz **600.00**

Coffeepot, 8" h, late 19th C, .833 fine, baluster form pot with allover scroll and foliage repoussé, windmill vignette on one side, scroll cartouche topped by crown flanked by putto on other side, legs topped by crowned human masks, four ball and claw feet, turned wood handle set at right angle to ram-horned grotesque spout, flattened lid with vertical ribbing, rampant lion finial, 11 troy oz **800.00**

Pitcher, 5-1/2" h, late 19th C, .833 line, baluster form, neck with band of fluting, repoussé to lower section of foliage, birds and putti, domed foot with vertical ribbing, spout with putto, beaded serpentine handle, lid with vertical reeding, repoussé and vegetal finial, base engraved "Esther Cleveland," 6 troy oz, descended in family of Grover Cleveland **260.00**

French, .950 fine

Coffeepot, 9-1/4" h, third quarter 19th C, pear-shaped, cast quadripartite scroll embellished serpentine spout and handle, heat stops, domed lid with flower form finial, 22 troy oz **460.00**

Dish, cov, undertray, Paris, 1819-38, "C. P." maker's mark, cylindrical body with acanthus and flat leaf

handles, rim with beading and flat leaf band, base with band of flat leaves, foot with band of laurel, lid with beaded edge, removable circular handle formed as cornucopia on leaf and flower base, fitted leather case, 30 troy oz **2,615.00**

Fish serving platter, 27-3/4" l, 11-1/2" w, oval, reeded rim, monogrammed, 66 troy oz **1,265.00**

Serving dish, 11-3/4" l, 2-1/4" h, third quarter 19th C, oval, two shell handles, vertical reeded border, 17 troy oz **490.00**

Sweetmeat dish, 5-1/2" l, 5" h, Odiot, Paris, maker, late 19th/20th C, shell form vessel drawn by sea creatures, reins held by two putti, flanking central standing putto poised as Neptune, holding trident-form fork, shaped rect base cast as water, 65 troy oz, pr **2,100.00**

Tray, 17-3/8" l, 13" w oval, late 19th C, partially obscured maker's mark, beaded edge, engraved initial in center, 34 troy oz **575.00**

Tureen, cov, 12-3/4" l, 10-1/2" h, third/fourth quarter 19th C, sprays of acorns and oak leaves to top, reeded rim, lid with flat leaf rim, stem with reeded shoulder, oval foot, flat leaf band, angular handles

with flat leaf to bottom, stylized corn finial about flat leaf and lotus ground. **1,840.00**

Wine taster, late 19th C, .950 fine, inset with crest to handle . . **125.00**

German, .800 fine

Basket, 14" l, shaped oval, paneled sides pierced with flowers, garlands, and scrolling foliage centering four vacant cartouches, center repoussé with flowers, foliage, and three putti at play, 15 oz, 8 dwt **200.00**

Beaker and underplate, 2-1/2" h cup, 5-7/8" d underplate, cylindrical cup stamped with cartouches of courting couples, everted rim, gold-washed int., plates with foliage and scroll rim, well for cup, monogrammed, 14 troy oz, pr **375.00**

Bottle, 15-1/2" h, figural peacock, various stamped hallmarks, "800," late 20th C **700.00**

Box, 5-1/4" x 3-1/4" x 1-1/2", rect, hinged lid, Roman chariot scene in relief, beaded edge, reeded sides with vine accents, marked "800 Germany" **200.00**

Bread tray, 15" x 10-1/2", repoussé, cartouches of courtship scene, imp German hallmarks and "800," c1920 . . . .**920.00**

Jewelry box, rococo style, late 19th C **1,300.00**

Kettle-on-stand, 16" h, compressed circular with lobed sides, four hoof feet, detachable cover with wooden finial, central swing partial wooden handle, multi-scroll stand with border, 48 oz, 8 dwt. . .**325.00**

Sauceboat, late 19th/early 20th C, 10-3/4" l, shape of open-mouthed fish, emb and engraved scales, open back with molded rim, tail shape handle, supported by cast fins, glass eyes, 13 troy oz **1,495.00**

Serving dish, 12" d, 3-1/2" h, Wilhelm T. Binder, c1900, rounded trefoil shape, three handles, repoussé leaf bud and line dec, scalloped, ribbed glass insert, imp "WTB, 800 fine" **1,150.00**

Wedding cup, 9" h, figural, beaded figure with chased and emb skirt, cup chased and emb with scrolls and grotesques, 15 troy oz **1,955.00**

Italian

Asparagus tongs, F. Broggi, Milan 20th C, 5-1/4" l, individual, plain, tapered form, set of six, 6 troy oz **115.00**

Punch bowl, 12-5/8" d, 10-1/2" h, late 19th/early 20th C, repoussé, bowl with band of flat leaves to base below further continuous hunt scene of men attacking various animals, domed foot with band of flat leaves below continuous hunt scene, removable liner, 146 troy oz **4,025.00**

Portuguese, .833 silver

Bowl, Oporto, 20th C, 11-3/4" d, molded scroll and shell rim, band of chased dec, molded circular foot, 14 troy oz **230.00**

Chalice, 12-1/2" h, domed lid with applied openwork foliate band,

Continental, Scandinavian, coffeepot, ivory heat stops at handle, marked "JOR" with hammer horizontal across text, two small dents, 8-1/2" h, $260. Photo courtesy of Cowan's Historic Americana

engraved bands and cruciform finial, bowl with engraved band with Latin inscription, applied gothic style openwork mounts, stem with beaded and engraved knop, stepped circular base, int. gilt, 31 troy oz **690.00**

Ewer, maker's mark "S&P," late 19th/early 20th C, 11-3/4" h, bulbous, molded shaped rim, body with chased stippled dec, emb foliate, scroll, and shell band, cast scroll handle, molded circular foot with emb dec, 33 troy oz... **815.00**

Kettle-on-stand, maker's mark effaced, second half 19th C, 14-1/4" h, inverted pear form, domed lid with cased foliates and wood urn finial, upright handle with cast silver acanthus mounts, body with allover chased and engraved foliates and scrolls, circular stand with four scroll legs and shell feet, chased and engraved burner with turned wood handle, 54 troy oz **920.00**

Salver, 11-5/8" d, molded openwork scroll and foliate rim, bright cut foliate dec on face, three cast legs with shell feet, 25 troy oz... **350.00**

Tray, maker's mark "GP," 20th C, 13-1/2" w, 22-5/8" l, rect, openwork raised rim with molded grape dec, cast foliate handles, face with engraved dec, 85 troy oz **1,265.00**

English

From the 17th century to the mid-19th century, English silversmiths set the styles which inspired the rest of the world. The work from this period exhibits the highest degree of craftsmanship. English silver is actively collected in the American antiques marketplace.

Basket, 6" d, 3-1/2" h, J. R. Hennell maker, London, 1884, Victorian, reticulated foliate pattern, circular banding, shaped edge with bead and flat leaf rim, four scroll and cylinder feet with husk swags, glass liner, 21 troy oz, pr **1,725.00**

Berry spoon, George III, marks partially obscured, later engraving, chasing and embossing, pr **200.00**

Bowl, 5-1/4" d, 1-1/2" h, W. Comyns & Sons maker, London, 1902, Edward VII, shallow bowl emb with shield-shaped panels, hand-hammered surface, low flower form foot, 7 troy oz...... **435.00**

Candelabra, pr, 12-1/2" h, maker attributed to Stephen Smith, London, 1875, Victorian, Renaissance

English, George III, cruet set by Stephen Ardesoif or Stephen Adams, London, 1800, seven original bottles, engraved flowerheads and ribbon, wreath reserve monogrammed JMM, curved feet, 10" h, $2,200. Photo courtesy of Sloan's Auctioneers & Appraisers.

Revival-style, convertible, two foliage scroll and foliate candle arms each with flat leaf nozzle, foliate and acorn finial between arms, stem and foot with stamped foliage, masks, and herms, applied openwork scroll detailing to stem, round foot raised on three scroll feet, small engraved device on foot, 59 troy oz, pr **4,600.00**

Castor

Attributed to Jabez Daniel, London, 1750, George II, pear shape, pierced domed lid, shoulder banded, spreading circular foot, 2 troy oz, 4" h, restorations. **230.00**

Hester Bateman, London, 1788, George III, urn form, engraved pierced lid with cast urn finial, engraved bands at shoulder, waist, and spreading circular foot, 2 troy oz, 5-3/4" h............. **690.00**

Caudle cup, 6" h, 10-1/2" l, Samuel Wastell maker, London, 1704, William III, Brittania Standard, tapered cylindrical body with single applied molded band, cast ear-shaped handles, spreading domed foot, engraved on one side, heraldic device in rococo-style cartouche, 26 troy oz **2,990.00**

Center bowl, 17" l, 5-1/2" h, Robert Garrard, London, 1811, George III, lobed ovoid body, two short scroll and acanthus handles, gadroon and shell border offset with two scroll details to

English, George III, centerpiece, London, 1795, maker's mark IS, possibly Joseph Scammell, pierced sides cast with bellflowers, two bow-tied monogrammed reserves, below aguilloche rim and above leaftip border, two ram's head and ring handles, ball feet, interior engraved with coat of arms, 45 oz 8 dwt, 12-1/2" w, **$3,000.** *Photo courtesy of Sloan's Auctioneers & Appraisers.*

each side, four cast paw feet topped by group of scrolls, 51 troy oz . . . **4,325.00**

Chamberstick, 4" l, 1-3/4" h, W. Comyns maker, London, 1888, Victorian, chased and emb with flowers and scrolls, removable bobeche, handle with monogrammed thumb-piece, 2 troy oz **115.00**

Charger, 11-3/4" d, Rebecca Emes and Edward Barnard, London, 1826, George IV, shaped edge, applied gadroon and shell border, engraved gartered heraldic device on rim, 29 troy oz **1,380.00**

Coaster, 4-3/8" d, Edward VII, Birmingham, 1904, "W.H.H." maker's mark, round, inset to center with George III Irish 10-pence bank tokens dated 1905, 4 troy oz, pr **115.00**

Coffeepot, 14-1/2" h, William Grundy maker, London, 1767, George III, baluster, spreading foot, scroll handle with ivory heat stops, serpentine spout with rocaille shell to base, flat leaf to spout, engraved monogram within foliate rococo-style cartouche, domed hinged lid with spiral reeded egg-shaped finial, 60 troy oz . **5,750.00**

Compote, 12-1/2" d, 7" h, Benjamin Smith maker, London, 1845, Victorian, bowl with shaped edge and vertical ribbing, everted rim with applied grapevine dec, tree-trunk form base with twining grapevine, 36 troy oz **1,150.00**

Cream jug, 5-1/4" h, Hester Bateman, London, 1782, George III, vasiform, chased beaded rim, body with repoussé farm scenes surrounding central cartouche, trumpet foot with

spreading rim, 3 troy oz, restoration **225.00**

Cup, 5-5/8" h, Samuel Godbeheve, Edward Wigan and J. Bolt makers, London, 1800, George III, baluster form, two handles, four drill holes in base, 11 troy oz **490.00**

Demitasse spoon, 5" l, John Wren maker, London, 1791, George III, bright cut engraved stem, fluted bowl, 3 troy oz, set of six **260.00**

Dish cross, 12" l, "BD" maker's mark, (Burrage Davenport), London, 1772, George III, pierced shell form feet and plate supports, burner with gadrooned rim, 15 troy oz **1,265.00**

Egg cup frame, Henry Nutting maker, London, 1800, George III, reeded central handle, four ball feet, six associated Sheffield egg cups, five associated demitasse spoons, 18 troy oz **550.00**

Entree dish, cov, 12-1/8" l, 5-3/4" h, "BS" makers mark, London, 1820, George IV, lid modified with later band of foliate repoussé and engraved with heraldic crest and monograms, base with gadroon and shell rim, removable leaf and shell handle, 67 troy oz **1,725.00**

Epergne, 10-1/2" l, 11-3/4" h, "GJ DF" maker's mark, London, 1913, George V, central stem below navette-shaped reticulated basket with applied border, flanked by smaller removable baskets on scrolled arms, ovoid reticulated base with applied scroll and shell border, four scroll feet, 76 troy oz **6,325.00**

Fish server, 11-1/4" l, attributed to John Neville, London, 1770, George III, reticulated blade with scrolling foliage, stem end with shell, handle, engraved

English, George III, London, 1763, maker's mark IWVL, shell form dish, two oz, two dwt, **$170.** *Photo courtesy of Sloan's Auctioneers & Appraisers.*

English, Victorian, stuffing spoon, by William Eaton, London, 1845, Fiddle pattern, engraved crest, six troy oz; 12-1/4" l, **$275.** *Photo courtesy of Sloan's Auctioneers & Appraisers.*

with gadrooned edge, central heraldic device, 4 troy oz **1,100.00**

Flower bowl, George III, Paul Storr, classical design based on Warwick vase, hallmarked London, 1808 . . . . **4,700.00**

Goblet, 6-1/2" h, maker's mark partially obscured (attributed to Henry Greenway), London, 1775, George II, beaded collar, tapered round funnel bowl, beaded trumpet foot, engraved coat of arms in roundel, 16 troy oz, pr **1,955.00**

Hot water kettle on stand, 12" h, John Emes maker, London, 1807, George III, lid partially reeded with wood finial, pot with ovoid body partially reeded with gadrooned edging, on tapered circular foot, fluted tap, upright silver and wood handle, stand with gadrooned rim with burner and cover, flat leaf legs, four hairy paw feet with wooden ball supports, pot engraved with mottoed coat of arms, small heraldic device on pot lid, burner lid, and burner, 83 troy oz **2,100.00**

Jug, cov, 7-3/4" h, "C. W." maker's mark, London, 1769, George III, later Victorian adaptations, stamped bands flanking convex band at rim, ovoid body with twisted reeding and fluting to lower section, central cartouche flanked by C-scrolls, serpentine handle, domed foot, short spout, domed hinged lid with Victorian hallmarks, twisted reeding, fluting on urn finial, 18 troy oz . . **400.00**

Meat skewer, 13" l, William Chawner, London, 1829, George IV, King's pattern, molded dec, engraved crest, 4 troy oz **230.00**

Mirror, 14-1/4" h, 10" d, "JR SJ" makers, London, 1887, Victorian, rect, curved top, reticulated with scrolls and flowers, mask center at base, grotesque beasts on either corner, beveled edge mirror, easel stand on back **980.00**

Muffineer, 8-1/2" h, Charles Stuart Harris maker, Brittania standard marks, London, 1899, tapered paneled lid with engraving, baluster form finial, paneled baluster form, tiered foot, 14 troy oz **800.00**

Mug, Richard Beale, London, 1731, George II, cylindrical, cast "S" scroll handle, molded circular foot, engraved crest, 6 troy oz, 3-3/4" h **980.00**

Mustard pot, attributed to William Barrett II, 1827, George III, circular, disk finial, reeded rim and base, reticulated sides with engraved foliates and urns, associated glass insert, 3 troy oz, 2-1/2" h **290.00**

Salt, open, 2-1/4" d, circular, London, 1787, Georgian, molded banded rim, three pad feet, monogrammed, cobalt blue glass liner, 4 troy oz, price for set of four **375.00**

Salver

9-3/4" l, 7" w, John Crouch & Thomas Hannan, London, 1813, George III, oval, banded molded rim, face with engraved band, central engraved coat of arms, four molded feet, 12 troy oz **915.00**

12-3/8" d, John Tuite maker, London, 1783, George II, shaped molded rim offset with shells, central engraved coat of arms in rococo cartouche, four scrolled leaf feet, 32 troy oz **2,185.00**

13-3/4" d, Robert Jones & John Schofield, London, 1777-78, round form, beaded and pierced foliate and anthemion rim border, four anthemion and scroll dec feet, later engraved floral and foliate

English, vinaigrette, oval, engraved, hinged lid with pierced and hinged interior grillwork for sponge with urn of flowing flowers, maker's mark "TB," London, 1800-01, 1-1/4" l, 3/4" d, **$315.** *Photo courtesy of Cowan's Historic Americana Auctions.*

decoration and inscription "This Salver is Presented by MR. COUSINS to MRS. TUCKER, As a token of his Respect and testimony of the high Estimation in which he holds the important Professional services rendered to him on various occasions by her Husband, 1st February 1838," imp maker's marks on reverse, light scratches, small base edge separation, approx. 40 troy oz **725.00**

16-1/4" d, John Cotton & Thomas Head maker, London, 1813, George III, beaded and ribbed border, four beaded and ribbed feet, center engraved with mottoed coat of arms, 64 troy oz.. **3,750.00**

17-1/4" d, Mappin & Webb makers, London, 1946, shaped edge with bead shell border, four scrolled feet, 60 troy oz **1,610.00**

22-7/8" h, Robert Abercomby maker, London, 1750, George II, shaped edge, engraved with wide band of florals, fruits, shells, scrolls, and diapered cartouches, four paw feet topped by shells, engraved central Chinoiserie-style coat of arms, 156 troy oz **4,320.00**

Sauce boat, 7-3/8" l, 5" h, George III, London, 1763, no maker's mark, shaped edge, flying scroll handle, engraved initials on one side, three hoof feet topped by shells, 11 troy oz **550.00**

Sauce tureen, cov, 9-1/4" l, 5-1/2" h, George Smith and Thomas Hayter makers, London, 1804, George III, domed lid with urn finial, boat shaped body with ribbed rim, loop handles, pedestal foot, lid and body monogrammed, 33 troy oz, pr **2,760.00**

Serving spoon, 11-3/4" l, William Eley and William Fearn, London, 1818, George III, engraved crest, 3 oz, 6 dwt **175.00**

Soup tureen, cov, 14-1/2" l, 10-1/4" h, William Elliott maker, London, 1819, George III, gadrooned rim, acanthus handles, four paw feet terminating in shell and acanthus leaves, lid with two bands of gadrooning and ribbed removable handle, engraved coat of arms on body and lid, 136 troy oz **7,475.00**

Standish, 11-3/8" l, 7-1/2" w, J. C. Vickery maker, London, 1906, Edward VII, rect, reeded border, two horizontal pen wells, two tapered inkwells with canted corners and hinged lids, central

ovoid covered well, hinged lid fitted with eight-day clock, four ball and claw feet, some restoration needed, 32 troy oz **2,100.00**

Sugar basket, 5-1/2" l, 3-1/2" w, Peter & Ann Bateman, London, 1798, George III, navette shape, molded banded rim and swing handle, engraved body with reticulated bands, banded oval foot, monogrammed, cobalt glass insert, 3 troy oz................... **920.00**

Sugar bowl, 6" l, 5-3/8" h, Georgian, marks rubbed, beaded rim, ovoid body with ribbon-tied floral sprays and swags, roundels on each side, heraldic device, spiraled loop handles, trumpet foot with bands of bright cut engraving, 5 troy oz................... **350.00**

Sugar tongs, Georgian, cast with shell, foliage, scrolls engraved with flowers, center vacant cartouche, 1 oz, 2 dwt **95.00**

Sweetmeat dish, 9-1/8" l, 5-5/8" w, 2-1/4" h, R & S Garrard maker, London, 1879, ovoid, flanked by male and female figure, auricular scroll and stylized shell handle, four periwinkle shell feet, 13 troy oz **1,495.00**

Tablespoon, 8-3/4" l, William Eley, London, 1826, George IV, fiddle pattern, monogrammed, pr, 6 troy oz **200.00**

Tankard, 7-3/4" h, John Longlands I maker, Newcastle, 1769, George III, tapered cylindrical form, plain body with engraved cartouche, serpentine handle with reticulated thumb piece, gadrooned foot rim, slightly domed lid with gadrooned rim, engraved presentation inscription, lacquered, 26 troy oz................. **1,265.00**

Tapersticks, pr, 4-1/4" h, Jas. Gould maker, London, 1737, George II, flattened knop, paneled step with ribbed shoulder, plain sconce, shaped

English, snuffbox, presentation type, silver box lined with gold, marked "FTC ? 1 Decbr. 1827-52," scroll and floral design engraved in lid, 3-1/8" l, **$250.** *Photo courtesy of Sanford Alderfer Auction Company.*

English, made in Birmingham, 1900, teapot and coffee pot, **$575.** *Photo courtesy of Joy Luke Auctions.*

stepped base, nozzles not present, 7 troy oz **1,035.00**

Tazza, 7-3/4" d, 3-1/4" h, Charles Stuart Harris maker, London, 1902, Edward VII, body with gadrooned rim and stamped border of faces and Chinoiserie-style motifs, tapered stem, domed foot stamped with band of foliage dec, center monogrammed, 14 troy oz **385.00**

Teapot
5" h, attributed to Augustus Le Sage, London, 1771, George III, cylindrical, disc finial, wood ear handle, engraved antelope crest on lid and side, 13 troy oz **1,100.00**

5-1/2" h, Andrew Fogelberg, London, 1796, George III, ovoid, domed lid with wood finial, body with engraved foliate bands, wood ear handle, 16 troy oz, restorations **550.00**

6-1/4" h, George Smith & Thomas Hayter, London, 1796, George III, fluted ovoid, engraved domed lid, bone mushroom finial and handle, engraved foliates and central crest, 15 troy oz, restorations **525.00**

Teapot stand, 7" l, Robert & David Hennell, London, 1795, Georgian, oval with beveled corners, molded rim engraved, face with engraved and bright cut foliate bands, central cartouche, four feet, 5 troy oz, 4-7/8" w **435.00**

Tea and coffee service, Rebecca Eames & Edward Barnard, London, 1814-15, George III, 8-3/4" h coffeepot with gadrooned pedestal, teapot, creamer, open sugar, sq bulbous form, emb lids with cast foliate finials, molded gadrooned rims, bodies with bands of spiral reeding, four ball feet, 73 troy oz **2,300.00**

Tea service
7-3/4" h teapot, Peter, Ann, and William Bateman makers, London,

1800, George III, ovoid teapot, helmet shaped cov creamer with angular handle, cov sugar with angular handles, all with partial vertical lobing, bands of bright cut engraving and engraved heraldic device, wooden pineapple finials, 33 troy oz **1,495.00**

9" h coffeepot, 16" h kettle on stand, Crichton Bros. makers, London, 1930, George V, coffee and teapots, kettle on stand, creamer, open sugar, cov sugar, all with ovoid body, arcaded and ribbed banding, teapot and coffeepot with wooden handles topped with silver flat leaves, lion's head roundels, reamer and sugar with curved handles terminating in lion's head roundels, 174 troy oz **2,990.00**

Tea urn, 15" h, maker's mark "I. R.," London, 1778, lid with tapered egg-shaped finial, beaded tape with ivory handle, beaded loop handles, four ball feet with stepped rect base and beaded edge, bright cut engraving throughout with husks, cartouches, and floral swags, 37 troy oz **2,100.00**

Tray, 25" l, 16-1/4" w, "EB" makers mark, London, 1822, George IV, rect, gadrooned border, handles with shells and leaves, four paw feet flanked by floral roundels and stylized wings, engraved allover pattern of flowers and leaves, center with mottoed crest and later monogram, 120 troy oz . . **2,760.00**

Waxjack, 6-1/2" h, attributed to Augustus Le Sage, London, third quarter 18th C, George III, cast handles, attached snuffer, spindle with spirally reeded bud form finial, domed base with beaded rim, supported by three cast claw and ball feet, inscription on base, 4 troy oz **980.00**

English, teapot, repoussé, allover flowers and scrolls, maker "ICWR," hallmarked, 1823, **$625.** *Photo courtesy of Joy Luke Auctions.*

Wine coaster, 5-3/4" d, 2-3/4" h, Joseph and John Angel makers, London, 1846, Victorian, applied scroll and shell rim, reticulated sides, engraved to base with scrolls, shells, and central heraldic crest, pr **5,465.00**

Irish
Fine examples of Irish silver are becoming popular with collectors.

Candlesticks, pr, George III/IV, Dublin, attributed to John Laughlin, Jr., larger gadrooned knob over gadrooned knob below partially vertically reeded stem with single horizontal beaded band, well with applied stylized wheat or grass fronds, domed gadrooned base, vertically reeded sconce, removable nozzle with gadrooned rim, small heraldic crest engraved on foot and nozzle, 49 troy oz **7,475.00**

Caudle cup, cov, 7-1/4" h, Dublin, mid-18th C, marked for John Hamilton, domed lid topped by ovoid finial, body with single molded band, crabstock handles, lobed spreading foot, no date mark, 37 troy oz, pr **5,175.00**

Cup, 4-7/8" h, mid-18th C, marked for John Letabliere, tapered cylindrical body with leaf cut card work, band of foliate engraving, domed spreading foot, scroll handles topped with flat leaves, engraved on one side with cartouche, no date marks, 44 troy oz, pr **5,465.00**

Salver, 6-1/2" l, George II/III, Dublin, William Townsend maker, shaped molded border, engraved center with heraldic crest in rococo cartouche, three pad feet with scroll legs, 8 troy oz **1,100.00**

Snuffer tray, George III, Dublin, 1798, William Doyle maker, octagonal boat shape, base with bright-cut engraved husk drops, heraldic crest within roundel flanked by leaves, sides reticulated with arcading, paterae, 4 troy oz **700.00**

Soup ladle, 13" l, John Power, Dublin, 1791, reeded bowl, engraved lozenge handle, 5 troy oz **435.00**

Scottish
Not to be outdone by their Irish and English neighbors, Scottish silversmiths also created fine objects.

Berry spoon, Edinburgh, 1820, George Fenwick maker **75.00**

Punch ladle
13-1/2" l, Edinburgh, 1789, maker's mark "CD," 6 troy oz **300.00**

14-1/2" l, Edinburgh, 1820, maker's mark "AH," ovoid bowl, twisted baleen handle, silver end cap **150.00**

Sheffield, English

Sheffield silver, or Old Sheffield Plate, has a fusion method of silver-plating that was used from the mid-18th century until the mid-1880s, when the process of electroplating silver was introduced.

Sheffield plating was discovered in 1743, when Thomas Boulsover of Sheffield, England, accidentally fused silver and copper. The process consisted of sandwiching a heavy sheet of copper between two thin sheets of silver. The result was a plated sheet of silver, which could be pressed or rolled to a desired thickness. All Sheffield articles are worked from these plated sheets.

Most of the silver-plated items found today marked "Sheffield" are not early Sheffield plate. They are later wares made in Sheffield, England.

Basket, 7-3/4" w, 13-3/4" l, S. Smith & Son, England, second half 19th C, oval, molded foliate rim, emb and reticulated sides, cast foliage handles, oval reticulated and engraved base, cobalt blue glass liner **460.00**

Biscuit box, 7" w, 7-1/2" h, oval, hinged lid, gadrooned trim, lion mask side handles, attached tray base on ball feet, late 19th C **120.00**

Carving set, 16-1/2" l, fork, knife, and steel, engraved image of Windsor Castle on knife blade, horn handles, silver plated crown finials, leathered case, late 19th C **350.00**

Claret jug, 11" h, cut glass body mounted at neck, hinged cover, baluster finial, multi-scroll foliate handle, c19435 .... **500.00**

Domed lid, 22" h, 11" l, engraved armorial whippet, oval handle, early 19th C **575.00**

Flatware service, Hanover pattern, William Hutton & Sons, England, late 19th C, service for six plus ladle,

English, Sheffield, tea and coffee service, 14" h tea kettle on stand, coffee pot, teapot, sugar, creamer, and waste bowl, 26" l two handled decorated oval tray by Rogers, $250. Photo courtesy of James D. Julia, Inc.

carving set, stuffing spoon, brass mounted wood case **550.00**

Plate, 9-3/4" d, circular, gadrooned rim, engraved Carlill crest, George III, price for pr **175.00**

Platter and meat cover, 26" l oval tree platter, four ball feet, two wooden handles, gadrooned rim, armorials on both sides, dome cover with gadrooned rim, reeded handles, engraved armorials **2,750.00**

Serving dish, cov, England, first half 19th C, rect, gadrooned rim and lid, cast branch and maple leaf handle, engraved coat of arms, 11-1/2" l, 8-5/8" w **230.00**

Tantalus, England, late 19th/early 20th C, central casket with two engraved hinged lids below handle, sides supporting two cut and pressed glass decanters, pedestal base supported by four column legs, 5-3/4" w, 15" l **490.00**

Tray, 18-1/2" x 7-1/2", kidney shape, gadrooned rim, pierced gallery of open lattice work, centered engraved lion crest, early 20th C **120.00**

Vegetable dish, cov, 13" l, plated, shaped rect, applied grapevine, scroll, and foliage handle, monogrammed **250.00**

Wine bottle holder, 16" l, wooden base, vintage detail, ivory casters **275.00**

Sheffield, teapot, warming stand, $625. Photo courtesy of Joy Luke Auctions.

Silver, plated

Englishmen G. R. and H. Elkington are given credit for being the first to use the electrolytic method of plating silver in 1838.

An electroplated-silver article is completely shaped and formed from a base metal and then coated with a thin layer of silver. In the late 19th century, the base metal was Britannia, an alloy of tin, copper, and antimony. Other bases are copper and brass. Today, the base is nickel silver.

In 1847, Rogers Bros. of Hartford, Connecticut, introduced the electroplating process in America. By 1855, a number of firms were using the method to produce silver-plated items in large quantities.

The quality of the plating is important. Extensive polishing can cause the base metal to show through. The prices for plated-silver items are low, making them popular items with younger collectors.

Bun warmer, 12-1/2" l, oval, cover chased with flowers and foliage, beaded rim, paw feet, liner, two reeded handles **275.00**

Candelabra, pr, 12" h, Continental, three-light, tapering stem issuing central urn-form candle-cup and two scrolling branches supporting wax pan and conforming candle-cup, oval foot with reeded border, vertical flutes **150.00**

Candle lamp shade, Tiffany Studios, Grapevine pattern, domed, pierced grapevine design, imp "Tiffany Studios New York," 6-1/2" d, 2" d fitter rim, 3-3/8" h, minor dents, price for four **1,265.00**

Candlesticks, pr, 7-1/2" h, Wurtembergishe Metallwarenfabrik, sq base applied with bow-tie garlands and foliage, rim with stylized leaves and beads rising to Corinthian column stems, detachable bobeches with beaded rims **375.00**

Claret jug, 9-1/2" h, eagle-form, textured cranberry glass body with realistic silver plate head and feet, set with glass eyes, hinged at neck, clear

Silver plated, carriage, standing female figure, movable wheels, ornate scrolls and flowers, Simpson, Hall, Miller Co., 16" l, 11" h, $650. Photo courtesy of Joy Luke Auctions.

Silver plated, creamer, steer, curved tail, bee on back, base engraved with grass and flowers, 6-1/2" w, $350. Photo courtesy of Sloan's Auctioneers & Appraisers.

draw handle, Continental, early 20th C **460.00**

Coffee urn

Continental, 19-1/2" h, vase form, body and lid fluted in sections, acanthus-capped handles, reeded spigot, sq pedestal base with ball feet **375.00**

Victorian, 16" h, baluster shape, repoussé grapevines centering two vacant cartouches, two handles in form of branch applied with similar dec, circular base pierced with scrolls at internals on four scroll, foliate, and beaded supports, detachable cover, grapevine finial **125.00**

Egg cup, 2-3/4" h, England, early 20th C, stems formed as cast kangaroos resting in circular underplates, price for pr **100.00**

Epergne, 13-1/2" h, three pale blue patterned glass vases with central reeded shaft, tripod base, winged sea horses supports, marked "HW & Co.," top insert missing **450.00**

Fish set, English, late 19th C, six forks, six knives with engraved blades, mother-of-pearl handles, wood case **320.00**

Flatware service, Marly pattern, Christofle, France, 20th C, service for 12 ....**990.00**

Game platter, 16" h, 26-1/2" l, English, late 19th C, well and three-platter base with attached hot water pan, raised on four medallion-capped feet, associated domed cov with beaded bands and engraved wide border of entwined circlets, applied open handle surrounded by conforming engraved dec, body with engraved griffin .**700.00**

Garniture, 6-1/4" h ftd compote with repoussé floral and foliate bands, each

side pc with conforming dec, Tiffany & Co. **350.00**

Hot water kettle on stand, 13" h, rounded kettle, partially reeded sides, scrolled silver, wood handle, detachable arming stand, marked "Made in England, Hand Chased" **150.00**

Inkwell, 11-1/2" h, England or America, 20th C, fence form, central fence supporting two urn form candle sconces, ends with three stakes bearing square cut glass inkwells with silver plated lids **195.00**

Lamp, table, 20-1/2" h, paneled shade, conical base, openwork silverplate grape vine designs, five panels of green and white slag glass, cast leaf finial, engraved leaves on base, base marked "Made and Guaranteed by the MB Co. USA," electrified, five sockets **1,200.00**

Monteith cooler, attributed to England, late 19th C, oval, shaped rims and cast loop handles, 7-3/4" w, 13" l, price for pr **815.00**

Punch cup, Lavigne, 1881 Rogers **25.00**

Sandwich box, 5-3/4" h, 4-1/8" h, English, early 20th C, rect, loop handle, hinged lid monogrammed, gilt int., leather carrying case **80.00**

Snuffbox, 2-3/4" l, English, late 19th C, foliate scroll engraved lid, set with central faceted purple stone, cowry shell body **300.00**

Silver plated, water cooler by Meriden Silver Plate Co., product number "8244," cylinder body with castle top supported by four columns, decorated base has band with birds and flowers, central cylinder has large repoussé horse with jockey, man walking horse, colt, chickens, birds and trees, standing horse finial (tail broken), full spigot with ivory handle, presentation plaque "Presented to S.S. Houghton by Chas Casper Jany 1st 1882," 11" d base, 21" h, $1,495. Photo courtesy of James D. Julia, Inc.

Plated, vase, white irid glass vase, silver plated holder with three-dimensional French Revolutionary War couple, square base, made by Derby, c1880, 8-5/8" h, $160.

Teapot, on base, 13" h, ribbing on bottom half, lid, and scrolled brass legs and burner, wooden scalloped finial, curved handle, two locking pegs on chains, marked "WH & SBP" ...**175.00**

Teapot, presentation type, 7" d, Mackay Cunningham & Co., Edinburgh, late 19th C, realistically modeled as curling stone, lid with bone and faux ivory handle, engraved reeded band on sides, engraved inscription, tapered circular silver plated stand.....**375.00**

Toast rack, 7" l, 2-5/8" w, England, late 19th/early 20th C, oval, central ring handle above cast cricket ball, rack formed as crossed cricket bats, four ball feet.....................**90.00**

Tray, 32" l, Victorian, oval, field engraved with floral and diaper medallions flanked by foliage with foliate garlands at intervals, beaded and geometrical design border and handles.....................**350.00**

Sheffield

Englishmen G. R. Elkington and H. Elkington are given credit for being the first to use the electrolytic method of plating silver in 1838.

Candlesticks, pr, 24" h, ornate columns with composite capitals, pale blue blown glass hurricane shades with cut floral designs **425.00**

Entree dish, 11" x 8", shaped rect, gadrooned rim, detachable handle with gadroon dec.................**75.00**

Hot water urn, 22-3/4" h, early 19th C, Philip Ashberry & Sons makers, urn-form body with flat leaf engraving at base, wide central band of engraved anthemion, round domed base with beaded rim, trumpet foot with band of guillouche centered by flowerheads and accented with husks, angular handles terminating in flat leaves, anthemion handle on top, domed lid with flat leaf engraving and foliage baluster finial, inner sleeve **750.00**

Sauceboat with underplate, rim applied with grapevines **95.00**

Soup tureen, 16" l, 10-3/4" h, early 19th C, ovoid body with applied gadroon and shell border, two fluted handles with leaf terminals, four scroll and flat leaf feet, domed lid with reeded band, leaf-form finial, body and lid with let-in engraved heraldic device, fitted drop-in liner, restorations, rosing **1,725.00**

Tankard, 5" h, Hy Wilkinson & Co. makers, tapered cylindrical form, plain ear handle, gold washed int., fitted leather case, 10 troy oz **235.00**

Tea and coffee service, baluster shaped coffeepot, 12-1/4" h kettle-on-stand, teapot, creamer, two handled open sugar, waste bowl, oval with canted corners, angular handles
. . . . **425.00**

SILVER OVERLAY

History: Silver overlay is silver applied directly to a finished glass or porcelain object. The overlay is cut and decorated, usually by engraving, prior to being molded around the object.

Glass usually is of high quality and is either crystal or colored. Lenox used silver overlay on some porcelain pieces. Most designs are from the Art Nouveau and Art Deco periods.

For more information, see this book.

Basket, 5-1/2" l, 6" h, deep cranberry body, allover floral and lattice design, sterling handle **600.00**

Decanter, 11-1/2" h, molded, pinched oval bottle, surface bamboo dec overall, base disk imp "Yuan Shun/Sterling," faceted crystal hollow stopper **375.00**

Flask, 5" h, clear bottle shaped body, scrolling hallmarked silver, hinged cov
. . . . **275.00**

Divided relish dish, mayonnaise bowl with underplate and ladle, small plate, $100. Photo courtesy of Joy Luke Auctions.

Inkwell, 3-3/4" x 3", bright green ground, rose, scroll, and lattice overlay, matching cov, monogram **650.00**

Jug, 9" h, colorless glass, tapered baluster form, star-cut base, silver cased applied draw handle, overlay of twining grapes and grape vines, plain cartouche beneath spout, stylized cobweb overlay below, Alvin Mfg Co., late 19th/early 20th C **1,380.00**

Perfume bottle

4" h, bulbed colorless glass bottle with engraved scrolled foliate silver overlay dec, initial "S" in cartouche, silver overlay on ball shaped glass stopper, Continental, wear, some loss to silver. **75.00**

5" h, baluster, elongated neck, colorless glass, scrolling foliage overlay, central monogrammed cartouche **225.00**

Tea set, 8-3/4" h, Lenox porcelain body, Reed & Barton silver overlay, three-pc set. **325.00**

Apple-green Lenox with Mauser silver overlay, salt and pepper shakers overlaid with violets, c1905; 4" h jam jar overlaid with apples, pre-1932, green stamp marks, $395. Photo courtesy of David Rago Auctions.

Flask, 3/16" pint, monogrammed, dated 1904, heavy overlay grape and leaf decoration, some dents, 5" h, $200. Photo courtesy of James D. Julia, Inc.

Vase, Heintz, sterling on bronze, cylindrical, rolled rim, cattail overlay on original verdigris patina, stamped mark and patent, 3" d, 6" h, $375. Photo courtesy of David Rago Auctions.

Vase, baluster, satin finished diamond quilted turquoise glass, Art Nouveau floral design silver overlay, marked "L Sterling," imperfections in glass, 10" h, $550. Photo courtesy of Sanford Alderfer Auction Company.

Vase

5" d, 12-1/4" h, bronze, sterling silver overlay of trees, verdigris patina, Heintz **850.00**

6" w, 10" h, baluster, mulberry glazed pottery, stylized tulip design applied in silver, marked "Spahr/800" **495.00**

7" h, Art Nouveau free-form irid blue body, applied silver overlay in iris pattern **1,100.00**

13-3/4" h, Art Nouveau ovoid cranberry glass body, flared rim supported by three applied clear glass handles, silver overlay on rim and body, waterlily and cattails design, marks obscured, minor losses to silver overlay . . **1,250.00**

SMITH BROS. GLASS

For more information, see this book.

History: After establishing a decorating department at the Mount Washington Glass Works in 1871, Alfred and Harry Smith struck out on their own in 1875. Their New Bedford, Massachusetts, firm soon became known worldwide for its fine opalescent decorated wares, similar in style to those of Mount Washington.

Marks: Smith Bros. glass often is marked on the base with a red shield enclosing a rampant lion and the word "Trademark."

Reproduction Alert: Beware of examples marked "Smith Bros."

Atomizer, 7" h, tan shading to cream opaque body, enameled amethyst and pink flowers, painted lion trademark, new hardware **260.00**

Biscuit jar

6" d, melon ribbed body shading from white to blue, polychrome enameled flowers **150.00**

7" h, opaque cream ground, sculptured diagonal swirl pattern, polychrome flower dec, red lion trademark **300.00**

7" d, 7-1/4" h, melon ribbed cream body, fall colored oak leaves, gold

Vase jar, melon ribbed, chrysanthemum decoration on pastel green background, gold beads around top, signed with rampant lion mark, repair to top of jar, 8-1/2" h, $100. Photo courtesy of James D. Julia, Inc.

acorns, metal lid stamped "S.B." **415.00**

7" d, 8-1/2" h, green and pastel brown tendrils of ivy wind around melon ribbed body, gold plated fittings, sgd "405" **885.00**

Bowl

3" d, lobed, pale pink ground, daisies dec, red rampant lion mark **150.00**

6" d, 2-3/4" h, melon ribbed, two shades of gold prunus dec, beaded white rim **375.00**

Sugar bowl, covered, melon ribbed, gold enamel blossoms, leaves, and branches, original metal hardware stamped "S. B.," 4-1/4" h, $230. Photo courtesy of James D. Julia, Inc.

9" d, 4" h, melon ribbed, beige ground, pink Moss Rose dec, blue flowers, green leaves, white beaded rim **675.00**

Bride's bowl, 9-1/2" d, 3" h bowl, 16" h overall, opal glass bowl, painted ground, 2" band dec with cranes, fans, vases, and flowers, white and gray dec, fancy silver-plated holder sgd and numbered 2117 . . . . **1,450.00**

Creamer and sugar, 4" d, 3-3/4" h, shaded blue and beige ground, multicolored violet and leaves dec, fancy silverplated metalware . . . **750.00**

Humidor, 6-1/2" h, 4" d, cream ground, eight blue pansies, melon-ribbed cov **850.00**

Jar, cov, 4" h, melon ribbed cream body, white daisies dec, red lion trademark **150.00**

Mustard jar, cov, 2" h, ribbed, gold prunus dec, white ground **300.00**

Plate, 7-3/4" d, Santa Maria, beige, brown, and pale orange ship . . . **635.00**

Rose bowl, 2-1/4" h, 3" d, cream ground, jeweled gold prunus dec, gold beaded top, sgd **285.00**

Salt and pepper shakers, silverplate napkin ring center on platform base, white shakers with blue floral trim, marked "Rockford #29" **750.00**

Vase, melon ribbed body, three enameled clusters of pastel blue raised gold outlined wisteria blossoms clinging to golden vines that meander across shoulder, pendants of old-gold-colored leaves, other pendants of gray shadow-like leaves in the distance, cream background, 6-1/2" d, 8-1/2", $1,000. Photo courtesy of Clarence and Betty Maier.

Salt, open, 2-1/2" d, 1-1/4" h, white ground, amber dec, sgd with trademark and lion shield **225.00**

Sugar shaker, 5-3/4" h, pillar ribbed, white ground, pink wild rose and pale blue leaves, blue beaded top, orig cov fair **495.00**

Toothpick holder

2-1/4" h, barrel shape, opaque white body, swag of single petaled blossoms **265.00**

2-1/2" h Little Lobe, pale blue body, single petaled rose blossoms, raised blue dots on rim. . . . **245.00**

Vase

5-1/4" h, 3-1/2" d, pinched-in, apricot ground, white wisteria dec, gold highlights, sgd **375.00**

5-1/2" h, petticoat shape, flared base, pink ground, multicolored foliage and herons, stamped mark on base, "Smith brothers-New Bedford, MA," pr **850.00**

7" h, soft pink ground, inverted dec of white pond lily, blue-green and black leaves, brown stems, maroon trim, c1870, pr **375.00**

8-1/2" h, double bulbed form, repeating molded foliate and panel motifs at top, hp chrysanthemum blossoms and leaves, cream and green ground, stamped "Smith Brothers" trademark in red on base **1,150.00**

10" h, 8" w, shaded rust, brown, yellow and gold ground, white apple blossoms, green leaves, and branches, painted beige int. **595.00**

12-1/2" h, Verona, colorless ground, deep purple and white irises, gold trim, green leaves and stems, int. vertical ribs. **550.00**

SNUFF BOTTLES

History: Tobacco usage spread from America to Europe to China during the 17th century. Europeans and Chinese preferred to grind the dried leaves into a powder and sniff it into their nostrils. The elegant Europeans carried their boxes and took a pinch with their fingertips. The Chinese upper class, because of their lengthy fingernails, found this inconvenient and devised a bottle with a fitted stopper and attached spoon. These utilitarian objects soon became objets d'art.

Snuff bottles were fashioned from precious and semi-precious stones, glass, porcelain and pottery, wood, metals, and ivory. Glass and transparent-stone bottles often were enhanced further with delicate hand paintings, some done on the interior of the bottle.

Hardstone, hand-carved agate, high-relief flowers and crane, Chinese, mounted on hardwood stand, domed lid glued down, chips, 3" h, $65. Photo courtesy of Cowan's Historic Americana Auctions.

Agate, Chinese

Baluster, blue, carved and incised birds amid flowering branches, conforming stopper with floral finial, 3" h **175.00**

Cameo, carved running horse. **80.00**

Carved, man rowing boat and pine trees **175.00**

Amber, landscape and figures, caramel inclusions, conforming id, Chinese, late 19th C, 4" l **1,265.00**

Celadon

Light jade, flattened ovoid short neck, 2-1/4" h **185.00**

Mottled jade, gray and brown inclusions, dog mask and ring form handles, Qing dynasty, Chinese **400.00**

Chrysoprase, flattened ovoid, light green, conforming stopper, 3" h . **215.00**

Cinnabar lacquer, ovoid, continual scene of scholars and boys in a pavilion landscape, dark red, conforming stopper, 3-1/4" h **230.00**

Cloisonné, auspicious symbols among clouds, yellow ground, lappet base border, ruyi head neck border, conforming stopper with chrysanthemum design, Qianlong four-character mark **185.00**

Coral, cylindrical, carved kylin, Chinese, 2-1/2" h **175.00**

Carved ivory, double, form of a Japanese lady with bouquet and Japanese man with walking stick and fan, colorful ink decoration, each container has its own ivory spoon attached to the heads of figures, 2-3/4" h, $275. Photo courtesy of Sanford Alderfer Auction Company.

Enameled glass, each side dec with deer beneath flowing trees, seal mark in red on base, 2-3/8" h **920.00**

Ivory, 3-3/4" l, curved ivory carved with bulrushes and crocodiles, flatleaf cap with ball finial, pebbled gilt-metal lid with glass-inset neck, mounted with short neck chain, Indian, late 19th/early 20th C **300.00**

Jade

Apple-green and celadon, silver mounted, Chinese **750.00**

Black, flattened rect form, relief carved mountains, applied white jade figural grouping on one side, rose quartz stopper, wood base, 2-1/2" h **255.00**

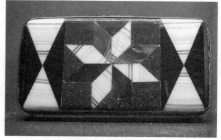

Snuffbox, agate quartz, brass trimmed, lid lined with slate, Inscription on slate reads "N.K. to W. B. Dance," mosaic star design on outside of lid, 1802, 2-1/2" l, $440. Photo courtesy of Sanford Alderfer Auction Company.

White jade, golden skin, D-shaped body, well hollowed, silver stopper mounted with amethyst, 19th C **300.00**

Lapis lazuli, ovoid, relief carved, figures beneath tree, Chinese, 4" h **115.00**

Malachite, carved, gourd, Chinese, 3" h **75.00**

Opal, carved sage seated before gourd, Ch'ing Dynasty, 3" h **125.00**

Overlay glass, seven colors, one side with floral designs in two archaic-form vases, reverse with immortal attending a crane and deer, bats flying above, each side with animal mask and ring handles, green, blue, mauve, coral, brown, and yellow, on white ground, 19th C....................**520.00**

Peking glass, Snowflake

Blue overlay, each side with prancing deer, head turned with a lingchi branch in mouth, 19th C, 2-1/2" h **490.00**

Red overlay, flattened ovoid, one side with serpent and tortoise, other with frog sitting under lily pad, 2-1/4" h **1,265.00**

Porcelain, Chinese, blue and white, floral dec, wood stand, Qianlong mark **450.00**

Rose quartz, flattened ovoid, relief carved leaves and vines, Chinese, 3" h **45.00**

Stag horn, flattened ovoid, one side with inset ivory panel with two laughing figures, reserve with inset panel with gold archaic script, 2-1/8" h **175.00**

Turquoise, flattened body, high shoulder, relief carved auspicious symbol, agate stopper, wood stand, 2-3/8" h **165.00**

Snuffbox, wood, bellows shape, decorated with brass tack lettering, reads "Forget Me Not," 4-3/4" l, $225. Photo courtesy of Sanford Alderfer Auction Company.

SOAPSTONE

History: The mineral steatite, known as soapstone because of its greasy feel, has been used for carving figural groups and designs by the Chinese and others. Utilitarian pieces also were made. Soapstone pieces were very popular during the Victorian era.

Vase, four openings, red tones, Chinese, c1900, 9-1/2" l, 6-3/4" h, $125.

Bookends, pr, 5" h, carved, block form, fu lion resting on top, Chinese.. **300.00**

Bullet mold, 6" l, inscribed "Don't Tread on Me," locations for Fort Lewis, Goshen, Buffalo Gap, Bull Pasture, Deerfield, Shenandoah Mt. **850.00**

Candlesticks, pr, 5-1/8" h, red tones, flowers and foliage **85.00**

Carving

3" h, even white color, servant kneeling before woman holding fan, China, 19th C **115.00**

4" w, 4-1/2" d, 3-1/2" h, dog's head, old darkened color, America, 19th C, chips, with stand **420.00**

8-1/2" h, man, standing, smiling, holding lotus flower **60.00**

9-1/4" h, Buddha, seated, praying, carved stone base **60.00**

12" h, woman, standing, wearing robe, restoration......... **120.00**

Hot plate, 16" l, 8-1/2" w **75.00**

Vase, carved peacock and chrysanthemums, stand, 15-1/2" h, $495. Photo courtesy of Joy Luke Auctions.

Plaque, 9-1/2" h, birds, trees, flowers, and rocks **125.00**

Sculpture, 10-1/4" h, 4-1/2" w, kneeling nude young woman, Canadian .. **95.00**

Sealing stamp, carved dec, 5" h, 1" d, curved scroll................. **95.00**

Toothpick holder, two containers with carved birds, animals, and leaves **85.00**

SOUVENIR AND COMMEMORATIVE CHINA AND GLASS

History: Souvenir, commemorative, and historical china and glass includes those items produced to celebrate special events, places, and people.

Collectors particularly favor China plates made by Rowland and Marcellus and Wedgwood. Rowland and Marcellus, Staffordshire, England, made a series of blue-and-white historic plates with a wide rolled edge. Scenes from the Philadelphia Centennial in 1876 through the 1939 New York World's Fair are depicted. In 1910, Wedgwood collaborated with Jones, McDuffee, and Stratton to produce a series of historic dessert-sized plates showing scenes of places throughout the United States.

Many localities issued plates, mugs, glasses, etc., for anniversary celebrations or to honor a local historical event. These items seem to have greater value when sold in the region in which they originated.

Commemorative glass includes several patterns of pressed glass that celebrate people or events. Historical glass includes campaign and memorial items.

Bust, Gillinder

Lincoln, frosted **325.00**

Napoleon, frosted and clear . **295.00**

Shakespeare, frosted **150.00**

Ashtray, New York City, blue and white transfer, Empire State Building, Statue of Liberty, Rockefeller Center, harbor scene, marked "Fine Staffordshire Ware, Enco, National, Made in England," $15.

Mug, ruby stained, "Souvenir of Blairsville," applied clear handle, $25.

Creamer

New Academy, Truro, multicolored image on white medallion, cobalt blue ground, gold and white dec
.... **30.00**

Wadsworth Atheneum, Hartford, CT, multicolored image on white medallion, lustered ground, 2" h, marked "Wheelock China, Austria"
.... **18.00**

Cup, Entrance to Soldier's Home, Leavenworth, Kansas, multicolored, beaded dec, 2-1/2" h, marked "Germany," slight wear to gold dec
.... **18.00**

Cup and saucer

Niagara Falls, cobalt blue ground, gold trim, 1-1/4" h x 1-3/4" d, 3-1/2" d saucer, scene of falls on saucer, marked "Made in Japan," matching wooden display stand
.... **20.00**

Souvenir of Edina, Missouri, white ground, rose dec, gold trim, 2-1/2" h x 3-3/4" w cup, 5-1/2" w cup, marked "Japan" **20.00**

Washington and Lafayette, transfer print portraits on cup of George Washington and Lafayette, saucer with portrait titled "Washington His Country's Father," 1-3/4" h, creamware, England, early 19th C
.... **490.00**

Demitasse cup and saucer

My Old Kentucky Home, 2" h x 2" w cup, 4" d saucer, marked "Handpainted, Made in Japan, NICO" **15.00**

Souvenir of Chicago, Ill, Victorian man and woman on inside of cup, 2" h x 2-1/2" w cup, gold trim, marked "Crest O Gold, Sabin, Warranted 22K" **17.50**

Dish

Beauvoir House, Jefferson Davis House, Biloxi, MS, 3-1/4" d, marked "Made by Adams, England for the Jefferson Davis Shrine" **20.00**

DeShong Memorial Art Gallery, Lester, PA, yellow luster ground, 3-3/4" x 3-1/4", marked "Made in Germany," wear to lettering and gold trim **12.00**

Dish, cov, Remember the *Maine*, green opaque glass **135.00**

Figure, souvenir of Atlantic City, two pigs having picture taken, green ground, marked "Germany" **150.00**

Goblet

G.A.R., 1887, 21st Encampment
.... **100.00**

Mother, Ruby Thumbprint pattern
.... **35.00**

Mug

Market Place and Town Hall, Preston, photos on front and back, pink luster ground, dated 1894, 3-1/2" h **35.00**

Ross Castle, Killarney, Ireland, orange luster ground, dec handle, 2-1/2" h, marked "G. H. O., Austria"
.... **25.00**

Paperweight

Moses in Bulrushes, frosted center
.... **145.00**

Plymouth Rock, clear........ **95.00**

Ruth the Cleaner, frosted.... **125.00**

Washington, George, round, frosted center **295.00**

Pitcher, 10" h, ironstone, shell molded oval form, wine-red ground, circular paneled sides enamel dec with landscape scenes, gilt trim, titled cartouche below spout "Senator Martin Wyckoff, of Warren County," imp mark "U Pottery," c1885, gilt wear.... **460.00**

Plate

Atlantic City, NJ, Rowland and Marcellus, 10-1/2" d **50.00**

Florida, Saint Augustine, Vernon Kilns, marked "Designed exclusively for J. Carver Harris"
.... **20.00**

Hogg, James Stephen, first native born governor of Texas, brown print, Vernon Kilns, marked "Designed for Daughters of the Republic of Texas" **25.00**

Marietta College 125th Anniversary, 1960, Wedgwood......... **25.00**

Nebraska, University of Nebraska, Vernon Kilns **30.00**

Oklahoma, Agricultural and Mechanical College, Vernon Kilns, marked "Designed especially for Creech's Stillwater, Oklahoma"
.... **32.00**

Remember the *Maine*, Spanish-American war, c1900, 8-1/2" d **240.00**

Sulphur Springs, Delaware, OH, light blue and black transfer, Staffordshire, NY retailer's label, 10-1/2" d, chip on table ring
.... **200.00**

Texas, Southwest Methodist University, Dallas, Vernon Kilns, marked "Made exclusively for Titche-Goettinger Co." **35.00**

Washington, Bellingham, green print, Vernon Kilns **60.00**

Tile, 4" d, Detroit Women's League, multicolored irid glass........ **135.00**

Tumbler, etched

Lord's Prayer.............. **15.00**

Niagara Falls, Prospect Point, gold rim **20.00**

Whittier birthplace, waisted, tall
.... **60.00**

Plate, memorial, Garfield center, clear pressed glass, 10" d, **$65.**

Plate, Boston department stores, founders in border, blue transfer, white ground, Wedgwood, 9-3/4" d, **$35.**

SOUVENIR AND COMMEMORATIVE SPOONS

History: Souvenir and commemorative spoons have been issued for hundreds of years. Early American silversmiths engraved presentation spoons to honor historical personages or mark key events.

In 1881, Myron Kinsley patented a Niagara Falls spoon, and in 1884, Michael Gibney patented a new flatware design. M. W. Galt, Washington, D.C., issued commemorative spoons for George and Martha Washington in 1889. From these beginnings, a collecting craze for souvenir and commemorative spoons developed in the late 19th and early 20th centuries.

Additional Listings: See *Warman's Americana & Collectibles* for more examples.

Basiwgstoke, red, blue, and orange enamel on shield, blade, unmarked, 5" l, **$12.**

Boulder, CO, name in bowl, Indian head handle **40.00**
B. P. O. E. Elks #896, marked "Reed & Barton Klitzner RI," silverplate, 4-1/2" l
. . . . **15.00**
Cawston Ostrich Farms, marked "Sterling," 3-1/4" l **15.00**
Denver, CO, sterling, gold washed bowl, acid etched pack mule, stem-end topped with winch with handle that turns, applied pick and shovel, stem entwined with rope, ending in bucket,

Lancaster, PA, city name engraved in bowl, sterling, **$30.**

Stratford on Avon, yellow enamel shield, 3-5/8" l, marked "EPNS," **$15.**

opposed by modeled rock, 1 troy oz, late 19th C **85.00**
Fort Dearborn, 1803-1857, marked "Sterling, Hyman Berg," 6" l **20.00**
Golden Gate Bridge, San Francisco, CA, marked "Holland 90" and hallmark, 5" l **15.00**
King Cotton **45.00**
Memorial Arch, Brooklyn, NY, round oak stove **40.00**
Palm Springs, Aerial Tramway, SP, John Brown, marked "Antico" . . **100.00**
Philadelphia, Independence Hall in bowl, SS **45.00**
Prophet, veiled **135.00**
Richmond, MO, SS **30.00**
Royal Canadian Mounted Police, "Victoria, British Columbia" in bowl, marked "Made in Holland," 4-1/2" l
. . . . **30.00**
Salem, MA, witch handle **45.00**
SS Momus, Westfield Pattern, Meridan Britannia, 1903, back engraved "L. P. Co.," 6" l **10.00**
St. Paul, The Tower, Houses of Parliament, West Minister, each marked "L. E. P. A1" on back, set of four in orig box **42.00**
Thousand Islands, fish handle, engraved bowl, SS, Watson **45.00**
Vista House, Columbia River, OR, detailed handle, marked "Sterling"
. . . . **32.00**
Windmill, detailed curved handle, movable blades on figural windmill, hallmarked **38.00**

SPANGLED GLASS

For more information, see this book.

History: Spangled glass is a blown or blown-molded variegated art glass, similar to spatter glass, with the addition of flakes of mica or metallic aventurine. Many pieces are cased with a white or clear layer of glass. Spangled glass was developed in the late 19th century and still is being manufactured.

Originally, spangled glass was attributed only to the Vasa Murrhina Art Glass Company of Hartford, Connecticut, which distributed the glass for Dr. Flower of the Cape Cod Glassworks, Sandwich, Massachusetts. However, research has shown that many companies in Europe, England, and the United States made spangled glass, and attributing a piece to a specific source is very difficult.

Basket, 7" h, 6" l, ruffled edge, white int., deep apricot with spangled gold, applied crystal loop handle, slight flake
. . . . **225.00**
Beverage set, bulbous pitcher, six matching tumblers, rubena, opalescent mottling, silver flecks, attributed to Sandwich, c1850-60 . . . . **250.00**
Bride's bowl, 10-1/2" d, ruffled rim, yellow and white mottled ground, overall silver mica flakes, yellow stemmed blue daisies dec **90.00**
Candlesticks, pr, 8-1/8" h, pink and whit spatter, green aventurine flecks, cased white int. **115.00**
Creamer, 3-1/4" d, 4-3/4" h, bulbous, molded swirled ribs, cylindrical neck, pinched spout, blue ground, swirled mica flecks, applied clear reeded handle **225.00**
Cruet, Leaf Mold pattern, cranberry, mica flakes, white casing, Northwood
. . . . **450.00**
Ewer, 9-1/2" h, raspberry pink ext., white int., mica flecks, twisted applied handle, rough pontil **250.00**
Jack-in-the-pulpit vase, 6-1/4" h, oxblood, green, and white spatter, mica flakes, c1900 . . . . **125.00**
Pitcher, 8-1/2" h, white, and amber cased to clear, mica flakes, applied amber reeded handle **550.00**
Rose bowl, 4" d, 3-1/4" h, pink cased body, Vasa Murrhina dec **50.00**

Barber bottle, red and white spatter, mica flecks, no stopper, 8-1/4" h, **$195.**

Salt shaker, cranberry, cased white int., molded leaf design, Hobbs, c1890
. . . . **125.00**
Sugar shaker, cranberry, mica flakes, white casing, Northwood. **115.00**
Toothpick holder, 2-1/4" h, alternating crimson and white mottled ground, gold mica, lattice stripes **65.00**
Tumbler, 3-3/4" h, pink, gold, and brown spatter, mica flecks, white lining
. . . . **90.00**
Vase
6-3/4" h, glossy pink cased satin, silver mica, two applied crystal handles. **75.00**
8-3/4" h, stick, cased satin glass alternating pink and blue panels, overall silver mica, crystal rigaree around neck **75.00**

SPATTER GLASS

History: Spatter glass is a variegated blown or blown-molded art glass. It originally was called "end-of-day" glass, based on the assumption that it was made from batches of glass leftover at the end of the day. However, spatter glass was found to be a standard production item for many glass factories.

Spatter glass was developed at the end of the 19th century and is still being produced in the United States and Europe.

For more information, see this book.

Reproduction Alert: Many modern examples come from the area previously called Czechoslovakia.

Basket, tortoiseshell, cream, tan, yellow, white, and brown spatter, white lining, rect, tightly crimped edge, colorless thorn handle. **120.00**
Berry set, master bowl and two sauces, Leaf Mold, cranberry vaseline
. . . . **300.00**
Bowl, 8-1/2" d, amber and brown mottled tortoiseshell **90.00**
Box, cov, cranberry ground, white spatter, clear knob finial **200.00**
Candlestick, 7-1/2" h, yellow, red, and white streaks, clear overlay, vertical swirled molding, smooth base, flanged socket **60.00**
Cologne bottle, 5-1/2" h, white spatter, enamel dec, orig stopper applicator,

Fairy lamp, orange, red, yellow, and white spatter, clear marked "Clarke's Patent" base, 4-1/2" h, $145.

marked "Made in Czechoslovakia," price for pr **115.00**
Creamer, Leaf Mold, cranberry vaseline
. . . . **250.00**
Darning egg, multicolored, attributed to Sandwich Glass **125.00**
Ewer, yellow ground, white spatter, tri-fold spout, flared applied clear handle, sharp pontil, 8-3/4" h **85.00**
Finger bowl and underplate, 6" d, 3-1/4" d, tortoiseshell, ruffled . . . **275.00**
Jack-in-the-pulpit, 5" h, 3-1/2" d, Vasa Murrhina, deep pink int., clear ruffled top **115.00**
Pitcher, 6-1/2" d, 8" h, burgundy and white spatter, cased in clear, ground pontil, clear reeded handle **395.00**
Rose bowl
Leaf Mold, cranberry ground, vaseline spatter. **250.00**
Mt. Washington, pink, blue, and white spatter on colorless ground, white opalescent scalloped top
. . . . **135.00**
Salt, 3" l, maroon and pink, white spatter, applied clear feet and handle
. . . . **125.00**

Pitcher, hand blown, multicolored spatter, interior cased in white glass, applied clear reeded handle, 8-1/2" h, $225. Photo courtesy of James D. Julia, Inc.

Sugar shaker, Leaf Umbrella pattern, cranberry. **495.00**
Tumbler, 3-3/4"h, emb Swirl pattern, white, maroon, pink, yellow, and green, white int. **65.00**
Vase
4" h, yellow ground, white spatter, floral dec **95.00**
7" h, 4-1/2" d, golden yellow and white, enameled bird and flowers, applied clear handles, colored enamel dec **180.00**
Watch holder, 3-3/4" x 4-1/4" dish, ruffled rim, blue spatter, 7" h ormolu metal watch holder **175.00**
Water set, Leaf Mold, cranberry vaseline. **1,495.00**

SPATTERWARE

History: Spatterware generally was made of common earthenware, although occasionally creamware was used. The earliest English examples were made about 1780. The peak period of production was from 1810 to 1840. Firms known to have made spatterware are Adams, Barlow, and Harvey and Cotton.

The amount of spatter decoration varies from piece to piece. Some objects simply have decorated borders. These often were decorated with a brush, requiring several hundred touches per square inch to achieve the spatter effect. Other pieces have the entire surface covered with spatter.

For more information, see this book.

Marks: Marked pieces are rare.

Notes: Collectors today focus on the patterns—Cannon, Castle, Fort, Peafowl, Rainbow, Rose, Thistle, Schoolhouse, etc. The decoration on flatware is in the center of the piece; on hollow ware, it occurs on both sides.

Aesthetics and the color of spatter are key to determining value. Blue and red are the most common colors; green, purple, and brown are in a middle group; black and yellow are scarce.

Like any soft paste, spatterware is easily broken or chipped. Prices in this listing are for pieces in very good to mint condition.

Reproduction Alert: Cybis spatter is an increasingly collectible ware in its own right. The pieces, made by the Polishman Boleslaw Cybis in the 1940s, have an Adams-type peafowl design. Many contemporary craftsmen also are reproducing spatterware.

Cup and saucer, handleless, green and red design, 2-3/4" d, **$120.**

Bowl, 5-1/2" d, Morning Glory flowers, red spatter, purple flowers, light overall crazing, small table rim chip **65.00**

Charger, 12" d, Persian Ware, marked "Allerton, Persian Ware, England," imp "10" **135.00**

Creamer

3-1/2" h, red and green rose, brown and black spatter, rim flake. **650.00**

3-3/4" h, Morning Glory, blue and green flower, red spatter . **2,750.00**

4" h, Rainbow Thumbprint, red, yellow, and blue peafowl, red, blue, and green spatter, damage and restoration **1,650.00**

5" h, red and green cockscomb design, blue spatter, paneled, stains on foot, minor flakes . **860.00**

5-5/8" h, Peafowl, red, green, and blue, paneled, unusual squiggly branches, minor enamel flake in blue **770.00**

Cup, blue stick spatter looping pattern, red, green, and blue long tulip . . . **75.00**

Cup and saucer, handleless

Dark blue, green, and red pomegranate, yellow dots, blue spatter, light stains, crazed saucer **800.00**

Light brown spatter, red and blue spray with green leaves, hairlines **385.00**

Peafowl, red, yellow, and blue, blue spatter, minor wear spot on tail **325.00**

Rainbow, Drape pattern, red, yellow, and green, small rim repair on cup, minor stains on saucer .. **3,080.00**

Red and green Christmas ball dec, light stains on cup **3,960.00**

Red, mustard, and green six-pointed star, stains on cup, foot chip **925.00**

Red, yellow, green, and blue tulip dec, blue spatter, cup has stained

area, filled-in flakes, hairline **110.00**

Miniature, handleless cup and saucer

Blue spatter, blue, mauve, and green dahlia **300.00**

Blue spatter, light green yellow, and red peafowl **350.00**

Red spatter **200.00**

Pitcher

4-3/4" h, blue drape with bands on shoulder, rim, and handle, hairlines, some stains, in-the-making separation at handle **460.00**

7-3/8" h, red rose, green leaves, paneled, molded spout, repaired handle with hairline **1,430.00**

7-7/8" h, paneled, molded fan under spout, red, green, and blue Peafowl, red spatter, stains, repaired spout **800.00**

8-1/2" h, Acorns, yellow and teal green, green and dark brown leaves, purple spatter, paneled, bubbles in brown and yellow, stains, rim repair **3,650.00**

Plate

7-1/2" d, Peafowl, red, yellow, and green, blue spatter border, rim chips **110.00**

8-3/8" d, blue border, blue, red, and green dahlia pattern **350.00**

8-1/2" d, blue border, center red and green flower, light stains. . . **150.00**

8-1/2" d, Peafowl, dark blue, green, and dark brown, long tail, red spatter, short hairline, in-the-making chip on table ring . **715.00**

8-1/2" d, Rainbow, light red, blue, and yellow border, rim flake **3,300.00**

Plate, Tulip pattern, yellow rim, wear, knife marks, 8-1/2" d, **$265.**

8-5/8" d, Rainbow, red, yellow, and blue spatter, few minor knife scratches **3,250.00**

8-3/4" d, red border, red, blue, and green flowers, minor enamel imperfections, minor stains . **110.00**

9-1/8" d, Rainbow, blue and yellow rainbow border, faded red and blue tulip with green leaves, hairlines, stains, filled in rim chip .. **4,400.00**

9-1/4" d, white center shield with blue stripes, red stars, blue spatter, back imp "Pekin China, T & Booth" **1,155.00**

9-1/2" d, Peafowl, red, yellow, and green, long tail extending into blue borer, three rim flakes, small burst bubbles **770.00**

10-1/2" d, Rainbow, red, blue, and green border, scalloped edge, imp "Adams," filled-in rim chip . **385.00**

10-3/4" d, blue flowers, red and blue flowers green leaves **150.00**

Platter

8-1/4" x 10-3/4", Peafowl, red, blue, and dark brown, appears to have been scoured, two hairlines, and flake on rim underside **615.00**

10-1/2" x 13-3/4", red and green rainbow border, large red and blue tulip with green and black foliage, imp anchor mark, restorations, hairline **4,510.00**

12-3/8" d, 15-7/8" w, light blue borders, rect white center panel, oblong, scalloped corners, minor rim flakes **220.00**

13-3/4" x 17-1/2", dark brown eagle and shield transfer center, blue spatter border, octagonal, stains and hairline **295.00**

Soup plate, 8-3/4" d, blue border, red, green, and yellow stripes, floral center **195.00**

Plates, 7-1/2" d, blue spatterware, green, yellow and red peafowl in center, marked "Stoneware/PW & Co.," 8-1/4" d, red spatterware, blue, yellow and green peafowl in center, **$425.** *Photo courtesy of Sanford Alderfer Auction Company.*

Sugar bowl, cov

5" d, 5" h, blue, green, and red designs, blue stripes, minor roughness on inside flange **250.00**

5-3/4" h plus lid, paneled, red school house, green spatter trees and grass, blue spatter, small crow's foot, restored handles, lid blue transfer replacement **715.00**

Teapot

5" h, Rainbow, green and yellow with purple loops, black spots, stains, filled-in rim chip, restoration to handle, spout, and lid. . . . **5,060.00**

7-5/8" h, Cockscomb, red and green design, blue spatter, hairlines in base, restored replaced lid **550.00**

9" h, Peafowl, red spatter, panel sides with arched panels, scrolled handle, domed lid, small chips on spout **1,980.00**

Tea set, 10-1/2" h cov teapot, 9" h cov sugar, 6" h creamer, blue on white, red roses, green foliage on both sides, ear-shaped handles with scalloped detail, old restorations to finials, repaired chip on teapot lid, minor handle chips **1,760.00**

Waste bowl, 6-1/4" d, 3-1/2" h, brown, red, and black Fort pattern, blue spatter, hairline **200.00**

SPONGEWARE

History: Spongeware is a specific type of decoration, not a type of pottery or glaze.

Spongeware decoration is found on many kinds of pottery bodies—ironstone, redware, stoneware, yellowware, etc. It was made in both England and the United States. Pieces were marked after 1815, and production extended into the 1880s.

Decoration is varied. On some pieces, the sponging is minimal with the white underglaze dominant. Other pieces appear to be solidly sponged on both sides. Pieces made between 1840 and 1860 have circular or horizontally streaked sponging.

Blue and white are the most common colors, but browns, greens, ochres, and a greenish blue also were used. The greenish blue results from blue sponging with a pale yellow overglaze. A red overglaze produces a black or navy color. Blue and red were used on

English creamware and American earthenware of the 1880s. Other spongeware colors include gray, grayish green, red, dark green on stark white, dark green on mellow yellow, and purple.

Bank, 5-1/2" l, figural, piggy, blue and cream, pierced coin slot on top . **155.00**

Bowl, 7" d, fluted, brown and blue sponge, cream ground **60.00**

Butter crock, 4-5/8" d, 3" h, blue and white, back labeled "Village Farm Dairy," chips, hairlines, crazing . **300.00**

Carpet ball, 3-1/4" d

Brown **85.00**

Green **75.00**

Red and white plaid **90.00**

Creamer, 3" h, green, blue and cream **100.00**

Cup and saucer, blue flower dec on cup **60.00**

Dish, 6-1/2" x 8-1/2", blue and white, serpentine rim **200.00**

Figure, rabbit, 4-1/2" l, blue and white, dark blue accent at eyes, initialed "JC," c1880, glaze flake at one ear and front paw **1,760.00**

Marble, 2" d, gray, blue sponge, late 19th C **220.00**

Milk pitcher, 7-1/2" h, black sponge, white ground **185.00**

Miniature

Bottle, 3-1/2" h, Bristol glaze, handle, red sponge dec, c1910 . . . . . **40.00**

Bowl, 2" x 4-1/2", blue and white **125.00**

Pitcher, 2-1/4" h, blue and white, minor surface wear at base. **100.00**

Sugar bowl, 4-7/8" h, blue and white, paneled body, crazing, stains, mismatched lid **95.00**

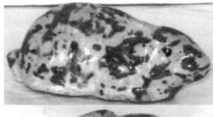

Figure, bunny, two views, dark cobalt blue at eyes, initialed "JC," c1880, 4-1/2" l, glaze flake at one ear and front paw, $1,760. Photo courtesy of Vicki and Bruce Waasdorp.

Jardinière, earthenware, blue greenish-brown sponge decoration over cream ground, hairline, imperfections, 10-1/2" d, 9-1/2" h, $210. Photo courtesy of Sanford Alderfer Auction Company.

Teapot, 4-1/8" h, blue and white dec, minor chips **850.00**

Mush cup and saucer, blue and white, worn gilt trim, slight hairline in cup base **85.00**

Pitcher

7-3/8" h, blue and white dec, minor chips on spout and rim **110.00**

9-1/2" h, blue and white, stamped "Uhl Pottery Co. Huntingburg, Ind.," some int. glaze crazing **550.00**

10" h, barrel shape, green, gold, and brown sponge **110.00**

Plate

8-3/4" d, red, yellow, and green tulip center, blue sponged border, imp

Miniature advertising jug, brown and white Bristol glaze, frame with black stenciling "Compliments of The Phoenix Bar, Los Angeles, CA 1911," back stenciled "Brook Hill None Superior," c1911, 3-3/4" h, $100. Photo courtesy of Vicki and Bruce Waasdorp.

"Cotton and Barlow," stains, filled-in rim chip, area of flaked glaze **85.00**

9-1/2" d, red, green, and black central flower dec, red and green sponged border **190.00**

Pitcher

6-1/2" h, blue and white, blue accent around rim, professional restoration to surface chip at spout, two short hairlines **155.00**

7-7/8" h, green and faded purple grapes, blue sponge dec, molded leaf spout, chips, handle glued **615.00**

9" h, navy blue and white, bulbous-shaped base **385.00**

Platter, 13-1/4" l, octagonal, central red and blue foliate chain, blue band border, cream ground, imp factory mark, Elsmore & Foster, Tunstall, 19th C **115.00**

Spittoon, 5" h, blue sponge, linear dec on white glazed ground, late 19th C **90.00**

Sugar bowl, cov, 4" h, floral reserve, brown sponge, English, 19th C . . **95.00**

Umbrella stand, 21" h, blue and white, two white accent bands, four blue accent bands, 6" u-shaped piece at top that was broken and reglued . . . **580.00**

Umbrella stand, blue and white, two white accent bands, four blue accent bands, 21" h, glued repair, $580. Photo courtesy of Vicki and Bruce

Wash bowl and pitcher, blue sponge underglaze dec, ironstone, 9" h pitcher, 12" d, 4" h bowl **415.00**

Water cooler, 18" h, blue and white, marked "Fulper Pottery Co. Flemington, NJ, Gate City Natural Stone Filter," stenciled "No. 6", two-pc construction, orig spigot, minor stone pig on front of filter top **385.00**

SPORTS CARDS

For more information, see this book.

History: Baseball cards were first printed in the late 19th century. By 1900, the most common cards, known as "T" cards, were those made by tobacco companies such as American Tobacco Co. The majority of the tobacco-related cards were produced between 1909 and 1915. During the 1920s, American Caramel, National Caramel, and York Caramel candy companies issued cards identified in lists as "E" cards.

During the 1930s, Goudey Gum Co. of Boston (1933 to 1941) and Gum Inc. (in 1939) were prime producers of baseball cards. Following World War II, Bowman Gum of Philadelphia (B.G.H.L.I.), the successor to Gum, Inc., led the way. Topps, Inc. (T.C.G.) of Brooklyn, New York, followed. Topps bought Bowman in 1956 and enjoyed a virtual monopoly in card production until 1981.

In 1981, Fleer of Philadelphia and Donruss of Memphis challenged Topps. All three companies annually produce sets numbering 600 cards or more. In the late 1980, the new-card industry expanded yet again, with Upper Deck, Score, Pacific joining the fray. Ultimately, the market for new cards would change dramatically from what it had been in the past, with about a half-dozen companies each producing dozens of cards sets in all four major sports, reducing the print runs to relatively miniscule numbers and elevating the wholesale and retail prices of the cards in the process.

Football cards have been printed since the 1890s. However, it was not until 1933 that the first bubble gum football card appeared in the Goudey Sport Kings set. In 1935, National Chicle of Cambridge, Massachusetts, produced the first full set of gum cards devoted exclusively to football.

Both Leaf Gum of Chicago and Bowman Gum of Philadelphia produced sets of football cards in 1948. Leaf discontinued production after its 1949 issue; Bowman continued until 1955.

Topps Chewing Gum entered the market in 1950 with its college-stars set. Topps became a fixture in the football card market with its 1955 All-American set. From 1956 thorough 1963, Topps printed card sets of National Football League players, combining them with the American Football League players in 1961.

Topps produced sets with only American Football League players from 1964 to 1967. The Philadelphia Gum Company made National Football League card

sets during this period. Beginning in 1968 and continuing to the present, Topps has produced sets of National Football League cards, the name adopted after the merger of the two leagues.

The expansion of the new-card industry noted above took place in a similar fashion in football, basketball and hockey cards, with many new licensees emerging after 1989.

Note: Prices shown are taken from the 2002 and 2003 editions of Krause Publications' Standard Catalogs of Baseball, Football and Basketball.

Baseball
American Caramel

E90-1, 1909-11, Keeler, throwing, Excellent (EX) **850.00**

T206 White Border 1909-11, Cobb, red background, Very Good (VG) **1,500.00**

Sporting News

1916 M101-4, No. 87, Jackson, VG-EX **2,750.00**

Bowman

1948

No. 1, Elliot, Near-Mint (NM) **125.00**

No. 8, Rizzuto, NM **255.00**

No. 14, Reynolds, NM. **40.00**

1949

No. 36, Reese, NM **150.00**

No. 50, Robinson, Near-Mint to Mint (NM-MT) **2,000.00**

No. 84, Campanella, NM . **350.00**

No. 131, Lehner, NM. **15.00**

1951

No. 1, Ford, NM **950.00**

No. 3, Roberts, EX **35.00**

No. 26, Rizzuto, NM-MT . . **375.00**

No. 253, Mantle rookie, NM **5,500.00**

1966 Topps, $100.

1957 Topps, **$190.**

1953, Color

> No. 6, Ginsburg, NM **35.00**
> No. 18, Fox, EX **45.00**
> No. 19, Dark, NM **30.00**
> No. 32, Musial, NM. **550.00**
> No. 33, Reese, EX **300.00**
> No. 59, Mantle, EX **675.00**

Cracker Jack

> 1914, No. 30, Ty Cobb, 1914, NM
> **5,000.00**

Diamond Stars

> 1935, No. 50, Mel Ott, NM .. **300.00**

Fleer, complete sets

> 1959, Ted Williams set, NM. **1,600.00**
> 1960, Greats, VG **235.00**
> 1961-62, Greats, EX **375.00**
> 1963, with checklist, NM... **1,300.00**
> 1982, MINT **45.00**
> 1984, NM **35.00**
> 1986, NM **25.00**

Goudey

> 1933, No. 75, Kamm, NM ... **260.00**
> 1933, No. 91, Zachary, NM... **60.00**
> 1933, No. 92, Gehrig, NM.. **3,500.00**
> 1933, No. 144, Ruth, NM .. **4,000.00**
> 1933 uncut sheet, NM **6,995.00**

Leaf

> 1948-49, No. 1, DiMaggio, EX
> **1,125.00**
> 1948-49, No. 4, Musial rookie, NM
> **1,350.00**
> 1948-49, No. 76, Williams, NM
> **825.00**

Play Ball

> 1939, No. 26, DiMaggio, EX. **500.00**
> 1939, No. 92, Williams, VG.. **660.00**
> 1939, No. 103, Berg, NM ... **190.00**
> 1940, No. 27, DiMaggio, NM
> **1,850.00**
> 1941, No. 14, Williams, NM. **1,900.00**
> 1941, No. 71, DiMaggio, NM
> **2,600.00**

Topps

> 1951, Red Backs
> > No. 1, Berra, NM **85.00**
> 1951, Blue Backs
> > No. 3, Ashburn, NM **95.00**

1954 Topps No. 1, **$800.**

> No. 20, Branca, EX **20.00**
> No. 50, Mize, NM **65.00**

1952

> No. 29, Kluszewski, PSA 9 (MINT)
> **8,750.00**
> No. 175, Martin, NM **375.00**
> No. 261, Mays, PSA 8 (NM-MT)
> **5,108.00**
> No. 311, Mantle, PSA 9 (MINT)
> **88,000.00**
> No. 356, Atwell, NM **220.00**
> No. 384, Crosetti, EX..... **200.00**
> No. 392, Wilhelm, PSA 9
> **7,760.00**

1953

> No. 1, Robinson, NM..... **675.00**
> No. 4, Wade, NM **25.00**
> No. 82, Mantle, NM.... **2,000.00**

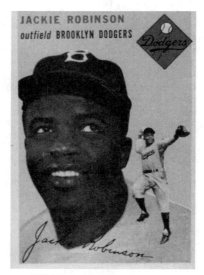

1954 Topps, **$225.**

1953 Bowman color, **$2,100.**

> No. 220, Paige, NM **500.00**

1954

> No. 1, Williams, NM **625.00**
> No. 22, Greengrass, NM .. **15.00**
> No. 94, Banks rookie, PSA 9
> **12,500.00**
> No. 128, Aaron rookie, PSA 9
> **30,200.00**
> No. 250, Williams, PSA 8
> **26,500.00**

1955

> No. 1, Rhodes, NM **290.00**
> No. 123, Koufax rookie, PSA 9
> **25,600.00**
> No. 124, Killebrew rookie, PSA 10
> (GEM MINT) **45,000.00**
> No. 220, Snider, NM..... **475.00**

Basketball

Bowman

> 1948
> > No. 2, Hamilton, NM **50.00**
> > No. 9, Philip, NM **140.00**
> > No. 32, Holzman, NM ... **425.00**
> > No. 66, Pollard, NM **400.00**

Topps

> 1957
> > No. 1, Clifton rookie, NM . **250.00**
> > No. 2, Yardley rookie, NM . **55.00**
> > No. 13, Schayes rookie, NM
> > **125.00**
> > No. 17, Cousy rookie, NM
> > **525.00**
> > No. 42, Stokes rookie, NM **120.00**
> > No. 77, Russel rookie, NM
> > **2,000.00**
> 1974-75
> > No. 1, Jabbar, NM **35.00**
> > No. 10, Maravich, NM **20.00**

Top row, 1933 Sport Kings: card at left is $275; card at right is $325. Middle row, 1948 Bowman: left: George Mikan rookie card, $4,500; center card, $100; card at right, $50. Bottom row, 1948 Bowman: right $100.

No. 39, Walton rookie, NM . **60.00**
No. 200, Erving, NM **55.00**

Football
Bowman, 1950
No. 1, Walker, NM **175.00**
No. 45, Graham rookie, NM. . **450.00**
Fleer, 1961
No. 30, Unitas, NM **70.00**
No. 41, Meredith, NM. **140.00**
No. 155, Kemp, NM. **155.00**
1963
No. 6, Long (short print), NM
. . . . **180.00**
No. 47, Dawson, NM. **250.00**

1986-87 Fleer, **$1,550.**

Topps
1955, All-American
No. 1, Herman Hickman rookie, NM. **90.00**
No. 12, Graham, NM **175.00**
No. 16, Rockne, NM. **325.00**
No. 20, Baugh, NM **200.00**
No. 27, Grange, NM. **350.00**
No. 37, Thorpe, NM **375.00**
No. 97, Hutson rookie, NM
. . . . **225.00**
No. 98, Feathers rookie, NM
. . . . **75.00**
1959
No. 10, Brown, NM. **125.00**
No. 44, Johnson, NM. **7.00**
No. 118, Cardinals team, NM
. . . . **5.00**
No. 126, Rams Pennant, NM
. . . . **4.00**
1960
No. 1, Unitas, NM. **80.00**
No. 4, Berry, NM **8.00**
No. 74, Gifford, NM **65.00**
1961
No. 166, Kemp, NM. **150.00**
1966
No. 96, Namath, NM **340.00**

SPORTS COLLECTIBLES

For more information, see this book.

History: People have been saving sports-related equipment since the inception of sports. Some was passed down from generation to generation for reuse; the rest was stored in dark spaces in closets, attics, and basements.

In the 1980s, two key trends brought collectors' attention to sports collectibles. First, decorators began using old sports items, especially in restaurant decor. Second, card collectors began to discover the thrill of owning the "real" thing. By the beginning of the 1990s, all sport categories were collectible, with baseball items paramount and golf and football running close behind.

Baseball
Baseball, autographed, sgd by members of team
American League All-Star Team, 1937, Foxx, Gehrig, DiMaggio
. . . . **7,000.00**

Shoeless Joe Jackson's favorite bat, affectionately referred to as "Black Betsy," was auctioned in August 2001 for $525,100. The historically significant bat, used for 13 seasons by Jackson, was auctioned by eBay for Real Legends. The hand-carved hickory bat had its one leather carrying case and is engraved with the Spaulding logo and the words "Old Hickory No. 150." The bat was kept in the Jackson family since Jackson's death in 1951.

Boston, 1964, Herman, Yastrzemski
. . . . **250.00**
National League All-Star Team, 1955, Musial **600.00**
New York, 1960, Stengel, Kubek, Maris, Howard, Berra, Ford. **700.00**
Oakland, 1981, Martin, Henderson
. . . . **200.00**
Baseball cap, autographed, game used
Bench, Johnny, 1970s Cincinnati Reds **450.00**
Jackson, Bo, 1994 California Angels
. . . . **85.00**
Walker, Larry, 1995 Colorado Rockies **165.00**
Baseball glove
Ashburn, Richie. **45.00**
Berra, Yogi. **100.00**
Reese, Pee Wee **65.00**
Bat
Mostil, Johnny, signed by Shoeless Joe Jackson **55,200.00**
Jackson, Shoeless Joe, Black Betsy
. . . . **525,100.00**
Calendar, Kist Soda, 1951, illus as Medcalf's Hall of Fame painting of young ball payer with Lou Gehrig watching from sky, full pad, 16" w, 33" l
. . . . **230.00**

Photograph, Brooklyn Base Ball Club— 1885 with names of team players, framed, some damage to base of border, 14" x 17", **$675.** *Photo courtesy of Joy Luke Auctions.*

Jersey, game used
    1955, Ken Griffey **2,800.00**
    1987, Reggie Jackson **700.00**
    1988, Mark McQwire. **1,500.00**
Magazine, *Baseball*, December 1926, cover with Ruby and Hornsby shaking hands during 1926 World Series **295.00**
Pennant, felt
    Brooklyn Dodgers, Ebbert Field, blue, 1940s. **190.00**
    Cooperstown, blue, multicolored Braves style Indian head, 1940s
    . . . . **75.00**
    Minnesota Twins A. L. Champs World Series, photo, 1965 . **125.00**
    New York Yankees, photo "M&M Boys Last Year Together!," 1966
    . . . . **95.00**
Photograph, Brandon Mill Braves, shows team and Shoeless Joe Jackson
. . . . **3,800.00**
Pinback button
    Peewee Reese, black and white real photo, Brooklyn Dodgers uniform
    . . . . **35.00**
    Sweet Cap Downey, Cincinnati Reds
    . . . . **20.00**
    Ted Williams, 1-3/4" d, black and white photo as youthful Boston Red Sox star, late 1930s **40.00**
    WBBM Radio Baseball Club, blue, white, and gold litho, crossed bats behind baseball, rim inscribed "Foley & Novak WBBM Amateur Club," Chicago, 1930s. **30.00**
Plate, 7-1/4" d, Base Ball, Caught on the Fly, center transfer print, white glazed ground, c1850 . . . . **920.00**

Photograph, Mickey Mantle Member, Advisory Staff Rawlings Sporting Goods Company, 10" x 8", **$20.** *Photo courtesy of Joy Luke Auctions.*

Presentation bat, 34" l, red painted bat, polychrome Odd Fellows symbols, incised in gold "West Lynn 15-3 Kearsarge West Lynn 23 East Lynn 5 Presented by H. W. Eastham, July 21, 1900, Aug. 18, 1900," (MA), with stand
. . . . **4,025.00**
Program
    All Star, Philadelphia, 1943 . . **495.00**
    All Star, St. Louis, 1948 . . . . . **325.00**
    New York Yankees, 1937 . . . . **195.00**
    New York Yankees, 1951 . . . . **195.00**
    World Series, 1950, at Philadelphia
    . . . . **250.00**
Roster sheet, Pirates, 1927 . . . . **175.00**
Tab
    Jerome "Dizzy" Dean, St. Louis Cards. **20.00**
    Wally Berger, New York Giants **15.00**

Basketball

Autograph, basketball
    Archibald, Nate **100.00**
    Bird, Larry **200.00**
    Bradley, Bill **150.00**
    DeBusschere, Dave. **125.00**
    O'Brien, Larry **125.00**
Autograph, photograph, 8" x 10"
    McGuire, Dick **20.00**
    Phillip, Andy. **20.00**
    Thurmond, Nate. **24.00**
Magazine, *Sports Illustrated*, Feb. 1949, Ralph Beard, Kentucky cover
. . . . **95.00**
Pin, Chicago Americans Tournament Championship, brass, 1935 . . . . . **75.00**
Program
    Basketball Hall of Fame Commemoration Day Program, orig invitation, 1961 . . . . **75.00**
    NCAA Final Four Championship, Louisville, KY, 1967 . . . . **175.00**
    World Series of Basketball, 1951, Harlem Globetrotters and College All-Americans **55.00**
Shoes, pr, game used, autographed
    Drexler, Clyde, Avais **225.00**
    Sikma, Jack, Converse **100.00**
    Webber, Chris, Nikes. **550.00**
Souvenir book, *Los Angeles Lakers,* with two records, Jerry West and Elgin Baylor on action cover **75.00**
Ticket
    NBA Finals Boston Celtics at Los Angeles Lakers, 1963 . . . . . . **95.00**
    San Antonio Spurs ABA Phantom Playoff, 1975, unused **15.00**
    St. Louis Hawks at San Francisco Warriors, Dec. 17, 1963 . . . . **50.00**

Print, Peoria Life Recreation—28 Billiard Tables, Peoria, Ill, Modern Venus, seated female nude figure draped with silk scarf, framed, 22" x 16-1/2", **$195.** *Photo courtesy of Joy Luke Auctions.*

Yearbook
    1961-62, Boston Celtics **150.00**
    1965-66, Boston Celtics **85.00**
    1969-70, Milwaukee Bucks . . **40.00**

Boxing

Autograph, photo, sgd
    Max Baer, 8" x 10". **180.00**
    Mike Tyson **60.00**
Badge, 4" d, Larry Holmes, black and white photo, red and black inscriptions, 1979 copyright Don King Productions
. . . . **25.00**
Boxing gloves, 35 readable autographs **380.00**
Cabinet card, 4" x 6"
    Corbett, James F., dressed in suit
    . . . . **375.00**
    Ryan, Paddy, full boxing post, dark brown border **395.00**
    Sullivan, John L., dark brown border, "John L. Sullivan, Champion of the World" **495.00**
Figure, 8" w, 20-1/4" h, carved fruitwood, fully carved figure throwing right jab, standing on continuation of trunk with tree bark intact, attributed to New Hampshire, c1900. . . . . . **1,955.00**
Plaque, 12-1/2" w, 16-3/4" h, carved pine, polychrome, figure of John L. Sullivan carved in relief against landscape in horseshoe-form, inscribed at base "J. L. Sullivan," old darkened crackled painted surface, New York, late 19th C. **2,185.00**

Fishing

Book, *McClane's Standard Fishing Encyclopedia and International Angling Guide*, A. J. McClaine, Holt, Rinehart, Winston, 1965, 2nd printing, 1,057 pgs, color and black and white illus by R. Younger, dj **22.00**

Catalog

Garcia Fishing Equipment & Supplies, Garcia Corp., Teaneck, NY, c1955, eight pcs, 7-1/2" x 11-1/4", accordian fold large 11-1/4" x 30" sheet **20.00**

Montague Rod & Reel Co., Montague City, MA, c1949, 16 pgs, 8-1/2" x 11", Catalog No. 49-M **55.00**

Penn Fishing Tackle Mfg., Philadelphia, PA, 1952, 32 pgs, 8-1/4" x 10-3/4", Catalog No. 17 of Penn Reels **32.00**

Shakespeare Co., Kalamazoo, MI, 44 pgs, 1951, 8-1/4" x 11", Catalog of Fine Wonerod Fishing Tackles **32.00**

Weber Lifelike Fly Co., Stevens Point, WI, 1941, 112 pgs, 6-1/4" x 9-1/4", Catalog No. 22, Flies & Fly Tackle **70.00**

White, E. M. & Co., Old Town, ME, c1922, 4 pgs, 4-5/8" x 7", E. M. White Builders of White Canoes **40.00**

Creel, 12" w, 6" d, 8-1/2" h, painted splint, carved wooden wire-hinged top, forest green, America, early 19th C **920.00**

Sign, "The Flatfish, World's largest selling fishing plug," Helen Tackle Co., Detroit, metal framed glass, 8" x 16" **350.00**

Tobacco tin, Forest & Stream, pocket size, 4-1/4" x 3" x 7/8" **600.00**

Football

Autograph, football

Bergey, Bill **70.00**

Ditka, Mike **125.00**

Flaherty, Ray **150.00**

Flask, sterling silver, figural golfer on front, 2-3/4" x 4-1/2", $600.

Green, Roy **70.00**
Long, Howie **75.00**

Autograph, helmet

Aikman, Troy, Dallas Cowboys **265.00**

Dawson, Len, Kansas City Chiefs **250.00**

Elway, John, Denver Broncos **275.00**

Autograph, photograph, 8" x 10"

Bradshaw, Terry **40.00**
Brown, Jim **30.00**
Thomas, Thurman **25.00**

Cartoon, 15" x 22" white art sheet, 14" x 19" orig sgd art in black ink and pencil by cartoonist Williard Mullin, blue pencil title "Theory vs Practice," blindfolded "All American Selector" attempting to select ideal college team and geographically correct, large center character "Pro Draft" who simply points to smiling footballer while deciding "Me For You," 1950s **125.00**

Game, Tom Hamilton's Navy Football Game, 1940s **45.00**

Pennant, felt, A.F.L.

Boston Patriots, white on red, multicolored Patriot **75.00**

Buffalo Bills, white on blue, pink buffaloes **95.00**

Houston Oilers, white on light blue **75.00**

Pin, Lehigh University, brown and gold ribbon, 4-1/2" l celluloid football player, c1950, $40. Photo courtesy of Julie Robinson.

Pinback button

Gustavus Homecoming, gold and black, cartoon art of Ole and Gus wearing football helmets while tugging at worm between them, 1929 . . . . **15.00**

Hail to Pitt, blue on yellow, cartoon of football player using coal bucket to catch football, inscribed "Scuttle The Lions," c1940 . . . . **15.00**

Philadelphia Eagles, green on white cello, orange suspended miniature football charm, c1950 . . . . . . **15.00**

Playoff guide, 1965 NFL, Green Bay Packers vs. St. Louis Cardinals . . **40.00**

Program

Army vs. Duke, at the Polo Grounds, 1946 . . . . **40.00**

Green Bay Packers, 1960 . . . . **30.00**

Heisman Trophy, 1957, John David Crow **30.00**

Rose Bowl, 1974, USC vs. Ohio State **40.00**

Golf

Autograph, photo, sgd, Tiger Woods **60.00**

Book

George Fullerton Carnegie, *Golfiana: or Niceties Connected with the Game of Golf*, Edinburgh, 1833, 18 pgs of poetry **21,850.00**

The Architectural Side of Golf, London, 1925 . . . . **14,950.00**

Golf club cane, 37-1/2" l, known as "Sunday Stick," 3" l x 3-1/2" h handle

Reel, brass P. A. Altmaire, Harrisburg, PA, Pat. Nov. 9, 1869, $2,145. Photo courtesy of Lang's Sporting Collectables, Inc.

fashioned as early driver, ivory foot held in place with four ebony pins, faux lead weight, marked "Addington" on top of handle, orig owner's initials, two ivory and one ebony separators, oak shaft, 7/8" burnished brass and iron ferrule, c1890 . . . . **1,075.00**

Magazine, *American Golfer,* June 1932 . . . . **10.00**

Noisemaker, 2-3/4" d, 6-1/2" l, litho tin, full-color image of male golfer, marked "Germany" on handle, 1930s . . . **35.00**

Print, Charles Crombie, *The Rules of Golf Illustrated,* 24 humorous lithographs of golfers in medieval clothes, London, 1905 . . . . . . **1,265.00**

Program, Fort Worth Open Golf Championship, Glen Garden Country Club, Ft Worth, TX, 1945 . . . . . . **100.00**

Hockey
Autograph
Orr, Bobby, photograph, 8" x 10" **50.00**
Smith, Clint, photograph, 8" x 10" **12.00**
Thompson, Tiny, puck **50.00**
Watson, Harry, puck **55.00**
Worsley, Gump, sgd 1968-69 Topps card **15.00**

Hockey stick, game used, autographed
Beliveau, Jean, 1960s CCM, cracked **700.00**
Cashman, Wayne, Sher-wood, uncracked **175.00**
LeBlanc, J. B., Koho, cracked **50.00**

Jersey, game used, Wayne Gretzky, Rangers, autographed **415.00**

Magazine, *Sport Revue,* Quebec publication, Feb 1956, Bert Olmstead, Hall of Fame cov **15.00**

Program, Boston Bruins, Sports News, 1937-38 . . . . **250.00**

Stick, game used, autographed
Bondra, Peter, Sherwood **90.00**
Lindros, Eric, Bauer Supreme **295.00**

Tobacco tin, Puck Tobacco, Canadian, tin litho, detailed image of two hockey players on both sides, 4" d, 3-1/4" h **190.00**

Hunting
Badge, Western Cartridge Co., plant type, emb metal, pin back, 1-3/4" x 1-3/8" **100.00**

Book, *The World of the White-Tailed Deer,* Leonard Lee Rue III, J. B. Lippencott, 1962, 134 pgs, black and white illus, dj **15.00**

Box, Peters High Velocity, two-pc cardboard shot gun shells, multicolored graphics, 25 16-gauge shells . . . **250.00**

Calendar top, Winchester, paper, man atop rock ledge, hunting rams, artist sgd "Philip R. Goodwin," metal top rim, 20" x 14" **125.00**

Print
"Life in the Woods-The Hunters Camp," published by Lyon & Co., printed by J. Rau, NY, five gentlemen in camp, two more fishing in lake, framed, 22" x 28", some foxing, center line burn, water stains in borders **150.00**
"Rabbit Catching-The Trap Sprung," lithographed by Currier and Ives, NY, two boys approaching box trap, winter setting, framed, 10" x 13", some toning, water stains at borders **495.00**

Sign
Paul Jones Whiskey, game-hunting scene, orig gold gilt frame, 43" x 57" **750.00**
Remington UMC, diecut cardboard
15" x 14", oversized shell next to box of ammunition **200.00**
15-1/2" x 9", Nitro Club Shells, English Setter atop pile of Remington Shotgun Shells **100.00**
L. C. Smith Guns, paper, two setters pointing to prey, 14" x 14-3/4" **1,200.00**
Winchester, diecut, cardboard, stand-up, Indian Chief with Winchester shotgun in one hand, additional barrels in other hand, 24" x 60" **200.00**

Trophy, 10-1/2" h, silverplate teapot, engraved in German "2nd Prize of the First Shooting Festival in Cincinnati held the 29th and 30th of September 1867 and won by Julius Lang," Eastlake style, some denting **295.00**

Watch fob, Savage Revolver, figural, metal **110.00**

Olympics
Badge, 1-3/4" x 2-1/4", enamel on brass, Winter Olympics, Albertville, red and blue on white, colored Olympic rings **25.00**

Brochure, 9-1/4" x 12-1/2", Official Pictorial Souvenir, 1932, issued by organizing committee, Los Angeles, stiff paper covers, lightly emb soft green cover design with silver and gold accents, 64 black and white pages **40.00**

Cartoon, 8-1/2" x 12-1/2", white art sheet centered by 6-1/4" x 12" orig art cartoon in black ink by Carl Hubenthal, Los Angeles Examiner, 1956, art and caption relate to first ever 7' high jump in Olympic trials by US athlete Charlie Dumas **45.00**

Key ring tag, clear Lucite plastic, paper insert for 1996 Summer Games, also encased is foot-shaped holder partially filled with red sand, back inscribed "Footwhere Acknowledges Where You've Set Foot, Foot Cavity Contains Genuine Soil of Atlanta Site of the Centennial Olympic Games," metal key ring **15.00**

Pinback button, 3" d, Minute Maid sponsor, orange and black cello, 1980 . . . . **25.00**

STAFFORDSHIRE, HISTORICAL

History: The Staffordshire district of England is the center of the English pottery industry. There were 80 different potteries operating there in 1786, with the number increasing to 179 by 1802. The district includes Burslem, Cobridge, Etruria, Fenton, Foley, Hanley, Lane, Lane End, Longport, Shelton, Stoke, and Tunstall. Among the many famous potters were Adams, Davenport, Spode, Stevenson, Wedgwood, and Wood.

For more information, see this book.

Notes: The view is the most critical element when establishing the value of historical Staffordshire; American collectors pay much less for non-American views. Dark blue pieces are favored; light views continue to remain under-priced. Among the forms, soup tureens have shown the largest price increases.

Prices listed below are for mint examples, unless otherwise noted. Reduce prices by 20 percent for a hidden chip, a faint hairline, or an invisible professional repair; by 35 percent for knife marks through the glaze and a visible professional repair; by 50 percent for worn glaze and major repairs.

The numbers in parentheses refer to items in the Armans' books, which constitute the most detailed list of American historical views and their forms.

Adams
The Adams family has W.ADAMS&SONS ADAMS been associated with ceramics since the mid-17th century. In 1802, William Adams of Stoke-on-Trent produced American views.

In 1819, a fourth William Adams, son of William of Stoke, became a partner with his father and was later joined by his three brothers. The firm became William Adams & Sons. The father died in 1829 and William, the eldest son, became manager.

The company operated four potteries at Stoke and one at Tunstall. American views were produced at Tunstall in black, light blue, sepia, pink, and green in the 1830-40 period. William Adams died in 1865. All operations were moved to Tunstall. The firm continues today under the name of Wm. Adams & Sons, Ltd.

Adams, plate, Mitchell & Freemans China & Glass Warehouse, Chatham Street, Boston, dark blue transfer, c1804-10, marked, 10-1/4" d, $715.

Bowl, 11" d, 2-1/2" h, English scenes with ruins, dark blue transfer, yellowed repair on back **155.00**
Creamer, 5-3/8" d, English scene, imp "Adams," dark blue **175.00**
Pitcher, 5-3/4" h, Eagle, Scroll in Beak, blue and white transfer, illegible imp mark for William Adams, Stoke, 1827-31, glaze scratches. . . . **1,320.00**
Plate, 10-1/4" d, Mitchell & Freeman's China and Glass Warehouse, Chatham St, Boston, blue and white transfer, imp marker's mark and printed title on reverse **715.00**
Teapot, Log Cabin, medallions of Gen. Harrison on border, pink (458) . . **450.00**

Clews

From sketchy historical accounts that are available, it appears that James Clews took over the closed plant of A. Stevenson in 1819. His brother Ralph entered the business later. The firm continued until about 1836, when James Clews came to America to enter the pottery business at Troy, Indiana. The venture was a failure because of the lack of skilled workmen and the proper type of clay. He returned to England, but did not re-enter the pottery business.

Bowl, Landing of Lafayette, 9" d, ext. floral design, rim repair. **410.00**

Clews, plates, left: Landing of General Lafayette, flowered border, dark blue transfer print, impressed Clews mark, 9" d, $400; right: View of Trenton Falls, shell border, dark blue transfer print, impressed "E. Wood & Sons," slight wear, light crazing, 7-1/2" d, $295. Photo courtesy of Cowan's Historic Americana Auctions.

Cup plate, Landing of Lafayette at Castle Garden, dark blue **400.00**
Pitcher
  6" h, Welcome Lafayette the Nation's Guest and Our Country's Glory, blue and white transfer, handle repair, int. staining **2,070.00**
  6-3/4" h, States Border pattern, scenic country vista with mansion on hill, river in foreground, blue and white transfer dec, minor int. staining. **980.00**
Plate
  7-3/4" d, Landing of Gen Lafayette, blue and white transfer, imp maker's mark for James and Ralph Clews, c1819-36, minor wear **500.00**
  8-3/4" d, Winter View of Pittsfield, Mass, medium blue transfer, imp

Clews, plate, Winter View of Pittsfield, Mass, vignettes of central scene in miniature on border, floral surround, dark blue transfer print, Clews mark, printed pattern mark, 8-1/2" d, $400. Photo courtesy of Cowan's Historic Americana Auctions.

label "Clews," surface wear, flake, stains visible on reverse . . . **225.00**
  10" d, Landing of General Lafayette, imp "Clews," dark blue, very minor wear **350.00**
  10-1/2" d, America and Independence, States border, America wears Mason's apron, holds portrait of Washington, dark blue transfer, scalloped edge, imp "Clews, Warranted, Staffordshire" **825.00**
  10-5/8" d, States series, America and Independence, fisherman with net, imp "Clews," dark blue, small rim flake. **440.00**
Platter
  Landing of Gen LaFayette at Castle Garden New York 16 August 1824, 11-3/4" x 15-1/4", blue and white transfer, imp maker's mark, minor glaze scratches. **2,200.00**
  States Border, center with vista of river with two swans, two men, rowboat on river bank, large country house surrounded by trees in background, blue and white transfer, imp marker's mark of James and Ralph Clews, Cobridge, 1819-36, glaze scratches **2,530.00**
  Winter View of Pittsfield Massachusetts, 14" x 16-1/2", blue and white transfer, imp maker's mark, glaze scratches. . . **3,450.00**
Soup plate
  10-3/8" d, Winter View of Pittsfield, Mass, imp "Clews," dark blue **440.00**
  10-1/2" d, Picturesque Views, Pittsburgh, PA, imp "Clews," steam ships with "Home, Nile, Larch," black transfer, chips on table ring **330.00**
Saucer, Landing of Gen. Lafayette, dark blue transfer, imp "Clews Warranted Staffordshire" **275.00**
Toddy plate, 5-3/4" d, Winter View of Pittsfield, Mass, scalloped edge, medium blue transfer, imp "Clews Warranted Staffordshire" **400.00**

J. & J. Jackson

J.&J. JACKSON Job and John Jackson began operations at the Churchyard Works, Burslem, about 1830. The works formerly were owned by the Wedgwood family. The firm produced transfer scenes in a variety of colors, such as black, light blue, pink, sepia, green, maroon, and mulberry. More than 40 different American views of Connecticut, Massachusetts, Pennsylvania, New York, and Ohio were issued. The firm is believed to have closed about 1844.

J. & J. Jackson, plate, The Race Bridge, Phila, American Scenery series, light blue transfer, Arman, #486, $175.

Deep dish, American Beauty Series, Yale College (493) 125.00
Plate, 10-3/8" d, The President's House, Washington, purple transfer . . . 275.00
Platter, American Beauty Series
   12" l, Iron Works at Saugerties (478) 275.00
   17-1/2" l, View of Newburgh, black transfer (463) 575.00
Soup plate, 10" d, American Beauty Series, Hartford, CT, black transfer (476) 150.00

Thomas Mayer

In 1829, Thomas Mayer and his brothers, John and Joshua, purchased Stubbs' Dale Hall Works of Burslem. They continued to produce a superior grade of ceramics.

Cream pitcher, 4" h, Lafayette at Franklin's Tomb, dark blue. 550.00
Gravy tureen, Arms of the American States, CT, dark blue (498) . . . 3,800.00
Plate, 8-1/2" d, Arms of Rhode Island, blue and white transfer, eagle back stamp, 1829, minor glaze scratches 790.00
Platter
   8-1/4" l, Lafayette at Franklin's Tomb, dark blue 525.00
   19" l, Arms of the American States, NJ, dark blue (503). 7,200.00
Sugar bowl, cov, Lafayette at Franklin's Tomb, dark blue (510) 850.00

Mellor, Veneables & Co.

Little information is recorded on Mellor, Veneables & Co., except that it was listed as potters in Burslem in 1843. The company's Scenic Views with

the Arms of the States Border does include the arms for New Hampshire. This state is missing from the Mayer series.

Plate, 7-1/2" d, Tomb of Washington, Mt. Vernon, Arms of States border 125.00
Platter
   14-1/2" x 19-3/4", European view, light blue and white transfer, imp and printed maker's mark, c1843, hairline, light wear 365.00
   15" l, Scenic Views, Arms of States border, Albany, light blue (516) 265.00
Sugar bowl, cov, Arms of States, PA, dark blue 350.00
Teapot, 9-1/2" h, Windsor pattern, dark blue. 200.00

J. & W. Ridgway and William Ridgway & Co.

John and William Ridgway, sons of Job Ridgway and nephews of George Ridgway, who owned Bell Bank Works and Cauldon Place Works, produced the popular Beauties of America series at the Cauldon plant. The partnership between the two brothers was dissolved in 1830. John remained at Cauldon.

William managed the Bell Bank Works until 1854. Two additional series were produced based upon the etchings of Bartlett's American Scenery. The first series had various borders including narrow lace. The second series is known as Catskill Moss. Beauties of America is in dark blue. The other series are found in light transfer colors of blue, pink, brown, black, and green.

Plate
   6" d, Catskill Moss, Anthony's Nose (925) 85.00
   7" d, American Scenery, Valley of the Shenandoah from Jefferson's Rock, brown (289) 120.00

J. W. Ridgway, platter, Beauties of America series, Deaf & Dumb Asylum, Hartford, CT, c1820-40, medium blue transfer, $925.

10" h, Beauties of America, City Hall, NY, dark blue (260) 225.00
Platter
   12-3/4" x 16-1/2", Beauties of America series, Alms House New York, blue and white transfer, printed title, scratches, scattered minor staining. 1,265.00
   19" l, Catskill Moss, Boston and Bunker's Hill, imp "William Ridgway Son & Co," medium blue, dated 1844, minor chips, knife marks, edge wear 525.00
Relish tray, 5-3/8" x 8-1/4", Savannah Bank, Beauties of America Series, blue and white transfer, printed title, c1814-30, minor imperfections . 750.00
Soup plate, 9-7/8" d, Octagon Church Boston, imp "Ridgway," dark medium blue 330.00
Wash bowl, American Scenery, Albany (279) 325.00

Rogers

John Rogers and his brother George established a **ROGERS** pottery near Longport in 1782. After George's death in 1815, John's son Spencer became a partner, and the firm operated under the name of John Rogers & Sons. John died in 1916. His son continued the use of the name until he dissolved the pottery in 1842.

Basket and undertray, 3" x 6-1/2" x 9-1/4", Boston State House, blue and white transfer, imp marker's mark for John Rogers and Son, Longport, 1815-50, hairline cracks 2,760.00
Cup and saucer, Boston Harbor, dark blue (441) 650.00
Cup plate, Boston Harbor, dark blue (441) 1,400.00
Deep dish, 12-3/4" d, Boston State House, blue and white transfer, imp marker's mark for John Rogers and Son, Longport, 1815-42, minor glaze scratches. 2,070.00
Plate, 9-5/8" d, The Canal at Buffalo, lace border, purple transfer, int. hairline 55.00
Platter, 16-5/8" l, Boston State House, medium dark blue (442) 1,000.00
Sauce tureen, cov, undertray, Boston State House, blue and white transfer, imp maker's mark for John Rogers and Son, Longport, 1815-42 . . . . . 2,900.00
Waste bowl, Boston Harbor, dark blue (441) 850.00

Stevenson

As early as the 17th century, the name Stevenson has been associated with the pottery industry. Andrew Stevenson of Cobridge introduced American scenes with the flower and scroll border. Ralph Stevenson, also of Cobridge, used a vine and leaf border on his dark blue historical views and a lace border on his series in light transfers.

The initials R. S. & W. indicate Ralph Stevenson and Williams are associated with the acorn and leaf border. It has been reported that Williams was Ralph's New York agent and the wares were produced by Ralph alone.

Bowl
8-3/4" d, Park Theater New York, blue and white transfer, printed mark, Ralph Stevens and Williams, Cobridge, 1815-40, minute scratches **2,530.00**
11" d, Capitol Washington, blue and white transfer, printed mark, Ralph Stevens and Williams, Cobridge, 1815-40, glaze imperfections **2,645.00**
Cup and saucer, New Orleans, floral and scroll border **95.00**
Jug, 8-1/4" h, dark blue print . . . **750.00**
Pitcher, 10" h, Almshouse, Boston, reverse with Esplanade and Castle Garden New York, blue and white transfer, unmarked **2,300.00**

Plate
6-1/2" d, Catholic Cathedral, NY, floral and scroll border, dark blue (395) **1,650.00**
6-7/8" d, Battery, NY, vine border (367) **800.00**
7-1/2" d, Columbia College, portrait medallion of President Washington, inset View of the Aqueduct Bridge at Rochester, blue and white transfer, Ralph Stevens and Williams, Cobridge, 1815-40, minor scratches **8,625.00**
8-1/2" d, Welcome Lafayette the Nation's Guest, portrait medallion of President Washington, City Hotel, New York, inset "entrance to the Canal into the Hudson at Albany," blue and white transfer, Ralph Stevens and Williams, Cobridge, 1815-40, minor scratches **4,600.00**
9" d, Boston Hospital, blue and white transfer, stamped title, maker's initials, imp maker's mark, minor glaze scratches **350.00**

Stevenson, platter, Alms House, Boston, vine border, dark blue transfer, impressed mark, 12-1/2" w, 16-1/4" l, $800.

10" d, Welcome LaFayette the Nation's Guest, Jefferson, Washington, Governor Clinton, Park Street Theater New York, vignette of View of Aqueduct Bridge at Little Falls, blue and white transfer, Ralph Stevens and Williams, Cobridge, 1815-40, minor scratches **3,740.00**
10-1/4" d, Harvard College, blue and white transfer, printed title, imp maker's mark **300.00**
10-1/4" d, New York from Brooklyn Heights, printed title, imp maker's mark, A. Stevenson, Cobridge, 1808-29 . . . . **900.00**
10-1/4" d, View of Governor's Island, printed title, imp maker's mark, A. Stevenson, Cobridge, 1808-29 . . . . **950.00**

Platter
7-1/4" x 9-1/4", Troy from Mount Ida, by W. G. Wallogy, landscape scene, floral border, blue and white transfer, back stamped with American eagle, marked "A. Stevenson Warranted Staffordshire" **1,550.00**
10-1/4" x 13", Battle of Bunker Hill, blue and white transfer, printed title, imp maker's mark, Ralph Stevenson, Cobridge, 1815-40, one scratch **8,625.00**
14-1/2" x 18-1/2", New York Esplanade and Castle Garden, blue and white transfer, printed title, imp maker's mark, Ralph Stevenson, Cobridge, 1815-40, minor glaze scratches . . . **5,750.00**

Soup plate
9" d, View on the Road to Lake George, printed title, imp maker's

mark, A. Stevenson, Cobridge, 1808-29 . . . . **1,100.00**
10" d, Erie Canal at Buffalo, lace border (386) **95.00**
Wash bowl, Riceborough, GA, lace border (388) **375.00**

Stubbs
In 1790, Stubbs established a pottery works at Burslem, England. He operated it until 1829, when he retired and sold the pottery to the Mayer brothers. He probably produced his American views about 1825. Many of his scenes were from Boston, New York, New Jersey, and Philadelphia.

Gravy boat, 4-1/4" h, Hoboken in New Jersey, Steven's House, blue and white transfer, printed title, Joseph Stubbs, Burslem, 1790-1829, minor imperfections **550.00**
Pitcher, 6" h, Boston State House, reverse with City Hall New York, blue and white transfer, unmarked, small chip on handle **980.00**

Plate
6-1/2" h, City Hall New York, floral and eagle border, medium blue transfer, unmarked, minor wear and small repair **225.00**
9" d, Upper Ferry Bridge of the River Schuylkill, blue and white transfer, printed title, Joseph Stubbs, Burslem, 1790-1829, imperfections **950.00**
10-1/4" h, Fair Mount near Philadelphia, floral border with eagles, medium blue transfer, imp "Stubbs" **475.00**

Joseph Stubbs, plate, Fairmont near Philadelphia, spread eagle border, dark blue transfer, 10" d, $195.

Platter

12" x 14-3/4", State House Boston, blue and white transfer, printed title, marked "Joseph Stubbs, Burslem," 1790-1829, minor scratches and crazing . . . **1,265.00**

13-3/4" x 16-3/4", Mendenhall Ferry, blue and white transfer, printed title, minor glaze scratches **2,185.00**

15-1/2" x 18-3/4", Upper Ferry Bridge over the River Schuylkill, well and tree, printed title on reverse, hairline **715.00**

Salt shaker, Hoboken in NJ, spread eagle border, dark blue (326) . . **700.00**

Wash bowl and pitcher, Upper Ferry Bridge Over the River Schuylkill, 12-5/8" d bowl, 10" h pitcher, blue and white, printed title, Joseph Stubbs, Burslem, 1790-1829 . . . . **1,840.00**

Unknown makers

Bowl, 11-1/8" d, 3-1/4" d, Franklin, scene of Ben flying kite, red transfer, minor wear **495.00**

Cup, handleless, dark blue transfer, Quadruped series, llama on both sides, floral border, scalloped rim **115.00**

Fruit bowl, undertray, 10-1/2" l, 5" h, reticulated, blue and white transfer, figures, cows, and manors in rural landscape, floral borders **765.00**

Jug, 6-3/4" h, pearlware, brown transfer print, commemorating British Admiral Nelson, portrait, ship *Victory,* various nautical devices, orange enamel highlights on rim and edges of handle, minor imperfections **1,650.00**

Pitcher, 5-7/8" h, dark blue transfer, View of the Erie Canal, floral borders, transfer slightly blurred, repairs **715.00**

Plate

7" d, Junction of the Sacandaga & Hudson River, black transfer, small rim glaze defect **95.00**

7-3/4" d, Near Fishkill, small chip on table ring **100.00**

8" d, View from Coenties-slip, scene of Great Fire, City New York, light blue transfer, wear, small edge flakes **385.00**

8-1/2" d, Court House Baltimore, blue and white transfer, fruit and flower border, printed title on reverse, light wear, hairline . **470.00**

8-3/4" d, Nahant Hotel near Boston, dark blue transfer, wear, chips on table ring **200.00**

9" d, "The Residence of the late Richard Jordon, New Jersey," brown, minor wear and stains **250.00**

9-3/4" d, City Hall, New York, dark blue transfer, minor wear . . . **275.00**

9-7/8" d, The Dam and Waterworks Philadelphia, blue and white transfer, fruit and flower border, printed title on reverse **650.00**

10" d, Exchange Baltimore, blue and white transfer, fruit and floral border, printed title on reverse **390.00**

10-1/4", Fulton's Steamboat, blue and white transfer, floral border, minor scratches and rim chips **890.00**

Platter, 16-5/8" l, Sandusky, dark blue, very minor scratches **8,525.00**

Saucer, 5-7/8" d, scene of early railroad, engine and one car, floral border, dark blue **275.00**

Teapot

Teapot, 8-1/4" h, The Residence of the Late Richard Jordan, New Jersey, brown transfer, small chip, stain and repair to lid **715.00**

Tea service, partial, Mount Vernon the Seat of the Late Gen Washington, blue and white transfer, floral border, three teapots, creamer, three cov sugar bowls, waste bowl, 13 tea bowls, 12 saucers, some with printed titles, imperfections **8,625.00**

Wood

Enoch Wood, sometimes referred to as the father of English pottery, began operating a pottery at Fountain Place, Burslem, in 1783. A cousin, Ralph Wood, was associated with him. In 1790, James Caldwell became a partner and the firm was known as Wood and Caldwell. In 1819, Wood and his sons took full control.

Enoch died in 1840. His sons continued under the name of Enoch Wood & Sons. The American views were first made in the mid-1820s and continued through the 1840s.

It is reported that the pottery produced more signed historical views than any other Staffordshire firm. Many of the views attributed to unknown makers probably came from the Woods.

Marks vary, although always include the name Wood. The establishment was sold to Messrs. Pinder, Bourne & Hope in 1846.

Creamer, 5-3/4" h, horse drawn sleigh, imp "Wood," dark blue, minor hairline in base **550.00**

Cup and saucer, handleless Commodore MacDonnough's Victory, imp "Wood & Sons," dark blue, pinpoints on cup table ring **355.00**

Unknown maker, platter, Vue Du Temple, scene of figures at temple looking across river, dark blue transfer, wear, chip, 13" x 16-1/2", $550. Photo courtesy of Sanford Alderfer Auction Company.

Unknown maker, plate, Fair Mount near Philadelphia, eagle and floral border, dark blue transfer 10-1/4" d, $225. Photo courtesy of Sanford Alderfer Auction Company.

Wood, plate, Erie Canal Aqueduct Bridge at Rochester, dark blue transfer, 7-5/8" d, $145.

Ship with American flag, Chancellor Livingston, imp "Wood & Sons" **770.00**

Gravy boat, 7-1/2" l, Catskill Mountains Hudson River, blue and white transfer, printed title, minor imperfections **650.00**

Pitcher, 6" h, Entrance of the Erie Canal into the Hudson River at Albany, reverse with View of the Aqueduct Bridge at Little Falls, blue and white transfer, printed title, scattered glaze loss to int. **1,725.00**

Plate

6-1/2" d, Cowes Harbour, blue and white transfer, shell border, imp maker's mark on reverse, light wear **245.00**

6-1/2" d, Mount Vernon, the Seat of the Late Gen'l Washington, blue and white transfer, imp maker's mark, 1819-46 . . . . **850.00**

6-1/2" d, Transylvania University, Kentucky, shell border, dark blue, label with eagle and banner and "E Pluribus Unim," imp "Wood" **775.00**

7-1/2" d, The Capitol Washington, blue and white transfer, imp maker's mark, 1819-46 . . . . **450.00**

8-1/4" d, Dartmouth, ships in harbor, irregular shell border, medium blue transfer, unmarked, knife scratches, minor stains **350.00**

8-1/2" d, Boston State House, blue and white transfer, imp maker's mark, 1819-46 . . . . **325.00**

9-1/4" d, The Baltimore & Ohio Railroad, (incline), imp "Enoch Wood," dark blue **770.00**

10" d, Table Rock Niagara, blue and white transfer, printed title, glaze scratches **550.00**

10-1/8" d, Cadmus at anchor, blue and white transfer, shell border, imp maker's mark, c1819-46, light scratches **500.00**

10-1/8" d, Chief Justice Marshall, Troy Line steamboat, blue and white transfer, shell border, imp marker's mark on reverse, minor wear **715.00**

10-1/8" d, Commodore MacDonnough's Victory, dark blue transfer, imp mark, wear, stains, crazing **385.00**

10-1/4" d, Pine Orchard House, Catskill Mountains, blue and white transfer, printed title, glaze scratches **575.00**

10-1/4" d, The Baltimore & Ohio Railroad, (straight), imp "Wood," dark blue, minor scratches **825.00**

10-3/8" d, Constitution and Guerriere, imp "Wood," dark blue minor scratches **1,760.00**

10-1/2" d, East Cowes Isle of Wright, shell border, blue and white transfer **765.00**

Platter

10" x 12-3/4", Highlands Hudson River, blue and white transfer, printed title, imp maker's mark, Enoch Wood & Sons, Burslem, 1819-46, minor roughness **3,335.00**

12-3/4" x 16-1/2", Lake George State of New York, blue and white transfer, printed title, partial imp marker's mark, c1819-46, minor glaze imperfections **2,585.00**

14-1/2" x 18-3/4", Christianburg Danish Settlement on the Gold Coast Africa, blue and white transfer, imp maker's mark, minor glaze imperfections **3,220.00**

Sugar bowl, cov, 7" d, 6" h, Wadsworth Tower, blue and white transfer, scalloped shaped handles, minor imperfections **265.00**

Tea service, partial, Wadsworth Tower, cov teapot, two large teacups, one large saucer, five teacups, six saucers, 15 plates, imperfections **2,645.00**

Toddy plate, 6-1/2" d, dark blue transfer, Catskill House, Hudson, imp "Wood," minor wear and stains . **525.00**

Tureen, cov, 7" h, Passaic Falls, State of New Jersey, blue and white transfer, repairs, glaze wear **200.00**

Undertray, 8-1/8" l, Pass in the Catskill Mountains, blue and white transfer, imp maker's mark, printed title, repair to handle **200.00**

Waste bowl, 6-1/4" d, 3-1/4" h, Washington standing at Tomb, scroll in hand, blue and white transfer, unmarked, Enoch Wood & Sons, Burslem, 1819-40, minor imperfections **750.00**

STAFFORDSHIRE ITEMS

History: A wide variety of ornamental pottery items originated in England's Staffordshire district, beginning in the 17th century and still continuing today. The height of production took place from 1820 to 1890.

For more information, see this book

Many collectors consider these naive pieces folk art. Most items were not made carefully; some even were made and decorated by children.

The types of objects are varied, e.g., animals, cottages, and figurines (chimney ornaments).

Note: The key to price is age and condition. As a general rule, the older the piece, the higher the price.

Reproduction Alert: Early Staffordshire figurines and hollowware forms were molded. Later examples were made using a slip-casting process. Slip casting leaves telltale signs that are easy to spot. Look in the interior. Hand molding created a smooth interior surface. Slip casting produces indentations that conform to the exterior design. Holes occur where handles meet the body of slip-cast pieces. There is not hole in a hand-molded piece.

A checkpoint on figurines is the firing or vent hole, which is a necessary feature on these forms. Early figurines had small holes; modern reproductions feature large holes often the size of a dime or quarter. Vent holes are found on the sides or hidden among the decoration in early Staffordshire figurines; most modern reproductions have them in the base.

These same tips can be used to spot modern reproductions of Flow Blue, Majolica, Old Sleepy Eye, Stoneware, Willow, and other ceramic pieces.

Chimney piece, cow and milk maiden, dark brown hair, orange and green trim, 7" l, 6-3/4" h, **$275.**

Bank, 5-1/4" h, cottage shape, repairs **195.00**

Bust, 8-1/4" h, Empress Maria Theresa, England, lead glaze creamware, underglaze translucent enamels, half bust mounted atop waisted socle, pierced hole to one shoulder factory made and apparently for holding additional ornament, late 18th C, slight glaze chip **1,175.00**

Cake stand, blue and white transfer, Wild Rose pattern, crazing, 12" d, 2-1/2" h **400.00**

Candlestick, lead glazed creamware

11-1/4" h, underglaze translucent colors, free form tree with leaf molded sconce and applied florets, late 18th C, restorations .. **1,175.00**

11-3/4" h, underglaze translucent brown, green, and blue enamels, molded tree form with applied foliage and shells, bird perched on branch, male figure standing on flat platform in center, late 18th C, restorations............. **650.00**

Cheese dish, cov, 9-3/4" l, 7-1/2" h, figural, cow head, enamel and pink luster detailing, shaped undertray **265.00**

Child's plate, 4-1/2" d, molded dressed goose, green, brown, and black enamel **55.00**

Creamer, 7" l, 2-1/2" h, cow, blue and dark red splotch polychrome dec, pearlware, early 19th C **235.00**

Cup and saucer, handleless, Gaudy floral design, blue, dark green, and gold, saucer imp "Clews Warranted Staffordshire," small rim flake on cup **250.00**

Figural group, older Quaker-type gentleman with little girl at his side, light post on right, shovel and pick-axe resting on lamp post, polychrome enamel decoration, Victorian, professional repair to top of lamp post, 10-1/4" h, $250. Photo courtesy of Cowan's Historic Americana Auctions.

Figure

3-3/8" h, barefoot girl in wingback chair, red plaid dress, yellow edging on chair, green base, some roughness on base **420.00**

4-5/8" h, Winter, canary, minor wear, small flakes **660.00**

5-1/2" h, 3-1/2" l, boy and girl under tree canopy, sheep and dog, oval base, two small nicks **90.00**

6-1/2" h, 3-1/4" d, lad up in tree, bird in hand, nest nearby, girl seated below, oval base, repairs ... **65.00**

7" h, squirrel, sitting upright holding nut, naturalistic stump base, ear repaired................ **125.00**

10-1/2" h, Benjamin Franklin, polychrome enamel, pink luster, standing, holding hat in one hand, documents in other, mid-19th C **2,000.00**

13" h, King Charles Spaniel, pr **375.00**

Hen on nest, 10-1/2" l, polychrome, good color, minor edge wear and chips on inner flange of base........ **715.00**

Jar, cov, 3-1/4" h, melon shape, alternating yellow and green stripes, cov with molded leaf, lead glaze, 18th C, hairline to cover, finial and rim chips.................... **4,315.00**

Jug, 8-1/2" h, Fair Hebe, high relief, modeled as tree trunk, creamware, lead glaze, attributed to Yoyez, c1788, rim chip and repair............. **998.00**

Figural group, Jolly Traveler Group, man with walking stick, mule, dog by their feet, impressed title to lozenge mounted to face of freeform oval base, applied with florets and encrusted grass, c1820, bocage missing, losses to applied leaves on basket and flowers on base, donkey's ears and man's arm with chips restored, 6-1/4" h, $450. Photo courtesy of Skinner Auctioneers and Appraisers.

Poodle with seated puppy, cobalt blue base, 7" h, $190. Photo courtesy of Cowan's Historic Americana Auctions.

Mantel ornament, 9" h, cottage, Potash Farm, hairlines.............. **175.00**

Miniature, tea set, Gaudy pink and green rose dec, 4-1/4" h teapot, creamer, sugar, waste bowl, two cups and saucers, few flakes, repairs **425.00**

Mug, 3-3/4" h, pearlware, black transfer print of Hope in landscape scene, silver luster highlights, minor imperfections **60.00**

Pitcher, 4-7/8" h, mask, pink luster rim, glaze wear, hairline to spout ... **175.00**

Plate, 10" d, feather edge, blue, emb rim design **55.00**

Platter, 21" d, blue and white transfer, "The Italian Pattern," attributed to Spode, early 19th C, unmarked, glaze wear, scratches............. **575.00**

Sauce boat, 7-7/8" l, fruit and flowers, molded feet and handle, dark blue, rim chips **330.00**

Sauce tureen, 7-1/2" l, blue transfer, pastoral scene, chips **345.00**

Teapot, cov, 9-3/4" l, black basalt, oval form, scalloped rim and classical reliefs centering columns with floral festoons, banded drapery on shoulder, incised brick banded lower body, unmarked, early 19th C, restored spout ... **360.00**

Tea service, Chinese Tree pattern, polychrome decorated puce transfer print, 6-1/2" h cov teapot; 8" d teapot stand; 4-3/4" h cream jug; 4-3/4" h cov sugar bowl; 7" d waste bowl; two serving dishes; seven coffee cups; 10

Pastile burner, cottage shape, applied green bocage, gold trim, white ground, open door and chimney, **$225.**

tea cups; 12 saucers, c1830, all with slight damage, hairlines, or chips **500.00**

Waste bowl, 5-5/8" d, Forget Me Not, red transfer, edge roughness **60.00**

Whistle, 3-1/2" h, overglazed enamel dec, modeled as bird perched on tree trunk, applied florets, c1820, tail restored **420.00**

STAFFORDSHIRE, ROMANTIC

History: In the 1830s, two factors transformed the blue-and-white printed wares of the Staffordshire potters into what is now called "Romantic Staffordshire." Technical innovations expanded the range of transfer-printed colors to light blue, pink, purple, black, green, and brown. There was also a shift from historical to imaginary scenes with less printed detail and more white space, adding to the pastel effect.

Shapes from the 1830s are predominately rococo with rounded forms, scrolled handles, and floral finials. Over time, patterns and shapes became

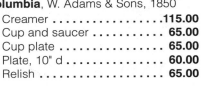

simpler and the earthenware bodies coarser. The late 1840s and 1850s saw angular gothic shapes and pieces with the weight and texture of ironstone.

The most dramatic post-1870 change was the impact of the craze for all things Japanese. Staffordshire designs adopted zigzag border elements and motifs such

For more information, see this book.

as bamboo, fans, and cranes. Brown printing dominated this style, sometimes with polychrome enamel highlights.

Marks: Wares are often marked with pattern or potter's names, but marking was inconsistent and many authentic, unmarked examples exist. The addition of "England" as a country of origin mark in 1891 helps to distinguish 20th-century wares made in the romantic style.

Caledonia, Williams Adams, 1830s

Plate, 9-1/2" d, purple transfer, imp "Adams" **60.00**
Platter, 17" l **500.00**
Soup plate, two colors **175.00**

Canova, Thomas Mayer, c1835; G. Phillips, c1840

Plate, 10-1/2" d **95.00**
Pudding bowl, two colors . . . **200.00**
Vegetable, cov **325.00**

Cheshire pattern, Burleigh Ware, cheese dish, cov, 9-1/4" l, 5" h, rect, sloped lid, underglaze blue ovoid finial, rect undertray, transfer printed green and blue, scenes of milkmaids and cheesemakers, aesthetic movement floral motifs, gilt accents, third quarter 19th C **115.00**

Columbia, W. Adams & Sons, 1850

Creamer **115.00**
Cup and saucer **65.00**
Cup plate **65.00**
Plate, 10" d **60.00**
Relish **65.00**

Coffeepot, by Enoch Wood & Sons, c1830, printed "HARP" and "EW&S," black transfer of house, urn, and bird in landscape, floral borders, spout printed with harp and sheet music laying by flowering urn, border at shoulder and cover printed upside down, 11" h, **$350.** *Photo courtesy of Sloan's Auctioneers & Appraisers.*

Soup bowl, Italian Villas, marked "J. & H. Co." for J. Heath, 8-3/4" d, **$45.**

Dado, Ridgways, 1880s

Creamer, brown **75.00**
Cup and saucer, polychrome . **80.00**
Plate, 7-1/2" d, brown **35.00**

Delzoni, plate, 8-3/4" d, brown transfer **60.00**

Dr. Syntax, James and Ralph Clews, Cobridge, 1819-36

Plate, 10-1/2" d, Dr. Syntax Disputing his Bill with the Landlady, blue and white transfer **125.00**
Platter, 14-1/4" x 19", Dr. Syntax Amused with Pat in the Pond, blue and white transfer, glaze scratches, scattered minor staining . **1,840.00**
Undertray, 10" x 5-3/4", Death of Punch, Dr. Syntax literary series, blue and white transfer, crazing on reverse **85.00**

India, plate, 9" d, red transfer scene, floral border **65.00**

Japonica, creamer and sugar . . **275.00**

Marmora, William Ridgway & Co., 1830s

Platter, 16-1/2" l **325.00**
Sauce tureen, matching tray . **350.00**
Soup plate **100.00**

Millenium, Ralph Stevenson & Son, 1830s, plate, 10-1/2" d **145.00**

Palestine, William Adams, 1836

Creamer and sugar **265.00**
Cup and saucer, two colors . . **135.00**
Cup plate **75.00**
Plate, 7" d **60.00**
Platter, 13" l **325.00**
Vegetable, open, 12" l **200.00**

Quadrupeds, John Hall, 1814-32

Plate, 10" d, central medallion with lion, printed maker's mark for John Hall, 1814-32, pattern mark in crown, price for pr **865.00**

Platter, 14-3/4" x 19", Quadrupeds pattern, central cartouche of elephant, printed maker's mark for John Hall 1914-32, pattern mark in crown, minor surface imperfections **4,315.00**

Shell pattern, Stubbs and Kent, Longport, 1828-30

Cream jug, 5" h, blue and white transfer, unmarked, imperfections **1,200.00**

Milk pitcher, 7" h, blue and white transfer, unmarked, imperfections **900.00**

Plate, 10" d, blue and white transfer, imp maker's mark, imperfections, price for eight-pc set **2,645.00**

Platter, 18-1/2" l, oval, blue and white transfer, imp maker's mark, repaired rim chip **1,955.00**

Soup plate, 10" d, blue and white transfer, imp maker's mark, wear, price for three........... **750.00**

Tea bowl and saucer, 2-1/2" h, blue and white transfer, imp maker's mark **450.00**

Vegetable dish, 12-1/4" d, 2-1/2" h, oval, blue and white transfer, imp maker's mark, scratches, wear **1,150.00**

Union, William Ridgway Son & Co., 1840s

Plate, 10-1/2" d **70.00**
Platter, 15" l.............. **165.00**

Unknown pattern

Cup and saucer, two dogs, flower and leaf border, imp maker's mark

Sugar bowl, covered, medium blue transfer, allover floral design with flowers in basket and blossom border, scalloped top rim, scrolled handles, marked "Stevenson Warranted Staffordshire, Stevenson Stone China," chips, rim repair, 6-1/2" w, 6" h, $250. Photo courtesy of Sanford Alderfer Auction Company.

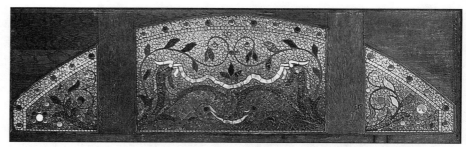

Window, Henry Belcher, mosaic and chunk jewel, original frame, 93" l, 29" h, $8,400. Photo courtesy of Fontaine's Auction Gallery.

for James & Ralph Clews, Cobridge, 1817-34, 2-1/4" h, 5-3/4" h, minor light wear... **150.00**

Tea set, partial, blue and white transfer

Bird in oval reverse, floral border, two teapots, creamer, small bowl, waste bowl, imperfections **1,265.00**

Three figures in landscape, manor house in distance, teapot, creamer, and two cov sugar bowls **1,610.00**

Venus, Podmore, Walker & Co., 1850s, plate, 7-1/2" d............... **50.00**

Yorkshire, soup plate, 10" d, light blue, slight glaze lines........... **200.00**

STAINED AND/OR LEADED GLASS PANELS

History: American architects in the second half of the 19th century and the early 20th century used stained-and leaded-glass panels as a chief decorative element. Skilled glass craftsmen assembled the designs, the best known being Louis C. Tiffany.

The panels are held together with soft lead cames or copper wraps. When purchasing a panel, protect your investment by checking the lead and making any necessary repairs.

Leaded

Firescreen, 48-1/2" w, 32" h, three panels, clear glass top half, hammered white glass lower half, central applied Art Nouveau floral design, green bull's eye highlights............ **2,750.00**

Panel, 96" h, 20" w, rect, rippled, and opaque glass, turquoise, white, and avocado, clear glass ground, stylized flowering plant motif, c1910, six panels **6,000.00**

Sketch for leaded glass window

Charcoal on paper, The Crucifixion, 26" d, America, c1920..... **170.00**

Watercolor, garden scene, mother and child before Christ figure, sgd on mat "Louis Comfort Tiffany," 6-3/4" x 4-1/2"......... **1,725.00**

Triptych, 34-3/4" h, 17-3/4" w, twining grapevines and grape clusters, green slag, textured purple and brown glass, amber border segments, textured colorless glass background, wood frame, cracks **1,380.00**

Window

17-3/4" d int., 19-1/4" d outside, bull's eye, beaded gilt-metal frame, octagonal surround, central beveled colorless glass octagon, surrounded by beveled diamonds, price for pr......... **1,035.00**

29-1/2" h, 18" w, attributed to Belcher Mosaic Glass Co., passion flower,

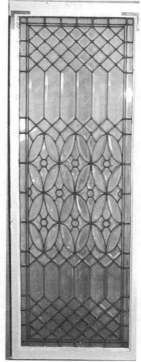

Door, bench leaded, clear glass, elongated with ornate part beveled glass inserts, 28" w, 78" h, $1,450. Photo courtesy of James D. Julia, Inc.

Window, stained and leaded, Heraldic panels, Europe, late 19th century, each shield shaped, 19-1/4" x 16-1/4" central shield divided with coats of arms, 22-5/8" x 14-7/8" with coat of arms topped by helmet, **$950.** *Photo courtesy of Skinner Auctioneers and Appraisers.*

pink ribbon, and rose bud against variegated amber ground, opalescent roundels, sea green and reddish umber frame of mosaic glass, unsigned **. 2,400.00**
36" h, 16-1/4" d, Prairie School, zinc caming, clear, white, green, and violet slag glass, stylized lilies and tulips, set of five, few minor cracks in glass **4,250.00**
53-1/2" h, seated cupid playing pipes for audience of birds in landscape, 19th C **11,160.00**

Stained
Panel
24" x 14", red, white, green, pink, and blue floral design, two layers of

striated and fractured glass, green patinated bronze frame, stamped "Tiffany Studios New York" pr **2,400.00**
26" x 21", Richard the Lion-Hearted on horseback, 1883 . . . . . . **675.00**
Transom window, 59" x 17", arched form, amber, green, and red, later walnut frame, brass plaque "Illinois Traction System Car Number 523" **260.00**
Window
35-1/8" w, 15-1/2" h, rect, arched top, brown glass border, gold glass panels, central stain pained medallion of bush of classical male, sgd "Louis Shuys," scrolled leaf surround, late 19th/early 20th C **425.00**
61-1/2" h, 61" l, over entry door type, blue and orange shield and geometric design, c1920 . . **490.00**

STANGL POTTERY BIRDS

History: Stangl ceramic birds were produced from 1940 until the Stangl factory closed in 1978. The birds were produced at Stangl's Trenton plant and either decorated there or shipped to its Flemington, New Jersey, outlet for hand painting.

For more information, see this book.

During World War II, the demand for these birds, and other types of Stangl pottery as well, was so great that 40 to 60 decorators could not keep up with the demand. Orders were contracted out to be decorated by individuals in their own homes. These orders then were returned for firing and finishing. Colors used to decorate these birds varied according to the artist.

Marks: As many as 10 different trademarks were used. Almost every bird is numbered; many are artist signed. However, the signatures are used only for dating purposes and add very little to the value of the birds.

Adviser: Bob Perzel.

Note: Several birds were reissued between 1972 and 1977. These reissues are dated on the bottom and are worth approximately the same as older birds, if well decorated.

3250, preening duck, natural colors **125.00**
3273, rooster, 5-3/4" h **800.00**
3274, penguin **500.00**
3276, bluebird **90.00**
3281, mother duck **600.00**
3285, rooster, 4-1/2" h, early blue green base **100.00**
3286, hen, 4-1/2" h, late lime green base **50.00**
3400, lovebird, old, wavy base **. 135.00**
3400, lovebird, revised leaf base **. 75.00**
3402, pair of orioles, revised . . . **115.00**
3402, pair of orioles, old **300.00**
3404, pair of lovebirds, old **400.00**
3404, pair of lovebirds, revised **. 125.00**
3405, pair of cockatoos, revised, open base **150.00**
3406, pair of kingfishers, blue . . **165.00**
3407, owl **350.00**
3430, duck, 22" **8,000.00**
3431, duck, standing, brown . . . **850.00**
3432, rooster, 16" h **3,500.00**
3443, flying duck, teal **250.00**
3444, cardinal, pink, glossy **90.00**
3445, rooster, yellow **185.00**
3446, hen, gray **300.00**
3450, passenger pigeon **1,800.00**
3451, William Ptarmigan **3,500.00**
3453, mountain bluebird **1,500.00**
3454, Key West quail dove, single wing up **275.00**

Window, stained, fruit and flower design, from west side Buffalo, NY, home, c1885, layered glass in ewer and some in fruit, waffle texture ribbon, 36" l, 22" h, **$4,200.** *Photo courtesy of Fontaine's Auction Gallery.*

Hummingbirds, #3599, marked, 10-1/2" h, **$325.** *Photo courtesy of David Rago Auctions.*

3454, Key West quail dove, both wings up **1,800.00**
3455, shoveler duck **2,000.00**
3457, walking pheasant **3,500.00**
3458, quail **2,000.00**
3459, falcon/fish hawk/osprey. **6,000.00**
3490, pair of redstarts **200.00**
3492, cock pheasant **225.00**
3518, pair of white-headed pigeons **950.00**
3580, cockatoo, medium **150.00**
3580, cockatoo, medium, white **600.00**
3581, group of chickadees, black and white **300.00**
3582, pair of green parakeets .. **225.00**
3582, pair of blue parakeets ... **250.00**
3584, cockatoo, large **275.00**
3584, cockatoo, large, matte white **1,075.00**
3590, chat **165.00**
3591, Brewers blackbird **160.00**
3595, Bobolink **150.00**
3596, gray cardinal **80.00**
3597, Wilson warbler, yellow **55.00**
3599, pair of hummingbirds ... **325.00**
3625, Bird of Paradise, large, 13-1/2" h **2,500.00**
3627, Rivoli hummingbird, with pink flower **175.00**
3634, Allen hummingbird **90.00**
3635, group of goldfinches **215.00**
3717, pair of blue jays **3,500.00**
3746, canary, rose flower **250.00**
3749, scarlet tanager **425.00**
3750, pair of western tanagers . **500.00**
3751, red-headed woodpecker, pink glossy **300.00**
3752, pair of red-headed woodpeckers, red matte **550.00**
3754, pair of white-winged crossbills, pink glossy **425.00**

Blue Jay with peanut, #3715, marked, 10-1/4", $920. Photo courtesy of David Rago Auctions.

3755, audubon warbler **475.00**
3756, pair of audubon warblers . **600.00**
3757, scissor-tailed flycatcher **1,100.00**
3758, magpie jay **1,400.00**
3810, blackpoll warbler **185.00**
3811, chestnut chickadee **145.00**
3812, chestnut-sided warbler ... **150.00**
3813, evening grosbeak **150.00**
3814, blackthroated green warbler **165.00**
3815, western bluebird **440.00**
3848, golden crowned kinglet .. **125.00**
3850, yellow warbler **135.00**
3852, cliff swallow **170.00**
3853, group of golden crowned kingfishers **780.00**
3868, summer tanager **750.00**
3921, yellow-headed verdin .. **1,700.00**
3922, European finch **1,200.00**
3924, yellow-throated warbler .. **680.00**
Bird sign **2,500.00**

STEIFF

History: Margarete Steiff, GmbH, established in Germany in 1880, is known for very fine-quality stuffed animals and dolls, as well as other beautifully made collectible toys. It is still in business, and its products are highly respected.

The company's first products were wool-felt elephants made by Margaret Steiff. In a few years, the animal line was expanded to include a donkey, horse, pig, and camel.

By 1903, the company also was producing a jointed mohair teddy bear, whose production dramatically increased to more than 970,000 units in 1907. Margarete's nephews took over the company at this point.

Newly designed animals were added: Molly and Bully, the dogs, and Fluffy, the cat. Pull toys and kites also were produced, as well as larger animals on which children could ride or play.

Marks: The bear's-head label became the symbol for the firm in about 1907, and the famous "Button in the Ear" round, metal trademark was added.

Notes: Become familiar with genuine Steiff products before purchasing an antique stuffed animal. Plush in old Steiff animals was mohair; trimmings usually were felt or velvet. Unscrupulous individuals have attached the familiar Steiff metal button to animals that are not Steiff.

Bear

3-1/2" h, honey blond mohair, black bead eyes, embroidered nose and mouth, fully jointed, padless style, c1950 .... **120.00**
5" h, blond mohair, rattle, no button, black shoe button eyes, fully jointed, embroidered nose and mouth, overall wear, stains, rip on arm, working rattle, excelsior

Bear, early, jointed, 12" h, $1,400. Photo courtesy of McMasters Harris Auction Co.

stuffing, no pad style, c1910 .... **415.00**
5-1/2" h, blond mohair, glass eyes, embroidered nose and mouth, no pad style, dressed in pink print dress with pink checked collar, yellow knit overalls, green corduroy jacket, red scarf, black felt hat and a bell around his neck, c1930 .... **345.00**
8-1/2" h, golden mohair, shoe button eyes, embroidered nose, mouth, and claws, fully jointed, excelsior stuffing, no pad arms, c1915, moth damage to foot pads **1,380.00**
12-1/2" h, light apricot, ear button, fully jointed, shoe button eyes, embroidered nose, mouth, and claws, excelsior stuffing, felt pads, c1905, fur loss, lower back and back of legs, slight moth damage on pads **1,610.00**
14" h, golden mohair, ear button, black embroidered nose and claws, mouth missing, black shoe button eyes, squeaker, fully jointed body, excelsior stuffing, original felt pads, c1905, one-inch fabric tear right front arm joint, very minor fur loss, overall soil **1,955.00**
14" h, light golden mohair, underscored ear button, black shoe button eyes, center seam, black embroidered nose, mouth, and claws, fully jointed, tan felt pads, c1905, holes in hand pads **4,890.00**
17" h, One Hundredth Anniversary Bear, ear button, gold mohair, fully

Three Steiff fish, one large, two small, $75. Photo courtesy of Joy Luke Auctions.

jointed, plastic eyes, black embroidered nose, mouth, and claws, peach felt pads, excelsior stuffing, certificate no. 3934, orig box **200.00**

20" h, golden long mohair, shoe button eyes, embroidered nose, mouth and claws, fully jointed, excelsior stuffing, c1905 . **8,920.00**

21" h, Zotty, long curly beige mohair, apricot chest, ear button, fully jointed glass eyes, airbrushed mouth, embroidered nose, peach felt pads, 1950s-60s **175.00**

30" h, blond mohair, script ear button, glass eyes, embroidered nose, mouth, claws excelsior stuffed, fully jointed, mid-19th C, felt feet pads have scattered moth holes, break at sides **1,955.00**

Beaver, 6" l, Nagy, mohair, chest tag, post WWII **95.00**

Bison, 9-1/2" l, mohair, ear button, chest tag, post WWII **200.00**

Boxer, 16-1/2" l, 15-1/2" h, beige mohair coat, black trim, glass eyes, leather collar marked "Steiff," head turns, minor wear, straw stuffing **165.00**

Boxer puppy, 4-1/4" h, paper label "Daly" **135.00**

Cat, 14" l, pull toy, white mohair coat, gray stripes, glass eyes, worn pink ribbon with bell, pink felt ear linings, button, cast iron wheels **1,980.00**

Cocker spaniel, 5-3/4" h, sitting, glass eyes, ear button, chest tag, post WWII **125.00**

Cocker spaniel puppy, 4-3/4" h, button **90.00**

Dalmatian puppy, 4-1/4" h, paper label "Sarras" **145.00**

Dog, 15-1/2" l, 14" h, pull toy, orange and white mohair coat, glass eyes, steel frame, cast iron wheels, one ear missing, button in remaining ear, voice box does not work **280.00**

Frog, 3-3/4" l, velveteen, glass eyes, green, sitting, button and chest tag **125.00**

Goat, 6-1/2" h, ear button **150.00**

Gussy, 6-1/2" l, white and black kitten, glass eyes, ear button, chest tag, post WWII **125.00**

Horse on wheels, 21" l, 17" h, ear button, glass eyes, white and brown, wear and breaks to fabric, on solid metal wheels, non-functioning pull-ring, c1930. . . . .**215.00**

Kangaroo and joey, 20-3/4" h mohair mother, 4" h velveteen baby both with glass eyes, embroidered nose, and mouth, ear button and tag, ...**395.00**

Koala, 7-1/2" h, glass eyes, ear button, chest tag, post WWII **135.00**

Lion, 21" l, 18" h, pull toy, worn gold mohair coat, glass eyes, worn streaked mane incomplete, no tail, ring pull voice box, steel frame, sheet metal wheels with white rubber treads marked "Steiff" **500.00**

Lizard, 12" l, Lizzy, velveteen, yellow and green, black steel eyes, chest tag **200.00**

Llama, 10" h, glass eyes, ear button, chest tag, post WWII **125.00**

Monkey, 5" h, Coco, glass eyes, ear button, chest tag, post WWII . . .**125.00**

Owl, 4-1/2" h, Wittie, glass eyes, ear button, chest tag, post WWII **95.00**

Palomino colt, 11" h, ear button, wear **330.00**

Panda, 6" h, black and white mohair, fully jointed, glass eyes, excelsior stuffing, felt open mouth and pads, c1950, some fur loss, moth damage on pads, button and tag missing . .**260.00**

Parakeet, 6-1/2" h, Hansi, bright lime green and yellow, airbrushed black details, plastic eyes, button tag, chest tag, plastic beak and feet **115.00**

Penguin, 5-1/2" h, Peggy, glass eyes, ear button, chest tag, post WWII.**95.00**

Pig, 15" l, pull toy, blonde mohair, button eyes, ear button, cast iron wheels, repairs, very worn mohair **330.00**

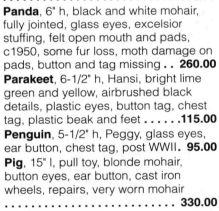

Three Steiff hand puppets: Mimic Biggie dog, rabbit, and Gaty alligator, $145. Photo courtesy of Joy Luke Auctions.

Rabbit, 9-1/2" h, unmarked, wear **220.00**

Soldier, 14" h, c1913, slight moth damage, hat and equipment missing **460.00**

Turtle, 7" l, Slo, plastic shell, glass eyes, ear button, chest tag, post WWII **85.00**

Walrus, 6-1/2" l, Paddy, plastic tusk, glass eyes, ear button, chest tag, post WWII **145.00**

Stein, Lea

History: Lea Stein, a French-trained artist born in Paris in 1931, began making her whimsical pieces of jewelry in 1969, after her husband, Fernand Steinberger, came up with a process of laminating layers of rhodoid (cellulose acetate) sheets with interesting textures and colors. The layers were baked overnight with a secret component of his creation and then cut into shapes for various designs of pins, bracelets, earrings, and shaped decorative objects. Some pieces have as many as 20 layers of cellulose bonded together.

The most easily recognizable Lea Stein pin is the 3-D fox, produced in a myriad of colors and designs. Often, lace or metal layers were incorporated into the celluloid, which produced an astounding number of unique textures. The 3-D fox's tail is looped from one piece of celluloid.

Many different styles of cats, dogs, bugs, bunnies, birds, ducks, and other creatures were introduced, as well as Art Deco-styled women, mod-styled children, flowers, cars, hats, purses, gold-encased and rhinestone encrusted designs, and lots of little "things," such as stars, hearts, rainbows, and even pins resembling John Travolta and Elvis Presley. In addition, collectors can find many bangles, rings, cuffs, earrings, barrettes, and rarer boxes, mirrors, and cigarette cases. The designs seem endless and to a Lea Stein collector, the ability to collect one of everything is almost impossible, because so many pieces were one of a kind. One particularly elusive piece is called "Joan Crawford" in the U.S. and "Carmen" in France. This piece was made in limited quantity and was always hard to find, but, a new cache has recently hit the market and they are not so difficult to find anymore.

These "vintage" pieces of jewelry were made from 1969 until 1981 and are identified by a V-shaped pin back, which is heat mounted to the back of each piece, as are the pin backs on her newer pieces. The pin back is always marked "Lea Stein Paris." Some of the later issues have riveted backs, but all of them are marked in the same way. At one time the age of a pin could be determined by the pin back, but because of many newly released pieces in the past few years, that no longer is always the case. Stein's workshop is still producing jewelry. While some of the vintage pieces are rare, it is virtually impossible to tell the difference between old and new releases, except with the knowledge of which designs were created at what time in Stein's career. Whether old or new, Lea Stein's jewelry is quite collectible.

Adviser: Judy Smith.

Bracelet, bangle, dark green and red swirled peppermint stick swirls . . **75.00**

Earrings, pr, clip, bright green swirls on pearly white, stamped on back, 1-3/8" d
. . . . **75.00**

Pin, all with signature Lea Stein-Paris V-shaped pin back

Bacchus, cat, pearly silver and black, 2-3/8" w, 1-1/8" h **65.00**

Bee, transparent wings with gold edge, faux ivory body and head, topaz colored glass edge eye, 2-3/8" wingspan **70.00**

Cat, standing, magenta lace, faux-mother-of-pearl ears and eyes, 3-3/4" l, 1-3/4" h **75.00**

Cicada, irid red wings, striped body and head, 3-3/8" l, 1-1/4" w . **75.00**

Double Totie, left in white lace, dark blue bow around neck with bright blue nose, right is magenta lace, black neck bow and nose, 2-1/4" w, 1-5/8" h **95.00**

Flamingo, pink, 1-7/8" w, 2-3/8" h
. . . . **55.00**

Fox, red tones **100.00**

Goldenberries, shades of plum, gold, and white, 2-3/8" w, 1-5/8" h
. . . . **65.00**

Golden Raptor, translucent blue body, golden overlay, topaz colored glass bed eye, 2-1/8" w, 2-1/4" h **80.00**

Joan Crawford **125.00**

Cat, Gomina, rusty faux-tortoise, shiny black eyes and ears, V-shaped Lea Stein Paris clasp, **$65.**

Mistigri Kitty, caramel, 4" 2, 3-7/8" h
. . . . **70.00**

Oriental girl, shades of blue and white, transparent light blue hat, faux-ivory face, transparent light blue eye, 2" w, 2-1/8" h **90.00**

Panther, pearly ivory harlequin, medium faux tortoiseshell, 4-1/4" l, 1-3/4" h **65.00**

Penguin, dark red brocade body and head, yellow lace beak, eye, neck, and feet, pearly harquelin lace body, 1-3/4" w, 3-1/8" h . **70.00**

Porcupine, irid gold and dark red body with black accents, black face and paws, dark red eye and nose, 3" w **80.00**

Ric, pearly ivory harlequin pattern, shiny black ears, nose, eye and collar **65.00**

Sailor, faux ivory face, neck, hands and feet, pearly purple suit and cap, pearly gray collar, 1-5/8" w, 2-3/8" h **80.00**

Swallow, pink and white lace wings, 2-3/4" w, 1-3/8" h **60.00**

Three ducks, orange lace bodies, dark royal blue heads, dark blue wings, 1" w, 2-1/4" h **75.00**

Geometric diamond, red outlined with mauve and gray, signed Lea Stein V-shaped clasp, 3-3/8" w, 1-1/4" h, **$70.**

Limo, crackly pink, highlighted by pearly pink and white moiré bumper, pink and white pearly wheels, small V-shaped Lea Stein signed clasp, 2-3/4" w, **$50.**

Book, silver glitter spine, pink plaid cover, shiny black pages, 3/8" thick including a faux-tortoise back, signed V-shaped clasp, 1-1/8" w, 1-3/4" h, **$45.** *Photos courtesy of Judy Smith.*

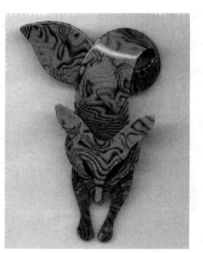

Fox, swirled red moiré, black eyes, V-shaped signature clasp, 2" w, 4" h, **$65.**

Ric the Terrier, faux ivory, black eye, nose, ears, and collar. 2-1/8" w, 3-5/8" h, **$65.**

STEINS

1892-1921

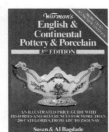

History: Steins, mugs especially made to hold beer or ale, range in size from the smaller 3/10 and 1/4 liter to the larger 1, 1-1/2, 2, 3, 4, and 5 liters, and in rare cases to 8 liters. A liter is 1.05 liquid quarts.

For more information, see this book.

Master steins or pouring steins hold 3 to 5 liters and are called krugs. Most steins are fitted with a metal-hinged lid with thumb lift. The earthenware character-type steins usually are German in origin.

Character

Beethoven, half liter, porcelain, lire on side of body and on porcelain inlaid lid, E. Bohne & Sohn **570.00**

Frederick III, in uniform, 1/2 liter, porcelain, porcelain lid, Schierholz, chips on lid repaired, int. color yellowing **1,735.00**

Indian, 1/4 liter, porcelain, inlaid lid, E. Bohne & Sohn **440.00**

L.A.W. high-wheel bicycle, half liter, porcelain, lithophane of man falling onto woman, inlaid lid, Schierholz... **440.00**

Monk, 1/3 liter, design by Frank Ringer, marked "J. Reinemann, Munchen" on underside of base, inlaid lid, 5" h **580.00**

Pug dog, Mettlach, #2018, 1/2 liter, character, pug dog, inlaid lid . **1,100.00**

Singing pig, 1/2 liter, porcelain, Schierholz, inlaid lid **580.00**

Skull, 1/3 liter, porcelain, large jaw, inlaid lid, E. Bohne & Sohn, pewter slightly bent **550.00**

Faience

Thuringen, 1 liter, 9-1/2" h, hp, floral design on front, purple trees on sides, pewter top rim and lid, pewter base ring, 18th C, tight hairline on side **1,155.00**

Glass

9-1/2" h, 1 liter, blown, wedding type, hp floral design and verse, pewter lid with earlier date of 1779, pewter brass ring, c1850. .... **925.00**

15-1/4" h, 6-1/2" d, amber, encased in fancy French pewter frame, ram's heads around stein, hinged top lid **495.00**

Ivory, hand carved, c1850-70

11-1/2" h, elaborate battle scene with approx. 100 figures, carving around entire body, silver top with figural knight finial, cherub bases and fruit in repoussé on lid, figural handle of man in armor, silver base with touch marks, discoloration to ivory **6,700.00**

13-1/2" h, elaborate hunting scene, four men on horseback, 15 dogs, ivory lid with various animals carved around border, 3-1/2" h finial of man blowing trumpet with dog, figural handle of bare breasted woman with crown, dog head thumb lift, left arm and trumpet missing **11,550.00**

Porcelain and Pottery

Delft, 1/2 liter, elaborate scene of two people playing lawn tennis, porcelain inlaid lid of sail boat, marked "Delft, Germany"................. **1,390.00**

Meissen, 1 liter, 7" h, hp, scene of three people in forest, floral design around sides, porcelain lid with berry finial and painted flowers, closed hinge, cross swords and "S" mark, c1820, strap repoured................. **3,100.00**

Mettlach

#1896, 1/4 liter, maiden on one side, cherub face on other, grape dec, pewter lift handle......... **350.00**

#2007, 1/2 liter, etched, black cat, inlaid lid................. **660.00**

#2057, 1/2 liter, etched, festive dancing scene, inlaid lid... **325.00**

#2093, 1/2 liter, etched and glazed, suit of cards, inlaid lid..... **700.00**

#2204, 1/2 liter etched and relief, Prussian eagle, inlaid lid... **780.00**

Salt glazed, White's Utica, mold #45, relief and blue accented tavern scene on one side, framed German verse on other, relief and blue accented gargoyle handle, conical pewter lid, matching thumb lift, small surface chip on base, 9-1/2" h, $180. Photo courtesy of Vicki and Bruce Waasdorp.

Mettlach, # 2382, 1/2 liter, knight drinking in cellar and riding off into night, conical lid, signed "H. Schlitt," 9" h, $865. Photo courtesy of James D. Julia, Inc.

Stoneware, German, half liter, decorated with dancing figures, pewter lid with porcelain inset decorated with portrait of lady, $95. Photo courtesy of Joy Luke Auctions.

Stoneware, Simon Peter Gerz German, three liter, decorated with relief panels of warriors with shields, marked "Saul, Holofernes & Sanherib," $125. Photo courtesy of Joy Luke Auctions.

#2580, 1/2 liter, etched, Die Kannenburg, conical inlay lid, knight in castle **695.00**

#2755, 1/4 liter, cameo and etched, three scenes of people at table, Art Nouveau design between scenes, inlaid lid **560.00**

Unknown maker, 1/4 liter, transfer and enameled, color, Ulmer Splatz!, The Bird from the City of Ulm, pewter lid **115.00**

Regimental, 1/2 liter, porcelain

2 Schwer. Reit. Regt. Erzh. Fz, Ferd u. Osterr-Este Esk Landshut 1899-02, named to Friederich Schmidt, two side scenes, lion thumb lift, old tear on lid repaired, minor scruffs, 11-1/2" h **675.00**

11 Armee Corps, Mainz 1899, names to Res. Doring, two side scenes, plain thumb lift, strap tear repaired, lines in lithophane, 10" h **485.00**

61 Field Artillery, Dartmstadt 1910-12, named to Kanonier Boxheimer, four side sides, roster worn, lion thumb lift **415.00**

120 Infantry, Ulm 1899-01, named to Tambour Wurst, two side scenes, Wurttemberg thumb lift, 10-1/2" h **520.00**

123 Grenadier, Ulm 1908-10, named to Grenadier Schindler, four side scenes, roster, bird thumb lift, open blister on int. base, finial missing **550.00**

Wood and pewter, Daubenkrug

1/2 liter, 6-1/2" h, pewter scene of deer, vines and leaves on sides, pewter handle and lid, c1820, some separations to pewter **925.00**

1/3 liter, 5-1/2" h, floral design on sides, oval with crown on front, pewter handle and lid, 18th C, splints in pewter and wood **1,270.00**

STEUBEN GLASS

1903–32

For more information, see this book.

History: Frederich Carder, an Englishman, and Thomas G. Hawkes of Corning, New York, established the Steuben Glass Works in 1904. In 1918, the Corning Glass Company purchased the Steuben company. Carder remained with the firm and designed many of the pieces bearing the Steuben mark. Probably the most widely recognized wares are Aurene, Verre De Soie, and Rosaline, but many other types were produced.

The firm is still operating, producing glass of exceptional quality.

Animals, colorless, NY, 20th C, inscribed "Steuben"

Dinosaur, 12-3/4" l, base wear **1,850.00**

Donkey, standing, 10-1/2" h **980.00**

Dove, on stand, 12-1/8" h, abrasion to side of dove **635.00**

Eagle, 4-3/4" h, imperfections . . **350.00**

Frog, sitting, 4-1/4" l, minor base wear **230.00**

Animal, elephant, trunk raised, signed, 7-1/4" h, $275. Photo courtesy of Sloan's Auctioneers & Appraisers.

Aurene, compote, base with script signature, 6" d, 8-1/4" h, $750. Photo courtesy of Joy Luke Auctions.

Seal, resting on flippers, 8-1/2" l **375.00**

Shore Bird, 8-3/8" l, light scratches to base **115.00**

Snail, 3-5/8" l, base scratch **115.00**

Squirrel, 4-1/8" h **350.00**

Aurene

Atomizer, 6" h, amber, gold irid finish, c1920, atomizer bulb missing . . **415.00**

Bowl, 10" d, amber, gold irid finish, sgd "Aurene 5061," orig triangular paper label, c1910 . . . . **460.00**

Bud vase, 3" d base, 10" h, blue, gold highlights, sgd "Steuben Aurene 2556" **700.00**

Cabinet vase, 2-9/16" d, 2-3/8" h, gold, ruffled rim, sgd "Aurene 2649," also sgd "F. Carder" across ground pontil **725.00**

Candlesticks, pr, 10-1/8" h, catalog #686, amber, twist stems on applied disc foot, strong gold luster, sgd "Aurene 686," c1920 . . . . **1,100.00**

Aurene, perfume bottle, shape #2183, iridescent gold with blue highlights, unsigned, 6" h, $635. Photo courtesy of James D. Julia, Inc.

Darner, 5-1/2" l, 2-1/4" d, gold, some nicks and scratches from use . . **850.00**

Lamp shade, 4-3/8" h, shape #2320, ribbed, bell shape, obscure silver fleur-de-lis paint stamp, pr **400.00**

Perfume, 6" h, amber, irid gold finish, sgd "Aurene 1818," c1915 . . . . . **650.00**

Planter, 12" d, blue, inverted rim, three applied prunt feet, engraved "Aurene 2586" **775.00**

Vase

5-3/4" h, amber, ftd, gold luster finish on ruffled rim, sgd "Aurene 167," c1910, wear to finish **425.00**

6" h, amber with bluish-gold irid finish, sgd "Aurene 148," c1920, wear to int. **460.00**

6-1/8" h, catalog no. 7447 variant, flared rim, double-bulbed ribbed body, gold irid, polished pontil, paper label "Steuben," inscribed "Steuben," light minor scratches **635.00**

8-1/2" h, amber, gold irid finish, classic shape, sgd "Steuben Aurene 2083," c1915. . . . **1,035.00**

11" h, irid green, gold hooked feather dec on bottom, fishnet dec at rim **5,750.00**

16-1/2" h, amber, irid finish shading from red gold at top to blue good foot, double sgd "Steuben Aurene," numbered 3285, c1920. . **3,165.00**

18-1/4" h, trumpet, amber, gold luster irid finish, sgd "Aurene 1213," c1915, wear to neck and foot **990.00**

Calcite

Bowl

8" d, ftd, opal, gold Aurene int., c1915 . . . . **230.00**

10" d, ftd, irid gold int. **350.00**

Aurene, vase, baluster, gold iridescent finish over blue, magenta shades at neck, signed "Aurene/F. Carder," 8" d, 15-3/4" h, $110. Photo courtesy of Sanford Alderfer Auction Company.

Compote, 8" h, amber bowl and foot, red and gold irid finish, irid blue rope twisted stem with gold finish . . **1,880.00**

Low bowl

5-3/4" d, irid gold int. **350.00**

8" d, irid gold int. **215.00**

10" d, gold irid int. **350.00**

12" d, rolled rim, irid gold int., c1915 . . . . **460.00**

Sherbet and underplate, 6" d, 4" h, calcite body, irid gold int., c1920, set of four **575.00**

Celeste Blue

Candlesticks, brilliant blue, applied foliate form bobeche and cups, bulbed shafts, c1920-33, set of four . . **2,300.00**

Center bowl, 16-1/4" d, 4-1/4" h, catalog #112, swirled optic ribbed broad bowl, rolled rim, applied fluted foot, partially polished pontil, c1925 . . . . **400.00**

Finger bowl, underplate, catalog #2889, 5" d flared bowl, 6-1/2" underplate, swirled ribbed design, c1925, set of 12, some chips . . **600.00**

Iced tea goblet, 6-1/2" h, catalog #5192, blue, flared, light ribbon, c1918-32, set of eight **400.00**

Juice glass, 4-1/2" h, catalog #5192, blue, flared, light ribbon, c1918-32, set of eight. **375.00**

Luncheon plate, 8-1/2" d, molded blue body, Kensington pattern variant, engraved border of leaves and dots, c1918-32, set of 12 . . . . **550.00**

Vase, 10" d, 12-1/4" h, clear glass handles **1,700.00**

Celeste Blue, candlestick, Celeste blue and amber, tulip candleholder, lily pad foot, 12" h, $1,495. Photo courtesy of James D. Julia, Inc.

Cluthra, urn, pink, allover bubbles, ground pontil, 6-1/2" h, $1,380. Photo courtesy of James D. Julia, Inc.

Cluthra

Lamp base, 12-1/2" h, ovoid, creamy white cluthra acid-etched Art-Deco flowers, acid-etched fleur-de-lis mark near base, orig gilded foliate bronze lamp fittings, c1925 . . . . **2,070.00**

Vase, 8" h, catalog #2683, rose, acid stamp script mark **2,600.00**

Wall pocket, 15-1/2" w, 8" h, half round flared bowl, black and white cluthra, cut and mounted to foliate gilt metal framework, polished pontil, c1930, slight corrosion to metal **490.00**

Crystal

Bowl, 10-7/8" d, 6-7/8" h, cylindrical hollow body, applied wave motifs on base, inscribed "Steuben" **490.00**

Calyx bowl, 9-1/2" d, 3-3/8" h, floriform oval, solid foot, inscribed "Steuben" **230.00**

Candelabra, two candle cups supported on scrolled shaft, inscribed "Steuben," 7-1/4" and 7-5/8" l, 4-1/4" and 4-3/4" h, base scratches, price for pr **490.00**

Center bowl, cov, 9" d, 12" h, dolphin and wave finial on cov, round bowl, applied wave motif on base, inscribed "Steuben," base scratches **690.00**

Cocktail set, 15" h cocktail shaker, six matching 2-1/2" h glasses, two applied red cherries, wheel-cut leaves, and stems on shaker, ruby stopper, same dec on glasses, some with fleur-de-lis marks, slight damage to stopper **3,700.00**

Goblet, 7-1/16" h, flared cylindrical vessel, knobbed stem, sq base, small

"S" inscribed on base, designed by Arthur A. Houghton, Jr., 1938, Madigan catalog #7846, set of six, two with small chips **260.00**

Paperweight, 2-1/2" d, sphere with randomly imp heart motifs, late 20th C **115.00**

Vase, 7-3/8" h, catalog #SP919, flared wing form, pedestal base, inscribed "Steuben" on base **330.00**

Grotesque

Bowl, 11-1/2" l, 6-1/4" h, blue jade, Frederick Carder design, minor int. surface wear, fleur-de-lis mark **3,850.00**

Vase, 9-1/4" h, amethyst, catalog #7090, pillar molded floriform body, ruffled rim shaded to colorless crystal at applied disk foot, acid script "Steuben" mark in polished pontil, c1930 . **525.00**

Jade

Bowl, 8" d, 6" h, two-line pillar, ftd, alabaster int., fleur-de-lis acid stamp mark..................... **800.00**

Bud vase, 7-3/4" h, green trumpet form vase with ruffled rim, supported on scrolled tripod hammered silver mount over round base, engraved "RAP" monogram, imp "Black Starr & Frost 7050 Sterling" on base **460.00**

Candlesticks, pr, 10" h, No. 2956, jade candle cup and base, alabaster shaft, gold foil labels **550.00**

Compote, 10" h, yellow, ftd... **1,450.00**

Lamp base

12" h, catalog #7001, urn form, plum jade, intricately etched in Belgrade pattern, gilt-metal lamp fittings, c1925, chips to rim under mounting **2,415.00**

13" h flared double gourd shaped dark amethyst body cased to alabaster int., overlaid with amethyst, cameo etched in Chinese pattern, double etched with scrolling design, gilt metal fittings with three scroll arms, shallow chip under fixture **1,850.00**

Parfait, 6" h, applied alabaster foot **350.00**

Rose bowl, 7" d, 7" h, spherical, smooth jade crystal **350.00**

Vase

3-1/2" d base, 8" h, catalog #1169, alabaster int., floral design **2,450.00**

8" d, 7" h, spherical, acid cut back Matsu pattern, alabaster int. **1,750.00**

10" d, 13" h, alabaster int., acid cut lattice design, fleur de lis mark, small rim chip **1,295.00**

Miscellaneous

Bowl, 6-1/2" h, Old Ivory, catalog #7307, pillar ftd, applied raised foot, c1930 .... **435.00**

Candlesticks, pr, 11-3/4" h, catalog #2956, amber glass baluster shaped stems, wide disk foot, c1925 ... **690.00**

Center bowl, 14" d, 8" h, ftd, topaz body, celeste blue rims, eight swirl cabochons **375.00**

Compote, 8-1/4" h, cobalt blue, flat bowl..................... **200.00**

Exhibition sculpture, 18" h, Salmon Run, designed by James Houston, engraved by George Thompson, number 14 in series of 20, orig red leather and velvet box...... **13,500.00**

Lamp base, 10-1/4" h, catalog #8023, urn form, swirled purple, blue, and red moss agate, gilt-metal lamp fittings, acanthus leaf dec, purple glass jewel at top, needs rewiring **2,415.00**

Paperweight, Excalibur, designed by James Houston, 1963, catalog #1000, faceted hand-polished solid crystal embedded with removable sterling silver sword, 18kt gold scabbard, base inscribed "Steuben" **1,955.00**

Parfait and underplate, 4-1/2" h, 5-1/4" d underplate, Calcite, gold, partial paper label........... **625.00**

Pitcher, 9" h, catalog #6665, Spanish Green, slightly ribbed oval, flared mouth, applied angled handle, raised disk foot, acid fleur-de-lis mark. **460.00**

Serving plate, 14-1/4" d, 2" h, catalog #3579, Bristol Yellow, board convex and folded rim, slight optic ribbing, wear scratches.................. **200.00**

Vase

6" h, Oriental Poppy, shape #6501 .... **3,200.00**

12-1/2" h, 9-1/4" d, catalog #7389, Strawberry Mansion, flared bulb form, colorless, sq plinth base, two applied "M" handles, designed by Frederick Carder, 1934, nick at base.................. **1,035.00**

Miscellaneous, amethyst, wine glasses, amethyst cut to clear bowls with lion head decoration, clear stems, signed, identically cut but different sizes, 9" h, 8" h, $2,130. Photo courtesy of James D. Julia, Inc.

Miscellaneous, vase, cranberry, shape #6030, spiral ribbed, polished pontil, faint acid stamp "Steuben" near edge of base, partly lost due to wear, c1925, 6-3/4" h, $295. Photo courtesy of Forrest D. Poston.

Miscellaneous, pair of vases, green opaque, rectangular vases, applied lion head medallions, unsigned, 7-1/2" h, $250. Photo courtesy of Woody Auctions.

Grotesque, fan vase, ruby shading to clear crystal, applied crystal foot, signed on base with fleur de lis acid insignia, 11-1/4", $525. Photo courtesy of James D. Julia, Inc.

Rosaline

Bowl

8" l, 7" w, 3-1/4" h, one end folded in, other pinched spout, inscribed "F. Carder Steuben 723" on edge of polished pontil **350.00**

9-3/4" d, rose shading to opal foot **200.00**

Compote, 4" h, ruffled, alabaster stem and foot **275.00**

Goblet, crystal foot **90.00**

Perfume, 5-3/8" h, catalog #6412, teardrop shape, cloudy pink, applied alabaster glass foot, c1925, pr . . **435.00**

Table setting, 7-1/2" h, four goblets with translucent rose bowl, clambroth

Acid cut back, vase, black amethyst, portrait medallions, floral garlands, 8" h, $3,140. Photo courtesy of Fontaine's Auction Gallery.

foot, four matching 8-1/2" d plates **1,260.00**

Ruby

Bowl, 9" d, tri-corner, rich color **260.00**

Candlesticks, pr

2-1/2" h, rich color **200.00**

12" h, rich color **1,100.00**

Center bowl, 13" d, rich color, ftd **230.00**

Compote, low, 12" d **150.00**

Vase, 9-3/4" h, sculptured Swirl pattern, sgd **435.00**

Verre De Soie

Bonbon, 6" h, compote form, overall irid surface, swirled celeste blue finial, twisted stem **850.00**

Perfume, 4-1/2" h, catalog #1455, ribbed body, celeste blue flame stopper, c1915 . . . . **400.00**

Vase

6-3/4" h, ftd, lime green body, Verre de Soie irid finish **250.00**

10" h, classic form, notched rim, allover floral motif **450.00**

STEVENGRAPHS

History: Thomas Stevens of Coventry, England, first manufactured woven silk designs in 1854. His first bookmark was produced in 1862, followed by the first Stevengraphs, perhaps in 1874, but definitely by 1879 when they were shown at the York Exhibition. The first portrait Stevengraphs (of Disraeli and Gladstone) were produced in 1886, and the first postcards incorporating the woven silk panels in 1904. Stevens offered many other items with silk panels, including valentines, fans, pincushions, and needle cases.

Stevengraphs are miniature silk pictures, matted in cardboard, and usually having a trade announcement or label affixed to the reverse. Other companies, notably W. H. Grant of Coventry, copied Stevens's technique. Their efforts should not be confused with Stevengraphs.

Collectors in the U.S. favor the Stevengraphs with American-related views, such as "Signing of the Declaration of Independence," "Columbus Leaving Spain," and "Landing of Columbus." Sports-related Stevengraphs such as "The First Innings" (baseball), and "The First Set" (tennis) are also popular, as well as portraits of Buffalo Bill, President and Mrs. Cleveland, George Washington, and President Harrison.

Postcards with very fancy embossing around the aperture in the mount almost always have Stevens's name printed on them. The two most popular embossed postcard series in the U.S. are "Ships" and "Hands across the Sea." The latter set incorporates two crossed flags and two hands shaking. Seventeen flag combinations have been found, but only seven are common. These series generally are not printed with Stevens' name. Stevens also produced silks that were used in cards made by the Alpha Publishing Co.

Stevens' bookmarks are longer than they are wide, have mitered corners at the bottom, and are finished with a tassel. Many times his silks were used as the top or bottom half of regular bookmarks.

Marks: Thomas Stevens' name appears on the mat of the early Stevengraphs, directly under the silk panel. Many of the later portraits and the larger silks (produced initially for calendars) have no identification on the front of the mat other than the phrase "woven in pure silk" and have no label on the back.

Bookmarks originally had Stevens' name woven into the foldover at the top of the silk, but soon the identification was woven into the fold-under mitered corners. Almost every Stevens' bookmark has such identification, except the ones woven at the World's Columbian Exposition in Chicago, 1892 to 1893.

Note: Prices are for pieces in mint or close-to-mint condition.

Bookmarks

Assassination, Abraham Lincoln **395.00**

Centennial, USA, 1776-1876, General George Washington, The Father of Our Country, The First in Peace, The First in War, The First in the Hearts of Our Countrymen!, few small stains . . **125.00**

Forget-Me-Not, Godden #441 . . **350.00**

I Wish You a Merry Christmas and a Happy New Year **75.00**

Lord Have Mercy **400.00**

Mail Coach **225.00**

Bookmarks, silk, both with George Washington, left marked "T. Stevens Coventry, England," right marked "Silk City," mounted in small glass display case, light staining, 9" h, $250. Photo courtesy of James D. Julia, Inc.

Mother and Child, evening prayers, 10-1/2" l, 2" w, 1-1/2" silk tassel . **400.00**

Mourning, Blessed Are They Who Mourn, 9-1/2" l, 2" w, 2" silk tassel ... **450.00**

My Dear Father, red, green, white, and purple ... **200.00**

Old Armchair ... **150.00**

Prayer Book Set, five orig markers attached with small ivory button, cream-colored tape fastened to orig frame, Communion, Collect, Lesson I, Lesson II, Psalms, gold lettering, gold silk tassels, orig mount, c1880-85 ... **3,400.00**

The Old Arm Chair, chair, full text, musical score, four color, 2" w, 11" l ... **125.00**

The Star Spangled Banner, U.S. flag, full text and musical score of song, red tassel, seven color, no maker's mark, 2-1/2" w, 11" l ... **185.00**

To One I Love, Love me little, love me long is the burden of my song, Love that is too hot and strong, burneth soon to waste, Still I would not have thee cold, not too backward or too bold; Love that lasteth till this old fadeth not in haste ... **175.00**

Postcard

RMS *Arabic*, Hands Across the Sea ... **465.00**

RMS *Elmina* ... **225.00**

RMS *Franconia* ... **225.00**

RMS *Iverina* ... **215.00**

USMS *Philadelphia* ... **225.00**

Stevengraph

Betsy Making the First United States Flag, Anderson Bros., Paterson, NJ, 5" x 8-1/2" ... **80.00**

Buffalo Bill, Nate Salsbury, Indian Chief, orig mat and frame, 8" x 7" ... **500.00**

Chateau Frontenac Hotel, Quebec, silver filigree frame ... **95.00**

Coventry, 7-1/4" x 13", framed . **100.00**

Death of Nelson, 7-1/4" x 2-1/2" ... **200.00**

Declaration of Independence . **375.00**

For Life or Death, fire engine rushing to burning house, orig mat and frame ... **350.00**

Good Old Days, Royal Mail Coach, 5-3/4" h, 8-1/2" l, orig frame **200.00**

God Speed the Plow ... **175.00**

H. M. Stanley, famous explorer . **300.00**

Kenilworth Castle, 7-1/4" x 13" framed ... **120.00**

Landing of Columbus ... **350.00**

President Cleveland ... **365.00**

Oxford, Cambridge, Are You Ready, 5-3/4" h, 8-1/2" l, orig frame **300.00**

The Water Jump ... **195.00**

Untitled, life-saving boat ... **175.00**

STEVENS AND WILLIAMS

History: In 1824, Joseph Silvers and Joseph Stevens leased the   Moor Lane Glass House at Briar Lea Hill (Brierley Hill), England, from the Honey-Borne family. In 1847, William Stevens and Samuel Cox Williams took over, giving the firm its present name. In 1870, the company moved to its Stourbridge plant. In the 1880s, the firm employed such renowned glass artisans as Frederick C. Carder, John Northwood, other Northwood family members, James Hill, and Joshua Hodgetts.

Stevens and Williams made cameo glass. Hodgetts developed a more commercial version using thinner-walled blanks, acid etching, and the engraving wheel. Hodgetts, an amateur botanist, was noted for his brilliant floral designs.

Other glass products and designs manufactured by Stevens and Williams include intaglio ware, Peach Bloom (a form of peachblow), moss agate, threaded ware, "jewell" ware, tapestry ware, and Silveria. Stevens and Williams made glass pieces covering the full range of late Victorian fashion.

After World War I, the firm concentrated on refining the production of lead crystal and achieving new glass colors. In 1932, Keith Murray came to Stevens and Williams as a designer. His work stressed the pure nature of the glass form. Murray stayed with Stevens and Williams until World War II and later followed a career in architecture.

For more information, see this book.

Additional Listings: Cameo Glass.

Basket, 5-1/2" d, 5" h, rect, translucent amber basket, applied green stemmed red strawberries, applied amber feet, amber handle ... **400.00**

Biscuit jar, cov, 7-1/2" h, 5-1/2" d, cream opaque, large amber and green applied ruffled leaves, rich pink int., SP rim, lid, and handle ... **300.00**

Bowl

4-1/2" d, 3-1/2" h, MOP satin, turquoise cased to yellow, Zipper pattern, engraved English registry mark, RD 55693 ... **700.00**

5-1/2" d, 3" h, cream cased to rose ground, applied amber-green fern leaves, applied rose-amber feet, raspberry pontil ... **200.00**

Box, cov, 4-1/2" d, 2-1/2" h, hinged, aventurine, green and red spatter, green metallic flakes, white lining, polished pontil ... **250.00**

Calling card receiver, 10" l, applied amber handle, rolled edge, translucent opalescent ground, three applied berries, blossoms, and green leaves, three applied amber feet ... **750.00**

Ewer, 8-1/2" h, 5" w, Pompeiian Swirl, deep rose shading to yellow, off white lining, frosted loop handle, allover gold enameled wild roses, ferns, and butterfly ... **1,500.00**

Jardinière, 6-1/2" d, 10" h, pink opalescent, cut back, two spatter flowers and sunflowers, three applied opalescent thorn feet, leaves, and stems, minor damage ... **350.00**

Perfume, 4-3/4" h, spherical, heat reactive dark amber shaded to green satin, spiraled air-trap switch, hallmarked and chased silver cap, c1890 ... **635.00**

Pitcher, 7" h, 4-1/2" d, mint green ext., robin's egg blue lining, three white and pink blossoms, amber leaves, twisting

Two bride's bowls, top is pink and white bowl with silver mica highlights, signed Pairpoint base, 11" x 10", $150; other is shell-shaped footed bowl with pink interior, white exterior, amber feet, Stevens & Williams, 10-1/2", $60. Photo courtesy of Woody Auctions.

Vase, reddish-amber clear ground, swirling white Osiris decoration, 5-1/2" h, **$1,350.** *Photo courtesy of Clarence and Betty Maier.*

clear amber glass tendril which twists to form handle, end of handle ground smooth **385.00**
Rose bowl, 4-1/2" d, 3-1/2" h, Cottage Ware, sea shell scalloped pattern, multicolored spatter over white lining, colorless ext. layer **150.00**
Vase
  5" h, opal glass cased in pink, applied large crystal leaf . . . **100.00**
  5-1/2" h, buttercup yellow body shading to cherry blossom-pink, cameo carved twisted Japanese

Vase, candy striped in light green and pink, ruffled, 8" h, **$225.** *Photo courtesy of James D. Julia, Inc.*

twisted, gnarled, cherry tree branch, pink borders, butterfly on reverse **1,450.00**
7" h, MOP satin, shading from deep rose to yellow, diagonal swirl pattern **1,150.00**
8" h, MOP satin, green shading to apricot, pink cased int., diagonal swirl pattern **2,530.00**
8-1/4" h, MOP satin, cased pink, air trapped diagonal swirl pattern, ground pontil **500.00**
10-1/2" h, ovoid body, elongated and bulbed neck, deep red overlaid in white, cameo etched and engraved grosbeak on flowering branch with two butterflies, central stylized floral border, c1890, chip on base border **2,185.00**

STIEGEL-TYPE GLASS

For more information, see this book.

History: Baron Henry Stiegel founded America's first flint-glass factory at Manheim, Pennsylvania, in the 1760s. Although clear glass was the most common color made, amethyst, blue (cobalt), and fiery opalescent pieces also are found. Products included bottles, creamers, flasks, flips, perfumes, salts, tumblers, and whiskeys. Prosperity was short-lived; Stiegel's extravagant lifestyle forced the factory to close.

It is very difficult to identify a Stiegel-made item. As a result, the term "Stiegel-type" is used to identify glass made during the time period of Stiegel's firm and in the same shapes and colors as used by that company.

Enamel-decorated ware also is attributed to Stiegel. True Stiegel pieces are rare; an overwhelming majority is of European origin.

Reproduction Alert: Beware of modern reproductions, especially in enamel wares.

Bottle, blown
  4-3/4" h, amethyst, daisy-in-diamond pattern, tiny interior pot stones **4,750.00**
  5-3/8" h, brilliant deep peacock green, 15 diamonds, pot stone in neck **440.00**
  5-7/8" h, hexagonal, colorless, enameled white dove, red rose,

Mug, enameled, center shield with carpenter's and blacksmith tools, floral decoration on sides, **$325.**

scroll work, red, blue, yellow, and white floral designs, flared lip **175.00**
Bride's or cordial bottle, 6-1/8" h, blue, "VIVAT, es leben alle miller 1764," (long live all Miller's) central floral motifs surrounding folklore symbols . **3,100.00**
Flip glass, colorless, sheared rim, pontil scar, form similar to McKearin plate 22, #2
  3-1/2" h, handle, engraved repeating swag motif around rim, lower body emb with graduated panels **210.00**
  6-1/4" h, engraved floral motif and sunflower **300.00**
  7" h, engraved bird in heart dec within sunburst motif **400.00**
  7-7/8" h, engraved pair of birds perched on heart within sunburst motif **475.00**
  8" h, engraved large flower and floral motif **325.00**
Flask
  4-3/4" h, amethyst diamond and daisy **495.00**
  5" h, amethyst, globular, 20 molded ribs, minute rim chip **1,380.00**
Jar, cov, 10-1/2" h, colorless, engraved sunflower and floral motifs, repeating dot and vine dec on cov, applied finial, sheared rim, pontil scar, form similar to McKearin plate 35, #2 and #3 . . **750.00**
Miniature, flip glass, 3" h, colorless, engraved bird within sunburst motif, seared mouth, pontil scar **325.00**
Tankard, handle, cylindrical, applied solid reeded handle, flared foot,

sheared rim, pontil scar, form similar to McKearin plate 22, #4

 5-1/2" h, milk glass, red, yellow, blue, and green enameled dec of house on mountain with floral motif, old meandering fissure around body of vessel **150.00**

 5-3/4" h, colorless, engraved with bird in elaborate sunburst motif **500.00**

Tumbler, 2-7/8" h, colorless, paneled, polychrome enameled flowers . **220.00**

STONEWARE

For more information, see this book.

History: Made from dense kaolin and commonly salt-glazed, stonewares were hand-thrown and high-fired to produce a simple, bold, vitreous pottery. Stoneware crocks, jugs, and jars were made to store products and fill other utilitarian needs. These intended purposes dictated shape and design—solid, thick-walled forms with heavy rims, necks, and handles and with little or no embellishment. Any decorations were simple: brushed cobalt oxide, incised, slip trailed, stamped, or tooled.

Stoneware has been made for centuries. Early American settlers imported stoneware items at first. As English and European potters refined their earthenware, colonists began to produce their own wares. Two major North American traditions emerged based only on location or type of clay. North Jersey and parts of New York comprise the first area; the second was eastern Pennsylvania spreading westward and into Maryland, Virginia, and West Virginia. These two distinct geographical boundaries, style of decoration, and shape are discernible factors in classifying and dating early stoneware.

By the late 18th century, stoneware was manufactured in all sections of the country. This vigorous industry flourished during the 19th century until glass fruit jars appeared and the use of refrigeration became widespread. By 1910, commercial production of salt-glazed stoneware came to an end.

Advertising bean pot, unsigned, attributed to Red Wing, 5-1/2" h, brown and white Bristol glaze, blue stenciled "Compliments of Fairway Market Larson & Elofson Cambridge, Minn, Tel. 24," orig lid, c1920, minor glaze wear **110.00**

Advertising crock, 8" h, unsigned, 1-1/2 gallon, stenciled rose design below imp and blue accented name, "Flint & Company, 132 & 136 Broad St., Prov. R.I.," c1860, age spidering in glaze **250.00**

Advertising jug

 9" h, unsigned, half gallon, Bristol glaze, stenciled under glaze "This Jug Not To be Sold Registered," blue script "Hollander Bros., 1-3-5 Main St, Paterson, NJ," c1880, glaze flakes throughout, glaze chipping at spout **440.00**

 9-1/2" h, unsigned, half gallon, blue stenciled on front "Gus Curry 15 & 17 Broad St, Utica,, NY," c1870, minor staining, glaze flake at spout **165.00**

 9-1/2" h, unsigned, half gallon, "J. F. Saxon" diagonally in blue script across front, c1880, couple of in the making pings. **125.00**

 10-1/2" h, J. Fisher, Lyons, NY, one gallon, blue script on front "Collins & Jordan 351 Elk St Buffalo, NY, c1870, minor wear and staining from use **315.00**

 13" h, C. W. Braun Buffalo, NY, two gallons, "Wm Craig, 48 & 50 Lloyd St, Buffalo, NY" in blue scrfipt on front, cinnamon cast, c1865 . . . . **250.00**

 16-1/2" h, unsigned, attributed to J & E Norton, three gallons, imp and blue accents, "A. P. Little Wholesale & Retail Dealer in Drugs, Medicine, & C/Canajoharie NY," imp name surrounded by stylized floral and leaf design, c1855, stained from use **580.00**

Advertising preserve jar, 12-1/2" h, S. Hart, three gallons, imp and blue accents," Crawfords & Murdock, Dealers in Dry Goods Groceries, Clothing Crokery & Hardware, Pulaskie, NY," blue script "3" surrounded by brushed plumes below store mark, c1875, professional restoration to rim chip at front **385.00**

Batter jug, 8-1/2" h, salt glaze, brushed cobalt blue tulip under spout, wire bale handle, applied handle near base, few rim flakes, small area of glaze discoloration **440.00**

Batter pail

 6" h, unsigned, attributed to White's, Utica, six qts, imp "6," oak leaf design under spout, orig bale handle, c1865, short tight hairline **330.00**

 8-1/2" h, unsigned, New York State origin, one gallon, orig bale handle, brush blue tulip design below spout, c1870, some very minor int. surface chipping at rim, minor staining from use. **315.00**

Batter pail, Cowden & Wilcox, Harrisburg, two gallons, large brushed floral design on back, large brushed plume all around pouring spout, original bale handle, minor use stains, c1870, 10" h, **$1,430.** *Stoneware photos courtesy of Vicki and Bruce Waasdorp.*

Butter churn, John Burger, Rochester, five gallons, ribbed double flower design, navy blue decoration at name and script gallon designation, original stoneware churn guide, c1865, 19" h, **$7,150.**

9" h, unsigned, attributed to Whites, Utica, one gallon, cobalt blue slip leaf below spout on front, orig bale handle, c1865 . . . . **615.00**

10" h, unsigned, attributed to Whites, Utica, six qts, navy blue hollyhock dec, c1865, professional restoration to rim chips and lug handle **360.00**

Bottle

9-1/2" h, imp and blue accented "C. F. Washburn," minor crow's foot at shoulder **35.00**

10" h, imp and blue accented "B. F. Haley California Pop Beer 1889," glaze drip at shoulder to right of imp name **135.00**

Cake crock

6-1/4" h, unsigned, PA origin, attributed to Remmey factory, flowers and vines all around, blue accents at handle, deep blue matching design on orig stoneware lid, imp "I" under applied ear, c1850, two nickel-sized surface chips at rim, dime size stone ping **715.00**

7-1/2" h, J. & E. Bennington, VT, brilliant blue thistle design, c1855, very minor glaze flaking at base on back **715.00**

9-1/2" h, Ottman Bros & Co., Fort Edward, NY, facing left bird perched on twig, c1870, professional restoration to some glaze flaking **600.00**

Canning jar, 9-1/2" h, unsigned, one gallon, four wide accent stripes across front, c1850, stack mark, glaze burns on left side **110.00**

Chicken waterer, 11" h, unsigned, probably PA origin, 1 gallon, imp "I" at

Cake crock, covered, unsigned, one gallon, brushed cobalt blue flowers repeated front and back, cobalt blue accents at handles, matching brushed design on lid, few chips at knob, c1850, 9" d, 6" h, $1,705.

shoulder, brushed blue accents at button top and inner and out rim of watering hole, c1840 . . . . **415.00**

Churn

13" h, unsigned, two gallons, table-top type, fitted carved wooden guide, brushed double plume design repeated front and back, c1870 . . . . **275.00**

16" h, Haxstun Ottoman & Co., Fort Edwards NY, four gallons, dotted peacock on stump, c1870, some chipping to stoneware guide, very tight spider on front **3,630.00**

16-1/2" h, Whites, Utica, four gallons, folky running bird, long neck extension as bird looks over his shoulder, strong cobalt blue application, c1865, minor stone ping on front, chip at rim on back **1,485.00**

17" h, Darrow & Sons, Baldwinsville, NY, five gallons, brushed double flower and gallon designation on front, light impression maker's mark, orig stoneware guide, c1860, 5" hairline and 3" hairline . . **500.00**

17" h, Hart Bros, Fulton, NY, four gallons, floral and plume dec, brush and slip application, c1880, some surface chipping to orig dasher guide **440.00**

17" h, J. Burger, Jr., Rochester, NY, four gallons, stoneware guide, dotted quail and jack in the pulpit flower, c1885 . . . . **5,500.00**

19" h, Burger & Co., Rochester, NY, six gallons, wreath design, factory name stamped upside down, orig stoneware guide, c1877 . . . **855.00**

19" h, John Burger, Rochester, five gallons, ribbed double flower design, deep navy blue color, blue at name and script gallon designation, orig stoneware churn guide, c1865, rim chip worn smooth from use. **7,150.00**

Cream pot

7-1/2" h, Roberts, Binghamton, NY, one gallon, bird on branch, c1860, ext. rim chip on back **770.00**

8" h, unsigned, attributed to NJ, one gallon, Bristol glaze, slip blue bird design, c1880, full length hairline on back, some surface chipping at rim **220.00**

8-1/2" h, Brady & Ryan, Ellenville, NY, six qts, singing bird on dotted branch, imp "6" below maker's name, c1885, extensive glaze

Crock, Ottman Bros & Co., Fort Edward, NY, four gallons, large signature bird on stump, cobalt blue at name, 1" hairline at rim, c1870, 11-1/2" h, $1,075.

flaking at rim and spots on back **180.00**

9-1/2" h, unsigned, attributed to Pruden Factory, Eliztown, NJ, name "Margaret" scripted in cobalt blue across front, "3" on opposite side, c1850 . . . . **800.00**

10-1/2" h, White & Co., Binghamton, three gallons, goony bird design, blue at name and gallon designation, c1866, minor surface chipping at rim int. **800.00**

Crock

7-1/2" h, N. A. White & Son, Utica, NY, 1-1/2 gallon, blue paddle tail running bird, looking backward, c1870, tight freeze line around base **360.00**

8" h, H. N. Ballard Burlington, VT, 1-1/2 gallon, stylized double floral dec, c1855 . . . . **1,540.00**

8-1/4" h, 12-1/4" d, double handles, incised lines, imp "3" with freehand spray of flowers below dark cobalt blue, int. with Albany slip glaze, shallow chips and flakes on rim and handles **330.00**

8-3/4" h, ovoid, prominent applied double handles, flared rim with lid flange, imp "2," label "I. M. Mead," (Portage County, OH), brushed cobalt blue on label and handles, some discoloration to salt glaze, minor wear, rim flake, short hairline **200.00**

9" h, J. A. & C. W. Underwood, Fort Edward, NY, two gallons, stylized floral spray dec, blue at name, c1865, some surface design fry, stone ping at base on side . **200.00**

Crock, Ottman Bros & Co., Fort Edward, NY, four gallons, large signature bird on stump, cobalt blue at name, 1" hairline at rim, c1870, 11-1/2" h, **$1,075.**

9" h, John Burger, Rochester, two gallons, unusual accents around gallon designation, c1855 **. 315.00**

10-1/2" h, Fort Edward Pottery Co., three gallons, navy blue bird on tree stump, blue at name, c1860, professional restoration to C-shaped through line at base **1,760.00**

11" h, Ballard & Brothers Burlington, VT, three gallons, triple flowering plant dec, blue at name and gallon designation, c1860, professional restoration to full length hairline, restoration to chip at right ear **180.00**

11" h, Fort Edward Pottery Co., four gallons, dotted wreath surrounding blue script date "1860," professional restoration to stone ping hole in bottom. **1,020.00**

11-1/2" h, Ottman Bros & Co., Fort Edward, NY, four gallons, large signature bird with filled in body, on stump, blue at name, c1870 . . . . **1,075.00**

11-1/2" h, T. Harrington, Lyons, five gallons, large signature starface dec, eight-point star covers front, c1850, professional restoration to full length hairline on left side **3,850.00**

11-1/2" h, unsigned, attributed to Ellenville factory, four gallons, large long tailed bird on tree stump, c1870, professional restoration to full length line on back and glaze flakes on front. **580.00**

12-3/8" h, 14-1/2" d, lug handles, cobalt blue peafowl perched on

floral spray, imp "Whites Utica" near rim, brownish discoloration **2,990.00**

12-1/2" h, imp label with cobalt blue highlights "J. A. & C. Underwood, Fort Edward, N.Y. 3," brushed cobalt blue bird perched on stump, glued crack around circumference, flakes. **360.00**

13" h, Burger & Co., Rochester, NY, five gallons, large triple fern dec, c1877, few minor surface chips from use **525.00**

14" h, stenciled dec "R. T. Williams, New Geneva, PA, 3," floral and line detail, double handles. **175.00**

16" h, J. Fisher, Lyons, NY, 10 gallons, brushed tulips cover entire front, brushed blue accent under applied ears, cobalt blue gallon designation, c1880, professional restoration to three full-length through lines **470.00**

25-1/4" h, stenciled signature "C. L. Williams and Company, Best Blue Stoneware, New Geneva, PA, 20," some freehand line dec, double handles, flared rim, cracks **. 495.00**

Flask, 6-1/2" h, unsigned, brushed blue tree dec, design repeated on both sides, incised reeded accents at neck, c1810, minor surface wear at base, stack mark **2,630.00**

Jar

10-1/2" h, J. Heiser, Buffalo, NY, two gallons, brushed flower design, blue at name, c1852, minor glaze spiders on side **440.00**

11-1/2" h, N. Clark & Co., Lyons, two gallons, ovoid, stoneware lid, double tulip dec, dots and lines accentuate vines, blue accents at ears and factory name, c1840, couple of surface chips at rim **800.00**

12" h, Edmunds & Co., two gallons, cobalt blue dotted bird perched on fence, trees, and grass, c1870, professional restoration to hairline **750.00**

13" h, unsigned, attributed to NY state, three gallons, cobalt blue Christmas tree dec, dots ornaments, star at top, slip blue "3" below tree, c1870, cinnamon clay color in the making, some surface roughness at rim from use **. 360.00**

15" h, unsigned, attributed to Frederick Carpenter, three gallons, light ochre accents at shoulder and handles, deep incised accent lines

Jug, G. Lent Troy, two gallons, ovoid, incised bird perched between double flower, accented by deep cobalt blue wash, repeated at maker's mark and handle, c1820, 14" h, **$10,725.**

at shoulder and rim, c1800, some surface chipping and staining from use **495.00**

Jug

7-1/4" h, ovoid, applied handle, incised lines around neck, incised "BLK 1802" with brushed cobalt blue highlights, paper label on front "George S. McKearin Collector of American Pottery No. 1258," some

Jug, A. O. Whittemore, Havana, NY, one gallon, beehive, cobalt blue decoration compote of fruit, c1870, professional restoration to neck hairline, 9" h, **$330.**

bruises and imperfections
.... **8,690.00**

9" h, A. O. Whittemore, Havana, NY, one gallon, beehive shape, blue dec compote of fruit, c1870, professional restoration to hairline on back **330.00**

10-3/4" h, ovoid, imp signature of "T. Reed," large cobalt blue tulip on one side, raised rings around spout, applied strap handle, shallow base chip **770.00**

11" h, N. A. White & Son, Utica, NY, one gallon, signature pine tree design, c1870 ....**250.00**

11" h, West Troy Pottery, one gallon, large bird on twig dec, c1880, professional restoration to chips in handle, chip on spout, minor glaze wear....................**440.00**

12" h, Binghamton, NY, one gallon, pine tree design, c1870, few glaze flakes at spout...........**275.00**

12" h, unsigned, attributed to Jonathon Fenton Boston, MA, one gallon, ovoid, cross-hatched brushed lollipop flower, c1790, some use staining **865.00**

12-1/2" h, T. Crafts & Co., Whatley, two gallons, ovoid, double floral dec, c1833, carved wooden stopper, stack mark on shoulder **580.00**

13" h, A. O. Whittemore, Havana, NY, two gallons, beehive shape, cobalt blue cross-hatched basket of flowers, dots and squiggles, c1870, glaze spider **460.00**

13-1/2" h, Harrington & Burger, Rochester, two gallons, large cobalt blue floral dec **650.00**

14" h, From Buchanan & McClure, 837 Market St, Philadelphia, two gallons.................**125.00**

14" h, L. Lehman & So., West 12th St., NY, two gallons, cobalt blue accent at name and gallon designation, long tailed prancing rooster on flowered branch, c1860, professional restoration to long hairline on left side **960.00**

14" h, N. Clark Jr., Athens, NY, two gallons, unusual sunburst dec, c1850, few stone pings....**525.00**

14" h, Swan & States Stonington, CT, two gallons, ovoid, deeply incised, cobalt blue accented plume design at shoulder, c1830, professional restoration to tight line on side.................**330.00**

14" h, unsigned, attributed to Fulper Bros, New Jersey, two gallons, applied Bristol glaze, singing bird on twig dec, c1880.......**330.00**

15" h, C. W. Braun, Buffalo, NY, three gallons, sunflower dec, c1870, professional restoration to base chips, handle replaced ... **190.00**

15-1/2" h, S. Blair Cortland, NY, three gallons, simple brushed flower at shoulder below imp name, c1830 ....**715.00**

16" h, I. Seymour & Co., Troy, NY, three gallons, ovoid, cobalt blue accents at name, nicely incised flower design at shoulder, c1825, minor stack mark on front.**1,075.00**

16" h, W. Hart, Ogdensburgh, three gallons, horse head design, blue at name, c1860, minor stone pings in the making **17,325.00**

Milk pitcher, 17" h, unsigned, Shenandoah Valley origin, attributed to Remmey factory, three gallons, brushed blue floral design fills entire front, c1850, professional restoration to handle, partially replaced **1,210.00**

Mug, 3-1/4" d, 4-3/4" h, applied handle, two brushed cobalt bands with incised edging....................**250.00**

Pitcher

7" h, ovoid, applied handle, brushed cobalt blue flower with long leaves, three flourishes around rim at

Pitcher, unsigned, one quart, two cobalt blue brushed double flower decorations, cobalt blue accents around rim and at handle, professional restoration to two through lines, c1850, 7" h, **$1,430.**

handle, interior with grown glaze, hairline at base **675.00**

brushed designs on either side of spout, imp "I" at shoulder, c1860 ....**1,815.00**

10" h, Whites Binghamton, incised line around middle, raised rim, cobalt blue polka dot floral dec **615.00**

10-1/2" h, unsigned, attributed to Lyons, NY, factory, one gallon, wreath surrounding floral design, blue accent at handle, cobalt blue has bled because of heavy application by potter, c1860, surface chip at spout may be in the making **330.00**

11" h, J. Burger, Rochester, NY, one gallon, blue accents at handle and imp name, bow tie dec, c1880 ....**615.00**

Preserve jar

9-1/2" h, Lyons, blue leaf and double blue "I's" for gallon designation, orig lid, c1860, few minor glaze spots on side...........**330.00**

10" h, Little West, 12th St. N. Pottery Works, 1-1/2 gallons, double dropping flower design, c1870, two short clay separation lines at rim probably occurred in making **495.00**

Preserve jar, Hamilton & Jones, Greensboro, PA, two gallons, striped cobalt blue accents above and below stenciled name, stenciled flower design around name and gallon designation, c1870, 11-1/2" h, **$310.**

10-1/2" h, E. & L. P. Norton, 1-1/2 gallons, stylized dotted floral design, c1880, very minor stone ping on side **275.00**

11" h, F. Stetzenmeyer & G. Goetzman Rochester, NY, two gallons, blue dec ribbed leaf and flower bud design, c1857, long galze spider on side. **990.00**

11" h, Harrington & Burger, Rochester, two gallons, bowed wreath design, script blue in canter of wreath, blue at name, c1853, int. short clay separation line at rim occurred in making **330.00**

11-1/2" h, John Burger, Rochester, two gallons, orig stoneware lid, triple fern design surrounds large "2," c1865, minor crow's foot glaze spider on side. **580.00**

11-1/2" d, N. Clark & Co., Rochester, NY, two gallons, stoneware lid, finely executed floral design, c1850, int. lime staining, couple of surface chips at rim, stone ping on side. **1,760.00**

12" h, Brady & Ryan, Ellenville, NY, two gallons, fitted stoneware lid, bushy tailed bird on dotted plume dec in bright blue, c1885, surface chip on lid, mottled clay color in the making **470.00**

12" h, Cortland, three gallons, brushed plume design, blue accent at name, c1850, minor surface chips from use. . . . **165.00**

13-1/2" h, N. A. White & Son, Utica, NY, three gallons, wide paddletail bird, c1868, very minor design fry to thick blue **3,520.00**

Water cooler

11" h, Gates City, six quarts, stoneware lid, orig spigot, cobalt blue bird dec, patented May 25, 1886 . . . . **935.00**

14" h, attributed to Robinson Clay Factory, three gallons, Bristol glaze, matching lid, orig spigot, relief Rebecca at the Well design on front, relief floral display on back, imp "3" in crown on bottom, c1880, 2" l glued chip in orig lid **360.00**

15" h, W. H. Farrar & Co., Geddes, NY, five gallons, ovoid, triple detailed flower, dotted tornadoes on either side, profuse use of dots, c1850, professional restoration to three hairlines. **1,020.00**

STRING HOLDERS

History: The string holder developed as a useful tool to assist the merchant or manufacturer who needed tangle-free string or twine to tie packages. The early holders were made of cast iron, with some patents dating to the 1860s.

When the string holder moved into the household, lighter and more attractive forms developed, many made of chalkware. The string holder remained a key kitchen element until the early 1950s.

Reproduction Alert: As a result of the growing collector interest in string holders, some unscrupulous individuals are hollowing out the backs of 1950s figural-head wall plaques, drilling a hole through the mouth, and passing them off as string holders. A chef, Chinese man, Chinese woman, Indian, masked man, masked woman, and Siamese face are altered forms already found on the market.

Figural wall lamps from the 1950s and 1960s also are being altered. When the lamp hardware is removed, the base can be easily altered. Two forms that have been discovered are a pineapple face and an apple face, both lamp-base conversions.

Advertising

Chase & Sanborn's Coffee, tin, 13-3/4" x 10-1/4" sign, 4" d wire basket string holder insert, hanging chain **825.00**

Dutch Boy Paints, diecut tin, Dutch Boy painting door frame, hanging bucket string holder, American Art Sign Co., 13-3/4" x 30". . . **2,000.00**

Dog, chalkware, 7" h, **$155.** *Photo courtesy of L & J Antiques & Collectibles.*

Jester, chalkware, 7-1/4" h, **$195.** *Photo courtesy of L & J Antiques & Collectibles.*

Es-Ki-Mo Rubbers, tin, cutout center holds string spool, hanging boot moves up and down on sign, 17" x 19-3/4" h **2,500.00**

Heinz, diecut tin, pickle, hanging, "57 Varieties," 17" x 14" . . **1,650.00**

Figural

Ball of string, cast iron, figural, hinged, 6-1/2" x 5" h **100.00**

Black man and woman, chalkware, matched pair **275.00**

Bonzo, blue, chalkware, 6-1/2" h **185.00**

Boy, top hat and pipe, chalkware, 9" h **125.00**

Bride, ceramic, marked "Made in Japan," 6-1/4" h **145.00**

Carrots, chalkware, 10" h . . . **225.00**

Cat, red rose on top of face, green bow under chin, chalkware **165.00**

Chef, multicolored, chalkware, 7-1/4" h **165.00**

Chipmunk, ceramic, 5-1/8" h **135.00**

Dutch girl, chalkware, 7" h . . **100.00**

Gourd, green, chalkware, 7-1/2" h **135.00**

Indian, 10-1/4" h, chalkware . **285.00**

Mammy, yellow blouse, blue apron, scissors in pocket, chalkware, 6-1/2" h **385.00**

Mammy, white dress, ceramic, 6-1/2" h **225.00**

Parrot, chalkware, 9-1/4" h . . **235.00**

Pineapple, face, chalkware, 7" h **165.00**

Porter, chalkware, 6-1/2" h . . **220.00**

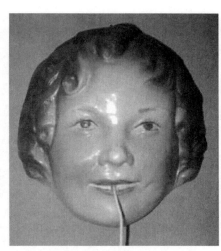

Shirley Temple, chalkware, 6-1/4" w, 6-3/4" h, $395. Photo courtesy of L & J Antiques & Collectibles.

Rose, red, green leaves, chalkware, 8" h **175.00**
Senorita, chalkware, 8" h **275.00**
Shirley Temple, chalkware, 6-1/4" w, 6-3/4" h **395.00**
Strawberry, chalkware, 6-1/2" h
. . . . **115.00**
Terrier, chalkware, gray and white, 8-1/2" h **195.00**
Woody Woodpecker, chalkware, copyright Walter Lantz, 9-1/2" h
. . . . **345.00**

SURVEYORS' INSTRUMENTS

History: From the very beginning of civilized cultures, people have wanted to have a way to clearly delineate what lands they owned. Surveying instruments and equipment of all kinds were developed to help in this important task. The ancients learned to use the sun and other astronomical bodies as their guides. Early statesmen like Washington and Jefferson used brass and ebony instruments as they surveyed the young America. A surveyor must know how to measure lines and angles of a piece of land, using the principles of geometry and trigonometry.

To accomplish this often-complicated mathematics, instruments of all types were invented and often patented. Accuracy is important, so many are made with precision components. A surveyor's level is an instrument that consists of a revolving telescope mounted on a tripod and fitted with cross hairs and a spirit level. It is designed to allow surveyors to find points of identical elevation. A transit is used to measure horizontal angles and consists of a telescope mounted at right angles to a horizontal east-west axis. English mathematician, Leonard Digges, invented an instrument called a "theodolite," used to measure vertical and horizontal angles. From a

simple compass to high-tech transits, today's collectors are finding these devices interesting. Fine examples of early instruments are coming into the antiques and collectibles marketplace as modern day surveyors now use sophisticated lasers and computers.

Alidade, cased, 11" l, W. & L. E. Gurley, Troy, NY, orig leather covered case, minor spots to lacquered finish . **440.00**
Anemometer, six register, eight blades, 2-5/8" d, fan drives 2-1/4" d silvered dial, brass, mounting bracket, softwood case, c1875 . . . . **345.00**
Astronomical Theodolite, 15-1/2" h, 10-1/2" l telescope, 5-1/2" d, two vernier vertical circle, 6", two vernier 20" horiz. circle, telescope and plate vials, microscope vernier readers, detachable alcohol lamp, detachable four-screw leveling base, trough compass on telescope, orig dovetailed mahogany box with accessories, marked "Stanley, Great Turnstile, Holborn, London, 7534," c1890, Heller & Brightly label mahogany ext. leg tripod **2,185.00**
Astronomical Transit, 20" h, 8-1/2" w, 15-3/4" telescope with rt. Angle prism eyepiece with removable strider level, 7" d double frame, two vernier, vertical circle with indexing vial and circle control, 6" d, two vernier, 15", silver horizontal scale, plate vial with ivory scale, tribrach leveling base, bright brass finish, pine case, marked "Blunt, New York," c1860 . . . . **7,500.00**
Circumferentor, 5-1/4" h, 9" d outside dia., 4-1/8" compass in center, attached to rotating sight vane/vernier arm, inset vial, silvered dial and outer ring, engraved with eight-point star, two outer fixed sight vanes, brass, marked "Dollond London," c1825 . . . . **1,955.00**
Drawing instruments, French, cased set, brass and steel instruments, wood scale, brass protractor, rosewood veneered case with warped lid . **220.00**
Flat plate transit, Edmund Draper, Philadelphia, #259, 13-1/2" h, 7-3/4" w, 10" telescope, 5" d vert. circle, 4-1/2" compass, 6" d single vernier, silver horiz. scale, two plate vials, four screw leveling, darkened brass finish, pine case, c1850 . . . . **1,725.00**
Nonius compass, 6 Inch, 15-1/8" x 6-7/8" x 7-1/8" h, 5-1/4" l detachable sight vanes, top designed to hold 7/8" d telescope, plate vials, silvered dial and edge engraved outer ring, unique 5' vernier moves the south sight vane by means of worn gear, mahogany case,

marked "J. Hanks," Troy, NY, c1825
. . . . **1,725.00**
Octant, 10-7/8", Riggs & Bro., Philadelphia, ebony, ivory inlaid signature panel, scale with brass trim
. . . . **550.00**
Pocket compass

1-1/2 inch, 2-1/4" x 2-1/4" mahogany case with hinged cov, 1-1/2" needle floats over engraved finely detailed mariner's star inside 2° increment quadrant outer ring, marked "T. T. Rowe, Lockport, N.Y.," c1825
. . . . **230.00**
2 inch, 2-5/8" d, brass, worn silvered dial, full circle, 180° cliometer scale, marked "Breiothaupt in Cassel," c1800 . . . . **565.00**

Reconnaissance transit, Buff & Buff Mfg. Co., Boston, 12007. 10-1/2" h, 5-1/4" w, 8 3/4" l telescope with rt. Angle solar eyep., 3-1/2" vial, 4" d vert. circle, crossed vials, 3" compass 4-1/2" d, two vernier, 1', silver horiz. scale, four-screw leveling, black leather finished brass, mahogany box, c1918 . . . . **920.00**
Saegmuller solar attachment, Fauth & Co., Washington, DC, Saegmuller's pat May 2, 81, 6-1/2" l, 4" h, brass and aluminum construction, level vial, sun lens, horiz. motion, c1885 . . . . . **920.00**
Solar transit, 17" h, Burt Solar Attachment, hour circle, 6.45" engineer's transit, 11" telescope, 3" rad vert. arc., 5" compass, telescope and plate vials, four-screw leveling, brass construction, rubbed bronze finish, detailed mahogany case, label, brass plummet, accessories, "W. & L. E. Gurley, Troy, NY," c1890 . . . . . **3,335.00**

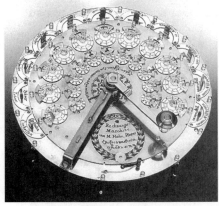

Replica of world's first working calculating machine for all four basic arithmetical operations, by German Philipp Matthäus Hahn, 1774, $25,100. Photo courtesy of Auction Team Breker.

Top left: Bausch, Lomb and Saegmuller level, brass and enameled brass, some wear, rings for tube have engine turnings, mahogany case, 8-3/8" x 21", $330; top right: W. & L. E. Gurley level, orig carrying case and tripod, 6-3/8" x 11-1/4", $300; middle row: left, Wm. Ainsworth & Sons, Denver, CO, level, enameled brass, some wear, dovetailed mahogany case with leather strap, $300; middle right: unidentified maker, level, tripod, and carrying case, with wear, 6-3/8" x 11-1/4", $275; bottom row: left: (scientific instrument) J. Dubosco & P. Pelin, Paris, colorimeter, brass, steel base, label "Arthur Thomas, Phila," minor surface rust, 15-1/2", $385; center: Sikes Hydrometer, inlaid mahogany case with label "Re-adjusted by W. R. Loftus Ltd. London," plate missing from ext. lid, 2" x 8" x 4", $110; left: small microscope, mahogany case, 3" x 8-3/4" x 3-1/2", $140. Photo courtesy of Garth's Auctions, Inc.

Surveying/astronomical theodite, 15-1/2" h, 10-1/2" l telescope, 5-1/2" d, two vernier vertical circle, 6", two vernier 20" horiz. circle, telescope and plate vials, microscope vernier readers, detachable alcohol lamp, detachable four-screw leveling base, trough compass on telescope, orig. dovetailed mahogany box with accessories, Heller & Brightly label, mahogany ext., leg tripod, "Stanley, Great Turnstile, Holborn, London, 7535," c1890 . . . . 2,185.00

Surveyor's compass

Davenport, Wm, Phila, 5" engraved face with tripod mount, plum bob, small magnifying glass, ivory scale, 14" l cherry case stenciled "A. C. Farrington" in gold and white 1,155.00

Patten, Richard, NY, 6" compass with engraved face, walnut case with litho label of eagle, ship, and signature, minor age cracks in lid, resoldered rim on brass cover, early tripod 990.00

Surveyors' and engineers' transit

Buff & Burger, Boston, #2149, 11" telescope wit vial, vert. arc., 6-1/4", 30" horiz. circle with inlaid silver scales, plate vials, four-screw leveling, green leather finish, orig dovetailed mahogany box with labels, c1890 . . . . 920.00

Paten, Richard, & Son, 6" d lens, 13-1/2" l, 8-5/8" h, brass, glass lens and level compass labeled "Richard Paten & Son, Baltimore," no tripod base 385.00

Pike, B. & Sons, 166 Broadway (N.Y.), 10-1/2" h, 8-3/8" w, 9-1/4" l telescope with vertical circle, 5" compass, 6-1/2" d horiz. scale (single vernier), telescope vial, plate vials, lacquered brass, orig

mahogany case with Gurley label, dated 11/11/1873 . . . . 980.00

Surveyors' vernier transit compass, 13-1/2" h, 11" telescope with vial, 3-1/2" d vert. circle, 5-3/4" compass, 4" rad. Declination vernier, two plate vials, cross sights, four-screw detachable leveling base, staff adaptor, stiff leg tripod, brass plumb bob, orig case with labels, bronzed brass, marked "W. & L. E. Gurley, Troy, NY," c1874 . . . . 1,840.00

Theodolite, Tackpole & Brother, New York, 1559, miniature, 8-1/2" h, 4-1/8" w, 7-1/8" l telescope with vial, 3-1/4" d, 1' vert. circle, 2" compass, 3-1/2" d, 2 vernier, 1' vert. circle, 2" compass, 3-1/2" d, two vernier, 1' silver horiz. scale, tribrach leveling base, black and brass finish, orig box, extension leg tripod, c1870 . . . . 1,495.00

Theodolite/Level, one-minute type, Wm Wurdemann, Washington, DC, 10" l telescope, 5-1/2" h, labeled "Gr. No. 5," 4" d, 1' vernier, silver metal horiz. scale, bull's eye-level vial, telescope motion screw, three-screw leveling base, telescope reversible in its yokes, c1860 . . . . 635.00

Theodolite with compass, Wm Wurdemann, Washington, DC, No. 155, 10-1/2" reversible telescope, 12-3/4" h, 6" d silver metal horiz. scale, two microscope read verniers, 4" compass, single-plate vial, telescope vial, three-screw leveling base and truss frame, c1865 . . . . 1,725.00

Vernier compass

Gurley, W. & L. E., Troy, NY, 13-1/4" h, 11" telescope, 6" compass with outside declination vernier, crossed plate vials, detachable four-screw leveling base, leveling adapter, sunshade, orig mahogany box with

label, bronzed finish brass, c1865 . . . . 2,300.00

Young, Wm. J, Maker 3694 Philadelphia, 13-3/4" l, 6-1/8" w, 9-1/4" h, detachable sight vanes, bull's eye vial (empty), outkeeper, non-reflecting dial and silver ring, 25º 5' vernier, brass cover and 6-1/8" l adapter, darkened brass, case and Jacob staff 1,725.00

Wye Level, 8-1/4" h, 4" w, 16-1/4" l, 1-3/8" d reversible telescope with 6-3/4" l, 4 screw leveling base, horiz. motion clamp and screw, eyepiece attachment, marked "Kuebler & Seelhorst Makers Philada, 597, Oct. 1, 1867 Patent" 500.00

SWORDS

History: The first swords used in America came from Europe. The chief cities for sword manufacturing were Solingen in Germany, Klingenthal in France, and Hounslow and Shotley Bridge in England. Among the American importers of these foreign blades was Horstmann, whose name is found on many military weapons.

New England and Philadelphia were the early centers for American sword manufacturing. By the Franco-Prussian War, the Ames Manufacturing Company of Chicopee, Massachusetts, was exporting American swords to Europe.

Sword collectors concentrate on a variety of styles: commissioned vs. non-commissioned officers' swords, presentation swords, naval weapons, and swords from a specific military branch, such as cavalry or infantry. The type of sword helped identify a person's military rank and, depending on how he had it customized, his personality as well.

Following the invention of repeating firearms in the mid-19th century, the sword lost its functional importance as a combat weapon and became a military dress accessory.

Note: Condition is key to determining value.

Cutlass, brass, scaled guard with pommel marked "CSN" on one side, anchor on opposite, period leather scabbard, blade exhibits light rusting, bend at tip with small chip to blade, leather on scabbard is dry and exhibits some separation to seam, 21" l blade, 26-1/2" l, $4,400. Photo courtesy of Sanford Alderfer Auction Company.

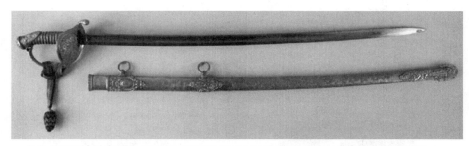

U.S. Model 1851 Staff & Field presentation sword, made by C. Roby to Colonel Harry Harris Davies, NY, slightly curved single edged blade signed "C. Roby & Co.,/W. Chelmsford, MASS" on ricasso, both faces of blade heavily decorated with etching of eagles, flags, stands of arms, florals, and "U.S.," half basket guard gilded cast brass with sprays of laurel, scrolls, and an inset rococo escutcheon surrounded by stars, all cast in very high relief and gold plated, grip also gold-plated cast brass simulating leather and wire wrap, heavy relief pommel with scroll and floral work overall, regulation black and gilt cloth sword knot attached to knuckle bow, gold-plated brass scabbard with engraved decoration over 80 percent of body, engraved with floral scrolls and flames, spread winged eagle and shield on a cloud with sunburst and arch of stars above, mountings cast in high relief with classical scrolls and floral work, Presented to/Col. Harry Harris Davies/by his numerous friends in New York City, Brooklyn/and Bayonne/U.S. of America, accompanied by notebook filled with information accumulated about Col. Davies, blade faded to gray, numerous dark spots, not affecting the etching, $6,325. Photo courtesy of James D. Julia Auctions.

Sword

Artillery, 25" l, Ames, 18-3/4" blade stamped with faint signature, U. S. and inspectors' markings, brass hilt with fish scale design, relief eagle **440.00**

Artillery officer's saber, 33" l, 27-1/2" l curved blade, wide fuller, eagle head pommel and hilt show most of orig fire gilding, replaced wooden handle, early 19th C **330.00**

Calvary saber

41" l, 35-1/2" l import blade with later date stamp of 1851, brass three branch hilt missing leather and wire wrapping, with scabbard . . **220.00**

41-1/2" l, Civil War, 35-3/4" blade stamped "Ames Mfg. Chicopee Mas, U.S.J.R. 1857," brass three-branch hilt with good patina, part of wire wrap and most of leather remains, iron scabbard **700.00**

42-3/4", Model 1860, Emerson & Silver, Trenton, NJ, signature on ricasso, inspector's initials and 1863 on other side, brass three branch hilt with good patina, dark leather wrapped handle missing its wire, browned steel scabbard **825.00**

43" l, 1840, stamped "U. S. 1862," brass three branch hilt with leather and wire wrapped handle, steel scabbard **660.00**

Foot officer, Cast brass helmet shaped pommel with single branch hilt, openwork detail on front of guard, leather and wire wrapped handle, 32" blade with "Clauberg," browned steel scabbard, nickel silver ring at entry, areas of orig etching on blade, some pitting, 41-1/2" l **330.00**

Infantry officer, Model 1850, Ames, 30-1/4" l etched and engraved blade with "Chicopee, Mass" address, cast hilt wash with open work, leather scabbard with brass bands and drag, engraved "Lt. Geo. Trembley, 174th N.Y.S.I.," 36-1/4" l **1,980.00**

Light artillery, 1842 pattern, moderately curved blade, 1-3/8" at ricasso, single wide fuller, left ricasso marked with early Ames logo, and right "1862," surcharged "Conn," handle leather wrapped with braided brass wire, large oval plain pommel cap, single D-guard with ball quillion, plain nickel plated scabbard with two hangers, 33" l **450.00**

Naval cutlass, 32" l, 26" blade, scroll signature "Ames Chicopee, Mass, 1862," brass hilt with minor dents, leather and wire wrap missing . . **250.00**

Officer

39" l, non-regulation, Civil War, 32" blade with fine etching including "U.S." eagle, and banner on opposite side, steel hilt with pierced "U.S." and detailed eagle with "E. Pluribus Unum," sharkskin cov grip with orig copper wire remaining, steel scabbard with minor pitting **1,200.00**

40" l, 19th C, import, 34" blade, sgd "Sargent & Son, Manufacturer to the East India Company," cast brass three-branch hilt with leaf designs, handle retains orig sharkskin and wire wrapping **150.00**

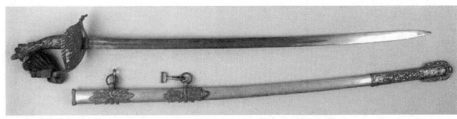

Civil War, Staff and Field Officers presentation, inscribed to Capt. Hitchcock, 153rd Illinois volunteers, unsigned European made non-regulation sword of presentation grade, 31" l single-edged blade with slight curve, faces are heavily etched with American trophies, floral sprays, spread winged eagle, and "U.S.," cast brass gold washed hilt, half basket guard with panoply of flags, tilted U.S. shield, drums, cannons, Liberty cap above, all resting on bed of oak leaves, edge of guard scalloped, single knuckle bow rising to fancy cast pommel with classical head on back and pineapple cap stain, cast German silver grip with acanthus leaf sprays top and bottom, laurel wrap, original gilt cloth sword knot at knuckle bow, steel scabbard, plated in German silver, brass top and middle mounts in leaf-like design, heavily engraved drag, casting of running flag bearer on face, scabbard is engraved: "Presented to/CAPT. C.H. HITCHCOCK/by Co. K 153 Regt. Ill. Vol. Inf./March 3, 1865," factory finish on blade, scabbard dirty, $5,175. Photo courtesy of James D. Julia Auctions.

European Cavalry saber, 19th C, sword with 35" slightly curved blade, wide unstopped fuller with 12" back grind at tip, flat iron, three-branch hand guard with ball quillion and tear-drop pommel cap, two-piece checkered hard rubber handle secured with 5 iron rivets, ricasso marked with crown over "L" over "8," original steel scabbard with two iron rings and drag, unit markings near the throat, blade has been cleaned with light surface pitting and several nicks to the cutting edge, wear to scabbard, $460. Photo courtesy of James D. Julia Auctions.

Staff and field officer, Model 1850, emb letter within two circles on ricasso "S. H.," etched and engraved 31" blade with stand of flags, eagle, "E. Pluribus Unum," scrolled foliage with "U.S," orig wire wrap with section of orig sword knot, blued steel scabbard with brass bands and drag, descended in family of Col. Edward Scovel, stationed at Johnson Island, some surface rust, 37" l **1,265.00**

TEA CADDIES

History: Tea once was a precious commodity and stored in special boxes or caddies. These containers were made to accommodate different teas and included a special cup for blending.

Around 1700, silver caddies appeared in England. Other materials, such as Sheffield plate, tin, wood, china, and pottery, also were used. Some tea caddies are very ornate.

Ivory tusk, 4-1/4" w, 5" h, formed as section of tusk, silver-plated mountings, flat hinged top with foliate finial, engraved scrolls, beaded and waved rim bands, 19th C **460.00**

Papier-mâché, 9-1/4" l, 6-3/4" d, 6" h, Regency Chinoiserie-style, rect case with canted corners, ornately dec with figural reserves within flower blossoms bordered by wide bands of gilding, conforming hinged lid opening to int. fitted with two removable pewter tea canisters with dec chasing **950.00**

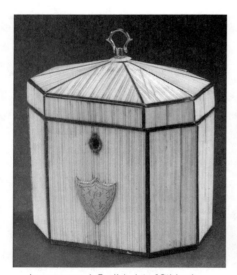

Ivory veneered, English, late 18th/early 19th C, octagonal, carved reeding, tortoise shell stringing, monogrammed shield form reserve, 5" h, **$1,800.** *Photo courtesy of Sloan's Auctioneers & Appraisers.*

Rosewood box, inlaid medallions, domed lid, ivory finial, **$200.**

Quillwork, 8-3/8" l, 4-3/4" d, 5-1/4" h, hexagonal, inlaid mahogany frames, blue and gilt quillwork panels covered with glass, floral vintage and leaf designs with crown and "MC 1804," two int. lidded compartments, replaced foil lining, English **2,750.00**

Silver, 7" h, lobed hexagonal form, lobed lid with filigree finial, allover Eastern style bird and foliate enamel dec, mounted with semi-precious stones, gilt int., approx 17 troy oz, Europe, late 19th/early 20th C . . **500.00**

Wood

Burl walnut veneer, 12-1/2" l, 6" d, 7-1/2" h, George III, rect case, hinged stepped domed lid, well

Mahogany, George III, late 18th C, octagonal bombe form, mounted brass handle and escutcheon, 7-1/4" w, **$1,900.** *Photo courtesy of Sloan's Auctioneers & Appraisers.*

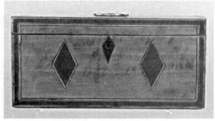

Satin wood, inlaid borders all around, diamond-shaped mahogany inlaid panels, two on front, one on each end and one large one on the top, silver ring pull, inlaid escutcheon, interior with two satin wood ivory handled lids, round center compartment with glass bowl, underside of lid quilted, 6" h x 12" w x 6" d, **$2,200.** *Photo courtesy of James D. Julia, Inc.*

fitted int. with two conforming veneered compartments, each opening to lead lined interiors, center section for mixing bowl, associated glass bowl **650.00**

Cherry, 10" l, Chippendale, mahogany cross banding, ogee feet, base and lid edge moldings, old finish, three int. compartments, orig brass escutcheon and bale with tooling, minor repairs **2,750.00**

Cherry veneer, 4-3/4" w, 3-3/8" d, 4-3/4" h, octagonal, banding inlay on lid and front panel, imitation fluting on corner panels, front with flower in oval medallion, conch shell inlay and oval medallion on lid, brass hinges and incomplete lock, brass keyhole escutcheon, age cracks and minor veneer damage **715.00**

Fruitwood, 6" h, figural pear, America or England, 19th century, wear, small crack **1,645.00**

Burl, striped inlay across top and along edges, ivory escutcheon, four brass claw feet, brass ring handles on ends, interior with two burl top hinged lid compartments, open round center compartment with glass bowl, glass bowl inside, 12-1/2" w, 6-1/2" d, 8" h, **$2,400.** *Photo courtesy of James D. Julia, Inc.*

Mahogany, 9-3/4" w, 5-5/8" d, 8" h, English, late 19th C, rect, slope-sided lid with brass handle, foliate brass escutcheon, lid opening to fitted int., three pewter canisters and lids, ogee bracket feet **690.00**

Rosewood veneer, 12" l, 6-1/4" d, 7-3/8" h, Federal, inlay, brass ring handles with cornucopia escutcheons and batwing keyhole escutcheon, int. with two lidded compartments and clear cut glass mixing bowl **990.00**

TEAPOTS

History: The origins of the teapot have been traced to China in the late 16th century. Early Yixing teapots were no bigger than the tiny cups previously used for drinking tea. By the 17th century, tea had spread to civilized nations of the world. The first recorded advertisement for tea in London is dated 1658 and called a "China drink…call Tcha, by other Nations Tay, alias Tee…" Although coffee houses were already established, they began to add tea to their selections.

While the Chinese had long been producing teapots and other tea items, the English were receiving these wares along with shipments of tea. By the early 1700s, British china and stoneware producers were manufacturing teapots. It was in 1706 that Thomas Twining bought his own coffee house and thwarted the competition of the many other such establishments by offering a variety of quality tea. Coffee houses were exclusively for males; thus, women would wait outside, sending their footmen inside for purchases. For the majority of the 1700s, teapots were Oriental imports. British factories continued experimenting with the right combination of materials that would make a teapot durable enough to withstand the daily rigors of boiling water. Chinese Export Porcelain was an inspiration to the British and by the end of the 1700s, many companies found the necessary combinations of china clay and stone, fired at high temperature, which could withstand boiling water needed to brew precious pots of tea.

From the very first teapots, figural shapes have always been a favorite with tea drinkers. The Victorian era saw a change from more utilitarian teapots toward beautiful, floral, and Rococo designs, yet figural pots continued to be manufactured.

Early American manufacturers mimicked Oriental and British designs. While the new land demanded sturdy teapots in the unsettled land, potteries were established steadily in the Eastern states. Rockingham teapots were produced by many companies, deriving this term from British companies manufacturing a strong, shiny brown glaze on heavy pottery. The best known is from the Bennington, Vermont, potteries.

By the 1800s and the turn-of-the-century, many pottery companies were well established in the U. S., producing a lighter dinnerware and china including teapots. Figural teapots from this era are highly desired by collectors, while others concentrate on collecting all known patterns produced by a company.

The last 20 years has seen a renewed interest in teapots and collectors desire not only older examples, but also high-priced, specialty manufactured teapots or individual artist creations commanding hundreds of dollars.

Adviser: Tina M. Carter.

Reproduction Alert: Teapots and other ware with a blurry mark of a shield and two animals, ironstone, celadon-colored body background, and a design made to look like flow blue, are new products, possibly from China. Yixing teapots have been reproduced or made in similar styles for centuries.

Basalt, 9-3/4" l, black, oval form, scalloped rim and classical relief centering columns with floral festoons, banded drapery on shoulder, incised brick banded lower body, unmarked, England, early 19th C, restored spout **360.00**

Cloisonné, panel with butterflies and flowers, Chinese, late 19th C. . . . **450.00**

Flow blue, Scinde pattern, Alcock, octagonal, 8 1/2" h. **950.00**

Graniteware, large teapot with pewter handle, lid and spout, Manning Bowman & Co. Manufacturers, called Perfection Granite Ironware, West Meriden, Connecticut **325.00**

Ironstone, Mason's Ironstone, Vista pattern, red and white scenic dec, matching trivet. **195.00**

Lenox, Art Deco, applied sterling silver dec, c1930, three-pc set. **400.00**

Majolica, fish, multicolored, Minton, no mark, late 1800s **2,000.00**

Yang-Tz-u, enameled, hexagonal 8-1/4" h teapot, bright polychrome painted mountainous landscapes on each panel, imitation famille rose and jaune decorated top and borders, surrounded by six matching nesting trays, each with lotus pod on underside, Chinese, made for export, 19th C, professional repairs on spout, lid, and handle, $250. Photo courtesy of Cowan's Historic Americana Auctions.

Royal Doulton, Dickensware, Little Nell, $195. Photo courtesy of Joy Luke Auctions.

Old Worcester, first period, Old Japan Star, 1765-70 . . . . **5,250.00**

Parian ware, Brownfield, Mistletoe pattern **450.00**

Porcelain, pink and gray luster swirls, Surf Ballet, by California artist, Sascha Brastoff, c1953. . . . . **265.00**

Rockingham glaze, 4-3/8" h, brown glaze,tree trunk form body, molded fruiting vines, branch handle, twig finial, imp Wedgwood, England, mark, c1870, chip to cover collar. **520.00**

Silver, 5-3/4" h, Hester Bateman, London, 1786, oval, domed lid with beaded rim, engraved bands, body with engraved bands and central cartouche, wood ear handle and finial, approx 13 troy oz **3,450.00**

Wedgwood, 7-1/4" l, Rosso Antico, Egyptian, applied black basalt hieroglyphs, crocodile finial, imp mark, early 19th C, slight chips to rim and spout **1,100.00**

Yixing, bamboo handle, Chinese "chop mark" or signature, c1880 . . . . . **450.00**

TEDDY BEARS

History: Originally thought of as "Teddy's Bears," in reference to President Theodore Roosevelt, these stuffed toys are believed to have originated in Germany. The first ones to be made in the United States were produced about 1902.

Most of the earliest teddy bears had humps on their backs, elongated muzzles, and jointed limbs. The fabric used was generally mohair; the eyes were either glass with pin backs or black shoe buttons. The stuffing was usually excelsior. Kapok (for softer bears) and wood-wool (for firmer bears) also were used as stuffing materials.

Quality older bears often have elongated limbs, sometimes with curved arms, oversized feet, and felt paws. Noses and mouths are black and embroidered onto the fabric.

The earliest teddy bears are believed to have been made by the original Ideal Toy Corporation in America and by a German company, Margarete Steiff, GmbH. Bears made in the early 1900s by other companies can be difficult to identify because they were all similar in appearance and most identifying tags or labels were lost during childhood play.

Notes: Teddy bears are rapidly increasing as collectibles and their prices are rising proportionately. As in other fields, desirability should depend upon appeal, quality, uniqueness, and condition. One modern bear already has been firmly accepted as a valuable collectible among its antique counterparts: the Steiff teddy put out in 1980 for the company's 100th anniversary. This is a reproduction of that company's first teddy and has a special box, signed certificate, and numbered ear tag; 11,000 of these were sold worldwide.

3-3/8" h, Schuco, golden mohair perfume bear, black steel eyes, embroidered nose and mouth, jointed at shoulders and hips, overall fur loss, soil, c1920. . . . . **150.00**

10" h, ginger mohair, fully jointed, black steel eyes, black embroidered nose, mouth, and claws, felt pads, Steiff, blank ear button, spotty fur loss **1,150.00**

10" h, light yellow short mohair pile, fully jointed, excelsior stuffing, black steel eyes, embroidered nose, mouth, and claws, felt pads, Ideal, c1905, spotty fur and fiber loss, pr **920.00**

11" h, blond mohair, fully jointed, excelsior stuffing, black steel eyes, open composition mouth with full set of teeth, c1908, fiber wear around mouth and nose, some fur wear at seams **750.00**

Boyds, Truman S. Bearington, jointed brown mohair, suede paws and feet, original box, 17" h, **$50.** *Photo courtesy of Joy Luke Auctions*

11-1/2" h, gold mohair, fully jointed, glass eyes, excelsior stuffing, Steiff, button missing, remnants of embroidered nose, mouth, and claws, spotty fur loss, extensive moth damage to pads **200.00**

12" h, yellow mohair, fully jointed, glass eyes, embroidered nose and mouth, excelsior stuffing, felt pads, Schuco, early 1920s, moth damage, spotty fur loss **350.00**

13-1/2" h, saffron rayon plush, fully jointed, excelsior stuffing, glass eyes, embroidered nose, mouth, and claws, felt pads, some fur loss, and fiber damage, c1930 . . . . **115.00**

15" h, mohair, gold plush, swivel head, brown glass eyes, shaved muzzle, black floss nose and mouth, excelsior stuffing, jointed at shoulders and hips, gold felt pads on paws and feet, unmarked, right paw pad damaged **150.00**

16" h, ginger mohair, fully jointed, excelsior stuffing, glass eyes, long arms, shaved muzzle, vertically stitched nose, felt pads, arrow ear button, Bing, c1907, very slight fur loss, head disk broken through front of neck . **2,300.00**

16" h, golden yellow mohair, fully jointed, glass eyes, brown still nose, embroidered mouth, excelsior stuffed, light fur loss, felt pads damaged, probably American, c1920. . . . . **260.00**

16-1/2" h, ginger mohair, fully jointed, black steel eyes, black embroidered nose, mouth, and claws, beige felt pads, excelsior stuffing, American, c1919, patchy fur loss, felt damage **800.00**

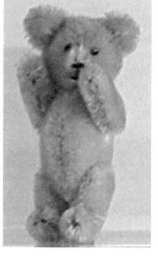

Yes/No Bear, gold plush, glass eyes, embroidered muzzle, slight wear to stomach, 5-1/2" h, **$250.** *Photo courtesy of James D. Julia, Inc.*

17" h, gray mohair, brown glass eyes, embroidered features, mouth redone, fully jointed, velveteen pads, some wear to lush pads, American, c1920 . **150.00**

18" h, possibly Ideal, worn and patched, replaced shoe button eyes, retains one glass eye, which may be original, c1915, accompanied by photo of orig child owner. **175.00**

19" h, brown tint gold mohair, fully jointed, glass eyes, shaved muzzle, black embroidered nose and mouth, excelsior stuffing, clipped mohair pads, Hermann, 1940s, fur slightly matted in spots **250.00**

21" h, brown-tipped blond long mohair, brown glass eyes, embroidered nose, mouth, claws shaved muzzle, and inner ears, crier, fully jointed, felt pads, mid-20th C **175.00**

24" h, black mohair, brown glass eyes, embroidered nose and mouthy, fully jointed, worn velveteen pads, America, c1920 . . . . **1,610.00**

24" h, golden brown mohair, fully jointed, glass eyes, embroidered nose and mouth, kapok and excelsior stuffing, felt pads, wearing dress, bonnet, and glasses, 1920s, spotty fur loss and felt damage. **350.00**

25" h, gold mohair, articulated body, glass eyes, ivory felt paw pads are worn, one replaced, wear **525.00**

25" h, yellow mohair, fully jointed, glass eyes, black embroidered nose, mouth, and claws, felt pads, excelsior stuffing, Ideal, 1920s, slight fur loss and matting **635.00**

26-1/2" h, gold mohair, articulated body, glass eyes, pink felt paw pads, some wear and repair **550.00**

27" l, light gold mohair, articulated body, glass eyes, very worn ivory felt paw pads, squeak voice box **360.00**

29" l, beige curly mohair, fully jointed, glass eyes, brown embroidered nose, mouth, and claws, excelsior stuffing, felt pads, Steiff, post WWII, ear button, some pad damage, wearing train engineer's outfit **575.00**

Teplitz China

History:
Around 1900, there were 26 ceramic manufacturers located in Teplitz, a town in the Bohemian province of what was then known as

Czechoslovakia. Other potteries were located in the nearby town of Turn. Wares from these factories were molded, cast, and hand decorated. Most are in the Art Nouveau and Art Deco styles.

Marks: The majority of pieces do not carry a specific manufacturer's mark; they are simply marked "Teplitz," "Turn-Teplitz," or "Turn."

Bust, 22-1/2" h, young woman, elaborate dress, fan, flowers, and hat with reticulated border, putto on shoulders, Ernest Wahliss, c1900, repaired **1,700.00**

Candlestick, 13" h, applied flowers, gold trim **125.00**

Creamer, hp, scene of bird in flight, gold trim **195.00**

Ewer, 10-5/8" h, gilt trimmed ivory ground, enameled birds in paneled sides, c1900 . . . . **300.00**

Figure

8" h, 8-1/2" l, two children, young boy in hat with pink ribbon, pushing young girl carrying umbrella and basket, soft beige ground, pink and blue highlights, sgd "Teplitz Bohemia," imp "4007" **450.00**

8-1/2" w, 17" h, nymph, standing on base with plants, muted greens, gold highlights, sgd "Whaliss" **2,500.00**

21" h, gentlemen, 18th century style dress **675.00**

Jar, 8-1/4" w, 6-1/2" h, hp, parcel gilt, molded dragon handles, marked "Alfred Shellmacher Teplitz" . . . **850.00**

Pitcher, 12" h, cylindrical, bulbous base, leaf-shaped handle, reticulated rim, ivory ground, iris and foliate dec, Ernst Wahliss Alexandra Porcelain Works, early 20th C, crown and shield mark on underside, hairline and crack at handle **110.00**

Urn, 14" h, ovoid, two delicate handles, textured neck, handles, and base, ivory and pale green, gilding, hp floral center, marked "Turn-Teplitz-Bohemia" in circle around vase mark, also marked "RS + K Made in Austria" **295.00**

Vase

5-3/4" d, 7" h, gourd shape, four handles, band of white and gold Glasgow roses, green leaves, gold details, gray-green leathering ground, stamped "Teplitz/Made in Austria/1174/18" **460.00**

6-1/4" h, Art Nouveau sand textured pod-form, scrolled leafage, matte green, tan, and ivory glaze, gilt highlights, printed maker's stamp on base, Paul Dachsel, c1905 . . . . **260.00**

8" h, Art Nouveau baluster form, slender neck, enamel dec, stylized wildflowers, gilt details, marked "Turin-Teplitz, Amphora Work Reissner," early 20th C **460.00**

10" w, 12" h, double handles, Art Nouveau floral design, burgundy ground, sgd "Julius Dresser, Teplitz" **750.00**

11-1/2" h, stylized blue and green scene of sun through trees, lower band with ivory and blue insect and blue floral dec, gold accents, stamped "Turn-Teplitz-Bohemia/RS+K/Made in Austria" **480.00**

12" h, lustered central panel with Art-Nouveau style female portrait, c1900 . . . . **575.00**

TERRA-COTTA WARE

History: Terra-cotta is ware made of hard, semi-fired ceramic. The color of the pottery ranges from a light orange-brown to a deep brownish red. It is usually unglazed, but some pieces are partially glazed and have incised, carved, or slip designs. Utilitarian objects, as well as statuettes and large architectural pieces, were made. Fine early Chinese terra-cotta pieces recently have sold for substantial prices.

Architectural fragment, 38" l, lintel supports, from Solomon Blumenfield Flats, 1884, pr **550.00**

Bowl, 6" d, 2" h, glazed **30.00**

Bust, 10-1/2" w, 10" h, good detail, dark red patina, hollow interior, firing separation noticeable from underside, nose restored **125.00**

Casino chip, 1-1/2" d, Club Forest, inlaid address, crest, 18 encrusted stars **25.00**

Pitcher, body decorated with red flower sprigs, molded dragon handle, fish spout, ink stamp mark, restoration, 12" h, $350. Photo courtesy of David Rago Auctions.

Teplitz vase, 13" h, Art Nouveau, two buttressed floriform handles, shaded amber and green matte glaze, marked, post-factory drill hole to bottom, small bruise to rim, $225; 6-1/2" d pie-crust dish, Rookwood, by E.P. Cranch, 1885, "Brer Bear and his Family," from Uncle Remus series, marked, $200. Photo courtesy of David Rago Auctions.

Figure, standing boy, book under arm, 22" h, $60. Photo courtesy of Joy Luke Auctions.

Figure

7-1/2" h, Aphrodite, dressed in tunic, open back, South Italian, third century B.C. **345.00**

11" h, St. Joseph, wearing long loose robes, black hat, polychrome dec, Spanish, 19th C **600.00**

18-3/4" l, reclining male figure with dog, inscribed "Claude Janin" **400.00**

Pedestal, 7" sq top, 24" h, price for pr **400.00**

Planter, 10-1/4" h, garland and mask motif. **100.00**

Statue, 55" h, Minera, woman in draped toga, grape and cable head dress, holding wine cup **2,000.00**

Tray, 9" x 7", hp, pilgrims resting, gilt dec, 1920 . . . . **85.00**

Urn, 29-1/2" h, molded putti and foliage dec, green glaze, waisted neck, two handles, circular base. **395.00**

Water pitcher, 13" h, c1810, base chip **325.00**

TEXTILES

History: Textiles is the generic term for cloth or fabric items, especially anything woven or knitted. Antique textiles that have survived are usually those that were considered the "best" by their original owners, since these were the objects that were used and stored carefully by the housewife.

Textiles are collected for many reasons—to study fabrics, to understand the elegance of a historical period, for decorative purposes, or to use as was originally intended. The renewed interest in antique clothing has sparked a revived interest in period textiles of all forms.

A big year for the sale of coverlets was 2002. Many large coverlet collections were auctioned at auction houses all around the country. When collectors have many great objects to choose from, they usually can find something to add to their collections at a more reasonable price. The prices of coverlets will surely rise again as they will always be popular with collectors and decorators.

Aubusson needlepoint rug, 45" x 71", oval central medallion with roses and 16 floral panels around edges, burgundy, red, pink, teal, beige, and white **250.00**

Bandana, printed on silk

Harrison and Morton, 1892 election **1,100.00**

Parker, Alton and Henry Davis, 1904, election. **415.00**

Bedspread

Embroidered candlewick, by Eliza Spink, (1807-77), Auburn, NY, white on white embroidered dec, central cartouche with floral urn, medallion above name and date surrounded by grapevine border,

further framed by grapevine and tulip border, central floral urn, 108" x 112", small holes, light staining, repairs **1,840.00**

Printed cotton toile, New England, late 18th/early 19th C, Cupid and several allegorical female figures in scenes of love, hand sewn, pieced and quilted in diamond pattern, backed with white homespun fabric, extended center panel, two pillow gussets, side drops, scalloped border on three sides, white binding, minor repair to backing, 109-1/2" l, 52-1/2" w center panel, 31-1/2" l side drops **1,295.00**

Coverlet, damask, two pcs, red, blue, and green on white ground, rose and star design, marked "made for P. Matthias by W. H. Gernand Damask Coverlet Manufacturer Westminster Carroll County, MD, 1871," 89" x 90" **1,125.00**

Coverlet, jacquard, one pc, Bierderwand, broad loom

Mustard, dark salmon, and navy blue stripes on natural, corner block "William & Rachel Guthrie" with poppy, overall floral designs, tulip-like medallions, added fringe, 84" x 96". **385.00**

Natural, dark navy blue, burgundy, and olive, "Latest Improvent P. Warranted M. by H. Stager, Mount Joy" on edge, star medallion with tulip center, surrounded by rose branches, Greek key and rose branch border, corner block with bird in tree branch, worn areas,

fringe loss, some edge damage, 69" x 77" **300.00**

Coverlet, jacquard, two pcs, Biederwand

Natural and navy blue, corner block "Daniel Lehr, Dalton, Wayne County, Ohio, 1847," leaf medallions, borders with backwards looking birds with tulips, minor stains and wear, some fringe loss, edge backed with blue cloth, 70" x 76" **450.00**

Coverlet, jacquard, woven in two pieces, American indigo blue and white wool, buildings and floral urns at bottom corner, spread-wing eagles, and "Liberty," white and blue side and bottom fringe, slight brown spots, very minor edge wear, 7'2" x 5'10", **$150.** *Photo courtesy of Cowan's Historic Americana Auctions.*

Noted Needlework

A very important textile was sold in Skinner's American Furniture & Decorative Arts auction on Feb. 24, 2002 for $12,925. The needlework picture done by J. Adams, New Orleans, Louisiana, in 1836, shows a minstrel couple in painted black face—a gentleman dressed in military uniform holding a sword, and a lady in period dress and bonnet holding a hankie—standing in a whimsical landscape of flowers, birds, and butterflies. He laments, "Tomorrow I go in a far distant land, To fight a battle unknown; Another will come and you will bestow, A happier peace to his hand." She replies, "Hush! Thy suspicion fair Emma Jane cried, It's hard for to love and to leave, For I swear by the Virgin that one in thy stead, Shall a Husband of Emma Jane's be." The figures are solidly stitched in silk threads of pinks, greens, pale blue, and brown, on a linen ground, and the piece is signed at lower right. It is 16-1/4" x 19-3/4", with minor staining at the margins. The needlework was from a private collection and accompanied with information from a University Press of Mississippi publication, titled *In Old New Orleans,* edited by W. Kenneth Holditch, containing an article by Kaye De Metz discussing "Minstrel Dancing" with references to "Oh Hush," and several other presentations performed by Big Daddy Rice on his visits to New Orleans in 1835 and 1836.

Coverlet, summer/winter, double weave, indigo and white, initialed "N. S." and dated "1839" in two corner blocks, woven in Double Rose and Tile pattern, tulip border, very minor seam separation, 90" x 75-1/2", **$600.** *Photo courtesy of Skinner Auctioneers and Appraisers.*

Natural and soft salmon, tan, and gold, corner block "Made by W. Moore 1848," (Newark, OH), rose medallion, grape vine border, another small diamond border, minor wear, fringe loss, some edge damage, two halves don't line up at center seam, 78" x 86"......**250.00**

Natural and tomato red, corner block for "John Klinhinz, Ohio, 1854," flowers and sunbursts with bird and rose border, some edge damage, added fringe, 70" x 84" **500.00**

Natural, navy blue, and tomato red, corner block "H. Petry, Canton, Stark County, Ohio, 1840," floral medallions with borders of potted tulips, eagles with trees and stars, fringe loss, minor stains, small hole, stitched repairs, 70" x 72" ..**425.00**

Natural, navy blue, mauve, and pale olive, flowers and stars, rooster border, corner block "Made by J. M. Kostner, Lewisvil, Coshoc. Co. Ohio 1846," some wear, fringe loss, 68" x 86"................**250.00**

Natural, navy blue, red, and golden olive, corner block "T. M. Alexander, Wayne County, S.C.T. Ohio 1845," floral motif, lions and sunbursts, borders of backwards looking birds with roses, grape vines, and diamonds, few stains, fringe loss, small hole, unbound top edge, 72" x 88" **650.00**

Natural, navy blue, salmon red, and olive brown stripes, corner block with four oak leaves "Peter Hartman, Wooster, Ohio, 1843," connected mirror images of potted flowers, alternating with bunches of grapes, border with eagles with shields sitting on grape vines and

roses, wear, few stains, some repair, fringe loss, 77" x 90" **300.00**

Navy blue and white, corner block "Jacob Snyder, Stark County, Ohio, 1848," oversize medallions with tulips and hearts surrounded by princess feathering, borders with potted tulips and vining leaves, fringe loss, minor edge damage, small stain, one end rebound with white cloth, 68" x 83" **250.00**

Navy blue, red, and olive green stripes, natural ground, corner block labeled "Gabriel Rausher, May 10, Delaware, Ohio, 1854," floral medallions, two vining floral borders, bottom border has backward looking parrots, one rolled edge, minor wear and fringe loss, some stitched repairs, 58" x 86" **440.00**

Navy blue, tomato red, and mixed green and yellow stripes with natural, corner block with fancy tulip and "F. Yahraus, Knox County, Ohio 1864," stars with flower and star medallions, one border with backward looking birds and flowers, two borders with grape vines, wear, small repair, edge damage, 74" x 88" **500.00**

Tomato red and navy blue bands on foundation of natural threads individually dyed light blue, border labeled "1848 Wove by J.S. for F.L.T.," quatrefoil corner block with bird under tree, diamonds alternating with wavy leaves, double borders of berry vines, worn edges with traces of blue calico binding, 74" x 90"...**385.00**

White/natural, blue, tomato red, and dark green, corner block with eagle "F. Yearous Loudonville, Ohil, 1855," floral medallions with sunbursts, border with vines, tulips, and trees, no fringe, seams, 71" x 90" **475.00**

Coverlet, jacquard, two pcs, double weave

Dark tomato red, navy blue, and natural, unusual geometric overshot type pattern, minor fringe loss, 68" x 78"...........**425.00**

Natural and dark blue, corner block "A. Smith, Lodi 1837," medallions of four roses each with stars in between, border with eagles, shields, two kinds of trees, worn, some damage, stitched repairs, 74" x 82" **330.00**

Natural and navy blue, corner block with house dated 1850, used by Craig family of weavers in Indiana, various medallions surrounded by seaweed and conch shells, two borders with well detailed flowers, other two with alternating urns, exotic birds, domed buildings, minor stains, 80" x 88".....**600.00**

Natural, navy blue, and salmon, conch shell corner block for Samel Balantyne, 1808-1861, Lafayette, IN, flowers in grid, borders of urns and pineapple with internal hearts, fringe missing some wear, edge damage, 75" x 86".........**365.00**

Natural, salmon, and navy blue, sunflower corner blocks, thistle medallions surrounded by roses, borders with grape vines, wear, minor stains, 72" x 78".....**600.00**

Natural, tomato red, and dark green, corner block with pinwheel and "Jas McLD" for James McLeran, Columbiana County, OH, after 1848, flower and leaf medallions on speckled background, pots of strawberries on border, bound edges, few areas of wear, 72" x 76" **425.00**

White and dark navy blue, geometric pattern, pine tree borders, overall light stains, one edge rebound with blue calico, 76" x 84"......**220.00**

Coverlet, overshot

One piece, broadloom, intricate optical pattern, natural, purple, and cinnamon, 74" x 106"......**495.00**

Two piece, optical pattern, natural, pink-red, and navy blue, some fringe trimmed, 68" x 78"...**450.00**

Two piece, tightly woven, natural, navy blue, and dark red, added red fringe, 80" x 90".........**250.00**

Coverlet, summer/winter, one pc, broad loom

Centennial, red, green, and navy blue stripes on natural, central medallion with star surrounded by flowers and eagles with shields in each corner, bound edge with checkered design, worn areas, fringe loss, 80" x 87" **125.00**

Hunter green and tomato red, central floral medallion surrounded by triangles, wide border with capitol building in center flanked by grape vines and flower urns, small stitched repair with minor damage at one of bound ends, 78" x 84" **450.00**

Natural, medium blue, salmon, golden olive stripes, narrow green stripe, border labeled "D. Cosley, Xenia, Ohio, 1851," delicate openwork design with star medallions, vines, and interlocking scrolls with feathers, one edge rolled, wear, fringe loss, 76" x 86" **250.00**

Natural, medium green, blue, and tomato red, corner block "Ettinger and Co. Arronsburg, Centre Co., 1865," central acanthus leaf medallion with floral corners, multiple borders including stars, diamonds, and grape vines, minor stains, one end cut down and rebound, 78" x 81" **350.00**

Natural, navy blue, red, dark green, corner block "Made by J. Hausman in Lobachsville for John Bechtol 1842," minor wear and stains, 76" x 100" **400.00**

Natural, red, blue, and yellow stripes, corner block "Emanuel Ettinger, Aaronsburg, Centre Co. 1846," quatrefoil leaf medallions alternating with stars and diamonds, tulip border, 76" x 91" **200.00**

Coverlet, summer/winter, two pcs, navy blue and pale salmon stripes, and natural, corner block "L. Rauch, fancy coverlet woven by G. Heilbronn, Lancaster O, 1850," branching floral medallions with borders of potted roses and backwards looking birds, minor wear, small stitched repair, fringe loss, light stains, 72" x 88" **275.00**

Draperies, Fortuny, early 20th C, four 19-1/4" w by 54" l panels, three 40" l by 54" l panels, large green fleur-de-lis patterns on taupe ground **2,990.00**

Handkerchief, printed on cotton, Democratic Party, donkeys from Jefferson to Truman, 1949 ..... **230.00**

Hooked rug

America, c1880, wool, two flower-filled, blue-striped cornucopias surrounded by stylized flowers and red scrolls, mottled tan and brown background, 43" x 73", minor wear **4,115.00**

America, 19th C, wool, center dec in pattern of alternating oak leaves and quatrefoil motifs, scrolled leaf border in shades of gray, green, red, tan, brown, pink, and black, 62" x 62", imperfections .. **1,175.00**

Hooked rug, winter landscape with sleigh and figures in village, framed, 26" x 37" sight, **$400.** *Photo courtesy of Sanford Alderfer Auction Company.*

America, 19th C, wool, house flanked by two trees, worked in shades of green, blue, red, and brown, mottled blue and tan ground, 16-1/2" x 26-1/2", mounted on wood frame **725.00**

America, 19th C, wool, reddish horse, black bridle, striped mane and tail, tan medallion, two tone brown with gold background, blue and ivory corner leaves, wreath around medallion with red berries, black cloth binding, minor wear and small hole at horse's back, 24-1/2" x 41" **315.00**

America, 19th C, wool, two center hearts, star in each corner, multicolored striped field, mounted on cotton backing, stretched onto wood frame, 30-3/4" x 40-1/8", minor losses **2,115.00**

America, early 20th C, country village with train in center, church and houses on the green, horse drawn carriages, people, and farm animals, flowering trees and shrubs, blue and purple border, 35" x 75", losses to center and border **1,530.00**

America, early 20th C, Oriental rug motif, rows of guls surrounded by multiple borders, worked in reds, blues, and cream on tan ground, 70" x 42-1/2", backed and repairs **765.00**

Frost, attributed to, tan ground, blue, pink, red, and purple center wheel design with multicolored diamonds on either end, outer border of purple, red, and tan line weaving between pink, blue, and red circles with crosses, medium brown outer border, hooked on burlap, minor wear, 31-1/4" x 51" **275.00**

Grenfell Industries, Newfoundland, Labrador, 1900-25, rescue scene with three figures, supply-laden dog sled, shades of brown, black, gray, green, blue, and yellow, brown border, 37-3/4" x 61-1/2", staining, fading **1,410.00**

Mourning picture, framed, silk threads, silk ground, central weeping willow tree, tombstone, obelisk, church in far left ground, never embroidered with names, 16-1/4" x 22", minor losses, deterioration of silk ground **600.00**

Needlework picture, framed

Attributed to Litchfield Female Academy, Litchfield, CT, unsigned, c1800, "Caroline, the Heroine of Litchfield," young girl seated in landscape beneath two willow trees, book in her lap, dog at her side, solidly stitched in silk and chenille threads, greens, golds, brown, and blue, watercolor features and background, round format, eglomise mat, period 18" x 17-1/2" frame, repairs..... **950.00**

Attributed to The Misses Patten School, Hartford, CT, 1800-10, silk needlework and watercolor, depiction of Biblical scene "Moses in the Bulrushes," surmounted by highly raised and padded metallic embroidered eagle holding floral swagged garland suspended from spangled bow knots at upper corners, oval format picture,

Needlework picture, Continental, 18th C, depicting adoration of Christ child, oval, framed, 7" x 5" sight, **$450.** *Photo courtesy of Sloan's Auctioneers & Appraisers.*

worked in chenille and solid stitches with hand painted figures and background, framed in spangles and partially surrounded by sheaves of wheat and other grains, padded and glued to cardboard, very minor toning, 17" x 13-3/4" **18,800.00**

Family record, Johnson family, Vassalboro, MA (now Maine), c1820, "Holman son of Lewis and Mary Johnson was born in Stoughton Massachusetts March 21 AD 1775 and was married Sept 12 1799 to Anna Daughter of Jonas and Martha Priest who was born in Vassalboro Mass Nov 12 AD 1780," listing of their nine children, wrought by "...A," rest unfinished, leafy branch in center, solidly stitched flowering border, worked in shades of blue, green, and pink, 26" x 22-1/2", toning, fading, minor staining at margins **450.00**

Family record, Thirza J. Hildreth Lynn 1836 Aged 12 Years, inscribed "Mr Samuel Hildreth Born Oct 9 1794, Miss Mary Morgan Born Sept 30 1796, Married Dec 16 1819" above vital records of their 7 children in central panel with sawtooth border, surrounded by solidly stitched meandering floral vine, 22" x 20-1/8", minor imperfections **3,820.00**

Memorial, picture centered with large monument, surrounded by grieving family, tablet inscribed "Mrs Fanny Spicer Ob't Aug 18th 1795, AE 20 Mrs. Mary Thayer Ob't Sept – 1806, AE 36 Mrs Sarah Clark Ob't Oct 12 1810 AE 24,"

Pillow, Arts & Crafts, stylized gold and red floral motif, beige ground, 20" x 20" $365. Photo courtesy of David Rago Auctions.

mourners, landscape, and sky painted in watercolor and gouache, monument, foliate tree, and shrubbery solidly stitched in silk and chenille threads, silk ground, eglomise mat, period frame, splits to silk inscriptions, some paint separation on glass, losses to mat and frame **4,700.00**

Memorial, Richardson family, c1820, two painted urn-topped monuments beneath willow tree, inscribed "Sacred to the Memory of Mrs. Hannah Richardson who died May 31st 1820 Aged 36," other "Sacred to the memory of John Gilson who died April 21st 1816 Ae 7 wks," two painted gravestones in solidly stitched foreground, flowering tree, small church, background with painted hills and blue sky, gilt and eglomise mat, 24" x 24-1/4" **4,700.00**

Mount Vernon, solidly stitched view of estate, General Washington standing on porch over looking hand painted Potomac River with sailing vessels, extending to pink and blue sky, foreground having tow ladies and a groomsman with hand painted features, horse and playful colt among flowers and tall grasses, foliate trees and shrubbery, 20" x 24-1/2", done from line engraving by Samuel Seymour, Philadelphia, March 15, 1812 . . . . **9,988.00**

Pillow, 15" h, 14" l, beadwork, central demi-lune beaded panel, white, gray, pink, and blue floral scene, gray velvet ground, blue, gray, and maroon silk trim, late 19th C **200.00**

Purse, 8" x 8" open, flame stitch needlework, shades of green, yellow, pink, and amethyst wool, lined in green linen, twill tape binding, two double pockets, identification "Simon Pinder April 23 1772" worked into borders **2,650.00**

Rag runner
  2' 10" x 10' 9", blue, rainbow stripes, yellow predominate, PA, stains **125.00**
  3' 1" x 12' 11", brown, tan, blue, and orange stripes **85.00**

Show towel
  14-1/2" w, 40" l, strong blue and dark pink cross-stitch geometric design, "Susanna Johnson 1839" . . **200.00**
  15-3/4" w, 54" l, homespun, pink and two shades of blue cross-stitch

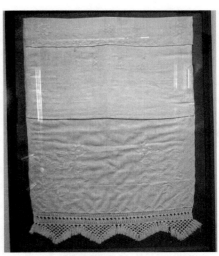

Show towel, signed "C. K.," dated 1822, geometric border, flowering vines with hearts in white embroidery on white linen, fish net type fringe at end of towel, framed, 17-1/2" w, 24" l sight, $125. Photo courtesy of Sanford Alderfer Auction Company.

needlework, urns of flowers, one with birds, hearts, diamond, and fretwork lines, "Elisabeth Schli 1810," fringed, few small holes, some repaired **440.00**

19" w, 62" l, homespun, dark brown finely stitched urns of flowers, one urn is heart shaped, "Betz Huhn 1808," woven decorative bands with pulled work and fringe at end, one end is bound **250.00**

19-1/2" w, 58" l, red, pale blue, pink, and yellow yarn crewel work flowers, potted tree, dark blue cross-stitched "ER 1840," decorative woven bands, wear to yarn border, stitch loss, very minor stains, added fringe **385.00**

Table cloth, 58" x 70", overshot linen, hand-tied fringe, some stains. . . **100.00**

Table mat, 41" x 53", pieced, red, green, black, white, and light blue wool, scalloped edges with diamond borders, star in each corner, large red and black checkered blocks within center panel surrounded by another band of diamonds, tacked blocks at each corner, smaller checkerboard blocks surround panel, black cloth backing and stretcher, minor damage and stains **1,155.00**

Table rug
  20" w, 42" l, appliqué, penny, mostly orange, blue, light green, and mauve wool, oblong with "tongue"

border, round blue cut-outs, light purple background, some stains
.... **250.00**

24-1/2" w, 15" h, wool yarn, two flowering plants, pink and beige blossoms, olive ground, New England, early 19th C, some losses
.... **2,875.00**

TIFFANY

For more information, see this book.

History: Louis Comfort Tiffany (1849-1934) established a glass house in 1878 primarily to make stained glass windows. In 1890, in order to utilize surplus materials at the plant, Tiffany began to design and produce "small glass," such as iridescent glass lampshades, vases, stemware, and tableware in the Art Nouveau manner. Commercial production began in 1896.

Tiffany developed a unique type of colored iridescent glass called Favrile, which differs from other art glass in that it was a composition of colored glass worked together while hot. The essential characteristic is that the ornamentation is found within the glass; Favrile was never further decorated. Different effects were achieved by varying the amount and position of colors.

Louis Tiffany and the artists in his studio also are well known for their fine work in other areas—bronzes, pottery, jewelry, silver, and enamels.

Marks: Most Tiffany wares are signed with the name "L. C. Tiffany" or the initials "L.C.T." Some pieces also are marked "Favrile," along with a number. A variety of other marks can be found, e.g., "Tiffany Studios" and "Louis C. Tiffany Furnaces."

Reproduction Alert: Tiffany glass can be found with a variety of marks, but the script signature is often faked or added later. When considering a purchase of Tiffany glass, look first to the shape, the depth of the iridescent coloring, then the signature.

Bisque
Pitcher, 5" d, 12-1/4" h, emb, tall leaves and cattails, speckled glossy green int., incised "LCT," short tight firing rim lines
.... **1,955.00**

Vessel, 7" d, 4" h, squatty emb seaweed and fish, smooth green glaze int., incised "LCT," several short tight rim lines **2,070.00**

Bronze
Bookends, pr, 4-3/4" w, 6" h, Zodiac, dark brown and green patina, imp "Tiffany Studios New York 1091"
.... **490.00**

Box, cov, 2" x 6-1/4" x 4", hinged, doré finish, lid dec with border of enameled blue-violet flowers, green leaves, stamped "Louis C. Tiffany Furnaces, Inc./Favrile/139," with monogram, repairs to both hinges **1,725.00**

Candelabra
9-1/8" h, two arms supporting cups with seven green and gold irid glass "jewels," brown and green patina, imp "Tiffany Studios New York" **2,760.00**

2-1/2" h, four bulbous cups with blown green Favrile glass on four curved arms, base with 16 green "jewel" inserts around platform base, imp "TG & D Co., Tiffany Studios New York D 887," corrosion, missing bobeches
.... **2,100.00**

Candlestick, 8" d, 24" h, tripod shaft, circular base, prong-set bobeche with flaring rim, orig dark verdigris patina, stamped "Tiffany Studios, New York, 1211" **4,315.00**

Cigar box, 6-1/2" l, 6" d, 2-1/2" h, rect hinged box, Zodiac pattern, multicolored enameling to each medallion, partial cedar liner, base stamped "Tiffany Studios New York 1655" **1,610.00**

Desk bell, 2-3/4" h, raised floral and foliate motif, gilt, imp "Tiffany Studios New York 1061" on clapper **750.00**

Bowl, oval, footed, blue iridescent, interior with etched vines, flowers, and leaves, base inscribed "L. C. Tiffany-Favrile #1895," 11" w, 4" h, $4,100. Photo courtesy of Joy Luke Auctions.

Candlestick, pulled feather shade, snuffer, original patina, signed, hairline crack to shade, $2,690. Photo courtesy of Fontaine's Auction Gallery.

Lamp, "Lily," seven amber/violet Favrile glass shades, bronze lilypad base, original patina, shades marked "L.C.T. Favrile" or "L.C.T.," base stamped "TIFFANY STUDIOS NEW YORK, 385," minor chips to flange of two shades, 20-1/2" x 9-3/4", $10,000. Photo courtesy of David Rago Auctions.

Desk set, American Indian pattern, 3-3/4" h inkwell, pr of blotter ends, pen tray, scissors, rocker blotter, all imp "Tiffany Studios New York" . . . **2,100.00**

Desk tray, 2-3/4" x 9-1/4" x 5-1/2", bronze and green slag, overlaid with grape vine pattern, attached penholder, cov inkwell, and match holder, stamped "Tiffany Studios New York," old cleaning to patina **2,870.00**

Frame, gilt, easel back, 10-1/4" w, 12" h, cast Heraldic pattern, lower recessed finished in patinated brown, imp mark "Louis C. Tiffany Furnaces Inc. 61" **1,035.00**

Glove box, 13-1/2" l, 4-1/2" d, 3-1/8" h, Grapevine pattern, striated green slag glass inserts, ball feet, imp "Tiffany Studios, New York" **980.00**

Magnifying glass, 8-7/8" l, gilt bronze, rosette pattern on handle, imp "Tiffany Studios 1788," imperfections . . . **750.00**

Paperweight, 1-1/2" h, 2-1/4" l, sphinx, orig patina, some gilt, stamped "Tiffany Studios New York" **275.00**

Plate, 9-3/4" d, 1" h, ftd, relief arts and crafts block designs around rim, sgd "Tiffany Studios New York, 1744" **475.00**

Thermometer, 8-3/4" h, Grapevine pattern, beaded border, green patina, green slag glass, easel stand, imp "Tiffany Studios New York" on reverse, minor corrosion **1,495.00**

Tray, 9-7/8" d, circular with extended rim and handles, etched, enameled blue, pink, and green floral cloisonné dec on handles, imp "Louis C. Tiffany Furnaces Inc., Favrile 512" under handle **460.00**

Twine holder, 3" h, Bookmark pattern, hexagonal form, hinged lid, reddish patina in lower recesses, imp "Tiffany Studios New York 905," minor spotting **1,035.00**

Glass, all Favrile
Bowl

4-1/8" d, ruffled rim, squat shouldered vessel, blue, polished pontil, inscribed "L.C. T./W56" **500.00**

4-3/8" d, 2-3/8" h, scalloped rim, small 10-ribbed bowl, gold, polished pontil inscribed "7373N 1104 L.C. Tiffany Inc., Favrile" **635.00**

4-1/2" d, scalloped rim, slightly ribbed vessel tapering to base, overall gold irid, polished pontil, inscribed "L.C.T.," light wear to irid **260.00**

7" d, wavy rim, 10-ribbed bowl, gold Favrile, inscribed "L.C.T. Favrile," light minor scratches **215.00**

7-3/4" d, wavy rim, 10-ribbed round body, gold Favrile, inscribed "L.C.T. Favrile" on base, polished pontil, minor scratches **815.00**

Bud vase, 13" h, 3-1/4" d, gold body, enameled green and gold circular base, stamped "Louis C. Tiffany Furnaces Inc" **900.00**

Cabinet vase, 2-1/2" h, bulbous, medial pulled green wave dec, gold irid, polished pontil, inscribed "L.C.T." on base, small scratches to irid . . **1,265.00**

Candlestick, 22-3/4" h, patinated bronze and favrile, ribbed floriform amber glass shade with shaded violet irid, fitted on circular knop, seven irid dark blue, purple, green, red, and amber irid turtle back cabochons, slender stem base, wide circular foot, imp "Tiffany Studios/New York/1213," shade inscribed "L.C.T." **9,750.00**

Carafe, 11" h, pinched ovoid body, elongated neck, topped with pinched and beaded stopper, ambergris, overall strong gold irid, polished pontil, base sgd "L. C. Tiffany Favrile 430," slight wear to rim **1,035.00**

Compote, 5-1/8" d, 2" h, stretched rim, shallow ftd bowl, blue **750.00**

Dish

5-1/4" d, 1-1/2" h, extended ruffled rim, round form, blue, inscribed "L. C. Tiffany Favrile 1034-1595m" **490.00**

Bud vase, floriform, bronze base and Favrile glass insert, ambers with pulled green and amber leaves, original patina, base stamped "TIFFANY STUDIOS, NEW YORK 1043," insert marked "LCT Favrile," 5" d, 12" h, $1,450. Photo courtesy of David Rago Auctions.

5-7/8" d, round rim, irid gold, inscribed "L.C.T.," paper label, polished pontil **215.00**

Finger bowl and underplate, 5-3/4" d bowl, 7" d underplate, eight-ruffled bowl, conforming underplate, fine gold stretched irid, both inscribed "L. C. T." **490.00**

Flower bowl, 12-1/2" d, circular, colorless body, brilliant gold irid vines and leaves, base inscribed "L. C. Tiffany Favrile 4034K" **980.00**

Jack-in-the-pulpit, lustrous amber gold irid body, flared and ruffled rim with stretched irid to edge, pink optic ribbed throat tapering to slender stem supported by bulbous base, inscribed "L. C. T. Y5472," paper label on button pontil, c1905 . . . . **14,950.00**

Nut dish, 4-1/8" d, 1-1/4" h, eight ribs and ruffled rim, irid gold, base inscribed "L. C. T." **375.00**

Rose bowl, 3-3/4" h, 10-ribbed form, ruffled rim, cobalt blue, overall blue irid luster, polished pontil sgd "L. C. Tiffany Favrile 1103-7725K," some scratches **865.00**

Salt, 2-3/8" h, swollen form, imp stylized floriform and zigzag border, gold, inscribed "L.C.T. Favrile" on base, polished pontil, price for pr **920.00**

Toothpick holder, irid glass, dimpled sides, etched "LCT" on base . . . **175.00**

Vase

4-1/4" h, stretched ruffled rim, bulbous bowl tapering to disk base, irid blue Favrile, inscribed "L.C. Tiffany Favrile 6128G" **2,185.00**

Desk set, Pine Needles pattern, green opalescent glass with bronze overlay, 16" l two-handled tray, letter-holder, inkwell with glass insert and hinged lid (#56), bronze match-pot, original patina, each stamped "TIFFANY STUDIOS, NEW YORK," cracks to glass in letter-holder and tray, chip to insert, $2,400. Photo courtesy of David Rago Auctions.

5" h, flared amber Favrile glass oval body, 25 tiny white cane blossoms among emerald green leaf leaves, amber stems, overall irid luster, inscribed "LCT Tiffany Favrile 2889C" around button pontil **2,415.00**

5-1/2" h, floriform, bulbous body, cobalt blue ground, wide flaring and ruffled rim, stretch irid to rim, strong blue luster, short stem, applied disk foot, inscribed "L. C. Tiffany, Favrile 9041E" **980.00**

6" h, floriform, blue, white and green hearts and vines dec, foot marked "5090 L. C. Tiffany Favrile" **4,800.00**

7" h, gold, high rounded shoulders with irid opal dec, marked "L. C. T. O1105" **3,250.00**

9" h, swollen body tapering to bulbed stem, amber, dec with trailing vines and heart leaves, applied dark foot, sgd "L. C. Tiffany - Favrile 5603G," bubbles below surface **1,840.00**

9-1/2" h, pale transparent amber crystal stem, peach-opal petal blossom, applied irid folded foot, marked "L. C. T. M1142," two folded blossom ribs **1,955.00**

10-1/4" h, 10-ribbed gourd form, flared and ruffled rim above bulbed top, round disk foot, blue irid, inscribed "L. C. Tiffany Favrile 1089-68201" **1,495.00**

13-1/2" h, cylindrical, amber gold irid glass, long green leaves, base marked "L. C. T.," inserted into elaborate dark and gold dore bronze holder stamped "Tiffany Studios New York 717" ... **1,495.00**

14-3/8" h, trumpet form, pulled green and irid gold feathers, inscribed "L.C.T. Favrile," gilt bronze acorn pattern mount imp "Tiffany Studios New York 1043" on base, crack and small chip near base .. **490.00**

Lamps

Boudoir, 15-1/2" h, dome shade, restored oviform base, irid gold glass dec with intricate intaglio carved green leaves, trailing budded vines, both sgd "L. C. Tiffany Favrile," shade also marked "5594L" **9,775.00**

Candle, 14-3/4" h, favrile, mismatched paneled shade with pink and blue accents, swirled ribs and bright gold with blue accents on base, peg candlestick with spring loaded socket fits into base, ring for shade, 1902

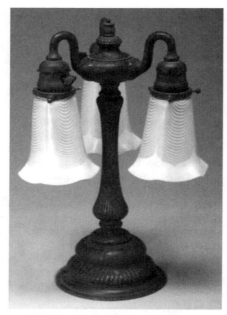

Table lamp, bronze, fluted base, three pendant fixtures, each with flaring white opalescent and green pulled feather art glass shade, base stamped "Tiffany Studios/New York," 17" x 11" $3,220. Photo courtesy of David Rago Auctions.

patent, etched label on shade "L. C. T. Favrle," base etched "L.C.T.," paper label "Tiffany Favrile, Registered Trademark," chip at top of shade **1,100.00**

Floor, 55" h, 10" d spun bronze shade, reflective white int., swing socket, shaft with stylized leaf motif, scroll foot circular base, base stamped "Tiffany Studios New York 425," pr ... **7,475.00**

Mantel lamp, 8" h, slight octagonal form, cream colored glass rising to bulbed top, caramel and gold pulled petal design, fitted gilt bronze and wood base **1,150.00**

Table

12-1/2" h, Nautilus, adjustable shell-form shade of striated green and white leaded glass segments, supported on bronze standard and cushion base, raised leaf dec, reddish-brown patina, base imp "Tiffany Studios New York 25891" and "Tiffany Glass and Decorating Company" mark, c1892-1902, 12-1/2" h **8,625.00**

22" w, 15-1/2" h, bronze, double branch, each branch with three irid glass shades, central bronze stem hollowed to one side to accept separate candle snuffer (missing), base imp "Tiffany Studios 10456"

on each glass shade, sgd "LCT" minor roughness on base of shades **12,500.00**

24" h, 16" d geometric mottled green glass tiles, band of irid favrile balls around center, shade sgd "Tiffany Studios, New York," bronze base with opaque medium green glass in latticework bottle shaped column, four leaf-shaped feet, stepped circular base, base sgd "Tiffany Studios, New York, #338", six small electric sockets, minor hairlines in a few glass tiles **77,500.00**

28-1/2" h, 22-1/2" d leaded glass globe shade, mottled green geometric slag glass segments progressively arranged, stamped "Tiffany Studios" on rim, four socket bronze standard, domed, stepped, circular base, stamped "Tiffany Studios New York 532" on base **19,550.00**

Silver
Bowl

5-3/4" d, 3" h, incised banding, everted rim, low domed foot, c1907-38, 11 troy oz **200.00**

9-1/4" h, 4-1/4" h, ftd, shaped edge with applied flowerhead and fern rim, stylized pad and paw feet with scrolled legs topped by acanthus leaves, center monogram, 1891-1902, 24 troy oz ... **1,610.00**

10-1/4" d, scalloped rim, foot ring marked "Tiffany & Co., Makers Sterling 23844, 26 troy oz . **660.00**

Trumpet vase, "Pulled Feather," with bronze stand, 12", $2,310. Photo courtesy of Jackson's.

Bread basket, 7" w, 10-3/4" l, oval, molded rim, center monogram, 1925-47, approx 12 troy oz **215.00**

Cake pate, 13-1/4" d, circular, shaped rim with molded foliate edge, face with reticulated and engraved bands, domed circular foot with engraved and reticulated dec, center monogram, c1908-1947, approx 47 troy oz
...................**1,955.00**

Candelabra, 12-1/4" h, three-light, cornucopia shoulder and central sconce, flanked by reeded scroll candle arms and further cornucopia sconces, plain columnar stem, foliate cornucopia and shell edge, round floral repoussé foot, removable beaded nozzles, sq base, 1902-07, 26 troy oz
...................**1,150.00**

Cigarette case, 3-3/8" x 2-1/4", rect, rounded corners, gold-washed ovoid push button clasp, gold-washed interior, engraved on front with name and date, suspended from silver link chain, c1907-38, 4 troy oz **90.00**

Cocktail set, 6-3/8" h cocktail shaker, six 4-1/8" cordial glasses, tapered ovoid shaker with hammered surface, engraved initials and date in base, glasses with conical bowl, baluster stem, plaint foot, monogrammed, c1875-91, 26 troy oz.........**865.00**

Compote, 15" w, 10" d, 5" h, wheat handles, engraved monogram **2,800.00**

Dresser set, 10 pcs, three brushes, comb, covered jar, receiving jar, hand mirror, shoe horn button hook, rect box, floral and scroll acid etched dec, gold-washed int. on jars and boxes, monogrammed, c1907-38, 23 troy oz
...................**1,850.00**

Flatware, silver gilt, English King pattern, 90 pcs...........**7,600.00**

Flask, 5-1/4" l, c1860-70, glass body, silver ball stopper, plain cap, monogrammed.............**175.00**

Asparagus server, footed square tray, lift-out pierced double handled serving tray, central monograms, marked "15158A Makers 2837" "C 1 and "2," 53 troy oz, 13" w, 10-1/2" d, 2-1/4" h, $1,450. Photo courtesy of James D. Julia, Inc.

Flower basket, flattened bell shape, flared sides, engraved husk drops and floral swags, reticulated to rim in guillouche pattern, overhead handle engraved with further husks, oval foot, 1907-38, pr, 26 troy oz......**2,645.00**

Iced tea spoon, 8" l, Bamboo pattern, molded bamboo form handles, set of four in Tiffany & Co. blue cloth bag in Tiffany box, mid-20th C.......**175.00**

Kettle on stand, 11-1/2" h, bulbous, domed lid, reeded bud finial, cast upright handle with leather mount, body with engraved band, circular stand with openwork skirt, three cast scroll legs with shell feet, 1916-47, 59 troy oz
...................**1,495.00**

Ladle, 11" l, Wave Edge, marked "Tiffany & Co., Sterling Pat 1884 M," 6 troy oz **320.00**

Muffiner, 7-1/2" h, 1891-1902, urn form body with bat's wing fluting below applied stylized leaf banding, spiral reeded stem, sq base, screw-in domed lid with paneled ball finial, 12 troy oz
...................**635.00**

Pitcher, 8-1/2" h, repoussé, waisted baluster form, ear handle, short spout, chased and emb all over with flowers and leaves, 1891-1902, 32 troy oz
...................**3,220.00**

Serving dish, 11-1/8" l, 5-1/2" h, crenelated banding, lid with ovoid handle flanked by anthemion, c1854-70, 41 troy oz.......**1,150.00**

Strawberry set, 11 strawberry forks, one sugar sifter, all gilt, twisted openwork handles and strawberry finials, early 20th C.........**1,800.00**

Stuffing spoon, 12-1/2" l, Chrysanthemum pattern, monogrammed, 8 troy oz **750.00**

Tea and coffee service, 8-1/2" h coffeepot, teapot, cov sugar, and creamer, all with Classical Revival-style embossing, paneled baluster coffeepot, angular handles, flattened urn finials, monogrammed, c1907-38, 69 troy oz
...................**3,750.00**

Tea service, Aesthetic Movement, 1895-91, 4-1/2" h teapot, creamer, cov sugar, three-molded cylindrical form, engraved Chinoiserie-style flowers, birds, and insects, rim border of stamped band of lozenges and flowerheads, teapot with short spout, foliate angular handle and ball finial, three foliate angular handles on sugar, engraved with Chinese-style letter monogram, 19 troy oz......**2,875.00**

Tray, 12-5/8" d, octagonal, ftd, molded guilloche rim, body with molded and engraved foliate scrolls with geometric panels, molded octagonal foot, monogrammed center, 1914-47, 35 troy oz...................**1,495.00**

Vase, cov, 16-3/4" h, flared rims, incised lines, stepped round bases, cov with wafers, elongated tear shaped finials, marked "Tiffany & Co. Makers, Sterling Silver," 65 troy oz, price for pr
...................**2,550.00**

TIFFIN GLASS

c1960

History: A. J. Beatty & Sons built a glass manufacturing plant in Tiffin, Ohio, in 1888. On January 1, 1892, the firm joined the U. S. Glass Co. and was known as factory R. Fine-quality Depression-era items were made at this high-production factory.

From 1923 to 1936, Tiffin produced a line of black glassware called Black Satin. The company discontinued operation in 1980.

Marks: Beginning in 1916, wares were marked with a paper label.

For more information, see this book.

Bowl, 10" l, 6-1/4" w, 4" h, Twilight, sq, ftd...................**290.00**

Bud vase, Fuchsia, crystal, 11" h
...................**100.00**

Celery, Flanders, pink........**140.00**

Champagne
    Cherokee Rose, crystal......**20.00**
    Flanders, pink.............**45.00**

Cocktail
    Byzantine, yellow...........**15.00**
    Cerise, crystal.............**28.00**
    Fuchsia, crystal............**20.00**
    June Night, crystal..........**20.00**

Compote, cov, #17523, Wisteria, crystal Cellini foot, two minute rim nicks
...................**395.00**

Console bowl, Fuchsia, crystal, flared, 12-5/8" d...................**135.00**

Cordial
    Cordelia, crystal **10.00**
    Flanders, pink.............**150.00**
    Fuchsia, crystal............**40.00**
    Persian Pheasant, crystal **45.00**

Cornucopia, Copen Blue, 8-1/4".**90.00**

Creamer, Flanders, pink, flat ...**230.00**

Cup and saucer, Flanders, yellow
...................**100.00**

Tumbler, #517 blown 12-ounce optic, classically influenced Eldorado etching, with griffin-like creature, c1920-29, 5" h, **$24.** *Photo courtesy of Michael Krumme.*

Close-up of Eldorado etching.

Decanter, Byzantine, crystal ... **600.00**
Goblet
　Cerise, crystal............. **25.00**
　Cherokee Rose, crystal...... **28.00**
　Flanders, crystal........... **88.00**
　Fuchsia, crystal............ **25.00**
Iced tea tumbler
　Cerise, crystal............. **28.00**
　Cherokee Rose, crystal, ftd .. **38.00**
Juice tumbler, ftd, Byzantine, crystal
.... **18.00**
Lamp, 8-1/2" h, 5" d, owl, rewired
.... **500.00**
Martini glass, 4-1/2" d, 3" h, Shawl Dancer, set of four........... **150.00**
Perfume bottle, 4" h, parrot, slate gray painted finish, enamel dec, orig label
.... **125.00**
Plate, Byzantine, yellow, 7-1/2" d **15.00**
Rose bowl, 5-1/2" x 5", Swedish Optic, citron green, c1960, mold #17430
.... **145.00**

Vase, Poppies, bulbous, bright blue frosted ground, 8" d, 8" h, **$115.**

Sherbet
　Cherokee Rose, crystal, tall... **24.00**
　Ramblin' Rose, crystal, low ... **23.00**
Sherry
　June Night, crystal.......... **30.00**
　Shawl Dancer, crystal **55.00**
Sugar
　Cerice, crystal............. **25.00**
　La Fleure, yellow **40.00**
　Vase 7-3/8" d, 14" h, crystal, artist sgd **400.00**
　8" h, Dahlia, cupped, Reflex Green, allover silver overlay **225.00**
　8-3/4" h, dark amethyst satin, poppy like flowers.............. **200.00**
Wall pocket, 9" l, 3-1/4" w, ruby. **175.00**
Water set, cov 12" h pitcher, Classic etch, Nile green handle, lid and foot, 11 8" h goblets with Nile green stem and foot, etched cameos of dancing girl
.... **1,750.00**
Wine
　Byzantine, crystal **18.00**
　Cherokee Rose, crystal **40.00**
　Fuchsia, crystal **35.00**

TILES

History: The use of decorated tiles peaked during the latter part of the 19th century. More than 100 companies in England alone were producing tiles by 1880.

By 1890, companies had opened in Belgium, France, Australia, c1875 Germany, and the United States.

Tiles were not used only as fireplace adornments. Many were installed into furniture, such as washstands, hall stands, and folding screens. Since tiles were easily cleaned

and, hence, hygienic, they were installed on the floors and walls of entry halls, hospitals, butcher shops, or any place where sanitation was a concern. Many public buildings and subways also employed tiles to add interest and beauty.

Notes: Condition is an important factor in determining price. A cracked, badly scuffed and scratched, or heavily chipped tile has very little value. Slight chipping around the outer edges of a tile is, at times, considered acceptable by collectors, especially if a frame can cover these chips.

It is not uncommon for the highly glazed surface of some tiles to have become crazed. Crazing is not considered detrimental as long as it does not detract from the overall appearance of the tile.

Art pottery, 6" h, 12" w, landscape with birds and moose in foreground, dark green high gloss glaze **175.00**
Arts & Crafts, 10" x 5-1/2", framed, scene of salt marsh landscape, blues, greens, and white, c1907 .... **2,100.00**
Batchelder, 6" h, 18" l, beige bisque clay with blue engobe, stamped "Batchelder/Los Angeles"
　Bouquet of flowers and birds, slight abrasion to surface **375.00**
　California desert landscape, abrasion to a few spots ... **850.00**
California Art, 8" h, 12" l scene of California courtyard with fountain, restored color and varnish, imp mark, mounted in Arts & Crafts frame **1,600.00**
Cambridge Art Tile, Covington, KY, 6" x 18"
　Goddess and Cherub, amber, pr
.... **250.00**
　Night and Morning, pr **500.00**
Claycraft
　6" x 12", horizontal, English thatched roof cottage next to foot bridge, semi-matte polychrome, mounted in period ebonized Arts and Crafts frame, covered stamp mark
.... **1,610.00**

Claycraft, 24-tile frieze depicting landscape in low relief, tall trees in shades of brown and green within half-round border, box frame, few small surface chips, 23" x 34" panel, **$7,475.** *Photo courtesy of David Rago Auctions.*

7-3/4" x 4", molded lone tree rising over ocean, matte polychrome glazes, stamped "Claycraft," mounted in new Arts & Crafts frame 815.00

13-1/4" h, 35" l, five tile faience panel, molded landscape of Mediterranean houses by sea, marks hidden by contemporary Arts & Crafts frame **2,400.00**

Grueby, 6-1/4" sq, mottled matte green glaze, mustard yellow blossom, ftd copper frame, raised indecipherable mark on base **1,100.00**

J. & J. G. Low, Chelsea, MA

4-1/4" sq, putti carrying grapes, blue, pr 75.00

6" d, circular, yellow, minor edge nicks and glaze wear 35.00

6" sq, woman wearing hood, brown 95.00

KPM, 5-3/4" x 3-3/8", portrait of monk, titled "Hieronymous of Ferrara sends this image to the prophet to God," small nicks to corners 245.00

Marblehead, 4-5/8" sq, ships, blue and white, pr 125.00

Minton China Works

6" sq, Aesops Fables, Fox and Crow, black and white 75.00

6" x 12", wild roses, polychrome slip dec .50.00

8" sq, Rob Roy, Waverly Tales, brown and cream 95.00

Minton Hollins & Co.

6" sq, urn and floral relief, green ground 45.00

Moravian, "Tempus," depicting Father Time, covered in blue and ivory glaze, red clay showing through, unmarked, small glaze flake to one edge, 10" x 7-1/4", $1,150. Photo courtesy of David Rago Auctions.

8" sq, Morning, blue and white 100.00

Moravian

10" x 7-1/4", Tempus, Father Time, blue and ivory glaze, red clay showing through, unmarked, small glaze flake on one edge. . 1,150.00

18" d, 1-1/2" h, Autumn, young man picking apples, basket at his feet, stamped "MR," made for Old Wicker Art School, Detroit, MI, 1920s, custom made wrought iron museum stand 5,750.00

Mosaic Tile Co., Zanesville, OH

6" sq, Fortune and the Boy, polychrome 80.00

8" sq, Delft windmill, blue and white, framed 55.00

Pardee, C.

4-1/4" sq, chick and griffin, blue-green matte 175.00

6" sq, portrait of Grover Cleveland, gray-lavender. 125.00

Providential Tile Works, Trenton, NJ, round, stove type, hold in center, flowered. 20.00

Rookwood Faience, 8" h, emb pink, ochre, and green geometric floral pattern, Arts & Crafts frame, stamped "RP," chips to corners 325.00

Sherwin & Cotton

6" sq, dog head, brown, artist sgd 100.00

6" x 12", Quiltmaker and Ledger, orange, pr. 145.00

Trent, 6" sq, head of Michelangelo, sea green glaze, sgd by Isaac Broome, imp mark. 115.00

U. S. Encaustic Tile Works, Indianapolis, IN

6" sq, wreath, flowered, emb, light green 20.00

6" x 18", panel, Dawn, green, framed 150.00

Wedgwood, England

6" sq, calendar, November, boy at seashore, peacock blue. . . . 95.00

8" sq, Tally Ho, man riding horse, blue and white 85.00

TINWARE

History: Beginning in the 1700s, many utilitarian household objects were made of tin. Because it is nontoxic, rust resistant, and fairly durable, tin can be used for storing food; and because it was cheap, tinware and tin-plated wares were in the price range of most people. It often was plated to iron to provide strength.

An early center of tinware manufacture in the United States was Berlin, Connecticut, but almost every small town and hamlet had its own tinsmith, tinner, or whitesmith. Tinsmiths used patterns to cut out the pieces, hammered and shaped them, and soldered the parts. If a piece was to be used with heat, a copper bottom was added because of the low melting point of tin. The industrial revolution brought about machine-made, mass-produced tinware pieces. The handmade era had ended by the late 19th century.

Anniversary top hat, 11" d, 5-3/4" h, 19th C. 1,150.00

Candle box, 14-1/2" h, cylindrical, hanging, some battering 220.00

Candle mold

12-1/2" l, 11-1/8" h, 24 tin tubes, double handles 350.00

17" w, 60 tubes, applied ear handles, minor corner break on base, couple spots resoldered . . . 495.00

Candle sconces, pr, 12-7/8" h, semicircular, candle socket and tall back with crimped crest, later white and green flowers, yellowed varnish, price for pr. 250.00

Cheese sieve, 6" h, heart shape, resoldered hanging ring. 360.00

Coffee pot, polychrome paint dec, America, mid-19th C, minor paint loss

8-3/4" h, straight spout, strap handle, green, yellow, and red floral dec, yellow flourishes at top and lid 865.00

10" h, goose neck spout, stylized floral dec front and back, embellishment on bottom . . 575.00

Cookie cutter

4-1/8" h, woman, long skirt, punched hole 90.00

Foot warmer, mortised and turned wood frame, punched tin sides with heart and circle design, wire bale handle at top, original tin tray for hot coals on interior, American, slight wear, 9" l, 7-3/4" w, 5-1/2" h, $200. Photo courtesy of Cowan's Historic Americana Auctions.

Snuffbox, oval, marked "Pat'd Jan. 24 1860 G. Parker," American, 3-1/4" l, $145. Photo courtesy of Sanford Alderfer Auction Company

4-3/4" l, tulip, scalloped edge **150.00**
6" h, stylized eagle **200.00**
7-1/4" l, elephant, seams loose
. . . . **100.00**
9-7/8" h, man with hat **195.00**
10" x 14-1/4", rocking horse, with handle **495.00**
12-5/8" h, Uncle Sam, full length, back marked "G.M.T. Co., Germany" **825.00**

Creamer, 4" h, polychrome spray of yellow, green, and red flowers beneath spout, attributed to New York, mid-19th C, minor paint loss . . . **200.00**

Foot warmer
7-3/4" x 9" x 5-3/4" h, punched panels with diamond designs, mortised frame with turned posts, wire bale handle, minor edge damage at post, wire latch missing
. . . . **110.00**
8-3/4" x 7-3/4" x 6" h, punched panels with heart in circle design, mortised wooden frame with turned posts and incised lines, wire bale handle, refinished **315.00**
9" x 7-1/2" x 5-5/8" h, punched panels with heart in circle design, mortised wooden frame with turned posts, old red stain, wire bale handle, traces of rust, penciled note inside **200.00**

Lamp
Grease, 1-5/8" h, colorful glaze
. . . . **165.00**
Petticoat, 4" h, orig whale oil burner, orig black paint **65.00**
Skater's, 6-3/8" h, light teal-green globe **225.00**

Lantern, 17-1/2" h, hanging, old dark green repaint, rococo detail, six panes of glass with reverse painted dec, candle socket in base, attributed to Ohio, one pane with corner missing
. . . . **420.00**

Quilt template, 4-5/8" d, star **30.00**
Shore bird, 9" l, 11-3/4" h, outstretched wings, curved tail, orig brown, white and black paint, some flaking, wooden base **295.00**
Tea bin, 8-3/4" w, 8" d, 10" h, painted red, litho portrait of pretty young lady, stenciled gold dec, America, 19th C, minor paint loss, price for pr . . . **750.00**
Teapot, 6-1/2" d, spout resoldered
. . . . **150.00**
Wall pocket, 6-3/4" w, 11-3/4" l, two tiers, extended round top back, punched hanging hole, America, 19th C, minor corrosion **115.00**
Wall sonces, pr, 8-1/4" d, 9-1/2" d, radiating mirrored segments on round tin reflector, crimped drip pan on single tin socket, American, 19th C, electrified, price for pr **1,120.00**

TINWARE, DECORATED

History: The art of decorating sheet iron, tin, and tin-coated sheet iron dates back to the mid-18th century. The Welsh called the practice pontypool; the French, tôle peinte. In America, the center for tin-decorated ware in the late 1700s was Berlin, Connecticut.

Several styles of decorating techniques were used: painting, japanning, and stenciling. Both professionals and itinerants did designs. English and Oriental motifs strongly influenced both form and design.

A special type of decoration was the punch work on unpainted tin practiced by the Pennsylvania tinsmiths. Forms included coffeepots, spice boxes, and grease lamps.

Box, cov, 13-3/4" l, 8-3/4" d, 9" h, dome top, wire and turned wooden handle on lid, yellow scrolled foliate designs, box with red and white swags, yellow leaf embellishments, black ground, America, 19th C **765.00**
Bread tray, 12-1/2" x 8-1/4", red, green, and yellow floral dec, yellow swag border, red edge, black ground, minor paint loss **345.00**
Canister, cylindrical, 6-1/4" h, 6" h, red cherries, green leaves, white border, yellow stylized leaves and swag borders, lid centered with leaf dec, red japanned ground, minor scratches
. . . . **400.00**
Coal scuttle, 15-1/2" l, 11-3/4" w, rect, sloped hinged lid, painted floral sprays and gold edging to three sides, top handle, coal scoop on back, four cast metal trefoil-paneled feet, removable

Coal hood, cast iron, brass, and ceramic mounts, S-curved lid, hp fight scene of European red deer, gilt stylized floral surround, top mounted cast white ware ceramic handle with brass mounts, cast iron feet with hidden casters, slot on rear for hand shovel, original hand shovel and interior liner (rusted) present, English, 30 percent gilt missing, painting with minor soil and scratches, 11-1/2" w, 17-1/2" deep, 17-1/2" h, $375. Photo courtesy of Cowan's Historic Americana Auctions.

liner, England/France, late 19th C
. . . . **245.00**
Coffeepot, cov, goose-neck spout, dome top
9-1/2" h, red, green, yellow, and white floral dec, black ground, crusty surface with some touch-up, rust on int., some battering **825.00**
10-1/2" h, yellow birds, red pomegranates, yellow stylized leaves, black ground, minor paint loss, lid unattached, repair to finial
. . . . **1,100.00**

Creamer, blue ground, red flowers, yellow details, wear, $225.

Fruit basket, Regency, japanned decoration, gilt decoration, black ground, English, some scratches, light fading, 12-1/4" l, 6-1/4" w, 3-1/2" h, $350. Photo courtesy of Cowan's Historic Americana Auctions.

10-5/8" h, flowers and foliage in shades of yellow, green, and red, black ground, America, 19th C, wear **765.00**

Creamer, hinged lid, 4-1/4" h, dark brown japanning, yellow, green, red, and white floral dec, some wear **525.00**

Deed box, dome top

6-3/4" w, 3-1/8" d, 3-5/8" h, orig dark brown japanning, white band on front panel, green leaves, red cherries, yellow border dec, wire bale handle, tin latch, slight wear **660.00**

8" w, 4" d, 4-3/4" h, black ground, yellow swags and lines, front with fruit, yellow, and green foliate, wire bale handle, tin hasp, minor wear, mostly to lid edges **250.00**

Document box, 11-1/2" w, 5" d, 6-1/4" h, dome top, brown japanning, red raped swags, yellow leaves, wavy lines, tin hasp, brass bale handle, int. lined with remnants of glue-on leaves, minor touch-up on front of lid and some edges, some wear **990.00**

Milk can, 8-1/2" h, black japanning, stenciled red and gold stylized floral design. **200.00**

Spice box, 7-1/4" d, round, seven int. containers, worn orig brown japanning, gold stenciled labels **175.00**

Sugar bowl, 3-1/2" h, worn orig red paint, brown and yellow comma type foliage, foot slightly battered . . . **190.00**

Tea caddy, 8-1/4" l, dark ground, worn stenciled bronze powder dec, int. lift-out tray fits over two lidded compartments, orig emb brass handle, minor damage **220.00**

Tray

20-3/8" x 28", three-masted ship *Red Jacket* at sea surrounded by ice floes, black ground, gilt border, cut-out handles, dent, minor wear **2,940.00**

28" l, oval, handles cut out to sides, scene of crags beside village painted in center, farmer and livestock in foreground, Europe, mid-19th C **500.00**

30" l, 24" w, oval, molded edge, large landscape scene painted in center, fruiting vine surround, *faux bois* woodgrained ground, mid-19th C **400.00**

Urn, cov13-1/4" h, slender stem, ovoid foot, gilt florals, birds, and butterflies, 19th C, pr **1,725.00**

Two handles, acorn finials, dec with floral sprays and birds, scalloped floral and repeating gilt leaf borders, weighted base, French, 19th C, some paint loss, minor dents, pr **575.00**

TOBACCO JARS

History: A tobacco jar is a container for storing tobacco. Tobacco humidors were made of various materials and in many shapes, including figurals. The earliest jars date to the early 17th century; however, most examples seen in the antiques market today were made in the late 19th or early 20th centuries.

Bear with beehive, 6-1/2" h, majolica, Continental **770.00**

Blackamoor, 6" h, majolica, marked "DEP" in circle, c1900, some restoration **330.00**

Black boy, red hat with tassel, majolica, repainted, nicks **275.00**

Bull dog, porcelain, German . . **275.00**

Hand painted by Florence Weaver, c1925, Indian bust, multicolored, gold trim and finial, initials on final, blank marked "Favorite, Bavaria," 7-1/4" h, $250.

White porcelain base with transfer decoration of pipes, cigarettes, cigars, matches, figural pipe on lid, 6-1/4" h, $90.

Creamware, 9" h, 6" d, plum colored transfers on side, one titled "Success to the British Fleet," striped orange, blue, and yellow molding, domed lid . **900.00**

Crystal, 7" h, hammered copper top, Roman coin dec, sgd "Benedict Studios" **250.00**

Dog's head, with pipe and green hat and collar, majolica **375.00**

Dwarf in sack, 8" h, terra cotta, multicolor dec, marked "JM3478," chips, wear. **255.00**

Girl on side, pipe on lid, majolica, Continental **75.00**

Indian, 5-1/2" h, black, majolica **330.00**

Jasperware, raised white Indian chief on cov, Indian regalia on front, green ground **195.00**

Majolica, 6" h, barrel shape, cobalt blue, green, gold, and brown, Doulton, Lambeth, England, #8481, artist's initials **225.00**

Mandarin, papier-mâché. **95.00**

Man with pipe, large bow tie, with match holder and striker, rim chips, hairline **165.00**

Man with top hat, majolica, Sarreguemines, hairline in base. **165.00**

Moose, porcelain, Austrian **200.00**

Owl, 11" h, majolica, brown, yellow glass eyes **825.00**

Rosewood, 12" l, 7-1/2" h, rect, four compressed bun feet, hinged lid, central compartment for mixing bowl flanked by two compartments for tobacco storage, removable lids, Continental, early 20th C **225.00**

Royal Winton, hp relief scene, marked "Royal Winton, England" **195.00**

Stoneware, 5" d, 6" h, applied Egyptian motif, brown ground, c1890 ... **130.00**

Toby type, Shorter and Sons ... **55.00**

Wave Crest, 5" sq, white opaque body, SP fittings.................. **450.00**

Wood, 7" l, 6-1/2" h, hand-carved walnut, knotty tree trunk, foreground of foliage, rabbit exiting his lair, flowering trumpet fine encircling vase, side inscribed "Viv Le Vin Lamour et le Tabac 1871," fitted lid with carved branch finial............... **320.00**

TOBY JUGS

History: Toby jugs are drinking vessels that usually depict a full-figured, robust, genial drinking man. They originated in England in the late 18th century. The term "Toby" probably is related to the character Uncle Toby from Tristram Shandy by Laurence Sterne.

Reproduction Alert: During the last 100 years or more, tobies have been copiously reproduced by many potteries in the United States and England.

Bennington type, 9-1/2" h, standing **175.00**

Delft, 11-1/4" h, man seated on barrel, green hat, green and black sponged coat, blue and yellow pants, old cork stopper, c19th C **365.00**

Luster ware, 6-1/2" h, blue coat, spotted vest, 19th C **175.00**

Majolica, 8-3/4" h, monk **165.00**

Royal Doulton, Neptune, D6652, 1960, 4" h, $75.

Minton, 11-1/4" h, majolica, Quaker man and woman, polychrome dec, imp mark, pr **4,600.00**

Portobello pottery, 10" h, standing, spatter enamel dec, orig cov, c1840 .... **275.00**

Pratt

9-1/4" h, pearlware glaze, typical blue, brown, and ochre palette, hat inset, small chips........ **425.00**

10-3/4" h, Hearty Good Fellow, blue jacket, yellow-green vest, blue and yellow striped pants, blue and ochre sponged base and handle, stopper missing, slight glaze wear, c1770-80............ **1,500.00**

Royal Doulton

2-3/4" h, The Fortune Teller .. **500.00**

4-1/2" h, Sam Weller, #d6265, "A" mark **190.00**

6-1/2" h, stoneware, blue coat, double XX, Harry Simson ..**395.00**

8-1/2" h, Falstaff, designed by Charles Noke, D6062, 1939-91 .... **175.00**

9" h, Winston Churchill, DT6171 .... **175.00**

Shaker, 5" h, polychrome dec, standing figure, yellow hat, blue coat, and red breeches with pink luster highlights, England, 19th C **150.00**

Staffordshire, seated man, tricorn hat, pitcher of ale on knee, polychrome decoration, indistinct mark, crack in lid, tiny rim flake on hat, 10-1/2" h, $745. Photo courtesy of Cowan's Historic

Shorter Son, Ltd., England, Long John Silver, 9-3/4" h **375.00**

Staffordshire

5-1/4" h, 4-1/4" h, seated, holding jug in one hand, glass in other, cobalt blue jacket, plaid vest, orange trousers, yellow hat, c1850 **235.00**

9" h, pearlware, seated figure, sponged blue jacket, ochre buttons, ochre and lavender speckled vest and trousers, brown hair and hat, green glazed base, shallow flake inside hat rim, attributed to Ralph Wood, c1770-80 .... **1,950.00**

9-1/4" h, Martha Gunn, translucent brown and ochre glazes, pearl body, brim repaired at hairline **1,265.00**

10-1/2" h, King Charles Spaniel, enamel dec, restored hat, late 19th C................. **275.00**

10-3/4" h, cat, enameled dec, holding letter, restored hat, late 19th C................. **300.00**

Stoneware, 6-1/2" h, blues, greens, and yellows, seated **75.00**

Whieldon, 9-1/2" h, pearlware, seated figure, yellow greatcoat, green vest, blue trousers, holding brown jug in left hand, raises foaming glass of ale towards mouth, lid missing, c1770-80 .... **1,600.00**

Wilkinson

10" h, Marshall Joffre, modeled by Sir Francis Carruthers Gould, titled "75mm Ce que joffre," printed mark, c1918, hat brim restored **345.00**

10-3/4" h, Field Marshall Haig, modeled by Sir Francis Carruthers Gould, titled "Push and Go," printed marks, c1917..... **460.00**

11-3/4" h, Winston Churchill, multicolored, designed by Clarice Cliff, black printed marks, number and facsimile signature, c1940 .... **825.00**

Yorkshire-Type, 7-3/4" h, caryatid form handle, Pratt palette dec, sponged base and hat brim int......... **750.00**

TOOLS

History: Before the advent of the assembly line and mass production, practically everything required for living was handmade at home or by a local tradesman or craftsman. The cooper, the blacksmith, the cabinetmaker, and the carpenter all had their special tools.

Early examples of these hand tools are collected for their workmanship, ingenuity, place of manufacture, or design. Modern-day craftsman often search out and use old hand tools in order to authentically recreate the manufacture of an object.

Broad ax, hand forged, early 1900s, 12-1/4" w blade, **$85.**

Anvil, hand forged, 8" **60.00**
Archimedian drill, bit, c1915 . . . **50.00**
Awl, bone, 5" l **25.00**
Bench press, Sherman, solid brass, 12 lbs, 9-1/2" x 6" **65.00**
Clamp, wood, jaws, 13-1/2" l, pr **115.00**
Chisel, blade stamped "E. Connor," 22-1/2" l **45.00**
Cooper's howel, L. & I. J. White, Buffalo, NY, No. 20, beechwood, 15" l
. . . . **225.00**
Drill, hand, Goodel and Pratt, brass ferrules **28.00**
File, half round, 20" l **15.00**
Hammer, claw type, Winchester . **55.00**
Key hole saw, British, 15-1/2" l . . **30.00**
Level, wood and brass
    Davis & Cook, patent "Dec, 1886"
    . . . . **45.00**
    Goodell-Pratt, brass bound mahogany, orig decal, 24" l . **225.00**
    Stanley, rosewood, patent 1896, 30" l
    . . . . **150.00**
Mallet, burl, hickory handle, 34" l
. . . . **200.00**
Mitre box, laminated maple, birch, and oak, graduated quadrant, Stanley
. . . . **45.00**
Plane
    Keen Kutter, K110 . . . . **45.00**

Sugar nips, wrought iron, engraved decoration, 9-3/4" l, **$165.** *Photo courtesy of Sanford Alderfer Auction Company.*

Ohio Tool Co., walnut, inscribed with carpenter's name, 9-1/2" l . . **25.00**
Stanley, #10-1/2 . . . . **120.00**
Varvill & Son, York, England, boxed bead molding planes, 9-1/2" l, 10-pc set **595.00**
Winchester Repeating Arms Co. No. 3208, smoothing, metallic, mahogany handles, 9" l . . . **185.00**
Router, Stanley, #71-1/2", patent date 1901 . . . . **40.00**
Rule, Stanley, #32, two-fold, 12" l, caliper **120.00**
Saw
    Band, mortised and pinned wood frame, orig red paint with blue and white striping, black and lade guides, laminated cherry and maple top, 76" **300.00**
    Buck, wood, worn varnish finish, marked "W. T. Banres," 30" . **45.00**
    Dovetail, Hague, Clegg & Barton, brass back, 9" l **95.00**
    Turning, W. Johnson, Newark, NJ, Richardson blade, 21" l . . . **165.00**
Screwdriver, flat wood handle, round sides, 9" blade **35.00**
Scribe, curly maple adjustable fence and arm, 21" l **75.00**
Shoot board, Stanley, No. 51/52, orig decal, 14" l **1,295.00**
Square, cherry, iron, brassbound blade, marked "Set Tray" **50.00**
Sugar auger, New England, 19th C, dual turned wooden handle, corkscrew-shaped wrought iron implement, black metal stand, 9-1/2" w, 15" h **230.00**
Wagon wrench **30.00**
Wheel measure, wrought iron, 14-1/2" l
. . . . **45.00**

TOOTHPICK HOLDERS

History: Toothpick holders, indispensable table accessories of the Victorian era, are small containers made specifically to hold toothpicks.

They were made in a wide range of materials: china (bisque and porcelain), glass (art, blown, cut,

Keyhole saw, British, 15-1/2" l, **$30.**

For more information, see this book.

opalescent, pattern, etc.), and metals, especially silver plate. Makers include both American and European firms.

By applying a decal or transfer, a toothpick holder became a souvenir item; by changing the decal or transfer, the same blank could become a memento for any number of locations.

Additional Listings: See *Warman's Americana & Collectibles* for more examples.

Bisque, skull, blue anchor-shape mark
. . . . **68.00**
Burmese, 2-1/2" h, shiny, soft peach blush fading to buttery-yellow, eggshell-thin body **425.00**
China
    Royal Bayreuth, elk **120.00**
    Royal Doulton, Santa scene, green handles **75.00**
    R. S. Germany, Schlegelmilch, MOP luster **40.00**
Glass
    Amberina, DQ, sq top **350.00**
    Cameo, Daum Nancy, winter scene, sgd **750.00**
    Cranberry, coralene beaded flowers
    . . . . **285.00**
    Cut, pedestal, chain of hobstars
    . . . . **145.00**
    Libbey, Little Lobe, hp violets, blue beading around top **250.00**
    Opalescent, Reverse Swirl, blue
    . . . . **85.00**

Amberina toothpick holder, inverted thumbprint type optic, made by New England Glass Company, Hobbs Bruckunier, or Libbey, late 19th century, hand-crimped ruffled edge, nice shading, ground pontil, and considerable wear on base, 3-1/4" d, 2-1/2" h, **$85.** *Photo courtesy of Michael Krumme.*

Burmese, Mt. Washington, flared painted blue rim, white blossoms with yellow centers, molded ferns and scrolls at base, 2-1/2" h, $1,085. Photo courtesy of Clarence and Betty Maier.

Pattern glass

Arched Fleur-De-Lis	45.00
Carnation, Northwood	75.00
Daisy and Button, blue	75.00
Delaware, rose stain, gold dec	175.00
Fandango, Heisey	55.00
Hartford, Fostoria	85.00
Jewel with Dewdrop	55.00
Kansas	45.00
Kentucky, green, gold trim	125.00
Michigan, clear, yellow stain	175.00
Paneled 44, Reverse, platinum stain	75.00

Texas, gold trim	50.00
Truncated Cube, ruby stained	75.00
US Coin, colorless, frosted Morgan one dollar coin, c1892	290.00

TORTOISESHELL ITEMS

History: For many years, amber and mottled tortoiseshell has been used in the manufacture of small items such as boxes, combs, dresser sets, and trinkets.

Note: Anyone dealing in the sale of tortoiseshell objects should be familiar with the Endangered Species Act and Amendment in its entirety. As of November 1978, antique tortoiseshell objects can be legally imported and sold with some restrictions.

Also see *Celluloid* for imitation tortoiseshell items.

Bellows, 20-1/8" l, 8" w, Continental, late 19th C, coromandel backing, front with premier part Renaissance-style scroll inlay, woven leather panel over brass tip 575.00

Box, cov, 2-1/2" d, 1" h, enamel insert on lid surrounded by gold band, hp enamel with seated woman in garden looking into mirror held by putti, French, loss to tortoise shell 450.00

Cane, 35-1/3" l, 2-1/3" w x 3-1/2" h carved handle, crook head of swan preening feathers, 1" gold-plated collar dec with diagonal lines and orig owner's initials, briarwood shaft, 1-1/3" white metal and iron ferrule, American, c1890, minor roughness to beak **700.00**

Cigar case

5-1/2" l, rect, case inlaid with three-color gold, reserve with vacant silver cartouche, hinged, pink silk lined int., fitted, expandable, Victorian, 19th C 450.00

5-5/8" x 2-7/8", rect, silver inlaid crane and foliate stalks, brass border with clasp, silk lined int., monogrammed, Continental, late 19th C 550.00

Cigarette case, 4-1/4" l, domed oval, applied central carved monogram, Continental, late 19th/early 20th C 325.00

Clock, mantel, 4-3/8" w, 3-1/2" d, 9-1/8" h, George III-style, early 20th C, balloon shape, enamel dial with Roman numerals, silver plated banding on front, four plated ball feet 950.00

Clock, travel, 4-3/8" l, 3-3/4" w case, 3-3/4" l watch, London, c1910, rect black morocco case with tortoiseshell panel on front in silver surround, enclosing nickel-cased watch with eight day movement 290.00

Comb and hairpin, gold lacquer dec, Japan 230.00

Diary, 3-3/4" x 2-5/8", silver inlaid floral bouquet and bird, silk lined int. fitted with pencil, monogrammed, French, late 19th C 400.00

Display case, 21" w, 11-1/2" d, 19-1/2" h, veneer and ebonized, pieced gallery with finials over single door, conforming base, ebonized compressed bun feet, Dutch . **1,080.00**

Dresser box, 4" l, 3-1/2" w, 2-1/8" h, Birmingham, England, 1901, maker's

California pattern, aka Beaded Grape, green, beaded edge, worn gold trim, 2-1/2" h, $65.

Bottle from traveling case, mushroom-shaped threaded tortoise shell lid, nickel and cork stopper, 19th C, 5" h, $170. Photo courtesy of Cowan's Historic Americana Auctions.

Hair comb, intricately carved 3-1/2" w band, 4" l prongs, $65.

Snuffbox, dark tortoise shell box, white beaded floral designs covered with glass and gold band edge, inscribed "Belonged to Jedida Dewer in 1784," losses, 3" d, $275. Photo courtesy of Sanford Alderfer Auction Company.

mark "L. & S.," heart shape, hinged lid with tortoiseshell inlaid with silver harp and ribbon tied husk swags, husk surround, velvet-lined interior, three short ball and claw feet **575.00**

Dressing table mirror, 7" w, 5-1/4" d, 8-1/4" h, Regency-style, mid-19th C, oval mirror plate in ivory surround, round ivory standards on tortoiseshell columns, ormolu finial, breakfronted with tortoiseshell and ivory base, four ormolu female herm supports **1,265.00**

Etui, 1-7/8" w, 1-1/2" d, 3-1/2" h, French, mid-19th C, tapered rect form, hinged

Tea caddy, two compartments on interior with tortoiseshell lids and ivory surround, pine frame covered with tortoise shell, satinwood bun feet, original foil lining, English, 19th C, 6" l, 3-1/2" d, 4-1/2" h, $2,600. Photo courtesy of Cowan's Historic Americana Auctions.

lid with sloping sides, scalloped silver mounts at edges, fitted int. with four utensils, glass perfume bottle . . **550.00**

Hair comb, row of rose-cut diamonds spaced by bezel-set oval rubies, mounted in silver-topped gold, Edwardian, French hallmarks, price for pr **1,645.00**

Lorgnette, 3-1/2" l closed, silver border with floral details, applied tortoiseshell over engine-turned ground, lever action, maker's mark rubbed, Continental, late 19th C **150.00**

Miniature, mandolin, 5-1/4" l, tortoiseshell, ivory, and mother-of-pearl, Continental **175.00**

Razor box, 7" l, 3" w, 1-3/4" h, rect box set with stylized monogram on lid, gold mountings, ebonized bun feet, William Comyns & Sons, London, c1904-5, sold with four ivorine straight razors (three Wilkinson, one German) **1,150.00**

Scent box, 2-1/4" h, trapezoid, blond tortoiseshell veneer, divided int. compartments, late Regency, c1825, scent bottles missing. **375.00**

Snuffbox, 3-3/8" l, 1-7/8" w, 1-1/8" d, book form, realistically modeled, tortoiseshell on front and back, cover set with oval silver plate formal miniature of 18th C boy and girl, sgd lower left "D. Drouris(?)" **350.00**

Tea caddy, English, late 18th/early 19th C

4-3/4" w, 3-3/8" d, 4-3/8" h, rect, hinged lid, small brass plate and escutcheon, int. fitted with tortoise shell veneered cover, some small losses **885.00**

Tea caddy, English, early 19th C, tortoise shell veneered, ivory mounts, silvered-copper ball feet, escutcheon and monogrammed reserve, interior with two covered compartments, 6-3/4" w, $1,800. Photo courtesy of Sloan's Auctioneers & Appraisers.

6-3/4" w, 3-5/8" d, 4-1/2" h, rect, light matched panels, domed lid with plain silvered plaque, plain sq escutcheon, hinged lid opening to two lidded wells **2,185.00**

7-5/8" w, 4" d, 4-1/4" h, rect, dark mottling, serpentine front, silvered escutcheon and lid with monogrammed silvered cartouche, hinged lid opening to two lidded compartments, bands of ivory veneer at perimeter, molded base **2,530.00**

TOYS

History: The first cast-iron toys began to appear in America shortly after the Civil War. Leading 19th-century manufacturers include Hubley, Dent, Kenton, and Schoenhut. In the first decades of the 20th century, Arcade, Buddy L, Marx, and Tootsie Toy joined these earlier firms. George Brown and other manufacturers who did not sign or label their work made wooden toys.

Nuremberg, Germany, was the European center for the toy industry from the late 18th through the mid-20th centuries. Companies such as Lehman and Marklin produced high-quality toys.

Today's toy collectors have a wonderful assortment to choose from. Many specialize in one company, time period, or type of toy, etc. Whatever their motivation, their collections bring joy. Individual collectors must decide how they feel about the condition of their toys, whether they prefer mint-in-the-box or gently played with examples or perhaps even toys that have been played with extensively. Traditionally, the toys in better condition have retained their values more than those in played-with condition. Having the original box, instructions, and/or all the pieces, etc., adds greatly to the collectiblity, and therefore the value.

Toy collectors can find examples to add to their collections at most of the typical antique and collectibles marketplaces, from auctions to flea markets to great antique shows, like Atlantique City, and even shows and auctions that specialize only in toys.

Additional Listings: Characters, Disneyana, Dolls, and Schoenhut. Also see *Warman's Americana & Collectibles* and *Warman's Flea Market* for more examples.

Notes: Every toy is collectible; the key is condition. Good working order is important when considering mechanical toys. Examples in this listing are considered to be at least in good condition, if not better, unless otherwise specified.

Arcade, USA
Ambulance, No. 187, 1932, 7-3/4" l
. . . . **400.00**
Auto, cast iron
Chevrolet, sedan, 1925, 7" l . **450.00**
Desoto, sedan, painted gray, nickeled grill and bumper, decal on trunk reads "Sundial Shoes," rubber tires, 4" l **130.00**

Arcade, Greyhound bus, Century of Progress, Chicago, 1933, cast iron, painted white and white, original label, rubber tires, 11-1/2" l, $425.

Ford coupe, Model A, No. 106, rumble seat, 1928, 6-3/4" l . **295.00**

Ford sedan, No. 1620X, 1933, 6-7/8" l **350.00**

Pontiac sedan, 1932, 6-1/2" l **350.00**

Dump truck, cast iron, International Harvester, painted green, red chassis, yellow pressed steel dump body, 11-1/4" l **275.00**

Fire trailer truck, red, blue fireman, detachable trailer, hose reel and ladder turntable, 16" l, ladders missing, paint loss **325.00**

Ice truck, cast iron, Mack, railed open bed body, rear platform, rubber tires, emb sides, painted blue, 6-7/8" l **275.00**

Milk truck, cast iron, Borden's, painted green, classic milk bottle design, rubber tires **1,430.00**

Pick-up truck, cast iron, "International" decals on door, painted bright yellow, black rubber tires, 9-1/4" l, some rust on left side **330.00**

Racer, Bullet, cast iron, classic bullet-shaped body, painted red, nickeled driver and mechanic, side pipes, and disc wheels, emb "#9" on side **550.00**

Stake truck
Chevrolet, 1925, 9" l **800.00**
Ford Model T, 1927, 9" l **600.00**
Mack, No. 246X, 1929, 12" l **1,400.00**

Arcade, Farmall tractor, driver, disc, cast metal, $740. Photo courtesy of Joy Luke Auctions.

Tank, cast iron, camouflage painting, large metal wheels, 7-1/4" l **330.00**

Taxi, cast iron, painted blue, black trim, emb luggage rack, seated driver and passenger, rubber tires, 8-1/4" l. **660.00**

Thresher, McCormick-Deering, gray and cream wheels, red lining, chromed chute and stacker, 12" l **320.00**

Tractor, cast iron
Farmall, "A", No. 7050, 1941, 7-1/2" l **475.00**
Fordson, No. 273, 1928, 3-7/8" l **95.00**
McCormick-Deering, No. 10-20, 1925, 6-3/4" l **300.00**

Trolley, Greyhound, New York World's Fair, blue and orange, nickel driver, decals, three cars with tinplate canopies, black tires, 16" l, some chipping and scratching **635.00**

Wrecker, cast iron
Ford Model T, 11" l, 1927.... **700.00**
Mack, No. 255, 1930, 12-1/2" l **1,500.00**
Plymouth, No. 1830, 1933, 4-3/4" l **350.00**

Arnold, USA

Cycle, turquoise, no longer sparks **650.00**

Ocean liner, twin funnels, white superstructure, black and red hull, tinplate, clockwork motor, lg. 13 in. **460.00**

Bing, Gebruder, Germany

Auto, tin, clockwork, center door model, black, seated driver, radiator cap ornament, spare tire on rear, 6-1/4" l **385.00**

Garage, litho tin, double doors, extensive graphics, houses sedan and roadster **550.00**

Limousine, litho tin wind-up, red, maroon and orange striping, orig driver, c1910, 5-1/4" l............... **690.00**

Open tourer, four seater, litho tinplate, gray-green, black and yellow lining, red button seats, black wings, front steering, orange and gray wheels, twin lamps, windscreen frame, hand-brake operated clockwork motor, c1915, 12-1/2" l, chauffeur missing, lamps detached **2,400.00**

Touring car, driver, tinplate, clockwork motor, front steering, 6-1/2" l.... **230.00**

Union ferry boat, hand-painted tin, clockwork, red hull, brown open deck, white deck housing, railing on side, window cut-outs on both sides, stack on roof, 12" l **1,200.00**

Borgfeldt, George, NY

Pluto the Pup, articulated wood, orig maker's box, 6" l **920.00**

Buddy L, USA

Airmail truck, black front, hood fenders, enc cab, red body and chassis, 1930, 24" l **675.00**

Airplane
Catapult airplane and hangar, 5000 Monocoupe, olive/gray hangar, 1930, 9-7/8" wingspan **950.00**
Four-engine transport, monoplane, green wings, yellow fuselage and twin tails, 1949, 27" wingspan **200.00**

Auto
Country Squire Wagon, off-white, brown woodgrain side panels, 1963, 15-1/2" l **85.00**
Flivver coupe, black, red spoke wheels, aluminum tires, 1924, 11" l **775.00**
Jr Camaro, metallic blue body, white racing stripes across hood, 1968, 9" l **50.00**

Cement mixer truck, red body, white side ladder, water tank, mixing drum, 1965, 15-1/2" l **75.00**

Dump truck
Flivver, black, drop-down endgate, 11" l, 1926 .... **700.00**
Husky, yellow hood, chrome one-pc wraparound bumper, 1969, 14-1/2" l **75.00**
Hydraulic Construction, medium blue front, large green dumper, 1967, 15-1/4" l **50.00**
Jr Dumper, avocado cab, tiltback dump section, 1969, 7-1/2" l **335.00**
Utility, done-tone slant design, red front, gray chassis, royal blue dump body, yellow seat, 1940, 25-1/2" l **175.00**

Electric Emergency Unit wrecker, white pressed steel, rear hoist, 16-1/2" l, paint wear and staining....... **215.00**

Buddy L, steam shovel, pressed steel, $285.

Express Line delivery truck, black pressed-steel, front steering and rear doors, 24" l **750.00**

Fire truck

Aerial truck, red, nickel ladders, 1925, 39" l **850.00**

Extension ladder, rider, duo-tone slant design, white front, red hood top, cab, and frame, red semi-trailer, white ladders, 1949, 32-1/2" l **150.00**

GMC fire pumper, red, aluminum finish ladders, chrome bar grille, horn, 1958, 15" l **150.00**

Ladder truck, red, bright metal grille and headlights, two white ladders, 1939, 24" l **100.00**

Greyhound bus, pressed steel, clockwork, bright blue and white, "Greyhound Lines" on sides, rubber tires, 16" l **275.00**

Outdoor railroad, No. 1000 4-6-2 locomotive and tender, No. 1001 caboose, No. 1003 tank, No. 1004 stock, No. 1005 coal cars (one with orig decal), 121-1/2" l, repainted . . **1,840.00**

Set

Fire department set, aerial truck, fire pumper with action hydrant, two plastic hoses, two plastic firemen, fire chief's badge, 1960 . . . . **250.00**

GMC Highway Maintenance Fleet, orange truck, trailer, sand and stone dump truck, scoop-n-load conveyor, sand hopper, steel scoop shovel, four white steel road barriers, 1957 . . . . **300.00**

Road builder set, green and white cement mixer, yellow and black bulldozer, red dump truck, husky dumper, 1963 . . . . **200.00**

Western Roundup set, turquoise fenders, hood, cab and frame, white flatbed cargo section, six sections of rail fencing, standing horse, cowboys, calf, steer, 1960 . . . . **175.00**

Steam shovel, No. 220, black, red corrugated roof and base, cast wheels, boiler, decal and winch, 14" h, surface rust, paint crazing on roof **115.00**

Telephone maintenance truck, No. 450, two-tone green, ladder, two poles, orig maker's box **350.00**

Tractor

Husky, bright yellow body, large rear fenders, black engine block, 1966, 13" l **50.00**

Ruff-n-Tuff, yellow grille, hood, and frame, black plastic engine block, 1971, 10-1/2" l **50.00**

Wrecker, orig condition **3,950.00**

Buffalo Toys

See-Saw, litho tin, boy and girl seated at each end of plank, 14" l **275.00**

Carette, Germany

Lighthouse, hand-painted tin, clockwork, central lighthouse, railed deck on each side hovers over tin water basin where boat with seated driver circles, 11" h, 10" d **715.00**

Cast iron, unknown American makers

Dump truck, green Mack style front, C-cab, red bed with spring lever, spoked nickel wheels, 7-3/4" l . . **490.00**

Gasoline truck, blue, Mack-style front, C-cab, rubber tires, one tire missing. 7" l **200.00**

Milk wagon, black cast-iron horse, gilt harness, yellow wheels, blue steel wagon body, 6-3/4" l **150.00**

Stake truck, Ford Model A, red, 7" l **200.00**

Champion

Auto, cast iron, coupe, painted red, nickeled grill and headlights, rumble seat, rubber tires, spare mounted on trunk, 7" l, repainted **250.00**

Gasoline truck, cast iron, painted red, Mack "C" cab, tanker body, emb on sides, rubber tires, 8-1/8" l **385.00**

Panel truck, cast iron, enclosed panel van, cast spare tires and headlights, traces of orig blue paint, spoked metal wheels, 7-1/2" l, poor condition . **180.00**

Racer, cast iron, painted red, silver trim, wind deflector on rear, separately cast driver painted blue, nickeled disc wheels, 8-1/2" l **1,815.00**

Stake truck, cast iron, painted red, Mack "C" cab, stake side body, nickeled spoke wheels, 7" l **660.00**

Truck, cast iron, "C" Mack cab, blue body, 7-3/4" l, replaced wheels . **195.00**

Wrecker, cast iron, red C-cab with crane, nickel plated crank and barrel, rubber tires, 8-1/4" l **330.00**

Chein

Barnacle Bill, tinplate, red hat, clockwork walking mechanism, 6-1/4" h **290.00**

Disneyland ferris wheel, clockwork motor, bell, six gondolas, litho Disney characters and fairgrounds scenes, 16-3/4" h, distortion and paint loss **350.00**

Chein, Popeye with parrot cages, litho tin windup, walks forward rolling cages at side, 8-1/2" h, $230. Photo courtesy of James D. Julia, Inc.

Hercules ferris wheel, clockwork motor, bell, six gondolas, litho children and fairground scenes, 16-1/2" l **325.00**

Wagon, horse-drawn, "Fine Groceries," tinplate, 12" l **290.00**

Chromolithograph paper on wood, unknown maker

Bagatelle game, two clowns with cup hats, patent date "March 7, 1895," 15" l **290.00**

Battleship *Texas*, sides printed with anchor, guns, and gangway, deck with two wood cannons, funnel, mast, one flag pole, second one detached, red flag, attached manuscript Christmas tag, 14" l **490.00**

Brownie Ten Pins, set of 10 different Palmer Cox Brownie figures, each with printed poem on reverse about their character, © Palmer Cox 1892, two mallets and three balls, wood box **1,150.00**

Noah's Ark, incised and applied dec, hinged roof, four carved humans, 40 animals, 19" l hull **750.00**

Trinity Chimes, eight chimes, cathedral scenes, upright case, 18" h **150.00**

Citroen, France

Aviation fuel truck, pressed steel, clockwork, painted red, enclosed cab with opening driver's door, tanker body with filler cap and brass drain valve, electric headlights, rear decal "AVIA," 18" l **1,350.00**

5CV, open tourer, two-seat, blue boat tail body, black wings and wheels, gray tires, front steering and clockwork motor, orig maker's box, 12" l . **2,070.00**

Fire engine, painted tin, clockwork, red, open bench seats, removable hose reel, ladders mount on rear body, disc wheels, rubber tires, orig box, 18" l **2,900.00**

Race car, pressed steel, clockwork, blue, molded seated figure with hand painted composition head, rubber tires, decal "Petite Rosalie," 12-1/4" l. **450.00**

Converse, USA

Heffield Farms delivery wagon, articulated horse, 21-1/2" l, considerable wear and paint loss **320.00**

Klondike Ice Co. delivery wagon, tinplate on wood, two litho horses, 17" l, paint poor **175.00**

Trolley, open sides, pressed steel, blue and mustard, stenciled dec, marked "City Hall Park 175" on both ends, reversible benches, large clockwork motor, 16" l, paint poor, destination boards missing **260.00**

Corgi

Ambulance, Chevrolet Superior, white body, orange roof, Red Cross decals, 4-3/4" l **30.00**

Auto

Chevrolet Impala, pink body, 4-1/4" l **50.00**

Corvette Sting Ray, metallic silver, 3-3/4" l **60.00**

Datsun 240Z, red body **15.00**

Ford Escort 13 GL, red, blue, or yellow body **8.50**

Ford Mustang Fastback, metallic lilac, metallic dark blue, silver, or light green body **30.00**

Ford Zephyr Estate Car, light blue, 3-7/8" **30.00**

Jeep CJ-5, dark metallic green body **10.00**

Mercedes-Benz 240D, silver, blue, or copper body, working trunk . **10.00**

MGA, red or metallic green body **60.00**

Porsche Carrera 6, white body, red or blue trim **30.00**

Renault 16TX, metallic blue body **20.00**

Volkswagen 1200 Driving School **25.00**

Camera van, Commer Mobile, metallic blue body, black camera on gold tripod, cameraman, 3-1/2" **60.00**

Car transporter, Bedford, black diecast cap, 10-1/4" l **100.00**

Character cars

Batmobile, glossy black body, gold tow hook **200.00**

Captain Marvel Porsche, white body, 4-3/4" l **20.00**

Hardy Boys Rolls-Royce, red body, yellow hood **70.00**

James Bond Aston Martin, metallic silver body, diecast base, red int., two figures, working roof hatch, ejector seat **100.00**

Kojak's Buick Regal, metallic bronze brown body **25.00**

Popeye's Paddy Wagon **195.00**

Saint's Volvo P-1800, white body, silver trim **55.00**

Supervan, silver, Superman decals, 4-5/8" l **15.00**

Helicopter, Chopper Squad, blue and white body **20.00**

Set

Agricultural, No. 55 Fordson Tractor, No. 51 Tipping Trailer, No. 438 Land Rover, No. 101 Flat Trailer, 1962-64 . . . . **280.00**

All Winners, No. 310 Corvette, No. 312 Jaguar XKE, No. 314 Ferrari, No. 324 Marcos, No. 325 Mustang, first series **100.00**

British Racing Cards, No. 152 Lotus, No. 151 PRM, No. 150 Vanwall, 1959 . . . . **150.00**

Corporal Missile, No. 112 missile, No. 1113 ramp, No. 1118 army truck **350.00**

Emergency set, No. 339 Land Rover police car, No. 921 police helicopter **30.00**

Tarzan, metallic green No. 421 Land Rover, trailer, dinghy, cage, five figures **100.00**

Tank truck, Mack Exxon, white cap and tank, red tank chassis, 10-3/4" l . . **15.00**

Taxi

Austin, London, black, yellow plastic int. **35.00**

Peugot 505, cream body, red int. **10.00**

Thunderbird Bermuda, white body, 4" l **50.00**

Tractor, Ford 5000, blue body, yellow scoop arm and controls, chrome scoop, 3-1/8" l **55.00**

Cor-Cor

Automobile, Graham, 1936, 20" l, pressed steel

Brown and beige, full running boards, black rooftop, electric headlights, spare disc wheels, emb "Cor-Cor Toys," chromed grill and rubber tires, restored **935.00**

Green, electric headlights, switch on side, rubber tires, metal wheels, chromed grill, restored **660.00**

Bus, sheet metal construction, green, orange wheels, "Inter City" decals on side, bench seats diecut from window wells, 23-1/2" l **990.00**

Dump truck, black body, orange bed and wheels, pressed steel, 23-1/2" l **260.00**

Stake truck, sheet-metal construction, black, brown stake body and rear platform, rubber tires, emb "Cor-Cor" on sides **770.00**

Truck, sheet-metal construction, enclosed black cab, green van body, rear platform, large painted metal wheels, 23" l **825.00**

Cragston

Robot, 10-1/2" h, battery-operated tinplate, silver-gray body, red arms and chest, domed clear-plastic head with visible mechanism, orig maker's box **1,725.00**

Shuttling freight train, locomotive, two wagons, accessories, orig box and wrapping **90.00**

Dayton Friction Co.

Patrol wagon, pressed metal and wood, friction driven, painted red, stenciled "Police Patrol" on front panel, seated driver on open bench seat, spoke wheels. 10" l **200.00**

Touring car, pressed metal, painted red, gold spoke wheels, open sides, friction driver, 12" l **470.00**

Dent, USA

Auto, sedan, 1930, cast iron, painted blue, partial black paint on roof, nickeled wheels, spare on rear, 7-1/2" l, repainted **330.00**

Cragstan, Mechanical Monkey Batter, painted tin windup, 7-1/2" h, original box, $750. Photo courtesy of Joy Luke Auctions.

Contractor's truck, cast iron, Mack, painted red, dual dump gondolas, open frame, nickeled disc wheels, painted centers, emb on sides, 7-1/2" l **1,050.00**

Dump truck, cast iron, green-gray, Mack-style front, C-cab, driver, red spoked wheels, spring-operated bed, swinging tailgate, 7" l, paint loss **320.00**

Fire patrol, cast iron, open-seat truck, rail sided open-bed body, rear platform, disc wheels, 5-3/4" l **220.00**

Taxi, cast iron, painted orange and black

Repainted seated driver, replaced painted disc wheels **315.00**
Seated figure, painted disc wheels, spare disc wheel on rear, 7-1/2" l **385.00**

Transfer wagon, cast iron, open seat, wagon painted orange, flared sides, seated driver on full width bench set and splash board sides, marked "Transfer," yellow spoked wheels, pulled by three horses, 18" l . . **1,100.00**

Dinky
Airplane
Autogyro, gold, blue rotor, 1934-41 . . . . **90.00**
Bristol Beinhem, 1956-63 . . . . **20.00**
Douglas DC3, silver, #60t, 1937-41 . . . . **125.00**
Lockheed Constellation, #66b, 1940 . . . . **70.00**
Percival Gull, camouflaged, #66c, 1940 . . . . **100.00**
Twin Engine Fighter, silver, #70d/731, 1946-55 . . . . **10.00**

Ambulance
Range Rover, #268, 1974-78 . . **25.00**
Superior Criterion, #263, 1962-68 . . . . **50.00**

Auto
Cadillac Eldorado, #131, 1956-62 . . . . **60.00**
DeSota, Diplomat, orange, F545, 1960-63 . . . . **70.00**
Ford Fairlane, pale green, #148, 1962-66 . . . . **30.00**
Jaguar XK 120, white, #157, 1954-62 . . . . **120.00**
Mustang Fastback, #161, 1965-73 . . . . **45.00**
Studebaker Commander, F24Y, 1951-61 . . . . **65.00**
Triumph TR-2, gray, #105, 1957-60 . . . . **60.00**
Volkswagen 1300 sedan, #129, 1965-76 . . . . **20.00**
Bulldozer, Blaw Knox, #561 . . . . . **45.00**

Bus
Routemaster, #289, 1964-80 . **75.00**
Silver Jubilee, #297, 1977 . . . **25.00**

Motorcycle
A. A. Motorcycle patrol, #270/44B, 1946-44 . . . . **30.00**
Police Motorcycle Partol, #42B, 1946-53 . . . . **30.00**

Police car
Citroen DS19, #F501, 1967-70 **75.00**
Plymouth, #244, 1977-80 . . . . **25.00**

Taxi
Austin, #40H, 1951-52 . . . . . . **60.00**
Ford Vedette, F24XT, 1956-59 **80.00**
Plymouth Plaza, #266, 1960-67 . . . . **60.00**

Tractor
David Brown, #305 . . . . **35.00**
Field Marshall, #37N/301 . . . . **60.00**
Massey-Harris, #27A/300 . . . . **50.00**

Truck
Austin Van, Nestle's, #471 . . . **60.00**
Citreon Milk Truck, #F586 . . . **145.00**
Foden Mobilgas Tanker, #941 **145.00**
Leland Tanker, Shell/BP, #944 **125.00**
Royal Mail Van, #260 . . . . . . **65.00**
Willeme Log Truck, #F36A/987 **75.00**

Fisher Price, USA
American Airlines plane, paper litho over wood, bright orange and blue, extensive graphics, two propellers, 20" wingspan **500.00**
Donald Duck Choo Choo, #450, 1940 . . . . **350.00**
Jack n Jill TV Radio, #148, 1956 **55.00**
Katy Kackler, #140, 1954 . . . . . . **45.00**

Fisher Price, Donald Duck, pull toy #185, copyright 1938 W.D.P., some wear to paint, one wooden wheel split, $275. Photo courtesy of James D. Julia, Inc.

Merry Mousewife, #473, 1949 . . **45.00**
Mickey Mouse, #748, 9" l **350.00**
Mother Goose Cart, #784, 1955 . **35.00**
Pony Express, #733, 1941 . . . . . **60.00**
Pushy Elephant, #525, 1934 . . **350.00**
Rock-A-Bye Baby Cart, #627, 1960 . . . . **15.00**
Sleepy Sue, #632, 1960 . . . . **30.00**
Streamline Express, #215, 1935 . . . . **350.00**
Sunny Fish, #420, 1961 . . . . **25.00**
Teddy Drummer, #775, 1936 . . **300.00**
This Little Pig, #910, 1963 . . . . . **25.00**
Uncle Timmy Turtle, #437, 1942 . . . . **100.00**
Wiggily Woofer, #640, 1957 . . . . **40.00**
Ziggy Zilo, #737, 1958 . . . . **50.00**

Gong Bell
Columbus bell, cast iron, Columbus standing, men rowing ornate ship mounted to spoke wheels, bell rings, emb on side "Landing of Columbus," 7-1/4" l, replaced figure **420.00**
See saw, pull type, cast iron, figures of black man on one end, clown on other end, spoked wheel platform, central bell rings when figures articulate, 6-1/2" l **660.00**

Hot Wheels, Mattel, vintage, MIP
'31 Doozie, #9649, orange, redline, 1977 . . . . **15.00**
'40 Ford, two-door, #4367, black, whit hubs, Real Rider, 1983 . . . . **50.00**

Gilbert, Uncle Sam, gravity toy, c1920, slight wear, 8" x 7", $460. Photo courtesy of James D. Julia, Inc.

'55 Chevy, #92, black, Real Rider, 1992 .... **30.00**

'57 Chevy, #9683, red, redline, 1977 .... **30.00**

'57 T-Bird, #9522, black, white hubs, Real Rider, 1986 .... **150.00**

Baja Bruiser, #8258, orange, 1974 .... **75.00**

Boss Hoss, #6406, 1971 .... **75.00**

Buzz Off, #6976, blue, 1974 .... **90.00**

Captain America, #2879, white, 1979 .... **175.00**

Cement Miser, #6452, 1970..... **60.00**

Circus Cats, #3303, white, 1975 . **75.00**

Custom Police Cruiser, #6269, 2969 .... **200.00**

Datsun 200XS, #3255, maroon, Canada, 1982 .... **175.00**

Dune Daddy, #6967, light green, 1975 .... **75.00**

El Rey Special, #8273, light blue, 1974 ....1,200.00

Emergency Squad, #7650, red, 1975 .... **65.00**

Fire Engine, #6554, red, 1970.. **100.00**

Flat Out 442, green, Canada, 1984 .... **150.00**

Fuel Tanker, #6018, 1971...... **200.00**

Heavy Chevy, #6408, 1970 .... **200.00**

Hot Heap, #6219, 1968 .... **65.00**

Incredible Hulk Van, #2850, white, 1979 .... **125.00**

Jet Threat, #6179, 1976........ **60.00**

Letter Getter, #9643, white, redline, 1977..................... **550.00**

Letter Getter, #9643, white, blackwall, 1977..................... **15.00**

Lotus Turbine, #6262, 1969..... **60.00**

Mantis, #6423, 1970 .... **60.00**

Maxi Taxi, #9184, yellow, blackwall, 1977..................... **60.00**

Motorcross Team Van, #2853, red, 1979 .... **125.00**

Neet Streeter, #9510, chrome, 1976 .... **40.00**

Olds 442, #6467, 1971 .... **800.00**

Poison Pinto, #9240, green, blackwall, 1977..................... **30.00**

Police Cruiser, #6963, white, 1973 .... **550.00**

Porsche 911, #6972, orange, 1975 .... **65.00**

Race Ace, #2620, white, 1968 .. **75.00**

Red Baron, #6963, red, blackwall, 1977 .... **25.00**

Rock Buster, #9088, yellow, blackwall, 1977..................... **15.00**

Sand Crab, #6403, 1970....... **60.00**

Sand Drifter, #7651, green, 1975 .... **375.00**

Silhouette, #6209, 1979 .... **90.00**

Sir Sidney Roadster, #8261, yellow, 1974 .... **90.00**

Six Shooter, #6003, 1971 ..... **225.00**

Super Van, #9205, chrome, 1976. **40.00**

Sweet 16, #6422, 1970........ **75.00**

Thor, #2880, yellow, 1979...... **30.00**

Tow Truck, #6450, 1970....... **55.00**

T-Totaller, #9648, brown, blackwall, 1977 .... **40.00**

Twinmill II, #8240, orange, 1976.. **35.00**

Vega Bomb, #7654, green, 1975 **800.00**

Volkswagen, #7620, orange, bug on roof, 1974 .... **60.00**

Warpath, #7654, white, 1975 ... **110.00**

Whip Creamer, #6457, 1970..... **50.00**

Z Whiz, #9639, gray, redline, 1977 .... **70.00**

Hubley, Lancaster, PA

Airplane, cast iron

American Eagle, WWII fighter 11" wingspan............... **150.00**

Lindy Glider, painted red, yellow wings, driver seated on front, emb wings, 6-1/2" l **1,210.00**

Navy WWII fighter, folding wings and wheels.................. **45.00**

Sea Plane, orange, and blue, two engines **35.00**

Auto, cast iron

Chrysler Airflow, battery operated lights, 1934 .... **1,250.00**

Coupe, 1928, 8-1/2" l....... **600.00**

Lincoln Zephyr and trailer, painted green, nickeled grill and bumper, 13-1/2" l **825.00**

Sedan and trailer, painted red sedan, trailer panted silver and red, rubber tires, factory sample tag, 9-1/2" l **715.00**

Streamlined Racer, 5" l...... **400.00**

Bell telephone, cast iron

8-1/4" l, painted green, silver sides, emb company name, Mack "C" cab, nickeled ladders, long handled shovels, pole carrier, spoked wheels, repainted.. **250.00**

*Hubley, racing car, cast metal, moveable cylinders, 1938, **$465.** Photo courtesy of Joy Luke Auctions.*

9-1/4" l, painted green, winch, auger, nickel water barrel on side, ladders, and pole carrier, fatigued rubber tires............ **660.00**

Boat, cast iron, painted red, emb "Static" on sides, sleet form, seated driver, hand on throttle of attached motor, chromed air cleaner, painted orange, three tires, clicker, 9-1/2" l, over painted **1,650.00**

Cement mixer truck, cast iron, red and green, nickel tank, rubber wheels, Mack, 8" l, restored **1,760.00**

Delivery truck, Merchants, 1925, 6-1/4" l.................. **400.00**

Fire truck, cast iron

Fire Engine, 5" l, 1930s...... **75.00**

Fire Patrol, 7-men, 1912, 5" l **3,575.00**

Hook and ladder, 1912, 23" l **1,850.00**

Ladder truck, 5-1/2" l **40.00**

Gasoline truck, cast iron, painted silver, red spoked wheels, cast figure, round tank body, rear facets, c1920, 6" l **495.00**

Milk truck, cast iron, painted white, emb "Borden's" on side panel, rear opening door, nickeled grill, headlights, and spoke wheels, 7-1/2" l, repaired headlights **1,980.00**

Motorcycle, cast iron

Harley-Davidson, 1932, 7-1/2" l **300.00**

Hill Climber, 1936, 6-1/2" l .. **375.00**

Indian Air Mail, 1929, 9-1/4" l **1,575.00**

Indian Four Cylinder, 1929, 9" l **1,700.00**

Motorcycle cop with sidecar **700.00**

Patrol Motorcycle, green, 6-1/2" l **275.00**

Popeye Patrol, 1938, 9" l ... **425.00**

Panama steam shovel, cast iron, painted red and green, large scale, nickeled shovel, cast people on trailer, dual rubbers on rear, 12" l..... **935.00**

Pull toy, Old Dutch Girl, cast iron, white and blue dress, holding yellow can of cleanser, rubber tires, c1932, 9" l, repaired stick, orig checker floor **4,100.00**

Racer, cast iron

Painted blue, painted red articulated pistons, seated driver, black tires, spoked wheels, 10-1/2" l . **1,760.00**

Painted green, red emb "5" on sides, hood opens on both sides to show extensively cast engine, disc

wheels, seated driver, replaced hood doors, 9-1/2" l..... **1,100.00**
Painted red, seated driver, emb "#1" on sides, rubber tires, 7-3/4" l **385.00**

Road roller, Huber, cast iron, painted green, large fancy spoke wheels painted red, figure stands on rear platform, 7-1/2" l.......... **1,320.00**

Stake truck, cast iron, two piece mold, chassis and hood painted red, stake body and cab painted blue, six rubber tires, 6-1/2" l.............. **375.00**

Steam shovel truck, cast iron, painted green and red, nickeled shovel, fatigued rubber tires, 8-1/4" l ...**385.00**

Taxi cab, painted orange and black, separate driver chassis and luggage rack, rubber tires, yellow cab stencil on rear doors, 8-1/4" l, professionally restored **470.00**

Tow truck, cast metal, Ford, 1950s, 7" l **50.00**

Wrecker, cast iron, 5" l **60.00**

Ives, Bridgeport, CT

Cuzner trotter, red tinplate carriage marked "Pat'd March 7, 1871," black spoked wheels, white horse with articulated legs, driver with striped trousers, black hat, brass clockwork motor, 11-1/2" l, some chipping **2,590.00**

Steamer, *King*, clockwork motor, black and red hull, brown superstructure with single funnel, 10-1/2" l, some wear **345.00**

Japanese

Haji, 8" l, car with boat trailer, friction powered, blue Ford convertible, red and cream Speedo motor boat with friction-powered motor, red trailer, orig packing and maker's box...... **400.00**

San, tugboat, 12-1/2" l, battery operated tinplate, red, cream, yellow, and blue, smoking mechanism, orig maker's box **200.00**

Japanese, San, painted tin toy friction operated truck "Children – Truck," truck bed decorated with Christmas items, 8" l, $115. Photo courtesy of Joy Luke Auctions.

Japanese, E.T. Co., painted tin toy friction operated Indianapolis Style racing car with driver, Champions Racer 98", 19" l, $1,750. Photo courtesy of Joy Luke Auctions.

T.N.

Dump Truck, 11" l, friction powered tinplate, red and cream, automatic side dump action, orig maker's box **150.00**

Great Swanee Paddle Wheeler, 10-1/4" l, friction powered tinplate, whistle mechanism, orig maker's box **175.00**

Space Patrol Car, 9-1/2" l, battery operated, litho, blue, cream, and silver, red astronaut, green laser, spinning antenna, orig maker's ox **1,265.00**

Y.H./Daiwa, car with sailboat, 6-1/4" l, friction powered tinplate, thunderbird style car, red body, black roof, red and cream sailboat with blue trailer . **435.00**

Kenton, Kenton, OH

Bus, Nile Coach, cast iron **750.00**

Elephant and clown chariot, remnants of silver paint and red blanket, yellow spoked wheels, detachable clown, 6-1/4" l, considerable paint wear and chips **130.00**

Farm wagon, cast iron, orig driver, one upright broken off, good paint, 11-1/2" l **165.00**

Kenton, fire pumper, horse drawn, cast iron, two black and one white horse attached to movable triple hitch, metal link reins that attach to driver seated on the top, removable 9" long rubber hoses with brass ends on each side, slight aging, 98 percent original paint, 22" l, 7" w, 8-1/4" h, $165. Photo courtesy of Hake's Americana & Collectibles.

Kenton, road scraper, #151, cast iron, green body, nickel plated blade, rubber tires, $150.

Fire pumper, cast iron, painted red, gold boiler top and lamps, driver, white tires, 10-1/4" l, some chipping .. **230.00**

Hose reel, cast iron, three white horses, white carriage and reel, driver, hose, and spoked wheels, 13-3/4" l, horses repainted, other paint poor **435.00**

Overland circus, cage wagon, red, yellow wheels, white horses, driver, and outrider, 14" l................ **425.00**

Sulky and driver, nickeled cast iron, red spoked wheels, 5" l **115.00**

Tractor trailer set, all cast iron, tractor painted red, orange tanker, two speed stake trailers, nickeled disc wheels, 22" l.................... **1,210.00**

Touring car, cast iron, painted white spoke wheels, cast headlamps and lanterns, 7-3/4" l, replaced figures **250.00**

Yellow cab, cast iron, painted orange and black, white disc wheels, orange centers, 6-1/2" l **495.00**

Keystone Mfg. Co., Boston

Air mail plane, olive green, three propellers, 25" **1,600.00**

Ambulance, canvas cover and stretcher, 27-1/2" l.......... **1,000.00**

Bus, Coast to Coast, blue, 31-1/4" l **1,200.00**

Fighter plane, "Ride 'Em," silver pressed-steel, red wings, propeller and seat, 25" l **520.00**

Moving van, black cab, red body, rubber tires, 26-1/4" **1,000.00**

Packard ride-on water tower, tower, nozzle, tank, and seat, lg. 32" l **1,035.00**

Police patrol truck, decals, 27-1/2" l **700.00**

Steam shovel, 20-3/4" l **75.00**

World's Greatest Circus truck, six removable animal cages, 26-1/4" l **2,500.00**

Kilgore, Canada

Airplane, cast iron, Seagull, painted red, nickeled wheels and wing mounted propeller, 7-3/4" l **880.00**

Auto, open roadster, 1928, cast iron, painted blue, nickeled wheels and driver, decal reads "Kilgore, Made in Canada," 6-1/8" l **825.00**
Delivery truck, cast iron, Toy Town, painted red, emb on side panels, gold highlights, silver disc wheels, 6-1/8" l, repainted **360.00**
Dump truck, cast iron, painted blue enclosed cab, red dump body, lever to lift, nickeled disc wheels, 8-1/2" l **330.00**
Ice cream truck, cast iron, enclosed cab painted blue, orange body, emb "Arctic Ice Cream" on sides, disc wheels, 8" l **420.00**

Kingsbury Toys, USA

Blue Bird racer, black details, U.S. and U.K. flags, 20" l **4,140.00**
Dump truck **200.00**
Streetcar, orange, black bumpers
No. 781, 9-1/4" l, scratching and chipping **200.00**
No. 784, clockwork motor, fixed turning and bell, 14" l, paint chipped **150.00**

Lehmann, Germany

Autin, coil-spring motor, wood grain litho cart, blue jacketed box, 3-3/4" l **290.00**
Beetle, spring motor, crawling movement, flapping wings, maker's box, one leg detached, but present, early Adam trademark **230.00**
Kadi, flywheel movement **290.00**
Na-Ob, red and yellow cart, blue eccentric wheels, gray donkey, marked "Lehmann Ehe & Co.," 6" l, front wheel missing **145.00**

Lehmann, donkey with clown cart, litho tin windup, earlier version with hand-painted tin arms and pants, flocked finish on Donkey, 7-1/2" l, $115. Photo courtesy of James D. Julia, Inc.

Oh-My Alabama coon jigger, lithograph tinplate, clockwork motor, 10" h **460.00**
Truck, tinplate, cream, red, and yellow, blue driver, fixed steering, clockwork motor, marked "Lehmann Ehe & Co.," 6-3/4" l **435.00**
Tut Tut motor car, white suited driver, horn, front steering, bellows, coil springs, paint loss, rust spotting, 6-1/2" l **635.00**
Walking Down Broadway, rack and pinion flywheel drive, litho couple, pug dog, orig lady's handbag, paint loss, 6-1/4" h **1,840.00**

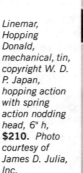
Linemar, Hopping Donald, mechanical, tin, copyright W. D. P. Japan, hopping action with spring action nodding head, 6" h, $210. Photo courtesy of James D. Julia, Inc.

Linemar, Japan

Donald Duck, Huey, Louey, and Dewey Marching Soldiers, clockwork motor, rubber titles, 11-1/4" l, scratches **375.00**
Gym toy, Donald Duck, clockwork motor, celluloid figure, red bar, doing acrobatics, 4-1/2" h **245.00**
Mickey Mouse with xylophone, litho, clockwork motor, black, red, and yellow, foliate dec on xylophone, orig box lid, 7" h, chips, tears to lid **750.00**
Popeye, rowboat, battery-operated tinplate, orig controller and maker's box **9,200.00**

Lineol, Germany

Armored car, litho tin clockwork, camouflage colors, revolving turret with gun, opening doors, spring lever for gun, wire guard covers vehicle, rubber tires, 10" l, symbols repainted, minor paint loss **935.00**
Cannon, 88MM, litho tin, camouflage colors, stabilizer arms, elevation cranks, four-tire open frame, tow hook, 14-1/2" l **935.00**
Motorcycle with side car, composition figures, tin fenders, disc wheels, 4-1/2" l **300.00**

Lionel, toy boats, top: wooden wind-up, marked "Miss America," 14-1/2" l, $185; bottom: painted tin wind-up speedboat, No. 44, 16-1/2" l, $350. Photo courtesy of Joy Luke Auctions.

Lionel

Mickey Mouse hand car, composition Mickey and Minnie figures and track **290.00**

Marx, Louis & Co., NY
Airplane
Airmail, monoplane, litho tin wind-up, two engines, 1930 . . . . **100.00**
American Airlines, flagship, pressed steel, wood wheels, 1940, 27" wingspan **200.00**
Bomber, metal, wind-up, four propellers, 14-1/2" wingspan **100.00**
Floor Zeppelin, 1931, 9-1/2" l **225.00**
Hangar with one plane, 1940s **150.00**
Lucky Stunt Flyer, litho tin wind-up, 1928, 6" l **150.00**
Pan American, pressed steel, four engines, 1940, 27" wingspan **90.00**

Marx, Merry Makers, litho tin windup, 1930s, four mice playing piano, 9-1/2" h, $660. Photo courtesy of James D. Julia, Inc.

Marx, Charlie McCarthy Car, litho tin windup, minor touch up to rear wheel, 8" l, $200. Photo courtesy of James D. Julia, Inc.

Pursuit Plane, one propeller, 1930s, 8" wingspan **125.00**

Sky Flyer, biplane and Zeppelin, 8-1/2" h tower, 1927 . . . . . . **225.00**

Trans-Atlantic Zeppelin, litho tin wind-up, 1930, 10" l **225.00**

Auto

Army car, battery operated . . . **65.00**

Crazy Dan car, litho tin wind-up, 1930s, 6" l **375.00**

Dippy Dumper, celluloid Brutus, litho tin wind-up, 1930s, 9" l **350.00**

Falcon, plastic bubble top, black rubber tires **50.00**

Jalopy, tin driver, friction, 1950s **150.00**

Leaping Lizzie, litho tin wind-up, 1927, 7" l **250.00**

Queen of the Campus, four college students, 1950 . . . . **250.00**

Rocket Racer, tin litho, 1935 . **275.00**

Siren police car, 1930s, 15" l . . **75.00**

Speed racer, 1937, 13" l **250.00**

Streamline Speedway, two litho tin wind-up racing cars, 1936 . **175.00**

Bulldozer/tractor, gold body, rubber treads, plow and farmer driver, blue and red stake wagons, hitch, two discs, plow, corn planter, harvester . . . **230.00**

G-Man pursuit car, pressed steel and tinplate, red and blue, armed agent, clockwork motor, 14-1/4" l, scratches **750.00**

Honeymoon Express, clockwork motor, circular base **100.00**

Lumar wrecker service truck, multicolored pressed steel, rear winch, 16" l, scratches and staining . . . **200.00**

Merrymakers Band, tinplate, one dancer missing **575.00**

Popeye and parrots, tinplate, clockwork motor, 8-1/4" h **350.00**

Royal Bus Lines, litho tin wind-up, 1930s, 10-1/4" l **135.00**

Set

Bulldog tractor, aluminum, litho wind-up, 1940, 9-1/2" l tractor **250.00**

Midget Road Building Set, litho tin wind-up, 1939, 5-1/2" l tractor **30.00**

Super Power Tractor and Trailer, litho tin wind-up, 1937, 8-1/2" l tractor **125.00**

Truck

Auto Transport, Mack, dark blue cab, dark green trailer, wind-up, 1932, 11-1/2" l **150.00**

Dump truck, yellow cab, blue bumper, red bed, 1950, 18" l **100.00**

Gravel truck, pressed steel cab, red tin dumper, 1930, 10" l **100.00**

Jalopy pickup, litho tin wind-up, 7" l **60.00**

Mack towing truck, dark green cab, wind-up, 1926, 8" l **175.00**

Pet shop truck, plastic, six compartments with vinyl dogs, 11" l **125.00**

RCA television service truck, plastic Ford panel truck, 1948-50, 8-1/2" l **175.00**

Royal Oil Co., Mack, dark red cab, medium green tank, wind-up, 1927, 8-1/4" l **200.00**

Searchlight, toolbox behind cab, 1930s, 10" l **150.00**

Stake bed, pressed steel, wooden wheels, 1936, 7" l **65.00**

U. S. Army division tank, No. 392, green, detailing, recoiling gun barrel, clockwork motor with start/stop action, 9-1/2" l **60.00**

Zippo the climbing monkey, multicolored litho tinplate, pull-string mechanism, 10" l **60.00**

Matchbox

Aston Martin DB2 Saloon, metallic light green, 1958 . . . . **20.00**

Atlantic Trailer, tan body, six metal wheels, 1956 . . . . **15.00**

Atlas truck, metallic blue cab, orange dumper, labels on doors, 1975 . . . **8.00**

Aveling Barford Road Roller, 1962 . . . . **8.00**

Benford Ton Tipper, gray cap, 1961 . . . . **10.00**

Boat and trailer, white full, blue deck, 1970 . . . . **3.00**

Case Tractor Bulldozer, red body, yellow base, 1969 . . . . **5.00**

Chevrolet Impala, taxi, orange, 1965 . . . . **10.00**

Commer pickup truck, 1958 . . . **35.00**

Daimler ambulance, silver trim, red cross on roof, 1958 . . . . **40.00**

Ferrari Berlinetta, metallic green body, 1965 . . . . **10.00**

Fiat 1500, 1965 . . . . **10.00**

Foden Ready Mix concrete truck, orange body, 1961 . . . . **65.00**

Ford Customline Station Wagon, yellow body, 1957 . . . . **20.00**

Ford GT, yellow or white body, 1965 . . . . **20.00**

Fork lift truck, red body, yellow hoist, 1972 . . . . **5.00**

Harta tractor shovel, orange, 1965 . . . . **20.00**

Hillman Minx, 1958 . . . . **15.00**

Horse drawn milk flat, orange body, 1954 . . . . **25.00**

Lambretta TV 175 motor scooter and sidecar, metallic green, 1961 . . . **25.00**

Land Rover Fire Truck, 1966 . . . **10.00**

Leyland Royal Tiger Coach, silver-gray, 1961 . . . . **10.00**

Marx, Popeye the Pilot, litho tin built-in key, copyright 1940 KFS, slight wear, 8" l, 7" w, 5-1/4" h, $525. Photo courtesy of Hake's Americana & Collectibles.

Ohio Art, Mickey Mouse Drum, litho tin, copyright Walt Disney, shows Mickey, Minnie, and Pluto playing and conducting, two wooden drumsticks, side strings replaced, 6-1/2" d, $170. Photo courtesy of James D. Julia, Inc.

London Bus, red body, 1965 .... **5.00**
Long Distance Coach, green body, No. 21 cast on base, London to Glasgow orange decals, 1958 .. **20.00**
Maserati, 1958 .... **10.00**
Mercedes Benz Coach, white, 1965 .... **30.00**
MGA sports car, white body, 1958 .... **50.00**
Morris Minor 1000, dark green, 1958 .... **20.00**
Plymouth Grand Fury police car, white body, black detailing, 1979 . **5.00**
Rolls-Royce Phamton V, 1964.. **15.00**
Scaffolding truck, silver body, green tinted windows, 1969.......... **5.00**
Setra Coach, #12, 1970 .... **5.00**
Snowtrac Tractor, red body, silver painted grille, 1964 .... **10.00**
Swamp Rat, green deck, plastic hull, tan soldier, 1976 .... **5.00**
Thames Trader, compressor truck, yellow body, black wheels, 1959. **20.00**
Thames Wreck, red body, 1961, 2-1/2" l **15.00**
Weatherhill Hydraulic Excavator, decal, 1956 .... **20.00**

Pratt & Letchworth
Dray wagon, cast iron, open bed wagon, single slat slides, wooden floor, standing figure, red spoke wheels, one horse, 10-1/4" l.............. **175.00**
Hook and ladder truck, cast iron, horse drawn, one red and one white horse, black frame with red detailing, spoked wheels, seated front driver, seated rear steerer, two wood ladders and bell, 23" l.............. **460.00**
Surrey, cast iron, open carriage, low splash board, two full width seams with arm and back rests, emb upholstering

mounted on two prs of spoked wheels, pulled by one horse, c1900, 14" l**990.00**

Schuco, trademark of Schreyer and Co., Germany
Acrobat bear, yellow mohair, glass eyes, embroidered nose and mouth, turns somersaults when wound, orig key, 1950s, 5" h **575.00**
Hopsta dancing monkey, red and yellow, baby mouse, clockwork motor, 4-1/2" h **175.00**
Mercedes Simplex, wind-up, 8-1/2" l **125.00**
Monkey bellhops, Yes/No monkey with painted metal face, metal eyes, ginger mohair head and tail, red and black felt outfit and hands, Acrobatic monkey with painted metal face, metal eyes, ginger mohair head, red and black felt outfit and hands, winds by rotating arms, oak Mission style settee, 1930s, 8-1/2" h, moth damage on both . **435.00**
Porsche microracer, No. 1037, red, key missing................. **55.00**
Set, Highway Patrol, squad car, 1958 .... **100.00**
Tank, keywind **40.00**
Teddy bear on roller skates, wind-up, beige mohair head, glass eyes, embroidered nose and mouth, cloth and metal body and legs, cotton shirt, felt overalls, hands, and boots, rubber wheels, marked "Schuco, U. S. Zone, Germany," clothes faded, key not orig **490.00**
Teddy bear on scooter, friction auction, yellow mohair bear, black steel eyes, embroidered nose and mouth, black felt pants, blue litho scooter, 1920s, 5-3/4" h **1,035.00**
Tumbling monkey.......... **100.00**
Van, battery operated, 4" l **75.00**

Skoglund & Olson, Sweden
Coupe, cast iron, painted gray, spare tire mounted on rear, rubber tires, red disc wheels, 8" l, repainted **550.00**
Farm tractor, cast iron, painted blue, red traction wheel, seated nickel driver, replaced steering wheel..... **1,100.00**
Ladder truck, cast iron, painted red, black cast side boxes, nickeled supports, rubber tires, removable house reel on open frame, one tin ladder, 16" l, repainted **715.00**
Pick-up truck, cast iron, painted yellow, enclosed cab, low side body, removable tailgate, rubber tires, red disc wheels, 10-3/4" l, repaired . **950.00**

Sedan and ramp, cast iron, green touring sedan with spare tire, resting in gray car ramp, 7-1/4" to 14-1/4" l, overpainted **1,870.00**
Wrecker, cast iron, painted white, red winch and crane on open body, rubber tires, painted red disc wheels, sides emb "Central-Garage," 11-3/4" l **1,540.00**

Strauss, Ham and Sam, litho tin windup, dated 1921, toy in good condition, original box in fair condition, 6-1/2" w, $635. Photo courtesy of James D. Julia, Inc.

Strauss, Ferdinard, Corp., New York City
Flying graf zeppelin, aluminum, clockwork mechanism, maker's box, 16" l, some tabs broken....... **290.00**
Jazzbo Jim, clockwork litho tinplate, banjo player, plaid jacket, cabin dec with caricatures, maker's box, hole in lid, 10-1/4" h **500.00**
Red cap porter, bulldog popping out of trunk, lid missing, uniform faded **230.00**
Santee Claus, lithograph tinplate with two reindeer and clockwork motor, arms missing **375.00**
Trolley car, litho tin wind-up, 6-1/2" l **210.00**

Structo
Bearcat Auto, 16" l, 1919..... **850.00**
Cement mixer truck, 18-1/2" l, 9" h **150.00**
Climbing military tank, green, 1929 .... **450.00**
Contractor truck, orange dump truck, 1924 .... **525.00**
Fire insurance patrol, 18" l, 1928 .... **250.00**
Fire truck, hydraulic hook and ladder, pressed steel, red, 3" l........ **175.00**
Lone Eagle airplane, monoplane, spring drive motor, 1928...... **600.00**
Motor dispatch, blue, decals, 1929, 24" **850.00**
Sky King airplane, blue, gray wings, 1929 .... **900.00**

Tinplate, unknown makers

Clown violinist, stilt-legs, striped trousers, clockwork motor, 9" h, poor condition **60.00**

Delivery carriage, litho, black, red, yellow, and pink, flywheel drive, 4-1/4" l **150.00**

Horse-drawn omnibus, attributed to Francis, Field and Francis, Philadelphia, 1850s, two white horses, black painted harnesses, wheel operated trotting, dark green roof with black fleur-de-lis and lining, emb gilt foliate surround, emb rear steps, door surround, driver's rear rest, emb window frames with painted curtains, red front, rear upper section, lower half with hand-painted polychrome floral and foliate dec, over blue-gray, ochre int. with ochre vis-a-vis bench seating along sides, wheels, 23" l, overall paint flaking, wheels detached, one window frame partially detached . . . **48,300.00**

Locomotive, attributed to Fallows, clockwork motor, cast wheels, high wings, cow catcher and bell, old repaint, 10" l **460.00**

Locomotive, Victory, red boiler, bell, black and gilt stack, red and blue cab with green roof, silver stenciled windows, yellow chassis, spoked wheels, 4-3/4" l, one wheel damaged, scratches and paint loss **990.00**

Porter and trolley, clockwork motor in hinged trunk, blue uniform, red and orange electric-type trolley, 4-1/2" l **145.00**

Steamer, three funnels, hand painted, red, cream, and gray hull, cream superstructure, 10" l **350.00**

Two-seater tourer, litho, red, yellow, and cream, driver, fly-wheel drive, 3" l **400.00**

Tonka

Boat transport, 1960, 38" l **250.00**

Construction

Bulldozer, #0300, 1962 . . . . . . **35.00**
Dump truck, #0180, 1949 . . . **100.00**
Dump truck and sand loader, #0616, 1963 . . . . **100.00**
Hydraulic dump, #0520, 1962 . **45.00**
Road grader, #0012, 1958 . . . . **75.00**

Fire truck

Aerial ladder truck, 1957 . . . . **200.00**
Rescue Squad, 1960 . . . . **100.00**
Suburban pumper, #0046, 1960 . . . . **100.00**

Mini

Camper, #0070, 1963 . . . . **75.00**
Jeep pickup, #0050, 1963 . . . . **35.00**

Livestock Van, 1964, 16" l **50.00**
Stake truck, #0056, 1963 . . . . **35.00**

Truck

Air Express, #0016, 1959 . . . **350.00**
Car Carrier, #0040, 1960 . . . **100.00**
Carnation Milk delivery van, #0750, 1954 . . . . **200.00**
Deluxe Sportsman, #0022, 1961 . . . . **100.00**
Farm state truck, 1957 . . . . . **190.00**
Green Giant Transport semi, 1953 . . . . **150.00**
Minute Maid Orange Juice van, #0725, 1955 . . . . **275.00**
Service truck, #001, 1960 . . . **100.00**
Wrecker truck, #0018, 1958 . **100.00**

Tootsietoy

Airplane

Aero-Dawn, 1928 . . . . **20.00**
Beechcraft Bonanza, orange . **10.00**
Curtis P-40, light green **120.00**
Navy Jet, 1970s, red **10.00**
Piper Cub, blue **10.00**
Stratocruiser **30.00**
Transport plane, orange, 1941 . . . . **40.00**

Auto

Andy Gump Car **75.00**
Bluebird Daytona Race Car . . **20.00**
Buick LaSabre, 1951 . . . . **25.00**
Buick Touring Car, HO series, 1960 . . . . **10.00**
Cadillac Coup, blue and tan . . **40.00**

Unique Art, Kiddy Cyclist, litho tin windup, bell rings as boy pedals, 9" h, $150. Photo courtesy of James D. Julia, Inc.

Chevrolet Roadster **20.00**
Corvair, 1960s **30.00**
Ford Fairlane Convertible, red . **10.00**
Ford V-8 Hotrod, 1940 . . . . . . **15.00**
International Station Wagon, red and yellow, 1939 . . . . **15.00**
Lincoln **20.00**
Oldsmobile 98, red, 1955 . . . . **20.00**
Packard, white, 1956 . . . . **25.00**
Plymouth, dark blue, 1957 . . . . **10.00**
Pontiac Fire Chief, red, 1959 . . **20.00**

Boat

Battleship **10.00**
Destroyer **10.00**
Transport **15.00**
Yacht **10.00**

Unique Art, Newark, NJ

Hee Haw, litho tinplate milk cart, clockwork motor, milk cans, donkey, and hillbilly, 10" l **350.00**

Kiddy cyclist, clockwork motor . . **90.00**

Jazzbo Jim, dancing figure, checkered jacket and trousers, log cabin dec with caricature figures, coil-spring motor, 9-1/2" h, some rust spotting and fading **260.00**

Wilkins

Ladder truck, pressed steel chassis, cast driver and operator, red spoked wheels, clockwork motor and ladder, 13-1/4" l, old repainting **230.00**

Steam pumper, cast iron, two black and one white horse, yellow frame, red wheels, nickeled boiler, 21" l . . . **690.00**

Wolverine Supply & Mfg. Co.

Car and trailer, press-and-go motor, litho tin, blue and orange 1940s style four-door sedan, four-wheel blue, white, and orange trailer, some scratches, dent in auto roof, 27-1/2" l **200.00**

Panama pile driver, gravity toy, falling ball-operated driver, patent date December 1905, seven clay balls, 15-1/2" h, paint flaking **230.00**

Zilotone, wind-up, figure plays tunes on xylophone, three interchangeable discs, repaired orig box lid, some paint chips **650.00**

Wyandotte, USA

Airplane

Army bombing plane, 8-1/2" wingspan **25.00**
Defense bomber, 9-1/4" l **70.00**
Stratoship mystery plane, 4-1/4" l **10.00**

Ambulance, painted pressed steel, nickeled grill, operating rear door, minor scratches, 11" l **150.00**

Wyandotte Toys, Humphreymobile, litho tin windup, copyright Ham Fisher, original box with tattered end flaps, 7" h, $420. Photo courtesy of James D. Julia, Inc.

Car and trailer, painted pressed steel, red, streamlined auto and travel trailer with operating rear door, replaced white rubber tires, paint worn, chips, and scratches, 25" l **215.00**
Circus truck and wagon, red and yellow, cardboard animals, 19" l **650.00**
Contractor truck, metal wheels, miniature wheelbarrow, 11-1/4" l . **70.00**
Gasoline truck, rubber wheels, 21" l **100.00**
Humphrey mobile, litho tinplate, fixed steering, clockwork motor, rear door, moving hat and arm, 9" l, some scratching **350.00**
Pan Am clipper, painted pressed steel, red and white, brass engines, nickeled propellers, 9" l **275.00**
Rocket racer, 6" l **50.00**
Streamlined Wagon, rubber wheels, 5-1/4" l **25.00**
Zephyr roadster, rubber wheels, 13-3/8" l **400.00**

TRAINS, TOY

History: Railroading has always been an important part of childhood, largely because of the romance associated with the railroad and the prominence of toy trains.

The first toy trains were cast iron and tin; wind-up motors added movement. The golden age of toy trains was 1920 to 1955, when electric-powered units and high-quality rolling stock were available and names such as Ives, American Flyer, and Lionel were household words. The advent of plastic in the late 1950s resulted in considerably lower quality.

Toy trains are designated by a model scale or gauge. The most popular are HO, N, O and standard. Narrow gauge was a response to the modern capacity to miniaturize. Today train layouts in gardens are all the rage and those usually feature larger scale trains.

Additional Listings: See *Warman's Americana & Collectibles* for more examples.

Notes: Condition of trains is critical when establishing price. Items in fair condition and below (scratched, chipped, dented, rusted, or warped) generally have little value to a collector. Accurate restoration is accepted and may enhance the price by one or two grades. Prices listed below are for trains in very good to mint condition, unless otherwise noted.

American Flyer

Boxcar, #33514, HO gauge, Silver Meteor, brown................ **45.00**
Caboose, #935, S gauge, 1957, brown **60.00**
Crane car, #944, S gauge, 1952-57, Industrial Brown hoist......... **30.00**
Flat car, #24558, S gauge, 1959-60, Canadian Pacific, Christmas tree load **145.00**
Gondola
 #941, S gauge, 1953-57, Frisco **10.00**
 #33507, HO gauge, D&H, brown, canister load **60.00**
Locomotive
 #345, S gauge, steam, 1954, Silver Bullet, Pacific, 4-6-2 ...... **200.00**
 #426, HO gauge, B&O, blue and gray................... **150.00**
 #3020, O gauge, electric, 4-4-4, c1922-25 .... **375.00**
Set, O gauge
 Freight, #476 gondola, #478 boxcar, #480 tank car, #484 caboose **130.00**
 Passenger, Railway Post Office car, Paul Revere coach, Lexington observation, orange **115.00**
Set, standard gauge, passenger
 #4331, #4331, #4332...... **300.00**
 #4340, #4341, two-tone red, brass trim **320.00**

#4653 electric locomotive, two Bunker Hill coaches, Yorktown observation car, orange, pre-war **865.00**

Bing, German

Locomotive, O gauge, pre-war
 Clockwork, cast iron, no tender, headlight missing......... **70.00**
 Live steam, 0-4-0, minor fire damage, no tender **815.00**
Set, O gauge, passenger, litho, #2395 combine, Winnegago coach, Lakewood observation, green with brown roofs **130.00**
Set, #1 gauge, passenger, litho, dark maroon, lettered "Pennsylvania Lines," combine #1250, coach #1207 . **435.00**

Ives

Baggage car
 #50, 1908-09, O gauge, four wheels, red litho frame, striped steps, white/silver body, sides marked "Limited Vestibule Express, United States Mail Baggage Co." and "Express Service No. 50," three doors on both sides, one on each end, black roof with celestory **150.00**
 #70, 1923-25, O gauge, eight wheels, red litho body, simulates steel, tin roof with celestory stripe, sliding center door, marked "The Ives Railway Lines, Express Baggage Service, 60, U. S. Mail" **30.00**
Caboose, #67, 1918, O gauge, eight wheels, red litho body, sliding door on each side, gray painted tin roof with red cupola, "The Ives Railway Lines" **45.00**
Gravel car, #63, 1913-14, O gauge, eight wheels, gray litho, rounded truss rods, marked "63" on sides..... **35.00**
Livestock car, #65, c1918, O gauge, eight wheels, orange-yellow litho body, type D trucks, gray painted roof with catwalk, sides marked "Livestock Transportation, Ives RR" **27.50**

Lionel, "O" Gauge locomotive, Santa Fe, #2333-20, 1949, silver and red, yellow trim, mint, original box, 3-1/2" x 13-1/4" l, 3-1/2" h, $55. Photo courtesy of David Rago Auctions.

Locomotive

#11, 1910-13, O gauge, 0-4-0, black boiler and cab, litho plates beneath arched cab windows, cast iron wheels, L. V. E. No. 11 tender
. . . .**165.00**

#19, 1917-25, O gauge, 0-4-0, black cast iron boiler and cab, two arched windows and "IVES No. 19" beneath, cast-iron wheels, NYC & HR No. 17 tender **225.00**

#25, 1906-07, O gauge, 4-4-2, black body, boiler tapers towards front, four separate boiler bands, three square windows on both sides of cab, gold frames and stripes, tin pony wheels, four-wheel L.V.E. No. 25 tender **275.00**

#3200, 1911, O gauge, 0-4-o, cast iron S-type electric center cab, green body, gold trim, cast iron six-spoke wheels, center door flanked by two windows, raised lettering "Ives" and "3200" below windows **250.00**

Parlor car

#62, 1924-30, O gauge, eight wheels, tin litho steel, red-brown, one-pc roof with clerestory stripe, five windows, two doors on each side, marked "The Ives Railway Lines" above windows **75.00**

#72, 1910-15, one gauge, eight wheels, white tin body, litho to simulate wood, tin roof with clerestory stripe, four double windows, three small windows, door at each end, marked "Twentieth Century Limited Express, No. 72, Chicago" .**490.00**

Set, O gauge, litho, freight, #3 cast iron stem locomotive, #1 tender, three #54 gravel cars, #56 caboose, c1910-14
. . . .**700.00**

Lionel, Mickey Mouse/Santa car, composition Santa, Mickey rides behind in Santa's toy sack, 10-1/2" l, **$350.** *Photo courtesy of James D. Julia, Inc.*

Tank car, #66, 1921-35, O gauge, eight wheels, gray painted body, black dome
. . . . **25.00**

Tender, #25, 1928-30, O gauge, diecast body, coal load, two four-wheel trucks. **150.00**

Lionel

Baggage car, #2602, O gauge, 1938, red body and roof **100.00**

Boxcar

#00-44, OO gauge, 1939 . . . . **45.00**

#HO-874, HO gauge, 1964, NYC
. . . . **25.00**

Caboose

#217, Standard gauge, 1926-40, orange and maroon **150.00**

#HO-841, HO gauge, 1961, NYC
. . . . **10.00**

Cattle car, #213, Standard gauge, 1926-40, cream body, maroon roof
. . . . **450.00**

Hopper car, #216, Standard gauge, 1926-40, silver, Sunoco decal . . **350.00**

Locomotive

#5, standard gauge, 0-4-0, steam, c1910-18, missing cow catcher, no tender. **415.00**

Marklin, No. TW 800, streamlined, blue, cream and silver, red wheels, celluloid windows, original box bottom, 15" l, **$2,300.** *Photo courtesy of James D. Julia, Inc.*

#10E, standard gauge, electric
. . . . **70.00**

#156, O gauge, electric, 4-4-4, dark green, c1917-23 . . . . **265.00**

Observation car

#322, Standard gauge, 1924 . **95.00**

#754, O gauge, 1934, streamliner
. . . . **70.00**

#2436, O27 gauge, 1954, Mooseheart. **45.00**

Pullman

#35, Standard gauge, c1915, orange
. . . . **65.00**

#607, O gauge, 1926 . . . . **45.00**

#2533, O gauge, 1952, marked "Silver Cloud" **85.00**

Refrigerator car, #214R, Standard gauge, 1929-40, ivory body, peacock roof **400.00**

Set, O gauge

Passenger, #252 electric locomotive, #529 coach, #530 observation, olive green, c1926 . . . .**175.00**

Passenger, Union Pacific, #752E power unit, #753 coach, #754 observation, silver, c1934 . .**350.00**

Set, standard gauge, freight

#11, #12, #14, #15, c1906-26
. . . .**175.00**

#13, #16, #17, c1903-23 . . . .**200.00**

#511, #512, #514R, #517, c1927-29
. . . .**140.00**

#513, #516, #517, c1926-32 .**290.00**

Set, standard gauge, passenger

#18, #19, #190, dark olive green, c1906-10. . . . .**230.00**

#10 electric locomotive, two #337 passenger cars, #338, c1925-29
. . . .**350.00**

#309, #310, #312, c1924-29 .**260.00**

#337, #337, #338, c1925. . . .**150.00**

TRAMP ART

History: Tramp art was an internationally practiced craft, brought to the United States by European immigrants. Its span of popularity was between the late 1860s to the 1940s. Made with simple tools—usually a pocketknife, and from scrap woods—non-reusable cigar box wood, and crate wood, this folk-art form can be seen in small boxes to large

Marklin, steam locomotive, rare green version, 1935, **$3,555.** *Photo courtesy of Auction Team Breker.*

pieces of furniture. Usually identifiable by the composition of thin-layered pieces of wood with chip-carved edges assembled in built-up pyramids, circles, hearts, stars, etc. At times, pieces included velvet, porcelain buttons, brass tacks, glass knobs, shards of china, etc., that the craftsmen used to embellish his work. The pieces were predominantly stained or painted.

Collected as folk art, most of the work was attributed to anonymous makers. A premium is placed on the more whimsical artistic forms, pieces in original painted surfaces, or pieces verified to be from an identified maker.

Bank, 6" h x 4" w x 4" d, secret access to coins **335.00**

Bird cage, 28" h x 22" w x 13-1/2" d, house with two compartments. . **775.00**

Box, cov

4-1/4" w, 3" d, 1-3/4" h, hinged cover, dove, heart, and anchor dec **200.00**

14" l, 7-1/8" d, 8-1/4" h, hinged top, cast brass pull, mounted pincushion on base, two concealed short drawers, painted blue and gold, c1890-1910 **815.00**

Cabinet, building shape, two towers, steeple roofline, small shelves. **3,600.00**

Chest of drawers, 40" h x 29" w x 20" d, scratch built from crates with four drawers, 10 layers deep **2,400.00**

Christmas tree, 25-1/2" h, carved wood, branching sections, painted cross finial, stepped polychrome base, sgd "D. Hafner," c1900 . . . . . . **2,070.00**

Clock, mantel, 22" h x 14" w x 7" d, red stain with drawers at base. **475.00**

Comb case, 27" h x 17" w x 4"d, adorned with horseshoes, hearts, birds, two drawers and mirrors **700.00**

Crucifix, 16" h x 7" w x 4-1/2" d, wooden pedestal base, wooden carved figure **185.00**

Document box, 14" h x 9-1/2" w x 9" d, diamond designs, sgd and date **375.00**

Box, three layers, green velvet, mirror inside, brass lion head pulls and paw feet, 12-1/2" x 7-1/2" x 8", $345.

Frame, five layers, diamonds and pyramids, 18-1/2" x 16-1/2", $275.

Doll furniture

Chair, 10" h, 7" w, 12" d, dec with brass tacks **450.00**

Bureau, 14" h x 12" w x 9" d, drawers and mirror **650.00**

Frame

9" h, 6-3/4" w, photograph of maker, signed and dated "1906" . . **275.00**

13" h x 12" w, horseshoe shape, light and dark wood **465.00**

14" h x 24" w, double opening frame with oval opening for photos **325.00**

16" h x 18" w x 4-3/4" d crown of thorns, multiple opening frame with minor losses, dark stain . . . **495.00**

25" h, 22" w, 13-1/2" x 15-1/2" opening five layers, hearts in each corner, orig gold and red speckled paint, minor wear. **715.00**

26" h x 24" w, velvet panels and sq corners **350.00**

Grotto, 12" w, 8" d, 29" h, carved and painted, carved cross steep on bell tower above grotto, applied floral, foliate, and geometric motifs, int. fitted with platform and drawer, two standing floral devices, painted red and green, cream-white ground, found in Ohio, late 19th/early 20th C **420.00**

Jewelry box

6" h x 11" w x 6" d, covered with hearts painted silver over gold, velvet lined **595.00**

8" h x 11" w x 7" d, hinged, pedestal, dark stain. **175.00**

9" h x 11-1/2" w x 7" d, large, dated "1898," metal lion pulls **300.00**

Lamp

24" h, 10" w, 10" d, table, double socket **550.00**

68" h, 17" w, 17" d, floor, heavy pedestal base, no shade **1,200.00**

Match safe, 9" h x 2" w x 2" d, strike surface, open holder for matches **75.00**

Medicine cabinet, 22" h x 18" w x 10" d, light and dark woods. **675.00**

Miniature

Chair, 8" h x 6" w x 5-1/2" d, crown of thorns **245.00**

Chest of drawers, 14" h x 5" w x 4" d, made of cigar boxes **375.00**

Music box, 3" h x 7" w x 6" d, velvet sides **425.00**

Night stand, 37" h x 22" w x 14" d, dark stain, drawer on top and cabinet on bottom, no losses **1,600.00**

Pedestal

14-1/2" h x 12" w x 8" d, multi-level, six draws **675.00**

16" h x 7" w x 4-1/2" d, polychromed in green and black paint . . **950.00**

Pedestal box

8-1/4" h x 9" w x 6-1/2" d, double, bar connecting top pyramids, velvet lined, precise notching . . . **325.00**

29-1/2" h x 16" w x 15" d, light and dark stained, made from fruit crates **1,850.00**

Plant stand, 22" h x 11" w x 11" d, painted gold, heavily layered . . **675.00**

Pocket watch holder, 9" h x 6-1/2" w x 5-1/2" d, ftd **375.00**

Radio cabinet, 50" h x 33" w x 16" d, box type radio encased behind doors, ornate **3,600.00**

Sewing box

8-1/2" h x 11-1/2" w x 8-1/2"d, velvet pin cushion on top **265.00**

9" h x 16-1/2" w x 8" d, painted red, white and blue sewing box, Uncle Sam cigar label under lid. **1,600.00**

Sewing cabinet, 27" h x 16" w x 9"d, lift top and three drawers made from crate wood **1,400.00**

Vanity mirror, 26" h, 14" d, 10" d, table top, heart on top and drawer . . **375.00**

Wall pocket

8" w, 3-1/2" d, 14" h, three pockets, hearts on crest, diamond and circle

Pin cushion box, seven layers, blue velvet interior, brass lion head pulls, 10-3/4" x 3-1/2" x 6" deep, $285.

dec, trim and dec painted orig medium blue and goldenrod **275.00**

14" h x 11" w x 7"d, painted with hearts and stars, pr.......**700.00**

TRUNKS

History: Trunks are portable containers that clasp shut and are used for the storage or transportation of personal possessions. Normally "trunk" means the ribbed flat- or domed-top models of the second half of the 19th century.

Early trunks frequently were painted, stenciled, grained, or covered with wallpaper. These are collected for their folk-art qualities and, as such, demand high prices.

Chinese, brass bound camphor wood, 19th C, minor imperfections

16" h, 36" w, 18" d, polychrome foliate dec on top, nailhead trim **1,035.00**

16-1/2" h, 36-1/4" w, 18-1/4" d, nailhead dec, monogrammed brass plaque............**865.00**

Dome top

6" l, 3-1/2" w, 2-5/8" h, paper-covered box green and red sponge dec, blue line and dot patterned paper-lined int., brass ring and iron latch, America, 19th C, wear **265.00**

11-1/2" h, 28" w, 14" d, paint dec, black painted ground, central vined pinwheel bordered by meandering floral and arched vines, front with tassel and drape border, central MA, early 19th C **1,035.00**

19" l, fabric on wood, worn painted dec in ivory and green, red border designs and flowers, interior lined with green marbleized paper, worn **425.00**

28-1/4" l, 13-3/4" w, 13-1/2" h, arched top with "L G" in scripted yellow

Dome top, wood rim, wooden slats, interior shelf, old lining, 20-1/4" x 32" x 25", **$120.**

paint, nail construction box, all grain painted to simulate mahogany, and outlined in yellow striping with yellow floral device centered under the lock, imperfections and repairs, New England, early 19th C..... **235.00**

33-1/4" w, 16-1/4" d, 18-3/4" h, black japanned brass mounts, gilt Chinoisiere dec of figures in garden landscape, side handles, late 18th/early 19th C, restoration **750.00**

44-1/2" w, 22-3/4" d, 19-1/2" h, hinged top, dovetailed box, white painted vine, floral and leaf dec over black painted ground, int. papered with early 19th C Boston area broadsides, attributed to MA, 19th C, some later paint..**1,035.00**

Flat top

14" x 8", Chinese, pigskin, red, painted Oriental maidens and landscapes within quatrefoils, brass loop handles and lock, 19th C................**125.00**

15-1/4" l, tooled leather on pine, iron straps, brass buttons and lock, lined with worn newspaper dated 1871, hinged replaced, some edge damage **385.00**

29-1/4" x 15-1/2" x 16-1/4", tin over wood, brass banded ends, wood rim, int. shelf missing **100.00**

Japanese, 18th C, lacquer, domed top, ext. painted with landscape scenes, base with ball feet, 35-1/2" w, 22" d, 33" h....................**2,100.00**

Military, 21-3/4" w, 17" d, 12-1/2" h, brass bound camphor wood, hinged rect top, storage well, brass bail handles, English, second half 19th C **200.00**

Flat top, black and red lacquered elm, square outline, two sections interior, Chinese, Qing dynast, 19-1/2" x 29" x 18", **$200.** *Photo courtesy of Sloan's Auctioneers & Appraisers.*

Portuguese Colonial, early 19th C, elaborately tooled and painted leather, with foliage and birds, wrought iron hardware, 35-1/2" l, 19" d, 15" h **1,100.00**

Vuitton, Louis, early 20th C, wardrobe, rect, wooden strapping, leather handles on ends, brass corners and clasps, int. with hanger bars, eight Vuitton hangers, 21-1/2" d, 15-1/2" d, 40-1/2" h **1,100.00**

VAL ST.-LAMBERT

History: Val St.-Lambert, a 12th-century Cistercian abbey, was located during different historical periods in France, Netherlands, and Belgium (1930 to present). In 1822, Francois Kemlin and Auguste Lelievre, along with a group of financiers, bought the abbey and opened a glassworks. In 1846, Val St.-Lambert merged with the Socété Anonyme des Manufactures de Glaces, Verres à Vitre, Cristaux et Gobeletaries. The company bought many other glassworks.

Val St.-Lambert developed a reputation for technological progress in the glass industry. In 1879, Val St.-Lambert became an independent company employing 4,000 workers. The firm concentrated on the export market, making table glass, cut, engraved, etched, and molded pieces, and chandeliers. Some pieces were finished in other countries, e.g., silver mounts were added in the United States.

Val St.-Lambert executed many special commissions for the artists of the Art Nouveau and Art Deco periods. The tradition continues. The company also made cameo-etched vases, covered boxes, and bowls. The firm celebrated its 150th anniversary in 1975.

For more information, see this book.

Ashtray, 6" w, hexagon, colorless crystal.....................**35.00**

Candlesticks, pr, 9-1/2" h, colorless crystal, orig paper labels......**250.00**

Compote, 3-1/2" d, amberina, ruby rim, mottled glass bow, applied amber foot and handles................**175.00**

Epergne, 19-1/4" h, 17" w, colorless crystal, marked "Val St Lambert Belgique," plated pot metal base **550.00**

Figure

3-1/2" d base, 7-1/4" h, parrot perched on bell, light cranberry, sgd "Val St Lambert, Belgique" **275.00**

Console set, pair 12-1/2" d cobalt blue shading to clear candle-sticks, 9-1/2" d, 6-1/2" h matching pedestal bowl, signed, $600. Photo courtesy of Woody Auctions.

6" l, 3-1/4" w, 3-1/4" h, cat, colorless crystal, acid script signature, artist's name, orig paper label **150.00**

Paperweight
4" h, apple, colorless crystal, acid etched script signature **85.00**
5-1/2" h, pear, colorless crystal, acid etched script signature **85.00**

Presentation vase, 14" h, green ground, cameo cut chrysanthemums, maroon enameling, c1900..... **500.00**

Vase
6-1/2" d, 7-3/4" h, free-form cylindrical shape, exterior moldings twisted around stylized foliate motif, colorless crystal with very slight yellow cast, orig paper label, acid etched script signature **175.00**
8-3/4" d, 12" h, emerald and colorless crystal **550.00**
11-1/2" h, cobalt blue ground, overlaid in copper, all over emb rosettes, emb "Val St Lambert Belgique," c1910 .... **575.00**

VALENTINES

History: Early cards were handmade, often containing both handwritten verses and hand-drawn pictures. Many cards also were hand colored and contained cutwork.

Mass production of machine-made cards featuring chromolithography began after 1840. In 1847, Esther Howland of Worcester, Massachusetts, established a company to make valentines that were hand decorated with paper lace and other materials imported from England. They had a small "H" stamped in red in the top left corner. Howland's company eventually became the New England Valentine Company (N.E.V. Co.).

The company George C. Whitney and his brother founded after the Civil War dominated the market from the 1870s through the first decades of the 20th century. They bought out several competitors, one of which was the New England Valentine Company.

Lace paper was invented in 1834. The golden age of lacy cards took place between 1835 and 1860.

Embossed paper was used in England after 1800. Embossed lithographs and woodcuts developed between 1825 and 1840, and early examples were hand colored.

There was a big revival in the 1920s by large companies, like R. Tuck in England, which did lots of beautiful cards for its 75th Diamond Jubilee; 1925 saw changes in card production, especially for children with paper toys of all sorts, all very collectible now. Little girls were in short dresses, boys in short pants, which helps date that era of valentines. There was an endless variety of toy types of paper items, many companies created similar items and many stayed in production until World War II paper shortages stopped production both here and abroad.

Adviser: Evalene Pulati.

Animated, large
Felix, half tone, German **25.00**
Jumping Jack, Tuck, 1900.... **65.00**
Bank True Love note, England, 1865
.... **75.00**
Bank of Love note, Nister, 1914. **38.00**
Charm string
Brundage, three pcs **45.00**
Four hearts, ribbon **45.00**

Comic
Sheet, 8" x 10", Park, London . **25.00**
Sheet, 9" x 14", McLoughlin Co., USA, 1915 .... **20.00**
Woodcut, Strong, USA, 1845 . **25.00**
Diecut foldout
Brundage, flat, cardboard ... **25.00**
Cherubs, two pcs **40.00**
Clapsaddle, 1911 .... **60.00**
Documentary
Passport, love, 1910........ **45.00**
Wedding certificate, 1914 ... **45.00**
English Fancy, from "Unrequited Love Series"
8" x 10", aquatint, couple, wedding **135.00**
8" x 10", aquatint, girl and grandmother **95.00**
Engraved
5" x 7", American, verse **35.00**
8" x 10" sheet, English, emb, pg **65.00**
8" x 10" sheet, English, hand colored **45.00**
Handmade
Calligraphy, envelope, 1885. **135.00**
Cutwork, hearts, 6" x 6", 1855 .... **250.00**
Fraktur, cutwork, 1800 ..... **950.00**
Pen and ink loveknot, 1820 . **275.00**
Puzzle, purse, 14" x 14", 1855 .... **450.00**
Theorem, 9" x 14", c1885 ... **325.00**
Woven heart, hand, 1840.... **55.00**
Honeycomb
American, kids, tunnel of love **48.00**
American, wide-eyed kids, 9". **40.00**

American, pull down, World War II, $25. Photo courtesy of Evalene Pulati.

Fancy layered pull down, 1914, **$175.**
Photo courtesy of Evalene Pulati.

German, 1914, white and pink, 11"
.... **75.00**
Simple, 1920, Beistle, 8" **18.00**
Lace paper
American, B & J Cameo Style
Large.............. **75.00**
Small, 1865............. **45.00**
American, layered, McLoughlin Co.,
c1880 .... **35.00**
Cobweb center, c1855 ..... **250.00**
English, fancy
3" x 5", 1865 .... **35.00**
5" x 7", 1855 .... **75.00**
8" x 10", 1840 .... **135.00**
Hand Layered, scraps, 1855.. **65.00**
Layered, in orig box
1875, Howland **75.00**
1910, McLoughlin Co..... **45.00**
Orig box, c1890............ **55.00**
Simple, small pc, 1875 ..... **22.50**
Tiny mirror center, 4" x 6"..... **75.00**
Whitney, 1875, 5" x 7"........ **35.00**
Novelty, American Fancy, c1900,
originally sold in a box
5" x 7-1/2", mat, fancy corners,
parchment, orig box **32.50**
7-1/2" x 10", rect, panel with silk,
celluloid, orig box **45.00**
10-1/2" x 10", star shape, silk
rusching, orig box........ **55.00**
16" x 10-1/2", oblong, satin, celluloid,
orig box **65.00**
Pulldown, German
Airplane, 1914, 8" x 14" **175.00**
Auto, 1910, 8" x 11" x 4"..... **150.00**
Car and kids, 1920s **35.00**
Dollhouse, large, 1935....... **45.00**
Rowboat, small, honeycomb paper
puff **65.00**
Seaplane, 1934, 8" x 9" **75.00**
Tall Ship, 8" x 16" **175.00**

German, pull down, 1920s, **$95.**
Photo courtesy of Evalene Pulati.

Silk fringed
Prang, double sided, 3" x 5".. **24.00**
Triple layers, orig box **38.00**
Standup novelty
Cupid, orig box........... **45.00**
Hands, heart, without orig box **35.00**
Parchment
Banjo, small, with ribbon .. **65.00**
Violin, large, boxed **125.00**

VALLERYSTHAL GLASS

History: Vallerysthal (Lorraine), France, has been a glass-producing center for centuries. In 1872, two major factories, Vallerysthal glassworks and Portieux glassworks, merged and produced art glass until 1898. Later, pressed glass animal-covered dishes were introduced. The factory continues to operate today.

For more information, see this book.

Animal dish, cov
Hen on nest, opaque aqua, sgd
.... **95.00**
Rabbit, white, frosted **85.00**
Swan, blue opaque glass....**110.00**
Box, cov, 5" x 3", cameo, dark green, applied and cut dec, sgd **950.00**
Butter dish, cov, turtle, opaque white, snail finial.................. **120.00**
Candlesticks, pr, Baroque pattern, amber **75.00**
Compote, 6-1/4" sq, blue opaque glass **75.00**
Dish, cov, figural, lemon, opaque white, sgd **70.00**

Honey dish, covered, opaque green, detailed thatch roof, embossed door and other details, **$350.**

Mustard, cov, swirled ribs, scalloped blue opaque, matching cover with slot for spoon **35.00**
Plate, 6" d, Thistle pattern, green **65.00**
Salt, cov, hen on nest, white opal **65.00**
Sugar, cov, 5" h, Strawberry pattern, opaque white, gold trim, salamander finial **85.00**
Toothpick holder, hand holding ribbed vessel, opaque blue........... **30.00**
Vase, 8" h, flared folded burgundy red rim, oval pale green body, matching red enamel berry bush on front, inscribed "Vallerysthal" on base **490.00**

VAN BRIGGLE POTTERY

History: Artus Van Briggle, born in 1869, was a talented Ohio artist. He joined Rookwood in 1887 and studied in Paris under Rookwood's sponsorship from 1893 until 1896. In 1899, he moved to Colorado for his health and established his own pottery in Colorado Springs in 1901.

The Art Nouveau schools he had seen in France heavily influenced Van Briggle's work. He produced a great variety of matte-glazed wares in this style. Colors varied.

Artus died in 1904. Anne Van Briggle continued the pottery until 1912.

Marks: The "AA" mark, a date, and "Van Briggle" were incised on all pieces prior to 1907 and on some pieces into the 1920s. After 1920, "Colorado Springs, Colorado" or an abbreviation was added. Dated pieces are the most desirable.

Advertising plaque, 11-1/2" l, 5-3/4" h, green and blue matte glaze, emb "VAN BRIGGLE POTTERY/COLORADO CLAY," 1/3" corner chip, few smaller edge chips **2,300.00**

Bowl, 4-1/2" d, 3-1/4" h, fine leathery robin's egg blue and charcoal glaze, incised mark, 1905 . . . . **690.00**

Cabinet vase, 2-1/2" d, 4-1/4" h, emb flowers in curved panels, covered in dark teal matte glaze, incised AA/Van Briggle/190?/186, with XXII/IV/33188 in ink, 1904 . . . . **1,610.00**

Chamberstick, 5-1/2" h, molded-leaf shape, hood over candle socket, green glaze **115.00**

Figure, 7" h, female nude holding shell, matte Persian blue glaze, incised "Van Briggle" **250.00**

Lamp base, 9" h, emb stylized florals under maroon glaze with blue over-spray, orig factory fittings, incised varnished bottom with logo, name, and Colo. Sprgs, c1920 . . . . **115.00**

Low bowl

6-1/2" h, shape no. "689," emb arrow root design, under matte green glaze, incised with logo, varnished bottom, Colo Sprgs, c1920 **260.00**

7" d, circular, rolled rim, maroon glaze with blue over-spray, incised marks, logo, and date 1916 **150.00**

8-3/4" d, 2-3/4" h, Dragonfly, closed-in rim, four molded dragonflies around rim, deep

Advertising plaque, c1930, embossed "VAN BRIGGLE POTTERY/COLORADO CLAY," green and blue matte glaze, small chip to one corner, few smaller edge chips, 5-3/4" x 11-1/2", $2,300. Photos courtesy of David Rago Auctions.

Bookends, pair, owls standing on books, Persian Rose glaze, one incised AA. 5" x 5", $200.

mulberry matte glaze, incised cipher, incised Van Briggle U.S.A., c1922-29 . . . . **350.00**

Night light, 8-1/2" h, figural, stylized owl, bulb cavity, light refracting glass eyes, turquoise blue matte glaze, unsgd **425.00**

Sconce, owl

3" d, 6" h, matte green glaze, incised mark, 1916, fittings missing, glaze scaling. **435.00**

3-3/4" d, 9-1/2" h, Persian Rose glaze, incised mark, rewired **400.00**

Tile, 18" x 12", six tile frieze, cuenca with stylized trees against blue sky, framed **250.00**

Vase

4" h, emb stylized florals, maroon glaze with blue over-spray, dirty bottom with incised "VB" logo and Colo Sprgs **225.00**

5-1/2" h, shape no. 833, molded stylized flowers, under brown glaze with green over-spray, dirty bottom with incised logo, name and Colo Sprgs, c1920. . . . . **230.00**

5-1/2" h, 5-1/4" d, bulbous, emb panels of stylized flowers and heart-shaped leaves in purple and green, matte blue ground, incised AA/Van Briggle/1905/?09/X, small glaze scale to one stem . **2,760.00**

Cabinet vase, 1904, embossed flowers in curved panels, dark teal (possibly experimental) matte glaze, Incised AA/Van Briggle/190?/186, with XXII/IV/33188 in ink, 2-1/2" d, 4-1/4" h, $1,610.

Paperweight, scarab, 1915, matte turquoise glaze, stamped VBP CO., 2-3/4" x 2", $350.

6" h, incised and molded stylized flowers, under blue/gray glaze with turquoise over-spray, "dirty bottom" incised with logo, name, and date "20," c1920 . . . . **375.00**

8" h, 3" d, closed-in rim, emb tulips, covered in matte ochre glaze, incised AA/Van Briggle/1904/V/141 . . . . **2,300.00**

8-1/4" h, 2-3/4" d, bulbous, crisply emb spade-shaped leaves, covered in mottled purple dripping over green matte glaze, incised AA/Van Briggle/Colo. Spgs./804/18/7, c1907-11, 3/4" rim bruise. **1,100.00**

8-1/2" h, 7" d, bulbous, emb panels of berries and leaves, covered in caramel, amber, and indigo matte glaze, incised AA/Van Briggle/1904/V/164 . . . . . **6,900.00**

9" h, 6" d, bulbous, cupped rim, two loop handles, emb leaves around base, covered in rare purple and

Vase, bulbous, 1907-11, crisply embossed spade-shaped leaves, mottled purple dripping over green matte glaze, incised AA/Van Briggle/Colo. Spgs./804/18/7, 3/4" bruise to rim, 8-1/4" x 2-3/4", $1,100.

Vase, bulbous, 1915, embossed trefoils, blue-green matte glaze, incised 695/AA/1915, 3-3/4" x 4-1/2", **$400.**

green matte glaze, incised AA/Van Briggle/1903/III/232 . . . . . **3,775.00**

9" h, 6" d, bulbous, emb poppy pods, rare dark blue-green leathery matte glaze, incised AA/Van Briggle/1903/III/18 . . . . . . **4,890.00**

10-1/4" h, 4-1/4" d, tapering, emb tobacco leaves, covered in matte ochre and umber glaze, incised AA, die-stamped 1915 and 45 . . . . **1,380.00**

11-1/4" h, 4" d, tapering, emb peacock fathers, covered in charcoal and chartreuse matte glaze, incised AA/Van Briggle/1905/III/174 . . . . . **5,750.00**

VENETIAN GLASS

History: Venetian glass has been made on the island of Murano, near Venice, since the 13th century. Most of the wares are thin walled. Many types of decoration have been used: embedded gold dust, lace work, and applied fruits or flowers.

Reproduction Alert: Venetian glass continues to be made today.

Beverage set, 10-1/2" h, pitcher, applied striped handle, eight flared tumblers, six spherical glasses, each striped with opaque orange, transparent yellow-amber, and clear crystal, design attributed to Fulvio Bianconi, 15-pc set **1,950.00**

Bowl, 7-1/2" w, 6-1/8" w, deep quatraform bowl, applied quatraform rim, blue, clear internal dec, trapped air

Vase, white latticinio, clear ground, clear handles with gold trim, 10-3/4" h, $225.

bubble square, circles, and gold inclusions, c1950 . . . . **360.00**

Candlesticks, pr, 8-3/8" h, white and black glass, formed as coat on twisted stem coat rack on tripod base, black domed foot, 20th C **275.00**

Centerpiece set, two 8-1/2" baluster ftd ewers, 78-1/2" ftd compote, red and white latticino stripes with gold flecks, applied clear handles and feet, three-pc set **150.00**

Decanter, 13" h, figural clown, bright red, yellow, black, and white, aventurine swirls, orig stopper **250.00**

Goblet, 6-1/2" h, ruby red, baluster stem, applied amberina rigaree, price for nine-pc set **250.00**

Sherry, amber swirled bowls, blue beaded stems, eight-pc set . . . **495.00**

Table garniture, two 14-1/4" h clear glass dolphins on white diagonally fluted short pedestals, six 5-3/4" h to 7-3/4" h clear glass turtle, bird, seahorse, dolphin, two bunches of fruit in bowls, figures on similar white pedestals, including 20th C . . . **550.00**

Vase, 8" h, handkerchief shape, pale green and white pulled stripe, applied clear rope base, attributed to Barovier, 1930s **65.00**

VILLEROY & BOCH

History: Pierre Joseph Boch established a pottery near Luxembourg, Germany, in 1767. Jean Francis, his son, introduced the first coal-fired kiln in Europe and perfected a water-power-driven potter's wheel. Pierre's grandson, Eugene Boch, managed a pottery at Mettlach; Nicholas Villeroy also had a pottery nearby.

In 1841, the three potteries merged into the firm of Villeroy & Boch. Early production included a hard-paste earthenware comparable to English ironstone. The factory continues to use this hard-paste formula for its modern tablewares.

Beaker, quarter liter, couple at feast, multicolored, printed underglaze **115.00**

Bowl, 8" d, 3-3/4" h, gaudy floral dec, blue, red, green, purple, and yellow, marked "Villeroy & Boch," minor wear and stains **50.00**

Charger, 15-1/2" d, gentleman on horseback, sgd "Stocke" **600.00**

Dish, cov, triangular, orange and black dec, marked "Villeroy & Boch, Mettlach," and "Made in Saar-Basin," molded "3865," c1880-1900 . . . **125.00**

Ewer, 17-3/4" h, central frieze of festive beer hall, band playing white couples dance and drink, neck and foot with formal panels between leaf molded borders, subdued tones, c1884, imp shape number, production number and date codes **900.00**

Figure, 53" h, Venus, scantily clad seated figure, ribbon tied headdress,

Pitcher, stoneware, #1726, panels decorated with stylized design and florets, 1-1/2 liter, $175. Photo courtesy of Joy Luke Auctions.

Plate, cobalt blue Delft-style design, back marked in blue "Villeroy & Boch, Dresden, Saxony," impressed "GR W 5," $45.

left arm raised across chest, resting on rock, inscribed "Villeroy & Boch," damage to foot and base **1,900.00**

Jardinière, 13" d, 12-1/2" h, maidens in field scene, marked "Villeroy & Boch" and Mettlach castle mark, early 1900s **895.00**

Platter

9-1/4" l, 8" w, white basketweave ground, blue fish and aquatic plants dec, marked "Villeroy & Boch, Delphin, Mettlach, Ceschutzt" **110.00**

12-3/4" d, Burgenland, dark pink transfer, white ground..... **165.00**

Stein, #2942, half liter, pewter lid, brown ground, beige earthenware cartouche "Braun ist meine Maid, Schaumt uber jeder-zeit," Jewish Star of David on reverse, marked "Villery & Boch/Mettlach, 7 02" **275.00**

Stein, stoneware, barrel shape, half liter, inlaid lid decorated with relief hops and leaves, $110. Photo courtesy of Joy Luke Auctions.

Tray, 11-1/4" d, metal gallery with geometric cut-outs, ceramic base with border and stylized geometric pattern, white ground, soft gray high gloss glaze, blue accents, base marked **200.00**

Tureen, cov, 11" w, Burgenland, dark pink transfer, white ground, marked "Mettlach, Made by Villeroy & Boch" **195.00**

Vase, 15" h, bulbous, cylindrical, deep cobalt blue glaze, splashes of drizzled white, three handled SP mount cast with leaves, berries, and blossoms, molded, pierced foot, vase imp "V" & "B," "S" monogram, numbered, c1900, price for pr **2,750.00**

Wall plaque, 13-1/4" d, stoneware, wide border with relief dec of fruit garlands, insects, and faces surrounding mythological center on black ground, marked #834, rim separations, minor scratching.................. **220.00**

WATCHES, POCKET

History: Pocket watches can be found in many places—from flea markets to the specialized jewelry auctions. Condition of movement is the first priority; design and detailing of the case is second.

Descriptions of pocket watches may include the size (16/0 to 20), number of jewels in the movement, whether the face is open or closed (hunter), and the composition (gold, gold filled, or some other metal). The movement is the critical element, since cases often were switched. However, an elaborate case, especially if gold, adds significantly to value.

Pocket watches designed to railroad specifications are desirable. They are between 16 and 18 in size, have a minimum of 17 jewels, adjust to at least five positions, and conform to many other specifications. All are open faced.

Study the field thoroughly before buying. There is a vast amount of literature, including books and newsletters from clubs and collectors.

Chatelaine, lady's

Edwardian, 18kt yg, brooch bezel-set with oval lapis in ribbed mount with seed pearl highlights framed by openwork bow and bellflowers, circular lapis connector, suspending open face watch, white enameled Roman numeral dial, jeweled movement, 0 size, key, French 18kt gold horology import mark **1,530.00**

Victorian, 14kt yg, white enamel dial, black Roman numerals edged by Arabic second numerals, fancy scrolled hands, textured back case dec with red enamel stars, suspended from 27-1/4" l curb and translucent red enamel baton link chain **235.00**

Lapel, lady's

Starr, Theodore B., NY, triple signed, Edwardian, 18kt yg, white porcelain dial, black Roman numerals, subsidiary seconds dial, jeweled nickel movement, inscribed dust cover, back case dec with pink guilloche and gold foliate motifs, 0 size, suspended from 14kt gold and pink enamel fleur-de-lis pin **715.00**

Unknown maker, 18kt gold and enamel, cream porcelain dial with Roman numerals, gold fancy scroll hands, jeweled gilt movement, cylinder escapement, back cover with cobalt blue enamel and gold fleur-de-lis, woven watch chain with enamel and seed pearl barrel-shape slides, onyx fob and key, back cover detached **450.00**

Pendant, lady's
Edwardian

Platinum and diamond, C. H. Meylan, Brassus, round white porcelain dial with black Arabic numerals, Louis XIV hands, scroll and foliate motif case bead-set with rose, single, and full-cut diamonds, high grade jeweled nickel diamond slide and swivel clasp ... **6,900.00**

Platinum and enamel, open-face engine-turned goldtone dial with black Arabic numerals, blue-steeled hands, blue-gray enamel guilloche case accented with collet and rose-cut diamonds, cabochon sapphire winder, rose-cut diamond bail and bow pendant, suspended from platinum chain **875.00**

Eterna, 18k yg, rushed gold, rect form, black line indicators, hallmark, 23.10 dwt...................... **230.00**

Figural, insect, 18k yg, rose-cut diamond accents, blue enamel hinged wings opening to reveal white dial, Roman numerals, flat 23-1/2" trace link chain **4,500.00**

Pocket, gentleman's

Audemars, 18 kt gold, hunting case, white enamel dial with Arabic numerals, Louis XIV hands, jeweled nickel movement, monogrammed case, 16 size.................... **980.00**

Baree, Neuchatel, No. 18332, 14k yg, repeater, Roman numerals, subsidiary dial for seconds, hairline to dial **500.00**

Bautte, Jq Fd. Geneve, 18k yg, white dial, Roman numerals, chased case

Gentleman's, Vacheron & Constantin, c1920, ultra thin platinum case, blue sapphires channel mounted around outside of case stamped 18J, eight adjustments, platinum 16" watch chain, $1,265. Photo courtesy of James D. Julia, Inc.

with bi-color floral bouquet on one side, mixed meal and enamel dec on other, scalloped edges, enamel damage
. . . .**260.00**

Bijou Watch Co., lady's label, 14k yg, dec dial with ornate hands, subsidiary seconds hand and dial, diamond-set engraved crescent moon and star on case, 14k yg ribbon shaped watch pin, c1900 . . . .**390.00**

Bourquin, Ami, Locle, #30993, 18 kt yg, key wind, white porcelain dial, black Roman numerals, subsidiary seconds dial, engraved case with black and blue enamel, accented with rose-cut diamonds, fitted wooden box with inlaid dec **1,100.00**

Boutte, #277389, 14k yg, 10 rubies, white dial, black Roman numerals, chased case with red and blue enamel star dec, Russian hallmarks, 29" l ropetwist chain, enamel loss . . .**300.00**

Caldwell, J. E., & Co., openface, 18 kt gold, white enamel dial, black Roman numerals, subsidiary seconds dial, Vacheron and Constantin jeweled movement, cavette dated June 5, 1900, verso monogrammed, 16 size . .**900.00**

Champney, S. P., Worcester, MA, 18k yg, openface, gilt movement, #8063, key wind, white dial, Roman numerals, subsidiary seconds dial, hallmarks, orig key, c1850, dial cracked, nicks to crystal. **250.00**

Elgin, 14kt gold, hunting case, white porcelain dial, black Arabic numerals, blue-steeled hands, subsidiary seconds dial, 15 jewel nickel movement, monogrammed, 16 size, suspended from 14kt gold curb link watch chain **300.00**

Howard, E., & Co., Boston, 18kt gold, hunting case, white enamel dial, black Roman numerals, blue-steeled scroll hands, subsidiary seconds dial, dust cover inscribed and dated June 6, 1872, monogrammed, 16 size. .**980.00**

Jacot, Charles E., 18k yg hunter case, nickel jeweled movement, #9562, numbered on dust cov, case and movement, white porcelain dial, Roman numerals, subsidiary dial for seconds, monogrammed case, orig wood case with extra spring, 14k yg chain .**750.00**

Jurgensen, J. Alfred, Copenhagen, #784, 18k yg hunter case, highly jeweled movement, patent 1865, white porcelain dial, subsidiary dial for seconds, fancy hands, elaborate monogram **3,300.00**

L'Epine, Paris, openface, white enamel dial, key wind, tri-color gold engraved case, 8 size, hand missing, chips to dial
. . . .**375.00**

Meylan, C. H., Brassus, openface, 18kt gold, white enamel dial, Arabic numerals, scrolled hands, subsidiary seconds dial, 19 jewel movement, 10 size **635.00**

Patek Philippe & Co., Geneve, 18k yg, open face, movement and case No. 161442, white dial, Roman numerals, bail missing **575.00**

Gentleman's, American Waltham, c1902, 14k yg, Riverside 17 jewel, open face, short watch chain, $300. Photo courtesy of James D. Julia, Inc.

Pocket, lady's

Meylan, C. H., 18kt gold and enamel, openface, white enamel dial with black Arabic numerals, fancy scrolled hands, gray guilloche enamel bezel, cover enameled with gold flowers set with diamonds, suspended from platinum and purple guilloche enamel baton link chain, crystal replaced, minor enamel loss. **850.00**

Unknown maker, retro, pink gold, hinged rect cover surmounted by rubies and diamonds, similarly set scroll and geometric shoulders, snake link bracelet, 6-1/4" l **750.00**

Vacheron & Constantin, 18kt gold, hunting case, white enamel dial, Roman numerals, gilt bar movement, cylinder escapement, sgd on cuvette, engraved case, 10 size **350.00**

Waltham, 14kt yg, hunting case, white enamel dial, Arabic numeral indicators, subsidiary seconds dial, Lady Waltham jeweled nickel movement by A.W.W. Co., floral engraved case no. 224709, 0 size, gold ropetwist chain **300.00**

Whipperman, A. J., Idaho Falls, Idaho, 14kt yg, hunting case, white enamel dial, black Arabic numeral indicators, subsidiary seconds dial, 15 jewel nickel movement by Rode Watch Co., floral engraved case dec with pale pink guilloche enamel, old mine-cut diamond in center, signed Gruen, dust cover inscribed, "Father to Elsie 1914," 0 size, fancy 14kt yg curb link and pink enamel baton link chain **180.00**

WATCHES, WRIST

History: The definition of a wristwatch is simply "a small watch that is attached to a bracelet or strap and is worn around the wrist." However, a watch on a bracelet is not necessarily a wristwatch. The key is the ability to read the time. A true wristwatch allows you to read the time at a glance, without making any other motions. Early watches on an arm bracelet had the axis of their dials, from 6 to 12, perpendicular to the band. Reading them required some extensive arm movements.

The first true wristwatch appeared about 1850. However, the key date is 1880 when the stylish, decorative wristwatch appeared and almost universal acceptance occurred. The technology to create the wristwatch existed in the early 19th century with Brequet's shock-absorbing "Parachute System" for automatic watches and Ardien Philipe's winding stem.

The wristwatch was a response to the needs of the entrepreneurial age with its emphasis on punctuality and planned free time. Sometime around 1930, the sales of wristwatches surpassed that of pocket watches. American makers quickly joined Swiss and German manufacturers.

The wristwatch has undergone many technical advances during the 20th century including self-winding (automatic), shock-resistance, and electric movements.

Gentleman's

Boucheron, dress tank, A250565, white gold, reeded bezel and dial, invisible clasp, black leather Boucheron strap, French hallmarks, orig leather pouch **2,150.00**

Buccellati, Gianmaria, dress, 18k yg, fancy engraved dial, black tracery enamel, black leather strap, 18k yg clasp, Italian hallmarks **6,900.00**

Cartier, 18k hg, rect convex white dial, black Roman numerals, round gold bezel, black leather strap **1,380.00**

Concord, Delirium, 18kt gold, round goldtone dial without indicators, flat rect bezel, quartz movement, Swiss hallmarks, 9" l orig crocodile band **1,265.00**

Garsons, 14kt gold, sq goldtone dial with simulated jewel indicators, 17-jewel nickel movement, subsidiary seconds dial, 8-1/4" l integrated mesh band **345.00**

Jurgensen, Jules, dress, 14k white gold, Swiss movement, silvertone brushed dial, abstract indicators, diamond-set bevel, black faux alligator strap **290.00**

Le Coultre, Futurematic, goldtone dial, subsidiary seconds dial, power reserve indicator, 10k yg-filled mount, lizard strap, 1950s **425.00**

Nardin, Ulysse, 14k yg, chronometer, goldtone dial, luminescent quarter

sections, applied abstract and Arabic numeral indicators, subsidiary seconds dial, lugs with scroll accents, leather strap, discoloration and scratches to dial **290.00**

Omega, 18k yg, round cream dial, goldtone Arabic numeral and abstract indicators, heavy mesh bracelet, mild soil to dial, 44.80 dwt **460.00**

Philippe, Patek, 18kt white gold, rect, silvertone dial, raised Arabic numerals, 18-jewel nickel movement, eight adjustments, subsidiary seconds dial, triple signed, leather band, c1930 . . . . **6,900.00**

Rolex, Oyster Perpetual

14k yg, goldtone dial, abstract indicators, sweep second hand, ostrich strap, slight spotting to dial **850.00**

Stainless steel, Air King, silvertone dial, applied abstract indicators, sweep second hand, oyster bracelet with deployant clasp, discoloration to dial, scratches to crystal **575.00**

Tiffany & Co., 18k yg, lapis lazuli color dial, stepped bezel, black crocodile strap **635.00**

Universal, Geneve, Uni-Compax, 18K yg, two-dial chronograph, silver-tone dial, sweep seconds hand, black lizard strap **980.00**

Vacheron & Constantin, 18kt gold, white round dial, abstract numeral indicators, 17-jewel nickel movements, 7-1/4" l associated 18kt gold brickwork band **1,495.00**

Lady's

Bueche Girod, 18k yg, elongated oval goldtone dial, rect bezel with stylized hinge lucks, satin band, c1970 . **980.00**

Bucherer, 18k yg, Swiss movement, 17 jewels, designed as double-hinged engraved bangle, center covered watch, cream dial, applied goldtone Arabic and abstract indicators, Swiss hallmarks **165.00**

Cartier, 18kt gold, Pathere, sq goldtone dial with diamond bezel, quartz movement, case and deployment buckle sgd "Cartier," flat rect link band **4,025.00**

Chopard, Geneva, 18kt gold, oval goldtone dial within larger oval crystal with seven floating collet-set diamonds, diamond-set dial, crystal, and shoulders, 8" l maroon leather band **2,760.00**

Elgin, 14k yg, MOP dial, black abstract and Arabic numeral indicators, hinged freeform cover with diamonds and cultured pearl accent, tapering link bracelet with mesh edges, 33.80 dwt **500.00**

Gruen, Art Deco, platinum, rect silvertone dial, black Arabic numerals, bezel enhanced with 32 circular-cut diamonds, mesh strap edged by box-set single-cut diamonds, highlighted by diamond-set floret shoulders, 6-1/4" l **4,225.00**

Hamilton Watch Co., dress, silvertone rect dial, applied Arabic numerals, flanked by four graduating collet set diamonds, diamond-set platinum bracelet, 2.16 cts **2,300.00**

Helbros Watch Co., 17 jewels, Art Deco, combination of old European and single cut diamonds, approx 1 ct, case hinged to allow better contour when worn, calibre French cut sapphires, curved crystal, platinum setting **995.00**

Le Coultre, Jaeger, 14kt gold, Reverso, silvertone dial with black Arabic numeral indicators, blue-steeled hands, case flips to reveal polished gold monogrammed cover, case sgd and numbered, 8" l tan ostrich leather strap **1,380.00**

Gentleman's, Rolex Oyster Perpetual, gold and stainless steel band, **$1,900.** *Photo courtesy of Joy Luke Auctions.*

Hamilton, lady's, 17 jewels, model 750, #72052A, 14K white gold decorated case framed with 17 single cut diamonds, white gold band decorated with 38 single-cut diamonds, replaced clasp, one stone missing, 10.6dwt., **$260.** *Photo courtesy of Sanford Alderfer Auction Co.*

Lady's, Movado, 14kt white gold, small square watch accented at top and bottom with two bands containing 14 diamond melees, engraved name on back plate, **$460.** Photo courtesy of James D. Julia, Inc.

Lehman, Retro, Uti movement, 18k yg, round goldtone dial with ruby indicators, one half framed in graduated calibre-cut channel-set rubies, snake like bracelet, French hallmarks, slight discoloration to dial **1,495.00**

Movado, 14kt gold, round, silvertone dial, diamond bezel and lugs, jeweled movement, black suede band . . **325.00**

Perraux, Retro, 14kt gold, sq white metal dial with gold indicators, lugs set with modified bullet-shaped aquamarines, flanked by diamonds, 17 jewel movement, black cord band with deployment clasp **635.00**

Philippe, Patek, 18kt, gold covered, sq, ivorytone dial with abstract indicators, 20-jewel nickel movement, 6-1/2" l integral mesh band, boxed . . **1,150.00**

Rolex, Oyster Perpetual, stainless steel, precision, cream dial, abstract indicators with phosphorescent, subsidiary seconds dial, slight discoloration to dial **1,380.00**

Swiss, 18k yg, Swiss movement, manual wind, domed bezel, goldtone dial, black Roman numerals, hallmark, leather strap **920.00**

Tiffany & Co., 14kt gold, oval white dial with black Roman numerals, diamond-set bezel, 6-3/4" l flexible flat rect link band **1,150.00**

Uti, Paris, Spritzer and Furhmann, lady's, 18k yg, silvertone dial, applied goldtone indicators, leather strap with keyhole form closure, hallmarks, wear to strap **575.00**

WATERFORD

History: Waterford crystal is high-quality flint glass commonly decorated with cuttings. The original factory was established at Waterford, Ireland, in 1729. Glass made before 1830 is darker than the brilliantly clear glass of later production. The factory closed in 1852. One hundred years later it reopened and continues in production today.

For more information, see this book.

Bowl, 9-3/4" d, Kileen pattern . . **260.00**
Cake plate, 10" d, 5-1/4" h, sunburst center, geometric design **85.00**
Cake server, cut-glass handle, orig box **80.00**
Champagne flute, 6" h, Coleen pattern, 12-pc set **450.00**
Christmas ornament, Twelve Days of Christmas Series, crystal, orig box, dated bag, orig sticker, brochure
    1982, Partridge in Pear Tree **450.00**
    1985, second, two turtle doves
    . . . . **250.00**

Decanter, Lismore pattern, 10-1/2" h, roughness on stopper, **$110.** Photo courtesy of Sanford Alderfer Auction Company.

Fruit bowl, turned down rim, pedestal base, 6-3/4" d, 5-3/4" h, **$295.**

    1986, three French hens **225.00**
    1987, four calling birds **200.00**
Compote, 5-1/2" h, allover diamond cutting above double wafer stem, pr **400.00**
Creamer and sugar, 4" h creamer, 3-3/4" d sugar, Tralee pattern **85.00**
Decanter, orig stopper
    10" h, ship's, diamond cutting
    . . . . **200.00**
    12-3/4" h, allover diamond cutting, monogram, pr **300.00**
Honey jar, cov **75.00**
Lamp, 23" h, 13" d umbrella shade, blunt diamond cutting, Pattern L-1122 . . . . **450.00**
Napkin ring, 2" h, 12-pc set . . . **225.00**
Old fashioned tumbler, 3-1/2" h, Comeragh pattern, pr **70.00**
Ring dish, 5" d, colorless, cut glass, price for three-pc set **110.00**
Tumbler, Colleen, set of six, orig box **400.00**
Vase, 6" h, diamond pattern, wreath around center, sgd **225.00**

WAVE CREST

WAVE CREST WARE

c1892

History: The C. F. Monroe Company of Meriden, Connecticut, produced the opal glassware known as Wave Crest from 1898 until World War I. The company bought the opaque, blown-molded glass blanks from the Pairpoint Manufacturing Co. of New Bedford, Massachusetts, and other glassmakers, including European factories. The Monroe company then decorated the blanks, usually with floral patterns. Trade names used were "Wave Crest Ware," "Kelva," and "Nakara."

For more information,
see this book.

Biscuit jar, cov, unmarked
  5-1/2" d, 5-1/2" h, pink and white
    background, melon ribbed, hp
    flowers **250.00**
  6-1/2" d, Helmschmied swirl opaque
    white and tan body, red enameled
    flowers **460.00**
  8" h, white ground, fern dec . **200.00**
Bonbon, 7" h, 6" w, Venetian scene,
  multicolored landscape, dec rim, satin
  lining missing **1,200.00**
Box, cov
  5-1/2" w, man on bended knee
    proposing to lady, roses, rococo
    swirls, orig lining **1,300.00**
  5-1/2" w, 4-3/4" h, white daisies,
    green leaves, earth tone details,
    unmarked **675.00**
  6" d, heart-shape, opaque tan glass
    body, dec with red and yellow
    mums, Belle Ware, #4625/10
    . . . . **460.00**
  7" w, pink florals, fancy ormolu
    fittings **800.00**
  7-1/4" d, 3-3/34" h, Baroque Shell,
    Moorish Fantasy design, raised
    pink-gold rococo scrolls, fancy
    Arabic designs of pale turquoise
    and natural opaque white, lace-like
    network of raised white enamel
    beads, satin lining missing
    . . . . **1,250.00**

*Dresser box, hinged, scenic panel of
Niagara Falls on lid, unsigned,
7" l, 4" h,* **$800.** *Photo courtesy of Joy
Luke Auctions.*

Cigar humidor, 8-3/4" h, blue body,
single-petaled pink rose, pink "Cigar"
signature, pewter collar, bail, and lid,
flame-shaped finial, sgd "Kelva" **685.00**
Cracker jar, 5-1/4" d, 10-1/2" h, blue
and white hp florals, green and brown
leaves, white Johnny jump-ups, puffy
egg crate mold **700.00**
Dresser box
  3" d, opaque ground, enameled
    cherub, married top and base
    . . . . **435.00**
  4" d, molded flowers, green and
    blue, enameled mill scene on
    cover, marked "Wavecrest" . **260.00**
  4" d, opaque blue body, red
    enameled flowers, orig lining
    . . . . **345.00**
  5" d, opaque rose and white body,
    blue and pink flowers, red banner
    mark **525.00**

*Dresser jar, hinged, lid decorated with
white daisies, unsigned, 4-3/4" d,* **$140.**
Photo courtesy of Joy Luke Auctions.

  5" d, 5-1/2" h, egg crate mold,
    alternating turquoise and opal
    panels, pink stemmed yellow
    flowers, four ftd emb metal holder
    . . . . **1,265.00**
  5-1/2" d, mottled red opaque ground,
    earthtone enameled flowers, red
    Kelva mark **690.00**
  6-3/4" d, Helmschmied swirl, blue to
    white opaque body, burgundy,
    rose, and yellow enameled violets
    . . . . **500.00**
  6-3/4" d, 6-3/4" h, egg crate mold,
    brown and tan, multitude of yellow
    mums, ormolu stand with three
    cupid feet, red banner Wavecrest
    mark **3,795.00**
  7" d, Baroque shell mold, opaque
    ground with pink hues, colorful
    pointillism design **525.00**

*Cracker jar,
Helmschmidt
swirl, pink
floral
decoration,
original metal
hardware,
original Wave
Crest label,
10" h,* **$350.**
*Photo courtesy
of James D.
Julia, Inc.*

*Left: 3" jewel
box, swirl mold,
light blue, pink
blossom
decoration,
signed,* **$200;**
*center: 2-1/2" x
4-1/4" powder
box, pink, blue
floral decoration,
unsigned,* **$75;**
*right: 3" h puffy
mold hinged
jewel box, white
shading to light
blue, pink and
white floral
branch
decoration,*
$100. *Photo
courtesy of
Woody Auctions.*

Left: 4-1/2" x 5" square box, pink and white, floral decoration, egg crate and scroll mold, signed, $400; center: 4-1/4" square jewel box, red mottled ground, white floral decoration, signed "Kelva," $300; right: 4-1/4" x 6" letter holder, light yellow, pink rose decoration, scroll mold, brass rim, signed, $225. Photo courtesy of Woody Auctions.

7" d, Baroque shell mold, opaque ground, red flowers framed by light and dark blue scrolling, red banner mark **850.00**

Ewer, lavender, figural woman on handle, ornate base **225.00**

Ferner, 6-3/4" d, egg crate mold, enameled blue flowers, four lion emb feet, orig liner **520.00**

Mustard jar, cov, spoon, green ground, floral dec, unmarked **140.00**

Pin dish, open

3-1/2" d, 1-1/2" h, pink and white, swirled, floral dec, unmarked **35.00**

4-1/4" d, 2" h, pink and white, eggcrate mold, blue violets dec, marked **80.00**

5" d, 1-1/2" h, white, scrolls, pink floral dec, marked **80.00**

Plate, 7" d, reticulated border, pond lily dec, shaded pale blue ground. **. 750.00**

Salt and pepper shakers, pr

Swirled, light yellow ground, floral dec, unmarked **75.00**

Tulip, brown and white ground, birds and floral dec **70.00**

Sugar shaker, 3-1/2" d, 5-1/4" h, Helmschmied Swirl, enameled pink florals, gray and brown foliage. **. 575.00**

Syrup pitcher, Helmschmied Swirl, ivory-colored body, blue and white floral dec, smoky-gray leafy branches, SP lid and collar **485.00**

Trinket dish, 1-1/2" x 5", blue and red flowers **175.00**

Vase, 10" h, pale pink accents on white, pink and orange chrysanthemums, enameled foliage, beaded white top **600.00**

WEATHER VANES

History: A weather vane indicates wind direction. The earliest known examples were found on late 17th-century structures in the Boston area. The vanes were handcrafted of wood, copper, or tin. By the last half of the 19th century, weather vanes adorned farms and houses throughout the nation. Mass-produced vanes of cast iron, copper, and sheet metal were sold through mail-order catalogs or at country stores.

The champion vane is the rooster—in fact, the name weathercock is synonymous with weather vane—but the styles and patterns are endless. Weathering can affect the same vane differently; for this reason, patina is a critical element in collectible vanes.

Whirligigs are a variation of the weather vane. Constructed of wood and metal, often by the unskilled, whirligigs indicate the direction of the wind and its velocity. Watching their unique movements also provides entertainment.

Reproduction Alert: Reproductions of early models exist, are being aged, and then sold as originals.

Arrow

31" l, 17" h, copper, sphere finial, old gilded surface, wear, minor dents **590.00**

36" l, 16" h, gilt copper, ball finial, weathered gilt surface, no stand, dents **360.00**

60" l, 29" h, copper, spire and belted ball finial, verdigris surface, no stand, dents, several bullet holes **950.00**

Banner

15-3/4" l, 37" h, sheet iron, iron ball finial on shaft above banner, heart and oval cutouts, weathered black paint, stand **1,645.00**

71-1/2" l, 17-3/4" h, pierced scrolled sheet copper, old surface, traces of gilt, no stand, minor dents **2,715.00**

Bird and fish, 18-1/2" w, 19" h, molded metal, full bodied, bird flies with aid of propellers above fish, marble eyes, unpainted weathered gray surface, Illinois, early 20th C, tall stand **1,150.00**

Eagle

15-1/2" l, 14-3/4" w, 9-1/8" h, gilt copper, outstretched wings perched on belted sphere over arrow directional, old gilt-copper verdigris surface, no stand, small loss on arrow feather. . . . **1,100.00**

21" wing span, 18-1/2" h, copper, full bodied, cast zinc feet, wooden base, one foot loose, arrow bent **250.00**

Ethan Allen, running horse, 25-1/2" l, 16-3/4" h, gilt copper and zinc, weathered gilded surface, including stand, restoration **2,585.00**

Fire wagon, 40" l, 29-1/4" h, painted copper, two horses, driver, steam fire engine, iron supports on underside, red, black, and gold paint, attributed to I. W. Cushing & Sons, Waltham, MA, late 19th C, including stand, imperfections **15,275.00**

Whirligig, faceless family, carved wood, painted green, brown, and white, $2,900.

Fish

12-3/4" l, 3-1/4" h, carved wood, full bodied, tail wrapped with lead sheeting, tacked button eyes, Midwestern U.S., late 19th C, remnant of post, minor losses, with stand **2,645.00**

26" l, 6-1/2" h, white painted carved wood and sheet metal, America, mid-20th C, tall stand **1,495.00**

27" l, 6" h, carved and painted wood, salmon orange, chamfered edge, tin reinforced carved bracket, Wakefield, MA, 19th C, inscribed "this set on a cedar tree near our farm before the Civil War," with stand **1,150.00**

Gamecock, 17-1/2" l, 18-1/2" h, molded copper, emb sheet copper tail, weathered gilt surface, no stand, repair on neck, bullet hole on breast . **4,995.00**

Heart and feather, 76-3/4" l, 13-1/4" h, sheet iron, found in New York state, late 18th C, fine rust and overall pitting, with stand **4,900.00**

Horse

17-3/4" h, running, copper, verdigris patina, traces of gilt, America, late 19th C, includes copper sphere, no stand, dents, small seam separations, 17-3/4" h . . . **2,350.00**

24" l, 18-1/2" h, zinc torso, copper ears, legs, and body, corrugated copper tail, attributed to J. Howard & Co., West Bridgewater, MA, third quarter 19th C, old surface with vestiges of gilt, no stand, old repair on one leg, wear, minor dents **7,650.00**

25" l, 19" h, molded zinc head and torso, copper body, tail, and legs, old surface, attributed to J. Howard

Running horse, copper, verdigris patina, traces of gilt, copper sphere, no stand, America, late 19th C, dents, small seam separations, 17-3/4" h, **$2,350.** *Photo courtesy of Skinner Auctioneers and Appraisers.*

& Co., West Bridgewater, MA, no stand, minor dents on ears **12,925.00**

26-1/4" l, 16" h, running, gilt copper, no stand, couple of small dents **2,470.00**

29" l, 14" h, running, molded copper and cast zinc, verdigris surface, attributed to A. L. Jewell & Co., Waltham, MA, 1850-67, no stand, minor dents, seam separation **4,625.00**

29-5/8" l, 18" h, running, molded copper, full bodied, verdigris surface, traces of gilt, no stand, wear, hole **3,410.00**

30" l, 20" h, running, gilded copper and zinc, full bodied horse, zinc head, stand, repair to tail, minor dents and seam separations **2,715.00**

31-1/8" l, 20-5/8" h, running, gilt copper and zinc, copper full bodied horse, zinc head, no stand, later gilt, replaced rod, wear **1,175.00**

32" l, 17" h, running, painted copper, flattened full bodied, older darkened putty painted surface, traces of gilt, no stand, dents, bullet hole repairs **1,410.00**

32" l, 18-3/8" h, running, copper, zinc ears, full-bodied, verdigris, yellow sizing, traces of gilding, body with imp maker's mark "A. J. Harris & Co., Boston," late 19th C, no stand, minor seam separation, repaired bullet hole **5,585.00**

32-1/2" l, 18-1/2" h, copper and zinc, full bodied, weathered silvered paint, traces of gold gilt, no stand, minor dents, repaired bullet holes **2,470.00**

32-1/2" l, 22" h, molded copper, running, old later painted surface, imp "A. J. Harris & Co." (Boston, MA,) late 19th C, no stand, wear, dents, seam separations . **2,350.00**

34" l, 25-1/2" h, prancing, molded copper, weathered gilt surface, vestiges of sizing, with stand, imperfections **4,115.00**

37-1/2" l, 63" h, running, copper, flattened full body with verdigris surface, traces of gilt, raised on cast iron directionals, copper sphere, pyramidal roof mount, repair to knee, dents **7,050.00**

41-1/2" l, 21" h, running, copper head, hollow molded full body, no

stand, gilt wear, minor dent **4,115.00**

61-1/2" l, 23-5/8" h, running, full-bodied, zinc, mounted on a hollow zinc rod with vestiges of gilt in the recesses, black metal stand, minor separations, repaired bullet holes, America, 19th C. . . **8,815.00**

Horse and jockey, 31-1/2" l, 22-3/4" h, copper, old yellow sizing surface, no stand, minor dents on ears and jockey's head **9,400.00**

Horse and rider, molded sheet iron, hollow body, orig mustard painted surface, wear, cracks **6,465.00**

Quill pen, 36-1/2" l, 23-1/2" h, iron and copper, spire and sphere finial with weathered regilded surface, attributed to L. W. Cushing & Sons, Waltham, MA, late 19th C, repaired, minor imperfections. **2,570.00**

Pig, 32" l, 20-1/4" h, molded copper, weathered dark verdigris surface, traces of gilt, stand, late 19th C, imperfections. **32,300.00**

Plow, 38-1/4" l, 13-1/2" h, iron and bronze, old surface, no stand . **3,415.00**

Pointing hand, 23" l, 35-1/4" h, sheet iron and wood, two wood finials on iron shaft, hand and sunburst sheet iron motif, no stand, imperfections. **2,235.00**

Rooster, 42" l, 26-1/2" h, sheet copper, old verdigris surface, traces of gilt, no stand, imperfections **5,585.00**

Schooner, 39" l, 23-3/8" h, wooden, hull painted red and black, cream colored sail, wire rigging, America, 20th C, wooden stand, wear **275.00**

Rooster, standing on directional arrow, gilded sheet copper, American, 75 percent original gilt intact, had been painted, normal bend, small 22-caliber bullet hole in tail, 34" l, 31" h, **$1,600.** *Photo courtesy of Cowan's Historic Americana Auctions.*

Sloop, gaff-rigged, molded copper, verdigris surface, America, early 20th C, no stand **4,415.00**

Stag, leaping

20" l, 19" h, molded copper, zinc antlers, old gilt surface, black metal stand, America, 19th C . . **8,225.00**

21-1/2" l, 17-3/4" h, molded copper, old regilded surface, mounted on wooden stand **5,290.00**

55-1/2" l, 41-5/8" h, molded copper, full body, attributed to A. I. Harris & Son, Waltham, MA, including stand, regilded old surface
. . . . **12,925.00**

Steer, 29-3/8" l, 20" h, zinc head, copper body, old painted surface, traces of gilt, no stain, wear, minor dents. **6,475.00**

Whirligig

Band leader, 9" w, 2-1/2" d, 20" h, polychrome carved pine, copper hat, bowtie and buttons, glass eyes, attributed to WI, late 19th C, stand, some paint wear **10,925.00**

Bicycle rider, 19" l, 4-1/2" d, 21" h, painted wood and sheet metal, man with metal wide brimmed hat, red body, high wheel green bicycle activated by blades in wheel, America, early 20th C
. . . . **3,450.00**

Cottage birdhouse, propeller on front, arrow tail in rear, painted cream, green and yellow trim, late 19th/early 20th C, 18" l, 8" w, 13" h **250.00**

Whirligig, Dutch mill, wood, gray and black paint, weathered surface, 16-1/2" h, **$175.**

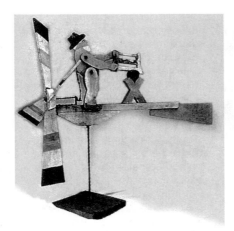

Whirligig, man sawing log, wood, red, white, and blue, c1930, 25-1/4" l, 24-3/4" h, **$150.**

Flying fish

17" l, 13-1/2" d, 5-1/2" h, carved and silver painted fish decoy, added tin wings and tail fin, rubber wheels, weathered surface, attributed to Minnesota, mid-20th C, with stand
. . . . **250.00**

25" l, 11" d, 6" h, painted wood and metal, painted blue-green, glass marble eyes, cut-out sheet metal fins and teeth, America, c1940, tall stand, weathered surface, eye missing. **575.00**

Policeman, 10" w, 18-1/8" h, polychrome carved pine and tin, mustache and beard, arms constructed with tin at elbows, orig painted surface, America, late 19th C, paddles missing
. . . . **11,500.00**

Soldier, 9-5/8" w, 13" h, painted wood, black, gray, and white, wooden stand, wear. **355.00**

Trotting horse, tin propeller, horse with articulated legs, painted white, weathered surface, metal stand, 28-1/2" l, 21-1/2" w, 28-1/4" h. . . **375.00**

Witch, 17" l, 22" h, painted wood, cut-out figure, rotating sheet iron paddle arms, weathered off-white paint, brown trim, stand. **4,410.00**

WEBB, THOMAS & SONS

History: Thomas Webb & Sons was established in 1837 in Stourbridge, England. The company probably is best known for its very beautiful English cameo glass. However, many other types of colored art glass were produced, including enameled, iridescent, heavily ornamented, and cased.

For more information, see this book.

Bowl

5-1/2" w, 5" h, Rainbow MOP satin, triangular, deep pink, yellow, blue, and white, applied thorn feet, raspberry prunt, sgd "Patent"
. . . . **1,500.00**

5-3/4" d, 4-1/2" h, avocado green, sapphire blue stripes, mica flakes, crystal applied fancy drippings on sides, applied crystal rigaree around top edge, applied clear feet, clear berry pontil **235.00**

12" d, 3" h, ruffled, blue ext., cased white int., sgd "Thomas Webb & Sons". **350.00**

Cologne bottle, 6" h, cameo, spherical, clear frosted body, overlaid white and red, carved blossoms, buds, leafy stems, and butterfly, linear pattern, hallmarked silver dec, molded and chased blossoms dec **3,200.00**

Cream pitcher

3-1/4" h, sepia to pale tan ground, heavy gold burnished prunus blossoms, butterfly on back, gold rim and base, clear glass handle with brushed gold **385.00**

3-3/4" h, 2-1/2" d, bulbous, round mouth, brown satin, cream lining, applied frosted handle **210.00**

Fairy lamp, blue shade with bird and branch decoration, clear Clarke's Cricklite insert, square blue satin base, 6-1/2" h, **$1,500.** *Photo courtesy of Woody Auctions.*

Ewer, 9" h, 4" d, satin, deep green shading to off-white, gold enameled leaves and branches, three naturalistic applies, applied ivory handle, long spout, numbered base **425.00**

Figure, 3" l, 1-1/2" h, pig, solid Burmese body, pink tint to hind quarters, curly tail, four feet, ears, and snout, Webb **750.00**

Flask, 11-5/8" h, fish shape, lemon yellow glass overlaid in white, wheel carved features, sterling silver fish tail screw lid, cameo carved "Rd. 15711," lid imp "Sterling," hairline and cameo loss at mouth **9,500.00**

Lamp, 3-1/4" h, 4-1/4" h, satin background, cameo cut rose shading to white sprig of cameo, three applied camphor feet, stamped "Thomas Webb and Sons" **1,265.00**

Perfume bottle, 4-1/4" h, undulating body, yellow overlaid in white, cut and carved as swimming dolphin, inscribed registry mark, "Rd. 18100," rim and cap missing **4,950.00**

Rose bowl

2-1/4" h, 2-1/2" d, Burmese, amethyst flowers, green and brown foliage, price for pr **690.00**

3" h, 3-3/4" d, Burmese, salmon shading to pink, dec with branch of pine cones, rim ground ... **200.00**

3-1/4" h, Burmese, salmon shading to pale yellow, amethyst flower leafy stem **260.00**

Vase

4-1/4" h, cameo, cased glass shading from deep rose to citron, cameo carved branch of flowers, sgd "Thomas Webb and Sons" **1,265.00**

4-1/4" h, 7" d, cases glass, pink fish scale cameo cutting, gold gilt rim and underwater scene **865.00**

4-3/4" h, flared rim, melon-ribbed body, shaded salmon pink overlay etched as fish scale pattern cased to ivory glass, gilt enamel flowering branch and butterfly dec, painted "Rd 39086" mark in rect on base, minor gilt wear **575.00**

5" h, cameo, white florals and tendrils dec, citron green ground **600.00**

5" h, 6" w, 18" circumference, shaded blue, sky blue to pale white cream, applied crystal edge, enameled gold and yellow dec of flowers, leaves, and buds, full butterfly, entire surface acid-cut in basketweave design **425.00**

5-1/4" h, 3-1/2" d, opaque ivory, cut leaves and berries, brown staining, circular cameo mark on base "Simulated Ivory English Cameo Glass," hallmarked silver rim and frosted ball feet **625.00**

5-7/8" h, cameo, raised rim, oval form, pale amber overlaid in white and blue glass, cameo etched dianthus blossoms and foliage, applied elbow-shaped arms cameo-etched in bamboo motif extending to rim, based sgd "Thomas Webb & Sons, Gem Cameo" **9,500.00**

7" h, MOP satin, purple shading to black air trapped body, gold trailing branches, two applied gold handles, registration numbers in gold **3,680.00**

7" h, 5" w, satin, basketweave mother of pearl, bulbous base shading from deep blue to pale blue, creamy lining............ **750.00**

7-1/4" h, 4" w at shoulder, Rainbow MOP satin, pink, yellow, blue, and white, DQ, flaring top, broad shoulder, tapered body, glossy white int., sgd "Patent" .. **1,250.00**

7-1/4" h, Japonesque, pale oval heat reactive body, white Burmese to pink at top, overall delicate oriental sepia scenes........... **345.00**

7-1/2" h, 5-5/8" d, shaded orange overlay, off-white lining, gold flowers and fern-like leaves, gold butterfly on back, applied bronze-colored glass handles **255.00**

8" h, 4" w, satin, pink and white stripes, fancy frilly top, bulbous base, unlined........... **425.00**

Whimsy, figural pig, lemon-yellow Burmese, shiny finish, curly tail, pink blushed ears, snout, and feet, 3" l, 1-1/2" h, **$750.** *Photo courtesy of Clarence and Betty Maier.*

Vase, peachblow, multicolored decoration, unmarked, 6-1/4" h, **$300.**

8-3/4" h, cased satin, shading from pale yellow to deep caramel, black and gold morning glories dec, registration numbers on base **250.00**

9" h, crystal ground, overlaid in blue, cameo-cut tulips, overall crystal stippling effect, sgd "Webb" in cameo **665.00**

10" h, 4" w, satin, pulled down edges, deep rose shading to pink, creamy lining, ruffled top, dome foot, pr **550.00**

10-1/2" h, gourd shape, satin, bright yellow shading to pale yellow, creamy white lining, bleed-through in pontil................ **285.00**

10-1/2" h, 4" w, bulbous, gold floral prunus blossoms, leaves, branches, pine needles, and insect, satin ground shaded brown to gold, creamy white lining, Jules Barbe dec **450.00**

11-1/2" h, peachblow, creamy int., enameled dogwood and branches dec................... **750.00**

WEDGWOOD

History: In 1754, Josiah Wedgwood and Thomas Whieldon of Fenton Vivian, Staffordshire,

 WEDGWOOD

WEDGWOOD
c1900

WEDGWOOD
c1759-1769

England, became partners in a pottery enterprise. Their products included marbled, agate, tortoiseshell, green glaze, and Egyptian black wares. In 1759, Wedgwood opened his own pottery at the Ivy House works, Burslem. In 1764, he moved to the Brick House (Bell Works) at Burslem. The pottery concentrated on utilitarian pieces.

Between 1766 and 1769, Wedgwood built the famous works at Etruria. Among the most-renowned products of this plant were the Empress Catherina of Russia dinner service (1774) and the Portland Vase (1790s). The firm also made caneware, unglazed earthenwares (drabwares), piecrust wares, variegated and marbled wares, black basalt (developed in 1768), Queen's or creamware, and Jasperware (perfected in 1774).

Bone china was produced under the direction of Josiah Wedgwood II between 1812 and 1822 and revived in 1878. Moonlight luster was made from 1805 to 1815. Fairyland luster began in 1920. All luster production ended in 1932.

A museum was established at the Etruria pottery in 1906. When Wedgwood moved to its modern plant at Barlaston, North Staffordshire, the museum was expanded.

Agate ware

Candleholder, 6-1/2" h, surface agate, applied creamware drapery swags, black basalt base, wafer Wedgwood & Bentley mark, c1775, restored chip to socle **1,495.00**
Vase, cov, 9-1/2" h, solid agate, creamware sibyl finials, traces of gilding, black basalt base, imp wafer Wedgwood & Bentley marks, c1770, gilt rim wear, covers with rim chips, nicks to bases, pr **7,500.00**

Basalt

Bough pot, cov, 7" h, scrolled handles terminating in ram's heads, pierced disc lid with removable candle nozzle,

Basalt, teapot, 8-1/2" h, $320.

imp mark, mid-19th C, restored nozzle and one handle **1,265.00**
Bowl, 10-1/8" d, engine turned dec, imp mark, early 20th C **230.00**
Bust, library type, mounted on waisted circular socle

    14" h, Watt, imp title, E. W. Wyon, F., and factory mark, c1877 . . **520.00**
    17-1/2" h, Minerva, imp title and mark, mid-19th C **2,415.00**
    18" h, Mercury, imp mark, mid-19th C **2,415.00**
Candlestick, 11-1/2" h, Ceres, modeled holding cornucopia form candle sconce and mounted to stepped circular base, imp title and mark, 19th C, restored candle nozzle, rim nicks to base **1,265.00**
Club jug, 5" h, enameled floral dec, imp mark, mid-19th C **350.00**
Creamer, 2-1/4" h, Dragon Kenlock Ware, enamel dec Chinese dragon design, imp and printed marks, c1895 . . . . **350.00**
Crocus pot and tray, 9-3/4" l, hedgehog shape, imp marks, c1800, repaired chips **920.00**
Cup and saucer, 5" d saucer, iron red and white banded palmette borders, Encaustic dec, imp lower case mark, late 18th C, slight enamel flake to saucer rim **1,265.00**
Figure

    10-1/4" h, Aphrodite, modeled seated atop cresting wave, imp mark, late 19th C, footrim chips **635.00**
    10-3/4" h, Voltaire, modeled holding book, imp title and mark on reverse, early 19th C **1,265.00**
    18-3/4" h, Venus on rock, after sculpture by Jean-Baptiste Pigalle, modeled to free form base, imp mark, mid to late 19th C . . **1,955.00**
Inkstand, 7" l, oil lamp form, attached to oval tray, applied rosso antico foliate decoration, insert inkpot, imp mark, c1820, restored nozzle **360.00**
Jug, 7-1/4" h, central putti-relief between bands of engine turning, mask head to handle terminal, metal mounts, imp lower case mark, late 19th C **2,875.00**
Lamp, 8-3/8" h, vestal and reading, cov, female figure seated on oval lamps, applied acanthus leaves and bellflowers, imp marks, 19th C, slight flake to book of reading lamp, ball finial reglued, finial and pitcher missing on vestal lamp, rim chip repair, price for pr **920.00**

Model

    2-3/4" h, bulldog, glass eyes, by Ernest Light, imp mark, c1915, imp nick to ear **345.00**
    11-1/4" h, Sphinx, female figure, lion body, stepped rect base, imp mark, early 19th C, chips to footrim and headdress **865.00**
Plaque, 5-1/2" x 7-1/4", oval, Hercules strangling Nemean lion, imp mark, set in ebonized wood frame, 19th C **815.00**
Slave Medallion, 1-1/8" x 1-1/4", oval, slave relief centering verse "Am I not a man and a brother?" imp mark and date, c1891 . . . . **635.00**
Rum kettle, 5-3/4" h, body with bacchanalian boys in relief above engine turned band, shaped bale handle, Sybil finial, imp lower case mark, late 18th C, restored chip on cov rim and finial **600.00**
Tankard, 4-1/4" h, cylindrical form, applied classical figures in relief, imp mark, restored rim chip, 19th C . **360.00**
Tea cup and saucer, Iris Kenlock Ware, enamel dec floral design, imp mark, c1895 . . . . **815.00**
Teapot, cov, 3-3/4" h, oval, molded arabesque floral body, sunflower finial, imp mark, early 19th C, rim nick to cover, tip of spout slightly ground **290.00**
Vase, cov

    12" h, lebes gamikos form, iron red and black classical Encaustic figures on one side, palmettes below handles, imp mark, early 19th C, slight chips to one cover rim, both finials off at joint, price for pr **11,500.00**
    13-1/4" h, two leaf molded scroll handles, engine turned, banded border with classical relief between arabesque floral designs, plinth with imp Wedgwood & Bentley wafer mark, 19th C, cover missing, relief loss **1,100.00**
Vase

    12-1/2" h, two handles, iron-red, black, and white classical figures on one side, stylized palmette design on reverse, gadroon and dot, palmette, laurel, and dot, and spearhead and dot borders, imp mark, c1800 . . . . **4,325.00**
    14" h, cov, serpent handles terminating to satyr masks, relief of Venus and Cupid, engine turning to base, shoulders, neck and cover, imp Wedgwood & Bentley wafer mark, c1775 . . . . **1,725.00**

Bone china, First period, c1820

Celery dish, gilt diamond border, printed mark, foot rim, light gilt war
. . . . **175.00**

Service plate, 10-5/8" d, each with hp floral center, scrolled foliate gilding to wide border, pale green ground printed marks, 20th C, price for set of 12 **980.00**

Tea set, Liberty Ware, 5-1/2" h silver shaped cov teapot, 6-1/2" h creamer, cov sugar, six cups and saucers, 7-3/4" d cake plate, gilt trim line and printed flag ensemble polychrome dec, c1917 . . . . **1,265.00**

Tureen, cov, underplate, 7-1/8" l, oval, polychrome floral dec, printed mark, rim chip to cov **346.00**

Caneware, Game pie dish and underplate, recumbent cow finial, floral scrollwork ground, shell-shaped handles, 6" dish, 7-1/4" shell scrollwork underplate, unmarked, early 19th C, horns chipped, tiny flake on lid, **$340.** *Photo courtesy of Cowan's Historic Americana Auctions.*

Caneware

Game pie dish, cov

8-1/4" d, round, applied fruiting grapevine banding, cauliflower finial, imp mark, mid-19th C, hairline, numerous chips to cov, no insert **230.00**

8-1/2" l, oval, hare finial molded dead game on cover, dish with dead game between fruiting grapevine festoons, imp mark, early 19th C, stained, missing liner **400.00**

9-1/4" l, oval, insert dish, relief of dead game between grapevine festoons, rabbit finial, imp mark, early 19th C **635.00**

Pie dish, 12" l, oval, liner, leaf molded cover, imp marks, 1863 . . . . . . **920.00**

Potpourri basket, 4-1/4" h, black basalt fruiting grapevine relief, imp mark, rim staining **575.00**

Tea set, 7-1/2" l cov teapot (restored body chip), 4-1/2" h creamer (handle restored), 4-1/4" cov sugar (cov restored), molded basketweave body, imp marks, c1840 . . . . **230.00**

Carrara

Bust, 14-3/8" h, Burns, raised circular socle, imp title, E. W. Wyon and factory mark, c1858 . . . . **520.00**

Figure, 20-1/4" h, Venus Victrix, seminude figure modeled standing on freeform base, inscribed title, imp mark, mid-19th C, shallow chip and nick to base **1,450.00**

Vase, cov, 7-1/2" h, trophy relief between floral festoons terminating at ram's heads, foliate borders, bronzed and gilt, imp and printed marks, c1900, cover restored **1,495.00**

Cream ware

Bowl

7-1/2" d, scalloped edge, cut-out design, imp "Wedgwood" . . **600.00**

8-1/8" l, reticulated, molded fiddleback ladle, imp "Wedgwood," stains, edge chip **160.00**

Plate, 9-1/8" d, scenic, little girl and mother buying buns from the Bun Man, back titled "Buns!, Buns!, Buns!," 1863 mark and artist sgd "Lessore" . . **335.00**

Vase, 6" h, molded grape vines and foliage, painted band of strawberries, mid-19th C **250.00**

Drabware

Club jug, 7-3/8" h, molded body, hunt subject, applied white fruiting grapevine border, imp mark, c1830, shallow rim chip **490.00**

Tea set, 6-1/2" h cov teapot (slight chips to spout and sibyl finial), 4-1/4" h creamer (rim chip), 5" h cov sugar, imp marks, c1830 . . . . **575.00**

Jasper

Barber bottle, 11" h, three colors, green ground, white relief and lilac ground medallions, bacchus head reliefs to shoulder, imp mark, mid-19th C, cover insert damaged
. . . . **2,100.00**

Biscuit jar

5-1/8" h, light green dip, applied white relief of fox hunting scene, silver plated rim, handle, and cov, imp mark, late 19th C **260.00**

5-1/8" h, three-color dip, central dark blue ground with applied white classical relief, bordered in bands of light blue, silver plated rim,

Fairyland Lustre, vase, square, scene of city with large tree in the foreground and bridge with figures in front of the city, concealed figures of fairies and animals at base of tree, other two sides show stylized trees, partially concealing stairway to city, opalescent luster glaze on outside, blue wash interior with band of butterflies decoration, 5-1/2" square top, 7-3/4" h, **$6,100.** *Photo courtesy of James D. Julia, Inc.*

handle, and cov, imp mark, late 19th C **415.00**

5-1/8" h, three-color dip, dark blue ground with applied relief alternating as bands of yellow trellis and white scrolls, silver plated rim, handle, and cov, imp mark, c1882, old repairs to rim lid, footrim chip **460.00**

5-1/8" h, three-color dip, dark blue ground with applied yellow zig-zags dec with white florets, between foliate frames, silver plated rim, handle, and cov, imp mark, c1882 . . . . **920.00**

5-1/4" h, dark blue dip, applied white birds in relief below laurel and berry banded border, silver plated rim, handle, and cov, imp mark, early 20th C **635.00**

5-1/4" h, lilac dip, applied white relief of fox hunting scene, silver plated rim, handle, and cov, imp mark, early 20th C **550.00**

5-1/4" h, three-color dip, central light green ground with applied white classical subjects below floral festoons terminating at ram's heads, foliage border, silver plated rim, handle, and cov, imp mark, 19th C **745.00**

5-1/4" h, three-color dip, green ground, applied vertical bands of white scrolls, yellow trellis, silver plated rim, handle, and cov, imp mark, c1882 . . . . **815.00**

5-1/2" h, lilac dip, applied classical figures, silver plated rim, handle, and cov, imp mark, late 19th C, light crazing to ground **375.00**

5-1/2" h, three-color dip, applied white classical figures on central black ground bordered by yellow ground, silver plated rim, cov, and handle, imp mark, c1900 . . **920.00**

5-1/2" h, yellow dip, applied black relief of fruiting grapevine festoons terminating at lion masks and rings, silver plated rim, cov, and handle, imp mark, c1930 . . . . **690.00**

5-5/8" h, yellow dip, applied black relief of muses below fruiting grapevine festoons terminating at lion masks and rings, silver plated rim, cov, and handle, imp mark, c1930, shallow footrim chips **550.00**

5-3/4" h, light blue dip, applied white classical figures, silver plated rim, handle, footrim, and cov, "biscuit"

Jasper, biscuit jar, covered, applied black relief of Muses below fruiting grapevine festoons terminating in lion masks with rings, grapevine border to foot, silver-plated rim, handle and cover, impressed mark, c1930, 5-3/4" h, $800. Photo courtesy of Skinner Auctioneers and Appraisers.

label to finial, no visible mark, late 19th C. **150.00**

5-3/4" h, three-color dip, central black ground with applied white classical relief, bordered in bands of yellow, silver plated rim, cov, and handle, imp mark, 19th C, shoulder nicks. **800.00**

5-7/8" h, black dip, applied white classical relief, silver plated rim, handle, footrim, and cov, imp mark, 19th C. **630.00**

6" h, dark blue dip, applied white classical relief, silver plated stand, rim, and hinged lid, imp mark, 19th C, footrim chip **375.00**

6" h, pale lilac dip, applied white classical relief, silver plated rim, handle, and cov, imp mark, c1900 . . . . **375.00**

6" h, three-color dip, central dark blue ground with applied white classical relief, bordered in bands of light blue, silver plated rim, handle, and cov, imp mark, late 19th C. **435.00**

6" h, three-color dip, dark blue ground with oval light blue medallions, applied white relief of classical figures on horseback between trophies and foliate borders, silver plated rim, handle, and cov, lion finial, imp mark, 19th C. **1,265.00**

6-1/8" h, three-color dip, light blue ground with oval green ground medallions and applied white relief of classical figures on horseback between trophies and foliate borders, silver plated rim, handle, and cov, imp mark, 19th C **1,265.00**

7-3/4" h, black dip, applied white classical relief, acorn finial, oak leaf relief on cov, imp mark, late 19th C, finial repaired at joint **200.00**

Bough pot, 11-1/8" l, oval, blue, applied white classical figures of amorini alternating with mask heads of bearded male, unmarked, missing pierced lid, rim chip repaired, hairlines to bottom **1,840.00**

Bowl

6-5/8" d, solid blue, basketweave body, imp mark, early 19th C **1,380.00**

7-1/8" d, dark blue dip, applied white Dancing Hours relief, imp mark, mid-19th C **920.00**

Jasper, brooch, oval carved chalcedony, mother and child, yellow gold border, signed "Wedgwood," $300. Photo courtesy of Sloan's Auctioneers & Appraisers.

10" d, black dip, applied white Dancing Hours relief, imp mark, c1981 . . . . **350.00**

Bracelet, 7" l, assembled group of six circular medallions, each with dark blue dip, applied white classical relief, imp marks, 19th C, gold mounts, one with chip repair **575.00**

Brooch, 1" x 1-1/4", octagonal, three-color, applied white classical relief on green ground, solid light blue medallion, gold mounted frame, imp mark, 19th C. **490.00**

Candlesticks, pr

6-3/4" h, dark blue dip, applied white classical relief, banded arabesque floral border, imp marks, late 19th C **460.00**

8" h, yellow dip, applied black acanthus leaves and bellflowers, fruiting grapevine borders, imp marks, c1930, one with slight stain **920.00**

Candy dish, cov

2-1/4" h, three-color dip, dark blue ground with applied yellow zigzags and white florets, foliage, and diamond border, silver plated rim, handle, and cov, imp mark, c1881, slight foot rim chip repaired **550.00**

2-5/8" h, lilac dip, applied white classical relief figures, silver plated rim, handle, and cov, imp mark, imp mark, c1877, light crazing, slight pitting to surface **690.00**

Canopic jar, cov, 9-1/2" h, primrose, applied terra-cotta jasper hieroglyphics and Zodiac signs in bands of relief, imp mark, 1978 . . . . **1,100.00**

Cistern, 6-3/8" h, light blue dip, applied white classical figures, hexagonal brass base, circular insert, two drop handles, imp mark, late 19th C. **575.00**

Claret jug, 11" h, dark blue jasper dip, applied white classical relief, silver plated spout, rim, and hinged cov, imp mark, 19th C, shallow foot rim flake **375.00**

Clock case, 6" h, rect, solid light blue, applied white classical relief, imp mark, c1900, shallow foot rim chips under base....................... **350.00**

Creamer, 2-3/4" h, three-color dip, Diceware, light green ground, applied yellow quatrefoils between white foliate trim, imp mark, mid-19th C, hairline **2,070.00**

Dish, 11-1/4" l, white, coiled ribbon border, classical relief of putti framed within band of entwined rings and florets, imp mark, early 19th C.. **400.00**

Dish on stand, cov, 3-3/4" h, dark blue dip, applied white classical foliate and fruiting grapevine relief, imp mark, c1870..................... **635.00**

Figure, 10-5/8" h, white, Rousseau, modeled standing and holding bouquet of flowers, inscribed title, imp mark, early 19th C.............. **5,465.00**

Hair receiver, 4-3/8" d, crimson dip, applied white classical relief and foliage designs, imp mark, c1920, slight loss to one figure................... **1,265.00**

Inkstand, 6-7/8" h, solid pale blue, sarcophagus form supporting two pots, applied white relief with central medallion of The Sacrifice to Hymen within drapery enclosure, impressed mark, late 18th C, missing covers, crazing throughout, old restorations to pots, backside of stand, and scrolled foliate relief **1,495.00**

Jam jar, cov, 3-3/4" h, three-color dip, central light green ground band bordered in lilac, applied white classical figures below floral festoons and foliate border, silver plated rim, handle, and cov, imp mark, mid-19th C **650.00**

Jardinière

4-1/2" h, light blue dip, applied white relief of classical figures below fruiting grapevine festoons, terminating in lion masks and rings, imp marks, 19th C, price for pr **260.00**

5-1/4" h, three-color, solid white ground, applied green floral festoons and foliate borders, lilac ram's heads and trophy drops, imp mark, 19th C.......... **1,035.00**

6-3/4" h, dark blue dip, applied central band of floral vine, imp mark, late 19th C **275.00**

8" h, light blue dip, applied white relief of classical figures below fruiting grapevine festoons, terminating in lion masks and rings, imp marks, late 19th C, slight rim line.................... **460.00**

Jewel box, cov, 4-1/2" h, dark blue dip, oval, classical subject medallion mounted to three of paneled sides, larger medallion set on hinged lid, gilt brass mountings, 19th C **1,100.00**

Jug

3-1/2" h, yellow dip, applied white classical relief, imp mark, c1900 .... **635.00**

3-3/4" h, crimson dip, tapering sides, rope handle, applied white classical relief, imp mark, c1920, restored footrim chip...... **490.00**

3-7/8" h, crimson dip, bulbous, applied white classical relief, imp mark, c1920, chip to spout, hairline in handle **460.00**

5-1/2" h, crimson dip, applied white classical relief within foliate frames, trophy drop below spout, imp mark, c1920, restored spout chip, loss to trophy relief **635.00**

5-3/8" h, yellow dip, applied black classical relief between bands of florets and rings, imp mark, c1930 .... **520.00**

6" h, black dip, applied white slip floral dec, artist sgd "Harry Barnard," imp mark, c1900 .... **2,645.00**

6-1/4" h, crimson dip, Etruscan, applied white classical relief, imp mark, c1920 .... **1,380.00**

Mantel luster, 13-1/2" h, drum shaped base, dark blue dip, applied white classical relief, cut glass bobeches and prisms, early 19th C, electrified, chips to glass and rims, relief loss, price for pr **920.00**

Match box, cov, 3-3/4" l, yellow dip, rect, applied white classical relief, imp mark, late 19th/early 20th C **550.00**

Match holder, 2-3/8" h, crimson dip, cylindrical, applied white classical relief, imp mark, c1920, relief loss **490.00**

Medallion, 3-1/4" x 4", solid black, applied white relief profile portrait of Josiah Wedgwood, incised "W.H." to truncation, self framed, imp mark and title on reverse, 20th C **200.00**

Miniature, dark blue dip
Jardinière on stand, 2-1/2" h, applied white classical relief, imp mark, c1890, both with int. rim staining,

one with hairlines and foot rim chip, price for pr **750.00**

Tea set, 2" h cov teapot (tip of spout restored), 1-1/4" h creamer, 2" h cov sugar, applied white classical relief, imp marks, c1893... **575.00**

Vase, 2-1/4" h, Portland shape, each with applied white crest in relief, titled "South Australia" and "Nairn," imp mark, c1900, price for pr **435.00**

Vase, 3-3/8" h, bottle form, applied white classical relief, imp mark, c1880, price for pr **865.00**

Mustard pot, 3" h, yellow dip, applied black fruiting grapevine festoons terminating at lion masks and rings, silver plated cover, imp mark, c1930 .... **320.00**

Necklace, 21" l, lilac dip, 21 assorted beads, each with applied relief, 14 teardrop-shaped with classical subjects, seven oval with stars and stiff leaves, unmarked, 19th C..... **920.00**

Oil lamp, 5-1/4" l, dark blue dip, applied white classical relief, Zodiac signs border, imp mark, early 19th C **1,265.00**

Perfume bottle, 1-7/8" d, solid light blue, applied white relief portraits of George III on one side, reverse with Queen Charlotte, each bordered by floral festoons, unmarked, late 18th/early 19th C, repair, chips to neck **490.00**

Plaque

5-1/2" w, 17-3/4" h, rect, three-color dip, applied white trophy relief, central green ground bordered in light blue, imp mark, 19th C, stained wood frame **2,990.00**

Jasper, oil lamp and cover, dark blue dip, applied white classical relief, cover with figure group above scrolled leaves, lamp with stiff leaf border, impressed mark, c1800, chip to cover, 5-1/4" l, $1,000. Photo courtesy of Skinner Auctioneers and Appraisers.

6" x 14-1/2", rect, black, white applied relief depicting groups of boys after designs by Lady Diana Beauclerk, impressed marks, set in ebonized wood frames, losses, 19th C, price for pr **3,450.00**

10" l, 4" h, rect, black dip, applied white Dancing Hours in relief, imp mark, late 19th C, ebonized wood frame **575.00**

11-1/2" l, 4-1/2" h, oval, green dip, applied white classical relief, imp mark, early 19th C, mounted in heavy brass frame, repairs . **550.00**

12" l, 6" h, rect, solid light blue, applied white Blind Man's Bluff in relief, foliate frame, imp mark, early 19th C **750.00**

15" l, 4-1/2" h, solid green, applied white relief of horses, modeled by Rosemary Barnett, unmarked, c1965, giltwood frame. . . **2,415.00**

18-1/4" l, 6-1/8" h, solid light blue, applied white classical relief of boys at play and gathering fruit, imp mark, and oval "O," attributed to Bert Bentley, c1925. . . **1,265.00**

19-1/2" l, 7" h, solid light blue, applied white Dancing Hours in relief, framed, marks not visible, 19th C, price for pr **4,600.00**

Portland vase

4" h, black dip, applied white classical figures, imp mark, date 1918, and "Marshall Field & Co." **415.00**

4-7/8" h, olive green dip, applied white classical relief, imp mark, c1920 . . . . **920.00**

6-1/4" h, crimson dip, applied white classical relief, imp mark, c1920 . . . . **3,110.00**

6-7/8" h, dark blue dip, applied white classical relief, imp mark, c1900 . . . . **375.00**

10" h, solid black, applied white classical relief, base with half length figure wearing Phrygian cap, imp mark, c1900 . . . **2,530.00**

10-7/8" h, dark blue dip, applied white classical relief, base with molded half figure wearing Phrygian cap, imp mark, 19th C, crack and hairline to body . **520.00**

Potpourri jar, cov

3" h, dark blue dip, two handles, pierced lid, applied white classical figures, imp mark, early 19th C, slight chips to pierced holes **690.00**

10-3/4" h, solid light blue, orange peel ground, applied white relief of Muses above band of music symbols, theatrical masks, and trophies, foliate borders, impressed marks, c1862, price for pr **3,750.00**

Salad bowl

5-3/4" d, dark blue dip, applied white classical relief below floral festoons terminating in ram's heads, foliate borders, silver plated rim, imp mark, 19th C. **375.00**

10-3/8" d, three-color dip, dark blue ground with applied relief alternating as bands of yellow trellis and white scrolls, silver plated rim, imp mark, c1882, old repairs to rim and foot rim chip **460.00**

Salad set, 7-1/2" d bowl, dark blue dip, applied white classical relief, silver plated rim, 11" l silver plate fork and spoon servers with dark blue handles, applied foliate relief, late 19th C **350.00**

Salt, open, 2-7/8" d, solid light blue, applied white Dancing Hours in relief, imp marks, 19th C, one with rim chip, other with relief loss to figure, price for pr. **750.00**

Slave medallion, 1-1/16" x 1-1/8", solid white, applied black jasper relief, unmarked, 19th C, rim chip restored, shallow surface rim chip **520.00**

Spill vase, 3" h, three-color dip, light blue ground, engine turned fluting below lilac ground medallions, applied white classical relief above floral festoons terminating at ram's heads, imp mark, mid-19th C **1,035.00**

Sugar bowl, cov, crimson dip, applied white classical relief, imp mark, c1920, restored chip on cover collar and two areas of relief. **290.00**

Syrup jug

6-1/4" h, dark blue dip, applied white birds in relief below oak leaf banded border, silver plated insert cov, imp mark, early 20th C **550.00**

7-3/4" h, three-color dip, dark blue ground with applied vertical bands of yellow trellis and white scrolls, hinged pewter lid, imp mark, late 19th C, restored **350.00**

Tea bowl and saucer, solid pale blue, applied white relief, children playing above band of engine turning on cup, 5" d saucer with acanthus and stiff

leaves bordering engine turned center, imp mark, late 18th C **980.00**

Tobacco jar, cov

4-1/4" h, lilac dip, applied white classical figures between foliate frames, lion masks and rings, silver plated replacement cov, imp mark, c1870, nick to festoon. **350.00**

5-7/8" h, light blue dip, applied white relief of male figures smoking and foliage, match strikes and holder on cover, weight insert, imp mark, late 19th C, small rim and foot rim chips **750.00**

9" h, light blue dip, applied white classical figures within foliate frames, lion masks and rings, candle sconce finial, imp, c1870, light staining to cov, foot rim chip, one ring of relief repaired, foot rim hairlines and nicks **260.00**

Trophy plate, 8-5/8" d, black dip, applied white relief with classical figures, trophies, floral festoons terminating at ram's heads, floral and foliate borders, imp mark, mid-19th C, white relief lightly stained, rim chip **970.00**

Tray, 10-1/2" l, crimson dip, rect, cut corners, applied white classical relief, imp mark, c1920, restored rim chip **520.00**

Vase, cov

6" h, solid light blue, applied white Dancing Hours figures, foliate borders, imp mark, 19th C . **690.00**

6-1/4" h, dark blue dip, flaring sides, applied white classical relief, pierced disc cov, imp mark, early 20th C **210.00**

6-3/4" h, crimson dip, two handles, applied white classical relief, imp mark, c1920, cover restored **1,380.00**

7" h, crimson dip, bottle form, applied white classical relief, imp mark, c1920 . . . . **2,185.00**

9-1/4" h, dark blue dip, two handles, applied white classical and foliate relief, imp mark, early 20th C **435.00**

9-1/4" h, three-color dip, light blue ground, lilac ground medallions of classical subjects, applied white floral festoons and foliate border, goat head handles, imp mark, mid-19th C, cover missing, horns on one handle restored, shallow footrim chips **575.00**

9-1/2" h, three-color dip, solid light blue body, lilac ground oval medallions, white relief of classical subjects, drapery swags, and foliate borders, imp mark, late 19th C, rim chip to shoulder . . . **1,610.00**

10-1/2" h, dark blue dip, applied white classical relief, imp mark, late 19th C, slight rim chip **435.00**

11-1/4" h, black dip, applied white relief of Muses centering floral festoon and foliate borders, imp mark, mid-19th C **2,100.00**

11-5/8" h, Australia, solid light blue, applied white relief, central portrait of Captain Cook on one side, classical group taken from Sydney Cove medallion on reverse, ribboned band at shoulder titled "Capt. Cook, Phillips, Banks, Solander," foliage border with fruiting festoons, crown finial, later plinth, imp mark, c1900, shallow rim chips on cov, loss to finial, one handle restored, marks on plinth partially removed **1,840.00**

12-1/4" h, solid light blue, engine turned bowl supported by three winged lions atop triangular plinth, applied white foliate relief, satyr mask beneath bowl, three Sybil figures as finial, imp mark, early 19th C **13,800.00**

Vase

3" h, three-color dip, green ground, applied lilac medallions, white portraits in relief between drapery swags, imp mark, 19th C, rim and foot rim chips **435.00**

6-1/4" h, green dip, applied white trellis and floral dec, imp mark, mid-19th C, light staining to foot rim **920.00**

6-1/2" h, black dip, applied white arabesque floral band centering foliate borders, imp mark, c1862, chips and relief loss to socle **575.00**

6-1/2" h, solid black, applied white relief of column and lion mask framed panels with medallions above flowering festoons, imp mark, c1890, restored rim chip **520.00**

Lusters

Box, cov, 4" x 7", Dragon, pattern Z4829, mottled blue glaze, mother-of-pearl int., printed mark, c1920 . . . . **1,850.00**

Bowl, 7" d, Dragon, pattern Z4829, fluted, scalloped, mottled blue ext. with dragons, mother-of-pearl int. with three jewel and guardian dragon center,

surrounding Bai-fuku and Waso-byo-ye, printed mark, c1920 . . . . **1,265.00**

Coffeepot, cov, 5-1/2" h, Moonlight, imp mark, c1810, small chips to spout and cover **690.00**

Cup, 2" h, three handles, Dragon, blue ext., gilt reptiles, eggshell int. with central dragon, printed mark, c1920 . . . . **275.00**

Dish, 4-3/4" d, Dragon, Daisy Makeig Jones marks, Z4831, c1914-31 . **675.00**

Malfrey pot, cov, 8-1/4" h, Fairyland, coral and bronze, printed mark, c1924, cov repaired, wear to glaze at top of shoulder **1,380.00**

Punch bowl, 11" d, Fairyland, Firbolgs, ruby ext., MOP Thumbelina int., printed mark and no., c1920 . . . . **3,600.00**

Teapot, cov, 3" h, Moonlight, drum form, imp mark, c1810, rim chips restored, nicks to spout rim **575.00**

Vase

9-3/4" h, Fairyland, black, trumpet, shape 2810, Z4968, Butterfly Women, printed marks, c1920, pr **4,000.00**

11" h, Dragon, pattern Z4829, mottled blue ext., mother-of-pearl int., Chinese pagoda panels, printed mark, c1920 . . . . **1,150.00**

Wall pocket, 10" l, Moonlight, nautilus shell, c1810, restorations, pr . . . **575.00**

Majolica, plate, brown rim, yellow trim, green center portrait, impressed mark, c1878, 8-3/4" d, $195.

Majolica

Barber bottle, cov, 11" h, cobalt blue ground, molded body with festooning fruiting grapevines between Bacchus mask heads applied to shoulder bordered in laurel and berries, imp mark, c1869, cover collar restored **1,840.00**

Biscuit jar, cov, 5-1/2" h, jar with molded dec of elephants within floral framed cartouches flanked by elephant masks, silver plated rim, bale handle and cover, imp mark, c1867, cover possibly married **1,250.00**

Bowl, 11" d, cauliflower, multicolored, cobalt blue, rim nick on back . . **495.00**

Compote, 8-1/2" d, 8-1/2" h, cherub, cattails and flowers **770.00**

Floor urn, 26" h, cobalt blue, ladies seated at top of bulbous vase, drapes of laurel wreaths and ladies head at base, turquoise, yellow, white, brown, green, and pink, repair to one base, minor nicks and repair to feet of ladies, pr **5,500.00**

Jug, 8-3/4" h, applied central fruiting grapevine band, imp marks, c1868, one with slight relief loss, price for pr **1,300.00**

Oyster plate, brown basketweave and shell **1,210.00**

Pitcher, 7" h, sunflower and urn, turquoise **770.00**

Plate

8-3/4" d, mottled, reticulated **165.00**

9" d, crane **690.00**

Salt, open, 5-1/2" h, modeled as scantily clad boy holding basket, freeform base, imp mark, c1889, slight hairlines to rim, glaze flakes, restored base chips **350.00**

Sugar, Argenta, bird and fan, repair to lid, hairline in base **125.00**

Umbrella stand, 24" h, Argenta Fan, hairlines **1,760.00**

Pearlware

Candlesticks, pr, turquoise glaze, modeled as classical female holding cornucopia form base, supporting leafy sconce, imp mark, c1872, glaze wear, nicks to glaze surface **1,380.00**

Fruit basket, 10-5/8" one stand, oval, basketweave molded center, pierced gallery, green enamel trim, imp mark, early 19th C, some damage to strapping of basket, glaze wear on stand **320.00**

Platter, well and tree, gaudy cobalt blue and rust Chrysanthemum pattern, c1800, repaired **595.00**

Potpourri vase, pierced cov, blue ground, white relief floral swags, band above engine-turned fluting, imp mark, c1800, body restoration, married cover **230.00**

Tea tray, 18-1/8" l, rect, cut corners, red/pink transfer printed border, c1886 . . . . **200.00**

Queen's Ware

Basket, 9" l, oval, undertray, basketweave molded bodies, pierced galleries, green and black enamel oak leaves and trim lines, imp mark, early 19th C **290.00**

Bidet, 21-1/2" l, fitted mahogany stand with cov, imp mark **425.00**

Bough pot, cov, 6" h, sq form, paneled sides, relief alternating with two figures representing Seasons and two urns, foliate molded sq disc lid and center insert, imp mark, mid-19th C, old repair to hairline on disc lid **460.00**

Box, cov, 3-3/4" d, flat cylindrical form, gilt trim to green transfer printed foliate design, imp mark, c1882, light wear **500.00**

Flemish jug, 8-1/4" h, molded body with majolica glazes, blue incised designs, relief portrait of Queen Victoria below spout, brown banded neck and foot, imp mark, 1877.......... **375.00**

Mold, 10-7/8" l, large oval shape, scalloped rim, molded design of fruit and foliate bouquet in ribbed pot, c1800, very slight rim line, several small chips................... **1,300.00**

Orange bowl, cov, 9-1/2" h, low pedestal foot, wide lobe-fluted flaring rim, high domed pieced cover with long tapering ovals framed by molded scroll lattice and floral designs, imp mark, 20th C..................... **635.00**

Plate, 8-3/4" d, molded border, enamel dec center with Cupid and Psyche, artist sgd "E. Lossore," imp mark, c1870 .... **635.00**

Platter, 15-3/4" x 20-3/8", oval, polychrome bird and floral dec in Chelsea style, imp mark, 1871.. **375.00**

Sauceboat, 8" l, molded trellis and scroll pattern after 19th C salt glaze stoneware model, imp mark, 19th C **460.00**

Slop pail, cov, 9-1/2" h, blue printed willow pattern, imp mark, c1912, missing straw bail handle...... **490.00**

Soup ladle, 11-1/4" l, bowl with yellow ground banding, black enamel foliate vine dec, imp mark, early 19th C **320.00**

Veilleuse, 3-3/8" h, cover and stand, iron-red and blue enamel banding, imp mark, early 19th C, staining, rim wear **460.00**

Rosso Antico, pair tripod vases, applied black basalt foliate relief, lion mask and ring terminals, impressed marks, early 19th C, rim nicks, restored chips, missing lids, 6-1/2" h, $1,175. Photo courtesy of Skinner Auctioneers and Appraisers.

Rosso Antico
Bowl

6-3/4" d, applied black basalt relief, fern dec, imp mark, early 19th C **850.00**

7-7/8" d, Egyptian, applied black basalt meander band above stylized foliate molded body, imp mark, early 19th C **1,300.00**

Box, cov, 3-1/2" d, flat cylindrical form, enamel painted flowers, imp mark, c1860, base rim chip........ **175.00**

Bust, 7-1/4" h, Matthew Prior, mounted on raised circular base, imp mark and title, restorations **420.00**

Candlesticks, pr, 7" h, polychrome floral sprays, imp mark, mid-19th C, each sconce restored **415.00**

Club jug, 6-1/4" h, polychrome floral sprays, imp mark, mid-19th C.. **520.00**

Cream jug, 2-1/4" h, hexagonal form, banded Greek key relief, imp mark, early 19th C............... **450.00**

Inkstand, 4" h, applied black basalt leaf and berry border on stand, supported by three dolphin feet, central pot insert, imp mark, early 19th C, foot rim restored **550.00**

Jug, 5-1/8" l, oval, molded lobed body, foliage, stem, and flower relief, imp mark, early 19th C, restored spout rim chip **675.00**

Oil lamp, cov, 5-1/4" l, applied black basalt relief with Zodiac signs, bordering central classical subject, imp mark, early 19th C, shallow chip to side of spout **815.00**

Plate, 8-1/2" d, Egyptian, applied black basalt hieroglyphs in relief, imp mark, early 19th C............... **490.00**

Sugar bowl, cov, 4-1/2" h, classical black basalt relief between foliate panels, widow finial, imp mark, c1820 .... **450.00**

Teapot, cov

3" h, Egyptian, octagonal shape, applied black basalt band of hieroglyphs in relief, imp mark, early 19th C, imp mark, small chips to cover rim, pot interior rim, old spout repair............. **395.00**

7-1/4" l, Egyptian, applied black basalt hieroglyphs, crocodile finial, imp mark, early 19th C, slight chips to rim and spout **1,100.00**

Tea set, 8-3/8" l cov teapot (spout shortened), 5-1/8" l creamer, 5-3/4" l cov sugar, applied white stoneware prunus dec, oval form parapet shape, crabstock handles, imp marks, early 19th C..................... **815.00**

Tray, 8-1/2" l, oval, Egyptian, applied black basalt hieroglyphs in relief, imp mark, early 19th C **1,100.00**

Stoneware

Dish, 9-3/8" l, leaf form, white, enamel floral sprays, imp mark, early 19th C, very slight rim nick.......... **230.00**

Portland vase, 10-1/4" h, glazed, granular blue/black ground, white classical relief, half length figure of man wearing Phrygian cap under base, imp mark, 19th C, slight crazing, shallow footrim chips............... **690.00**

Victoria ware, portrait vase, 7-5/8" h, color slip dec, portrait medallions in relief above laurel festoons, mounted on raised drum base with ram's heads and laurel festoons, imp mark, c1880 .... **1,100.00**

WELLER POTTERY

History: In 1872, Samuel A. Weller opened a small factory in Fultonham, near Zanesville, Ohio. There he produced utilitarian stoneware, such as milk pans and sewer tile. In 1882, he moved his facilities to Zanesville. Then in 1890 Weller built a new plant in the Putnam section of Zanesville along the tracks of the Cincinnati and Muskingum Railway. Additions followed in 1892 and 1894.

In 1894, Weller entered into an agreement with William A. Long to purchase the Lonhuda Faience Company, which had developed an art pottery line under the guidance of Laura A. Fry, formerly of Rookwood. Long left in 1895, but Weller continued to produce Lonhuda under the new name "Louwelsa." Replacing Long as art director was Charles Babcock Upjohn. He, along with Jacques Sicard, Frederick Hurten Rhead, and Gazo Fudji, developed Weller's art pottery lines.

At the end of World War I, many prestige lines were discontinued and Weller concentrated on commercial wares. Rudolph Lorber joined the staff and designed lines such as Roma, Forest, and Knifewood. In 1920, Weller purchased the plant of the Zanesville Art Pottery and claimed to produce more pottery than anyone else in the country.

Art pottery enjoyed a revival when the Hudson Line was introduced in the early 1920s. The 1930s saw Coppertone and Graystone Garden ware added. However, the Depression forced the closing of the Putnam plant and one on Marietta Street in Zanesville. After World War II, inexpensive Japanese imports took over Weller's market. In 1947, Essex Wire Company of Detroit bought the controlling stock, but early in 1948, operations ceased.

Additional Listings: See *Warman's Americana & Collectibles* for more examples.

Bank, apple, figural. **750.00**
Candlestick
 9-3/8" h, round rim, sq pyramid form, reticulated arches near base, raised flowers and berries on vine, matted brown glaze, pink, blue, and highlights, one imp "Weller" on base, late 1920s, price for pr
 . . . . **150.00**
 13-1/2" h, Glendale, owl dec. **520.00**

Boudoir lamp base, Blue Louwelsa, painted clover blossoms, stamped Louwelsa Weller, 6-1/2" h pottery base, $500. Photo courtesy of David Rago Auctions.

Jardinière, gray, lavender iris decoration, signed, 8", $100. Photo courtesy of Woody Auctions.

Compote, Bonito, 4" h **65.00**
Console bowl, Sydonia, 17" x 6" . **90.00**
Console set, Glendale, 15-1/2" d flaring center bowl, flower frog, pair of low candlesticks, bruise to flower frog, kiln mark **1,100.00**
Cornucopia
 Lido, mauve. **55.00**
 Wild Rose, peach and green. . **45.00**
Ewer, Barcelona Ware, orig label
 . . . . **250.00**
Frog tray, 15-1/2" l, oval, raised edge, frog and water lily on one side, lily pads on other, blotchy semi-gloss green glaze, "Weller Pottery" ink stamp
 . . . . **635.00**
Garden ornament, swan, ivory glaze, 20" x 18", minor flakes **6,500.00**
Jardinière
 Aurelian, brown glaze, painted fruit, sgd "Frank Ferrell" **1,100.00**
 Orris, 13-1/4" d, 11-1/2" h, thick rim, band of stylized flowers and leaves over fluted sides, matte green glaze, unsigned, c1920-30 . **250.00**
Lamp base
 5" d, 11-1/4" h, Forest, unmarked, 2" chip next to hole at base. . . **460.00**
 10" d, 13-1/4" h, Louwelsa, by Hattie Mitchell, gourd shape, painted yellow cherry blossoms, stamped "Weller Louwelsa," sgd "H. Mitchell" on body **460.00**
Mug, Dickensware, dolphin handle and band, sgraffito ducks **250.00**
Pitcher
 Coppertone, figural fish handle
 . . . . **2,100.00**
 Louwelsa, 14" h, artist sgd, #750
 . . . . **650.00**
Planter, Forest Tub, 4" **135.00**

Vase, Dickensware, monk drinking ale, stamped X356/6, 4-1/4" d, 9" h, $410. Photo courtesy of David Rago Auctions.

Towel rack, 11-1/2" l, molded lovebirds and roses **850.00**

Vase

 5-1/4" h, hexagonal shape, indented panels, matte green, incised "Weller," c1900-25, glaze chip at base. **175.00**

Vase, faceted, smooth matte green glaze, unmarked, 3-3/4" d, 8-1/2" h, $325. Photo courtesy of David Rago Auctions.

WHALING

History: Whaling items are a specialized part of nautical collecting. Provenance is of prime importance since collectors want assurances that their pieces are from a whaling voyage. Since ship's equipment seldom carries the ship's identification, some individuals have falsely attributed a whaling provenance to general nautical items. Know the dealer, auction house, or collector from whom you buy.

Billet head, 18-1/4" l, carved and painted wood, scrolling design, 19th C
.... **920.00**

Block, carved whalebone, 19th C, pr

2-1/2" l................. **575.00**

3-1/4" l............... **1,095.00**

Blubber mincing knife, 36" l, two handles, orig wood scabbard, America, 19th C, wear, partial loss to scabbard
.... **470.00**

Broadside

"Land of the West, Greenland Whale Fishery," 12-stanza poem, London, second half 19th C....... **120.00**

List of Shipping Owned in the District of New Bedford, Jan 1, 1832, Employed in the Whale Fishery and Foreign Trade, lists vessels, tonnage, managing owners, New Bedford, 1832 .... **575.00**

Chart square, 29-7/8", brass and wood, inscribed "MST," 19th C **200.00**

Club, 11-7/8" l, whalebone, 19th C
.... **950.00**

Cutting spade, 56-1/2" l, iron, orig wood handle, America, 19th C, rust pitting, wear............... **150.00**

Dipper, 9-1/4" l, turned mahogany handle, ivory attachment, and coconut shell bowl with incised rosette, chain, and liner dec **550.00**

Vase, Minerva, amber trees, brown background, Imp WELLER, 3/4" rim chip, small chip and nicks to base, 13-1/2" h, $2,100. Photo courtesy of David Rago Auctions.

7-1/2" h, elongated sq form, Klyro pattern, reticulated rectangles around rim above raised flowers on rect panels, matte green glaze with pink and brown highlights, imp "Weller" on base **225.00**

8" h, Coppertone, figural leaping trout................ **1,900.00**

8" h, Coppertone, molded leaves, figural frog handles **1,200.00**

8-1/4" h, flared rim, cylindrical, Forest pattern, raised woodland scene, matte brown and green glaze, unmarked, c1920, hairline.. **230.00**

8-3/8" h, round bowl dec with raised leaf blades raised on column with three angled supports and round stepped base with similar leaf blade dec, matte green glaze, imp "Weller" on base, minor base chip
.... **635.00**

8-1/2" h, Etna, underglaze slip dec florals, c1915........... **260.00**

10-3/4" h, cylindrical, raised band of stylized flower buds on stems around rim, unmarked, hairlines
.... **285.00**

15" h, Hudson, painted irises, sgd "McLaughlin".......... **1,000.00**

Wall pocket, Glendale, owl in tree trunk, c1920, 11" h **350.00**

Whale's tooth, engraved portrait of gentleman and lighthouse, Lady Liberty holding globe and shield surmounted by vines, billowing flag, and angel on reverse, red and black decoration, inscribed "Warren," 19th C, 6-1/4" l, $2,350. Photo courtesy of Skinner Auctioneers and Appraisers

Whale's tooth, scrimshawed three-masted schooner surrounded by fine vine patterns, reverse side is inscribed "TAKEN/FROM A DEAD/WHALE/BY L.B.MORSE/1850," mellow patina, 2-3/4" w, 7" l, $690. Photo courtesy of James D. Julia Auctions.

Fid, 16" l, whalebone, 19th C, minor cracks..................... **490.00**

Figure, 16-3/8" l, carved baleen, whale, whalebone inlaid eye, 19th C, repair to tail........................ **865.00**

Harpoon

60" l, double-tined, cracks, loss to pole................... **285.00**

99-1/2" l, toggle, mounted on pole, 19th C **1,265.00**

Killing iron, 84" l, wood and iron, rope, shaft marked "A. J. Atwood," America, 19th C.................... **325.00**

Lance, 55" l, iron, America, 19th C, rust, pitting **200.00**

Log book

Journal of a Voyage to the North West Coast in the Ship Issac Hicks of New London by Freeman Lathrop sailed Sept 25th/44, 133 pages, written in blue ink, illus with watercolor pen and ink portrait of the chip, two depictions of whaling activities, four whale stamps
.... **9,200.00**

Whaling gun with lance, unmarked, cal. 7/8", 20" part oct. bbl, wooden stock, 17" l iron lance, remains of wire wrap on tail, metal surfaces heavily pitted, very dark patina, wood badly damaged, shows numerous repairs with copper strap overlays, some wood filler, $2,185. Photo courtesy of James D. Julia Auctions.

The Ship Indian Chief, John Hempstead Master, whale cruise towards Pacific Ocean North West Coast, sailed July 1, 1844, out of New London, owned by Frank Chew and Co., returned to New London, March 7, 1847, with 130 barrels of sperm oil, 3,070 barrels of sperm oil on board, illus with 65 whale stamps, 67 ship stamps, binding spine broken, marbleized cover worn, some toning to paper **17,250.00**

Marking gauge, 9-1/8" l, whalebone, 19th C **1,035.00**

Pan bone, 2-1/4" x 3-1/4", double sided engravings of three-masted ships under sail, 19th C, crack, gouges **375.00**

Parceling tool, 5-7/8" l, whale ivory, crossbanded design, engraved "N. D. 1829," repair **175.00**

Print, lithograph with hand coloring

16" x 32-1/4", *Sperm Whaling with Its Varieties,* J. H. Bufford, lithographer and publisher, after Benjamin Russell, framed, minor abrasions, foxing, toning **690.00**

21-1/2" x 32", *Private Signals of the Whaling Vessels Belonging to the Port of New Bedford,* Charles Taber & Co., identified in inscriptions in center of sheet, laid down on canvas, losses, tears, overall toning, scattered stains . . **1,380.00**

Rubber, whalebone, 19th C . . . **425.00**

Toggle harpoon, 67" l, wood and iron, rope, America, 19th C **300.00**

WHIMSIES, GLASS

History: During lunch or after completing their regular work schedule, glassworkers occasionally spent time creating unusual glass objects known as whimsies, e.g. candy-striped canes, darners, hats, paperweights, pipes, and witch balls. Whimsies were taken home and given as gifts to family and friends.

Because of their uniqueness and infinite variety, whimsies can rarely be attributed to a specific glass house or glassworker. Whimsies were created wherever glass was made, from New Jersey to Ohio and westward. Some have suggested that style and color can be used to pinpoint region or factory, but no one has yet developed an identification key that is adequate.

Glass canes are among the most collectible types of whimsies. These range in length from very short (under one foot) to 10 feet or more. They come in both hollow and solid form. Hollow canes can have a bulb-type handle or the rarer C- or L-shaped handle. Canes are found in many fascinating colors, with the candy striped being a regular favorite with collectors. Many canes are also filled with various colored powders, gold and white being the most common and silver being harder to find. Sometimes they were even used as candy containers.

Bracelet

2" to 3" d, Lutz type, clear, multicolored twists and spirals, gold **85.00**

3" d, solid glass, varied colored stripes **65.00**

Buttonhook

5" to 10" l, plain

Bottle green **35.00**

Colorless **25.00**

7" h, bottle green, elaborately twisted body, amber ends **75.00**

Cane

35" h, colorless, rainbow threading **100.00**

For more information, see this book.

Cane, colorless, cobalt blue, white, and maroon spirals, knob head, fire-polished tip, early to mid-19th C, 45" l, $250. Photo courtesy of Pacific Glass Auctions.

46-1/2" l, aqua, spiraled, mid-19th C **175.00**

48" l, cobalt blue, shepherd's crook handle **265.00**

60" l, bottle green, finely twisted, curved handle **150.00**

Darner

5" l, amber head, applied colorless handle **200.00**

7" l, white ground, blue Nailsea loopings **165.00**

Egg, 4-1/2" h, hollow, milk glass, various colored splotches **85.00**

Horn

8-1/2" l, French horn type, candy stripes **300.00**

20" l, trumpet type, red, white, yellow, purple, and green candy stripes **175.00**

Ladle, 10" l, hollow, gold powder filled, colored splotches, curved handles **70.00**

Pen, green, finely twisted applied bird finial **85.00**

Pipe

20" l, spatter, large bowl, English **250.00**

36" l, long twisted stem, small hollow bowl, aqua, America, c1900 . . . . **120.00**

Potichomanie ball, 12" d, blown, aqua, paper cut-outs of flowers, etc., matching 24" h stand, attributed to Lancaster NY **600.00**

Rolling pin

14" l, black or deep olive green, white dec, early Keene or Stoddard **150.00**

15" l, Nailsea type, cobalt blue ground, white loopings . . . **175.00**

Top hat, 7" h, 15" d, colorless, folded rim, polished pontil **75.00**

Witch ball, 3-1/2" d, freeblown, attributed to Boston and Sandwich Glass Works, 1850-80, rose and green loops on white milk glass background, ground moth, smooth base **375.00**

Witch ball holder, 3-1/2" d, 6" h, dark amber, blown, sickness with small broken blister **440.00**

WHITE-PATTERNED IRONSTONE

History: White-patterned ironstone is a heavy earthenware, first patented under the name "Patent Ironstone China" in 1813 by Charles Mason, Staffordshire, England. Other English potters soon began copying this opaque, feldspathic, white china.

All-white ironstone dishes first became available in the American market in the early 1840s. The first patterns had simple Gothic lines similar to the shapes used in transfer wares. Pattern shapes, such as New York, Union, and Atlantic, were designed to appeal to the American housewife. Motifs, such as wheat, corn, oats, and poppies, were embossed on the pieces as the American prairie influenced design. Eventually, more than 200 shapes and patterns, with variations on finials and handles, were made.

White-patterned ironstone is identified by shape names and pattern names. Many potters only identified the shape in their catalogs. Pattern names usually refer to the decorative motif.

Butter dish, cov, Athens, Podmore Walker, c1857 . . . . **95.00**

Cake plate, 9" d, Brocade, Mason, handled **180.00**

Chamber pot, cov, emb Fleur-De-Lis & Daisy o handle, 1883-1913, marked "Johnson Bros." **165.00**

Coffeepot, cov

  Laurel Wreath **275.00**

  Wheat and Blackberry, Clementson Bros. **220.00**

Compote, ftd, Taylor & Davis, 10" d, 6" h **220.00**

Creamer

  Fig, Davenport **95.00**

  Wheat in the Meadow, Powell & Bishop, 1870 . . . . **85.00**

Creamer and sugar, Scroll pattern, E. Walley, repaired finial, luster dec **170.00**

Cup and saucer

  Acorn and Tiny Oak, Parkhurst **35.00**

  Grape and Medallion, Challinor **40.00**

  Laurel Wreath, handleless, set of 13, some chips **350.00**

  Wheat, Brockhurst, handleless, luster dec **25.00**

Ewer, Scalloped Decagon, Wedgwood **150.00**

Gravy boat

  Bordered Fuchsia, Anthony Shaw **75.00**

  Wheat & Blackberry, Meakin . . **65.00**

Milk pitcher, Leaf, marked "Royal Ironstone China, Alfred Meakin, England," 9" h **245.00**

Nappy, Prairie Flowers, Livesley & Powell **20.00**

Pitcher

  Berlin Swirl, Mayer & Elliot . . . **120.00**

  Japan, Mason, c1915 . . . . . . **275.00**

  Syndenhaum, T. & R. Boote . . **195.00**

  Thomas Furnival, 9" w, 9-1/2" h **220.00**

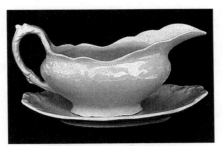

Gravy boat, underplate, marked "Royal Ironstone China, Johnson Bros, England," 4" l, 4-1/2" h gravy, 5" w, 8-1/2" l underplate, **$45.**

Plate

  Ceres, Elsmore & Forster, 8-1/2" d **15.00**

  Corn, Davenport, 10-1/2" d . . . **20.00**

  Fluted Pearl, Wedgwood, 9-1/2" d **15.00**

  Gothic, Adams, 9-1/2" d **20.00**

  Laurel Wreath, 10", set of 13. **325.00**

  Prairie, Clemenston, Hanley, 6-5/8" d **15.00**

  Scroll pattern, E. Walley, 8" d . **55.00**

  Wheat and Clover, Turner & Tomkinson **20.00**

Platter

  Columbia, 20" x 15" **125.00**

  Laurel Wreath, three graduated sizes **325.00**

  Wheat, Meakin, 20-3/4" x 15-3/4" **95.00**

Punch bowl

  Berry Cluster, J. Furnival. . . . **175.00**

  Rosettes, handles, Thomas Furnival & Sons, c1851-90, 9-1/2" 3, 6" h **315.00**

Relish

  Laurel Wreath, diamond shape **25.00**

  Wheat, W. E. corn **30.00**

Salad plate, Laurel Wreath, set of eight **90.00**

Sauce tureen, cov

  Columbia, underplate, Joseph Goodwin, 1855 . . . . **315.00**

  Prize Bloom, T.J. & J. Mayer, Dale Hall Pottery **320.00**

  Wheat & Blackberry, Clementson Bros. **275.00**

Soap dish, Bordered Hyacinth, cov, insert, W. Baker & Co., 1860s . . **150.00**

Soup plate, Fig, Davenport, 9-1/2" d **25.00**

Sugar bowl, cov

  Hyacinth, Wedgwood **145.00**

  Fuchsia, Meakin **140.00**

  Livesley Powell & Co., registry mark, 8" h **295.00**

Teapot, cov, T & R Boote, Burslem, registry mark for Nov. 26, 1879, 9-1/2" h **240.00**

Toothbrush holder

  Bell Flower, Burgess **50.00**

  Cable and Ring, Cockson & Seddon **40.00**

Tureen, cov, underplate

  Grape, matching ladle, chips **135.00**

  Laurel Wreath, large **2,100.00**

Vegetable, cov

  Blackberry **95.00**

  Lily of the Valley, pear finial . . **110.00**

Vegetable, open, Laurel Wreath, pr **200.00**

Waste bowl, Laurel Wreath **45.00**

WILLOW PATTERN CHINA

History: Josiah Spode developed the first "traditional" willow pattern in 1810. The components, all motifs taken from Chinese export china, are a willow tree, "apple" tree, two pagodas, fence, two birds, and three figures crossing a bridge. The legend, in its many versions, is an English invention based on this scenic design.

By 1830, there were more than 200 makers of willow pattern china in England. The pattern has remained in continuous production. Some of the English firms that still produce it are Burleigh, Johnson Bros. (Wedgwood Group), Royal Doulton (continuing production of the Booths' pattern), and Wedgwood.

By the end of the 19th century, production of this pattern spread to France, Germany, Holland, Ireland, Sweden, and the United States. Buffalo Pottery made the first willow pattern in the United States beginning in 1902. Many other companies followed, developing willow variants using rubber-stamp simplified patterns, as well as overglaze decals. The largest American manufacturers of the traditional willow pattern were Royal China and Homer Laughlin, usually preferred because it is dated. Shenango pieces are the most desirable among restaurant-quality wares.

Japan began producing large quantities of willow pattern china in the early 20th century. Noritake began about 1902. Most Japanese pieces are porous earthenware with a dark blue pattern using the traditional willow design, usually with no inner border. Noritake did put the pattern on china bodies. Unusual forms include salt and pepper shakers, one-quarter pound butter dishes, and canisters. The most desirable Japanese willow is the fine quality NKT Co. ironstone with a copy of the old Booths pattern. Recent Japanese willow is a paler shade of blue on a porcelain body.

The most common dinnerware color is blue. However, pieces can also be found in black (with clear glaze or mustard-colored glaze by Royal Doulton), brown, green, mulberry, pink (red), and polychrome.

The popularity of the willow design has resulted in a large variety of willow-decorated products: candles, fabric, glass, graniteware, linens, needlepoint, plastic, tinware, stationery, watches, and wall coverings. All this material has collectible value.

Marks: Early pieces of Noritake have a Nippon "Royal Sometuke" mark. "Occupied Japan" may add a small percentage to the value of common tablewares. Pieces marked "Maruta" or "Moriyama" are especially valued.

Reproduction Alert: The Scio Pottery, Scio, Ohio, currently manufactures a willow pattern set sold in variety stores. The pieces have no marks or backstamps, and the transfer is of poor quality. The plates are flatter in shape than those of other manufacturers.

Note: Although colors other than blue are hard to find, there is less demand; thus, prices may not necessarily be higher priced.

Berry bowl, small
    Blue, Homer Laughlin Co...... **6.50**
    Pink, marked "Japan"........ **5.00**
Bowl, 9" d, Mason............ **45.00**
Cake plate, Newport Pottery Ltd., England, SP base, c1920 ..... **300.00**
Charger, 13" d............... **55.00**
Coffeepot, cov, 10" h, 3" h warmer stand **165.00**
Creamer, round handle, Royal China Co......................... **10.00**
Cup and saucer
    Booths................... **30.00**
    Buffalo Pottery **25.00**
    Homer Laughlin **10.00**
    Japanese, decal inside cup, pink **25.00**
    Shenango **15.00**
Dinner plate
    Allerton, 10" d............. **25.00**
    Buffalo Pottery, 9" d........ **20.00**

Grill plate, three sections, Royal China, **$24.**

Platter, blue, Allterton, 9-1/4" w, 11-1/4" l, **$70.**

    Johnson Bros., 10" d........ **15.00**
    Royal China Co............ **10.00**
Egg, transfer printed pattern on ceramic body, early 20th C
    4-1/2" l, gray ground **95.00**
    5" l, white ground.......... **90.00**
    5-1/2" l, light blue ground **85.00**
Gravy boat, 5" x 6-1/2", Royal China Co. **25.00**
Pie plate, 10" d............... **50.00**
Platter, 19" x 14-1/2", marked "Copeland, Made in England," c1940 .... **195.00**
Sugar, cov
    Allerton **65.00**
    Royal China Co., handleless .. **40.00**
Tea cup and saucer, scalloped, Allerton..................... **45.00**
Tea set, 5" h hexagonal teapot, creamer, cov sugar, tray, seven cups, six saucers, 20-3/4" d round tray with scalloped rim, gilt foo dog lid finials, gilt handles and rims, pattern registered January, 1879, printed at rim with quotation from Robert Burns' "Auld Lang Syne," Spode, late 19th C, retailed by Tiffany & Co., price for 17-pc set **950.00**
Toby jug, 6" d, overall crazing.. **930.00**
Wash bowl and pitcher, 7-1/2" h pitcher, 12" d bowl, Adderlys Ltd., Staffordshire, c1906, age crack in pitcher **375.00**
Water set, 9" h pitcher, six 3-5/8" h tumblers, c1940-50 .... **195.00**

WOODENWARE

History: Many utilitarian household objects and farm implements were made of wood. Although they were subjected to heavy use, these implements were made of the strongest woods and well cared for by their owners. Today collectors and decorators treasure their worn lines and patina. Collectors often consider their hand-made wooden items as folk art, elevating what once might have been a common utilitarian item to a place of honor.

Bag stamp, 5" h, pine, relief carved tulip in heart-dec urn, PA, c1750 .... **2,100.00**
Bank, 4-1/2" w, 3-13/16" d, 3-5/8" h, rect, carved gardenia blossoms and leaves on top and sides, dark blue painted ground **525.00**
Bas-relief carving
    5" w, 6-3/4" h, woman holding bird, found in Iowa **525.00**
    6-1/8" l, 4-1/8" h, basket of fruit, repaired **435.00**
Basket, 10-3/4" l, 5-3/4" h, carved freeform burl, America, 19th C **1,120.00**
Bowl, burl, 18-1/2" d, 6-1/2" h, large ash burl, nut brown color, tight figure, incised dec line below lip, turned foot, short age cracks at rim **3,100.00**
Bowl, carved
    5" d, 1-1/2" h, burl, good figure, dark patina, int. with few scorch marks **880.00**
    6-1/4" w, 2-1/2" d, 4" h, double carved horse heads, incised eyes, carved ears, mouths, and forelocks, wear from use .. **450.00**
    8-1/2" w, 17" l, 2-1/2" h, double molded rim, inscribed and dated "Kenai Indian Alaska, 1886" **1,150.00**
    11-1/2" d, 4" h, burl, ash, very good figure, old scrubbed surface, incised ring detail around base, ext. with raised rim, rim split **880.00**
    12" d, 4-1/4" h, burl, banded rim tapering to base, old surface, America, 19th C......... **635.00**
    13-3/8" d, 4-1/4" d, burl, very good figure, dark brown patina, thinly turned, turned foot, raised rim ring, couple of old minor splits. **1,210.00**
    14-11/16" d, 8" h, burl, deep oval form, handled, ftd, 18th C **5,750.00**

Trencher bowl, softwood, lip indistinctly stamped "L. Goodard" in block letters, American, wear on interior and bottom, one tight short crack in lip, 20-1/2" l, 12" w, 5" h, **$245.** *Photo courtesy of Cowan's Historic Americana Auctions.*

17" d, 13-1/2" d, 7" h, burl, vestiges of handles, red paint, Eastern Woodlands, New England, early 19th C **1,100.00**

19" d, 4-3/4" h, ash burl, very good figure, thinly turned, scrubbed surface, low sides, turned foot, incised rings, slanted groove treatment along outer rim, slightly misshaped, small areas of filler on ext. **1,650.00**

Bowl, turned, 15-5/8" d, 4-1/2" h, painted salmon, America, 19th C, minor wear **1,530.00**

Box, cov

5-1/4" d, 3-3/8" h, oval, bentwood, single finger construction with opposite directions on lid and base, iron tacks, old dark green paint shows lighter under lid, minor wear to paint **2,420.00**

5-3/4" w, 4" d, 1-3/4" h, book shape, spruce, inland bands, star, crescent boon, hearts, and leaves, one end with sliding lid, minor alligatoring to varnish, short age cracks **200.00**

6-3/8" w, 3" d, 1-7/8" h, book shape, Frisian carved, made from solid piece of wood, sliding lid, overall geometric carving, matching patterns on front and back, hearts and pinwheel on spine, good patina, int. with ivory paint, yellowed varnish, minor edge damage, few worm holes . . **220.00**

8-1/4" w, 6-1/4" d, 4-1/4" h, oval, bentwood, single finger on lid, overlapping seams on base, steel tacks, old medium blue paint, wear to lid. **495.00**

12" w, 6-1/4" d, 5-3/4" h, pine and poplar, orig red paint, applied molding on lid, dovetailed case, molded base, int. slotted for divider (missing) **550.00**

Boxes, covered, burl wood, dovetailed construction, square, corners with chips and repairs, 4-3/4" square, 3-1/2" h, $550. Photo courtesy of Sanford Alderfer Auction Company.

Bucket, cov, tongue and groove stave construction

4-3/4" d, 3-7/8" h, old gray paint, brass bands, wood and wire bale handle, base imp "Washington Mfg Co. Troy, NY" **220.00**

8-3/4" d, 8-1/2" h, faded orig red paint below center band, black iron bands and finial, slightly tapered sides, fittings for bale handle stamped "Pat. Oct. 27, 85" **220.00**

Bucket, open, 11-1/2" d, 12-1/4" h, stave construction, wood bands, bentwood swing handle, layers of old red paint, some water damage on bottom **550.00**

Busk, 12" h, carved maple, engraved with Indian smoking pipe, chip-carved geometric compass designs, attributed to New England, early 19th C, stand **980.00**

Canoe cup, 5-3/4" l, 2-1/4" h, cup with elongated bowl, carved beaver, New England, 19th C, with stand . . . **520.00**

Charger, 21-3/4" d, treenware, scribed dec, late 18th/early 19th C, minor imperfections **1,035.00**

Churn, 49-1/2" h, stave construction, refinished pine, lollipop handle, tapered sides, turned lid with dasher, replaced copper bands **165.00**

Firkin

9" d base, 7" h, staved construction, four wooden bands, hand forged iron bail handle, wooden stopper, painted red, America, early 19th C, minor wear **265.00**

12" d, 12-1/2" h, staved construction, green lapped bands, swing handle fastened with pegs, painted red, "Cassia" inscribed in white letters, matching cover, America, mid-19th C, wear. **530.00**

Flax wheel, 45" h, upright type, mixed hardwoods, four turned legs, single treadle, double flyers with bobbins, single wheel at top with turned spokes, few replacements **250.00**

Glove box, 13-1/2" l, sandalwood, lid and sides pierced carved with animals, deities, and flowers, supported by figures of ducks, India, 19th C . **345.00**

Jar, cov

3-1/2" d, 6" h, Peaseware, bulbous, shaped finial, incised ring dec on lid and body, low foot. **325.00**

8-3/4" d, 9" h, treenware, fan shaped sponged vinegar dec in red over mustard, wide sloping rim and base, glued repair, edge damage on lid flange, age crack . . **1,210.00**

Mortar and pestle, early, turned oak, 5" w, 9" h mortar, $50. Photo courtesy of James D. Julia, Inc.

Measuring device, carved and inlaid shoe-form, carved head of gentleman, ivory inlaid eyes, inlaid metal buckle, two ivory inlaid panels each dec with two engraved shoes, Holland, late 18th C, minor losses, wear, crack **920.00**

Mortar and pestle, 6-1/4" d, 18-1/4" h, turned maple, acorn-shaped knop, three incised lines on cylindrical pestle, mortar with molded base, 19th C, cracks. **90.00**

Pantry box, 6-1/4" d, 2-1/4" h, round, painted black, top carved with central star within medallion and leafy border, cross hatch swags on side, int. lined with partial advertising lithographs, New England, mid-19th C, minor imperfections **715.00**

Pewter rack, hanging, 35" w, 3-3/4" d, 29-3/4" h, oak, dark finish, two shelves, stylized lion finials on tops, wire nail construction, English **150.00**

Picture frame

13-3/8" w, 15-1/2" h, stenciled and painted, rect, gold floral dec on black ground, remnants of paper label on reverse **375.00**

13-3/4" w, 17-5/8" h, painted pine, black half round frame, meandering fruited vine and plant border, 19th C, finish alligatored **520.00**

19-5/16" w, 22" h, rect, reticulated scalloped edge, compass star corner rosettes, painted black, 19th C, finish alligatored**. . . 550.00**

Quilt rack, folding

34-3/4" w, 64" h, two sections, pine, old natural finish, three cross pcs mortised into frame **. 95.00**

108" w, 66" h, three sections, each fitted with three cross pcs mortised into frame, cast iron hinges, old putty colored paint **. 120.00**

Saffron container, 2-1/2" d, 4-5/8" h, Lehnware, turned wood, knob on lid, salmon ground, white, red, and green flowers around base, strawberries on lid, minor edge chip on base**. . 1,980.00**

Salver, 10-3/4" d, mahogany, molded pie-crust edge, America, 19th C, staining, edge loss **. 2,820.00**

Scoop, 9-3/4" l, carved, America, 19th C **. 210.00**

Scrub box, wall type, 7-1/2" w, 11-3/4" h, pine, painted green, America, 19th C, wear **. 715.00**

Shelves, 30" w, 10" d, 37-3/4" h, walnut, orig dark finish, four graduated shelves with rounded edges, shaped corners, turned shelf supports and finials, scalloping and cut-outs on center backboard including pinwheel and medallion top, sq cut nail construction **. 600.00**

Snuffbox, cov, 4-1/2" l, 1-7/8" w, 1-1/4" h, hand painted, black lacquer ground, oblong lid with husband rocking baby in cradle, wife in bed, surrounded by dog, cat, wood stove with kettle, gilt border, England, early 19th C, wear **. 2,235.00**

Spice box, 9" d, 3-3/8" h, round box, lapped construction, eight small cylindrical cov wood containers, stenciled spice label on each, America, 19th C **. 250.00**

Sugar bowl, cov, 8" d, 7-1/2" h, turned maple, acorn finial on flaring domed lid, bulbous body, flaring foot, old refinish, loss to inside rim **. 690.00**

Sugar bucket, cov

13-1/2" h, orig dark green paint, faint signature "C. Wilder & Son, So. Hingham, Mass" on lid, tapering sides, lapped staves, copper tacks, arched bentwood handle, minor edge chips **. 550.00**

15" h, orig blue paint, old hand plane marks, copper and steel tacks, arched bentwood handle, stenciled "E. F." on bottom, chips **. . . 450.00**

Toddy ladle, 14-1/4" l, carved, notched handle, round bowl, dark brown patina, America, early 19th C, wear **. . . 440.00**

Trencher, 23" l, 10-3/4" w, 3-1/4" h, rect, canted sides, rough hewn from pine, good patina **. 65.00**

Trivet, 4-1/4" x 7-7/8" x 4-3/8" h, pine, wire nails, cut-out feet and ends on apron, old robin's egg blue with red stripes, hand painted decoupaged print of Mt. Vernon on top, minor flaking, multiple nail holes in one area **. . 350.00**

Tub, 3-5/8" d, 2-1/2" h, Treenware, chip carved edge, two handles, heart cut-outs, dark green (black) ext., yellowed ivory paint int., split **. 1,375.00**

Ventriloquist's head, mounted on later stand

5" w, 6" d, 8" h, carved pine, natural surface, America, c1930, eyes missing **. 375.00**

5-1/2" w, 5" d, 8-1/2" h, carved yellow pine, fixed eyes, spring-activated mouth with pull string, old patina, attributed to southern U.S., last quarter 19th C **. 1,150.00**

Wall shelf, 38-1/2" l, 6-1/2" d, 16" h, bird's eye maple, carved, shaped and slightly bowed top shelf with incised front on pierced, shaped, scrolling supports, each with three circular bosses joined by incised medial bar, lower shaped shelf, old finish, New England, mid-19th C, minor imperfections **. 920.00**

Wand, 21-5/8" h, carved wood, upright hand, traces of red paint, attributed to Penitente, American Southeast, c1890 **. 1,265.00**

Wash tub, 23-3/4" d, 16-1/2" h, painted pine, circular, pierced handle, stave and metal band construction, old red paint, America, late 19th C, wear, loose bands **. 260.00**

World's Fairs and Expositions

History: The Great Exhibition of 1851 in London marked the beginning of the World's Fair and Exposition movement. The fairs generally featured exhibitions from nations around the world displaying the best of their industrial and scientific achievements.

Many important technological advances have been introduced at world's fairs, including the airplane, telephone, and electric lights. Ice cream cones, hot dogs, and iced tea were first sold by vendors at fairs. Art movements often were closely connected to fairs, with the Paris Exhibition of 1900 generally considered to have assembled the best of the works of the Art Nouveau artists.

Crystal Palace, 1851

Pipe, white clay Pipe, 6" l, Crystal Palace on bowl **. 100.00**

Pot lid, Pratt, 5" d **. 200.00**

Crystal Palace, NY, 1853

Dollar, so called, 1-3/4" d, shows seated Liberty and Crystal Palace **. 75.00**

Print, Currier and Ives, Crystal Palace **. 400.00**

Centennial, 1876

Bank, still, cast iron, Independence Hall, 9" h x 7" w **. 350.00**

Glass slipper, Gillinder

Clear**. 35.00**

Frosted **. 40.00**

Medal, wooden, Main Building, 3" d **. 60.00**

Scarf, 19" x 34", Memorial Hall, Art Gallery colorful **. 100.00**

New Orleans World's Industrial and Cotton Expo, 1885, program, cover stamped "April 1885" **. 45.00**

Columbian Exposition, 1893

Album, 5-3/4" x 9", hardcover, gold emb "World's Fair Album of Chicago 1893"**. 50.00**

Book, *History of the World's Fair Being A Complete Description of the World's Colombian Exposition from Inception,* Major Ben C. Truman, illus, 592 pgs **. 60.00**

Cup, 2-1/2" h, peachblow glass, double handles, ribbed, shading from pink to white, gilt dec "World's Fair-1893 Chicago," minor crack at handle **300.00**

Medal, 1-1/2", brass luster finish white metal, bust portrait of Christopher Columbus on one side, other side

Columbian Expo, 1893, jack-in-the-pulpit, vase, peachblow, raspberry shading to white glass with gold enameling "WORLD'S FAIR 1893," 7-1/2" h, $750. Photo courtesy of James D. Julia, Inc.

Columbian Expo, 1893, stevensgraph with five colors, showing Mrs. Potter Palmer, President of the Board of Lady Managers, graphic portrait of her and view of Woman's Building, mounted on original paper and produced by John Best & Co., Patterson, NJ, 10" x 2-1/2", **$100.** *Photo courtesy of Sanford Alderfer Auction Company.*

"400th Anniversary of The Discovery of America," 1492-Oct-1892 . . . . **20.00**
Mug, 4-3/4" h, salt glazed stoneware, imp, blue accents "World's Fair Chicago 1893" **165.00**
Photo booklet **25.00**
Souvenir spoon **25.00**
Ticket **30.00**
Watch case opener, Keystone Watch Case Co. **15.00**

Trans-Mississippi, 1898

Change purse, leather and mother of pearl, showing fair name on side . **45.00**

Pan American, 1901

Cigar case, hinged aluminum 2-1/2" x 5-1/2" **35.00**
Frying pan, pictures North and South America, 6" long **75.00**
Medallion, bright luster brass, profile of buffalo between "Souvenir" and "1901," reverse marked "Pan-American Exposition/May-November Buffalo, NY" **15.00**
Pinback button
  Swifts Pig, multicolored plump pig seated in frying pan, tiny inscription "Pan-American Souvenir," black lettering "Swift's Premium Hams and Bacon-Swift & Co., U.S.A." **25.00**
  Temple of Music, multicolored art view of building exterior **25.00**
  The Propylea, multicolored art view of building exterior **25.00**
Plate, frosted glass, three cats painted on dec, 7-1/2" d **35.00**

Automata, blue uniformed character, standing on orange platform with Trylon and Perisphere behind him. He was for sale at the October 2002 Atlantique City show for **$10,000.**

St. Louis, 1904

Match safe and cigar cutter, 2-3/4" w, 1-1/2" h, detailed drawing of Palace of Varied Industries on one side, picture of Gardens and Terraces of States on other, tarnished **150.00**
Medal, silvered brass, 2-3/4" d . . **60.00**
Photo album, eight pgs, 15 orig photos **45.00**
Pinback button, KY home, multicolored exhibit building of Kentucky against upper half gold background, inscribed "Ky. Home World's Fair," bottom margin inscription "It's Part Mine" **25.00**
Plate, 7-1/4" d, scene in center, lacy border **25.00**
Stamp holder, aluminum, 1-1/8" x 1-3/8" **35.00**
Souvenir mug, bronze, emb scene of Palace of Electricity, 6" h **115.00**
Souvenir plate, 7" d, Festival Hall, Cascade Gardens **55.00**
Tumbler, 4" high, copper plated base, metal, shows Louisiana Purchase Monument, Cascades, Union Station and Liberal Arts Bldg **35.00**

Alaska-Yukon, 1909

Watch fob, three pcs, State Building, Totem Pole, Fair Logo in Center, 4" l **75.00**

Chicago, 1933, mug, green glaze, molded figures "A Century of Progress – World's Fair Chicago 1933" nude female handle, minor chip in glaze near base, **$165.** *Photo courtesy of Joy Luke Auctions.*

Hudson-Fulton, 1909

Pin back, color pictures profiles of Hudson and Fulton, 1-1/4" d **25.00**

Panama-Pacific, 1915

Pocket watch, official, silver plated, 2" d **300.00**
Postcard **5.00**

Century of Progress, Chicago, 1933

Employee badge, round medallion with "A Century of Progress" around perimeter, "International Exposition Chicago 1933" and employee number below **55.00**
Menu, Walgreens **45.00**
Pinback button
  I Was There, red, white, and blue **20.00**
  New York Visitor, red, white, and blue **20.00**
Playing cards, full deck, showing views of the fair, all different, black and white **45.00**
Ring, adjustable, silvered brass, miniature exhibit building on blue enamel background, inscribed "Chicago, 1934" **25.00**
Souvenir key, bright silver luster brass, sponsored by Master Lock Co., "Master Laminated Padlocks Sold All Over the World," opposite side with miniature form image of exhibit buildings and "World's Fair 1933," tiny horseshoe and four-leaf clover, inscribed "Keep Me For Good Luck" **28.00**
Tape measure, silver, blue, and white official logo, other side with black and white photo of Paris replica village exhibit **32.00**
Toy wagon, red, white wheels, decal of Transportation Bldg in middle approx 3-1/2" l **175.00**

Great Lakes, 1936
Pinback, Florida, with state flag on the face, 1-1/2" d **18.00**

Texas Centennial, 1936
Playing cards, colorful with Texas state flag on back, boxed **40.00**

Golden Gate, 1939
Bookmark, typical view, 4" l **20.00**
Match book, orig matches, pictures Pacifica **10.00**
Token, shows Sun Tower and Bridge, 1-1/8" d **15.00**

New York, 1939
Bookmark, 3-3/4" l, diecut and silvered thin brass spear page marker and letter opener, applied metal disk with blue and dark orange accents on silver luster "New York Worlds Fair, 1939," plus images of Trylon and Perisphere **20.00**
Candy tin, miniature, by Bagatele, very colorful, 4-1/4" x 6-1/2" **65.00**
Folder, 6-1/4" x 12", printed paper, blue, white, and orange, one side with three images of Borden's Elsie, Trylon, and Perisphere, reverse with blue and white printing, pictorial family endorsement, recipe, and text relating to Borden's Chateau cheese, August 1939 publication date **20.00**
Pencil sharpener, bakelite **45.00**
Pin
   Brass, diecut, miniature twin engine airplane, upper wing inscribed "World's Fair U.S.A.," lower wing inscribed "Flight 1939 NX 18973," tiny Trylon and Perisphere on brass pendant on nose **25.00**

New York, 1939, busts, pair, white porcelain Art Deco heads of man and woman, green Lenox/USA stamps, 8-3/4" x 4", $650. Photo courtesy of David Rago Auctions.

New York, 1939, clock, plastic Deco style case, art image of Trylon and Perisphere in front of General Electric Exhibit Building on face, 4" d, 4-1/4" h, $475. Photo courtesy of Hake's Americana & Collectibles.

   Brass, formed as slightly concave seashell, soft white paint blending to soft blue, applied brass miniature Trylon and Perisphere, scroll style bottom margin . . . **65.00**

   Syroco, brown composition wood pin, formed in relief cloud formations above Trylon and Perisphere, landscaping trees on right and left, yellow, blue, and green accents, inscribed "New York World's Fair," tiny copyright and authorization, brass fastener **35.00**

Pinback button, 1-1/4" d, gold and blue cello, blue fabric ribbon inscribed in gold for May 1, 1939 event, Revolutionary War soldier behind inscription "New Haven Advertising Club, Inc./Vigilance," outer rim inscribed "New Haven Day-New York World's Fair" **125.00**

Pocketknife, 2" l steel knife based on each side by pearl-like plastic panels, one with tiny blue Trylon and Perisphere, plus inscription "New York World's Fair 1939," two steel blades **40.00**

Postcard, photo type **6.00**

Ring, adjustable, silvered brass, inscribed "World's Fair" over "NY," flanked by numeral "19" on one left, "39" on right **25.00**

Souvenir spoon, 7" l, Theme Building on front, "Pat. Pend., Wm Rogers Mfg. Co." **25.00**

Brussels, 1958
Paperweight, Atomaton, chrome plated on marble base, 4-1/2" x 4-1/2" x 4-1/2" **75.00**

New York, 1964
Dime, circular plastic case with 1946 Eisenhower dime in center, reads "NY World's Fair, 1964-1965 Neutron Irradiated Dime," back reads "Atomic Energy Commission, United States of America," 2" d **40.00**
Fork and spoon display, 11" l, mounted on wooden plaque, Unisphere decals on handles **45.00**
Hat, black felt, Unisphere emblem, white cord trim, feather, name "Richard" embroidered on front **25.00**
Lodge medallion, bronze luster finish, image of Unisphere and two exhibit buildings, brass hanger loop, inscribed "The Grand Lodge I.O.O.F. of the State of New York" **15.00**
Paperweight, panoramic scenes **40.00**
Postcard, 10 miniature pictures, 20 natural color reproductions, unused **20.00**
Puzzle, jigsaw, 2" x 10" x 11", Milton Bradley, 750 pcs, unopened **20.00**
Salt and pepper shakers, pr, Unisphere, figural, ceramic **50.00**
Souvenir book, *Official Souvenir Book of the New York World's Fair,* 1965 **25.00**
Yo-yo **45.00**

YARD-LONG PRINTS

History: In the early 1900s, many yard-long prints could be had for a few cents postage and a given number of wrappers or box tops. Others were premiums for renewing a subscription to a magazine or newspaper. A large number were advertising items created for a store or company and had calendars on the front or back. Many people believe that the only true yard-long print is 36 inches long and titled "A Yard of Kittens," etc. But lately collectors feel that any long and narrow print, horizontal or vertical, can be included in this category. It is a matter of personal opinion.

Values are listed for full-length prints in near-mint condition, nicely framed, and with original glass.

Reproduction Alert: Some prints are being reproduced. Know your dealer.

Note: Numbers in parentheses indicate C. G. and J. M. Rhoden and W. D. and M. J. Keagy, *Those Wonderful Yard-Long Prints and More,* Book 1 (1989), Book 2 (1992), Book 3 (1995), book number and page on which the item is illustrated, e.g. (3-52) refers to Book 3, page 52.

Advisers: Charles G. and Joan M. Rhoden, and W. D. and M. J. Keagy.

Animals
At the North Pole, copyright 1904, Jos. Hoover & Son, Philadelphia (Bk 2-29) **350.00**

Four kittens climbing tree, Helena Maguire (Bk 3-23)............**350.00**

In Sunny Africa, #1038, copyright 1904, Jos. Hoover & Son, Philadelphia (Bk 3-28)...................**450.00**

Kittens with mother, eight kittens, one reading book, one playing with spool (Bk 2-25)...................**275.00**

Yard of Dogs, copyright 1903, eight dogs, one with bird in mouth, one with bandage on head covering eye (Bk 2-21)...................**300.00**

Calendar

1906, Pabst Extract, Indian, by C. W. Henning, "Hiawatha's Wooing" poem on back of print (Bk 2-101)......**500.00**

1909, Pabst Malt Extract, Rose Girl, calendar at bottom (Bk 3-57)...**400.00**

1910, Clay, Robinson & Co., American Beauty Souvenir, adv and calendar on front, (Bk 3-44)..............**450.00**

1914, Pabst, American Girl, lady in full-length gown, muted shades of tangerine, yellow, and green (Bk 1-17)........................**400.00**

1915, Pompeian, lovely lady with handsome young man, grandfather clock in background (Bk 1-23)..**325.00**

1918, American Farming Magazine, sgd "W. H. Lister," lady in light gray and pale yellow dress, parasol, carrying basket of flowers (Bk 1-9)......**400.00**

1929, Seiz Good Shoes, sgd "Earl Chambers," calendar at bottom (Bk 2-85)...................**350.00**

Framed yard long print of girl in red evening dress, holding opera glasses, 36" x 11-1/2", $275. Photo courtesy of Joy Luke Auctions.

Children

A Yard of Kids, black and white, 11 stages of "hatching" (Bk 3-121) **300.00**

Cupid's Festival, copyright by Art Interchange Co. of New York (Bk 3-109)........................**375.00**

Easter Greetings, copyright 1894 by Knopp Co., Paul DeLongpre (Bk 3-107)........................**425.00**

Morning Glories, copyright 1892 by Mast, Crowell & Kirkpatrick, Springfield, Ohio, Maud Humphrey (Bk 2-105)........................**400.00**

Flowers and fruits

A Yard of Baby's Breath & Roses (Bk 1-52)...................**275.00**

Carnations, Grace Barton Allen (Bk 2-30)...................**250.00**

Chrysanthemums, C. Klein (Bk 2-34)........................**250.00**

Dogwood and Violets, Paul DeLongpre (Bk 3-28).........**300.00**

Yard of Cherries and Flowers, LeRoy (Bk 2-70)..................**250.00**

Yard of Roses, V. Janus, copyright by Perry Mason & Co. (Bk 2-51)..**250.00**

Long ladies

Lady in wide brim hat, seated with dog at her knees, 1916, sgd "H. Dirch," The Clay Robinson & Co. Army of Employees shown on back (Bk 2-91)........................**350.00**

Lady on balcony, facing moonlit waters, flowers in her hand (Bk 2-89)........................**300.00**

Lovely lady in long pale blue dress, seated, holding fan in her gloved hand, roses at her feet (Bk 3-96).....**500.00**

Lovely lady in red dress, seated in chair, carved lion's heads on chair arms, several roses at her feet (Bk 2-87)........................**350.00**

Pompeian Art Panel, titled "Irresistable," by Clement Donshea, dated 1930, lovely blond lady, handsome young man, rose garden (Bk 3-63)..................**350.00**

Stockman Bride, for National Stockman and Farmer magazine, dated 1911, beautiful dark haired lady in floor length white gown, holding long stem red roses (Bk 3-53)..........**450.00**

The Girl with the Laughing Eyes, copyright 1910 by F. Carlyle, lady in long off-shoulder gown, holding paper lantern (Bk 2-92)............**300.00**

Walk-Over Shoe Co., pretty girl dressed in cowgirl outfit, standing behind tree where she has carved "Walk-Over" (Bk 1-47).........**450.00**

YELLOWWARE

For more information, see this book.

History: Yellowware is a heavy earthenware which varies in color from a rich pumpkin to lighter shades, which are more tan than yellow. The weight and strength varies from piece to piece. Although plates, nappies, and custard cups are found, kitchen bowls and other cooking utensils are most prevalent.

The first American yellowware was produced at Bennington, Vermont. English yellowware has additional ingredients that make its body much harder. Derbyshire and Sharp's were foremost among the English manufacturers.

Bank, 3-5/8" h, house shape, molded detail highlighted in black, roof marked "For My Dear Girl," firing crack at chimney...................**660.00**

Bean pot, cov, 6-1/2" h, three white slip accent bands, bands repeated on orig matching lid, relief lines on both, Watt pottery logo on base, orig lid has been broken and reglued, bowl has some staining from use............**165.00**

Bowl, 13" d, 6" h, two wide white accent bands....................**165.00**

Candleholders, pr, 2-1/2" h, Rockingham glaze, attributed to Bennington, replaced glass chimneys, c1850.....................**615.00**

Canning jar, relief draped design, some crazing to glaze, surface chips, $125. Photos courtesy of Vicki and Bruce Waasdorp.

Miniature, bowl, three bold white slip accent bands, 4-1/2" d, 2" h, Lot , $150.

Canning jar, 6-1/2" h, relief draped design, some crazing to glaze, rim surface chips 125.00
Coffeepot, 8-1/2" h, Rockingham glaze, relief of woman snorting snuff on one side, man smoking pipe on other side, matching lid, c1850 . . . . 50.00
Creamer, 4-3/4" h, brown stripes, white band, blue seaweed dec, shallow flake on inside edge of table ring 440.00
Figure, 12" h, seated spaniel, open front feet design, attributed to Bennington factory, Rockingham glaze, c1850, few minor glaze flakes on base 275.00
Flask, 7-3/4" h, book shape, Rockingham glaze, c1850, two unglazed spots on one side . . . 275.00
Food mold
   3-3/4" d, 1-1/4" h, miniature, Yellow Rock, Phila mark 185.00
   7-1/2" d, 2-3/4" h, turk's head 145.00
Foot warmer, 9" h, Rockingham glaze, relief scroll design at shoulder, c1850 . . . . 440.00
Lamp base, 8-1/2" h, prominent rings, running brown and yellow/green glaze, partial lamp parts 115.00
Measure, 5-3/4" h, 6-1/2"d, Spearpoint & Trellis 300.00
Miniature
   Bowl, 4-1/2" d, 2" h, three bold white slip accent bands, some use stains 145.00
   Chamber pot, 2" h, three white slip accent stripes 155.00
Mug, 3-3/4" h, adv, red stencil on one side: "Fenton's Pekin Buffalo, NY," black stencil on reverse: "If drinking interferes with your business, give up business," two gilt-relief accent bands 70.00
Nappy, 9-1/2" d, 2-3/4" h, applied copper luster design in Pennsylvania-style floral design, c1860, very light 1" hairline extending from rim, overall wear to copper luster at int. rim 275.00

Wine glass, footed, Rockingham glaze, darker accents at rim, c1870, 4" h, $275.

Pepper pot, 4-1/2" h, blue seaweed dec, band dec 475.00
Pie funnel, 2-1/2" h, unmarked . 125.00
Pie plate, 10" d, unmarked 90.00
Pitcher, 4-1/4" h, brown and green Rockingham glaze, relief ribbed design, "Wetsch's Store, Wishek" in relief on front, some age crazing 100.00
Rolling pin, 8" l, very minor glaze age crazing 470.00
Spittoon, 8" d, Rockingham glaze, overall relief vine pattern 30.00
Sugar bowl, cov, 4-1/2" h, Rockingham glaze, relief vine and floral design 65.00
Teapot, 5" h, applied brown/green sponged glaze, orig lid, small glaze flake 110.00
Wash board, 5" w, 12" l, mottled Rockingham glaze, c1880, wooden frame with dry worn surface 615.00
Wash bowl and pitcher, 9-1/2" d bowl, 7-3/4" h pitcher, brown and blue sponged dec, brown stripe on pitcher 335.00
Wine glass, 4" h, Rockingham glaze, darker accents at rim, c1870 . . . 275.00

ZANE POTTERY

History: In 1921, Adam Reed and Harry McClelland bought the Peters and Reed Pottery in Zanesville, Ohio. The firm continued production of garden wares and introduced several art lines: Sheen, Powder Blue, Crystalline, and Drip. The factory was sold in 1941 to Lawton Gonder.

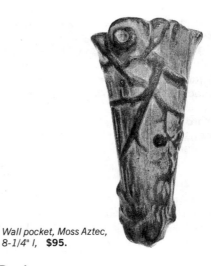

Wall pocket, Moss Aztec, 8-1/4" l, $95.

Bowl
   5" d, brown and blue 45.00
   6-1/2" d, blue, marked "Zanesware" 35.00
Figure, 10-1/8" h, cat, black, green eyes 500.00
Jardinière, 34" h, green matte glaze, matching pedestal, artist sgd "Frank Ferreu" 375.00
Vase
   5" h, green, cobalt blue drip glaze 30.00
   7" h, flowing medium green over dark forest green ground . . . 85.00
   8" h, ivory glaze, emb flowers and leaves 75.00

ZANESVILLE POTTERY

History: Zanesville Art Pottery, one of several **LA MORO** potteries located in Zanesville, Ohio, began production in 1900. At first, a line of utilitarian products was made; art pottery was introduced shortly thereafter. The major line was La Moro, which was hand painted and decorated under glaze. The firm was bought by S. A. Weller in 1920 and became known as Weller Plant No. 3.

Marks: The impressed block-print mark "La Moro" appears on the high-glazed and matte-glazed decorated ware.

Bowl, 6-1/2" d, fluted edge, mottled blue glaze 65.00
Coffeepot, cov, 8" h, stoneware, Bodine Pottery Co., sand colored, unglazed ext., Albany slip int., tin wire straps, handle, spout, lid, and wire bale handle, c1880 . . . . 1,020.00

Jardinière

7-1/8" h, 8-1/2" d, waisted cylindrical form, landscape scene, blue, green, and maroon matte glaze, c1908 . . . . **175.00**

8-1/4" h, ruffled rim, cream to light amber peony blossoms, shaded brown ground **75.00**

Plate, 4-1/2" d, applied floral dec **25.00**

Vase

8" h, mottled green matte glaze **150.00**

8-3/4" h, cone shaped top, bulbous base, La Morro, marked "2/802/4" **350.00**

10-1/4" h, light gray horse portrait, light olive green to blue-green ground, matte ext., glossy brown int., sgd "R. G. Turner" **825.00**

ZSOLNAY POTTERY

History: Vilmos Zsolnay (1828-1900) assumed control of his brother's factory in Pécs, Hungary, in the mid-19th century. In 1899, Miklos, Vilmos' son, became manager. The firm still produces ceramic ware.

The early wares are highly ornamental, glazed, and have a cream-colored ground. Eosin glaze, a deep rich play of colors reminiscent of Tiffany's iridescent wares, received a gold medal at the 1900 Paris exhibition. Zsolnay Art Nouveau pieces show great creativity.

Marks: Originally, no trademark was used; but in 1878 the company began to use a blue mark depicting

Figure, dog, sitting, modern, $90. Photo courtesy of Jim and Susan Harran.

the five towers of the cathedral at Pécs. The initials "TJM" represent the names of Miklos' three children.

Note: Zsolnay's recent series of iridescent-glazed figurines, which initially were inexpensive, now are being sought by collectors and steadily increasing in value.

Bowl, 6-1/2" l, 2-1/2" h, sea shell shape, hp florals, gold highlights and edging, blue mark "Zsolnay Pecs," castle mark, "Patent," imp factory mark and numbers **160.00**

Cache pot, 13" d, young girls dance holding hands around stylized tree form, blue, pale silver, and pale lilac glazes **4,250.00**

Chalice, 6" h, four flower stems as handles attached to upper body, flowers and berries in relief as terminals, green and blue Eosin glazes, red int., form #5668, c1899, millennium factory mark, ext. rim chip repaired **1,650.00**

Coffee set, 8-1/2" h cov coffeepot, creamer, sugar, cake plate, six cups, saucers, and dessert plates, cobalt blue and gold trim, white ground **600.00**

Compote, 11" d, ribbed, four caryatids molded as angels supports, blue-green irid glaze **1,100.00**

Creamer, 6-1/2" l, fierce dragon handle **250.00**

Figure

Bears, pair, emerald green glaze, 7-1/2" l, 5" h **695.00**

Vase, classic shape, flaring rim, nacreous chartreuse glaze, stylized suns and flowers, gold stamp mark, 11" x 5", $495. Photo courtesy of David Rago Auctions.

Mallard ducks, 7" l, 7" h **195.00**

Spaniel, artist sgd, 5" h **95.00**

Woman, 9-3/8" l, 4-3/4" w, 5-1/2" h, irid blue and green glaze, brown manufacturer's stamp "Zsolnay PECS Made in Hungary," repaired base chips **460.00**

Garden seat, 18-1/2" h, form #1105, c1882, wear to top surface, repairs to applied dec **1,850.00**

Jardinière, 16" l, ovoid, multicolored florals, protruding pierced roundels, cream ground, blue steep mark. **450.00**

Jug, 10-1/2" h, yellow glaze, worn gilt highlights, form #109, c1882 . . . **500.00**

Pitcher, 7-1/2" h, form #5064, red/maroon metallic Eosin ground, cream and pale brown flower dec, c1898, millennium factory mark . **750.00**

Puzzle jug, 6-1/2" h, pierced roundels, irid dec, cream ground, castle mark, imp "Zsolnay" **195.00**

Vase

3-3/4" h, allover hp flower and leaf design, red, cream and gold-green metallic Eosin glazes, sgd "Flora Nici," dated Nov. 14, 1923 . . . . **1,200.00**

4-1/4" h, form #2289, hand-drawn factory mark and name, c1882 . . . . **1,500.00**

9" h, tapering reeded baluster, gold and cobalt blue irid finish . . **225.00**

9-1/4" h, quatrefoil rim, elongated neck, figure of woman wearing diaphanous dress seated on shoulder, irid gold, green and blue shaded glaze, irid stamped mark "Zsolnay PECS Made in Hungary" **460.00**

Wine flask, 6-1/2" h, relief dec, putty ground, c1902 . . . . **450.00**

Vessel, two-headed dragon, four legs, green, brown, gold, impressed mark, 7-3/4" h, 11-1/2" w, $225.

INDEX